Legal Studies in International, European and Comparative Criminal Law

Volume 2

The main purpose of this book series is to provide sound analyses of major developments in national, EU and international law and case law, as well as insights into court practice and legislative proposals in the areas concerned. The analyses address a broad readership, such as lawyers and practitioners, while also providing guidance for courts. In terms of scope, the series encompasses four main areas, the first of which concerns international criminal law and especially international case law in relevant criminal law subjects. The second addresses international human rights law with a particular focus on the impact of international jurisprudences on national criminal law and criminal justice systems, as well as their interrelations. In turn the third area focuses on European criminal law and case law. Here, particular weight will be attached to studies on European criminal law conducted from a comparative perspective. The fourth and final area presents surveys of comparative criminal law inside and outside Europe. By combining these various aspects, the series especially highlights research aimed at proposing new legal solutions, while focusing on the new challenges of a European area based on high standards of human rights protection.

As a rule, book proposals are subject to peer review, which is carried out by two members of the editorial board in anonymous form.

More information about this series at http://www.springer.com/series/15393

Serena Quattrocolo • Stefano Ruggeri
Editors

Personal Participation in Criminal Proceedings

A Comparative Study of Participatory
Safeguards and *in absentia* Trials in Europe

Springer

Editors
Serena Quattrocolo
Department of Law, and Political,
Economic and Social Sciences
University of Piemonte Orientale
Alessandria, Italy

Stefano Ruggeri
Law Department
University of Messina
Messina, Italy

ISSN 2524-8049 ISSN 2524-8057 (electronic)
Legal Studies in International, European and Comparative Criminal Law
ISBN 978-3-030-01185-7 ISBN 978-3-030-01186-4 (eBook)
https://doi.org/10.1007/978-3-030-01186-4

Library of Congress Control Number: 2019930286

Cover illustration: Maria Isabel Ruggeri

This Springer imprint is published by the registered company Springer Nature Switzerland AG
The registered company address is: Gewerbestrasse 11, 6330 Cham, Switzerland

Contents

List of Contributors

Lorena Bachmaier Winter University Complutense Madrid, Madrid, Spain

Marco Bassini Bocconi University, Milano, Italy

Emmanouil Billis Max Planck Institute for Foreign and International Criminal Law, Freiburg, Germany

Bárbara Churro Portuguese Constitutional Court, Lisbon, Portugal

Flaviu Ciopec Faculty of Law, West University of Timişoara, Timişoara, Romania

Vânia Costa Ramos Research Centre for Criminal Law and Criminal Sciences, University of Lisbon, Lisbon, Portugal

Valentina Covolo University of Luxembourg, Luxembourg, Luxembourg

Elena D'Alessandro University of Turin, Turin, Italy

Eduardo Demetrio Crespo Castilla-La Mancha University, Toledo, Spain

Barbara Drevet University of Bordeaux, Bordeaux, France

Anett Erzsébet Gácsi University of Szeged, Szeged, Hungary

Panagiotis Gkaniatsos Criminal Law Department, University of Göttingen, Göttingen, Germany

Felix Golser Department of Criminal Law and Criminal Procedure, University of Salzburg, Salzburg, Austria

Krisztina Karsai Institute of Criminal Law and Criminal Science, University of Szeged, Szeged, Hungary

Kate Leader University of York, York, UK

Annalisa Mangiaracina University of Palermo, Palermo, Italy

Aneta Petrova Bleiwäsche, Germany

Oreste Pollicino Bocconi University, Milano, Italy

Serena Quattrocolo Department of Law, and Political, Economic and Social Sciences, University of Piemonte Orientale, Alessandria, Italy

Magdalena Roibu Faculty of Law, West University of Timişoara, Timişoara, Romania

Stefano Ruggeri Messina University, Messina, Italy

Ágata María Sanz Hermida Castilla-La Mancha University, Toledo, Spain

Anne Schneider University of Mannheim, Mannheim, Germany

Zsolt Szomora Institute of Criminal Law and Criminal Science, University of Szeged, Szeged, Hungary

María Luisa Villamarín López University Complutense Madrid, Madrid, Spain

Benjamin Vogel Max Planck Institute for Foreign and International Criminal Law, Freiburg im Breisgau, Germany

Part I
Introduction to the Research

Preliminary Issues

Serena Quattrocolo and Stefano Ruggeri

Abstract This first chapter presents the background for the research, rooted in the most recent developments in in absentia trials in Europe. Moreover, it explains the goals and the method of this comparative investigation, covering 12 legal orders, with several, different approaches to comparison. The comparative-law examination of the national jurisdictions shall pose the basis for further analysis on an interdisciplinary layer, from the viewpoint of constitutional law, civil procedure law, substantive criminal law, international (human rights) law and EU Law.

Abbreviations

EAW   European arrest warrant
ECHR   European Convention on Human Rights
ECtHR   European Court of Human Rights
EU   European Union

Although this contribution is the result of a joint discussion, *Serena Quattrocolo* is the author of paragraph 1, while *Stefano Ruggeri* is the author of paragraphs 2 and 3.

S. Quattrocolo (✉)
Department of Law, and Political, Economic and Social Sciences, University of Piemonte Orientale, Alessandria, Italy
e-mail: serena.quattrocolo@uniupo.it

S. Ruggeri
Department of Law 'Salvatore Pugliatti', Messina University, Messina, Italy
e-mail: steruggeri@unime.it

© Springer Nature Switzerland AG 2019   3
S. Quattrocolo, S. Ruggeri (eds.), *Personal Participation in Criminal Proceedings*, Legal Studies in International, European and Comparative Criminal Law 2, https://doi.org/10.1007/978-3-030-01186-4_1

1 The Problem

In the last decades, a number of important developments, which have taken place in Europe, both in the case-law and legislation at different levels, have drawn the focus on the presence of private parties, mainly on the attendance of the accused, in criminal proceedings, in the field of both transnational and domestic criminal justice. Traditionally, international law instruments of international cooperation did not ensure specific safeguards to the individuals tried *in absentia* and involved in surrender procedures. In Europe, the 1957 European Convention on Extradition provided nothing in this regard, and it took more than 20 years before the 1978 Second Additional Protocol dealt with this problem. Moreover, the approach adopted was still rather minimalist. The requested country could discretionarily reject a request for surrender aimed at the enforcement of a sentence or detention order imposed by a judgment issued *in absentia* only if it considered that the minimum defence rights due to any person charged with a criminal offence had not been satisfied in the relevant proceedings. Furthermore, refusal of surrender was excluded where the requesting State offered sufficient assurance to guarantee to the individuals concerned the right to a retrial aimed at safeguarding their defence rights.[1]

Without a doubt, this approach had enormous influence on subsequent case-law and legislation, going far beyond the sphere of international law. The jurisprudence elaborated by the Strasbourg Court since the 1984 leading judgment *Colozza v. Italy* provides a clear example of how international human rights case-law has transposed the logic of subsequent mechanisms into the field of domestic criminal justice to save the lawfulness of convictions held in the absence of the accused.[2] Almost a quarter century after the 1978 Protocol to the Extradition Convention, the Framework Decision on the European arrest warrant enacted the typical solutions of the so-called 'conditional extradition' into the new surrender procedures among EU countries.[3] Despite the clear attempt to align the EAW procedures with the Strasbourg case-law and with the traditional approach of international law instruments on extradition, the arrangements of the EAW Framework Decision inevitably weakened the protection of the defendants tried *in absentia*. EU institutions, in particular, made no reference to the need to preserve 'minimum defence rights', laid down instead by the 1978 Protocol. Moreover, the strongly mutual-recognition-based approach of the EAW legislation imposed on the executing authority a general obligation to enforce the warrant issued by a foreign authority, without enabling it to call into question the quality of the assurances offered by the issuing country.

This heritage has produced further developments in more recent years. The Strasbourg case-law has played a decisive role in the adaptation of domestic legislation in various countries to international law standards. The Italian legislative reform carried out by Law 67/2014, which abolished the old default proceedings

---

[1] Art. 3(1) ECE.
[2] ECtHR, *Colozza v. Italy*, judgment of 12 February 1985, Appl. No. 9024/80.
[3] Art. 5 FD EAW.

and provided for specific safeguards for absent defendants, is an enlightening example of the in-depth changes that have taken place in national law under the influence of European jurisprudence.[4] Moreover, we have witnessed the increasing attention by EU institutions to the problem of participatory rights in relation to *in absentia* trials. Here also, a new approach was first adopted in the field of international cooperation. Framework Decision 2009/299/JHA, amending *inter alia* the EAW Framework Decision to reduce the margin of discretion of national authorities and to drop the uncertain requirement of assurances, laid down the specific conditions under which individuals could be surrendered to other Member States for the enforcement of a sentence or a detention order rendered *in absentia*.[5] Seven years later, Directive 2016/343/EU extended a similar approach to domestic criminal proceedings, while dangerously softening, however, some important requirements, such as that of legal assistance provided by a lawyer mandated by the absent defendant.[6] It is probable that the strong confrontation that divided the CJEU case-law and domestic (constitutional) courts on the relationship between the 2009 EU legislative set-up and constitutional law[7] contributed to the legislative arrangements made in 2016, which provide for minimalist harmonisation in such delicate area.

Interestingly, most of these developments reveal an approach that still largely looks at participatory rights in a rather negative form. In Spain, for instance, *in absentia* trials still have a reduced scope of application and the judicial declaration of *rebeldía* entails as a rule the suspension of the proceedings.[8] On the contrary, the new Italian procedure for absent defendants has inherited several dangerous aspects of the default proceedings, which allow criminal proceedings to be instituted on the basis of weak presumptions of awareness of the trial and submits the defendant to cumbersome burden of proof to challenge the conviction rendered *in absentia*.[9] At a deeper level still, both EU legislation and the Strasbourg case-law highlight an understanding of participation in criminal trials in terms of absence, while overlooking the values underpinning the defendant's presence. The EU Directive 2016/343 provides a clear example, focusing, after the solemn acknowledgment of the right to be present at trial, on the requirements governing a criminal law action *in absentia*.[10]

Certainly, the European case-law's understanding of the accused's presence at trial as equivalent to his involvement in a subsequent trial or a higher instance[11] has largely influenced the developments occurred in both domestic and EU law.

---

[4] Mangiaracina, in this volume, Sect. 5.2.

[5] Schneider, in this volume, Sects. 3.2.1.1–4.

[6] See Bachmaier Winter, in this volume, Sect. 4.1.3.

[7] Cf. Demetrio Crespo and Sánz Hermida, in this volume, Sect. 3.1; Pollicino and Bassini, in this volume, Sects. 5 and 6.1; Schneider, in this volume, Sect. 3.3.2.

[8] See Villamarín López, in this volume, Sect. 3.1.

[9] Mangiaracina, in this volume, Sect. 5.2.

[10] Art. 8 of Directive 2016/343/EU.

[11] Cf. Ruggeri, in this volume, Sect. 3.1.1.

Furthermore, attendance in court is widely dealt with in terms of physical presence,[12] and neither EU legislation nor domestic laws have still generally developed a coherent set of safeguards governing the personal involvement of private parties in criminal proceedings. A look at the criminal justice systems within the Council of Europe's area, moreover, reveals highly different approaches to the defendant's participation in court proceedings, which cannot be traced back to the traditional distinction between a right to attendance and a duty to be present at trial.[13] Indeed, right and duty not only tend to overlap in the majority of national jurisdictions, but also in the Strasbourg case-law, which, although discouraging unjustified absences, has never clarified the extent to which the defendant's choice of steering away from the trial can legitimately be sanctioned.[14]

2 Subject and Goals of the Investigation

Against this background, this study aims at providing a wide-ranging analysis of personal participation in criminal proceedings. The focus of this research, therefore, is neither limited to the *in absentia* trials nor to the defendant's physical attendance at court hearings. On the one hand, absence should not only be analysed in relation to default proceedings and their implications in the field of international surrender procedures, but also with regard to further proceedings excluding participation of defendants, such as *inaudito reo* procedures, as well as proceedings that entail restrictions on their participatory rights (*e.g.*, *in camera* hearings). On the other, personal participation shall be examined in the light of the fair trial safeguards that should enable private parties to be effectively involved in criminal proceedings and make their own contribution to fact-finding. Doubtless, personal participation does not only hold relevance in court proceedings and a public trial, but also deserves in-depth analysis in the pre-trial inquiry and particularly in the context of interim decisions that can lead to the adoption of intrusive investigations and measures impinging on individual rights (*e.g.*, pre-trial detention, wiretaps, and so on).

The adoption of such wide-ranging viewpoint, moreover, has led us to further broaden the perspective of this research in a double way. First, the wide understanding of criminal proceedings by Strasbourg case-law, in particular, suggests extending the analysis to the problems concerned with *in absentia* trials and the participatory guarantees acknowledged in the field of civil justice with specific regard to civil proceedings imposing pecuniary penalties.[15] Second, but not less interestingly, this study also encompasses the personal role that individuals other than the accused, as

---

[12] See Quattrocolo, in this volume, Sect. 3.1.

[13] *Ibid.*, Sect. 3.1.

[14] Cf. Ruggeri, in this volume, Sect. 3.1.1.

[15] D'Alessandro, in this volume.

long as they are involved in criminal proceedings, can play in procedural activities and criminal-law hearings.

The goals of this research, however, are not exclusively of a diagnostic nature. Certainly, the solution models emerging from human rights law provide a basis of utmost importance for a critical re-assessment of national law, as well as for the examination of the steps forward that can still be made in statutory and/or case-law *de jure condendo*. Furthermore, the different approaches of the selected national jurisdictions constitute a fundamental point of reference to test the consistency of ECHR and EU law. The ultimate goal of this study, therefore, is to provide a set of essential guarantees aimed at governing the personal involvement of private parties in a European judicial area based on the highest standards of protection of fundamental rights.[16]

3 Methods and Structure of the Research

The present study deals with these problems through a comparative-law analysis of personal participation in criminal proceedings. Comparison shall be conducted at two main levels.

The first one focuses on the different approaches of twelve domestic criminal justice systems to the issues listed in the Attachment, which appears at the end of this book.[17] Following the general approach of this research, both national reports and the comparative-law analysis firstly focus on the participatory rights of the accused and other individuals involved in criminal proceedings. Personal participation, however, shall not be examined with exclusive regard to the trial phase, but with comprehensive focus on several stages of the proceedings (from the pre-trial inquiry to higher instances), as well as on different types of proceedings (from the public trial to alternative proceedings and *in camera* and closed hearings).[18] The proceedings excluding the involvement of the accused shall be analysed at a second level, with an approach that, moreover, does not only look at *in absentia* trials, but also at *inaudito reo* procedures.[19] This systematic approach shall be extended to the field of transnational criminal justice, with the aim of assessing the participatory safeguards that the selected jurisdictions acknowledge in the two main areas of EAW proceedings and transborder investigations and evidence-gathering procedures,[20] as well as the relevance that the accused's absence holds particularly in the context of international surrender proceedings.[21]

---

[16] *Ibid.*

[17] Quattrocolo, in this volume.

[18] *Ibid.*, Sect. 3.3.

[19] *Ibid.*, Sect. 5.3.

[20] *Ibid.*, Sect. 6.1.

[21] *Ibid.*, Sect. 6.2.

The national countries examined in this study have been selected according to different criteria. Some of them—such as, as noted, Italy and Spain—deserve comparative examination because of the different legal statute on the proceedings based on the accused's absence.[22] The very notion of *in absentia* trials, moreover, is not at all uniform. In contrast to some jurisdictions that in any case ensure legal assistance to the accused tried in their absence (*e.g.*, Italy), others conceive of genuine *in absentia* trials in relation to those proceedings in which not only is the accused absent but also no defence counsel was appointed (*e.g.*, Greece).[23] Moreover, comparison shall also be extended to the increasing tendency to maintain or even introduce new procedures that exclude or considerably restrict participation of defendants and other private parties. Italian law, although introducing a new trial for absent defendants, has left unchanged another procedure that rules out any involvement of private parties, namely the penal order proceeding.[24] In 2015, Spanish legislature has even enacted an unprecedented penalty order procedure, which, however, remarkably involves the accused prior to the rendering of the guilty verdict.[25] In England and Wales, the traditional approach against trials *in absentia* has been overcome since 2001, and state-related concerns oriented toward efficiency in criminal justice have allowed their increasing use (also on the basis of dangerous presumptions of knowledge) over last years.[26] Another field in which this tendency can be observed is that of *in camera* and closed hearings, which notions also are not unified as they relate to a group of different types of proceedings that may not only exclude the right to a public trial, but can also affect the right to access evidence. It is interesting to note that in various jurisdictions, constitutional case-law has set limits to the use of such proceedings. In some countries (*e.g.*, Germany), constitutional case-law does not still allow proceedings entailing non-disclosure of sensitive evidence,[27] while in others (*e.g.*, Hungary) the Constitutional Court has reacted to the legislature's failure to enact clear rules on the forms of court procedures, particularly at higher instances.

Furthermore, the choice of the selected jurisdictions allows a comparative analysis of the extent to which participatory rights have been enhanced in the last years in Europe, a result is largely due to the strong influence of ECtHR case-law and the harmonisation process of criminal justice made at the EU level. Moreover, it is noteworthy that in some jurisdictions (*e.g.*, Portugal and Italy) constitutional law provides binding indications regarding specific participatory guarantees that must be ensured, in particular, to the accused.[28] Among these jurisdictions, Portuguese

---

[22] See respectively Mangiaracina, in this volume, Sect. 5.2; Villamarín López, in this volume, Sect. 5.2.

[23] Billis and Gkaniatsos, in this volume, Sect. 5.2.

[24] Mangiaracina, in this volume, Sect. 5.3.

[25] Villamarín López, in this volume, Sect. 5.3.

[26] Leader, in this volume, Sect. 5.1.

[27] Vogel, in this volume, Sect. 3.3.

[28] Cf. Mangiaracina, in this volume, Sect. 1; Costa Ramos and Churro, in this volume, Sect. 1.2.

Constitution provides a rather unique provision that explicitly allows for procedural activities to be carried out in the absence of the accused, while charging the legislature to define the cases and provided that defence rights are ensured in these situations.[29] In several countries, the lack an explicit constitutional acknowledgment of participatory safeguards has been compensated for in various ways. In some jurisdictions, participatory rights have gained constitutional relevance by means of general clauses, such as that regarding the access to justice (*e.g.*, Romania),[30] or the right to an effective defence (*e.g.*, Bulgaria).[31] In other countries, such as Austria and Luxembourg, the constitutional status recognised to the European Convention has enabled the acknowledgment of the solutions provided by the Strasbourg case-law.[32]

Altogether, the wide-ranging selection of these countries also enables us to assess the consistency solutions elaborated by the Strasbourg case-law and the harmonisation provided by EU law from the perspective of jurisdictions belonging to different criminal justice traditions.[33] As noted, this critical examination among the ultimate aims of this research.

The second comparative-law analysis focuses on the perspective of human rights law, cutting across the critical examination conducted in relation to both domestic and transnational criminal justice of constitutional law, substantive criminal law, ECHR law and EU law.[34] The main purpose of this comparison is twofold. First, it aims at providing a crosscutting diagnosis of the main principles underpinning personal participation in constitutional and substantive criminal law, as well as in ECHR and EU law. Particular attention shall be devoted to the solutions elaborated by domestic (constitutional) case-law, and by Strasbourg and Luxembourg jurisprudences on specific problematic issues, particularly on the proceedings that exclude or restrict participation in criminal trials.[35] The procedural safeguards acknowledged at these different levels shall be critically examined in the light of the requirements posed by the selected criminal justice systems.[36] Yet the goal of human rights comparison, as noted, is not limited to diagnosis. The identification of the human rights requirements of personal participation in criminal proceedings shall enable us to a critical evaluation of domestic law in the light of the European Convention and its developments resulting from EU harmonisation. This evaluation shall constitute the basis for the establishment of the essential guarantees with a view to a participatory understanding of criminal justice in Europe.

---

[29] Costa Ramos and Churro, in this volume, Sect. 4.1.

[30] Ciopec and Roibu, in this volume, Sect. 1.

[31] Petrova, in this volume, Sect. 1.

[32] See Golser, in this volume, Sect. 1; Covolo, in this volume, Sect. 1.

[33] Quattrocolo and Ruggeri, in this volume.

[34] Ruggeri, in this volume.

[35] *Ibid.*, Sect. 3.1.4.

[36] *Ibid.*, Sect. 4.1.3.

Part II
Personal Participation in Court Proceedings and *In Absentia* Trials in Domestic and Transnational Criminal Justice. The Perspective of National and Comparative Law

Report on Austria

Felix Golser

Abstract The comprehensive rights to personal participation in Austrian criminal procedure fulfil international human rights standards. *In absentia* proceedings are only allowable in certain proceedings on offences which are punishable with no more than 3 years imprisonment and only if strict criteria are met. In EAW and surrender proceedings the accused has the right to be heard in a public trial. Penal order proceedings are only allowable if they have been interrogated and have explicitly waived the trial. The proceedings on surrender based on *in absentia* verdicts possibly require some minor changes to fulfil ECHR requirements. Relevant European directives made only minor changes in domestic law necessary.

Abbreviations

ARHG	Austrian code on surrender and legal assistance in criminal matters
CCP	Austrian code of criminal procedure (Strafprozessordnung)
EAW	European Arrest Warrant
ECHR	European Convention of Human Rights
ECtHR	European Court of Human Rights
EU	European Union
EU-JZG	Austrian code on the judicial cooperation in criminal matters with member states of the EU
JGG	Jugendgerichtsgesetz—Austrian law on criminal proceedings of juvenile offenders
PC	Austrian criminal code (Strafgesetzbuch)
ZustG	Zustellgesetz—Austrian law for the delivery of letters by courts and authorities

F. Golser (✉)
Department of Criminal Law and Criminal Procedure, University of Salzburg,
Salzburg, Austria
e-mail: felix.golser@sbg.ac.at

© Springer Nature Switzerland AG 2019
S. Quattrocolo, S. Ruggeri (eds.), *Personal Participation in Criminal Proceedings*, Legal Studies in International, European and Comparative Criminal Law 2, https://doi.org/10.1007/978-3-030-01186-4_2

1 Constitutional Requirements of the Involvement of Private Parties in Criminal Justice

The most important source of constitutional rights of private parties in Austrian criminal law is article 6 ECHR. The ECHR was accorded constitutional status in Austria and guarantees the individual right to a fair trial. Criminal courts have to apply article 6 ECHR in the same way as other constitutional rights and have to interpret procedural rights according to it. If a law would infringe it, the constitutional court could rescind it. The direct application of article 6 ECHR guarantees is not free from preconditions, though. If article 6 ECHR is infringed by a court decision during trial, defendants or their lawyers have to object to it during trial in order to be able to use this as ground for appeal or a plea of nullity (§ 281(1)4 CCP). If they fail to do so, they have no remedy to enforce their rights guaranteed by article 6 ECHR.[1]

2 Personal Participation of Private Parties and Legal Assistance

Legal assistance is crucial for the proper exercise of participation rights. Defendants have the right to make use of legal assistance in every stage of the proceedings. In some proceedings, they are even required to nominate a defender. This applies for the whole proceedings if the accused are in pre-trial custody or the proceeding is about the accommodation in an institution for mentally abnormal offenders. In most cases, they are only required to be represented by a lawyer during the trial. This applies, for example, if they are accused of an offence which is punishable with more than 3 years imprisonment or when the court has to decide about the accommodation in an institution for addicts or dangerous recidivistic offenders (§ 61 CCP). If defendants are required to be represented by a lawyer but do not nominate one, the court can assign one. If they are financially unable to afford one, the state will cover the costs. This is not only the case if they are required to be defended by a lawyer, but also if it is in the best interest of the administration of justice. The law mentions as examples for this, complicated cases, particular remedy proceedings, handicapped defendants and those who are not proficient in the official language used in court (§ 61(2) CCP).[2]

---

[1] If they do not object to the court decision, they have not exhausted the domestic remedies and cannot appeal to the European Court of Human Rights (ECtHR, *Batista Laborde v. Austria*, judgement of 2 February 2016, Appl. No. 41767/09).

[2] The official language used in court is usually German. The Croatian, Slovenian and Hungarian minorities have the right that in certain courts the proceedings are held in their native language. (Bachner and Foregger in Fuchs and Ratz 2014, § 56 para 7).

Contact with the lawyer can only be limited to a general information on the rights of the defendant if they were arrested, have not yet been transferred to court and it is necessary to prevent an obstruction of the investigation or the suppression of evidence (§ 59(2) CCP).

Defence lawyers have the right and duty to express everything useful for the defence of the accused. They also have to use every permissible mean of defence, only limited by law, their mandate and their conscience (§ 57(1) CCP). Every right defendants have can also be exercised by their defence lawyers. They can also question witnesses, access records and make their own investigations. While making private investigations, defendants and their lawyers do not have more power than any other private person and do not get support by the police. Therefore, they can visit witnesses and ask questions but cannot summon them or oblige them to say the truth. Defence lawyers are obliged to partiality and can lie in court without facing consequences, if necessary.[3]

Defendants who do not speak or understand German have the right to language assistance. This assistance has to be oral, if possible. Defendants also have the right to a written translation of "relevant files", if this is necessary to guarantee a fair trial. "Relevant Files" comprises certain documents mentioned in the law, e.g. the indictment, decisions on pre-trial custody and non-final judgments. Other relevant files are those which they need to understand to defend against the accusations by showing their point of view (§ 56 CCP).[4]

Defendants and their lawyers have access to the records on the investigation and trial of the police, the prosecutor and the court. They can also examine collected evidence if this is possible without disadvantage to the investigation. These rights can be limited to protect personal information on anonymous witnesses. Access to records can also be limited until the end of the investigation procedure if there are special circumstances which indicate that immediate access to certain records could endanger the investigation (§ 51 CCP). If they are in pre-trial custody, access to files which are relevant for the evaluation of the suspicion and the reasons for arrest cannot be limited. In case a settlement by diversion is indicated, the access to the records cannot be limited as defendants have to know which incriminatory evidence exists to meet an informed decision on whether they should accept the diversion.[5]

---

[3] Bertel and Venier (2012), § 57 para 2.
[4] Bachner and Foregger in Fuchs and Ratz (2014), § 56 para 16.
[5] Seiler (2016), para 195.

3   Personal Participation of the Accused in Criminal Proceedings

3.1   General Features of Personal Participation: Absolute Individual Right or Duty of Diligence?

Personal participation is an absolute individual right but also a duty in first instance trials. With certain exceptions, if defendants do not appear in court, the trial has to be rescheduled. They have to be summoned by a letter with information on the subject, time and date of the trial and their relevant rights. If defendants fail to appear in court and it was threatened in the summon, their appearance can be enforced (§ 427(2) CCP).[6] The cost of rescheduling the trial has to be covered by the defendant (§ 389(3) CCP). Defendants have to be summoned early enough to have at least 8 days for the preparation of their defence. This is reduced to 3 days for proceedings at the district court (§ 455(1) CCP). If it has to be expected that the trial will take long, they are required to have at least 14 days preparation time (§ 221 CCP).

Trials in the first and in higher instances and in surrender proceedings generally have to be public. Therefore, the trial has to be publicly announced and can be attended by anybody. Audio and video recordings are prohibited (§ 228 CCP). The public can only be excluded on certain grounds mentioned in the law (§ 229(1) CCP). The pronouncement of the judgement always has to be public (§ 229(4) CCP). Defendants have the right and duty to attend it. If they become unable to attend the trial due to illness, the trial has to be rescheduled unless they agree that it can be continued without their attendance (§ 275 CCP). If they disturb it with inappropriate behaviour, the chairman of the court has to warn them that they can be removed from the trial. If they continue their behaviour, the court can decide to exclude them for some time or the whole trial (§ 234 CCP). In a controversial decision, the refusal of an Islamic defendant to remove her full-face veil was seen as disrespect to the court and led to her exclusion.[7] Defendants can even be excluded during the pronouncement of the verdict. In this case, a member of the court and the clerk of the court have to pronounce it to them after the trial (§ 234 CCP).

3.2   Personal Participation in the Pre-Trial Inquiry (with Particular Regard to the Interim Decisions on Coercive Measures)

Defendants have to be informed about an investigation against them and their rights in the investigation proceedings as soon as possible. If the investigation indicates that they have committed a different or an additional crime, they have to be informed

---

about this. This can only be deferred if it would endanger the investigation (§ 50 CCP).

During the investigation proceedings, witnesses are usually questioned without participation of the defendant. An exception is the adversarial interrogation (§ 165 CCP) which is used when a witness will possibly be unable to give evidence during trial. It also has to be applied on victims who are particularly protective, e.g. less than 14 years old or violated in their sexual sphere (§ 66a CCP). Defendants, their lawyers, prosecution and victims have the right to participate and ask questions. It is possible to let the participants watch the interrogation by image transmission and let an expert (e.g. a psychologist) ask the questions to prevent the witness or victim from facing the defendant. A Video of the interrogation can be shown or a protocol can be read out at the trial.

The police can confiscate objects during the investigation proceedings, if this is necessary to secure evidence, private rights or forfeiture (§ 110 CCP). The prosecution has to request a court order as soon as possible (§ 113 CCP). The concerned person can appeal against the decision (§ 87 CCP). The parties have no right to personal participation in these proceedings. The final decision on confiscation and forfeiture is made in the main trial (§ 443 CCP).

The decision about pre-trial custody is made in a non-public hearing with participation of the parties. Defendants have the right and duty to personally participate in the hearing except if it is impossible due to an illness. If they are not imprisoned in the remand prison of the responsible court, it is permissible to connect them by video conference (§ 176(3) CCP). They are obliged to be assisted by a lawyer during the hearing. Failing to inform defendants or their lawyers about the hearing would be a violation of their constitutionally guaranteed right to freedom and could be used as grounds for appeal against the decision. If the court summons witnesses, the defendant and their lawyer can ask them questions. Since defendants can be connected by video conference and the hearing does not have to be rescheduled if they cannot attend due to medical reasons, their participation rights do not go as far as during the trial (§ 176 CCP).

Defendants can object to coercive measures violating their rights set by the prosecution. Within 4 weeks after the measure was executed, they have to address their objection to the prosecution which can allow it. Otherwise, it has to defer it to the court. If it deems it necessary for evidence-gathering, the court can set a non-public hearing. While defendants have the right to encourage such a hearing, they cannot enforce it. Their right to be heard can therefore be limited to their written objection (§ 106 CCP). The defendant can appeal against a coercive measure ordered by the court within 2 weeks. The court of appeal then decides on the case without a hearing based on the files and the defendant's appeal (§ 107 CCP).

3.3 Personal Participation in Proceedings in Camera

There are no *in camera* proceedings in Austrian criminal procedure.

3.4 Personal Participation in Alternative Proceedings

Austrian law knows diversion as alternative to traditional criminal proceedings. For it to be applicable the circumstances have to be sufficiently clarified and a conviction of the suspect has to appear highly likely. Therefore, the defendant and the victim have to be heard. It is only permissible, if the offence is punishable with no more than 5 years imprisonment, has not lead to the death of someone and the guilt of the offender has not to be considered serious. The prosecutor can then abstain from prosecution (1) under a probation period, (2) if the offender pays a certain amount of money, (3) if they do public service hours or (4) participate in a conflict resolution with the victim. Conflict resolution is a meeting with the victim where defendants have to show responsibility for their actions and offer compensation. There is no formal trial for a diversion by the prosecution. This does not infringe the constitutional rights of the defendant since the diversion is voluntary; the defendant has the right to demand a criminal trial.[8] After the indictment was submitted, diversion by the court is possible. This is permissible until the end of the trial. In this case, the procedural laws of normal criminal trials apply.[9]

3.5 Personal Participation at Trial

3.5.1 Personal Involvement in the Evidence-Gathering

After the initial pleading of the prosecution, the evidence-gathering begins with the hearing of the accused. They can give a counterstatement to the speech of the prosecutor and show their point of view on the facts of the case. This statement can be used as evidence in favour or to the disadvantage of the defendant (§ 245(1) CCP). Then, the actual evidence-gathering begins. The prosecutor and defendants or their lawyers can make requests for evidence. Such a request can be a motion to take evidence, a request to omit the taking of certain evidence or to take the evidence in a certain order. The other party can counter such a request with a founded objection.[10] A motion to take evidence has to comprise (1) which piece of evidence has to be taken, (2) what it is meant to proof (the topic of the evidence), (3) why the evidence is suitable to proof this and (4) the necessary information for the taking of the evidence (§ 55(1) CCP). The applicant has to clearly define the evidence, e.g. by giving the location of an object or naming the mayor of a certain town as witness. The topic of the evidence is the fact which it is meant to proof, e.g. the witness met the defendant Tuesday evening at a restaurant. Only naming the aim of the evidence, e.g. proofing that the defendant did not commit a murder Tuesday evening at a ware-

---

[8] Schroll in Fuchs and Ratz (2016), § 198 para 9.
[9] Schroll in Fuchs and Ratz (2016), § 199 para 2.
[10] Kirchbacher in Fuchs and Ratz (2009), § 246 para 15 ff.

house, is not sufficient. If it is not obvious, the applicant has to explain why the evidence is suitable to clarify the topic of the evidence and why this is relevant for the judgement, e.g. the testimony of the witness will show that the accused was at the restaurant that evening, was therefore unable to commit the murder, hence he is not guilty. They also have to give the information the court needs to gather the evidence, e.g. if they request the reading out of a document, they have to tell the court where it can be found. If these criteria are not met, the request is no formal motion to take evidence and has to be rejected by the court.[11] A formally correct motion to take evidence can be rejected only if it is impossible due to factual or legal reasons or if the evidence is not suitable to proof a relevant fact. It can also be rejected if its results are already obvious, its topic is already sufficiently proofed or of no relevance to the case (§ 55(2) CCP). The evidence-gathering usually starts with the evidences of the prosecutor (§ 246(1) CCP). The defendant has the right to comment on every evidence taken (§ 245 (1) CCP).

3.5.2   Personal Contribution to the Fact-Finding

Defendants or their lawyers have the right to question witnesses and expert witnesses. The chairman of the court can reject impermissible or inadequate questions. After every testimony of a witness or expert witness, the defendant can give a statement (§ 248(3) CCP). When questioning an expert witness, the defendant can call in an expert to support them. The expert can either ask the expert witness themselves or give advice to the defendant or their lawyer (§ 249(3) CCP). Protocols on the questioning of witnesses can only be read out and videos of their questioning can only be showed in exceptional cases mentioned in the law. This is permissible, if the appearance of the witness in court is impossible due to factual reasons. It is also possible, if witnesses diverge from an earlier testimony or if they refuse to testify without being entitled to do so. It is also permissible if the witness was heard in an adversarial interrogation. If defendant and prosecutor both agree, reading out a testimony is permissible without additional requirements (§ 252(1) CCP). The reading out of protocols is strictly limited as it makes it considerably more difficult to judge the credibility of the witness. It also makes it impossible for the parties to ask questions during the questioning; therefore, it is also limiting the participation rights of the defendant.

3.6   Personal Participation in Higher Instances

The regional court decides on appeals against verdicts of district courts. The court of appeal decides on appeals against judgements of single judges at the regional court. The supreme court decides on pleas of nullity against the conviction or

---

[11] Schmoller in Fuchs and Ratz (2011), § 55.

acquittal by a court with a jury and courts with lay assessors. The court of appeal decides also on appeals against the amount of the sentence imposed by these courts. The appeal of nullity can only be based on certain grounds listed in the law and can challenge fact-finding and evaluation of evidence only when errors are severe and obvious from the files. In proceedings on a plea of nullity, new evidence cannot be presented. To make use of any of these remedies, appellants have to submit a pleading to the court which can be countered by the opposing party. The remedy has to be announced within 3 days of the end of the trial and can be submitted within 4 weeks after they have received the written verdict. (§§ 284(1), 285(1), 294(1) CCP).

In proceedings on a plea of nullity, the first instance court has to examine the remedy with regard to formal requirements. If those are not met, it has to reject the plea of nullity (§ 285a CCP). The appellant can object to this decision at the supreme court (§ 285b CCP). The parties have no right to personal participation in these preliminary proceedings. In certain cases, if the procurator general or the correspondent (one of the judges) proposes, the supreme court can decide in a non-public session. This applies for example if it is clear that the first instance court has to hold a new trial or if the plea concerns formal errors at the trial and the court unanimously decides that those are not given. It also applies, when the supreme court rejects the plea on formal grounds (§ 285d CCP). This often happens, when the court decides that the appellant has not sufficiently elaborated a ground of nullity.[12] Literature often criticises, that the requirements the supreme court sets towards the elaboration of grounds of nullity are too high and that it even rejects unsubstantial pleas by interpreting them as not sufficiently elaborated.[13] The high frequency of such decisions in non-public sessions without participation of the parties erodes the right to personal participation. If the court does not decide in such a non-public session, a public trial has to be held. The defendant has to be informed about the trial and has to be given at least 8 days for preparation but is not obliged to attend it (§ 286 CCP). If the court finds formal errors or insufficient fact finding, a re-trial has to be held at the first instance court. Otherwise, it can decide on the case itself (§ 288 CCP).

Courts deciding on an appeal can only do so in a non-public trial if they have to reject it on formal grounds (§ 294(4) CCP) or, when a regional court decides, if it is obvious that the first instance verdict has to be lifted (§ 470 CCP). Otherwise, a public trial has to be held which follows the rules of first instance trials, if no divergent rules apply (§ 473(1) CCP). The defendants have to be summoned to the trial and has to be given at least 8 days for preparation (§ 294(5) CCP). If they are unable to attend, the trial has to be rescheduled. Unlike at the proceeding at the supreme court, they have an absolute right to attendance. If the court doubts the facts found by the first instance, it can question witnesses or gather new evidence (§ 294(5) CCP).[14] The parties can also take motion to take new evidence under the same

---

[12] Seiler (2016), para 1150.

[13] Bertel and Venier (2012), § 285d para 5; Seiler (2016), para 1150.

[14] Bertel and Venier (2012), § 294 para 8.

conditions as during the first instance trial (§ 467(1) CCP). Witnesses and expert witnesses only have to be heard again if the court doubts the correctness of their testimony or expertise or the conclusions of the first instance based on them (§ 473(2) CCP).[15]

3.7   Special Rules in the Field of Serious Organised Crimes

Austrian criminal procedure does not have special laws to fight serious organised crime. Though, there are some norms which are especially applicable when fighting criminal organisations. Witnesses whose life, physical integrity or freedom would otherwise be threatened, can make an anonymous testimony. The effectivity of this ruling is limited, as the witnesses still have to appear in court and cannot cover their face since facial expressions are important to judge the credibility of a witness (§ 162 CCP). Most of these norms do not have direct impact on personal participation, however. The investigation on criminal organisations allows the use of undercover policemen and optical and acoustical observation (§§ 131(2), 136(1) CCP). It is possible to abstain from the prosecution of key witnesses in cases on organised crime (§ 209a CCP). The possibility to exclude the public from the trial can also become relevant in proceedings on organised crimes.[16]

4   Personal Participation of Private Parties Other Than Defendants (in Particular, the Contribution of the Victim to the Fact-Finding)

§ 65 CCP defines victim as someone whose legally protected interests have been infringed or certain relatives of someone who was killed by an offence. Victims have the right to access records, be informed about their rights and the status of the trial and to be supported by an interpreter. If the prosecution decides to suspend the investigation, they can complain to the court. They can attend the trial and ask questions to the accused, witnesses and expert witnesses. They have the right to get psychological and legal assistance, if necessary (§ 66 CCP). Victims who were violated in their sexual or bodily integrity can be questioned using audio and video transmission. The prosecution and defendants can then ask victims questions without being physically present e.g. by letting a psychologist ask the questions (§ 165 CCP). If they were violated in their sexual sphere they can reject questions they deem unreasonable and have the right to be questioned by a person of their gender (§ 70(2) CCP).

---

[15] Seiler (2016), para 1187.
[16] For this see Sect. 3.1.

If they want to get compensation for their damages caused by the offence, they can join the proceedings as private party concerned. They can make motions to take evidence during the investigation or trial. The court has only to decide on the compensation if this does not require additional evidence-gathering which would slow down the proceedings considerably (§ 366 (2) CCP). If the prosecutor decides to drop the charge during the trial, they can continue it (§ 67 CCP). Certain less serious offences can only be prosecuted if the victims prosecute by themselves, taking the place of the public prosecution (§ 71 CCP).[17]

If someone else than the accused is concerned by confiscation or forfeiture during the investigation proceedings or trial, concerned persons have the same rights as defendants as far as their property rights are concerned (§ 64 CCP). They have to be summoned to the trial, but if they fail to appear, the trial does not have to be rescheduled (§ 444(1) CCP).

5   *In Absentia* Proceedings

5.1   *Information Rights and Conditions of Waiver of Personal Participation in Criminal Proceedings*

In absentia proceedings are only permissible under certain strict criteria if defendants do not appear in court. It is necessary that the summon has been personally delivered to the defendants (§ 427(1) CCP). Deposition at the post office is only sufficient if they are currently present in their hometown and have been informed about it (§§ 17 ZustG). The summon has to contain the offenses defendants are accused of (it can refer to the bill of indictment for this) and has to inform them about the consequences of failing to appear in court.[18] It is only permissible in proceedings on offences which are punishable with no more than 3 years imprisonment. Defendants must have been heard on the accusation in a formal interrogation. An accused who refused to give evidence still counts as heard.[19] If these criteria are met, the judge can decide whether they deem the attendance of the accused necessary to decide on the case or if they want to pass a judgment without their attendance (§ 427(2) CCP). The written verdict has to be delivered to the defendant (§ 427(1) CCP). *In absentia* proceedings are not permissible against offenders under the age of 21 (§§ 32 (1), 46 (2) JGG).

If defendants do not want to attend a trial at the district court, they can send their lawyer as representative. In this case, the lawyer gets the legal position of the defendant during the trial. They can even give evidence instead of the accused. If the

---

[17] This includes offences like libel (§ 115 PC) or violation of the privacy of correspondence (§ 118 PC).

[18] Bauer and Jerabek in Fuchs and Ratz (2009), § 427 para 9.

[19] Seiler (2016), para 823.

judge deems it necessary for the fact finding, they can still summon the defendant. (§ 455 CCP).

5.2   Default Proceedings and Subsequent Remedies (e.g., Retrial or Judicial Review in a Higher Instance)

Defendants can object to the verdict of an *in absentia* trial within 2 weeks of personal service.[20] The objection has to be allowed if defendants were deterred from attending the trial by an unavoidable hindrance (§ 427(3) CCP). A hindrance is unavoidable if it would have deterred a diligent person in the situation of the defendant from attending the trial. This includes accidents or sickness of defendants.[21] They have to proof the hindrance. District courts can decide on objections against their verdicts on their own after hearing the defendant. If the court rejects the objection, they can appeal to the regional court (§ 478 CCP). The court of appeal decides on objections against verdicts of regional courts in non-public hearings without personal participation of the defendant (§ 427(3) CCP). They can also submit an appeal or plea of nullity against the verdict. It can be used as ground of nullity or appeal if one of the requirements of an *in absentia* judgment is not fulfilled (§ 427 CCP). These two remedies can also be combined. If the objection is allowed, a retrial in the first instance will take place (§ 427(3) CCP).

5.3   Inaudito Reo Proceedings (e.g., Penal Order Procedure)

The court can allow a request by the prosecution for a penal order procedure only in proceedings on offences which are punishable with no more than 3 years imprisonment. Defendants must have been heard on the accusation in a formal interrogation. They must have been informed about the consequences and explicitly waived the trial. The results of the investigation and hearing have to be sufficient to decide on the guilt and punishment of the offender and the interests of the victim may not be neglected. The penal order procedure is not applicable if the requirements of diversion are met (§ 491(1) CCP).[22] The punishment can only be a fine or, as far as the defendant is represented by a lawyer, a suspended prison sentence of no more than 1 year (§ 491(2) CCP). Penal orders are not allowable against offenders under the age of 21 (§§ 32 (1), 46 (2) JGG). The defendant, their lawyer, the victim and the prosecution have to receive the order. They can object to it within 4 weeks of receiving it without the need for certain grounds. It can only be rejected if it was submitted

---

[20] See Austrian supreme court judgement of 10. May 2015, No. 14Os37/05f.

[21] Bauer and Jerabek in Fuchs and Ratz (2009), § 427 para 19.

[22] For diversion see Sect. 3.4.

too late or by someone who is not entitled to it. The appellant can appeal against this decision to a higher instance. A successful objection leads to a normal trial (§ 491 CCP). If only the accused objected to the order, their punishment cannot be increased in the subsequent trial (§ 16 CCP). If no objection is submitted, the penal order becomes a final verdict.

6 Participatory Rights in Transnational Criminal Justice

6.1 Participatory Safeguards in EAW Proceedings

6.1.1 Participatory Rights in the Decision on Surrender

The surrender proceeding is initiated by the prosecution. As soon as concerned persons are arrested, they have to be informed about the content of the EAW, about their right to a translation of the EAW and to be represented by a lawyer. They also have to be informed about the possibility to agree to a simplified proceeding at the earliest in the first hearing on the continuation of the custody after consulting a lawyer (§ 16a EU-JZG). The single judge at the regional court has to decide on the EAW (§§ 13 EU-JZG, 26 ARHG). They have to examine the requirements for surrender based on the content of the EAW. They only have to investigate if the suspicion in the EAW is sufficient, if they have serious doubts about it or evidence which refutes the suspicion without delay is accessible (§ 19(1) EU-JZG). The judge has to hear the concerned person on the EAW and inform them about the accusation. If they or the prosecution request it or the judge deems it necessary, a public trial has to be held (§ 31(2) ARHG). Despite such a request, the judge can reject the EAW without public trial. The concerned person has to be represented by a lawyer (§ 61(1) CCP). They have to be given at least 8 days for preparation. If they are unable to attend the trial due to health reasons, they can by connected by video conference.[23] The procedure of normal criminal trials applies, if there are no special laws (§§ 1(2) ARHG, 9 (1) EU-JZG). The judge has to sum up the content of the files and proceeding to date and the prosecutor can give a statement. Concerned persons have the right to comment on the statement of the prosecutor and the EAW and have the right to the last word. The decision has to be made within 30 days of the arrest of the concerned person (§ 21 EU-JZG). If concerned persons or the prosecution announce a remedy within 3 days of the trial, they can object to the court of appeal within 2 weeks of receiving the written decision. The court of appeal has to decide in a public trial within 60 days of the arrest of the concerned person (§ 31 ARHG). If concerned persons agree and the requirements for surrender are met, the court can immediately allow it. Concerned persons or the prosecution can object to this decision within 3 days in which case the court of appeal has to decide (§ 20 EU-JZG).

---

[23] Hinterhofer and Schallmoser in Höpfel and Ratz (2015), WK EU-JZG § 21 para 16 ff.

6.1.2   *In Absentia* Proceedings in the Trial Country and Its Relevance in the Surrender Procedure

Surrender of the concerned person for the execution of a prison sentence or imprisonment as a preventive measure imposed in an *in absentia* proceeding is only permissible if the EAW shows that certain criteria are met (§ 11 EU-JZG). Austrian law recognizes four different cases in which these criteria are met. It is permissible if concerned persons became aware of the time and place of the trial in due course by summon or in another way and were informed that a verdict can be passed in their absence (§ 11(1)1 EU-JZG). The surrender is also possible if, with knowledge of the scheduled trial, they entrusted a freely chosen or by the court assigned lawyer with their representation at the trial and the lawyer actually represented them at the trial (§ 11(1)2 EU-JZG). It is also permissible if they received the verdict and were informed about their right to a retrial or a remedy which leads to a new examination of the facts in their presence, including the consideration of new evidence. They also have to either have waived this right or not to have it executed in time (§ 11(1)3 EU-JZG). It is also sufficient if the state they are surrendered to guarantees that they will receive the verdict without delay after the surrender together with information on the aforementioned rights (§ 11(1)4 EU-JZG).

6.2   *Participatory Safeguards in Transborder Inquiries and the Taking of Overseas Evidence*

The Austrian prosecution is responsible for the execution of requests for judicial assistance, for which it can utilize the criminal police (§ 50(1) ARHG). They have to follow Austrian criminal procedural law. If it demands methods which are foreign to Austrian procedural law they still can be applied if they do not violate the principles of Austrian criminal law (§ 58 ARHG). Parties of foreign proceedings have the right to participate in the execution of the request if this is necessary for the proper execution. This would be the case in an adversarial interrogation. They may not be prosecuted or imprisoned for actions previously committed to their entry in Austria (§ 59 ARHG). Therefore, foreign private parties have the same participation rights Austrian parties would have in the same proceedings. Foreign summons can only be delivered to people in Austria if they are guaranteed not to be imprisoned for actions they committed before leaving Austria, except if they are summoned as defendants. They have to contain the information that Austrian authorities will not enforce the summon (§ 53 ARHG). Concerning participation rights, there are no differences between requests of EU members and non-members (§ 55 EU-JZG). The decision on requests for confiscation by EU members is made by a single judge within 24 h, without personal participation of private parties (§ 46 EU-JZG).

Foreign authorities taking evidence for Austrian authorities are applying their own procedural law. Therefore, the right to personal participation in these proceedings depends on foreign law. If the principles of a fair trial are violated by these proceedings, this could be used as ground of nullity (§ 281(1)4 CCP).

7 Requirements of Personal Participation and *in Absentia* Proceedings. The Perspective of Supranational and International Human Rights Law

7.1 The Perspective of International Human Rights Law. Critical Remarks on Domestic Law in the Light of the European Convention

§ 11(1)4 EU-JZG could infringe article 6(3)a ECHR. Regarding the EAW, the state which convicted the accused only has to guarantee that they will receive the *in absentia* verdict and that they will be informed about their right to a retrial or judicial review. As a result, Austria always has to surrender defendants who have not yet received their verdict. According to 6(3)a ECHR, defendants have the right to be informed promptly on the accusation against them. Therefore, *in absentia* judgements should be only executable if the issuing state proves that the defendants had knowledge about the trial.[24] It would be preferable, if the norm was changed in a way that defendants have to receive the verdict and get the opportunity to request a retrial or judicial review before being surrendered.[25]

7.2 The Perspective of EU Law. Developments in Domestic Law as a Result of EU Law

Directive 2013/48/EU on the right to access a lawyer made some changes in Austrian criminal procedure law necessary. It is no more permissible to monitor the contact between defendants and their lawyers (§ 59(2) CCP). Defence lawyers can now give statements after thematically coherent sections during interrogation (§ 164(2) CCP).

Directive 2012/13/EU on the right to information in criminal proceedings only led to minor changes. § 50 CCP now specifies that the information has to be given in a language and way the defendant understands. It also makes clear, that defendants have to be informed when the investigation indicates that they have committed a different or an additional offence.

Directive 2014/42/EU on the freezing and confiscation of instrumentalities and proceeds of crime led to changes in the proceedings on confiscation. It is now

---

[24] ECtHR, *Sejdovic v. Italy*, judgement of 10 November 2004, Appl. No. 56581/00.
[25] Hinterhofer and Schallmoser in Eilmansberger and Herzig (2010), p. 365.

possible to confiscate objects which were used to commit a crime in a trial without attendance of the accused if they cannot attend due to illness or being fugitive, have been heard on the accusation and requirements for confiscation and a confiscation seems highly likely in case of a conviction (§ 445(1) CCP). Since this does not only include particularly dangerous objects, but everything used for the crime (e.g. the getaway car), it is considered a punishment.[26] That a conviction is more or less presumed could be problematic with regards to the presumption of innocence.[27]

8 Concluding Remarks

The comprehensive rights to personal participation in Austrian criminal procedure fulfil international human rights standards. *In absentia* proceedings are only allowable in certain proceedings on offences which are punishable with no more than 3 years imprisonment and only if strict criteria are met. In EAW and surrender proceedings the accused has the right to be heard in a public trial. Penal order proceedings are only allowable if they have been interrogated and have explicitly waived the trial. The proceedings on surrender based on *in absentia* verdicts possibly require some minor changes to fulfil ECHR requirements. Relevant European directives made only minor changes in domestic law necessary.

References

Bertel C, Venier A (2012) Kommentar zur StPO. Jan Sramek Verlag, Vienna
Fuchs H, Ratz E (2009–2016) Wiener Kommentar zur Strafprozessordnung. Manz, Vienna
Hinterhofer H, Schallmoser N (2010) Europäisches Strafrecht. In: Eilmansberger T, Herzig G (eds) Europarecht. NWV, Vienna
Höpfel F, Ratz E (2012–2015) Wiener Kommentar zum Strafgesetzbuch. Manz, Vienna
Seiler S (2016) Strafprozessrecht, 15th edn. Facultas, Vienna
Wirth B, Schallmoser N, Hinterhofer H (2015) Europäisches Strafrecht. In: Herzig G (ed) Europarecht. NWV, Vienna

---

[26] Fuchs and Tipold in Höpfel and Ratz (2012), § 19a para 17.

[27] Wirth et al. in Herzig (2015), p. 376 on Directive 2014/42/EU; different the explanations in the draft of the government (RV 689 BlgNR XXV. GP, 52).

Report on Bulgaria

Aneta Petrova

Abstract In this chapter, I will first discuss the Bulgarian criminal justice system and provide an introductive assessment of the third CCP (The last revision was completed in 2005, Penal Procedure Code of the Republic of Bulgaria 2005, State newspaper 86/28.10.2005. It is subject to legislative amendments (most recently in 2014)) and then explore to what extent a defendant's absence can affect the procedural integrity. In order to fully understand *in absentia* judgements in Bulgaria, it is necessary to briefly explain the jurisdiction status.

This chapter considers an aspect of personal participation in criminal proceedings—*in absentia* judgments in Bulgaria—and analyses under which circumstances defendants are prosecuted and convicted without any—or insufficient—regard to article 55 CCP.

A complete enquiry on personal participation in criminal proceedings would also require a detailed analysis of extraterritorial prescriptive, enforcement and adjudicative jurisdiction. In this chapter, however, I will only examine the applications of personal participation in criminal proceedings in Bulgaria.

Abbreviations

CCP   Code of Criminal Procedure of the Republic of Bulgaria
EAW   European Arrest Warrant
ECHR   European Convention for Human Rights
ECtHR   European Court of Human Rights

A. Petrova (✉)
Bleiwäsche, Germany

© Springer Nature Switzerland AG 2019
S. Quattrocolo, S. Ruggeri (eds.), *Personal Participation in Criminal Proceedings*, Legal Studies in International, European and Comparative Criminal Law 2, https://doi.org/10.1007/978-3-030-01186-4_3

1   Constitutional Requirements of the Involvement of Private Parties in Criminal Justice

The constitutional design of the Bulgarian criminal justice system provides the overall context of this topic. It can be seen as "the door" into Bulgarian justice, allowing to study the requirements and implications of the criminal procedure by default. Nevertheless, I assume that it is necessary to move beyond the term "criminal procedure by default", as it does not fully exhaust the array of possible theoretical frameworks concerning the *in absentia* proceedings.

The 1991 Constitution of the Republic of Bulgaria did not address directly the issue of the involvement of private parties in criminal justice. Nowhere does it mention private parties or involvement in criminal justice. The Bulgarian pays little attention to the role of private parties, despite the fact that it is now widely accepted that they play a crucial role in modern criminal proceedings.[1] Nevertheless, the constitutional right of a private party to involve in criminal proceeding has been described as a right of defense. Article 122(1) of the Constitution of the Republic of Bulgaria provides that individuals and legal entities have the right of defense in every procedural stage. In other words, not only the defendants, but all individuals, including the victims are entitled to the protection of the Constitution of the Republic of Bulgaria.

The right of defence is a possibility for actively participating in criminal proceedings and this is known as "dispositive".[2] There is an opinion of the Appellate Courts suggesting that the right of defence is mandatory.[3] That would mean that the principle of self-incrimination would be abolished.[4] Nevertheless, the right of defence is being defined by numerous court decisions specifying which guarantees must be granted to citizens.[5] As Radka Radeva stated, there has been a reciprocal relationship between defendant's rights and obligations of the investigative bodies, prosecutors, and judges. For example, the subpoena stems from the defendant's right to participate at any stage of the criminal proceedings.[6]

---

[1] See about the role of the victim in criminal proceedings Radeva (1971), p. 6; Bednarova (2011).

[2] Pavlov (1986), pp. 14, 24, 34; Radeva (1985), p. 7; Trendafilova (2000), p. 251.

[3] Decision 1088-1959-II.

[4] Radeva (1985), p. 32.

[5] There are many cases involving *in absentia* issue has arisen both in the Bulgarian Supreme Court and in the district courts. See for example: Decision 299-1975-I; Decision 83-1977-I; Decision 305-1977-II; Decision 320-1977-II; Decision 328-1978-II; Decision 582-1978-II; Decision 576-1980-I; Decision 243-1982-II; Decision 551-1982-II; Decision 357-1984-II; Decision 358-1984-II; Decision 51-1985-II; Decision 61-1985-II; Decision 442-1985-I; Decision 361-1986-II; Decision 172-1987-II; Decision 406-1988-I; Decision 226-1990-II; Decision 836-1990-I; Decision 230-1991-I; Decision 460-1991-I; Decision 145-1992-II; Decision 30-1992-II; Decision 474-1992-I; Decision 747-1992-I; Decision 537-1993-II; Decision 624a-1993-I; Decision 72-1994-I; Decision 110-2000-II; Decision 32-2003-III; Decision 205-2003-II.

[6] Another example concerns the confession. See Radeva (1985), p. 24.

It is fitting for an essay regarding the criminal default under the Criminal Procedure Code of the Republic of Bulgaria (CCP) to briefly discuss the structure of the Bulgarian criminal justice system. Bulgaria has three different court systems: judicial courts, which deal with law violations within two trial instances (Courts of first instance, which operate at two levels: District Courts and Appellate Courts, Courts of second instance and one review instance, the Supreme Court of Cassation); a Specialized Criminal Court, which deals with serious organised crimes, and six military courts.

The CCP covers a wide range of topics within the Bulgarian jurisdiction. It concerns, for example, the functional jurisdiction, the chronology of the process, and so forth.

Nevertheless, to gain a comparative knowledge of personal participation in criminal proceedings, I must use the sequence of procedural steps followed in the ordinary criminal trial, and appreciate the procedural framework from the defendant's point of view involved in criminal proceedings.[7]

The Bulgarian criminal justice system has enshrined overwhelmingly the inquisitorial model in pre-trial investigation.[8] The pre-trial proceedings are conducted by an investigating magistrate (следовател) or investigating police officers (разследващ полицаи), art. 52 CCP. They order searches, seizures, and so forth; they interrogate the defendant.[9] The office of the examining magistrate was reduced; an investigating magistrate carries out investigations only for the most serious crimes, e.g., arts. 95–110, arts. 357–360, and arts. 407–419a Criminal Code.[10] The role of the prosecutor at the pre-stage is to ensure that the procedural actions are conducted legally. As a matter of fact, the conduct in the proceeding is subject to elements and institutes regarding hearsay, admissions of a party-opponent, allocating the burdens of proof, and so forth. These rules promote the objectives set forward by the principle of adversariality (Art. 121(1) of the Constitution of the Republic of Bulgaria, art. 12 CCP), immediacy (art. 18 CCP), orality (art. 19 CCP), and publicity of hearings (art. 20 CCP). The CCP follows the doctrine of objective truth (art. 13 CCP). Nevertheless, the court fulfills two purposes: one the one hand, the judge should know the law, and on the other hand, he helps to search the objective truth, e.g., the facts (arts. 277(4), 280(2), 28(2), 285 CCP). For example, he prevents a subject from wrongfully filing a claim. The process ought to be guided by the judge as he is the major subject of the process.[11] Articles 276, 286 CCP provide a guidance as a rational methodology which concerns the procedural activity.

The Bulgarian criminal justice system was modernized during the last two decades. Three influences became visible: the first relies on the functional legitimacy,

---

[7] About the personal participation at any stage of the criminal proceedings see Pavlov (1986), p. 93.

[8] Trendafilova (1999), p. 132.

[9] See about the statutory amendments and doctrinal evaluation in the investigative phase of the criminal proceedings in comparative context Trendafilova (2000), p. 17; Trendafilova (1999), p. 132.

[10] Art. 194 CCP.

[11] Petrova (2005), p. 138. See also Decision 92-2002-I.

the second and third on the European institutional influence (ECHR and EU-influence).[12] This subsection addresses the first of these influences.

The most important influence on the contemporary Bulgarian criminal justice system has been the expansion of the adversariality.[13] The criminal justice norms, which are arising from the process of the liberation and democratization, are arts. 7(1), 12, 20 CCP.[14] My starting point will be article 7(1) CCP: "The heart of the Bulgarian criminal justice system is the trial process." The procedural rules include the principle of adversariality, art. 12(2) CCP.

The following two influences on contemporary Bulgarian criminal justice reflect the institutional developments in Europe. They refer to the interaction between the Bulgarian criminal justice system and the ECMR, European Criminal Law,[15] and ought to comply with the requirements and structure of Bulgarian's criminal procedure theory.[16]

The concept of involvement plays a central role in Bulgarian criminal procedure. Following more than a hundred years of discussions, the "disk"-concept of involvement has achieved acceptability.[17] Scholars distinguish three disks of involvement in the Bulgarian criminal justice system: participants in criminal proceedings (участници в наказателното производство), subjects (субекти), and parties (страни).[18] The biggest disk entails the participants in criminal proceedings, the middle the subjects, and the little the parties. These functions come from concrete procedural figures.[19] They are useful to distinguish certain procedural roles.[20] For example, as far as criminal procedural parties are concerned, the following options are possible:

1. Parties to the court proceedings are: the prosecutor; the defendant and the defence counsel; the private complainant and private prosecutor; the civil claimant and civil respondent who, under art. 253 CCP, fulfill prosecution, and defence function.
2. Subjects are the parties and the trial, they fulfill all three functions.
3. The witnesses, expert witness, translator or interpreter parents or guardians of the underage accused party, in trial of young offenders: a pedagogue or psychologists

---

[12] Trendafilova (2000), p. 9.

[13] Vogler (2008), pp. 1 ff.; Pavlov (1966), p. 16; Trendafilova (1999), at 139; Trendafilova (2000), pp. 56, 239.

[14] For a discussion of the evidence law and exclusionary rules see Turner (2014), p. 821.

[15] See Section F concerning the requirements of personal participation and *in absentia* proceedings from of supranational and international human rights law perspective.

[16] Trendafilova (2000), p. 8.

[17] See interpretative decision 2-2002-Criminal Senats' Meeting, Supreme Court of Cassation.

[18] See Court Proceedings Act, State newspaper 77/07.04.1897, art. 367.

[19] Pavlov (1986), p. 32.

[20] Radeva (1971), p. 24.

are participants in the criminal proceedings. These individuals take part in the procedure; they should not fulfill other tasks.[21]

Having explained the structure of the Bulgarian criminal justice system, I will now analyse three issues in the relationship with personal participation in criminal proceeding: first, whether the defendant should assist to the proceedings; second, which consequences are triggered by the defendant's default; and third, which procedural guarantees are provided.[22] The main participatory guarantees are articulated in the CCP.

The first question is, should the defendant assist to the proceedings. As I mentioned, the defendant has no obligation to take an active role in the criminal proceedings. That is does not mean that his participation at the pre-trial stage is not necessary in exercising of concrete procedural actions such as the involving of defendant, for example. According to art. Art 219(4) CCP "The body of investigation shall submit the decree of involving to the defendant and to his/her defender, and shall give them opportunity to become acquainted with the complete contents of it, and in case of necessity shall give additional clarifications."

At the pre-trial stage the CCP failed to recognize that gravity requirements outlined in Art. 269(3). Here it does not play a role.[23] The rationale is that the pre-trial stage plays a preparatory role in the proceedings, art. 7(2) CCP.[24] It should be met rational legitimacy through communicating to the defendant. In contrary, at the trial stage the defendant may not participate at hearing except in "cases of indictment in a grave crime".[25] The trial stage performs and embodies the adversariality. This is based on functionalism and therefore on allocation between prosecuting, defending, and adjudicating.[26]

Secondly, the default of the defendant brings either to in absentia proceedings or to the suspension of criminal proceedings.[27] The relationship between the public safety by investigating crimes in absentia and the rights of the defendants is shaped by choices made by the prosecutor.

Thirdly, the proceedings may be suspended when "trying the case in the absence of the trial defendant would prevent discovering the objective truth," art. 25(2) CCP. This requirement ought to give the necessary guarantees for a fair trial.[28]

---

[21] For a similar distinction, see Pavlov (1996), pp. 5, 48, 149, 254.

[22] Pavlov (1986), p. 16.

[23] Compare with the trial stage in Decision 61-1992-Military Court.

[24] Saranov (1937), II, p. 476; Trendafilova (1999), p. 131; Trendafilova (2000), p. 14.

[25] Art. 269(1) CCP.

[26] Pavlov (1966), p. 7.

[27] Arts. 269(3), 25(2) CCP 1999.

[28] See Section F point I concerning other guarantees such as mandatory council, art. 94(1)(8) CCP; *Inaudito reo* proceedings, art. 423 CCP, and so forth.

2 Personal Participation of Private Parties and Legal Assistance

This section seeks to examine the participation of private parties and legal assistance in criminal proceedings. The substantial claim is that in absentia judgments can be exploited by a normative theory only if personal participation is supported by an acceptable normative foundation. Considering the issue of in absentia proceedings[29] and the possibility of judicial review[30] can be considered as the framework which legitimates these proceedings and explains why the normative account is necessary in providing concrete implications.[31] The personal participation of private parties and legal assistance are fundamental principles in contemporary criminal justice studies.

The private parties can be present; their participation must never be mandatory.[32] Clearly, if they are called into a proceeding, the principle of personal participation is limited to those cases in which they participate.[33] In other words, articles 74, 75 CCP refer to a party which has made requests for participating in the procedure or has otherwise developed a sufficient connection with the proceeding (for example, as a subject of a criminal proceedings or as witness) to be considered part of that process.[34]

Under Bulgarian criminal procedural law, a victim does not become a party until his constitution. The mandatory regulation of his participation has two implications, depending upon the type of crime. Thus, the chronology of the process relies on a substantive law's distinction between misdemeanour and felony.

The victim of a crime may be involved in a prosecution under the following alternatives: the first one occurs in proceedings "in publicly actionable criminal cases" (дела от общ характер), and the second one in proceedings "in privately actionable cases" (дела от частен характер).[35] Firstly, if they are constituted as private prosecutors, they "may continue the charges also after the prosecutor has made a statement that he/she will not maintain any further".[36] Secondly, the victim of ordinary crimes may bring charges and prosecution before court as a private prosecutor and file, during the proceedings, a civil claim for compensation of the damages and therefore the person has made requests for participating in the procedure as civil claimant. The same rules are applicable to crimes prosecuted on the grounds of complaints by the victim. The different circumstances are set out in the

---

[29] Arts. 206, 269 CCP.

[30] Art. 423 CCP.

[31] See decision 11.03.2014г./II, Court of Appeals, Pleven.

[32] Petrova (2005), p. 163.

[33] Radeva (1971), p. 16.

[34] Radeva (1971), p. 18.

[35] Compare with art. 103 CCP.

[36] Art. 78(2) CCP.

Special Part of the Criminal Code.[37] In this situation the ex officio principle is not relevant. Since the private prosecutors are directly concerned with their individual interests,[38] no authority (pre-trial investigation bodies or public prosecutors) can engage in privately actionable cases. Thus, there is no pre-trial stage,[39] i.e., the situations are referred direct to the trial. The private prosecutor is bound only to make the facts public.[40]

Thirdly, the victim can be constituted as a civil claimant; this constitution would implicate to fulfil another function which is complementary: Civil action by the civil claimants.[41] Both procedural roles are compatible because they are based on different claims: criminal and/or civil.

The CCP does not explicitly use the term "private parties". It is a result of doctrinal analysis. Let us briefly characterize each of these private parties as they are defined by scholars.[42] First, a lawsuit may involve dispute resolution of criminal law issues not only between individuals and prosecutors, but also legal persons such as business entities or non-profit organizations (e.g., corporate, state interests could be involved). The legal person may only bring a civil action.[43] Thus, it may file requests to be constituted as a civil claimant, art. 255(2) CCP.

In addition, the obligation for the victims of a crime to explain their procedural rights is of general nature, art. 73(1) CCP. The absence of private complainant precludes the possibility to prosecute criminal conduct.[44] In privately actionable cases the attendance of defendants is not mandatory.[45]

The second important issue concerns legal assistance in criminal proceedings. The right to legal assistance is embodied in constitutional provisions. Pursuant to Article 30(4) of the Constitution of the Republic of Bulgaria, anyone who is arrested or accused has a right to access a lawyer in criminal proceedings. Article 97(1) CCP, however, also provides that the defence counsel may join criminal proceedings from the moment an individual is detained or has been called as a defendant.[46] The right to legal assistance is considered fundamental in view of the attendance of defendants in criminal proceedings, i.e., the right of defence applies equally to all defendants.[47] In the procedural context this applies regardless of the defendant wishes to

---

[37] Arts. 161, 175, 193a, 218c Criminal Code.

[38] Pavlov (1986), p. 17.

[39] Art. 84(1) CCP.

[40] Decision 472-2001-II.

[41] Art. 84(1) CCP.

[42] Petrova (2005), pp. 130, 162, 169.

[43] Radeva (1971), p. 4. Decision 820-1997-II.

[44] Radeva (1971), pp. 2, 7, 18; Pavlov (1996), II, p. 116; Decision 621-2002-III.

[45] Decision 136-1993-II.

[46] Pavlov (1986), p. 163.

[47] Pavlov (1986), p. 153; Pavlov (1996), p. 124; Decision 8-1972-I. Decision 481-1981-II; Decision 319-1983-II; Decision 280-1984-I.

authorize a defence counsel or not.[48] The lawyer's defence concerns the question what its terms should be. If the doctrine presents the distinction between adjudication (guidance and disposal), prosecution, and defence as essential,[49] then a reasonable explanation of the modern Bulgarian lawyer's function must identify an efficiency principle.

The right of the accused should be exercised effectively. As a matter of fact, scholars and practice seek to unify diverse considerations under the principle of efficiency by emphasizing how different guarantees are required to justify procedural structures.

The Courts adopts a mandatory rule which requires an effective legal assistance at the beginning of the criminal procedure.[50] This guarantee is designed to maximize compliance with the rules governing arrest. The case law developed criteria to guide how the obligations should provide the "necessary" "необходимата" and "really" "действителна" defence.[51] Thus, the legal standards rely on article 55(1) CCP: The defendant shall have "a defence counsel. The defendant shall have the right for his/her defence counsel to take part when investigative actions are taken, as well as in other procedural actions requiring the attendance thereof, unless he has expressively waved this particular right." This general rule can be assessed by reference to concrete procedural actions (процесуални действия). For example, art. 219(4) CCP requires that "the investigative body shall present the citation decree to the defendant and his/her defence counsel, allowing them to gain knowledge of its full content and, where needed, giving additional explanations. The investigative body shall serve against a signature a copy of the decree on the defendant."

The purpose of legal assistance is determined by its applications. The specific rule is well stated in art. 99(1) CCP, as follows: "The defence counsel shall have the right to take part in all investigative actions involving the defendant, his failure to appear not being an obstacle to their progress," i.e., not all the procedural actions need to be communicated by the legal assistance.

In other words, legal assistance is an unavoidable corollary of the prosecution and court to enforce criminal law. Defendants in absentia proceedings, i.e., who are not present in court, are individuals who are entitled to the same constitutional and procedural protection.[52]

---

[48] See the hypothesis in art. CCP "Mandatory participation of defense counsel".

[49] Pavlov (1986), p. 25; Pavlov (1966), pp. 14, 149, 154, 181; Zonkov (1994), p. 92.

[50] Decision 120-2001-II.

[51] Decision 1122-1958-II.

[52] Trendafilova (1992), p. 165.

3 Personal Participation of the Accused in Criminal Proceedings

3.1 General Features of Personal Participation: Absolute Individual Right or Duty of Diligence?

The personal participation in criminal proceedings belongs to the general topics of legal and judicial reasoning. It optimizes the ordinary process of reasoning. For example, the participation of the defendant may be a good reason for making a confession, or the attendance of the witness may help for assessing a credibility of another testimony.

An individual in criminal proceedings is a subject. This claim brings to concrete conclusions. First, the defendant is subject to the right of defence.[53] Second, he is subject to formally established procedural codes of conduct. There is a necessity both for objectivity and protection of individual rights.[54]

This consideration may be influenced by two questions: why is the government justified in exercising coercion to guarantee the defendants' attendance at the pre-trial stage and why do judges decide cases in absentia. The first response is an accurate description and a successful enforcement in providing an account of a basis for predictions (e.g., Legal decisions in general),[55] enforcement, and judicial overview (i.e., Case outcomes in particular), i.e., CCP stipulates oversight in this context. To prove whether a detention is reasonable, the courts examine during a hearing the circumstances to dispose a remand in custody as part of an ongoing investigation. Article 65(3) CCP prescribes that "The hearing of the case shall be scheduled within 3 days after the file has been received by the court on the occasion of a public court hearing attended by the prosecutor, the defendant and his/her defence counsel. The case shall be heard in the absence of the defendant when he/she does not wish to appear, having made a statement to this effect, or his/her participation is impracticable due to his/her health condition."

Furthermore, an explanation of procedural activity might be given in terms of adjudicative legitimacy, e.g., explaining how a case outcome is based on the relationships between the parties, and on the interactions between specific variables such as probative value, beyond reasonable doubt, and so forth. In other words, procedural participation may be described as a communicative process. The exchange of information among parties can increase awareness about the universal values such as legality, participation, accountability, and fundamental human rights.

The role of personal participation of the defendant in criminal proceedings is a study concerning both absolute individual right. On one hand, the rationale for in absentia proceedings is that an effective justice must be delivered for the majority's

---

[53] Radeva (1985), p. 29; Trendafilova (1995), p. 14.

[54] Pavlov (1986), p. 17.

[55] E.g. art. 63 CCP.

interest.[56] On the other hand, the right to take part in criminal proceedings according to article 55(1) CCP must be considered, i.e., the rights of the defendant should be protected.[57] The system ought to guarantee equality of "citizens who take part in criminal proceedings" before the law, art. 11(1) CCP. For example, art. 254(4) CCP requires the judge-rapporteur to inform the defendant of the charges' nature.

Because of his absence the defendant cannot exercise his rights. Art. 94(1)(8) CCP provides mandatory participation of the defence counsel.[58] The defence in absentia proceedings operates alone. Prosecutors and defence counsels make the case without the defendant's participation. In practice, however, the accused does not have a right to make a request to answer to interrogatories, a request for production of documents, a request for admissions and depositions, and so on. The defendant does not transfer any rights to their lawyer. For example, the defendant has the right to be represented by counsel, in procedure by default the prosecutor and judge should conduct the procedure with participation of the counsel, art. 94(1)(8) CCP. The right to be represented by counsel could be seen as a procedural guarantee which is apart from the CCP normative construct.[59] The Court held that in privately actionable cases the counsel may not represent the defendant.[60] The mandatory participation of defence counsel indicates that this guarantee should apply both in in absentia proceedings and in proceeding in publicly actionable criminal case.

The law evidence scholarship and theory as well as in absentia proceedings are permanently misconceived by the Bulgarian courts.[61] For example, art. 281(1)(5) CCP provides that "depositions of witnesses which were stated in the same case at the pre-trial phase before a judge or before another court panel, shall be read out where the witness fails to appear, and the parties agree with that." The court found that the agreement by defence counsel is identical with this one by the defendant.[62] The argument is based on two different assumptions—that the defence counsel acts as a representative and as a party.[63] This is a mistaken judgment and I criticize this practice. The extension of the institute "Reading out depositions of witnesses"[64] is inappropriate because of the violation of procedural rights of the defendant in terms of art. 348(3)(1) CCP and art. 6(3)(c) ECHR. Indeed, this decision can explain why the case practice falls short of providing a concrete relationship between guarantees and coercive measures, e.g., art. 5 and 6 ECHR.[65]

---

[56] Pavlov (1986), p. 61.

[57] Pavlov (1986), p. 17; Radeva (1985), p. 23.

[58] Decision 729-1998-II; interpretative decision 48-1987-Criminal Senats' Meeting, Supreme Court of Cassation.

[59] See decision № 105/10.10.2012г., Court of Appeals, Sliven.

[60] Decision 136-1993-III.

[61] Decision 723-2004-I; Decision 172-2007-III; Decision 258-2010-III; Decision 156-2012-I; Decision 181-2013-I; Decision 169-2015-III.

[62] See decision № 371/22.06.2012, District Court, Razgrad.

[63] Pavlov (1986), p. 38.

[64] Art. 281 CCP.

[65] ECtHR, *Stoichkov v. Bulgaria*, judgment of 24 March 2005, Appl. No. 9808/02.

It is then safe to say that the right to be present at court, although important, is not fundamental.[66] Article 269(3) CCP provides some guidance on the question whether the balancing between defendant's personal rights and effective justice justifies in absentia proceedings.[67] In case 1512/2011, for example, the court concluded that the case could not be tried in absentia because the requirement of Article 269(3) CCP and therefore the case is tried in violation of the participatory guarantees.[68]

How should the Bulgarian criminal justice system and its legal framework manage the tension between the parties' rights? Is the Bulgarian criminal procedure law applied equally and fairly to all participants? To what extent, if any, is personal participation inconsistent with the defendants and other participants' rights in criminal proceedings? I am looking for the institute or institutes which can compensate the failure of exercising personal rights.

The question, therefore, is: What happens when a defendant's absence from a court proceeding influences the gravity of the conduct and circumstances concerning the finding of an objective truth.[69] Defendants should attend and appear in a criminal proceeding. But he may change his address in other country different from the forum's one over time, e.g., he may live outside the forum state's borders. In the case of criminal default, his depositions "given in the same case at the pre-trial proceedings before a judge or before another court panel, shall be read out."[70]

In a doctrinal discussion, it is important not only to observe, but also to prevent these situations because this legislative solution does not alter the significance of securing attendance of defendants in criminal proceedings. For these cases, the CCP provides coercive measures. The following section looks at the discussions on issues related to personal participation in the pre-trial inquiry.

3.2 Personal Participation in the Pre-trial Inquiry with Particular Regard to the Interim Decisions on Coercive Measures

This section provides an overview of the defendant's obligations in a criminal investigation. It relies on the defendant's procedural position, and especially his participation in criminal proceedings, as well as on the criminal proceedings' character as a public organized activity.[71] The notes explain how the coercive measures impact the personal participation in a criminal investigation.

---

[66] Pavlov (1986), II, p. 239. 607/22.12.2008.

[67] See decision 275/11.05.2016, District Court, Sofia.

[68] Decision 1512-2011-III; 646-2008-I.

[69] See arts. 25(2), 269 (3) CCP.

[70] See art. 279(1)(2) CCP.

[71] Pavlov (1996), I, p. 32; Petrova (2005), p. 8.

The Constitution of the Republic of Bulgaria guarantees the right to respect of private life. Article 30(1) of the Constitution of the Republic of Bulgaria provides that everyone is entitled to personal freedom and inviolability.[72] A most fundamental part of this idea involves going back to the analysis of the measures and evidence in general.

In order to understand the debate surrounding the personal participation in the pre-trial inquiry, it is important to understand the context of the arts. 206, and 269 CCP.[73]

The pre-trial stage is aimed at gathering the evidence for the accusation before the trial. The CCP is the source imposing coercive measures which should guarantee the defendant's attendance during a criminal investigation, arts. 66(1), 71(2) CCP. The mandatory participation at the pre-trial stage justifies the exercise of state coercion.[74]

Article 56(2) CCP provides: "Where charges are pressed in pursuance of Article 269, para 3, items 2 and 3, a restraining measure shall be imposed once the accused party is found."

The restraining measure is measures of procedural coercion.[75] The right not to be coerced into participation in the pre-trial stage does not exist.[76] The defendant is "sought" to participate in a criminal investigation. For example, the prosecutor ought to obtain the pursued person in a criminal prosecution under art. 219 CCP.[77] One way to obtain the person for the criminal proceedings' purposes is to go through the process of search operations, art. 245 CCP. Art. 245(1)(1) CCP provides: "Where criminal proceedings have been suspended because the perpetrator had not been discovered, the prosecutor shall remit the case … in order to continue searching for him/her." The authorities ought to take every necessary measure for a lawful capture of the person.[78] The detention is procedural and follows the factual capture of the person. The difficulty doesn't rely on how to insure the defendant's participation but on a far more procedural issue. In the context of the CCP the Bulgarian authorities ought to search and seize persons from their home either in Bulgaria or abroad and deliver them to the prosecutor to face charges.[79] The Supreme Judicial Court is called Supreme Court of Cassation. It finds violation when the authorities do not

---

[72] See also about other constitutional rights, art. 33(2), 34(2), 40(2) of the Constitution of the Republic of Bulgaria. Trendafilova (1996), p. 9; Chinova (1998), p. 24; Pavlov (1986), p. 24.

[73] See also the equivalent rules, art. 217a and 268 CCP 1974.

[74] See for example art. 219 CCP ("Constituting the accused party and presentation of the decree to this effect"), art. 225 CCP ("New constitution of the accused party"), art. 227 CCP ("Presentation of the investigation").

[75] See measures of coercion and the defendant's obligation in context of his attendance, Decision 597-2001-I.

[76] See also Court Proceedings Act, State newspaper 77/07.04.1897, arts. 188, 197, 199.

[77] See decision No. 6770/23.06.2016r., District Court, Varna.

[78] For a critical introduction to material aspects of the seizure, see Filchev (1995), pp. 68–72.

[79] See decision No. 371/22.06.2012r., District Court, Razgrad.

take all measures for searches and seizures[80] and it hears cases raising constitutional issues.

During a criminal proceeding CCP requires searching for objective truth. The law furnishes no test of objective truth. This requirement goes to the status of the defendant as a subject of the criminal proceeding.

Law enforcement agents and prosecutors issue a subpoena for the attendance of a defendant in any proceeding.[81] The CCP provides when and by whom[82] the subpoena may be issued and it sets out the guidance for issuing a subpoena: it must be made according to the criminal procedure law and rules (arts. 178 - 182 CCP).[83]

When a case is in pre-trial, the analysis is different because art. 206 CCP applies. Only out of four situations are applicable in the pre-trial, arts. 269(3)(1, 2, 4) CCP.

In absentia proceedings are conducted under CCP in three circumstances. Each of these alternatives should implement with searching for the objective truth. First, the case may be tried in the absence of the accused, if the person could not be found at the address he/she specified, or he has changed his/her address without notifying the appointed body.[84] Second, his/her place of residence in this country is not known and has not been identified after a thorough search; art. 269(3)(2) CCP. Third, art. 269(3)(4) CCP provides a subpoena for defendants who live outside Bulgarian borders. The purpose of this rule is to regulate subpoenas abroad.[85] Defendants who live abroad or in Bulgaria receive equal procedural protections. CCP is intended to cover both situations. In other words, subpoena is authorized under CCP in three circumstances: (1) if the defendant lives abroad and his/her place of residence is not known; (2) if the defendant lives abroad and may not be otherwise summonsed; (3) when the defendant has been validly summonsed, but has failed to specify good reasons for his/her non-appearance.[86]

3.3   *Personal Participation in Proceedings* **In Camera**

The trial process in Bulgaria is public, art. 20 CCP. Society has to be convinced that judicial conflicts are being well handled. Nevertheless, the courts meet in a closed session under one rule: the defendant should be present during trial proceedings in camera.

---

[80] Decision 720-1992-I; Decision 473-2002-III; Decision 43-2011-I; Decision 15-2013-III; Decision 19-2013-II; Decision 339-2014-II; Decision 99-2016-I; See interpretative decision 1602-2011-Criminal Senats' Meeting, Supreme Court of Cassation.

[81] See also Chinova (2007), p. 8.

[82] See art. 178 CCP.

[83] See Decision 372-2002-I.

[84] Art. 269 (3)(1) CCP.

[85] See also Chinova (2007), p. 13.

[86] See also Decision 399-2003-I; Decision 447-2002-I; Ruling № 348/18.09.2012г., Court of Appeals, Plovdiv.

The exceptions of publicity are enforced to prevent revelation of confidential matters within the context of judicial proceedings.[87] These exceptions of publicity of hearings have two features. First, the rules regarding the principle of confidentiality in Bulgarian justice system are stricter in the pleading rules. For example, the confidential character of disclosure, e.g., evidence gathering, fact-finding, art. 263(1) CCP. In contrast, "decisions shall be announced publicly in all cases", art. 263(4) CCP.[88] Second, the applicability of the article 20 CCP depends on three restrictions: state secret, public morals and anonymity of the witness pursuant article 123(2)(2) CCP or preventing divulgation of facts related to the intimate life of citizens, art. 263(2) CCP. In these situations, the criminal proceedings are always held in closed session.[89] The publicity of hearings in court comes also with some relative practical constrains: The juvenile proceedings[90] or interrogation of children can be conducted *in camera*, art. 263(3) CCP. The courts differ on whether to allow children into the courtroom during hearings.

Another restriction is provided by the limitations to publicity of the court hearing. According to article 409(1)(2) of the CCP "the court may request from the defence counsels, the witnesses and the other persons in the courtroom, to declare that they shall not divulge the circumstances presented in the court hearing in consideration of the classified information discussed in it. When examining cases against officers, no sergeants and privates shall be allowed in the courtroom as listeners." Court hearings behind closed doors may be attended by individuals whom the presiding judge authorities to do so, as well as one individual indicated by each accused party, art. 264(1) CCP.[91]

The judgment must be delivered in the presence of the defendant, art. 263(4) CCP. This circumstance raises issues of whether the trial court has obligation to notify a defendant for scheduling the case for new examination. The Supreme Court of Cassation held that the publicity of hearings provides an adequate guarantee for the notification of the person.[92]

---

[87] See for example, Decision 402-2002-III.

[88] See also article 310(1) CCP.

[89] Petrova, Aneta, Major ways in the criminal proceedings' evaluations at the pre-trial, in: European Criminal Law, 2008, 353 at 409.

[90] Arts. 385-395 CCP.

[91] Pavlov (1996), I, p. 124.

[92] See for example, Decision 369-2002-II.

3.4 Personal Participation in Alternative Proceedings

A criminal charge is an *ultima ratio* of a series of attempts to resolve a conflict.[93] This is a community response for wrongdoings committed by citizens. Criminal proceedings following the general procedure are not characterised by efficiency. In contrary, CCP provides six forms of alternative proceedings at the pre-trial and trial stage. These special forms of procedure in the Bulgarian criminal justice system are expressed as being intended to ensure effectiveness and, at the same time, they intend to protect the defendant. There are: Examination of the case in court upon request of the accused party "разглеждане на делото в съда по искане на обвиняемия, arts. 368-369 CCP"; Reduced judicial trial in proceedings before the first instance court "съкратено съдебно следствие в производството пред първата инстанция, arts. 369a-374 CCP"[94]; Exemption from criminal responsibility with the imposition of administrative sanction "освобождаване от наказателна отговорност с налагане на административно наказание, arts. 375-380 CCP"; Concluding a proceeding because of an agreement between the parties "(решаване на делото със споразумение, arts. 381-384 CCP". Variations to the forms and chronology of the Bulgarian criminal justice process exist not only at the trial stage, but also at the prosecution stage. The division between summary proceedings "бързо производство", arts. 356-361 CCP, and immediate proceedings "незабавно производство", arts. 362-367 CCP relies on the timing of the intervention of the investigative bodies which reflects different approaches of the Bulgarian criminal investigation.

The problem of personal participation in alternative proceedings is generated by their substantial differences between different stages. I will try to explain why these alternatives forms fall short of providing concrete rights to the participants in criminal proceedings. For example, in summary and immediate proceedings the private parties have no right to know the nature of the allegation against the defendant, arts. 356(5), and 362(5) CCP.

The in absentia proceedings do not exist as a well established institution. I will focus only on the legal basis, e.g., the procedural safeguards which affect the procedural integrity. A reason for concern in criminal proceedings is that in situations where the defendant has not responded to a summons or has failed to appear before a court of law, some of his personal rights are precluded. For example, if the defendant could not participate in an agreement, because of this situation he wouldn't be able to exercise his personal rights.[95] The situation is the same in the case of reduced judicial trials in proceedings before the first instance courts. When the defendant has not responded to a summons or has failed to appear before a court of law, he wouldn't be able to challenge the accusation. These forms are designed as alterna-

---

[93] Zonkov (1994), p. 57.

[94] See interpretative decision 1-2009-Criminal Senats' Meeting, Supreme Court of Cassation.

[95] Decision 449-2002-III; Decision 350-2003-II. See also Chinova, supra note 73, at 17; Trendafilova, supra note 54, at 44.

tives to the formal proof. The operational consequences are disputes between parties (in the first case) or the acceptance of criminal charges (in the second case).

Another example: The "Examination of the case in court upon request of the accused party" was incorporated within arts. 368-369 CCP; since 2010, there have been restrictions on the length of the investigations.[96] The rationale of these procedural rules is not intended to facilitate the fact-finding process or to safeguard the procedural integrity, but to protect the interests of the defendant. How will these interests be protected when the defendant has not responded to a summons or has failed to appear before a court of law? A defendant can request the examination of his/her case in court. These alternative proceedings provide no protection to defendants which are, for example, compelling with the time limits of art. 269(3)(4) CCP, lacking a personal connection to the case. Giving these considerations, the practitioners always apply the general rules if the defendant fails to appear in court.[97]

3.5　Personal Participation at Trial

3.5.1　Personal Involvement in the Evidence-Gathering

The procedural fact-finding is built on the law of evidence.[98] The defendant's statement (Explanations of the accused party, art. 115 CCP) is a main source of evidence.[99] The CCP provides a wide range of possibilities to use evidence gathered in specified circumstances. The explanations of the defendant given during the pre-trial proceedings before a judge or before another court panel, for example, shall be read out whenever the case is being tried in the absence of the defendant, art. 279(1)(2) CCP. In this case, the balance between efficiency and protection of individuals is weighted in favour of admissibility of the defendant's declarations. By doing so, the court goes back in time, discloses this evidence, takes it for granted and proceeds to assess it.

Nevertheless, the legislator stressed a threshold requirement for the defendant's presence. This requirement affects not only the rules of evidence in a common (general) criminal procedure model, but also in different simplified criminal procedure models which were enacted over the years.[100]

The involvement in the evidence-gathering faces a treacherous dynamic: The defendant must be present at pre-trial stage (the investigation (arts. 207, 235 CCP: "Institution of pre-trial proceedings and conduct of the investigation", "Records for

---

[96] After the 2010 reforms.

[97] 100-2012-Razgrad Appellate Court.

[98] See Petrova (2016).

[99] See in context of the *in absentia* proceedings interpretative decision 70-1974-Criminal Senats' Meeting, Supreme Court of Cassation.

[100] The summary and immediate proceedings (arts. 356-361 CCP) was introduced in 1993 (State newspaper, 110/93).

investigative actions"), during the action taken by the prosecutor following completion of the investigation (arts. 242-246 CCP) and trial stage. The trial stage is separated in five sections (arts. 271-310 CCP):

1. Actions to allow the case to progress at court hearing, arts. 271-275 CCP;
2. Judicial trial, arts. 276-290, CCP;
3. Court debates, arts. 291-296, CCP;
4. Final plea of the defendant, arts. 297-299, CCP;
5. Sentencing, arts. 300-310 CCP.

In taking this step, the law maker rejected an approach to the institutes such as self-incrimination, confessions, and unlawfully obtained evidence.

This need to support the evidence-gathering creates an obligation to bring cases forward. The trials in absentia set forth in the CCP are demanding on the magnitude or gravity of crimes, art. 269(1) CCP. For example, the prosecutor relied on national procedural rules relating to gravity of the underlying conduct to initiate his in absentia criminal proceeding. When the situation refers to a serious crime and "the case in the absence of the trial defendant would impede discovering the objective truth" (art. 25(2) CCP), the criminal proceedings shall be suspended. The courts prefer to apply the stricter test.[101] In other words, we have to cumulate two criteria: objective, and subjective. The prosecutor must keep legal criteria of gravity in mind. The criminal law stressed a threshold requirement for the most serious crimes. In contrast, the second criteria relies on the prosecutorial discretion in deciding whether to proceed with the investigation or not. Article 25 CCP is referred to the criminal proceeding as a whole.

Once again, the accused person should be present from the beginning to the end of the criminal proceeding: at the pre-trial (the initial appearance, the initial arraignment, discovery, pre-trial detention, voir dire examination, and the plea) and trial stage (especially permanence of the court panel, art. 258 CCP, the return of the verdict; sentencing).

Pre-trial proceedings include the investigation and action taken by the prosecutor following the completion of investigations. Article 224 CCP requires presence during the performance of investigative actions.

In two cases the defendant may not participate in the gathering of evidence: Reduced judicial trial in proceedings before the first instance (съкратено съдебно следствие в производството пред първата инстанция), arts. 369a-374 CCP,[102] and Disposing of the case by virtue of an agreement (решаване на делото със споразумение), arts. 381-384 CCP. The first case is an alternative form to judicial trial, arts. 276-290, CCP.

Art. 371 CCP provides:

In the preliminary hearing of the parties:

---

[101] Decision 797-2005-III; Decision 399-2003-I.

[102] See interpretative decision 1-2009-Criminal Senats' Meeting, Supreme Court of Cassation.

1. the defendant and his/her defence counsel, the civil claimant, the private prosecutor and their counsels may agree not to conduct an interrogation of all or some of the witnesses and expert witnesses, while in the issuance of the ruling, the content of the respective records and experts conclusions at the pre-trial stage of proceedings will be used;
2. the defendant may fully admit the facts stated in the factual section of the indictment, agreeing not to collect evidence in respect thereof.

The situation of personal involvement during the evidence gathering in case of disposing of the case by virtue of an agreement is analogous. These forms are alternatives to formal proof, where all the matter of fact needs to be discussed by the court and the parties. There are two ways an evidence law might respond to the problem of searching for the truth in criminal proceedings: the consensual agreement about the facts and the ordinary findings of facts. Thus, this distinction is essential to understanding the personal contribution to the fact-finding.

3.5.2 Personal Contribution to the Fact-Finding

Can a trial in proceedings by default under the conditions of the CCP plausibly articulate the reasons why certain facts are considered to have been proved? Concretely speaking, testimony is presented according to CCP. The defendant cannot participate in the formal procedure of questioning and cross-questioning. He cannot present evidence supporting his case. For example, he cannot exercise the right to defend himself. Therefore, the waiver of the defendant's right of participation in the trial court is linked to the waiver of a set of constitutional and procedural rights. This situation is problematic for the balance between protection of public and individual interests for several reasons. Firstly, it is worth pointing out that it is necessary not only to inform people about their procedural rights, but it is also fundamental to ensure the possibility to exercise them.[103] Secondly, knowing the implications *in concreto* requires defendants to waive their right to confront and cross-examine witnesses as well as other defendants and so on. Thirdly, this count is relevant not only to the fairness of the trial's hearing but also in order to find the truth in criminal proceedings. It is woven into the structure of the material constitutive elements of personal contribution to the fact-finding.

I do not believe that in absentia proceedings are unnecessary. I argue that the Bulgarian jurisdiction status of in absentia proceedings is insufficient and meets state consent, structural and functional requirements of legitimacy. As a consequence, I must record that the absence of a formal model of in absentia trials reduces the integrity of this kind of proceedings. As a matter of fact, these proceedings should emerge as an individual legal category.

---

[103] Arts. 15(3) CCP.

3.6 Personal Participation in Higher Instances

The CCP provides a legal framework for the investigation, prosecution, and punishment of crimes. As a part of each criminal justice system there are trial courts, appellate review instances (first case) and cassation instances (second case). In the first case the competent courts are the district courts and appellate courts, in the second one the Supreme Court of Cassation, art. 45 CCP. The appellate courts and the Supreme Court of Cassation have a controlling function. It is a third sub-stage in the court trial proceedings.[104] The subject of the review is "the correctness of the decision", art. 313 CCP. The defendant's right to participate is guaranteed. The district, appellate courts and Supreme Court of Cassation should issue a subpoena for the attendance of a defendant in any criminal action or proceeding in such court, i.e. it is mandatory at any stage of the criminal proceeding.[105] For example, at the appellate review "the parties and the other persons taking part in the intermediate appellate review proceedings shall be summoned pursuant to the procedure set forth under Articles 178–182, CCP unless they have been informed by the first instance court of the date on which the case would be examined", art. 328 CCP.

Under the terms of the CCP, the participation of a prosecutor both in appellate and cassation proceedings is mandatory.[106] Both the appellate and cassation instance ensure an opportunity for defendants to participate in a public court's hearing. Failure of the other parties in appellate proceedings to appear without a valid reason shall not be an obstacle to the examination of the case, art. 329(2) CCP. During cassation proceedings: Failure of the other parties to appear without valid reasons shall not be an obstacle to the examination of the case. The case shall be examined in the absence of a party, where the latter has not been located at the address he/she had provided, art. 353(2) CCP.

3.7 Special Rules in the Field of Serious Organised Crimes

The CCP provides special rules in the field of serious organised crimes.[107] They are included under the definition "in cases with indictment in serious crimes." The Specialized Criminal Court has jurisdiction to try defendants convicted for crimes under art. 411a (1)(2) CCP, and for crimes committed abroad, art. 411a (3) CCP. It hears disputes regarding serious crimes involving the State.

---

[104] The first sub-stage is the preparatory action prior to examination of the case at a court hearing (arts. 247-257 CCP) and the second one trial hearing (arts. 248-312 CCP).

[105] Decision 373a-1985-III.

[106] Arts. 329(1), 353(2) CCP.

[107] Arts. 321, 321a Criminal Code and for crimes enumerative ruled in art. 411a(2) CCP such as arts. 116(1)(10), 131(1)(8), 142(2)(6)(8) Penal Code, and so forth.

The CCP precludes trials in absentia in cases with indictment in serious crimes, art. 269(1) CCP. When the defendant has not responded to a summons or has failed to appear before a court of law, the general rules are applicable (art. 411e CCP).

4 Personal Participation of Private Parties Other Than Defendants (in Particular, the Contribution of the Victim to the Fact-Finding)

The Bulgarian criminal justice system is a defendant focused model: personal participation of the victim is separate from, and applies to, the victim's role in fact-finding process. It is accessory; they are responsible for protection of their interests.[108] The position of the victims in criminal proceedings has been a source of controversy during recent history. According to Stephen Trechsel, none of the original Human Rights Conventions make any mention of victim's rights.[109] Their representation in the process as a party alongside the prosecution and defense is not mandatory.[110] In contrary, the victim's participation under the regime of the CCP 2005 creates conditions that diminish efficiency in criminal proceedings.[111] Through the instrument "Return the file to the prosecutor", the judge-rapporteur returns the case file to the prosecutor for further investigation", arts. 249(2), 248(2)(3) CCP.

Regarding victims' participation, the law maker was driven by an understanding that conceived the non-mandatory participation as a way of protecting freedom. Victims have a free choice to participate or not in criminal proceedings within the context of prosecution, and civil action functions, art. 49(3) CCP, and right to the assistance of counsel, art. 100(1) CCP. Thus, the private parties' role is accessory. They became a subject of a criminal process after their formal constitution, art. 74(3) CCP, i.e. they can be joined as a party.[112]

The court, the prosecutor and investigative bodies must guarantee to the private parties the opportunity to participating in the proceedings.[113] An example is provided by article 15(3) CCP which forces the court, the prosecutor and the investigative bodies to explain the procedural rights of persons affected by their decisions. They shall ensure the possibility to exercise them. The special part of the CCP contains concrete references to this context. For example, "Prior to presenting the investigation, the investigative body shall explain to the attending persons their rights", art. 227(7) CCP, and "the victim and his/her counsel, provided they have

---

[108] See interpretative decision 2-2002-Criminal Senats' Meeting, Supreme Court of Cassation.

[109] Trechsel (2006), p. 36.

[110] Decision 228-2001-III.

[111] For other arguments see Trendafilova (2000), p. 41.

[112] See also article 75(3) CCP.

[113] Victim's participation in alternative proceedings "Disposing of the case by virtue of an agreement", Decision 741-2001-II.

submitted a request to this effect, shall be summoned for the conclusion of the investigation" art. 227(2) CCP.[114] This could happen at any stage of the criminal proceedings, in pre-trial proceedings and during the investigation,[115] in proceedings before the first instance court, in preparatory actions for examination of the case at a court hearing,[116] in the actions to allow the case to progress at a court hearing,[117] and in a judicial trial.[118] The presence of the private parties at investigative actions is not required. For example, "where the provisions of this Code[119] do not provide for attendance of the accused party, of his/her defence counsel or of the victim and his/her counsel in conducting the respective investigative actions, the pre-trial body may allow them to attend, provided this will not obstruct the investigation."[120] The victims can choose to follow these routes or not. Rather, the private parties should operate through different level of engagement with the mandatory participants, e.g., prosecutor, judge and so forth. Nevertheless, the victims are under obligation to testify, i.e. they give testimony upon all relevant facts inquired of in a court as a citizen's obligation. The foundation of these procedural rules is designed or intended to facilitate the fact-finding process or to safeguard the integrity of the criminal proceeding.

5   *In Absentia* Proceedings

5.1   *Information Rights and Conditions of Waiver of Personal Participation in Criminal Proceedings*

For the purpose of this essay, I will analyse three junctures which concern the *in absentia* proceedings at the trial stage: in the first place, the gravity requirement is central to in absentia proceedings; secondly, the judicial discretion to suspend, and finally the conditions of waiver of personal participation in criminal proceedings. In other words, three structural features of the Bulgarian criminal justice system characterize the *in absentia* proceedings. First among these, is the difference between the pre-trial and trial stage, as well as the relationship between them. Both the prosecutor and the judge permit defendants to forego participation by entering *in absentia* proceedings. But the conditions are different. For example, the gravity of the

---

[114] In contrast to the summary and immediate proceedings, arts. 356(5) CCP, and 362(5) CCP.

[115] Article 224 CCP.

[116] Articles 255, 257 CCP.

[117] Article 271(5) CCP.

[118] Article 287(5)(6)(7) CCP.

[119] CCP.

[120] Art. 224 CCP: "Presence during the performance of investigative actions". See also Art. 248(2)(3) CCP.

underlying crimes is irrelevant during the pre-trial.[121] The conditions of *in absentia* proceedings differ in both stages only regarding the normative prerequisites each of them employs.

Secondly, the absence of a defendant gives prosecutors and judges leeway in deciding *in absentia* proceedings or the suspension of criminal proceedings. Criminal proceedings are suspended if trying the case in the absence of the defendant would obstruct discovering the objective truth, art. 25(2) CCP. Third, the judge must be convinced that there is substantial basis for the *in absentia* proceedings. They are grounded on some notion of efficiency. But the criminal proceedings require weighing the public interests against the individual interests of the defendant. The rights of the defendant can be seen in this regard as correlative.

In this sub-section these three junctures are evaluated in the context of information rights and conditions of waiver of personal participation in criminal proceedings. The information rights should guarantee the defendant's participation in criminal proceedings.

5.1.1 Information Rights

The first debate on in absentia proceedings concerns the issue of information rights. Together with the presumption of innocence, compliance with the procedural form and inviolability of the person, the information rights are a fundamental guarantee for the right to defence and safeguard for objective truth. These guarantees are constitutionally protected and provided in criminal proceedings, art. 15(3) CCP. The guidelines established for the court hearing, providing that the judge must explain to the parties their rights, can be considered as an example of it, 274(2) CCP. The prosecutor has the same obligation at the pre-trial stage, 227(7) CCP.

5.1.2 Conditions of Waiver of Personal Participation in Criminal Proceedings

A failure to appear may have two consequences, the prosecution and investigation may be suspended during the absence of the defendant or the case may be tried in the *in absentia* manner. In absentia proceedings require adequate trial preparation.[122] The conditions of in absentia trials are governed by the statutory law—not merely defences, but also, for example, victims participating.

Article 269(3) CCP provides the conditions of waiver of personal participation in criminal proceedings. It enumerates four alternative material requisites. They must be considered together with the searching for the objective truth and the gravity of the underlying crime.

---

[121] See arts. 206, 269 CCP.

[122] See for example Art. 254 (4) CCP.

The legislator stressed a threshold requirement for the judgement *in absentia*. The case law has consistently argued for a strict reading of this materiality standard.[123] It implies the two cumulative provisions, arts. 269(1) and 269(3) CCP. Article 269(1) CCP provides that the presence of the accused party at the court hearing is mandatory in all cases with indictment for serious crimes. As I have stated, this prerequisite applies only to the trial stage. According to art. 269(3) CCP, the judge should consider the following four factors:

Firstly, the case may be tried in the absence of the accused, if the person could not be found at the address specified by him, or he has changed his/her address without notifying the respective body.[124] Secondly, his/her place of residence in the country is not known and has not been identified after a thorough search; arts. 269(3)(2) CCP.[125] Thirdly, the defendant has been validly summonsed,[126] but has failed to specify good reasons for his/her non-appearance.[127] The defendant shall be notified of the scheduled court hearing and of the consequent *in absentia* trial.[128] Finally, art. 269(3)(4) CCP provides subpoena for defendants when they live outside Bulgarian borders, and

(a) his/her place of residence is not known[129];
(b) may not be otherwise summoned[130];
(c) has been validly summoned, but has failed to specify good reasons for his/her non-appearance.[131]

The four requirements mentioned above deal with the reason and the purpose of the rule, which is to conduct *in absentia* proceedings when the non-attendance of the defendant throughout the pre-trial and trial stages doesn't violate his rights. The determination of whether the proceedings are *in absentia* depends on the substantive terms and discretion, e.g., there is a combination of the two groups of prerequisites. On the one hand, the substantive prerequisites under art. 269(1) CCP and art. 269(3) CCP are beyond question.[132] If the court is of the opinion that these requirements exist, the question is: What is the role of searching for objective truth for the case's outcome? The detailed prescriptions are based on the legislative assumption that courts cannot venture deeply into this area.

---

[123] Art. 269 (1) CCP and art. 269(3) CCP.

[124] Art. 269 (3)(1) CCP.

[125] Decision 423-1993-I.

[126] Art. 269 (3)(3)(a) CCP.

[127] Art. 269 (3)(3)(b) CCP.

[128] Art. 269 (3)(3)(c) CCP.

[129] Art. 269 (3)(4)(a) CCP.

[130] Art. 269 (3)(4)(b) CCP.

[131] Art. 269 (3)(4)(c) CCP.

[132] Decision 50-1993-II.

On the other hand, the judge faces the final choice by exercising his discretionary authority. For example, the procedural prerequisite (searching for the objective truth) is a matter of inner conviction throughout the decision-making process.

This survey leads to the following: Though the obligatory compliance with one of the substantive conditions pursuant art. 269(1) CCP and 269(3) CCP, the judge must inquire into the factual basis for searching the objective truth. This institute becomes important in assessing how in absentia proceedings should be conducted. The judge can dispense with the presence of the accused if this shall not obstruct the discovery of the objective truth. Thus, searching for the objective truth determines the results in the particular case, art. 269(2) CCP.

If a court considers a criminal default in violation of these requirements, the remedy is to return the case-file to the prosecutor, art. 288(1), 335(1)(1), 348(2), 358(3) CCP.[133] When starting these actions again is impossible, the courts nullify those procedural actions that infringed procedural rules.[134]

5.2 Default Proceedings and Subsequent Remedies (e.g., Retrial or Judicial Review in a Higher Instance)

Default proceedings and subsequent remedies should recover damages suffered through the insufficient or wrong application of the procedural requirements or guarantees, resulting from the defendant's failing to appear before a court of law. In this situation, there are three possibilities through the first instance, appellate and cassation instance as well as retrial. I will analyse them in order.

It is necessary to first consider the damages that may occur during trial hearings. In this case, the remedy is to suppress the evidence gathered by precluding the prosecution from using it. This instrument is stated in many provisions such as arts. 234(4), 177(2) CCP.

Secondly, the review instances, in which the courts determinate if the requirements described above, are met. These requirements are designed to protect the defendant and to ensure a substantial opportunity for him to participate in a public court's hearing.

The examination of a case can refer to a procedural inquiry into whether the defendant's rights are respected. It differs from the appellate instance, cassation and retrial. The fact-finding and evaluation of the situation on factual basis are only found in the appellate trials. In contrary, the Bulgarian Court of Cassation should repeal judgments when the records from the previous instances reveal that individual rights of the parties were not correctly articulated, art. 348(3) CCP.[135]

---

[133] Decision 299-1983-II.

[134] See also interpretative decision 2-2002-Criminal Senats' Meeting, Supreme Court.

[135] Decision 55-2003-I.

The criminal procedure order follows the same revision grounds. The following section look at the main junctures on issues related to criminal order procedure.

5.3   Inaudito Reo *Proceedings*

Inaudito reo proceedings implies the right of the defendant to reopen a proceeding in front of the Supreme Court of Cassation.[136] Article 423 CCP ("Re-opening of a criminal case upon request of an individual sentenced by default") provides the criminal order procedure.[137]

In the procedure for a criminal order, the factual situation is indisputable. The supreme judge analyses only the legal conclusions, e.g., if the procedural rules are applied legally and fairly because "justice must not only be done but also be seen to be done."[138] For example, obtaining in absentia judgments without the defendant having ever been summoned is a procedural infringement ("substantial breach of procedural rules").[139] In other words, the violation of the procedural right of participation is a consequence of that procedural action. The rules of the appellate trial are applicable here, e.g., there is no trial hearing (witnesses are not heard, evidence is not collected) differently from first and appellate instances. The Supreme Court of Cassation is concerned only with questions of law, e.g., it does not conduct substantial trials.

The lack of knowledge of a pending case or file provides the most straightforward argument underlying the particular applications. The Court must determinate "whether the individual had been aware of the criminal prosecution against him/her."[140]

The defendant knows about the criminal proceedings after having been charged at the pre/trial stage.[141] The Supreme Court of Cassation explained that in this case there is no violation of the procedural rules and the fairness is satisfied. In the case analysed by the Supreme Court of Cassation, Bulgarian officials had attempted to ensure presence of the defendant but he was not brought to trial[142] or he waived his right to participate in the proceeding.[143] This requirement is irrelevant "when a request has been made by a convict sentenced in absentia, surrendered by another

---

[136] Petrova (2008), p. 470.

[137] The same rules were provided in Court Proceedings Act, State newspaper 77/07.04.1897, art. 587(5), art. 254(d) CCP 1952, and with the amendments 1999, State newspaper 70/99, in art. 362a CCP 1974. See interpretative decision 32-1975-Criminal Senats' Meeting, Supreme Court.

[138] van den Wyngaert (1993), p. 13.

[139] Decision 729-1998-II; Decision 156-99-II; Decision 723-2004-I. See also Art. 348 (1)(2) CCP and Art. 348 (3)(1) CCP.

[140] See art. 423(5) CCP. See also Decision 447-2002-II.

[141] Decision 651-2001-II; Decision 348-2000-II. See also Decision 155-2000-II.

[142] Decision 183-2000-II; Decision 651-2001-II; Decision 182-2001-II; Decision 549-2002-II.

[143] Decision 209-2000-I.

state to the Republic of Bulgaria,"[144] i.e. the *in audito reo* proceedings rely on the probable cause requirements which depend upon whether the defendant was surrendered.

The second question is "how", i.e. the procedural aspects.[145] Giving the formal structure of the criminal order procedure, legislator provides the most straightforward accommodation. For example, within 6 months from the date of the conviction by default, when the defendant gains knowledge of a decision that has entered into force, he may file a request for re-opening the criminal case, but only if he wasn't aware of the sentence issued against him, art. 423(1) CCP.[146] Proceedings for reopening of the criminal case are terminated if the convicted person by default failed to appear at the court hearing without valid reason, art. 423(3) CCP.[147]

6 Participatory Rights in Transnational Criminal Justice

The Extradition and European Arrest Warrant Act 2005 (Extradition Act 2005) was adopted by Bulgaria's parliament on June 3, 2005.[148] It is structured to present two complementary regimes: surrender of the requested person by European Arrest Warrant (EAW) to the issuing Member State of the European Union according to arts. 35-66 Extradition Act 2005 and an extradition from Bulgaria to other countries.[149] In decision 3,[150] the Constitutional Court interpreted the provision of art. 25(4) of the Constitution of the Republic of Bulgaria and made a difference between the both regimes which are supplemented by the provisions found in arts. 2 and 3 Extradition Act 2005.

The following two sections and two undersections discuss the participatory safeguards in EAW proceedings and in transborder inquiries in context of the intersections of the application of the EAW and the protection of fundamental rights, including participatory rights in the decision on surrender, *in absentia* proceedings in the trial country and its relevance in the surrender procedure, and the taking of overseas evidence. I will discuss below to each in turn.

---

[144] See art. 423(5) CCP; Decision 155-2000-II.

[145] Decision 209-2000-I; Decision 651-2001-II.

[146] Decision 209-2000-I; Decision 155-2000-II.

[147] Decision 729-1998-II;156-99-II; 723-2004-I. See also Art. 348 (1)(2) CCP and Art. 348 (3)(1) CCP.

[148] The *Law of the Extradition and the European Arrest Warrant*: Prom. SG. 46/03.03.2005, amend. SG. 86/28.10.2005, amend. SG. 52/06.06.2008, amend. SG. 49/29.06.2010, amend. SG. 55/19.07.2011, amend. SG. 53/27.06.2014.

[149] See decision No. 193/21.12.2015, Appellate Court, Plovdiv.

[150] Constitutional Decision 5-2004.

6.1   Participatory Safeguards in EAW Proceedings

6.1.1   Participatory Rights in the Decision on Surrender

Implementing the European Arrest Warrant framework decision,[151] Extradition Act 2005 applies to extradition from Bulgaria to another EU Member State and from another EU Member State to Bulgaria. Part 5 of the Extradition Act 2005 (arts. 35-66) includes the surrender procedures. In conducting an EAW proceedings should be taken four steps: EAW submission and screening, arts. 38b, 42 Extradition Act 2005; arrest, art. 43 Extradition Act 2005; surrender hearing, arts. 44 Extradition Act 2005; and appellation, art. 48 Extradition Act 2005. How these steps are procedural organised? The district Court at the place of residence of the requested person shall check if the EAW meets the requirements under arts. 37 and 38 Extradition Act 2005 and according art. 42 Extradition Act 2005 render detention. The detention is a subject of a hearing conducted by a judge. Following the first appearance, the next step is the surrender hearing. Within 7 days the requested person shall be tried in an open session. It is important to know which participatory rights apply in the decision on surrender. The set of safeguards in surrender proceedings comprises six main components:

- Screening of the EAW by a neutral body, namely the district Court at the place of residence of the requested person, art. 42 Extradition Act 2005.
- A surrender hearing within 7 days is required. It could be waived by the requested person if he/she "gives his/her consent for being turned over", art. 45 Extradition Act 2005. If the surrender hearing is not waived, the requested person is brought before three judges from the respective district Court, art. 44 I, II Extradition Act 2005.
- Fundamental trial rights of criminal proceedings, such as a right of defense and translation are guaranteed, art. 44(3) Extradition Act 2005.
- Requested persons shall be informed of their right to grant consent for surrender, art. 44(3) Extradition Act 2005.
- Consent justifies surrender without hearing; in these cases, the requested person has agreed in advance to be surrendered. The court has used language reminiscent of well/known accounts of *in absentia* justification.
- Control mechanism through appeals, art. 48 Extradition Act 2005.

When requested person is a non-European citizen, the considerations are different because the Part II Extradition Act 2005 applies. Part II includes the following steps: a request for extradition presented by a third country: submission and screening, art. 9, 10 Extradition Act 2005; arrest, arts.13-15 Extradition Act 2005; extradition hearing, arts. 16-19 Extradition Act 2005; and appellation, art. 20 Extradition Act 2005.

---

[151] European arrest warrant under Council Framework Decision 2002/584/JHA.

6.1.2 *In Absentia* Proceedings in the Trial Country and Its Relevance in the Surrender Procedure

The surrender occurs within the framework of an Extradition Act 2005 and when the purpose is to enable the requesting state to place the requested person on trial. At the same time, *in absentia* proceedings in the trial country could have many different outcomes. For example, there are criminal cases against absent defendants with little likelihood that sentences will be imposed or judgements will be enforced. Other cases could be materialised in surrender procedures. This second case is subject of the following subsection.

In determining whether to accept the request for surrender, courts are required to make evaluations regarding the issue is there enough guarantees about the possibility to secondary truing of the cases against defendants, art. 8(4) Extradition Act 2005. Courts are free, but not obligated to respond affirmative in deciding whether guarantees provided. Moreover, the court evaluates the fairness in the criminal procedure of a requesting state. More specifically, the request should be evaluated in terms of defendants' rights and guarantees, art. 7 Extradition Act 2005. The Extradition act provides that "surrender request should be denied if the requested state cannot ensure a fair trial, art. 7(5) Extradition Act 2005.

Article 40a Extradition Act 2005 provides that EAW must include a certified copy of a sentence if the requested person is sentenced *in absentia*. According to article 422(1)(6) CCP "[t]he penal case shall be re-established, where extradition is admitted in the case of verdict by default against provided by the Bulgarian State bails for the revival of the suit – for the crime for which the extradition has been admitted." The restrains of the form of surrender proceedings have been rarely been tested in many cases.[152]

In the next section, we would like to provide an overview of how the participatory safeguards prescribed by the Bulgarian CCP impact the transborder inquiries and the taking of overseas evidence.

6.2   Participatory Safeguards in Transborder Inquiries and the Taking of Overseas Evidence

This undersection considers participatory safeguards in transborder inquiries and the taking of overseas evidence. In the quickly evolving area of transnational crimes the transborder inquiries and taking of overseas criminal evidence are indispensable. With inquiries and the taking of evidence I am concerned the process of formal proof underlying searches (for example, evidence seized during the searches) or interrogations (oral declarations). The notions of *"transborder" and "overseas"* refer to actions such as interrogations, searches, seizures, and so forth, taken outside

---

[152] See Decision 21-2014-III.

the borders of Bulgaria (for example, searches of property that is located in a foreign country). More specifically, the notion "*transborder*" suggests commitment of transnational crimes.

The suspect, the defendant or the witness has developed substantial connections with a country different to trial one. For example, he or she could be a foreign citizen, victim of theft. This situation raises a set of issues. When the inquiry is conducted abroad are applicable the provisions and safeguards which may be quite different in compare with the Bulgarian ones. Are the results of the inquiry transferable in the Bulgarian adjudicative system?

In criminal procedure, there can be question about things which are necessary to hear the cause. In this sense, the fact-finding process is communicative and disputable. The inquiries reflect the formal necessity for proof. There are inquiries at pretrial and trial stage. The issue is how the participatory safeguards afforded by the Constitutions of Republic Bulgaria and CCP impact the transborder inquiries of transnational crimes.

The transborder inquiries akin to the domestic ones reflect many participatory safeguards. Yet I will address this issue in the context of the privilege against self-incrimination. Coerced statements and sentencing on ground of self-incriminations are not permitted, art. 31(2) of the Constitution of the Republic of Bulgaria. The goal of this provision is to prevent the defendant from inducing a false result. The both constitutional safeguards apply equally to Bulgarian and foreign person being inquired, i.e. everybody is protected by equal protection provision. As a result, important is only the difference between involuntary statements and unwarned because of their use at trial to prove the defendant's guilt. The torture makes the results of the inquiries unusable. The law enforcement authorities and judiciary are obligated to inform the person about the right to remain silent, art. 103(3) CCP. Another example concerns the constitutional limitations provided by art. 165(2) of the Constitution of the Republic of Bulgaria. Art. 165(2) CCP provides that "Interception and seizure of correspondence shall be allowed only when it is necessary for the detection and prevention of serious crimes." Aliens receive on the territory of the Republic of Bulgaria the same participatory rights.

The second set of issues concerns the participatory safeguards in the taking of overseas evidence. Each EU Member State is bound to follow its evidence rules (art. 102-190 CCP) as a matter of law. In case of detection of transnational crime, the investigations should be extended to intersections among two or more states.

Evidence are transferred, requested persons are extradited, and so forth. Actually, a EU Member State does not make anything different from what it would do on their territory, i.e. on their own (for example, evidence gathering). The question is how to interrogate an individual who is temporarily present in a state (a tourist, for example) but has no other connection with it or could we use the evidence gathered abroad or when the investigation is conducted abroad. Yet it will be determined whether and to what extent the participatory safeguards apply to taking of overseas evidence in criminal proceedings involving Bulgarian citizens. This issue interdepends with the consequences for Bulgaria in conducting investigations beyond its boundaries.

The issue of taking of overseas evidence is concerned in horizontal, state-to-state context. The Bulgarian judges have no authority on the territory of another state. Art. 471(1), 1st sentence CCP, provides the basis for the international legal assistance in penal cases: "International legal assistance in penal cases of another state shall be rendered on the terms of a concluded international treaty to which the Republic of Bulgaria is a party, or on the principle of mutuality." For example, the witness's knowledge or that he saw, heard or otherwise perceived. He should accept some social obligations such giving of testimony according to art. 473 CCP. In the event of a refusal to appear, no coercive measures may be applied to them. This is accomplished with the obligation to speak the truth. The witness could be required to speak through video conference or telephone conference pursued to art. 474 CCP.

Transfer of penal procedure by another state is possible as provided by art. 478 CCP. The transfer applies to trials without juries. Three professional judges take the decision. Pursuant article 478(2)(3, 4) CCP the Supreme Cassation Prosecution—for pre-trial procedure, and the Ministry of Justice—for Court procedure "shall immediately forward the application for transfer of the penal proceedings to another state to the competent authority in respect of the penal proceedings according to the provisions of this Code, and when the jurisdiction may not be determined under the rules of Art. 37– to the Courts in Sofia. The application for transfer of the penal proceedings from another state shall be received by the penal proceedings authority, if several of the following grounds are present the perpetrator has permanent residence in the territory of the Republic of Bulgaria; and the perpetrator is citizen of the Republic of Bulgaria." The absence of an each of the prerequisites listed in art. 478(2) CCP is a valid basis for rejecting by the court.

There are many reasons for the existence of the participatory guarantees. One suggested argument is the possibility through confrontation to avoid untrustworthiness due mistake or inaccuracy. The purpose is the protection of the suspect, the defendant, the victim, i.e. the party against whom the transfer is requested. With other words, it should be applied every participatory safeguard wherever Bulgaria low enforcement bodies and adjudicative exercises their powers.

It is important which participatory rights *in concreto* are guaranteed in transborder inquiries and the taking of overseas evidence. For example, a testimony which is made outside the presence of the requested person against whom it is being offered is admissible in trial only if his participatory rights are guaranteed.

Whether the evidence is admissible depends on mode, source, and form of the evidence as provided by the rules of evidence in each jurisdiction. For example, information obtained by usage of special intelligence devices is insufficient by itself to establish probative value, art. 177(1) CCP. With other words, the evidence has probative value pursuant to statutory authority of each EU Member State. Participatory safeguards are intertwined with the question of how the judges obtain evidence. The connection between reasoning and outcome should not fail short. Moreover, each participatory safeguard could be properly assessed in the context of the particular circumstances of a case.

7 Requirements of Personal Participation and In Absentia Proceedings. The Perspective of Supranational and International Human Rights Law

7.1 The Perspective of International Human Rights Law. Critical Remarks on Domestic Law in the Light of the European Convention

The Bulgarian criminal law justice system was developed by and through the European Convention, especially the case law on arts. 5 and 6 represented more than any other a fundamental influence. The basic CCP procedures and institutes have repeatedly been upheld against European challenges because of the democratization of the Bulgarian state and community after 45 years totalitarian regime.

In absentia proceedings require certain protections above and beyond the ones provided for the defendant participating in the proceedings. Three different procedural guarantees exist in Bulgaria. Some of them such as *inaudito reo* proceedings pursuant art. 423 CCP take into account the nature and the implementation of art. 6(3)(a)(b)(c) ECHR.[153]

1. There are strong reasons for the mandatory council: this procedural guarantee should ensure that in absentia proceedings are conducted fairly, art. 94(1)(8) CCP.[154]
2. *Inaudito reo* proceedings, art. 423 CCP.
3. In absentia proceedings are not applicable in special rules for alternative proceedings such as "Reduced judicial trial in proceedings before the first instance" (съкратено съдебно следствие в производството пред първата инстанция), arts. 369a-374 CCP,[155] "Disposing of the case by virtue of an agreement" (решаване на делото със споразумение), arts. 381-384 CCP.[156]

During the last 24 years, the Bulgarian criminal justice system, legislation and case law has undertaken steps to adopt the ECHR-standards. The most visible influence of the ECHR law is the right to a trial within a reasonable time, art. 6(1) ECHR. It was first introduced by Bulgarian Criminal Procedure Code 2006 in art. 22(1) CCP. These procedural guarantees appear to meet the ECHR's standards.

The European Court of Human Rights (ECtHR) has published a decision concerning violations against defendant's participation in investigations and in trials. In Stoichkov v. Bulgaria,[157] the defendant was charged and convicted on September the

---

[153] Decision 209-2000-I; Decision 155-2000-II.

[154] Decision 729-1998-II.

[155] See interpretative decision 1-2009-Criminal Senats' Meeting, Supreme Court of Cassation.

[156] Decision 350-2003-III.

[157] ECtHR, *Stoichkov v. Bulgaria*, judgment of 24 March 2005—Appl. no. 9808/02.

3rd, 1988. Stoichkov v. Bulgaria is a "clear case of illegality."[158] On March 24, 2005, the ECtHR ruled in Stoichkov v. Bulgaria that in absentia judgements violated the defendant's right to a fair trial under Art. 6 of the ECHR because the Supreme Court of Cassation did not reopen the criminal proceedings. The ECtHR held that protection of defendant's rights could be insured by requiring a judge's review of the legal issues. The interaction between Art 6(3)(d) and Bulgarian law is explained.[159]

7.2   The Perspective of EU Law. Developments in Domestic Law as a Result of EU Law

The Bulgarian criminal justice system shares the theoretical understandings of the European criminal law tradition. The EU criminal law has influenced national law both directly and indirectly. One of these indirect implications are the special rules for examination of cases for crimes committed by people who do not speak Bulgarian, arts. 395a-395i CCP. The right to a trial within a reasonable time was guaranteed with the special rules for examination of the case in court upon request of the accused party, arts. 368-369 CCP.

Other involvements of rules in criminal proceedings under European influence concern a particular kind of institutes. The national criminal justice has become European's central instrument for dealing with problems such as protection of financial interests. At a first glance this account may seem challenging to the relationship between European and domestic authorities. However, art. 127 CCP provides that the reports of the European Anti-Fraud Office (OLAF) are written with objectives forms of evidence together with the "records of action taken for investigation at judicial trial and of other procedural action, as well as records for the preparation of material objective forms of evidence and other documents." The bodies of pre-trial proceedings may request for the director of OLAF the reports and other documents enclosed with respect to their investigations.[160]

8   Concluding Remarks

The Bulgarian criminal justice remains caught between its desire to pursue effective representation in criminal proceedings, investigation activity of the law enforcement authorities, and its EU commitments. The challenge for the Bulgarian doctrine and theory is to explain how their explanations and justifications can be defended in

---

[158] Harris et al. (1995), p. 107.
[159] Renzikowski (2008), pp. 124–135.
[160] See also art.159(2) CCP.

absence of a normative concept. This essay has had two goals: to show the short-comings in dealing with ordinary crimes in trial *in absentia* and to give the basis for interdisciplinary analysis, e.g., this chapter serve as an instrument for comparative analyse. It offered important insights into the way the *in absentia* proceedings are interacting with personal participation.

The Bulgarian criminal justice system is extensively structured according to the principle of adversariality. The participants in criminal procedure are bound by the participatory guarantees. The criminal default is an institute of the effectiveness lies in a consensus on the procedural integrity as a whole. The victim and defendant to participate in criminal proceedings are entitled to the protection of the CCP. Thus, the victim of ordinary crimes has three possibilities to participate in criminal proceedings. Two of these forms are alternative. They rely on the structural division between the process applicable to major and minor crimes.

The *in absentia* proceedings show a preventive potential because the legal threshold for investigation, prosecution, and adjudication in cases of ordinary crimes is lowered. Under the terms of the CCP, the prosecutor,[161] the judge-rapporteur[162] or the judge[163] have the authority to suspend the criminal proceedings. If it is necessary for the investigation, "the suspended criminal proceedings shall be reopened by the prosecutor", art. 245(2) CCP.

The Bulgarian policy makers appear to understand the effectiveness only in context of the interests of justice (for example, effective criminal prosecution). As we know, the effectiveness means also effective judicial protection, for example, the right to effective assistance of counsel, and so forth. However, the effectiveness and legitimacy would be taken into account in context of the substantive fundamental rights of the defendant or others involved in criminal proceedings. The grave ones are not subject of the pre-trial stage of criminal proceedings.

The assumption in this essay is that an *in absentia* proceedings raise substantial procedural rights concerns. This assumption is based on two arguments. First, the CCP contains a limited legal basis for *in absentia* proceedings. Complicating the provisions is a differential between the attendance of defendants, witnesses, and other participants in criminal proceedings. Second, the shortcomings of the criminal procedure by default described above were arisen in fairness context.

We can summarize, *in absentia* proceedings the defendant is in a weak position to exercise his rights. He is absent. He cannot defend himself. The concept of the proceedings by default must meet procedural requirements. The law enforcement authorities only had power to proceed to try defendants in his absence if the provisions of art. 269 CCP exist. For example, if they don't know his/her permanent address pursuant art. 269 (3)(1) CCP.

In absentia proceedings extend to pressing for reforms that would strengthen the guarantees under which the accused will be convicted. The CCP contains expressly

---

[161] Art. 244(1)(1) CCP.

[162] Art. 251(1) CCP.

[163] Art. 290(1) CCP.

additional limits. Paragraph 3 of article 269 contains three separate preconditions that must be alternatively satisfied. The Bulgarian Supreme Court of Cassation has held in several instances that the criminal trial *in absentia* should be provided under the requirements of the art. 269(3) CCP.

The Bulgarian criminal justice system requires mandatory participation of the defence counsel in trials *in absentia*. The guarantee is provided in art. 94(1) (8) CCP. The participation of the defense counsel is a part of the CCP normative framework. It is a mandatory prerequisite for representation under the CCP.

The Bulgarian Law of the Extradition and the European Arrest Warrant (Extradition Act 2005) was adopted on June 3, 2005 (SG 46/05). It includes two procedural regimes: extradition procedure according to arts. 5-34 Extradition Act 2005, and surrender from Bulgaria to another EU Member State. Part 5 of the Extradition Act 2005 implements the European Arrest Warrant (EAW) framework decision. Surrender follows a formal procedure set forth in arts. 35-65 Extradition Act 2005. It concerns the following four steps: submission and accession of the EAW (art. 42 Extradition Act 2005), arrest and hearing (art. 43 Extradition Act 2005), surrender hearing (art. 44 Extradition Act 2005) and appellation (art. 48 Extradition Act 2005). The requested person may be arrested without a warrant for 72 h. The detention should assure his appearance in accordance to art. 43(5) Extradition Act 2005. Competent to enact surrender is the district Court at the place of residence of the requested person. The requested person has a right of translator and defense counsel. He should be also informed about the ground for the arrest, the content of the EAW, and the possibility to surrender without hearing according to art. 43(4) Extradition Act 2005. Restraints could be imposed after adversatory hearing. The waiver of hearing is supplemented by the provisions found in art. 45 Extradition Act 2005. According to art. 44(2) Extradition Act 2005 the surrender hearing provides the following guarantees:

- Hearing in open sitting of three judges with the participation of the prosecutor.
- Right of translator and defense counsel.
- Right of waiver of hearing.
- The surrender case shall be heard in a body of three judges in open session with the participation of the prosecutor, art. 44(2) Extradition Act 2005.

The transfer is governed by the requirements of the art. 478 CCP.

When Bulgarian law enforcement bodies are involved in transborder inquiries and the taking of overseas evidence, the rationale is investigation, prosecution, and adjudication of the defendant. However, the results of actions, such as an overseas interrogation, needs to be communicated by the defendant as a party in the criminal proceeding.

In absentia proceedings are also a common mechanism for expediting adjudicative jurisdiction. I believe that under current challenges and influences the rules about *in absentia* proceedings should be changed.

References

Bednarova J (2011) The heart of the criminal justice system: a critical analysis of the position of the victim. Internet J Criminol:1–46 www.internetjournalofcriminology.com

Chinova M (1998) Coercive measures and the inviolability of the person, Сиби.

Chinova M (2007) Proceedings by default under criminal procedure code. Contemp Law: 7–18

Filchev N (1995) The crime in the transition to a market economy and criminal legislation. Contemp Law 6, Сиби

Harris OJ, O'Boyle M, Warbrick C (1995) Law of the European Convention of human rights. Oxford University Press, Oxford

Pavlov S (1966) Problems of major functions in socialist criminal proceedings. Bulgarian State University Press, Bulgaria

Pavlov S (1986) Citizens' rights of defence. Bulgarian State University Press, Bulgaria

Pavlov S (1996) Criminal proceedings of Republic of Bulgaria. Bulgarian State University Press, Bulgaria

Petrova A (2005) Criminal justice, Makros

Petrova A (2008) Major ways in the criminal proceedings' evaluations at the pre-trial. Eur Crim Law:353–499

Petrova A (2016) When fictions rule the trial: how to explan the dichotomy of fact-finding to criminal defendants? Revista General de Derecho Público Comparado (19)

Radeva R (1971) The victim as a prosecutor in criminal proceedings. Bulgarian State University Press, Bulgaria

Radeva R (1985) The right of defence of the accused in Bulgarian criminal procedure. Bulgarian State University Press, Bulgaria

Renzikowski J (2008) Der schwere Weg zum Rechtsstaat – die Umsetzung von Art. 5 EMRK in Bulgarien. In: Petrova A (ed) European criminal law, University Press of the University of Plovdiv, pp 124–160.

Saranov N (1937) Bulgarian criminal procedural law. Bulgarian State University Press, Bulgaria

Trechsel S (2006) Human rights in criminal proceedings. Oxford University Press, Oxford

Trendafilova E (1992) The councel for the defence in the criminal procedure of Bulgaria. Bulgarian State University Press, Bulgaria

Trendafilova E (1995) The judicial control on the pre-trial German criminal proceedings. Bulgarian State University Press, Bulgaria

Trendafilova E (1996) The prosecution and investigation authorities and the human rights in criminal proceedings. Contemp Law: 7–14

Trendafilova E (1999) The necessary amendments in criminal proceedings. Juridicheski svjat: 130–160

Trendafilova E (2000) The Criminal procedure code' amendments as of 1999: theoretical principles, legislative decisions, tendencies. Bulgarian State University Press, Bulgaria

Turner JI (2014) The exclusionary rule as a symbol of the rule of law. SMU Law Rev 67:82 ff

van den Wyngaert C (1993) Criminal procedure systems in the European Community. Bloomsbury Professional, Belgium

Vogler R (2008) Introduction. In: Vogler G, Huber B (eds) Criminal procedure in Europe. Duncker & Humblot GmbH, Berlin, pp 1–38

Zonkov I (1994) Problems concerning criminal procedure functions. Leg Thought: 88–94

Report on England and Wales

Kate Leader

Abstract This chapter describes the participatory rights of a defendant in domestic criminal proceedings in England and Wales in both the pre-trial and trial period. The chapter also considers the law in England and Wales relating to trials in absentia, before considering participatory rights at a transnational level. As I outline in this chapter, recent policy developments in England and Wales have resulted in a number of "efficiency" initiatives theoretically designed to expedite decision making but which have resulted in the potential undermining of participatory rights for a defendant. In addition, recent changes to legal aid have made it increasingly difficult for individuals to access legal representation at different stages of the criminal process. Finally, and most significantly, the United Kingdom remains in a transitional period post "Brexit" referendum in terms of its criminal justice arrangements. The Conservative government made the repealing of the *Human Rights Act* and its replacement with a British Bill of Rights one of their election policies and although this has not yet materialised (indeed, it has been repeatedly delayed), as of January 2018 parliament has voted not to retain the EU Charter of Fundamental Rights in domestic law when it leaves the EU. This context means that many questions of participatory rights, particularly those linked to the future of the *Human Rights Act*, therefore remain unresolved and a source of concern.

Abbreviations

CICA   Crime (International Co-operation) Act 2003
CJA   Criminal Justice Act 2003
CPS   Crown Prosecution Service
DPP   Director of Public Prosecutions
EAW   European Arrest Warrant

K. Leader (✉)
York Law School, Freboys Lane, University of York, Heslington East, York, UK
e-mail: Kate.leader@york.ac.uk

© Springer Nature Switzerland AG 2019
S. Quattrocolo, S. Ruggeri (eds.), *Personal Participation in Criminal Proceedings*, Legal Studies in International, European and Comparative Criminal Law 2, https://doi.org/10.1007/978-3-030-01186-4_4

ECtHR   European Court of Human Rights
HoC   House of Commons
HRA   Human Rights Act 1998
IDPC   Initial Details of the Prosecution's Case
LASPO   Legal Aid, Sentencing and Punishment of Offender Act 2012
LOR   Letter of Request
MLA   Mutual Legal Assistance
MoJ   Ministry of Justice
NCA   National Crime Agency
PACE   Police and Criminal Evidence Act 1984
YJCEA   Youth Justice and Criminal Evidence Act 1999

1   Constitutional Requirements of the Involvement of Private Parties in Criminal Justice

The United Kingdom, along with only two other democratic states, has no formal written constitution, a situation Robert Blackburn has described as "extraordinary."[1] The lack of a written document does not, however, denote an absence of constitutional arrangements. Rather, as Martin Loughlin puts it, this means that in the United Kingdom, the constitution can be understood as "an expression of the laws, institutions, and practice which make up the tradition of governing" and that it is "in this sense that we might refer to Britain's distinctive political constitution."[2] The constitutional requirements governing criminal justice in England and Wales, then, are to be found through a variety of sources including Acts of Parliament, case law and "unwritten conventions."[3]

The most important provision relating to participatory rights is of course the *Human Rights Act 1998*, which incorporates, amongst other things, Article 6 of the European Convention of Human Rights into domestic law. This act provides a defendant with the right to a fair and open trial, the presumption of innocence, the right to legal representation, the right for adequate time and resources to prepare a defence, the right to test the evidence against her and the right to an interpreter if required.[4] Of course, the passage of the *Human Rights Act* by no means created any

---

[1] Blackburn (2015), p. 1.

[2] Loughlin (2003), p. 44, explains that the constitution can best be understood as "a translation of the Greek politeia [...] a descriptive term for the entire body politic."

[3] Blackburn notes in his arguments for a written constitution that the multiple sources of a UK constitution are confusing and inaccessible: "The present mass of common law rules to be gleaned in law reports, convoluted Acts of Parliament that are unreadable to most people, and unwritten conventions some of which are unclear even to politicians, is utterly impenetrable to most people." Blackburn (2015), p. 3.

[4] In addition, the right to silence is also implicitly recognized within this "Although not specifically mentioned in Article 6 of the Convention, the right to silence and the right not to incriminate oneself [...] are generally recognised international standards which lie at the heart of the notion of a

of the above rights, many of which have been long recognized in England and Wales.[5] However prior to the passage of this act:

> procedural approaches to the protection of individual rights—democratic accountability, checks and balances, and the rule of law—were clearly favoured over the more substantive approach associated with a formal statement of entrenched individual liberties that are legally enforceable in the courts and supreme to ordinary legislation.[6]

So, in this respect it may be argued that the main change effected by the passage of the Human Rights Act has been the adoption of a more substantive approach to individual liberties. In addition, as Federico Picinali and others observe, the passage of the *Human Rights Act* has to a degree given "constitutional" weight to these rights.[7]

Beyond the *Human Rights Act,* though, there are also derived rights and conventions for participants in criminal proceedings in England and Wales developed from common law and other statutes. Dinah Rose QC calls these "roast beef" rights: "the 'robust, stout and strong' rights that are and always have been fundamental principles underpinning the common law, and upheld by English courts, and which may properly be called constitutional rights."[8] Rose argues that one of these fundamental rights is "access to justice" for participants in criminal proceedings, including trial by judgment of one's peers[9] and the avoidance of selling, denying or delaying justice.[10] However, the lack of a written constitution means that which rights and laws are to be considered "constitutional" (if any) remain contested.[11]

---

fair procedure under Article 6." ECtHR, *Saunders v. United Kingdom*, judgment of 17 December 1996, Appl. No. 19187/9, 23 EHRR 313, paragraph 68.

[5] For example, the presumption of innocence has long been considered the "golden thread" running through common law in England and Wales. See Woolmington v. DPP [1935] AC 462.

[6] Vick (2002), p. 346.

[7] Picinali (2014), p. 2.

[8] Rose (2011), p. 3.

[9] "Judgment by one's peers" is a particularly important right for defendants in England and Wales, as it is not one provided for in Article 6. In England and Wales a defendant charged with an indictable offence will automatically be entitled to a trial by jury, and a defendant charged with a triable either way offence has the right to opt for a trial by jury.

[10] Both provisions can be derived ultimately from the *Magna Carta*. The importance of the *Magna Carta* itself to criminal proceedings has been questioned by some scholars (one of whom described it as a 'failed peace treaty written in Latin'). However, those who argue for *Magna Carta*'s importance emphasise that these two clauses in particular have been fundamental to formulating the concept of a fair trial in England. See Jennings (1965).

[11] For example, some would argue an individual's right in law to pursue a private prosecution was a 'constitutional safeguard', but others would not include it in the provisions they considered constitutional. The House of Commons [HoC] briefing includes reference to its constitutional authority (file:///H:/SN05281.pdf), but it goes unmentioned in the summary of constitutional laws. Picinali also notes the contested nature of what is constitutional when discussing the presumption of innocence. As he expresses it: "the Act has bestowed upon [the presumption of innocence] – or, at the least, has reinforced its – constitutional status." 2014, p. 2.

In addition, parliamentary sovereignty underpins all constitutional arrangements in the United Kingdom. So even though a piece of legislation such as the *Human Rights Act* may be considered constitutional, it still theoretically has no special legal status. As Lord Hoffman notes:

> Parliamentary sovereignty means that Parliament can, if it chooses, legislate contrary to fundamental principles of human rights. The Human Rights Act 1998 will not detract from this power. The constraints upon its exercise by Parliament are ultimately political, not legal.[12]

It is perhaps misleading to say there is no special legal protection offered to human rights in the United Kingdom: Lord Hoffman explicitly states that unless parliament explicitly seeks to overturn protections, "laws will be read to assume they are subject to individual rights."[13] However, as Lord Hoffman goes on to note, the only protection from such legislation is the "principle of legality" where "Parliament must squarely confront what it is doing and accept the political cost."[14] For Lord Hoffman, and other scholars, this protection brings the United Kingdom into line with other countries with a written constitution. It remains the case, however, that whilst there are constitutional safeguards for private participation in criminal proceedings, such as those contained in the *Human Rights Act*, these are not protected from change via parliament.

This is certainly not an idle observation in the current climate: since 2012, the Conservative government has been in the process of formulating a "British Bill of Rights" that would replace the *Human Rights Act*: this formed part of the party's election manifesto in 2015.[15] This political move indicates the degree to which the *Human Rights Act*, although entrenched law, is perceived in the UK by Conservative policy makers, and, post "Brexit" referendum, perhaps a fair proportion of the general public, as suspect due to its connection with Strasbourg, with whom the relationship could at its most generous be described as troubled.

So, what might a British Bill of Rights look like, and how might it change participatory safeguards in criminal proceedings? Leaving aside the political football the *Human Rights Act* has become, it is widely expected that the new Bill of Rights

---

[12] Ex Parte Simms [2000] AC 115, p. 131.

[13] A 2004 Joint Committee investigating parliamentary emergency powers argued that "fundamental parts of constitutional law" could be found in certain statutes, making the argument that any powers enabling parliament to overturn these statutes was problematic. See First Report of the Joint Committee on Draft Civil Contingencies Bill 2003, para 183.

[14] "Fundamental rights cannot be overridden by general or ambiguous words. This is because there is too great a risk that the full implications of their unqualified meaning may have passed unnoticed in the democratic process. In the absence of express language or necessary implication to the contrary, the courts therefore presume that even the most general words were intended to be subject to the basic rights of the individual. In this way, the courts of the United Kingdom, though acknowledging the sovereignty of Parliament, apply principles of constitutionality little different from those which exist in countries where the power of the legislature is expressly limited by a constitutional document." *Ex parte Simms* [2000] AC 115, p. 131.

[15] Whether this will happen and how continues to be argued as, despite multiple timeframes proposed from 2012 onwards, no actual draft bill has yet surfaced.

would most probably retain all rights relating to a fair trial, as well as potentially incorporating some of the "roast beef rights" outlined above, including, perhaps, a provision relating to trial by jury.[16] The proposers of the "British Bill of Rights" argue that giving constitutional rights a special recognition in law would help protect these rights; critics argue that this is an unnecessary and retrograde step based on a xenophobic attitude to human rights as a perceived foreign intrusion into British law making.[17] The intended direction of this government post-Brexit has been made explicit in the draft *EU Withdrawal Bill*, published in July 2017, which makes clear that the UK is not planning on incorporating the EU's Charter on Fundamental Rights. An amendment tabled by the opposition leader, Jeremy Corbyn, that attempted to retain the Charter was defeated in the House of Commons in January 2018.[18]

2 Personal Participation of Private Parties and Legal Assistance

In England and Wales, any defendant accused of a crime has the right in law to legal representation and, if she cannot afford to pay a lawyer, to have access to an appointed representative for free. However, in practice this right is arguably being undermined. The right to free representation through the provision of legal aid has been means tested since 2006 in the Magistrate's Court (which hears less serious matters) and 2010 in the Crown Court (which hears the more serious offences).[19]

In addition to means testing, defendants are also only granted legal aid in England and Wales if they pass the "Interests of Justice" test which assesses the kind of case being dealt with, the history of the offender and whether the consequences are sufficiently serious to warrant legal aid.[20] The considerable complexity of applying

---

[16] It should be noted, of course, that jury trials are vanishingly rare in England and Wales. Although guaranteed to any defendant accused of an indictable offence, or triable either way offence, court reforms increasingly seek to avoid trial at all. See Galanter (2004).

[17] Gearty (2016), describes Brexit as an "act of self-harming isolationism by the UK." For arguments for a British Bill of Rights, see the Conservatives' 2010 Publication, rather dubiously named *Protecting Human Rights in the UK*.

[18] European Union withdrawal Bill, draft available at: file:///H:/18005.pdf.

[19] Hurdles to obtaining legal aid in England and Wales have also been aggravated by threatened changes to legal aid funding for representatives. The government attempted to introduce a criminal legal aid tender whereby law firms would have to bid for government contracts to provide legal aid and the available contracts would be cut from 1200 to 527 which would have significantly reduced the firms able to offer legal aid to individuals. However, after intense criticism and significant protests from the legal profession, the government have retreated for the moment. For more information see the report from Legal Action Group 2015.

[20] See https://www.gov.uk/guidance/work-out-who-qualifies-for-criminal-legal-aid. The interests of justice test is ultimately skewed towards individuals being tried for more serious offences, with the possibility of loss of liberty being a strong argument for legal aid being found by the Legal Aid

for legal aid, and delay in processing applications, may mean that in England and Wales a defendant at a first hearing may still be waiting the outcome of their application for legal aid. This can have a significant impact on an individual's rights, particularly in Magistrates' Courts, where defendants are expected to enter a plea at their first hearing.[21]

Defendants may also choose to represent themselves, should they waive their right to counsel, or dismiss their representation, or not meet the criteria for legal aid and not be able to afford to hire representation privately.[22] Self-representation is a recognized right in all courts in England and Wales, including higher courts.[23] However, although there are an increasing number of unrepresented defendants, this is more likely to be indicative of the potential hurdles faced by individuals charged with a criminal offence accessing their right to legal representation, nominally protected under the *Human Rights Act*.[24]

Whilst I have up until now only spoken of defendants, other individuals also have some legal rights in pursuing criminal proceedings. This includes the right of private parties to commence a private prosecution, protected under section 6(1) of *the Prosecution of Offences Act 1985*. Private prosecutions are usually seen as another option for victims of crimes where the police fail to investigate or the Crown Prosecution Service (CPS) declines to prosecute.[25] Although private prosecutions undertaken successfully by individuals are relatively rare, private prosecutions form a part of the landscape in England and Wales, most commonly being undertaken by

---

Agency to be in the interests of justice. This is arguably another reason why Magistrates' Courts have increasing numbers of unrepresented defendants.

[21] A defendant should also be able to access a duty solicitor at the court itself if facing an imprisonable offence, however provision does not currently meet demand and even if available, a duty-solicitor is being asked to represent a defendant with minimal information available.

[22] A defendant is not permitted to change legally appointed representatives unless a compelling reason is given, which means that if a defendant is dissatisfied with their representation but the judge refuses their application to change representatives, then she may find herself without representation. For more information see Padfield (2012).

[23] The only exception to a defendant's right to represent herself is the explicit ban on a defendant directly cross examining a child witness, or a complainant in sexual assault proceedings.

[24] In civil proceedings, the courts express this in *R (Kigen) v Secretary of State for the Home Department* [2015] All ER (D) 132 decided that a delay in legal aid application was not a sufficient excuse for postponing court proceedings. Whilst there has been no such explicit decision in criminal proceedings thus far this decision is arguably indicative of the overriding emphasis on avoiding delay which trumps any potential undermining of rights for a defendant during the pretrial stage.

[25] "The individual, in such situations, who wishes to see the law enforced has a remedy of his own: he can bring a private prosecution. This historical right which goes right back to the earliest days of our legal system, though rarely exercised in relation to indictable offences… remains a valuable constitutional safeguard against inertia or partiality on the part of authority". Lord Wilberforce in Gouriet v. Union of Post Office Workers [1977] UKHL 5. A notable example of a private prosecution is the attempt by the families of victims of the Hillsborough disaster, where 96 people died after being crushed at a football game, to privately prosecute David Duckenfield, the Chief Superintendent responsible for crowd control, after an inquest ruled the deaths accidental and the CPS declined to prosecute.

private organisations, such as the Royal Society for Prevention of Cruelty to Animals (RSPCA) and for protection of copyright.[26]

To initiate a private prosecution, an individual must provide the relevant information to a magistrate who can, if they accept the validity of the information given, then issue a summons or a warrant for arrest.[27] If a summons is issued and the matter progresses to trial, the Crown Prosecution Service has the right to take over the prosecution and to either take it to trial or potentially discontinue it, should they decide there is insufficient evidence, or that it is not in the public interest to proceed. It should be noted, however, that legal aid is *not* available to individuals instituting private prosecutions and consequently its application is arguably limited to those with the means to do it.[28]

3 Personal Participation of the Accused in Criminal Proceedings

In England and Wales, a defendant charged with an indictable offence is required to attend her own trial. This requirement is also seen as part of fulfilling a defendant's right to effective participation in her own defence. As Lord Bingham outlines in the leading case on trials in absentia, *R v Jones*:

> For very many years the law of England and Wales has recognised the right of a defendant to attend his trial and, in trials on indictment, has imposed an obligation on him to do so. The presence of the defendant has been treated as a very important feature of an effective jury trial.[29]

This summary, however, skates over much more difficult questions about defendant participation at trial in England and Wales, specifically (a) whether a defendant

---

[26] There has been a recent move to remove the right of private prosecution from organizations such as the RSCPA, the argument being that this enlarges criminalization with private parties being more likely to unnecessarily prosecute individuals for whom an alternative disposal might be more appropriate. See: http://www.bbc.co.uk/news/uk-37987213.

[27] This quite archaic process is called 'laying an information' and involves laying out the alleged charge and sufficient evidence for a magistrate to decide that a prosecution is warranted. It is important to note that the kinds of proceedings that permit the institution of private prosecutions are limited. Private prosecutions must be approved by the Attorney General in instances of pursuing crimes of universal jurisdiction such as war crimes, and the DPP must approve a prosecution in alleged cases of assisted suicide.

[28] Private prosecutions are not without controversy, however, with the case of Eleanor de Freitas highlighting the potential issues of enabling private parties to pursue prosecutions. De Freitas reported being raped by her then partner in 2013. The police, after initial investigation, decided there was insufficient evidence and dropped the case. Her ex-partner then initiated a private prosecution against her, which the CPS took over. De Freitas committed suicide just before she was due to stand trial for a false rape claim. The suitability of the prosecution, in light of Miss De Freitas' known mental illness, has drawn attention to the issues that can arise from private prosecution.

[29] Lord Bingham in R v Jones [2002] UKHL 5, p.

indicted of a criminal offence must always be present, and (b) most importantly, why the presence of the defendant is considered so important.

To begin by addressing (a), it is important to stress that whilst the defendant has the right to attend her own trial on indictment in the Crown Court, it is not always legally necessary for a defendant to be present for the trial to go ahead. As I will outline below, trials in absentia for indictable offences have been legally permitted in England and Wales since 2001. So, whilst a defendant's presence is considered desirable (as a "very important feature of an effective jury trial"), a defendant's presence is not deemed necessary to achieve a just outcome, nor is the absence of the defendant necessarily held to have breached that individual's rights (although only under certain conditions outlined below). In addition, should a defendant behave in a disruptive or aggressive manner, she may be removed from the court-room whilst the trial proceeds in her absence, again without this being deemed to offend a defendant's participatory rights at trial.[30]

However, although the right of access for a defendant at her own trial is not unfettered, there remains, as Lord Bingham outlined above, a longstanding and deep-seated belief that a defendant generally should be present at her own trial. But why this should be the case is less easy to establish. Lord Bingham notes in *Davis* that it is "a long-established principle of the common law that the defendant in a criminal trial should be confronted by his accusers."[31] The suggestion here, then, is that the compelling reason for a defendant's presence is that it invokes the principle of "confrontation", where a defendant has the right to confront the accusers against her.

This right of "confrontation," though, where a defendant has the right to confront the witnesses against them, is not a right recognized to the same extent in England and Wales as it is in other jurisdictions. Whilst the *Human Rights Act* protects a defendant's right to examine witnesses against her, or to have them examined, there is no explicit recognition of confrontation in and of itself. Mike Redmayne has argued that this is indicative of confrontation being a "weak" right in England and Wales, as opposed to a "strong right" in Europe and the US where such a principle is outlined explicitly in ECtHR case law, as well as in the Sixth Amendment of the US Constitution.[32]

In addition, the meaning of confrontation is arguably rather unclear, and why it should be a necessary right in England and Wales is debated. Some argue that con-frontation is linked to maintaining an open trial, where a defendant confronting her accusers guarantees a public process.[33] Others argue that confrontation is about the right to cross-examination of a defendant's accusers.[34] Others still argue confronta-

---

[30] See R v. Abrahams [1895], 21 VLR 343, p. 347.

[31] R v. Davis [2008] UKHL 36 at para 5.

[32] ECtHR, *Al-Khawaja and Tahery v United Kingdom*, judgment of 15 December 2011, Appl. Nos. 26766/05 and 22228/06, 2127. See also Redmayne (2010).

[33] Spigelman (2005), p. 148.

[34] See Friedman (2002), pp. 247–248.

tion protects the preference for oral testimony over the admission of hearsay evidence.[35] In addition, confrontation has been argued to be necessary for effective demeanour assessment or to help the jury to make an informed decision. It has also been argued that the gathering together at criminal trial is about less tangible concerns and more about the belief that something happens when people gather together, live, that could not happen as well any other way, expressing, as the US Supreme Court in *Coy v Iowa* explained, "something deep in human nature."[36]

Ian Dennis, outlining some of these possibilities, concludes that "confrontation can best be seen as a bundle of rights" rather than a single right.[37] In this respect, whilst England and Wales approach confrontation differently to the ECHR, they share the same vagueness about what confrontation means. As Mike Redmayne observed in 2010: "The scholarly literature is somewhat more helpful, but scholars have offered a range of ways of theorising confrontation, and these theories tend to have different implications for the scope of the confrontation right."[38]

However, whilst legal scholarship and jurisprudence about confrontation often privileges a rights based argument, it is worth noting that a considerable amount of scholarship argues that the compelling reasons for the presence of a defendant at her trial relate to different, and darker reasons, such as the imprinting of judicial authority over the body of the defendant, the public submission of a defendant to the process through their physical presence and other factors that are more to do with the effective claiming of authority of the law over the body of the defendant than to do with any protection of her procedural rights.[39] This argument is arguably given weight by the continued use of the dock in *all* criminal trials in England and Wales, despite empirical evidence that placing the defendant in the dock serves to undermine the presumption of their innocence in the eyes of a jury.[40]

Whilst there is no doubt, then, that *part* of the need for a defendant's presence is about protecting her rights, this is clearly not the only, or even the main reason of requiring a defendant's presence in England and Wales. Indeed, English law departs from ECtHR jurisprudence explicitly here. In *Al Khawaja and Tahery v United Kingdom*, the Strasbourg court found that the United Kingdom had violated the

---

[35] O'Brian (2005), p. 494.

[36] Redmayne is here referring to William O'Brian's work as well as referring to the US case of Coy v Iowa 487 US 2012 [1988] where the court argued that: "There is something deep in human nature that regards face-to-face confrontation between accused and accuser as essential to a fair trial in a criminal prosecution [...] It is always more difficult to tell a lie about a person "to his face" than "behind his back".

[37] Dennis (2010), p. 2.

[38] Redmayne (2010), p. 3.

[39] Goodrich (1984), Halewood (1997) and Leader (2007; 2010).

[40] Rossner (2016). Use of the dock has now been extended, in some cases, to include juvenile criminal proceedings. Previously, proceedings for those under 18 were deliberately made less adversarial and the defendant was able to sit with a parent or guardian, and a legal representative. Whilst this remains the case for many young defendants, the extension of the use of enclosed docks for underage defendants continues.

defendants' rights of confrontation, by permitting hearsay evidence.[41] However, the UK Supreme Court in *Horncastle* made explicit that they did not accept, and would not follow, the ECHR approach to confrontation.[42] Whilst the question at stake in these cases related to absent witnesses, rather than an absent defendant, it remains significant in evidencing the attitude in England and Wales towards confrontation and, through this, defendant presence: that whilst it is desirable a defendant and the witnesses against her share a room, it is not an absolute right.

Whilst what confrontation means and to what extent it is required continues to be debated in England and Wales, one other corollary question less often asked is the degree to which the presumption in favour of defendant presence includes specific physical presence *in person*, or whether presence can be facilitated through technology. This question is increasingly pertinent in the context of an increased use of technology to replace live witnesses, which is a growing feature of courts in England and Wales. It is now becoming an increasingly commonplace occurrence for defendants remanded in custody to appear at a first hearing, or for a bail hearing via video-link from prison, and not in person. Pre-trial hearings and sentencing are also often performed with the defendant watching via video-link.

A tentative answer to whether a defendant needs to physically be there can perhaps be seen in the recent developments in criminal trial proceedings to protect vulnerable and intimidated witnesses. Over the past 15 years in England and Wales, growing recognition of the problematic aspects of adversarial trial for those under 18 and for those who are victims of specific kinds of crimes, such as rape and sexual assault, has led to the introduction of 'special measures' to reduce the potential trauma that may result from the defendant and the witness sharing the same space.[43] The most significant special measure is the introduction of remote testimony, whereby a rape complainant, for example, is automatically entitled to testify from another room, and her testimony to be beamed live into the courtroom. This permits the inference that there is still a presumption that a defendant should be physically present in the courtroom. However, the recent trial of Rolf Harris on historical child sex offences signifies an important departure from this presumption. Harris spent the majority of the trial being beamed in remotely from the prison where he was remanded. This is the first time in British legal history that a defendant has appeared via video-link in his own trial. Whilst the judge in the trial emphasised that Harris's case was an exception, it remains to be seen whether a precedent has been established for future 'exceptions', undermining the long-held practice of ensuring a defendant's physical presence in the courtroom. Ultimately, it is contested as to why this preference for live presence remains, particularly in the absence of any conclusive arguments as to the value of confrontation in England and Wales, and the Harris trial suggests that it is possible practices may change in the future, having unknown,

---

[41] For a discussion of the decisions in both *Horncastle* and *Al Khawaja,* see Dennis (2010) and Redmayne (2010).

[42] R v. Horncastle [2009] UKSC 14.

[43] Ss16,17 Youth Justice and Criminal Evidence Act [YJCEA] 1999.

but potentially troubling, implications for defendants' participatory rights. It is important to note, however, that whilst remote hearings are increasingly routine for prisoners on remand, there are no plans in place to expand this further for the time being.

3.1   Personal Participation in the Pre-Trial Inquiry

The pre-trial period is of considerable importance when considering the participatory rights of defendants in criminal proceedings in England and Wales. As outlined above, the protected rights of a defendant all relate to a fair trial, but many potential breaches of Article 6 can of course occur prior to trial. Whilst the courts in England and Wales have been willing to recognise the contravention of Article 6 through the breaching of some pre-trial procedures, such as improper evidence gathering, much of the difficulties that defendants now face are to do with being expected to enter a plea in the absence of advance information about the prosecution's case, as well as being expected to enter a plea in the potential absence of legal representation or assistance.[44] This is again particularly the case for individuals accused of less serious offences and whose cases are heard in Magistrates' Courts, rather than Crown Courts.

As outlined above, access to legal aid is difficult and it is likely—although we currently lack sufficient empirical research in the area—that many individuals, particularly those in Magistrates' Courts, are going without legal representation, and not necessarily doing so out of choice. In addition, recent efficiency measures, including new streamlined hearings to avoid any unnecessary delays, means that defendants in Magistrates' Court proceedings are expected to give their plea at a first hearing. This means entering a plea can take place before the defendant has received approval for legal aid funding and, potentially, even before a defendant has had any contact with a duty solicitor.[45]

In addition, as the Crown Prosecution Service explicitly outlines in their guidance on Advance Information:

---

[44] The courts have long recognised in England and Wales that pre-trial breaching of fairness can undermine a fair trial overall; for example, improperly gathered evidence by the police can be held to undermine this right (see R v. Chalkley and Jeffries [1998] 2 All ER 155). However, in England and Wales there is still a presumption that evidence be permitted, however gathered, unless it would contravene the fairness of the trial or if it is itself unreliable. The breaching of a defendant's rights, or the violation of the codes governing policing (PACE codes) will not necessarily result in the exclusion of the evidence at trial.

[45] Nicola Padfield's (2012) article into self-representation in criminal proceedings found there were several defendants who had had no access to legal representation, saying they had not been able to obtain the services of a lawyer. Whilst the reasons for this are unclear, given that duty solicitors are theoretically meant to be available at all courtrooms, it is clearly the case that there is a substantial minority of defendants who never obtain legal advice, and that this is not voluntary.

> The right to a fair trial under Article 6 of the ECHR does not require that prosecution wit-
> ness statements in summary proceedings have to be disclosed to the defence before trial.[46]

Whilst the prosecution are meant to disclose advance information about their case (The Initial Details of Prosecution Case, or IDPC), this is only required under the *Criminal Procedure Rules* "as soon as practicable" and in any event no later than the "beginning of the day of the first hearing."[47] At the point of a plea hearing, the prosecution only needs to provide a bare outline of the charges and the entering of a plea "does not depend on the extent of advance information, service of evidence, disclosure of unused material or grant of legal aid."[48] This means that today in England and Wales a defendant in a Magistrates' Court may enter a plea in the absence of any information about the evidence against her, beyond a bare recital of the charges, and that she may do so without having had any legal advice about how to plead.

Adding to this situation, defendants are also incentivized to plead guilty through the offering of automatic sentencing reduction. This is designed to limit the number of cases going to trial. Any individual pleading guilty at a first hearing will automatically have their sentence "discounted" by a third. Thereafter the reduction drops to one-quarter once a trial date is set and one-tenth if the defendant pleads guilty at the door of the trial or during the trial itself.[49] For an individual facing court, especially those who cannot access legal advice, this kind of incentivization can arguably potentially act as a form of pressurisation into entering a guilty plea. It is currently estimated that more than 90% of defendants plead guilty at a first hearing in a Magistrates' Court.[50] Nicola Padfield, drawing on a 2009 study by Souza and Kemp, argues there is evidence that the chances of pleading guilty are increased by not having legal representation.[51]

Finally, as mentioned earlier, more defendants are appearing remotely from custody, particularly for first hearings and bail decisions.[52] This can arguably be significant in that appearing from a prison may affect how the accused is perceived by the court, and may make a magistrate more likely to perceive such an individual as a threat, which is prejudicial to her right to a presumption of innocence.[53] This can

---

[46] See http://www.cps.gov.uk/legal/a_to_c/advance_information/.

[47] Criminal Procedure Rules 8.2.

[48] Leveson LJ (2009) cited in CPS guidance on disclosure, Appendix E, available http://www.cps.gov.uk/legal/d_to_g/disclosure_manual/annex_k_disclosure_manual/ (accessed 10 January 2017).

[49] Sentencing Council 2007.

[50] Maguire (2012). Alternatively, conversely, this may also lead some individuals charged with triable either way offences to take their chances in crown court before a jury and risk a longer sentence in the absence of effective legal advice.

[51] Padfield (2012), Souza and Kemp (2009). It is also notable that the latter research was done prior to further alterations to legal aid. Whilst there is no recent empirical research available, one can expect that the situation would have worsened in regards to access to representation for defendants in Magistrates' Courts.

[52] Rowden (2013) and Ridout (2010).

[53] There has been much interesting scholarship done into the procedural safeguards around the presumption of innocence and how it is protected, however, most of it is focused around the analy-

undermine a defendant's chances of obtaining bail.[54] All of these pre-trial features clearly potentially conflict with or undermine a defendant's right to a fair trial and their rights of effective participation, may be difficult to use as a basis for a subsequent appeal in terms of breaches of Article 6.

3.2   Personal Participation in Proceedings in Camera

The right to an open trial for a defendant accused of criminal conduct is subject to certain limitations dependant on the type of offence in England and Wales. Cases involving children as victims, and sexual assault proceedings, are automatically closed to the public. In addition, other kinds of hearings relating to "sensitive material" may also be closed to the public. This has most recently come to public attention in the case of Errol Incedal, who was charged with terrorism related offences, and whose case was one of several recent attempts in England and Wales to hold cases involving terrorism charges in secret.

In the *Incedal* case, the Director of Public Prosecution [DPP] made an application to the court to hold the trial in camera as well as made an application for non-disclosure of sensitive material, in addition to an application to keep the defendant anonymous. This application was supported by the Secretary of State for Home Department and the Secretary of State for Foreign and Commonwealth affairs who each provided certificates and schedules of evidence supporting the DPP's application for secrecy.[55] A challenge from the *Guardian* newspaper and others prevented the trial from taking place entirely secretly, and resulted in certain parts of the trial being open to journalists and the name of the defendant being disclosed.[56] Had the full application of the DPP succeeded, however, the trial would have been closed to the public, closed from all reporting, the defendant would have remained unnamed and any evidence relating to the case would have gone unreported. As it was, the defendant was named, and journalists were able to attend some of the proceedings and provide some coverage.

But what effect does the advent of the "secret" trial have for a defendant's participatory rights? In this case, it meant that the defendant and his legal representative

---

sis of reverse burdens in law (see, for example Picinali 2014). There is less done into the degree to which interim measures prior to trial can undermine such a presumption. Jenni Ward's (2015) article on changes to pretrial provides a good overview of scholarship into virtual courts and their contested problems and benefits.

[54] In addition, should the defendant have legal representation and appear remotely, that legal representative must choose to either be in the courtroom, and therefore be separated from their client, or to be with their client and therefore remote from the courtroom.

[55] When considering whether to hold proceedings in camera, the court in England and Wales makes the final decision, but does so with 'the highest regard' to the Secretary of State and it is generally expected that the court should 'not depart from their view'. Guardian News and Media Ltd & Ors v R. & Incedal [2016] EWCA Crim 11, para 51, 52.

[56] *ibid.*

were only entitled to receive redacted certificates from the Secretary of State that laid out the need for secret proceedings. Incedal and his representative were not entitled to the schedules of information about the protected evidence, which obviously impeded their ability to adequately prepare a defence. However, during the trial itself, Incedal and his representative had the right to hear the evidence against him and to test it. As the presiding judge in the *Guardian* appeal noted:

> It is important to reiterate that a defendant's rights are unchanged whether a criminal trial is heard in open Court or in camera and whether or not the proceedings may be reported by the media: thus, the defendant in such a hearing has the right to know the full case against him and to test and challenge that case fully. This is a very proper consideration but it does not, in any way, lessen the need for close scrutiny of any suggested departure from the principle of open justice.[57]

Whilst a defendant's procedural rights do not markedly differ under such circumstances, it is arguably overly optimistic to argue that a defendant's rights are "unchanged" in such circumstances. Leaving aside the lack of information provided prior to trial, the attempt to ban all reportage from the trial also undermines the "openness" of the criminal proceedings protected under Article 6. Secondly, a defendant's rights in such circumstances to know the "full case" against him does not include the disclosure of identity or source of any sensitive witnesses or information who can remain protected. Overall, the courts in England and Wales have made it clear that there is no overriding right to an open trial, or to disclosure, that cannot be overridden by the interests of national security, and that trials can be deemed fair by a court under the Human Rights Act even if that trial is held entirely in secret. This suggests a clear limitation on participatory rights for defendants in any case that involves "sensitive material."[58]

3.3   Personal Participation in Alternative Proceedings

One alternative method of proceedings with growing use in England and Wales is that of restorative justice, currently being used as both an alternative to prosecution and an alternative form of sentencing.[59] In each instance, the accused must admit their guilt before the process can take place. The victim and/or victim's representative then gather with the defendant, facilitators and other interested parties to discuss ways in which the guilty party can make amends for their wrongdoing to the victim and within the community and provides an opportunity for the victim to

---

[57] Guardian News And Media Ltd & Ors v R. & Incedal [2016] EWCA Crim 11, para 36.

[58] See ECtHR, *Kennedy v UK,* judgment of 18 May 2010, Appl. No. 26839/05, 682; Home Office v Tariq [2011] UKSC 35. As Dinah Rose points out, this means that: "A statutory claim seeking compensation for race discrimination may be held entirely in secret, in the absence of the claimant, if the government considers that disclosure of the relevant evidence would harm national security, and such a trial is not incompatible with article 6 of the Convention." Rose (2014), p. 10.

[59] For more information on restorative justice, see Rossner (2013).

explain the impact the crime committed by the individual has had on them.[60] These restorative justice methods are most commonly used for youth offenders, as the emphasis is on restoration and reintegration into the community.[61] Certain types of offences, particularly the more serious, any violent and any sexual offences are not considered appropriate for restorative methods. Advocates of this process argue that an emphasis on reintegration and restoration avoids the marginalisation or ritual shaming of traditional criminal proceedings and potentially lowers the risk of recidivism. In addition, this form of proceedings enable the victim to take a more active role than allotted to them in traditional adversarial trial. In any form of restorative justice, both the offender and the victim must consent.[62] Regardless of the form restorative justice takes, the offender will personally participate in the proceedings, rather than through a legal representative, although she has the right to have people attend the conference with her for support.

3.4 Personal Participation at Trial

Whilst debate remains as to the value of a defendant's physical presence in the courtroom at trial, the defendant occupies a largely passive role in criminal proceedings in England and Wales. This has historically been argued to be the result of the introduction of defence counsel in the late eighteenth and nineteenth century. Prior to this time, legal representation for the accused was banned and the accused had to represent herself. Historically, legal representation was seen as undesirable as it was argued that a defendant telling her own story was more persuasive and convincing than that of an intermediary party telling her story for her. William Hawkins, writing in 1716, commented in *Pleas of the Crown:*

> Every one of common Understanding may as properly speak to a Matter of Fact, as if he were the best Lawyer. It requires no manner of Skill to make a plain and honest Defence. The Simplicity and Innocence artless and ingenuous Behaviour of one whose conscience acquits him, has something in it more moving and convincing than the highest Eloquence of persons speaking in a Cause not their own.[63]

---

[60] This process can be done face-to-face, virtually and through 'shuttling' letters. For more details on when and how restorative justice is used, see the CPS's Restorative Justice Guide at: http://www.cps.gov.uk/legal/p_to_r/restorative_justice/.

[61] In this respect, youth justice in England and Wales is compatible with the European Convention of the Rights of a Child where '[t]he protection of the best interests of the child means…that the traditional objectives of criminal justice, such as repression/retribution, must give way to rehabilitation and restorative justice objectives in dealing with child offenders. This can be done in concert with attention to effective public safety.' UN CRC, para 10, gen comment 10.

[62] Although in some cases, if the victim does not consent, another affected community member may participate, if appropriate.

[63] Hawkins 1724 (re-edited in 1978), p. 34.

The introduction of defence counsel had the concomitant effect of silencing the defendant. Once a defendant was not required to tell their own story, this left them little to do at their own trial.[64] Charles Cottu, a French visitor to the English courts in the 1820s, commented that in England and Wales "the accused does so little in his own defence that his hat on a pole might without inconvenience be his substitute at trial."[65] This is still the case today: a defendant plays no role in evidence gathering, or fact-finding unless she chooses to represent herself. In addition, until relatively recently defendants were also not allowed to testify under oath. It is still common for a defendant to not offer testimony, although since 1994 there has been the right to draw inferences from a defendant's silence. This passivity of the defendant adds weight to sociological claims that the primary value of a defendant's presence at trial lies in the symbolic weight of their presence in the dock, emphasising the authority of the law and their submission to the process.

3.5 Personal Participation in Higher Instances

As mentioned earlier, a defendant has a right to represent herself in all courts, including the higher courts, but whilst it is possible for a defendant to represent herself at trial, it is highly unusual for an individual to be unrepresented at appeal, and a represented appellant's presence is not required in the higher courts.

3.6 Personal Participation of Private Parties Other Than Defendants

In adversarial trial, there is no recognized role for a victim. Unlike the defendant (who usually has representation) the crime is prosecuted by the state, who does not represent the victim or the victim's interest. The victim's primary importance is that of a source of evidence and if he or she does give evidence, they will be treated similarly to any other witness, and they make no contribution to fact finding. This state of affairs has prompted much criticism from victim's campaigners over the last 30 years, most notably in cases of rape and sexual assault where the complainants, who are often the only source of evidence, have been gruellingly or brutally cross examined for hours, and sometimes even days, on the stand in court.[66]

In the first instance, this has led to the introduction of special measures for what are known as "intimidated" or "vulnerable" witnesses. These are witnesses, such as

---

[64] See Langbein (2003), for a comprehensive overview of the introduction of defence counsel into criminal proceedings in England and Wales.

[65] Cottu quoted in Langbein (2003), p. 6.

[66] Zydervelt et al. (2016).

sexual assault victims or children, which a court deems likely to be negatively affected by the court setting to the point that it will adversely affect their ability to give evidence.[67] There are a number of "special measures" available as alternatives for vulnerable or intimidated witnesses, including the option of testifying remotely, the option of testifying behind screens, having the opportunity to see the courtroom beforehand and excluding the public from the courtroom (which is automatic in cases of rape, sexual assault and cases involving children).

However, whilst these reforms sought to ameliorate the traumatic experiences of testifying at adversarial trial, many victim's groups argued that more needed to be done to involve the victim more in the prosecutorial process. Victims of crime complained they were frequently left uninformed by police and the CPS about major decisions in their case, or were not told about court dates, or were not told why their cases were dropped. This has led to the Victims Right of Review, where victims have the right to review decisions taken in their case, including where the CPS has declined to prosecute, the right to review of police decisions to drop a case, the right to be informed about any significant development in an investigation, and being notified when a suspect has been arrested, or released.[68]

In addition, those who are victims or the family of victims have the right to make a Victim Personal Statement [VPS] prior to the sentencing of a convicted offender. This statement is an opportunity for the victim to explain to the court the impact the crime has had on them or on their family. The VPS can be read aloud in a courtroom but cannot affect sentencing. As above, victims are also now, where appropriate, given the opportunity to participate in alternative restorative justice proceedings, enabling them to play a more concrete role as well as giving them the opportunity to express to the offender the impact the crime has had on them.[69]

4   *In Absentia* Proceedings

Trials in absentia have been permitted in England and Wales since 2001, but they are meant to only be held when in the "interests of justice" and should be "exceptionally rare".[70] *R v Jones*, the leading case on the subject, established the test for permitting such absentia trials, where:

(b) the court must not proceed if the defendant is absent, unless the court is satisfied that—

---

[67] ss16–17, Youth Justice and Criminal Evidence Act 1999.

[68] See CPS Victim Right To Review, http://www.cps.gov.uk/victims_witnesses/victims_right_to_review/.

[69] The value of the VPS has been debated. On the one hand, there was recent controversy over a judge being heard by a victim's family describing the VPS as making 'no difference' (BBC 2014); on the other hand, a judge who took into account a victim's plea for clemency for a defendant had his sentencing decisions criticized.

[70] See R v Hayward and Ors. [2001] EWCA Crim 168.

(i) the defendant has waived the right to attend, and
(ii) the trial will be fair despite the defendant's absence[71]

The court is therefore not permitted to *assume* that a defendant has waived her rights if she is not in attendance; rather the circumstances must indicate that the defendant has deliberately waived them. Having said that, though, whilst the assumption derived from *Jones* might mean that evidence of a waiver needs to be an explicit renunciation of rights, this is in fact not the case.[72] As *R v O Hare* outlines:

> for an accused to be taken to have waived his right to be present at his trial, it must be proved that he knew of, or was indifferent to, the consequences of being tried in his absence and without legal representation; a direction from the court upon the grant of bail, explaining the consequences of non-attendance at trial, and the provision to the accused of a written statement to the same effect would, therefore, generally provide an incontrovertible means of proof.[73]

Whilst it is therefore insufficient for a court to decide that a defendant "must have known", it seems that the "opportunity" for a defendant to decline to be there is satisfied by there being evidence that the defendant received a standardized written statement informing her of the consequences of non-attendance at trial.[74] However, whilst such a situation may give rise to the existence of a "waiver", the court is still not entitled to proceed on this basis alone. Instead, the court must then consider the question of the overall fairness of the proceedings, should it continue in the absence of the defendant. This overall fairness is tested by considering:

> the extent of the disadvantage to the defendant in not being able to give his account of events; whether an adjournment might assist in securing the defendant's attendance, and whether the defendant wished to be legally represented at the trial or whether he had waived his right to representation.[75]

This means that whilst it is possible for a defendant to be tried in her absence, it is less likely if the defendant does not have legal representation. It is theoretically

---

[71] *R v Jones* [2002] UKHL 5, [2003] 1 A.C. 1.

[72] "The decision to try a defendant in his absence had to be exercised with the utmost care and caution. It was important for the court to determine whether the defendant deliberately and consciously chose to absent himself. If that was the case, the court then had to consider all the relevant circumstances, including: the seriousness of the offence; the extent of the disadvantage to the defendant in not being able to give his account of events; whether an adjournment might assist in securing the defendant's attendance, and whether the defendant wished to be legally represented at the trial or whether he had waived his right to representation." R. v Jones [2002] UKHL 5, [2003] 1 A.C. 1.

[73] *R. v. O'Hare* [2006] Crim.L.R. 950, CA.

[74] See for example *R v. Folarin* [2014] EWCA Crim 3033 where the defendant was considered to have been given 'ample notice' and therefore his non-attendance was considered to be a waiving of his right to attend.

[75] R v Jones [2002] UKHL 5, [2003] 1 A.C. 1. The initial *Jones* test included the seriousness of the offence, however this has discounted with the House of Lords stating that a just outcome and a fair trial was of equal importance, regardless of the seriousness of the offence being tried. See *Guttentag v. DPP* [2009] EWHC 1849.

possible, though, for a trial to proceed in the absence of a defendant who has waived her rights to representation.

The above guidance for trials in absentia applies in Crown Courts only. The situation for trials in absentia is different for a defendant in the Magistrates' Courts where procedural safeguards are less thorough. In Magistrates' Courts, the magistrates can proceed without a defendant under Section 54 of the *Criminal Justice and Immigration Act 2008* which "creates a presumption that, if defendants fail to attend for trial without good cause, magistrates will use their powers to try them in their absence and sentence them if convicted."[76] Prior to this act, the court could only proceed in the absence of a defendant if:

> it is proved to the satisfaction of the court, on oath or in such other manner as may be prescribed, that the summons was served on him within what appears to the court to be a reasonable time before the hearing or adjourned hearing or the defendant has appeared on a previous occasion to answer to the complaint.[77]

The new provision explicitly states that "if the accused has attained the age of 18 years, the court shall proceed in his absence unless it appears to the court to be contrary to the interests of justice to do so", and the passage of the bill is emblematic of the concerted pushes towards enhancing the "efficiency" of criminal proceedings.[78]

The only check on the right of a Magistrates' Court to proceed in a defendant's absence is if there is an "acceptable reason for his failure to appear." What this acceptable reason is, however, is up for debate. In *R v Ealing*, a defendant repeatedly failed to attend court and provided medical certificates for his absence. Tuckey, LJ, in permitting the court to proceed despite this argued that:

> includes a fair opportunity to be present at his trial to hear and test the evidence against him and give evidence on his own behalf. However, the words are "fair opportunity" not "unlimited opportunity", otherwise it would never be possible to proceed in a defendant's absence and a defendant would be able to postpone trials indefinitely without the risk that the court would eventually be able to say, "enough is enough, we will proceed in his absence".[79]

Whilst it seems reasonable that such a provision would be of utility where a defendant is seemingly avoiding trial for an extended period, this discretion is illustrated more problematically in *R v Solihull* where a defendant was not allowed into the courtroom as he had been making a scene outside court.[80] The Magistrates in that case decided that despite him being physically prevented from being present, he was "voluntarily absent," and they tried him in his absence. This decision was over-

---

[76] s54, Criminal Justice and Immigration Act 2008.

[77] S55(3) Magistrates Court Act 1980.

[78] This efficiency push has been notably undertaken by the government since 2010 as part of their plans for "Swift and Sure Justice Ministry of Justice [MoJ] 2012, however this bill predates the coalition government and is a product of the previous Labour administration.

[79] Magistrates Court Ex p. Burgess [2001] 165 J.P. 82.

[80] R. (on the application of Davies) v Solihull Justices [2008] EWHC 1157.

turned at appeal where the judges argued that a defendant must have "control" over the reasons why he may be absent; if it is outside of his control, then this does not count.[81] Whilst the appeal decision illustrates that there are limits to the circumstances in which magistrates may "presume" a defendant voluntarily absented herself, the wideness of the presumption under S54 underlines the discretion magistrates are permitted in determining whether to proceed without a defendant.

Indeed, whilst trials in absentia are argued to be justified only in exceptional circumstances, they are becoming increasingly more commonplace in Magistrates' Courts. Whilst statistics on trials in absentia are not published by the Ministry of Justice, a 2006 estimate found that at least 15% of trials proceeded in a defendant's absence in the lower courts, with these cases mostly situations of low level motoring offences.[82] Given the change in the law in 2008 that enables a presumption for a court to proceed in a defendant's absence, it is reasonable to expect that the amount may now be higher. Because the courts are not required to provide a reason for a decision to proceed without the defendant under S54, there is a potential risk that trials will proceed without sufficient investigation into the reasons for a defendant's absence. This could lead to situations where defendants unaware of their trial, or unable to access the courts, have trials held in their absence. Whilst legal representatives of absent defendants in both Magistrates' and Crown Court may argue against the trial proceeding in their client's absence, a bigger issue is that of unrepresented parties who have no one to argue for them in these circumstances.

4.1   Default Proceedings and Subsequent Remedies

If a defendant is tried and convicted in absentia in England and Wales in a Magistrates' Court, she may lodge a statutory declaration to the Magistrates' Court under the Criminal Procedure Rules 37.11 stating that she was unaware of their trial until after it took place. If this is done within 21 days of the trial, "the hearing must be treated as if it had not taken place at all."[83] But this provision is rarely taken up in practice and this suggests that there is limited awareness of such a right. In addition, it is likely that many individuals convicted in their absence remain unaware of this fact for a considerable period, which is problematic when appeals must be lodged within 21 days of the conviction (although the court has discretion to extend the time allowed). These factors call into question how easy it is to obtain a remedy in such circumstances. It should be noted, however, that all individuals convicted of an offence in a Magistrates' Court have a right of re-hearing in a Crown Court. For defendants tried and convicted in absentia in a Crown Court, however, there is no

---

[81] R v. Thames Youth Court [2002] 166 J.P. 711, QBD (Pitchford J.). and R. (M.) v. Burnley, Pendle and Rossendale Magistrates' Court, [2009] 174 J.P. 102, QBD (Langstaff J.).

[82] National Audit Office (2006), p. 9.

[83] s37.11 Criminal Procedure Rules.

automatic right of rehearing and one will only take place if the court finds the initial conviction unsafe. Again, it is important to note that protection of these rights is likely to be stronger where the defendant in question has legal representation.

5 Participatory Safeguards in EAW Proceedings

5.1 Participatory Rights in the Decision on Surrender

The arrangements governing extradition proceedings through the European Arrest Warrant in England and Wales are outlined in s1 of the *Extradition Act* 2003 which implements the 2002 European Union Framework decision.[84] Under these current arrangements, all EAW warrants are received and certified by the National Crime Agency [NCA]. Once this is done a warrant can be issued for the individual sought. Once an individual is detained, they must be brought 'as soon as practicable' to Westminster Magistrates' Court where all hearings of extradition are held. This will involve an initial hearing, which deals with preliminary matters and sets a date for the next hearing, and the Extradition hearing proper where the decision as to extradition will be made.

There are a number of procedural safeguards for participants built into the extradition process into England and Wales. These involve both protection of participatory rights in the hearings themselves, as well as other forms of protection against unjust treatment that may result from the execution of the extradition request itself. In terms of participatory rights, an individual must be brought to Westminster Magistrate's Court within 48 h of being detained. Once at the Magistrates' Court, the individual has the right to know about the content of the EAW, which must be explained to her by a judge at the initial hearing. In addition, the individual must be informed in detail about the possibility of consenting to extradition and the full consequences of this decision. The individual may also not be remanded in custody without a hearing as to the suitability of bail.

The individual also has the right to legal representation for these hearings and can make an application for legal aid. If she is unsuccessful in obtaining legal aid she may represent herself. It is notable that if an individual does not have legal representation, the judge is not allowed to accept her consent until ensuring that she has been made thoroughly aware of the consequences of this consent. In addition, an interpreter must be provided throughout the proceedings for the individual. Should the extradition order be granted, the individual at this point also has the right to appeal this, although this is subject to having the appeal accepted by the higher court.

---

[84] As I will discuss later, the UK opted out of the Framework Decision, along with 130 other EU policing and criminal justice measures, in July 2013. It opted back into the Framework Decision on the EAW in November 2014. Dawson and Lipscombe (2015).

Beyond the procedural rights an individual has at their surrender hearing, the court itself in England and Wales has powers to refuse extradition via an EAW if they do not accept certain facts about the extradition claim:

> In England and Wales, at the extradition hearing the appropriate judge has the same powers (as nearly as may be) as a magistrates' court would have if the proceedings were the summary trial of an information against the person in respect of whom the Part 1 warrant was issued.[85]

This power of scrutiny can lead to the court discharging an EAW and refusing to proceed with extradition. This could happen for several reasons. Firstly, should the Westminster Court find that the extradition would breach the human rights of the individual, they can discharge the extradition application. Secondly, the Westminster court may enquire into the circumstances under which the individual was convicted and whether her rights were protected in the trial. If the court finds that the trial was not fair, this can be another reason to discharge the EAW. The courts can also decline an extradition request if the offence for which the individual is either wanted, or has been convicted of, is not a recognized offence in the United Kingdom. All of these situations above are recognized as optional refusal grounds under Article 4 of the 2002 Framework decision.

In addition, though, the courts in England and Wales have arrogated for themselves power to refuse extradition on other grounds as well. This includes the option to refuse an application for extradition if the court finds the request has been unnecessarily delayed, and is therefore "unjust or oppressive." This has most recently been seen in *Cieczka v Poland* [2016] where the court declined to extradite an individual due to a 6-year delay between the home country knowing the whereabouts of an individual and requesting their extradition.[86] Most recently, the *Anti-Social Behaviour, Crime and Policing Act 2014* has inserted a proportionality test into the Extradition Act whereby, under the new provision of s21a), a judge may consider not only whether the extradition may breach an individual's human rights but also whether the extradition is proportionate to the extradition offence and enables a judge to refuse extradition on these grounds. Each of these grounds have been criticized as undermining the principle of mutual recognition and as being incompatible with the Framework.

***In Absentia* Proceedings in the Trial Country and Its Relevance in the Surrender Procedure**   Section 20 of the Extradition Act 2003 covers the procedure that judges must go through when the EAW issued concerns an individual convicted of an offence in another country. In this circumstance, the judge must first consider, under s20.1, "whether the person was convicted in his presence." If the judge is satisfied that the individual was present at her own trial, the extradition may proceed (presuming the EAW does not fall foul of the other stipulations listed above that may prevent extradition taking place). If, however, the judge determines that the

---

[85] Ss9.1, Extradition Act 2003.
[86] *Cieczka v Poland* [2016] EWHC 3399 (Admin).

individual was not present at her own trial and that it was conducted in absentia the court must then consider if the individual voluntarily absented herself from her trial. If the court finds that this is the case, then extradition may proceed (again excluding situations outlined above where the court deems an individual's human rights to be at risk, or any other related justification to discharge the warrant). If the court decides that an individual was not voluntarily absent, extradition may only proceed if the judge is satisfied that the individual in question is "entitled to a retrial or (on appeal) to a review amounting to a retrial". This review must have the following basic rights requirements protected under Article 6:

(a) the right to defend himself in person or through legal assistance of his own choosing or, if he had not sufficient means to pay for legal assistance, to be given it free when the interests of justice so required;
(b) the right to examine or have examined witnesses against him and to obtain the attendance and examination of witnesses on his behalf under the same conditions as witnesses against him.[87]

If the Westminster court finds that no such remedy is available to an individual, a judge must not allow the extradition to proceed and instead must order the individual's discharge.

6 Participatory Safeguards in Transborder Inquiries and the Taking of Overseas Evidence

Richard Vogler argues that until "comparatively recently, the United Kingdom had adopted a very negative attitude towards investigative co-operation between police forces" with a marked history of failure to opt into European agreements to facilitate transborder enquiries.[88] However, this has shifted significantly in the last decade or so, with the UK fully participating in the Schengen Agreement, including judicial cooperation provisions, by 2004.

The Home Office in the UK issues guidelines on Mutual Legal Assistance, explaining how and why it will consider requests for cooperation and assistance. In the first place, such requests must be lodged via a formal International Letter of Request (ILOR). Requests for MLAs may be refused on *de minimis* grounds (where the offence concerns a financial loss of less than £1000, or the offence occurred over 10 years prior with no good explanation for the delay), or for a host of other reasons, including the absence of dual criminality, or if there is reason to believe the request was made:

---

[87] Ss20.8a), b), Extradition Act 2003.
[88] Vogler (2013), p. 389.

for the purpose of investigating, prosecuting or punishing a person on account of his/her race, gender, sexual orientation, religion, nationality, ethnic origin or political opinions or that person's position may be prejudiced for any of those reasons.[89]

Should the MLA requests be acceded to, any investigations undertaken by the police here are subject to the PACE codes, which outline extensive and detailed limits on policing powers. This includes the 'detention clock' specifying how long an individual may be detained upon being arrested before he or she must be charged or released. This also includes detailed provisions on interviewing, including the suspect's right to a copy of the interviewing audio or videotape. A detailed record must be made of the individual's custody as well, and this must be made available to the suspect. The individual must also be allowed access to legal representation.[90]

In terms of the participatory safeguards for defendants with regards to the use of overseas evidence, s78 of PACE 1984 stipulates that evidence that would contravene the fairness of the trial should be excluded. This means the refusal to accept any forced confessions or evidence that may have been obtained under torture. However, evidence taken overseas in a manner different to the methods of evidence gathering in the United Kingdom will not necessarily be excluded. [91]

7   Requirements of Personal Participation and *In Absentia* Proceedings. *The Perspective of International Human Rights Law and EU Law*

There are a number of areas of criminal proceedings in England and Wales that demonstrate a trend towards the undermining of participatory rights. In the first instance, there is the continued use of the dock in all criminal proceedings, whereby a defendant is isolated in the courtroom. Not only does this separate her from her legal representative at her trial but in addition, the effect of the dock on perceptions of innocence has been documented.[92] More recent developments that can potentially affect the presumption of innocence have resulted from the growing use of video-link technology. As outlined above, individuals are increasingly appearing for bail hearings and sentencing remotely. Not only does this again potentially separate defendants from their legal representatives, thus potentially compromising their ability to make representations but it also means that they are not afforded the opportunity to be in the same room with the judge in question. The effect this may have on how they are perceived is not yet known, but scholars have hypothesised

---

[89] s2, MLA Guidelines 2015.

[90] PACE Code G (Arrest and Interviewing).

[91] The question of hearsay evidence is particularly pertinent here as much of the evidence submitted under the LOR may be in written form. Generally, under the CICA 2003, such written evidence can be admitted if the court believes the witness's justification for their absence.

[92] Rossner (2016).

that there is a potential for this kind of "dehumanised" contact to undermine the potential for empathy and affect the perception of their innocence.[93] In addition, the ongoing sentencing reduction for guilty pleas potentially creates a situation that may be encouraging individuals to falsely plead guilty.

Other areas that compromise defendants' participatory rights have resulted from the Coalition and Conservative governments' "Stop Delaying Justice" initiatives since 2012. This involves measures that are designed to avoid unnecessary hearings and delays but which has resulted in potentially compromising a defendant's rights. These measures include an emphasis on taking a plea at a first hearing in a Magistrates' Court even in situations where advance information has not been disclosed.[94]

In terms of provisions for trials *in absentia*, the increased emphasis since 2008 on enabling trials to proceed in the lower courts without any requirement for the courts to do any investigation as to why a defendant is not present is a potentially problematic provision, particularly where the remedy in question, the statutory declaration, is also potentially unsatisfactory in terms of how infrequently it is taken up, although here again we lack adequate research to know the full picture. This issue can however be potentially linked to the wider problem of lack of access to legal aid and lack of free legal advice meaning that very few individuals without representation in a situation where a trial has proceeded in their absence will be aware of what they should do and who to ask for help. In addition, whilst in the higher courts, the courts are not allowed to proceed without some enquiry into why the defendant is absent, it should be of concern that there is no rehearing right for those who are absent from indictable trials unless the conviction is deemed to be potentially unsafe.

Of most concern, of course, is the question of whether or not the United Kingdom will repeal the *Human Rights Act* altogether. Some, including the current Prime Minister Theresa May, have suggested withdrawing from the ECHR altogether and the jurisdiction of the ECtHR, although it should be emphasised that this is a minority view and not one endorsed by the Conservative government. However, whilst the replacement of the *Human Rights Act* with a British Bill of Rights is the only announced policy, it is of concern that some individuals at a high level in government would consider removing the right of appeal to Strasbourg for those who have had their right to a fair trial undermined. The publication of a draft *EU (Withdrawal) Bill* that fails to incorporate the EU Charter of Fundamental Rights is a troubling sign of the direction in which the UK may head in regard to rights protection.

In addition, the United Kingdom, even prior to the Brexit referendum, has form for behaving slightly reluctantly when it comes to implementing EU criminal justice policy. In 2013, the UK gave notice of its intention to opt out of a mass of criminal justice policy directives, although it has subsequently opted back into some of

---

[93] Rowden (2013).

[94] It should be noted as well that legal aid cuts not only affect the participatory rights of unconvicted defendants. Changes in legal aid provision to prisoners mean that those who have been convicted cannot obtain legal representation to protest about their conditions of imprisonment.

these, including the EAW. Post-Brexit decision, but prior to the actual leaving of the European Union, any speculation as to the future is very difficult to pin down. Whilst the draft *EU (Withdrawal Bill)* plans to incorporate current EU law into domestic law, which would include criminal justice policy, it is clear from a number of areas outlined above that the United Kingdom is keen to go its own way in the area of criminal justice. This is clear from the Supreme Court's reluctance to recognize the principle of confrontation as provided for in the ECtHR jurisprudence, parliament's 2014 insertion of its own proportionality tests for the execution of the EAW as well as other grounds of refusal not outlined in the Framework, despite this undermining the principle of mutual recognition. It is also evident in the ongoing difference of opinion of parliament with some rulings from Strasbourg, such as the decision on prisoner voting rights. It is, of course, most evident in the UK's desire to withdraw from the EU Charter of Fundamental Rights.

8 Concluding Remarks

As outlined above, there are a number of recent developments in criminal justice policy in England and Wales to cause concern for participatory rights. These include efficiency measures that limit access to information for defendants about the evidence against them, that limit time in which defendants can make a decision that can affect their future, and which also restrict access to legal representation, undermining defendants' ability to defend themselves. In addition, the push towards holding more trials without a defendant present (particularly in trials that deal with less serious offences) has the real potential of causing considerable injustice as the lower courts now have the power to proceed without enquiry as to a defendant's whereabouts.[95]

However, in concluding this chapter, whilst all of the above continues to cause concern, the larger shifts in criminal justice policy in England and Wales, and the concomitant effect shifts in policy will have on the participatory rights of defendants, remain up in the air. We are living through a critical time, the interstice between the triggering of Article 50 and the concluded arrangements, so we can only speculate as to what will happen in the future with regards to criminal justice policy. It seems almost certain that the EU Charter on Fundamental Rights will not be incorporated into domestic law after the UK leaves the EU. It is likely that the *Human Rights Act* will be repealed (this is certainly a key policy goal of the current government) and will be replaced by a British Bill of Rights, although the continuous delay of publication of this draft bill suggests it is proving a problematic promise to implement. If it does go ahead, however, this bill of rights is unlikely to be

---

[95] It is of course important to note, however, that whilst the Magistrates' Courts do not have to conduct an enquiry into a defendant's absence, this does not mean that they do not in practice. Again, we lack empirical research here to do more than speculate. Clearly, further research into Magistrates Courts proceedings is of critical importance in understanding how the policy shifts are working in practice.

radically different to the *Human Rights Act*, and is expected to retain most of the rights outlined in Article 6. However, a worst-case scenario is that such an introduction is a step towards an attempt to withdraw the United Kingdom from the ECHR and the jurisdiction of the ECtHR. It is important to stress that this is *not* government policy: the Conservatives dropping their pledge to withdraw from the ECHR before the last general election, meaning that until the end of the current parliament, 2022, any developments in this direction are off the table. However, our current Prime Minister has actively called for it until mid-2017 and so it remains a future possibility. There is also no doubt, on review, that there has been a ring of isolationism in the United Kingdom's approach to criminal justice policy from the EU for some time. What effect Brexit, and what Conor Gearty calls our "self-harming isolationism" will have on criminal justice policy and participatory rights in the future remains to be seen, but it is a source of deep concern.

References

BBC (2014) Family hears judge say victim statements make 'no difference'. 5 August 2014. http://www.bbc.co.uk/news/uk-28644799. Accessed 31 July 2018

Blackburn R (2015) Enacting a written constitution for the United Kingdom. Statute Law Rev 36(1):1–25

Dawson J, Lipscombe S (2015) Briefing Paper: the European Arrest Warrant. House of Commons Library, London

Dennis I (2010) The right to confront witnesses: meanings, myths and human rights. Crim Law Rev 4:255–274

Friedman RD (2002) The conundrum of children, confrontation and hearsay. Law Contemp Probl 65:249–252

Galanter M (2004) The vanishing trial: an examination of trials and related matters in federal and state courts. J Empir Leg Stud 1(3):459–570

Gearty C (2016) The Human Rights Act should not be repealed. https://ukconstitutionallaw.org/2016/09/17/conor-gearty-the-human-rights-act-should-not-be-repealed/. Accessed 31 July 2018

Goodrich P (1984) Law and language: an historical and critical introduction. J Law Soc 11(2):263–323

Halewood P (1997) Violence and the international word: conceptualizing violence: presence and future developments in international law. Albany Law Rev 60(3):565–570

Jennings I (1965) Magna Carta: and its influence in the world today: Private Publication, London

Langbein J (2003) Origins of the adversarial criminal trial. Oxford University Press, Oxford

Leader K (2007) Bound and Gagged: the Role of Performance in the Adversarial Criminal Trial. Philament 11

Leader K (2010) Closed-circuit television testimony: liveness and truth-telling. Law Text Cult, 14

Loughlin M (2003) The idea of public law. Oxford University Press, Oxford

Maguire M (2012) Criminal statistics and the construction of crime. In: Reiner R, Morgan R, Maguire M (eds) Oxford handbook of criminology. Oxford University Press, Oxford, pp 206–244

Ministry of Justice (2012) Swift and Sure Justice: The Government's Plans for Reforms of the Criminal Justice System. Stationery Office, London. https://www.gov.uk/government/uploads/system/uploads/attachment_data/file/217328/swift-and-sure-justice.pdf. Accessed 31 July 2018

National Audit Office (2006) Effective use of magistrates' courts hearings. Report by the Comptroller and Auditor General. HC 798 Session 2005–2006

O'Brian W (2005) The right of confrontation: US and European perspectives Law Q Rev 121:481, 494

Padfield N (2012) The right to self-representation in English criminal law. Revue internationale de droit pénal 83(3):357–375

Picinali F (2014) Innocence and burdens of proof in English criminal law. Law Probab Risk 13:243–257

Ridout F (2010) Virtual Courts, Virtual Justice. Criminal Law and Justice Weekly. 24th September 2010.   https://www.criminallawandjustice.co.uk/features/Virtual-Courts---Virtual-Justice (available on LexisNexis since April 2018)

Redmayne M (2010) Confronting Confrontation. LSE Law, Society and Economy Working Papers 10/2010

Rose D (2011) Beef and liberty: fundamental rights and the common law. Atkin Memorial Lecture. http://pgil.pk/wp-content/uploads/2014/12/Atkin_Memorial_Lecture_Final_version1.pdf. Accessed 31 July 2018

Rossner M (2013) Just emotions: rituals of restorative justice. Oxford University Press, Oxford

Rose D (2014) Beef and liberty: fundamental rights and the common law. Atkins Memorial Lecture. Full text available at: http://pgil.pk/wpcontent/uploads/2014/12/Atkin_Memorial_Lecture_Final_version.pdf

Rossner M (2016) Does the placement of the accused at court undermine the right to a fair trial? LSE Law Policy Briefing. http://eprints.lse.ac.uk/68977/. Accessed 31 July 2018

Rowden E (2013) Virtual courts and putting 'Summary' back into 'Summary Justice': Merely Brief, or unjust? In: Simon J, Temple N, Tobe R (eds) Architecture and justice: judicial meanings in the public realm. Ashgate, Farnham, Surrey

Souza K, Kemp V (2009) Study of defendants in Magistrates' Courts. Ministry of Justice, London

Spigelman J (CJ) (2005) The principle of open justice. Univ N S Wales Law J 29(1):147–166

Transform Justice (2016) Justice denied? The experience of unrepresented defendants in the criminal courts. http://www.transformjustice.org.uk/wp-content/uploads/2016/04/TJ-APRIL_Singles.pdf. Accessed 10 Jan 2017

Vick DW (2002) The human rights act and the British Constitution. Texas Int Law J 37:329–372

Vogler R (2013) Report on England and wales. In: Ruggeri S (ed) Transnational inquiries and the protection of fundamental rights in criminal proceedings. Springer, London

Ward J (2015) Transforming 'Summary Justice' through police-led prosecutions and "Virtual Courts": is "Procedural Due Process" being undermined? Br J Criminol 55(2):341–358

Zydervelt S, Zajac R, Kaladelfos A, Westera N (2016) Lawyers' strategies for cross-examining rape complainants: have we moved beyond the 1950s? Br J Criminol 57(3):551–569

Report on France

Barbara Drevet

Abstract Personal participation can be understood as the right to be involved in criminal proceedings going on against oneself. Participation in French criminal proceedings has, for the most part, been shaped by decisions made by the courts, the French *Cour de cassation* and *Conseil constitutionnel* or by the European Court of Human rights. Most notably, following many condemnations by the European Court of Human Rights, the contumacy rules have been replaced by the criminal default rules which are far more protective of the accused's fundamental rights.

This study provides an examination of the efforts made by French legislation to ensure personal participation at each stage of the criminal proceedings.

Abbreviations

Ass. plén.	Assemblée plénière de la Cour de cassation
Cass. crim.	Chambre criminelle de la Cour de cassation
CCP	Code of criminal procedure
CJEU	Court of Justice of the European Union
Cons. const.	Conseil constitutionnel
ECHR	European Convention on Human Rights
ECtHR	European Court of Human Rights

B. Drevet (✉)
Institut de Sciences Criminelles et de la Justice, Université de Bordeaux, Bordeaux, France

© Springer Nature Switzerland AG 2019   93
S. Quattrocolo, S. Ruggeri (eds.), *Personal Participation in Criminal Proceedings*, Legal Studies in International, European and Comparative Criminal Law 2, https://doi.org/10.1007/978-3-030-01186-4_5

1 Constitutional Requirements of the Involvement of Private Parties in Criminal Justice

Since 1971 and the decision *"Liberté d'association"* made by the *Conseil constitutionnel*,[1] French constitutional rules involve not only the Constitution itself but also both the Preambles of the Constitutions of 1958 and of 1946, the Declaration of the Rights of Man and of the Citizen of 1789 and laws consecrating "fundamental principles recognized by the laws of the Republic". Consequently, constitutional judges have to check whether the law they are reviewing is compatible with the principles contained by those texts.

Using article 16 of the Declaration of the Rights of Man and of the Citizen according to which "any society in which the guarantee of rights is not assured, nor the separation of powers determined, has no Constitution", the *Conseil constitutionnel* consecrated the right to an effective remedy as a constitutional principle, first implicitly,[2] then more clearly.[3] Therefore, every citizen has the right to have access to a judge, which, in criminal justice, applies to every private party,[4] meaning that both the victim and the accused must be able to have their case heard before a judge.

The involvement of the accused in criminal justice seems to be obvious since she is the reason why the process started in the first place. However, as she is involved mostly against her will, she has the right not to participate actively in the procedure. More precisely, she has the right not to contribute to incriminating herself, in other words, to stay silent. It has taken a very long time for the *Conseil constitutionnel* to recognize the constitutional value of the right to stay silent. In a landmark decision, it abrogated the provisions regarding police custody, in part because the person kept in custody wasn't informed that she had the right to stay silent,[5] but without giving it any constitutional character. However, in November 2016, the *Conseil constitutionnel* stated for the first time that the right to stay silent was a constitutional principle linked to article 9 of the Declaration of the Rights of Man and of the Citizen.[6] Therefore, the accused is protected, whether she chooses to be actively involved in the criminal procedure or not to participate.

If, generally speaking, the involvement of the accused in criminal justice has never really been problematic, the involvement of the victim, and more precisely the civil party, has proved to be more of a challenge. The *Conseil constitutionnel* had to

---

[1] Cons. const. 16 July 1971 "Liberté d'association", n° 71-44 DC.

[2] Cons. const. 21 January 1994, n° 93-335 DC, para. 4.

[3] Among many decisions, see Cons. const. 23 July 1999, n°99-416 DC, para. 37; Cons. const. 11 April 2014, n°2014-390 QPC, para. 3 regarding criminal law. For a summary of the appropriate decisions, see Vandermeeren (2005), p. 1102.

[4] Pradel (2015), § 381–382.

[5] Cons. const. 30 July 2010, n° 2010-14/22 QPC, § 28. On this issue, see Giudicelli (2011), p. 139; De Lamy (2011a), p. 168.

[6] Cons. const. 4 November 2016, n° 2016-594 QPC, § 5. See Combles De Nayves and Mercinier (2017), p. 27.

intervene in 2010[7] to give a "constitutional dimension to the civil party's rights".[8] The case was about article 575 CCP which prevented the victim from appealing before the *Cour de cassation* against a decision made by the Investigation Chamber if the prosecutor wasn't appealing before the *Cour de cassation* as well. As a result, the civil party did not have an autonomous access to the *Cour de cassation*. The constitutional judges based their decision on article 6[9] and article 16[10] of the Declaration of the Rights of Man and of the Citizen and explained that even if the civil party's situation was not identical to that of the accused or of the public prosecutor, article 575 meant that the civil party would not have access to the *Cour de cassation* if the public prosecutor chose not to appeal before it.[11] Consequently, the judges ruled that by preventing a party from effectively using its rights before the Investigation Chamber, article 575's restriction on the rights of the defence was unjustified.[12] Therefore, article 575 CCP was abrogated.

Interestingly enough, the same article had been examined by the European Court of Human Rights in 2002[13] and the judges concluded that article 6§1 of the European Convention on Human Rights had not been violated by the limit placed on the civil party. The European judges explained that "having regard to the role accorded to civil actions within criminal trials and to the complementary interests of civil parties and the prosecution, the Court cannot accept that the equality-of-arms principle has been infringed in the instant case (…) A civil party cannot be regarded as either the opponent—or for that matter necessarily the ally—of the prosecution, their roles and objectives being clearly different".[14] The difference between the two decisions might be explained by looking at the principles used by the *Conseil constitutionnel* and by the European Court of Human Rights. The former decision was based on the rights of the defence coupled with the equality of arms principle whereas the latter was only based on the equality of arms principle.[15]

In any case, the decision made by the *Conseil constitutionnel* in 2010 proved that the rights of the defence apply to the civil party, which is worth mentioning

---

[7] Cons. const. 23 July 2010, n° 2010-15/23 QPC.

[8] Bonfils (2016), §169.

[9] According to which the law "must be the same for all, either that it protects, or that it punishes".

[10] According to which "Any society in which the guarantee of rights is not assured, nor the separation of powers determined, has no Constitution".

[11] Cons. const. 23 July 2010, para. 8: "*si la partie civile n'est pas dans une situation identique à celle de la personne mise ne examen ou à celle du ministère public […], la disposition contestée a pour effet, en l'absence de pourvoi du ministère public, de priver la partie civile de la possibilité de faire censurer, par la Cour de cassation, la violation de la loi par les arrêts de la chambre de l'instruction…*".

[12] Cons. Const. 23 July 2010 para. 8: "*en privant une partie de l'exercice effectif des droits qui lui sont garantis par le code de procédure pénale devant la juridiction d'instruction, cette disposition apporte une restriction injustifiée aux droits de la défense*".

[13] ECtHR, *Berger v. France*, judgment of 3 December 2002, Appl. No. 48221/99.

[14] *Berger v. France* para. 38.

[15] See De Lamy (2011b), p. 188; Lacroix (2010), p. 2686; Touillier (2010), p. 10.

considering that according to the European Convention on Human Rights, the rights of the defence only apply to a person "charged with a criminal offence". Under French national law, those rights are regarded as a fundamental principle of the Republic[16] and apply to all the private parties. They include notably the adversarial principle, the right to an interpreter and the right to legal assistance.

2 Personal Participation of Private Parties and Legal Assistance

As a part of the rights of the defence, the right to legal assistance has long been recognized as a constitutional principle by the *Conseil constitutionnel.*[17] In 1995, the *Cour de cassation* even considered that the defence constituted a fundamental right with a constitutional character for everyone.[18] It means that the lawyer is constitutionally protected[19] and that every party involved in criminal justice, that is to say the accused and the victim, has to be able to have a lawyer. However, it does not mean that the parties must have a lawyer and they can choose not to be assisted by one.[20] In that case, no difference should be made between a party assisted by a lawyer and a party not assisted by one. The *Conseil constitutionnel* had to intervene twice to sanction two articles of the code of criminal procedure that made it impossible for a private party, whether the accused or the civil party, to have access to an information without a lawyer. In 2011, the constitutional judges decided that communicating the public prosecutor's requisitions following the end of the investigation only to the lawyers and not to the parties themselves violated the adversarial principle and the rights of the defence.[21] The following year, the constitutional judges made the same decision regarding the communication of the Investigation Chamber's decision to order an expertise to the parties' lawyers only.[22] More generally, the 2014 Act transposing the European Directive on the right to information in criminal proceedings[23] tried to make sure that the parties could have a direct access to all the information regarding their case. For instance, a second paragraph was

---

[16] Cons. const. 19–21 January 1981 "Sécurité et liberté", n° 80-127 DC.

[17] Cons. const. 19–21 January 1981 "Sécurité et liberté", n° 80-127 DC according to which the lawyer "*fait partie des droits de la défense qui résultent des principes fondamentaux de la République*".

[18] Ass. plén. 30 June 1995: "*la défense constitue pour toute personne un droit fondamental à caractère constitutionnel*".

[19] See Krikorian (2007), p. 3.

[20] Except before the assize court.

[21] Cons. const. 9 September 2011, n° 2011-160 QPC, §5.

[22] Cons. const. 23 November 2012, n° 2012-284 QPC, §4.

[23] *Loi n° 2014-535 du 27 May 2014 portant transposition de la directive 2012/13/UE du Parlement européen et du Conseil, du 22 May 2012, relative au droit à l'information dans le cadre des procédures pénales.*

included in article 63-4-1 CCP to add that the person kept in custody could have access to her file himself.

Consequently, both the accused and the victim can be assisted by a lawyer during criminal proceedings.

2.1   Accused and Legal Assistance

The French procedure is divided into several stages that involve different degrees of coercion on the accused. However, whatever the stage, the lawyer can always be present.

During the police inquiry, the less coercive measure is the *audition libre*. At this point, the police are suspicious but they do not have enough elements to take the person into custody. However, the person can choose to be heard by the police. Before 2014, the measure did not have any legal basis in the code of criminal procedure but was introduced by the *Conseil constitutionnel* in 2011. It considered that the person heard under that measure had to be informed of the nature and date of the offence she is suspected of and of her right to leave the police station at any moment.[24] The idea was that the person was here on her own will. The *audition libre* was given legal basis by the 2014 Act, which introduced article 61-1 CCP. According to the new article, the person subject to the *audition libre* has the right to have a lawyer when the offense she is suspected of is punishable by imprisonment and she has to expressly accept to be heard without legal assistance. The lawyer can ask questions during the hearing and make written observations at the end. However, the lawyer does not have any access to the file.

That point constitutes a difference between the *audition libre* and police custody, that is to say the point during the inquiry when the person suspected of an offense is being kept into custody for no more than 48 h. Regarding that measure, the *Conseil constitutionnel* decided as early as 1993 that the accused had the right to have a lawyer during her time in custody.[25] Then, following the European Court of Human Rights' decisions,[26] the *Conseil constitutionnel* abrogated the rules regarding police custody.[27] They were re-written in 2011[28] to include the right to see a lawyer at the beginning of custody.[29] That right is deemed so important that the *Cour de cassation*

---

[24] Cons. const. 18 November 2011, n° 2011-191/194/195/196/197 QPC, §20.

[25] Cons. const. 11 August 1993, n° 93-326 DC, §12.

[26] Most notably ECtHR, *Salduz v. Turkey, judgment of* 27 November 2008, Appl. No. 36391/02 and ECtHR, *Dayanan v. Turkey, judgment of* 13 October 2009, Appl. No. 7377/03.

[27] Cons. const. 30 July 2010 cited in Sect. 1.

[28] *Loi n° 2011-392 du 14 April 2011 relative à la garde à vue.*

[29] Art. 63-3-1 CCP.

even considered that the lawyer must be present, even if the person kept in custody waived her right.[30]

However important that right is, it is not absolute. Indeed, the prosecutor can postpone the lawyer's presence to 12 h at the most, if she thinks either that it is essential regarding the circumstances of the inquiry, that it will enable urgent inquiries to collect or preserve evidence, or that it will prevent an imminent threat to someone's life or physical integrity.[31] In case of an offense punishable by a prison-term of at least 5 years, the postponement can go up to 24 h but has to be decided by the "liberty and custody" judge.

For some offences, a judicial investigation stage is possible[32] and sometimes mandatory.[33] In that case, an investigating judge directs the investigations. At that stage, the accused cannot be interrogated without her lawyer.[34] Before each questioning, the lawyer has access to the accused's file[35] in order to be able to protect her rights of the defence. In some precise cases,[36] the investigating judge can ask the "liberty and custody" judge to place the accused under custody on remand. According to article 145 CCP, the accused has to be assisted by a lawyer. The latter can apply for the accused's release at any time.[37]

At last, at trial the lawyer's presence is mandatory before the assize court,[38] that is to say when the offence considered is a crime. Her presence is also mandatory when the procedure of *comparution sur reconnaissance préalable de culpabilité* is open. That procedure is pretty close to the plea bargaining known in *Common law* systems: for most misdemeanours, the prosecutor can put that procedure into action if the accused confesses. The lawyer must be present when the accused and the prosecutor agree on a sentence[39] and when the judge approves the agreement.[40]

On the contrary, before the criminal court, the lawyer's presence is not mandatory and the accused can represent himself. Nevertheless, the right to legal assistance is a fundamental right and it has to be effective. Therefore, the *Cour de cassation* used article 16 of the Declaration of the Rights of Man and of the Citizen to say that in order for the right to legal assistance to be effective, the judge must inform the accused that she can ask for a lawyer even during the trial.[41]

---

[30] Cass. Crim. 5 November 2013 n° 13-82-682, Bull. N°213.

[31] Art. 63-4-2 CCP.

[32] When the offence is a misdemeanour.

[33] When the offence is a crime.

[34] Art. 114(1) CCP.

[35] Art. 114(3) CCP.

[36] Arts. 143-1 and 144 CCP.

[37] Art. 148 CCP.

[38] Art. 317 CCP.

[39] Art. 495-8(4) CCP.

[40] Art. 495-9(2) CCP.

[41] Cass. Crim. 24 November 2010 n° 10-80551, *Bull.* 188.

2.2   Victim and Legal Assistance

Similarly to what happens for the accused, whatever the stage of the criminal procedure is, the victim has a right to legal assistance.

During police inquiry, a lawyer can assist the victim when she is confronted to the accused, whether the latter is under a measure of *audition libre*[42] or in custody.[43] In that case, the lawyer can even see the victim's statement.[44]

During judicial investigation, according to article 114 CCP, the victim civil party must be assisted by a lawyer when she is heard or questioned by the investigating judge. She can also ask for her lawyer's presence when a witness or another civil party is heard or during the accused's questioning.[45]

Lastly, a lawyer can always represent a civil party before the criminal court[46] in which case the decision is adversarial. The civil party has a right to legal assistance before the assize court as well.[47]

3   Personal Participation of the Accused in Criminal Proceedings

3.1   General Features of Personal Participation: Absolute Individual Right or Duty of Diligence?

Personal participation can be understood as the right to be involved in criminal proceedings going on against oneself. The right to personal participation includes the right to be informed of such proceedings, the rights of the defence and the right to be present at trial. However, whether or not that right is absolute, that is to say cannot be infringed under any circumstances, remains an issue. It goes back to the classic question of the balance between the rights of the individuals and the protection of public order. The latter calls for effective criminal proceedings, from the inquiry to the court's decision on one's guilt, which sometimes requires the individual not being informed or present. As a result, it seems that personal participation cannot be an absolute right and limits are found throughout criminal proceedings.

The inquiry cannot always involve the suspect and in order to be effective, some measures are even based on her ignorance of the proceedings, such as geolocalisation[48]

---

[42] Art. 62-2 CCP.

[43] Art. 63-4-5 CCP.

[44] Art. 63-4-5(2) CCP.

[45] Art. 82-2 CCP.

[46] Art. 424 CCP.

[47] Art. 306 CCP mentions the lawyer of the parties, that is to say, the accused's lawyer and the civil party's lawyer.

[48] Art. 230-32 CCP.

or interception of communications.[49] However, it does not mean that the suspect's rights are not to be taken into account and police officers must respect code of criminal procedure rules. There is a duty of diligence on them not to gather evidence illegally or without respecting the suspect's fundamental rights. As a result, it is possible for the suspect to intervene later on during the criminal proceedings, either during the judicial investigation if there is one or directly at trial, by making motions to suppress evidence obtained illegally during the inquiry. In that case the individual enjoys all of her rights of the defence and can actively participate in the proceedings. Regarding measures made without the suspect's knowledge during the inquiry, it can be said that personal participation isn't totally disregarded but postponed.

Personal participation is stronger when the proceedings become judicial, that is to say when a judge is involved. Indeed, as soon as the judicial investigation starts, the accused must be informed, can be assisted by a lawyer and can ask the judge to order measures necessary to the establishment of the truth.[50] Nevertheless, measures possible during police inquiry are also possible during judicial investigation, resulting in the postponement of the accused's knowledge of them.

Lastly, at trial, the accused's presence is mandatory but balance between her rights and the need for justice and criminal proceedings to go on still need to be addressed. In that regard, it seems necessary to provide the possibility for *in absentia* proceedings. According to the European Court, "the impossibility of holding a trial by default may paralyse the conduct of criminal proceedings, in that it may lead, for example, to dispersal of the evidence, expiry of the time-limit for prosecution or a miscarriage of justice".[51] As a result, a trial can be held in the accused's absence, as long as remedies are provided to the convicted.[52]

Consequently, personal participation of the accused in criminal proceedings cannot be an absolute right. Even though the authorities have to do whatever they can to make sure the accused is involved in the proceedings, they can still proceed without him in order to ensure public order.

3.2 Personal Participation in the Pre-Trial Inquiry (with Particular Regard to the Interim Decisions on Coercive Measures)

In French criminal procedure, pre-trial inquiry is divided into two stages: police inquiry and judicial investigation.[53]

---

[49] Art. 706-96 CCP.

[50] Art. 82-1 CCP.

[51] EctHR, *Colozza v. Italy*, judgment of 12 February 1985, Appl. No. 9024/80, para. 29.

[52] See Sect. 5.

[53] See Sect. 2.

First, during police inquiry, there are two ways of questioning a suspect, using either *audition libre* or police custody. Contrary to the latter, the former is not coercive and the suspect can leave the police station whenever she wants. That is the only difference regarding the suspect's rights. When the 2014 Act[54] introduced the *audition libre* into the code of criminal procedure, it made sure to match the provisions regarding the suspect's rights to the ones related to custody. Consequently, the rights of the defence are nowadays linked to suspicion and not to coercion. In any case, whether the suspect is subject to *audition libre* or to police custody, she has to be informed of the nature, the date and place of the presumed offence.[55] She also has the right to see a lawyer[56] or an interpreter[57] and can make declarations, answer the questions asked by the police or stay silent.[58] Since 2014, the suspect in police custody has a direct access to her file,[59] even if the access is still limited to specific elements only.[60]

Secondly, during judicial investigation, the suspect can make declarations, answer questions or stay silent.[61] According to article 82-1 CCP, the parties, that is to say both the suspect and the victim, can ask the investigating judge to be heard, questioned or even taken to the place where the event took place. They can also ask for a witness to be heard of for a confrontation to take place. Article 82-1 even uses general wording, allowing the parties to ask for every measure necessary to the establishment of the truth. Their requests have to be written and motivated and the investigating judge has a month to decide whether or not to authorize the measure. If the liberty and custody judge wants to put the suspect under custody on remand, she must inform him that the measure can only be decided after an adversarial debate and that she can ask for a delay to prepare her defence.[62]

More generally, and since the 2014 Act, every suspect in custody, whether police custody or custody on remand, must be given a document summarizing all of her rights.[63] With this new provision, the issue was to know what would happen if the document wasn't given. Interestingly enough, the judges didn't reach the same conclusion. Regarding custody on remand, the *Cour de cassation* decided that not giving the document to the suspect had no incidence on the procedure.[64] On the contrary, regarding police custody, they considered that the rights' notification was a condition of their effectivity. As a consequence, the document had to be given again if the

---

[54] See Sect. 2.

[55] Art. 61-1 CCP regarding *audition libre* and article 63-1 §1 2° regarding police custody.

[56] See Sect. 2.

[57] Art. 61-1(13) CCP regarding *audition libre* and article 63-1 §1 3° regarding police custody.

[58] Art. 61-1(14) CCP regarding *audition libre* and article 63-1 §1 3° regarding police custody.

[59] Art. 63-1(13) CCP.

[60] See Botton and Taupiac-Nouvel (2014), pp. 1351–1357.

[61] Art. 116 CCP.

[62] Art. 145(4) and (5) CCP. On the suspect's right to a lawyer, see Sect. 2.

[63] Art. 803-6 CCP.

[64] Cass. Crim. 14 October 2014, n°14-85-555, Fonteix (2014).

police wanted to extend custody, otherwise the measures taken after would not be valid.[65]

3.3 Personal Participation in Proceedings in Camera

In French criminal procedure, the judicial investigation is directed by a judge who can hear and question suspects, victims and witnesses. In order to respect the secrecy of the judicial investigation principle, those hearings or questioning happen *in camera*, that is to say in the investigating judge's chambers, without the press or the public. However, when she wants to put the suspect under custody on remand, she has to take the case before the liberty and custody judge, in which case, the proceeding takes place publicly.[66]

The same principle of secrecy applies before the Investigation Chamber where the decisions are made *in camera*, unless the accused asks for the proceeding to be public.[67] By exception, decisions regarding custody on remand,[68] European arrest warrant[69] and extradition[70] have to be made in open court. Nevertheless, as far as custody on remand proceedings are concerned, the public prosecutor, the accused, the civil party or their lawyers, can ask for the proceeding to take place *in camera*. Indeed, they can argue that the publicity would hinder the investigations, breach the presumption of innocence, breach the serenity of the debates or harm the person's dignity in case of organised crimes. In that case, the Investigation Chamber's decision regarding their request is reached *in camera* and can be appealed in cassation only with the decision regarding the main claim.[71]

Contrary to the judicial investigation stage, the trial stage is by principle public, whether the trial takes place before the criminal court or before the assize court. However, there are exceptions to publicity before both courts.

Before the criminal court, if the court itself considers that publicity would be dangerous for the serenity of the debates, the person's dignity or a third party's interests, they can order for the trial to take place *in camera*.[72] Here there is no mention of the accused who cannot oppose the decision. The assize court has the same prerogative if it considers that publicity would be dangerous for the order or

---

[65] Cass. Crim. 1 December 2015, n°15-84-874, Collot (2016).
[66] Art. 145(6) CCP.
[67] Art. 199(1) CCP.
[68] Art. 199(2) CCP.
[69] Art. 695-30(2) CCP.
[70] Art. 696-13(3) CCP.
[71] Art. 199(2) CCP.
[72] Art. 400(2) CCP.

morals.[73] Moreover, for certain crimes listed restrictively by article 306,[74] the victim civil party can ask for the case to be heard *in camera*, in which case the application has to be granted. For these offences, the right to ask for the trial to happen *in camera* or to oppose such a measure belongs to the victim civil party only and there is no mention of the accused whose consent is irrelevant. As a result, when a request is made by the accused, if the victim civil party does not oppose it, the assize court can decide freely whether or not to grant the request.[75] On the contrary, if the victim civil party opposes the request, her opposition binds the assize court and the *in camera* proceeding cannot be granted.[76]

3.4 *Personal Participation in Alternative Proceedings*

In France, it is for the public prosecutor to decide how a criminal case should go and if the tribunal's intervention is needed. If she does not think it is necessary, the prosecutor can use alternative proceedings to avoid taking the case to court.

It is possible for the prosecutor to organize a measure of criminal mediation[77] if she considers that the measure would likely compensate the victim, put an end to the trouble caused by the offence or help rehabilitate the offender.[78] Before 1999, the measure had to be agreed by both the victim and the offender to happen but since 1999, only the victim's consent is mentioned by article 41-1, which could mean that the offender's consent doesn't matter. However, and even though the law doesn't mention it, it would be impossible for a mediation measure to work without the offender's consent. In that sense, the article's wording seems to be unfortunate. What is more unfortunate is that even if the measure did work, it would not extinguish the prosecution. As a result, an offender could be confronted to a measure of criminal mediation and be brought before a court of law. It raises the issue of the weight to put on an admission of guilt during the criminal mediation, and whether it can be used against the offender if the mediation fails.[79]

The admission of guilt is also at the core of two other alternative proceedings: the *composition pénale* and the *transaction pénale*. However, and contrary to the criminal mediation, their success implies the termination of the prosecution.

The *composition pénale* was created in 1999, after its ancestor, the *injonction pénale*, had been abrogated by the *Conseil constitutionnel* due to a lack of judicial

---

[73] Art. 306(1) CCP.

[74] Torture, barbarous acts including sexual assaults, slavery or procuring.

[75] Cass. Crim. 6 December 2000, n°00-82-691, *Bull.* N°364.

[76] Cass. Crim. 30 October 1985, n°85-92109, *Bull.* N°337.

[77] Art. 41-1(5) CCP.

[78] Art. 41-1(1) CCP.

[79] On that point see Dreyer (2008), p. 131.

intervention.[80] According to article 41-2 CPP-France, if the offence is punishable by a prison-term inferior or equal to 5 years,[81] the prosecutor can suggest such an alternative to the offender who admits her guilt. This admission of guilt is essential and the procedure cannot go on if it is missing. Then, the offender and the prosecutor settle on one or several measures listed by the text and their settlement must be ratified by a judge. If she doesn't ratify the settlement, she has to notify her decision to the victim and the offender, and none of them can form an appeal. If the *composition pénale* is ratified by the judge and executed by the offender, the prosecution is extinguished. But if the offender doesn't fulfil the measure, the prosecution is initiated.

On the other side, the *transaction pénale* was created in 2014 and makes it possible for police officers, for particular offences[82] and with the prosecutor's authorization, to propose a fine to the offender. If she agrees, the *transaction* must be ratified by the judge. In that case and if the offender executed the *transaction pénale*, the prosecution is extinguished, which brings the alternative closer to the *composition pénale*.[83] However, the *transaction pénale* raised concerns and was brought before the *Conseil constitutionnel* in 2016 by magistrates and lawyers unions.[84] They argued that the offender couldn't give her consent freely because she was exposed to police pressure, especially if the measure was proposed during police custody. Besides, they considered that the rights of the defence were violated because article 41-1-1 didn't mention the offender's right to be assisted by a lawyer. The constitutional judges ruled that there was no violation of the rights of the defence but they added a *réserve d'interprétation*. According to them, in order for a *transaction pénale* to be concluded, the offender must be informed of her right to legal assistance.[85] As a consequence, article 41-1-1 doesn't violate any constitutional principle as long as it is interpreted the way the *Conseil constitutionnel* interpreted it.[86]

3.5 Personal Participation at Trial

The trial being the crucial point of criminal proceedings, it is of utmost importance for the accused to be involved. As a result, she has to appear personally before the court[87] and enjoys different rights. First, whatever the court, the accused can always

---

[80] Cons. Const. 2 February 1995 n° 95-360 DC. The constitutional judges considered that the absence of a judge violated the presumption of innocence and the rights of the defence.

[81] Except in case of press offences, manslaughter and political offences.

[82] Mostly fines and small misdemeanour punishable by a prison-term of 1 year at the most.

[83] Some authors even consider that there is no real difference between the two. See Robert (2014), étude 16; Perrier (2014), p. 2182; Jeanne (2016), p. 1.

[84] Cons. Const. 23 September 2016 n°2016-569 QPC.

[85] para. 9.

[86] For a commentary of the decision, see Bonis-Garçon (2017).

[87] See exceptions Sect. 5.

be assisted by a lawyer.[88] Secondly, like during the judicial investigation, the accused can answer questions, make declarations[89] or stay silent. It can lead to situations where the accused made declarations to police officers but refuses to confirm them before the judge. In that case, the judge cannot substitute the accused's silence by the declarations she made before the beginning of trial and must offer her a chance to respond each time she mentions the accused's past declarations.[90] In any case and regarding the importance of the right to stay silent, silence itself cannot be considered as an admission of guilt, nor can it be the sole basis of the conviction.

Thirdly, the accused can ask the judge to hear witnesses, even if they have not been regularly subpoenaed.[91] Both the accused and her lawyer can question witnesses or experts. However, whereas the lawyer can question the witness or the expert directly,[92] the accused cannot question them by herself and must ask the judge to do so for her.[93] As a result, it is for the judge to decide discretionarily whether or not to grant the accused's request. On the contrary, the judge must grant the accused's request to be confronted to a witness, except if the confrontation already happened during the judicial investigation.[94]

Lastly, according to article 341 CCP, before the assize court, the accused must be showed exhibits if the judge considers it necessary. In that case, the accused can make observations. Besides, every party, that is to say the public prosecutor, the civil party and the accused, can bring every piece of evidence they deem useful.[95]

3.6 Personal Participation in Higher Instances

At the European level, Protocol 7 to the Convention for the Protection of Human Rights and Fundamental Freedoms protects the right of appeal in criminal matters and considers that "everyone convicted of a criminal offence by a tribunal shall have the right to have his conviction or sentence reviewed by a higher tribunal".

However, France has not always recognized this principle and used to make a difference between the possibility to appeal and the possibility to appeal in cassation.[96] Whereas the latter was possible for every judgment made by a criminal court,

---

[88] On the point see Sect. 2.

[89] Art. 442 CCP for the criminal court.

[90] Cass. Crim. 30 April 1960.

[91] Art. 444(3) CCP for the criminal court and art. 329 for the assize court.

[92] Art. 442-1(1) CCP for the criminal court and art. 312(1) for the assize court.

[93] Art. 442-1(2) CCP for the criminal court and art. 312(2) for the assize court.

[94] Cass. Crim. 20 September 2006 n°06-81311.

[95] Cass. Crim. 17 June 1976 n°76-900888, *Bull.* 219.

[96] In case of an appeal, the judges are judges of fact and of law whereas in case of an appeal in cassation, the judges are only judges of law.

the former was not possible for judgements made by the assize court.[97] As a result, someone convicted of a crime could only appeal in cassation. The presumption of innocence and victims' rights Act of 2000[98] consecrated the right for every convicted to have their conviction reviewed by another jurisdiction[99] which globalized the right of appeal in criminal matters.

Even before 2000, the *Conseil constitutionnel* protected the access to a higher instance by using the right to equality between citizens. For instance, the constitutional judges suppressed parts of a law that made the accused's access to a higher instance dependant on the civil party's attitude.[100] The *Conseil constitutionnel* even protects the access to a higher instance at the judicial investigation stage. In 2010, they considered that parts of article 207 CCP violated article 6 and article 16 of the Declaration of the Rights of Man and of the Citizen because they made it possible for the Investigation Chamber to prevent the accused from accessing an appeal court in custody on remand matters.[101]

As a result, the right of appeal is protected at every stage of the criminal proceedings.

3.7 Special Rules in the Field of Serious Organised Crimes

The most notable rule regarding organized crimes deals with the right to legal assistance during police custody. Indeed, it is possible to postpone that right to 48 h at the most if the offence involves organized crimes and to 72 h if the offence involves drug trafficking or terrorism.[102] During the first 24 h, the decision can be made by the prosecutor but then only the liberty and custody judge[103] can decide if the postponement is to go on or not.[104] Based on the importance of the right to legal assistance,[105] article 706-88 CCP was brought before the *Conseil constitutionnel*.[106] The constitutional judges decided that even if the rights of the defence imposed the right to legal assistance, it could be postponed by a judicial authority in case of grave and complex offences committed by people belonging to organized crimes,

---

[97] The assize court is competent to judge crimes and is the only French jurisdiction where the decisions are made by a jury.

[98] *Loi n° 2000-516 du 15 June 2000 renforçant la protection de la présomption d'innocence et les droits des victimes.*

[99] Preliminary article, §1, CCP.

[100] Cons. Const. 19–21 January 1981 "Sécurité et liberté", n° 80-127 DC.

[101] Cons. Const. 17 déc. 2010 n°2010-81 QPC.

[102] Art. 706-88(6) CCP.

[103] Or the investigating judge if the custody happens during the judicial investigation phase.

[104] Art. 706-88(7) CCP.

[105] On that point see Sect. 2.

[106] Cons. Const. 21 November 2014 n°2014-428 QPC.

when such a postponement is necessary to preserve evidence or prevent attacks on individuals.

4   Personal Participation of Private Parties Other Than Defendants

The concept of civil party is definitely one of the most distinctive feature of the French system. According to article 2 CCP, "anyone who has personally suffered damage directly caused by a criminal offence may bring civil-party proceedings to seek compensation for such damage". Since 1989, the *Cour de cassation* even considers that the notion of civil party applies to the victim itself but also to the victim's close relatives.[107]

However, the concept raised the issue of the applicability of article 6 paragraph 1 of the European Convention to civil parties which led to chaotic decisions by the European Court. The Court itself considered that its case-law "present[ed] a number of drawbacks, particularly in terms of legal certainty for the parties".[108] In a landmark decision, the European Court tried to simplify its jurisprudence by considering that "there can be no doubt that civil-party proceedings constitute, in French law, a civil action for reparation of damage caused by an offence".[109] As a consequence, article 6 paragraph 1 is applicable unless civil party proceedings were launched only for purely punitive purposes,[110] that is to say if the civil party didn't ask any compensation or if the criminal proceedings weren't necessary to obtain said compensation.

In any case, the civil party is considered as a party to the criminal trial and as such, must be kept informed of the steps of the proceedings,[111] can be assisted by a lawyer,[112] can obtain compensation from criminal courts themselves and can even appeal decisions. During the judicial investigation, the civil party has the same prerogatives as the suspect[113] and can therefore ask the investigating judge to be heard, questioned or even taken to the place where the event took place, ask for a witness to be heard of for a confrontation to take place and ask for every measure necessary to the establishment of the truth.

The civil party can even participate more actively in the establishment of the truth by collecting evidence by himself. It raises the issue of the loyalty in

---

[107] Cass. Crim. 9 February 1989 n°87-81359, *Bull.* 63.

[108] ECtHR, *Perez v. France,* judgment of 12 February 2004, App. No. 47287/99, para. 54.

[109] *Perez v. France* para. 62.

[110] *Perez v. France* para. 70. On the decision itself, see Roets (2004), p. 2943; Divier (2004), p. 2948.

[111] Art. 90-1 CCP.

[112] On that point see Sect. 2.

[113] See Sect. 3.2.

establishing proof. The *Cour de cassation* has subjected public authorities to that principle since 1888[114] but has always been more lenient towards victims. Indeed, judges allow them to be disloyal to obtain a piece of evidence. The most famous case-law deals with the "testing" process used by members of associations to prove discrimination. Coloured people tried to enter night clubs but couldn't because the club was supposedly full. Then, white people of the association *SOS racisme* tried to enter as well and got in. The whole scene was secretly filmed and photographed and the association used the films and photos as evidence before the criminal court to prove racial discrimination. In 2002 the *Cour de cassation* considered that the method was acceptable and that the evidence couldn't be put aside on the sole reason that they had been obtained illicitly or unfairly.[115] The *Cour de cassation* considered that the testing process didn't violate the rights of the defence nor the right to a fair trial.[116] The testing process has even been ratified.[117] Consequently, it is possible to say that loyalty in establishing proof doesn't apply to victims, as long as the adversarial principle is respected, that is to say as long as the evidence can be discussed by both the victim and the accused at trial.

5   *In Absentia* Proceedings

According to the European Court of Human Rights, "it is of capital importance that a defendant should appear, both because of his right to a hearing and because of the need to verify the accuracy of his statements and compare them with those of the victim - whose interests need to be protected - and of the witnesses".[118] However, in case of *in absentia* proceedings, it is possible for a trial to take place and for a decision to be made in the accused's absence. As they represent a threat to many of the accused's rights, such proceedings are strictly framed by the law.

5.1   *Information Rights and Conditions of Waiver of Personal Participation in Criminal Proceedings*

In French law the trial court depends on the offence charged. If the offence is punishable only by a fine, the proceedings take place before the *Tribunal de police*. If it is punishable by a prison-term of 10 years at the most, the case is brought before the criminal court and if it is punishable by a prison-term of more than 10 years, the

---

[114] Cass. Crim., 31 January 1888 *Wilson*, S. 1889, I, p. 241.

[115] Cass. Crim., 11 June 2002, n°01-85559, *Bull.* 131.

[116] Cass. Crim., 4 February 2015, n°14-90-048, *Bull.* 26.

[117] Art. 225(3)(1) CCP.

[118] ECtHR, *Poitrimol v. France*, judgment of 23 November 1993, Appl. No. 14032/88, para. 35.

case is brought before the assize court. Whatever the court, by principle the accused must appear personally before them. However, the law admits some exceptions.

Before the *Tribunal de police*, if the accused incurs only a fine, she can be absent and represented by a lawyer or grant a special proxy to someone.[119] But if the offence is not only punishable by a fine, the accused cannot grant any special proxy and can only be represented by a lawyer.[120] In any case, the rules applying before the criminal court regarding judgements by default can apply before the *Tribunal de police*.

Article 410 CPP-France makes it mandatory for the accused to appear personally before the criminal court except if she has an acceptable excuse, in which case the decision cannot be adversarial. On the contrary, if the accused's excuse is not acceptable, the decision is *contradictoire à signifier*.[121] Before the *Perben II* Act of 2004, if the accused was absent without a valid excuse, her lawyer couldn't be heard. The European Court ruled that such a restriction violated article 6 of the European Convention and considered that the accused shouldn't lose the benefit of legal assistance because of her absence at trial.[122] The French *Cour de cassation* followed that decision and ruled that in case of an accused absent at trial without any valid excuse, not hearing her lawyer violated the right to fair trial and the right to legal assistance.[123] As a consequence, the *Perben II* Act of 2004 introduced a third paragraph to article 410 CCP, imposing the lawyer's hearing.

Besides, before the criminal court, it is always possible for the accused to apply, by letter to the presiding judge, to be tried *in absentia*, in which case she has to be represented by a lawyer.[124] Even if the accused did not send a letter to the presiding judge, a lawyer provided with a proxy can still defend her at trial, the proxy implying the accused's consent to being judged *in absentia*.[125] As long as a lawyer is present and heard by the criminal court, the decision is adversarial. However, if the lawyer himself is absent, the decision is *contradictoire à signifier*.[126] In any case, if the criminal court considers that the accused's presence is necessary, it can fix a new date and summon the accused. If the latter still doesn't appear before the court, the judge can either postpone the hearing again or rule in a decision *contradictoire à signifier*.

---

[119] Art. 544(2) CCP.

[120] Cass. Crim. 22 June 2011 n°11-80070, *Bull.* 151.

[121] Art. 410(2) CCP. It means that the accused is tried as if she were present but she must be notified of the decision.

[122] ECtHR, *Van Pelt v. France,* judgment of 23 May 2000, Appl. No. 31070/96 para. 67.

[123] Ass. Plén. 2 March 2001, n° 00-81388, *Bull.* 56.

[124] Art. 411(1) CCP.

[125] Cass. Crim. 30 January 1992, n° 91-80639, *Bull.* 43.

[126] Art. 411(5) CCP.

5.2   Default Proceedings and Subsequent Remedies

The rules regarding default proceedings depend on the court the case is heard before.

5.2.1   Criminal Court and Default Proceedings

Before the criminal court, in order for default rules to apply, the accused must be totally absent. As a result, if she was present at the beginning of the trial, the default rules cannot apply.[127]

In any case, for a judgement to be made *in absentia*, three cumulative conditions must be fulfilled: the summons must not have been served personally to the accused, it must not have been established that she knew of said summons and she must not be represented by a lawyer.[128] If a lawyer is present at trial, the judgment is not made *in absentia* but is *contradictoire à signifier.*[129] Such a decision must be notified by a bailiff and cannot be executed as long as the opposition period runs.[130]

Indeed, in case of a judgement *in absentia*, the accused can choose between two remedies: appealing the decision or filing an opposition. However, if the accused chooses to appeal the decision, she definitely gives up on the opposition.[131] While the former is a general remedy that sends the case to a higher court, the latter is exclusively for judgments *in absentia*. If said judgement has been notified to him, the accused has 10 days to form an opposition.[132] However, if the notification has not been made to the accused himself, the 10 days' period runs only if the accused's knowledge of such a notification has been proved. If not, the opposition can be formed until the limitation period of the penalty expires.[133]

Once an opposition is formed, the time-limit for court action is interrupted and, according to article 489 CCP, the judgment *in absentia* is null and void in all its provisions. As a consequence, the court which gave said judgement sets it aside and rehears the case, which gives the accused the possibility to file motions against evidence established during the first trial.[134] Nevertheless, the accused must appear personally before the court or be represented by her lawyer. If she does not, the case falls in the hypothesis of repeated default. Consequently, the opposition itself is declared null and void and the judgement *in absentia* goes back into force.[135]

---

[127] Art. 413 CCP.

[128] Art. 412(1) CCP.

[129] Art. 412(2) CCP.

[130] Art. 488 CCP.

[131] Cass. Crim. 7 February 1984, n° 83-91104, *Bull.* 44.

[132] Art. 491 CCP.

[133] Art. 492 CCP. For offences brought before the criminal court, the limitation period of the penalty is 5 years.

[134] ECtHR, *Abdelali v. France,* judgment of 11 October 2002, Appl. No. 43353/07.

[135] Art. 494 CCP.

Moreover, the accused cannot form an opposition against a repeated default measure.

5.2.2   Assize Court and Default Proceedings

Before the assize court and contrary to what happens before the criminal court, the rules regarding default proceedings apply to the accused who is absent without any valid excuse and to the accused whose absence is noticed during the trial itself, if it is not possible to suspend the debates until she returns.[136] It is for the judge, without the jury, to decide whether or not the excuse is valid. Like the criminal court, the assize court can postpone the trial or decide to judge the accused *in absentia*, in which case it does so without the jury.[137] The same rule applies to the accused who has fled or absconded.[138]

Before the assize court, the accused cannot appeal a judgement *in absentia*[139] nor can she form an opposition. Here the remedy has more of an automatic effect and depends on the accused being arrested or surrendering. In such a case, the judgement *in absentia* is automatically null and void and the case is reheard by the assize Court,[140] leaving the accused with no possibility to consent to the former judgement.

5.3   Inaudito reo *Proceedings*

French law admits criminal procedures that avoid going before a court and, as a consequence, avoid the adversarial debate that would have taken place here. Those procedures called simplified procedures, are a special way of exercising public action and imply a judicial process that is strictly written and not adversarial but that lead to a conviction similar to one made by a judgment *in absentia*. Considering their exceptional character, those procedures are only available in case of contraventions or small misdemeanours. Except for small differences, the two penal order procedures are quite similar.

Penal order procedures are possible for all contraventions[141] and for misdemeanours listed by article 495 CCP. In order for the simplified procedure to happen, a prison-term or a fine superior to 5000 euros must not be necessary according to the facts. In any case, if the judge considers that an adversarial debate is necessary, she

---

[136] Art. 379-2(1) CCP.
[137] Art. 379-3 CCP.
[138] Art. 270 CCP.
[139] Art. 379-5 CCP.
[140] Art. 379-4(4) CCP.
[141] Art. 524 CCP.

has to give the case back to the public prosecutor in order for her to proceed in the usual way.[142] Otherwise the judge pronounces a penal order. In case of a contravention,[143] the penal order doesn't have to be justified whereas it must be in case of a misdemeanour.[144]

Once the penal order has been notified to the accused, she has 30 days to form an opposition in case of a contravention[145] and 45 days in case of a misdemeanour.[146] Then, both procedures have the same effect: the case goes back to the usual procedure and the adversarial debate is re-established. It can even lead to a judgment *in absentia*, in which case it is possible for the accused to form an opposition.[147] If the accused doesn't form an opposition, the penal order is final.[148]

Prior to her introduction in the code of criminal procedure, the possibility for misdemeanours to be subjected to penal orders was questioned and led to a decision by the *Conseil constitutionnel* in 2002.[149] The main grief made against the new simplified procedure was that it contradicted the right to equality between citizens because the judge could make a discretionary decision to resort to it. However, the constitutional judges reminded that different situations, facts and people could be subjected to different laws as long as the differences were justified and didn't violate the rights of the defence and the right to fair trial. Then, after having examined the rules governing penal orders in case of misdemeanours, they ruled that the procedure was not violating those principles and was compatible with the right to equality between citizens.

6 Participatory Rights in Transnational Criminal Justice

6.1 Participatory Safeguards in EAW Proceedings

The European arrest warrant was introduced into French law in 2004 by the *Perben II* Act[150] which transposed the Council Framework decision of 13 June 2002 on the European arrest warrant and the surrender procedures between Member States. It aimed at replacing the extradition procedure in order for surrenders to be faster and to implement the principle of mutual recognition of criminal decisions. Nevertheless,

---

[142] Art. 525(3) CCP for contraventions and 495-1 for misdemeanours.

[143] Art. 526(2) CCP.

[144] Art. 495-2 CCP.

[145] Art. 527 CCP.

[146] Art. 495-3 CCP.

[147] Art. 528(1) CCP for contraventions and 495-4 for misdemeanours. See Sect. 5.2 for the rules regarding default proceedings.

[148] Art. 528-1(1) CCP for contraventions and 495-5 for misdemeanours.

[149] Cons. const. 29 August 2002, n° 2002-461 DC.

[150] *Loi n°2004-204 du 9 mars 2004.*

safeguards were introduced to protect the person subjected to a European arrest warrant.

6.1.1 Participatory Rights in the Decision on Surrender

Once a European arrest warrant is issued, the idea is for the authorities of the executing Member State to surrender the person as quickly as possible. That is why article 695-27 requires the requested person to be brought in front of the Attorney general in the 48 h of her arrest. During that time, the rules regarding police custody apply.[151] Besides, the Attorney general has to inform the requested person of the existence and content of the EAW and of her right to legal assistance. Mostly, the requested person has to be informed of her right to consent to the surrender or to oppose it and of her right to give up on the speciality rule.[152]

Article 695-28 CCP adds that the Attorney general can ask the judge to incarcerate the requested person until the surrender decision is reached by the Investigation Chamber. The article's wording seemed to prevent the judge from letting the requested person free without any control measures and the argument was made before the *Cour de cassation*. It was also argued that the rights of the defence were violated by the lack of mention of the lawyer by article 695-28. In a decision of December 2016,[153] the constitutional judges ruled that article 695-28 CCP didn't violate neither the right to liberty nor the rights of the defence but they added two *réserves d'interprétation*. As a consequence, article 695-28 doesn't violate the right to liberty as long as it is interpreted as permitting the judge to let the requested person totally free[154] and it doesn't violate the rights of the defence as long as it is interpreted as permitting the requested person to be assisted by a lawyer.[155]

Whether or not the requested person has been subjected to incarceration, she has to appear before the Investigation Chamber 5 days at the most after her audition by the Attorney general.[156] Once before the Chamber, the requested person can make declarations, be assisted by a lawyer or by an interpreter[157] and has to be asked again whether or not she consents to the surrender. On one hand, if she consents, the Investigation Chamber must remind him of the consequences of her choice and of its irrevocability and must ask if she wishes to renounce the speciality rule. Then the Chamber has 7 days to rule on the surrender and its decision cannot be appealed.[158] That simplified procedure aims at going even faster when the requested person

---

[151] See Sect. 3.2.

[152] Art. 695-21(6) CCP.

[153] Cons. const. 9 December 2016 n°2016-602 QPC.

[154] para. 15.

[155] para. 16.

[156] Art. 695-29 CCP.

[157] Art. 695-30 CCP. France.

[158] Art. 695-31(3) CCP.

consents. However, the *Cour de cassation* pointed out that in case of a protected adult, that procedure cannot be used because her consent can never be given irrevocably.[159] On the other hand, if the requested person doesn't consent to her surrender, the Investigation Chamber has 20 days to rule and its decision can be appealed in cassation.[160] If needs be, the *Cour de cassation* must rule in 40 days.

6.1.2 *In Absentia* Proceedings in the Trial Country and Its Relevance in the Surrender Procedure

The first Framework Decision regarding the European arrest warrant made no specific mention of the way to deal with *in absentia* proceedings in the trial country. This situation was tackled by Framework Decision of 26 February 2009 enhancing the procedural rights of persons and fostering the application of the principle of mutual recognition to decisions rendered in the absence of the person concerned at the trial. It was transposed into French law by the 2013 Act[161] which introduced article 695-22-1 CCP. Interestingly enough, what was introduced as a ground for optional non-execution of the European arrest warrant in the Framework Decision of 2009 became a ground for mandatory non-execution of the European arrest warrant in French law. As a result, if the requested person did not appear in person at the trial resulting in the custodial sentence or detention order, the French authorities must refuse to execute the European arrest warrant.[162] However, article 695-22-1 provides four exceptions to the mandatory refusal.

First, the European arrest warrant can be executed if the requested person was effectively and unequivocally informed, in due time, by being summoned or by any other means, of the date and place of the trial and that a decision could be handed down if she didn't appear for the trial.

Second, the European arrest warrant can be executed if the requested person was aware of the trial and was actually defended by a lawyer she had given a mandate to, whether the lawyer was appointed by the person concerned or by the State. Even if the requested person was actually defended by a lawyer, the *Cour de cassation* considers that the Investigation Chamber must make sure that the lawyer was given a mandate and that the requested person could still appeal the decision.[163]

Third, the execution of the European arrest warrant can be made if the requested person, who had been served with the decision and was expressly informed of her right to a retrial in which she has the right to participate and which may lead to the original decision being reversed, expressly stated that she does not contest the decision or did not request a retrial within the applicable time frame.

---

[159] Cass. crim. 17 February 2016 n°16-80653, *Bull.* 58.

[160] Art. 695-31(4) CCP.

[161] Loi n°2013-711 du 5 août 2013.

[162] Art. 695-22-1(1) CCP.

[163] Cass. crim. 25 March 2014, n°14-81430.

Fourth, the execution of the European arrest warrant can be made if the requested person will be personally served with the decision as soon as she is surrendered and will be informed of her right to a retrial in the same conditions as in the third exception. That exception was applied by the Investigation Chamber in a case where the requested person had not been present to her trial in Italy but could ask for a retrial in the 30 days following her surrender.[164]

Those four exceptions are so wide that it is possible to wonder if the mandatory non-execution of article 695-22-1 will ever be applied.

6.2 Participatory Safeguards in Transborder Inquiries and the Taking of Overseas Evidence

With the evolution of transnational criminality came the evolution of laws to make transborder inquiries possible and to make sure that judicial systems would be effective enough in tackling that particular form of criminality. At the European level, the Council of Europe adopted the Convention on mutual assistance in criminal matters between Member States "in order to improve the speed and efficiency of judicial cooperation".[165] However, there is still a need to protect the individuals suspected, whether France is the State executing a request for mutual assistance or the State requesting such a measure.

On one hand, if France is the requested State, the measure has to be executed in accordance with the code of criminal procedure.[166] However, the measure can be executed following the requesting State's rules if the latter wants to, as long as those rules do not limit the safeguards accorded to parties by the Criminal procedure code.[167] Consequently, French authorities have to effectively control any measure requested by another State and it is possible for an accused to launch a motion to suppress evidence obtained by French authorities executing an international letter rogatory, as long as the judge can have the evidence to control it.[168]

On the other hand, if France is the requesting State, questionings, hearings and confrontations taking place abroad have to be executed in compliance with rules established by the Criminal procedure code[169] and the accused cannot be questioned or confronted to someone without her consent.[170] As a result, even if French authorities are not the ones executing the measure, they still have to make sure that it was executed in accordance with French rules and safeguards. The European Court

---

[164] Cass. crim. 25 October 2013, n°13-86329, *Bull. 190.*

[165] Council Act of 29 May 2000.

[166] Art. 694-3(1) CCP.

[167] Art. 694-3(2) CCP.

[168] Cass. crim. 3 June 2003, n° 02-87484, *Bull.* 2003.

[169] Art. 694-5(2) CCP.

[170] Art. 694-5(3) CCP.

considers that it is for French authorities to ensure that the measure has been executed without any violation of the rights of the defence and to protect the fairness of the criminal procedure they are in charge of.[171]

Besides, following the European Directive regarding European Investigation Order in criminal matters,[172] an executive order of December 2016[173] and a decree of April 2017[174] introduced European investigation orders into the code of criminal procedure.[175] The new rules include safeguards for the individuals concerned with the order, especially for individuals in custody. If a person is to be temporary transferred to the issuing State, the person must consent to such a measure[176] and it is for the executing State to order her release.[177] Most importantly, the person cannot be prosecuted or convicted in the issuing State for acts committed before her departure from the executing State if the acts or convictions are not mentioned in the European investigation order.[178]

Lastly, it is possible for French authorities to obtain evidence gathered in a country that is not part of the European Union. In that case, general principles framing French criminal procedure must be applied. Under French law, public authorities, that is to say judges, prosecutors and police officers, must respect the loyalty in establishing proof principle,[179] which means that they cannot gather proof illicitly or unfairly. In that regard, and in order for police inquiries to be effective, a difference is made between provocation to commit an offence[180] and provocation to gather evidence.[181] While the former is considered as violating the loyalty in establishing proof principle, the latter is admitted. For instance, a police officer cannot ask a person to fake-buy paedophile photos on the internet in order to prove the offence because such a method constitutes a provocation to commit an offence.[182] However, the issue of what to do with a piece of evidence obtained that way in the United States was raised before the *Cour de cassation*. The court considered that even

---

[171] ECtHR, *Stojkovic v. France and Belgium*, judgment of 27 October 2011, Appl. No. 25303/08 in which following a French request, a suspect has been heard in Belgium without being assisted by a lawyer. On that decision see Herran (2013), p. 735.

[172] Directive 2014/41/EU of the European parliament and of the council of 3 April 2014 regarding the European Investigation Order in criminal matters.

[173] Ordonnance n° 2016-1636 du 1er décembre 2016 relative à la décision d'enquête européenne en matière pénale.

[174] Décret n° 2017-511 du 7 avril 2017 relatif à la décision d'enquête européenne en matière pénale.

[175] The new rules came into force on the 22th May 2017.

[176] Art. 695-25 CCP.

[177] Art. 695-26(1) CCP.

[178] Art. 695-26(2) CCP.

[179] Cass. crim., 31 January 1888 *Wilson*, S. 1889, I, p. 241. On the contrary, that principle doesn't apply to the victim. On that point see Sect. 4.

[180] Here police officers encourage the suspect to commit an offence in order to be able to prove it.

[181] Here police officers use different tricks and manoeuvers to be able to prove that someone committed an offence, without encouraging him to do so.

[182] Cass. crim. 11 May 2006, n°05-84837, *Bull.* 132.

though such evidence is admissible in the United States, it cannot be admissible before French courts insofar as the method used violates the loyalty in establishing proof principle.[183]

Consequently, it seems that evidence gathered abroad are considered as if they have been gathered in France and must be subjected to the same safeguards.

7 Requirements of Personal Participation and *In Absentia* Proceedings. The Perspective of Supranational and International Human Rights Law

7.1 The Perspective of International Human Rights Law. Critical Remarks on Domestic Law in the Light of the European Convention

According to the European Court of Human Rights, "it is of capital importance that a defendant should appear, both because of his right to a hearing and because of the need to verify the accuracy of his statements and compare them with those of the victim - whose interests need to be protected - and of the witnesses".[184] However, the Court has never been opposed to *in absentia* proceedings, as long as some safeguards are respected and as long as the accused can have the case retried.[185] France has been subjected to numerous decisions regarding its laws on *in absentia* proceedings and was often found to be violating the European Convention. The main issue seemed to be the representation by a lawyer.

Indeed, in *Poitrimol*, the European Court considered that the accused's absence doesn't mean that she cannot be represented by a lawyer.[186] It led to two other condemnations where the European Court ruled that the lawyer had to be heard by the criminal court, even if the accused was absent.[187] As a result, in 2001 the French *Cour de cassation* reversed its case-law to follow the European decisions and considered that the right to fair trial and the right to legal assistance included the right for the accused to be represented by a lawyer, even in her absence at trial.[188] It ultimately led to the addition, by the *Perben II* Act, of a third paragraph to article 410 CCP, according to which if a lawyer is present at trial, the court cannot rule *in*

---

[183] Cass. crim. 4 June 2008, n°08-81045, *Bull.* 141.

[184] ECtHR, *Poitrimol v. France*, judgment of 23 November 1993, Appl. No. 14032/88, para. 35.

[185] *Poitrimol*, para. 31.

[186] para. 34.

[187] ECtHR, *Van Pelt v. France*, judgment of 23 May 2000, Appl. No. 31070/96 and ECtHR, *Karatas et Sari v. France*, judgment of 16 May 2002, Appl. No. 38396/97.

[188] Ass. plén. Dentico, 2 March 2001, n°00-81.388, *Bull.* 56.

absentia.[189] Following another condemnation by the European Court,[190] the Act also abolished the contumacy rules before the assize court and replaced them by the criminal default rules.[191]

Legal assistance was also an issue in the accused's right to legal remedy. Indeed, before the assize Court, the accused had to surrender before being able to appeal the decision and the lawyer could not appeal for him if she refused. After numerous condemnations by the European Court,[192] the presumption of innocence and victims' rights Act of 2000 abrogated article 583 CCP and allowed lawyers the possibility to appeal for their clients. Before the criminal court the issue was dealt with by the judges who used to consider that the accused had to be the one to appeal personally. However, the case-law was overturned following the European Court's decisions.[193]

According to the European Court, "when domestic law permits a trial to be held notwithstanding the absence of a person" charged with a criminal offence"(…) that person should, once she becomes aware of the proceedings, be able to obtain, from a court which has heard him, a fresh determination of the merits of the charge".[194] In that regard, it seems that the rules related to *in absentia* proceedings, both before the criminal court and the assize court, are compatible with the European Convention. Nevertheless, the automatic retrial in case of *in absentia* proceedings before the assize court might be an issue in that it is not possible for the accused to waive her right to be present at trial, nor it is possible for him to agree with the judgement made *in absentia*. However, it seems that the European Court doesn't make the possibility to waive her right to be present at trial mandatory and allows for retrial to be automatic. As a result, the French rules regarding *in absentia* proceedings should be deemed compatible with the European Convention.

7.2 The Perspective of EU Law. Developments in Domestic Law as a Result of EU Law

Up until now and except for the Directive on the European arrest warrant, the European union has never really been interested in *in absentia* proceedings. In 2015, the European Court of Justice could have used the opportunity offered by the Covaci

---

[189] On that point see Sect. 5.1.

[190] ECtHR, *Krombach v. France*, judgment of 13 February 2001, Appl. No. 29731/96.

[191] See Sect. 5.2.

[192] ECtHR, *Guérin v. France*, judgment of 29 July 1998, Appl. No. 25201/94; ECtHR, *Omar v. France*, judgment of 29 July 1998, Appl. No. 53613/99; ECtHR, *Papon v. France*, judgment of 25 July 2002, Appl. No. 54210/00; ECtHR, *Walser v. France,* judgment of 1st July 2004, Appl. No. 56653/00.

[193] Cass. crim. 24 November 1999, n°97-85694, *Bull.* 273.

[194] ECtHR, *Colozza v. Italy*, judgment of 12 February 1985, Appl. No. 9024/80, para. 29.

case[195] to at least give an opinion on *in absentia* proceedings, and more precisely on *inaudito reo* proceedings. However, they chose not to do so and focused on the right to interpretation and translation and the right to information in criminal proceedings recently consecrated in two Directives.[196] They considered that those rights did not make it mandatory for States to translate every document used during the proceedings but only those considered as essential "in light of the proceedings concerned and the circumstances of the case".[197] The judges even refused to decide whether or not the objection to a penal order constituted an essential document to the proceedings, leaving Member States some margin of appreciation. It seems that the peculiarity of penal orders, and more generally of *inaudito reo* proceedings, was completely ignored by the European Court of Justice.

However, in 2016 the European union approved the Directive on the strengthening of certain aspects of the presumption of innocence and of the right to be present at the trial in criminal proceedings.[198] The latter is dealt with in Chapter 3 composed of articles 8 et 9. According to the first one, the State "shall ensure that suspects and accused persons have the right to be present at their trial"[199] but it is still possible for a trial to be held *in absentia* if "the [accused] has been informed, in due time, of the trial and of the consequences of non-appearance"[200] or if, "having been informed of the trial, [the accused] is represented by a mandated lawyer".[201] If those alternative conditions are not met, the accused must be given the opportunity to have a new trial.[202] Though it is still early to know how the European Court of Justice will use this new Directive, it seems that the conditions it sets are almost identical to the ones set by the European Court of Human Rights. As a consequence, French rules regarding *in absentia* proceedings seem to be compatible with EU law.

8   Concluding Remarks

French *in absentia* rules are the product of numerous decisions, both at the national and at the European level. They had to be changed to make way to lawyer's representation and legal remedy, two safeguards against unfair trial consecrated first by the European Court of Human Rights and then by the European union. The right to have a new trial is provided regardless of the offence and is even taken to the next

---

[195] CJEU, *Covaci*, 15 October 2015, n°C-216/14.

[196] EU Directive on the right to interpretation and translation, 2010/64/EU and EU Directive on the right to information in criminal proceedings, Directive 2012/13/EU.

[197] *Covaci para. 51.*

[198] Directive on the strengthening of certain aspects of the presumption of innocence and of the right to be present at the trial in criminal proceedings, 9 March 2016, n°2016/343 EU.

[199] Art. 8(1) CCP.

[200] Art. 8(2)(a)CCP.

[201] Art. 8(2)(b)CCP.

[202] Art. 9 CCP.

level in case of a crime where a retrial is automatic as soon as the accused is found
or surrenders. Consequently, it is possible to argue that the current *in absentia* system is quite well balanced and takes into account both the accused's rights and the
need for justice and public order. It could explain why the new Directive on the
presumption of innocence and the right to be present at trial has not raised concerns
in France yet.

However, the right to information and more specifically one's right to have access
to her file proves to be more of a challenge in France. During police inquiry, it is still
impossible for a suspect or her lawyer to have access to all the documents in the file,
making her personal involvement more problematic at this stage of the proceedings.
Progress could definitely be made at this stage by granting such an access and the
possibility to discuss the elements contained in the file. In the same way, the lawyer's role of effectively protecting the rights of the defence would by strengthened
by such an access. On the other hand, in order for such an evolution to be truly possible, some *juridictionnalisation* would have to be introduced into the police inquiry
stage. Allowing debates before a judge to discuss every element of the procedure as
early as during police inquiry might not be in harmony with fast and effective investigations. Once again, the balance between people's rights and the need for justice
and criminal proceedings to be effective has to be found.

References

Angevin H. Défaut en matière criminelle. Jurisclasseur procédure pénale, fasc. 20
Bonfils Ph (janvier 2016) Partie civile. Répertoire Dalloz
Bonis-Garçon E (2017) La transaction pénale de l'article 41-1-1 du Code de procédure pénale. Les
    nouveaux cahiers du Conseil constitutionnel, n°54
Botton A, Taupiac-Nouvel G (2014) La réforme du droit à l'information en procédure pénale.
    J.C.P.G, pp 1351–1357
Caron D (mise à jour du 5 février 2018) Tribunal correctionnel - Débats - Comparution et citation.
    Jurisclasseur procédure pénale, fasc. 20
Combles De Nayves P, Mercinier E (2017) Le silence est d'or. AJ pénal, p. 27
Collot L (2016) Garde à vue: l'absence d'une nouvelle notification des droits emporte la nullité de
    la prolongation. Dalloz actualité, 6 January
De Lamy B (2011a) Inconstitutionnalité de l'article 575 du code de procédure pénale: la partie
    civile promue par le Conseil constitutionnel. R.S.C., p 188
De Lamy B (2011b) L'avancée des garanties en matière de garde à vue ou la consécration d'un
    basculement de la procédure pénale vers la phase policière ? R.S.C., p 168
Divier P-F (2004) L'instruction pénale française à l'épreuve du "procès equitable" européen.
    Dalloz, chron. 2948
Dreyer E (2008) La médiation pénale, objet juridique mal identifié. J.C.P.G, n°14, doctr. 131
Fonteix C (2014) Détention provisoire: premières précisions relatives à la « déclaration des droits.
    Dalloz actualité, 8 December
Giudicelli A (2011) Le Conseil constitutionnel et la garde à vue: puisque ces mystères nous dépas-
    sent, feignons d'en être l'organisateur. R.S.C., p 139
Herran Th (2013) L'emprise de la Cour européenne des droits de l'homme sur l'entraide répressive
    internationale. R.S.C. p 735
Jeanne N (2016) Réflexions sur la transaction pénale par officier de police judiciaire. R.S.C., p 1

Krikorian Ph (2007) Le statut constitutionnel de l'avocat défenseur. Gaz Pal 338:3

Lacroix C (2010) Les parties civiles à l'assaut de la chambre criminelle de la Cour de cassation, *D.*, p 2686

Perrier J-B (2014) La transaction pénale de l'article 41-1-1 du Code de procédure pénale. Bonne idée ou outil dangereux?, *D.*, 2182

Pradel J (2015) Procédure pénale, Cujas, 18th éd.

Robert J-H (2014) Punir dehors – Commentaire de la loi n°2014-896 du 15 August 2014, *Dr. pén.*, étude 16

Roets D (2004) Le contentieux de l'action civile et l'article 6§1 de la Convention européenne des droits de l'Homme: une tentative de clarification de la Cour de Strasbourg, *D.*, chron. 2943

Touillier M (2010) Le Conseil constitutionnel sonne le glas de l'article 575 du Code de procédure pénale. Gaz Pal 224:10

Vandermeeren R (2005) Permanence et actualité du droit au juge. AJDA, p 1102

Report on Germany

Benjamin Vogel

Abstract German constitutional jurisprudence emphasizes a close link between the truth-finding purpose of the criminal trial and the presence of the accused. As the latter's individual culpability is of key importance to the imposition of criminal sanctions, procedural law attaches great value to the defendant's presence at the trial, laying down both a right and a duty to this effect. It is only for crimes of minor severity that a sanction can be imposed without giving the defendant the opportunity to personally comment on the charges before a judge in advance—and even then, he or she can demand a subsequent trial. In any case, the defendant must have the opportunity to comment on the charges in an oral hearing. Furthermore, as the trial serves to ascertain the truth in the best possible way, accused persons have very limited options to waive their right to be present at trial, even after having been heard on the charges. Within narrow limits, the defendant can be temporarily removed from the trial, particularly for the purpose of maintaining order or enabling the examination of a witness. Beyond that, and with the exception of some alternative proceedings such as private prosecutions, German law broadly presupposes the personal presence of the defendant throughout the trial. In contrast, the accused's personal participation at the pre-trial stage remains limited and is then primarily relevant for the judicial interrogation of witnesses and in judicial review proceedings against pretrial detention. The right to be present at one's trial recently gained special significance in European Arrest Warrant proceedings following an *in absentia* trial in the requesting state where the convicted person had not unequivocally waived the right to be present. The Federal Constitutional Court stipulates special requirements in this regard in order to ensure that the right to a retrial in the requesting state is effective.

B. Vogel (✉)
Max Planck Institute for Foreign and International Criminal Law,
Freiburg im Breisgau, Germany
e-mail: b.vogel@mpicc.de

© Springer Nature Switzerland AG 2019
S. Quattrocolo, S. Ruggeri (eds.), *Personal Participation in Criminal Proceedings*, Legal Studies in International, European and Comparative Criminal Law 2, https://doi.org/10.1007/978-3-030-01186-4_6

Abbreviations

AICCM	Act on International Cooperation in Criminal Matters
BeckRS	Beck online case law report
BGHSt	Decisions of the Federal High Court (criminal matters)
BT-Drucks.	Parliamentary documents of the Bundestag
BVerfGE	Decisions of the Federal Constitutional Court
CC	German Criminal Code (StGB)
CCP	German Code of Criminal Procedure (StPO)
CJEU	Court of Justice of the European Union
ECHR	European Convention of Human Rights
ECtHR	European Court of Human Rights
NJW	Neue Juristische Wochenschrift (journal)
NStZ	Neue Zeitschrift für Strafrecht (journal)
NStZ-RR	NStZ case law report
OLG	Oberlandesgericht
RhPfVerfGH	Constitutional Court of Rhineland-Palatinate

1   Constitutional Requirements for the Involvement of Private Parties in Criminal Justice

In German law, the participation of the accused in criminal proceedings is rooted in the constitutional obligation of the state to respect human dignity and, following from that, in the right to a fair hearing and in the principle of culpability. According to the domestic constitutional law understanding of the rule of law, and as notably expressed by the constitutional right to a fair hearing, nobody can be made a mere object of public proceedings that directly affect him. From this, it follows that defendants in criminal proceedings must have an effective opportunity to influence their trial, to personally comment on the charges, to present exonerating circumstances, and to initiate a comprehensive and exhaustive inquiry into such circumstances.[1] In contrast, constitutional jurisprudence defines the principle of culpability as an expression of the Basic Law's guarantee of "dignity and responsibility for oneself" (*Eigenverantwortlichkeit*), i.e., the "responsibility of the person, who can decide on his or her actions him- or herself" and who is "a spiritual and moral being who is predisposed to freely define and develop him- or herself."[2] Individual blame-worthiness of the accused is thus central to the criminal law. There must be a "just proportion between the punishment on the one hand and the gravity of the offence,

---

[1] BVerfGE 63, 332 = BVerfG NJW 1983, 1726, 1727; BVerfG NStZ-RR 2004, 308, 309.

[2] BVerfGE 140, 317 = Federal Constitutional Court, Order of the Second Senate of 15 December 2015—2 BvR 2735/14, at para. 54. Citations refer to translations of the Federal Constitutional Court's decisions available on its website: www.bundesverfassungsgericht.de.

and the culpability of the offender, on the other hand."[3] Consequently, in order to establish the true facts of the case, the personality of the accused individual is of paramount importance. The Federal Constitutional Court stresses "that a criminal sanction that does not comprehensively take into account the personality of the offender cannot be a criminal sanction that is appropriate with regard to the dignity of the accused." From this, the Constitutional Court states "as a rule, that a court, in an oral hearing in the presence of the accused, gains an insight into the accused's personality, his motifs, his perspective on the offence, on the victim and the circumstances of the offence. It has to be ensured that the accused at least has the right to personally present circumstances to the court, in particular such of a justifying, excusing, or mitigating nature, the judge and the accused being face to face."[4]

The personal participation of the accused thus not only raises issues with regard to the constitutional right to a fair hearing.[5] This right reflects the state's obligation to respect human dignity, as it prevents individuals in criminal proceedings from being treated as mere objects.[6] The principle of culpability goes beyond this procedural aspect, as it concerns the essence of the criminal sanction. Not only must accused have the opportunity to influence the outcome of proceedings by questioning inculpatory evidence and by presenting exculpatory evidence, but they must also be allowed to present their perspective on events to the court. Under the principle of culpability, the uncovering of the accused's perspective constitutes a key purpose of the proceedings. Thus, the personal participation of the accused in criminal proceedings not only serves to ensure defence rights, and thereby a more reliable establishment of facts, but it also reflects the constitutional idea that the accused's perspective is an essential part of the court's fact-finding.[7] While the Constitution also guarantees the accused's right to remain silent,[8] it follows from the above that criminal proceedings in which the accused are not given the opportunity to tell their version of events do not conform to the principle of culpability.

---

[3] BVerfGE 140, 317, 343 f.= Federal Constitutional Court, 2 BvR 2735/14, at para. 54 f.

[4] BVerfGE 140, 317, 345 f. = Constitutional Court, 2 BvR 2735/14, at para. 58.

[5] Cf. Article 103 section 1 of the Basic Law; BT-Drucks. 18/3562, p. 47; BGHSt 55, 87 = BGH NJW 2010, 2450.

[6] BVerfGE 63, 332, 337 f. = NJW 1983, 1726, 1727; BVerfG NJW 1991, 1411; Böhm (2015), p. 3132; Laue (2010), p. 295.

[7] Cf. BVerfGE 118, 212 = BVerfG NJW 2007, 2977, 2979; BGHSt 26, 84, 90 = BGH NJW 1975, 885, 886; BGH NStZ 2011, 233, 234; Deiters (2015), § 230, para. 1e; Diemer (2013), § 247, para. 2; Laue (2010), p. 295; Meyer-Goßner (2016), § 230, para. 3; Roxin and Schünemann (2014), p. 354; Trüg (2011), p. 3256; Zehetgruber (2013), p. 398; more sceptical towards the "truth-seeking" rationale: Eisenberg (2012), p. 64.

[8] BVerfGE 56, 37 = BVerfG NJW 1981, 1431; BVerfGE 133, 168 = BVerfG NJW 2013, 1058, 1061.

2   Personal Participation of Private Parties and Legal Assistance

2.1   Mandatory Defense Counsel

The accused is entitled to have the assistance of defence counsel at any stage of the criminal proceedings.[9] However, the assistance of defence counsel is mandatory only if this "appears necessary because of the seriousness of the offence, or because of the difficult factual or legal situation, or if it is evident that the accused cannot defend himself", in particular if the offence is punishable by a minimum sentence of 1 year, if the first-instance trial is conducted before the Regional Court (*Landgericht*),[10] if the accused has been remanded in custody, or if it may be necessary to bring the accused to a psychiatric hospital to be held under observation there.[11] In exceptional circumstances, the assistance of defence counsel may also be mandatory (if not already so for other reasons) when the defendant is temporarily removed from the main hearing during examination of a witness who would not testify or tell the truth in the presence of the defendant. Depending on the seriousness of the charges and the importance of the witness, this can then become necessary with respect to Article 6 paragraph 3 lit. d ECHR.[12]

2.2   Representation of Private Parties

The presence of a defence counsel at the hearing does not, in principle, constitute a substitute for the presence of the defendant.[13] Defendants are entitled to be represented by a defence counsel only in cases in which the main hearing may be held in their absence.[14] Procedural law thus clearly differentiates between the responsibilities of a defence counsel, on the one hand, and representation of the defendant, on the other. While a defence counsel is meant to assist the defendant,[15] he or she is

---

[9] Section 137 para. 1 CCP.

[10] Note that the Regional Court is the first-instance court, in particular when a sentence of imprisonment exceeding 4 years or placement of the accused in a psychiatric hospital is to be expected; section 74 para. 1 Courts Constitution Act.

[11] Section 140 para. 1 no. 1, 2, 6, para. 2 CCP. Citations of German statutes refer to translations provided by the Federal Ministry of Justice and Consumer Protection, available under www.gesetze-im-internet.de.

[12] Cf. OLG Zweibrücken, NStZ 1987, 89; OLG Frankfurt, NStZ-RR 2009, 207, 208; Frister (2016), § 247, para. 17.

[13] OLG Hamburg, Order of 3rd December 2013—1-25/13 -, BeckRS 2014, 00512.

[14] Section 234 CCP; Gmel (2013), § 234, para. 1; Meyer-Goßner (2016), § 234, para. 1; Roxin and Schünemann (2014), p. 359.

[15] Section 137 para. 1 CCP.

only allowed to represent the defendant by performing the latter's procedural acts if the defendant authorised the defence counsel to do so and if the law allows such delegation.[16] If such representation is possible, i.e., when the main hearing may be held in the defendant's absence and defence attorney has received power of attorney from the defendant, the former is entitled to execute all procedural rights of the defendant, in particular to make a statement on the charges in the name of the defendant.[17] The defence counsel is authorised to represent the defendant without power of attorney only in conjunction with a limited number of procedural rights (in particular the waiver of taking evidence).[18]

In contrast, victims or their next of kin, to the extent that they are entitled to participate in criminal proceedings as a "private prosecutor" or as a "private accessory prosecutor," can always choose to be represented by an attorney.[19]

3 Personal Participation of the Accused in Criminal Proceedings

3.1 General Features of Personal Participation: Absolute Individual Right or Duty of Diligence?

3.1.1 Right and Duty to Attend

The German law of criminal procedure assumes both a right and a duty of the defendant to attend the entire main hearing,[20] explicitly stipulating the principle: "No main hearing shall be held against a defendant who fails to appear."[21] This includes instances in which the court takes evidence by examining objects outside the courtroom.[22] Defendants are also regarded as having failed to appear where they are physically present, but unfit to stand trial and therefore unable to reasonably represent their interests.[23] Beside fair trial concerns, the accused's presence is meant to provide the court with direct knowledge of his or her personality and explanations,[24] thereby reflecting the constitutional requirement, originating from the principle of

---

[16] BT-Drucks. 18/3562, p. 67; Deiters (2015), § 234, para. 1.

[17] BT-Drucks. 18/3562, p. 72 f.; BGHSt 9, 356 = BGH NJW 1956, 1727 f.; Deiters (2015), § 234, para. 5; Gmel (2013), § 234, para. 5; Meyer-Goßner (2016), § 234, para. 9 f.

[18] Section 234a CCP; cf. Deiters (2015), § 231, para. 33; Gmel (2013), § 234a, para. 4.

[19] See below Sects. 3.4.1 and 4.

[20] BGHSt 26, 84, 90 = BGH NJW 1975, 885, 886; BGHSt 55, 87 = BGH NJW 2010, 2450, 2451; Meyer-Goßner (2016), § 230, para. 3 f.

[21] Section 230 para. 1 CCP.

[22] Deiters (2015), § 230, para. 4.

[23] BGHSt 23, 331 = BGH NJW 1970, 2253, 2254 f.; Meyer-Goßner (2016), § 230, para. 8.

[24] Beulke (2012), p. 251.

culpability that the purpose of the criminal trial is to uncover the truth. German criminal procedure is thus, in principle, reluctant to allow *in absentia* trials.[25] A duty to attend the main hearing is especially ruled out and therefore basically prevents a trial if there is an obvious and imminent danger that defendants would lose their life or suffer grave impairment to their health.[26] If defendants do not appear without sufficient excuse, the court can order them to be brought before it or have them arrested for the duration of the trial; in the written summons to the hearing, however, they must already be informed about the possible consequences of their non-appearance.[27] Otherwise, the court must adjourn the hearing. Furthermore, once the defendant has appeared, the court may take "appropriate measures to prevent the defendant from absenting himself."[28] As will be shown below,[29] the court can conduct a main hearing against a defendant who did not appear before it (or did not reappear at its resumption) only under narrow conditions.

3.1.2 Removal of the Defendant to Maintain Order

In some instances, even a defendant who has appeared at the main hearing and is fit to stand trial can be removed from the courtroom. One of these exceptions results from the court's power to remove the defendant from the courtroom for the purpose of maintaining order if he or she seriously disrupts the hearing.[30] Such disruption must normally go beyond a one-time incident.[31] In this case, "the hearing may be conducted in his absence if the court does not consider his further presence to be indispensable" for assessing the value of evidence "and as long as it is to be feared that the defendant's presence would be seriously detrimental to the progress of the main hearing." In any case, the trial court must give the defendant the opportunity to comment on the charges.[32] As soon as the defendant is allowed back into the courtroom, the court is required to "inform him of the essential contents of the proceedings during his absence."[33]

---

[25] Cf. BT-Drucks. 18/3562, p. 47; BVerfG, Order of 27th December 2006—2 BvR 1872/03 -, BeckRS 2012, 54108; OLG Hamburg, Order of 3rd December 2013—1-25/13 -, BeckRS 2014, 00512; Deiters (2015), § 231a, para. 4; ZehetGruber (2013), p. 398.

[26] BVerfGE 51, 324 = BGH NJW 1979, 3249 f.

[27] Section 230 para. 2, section 216 para. 1 CCP; Roxin and Schünemann (2014), p. 355.

[28] Section 231 para. 1 CCP.

[29] Cf. Sect. 5.1.

[30] Meyer-Goßner (2016), § 231b, para. 6.

[31] BGHSt 39, 72 = BGH NJW 1993, 1343; Deiters (2015), § 231b, para. 3.

[32] Section 231b para. 1 CCP; cf. BGHSt 9, 77 = BGH NJW 1956, 837, 838; Deiters (2015), § 231b, para. 3 f.

[33] Section 231b para. 2, section 231a para. 2 CCP; cf. BGH NStZ-RR 2010, 283.

3.1.3 Temporary Removal of the Defendant During Examination of Witness or Co-defendant

The law also allows for removal of the defendant from the courtroom during parts of the hearing in the interest of discovering the truth or to protect witnesses or defendants themselves. The defendant can be ordered to leave the courtroom during an examination if, on the basis of specific facts, it is to be feared that a witness or co-defendant will not tell the truth or refuse to give evidence in the presence of the defendant.[34] Such removal is also possible "if on examination of a person under 18 years of age as a witness in the defendant's presence, considerable detriment to the well-being of such witness is to be feared or if an examination of another person as a witness in the defendant's presence poses an imminent risk of serious detriment to that person's health."[35] For adult witnesses, this requires a high probability of grave detrimental consequences (e.g., an expected nervous breakdown or revenge if the identity of the witness were to be revealed[36]); in the case of a minor, probable detrimental effects on the personal development suffice.[37] In the interest of the defendant, removal can also be ordered "for the duration of discussions concerning the defendant's condition and his treatment prospects, if substantial detriment to his health is to be feared."[38] In order to safeguard defence rights, the presiding judge is obliged to inform the defendant "of the essential contents of the proceedings, including the testimony, during his absence" immediately after the defendant returns to the courtroom[39] or ensure that the defendant can, during his absence, follow the hearing by means of an audio-video link.[40] In case documents or objects were examined during the defendant's absence, they have to be shown to defendants after their return to the courtroom.[41] Once they have been informed about the essential content of the proceedings during their absence, or during/after following the hearing via an audio-video link, defendants must be given the opportunity to directly question the witness or submit questions to him or her.[42]

---

[34] Section 247 s. 1 CCP; BGH NStZ 2001, 608; BGH NStZ 2002, 44, 45; BGH BGH NStZ-RR 2004, 116, 118; BGH NStZ 2010, 53; BGH NStZ 2015, 103, 104; Diemer (2013), § 247, para. 5; Frister (2016), § 247, para. 20 f., 24; Meyer-Goßner (2016), § 247, para. 3 f.; Metz (2017), p. 446 f.

[35] Section 247 s. 2 CCP; Frister (2016), § 247, para. 34.

[36] In the latter case, a witness examination via video link will usually be more appropriate; see below Sect. 3.7; cf. Frister (2016), § 247, para. 46.

[37] Diemer (2013), § 247, para. 10 f.; Frister (2016), § 247, para. 34–40; Meyer-Goßner (2016), § 247, para. 12.

[38] Section 247 s. 3 CCP; Diemer (2013), § 247, para. 12; Frister (2016), § 247, para. 47.

[39] Section 247 s. 4 CCP; BGH NStZ 1998, 263; BGH NStZ-RR 2007, 85; Diemer (2013), § 247, para. 14; Frister (2016), § 247, para. 69; Meyer-Goßner (2016), § 247, para. 15 f.; Widmaier (1998), p. 263.

[40] BGHSt 51, 180 = BGH NJW 2007, 709; BGH NStZ 2011, 534; Diemer (2013), § 247, para. 15; Frister (2016), § 247, para. 67.

[41] BGHSt 54, 184, 187 = BGH NJW 2010, 1010, 1011; BGH NStZ-RR 2008, 315; NStZ-RR 2014, 53 f.; Diemer (2013), § 247, para. 8; Erb (2010), p. 347; Frister (2016), § 247, para. 61.

[42] BGH NStZ 2011, 534; Frister (2016), § 247, para. 76.

3.2   Personal Participation in the Pre-trial Inquiry (with Particular Regard to Interim Decisions on Coercive Measures)

3.2.1   Judicial Examination of Witnesses and Experts

Right to Attend

At the pre-trial stage, the accused and defence counsel are, in principle, "permitted to be present during the judicial examination of a witness or an expert." However, the judge "may exclude an accused from being present at the hearing if his presence would endanger the purpose of the investigation." Such endangerment is presumed "in particular if it is to be feared that a witness will not tell the truth in the presence of the accused."[43] A similar endangerment must be assumed if the accused would, with substantial likelihood, use information obtained on the occasion of the judicial examination to obstruct the investigation.[44]

An accused who has been remanded in custody and has a defence counsel is "entitled to be present only at such hearings held at the place where he is in custody." If this were to endanger the success of the investigation, the accused and defence counsel are not even given prior notice of the dates of a pre-trial hearing.[45] Such endangerment of the investigation can result from a delay caused by service of the notice that could lead to a loss of the witness, but also from the substantiated expectation that the accused, if he or she were to be informed about the examination in advance, could push the witness to provide untruthful testimony or coerce the witness to refuse testimony.[46] Apart from that, the accused or defence counsel are not entitled to be present at an examination of witnesses and experts by the state prosecution office or the police.

Mandatory Defence Counsel

If the accused is excluded from a judicial examination in line with the forgoing and does not yet have a defence counsel, this can pose problems with regard to Article 6 para. 3 lit. d of the ECHR. As a result, the jurisprudence of the Federal High Court requires the court to appoint a defence counsel before the judicial examination of a key prosecution witness if the participation of a defence counsel at the future main hearing seems likely (which applies, in particular, in cases in which the accused is remanded in custody or is accused of a crime punishable by imprisonment of at least

---

[43] Section 168c para. 1, 2 CCP.

[44] Schmitt (2016), § 168c, para. 3.

[45] Section 168c para. 4, 5 CCP.

[46] BGHSt 29, 1 = BGH NJW 1980, 1056; BGH NJW 2003, 3142 f.; Schmitt (2016), § 168c, para. 5.

1 year[47]).[48] This ensures respect for the accused's rights in that it enables the defence counsel to ask the witness questions and thus represent the interests of the accused if the latter is excluded from the judicial examination.[49] This requirement is of particular importance when the witness, due to insurmountable impediments, does not appear at the subsequent main hearing; the examination of a witness, expert, or co-accused at the main hearing can then be "replaced by reading out the written record of his previous examination by a judge."[50]

3.2.2   Coercive Investigative Measures

Proceedings Following Apprehension of the Accused

An interim decision on coercive measures at the pre-trial stage does not require a prior hearing if this were to endanger the purpose of the measure,[51] which is typically the case for the initial judicial decision on remand detention. However, the law provides subsequent judicial remedies against interim coercive measures. If the accused has been apprehended on the basis of an arrest warrant, he or she must be brought before the competent judge without delay.[52] The judge must examine the accused in person. If the accused cannot be brought to the court due to ill health, a judge must visit him in hospital.[53] At this hearing, the accused must be given the opportunity to refute the grounds for suspicion. The accused can also apply for the taking of exonerating evidence. If accused use their right to first consult a defence counsel,[54] the hearing has to be postponed in order to enable counsel to attend.[55] Defence counsel must normally be allowed access to the case file. If such access might endanger the purpose of the investigation, access to the file can be restricted, but the defence counsel must at least receive access to the information that is relevant for assessing the lawfulness of the deprivation of liberty.[56] The court is not allowed to confirm the lawfulness of the arrest warrant on the basis of parts of the file to which the defence counsel had no prior access.[57] Furthermore, the competent judge must "so far as he considers it of importance, take such evidence if loss of

---

[47] Cf. Sect. 2.1 above; section 140 para 1 no. 1, 4 CCP; section 74 para. 1 Courts Constitution Act.

[48] BGHSt 46, 93 = BGH NJW 2000, 3505.

[49] Regarding the possibility to substitute the accused's presence by the presence of a defense counsel at the examination of a witness in order to conform with Article 6 ECHR, cf. ECtHR, *Doorson v. Netherlands,* judgement of 26th March 1996, Appl. No. 20524/92.

[50] Section 251 para. 2 no. 1 CCP.

[51] Section 33 para. 4 CCP.

[52] Section 115 para. 1, 115a para. 1 CCP.

[53] Schmitt (2016), § 115, para. 7.

[54] Cf. sections 137 para. 1, 168c para. 1 CCP.

[55] RhPfVerfGH, NJW 2006, 3341, 3343; Schmitt (2016), § 115, para. 8.

[56] Section 147 para. 2 CCP; Schmitt (2016), § 147, para. 25a.

[57] Deutscher Bundestag, Drucksache 16/11644, p. 34; Schmitt (2016), § 147, para. 25a.

evidence is to be feared or if the taking of the evidence may justify the release of the accused."[58] Thus the taking of exonerating evidence might be particularly appropriate where there are substantiated indications that a witness or co-accused could revoke their incriminatory testimony or when there is a specific expectation that the examination of witnesses in person would strengthen doubts about their credibility. This right to apply for the taking of evidence ultimately finds its limits in the legislative intention that the pre-trial judicial examination is not meant to comprehensively investigate the case.[59]

Subsequent Review of Pre-trial Detention

While the accused remains remanded in custody, he or she is at any time entitled to apply for a court hearing to challenge the arrest warrant[60] before the court that issued the initial arrest warrant.[61] In this case, "a decision shall be given after an oral hearing upon application by the accused, or at the court's discretion *proprio motu*."[62] The accused has a right to a "further oral hearing only if remand detention has continued for at least three months and at least two months of remand detention have elapsed since the last oral hearing."[63] Furthermore, this right to a separate oral hearing does not apply "as long as the main hearing is in process."[64] The oral hearing is to be held without delay, at most no later than 2 weeks after the application, except when the accused agrees to a postponement.[65] The accused is entitled to attend the hearing in person, "unless great distance or sickness" or "other insurmountable obstacles prevent his being brought to the hearing."[66] If accused waive their right to attend in person or if insurmountable obstacles prevent their personal attendance, the court can conduct the oral hearing "in such a way that the accused is located in another place than the court and the hearing is simultaneously transmitted audio-visually to the place where the accused is located and to the courtroom." Otherwise, if the accused is neither attending in person nor by means of the aforementioned audio-visual transmission, the rights of the accused at the hearing shall be safeguarded by the defence counsel. If the accused does not yet have such counsel, the court has to appoint one.[67] Regarding the possible taking of evidence, the aforesaid applies.[68]

---

[58] Section 166 para. 1 s. 1 CCP.

[59] OLG Köln, NStZ-RR 2009, 123 f.

[60] Section 117 para. 1 CCP.

[61] Cf. Section 126 para. 1 CCP.

[62] Section 118 para. 1 CCP.

[63] Section 118 para. 3 CCP.

[64] Section 118 para. 4 CCP.

[65] Section 118 para. 5 CCP.

[66] Section 118a para. 2 CCP.

[67] Section 118a para. 2 CCP.

[68] Cf. Schmitt (2016), § 118a, para. 4.

Review of Other Coercive and of Clandestine Measures

With respect to searches, seizure, and attachment of property, the accused can file a complaint (*Beschwerde*) to a higher-instance court.[69] The higher court assess the lawfulness of the measure on questions of both law and facts. To this end, it "may order investigations or conduct them itself."[70] The court decides without oral hearing.[71] Yet, it may not make its decision to the detriment of the accused on the basis of evidence or information in respect of which the accused has not been heard.[72]

The procedural law also provides for a judicial remedy against clandestine investigative measures, in particular regarding the seizure of postal items (section 99 CCP), telecommunications interception (section 100a CCP), interception of speech on private premises (section 100c CCP), acquisition of telecommunications traffic data (section 100g CCP), use of undercover investigators (section 110a CCP), and police observation (section 163e CCP). Individuals directly affected by those measures shall be notified about them if notification does not endanger the purpose of the investigation.[73] After such notification or after otherwise becoming aware of the measure, the affected person can apply to the court that issued the initial authorisation to review the lawfulness of the measure and of the manner of its implementation.[74] This review also does not entail an oral hearing. In order to prepare the application, defence counsel is, in principle, entitled to access the investigative file.[75] However, unless the investigation has been concluded, pre-trial access to the file can be denied to the extent that this may endanger the purpose of the investigation.[76]

3.3 *Personal Participation in Proceedings* In Camera

The Federal Constitutional Court has stressed that judicial in camera proceedings (i.e., court proceedings in which the decision is taken on the basis of evidence that is not disclosed to the accused and defence counsel) are not permitted in criminal procedure. Even in judicial complaint proceedings against coercive and clandestine investigative measures, the evidence underlying the investigative measure must be accessible to the applicant in the same way as it is for the court of review. The initial

---

[69] Sections 304 para. 1, 306 CCP; Schmitt (2016), § 98, para. 31; § 105, para. 15; § 111e, para. 20.

[70] Section 308 para. 2 CCP.

[71] Section 309 para. 1 CCP.

[72] Cf. section 33 para. 3 CCP.

[73] Section 101 para. 4, 5 CCP.

[74] Section 101 para. 7 CCP. After an indictment has been filed, the court entrusted with the matter is competent to review the investigative measure when issuing its concluding decision.

[75] Schmitt (2016), § 101, para. 25d.

[76] BGH—Order of 22nd September 2009—StB 28/09—BeckRS 2009, 86260; sections 147 para. 2, 477 para. 2 CCP.

court authorisation of such investigatory measures is normally issued without prior hearing of the suspect. However, judicial review of such authorisation cannot, according to the Constitutional Court, be decided without granting the accused prior access to the parts of the investigative file that are relevant for assessing the lawfulness of the initial authorisation.[77] For complaint proceedings against past investigative measures that are no longer being executed—in particular against an already executed search warrant or terminated telecommunications surveillance—the Constitutional Court allows the following: if access to relevant parts of the investigative file would endanger the purpose of the investigation and is therefore lawfully denied, judicial review of the initial authorisation can be postponed until such time as defence counsel can be granted access to the file,[78] i.e., at the latest at the time the investigation is concluded.[79] In contrast, the postponement of such access to the file is not possible if, during the complaint proceedings, the coercive measure—particularly a continuing seizure or attachment of property—is still being enforced.[80]

3.4 Personal Participation in Alternative Proceedings

3.4.1 Private Prosecutions

For a limited number of comparatively less serious offences (such as trespassing, defamation, non-aggravated bodily injury, and stalking), German criminal procedure provides for private prosecutions, thereby allowing an aggrieved person to bring a prosecution without taking recourse to the public prosecution office. In this case, the defendant can be assisted at the main hearing by an attorney or be represented by an attorney and is thus not required to be present in person. The court can, however, order the personal appearance of the defendant,[81] in particular when this seems necessary for fact-finding purposes.[82]

3.4.2 Proceedings Before the Juvenile Court

Furthermore, special requirements apply for exceptions to the defendant's personal participation at the main hearing before the juvenile courts, i.e., criminal courts that deal with crimes committed by youths (aged 14–17) and, under certain

---

[77] BVerfG, NJW 2004, 2443; NJW 2006, 1048; NStZ-RR 2008, 16; 2013, 379.

[78] BVerfG NStZ 2007, 274, 275; NStZ-RR 2008, 16, 17; NStZ-RR 2013, 379, 380; Schmitt (2016), § 101, para. 25d.

[79] Cf. section 147 para. 2 CCP.

[80] Cf. BVerfG NJW 2004, 2443; NStZ-RR 2008, 16, 17; NStZ-RR 2013, 379, 380; LG Kiel, NStZ 2007, 424.

[81] Section 387 CCP.

[82] Meyer-Goßner (2016), § 287, para. 6.

circumstances, young adults (aged 18–20).[83] Due to the primarily educational purpose of juvenile courts,[84] the law is particularly reluctant to allow for proceedings against absent defendants. "The main hearing may take place in the absence of the defendant only if this would be permissible in the general proceedings, if there are special reasons to do so and with the assent of the public prosecutor." Special reasons are only given in cases of less serious crimes, provided that the court already has sufficiently detailed information about the defendant's personality and provided that the defendant's appearance would not have a detrimental impact, e.g., on his or her employment situation. Under such circumstances, it may often be appropriate to dispense with prosecution or discontinue proceedings.[85] Still, the accused in the juvenile court can temporarily be excluded from the main hearing to the extent that discussions could be disadvantageous to the accused's education and development; in this case, the court must inform the accused of the content of deliberations held in his or her absence as far as this is necessary for the defence.[86]

3.4.3 Preventive Detention Proceedings

German criminal law also allows for preventive detention without the instigation of criminal proceedings in cases in which the perpetrator cannot be held criminally responsible or is unfit to stand trial. This particularly applies to the court's power to issue a mental hospital order if a person "has committed an unlawful act in a state of insanity" and "a comprehensive evaluation of the offender and the act leads to the conclusion that as a result of his condition, future serious unlawful acts can be expected of him and that he therefore presents a danger to the general public."[87] A court can also issue a custodial addiction treatment order if a person is addicted to alcohol or other drugs and is not convicted of an offence only because he has been found to be insane, provided that "there is a danger that he will commit future serious unlawful acts as a consequence of his addiction."[88] Likewise without the instigation of criminal proceedings, the court can also issue driving disqualification and professional disqualification orders.[89] In preventive detention proceedings, the accused must be assisted by a defence counsel.[90] If the accused's appearance in court is "impossible due to his condition or is inappropriate for reasons of public order or security," the court can conduct the main hearing in the absence of the

---

[83] Section 1 Youth Courts Act.

[84] Section 2 Youth Courts Act.

[85] Section 50 para. 1 Youth Courts Act; cf. Eisenberg (2012), p. 65; id. 2016, § 50, para. 16 ff.; Laue (2010), p. 296.

[86] Section 51 para. 1 Youth Courts Act.

[87] Section 63 CC.

[88] Section 64 CC.

[89] Section 71 para. 2 CC.

[90] Section 140 para. 1 no. 7 CCP.

accused.[91] The accused's appearance may, in particular, be impossible due to the acute danger of suicide or danger that his or her health condition might otherwise deteriorate.[92] Reasons of public order or security can be the expectation that the accused could commit acts of violence during his transport or the hearing.[93] If the court anticipates such impediments, the accused must "be examined prior to the main hearing by a commissioned judge with the assistance of an expert."[94] Such examination is meant to enable the court to gain at least indirect knowledge of the accused's personality and to offer the accused an opportunity to comment on the accusations. In contrast, if the court has already examined the accused on the charges, it may conduct the main hearing in the (permanent or temporary) absence of the accused if "the condition of the accused so requires" or a proper main hearing is otherwise not possible—in particular if the accused would constantly disrupt the hearing.[95]

3.4.4 Proceedings to Preserve Evidence

Special proceedings exist for the purpose of preserving evidence when the accused's whereabouts are unknown or the accused is otherwise out of reach for the German authorities.[96] In such proceedings, the accused may be represented by a defence counsel and even by relatives. If charges have already been filed against an absent accused, the entirety of the accused's property, to the extent that it is located within Germany, may be seized by the court in order to force his or her appearance should the grounds for suspicion justify the issuing of an arrest warrant.[97]

3.4.5 Confiscation Proceedings

In addition, procedural law provides for participation of persons at the main hearing that are not accused themselves, but who might be negatively affected by the criminal court's confiscation order because they own the property in question or have some other right to it. In this case, the court orders such person to participate in the proceedings.[98] If such person "fails to appear at the main hearing despite being properly informed of the date of the hearing, the hearing may be conducted in his

---

[91] Section 415 para. 1 CCP; cf. BGH NJW 2001, 3277, 3278.

[92] Meyer-Goßner (2016), § 415, para. 2.

[93] Meyer-Goßner (2016), § 415, para. 3.

[94] Section 415 para. 2 CCP.

[95] Meyer-Goßner (2016), § 415, para. 8.

[96] Section 276, section 285 CCP.

[97] Section 290 para. 1 CCP, Börner (2005), p. 547 f. Roxin and Schünemann (2014), p. 508.

[98] Section 431 para. 1 CCP; BGH NJW 2016, 3192 f.

absence."[99] Such person may also chose to be represented by an attorney.[100] However, if persons with an interest in the confiscation were unable to attend the proceedings through no fault of their own, in particular if they were not informed of it, they can apply for a review of the confiscation decision.[101]

3.4.6 Objection Proceedings Against Regulatory Fines

Lastly, special rules apply in proceedings for regulatory offences, i.e., such offences for which the law does not provide imprisonment, but only the imposition of a regulatory fine by an administrative body. Persons concerned can file an objection against such fine with the court. In the course of the resulting proceedings, they can apply to be exempted from their obligation to appear before the court if they have already made a statement on the matter or declared that they will not comment on the matter at the main hearing, provided that their presence is not necessary to clarify factual questions. If such exemption is granted, the person concerned can authorise a defence counsel to represent him or her at the main hearing.[102] However, if the person concerned fails to appear despite not having been exempted from the obligation to do so and without sufficient excuse, the court must reject the objection without a hearing on the merits.[103]

3.5 Personal Participation at Trial

3.5.1 Personal Involvement in the Evidence-Gathering

Right to Apply for the Taking of Evidence at the Main Hearing

While the taking of evidence is primarily conducted by the court, the defendant is entitled to apply for the taking of further evidence. In principle, the court has no discretion to reject an application for the taking of evidence. An application can only be denied if such evidence would be inadmissible or if "such evidence is superfluous because the matter is common knowledge, the fact to be proved is irrelevant to the decision or has already been proved, the evidence is wholly inappropriate or unobtainable, the application is made to protract the proceedings, or an important allegation which is intended to offer proof in exoneration of the defendant may be

---

[99] Section 436 para. 1 CCP.

[100] Section 434 para. 1 CCP.

[101] Section 439 para. 1 CCP; cf. BGH Order of 2nd August 2012—5 StR 408/11, BeckRS 2012, 18236.

[102] Section 73 Act on Regulatory Offences.

[103] Section 74 para. 1, 2 Act on Regulatory Offences.

treated as if the alleged fact were true."[104] However the court is not allowed to reject an application on the basis of anticipation of the outcome of the requested taking of evidence. Thus, an application cannot be rejected because the court believes that the opposite of the fact that the application seeks to establish has already been proven, or because it anticipates that the requested evidence would be untrustworthy.[105] The application can be rejected for relying on "wholly inappropriate" evidence if it appears impossible (and not merely unlikely) that the evidence would substantiate the underlying factual claim from the outset.[106] Evidence is considered "unobtain-able" if the court, despite appropriate efforts, was unable to obtain it, and there is no reasonable expectation that the court might obtain it in the foreseeable future.[107] Further limitations on the right to request the taking of evidence apply with regard to the examination of experts. Such applications can be denied if the court itself already possesses the sought after specialist knowledge.[108] The hearing of another expert on the same factual point "may also be refused if the opposite of the alleged fact has already been proved by the first expert opinion." This rule, however, does "not apply to cases where the professional competence of the first expert is in doubt, where his opinion is based upon incorrect factual suppositions, where the opinion contains contradictions, or where the new expert has means of research at his disposal which seem to be superior to the ones of an earlier expert."[109] Courts have even more discretion to reject applications for inspections *in loco*. They can be rejected if the court "deems the inspection not to be necessary". The court has the same discretionary power with regard to an application to examine a witness if the witness has to be summoned from abroad. Under this discretionary power, the court can reject an application particularly if, in view of other evidence, it is already reasonably convinced that the evidence sought will not confirm the applicant's factual assertion.[110] In contrast, upon application by the defendant, the court is obliged to extend the taking of evidence to such witnesses and experts who were summoned by the defendant and appeared at the trial. It must also consider other evidence (i.e., documentary evidence and objects) that has already been brought before the court by the defendant. In these cases, an application for the taking of evidence can only be rejected if such evidence is inadmissible or "if the fact for which evidence is to be furnished has already been proved or is common knowledge, if there is no connection between the fact and the matter being adjudicated, if the evidence is completely unsuitable, or if the application has been filed for the purpose of protracting

---

[104] Section 244 para. 3 CCP.

[105] BGH StV 2001, 95; BGH NStZ-RR 2008, 205; BGH NStZ-RR 2010, 211, 212; Beulke (2012), p. 299.

[106] BGH NStZ-RR 2002, 242 f.; BGH NStZ-RR 2010, 211, 212; BGH NStZ-RR 2012, 51, 52.

[107] BFGSt 22, 118, 120 = BGH NJW 1968, 1485; BGH StV 1987, 45; Beulke (2012), p. 300.

[108] BGH NStZ 2010, 100, 101; NStZ 2010, 586; NStZ 2017, 300 f.

[109] Section 244 para. 4 CCP; cf. BGH NStZ 2002, 653, 654; NStZ 2005, 159; NStZ 2010, 405 f.

[110] BGHSt 40, 60, 62 = BGH NStZ 1994, 351, 352; BGH NStZ 2005, 701, 702 f.; Beulke (2012), p. 302.

the proceedings."[111] However, a witness or expert directly summoned by the defendant is obliged to appear only if the defendant beforehand offers reimbursement for travel expenses and absence from work in cash or proves that they have been deposited at the court's registry in advance.[112]

Defence Counsel's Right to Apply for the Taking of Evidence

If the main hearing can be held in the defendant's absence, a defence counsel who is present can still apply for the taking of evidence under the aforementioned conditions. To the extent that the taking of certain evidence is subject to the defendant's approval—which is required especially in specific cases in which the court wishes to substitute the examination of a witness, expert, or co-defendant by the reading of a prior examination record[113]—the absent defendant loses the right to object. The defence counsel who is present can still raise objections.[114]

Application for the Taking of Evidence Before the Main Hearing

Furthermore, after proceedings have been opened by the trial court, yet before the main hearing, the defendant can apply for the summoning of witnesses and experts and for the production of other evidence to be examined at the main hearing; applications to this effect can only be denied for the abovementioned reasons.[115] Applications for the taking of evidence can be made, in particular, when the absent defendant is examined by a judge outside the main hearing, which is required as a precondition for conducting the main hearing in the defendant's absence in some cases.[116]

3.5.2   Personal Contribution to the Fact-Finding

Before it commences with the taking of evidence, the court will inform the defendant that he or she may make any statement on the charges. If the defendant is prepared to do so, the court shall examine him or her.[117] Furthermore, the defendant is

---

[111] Section 245 para. 2 CCP.

[112] Section 220 para. 2 CCP.

[113] Cf. section 251 para. 1 no. 1, para. 2 no. 3 CCP.

[114] Section 234a CCP; BGHSt 3, 206 = BGH NJW 1952, 1345 f.; Gmel (2013), § 231, para. 9; Meyer-Goßner (2016), § 234a, para. 4 f.

[115] Section 219 CCP; Meyer-Goßner (2016), § 219, para. 3.

[116] Gmel (2013), § 231a, para. 21; Gmel (2013), § 233, para. 18; see above Sect. 3.1, and below Sects. 5.1.2 and 5.1.5.

[117] Section 243 para. 5 CCP.

entitled to address questions to witnesses and experts.[118] After each examination of a co-defendant and each taking of evidence, the court will ask defendants whether they have anything to add.[119] Following the taking of evidence, defendants are given the opportunity to present their arguments. Even if the defence counsel has spoken for them, the court shall ask defendants whether they wish to add anything to their defence.[120]

Naturally, the absent defendant loses the opportunity to contribute to the fact-finding at the main hearing.[121] However, a defence counsel who is present can avail himself of most of these participatory rights independently of the defendant, in particular the right to ask the witnesses and experts questions[122] and to make a statement after each taking of evidence.[123] Furthermore, if the defendant authorises defence counsel to this effect, the latter can make a statement on the charges and respond to the court's questions in the name of the defendant.[124]

3.6   Personal Participation in Higher Instances

In addition to the general rules pertaining to the defendant's absence at the main hearing,[125] some special rules apply to the defendant's participation in *Berufung* proceedings (i.e., an appeal on points of fact and law). If at the beginning of the main *Berufung* hearing neither the defendant nor a defence counsel whom the defendant has authorised to be present has appeared, and if there is no sufficient excuse for the failure to appear, the court can dismiss an appeal by the defendant on fact and law without hearing the merits of the case. The law then assumes that the defendant has no further interest to proceed with the appeal.[126] The same applies when the continuation of the main hearing is prevented due to one of the following circumstances: (1) if defence counsel absents him or herself without sufficient excuse and the absence of the defendant is not sufficiently excused or if the defense counsel refuses to further represent the absent, insufficiently excused defendant; (2) if the defendant absents him or herself without sufficient excuse and no defense counsel authorised by the defendant is present; (3) if the defendant wilfully and

---

[118] Section 240 para. 2 CCP.

[119] Section 257 para. 1 CCP.

[120] Section 258 para. 3 CCP.

[121] Gmel (2013), § 231, para. 9.

[122] Section 240 para. 2 CCP.

[123] Section 257 para. 2 CCP.

[124] See above under Sect. 2.2.

[125] Cf. section 332 CCP; see above under C., I. and below under E, I., with the exception of sections 231 and 231a CCP; BT-Drucks. 18/3562, p. 74.

[126] BT-Drucks. 18/3562, p. 67; Meyer-Goßner (2016), § 329, para. 2.

culpably places him- or herself in a condition precluding fitness to stand trial and no defence counsel authorised by the defendant is present.[127]

To the extent that the defendant's presence is not necessary in view of the court's duty to uncover all relevant facts, the main hearing is conducted without the defendant if he or she is represented by a defence counsel whom he or she has authorised to this effect. To the extent that the defendant's presence is not necessary, the main hearing is also conducted without the defendant—even in the absence of a defence counsel—if the defendant's absence has not been sufficiently excused and the appeal was filed by the prosecution[128]; in this case, the court shall inform the defendant or defence counsel of the essential contents of the proceedings during their absence once one of them appears, unless the pronouncement of the judgement has already commenced.[129] If, following an appeal by the prosecution, the main hearing cannot be concluded in the absence of the defendant, the court shall, to the extent necessary to uncover relevant facts, order the defendant to be brought before it or to be arrested.[130] If, following an appeal by the defendant and despite a defence counsel being present, the presence of the defendant is necessary, the court shall summon the defendant to appear before it; if the defendant then does not appear without sufficient excuse and his or her presence continues to be necessary, the court shall dismiss the appeal. In the summons, defendants must be informed that the appeal may be dismissed in their absence.[131] After service of the appeals judgement issued in their absence, defendants may lodge an objection within 1 week to the effect that they were prevented from attending the appeals hearing through no fault of their own Defendants are granted restoration of the *status quo ante* upon application, in particular if they had not been properly summoned to the main hearing.[132]

Thus, German law does provide for *in absentia* main hearings in *Berufung* proceedings if the defendant is represented by a defence counsel or the appeal has been filed by the prosecution. As already mentioned, however, such *in absentia* hearings are permitted only to the extent that the defendant's presence is not deemed necessary in light of the court's comprehensive duty to uncover all relevant facts.[133] Consequently, the presence of the defendant at the *Berufung* hearing will normally be necessary, in particular if it is to be expected that the defendant's contribution would contribute to the discovery of the truth, because the defendant's presence

---

[127] Section 329 para. 1 CCP; Meyer-Goßner (2016), § 329, para. 17–18.

[128] Section 329 para. 2 CCP.

[129] Section 329 para. 5 CCP; Meyer-Goßner (2016), § 329, para. 35.

[130] Section 329 para. 3 CCP.

[131] Section 329 para. 4 CCP; Meyer-Goßner (2016), § 329, para. 10.

[132] Section 329 para. 7, section 44 para. 1 CCP; Meyer-Goßner (2016), § 329, para. 15a.41.

[133] BGHSt 17, 391 = BGH NJW 1962, 2020, 2021; Böhm (2015), p. 3133 f.; Meyer-Goßner (2016), § 329, para. 36.

seems appropriate in light of the gravity of the expected sentence[134] or because the court considers it crucial to gain a personal impression of the defendant.[135] In contrast, *in absentia Berufung* hearings are allowed particularly when, in view of the issues raised by the appeal, the defendant's presence is clearly irrelevant, e.g., in cases in which procedural law requires proceedings to be stayed in any case or when substantive law precludes a conviction in view of the facts.[136] Accordingly, the presence of the defendant might be required for parts of the main hearing, but not for other parts.[137]

In *Revision* proceedings (i.e., an appeal on points of law only), the defendant may "appear at the main hearing or may be represented by defence counsel." However, if the defendant is remanded in custody, he or she is not entitled to be present.[138]

3.7 Special Rules in the Area of Serious Organised Crime

In response, especially to the challenges posed by the prosecution of organised crime, German procedural law contains special rules to protect a witness's anonymity and shield a witness from the defendant. As already mentioned above,[139] the defendant can be temporarily removed from the main hearing if it is to be feared that a witness will not tell the truth when examined in the presence of the defendant. This possibility is complemented by the right of witnesses not to reveal their identity if this were to endanger their or another person's life, limb, or liberty[140] or were to jeopardize the continued use of the witness as an undercover agent.[141] Furthermore, a witness may remain in another location and be examined by means of an audio-video link to the courtroom if there is an "imminent risk of serious detriment to the well-being of the witness were he to be examined in the presence of those attending the main hearing."[142] To protect the witness, the audio-video link may be acousti-

---

[134] Note that *Berufung* is admissible only against judgements of the Local Court, which may not impose a sentence of imprisonment of more than 4 years; cf. section 312 CCP and section 24 para. 2 Courts Constitution Act. First-instance judgements of higher criminal courts (dealing with more serious crimes) can be appealed on points of law only.

[135] BT-Drucks. 18/3562, p. 73 f.; BGHSt 17, 391 = BGH NJW 1962, 2020, 2021; Böhm (2015), p. 3133; Frisch (2015), p. 72 f.; Meyer-Goßner (2016), § 329, para. 36; cf. OLG Karlsruhe, NStZ-RR 2004, 21, 22.

[136] Frisch (2015), p. 71; Meyer-Goßner (2016), § 329, para. 36.

[137] BT-Drucks. 18/3562, p. 74.

[138] Section 350 para. 2 CCP; Deiters (2015), § 230, para. 2.

[139] Cf. 3.1.3.

[140] Section 69 para. 3 CCP; cf. section 110b para. 3 CCP; Eisenberg (1993), p. 1035 f.

[141] Section 110b para. 3 CCP.

[142] Section 247a para. 1 CCP; BGH NStZ 2017, 372 f.; cf. Leipold (2005), p. 471 f.; Roxin and Schünemann (2014), p. 358.

cally or visually altered,[143] and the defendant can be removed from the hearing during its transmission.[144]

4 Personal Participation of Private Parties Other Than Defendants (in Particular, the Contribution of the Victim to the Fact-Finding)

After submission of the indictment to the court, aggrieved persons (or, in case of an unlawful killing, their next of kin) can, for a number of offences, notably violent crimes and criminal infringements of copyright law, join the public prosecution as private accessory prosecutors.[145] In this case, they have the right to be present at the main hearing even if they are to be examined as a witness. The private accessory prosecutor is also entitled to challenge a judge or an expert (in particular for fear of bias); to ask the defendant, witnesses, and experts questions; to object to orders by the presiding judge and to particular questions; and to apply for evidence to be taken. The private accessory prosecutor can also make statements following the examination of the defendant and following each individual taking of evidence. Private accessory prosecutors can further avail themselves of the assistance of an attorney or choose to be represented by such attorney.[146] Lastly, they can appeal decisions of the court independently of the public prosecution office.[147]

5 *In Absentia* Proceedings

5.1 *Information Rights and Conditions of Waiver of Personal Participation in Criminal Proceedings*

5.1.1 Defendant Absenting Himself or Failing to Reappear Without Permission

In principle, defendants cannot waive their right to attend the main hearing.[148] However, *in absentia* proceedings are permitted in certain, albeit narrow circumstances. To prevent the defendant from impeding or unduly delaying proceedings,

---

[143] BVerfG NStZ 2007, 534; BGH NJW 2003, 74.

[144] BGH NStZ 2003, 274; BGH NStZ 2006, 648.

[145] Section 395 CCP.

[146] Section 397 CCP.

[147] Section 401 para. 1 CCP.

[148] BGH NJW 1973, 522; NJW 1976, 1108; NStZ-RR 2015, 51; Frister (2016), § 247, para. 4; Meyer-Goßner (2016), § 230, para. 2; Roxin and Schünemann (2014), p. 358.

the main hearing can be concluded in the defendant's absence if the defendant absents him- or herself, or fails to appear when an interrupted main hearing is continued. This, however, requires that the trial court has already examined the defendant on the charges, in the sense that the defendant had been given the opportunity to respond to the indictment after it was read at the beginning of the main hearing and the court does not consider the defendant's presence necessary for fact-finding purposes.[149] This exception from the defendant's duty to attend furthermore requires that the absence of the defendant involves culpability on his or her part, i.e., the court must be convinced that the defendant consciously disregarded the duty to attend without legitimate justification or excuse.[150] This requirement is not fulfilled for example, if the defendant has fallen ill, arrives late due to a train delay[151] or overslept,[152] trusted the erroneous advice of defence counsel that he or she is under no obligation to attend,[153] or if defendants find themselves under significant pressure not to attend, in particular if they would risk losing their employment.[154] In contrast, defendants' absence is considered culpable if, after having been examined on the indictment, they placed themselves in a condition precluding fitness to stand trial, e.g., through the consumption of alcohol or—according to a controversial ruling of the Federal High Court—due to a suicide attempt that was committed with the expectation of thereby avoiding the main hearing.[155] If the court, in the course of the main hearing, considers the defendant guilty of an offence different from the one specified in the original charges, it can convict the defendant only after having informed him or her to this effect. If a defence counsel is present, however, it suffices that the court inform defence counsel about the change in its legal assessment.[156] If defendants return to the main hearing before the pronouncement of the judgement, they regain all their procedural rights,[157] in particular the right to apply for the taking of specific evidence and to deliver a closing statement. It is not necessary to repeat procedural acts performed during defendants' prior absence; however, if defendants are not assisted by a defence counsel, the court's duty of care for

---

[149] Section 231 para. 2 CCP; BGHSt 46, 81 = BGH NJW 2000, 2830; Deiters (2015), § 231, para. 11 f.; Gmel (2013), § 231, para. 7 f.; Meyer-Goßner (2016), § 231, para. 19; Roxin and Schünemann (2014), p. 356.

[150] BGHSt 37, 249 = BGH NJW 1991, 1364, 1365 f.; BGH NStZ-RR 2001, 333; BGHSt 56, 298 = BGH NJW 2011, 3249, 3252; Deiters (2015), § 231, para. 16 f.; Eisenberg (2012), pp. 65, 69; Gmel (2013), § 231, para. 3; Meyer-Goßner (2016), § 231, para. 9 f.

[151] BGH NStZ 2003, 561 f.

[152] BGH NJW 1991, 1367.

[153] OLG Bremen StV 1992, 558.

[154] BGH NJW 1980, 950 f.; BGH NStZ 1985, 13, 14.

[155] BGH NJW 1981, 1052; BGH NStZ 1986, 372; BGH NJW 1991, 2917 f.; BGH NStZ 2002, 533, 535; BGHSt 56, 298 = BGH NJW 2011, 3249, 3252; Arnoldi (2012), p. 109 f.; Deiters (2015), § 231, para. 28a; Eisenberg (2012), p. 67; Gmel (2013), § 231, para. 3, 5; Meyer-Goßner (2016), § 231, para. 17; Roxin and Schünemann (2014), p. 356; Trüg (2011), p. 3256.

[156] Cf. Section 234a, section 265 para. 1, 2 CCP; Gmel (2013), § 231, para. 10.

[157] BGH NStZ 1986, 372; BGH NStZ 1990, 291; OLG Stuttgart NStZ-RR 2015, 285, 286; Deiters (2015), § 231, para. 37.

defendants may require it to inform them about the essential contents of the proceedings during their absence.[158]

5.1.2 Defendants Compromising Their Fitness to Stand Trial

In contrast, requirements for an *in absentia* main hearing are more demanding if, due to the defendant's unfitness to stand trial, the trial court was not even able to examine him on the charges at the main hearing. The law here is motivated by the desire to prevent a defendant from undermining proceedings once he or she is physically within reach of the authorities. If the defendant, before having been heard on the charges, "wilfully and culpably placed himself in a condition precluding his fitness to stand trial, and if, as a result, he knowingly prevents the proper conduct or continuation of the main hearing in his presence, the main hearing shall […] be conducted or continued in his absence, unless" exceptionally—in particular for assessing the value of evidence[159]—"the court considers his presence to be indispensable." In addition, this requires that the defendant, after the trial court has received the indictment and allowed the case to proceed to trial, is given the opportunity to make a statement on the charges before the trial court or before a single member of the trial court outside the main hearing,[160] even if the defendant does not comment despite being mentally able to do so.[161] Even then, an *in absentia* hearing shall only exceptionally be permitted.[162] This provision is not only applicable when the defendant is permanently unfit to stand trial, however, but also covers cases of temporary unfitness that would render it impossible to conclude the main hearing within a reasonable time frame.[163] It applies, in particular, to cases in which the defendant attempts to subvert the hearing through a hunger strike, other forms of self-harm,[164] or the abuse of medication or narcotics.[165] In contrast, defendants are normally not required to undergo medical treatment to restore their health,[166] at least

---

[158] Cf. BGHSt 3, 187 = NJW 1952, 1306; BGH NStZ-RR 2003, 1, 2; Deiters (2015), § 231, para. 38; Gmel (2013), § 231, para. 12; Meyer-Goßner (2016), § 231, para. 23.

[159] Deiters (2015), § 231a, para. 31; Gmel (2013), § 231a, para. 11; Meyer-Goßner (2016), § 231a, para. 14.

[160] Section 231a para. 1 CCP; cf. BVerfGE 41, 246 = BGH NJW 1976, 413; Gmel (2013), § 231a, para. 13.

[161] Deiters (2015), § 231a, para. 28; Gmel (2013), § 231a, para. 14 f.; Meyer-Goßner (2016), § 231a, para. 12.

[162] Deiters (2015), § 231a, para. 6.

[163] BVerfGE 41, 246 = BGH NJW 1976, 413, 414; Deiters (2015), § 231a, para. 10; Gmel (2013), § 231a, para. 2; Meyer-Goßner (2016), § 231a, para. 9.

[164] BGHSt 26, 228 = BGH NJW 1976, 116, 117; Deiters (2015), § 231a, para. 16; Gmel (2013), § 231a, para. 3a; Meyer-Goßner (2016), § 231a, para. 5.

[165] BVerfGE 51, 324 = BGH NJW 1979, 3249; Deiters (2015), § 231a, para. 14; Meyer-Goßner (2016), § 231a, para. 7.

[166] Cf. BVerfGE 89, 120 = BVerfG NJW 1994, 1590, 1591; Deiters (2015), § 231a, para. 16; Gmel (2013), § 231a, para. 3; Meyer-Goßner (2016), § 231a, para. 7.

not if such treatment could have significant detrimental side-effects.[167] With regard to defendants' required intent, it suffices that they consciously accept that their unfitness to stand trial could be the consequence of this behaviour, even if this was not the only or primary goal.[168] It should be emphasized that the aforementioned only concerns the defendant's unfitness to attend trial and does not extend to the defendant's absence due to flight.[169] The decision to conduct the hearing without the defendant requires prior expert testimony by a physician. It can be challenged by means of a complaint (*Beschwerde*) to a higher-instance court; this challenge has a suspensive effect.[170] If the defendant is not yet assisted by a defence counsel, the court shall appoint one as soon as a hearing in the absence of the defendant is being considered.[171] Should defendants regain their fitness to attend trial at a later point in the hearing, the law requires the court to inform them of the essential contents of the proceedings during their absence unless it has already commenced with the pro-nouncement of the judgement.[172]

5.1.3   Excusing Defendant from Attending Parts of the Hearing

A further—only narrowly applicable—exception to the defendant's duty to attend exists for main hearings with multiple defendants, when parts of the hearing do not affect one of the defendants. Since these parts would neither directly nor indirectly affect the charges against this particular defendant, they cannot have an impact on the verdict or on sentencing.[173] This can particularly be the case when some of the charges do not concern all defendants.[174] Upon application, the court may then per-mit an individual defendant and also his or her defence counsel to excuse them-selves during those parts of the hearing that are irrelevant for them.[175]

---

[167] Cf. OLG Nürnberg NJW 2000, 1804; 1805; OLG Düsseldorf, NStZ-RR 2001, 274; LG Lüneburg, NStZ-RR 2010, 211.

[168] BGHSt 26, 228 = BGH NJW 1976, 116, 118; Gmel (2013), § 231a, para. 5; Meyer-Goßner (2016), § 231a, para. 8.

[169] Cf. Deiters (2015), § 231a, para. 4.

[170] Section 231a para. 3 CCP; Deiters (2015), § 231a, para. 41 f.

[171] Section 231a para. 4 CCP; Deiters (2015), § 231a, para. 29; Gmel (2013), § 231a, para. 17; Meyer-Goßner (2016), § 231a, para. 13.

[172] Section 231a para. 2 CCP; Meyer-Goßner (2016), § 231a, para. 19.

[173] BGH NStZ 2009, 400; BGH NStZ 2010, 227; BGH NStZ 2012, 463; BGH NStZ 2013, 666, 667; Deiters (2015), § 231c, para. 5; Gmel (2013), § 231c, para. 4.

[174] Cf. BGHSt 32, 100 = BGH NJW 1984, 501, 502.

[175] Section 231c CCP.

5.1.4 Unauthorised Non-appearance of Defendant in Cases of Low-Level Charges

Beyond that, a complete main hearing against absent defendants is permissible in the interest of protecting the functioning of the criminal justice system if they were properly summoned—which requires that defendants' whereabouts are known to the court[176]—and thereby explicitly warned that the hearing may take place in their absence. This is only allowed, however, if, in view of the facts of the specific case, "a fine up to 180 daily units, a warning with sentence reserved, a driving ban, forfeiture, confiscation, destroying or making an item unusable, or a combination thereof" would constitute an appropriate response to the offences charged. A higher penalty or a measure of reform and prevention than that previously stated may not be imposed, in particular not a custodial sentence.[177] Furthermore, the defendant must have consciously and culpably been absent.[178] The existence of these conditions does not, however, authorise the defendant not to appear, but only authorises the court to conduct the main hearing in the defendant's absence.[179] If a record of a prior judicial examination of the defendant is available, it must be read out at the main hearing,[180] except when the absent defendant is represented by defence counsel, as the latter can make a statement on the charges in the name of the defendant.[181] Should the court, at the main hearing, find that the defendant is guilty of an offence different from the one mentioned in the indictment, it can proceed with the hearing only if the absent defendant is represented by a defence counsel.[182] Even if the aforementioned conditions for an *in absentia* hearing are fulfilled, the court can order the defendant to be brought before it,[183] especially if the court assumes that the defendant's presence is necessary for discovering the truth.[184] If the main hearing is conducted in the defendant's absence, the judgement must be served on the defendant personally or on his or her defence counsel.[185] Defendants can apply for restoration of the *status quo ante* within 1 week of service of judgement if they were prevented from attending the hearing through no fault of their own. They may at any time, even after the aforesaid 1-week time limit, request restoration of the *status quo ante* if they were not informed of the summons to the main hearing.[186]

---

[176] Deiters (2015), § 232, para. 8; Meyer-Goßner (2016), § 232, para. 4.

[177] Section 232 para. 1 CCP; Gmel (2013), § 232, para. 6; Meyer-Goßner (2016), § 232, para. 7.

[178] Cf. section 235 CCP; OLG Karlsruhe NStZ 1990, 505, 506; Gmel (2013), § 232, para. 9; Meyer-Goßner (2016), § 232, para. 11.

[179] Gmel (2013), § 232, para. 1.

[180] Section 232 para. 3 CCP.

[181] Deiters (2015), § 232, para. 12; Gmel (2013), § 232, para. 14; Meyer-Goßner (2016), § 232, para. 15.

[182] Cf. section 265 para. 1, section 234a CCP; Meyer-Goßner (2016), § 232, para. 18.

[183] BGHSt 25, 165 = BGH NJW 1973, 1006, 1007; Meyer-Goßner (2016), § 232, para. 1.

[184] Meyer-Goßner (2016), § 232, para. 13.

[185] Section 232 para. 4 CCP; Deiters (2015), § 232, para. 19; Gmel (2013), § 232, para. 18 f.

[186] Section 235, section 44 CCP.

5.1.5   Excusing Defendant from Attending Main Hearing in Cases of Low-Level Charges

Lastly, the law provides for a formal waiver of the duty to attend in order to take legitimate interests of the defendant into account.[187] He can lodge an application to the court to be released from the obligation to appear at the main hearing if, in view of the facts of the case, "only imprisonment up to six months, a fine up to 180 daily units, a warning with sentence reserved, a driving ban, forfeiture, confiscation, destroying or making an item unusable, or a combination thereof, is expected to be imposed." "A higher penalty or a measure of reform and prevention may not be imposed in his absence."[188] Such an application can be especially useful if the defendant would prefer to refrain from appearing personally because of the great distance between his or her residence and the court, for reasons of ill health, for professional reasons, or for private reasons.[189] The court may withdraw its authorisation at any point, however, in particular if it considers the aforementioned sentencing powers to no longer be adequate or if the defendant's presence is necessary, especially for fact-finding purposes.[190] Furthermore, the law provides safeguards to protect accused from making an insufficiently informed application and to provide them with the opportunity to present their perspective before a judge.[191] To these ends, if the court grants the defendant's application to be released from the obligation to appear, he or she must be examined on the charges by a judge of the trial court or by a commissioned judge of another court. On this occasion, the defendant must also "be advised of the legal consequences admissible at the hearing in his absence and be asked whether he maintains his application to be released from the obligation to appear at the main hearing." To facilitate the aforementioned application, and lieu of an examination of the accused by a requested or a commissioned judge, the court may also conduct the examination on the charges outside the main hearing by means of video link, thus allowing the defendant to be in another location than the court.[192] The record of the defendant's examination must be read out at the main hearing.[193] Should the court, at the main hearing, find that the defendant is guilty of an offence different from the one mentioned in the indictment, or should the court wish to rely on inculpatory evidence not yet presented to the defendant, he or she must again be examined by a judge[194]; alternatively, the court can summon the defendant to the main hearing and examine him or her there.

---

[187] Deiters (2015), § 233, para. 1; Gmel (2013), § 233, para. 1.

[188] Section 233 para. 1 CCP.

[189] Deiters (2015), § 233, para. 10; Meyer-Goßner (2016), § 233, para. 1.

[190] Deiters (2015), § 233, para. 10; Gmel (2013), § 233, para. 5; Meyer-Goßner (2016), § 233, para. 12.

[191] BGHSt 25, 42 = BGH NJW 1973 2004, 205; Gmel (2013), § 233, para. 12; Meyer-Goßner (2016), § 233, para. 15.

[192] Section 233 para. 2 CCP; cf. Deiters (2015), § 233, para. 13.

[193] Section 233 para. 3 CCP; Deiters (2015), § 233, para. 22.

[194] Deiters (2015), § 233, para. 15; Gmel (2013), § 233, para. 12; Meyer-Goßner (2016), § 233, para. 16.

5.2   Default Proceedings and Subsequent Remedies (e.g., Retrial or Judicial Review in a Higher Instance)

5.2.1   Appeal on Points of Law and Retrial Options

When a main hearing in the (permanent or temporary) absence of the defendant is allowed, subsequent judicial remedies against the judgement are the same as those applicable to judgements following an ordinary main hearing: *Revision* (i.e., an appeal on points of law only) and in some cases[195] *Berufung* (i.e., an appeal on points of fact and law). Particularly in those cases in which the law allows for *in absentia* proceedings in view of the minor severity of the expected sentence, the defendant normally has the opportunity to appeal the first-instance judgement on points of fact and law. To the extent that the first judgement is appealed, this leads to a full retrial before a higher-instance court.[196]

As already stated, the law provides additional remedies in two cases (trials on minor charges where no custodial sentence is expected and *Berufung* proceedings) in which defendants were unable to attend the main hearing through no fault of their own, including the situation of not having been previously warned that a judgement could also be rendered in their absence. These remedies lead to a complete retrial in the same instance.[197]

5.2.2   Defendant's Absence at Main Hearing as Ground for Annulment of Judgement

The great significance that German criminal procedure ascribes to the defendant's presence is demonstrated by the fact that the defendant's unlawful absence from a significant part of the trial constitutes an "absolute ground for appeal," i.e., the conviction must be set aside irrespective of whether this absence has had a material effect on the judgement or not.[198] Accordingly, if the court conducted the entire trial or parts of the trial in the absence of the defendant, but the conditions for such an *in absentia* trial were not given, the judgement will be quashed, in particular if the defendant had a legitimate justification or excuse not to attend. The quashing can lead to a partial or complete retrial in a lower-instance court, depending on whether the defendant has limited the appeal to only parts of the judgement or is contesting it in its entirety.[199] The jurisprudence of the Federal High Court has adopted a rather

---

[195] See note 126.

[196] Section 312, section 327 CCP.

[197] Sections 232, 235, 329 para. 7 CCP; cf. Meyer-Goßner (2016), § 235, para. 8, § 329, para. 44.

[198] Section 338 no. 5 CCP; BGHSt 55, 87 = BGH NJW 2010, 2450, 2451; Deiters (2015), § 230, para. 37; Roxin and Schünemann (2014), p. 355.

[199] Cf. section 353 para. 1; BGH NJW 1995, 1910 f.; BGH NJW 2003, 597, 598; Meyer-Goßner (2016), § 353, para. 6.

strict approach when determining whether the relevant part of a hearing was significant and therefore justifies a quashing of the judgement. Any exclusion of the defendant from the hearing must be limited to what is strictly necessary to safeguard
other important interests. Thus, e.g., while the defendant may lawfully be excluded
from the hearing during the examination of a witness in order to protect this witness,
the defendant must, in principle, return to the courtroom and be informed about the
relevant content of the witness's testimony before the witness is discharged. The
defendant's absence is then no longer strictly necessary, as the witness can well be
removed from the courtroom before being discharged. Should the defendant wish to
submit questions to the witness after being informed about the content of the testimony, the latter can be brought back to the courtroom and the defendant simultaneously removed again. As the interval between the witness's testimony and the
witness's discharge enables the defendant to promptly respond to the testimony
made in his or her absence, it is considered a significant part of the main hearing.
Therefore, the defendant's absence at this stage would lead to the quashing of the
judgement, except if the defendant declares that he or she does not intend to submit
further questions to the witness or if the same witness is subsequently examined
again.[200] Similarly, the defendant cannot be excluded from the hearing interval during which an application for his or her exclusion is discussed and from the pronouncement of the court's decision to this effect; otherwise the judgement will be
quashed, even if the defendant had voluntarily agreed to leave the courtroom.[201]

5.3   Inaudito Reo *Proceedings (e.g., Penal Order Procedure)*

In case of misdemeanours, a court can impose the legal consequences of an offence
by means of a written penal order without a main hearing. The public prosecution
office can file an application to this end if, in view of the results of its investigation,
it does not consider a main hearing to be necessary. A penal order cannot, however,
lead to the imposition of a custodial sentence if the indicted person has no defence
counsel. If the accused has a defence counsel, a penal order can also impose imprisonment for up to 1 year, provided that its execution is suspended on probation.[202]
Before issuing the penal order, the court is not required to offer the indicted person
a prior hearing. The court may issue a penal order if, on the basis of the file submitted by the prosecutor, there appear to be sufficient grounds to suspect that the
indicted accused has committed a criminal offence. Thus, for a penal order to be
issued, it is not necessary that the judge is fully convinced of the accused's guilt.[203]

---

[200] BGHSt 55, 87 = BGH NJW 2010, 2450, 2451 f.; BGH NStZ 2006, 713; 2011, 534; 2014, 532,
533; NStZ 2015, 104 f.; Diemer (2013), § 247, para. 7 f.; Fezer (2011), p. 77, 86; Meyer-Goßner
(2016), § 247, para. 20c.

[201] BGH NStZ-RR 2015, 51; Diemer (2013), § 247, para. 16.

[202] Section 407 para. 1 CCP.

[203] Meyer-Goßner (2016), § 408, para. 7.

However, the judge must open a "main hearing, if he has reservations about deciding the case without a main hearing, if he wishes to deviate from the legal assessment in the application to issue the penal order, or if he wishes to impose a legal consequence other than those applied for and the public prosecution office insists on its application."[204] In addition, in proceedings before a single criminal court judge (*Strafrichter*) and in proceedings before a court with lay judges (*Schöffengericht*)— i.e., in cases of low-level crimes or those of medium gravity—if the main proceedings have already been opened, the prosecutor can apply for a penal order if the defendant fails to appear or if a main hearing is impeded for other important reasons (such as the absence of an important witness[205]), provided that the aforementioned conditions for issuing a penal order are fulfilled. The judge shall grant the application if he or she has no reservations.[206] If the accused does not yet have a defence counsel and if the judge is considering the issuing of a penal order with a suspended prison sentence of up to 1 year, he must first appoint a defence counsel for the defendant.[207] The penal order must be served to the defendant, e.g., personally or by placing it in the letterbox of the effective residence or at the business premises where the defendant is employed,[208] or to defence counsel.[209]

"Within two weeks following service of the penal order the defendant may lodge an objection against the penal order at the court which issued it."[210] In this case, the court will then proceed with a full main hearing that follows the general rules. At this hearing, the defendant can be represented by a defence counsel; the defendant is not required at attend in person.[211] If the defendant does not appear at the main hearing, is not sufficiently excused, and is not even represented by a defence counsel, the court shall dismiss the objection without hearing its merits.[212] When this happens, or an objection is not lodged in time, the order becomes equivalent to a judgement that has entered into force.[213] However, if the defendant was prevented from observing the 2-week time limit for lodging an objection "through no fault of his own, he shall be granted restoration of the *status quo ante* upon application."[214] This holds especially true if defendants can prove that they were temporarily absent from home and had no reason to anticipate that they would be served with a penal order during their absence.[215]

---

[204] Section 408 para. 3 CCP.

[205] Meyer-Goßner (2016), §408a, para. 4.

[206] Section 408a CCP.

[207] Section 408b CCP.

[208] Section 37 para. 1 CCP, sections 177 ff. Code of Civil Procedure.

[209] Section 145a para. 1 CCP.

[210] Section 410 para. 1 CCP.

[211] Section 411 para. 1, 2 CCP.

[212] Section 412, section 329 para. 1 CCP.

[213] Section 410 para. 3 CCP.

[214] Section 44 para. 1 CCP; cf. Meyer-Goßner (2016), § 411, para. 2.

[215] BVerfG, NJW 1969, 1531.

6 Participatory Rights in Transnational Criminal Justice

6.1 Participatory Safeguards in EAW Proceedings

6.1.1 Participatory Rights in the Decision on Surrender

According to the Act on International Cooperation in Criminal Matters (*Gesetz über die internationale Rechtshilfe in Strafsachen*), after reception of the extradition[216] request, the single criminal court judge (*Strafrichter*) shall advise the person sought of his rights and "ask him whether and if so on what grounds he wishes to object to the extradition."[217] Counsel is entitled to attend the hearing.[218] The single judge does not, however, decide on the admissibility of extradition, but only records the sought person's statements.[219] In fact, if the person sought does not consent to the extradition or the public prosecution service applies for a judicial decision, the admissibility of extradition shall be decided by the Higher Regional Court (*Oberlandesgericht*), i.e., by the highest court at the federal state level (*Bundesland*). This court may examine the person sought and may take further evidence beyond the documents offered by the requesting state.[220] The Higher Regional Court may also hold an oral hearing,[221] but this rarely occurs in practice.[222] While the Higher Regional Court, in principle, has discretion to examine the person sought, it may be particularly bound to do so, especially if the court's personal impression of the sought person is deemed necessary to assess whether extradition might violate fundamental rights.[223] It may also be considered necessary if the person's prior statements indicate that the act might be justified or excused under German criminal law and the extradition request does not address this possibility.[224] Even without an oral hearing, the court must respect the right of the person sought to a fair hearing, i.e., it must provide the person sought or counsel with the opportunity to at least submit written statements regarding the evidence and the applications filed by the public prosecution service.[225] The person sought and counsel are further entitled to attend any taking of

---

[216] The official English translation of the Act on International Cooperation in Criminal Matters by the Federal Ministry of Justice uses the term "extradition" even with regard to EAW proceedings. Therefore, while the English-language version of Framework Decision 2002/584/JHA refers to the term "surrender," the present text continues to use the term "extradition."

[217] Section 28 para. 2 AICCM.

[218] Section 77 AICCM, section 168c CCP; Köberer (2015), § 28, para. 354; Lagodny (2012), § 28, para. 6.

[219] Lagodny (2012), § 28, para. 1.

[220] Section 30 para. 2 AICCM; OLG Zweibrücken, NStZ 2008, 639.

[221] Section 30 para. 3 AICCM.

[222] Köberer (2015), § 30 IRG, para. 390; Lagodny (2012), § 28, para. 3.

[223] Lagodny (2012), § 30, para. 30.

[224] Köberer (2015), § 30 IRG, para. 380; Lagodny (2012), § 30, para. 20.

[225] Section 33 para. 3 CCP, section 77 para. 1 AICCM; Köberer (2015), § 30 IRG, para. 389.

evidence by the court.[226] In the case of an oral hearing, the person sought and counsel are entitled to attend and are to be informed of the time and place of the hearing.[227] If the person sought is in custody, he or she has to be brought to the hearing, unless he or she waives the right to attend or insurmountable obstacles like illness prevent attendance. If persons sought are not brought to the oral hearing, counsel must represent them. In this case, if persons sought do not already have a counsel of their choice, it shall be appointed for their defence.[228] If persons sought are not in custody, the court can order their personal attendance and, if they have been properly summoned and are not sufficiently excused, order them to be brought before the court.[229] In any case, the parties present at the oral hearing have a right to be heard.[230]

6.1.2 *In Absentia* Proceedings in the Trial Country and Its Relevance in the Surrender Procedure

As a principle, the law provides that extradition to EU Member States for the purpose of enforcement is not admissible if the convicted person did not personally attend the hearing that led to the judgement.[231] This includes the case when the accused did not attend substantial parts of the hearing.[232] Notwithstanding this principle, and thereby largely following Council Framework Decision 2009/299/JHA, extradition following an *in absentia* judgement is admissible in the following cases: (1) if the convicted person had, in due time, been personally summoned to the hearing that led to the judgement or had otherwise officially been informed about the place and date of said hearing, so that it is established beyond doubt that the person knew about the scheduled hearing, provided, in both cases, that the person had been informed that a judgement could also be issued in his or her absence[233]; (2) if—insofar not mandated by the Framework Decision[234]—defence counsel had been attending the proceedings and the convicted person avoided the service of a summons by fleeing in the knowledge of the proceedings against him or her[235]; or (3) if the convicted person, being aware of the scheduled hearing, had appointed defence counsel to defend him or her at the hearing and was then effectively defended by this defence

---

[226] Köberer (2015), § 30 IRG, para. 390; Lagodny (2012), § 30, para. 29.

[227] Section 31 para. 1 AICCM.

[228] Section 31 para. 2 AICCM; Köberer (2015), § 31 IRG, para. 396; Lagodny (2012), § 31, para. 9 f.

[229] Section 31 para. 3 AICCM.

[230] Section 31 para. 4 AICCM.

[231] BT-Drucks. 18/3562, p. 78.

[232] Cf. BT-Drucks. 18/3562, p. 79.

[233] Section 83 para. 2 no. 1 AICCM; BT-Drucks. 18/3562, p. 79; Böhm (2017), pp. 77, 80.

[234] Cf. BT-Drucks. 18/3562, p. 81; cf. BVerfG NJW 1991, 1411.

[235] Section 83 para. 2 no. 2 AICCM; OLG München NStZ 2017, 50.

counsel at the hearing.[236] Furthermore, extradition for the purpose of enforcement of an *in absentia* judgement is also admissible if the convicted person expressly declared that he or she would not contest the judgement or did not file an application for a retrial, or a (higher-instance) appeal, within the applicable time limit. In both cases, that the convicted person has to have previously been expressly advised about the right to a retrial or appeal against the judgement and that he or she is entitled to attend the retrial or appeals hearing where the facts of the case, including new evidence, can again been examined, and that, as a result, the prior judgement can be overturned.[237] Lastly, extradition for the purpose of enforcement of an *in absentia* judgement is admissible if the convicted person, immediately after transfer to the requesting Member State, is personally served with the judgement and is advised as to the right to a retrial or appeal that correspond to the aforementioned standards, and on the relevant time limits.[238] In any case, even if a conviction fulfils one of the aforementioned conditions, an extradition might still be inadmissible if the hearing violated Article 6 of the European Convention of Human Rights, in particular if convicted persons were summoned to the hearing or advised about their right to a retrial in a language that they could not understand and were not provided with an adequate translation, if convicted persons were summoned to the hearing but did not attend through no fault of their own, or if the applicable time limits for a retrial were inadequate.[239]

6.2   Participatory Safeguards in Trans-Border Inquiries and the Taking of Overseas Evidence

In line with Article 4 para. 1 of the Convention on Mutual Assistance in Criminal Matters between the Member States of the European Union,[240] mutual assistance within the EU shall comply with the procedures required by the law of the requesting Member State, unless that would be contrary to fundamental principles of law in the requested Member State. In a similar vein, according to Art. 9 para. 2 of the Directive 2014/41/EU regarding the European Investigation Order in criminal matters, "The executing authority shall comply with the formalities and procedures expressly indicated by the issuing authority [...] provided that such formalities and procedures are not contrary to the fundamental principles of law of the executing

---

[236] Section 83 para. 2 no. 3 AICCM.

[237] Section 83 para. 3 AICCM; BT-Drucks. 18/3562, p. 83.

[238] Section 83 para. 4 AICCM; Böhm (2017), pp. 77, 81.

[239] Cf. section 73 AICCM; BT-Drucks. 18/3562, p. 80 f., 83.; cf. BVerfGE 63, 332 = BVerfG NJW 1983, 1726 f.

[240] Council Act of 29 May 2000 establishing in accordance with Article 34 of the Treaty on European Union the Convention on Mutual Assistance in Criminal Matters between the Member States of the European Union [2000] OJ C197/01.

State."[241] This rule is also of relevance when, according to the law of the requesting Member State, the defendant and defence counsel have a right to attend the performance of an investigative measure, particularly the examination of a witness. Within the confines of German procedural law,[242] in particular the condition that such participation does not undermine safeguards of German procedural law, the German authorities will, in principle, have to comply with the foreign authority's request to allow the defendant and defence counsel to attend.[243]

In line with the preceding observations, investigative measures performed abroad by foreign authorities on the request of German judicial authorities must respect the right of the defendant to attend the performance of such measures. Subject to certain exceptions,[244] German law does provide a right for the defendant as well as the defence counsel to attend the examination of witnesses by a judge. This right also applies when, following a German request for legal assistance, a witness is examined abroad by a foreign judge if, and only if, the applicable foreign law allows the defendant's attendance. In this case, the German request for assistance must call on the requested authority to inform the requesting authority of the date of the judicial examination in a timely manner, so that the defendant and the defence counsel are informed accordingly and their attendance thus enabled.[245]

7 Requirements of Personal Participation and *In Absentia* Proceedings: Supranational and International Human Rights Law

7.1 *International Human Rights Law: Critical Remarks on Domestic Law in the Light of the European Convention*

7.1.1 Participation at the Pre-trial Stage

With regard to the right to a fair trial, in particular the right to confront prosecution witnesses according to Article 6 para. 3 lit. d ECHR, problems can arise as to the judicial examination of witnesses in the absence of the defendant at the pre-trial stage if neither the latter nor defence counsel have been notified of the court hearing.[246] A 2015 Grand Chamber judgement of the ECtHR found that Germany violated Article 6 ECHR when two key prosecution witnesses did not testify at the

---

[241] Directive 2014/41/EU of the European Parliament and of the Council of 3 April 2014 regarding the European Investigation Order in criminal matters; OJ EU no. L 130 of 1 Mai 2014, p. 10.

[242] Güntge (2015), p. 24; Lagodny (2012), § 59, para. 38; Wahl (2016), p. 589.

[243] Cf. BGH NStZ 2007, 344; Güntge (2015), § 59, para. 23 f.

[244] Above under Sect. 3.2.1.

[245] BGHSt 42, 86 = BGH NJW 1996, 2239, 2240; Schmitt (2016), § 168c, para. 8.

[246] Cf. Sect. 3.2.1.

main hearing and neither the defendant nor the defence counsel were present during their pre-trial examination by a judge. Despite this, the trial court based the defendant's conviction on the record of the judicial pre-trial examination to a decisive extent. The Grand Chamber held that, in view of the evidentiary importance attributed to the witnesses by the trial court, sufficient counterbalancing factors had been missing to compensate for the lack of opportunity to directly cross-examine the witnesses at the trial. In particular, despite it already having been reasonably foreseeable for the authorities at the moment of the witnesses' examination that the latter would not attend the main hearing, no defence counsel was appointed at the pre-trial stage to question the witnesses at their judicial examination,[247] no video recording of this examination was produced[248] to allow an observation of the witnesses' demeanour, and neither the defendant nor the defence counsel ever had the opportunity to put questions to the witnesses, not even indirectly.[249] Despite acknowledgment that the trial court had examined the reliability of the evidence in a careful manner, the Grand Chamber nevertheless concluded that the lack of sufficient counterbalancing factors rendered the trial unfair as a whole.[250] This essentially confirms and further reinforces the criticism expressed in a 2012 Chamber judgement in which the ECtHR already found a violation of Article 6 ECHR in that, contrary to the Code of Criminal Procedure, no defence counsel had been appointed to attend the pre-trial examination of a decisive prosecution witness by a judge, and this witness then did not testify at the main hearing.[251] Existing German procedural law arguably provides prosecutors and courts with sufficient instruments to counterbalance a curtailment of Article 6 para. 3 lit. d ECHR, but leaves them with too much leeway to apply those instruments, in particular when assessing whether the appointment of a defence counsel is mandatory.[252] The aforementioned jurisprudence indeed suggests the need for a further strengthening of defence rights at the pre-trial stage, particularly by enhancing the role of the defence counsel at the judicial examination of witnesses.[253]

---

[247] Despite this having been possible, cf. section 141 para. 3 CCP; cf. 2.1.

[248] This possibility is provided for by section 58a para. 1 CCP, according to which the witness examination shall, depending on the circumstances, be conducted by a judge and recorded "if there is a concern that it will not be possible to examine the witness during the main hearing."

[249] According to section 223 para. 1 CCP, a witness can be examined by a member of the trial court or a commissioned judge outside the main hearing when insurmountable obstacles prevent him from appearing at the trial. An examination of a witness abroad can be conducted by a German consul; cf. section 15 para. 4 Act on Consular Officers; Meyer-Goßner (2016), § 251, para. 33.

[250] ECtHR, *Schatschaschwili v. Germany*, judgement of 15 December 2015, Appl. no. 9154/10, para. 146 ff.; Thörnich (2017), p. 48 ff. Cf. also ECtHR, *Al-Khawaja and Tahery v. United Kingdom*, judgement of 15 December 2011, Appl. no. 26766/05 and 22228/06.

[251] ECtHR, *Hümmer v. Germany*, judgement of 19 October 2012, Appl. No. 26171/07, para. 48 ff.; Thörnich (2017), p. 50.

[252] Cf. Sect. 3.2.1.

[253] Thörnich (2017), p. 55.

7.1.2 *In Absentia* Proceedings

According to the ECtHR jurisprudence regarding Article 6 para. 1 ECHR, defendants may, of their own free will, waive the right to appear in person at their trial, either expressly or tacitly, provided that the waiver is established in an unequivocal manner and that defendants could reasonably foresee the consequences of their non-attendance. In particular, there is no violation of Article 6 ECHR if defendants had been officially informed about the date and place of the trial and did not attend without valid excuse or if they were defended by a legal counsel to whom they had given mandate to this effect.[254] Given its stringent requirements regarding *in absentia* criminal proceedings, German law seems to be mostly in line with those ECHR standards as regards first-instance trials.[255] Under German law, a main hearing is only allowed if the defendant has been properly summoned (which requires that the court is aware of the actual whereabouts) and informed about the charges and the trial's date and place. As seen above,[256] German law provides for an express waiver of the defendant's duty to attend in case of minor charges as well as a waiver for parts of the main hearing that only concern a co-defendant. For all other instances in which the court can conduct the main hearing against defendants who did not appear or are unfit to stand trial, German law assumes that defendants have tacitly waived the right to attend, as the law requires that they must have been aware of the charges and of the date and place of the main hearing and culpably chose not to attend. One might, however, question the Federal High Court's jurisprudence according to which defendants are deemed as having waived their right to attend where they did not attend due to a suicide attempt committed with the expectation to thereby avoid the main hearing.[257]

Looking beyond first-instance trials, an ECtHR judgement of 2012 found a violation of Article 6 para. 3 lit. c ECHR with regard to proceedings following an appeal on points of fact and law (*Berufung*). According to the procedural rules at the time, the appeals court was bound to dismiss an appeal lodged by the defendant without deciding on its merits if the defendant did not appear at the appeals hearing and was not sufficiently excused.[258] The ECtHR considered this to be a disproportionate curtailment of Article 6 para. 3 lit. c ECHR to the extent that this automatic

---

[254] ECtHR, *Sejdovic v. Italy*, judgement of 1 March 2006, Appl. No. 56581/00, at para. 86–88; ECtHR, *Medenica v. Switzerland*, judgement of 14 June 2001, Appl. No. 20491/92, at para. 56–59; ECtHR, *Haralampiev v. Bulgaria*, judgement of 24 April 2012, Appl. No. 29648/03, at para. 32–34.

[255] Cf. Laue (2010), p. 297.

[256] Cf. Sects. 5.1.3 and 5.1.5.

[257] BGH NJW 1981, 1052; BGH NStZ 1986, 372; BGH NJW 1991, 2917 f.; BGH NStZ 2002, 533, 535; BGHSt 56, 298 = BGH NJW 2011, 3249, 3252; Arnoldi (2012), p. 109 f.; Deiters (2015), § 231, para. 28a; Eisenberg (2012), p. 67; Gmel (2013), § 231, para. 3, 5; Meyer-Goßner (2016), § 231, para. 17; Roxin and Schünemann (2014), p. 356; Trüg (2011), p. 3256.

[258] BVerfG, Order of 27th December 2006—2 BvR 1872/03 -, BeckRS 2012, 54108; OLG Hamburg, Decision of 3rd December 2013—1-25/13 -, BeckRS 2014, 00512; Zehetgruber (2013), p. 398.

dismissal of the appeal also applied where defence counsel was present at the appeals hearing. It noted that "the legitimate requirement that defendants had to attend their trial had to be met by other means than a deprivation of the defence rights of the person concerned."[259] Following the 2012 decision of the ECtHR, the German legislator modified the procedural rules on *Berufung* proceedings, allowing for an *in absentia* hearing on the appeal particularly if the defendant is represented by defence counsel and the presence of the defendant does not seem necessary for uncovering the truth.[260] Even though the ECtHR stressed that the procedural framework of *in absentia* proceedings should prioritize defence rights over a defendant's duty to attend the hearing, the new rules can still be problematic: they allow the court to dismiss an appeal lodged by the defendant on the sole grounds of his or her absence, even if defence counsel is present, provided that the court assumes that the presence of the defendant is necessary for uncovering the truth. It thus appears that, in order to comply with the ECtHR, courts will need to adopt a narrow reading of what makes the presence of the defendant "necessary."[261] A dismissal of the appeal due the absence of the defendant should be allowed only when, despite the presence of defence counsel, it appears that the attendance of the defendant is clearly indispensable for reaching a verdict on appeal.[262] Based on this standard, it would even appear that the presence of a defendant who remained silent at the first instance hearing and who then, without sufficient justification or excuse, is not present at the *Berufung* hearing, is not necessary.[263] In contrast, the defendant's presence at the *Berufung* hearing seems to be necessary particularly when the appeals court is called on to reach a new sentencing decision.[264] This also seems to be that case when the defendant has extensively testified at the first instance hearing and new evidence presented by the defence counsel makes it necessary to broadly reassess the value of the defendant's prior testimony. Furthermore, the new rules on *Berufung* appear problematic in light of ECtHR jurisprudence, as they oblige the appeals court to automatically dismiss the appeal lodged by the defendant if the latter was initially present at the beginning of the *Berufung* hearing, but is absent at a later point without sufficient excuse and no defense counsel is present.[265] Such automatic dismissal appears unreasonable if a defendant has already told the appeals court everything he or she wanted to say, so that a further presence seems redundant—even if without sufficient excuse.[266]

---

[259] ECtHR, *Neziraj v. Germany,* judgement of 8 November 2012, Appl. No. 30804/07, para. 52 ff. = NStZ 2013, 350; cf. Böhm (2015), p. 3133; Gerst (2013), p. 310 ff.; Zehetgruber (2013), p. 401.

[260] Cf. above Sect. 3.7.

[261] For an extensive reading, see OLG Hamburg, NStZ 2017, 607 f.

[262] Böhm (2015), p. 3133; Meyer-Goßner (2016), § 329, para. 15a.

[263] Cf. Böhm (2015), p. 3133.

[264] Frisch (2015), p. 72 f.; Meyer-Goßner (2016), § 329, para. 36.

[265] Section 329 para. 1 CCP.

[266] Frisch (2015), p. 72.

7.2 The Perspective of EU Law: Developments in Domestic Law as a Result of EU Law

7.2.1 Rights to Translation and Information

In 2013, Germany transposed Directive 2012/13/EU[267] on the right to information in criminal proceedings and Directive 2010/64/EU on the right to interpretation and translation.[268] Relatively few changes were considered necessary in order to bring national law in line with the new European instruments. In particular, with regard to the assistance of an interpreter at both the trial and pre-trial stage, the national legislator considered established practice to already conform to the European requirements.[269] In order to transpose Article 3 of Directive 2010/64/EU, the new law, however, contains an explicit provision on the translation of relevant documents, thereby essentially codifying established domestic jurisprudence.[270] It provides that, in principle, "a written translation of custodial orders as well as of bills of indictment, penal orders and non-binding judgements shall be necessary for the exercise of the rights under the law of criminal procedure of an accused who does not have a command of the German language."[271] Yet, following the already established balancing approach of the domestic courts,[272] the new law then qualifies this principle in that the translation of merely an excerpt of such document suffices it safeguards the defence rights of the accused. Moreover, an oral translation of such documents or an oral summary thereof can be substituted for a written translation if it enables safeguarding of the defence rights of the accused. As the law explicitly states, this can be assumed as a rule if the accused has defence counsel.[273] Following Article 3 para. 1 d of Directive 2012/13/EU, the law also provides that a court must "advise the accused in a language he understands that he may" to the extent that this is necessary to exercise his rights "demand that an interpreter or a translator be called in for the entire criminal proceedings free of charge."[274] Furthermore, in line with Article 3 para. 1 b of this Directive, the accused must be informed about the conditions under which he or she may request the appointment of a free-of-charge man-

---

[267] Directive 2012/13/EU of the European Parliament and of the Council of 22 May 2012 on the right to information in criminal proceedings; OJ EU no. L 142 of 1 June 2012, p. 1; cf. Ruggeri (2016), p. 581 ff.

[268] Directive 2010/64/EU of the European Parliament and of the Council of 20 October 2010 on the right to interpretation and translation in criminal proceedings; OJ EU no. L 280 of 26 October 2010, p. 1; cf. Ruggeri (2016), p. 585 ff.

[269] Christl (2014), p. 377.

[270] Cf. BGH NStZ 2017, 63 f.; Christl (2014), p. 379.

[271] Section 187 para. 2 s. 1 Courts Constitution Act.

[272] BVerfGE 64, 135 = BVerfG NJW 1983, 2762, 2764 f.; HansOLG Hamburg, NStZ 1993, 53; OLG Düsseldorf, NJW 2003, 2766 f.; Christl (2014), p. 378.

[273] Section 187 para. 2 s. 2–5 Court Constitution Act.

[274] Section 187 para. 1 s. 2 Courts Constitution Act. Broadly, the same obligation already existed with regard to an accused at the moment of his arrest; section 114b para. 2 s. 2 CCP.

datory defence counsel during his first examination by a court, prosecutor, or the police[275]; formerly, German jurisprudence had limited such an information duty to cases in which the defendant was accused of crimes punishable by imprisonment of at least 1 year.[276] In order to conform to Article 4 of Directive 2012/13/EU, the previous content of the "Letter of Rights" that is to be handed to an accused upon his or her arrest had to be expanded and now also contains information about the conditions for the appointment of a mandatory defence counsel, about judicial remedies against his detention, and about the right to access the investigative file.[277]

7.2.2   *In Absentia* Proceedings

In 2015, Germany transposed Council Framework Decision 2009/299/JHA[278] by amending its Act on International Cooperation in Criminal Matters, as already discussed above.[279] Since then, the Federal Constitutional Court has further clarified the relevant law and thereby confirmed and even reinforced German law's reluctance towards *in absentia* main hearings. As mentioned earlier, the accused's participation in the main hearing finds its primary normative foundation in the constitutional guarantee of the principle of culpability. Rooted in human dignity, the principle of culpability forms part of Germany's "constitutional identity," according to the Constitutional Court—it can neither be changed by constitutional reform nor by supranational authority, in particular not by European Union legislation.[280] According to the Court, the extradition of a person for the purpose of enforcing a criminal sentence constituted in itself an enforcement of this sentence.[281] The Constitutional Court critically assessed the jurisprudence of the Court of Justice of the European Union in the *Melloni* case, according to which Article 4a of the Framework Decision on the European Arrest Warrant "must be interpreted as precluding the executing judicial authorities, in the circumstances specified in that provision, from making the execution of a European arrest warrant issued for the purposes of executing a sentence conditional upon the conviction rendered *in absentia* being open to review in the issuing Member State."[282] The Constitutional Court

---

[275] Section 136 para. 1 s. 3, section 163a para. 3 s. 2, para. 4 s. 2 CCP.

[276] BGH NStZ 2006, 236, 237.

[277] Section 114b para. 2 s. 1 no. 4a, s. 2 CCP.

[278] Council Framework Decision 2009/299/JHA of 26 February 2009 amending Framework Decisions 2002/584/JHA, 2005/214/JHA, 2006/783/JHA, 2008/909/JHA and 2008/947/JHA, thereby enhancing the procedural rights of persons and fostering the application of the principle of mutual recognition of decisions rendered in the absence of the person concerned at the trial; OJ EU no. L 81 of 27 March 2009, p. 24; cf. Ruggeri (2016), p. 596 ff.

[279] BT-Drucks. 18/3562, p. 53 ff.; cf. 6.1.2.

[280] BVerfGE 140, 317, 341 = Federal Constitutional Court, 2 BvR 2735/14, at para. 48.

[281] BVerfGE 140, 317 = Federal Constitutional Court, Order of the Second Senate of 15 December 2015—2 BvR 2735/14, at para. 52.

[282] Cf. CJEU, Judgement of 26 February 2013, Melloni, C-399/11, para. 46; cf. Safferling (2014), p. 549 f.

emphasized that this would "not relieve German authorities or courts of their obligation to ensure that the principles of Art. 1 sec. 1 GG", i.e., the obligation to respect human dignity, "are complied with in the context of extraditions executing a European arrest warrant." When executing a European Arrest Warrant, the German authorities must therefore ensure that the minimum guarantees of the rights of the accused required by respect for human dignity will also be observed in the requesting Member State or they must otherwise refrain from extraditing the person.[283] The Framework Decision on the European Arrest Warrant and relevant domestic law had to be interpreted in this sense. Finding that the requirements under Union law for the execution of a European Arrest Warrant were not lower than those required by the German Constitution, the enforcement of a criminal sentence issued following an *in absentia* trial is, on the one hand, admissible in "cases in which the person, of his or her own free will, and unequivocally, waived his or her right to be personally present at trial." On the other hand, extradition would also respect the dignity of the accused in cases where "the accused is offered the opportunity to have a court review the facts pertaining to the charges brought against him or her" and "the court competent for potential appeal or retrial proceedings also hear[s] the accused" and "examine[s] not only the law but also the facts." Referring to the eleventh recital of Framework Decision 2009/299/JHA and ECtHR case law, the Constitutional Court requires Article 4a section 1 letter d of the EAW Framework Decision to be interpreted to the effect that the courts dealing with an appeal or retrial have no discretion to reexamine the merits of the case and that, consequently, Article 4a section 1 letter d of the Framework Decision required that the accused "had a right to the evidence presented by him or her for his or her exoneration to be examined or re-examined."[284] Furthermore, this right had to be effective, which is especially not the case when the accused, as a precondition of an appeal or retrial, is "left with the burden of proving that he or she was not seeking to evade justice or that his or her absence [at the prior trial] was due to *force majeure.*"[285] The constitutional jurisprudence thus specifies the reading of both Article 4a section 1 letter c and d of the EAW Framework Decision and of the relevant implementing legislation, i.e., section 83 paragraph 3 of the Act on International Cooperation in Criminal Matters.[286] The wording would seem to allow for a more restrictive interpretation of the scope of the examination of exonerating evidence.[287]

---

[283] BVerfGE 140, 317, 355 = Federal Constitutional Court, 2 BvR 2735/14, at para. 83; Sauer (2016), p. 1138.

[284] BVerfGE 140, 317, 357 f. = Federal Constitutional Court, 2 BvR 2735/14, at para. 88 f., 100–102; cf. Böhm (2015), p. 3132 f.; Laue (2010), p. 297.

[285] BVerfGE 140, 317, 364 = Federal Constitutional Court, 2 BvR 2735/14, at para. 103, relying on ECtHR, *Colozza v. Italy*, judgement of 12 February 1985, Appl. no. 9024/80, para 30.

[286] See Sect. 7.1.

[287] Cf. article 4a of Framework Decision 2002/584/JHA as amended by Framework Decision 2009/299JHA ("retrial, or an appeal [...] which *allows* the merits of the case, including fresh evidence, to be re-examined"; emphasis added) and section 83 para. 3 sentence 2 AICCM ("Recht auf Wiederaufnahme des Verfahrens oder auf ein Berufungsverfahren [...] bei dem der Sachverhalt, einschließlich neuer Beweismittel, erneut geprüft [...] *werden kann*"; emphasis added).

8   Concluding Remarks

As has become clear, German law attaches great importance to the personal participation of the defendant in criminal proceedings. The prosecution of crime might
well be rendered more effective by a procedural mechanism that precludes a defendant from relying on exonerating evidence if he or she has consciously obstructed
his trial through flight. However, if the idea of such preclusion constitutes a main
attraction of *in absentia* trials, it necessarily conflicts with German constitutional
law. It was already mentioned that German constitutional law requires a "just proportion between the punishment on the one hand and the gravity of the offence, and
the culpability of the offender, on the other hand."[288] Following from this, constitutional jurisprudence has set strong limits for legislative instruments that allow for
greater procedural flexibility in exchange for enhanced effectiveness of criminal
trials. While the Federal Constitutional Court also stresses the importance of the
state in ensuring the effective functioning of the criminal justice system, this does
not allow the criminal courts to adopt a sentence that is no longer commensurate
with the crime before them.[289] From this requirement, constitutional jurisprudence
deduces that the trial's purpose is to ascertain the substantive truth in the best possible way.[290] As the defendant's perspective is considered as a central element of this
truth,[291] German criminal procedure only has limited options to allow for *in absentia* proceedings, even when absent defendants were well aware of criminal proceedings against them and could therefore be considered to have unequivocally waived
their right to be present and defend themselves in person. In view of the aforesaid
constitutional requirements, the sincerity of a waiver of defence rights is only one
element to be considered. Beyond that, the admissibility of *in absentia* trials also
depends on whether such proceedings would still be guided by the requirement that
the trial must serve to find the substantive truth to the best extent possible. This, in
turn, depends on whether the court can assume with reasonable certainty that the
defendant's presence would not improve the quality of fact-finding. The defendant's
awareness of mere prosecutorial suspicion at the pre-trial stage does not allow the
conclusion that an attempt to evade prosecution through flight demonstrates an
unwillingness on his or her part to contribute to the fact-finding at trial. Only
once the charges have been presented to the defendant in the summons to/at the
main hearing, or by a member of the trial court, or by another judge commissioned
by the trial court can the latter foresee with reasonable certainty whether the defendant would add anything substantial to the fact-finding. Thus, only at this point, it
can be assessed whether the trial—even when conducted in the defendant's

---

[288] BVerfG NJW 2016, 1149, 1153 = Federal Constitutional Court, Order of the Second Senate of
15 December 2015—2 BvR 2735/14, at para. 54 f.

[289] Cf. BVerfGE 133, 168 = BVerfG NJW 2013, 1058, 1060.

[290] BVerfGE 133, 168 = BVerfG NJW 2013, 1058, 1067.

[291] Cf. BVerfG NJW 2016, 1149, 115 3f. = Constitutional Court, Order of the Second Senate of 15
December 2015—2 BvR 2735/14, at para. 58.

absence—would continue to be guided by its objective to ascertain the truth in the best possible way. Even then, the trial court must always remain alert to the possibility that the defendant's presence could improve the quality of fact-finding and might therefore again be required, particularly if new evidence emerges that the defendant did not initially anticipate.

In some instances, German law might not yet provide for a sufficient level of participation of the accused and defence counsel at the pre-trial stage, in particular with regard to the examination of prosecutorial witnesses. It is noteworthy, however, that constitutional jurisprudence stresses the involvement of the accused with regard to the imposition of provisional restrictive measures. In principle, access to the investigative file can, to a large extent, be restricted until the conclusion of the investigation.[292] As has been shown,[293] however, according to the Federal Constitutional Court, the gravity of rights infringements that result from measures such as pre-trial detention or provisional seizure of property makes it necessary to apply disclosure standards to these measures equivalent to the standards required at the main hearing. Accordingly, judicial review of such provisional measures at the pre-trial stage requires full disclosure, both to the court and to the defendant, of the evidence on which imposition of the provisional measure is based.[294] Such extensive disclosure requirements effectively limit the attractiveness of those criminal policy concepts that would like to shift crime control away from conviction-based measures towards preventive pre-trial measures. The key role of the main hearing and, ultimately, the importance of the defendant's personal participation are thus strengthened.

References

Arnoldi O (2012) Anmerkungen zu BGH. NStZ, 105, ibid, p 108

Beulke W (2012) Strafprozessrecht, 12th edn

Böhm KM (2015) Die strafrechtliche Abwesenheitsverhandlung im Berufungsverfahren. NJW, p 3132

Böhm KM (2017) Aktuelle Entwicklungen im Auslieferungsrecht. NStZ, p 77

Börner R (2005) Die Vermögensbeschlagnahme nach §§ 290 ff. StPO. NStZ, p 547

Christl E (2014) Europäische Mindeststandards für Beschuldigtenrechte – Zur Umsetzung der EU-Richtlinien über Sprachmittlung und Informationen im Strafverfahren. NStZ, p 376

Deiters M (2015) In: Albrecht AH et al (eds) Systematischer Kommentar zur Strafprozessordnung, vol 4, 5th edn. §§ 198–246, StPO

Diemer H (2013) In: Hannisch R (ed) Karlsruher Kommentar zur Strafprozessordnung, 7th edn

Eisenberg U (1993) Straf(verfahrens-)rechtliche Maßnahmen gegenüber "Organisiertem Verbrechen". NJW, p 1033

Eisenberg U (2012) Sich-Entfernen bzw. Fernbleiben während der Hauptverhandlung. NStZ, p 63

Erb V (2010) Anmerkungen zu BGH. NStZ, 162, ibid, p 347

Fezer G (2011) Anmerkungen zu BGH. NStZ, 47, ibid

---

[292] Section 147 CCP.

[293] See Sects. 3.2.2 and 3.3.

[294] BVerfG, NJW 2004, 2443; NJW 2006, 1048; NStZ-RR 2008, 16; 2013, 379.

Frisch W (2015) Verwerfung der Berufung ohne Sachverhandlung und Recht auf Verteidigung –
Zur Änderung des § 329 StPO. NStZ, p 69

Frister H (2016) in: Albrecht AH et al (eds) Systematischer Kommentar zur Strafprozessordnung,
vol. 5, 5th edn., §§ 246a–295, StPO.

Gerst HJ (2013) Die Konventionsgarantie des Art. 6 III c und die Abwesenheitsverwerfung gemäß
§ 329 I 1 StPO – Ein kleiner Schritt für Straßburg, ein zu großer für Deutschland?. NStZ, p 310

Gmel D (2013) In: Hannisch R (ed) Karlsruher Kommentar zur Strafprozessordnung, 7th edn

Güntge GF (2015) In: Ambos K, König S, Rackow P (eds) Rechtshilferecht in Strafsachen

Köberer W (2015) In: Ambos K, König S, Rackow P (eds) Rechtshilferecht in Strafsachen

Lagodny O (2012) In: Schomburg W, Lagodny O, Gleß S, Hackner T (eds) Internationale
Rechtshilfe in Strafsachen, 5th edn

Laue C (2010) Die Hauptverhandlung ohne den Angeklagten. JA, p 294

Leipold K (2005) Die Videovernehmung. NJW-Spezial, p 471

Metz J (2017) Entfernung des Angeklagten nach § 247 StPO. NStZ, p 446

Meyer-Goßner L (2016) In: Meyer-Goßner L, Schmitt B (eds) Strafprozessordnung, 59th edn

Roxin C, Schünemann B (2014) Strafverfahrensrecht, 28th edn

Ruggeri S (2016) Right to personal participation in criminal proceedings and in absentia procedures in the EU area of freedom, security and justice. ZStW, p 578

Safferling C (2014) Der EuGH, die Grundrechtecharta und das nationale Recht: Die Fälle Akerberg
Fransson und Melloni. NStZ, p 545

Sauer H (2016) "Solange" geht in Altersteilzeit – Der unbedingte Vorrang der Menschenwürde vor
dem Unionsrecht. NJW, p 1134

Schmitt B (2016) In: Meyer-Goßner L, Schmitt B (eds) Strafprozessordnung, 59th edn

Thörnich D (2017) Art. 6 Abs. 3 lit. d EMRK und der unerreichbare (Auslands-)Zeuge:
Appell zur Stärkung des Konfrontationsrechts bei präjudizierender Zeugenvernehmung im
Ermittlungsverfahren. ZIS, p 39

Trüg G (2011) Anmerkungen zu BGH. NJW, 3249, ibid, p 3256

Wahl T (2016) In: Sieber U, von zur Mühlen N (eds) Access to telecommunication data in criminal
justice

Widmaier G (1998) Anmerkungen zu BGH. NStZ, p 263, ibid

Zehetgruber C (2013) Zur Unvereinbarkeit von § 329 Abs. 1 S. 1 StPO mit der EMRK. HRRS,
p 397

Report on Greece

Emmanouil Billis and Panagiotis Gkaniatsos

Abstract This chapter examines issues of personal participation in criminal proceedings and issues related to *in absentia* trials from the perspective of the law of Greece.

Abbreviations

CCP	Greek Code of Criminal Procedure
CISA	Convention on the Implementation of the Schengen Agreement
Const.	Constitution
EAW	European Arrest Warrant
ECHR	European Convention for the Protection of Human Rights and Fundamental Freedoms
ECtHR	European Court of Human Rights
EIO	European Investigation Order
ETS	European Treaty Series (Council of Europe)
EU	European Union
FD	Framework Decision
ICCPR	International Covenant on Civil and Political Rights
OJEU	Official Journal of the European Union
PC	Penal Code
UN	United Nations

E. Billis (✉)
Max Planck Institute for Foreign and International Criminal Law, Freiburg, Germany
e-mail: e.billis@mpicc.de

P. Gkaniatsos
University of Göttingen, Criminal Law Department, Göttingen, Germany

© Springer Nature Switzerland AG 2019
S. Quattrocolo, S. Ruggeri (eds.), *Personal Participation in Criminal Proceedings*, Legal Studies in International, European and Comparative Criminal Law 2, https://doi.org/10.1007/978-3-030-01186-4_7

1 Constitutional Requirements for the Involvement of Private Parties in Criminal Justice

The criminal law and criminal justice system of Greece belong to the civil law family.[1] The heart of Greek criminal law is the systematic codification of written norms with ordinary force concerning principal issues of crime and procedure in the Penal Code (*Ποινικός Κώδικας, Poinikos Kodikas*, PC-Greece)[2] and the Code of Criminal Procedure (*Κώδικας Ποινικής Δικονομίας, Kodikas Poinikis Dikonomias*, CCP)[3] respectively.[4] At supra-statutory level, provisions relevant to criminal law are included in the Constitution of the Hellenic Republic (*Σύνταγμα, Syntagma*, Const.).[5] The fundamental law of Greece regulates the system of government (parliamentary republic) on the basis of the separation of powers principle. According to art. 26 Const., judicial powers shall be exercised by the courts, whose decisions shall be executed in the name of the Greek people.[6] Courts are composed of regular judges who, in the discharge of their duties, are subject only to the Constitution and the laws. The jurisdiction of ordinary criminal courts comprises the punishment of criminal offences and the imposition of all measures provided by criminal laws.[7]

The Greek criminal process, overseen by the competent state authorities (prosecutors and judges as objective and impartial judicial officials), is mainly "inquisitorial"[8] and its central objective is the search for the substantive truth.[9] As in most other continental European systems, jury trials in their pure form do not exist (any more) in Greece. In practice, the participation of lay judges in "mixed jury courts" is limited to specific cases of serious offences and always involves the co-participation of professional judges. Moreover, according to the Constitution, all judgments (judicial decisions), including those of the mixed jury courts, must always be specifically and thoroughly reasoned.[10]

---

[1] See with further references Billis (2013), pp. 213–215.

[2] Law 1492/1950 (in conjunction with Presidential Decree 283/1985). For the translation of the Greek Penal Code, see Chalkiadaki and Billis (2017), pp. 63–226.

[3] Law 1493/1950 (in conjunction with Presidential Decree 258/1986).

[4] For more details, also with respect to the modern developments in Greek criminal law, criminal procedure, and the execution of punishment, see Billis (2013), pp. 245–288.

[5] The English translation of the Greek Constitution of 1975/1986/2001/2008 is available on the website of the Hellenic Parliament (http://www.hellenicparliament.gr/en/Vouli-ton-Ellinon/To-Politevma/Syntagma, last accessed 31.7.2018).

[6] See with further references Billis (2013), pp. 192–195.

[7] Arts. 93(1), 96(1) Const.

[8] On this concept, see Billis (2015), pp. 13–140.

[9] On the principles and rights of the Greek criminal procedure, see Androulakis (2012), pp. 23–97, 133–246; Karras (2011), pp. 20–64, 245–250, 352–363, 372–430, 627–732, 804–814. See also Anagnostopoulos and Magliveras (2000), pp. 131–191; Billis (2017), pp. 11–12; Mylonopoulos (1993), pp. 169–175; Spinellis and Spinellis (1999), pp. 18–26, 31–32.

[10] Art. 93(3) Const.

Furthermore, by treating the individual as a citizen and bearer of rights and obligations *vis-à-vis* the state, the Constitution establishes the elements necessary to operate a legal system in an effective protective, and fair manner. These elements include the state's primary obligation to respect and protect human dignity by guaranteeing equality, personal freedom, and the protection of fundamental rights,[11] as well as the principles of the rule of law and proportionality.[12] In this context, the Greek Constitution does not expressly address issues regarding the personal participation and active involvement of the accused and other private parties in criminal proceedings. Nevertheless, in accordance with art. 2(1) Const. (respect and protection of human dignity) and art. 6(2) ECHR (presumption of innocence), the accused must never be treated as an object of the criminal process and trial but as its central and most important subject. This means that the accused is the holder of individual participation and information rights provided for in the law (most importantly the Code of Criminal Procedure) and that these constitutionally protected rights cannot be set aside due to other procedural objectives such as the search for the substantive truth. Additionally, of importance in the context of the personal participation in criminal proceedings are the following constitutional rights and guarantees: the right to legal protection by the courts and to a judicial hearing, which is enshrined in art. 20 Const. and in various provisions of the Code of Criminal Procedure (e.g., art. 333(2) CCP); the guarantees of "natural judge" (art. 8 Const., i.e., the law establishes *a priori*, according to general and abstract criteria, the judges and courts competent to try the various kinds of offences) and of judicial impartiality and independence (arts. 87–90 Const.); the due process guarantees in the context of deprivation of liberty and illegal detention (art. 6 Const.); as well as the public nature of court hearings (art. 93 Const.).[13]

The Greek legal order may also adopt, at the supra-statutory level, rules of international origin. More specifically, these include, according to the Constitution, generally recognised rules of international law as well as international conventions as of the time they are ratified by law (act of parliament) and become operative according to their respective conditions, which are an integral part of domestic law and prevail over any contrary provision of law (art. 28(1) Const.).[14] Hence, these kinds of norms are located in the hierarchy between the Constitution and ordinary acts of parliament.

This means, for example, that, with regard to principles of criminal law and procedure and to human rights guarantees, the provisions of the European Convention for the Protection of Human Rights and Fundamental Freedoms of 1950 (ECHR)[15] must always be applied directly by the domestic courts in a way that prevails over

---

[11] Arts. 1(3), 2(1), 4–25, 29, 51, 55 Const.

[12] Art. 25(1) and arts. 7, 8, 10, 20, 26, 93, 95 Const.

[13] For a more detailed overview, see Billis (2013), pp. 237–241 with further references. See also Androulakis (2012), pp. 23–24; Karras (2011), pp. 217–221; Mylonopoulos (1993), pp. 163, 168.

[14] See also art. 36 Const.

[15] See Law 2329/1953 and Legislative Decree 53/1974.

any contrary statutory provision.[16] Greece, as a Member State of the Council of Europe, is bound by decisions of the European Court of Human Rights (ECtHR) involving violations by States of the rights provided in the Convention.[17] As regards the involvement of the parties, and especially the accused, in the criminal process, of particular importance are the fair trial principle and the special due process, procedural, and defence guarantees expressly provided in arts. 5 (right to liberty and security) and 6 (right to a fair trial) ECHR. In the same context, the respective provisions of the International Covenant on Civil and Political Rights of 1966 (ICCPR)[18] are also an integral part of the Greek legal system.[19]

Moreover, art. 28(2–3) Const. provides that, under strict conditions, powers granted by the Constitution may be vested, by treaty or agreement, in agencies of international organisations if this serves an important national interest and promotes cooperation with other states; Greece can also limit the exercise of national sovereignty, provided this is dictated by an important national interest. As a whole, art. 28 Const. establishes a national legal basis for Greece's participation in the European integration process and, at the same time, the supremacy of European law over domestic statutory law.[20] In this context, Greece has already become a Member State of the European Community (1981) and the European Union (EU, 1992)[21] that succeeded and replaced the European Community in 2009.[22] Hence, Greece is subject to the rules, rights, freedoms, and principles set out in the Treaty on the European Union, the Treaty on the Functioning of the European Union, and the secondary legal acts (regulations and directives) of the Union,[23] as well as the Charter of Fundamental Rights of the EU (2000, 2007).[24]

---

[16] See also art. 1 ECHR.

[17] See in that respect the ECHR-Protocol No. 11, ratified by Greece, and art. 525(1) CCP; also, art. 46 ECHR.

[18] Law 2462/1997.

[19] For more details, see Billis (2013), pp. 216–217, 226–228.

[20] On the controversy about the question of supremacy of European laws over the Constitution, see Christianos (2008), pp. 66–68; Spyropoulos and Fortsakis (2009), pp. 63, 79–80.

[21] For more details and references, see Dagtoglou (2008), pp. 25–26.

[22] See Law 3671/2008 ratifying the Treaty of Lisbon (2007, in force since 1 December 2009), which amended the former European Union and European Community Treaties; also art. 1 of the current Treaty on European Union.

[23] See especially arts. 2, 4, 6 Treaty on European Union and arts. 82–89, 288, 291 Treaty on the Functioning of the European Union.

[24] See art. 6(1) Treaty on European Union.

2 Personal Participation of Private Parties and Legal Assistance

In Greece, the investigation of crimes, the prosecution, and the supervision and continuation of fact-finding procedures are typically *ex officio* competences of state officials who are committed to legality, objectivity, and impartiality.[25] Nevertheless, the code of criminal procedure provides exceptions to this rule, for example in the form of norms that, with regard to specific (minor) offences, require a prior criminal complaint[26] by the victim for initiating criminal proceedings and of norms addressing the active participation of the victim in the process as a "civil action party" with independent rights to legal assistance and legal representation.[27]

The accused has in the state-driven criminal proceedings, during both the pre-trial and trial phase,[28] the rights to a defence counsel and to unlimited communication with him/her, to legal representation, to appoint an expert advisor, as well as (if necessary) to the free assistance of an interpreter.[29] Also provided are the mandatory (upon request or *ex officio*) appointment of defence counsel by the state in felony cases[30] and, in general, the free legal assistance to citizens in need (based on economic criteria and the seriousness of the charges).[31]

With respect to all types of crimes,[32] the accused must, and has the right, to be present at the various stages and types of the public judicial proceedings, alone or accompanied by his/her lawyer, but he/she may also be represented by a lawyer (in his/her absence); in the latter case, however, the trial court may order the personal appearance of the accused at any time if it finds this necessary for the purpose of finding the truth.[33] Particularly in felony cases, and especially those before the court of first instance, the presence of, or the representation by, a lawyer is mandatory, with the exception of cases where the accused has repeatedly rejected the *ex officio* appointment of counsel and of trials *in absentia*, where an accused, although formally summoned, neither appeared personally before the court nor was represented

---

[25] See Karras (2011), pp. 25–26, 244–247.

[26] See arts. 117–120 PC and arts. 46–53 CCP.

[27] See arts. 83, 84, 96, 97, 99, 108 CCP and Law 3226/2004.

[28] For an introduction to the general system of criminal proceedings in Greece, see Billis (2017), pp. 8–12.

[29] See especially arts. 31(2), 96, 100, 104–105, 204, 233, 340, 376 CCP; art. 6(3) ECHR. See also Anagnostopoulos and Magliveras (2000), pp. 153–155.

[30] See arts. 100(3), 308B(1), 340, 376 CCP. On the obligatory (upon request) appointment of defence counsel in summary proceedings for perpetrators of misdemeanours caught in the act, see art. 423 CCP. On the *ex officio* appointment of counsel in cases of psychiatric evaluation of the accused, see art. 200 CCP.

[31] See Law 3226/2004.

[32] On the different crime categories (felonies, misdemeanours, petty violations), see Billis (2017), pp. 22–24.

[33] See art. 340 CCP.

by appointed lawyer. In these cases, the felony trial shall continue as usual in the absence of a lawyer and in the absence of the accused and a lawyer, respectively.[34]

3 Personal Participation of the Accused in Criminal Proceedings

3.1 General Features of Personal Participation: Absolute Individual Right or Duty of Diligence?

The Greek criminal process is mainly "inquisitorial" and governed by the principle of the search for the substantive truth. The institutions vested with the competence for this purpose are the state authorities, that is, the prosecutors and judges as objective and impartial judicial officials (e.g., art. 239 CCP).[35] The accusatory principle (i.e., accusation and trial in the hands of separate authorities) governs the prosecution of every crime. Furthermore, the prosecutor is bound by the principle of mandatory prosecution as long as there are legal and substantive grounds for initiating and continuing a prosecution, whilst the provisions in favour of discretionary prosecution are limited (e.g., to cases involving minors accused of petty violations or misdemeanours).[36] In general, the state's judicial officials must always consider all the facts of each case (in favour of and against the accused) and their correlation to the criminal charges.[37]

Besides the state authorities (in particular, judges and prosecutors, who are not parties in the strict sense),[38] main parties in the criminal process are the defence and the civil action party. The Code of Criminal Procedure gives victims (harmed persons), under specific conditions, the right to actively participate in the criminal proceedings as damaged parties by bringing a civil action.[39] The accused, as the central and most important subject of the process, is also the explicit holder of individual participation and information rights; in accordance with art. 2(1) Const. (respect and protection of human dignity as the state's primary obligation) and art. 6(2)

---

[34] See arts. 340, 432 CCP. Art. 340(1) CCP, as amended by Law 4509/2017, provides that the accused can remove only one of the two or three *ex officio* appointed counsels. It also provides that after its first session trial shall continue in the absence of the accused and his/her lawyer(s) even in those cases that the absence is due to the fact that the counsel has resigned or the accused has revoked the mandate. As this provision was amended after the present text was drafted, the controversy caused thereby cannot be examined further in this chapter.

[35] For more details, see Billis (2017), pp. 6, 11–12.

[36] See especially arts. 36–45A CCP. For more details, see Karras (2011), pp. 247–250.

[37] See arts. 239, 274, 327(1), 490 CCP; also Karras (2011), pp. 21–25.

[38] Although the trial prosecutor represents the prosecution, as a judicial authority he/she is not a party to proceedings in the strict sense: He or she may also plead for an acquittal, must summon all necessary prosecution and defence witnesses, and may lodge appeals in favour of, or against, the defendant. See also below, Sect. 3.5; Billis (2013), pp. 196, 200 with further references.

[39] For more details, see below, Sect. 4.

ECHR (presumption of innocence), the accused must never be treated as an object of the criminal trial.

Accordingly, the accused and his/her defender have, not only in court but also during the pre-trial investigations, the following rights: to be informed of the nature and cause of the accusations; to access the case file before stating (orally and/or in writing) the defence arguments and prepare the defence; to be present at most proceedings and participate actively in the evidentiary process; to be heard, (to be called to) address questions, and to comment on the investigation material and all the evidence, as well as to present or suggest further defence strategies and evidence.[40] During all proceedings, the accused also has the right not to answer any accusations and to remain silent.[41] The accused must be informed promptly and explicitly of his or her rights by the state officials.[42]

3.2 Personal Participation in the Pre-trial Inquiry (with Particular Regard to the Interim Decisions on Coercive Measures)

The ordinary criminal process is divided into a pre-trial and a trial phase. The pre-trial phase mainly consists of the prosecution (in the hands of the prosecutor) and the investigation (in the hands of the prosecutor and/or the investigating judge) of criminal offences.[43] Pre-trial inquiries, especially in cases of serious offences, are extensive, judge-ruled, non-public, and basically non-adversarial.[44] The pre-trial evidentiary results are documented and gathered into a dossier, which consists of the case file and may be used by the trial court.[45]

In all felony cases (e.g., homicide) and, under exceptional conditions, in cases of more serious misdemeanours, an "ordinary investigation" shall be initiated by the public prosecutor.[46] The ordinary investigation is conducted exclusively by an ordinary judge who must undertake all investigative measures necessary (e.g., home search) to detect the specific crime as described by the public prosecutor, as well as all perpetrators.[47] Moreover, in cases of serious offences, the investigating judge is responsible for issuing arrest warrants, ordering restrictive conditions (e.g., bail),

---

[40] See arts. 31(2), 97, 99, 101, 104–105, 273(2), 274 CCP; art. 6(1, 3) ECHR.

[41] Arts. 31(2), 273(2), 366(3) CCP; art. 6(1) ECHR.

[42] Arts. 31(2), 99A, 103, 104–105, 273(2), 342 CCP. See also below, Sect. 5.1.

[43] On the various stages and organs of prosecution and investigation, see Billis (2013), p. 197.

[44] See, however, art. 219(2) CCP regarding the *inter partes* examination of witnesses not able to give evidence in court.

[45] See arts. 241, 364–365 CCP; also Karras (2011), pp. 352–353.

[46] See arts. 43, 246, 282 CCP and arts. 111–115 CCP. For more details, see Spinellis (2008), pp. 479–480; Spinellis and Spinellis (1999), pp. 18–20, 26–27. See also Anagnostopoulos and Magliveras (2000), pp. 135–140; Billis (2017), pp. 8–9.

[47] Arts. 246–250 and 13 CCP.

and for issuing, under specific conditions, that is, only with agreement of the public prosecutor and—with very few exceptions—only in felony cases, a pre-trial detention warrant.[48]

The defence has the right to be present at all pre-trial and out-of-court investigative activities and evidentiary hearings, and to submit comments thereon, with the exception, however, of most pre-trial examinations of witnesses and co-defendants, in which the defence is called to participate only if the witness is considered unable to attend trial.[49] Furthermore, the accused must be called and has the right (but not the obligation) to answer the charges before the investigating authorities; prior to answering the charges, he/she can take 48 h (or more, under special circumstances) to prepare his/her defence.[50]

Regarding interim judicial decisions imposing coercive measures during the pre-trial phase, the accused (and/or the defence counsel) may exercise, under specific conditions and, occasionally, within pre-determined time limits depending on the procedural stage, *inter alia*, the following rights:

- to be present during home searches (art. 256 CCP);
- to complain against an expired arrest warrant (art. 279 CCP);
- to apply for the imposition of the restrictive condition of home confinement with electronic monitoring instead of the more severe measure of pre-trial detention (arts. 282, 283A CCP);
- to be heard and present arguments before the prosecutor prior to the issuance of the latter's written proposal to the investigating judge regarding the imposition of pre-trial detention (art. 283 CCP);
- to submit a (written) request to the investigating judge for the abrogation of the imposed coercive measures, the replacement of the measure of pre-trial detention with restrictive conditions (e.g., bail or residence and travel restrictions), or the replacement of the imposed restrictive conditions with other (less severe) restrictive conditions (art. 286 CCP);
- to submit a written appeal to the competent judicial council (*in camera* proceedings) against decisions of the investigating judge imposing restrictive conditions or pre-trial detention, against decisions of the judge denying a request for the abrogation of these coercive measures or the replacement of the pre-trial detention with restrictive conditions, and against decisions of the judge replacing the imposed restrictive conditions with pre-trial detention or other (more severe) conditions (arts. 285, 286 CCP)[51]; and

---

[48] On the basic investigative and coercive measures, see arts. 251–275, 276, 282–283 CCP. On the requirement of a judicial decision or of the presence of a judge when severe coercive measures, such as pre-trial detention, home search, or electronic surveillance are to be taken, see, e.g., arts. 6, 9, 19 Const. For more details, see Anagnostopoulos and Magliveras (2000), pp. 165–178; Karras (2011), pp. 458–564; Mylonopoulos (1993), pp. 175–177; Spinellis and Spinellis (1999), pp. 20–23. See also Billis (2013), pp. 197–198 with further references.

[49] Arts. 97, 99, 100, 309(2); see, however, arts. 219(2), 328, 354 CCP.

[50] Arts. 31(2), 100, 102, 104, 270, 274 CCP.

[51] See also arts. 302–303 CCP regarding bail.

– to file written submissions to the competent judicial council regarding the discontinuation of the pre-trial detention after 6 months and (in case of previous continuation) 12 months of detention have passed,[52] and, if the council finds it necessary, to present oral arguments thereon before the judges in the *in camera* proceedings (art. 287 CCP).

3.3 *Personal Participation in Proceedings* In Camera

As seen above, the pre-trial phase also includes proceedings held before judicial councils composed of professional judges. As a rule, these proceedings are non-public and the deliberations take place *in camera* after the prosecutor has submitted a written proposal and (where provided) has expressed his/her arguments orally and left the judicial chambers; in most proceedings before judicial councils, the accused does not participate in person but may file written submissions.[53]

Particularly in the so-called intermediate proceedings, the judicial councils are, *inter alia*, competent to decide on the basis of the investigation results whether a felony case should be further referred to trial or dismissed; for minor offences, however, the public prosecutor may refer the case directly to trial.[54] The intermediate proceedings take place in the absence of the prosecutor and the parties (defence and civil action party); however, the council may, in exceptional cases, order the personal appearance of all parties and of the prosecutor, and it must invite the parties to comment on relevant documents and evidence submitted to the council after ordinary investigations have concluded.[55]

3.4 *Personal Participation in Alternative Proceedings*

Apart from the ordinary proceedings, Greek criminal procedure also provides special forms of proceedings.[56] These (simplified) proceedings exclude either the extended pre-trial investigation phase or the trial phase (fully or partially). Such proceedings include: "summary proceedings" (mainly for perpetrators apprehended

---

[52] The maximum limit of pre-trial detention is 18 months (art. 6 Const.).

[53] See arts. 138, 287, 306, 308, 308A, 309(2), 316 CCP.

[54] See especially arts. 245, 308, 308A, 322 CCP.

[55] Arts. 309(2), 316 CCP.

[56] On the rules and principles of the proceedings before judicial councils, the trial phase (including the appeal proceedings), and the special and summary proceedings, see arts. 305–319, 320–373, 409–435, 462–532 CCP; Karras (2011), pp. 565–600, 601–766, 767–787, 801–982. See also the older overviews by Anagnostopoulos and Magliveras (2000), pp. 134–135, 147–152, 159–164, 179–191; Mylonopoulos (1993), pp. 167, 174–175, 177–183; Spinellis and Spinellis (1999), pp. 18–26.

during the commission of the offence); extradition proceedings[57]; as well as "penal mediation proceedings" in domestic violence cases and "penal conciliation proceedings" in economic crime cases, which provide a model for the future development of plea arrangements in the law of criminal procedure.[58]

In particular, for perpetrators of petty violations and misdemeanours apprehended during the commission of the crime or on the following day, the Code establishes summary proceedings, which take place immediately and (in the case of misdemeanours) at the latest 15 days after the arrest. Not unlike the ordinary criminal trial, these proceedings are public and, for the most part, oral. However, in this case, there are no pre-trial investigations and written preparatory proceedings, and the accused has no or only limited time to prepare his/her defence. The judgment of the court is primarily based on evidence and the testimony of witnesses found at the crime scene, or of witnesses named by the accused and the civil action party without prior notice, as well as on the trial testimony of the accused (if he/she decides to testify). During trial, the defence has the same legal representation and participation rights as in the ordinary criminal proceedings. If the court where the summary proceedings are pending finds that the evidence gathered so far is insufficient, it orders the case to be tried at a later time before a court applying ordinary proceedings.[59]

Furthermore, in 2010 the newly drafted art. 308B CCP introduced the so-called penal conciliation proceedings, i.e., a mixed kind of plea-bargaining and mediation process, which may only apply to felony acts of misappropriation (art. 375 PC-Greece), fraud (art. 386 PC- Greece), computer fraud (art. 386A PC-Greece), abuse of trust (art. 390 PC-Greece), and usury (art. 404 PC-Greece) against natural or legal persons of private law.[60] Pursuant to art. 308B CCP, these proceedings may only be initiated upon request of the accused to the competent prosecutor until the end of ordinary investigations. The out-of-court discussions between the accused and the harmed person (and/or their legal counsels), which take place before the prosecutor, aim at reaching an agreement regarding the return of the misappropriated objects or money in exchange for a mitigated punishment. If such a written settlement between the accused and the victim is reached, it must be formally validated in a public hearing in the presence of the accused by the competent criminal

---

[57] See arts. 436–456 CCP, which, *inter alia*, provide for possibilities of the interested party to be personally heard and to appeal. However, nowadays, the proceedings for most extradition cases are autonomously regulated by international instruments and multilateral or bilateral treaties. See especially below, § F.I., with regard to Law 3251/2004 implementing the provisions (including those referring to the personal participation and the rights of the person in the relevant proceedings) of the Framework Decision 2002/584/JHA on the European Arrest Warrant. See also, e.g., the Convention on Simplified Extradition Procedure between the Member States of the European Union of 1995 (ratified with reservations in 2000), the Convention Relating to Extradition between the Member States of the European Union of 1996 (ratified with reservations in 1999), and the European Convention on Extradition of 1957 (signed in 1957, ratified in 1961).

[58] See also art. 122(1ε) PC introducing the possibility of out-of-court settlements between juvenile offenders and their victims.

[59] See arts. 105, 242, 243(2), 273–275, 279, 409–413, 417–426 CCP.

[60] See Law 3904/2010; Karras (2011), pp. 584–586.

court, which, for that purpose and without hearing further arguments and evidence, finds the accused guilty and imposes the mitigated punishment (or, in some cases, no punishment at all).

Finally, in 2006, the procedure of "penal mediation" was introduced, which addresses the possibility of an out-of-court settlement of misdemeanour disputes in domestic violence cases.[61] These proceedings take place before the competent prosecutor in the presence and with the participation of the parties. A successful penal mediation presupposes the explicit acceptance of the settlement by all parties. Under specific conditions (e.g., attending a therapeutic programme and restoring the harm done to the victim), with which the accused must comply for at least 3 years, penal mediation can result in permanently ending criminal prosecution by way of a prosecutorial order (without the interference of a criminal court).

3.5   *Personal Participation at Trial*

The ordinary trial[62] before the Greek criminal courts consists of two stages: the "preparatory proceedings" and the "main court proceedings." In terms of the personal participation of the accused at trial, a distinction is drawn between his/her involvement in the formal gathering of evidence (below under Sect. 3.5.1), which takes place mainly during the preparatory proceedings, and his/her participation in the finding of facts (below under Sect. 3.5.2.), which takes place during the main court proceedings.

3.5.1   Personal Involvement in the Gathering of Evidence

If, following the conclusion of the pre-trial investigations, the commencement of the trial phase is ordered, formal evidence-gathering is continued in the preparatory proceedings. These are in the hands of the prosecutor and aim, *inter alia*, at ensuring the presence of the participants (defence and civil action party) and of all necessary witnesses[63] at the main court proceedings, and at giving the participants the possibility to prepare for the trial.[64] To this end, the prosecutor must summon the accused[65] and (at least for the more serious crimes) disclose to him/her, within specific time limits, a list with all the witnesses for the prosecution summoned to testify at trial

---

[61] See arts. 11–13 Law 3500/2006.

[62] For the alternative proceedings, see above, Sect. 3.4.

[63] On witness summons, see arts. 213, 326–327 CCP; see also Karras (2011), pp. 609–614.

[64] See Karras (2011), p. 601.

[65] See arts. 320–321 CCP.

(art. 326(1) CCP),[66] as well as the documents to be examined at trial.[67] The civil action party is subject to the same obligation of prior disclosure of summoned witnesses but, as a rule, this does not apply to the accused (art. 326(2) and (3) CCP).[68] Subject to specific conditions and time limits, the accused, in addition to the witnesses he/she may call at his/her own expense (defence witnesses), also has the right to request the prosecutor during the preparatory proceedings (art. 327(2) CCP) or the presiding judge during the main trial (arts. 355–356 CCP) to mandatorily summon additional relevant witnesses (primarily those residing in Greece), and, in fact, as many on his/her behalf as are summoned against him/her.[69] During the preparatory proceedings and the main trial, the defence, the prosecutor, and the civil action party may also request the presiding judge to conduct the out-of-court examination of witnesses unable to give evidence in court (e.g., due to illness), which (if approved) is conducted by a judicial official in the presence of all the participants or their attorneys.[70] Finally, the accused has the right to request the court to appoint experts and to exclude experts appointed by other participants in the proceedings. In cases where experts have been appointed by the court, the accused may also appoint experts on his/her behalf as technical consultants.[71]

3.5.2 Personal Contribution to the Finding of Facts

The main trial proceedings are under the direction of, and controlled by, the presiding judge (art. 333 CCP). However, there are also adversarial elements in the Greek criminal trial. Especially the hearings are, in principle, oral (art. 331 CCP) and public (arts. 93(2) Const. and 329 CCP). As a rule, all evidence, witness

---

[66] According to art. 327(1) CCP, the prosecutor must summon all essential witnesses necessary for finding the substantive truth, see thereon Androulakis (2012), p. 394; on the substantive truth as the central objective of the criminal proceedings, see already above, Sect. 1. Consequently, the prosecutor, who as a judicial authority is bound by the principle of objectivity (see above, Sect. 2.), has the *obligation* to summon not only incriminating but also exculpatory witnesses, as well as the *discretion* to summon new witnesses (who did not testify at a prior stage of the proceedings) and submit new evidence (apart from the evidence gathered during the investigation) (art. 327(1) CCP); on the use of this discretion only exceptionally, as one violating the right of the accused to have adequate time to prepare his defence, see Karras (2011), p. 610.

[67] Although this disclosure obligation regarding the list of documents is not explicitly provided for, the right of the accused to prepare his/her defence calls for an analogous application of art. 326(1) CP; see Karras (2005), p. 759.

[68] See Androulakis (2012), pp. 405–406.

[69] Art. 327(2) CCP provides for only one additional witness in misdemeanour cases and up to two in felony cases. However, the provision should be interpreted in conjunction with art. 6(3)(d) ECHR providing that everyone charged with a criminal offence has the right to the attendance and examination of witnesses on his behalf under the same conditions as witnesses against him; see also art. 14(3)(e) ICCPR; Karras (2011), pp. 610–611; Androulakis (2012), pp. 405–406.

[70] See arts. 328 and 354 CCP in conjunction with art. 219(2) CCP. See also Karras (2011), p. 624.

[71] See arts. 183–208 CCP. On expert witnesses either appointed by the court or by the parties as consultants, see Androulakis (2012), pp. 310–314; Karras (2011), pp. 461–487.

testimonies, and documents must be presented orally during the trial before the judge(s). Nevertheless, the principle of immediacy in its substantive sense (i.e., the preference for direct evidence) is not absolutely guaranteed. Under certain conditions, the admission in trial and evaluation of hearsay evidence or of the documented preliminary testimony of an absent witness are neither prohibited nor rare. This is also in accordance with the principle of free evaluation of evidence, which prevails in the Greek criminal process (art. 177(1) CCP),[72] pursuant to which the judges must always follow their conscience in evaluating the evidence and are not bound in their rulings by formal rules of evidence.[73]

The defence enjoys, in accordance with the principle of equality of arms or opportunities, the right to participate actively in the evidentiary process.[74] One prerequisite for active participation is, apart from being present in the sense already described above,[75] that the accused be informed of the accusations and the evidence against him/her and be able to understand them.[76] Moreover, the accused has the right to be heard, to rebut the charges against him/her and submit arguments, to file applications and raise objections regarding any matter relevant to the case at hand, to directly address questions (himself/herself or through his/her lawyer) to all the witnesses and experts and comment thereon, to comment on the credibility of the examined witnesses and pieces of evidence, to call new witnesses, and to present evidence of his/her choice and in his/her favour.[77] These rights are not absolute and may be subject to limitations, for example for reasons of witness and victim protection.[78] Notwithstanding the right of the accused to remain silent, the defendant's (personal) statement, where he/she is called to answer the charges orally and without interruption, assumes a central role at trial (art. 366 CCP). Furthermore, the accused always has the right to the last word, not only at the end of the evidentiary proceedings, where he/she or the defence counsel is the last to make a closing statement but also after the examination of each piece of evidence or witness.[79]

---

[72] Limits on this principle are established by the rule of the non-evaluation (exclusion) of evidence acquired through criminal behaviour (art. 177(2) CCP) as well as by the obligation of the court to give specific and full reasons for every judgment (arts. 93(3) Const. and 139 CCP). For more details, see Karras (2011), pp. 686–704.

[73] See thereon Androulakis (2012), pp. 193–200.

[74] In the opinion of Androulakis (2012), p. 434, the active participation of the accused in the evidentiary process is a concrete manifestation in the criminal process of the constitutional right to a judicial hearing (art. 20 Const.).

[75] See above, Sect. 2.

[76] On the right to be informed of the accusation, see especially arts. 320–321, 343 and 403 CCP, and art. 6(3)(a) ECHR; on the interdependent rights to be informed in a language that the accused understands and to free assistance of an interpreter, see arts. 233–238 CCP and art. 6(3)(e) ECHR.

[77] See especially arts. 138(2), 274, 333(2, 3), 342, 357(2, 3), 358, 360, 362, 364–366, 368 CCP and art. 6(1, 3) ECHR.

[78] See, for example, arts. 226A and 226B CCP.

[79] See especially art. 369 CCP.

3.6 Personal Participation in Higher Instances

Besides the first-instance trials, there is one more instance of jurisdiction in the Greek criminal procedure, which is the appellate proceedings (second instance). The courts of second instance (courts of appeal)[80] are usually composed of more experienced or qualified judges. They have jurisdiction to decide both on the merits (facts) and the law that was applied by the first-instance courts, provided an appeal is statutorily permitted and formally filed. The Supreme Court *Areios Pagos (Άρειος Πάγος)*[81] does not serve as a third instance in the strict sense, since it only assesses and decides upon the (substantive and procedural) law applied in criminal proceedings by the lower courts. The decisions of *Areios Pagos* must relate to specific grounds for appeal (cassation),[82] and can ultimately lead to the complete re-trial of a case by the trial court.

As far as the participation of the defendant in second-instance proceedings is concerned, it depends first on the extent of his/her right to appeal.[83] Both convictions (art. 489 CCP) and acquittals (art. 486 CCP) may be appealed by the defendant, but subject to the conditions and limitations set out in the respective provisions.[84] As long as a judgment is formally appealable and the defendant lodges an appeal, he/she (as an appellant) has, apart from all the aforementioned general defence rights, similar rights in evidence-gathering and fact-finding to the ones in first-instance trials, most notably the right to be present, either personally or (in his absence) through his/her defence counsel, to be duly summoned, and to call new witnesses who have not been previously examined.[85] Nevertheless, technical reasons and the nature of the appellate review may impose exceptions and limitations to this participation. Convicted appellants who serve their sentence in prisons away from the seat of the competent court of appeal shall not be brought before it, but they may express their position through written submissions or be represented by a counsel (art. 497(9) CCP). Moreover, the non-appearance of a duly summoned

---

[80] Depending on the court that decided in the first instance, the courts with jurisdiction to hear an appeal are: the "misdemeanours courts" (composed of one or three professional judges); the *Efeteia (Εφετεία, "courts of appeal" stricto sensu)* acting as second-instance courts (composed of three or five professional judges); the "mixed jury courts of appeal" (composed of three professional judges and four jurors); the "juvenile courts" (composed of one professional judge); and the "juvenile courts of appeal" (composed of three professional judges). For more details, see Billis (2017), pp. 10–11.

[81] *Areios Pagos* is composed of 5, or in the case of (ordinary) plenary hearings, at least 17 higher judges.

[82] Cassation grounds comprise, for example, the erroneous interpretation and application of the substantive law by the trial court, the violation of the rights of the defendant, or the disregard of the principle of double jeopardy. For more details, see art. 510 CCP; Androulakis (2012), pp. 489–506; Karras (2011), pp. 938–974.

[83] For the right and the possibilities to appeal, see art. 2 of Protocol No. 7 to the ECHR and arts. 462–530 CCP.

[84] See arts. 486–498 CCP.

[85] See especially arts. 497(9), 500, and 502 CCP.

appellant at the appellate proceedings, either personally or through his/her legal counsel (if one is appointed), is considered a waiver of the appeal, which shall then be rejected.[86] Finally, the appellate review shall only extend to those parts of the first-instance judgment to which the grounds for appeal mentioned in the notice of appeal refer (art. 502(2) CCP).

Compared to the first and second-instance proceedings, the participation of the defendant in proceedings before the Supreme Court *Areios Pagos* is subject to more limitations, dictated by the very nature of the cassation review (review of law based on very specific grounds for appeal). Therefore, the defendant who has formally filed a cassation appeal[87] and has been duly summoned to the hearing (art. 513(1) CCP) is not allowed to represent himself and be personally heard but only to be represented by a defence counsel (art. 513(3) CCP). The non-appearance of the defence counsel has the same effects as before the second instance courts, that is, rejection of the cassation appeal and of any further cassation appeal; in addition, a fine may be imposed (art. 514 CCP).[88]

3.7   Special Rules in the Field of Serious Organised Crime

The legal position of the accused regarding his/her rights and the possibilities to participate in the criminal process may change to some extent in the context of the fight against serious organised crime. Special rules for the investigation and prosecution of violent acts of terror and criminal organisations, which have been introduced in the Greek legal order as a response to the rise of terrorism and the ongoing transnationalisation of modern organised crime, may lead to further restrictions and limitations on the participation rights of the defence. For example, art. 253A CCP introduced special investigation methods with respect to specific serious organised crimes, including the judicial suspension of the (constitutionally protected) secrecy of free correspondence and communication, the extended use of undercover agents, the taping of suspected activities through advanced surveillance technologies, and the extended processing and use of personal data by the authorities.[89] Due to the severely coercive and not fully transparent nature of these measures, the possibilities of the accused to participate actively and effectively in the

---

[86] See art. 502(1) CCP. See also Androulakis (2012), pp. 476–480; Karras (2005), p. 1078.

[87] The defendant may appeal by way of cassation against final judgments of conviction (arts. 505, 473 CCP), an acquittal if it was based on grounds of remorse (art. 506 CCP), or a decision of a court that declined its *ratione materiae* competence and referred the case to the competent court, if said decision cannot be challenged before an appellate court (art. 504 CCP).

[88] On the problem of the conformity of this provision with art. 6(3)(c) ECHR, see Karras (2011), pp. 974–975.

[89] See in conjunction with Laws 2928/2001, 3251/2004, and 4049/2012; also arts. 9, 9A, 19 Const. and Laws 2225/1994, 2472/1997, 2713/1999, 3115/2003, 3471/2006, 3674/2008, 3783/2009, 3917/2011, as well as Presidential Decree 47/2005.

criminal investigations at hand may be practically limited. Furthermore, art. 200A CCP regulates the coercive collection and analysis of DNA-data for the purpose of investigating serious criminal offences.[90] This examination, which must be conducted in a manner respectful to the subject, may request not only the investigating authorities but also the accused himself/herself, who, moreover, has extensive possibilities for reviewing (e.g., with the help of experts appointed by him/her) the results of the DNA analysis.

The accused may face practical restrictions of his/her participation rights also in the case of corruption related crimes. For the investigation and prosecution of such crimes, art. 253B CCP also provides, apart from the aforementioned special investigation methods, the possibility of undercover investigations conducted either by the traditional investigating authorities or by private persons acting as covert agents.[91] The latter possibility is not without problems in a procedural system where the state has exclusive competence to investigate and prosecute crimes, which makes it necessary to clarify further the defence guarantees and the framework in which these investigations are to take place.

Besides the provisions introducing new investigation methods, limitations to the defendant's participation in the proceedings may arise from special rules concerning the protection either of vulnerable groups of witnesses[92] or of the so-called "public interest witnesses," that is, persons who report or contribute to the disclosure of corruption crimes (e.g., whistle-blowers).[93] In such cases, redacted witness testimonies, secret witness identities, or examinations employing modern telecommunication technology (e.g. videotaped testimony, examination by video link) limit the possibilities of the accused to know, examine, and challenge the credibility of the evidence against him/her.

4 Personal Participation of Private Parties Other Than Defendants (in Particular, the Contribution of the Victim to the Fact-Finding)

In the Greek criminal procedure, proceedings may be initiated by complaint of the victim of the offence (harmed person),[94] who may also participate in the criminal proceedings as a "civil action party."[95] The civil action party has a central position

---

[90] See also Laws 2928/2001, 3783/2009, 4274/2014, 4322/2015.

[91] See art. 253B CCP and Law 4254/2014.

[92] For more details, see, e.g., arts. 226A, 226B CCP and art. 9 Law 2928/2001, as well as the analysis below, Sect. 4.

[93] See art. 45B CCP introduced by Law 4254/2014.

[94] See especially arts. 27, 36–43, 46–53 CCP.

[95] See arts. 63–70, 82–88 CCP. On victim and civil action issues, see also Karras (2011), pp. 258–298, 403–430. See also Anagnostopoulos and Magliveras (2000), pp. 140–146, 155–158;

in the criminal proceedings opposite to the defendant, justified by the mixed nature of the civil action, which is not only *civil* but also *criminal*.[96] This is manifested, for example, in art. 64(2) CCP, which provides for the right of the civil claimant to participate in the criminal proceedings merely for the purpose of supporting the criminal charges against the defendant, even if a third person (not the accused) is liable for restitution, monetary compensation, or pecuniary satisfaction for the moral harm suffered or the distress caused by the offence (the usual grounds for a civil action, art. 63 CCP). The mixed nature of the civil action may also explain the extended rights vested in the civil action party, which, to some extent, are similar to those of the accused: most notably the right to counsel, to present evidence, to call witnesses, to appoint experts, to examine witnesses and submit observations, to request the out-of-court *(inter partes)* examination of witnesses not able to give evidence in court, and to make final statements (which, however, should not address the issue of sentencing).[97]

Obviously, crime victims also participate in most criminal proceedings as witnesses. Under the influence of international and European legislation, provisions have recently been adopted for the participation in criminal proceedings and the enhanced protection of sensitive groups of witnesses, such as the victims of trafficking or minors who are victims of sexual offences.[98] The presence and support of a specialised psychiatrist or psychologist during the examination of the victim witness or the videotaping of the examination as a substitute for the physical presence of the vulnerable witness at court exemplify some of the new possibilities.[99] Furthermore, provisions have also been adopted for the protection of victims of organised crime (art. 187 PC-Greece), who have decided to testify as witnesses, from acts of retaliation or intimidation. These include new measures such as physical protection, relocation, new identities, redacted personal data in witness statements, and the use of the (tele)communication technologies for witness testimony or examination.[100]

Another private party with participation rights in the criminal proceedings, apart from the civil action party, is the "civil responsible" party,[101] that is, a person (other than the criminal defendant) who, in the criminal case at hand, is liable under civil law for the compensation of the civil action party or the payment of imposed fines

---

Mylonopoulos (1993), pp. 169–171; Spinellis (1986), pp. 405–418; Spinellis and Spinellis (1999), pp. 33–35.

[96] On the mixed nature of the civil action in criminal proceedings, see Androulakis (2012), pp. 83–86.

[97] See especially arts. 96, 97, 98, 99, 108, 108A, 138, 309, 326, 328, 333, 343, 357, 358, 369 CCP. See also above, Sect. 2.

[98] See, e.g., Law 3064/2002 in conjunction with Presidential Decree 233/2003 and Law 3875/2010, as well as Laws 2298/1995, 3811/2009, 3860/2010, 3875/2010, 4198/2013, and 4267/2014.

[99] See especially arts. 226A and 226B CCP.

[100] See for instance art. 9 Law 2928/2001.

[101] The institution has its origins in the Italian *responsabile civile*, see arts. 83–88 CCP-Italy.

and expenses.[102] Unlike the civil action party, the genuinely civil nature of the institution of the civil responsible party raises questions regarding the role of such actors in criminal proceedings, particularly since they are vested with all the rights of the defendant (art. 107 CCP).[103]

5   *In Absentia* Proceedings

5.1   *Information Rights and Conditions of Waiver of Personal Participation in Criminal Proceedings*

As far as the information rights of the accused are concerned, the newly added art. 99A CCP[104] has introduced into the Greek criminal procedure law an extensive *right to information about rights*, which enhances and complements the protection vested by pre-existing provisions.[105] Most notably, this provision extends the protective scope of the information right, on the one hand, *ratione temporis,* as it is triggered at an early point in the proceedings and "at the latest before the first official interview of the suspect or accused person by the police or by another competent authority."[106] On the other hand, the provision has an extensive *ratione materiae* application, including criminal proceedings not only for felonies but also for misdemeanours and petty violations.[107] Generally, the suspects or accused persons shall be informed, orally or in writing and in simple and accessible language, about their right to access a lawyer,[108] to obtain free legal advice, to be informed of the

---

[102] See especially arts. 89–95, 107, 167, 221, 320(2), 367, 467 CCP.

[103] Critical thereon, Androulakis (2012), pp. 369–370.

[104] Art. 99A CCP was introduced by Law 4236/2014, transposing into the Greek legal system the Directive 2012/13/EU of the European Parliament and of the Council of 22 May 2012 on the right to information in criminal proceedings, OJEU L 142–10 (1 June 2012) and the Directive 2010/64/EU of the European Parliament and of the Council of 20 October 2010 on the right to interpretation and translation in criminal proceedings, OJEU L 280/1–7 (26 October 2010).

[105] See especially arts. 100 (access to, and representation by, lawyer), 101 (information of the accusation and access to the materials of the case), and 102 CCP (extension of time limit to answer the charges), as well as arts. 103 and 104 CCP (obligation of the investigating authorities—investigating judge and investigating officers—to explain to the accused the rights provided for in arts. 100–102 CCP).

[106] See recitals 19 and 28 Directive 2012/13/EU. See also the terms used in the text of art. 99A CCP and the Greek text of the Directive ("αμέσως", i.e., immediately, promptly), and in the English (*promptly*), German (*umgehend*), French (*rapidement*), or Italian (*tempestivamente*) texts of the Directive, all expressing a notion of "as soon as possible" and without undue delays.

[107] Cf. in this regard, the provisions of arts. 103 and 104 CCP limiting this obligation of the investigating authorities only in cases of ordinary investigations (art. 103 CCP) and pre-investigations (art. 104 CCP).

[108] On the right to appoint a defence counsel or have one appointed *ex officio* by the investigating judge, see also art. 100 CCP. See also above, Sect. 2.

accusation,[109] to remain silent, and their right to interpretation and translation.[110] Those rights are considered essential for safeguarding the fairness of the proceedings.[111]

If the person concerned (suspect or accused) is arrested or detained,[112] further safeguards shall be ensured.[113] For one, an oral information of the persons concerned about their rights is insufficient.[114] Instead, they should be given a *Letter of Rights*, written in a simple and accessible language, which they can understand. In addition to the aforementioned rights, this Letter shall provide information about any rights relevant to the current status of deprivation of liberty, *inter alia*, about the right to access the materials of the case,[115] the possibilities, under national law, to challenge the lawfulness of the arrest or detention, the suspect's or accused's right to have consular authorities and one other person informed, to access urgent medical assistance, and the maximum number of hours or days suspects or accused persons may be deprived of liberty before being brought before a judicial authority.[116]

Those information rights also dictate that the accused be formally and in due time notified of any important development in the proceedings (e.g., issuance of judicial decisions, or the obligation or possibility to appear before the investigating judge or the court). In this regard, art. 273(1) CCP provides for the obligation of the investigating authorities, when the accused appears before them to answer the charges, to ask him/her to state an address of domicile or residence, where all judicial documents shall be served throughout the whole proceedings.[117] Furthermore, arts. 320 and 321 CCP provide for the notification of the accused of the forthcoming trial by formal summons. Pursuant to art. 321(1, 2) CCP, the summons must entail, *inter alia*, the particulars of the scheduled trial (date, time, competent court) and the

---

[109] In conjunction with arts. 101 and 273(2) CCP.

[110] Art. 99A(1) CCP and art. 3 Directive 2012/13/EU; on interpreters, see also the provisions of arts. 233–238B CCP.

[111] See recital 19 Directive 2012/13/EU. On the fair trial as an "umbrella term covering procedural rights", see Ambos (2016), pp. 60–96; Ambos (2018), pp. 86–88, with further references.

[112] Arrest or detention shall be interpreted widely, including any deprivation of liberty of the suspect or the accused in the course of criminal proceedings, within the meaning of art. 5(1)(c) ECHR, as interpreted by the ECtHR case-law; see recital 21 Directive 2012/13/EU.

[113] See art. 99A(3) CCP and art. 4 Directive 2012/13/EU.

[114] See, however, art. 99A(4) CCP and art. 4(5) Directive 2012/13/EU providing for the possibility of an oral enlightenment of the arrested or detained persons in a language that they understand when a Letter of Rights is not available in the appropriate language. Nevertheless, even in these cases a Letter of Rights in a language that the persons understand shall be given to them without undue delay.

[115] In conjunction with art. 101 CCP.

[116] See art. 99A(3) CCP and art. 4(2,3) Directive 2012/13/EU.

[117] See also arts. 154–165 CCP regulating the legal framework for notice and service of judicial documents (e.g. summons, judgments) throughout the proceedings.

charged offences in order for the accused to be able to exercise his/her right to be present at, and participate in the trial.[118]

The presence and participation of the accused in the proceedings constitute fair trial guarantees. The Greek law does not provide for the possibility of an explicit waiver with regard to the respective rights. If anything, one may speak of an implicit waiver by interpreting the conduct of the accused (his/her absence) as such (waiver).[119] In addition, there is, apart from a fair trial right, the presence requirement, as explicitly provided in art. 340(1) CCP, which also serves other interests of the criminal procedure, most notably the objective of finding the substantive truth.[120] Even if the accused has "waived" his/her right to be personally present at trial (e.g., by being represented instead by a lawyer), the court may always order his/her personal appearance before it if it deems it necessary for finding the substantive truth (art. 340(2) CCP). From this perspective, the presence requirement in the Greek criminal procedure should be considered as an obligation allowing for some exceptions rather than a right that can be waived.

Art. 340 CCP establishes three exceptions from the presence requirement, where the accused may implicitly "waive" his/her right to personal appearance. Only in one of these cases, however, is there a full waiver of the right to be present and participate, resulting in a real *in absentia* trial: This is the case of an accused who was formally summoned to trial with his/her *residence being known to the authorities*[121] but neither appears in person at trial nor appoints a defence counsel to represent him/her.[122] In the other two exceptional situations, the absent accused is replaced and represented by a defence counsel, appointed by a written statement from the accused: Art. 340(2) CCP provides for the general discretion of the accused to be represented by a defence counsel, while art. 340(4) CCP covers those cases where the accused has already been convicted and his/her personal appearance would mean his/her subjection to the execution of the punishment.[123] In all these cases the accused albeit absent is tried *as if he/she were present*. The same may occur (representation by defence counsel and trial as if the accused were present) if the accused is detained and, due to *force majeure* or because of insurmountable obstacles, is unable to appear in person and the court does not make use of its discretion to postpone the trial (art. 346 CCP). Apart from the cases where the right to be present is

---

[118] See also art. 6(3)(a) ECHR; Androulakis (2012), pp. 395–397; Karras (2005), pp. 744–747.

[119] An exception to the rule that says it is permitted that the absence of the accused be interpreted by the court as a waiver of his/her right to be present are felony trials, provided that the accused has a residence unknown to the authorities and has neither appeared before the authorities nor is arrested; in such cases, the trial may not continue until the accused is arrested or appears before the court, see art. 432(1) CCP.

[120] See already above, Sect. 2; see also Karras (2011), pp. 637–643.

[121] On the summons of persons with known or unknown residence, see arts. 155–156 and 273 CCP.

[122] See arts. 340(3) and 432(2) CCP.

[123] This provision includes motions to annul the procedure or the judgment, motion to suspend the enforcement of the judgment if notice of appeal or cassation has been lodged, and motion to determine a total sentence.

waived for the whole trial, arts. 344, 347, and 348 CCP provide for the (partial) absence of an accused who was initially present at trial.[124] As a rule, such absence shall not obstruct the progress of the trial and the court may permit the representation of the accused by defence counsel or adjourn the trial.

5.2   Default Proceedings and Subsequent Remedies (e.g., Retrial or Judicial Review at a Higher Instance)

Under the Greek law of procedure, in specific (exceptional) cases, a criminal trial can take place *in absentia* of the accused. In these cases, the distinction is between situations where the accused is personally absent but represented by a defence counsel and situations where the accused is absent and no defence counsel is appointed. Only the latter cases are considered genuine *in absentia* trials (and will be the object of the following analysis), for in the former cases the accused is tried as *if he/she were present*.[125]

Another important distinction involves the type of offence under consideration. With respect to felonies, the gravity of the offence dictates that the accused be present or represented by counsel and that he/she must have been formally notified of the trial. An exception is introduced in art. 432(2) CCP,[126] which allows for *in absentia* felony trials, provided that the absent accused was summoned as a person of known residence. In this case, the accused is tried *in absentia* even without the necessity of the court appointing a defence counsel *ex officio*.[127] If, however, the accused was summoned as a person of unknown residence and does not appear, the court must suspend the trial until the accused is arrested or appears before it by other means (art. 432(1) CCP). In misdemeanours cases, any judgment resulting from a trial in the absence of the accused and with no representation by a defence counsel is considered a legally binding *in absentia* judgment, regardless of how the accused was summoned (as a person of known or unknown residence). This last fact is only important with regard to the legal remedies a convicted person has against such *in absentia* judgments.[128]

The Greek criminal procedure provides two legal remedies against genuine *in absentia* judgments, depending on the type of the offence and the way the convicted person was summoned. Regarding non-appealable misdemeanours (art. 341 CCP) and felonies (art. 435 CCP), the convicted may file a motion *to annul the in absentia*

---

[124] In particular, this partial absence may be due to medical emergency, the exercise of the defendant's right to remain silent or tried in his/her absence, or may be ordered by the court if the accused obstructs the conduct of the trial.

[125] See arts. 340(3), 346(2), 432(2) CCP, and above, Sect. 5.1.

[126] In conjunction with art. 340(3) CCP.

[127] See art. 432(2) CCP.

[128] See especially arts. 340(3), 341, 428, 429 CCP.

proceedings if he/she was summoned as a person of known residence and, due to *force majeure* or other insurmountable obstacles, he/she was unable to appear before the court or notify it by any other means and ask for the postponement of the trial. If the court grants this motion, the *in absentia* judgment is rendered void and a retrial is ordered.[129] No special remedies are provided for misdemeanours tried *in absentia* with regard to which the accused was summoned as of known residence, and he/she can still lodge an appeal. The only option for the accused who was thus deprived of the first instance of jurisdiction is to file the ordinary legal remedies (appeal, cassation). For misdemeanours with regard to which the accused was summoned as a person of unknown residence, the convicted may file a motion to *annul the in absentia judgment*, claiming that he/she actually has a residence known to the authorities (art. 430 CCP). If the motion is granted, the judgment is rendered void and a retrial is ordered by the court (art. 431 CCP).[130]

5.3   Inaudito reo *Proceedings (e.g., Penal Order Procedure)*

The Greek criminal procedure provides for *inaudito reo* proceedings where the personal participation of the accused can occur only after the judgment was rendered. This kind of *in absentia* proceeding is reserved only for cases of petty violations (arts. 414–416 CCP) and minor misdemeanours for which the single-judge misdemeanour courts are competent and the judge deems it appropriate to impose only a fine (art. 427 CCP).[131] The procedure is conducted in writing and a public hearing is only held for the pronouncement of punishment, in the absence of the accused who is not summoned.

The possibility of an actual hearing, where the accused convicted *in absentia* can be present and heard, depends on the filing of objections by him/her against the judgment within specific time limits. The short time limit for filing the objections (8 days from the date the judgment was served to the convicted) and the subsequent execution of the judgment after the expiration of this deadline (only the timely filing suspends the execution of the judgment, art. 416 CCP) raises fair trial issues, especially in terms of misdemeanours.[132] Against the decision of the first instance court to which no objections were filed (in time), the convicted has the right to appeal and cassation under the general provisions (art. 416(2) CCP). The same applies with regard to the judgment issued by the court after objections were filed and a hearing was held (art. 416(1) CCP).

---

[129] See arts. 435(2) and 341(2) CCP.
[130] See Androulakis (2012), pp. 426–431.
[131] See Karras (2005), pp. 905–908, 924–925.
[132] See Karras (2005), pp. 924–925.

6   Participatory Rights in Transnational Criminal Justice

6.1   Participatory Safeguards in EAW Proceedings

6.1.1   Participatory Rights in the Decision on Surrender

Greece has implemented the EU Council Framework Decision of 13 June 2002 on the European Arrest Warrant and the surrender procedures between Member States (FD EAW)[133] with Law 3251/2004. Pursuant to this law, the Greek Ministry of Justice is the designated central authority for assisting the competent judicial authorities in EAW issues (art. 3). The prosecutor appointed to the competent Court of Appeal is not only the authority responsible for issuing the EAW in Greece (art. 4) but also the executing judicial authority responsible for receiving the EAW, arresting and detaining the requested person, introducing the case to the competent judicial council, and executing the decision on the surrender of the person under consideration. In case the arrested person consents to surrender, the judicial authority responsible for deciding on the execution of a EAW is the competent President of the Court of Appeal. If the arrested person does not consent, the competent Judicial Council of the Court of Appeal (art. 9) is responsible for deciding on the execution of a EAW.

According to art. 15 Law 3251/2004, the requested person arrested for the purpose of executing the EAW is provided promptly with an appropriate Letter of Rights containing information on his/her rights.[134] The person is then, without delay, brought before the competent prosecutor appointed to the Court of Appeal. The prosecutor shall inform the requested person of the European arrest warrant and its contents, of his/her right to assistance by a legal counsel and by an interpreter,[135] as well as of the possibility of consenting to surrender to the issuing judicial authority.[136] It must be noted that Greece has not yet fully implemented the Directive 2013/48/EU on the right of access to a lawyer in criminal proceedings and in European arrest warrant proceedings.[137] In any case, the arrested person has the right, at his/her own expense, to request (either personally or through the legal counsel) copies of the case file, as well as the right to appeal before the Judicial Council of the Court of Appeal

---

[133] FD 2002/584/JHA, OJEU L 190 of 18 July 2002, 1.

[134] See art. 5 Directive 2012/13/EU on the right to information in criminal proceedings in conjunction with art. 99A CCP, and above, Sect. 5.1.

[135] On the right to an interpreter, see also arts. 233(1) and 236A CCP in conjunction with arts. 2(7) and 3(6) Directive 2010/64/EU on the right to interpretation and translation in criminal proceedings, and below, Sect. 7.2.

[136] See also art. 17 Law 3251/2004.

[137] Directive 2013/48/EU of the European Parliament and of the Council of 22 October 2013 on the right of access to a lawyer in criminal proceedings and in European arrest warrant proceedings, and on the right to have a third party informed upon deprivation of liberty and to communicate with third persons and with consular authorities while deprived of liberty, OJEU L 294/1-12, 6 November 2013.

regarding issues related to the identity of the requested person. The opportunity for appeal exists also against decisions ordering the detention of the arrested person until a decision on the execution of the EAW is issued (art. 16).

Most importantly, according to art. 18 Law 3251/2004,[138] if the requested person does not consent to his/her surrender and the case is, therefore, referred to the Judicial Council of the Court of Appeal competent for deciding on the execution of the EAW, the person has the right to be personally (and, as a rule, publicly) heard by the Council, assisted by his/her legal counsel and an interpreter. The person may also ask for the appointment of a counsel by the President of the Court of Appeals. Against the decision of the Judicial Council of the Court of Appeal on the surrender, the requested person and the prosecutor may lodge an appeal before the Supreme Court *Areios Pagos*; the requested person is then summoned to appear in person before the Judicial Council of the Supreme Court (art. 22).[139]

6.1.2   *In Absentia* Proceedings in the Trial Country and Its Relevance in the Surrender Procedure

According to art. 13(1) Law 3251/2004, where the EAW has been issued for the purposes of executing a sentence or a security measure imposed by a decision rendered *in absentia* and if the person concerned had not been summoned in person or otherwise informed of the date and place of the hearing which led to the decision rendered *in absentia*, the execution of the EAW by the competent judicial authority may be subject to the condition that the issuing judicial authority gives adequate guarantees that the requested person will have an opportunity to apply for a retrial of the case in the issuing Member State and to be present at the judgment. It should be noted, however, that Greece has not yet fully implemented the Framework Decision 2009/299/JHA of 26 February 2009 amending Framework Decision 2002/584/JHA, thereby enhancing the procedural rights of persons and fostering the application of the principle of mutual recognition to decisions rendered in the absence of the person concerned at the trial.[140]

Art. 1(2) Law 3251/2004 introduces a human rights clause, providing that the application of the EAW provisions shall not have the effect of violating fundamental rights and fundamental legal principles as those are enshrined in the Greek

---

[138] In conjunction with art. 448 CCP.

[139] On a situation pending the decision, where the EAW has been issued for the purpose of conducting a criminal prosecution, the requested person may be heard by the executing judicial authority under specific conditions or be temporarily transferred to the issuing State, see art. 23 Law 3251/2004 and arts. 18–19 FD EAW.

[140] See art. 2 Council Framework Decision 2009/299/JHA of 26 February 2009 amending Framework Decision 2002/584/JHA, 2005/214/JHA, 2006/783/JHA, 2008/909/JHA and 2008/947/JHA, thereby enhancing the procedural rights of persons and fostering the application of the principle of mutual recognition to decisions rendered in the absence of the person concerned at the trial.

Constitution[141] and in art. 6 of the Treaty on European Union. Moreover, no person shall be removed, expelled, or extradited to a state where there is a serious risk that he or she would be subjected to the death penalty, torture, or other inhuman or degrading treatment or punishment.

6.2 Participatory Safeguards in Transborder Inquiries and the Taking of Overseas Evidence

Apart from the FD EAW, in the field of legal assistance, Greece has signed and ratified not only bilateral treaties extensively regulating matters of extradition, transborder inquiries, and the taking of overseas evidence between national legal orders (e.g., the Treaty between the USA and Greece on Mutual Legal Assistance in Criminal Matters of 26 May 1999)[142] but also a great number of international and supranational legal instruments within the framework of the Council of Europe and the European Union. The most notable examples are the European Convention on Extradition of 13 December 1957,[143] the Convention on Simplified Extradition Procedure between the Member States of the EU of 10 March 1995,[144] the Convention on Extradition between the Member States of EU of 27 September 1996,[145] the European Convention on Mutual Assistance in Criminal Matters of 20 April 1959,[146] the Convention on Laundering, Search, Seizure and Confiscation of the Proceeds from Crime of 8 November 1990,[147] the UN Convention against Corruption,[148] the UN Convention against Transnational Organized Crime,[149] the Convention

---

[141] See above, Sect. 1.

[142] Treaty between the Government of the United States of America and the Government of the Hellenic Republic on Mutual Legal Assistance in Criminal Matters of 26 May 1999, ratified with Law 2804/2000; see also Law 3771/2009 ratifying the Protocol of 2003 to the Treaty of 1999.

[143] ETS No. 24, entry into force 18 April 1960; Greece ratified it with Law 4165/1961.

[144] OJEU C 78 of 30 March 1995, 2; Greece ratified it with Law 2780/2000.

[145] OJEU C 313 of 23 October 1996, 11; Greece ratified it with Law 2718/1999.

[146] ETS No. 30; entry into force 12 June 1962. Greece ratified it with Legislative Decree 4218/1961. This Convention is complemented by two Additional Protocols of 17 March 1978 (ETS No. 99; entry into force 12 April 1983) and of 8 November 2001 (ETS No. 182; entry into force 1 February 2004); Greece has signed both of them, but ratified only the first one with Law 1129/1981. Note, however, that Greece has not ratified the respective EU Mutual Assistance Convention (Convention on Mutual Assistance in Criminal Matters between Member States of the EU of 29 May 2000, OJEU C 197 of 12 July 2000, 3) and its Additional Protocol of 16 October 2001 (OJEU C 326 of 21 November 2001, 1), being one of the few Member States not bound by it.

[147] ETS No. 141, entry into force 1 September 1993; ratified with Law 2655/1998. See also the Council of Europe Convention on Laundering, Search, Seizure and Confiscation of the Proceeds from Crime and on the Financing of Terrorism of 16 May 2005 (ETS No. 198, entry into force 1 May 2008), which has been signed by Greece, but not yet ratified.

[148] General Assembly Resolution 58/4 of 31 October 2003; Greece ratified it with Law 3666/2008.

[149] General Assembly Resolution 55/25 of 15 November 2000; Greece ratified it with Law 3875/2010.

Implementing the Schengen Agreement of 19 June 1990,[150] the Europol Convention,[151] the Council Decisions regarding Eurojust,[152] and the FD 2002/465/JHA of 13 June 2002 on joint investigation teams.[153] On the other hand, one cannot overlook the fact that Greece has so far failed to implement in its national law, demonstrating considerable delays, most of the major more recent EU secondary legislative acts in the field of legal assistance, such as the FD 2003/577/JHA on the Execution of Orders Freezing Property or Evidence,[154] the FD 2006/783/JHA on the Mutual Recognition of Confiscation Orders,[155] and the FD 2008/978/JHA on the European Evidence Warrant for the Purpose of Obtaining Objects, Documents and Data for Use in Proceedings in Criminal Matters.[156] Finally, the Directive 2014/41/EU of the European Parliament and of the Council of 3 April 2014 regarding the European Investigation Order in criminal matters was implemented in September 2017.[157]

Furthermore, this legal framework is complemented by provisions of national law: arts. 436–456 CCP address issues of extradition and arts. 457–461 CCP regulate other forms of mutual assistance in criminal matters (e.g., questioning of accused persons and witnesses, gathering and confiscation of evidence).[158] However, these provisions apply only complementary to, and as long as they comply with, the respective multilateral or bilateral agreements.[159] Regarding extradition, the provi-

---

[150] The Schengen acquis—Convention implementing the Schengen Agreement of 14 June 1985 between the Governments of the States of the Benelux Economic Union, the Federal Republic of Germany and the French Republic on the gradual abolition of checks at their common borders OJEU, L 239 of 22 September 2000, 19–62. Greece ratified it with Law 2514/1997.

[151] Convention based on Article K.3 of the Treaty on European Union, on the establishment of a European Police Office (Europol Convention) (OJEU, C 316 of 27 November 1995, 2) and the three Protocols amending it; ratified with Laws 2605/1998, 3294/2004, 3295/2004. The Council Decision 2009/371/JHA of 6 April 2009 establishing the European Police Office (Europol) (OJEU, L 121 of 15 May 2009, 37) that replaces the Europol Convention has not yet been transposed into Greek law.

[152] Council Decision 2002/187/JHA of 28 February 2002 setting up Eurojust with a view to reinforcing the fight against serious crime (OJEU, L 63 of 6 March 2002, 1); Council Decision 2003/659/JHA of 18 June 2003, amending Decision 2002/187/JHA (OJEU, L 245 of 29 September 2003, 44); Council Decision 2009/426/JHA of 16 December 2008 on the strengthening of Eurojust and amending Decision 2002/187/JHA (OJEU, L 138 of 4 June 2009, 14). Greece implemented them with Law 3663/2008.

[153] OJEU, L 162 of 20 June 2002, 1–3. Greece implemented it with Law 3663/2008.

[154] OJEU L 196 of 2 August 2003, 45.

[155] OJEU L 328 of 24 November 2006, 59.

[156] OJEU L 350 of 18 December 2008, 74. This FD has been repealed by Regulation (EU) 2016/95 (see recital 11 and Art. 1 Regulation (EU) 2016/95 of 20 January 2016 repealing certain acts in the field of police cooperation and judicial cooperation in criminal matters, OJEU L 26 of 2 February 2016, 9–12).

[157] OJ EU L 130, 1 May 2014, 1. See Law 4489/2017. For an analysis of the major EU secondary legislative acts in the field of legal assistance, see Ambos (2018), pp. 453–461.

[158] On the threefold distinction of legal assistance in extradition, other mutual legal assistance, and enforcement assistance, see Ambos (2018), p. 415 with further references.

[159] See Triantafyllou (2009), pp. 67–71.

sions of the CCP apply only to cases where the law on EAW does not apply and provide for the requirement of dual criminality as well as for the prohibition of the extradition of Greek nationals. According to art. 447 CCP, for the purpose of extradition the arrested person has the right, at his/her own expense, to request (either personally or through the legal counsel) copies of the case file. Regarding the extradition hearings, the requested person has the right under arts. 448, 450 CCP to be personally (and, as a rule, publicly) heard by the Judicial Council of the Court of Appeal, assisted by his/her legal counsel and an interpreter. The person may also ask for the appointment of a counsel by the President of the Court of Appeals. Against the decision of the Judicial Council of the Court of Appeal on the extradition, the requested person and the prosecutor may lodge an appeal before the Supreme Court *Areios Pagos*; the requested person is then summoned to appear in person before the Judicial Council of the Supreme Court (art. 451 CCP).

In terms of other types of mutual legal assistance, the enumeration of the investigating measures in art. 457 CCP, regarding outgoing requests from the Greek judicial authorities for the gathering of evidence, is not restrictive.[160] As for the incoming requests by foreign judicial authorities, they may be granted in accordance with the principle of reciprocity for any investigating measure and under the specific conditions set by the CCP, as long as the measure is allowed by Greek law (art. 458 CCP). Issues may arise regarding requested *coercive* measures not covered by the wording of art. 458 CCP.[161] The requests are usually transmitted through the Ministry of Justice to the competent prosecutor of the Court of Appeal, and forwarded to the locally competent investigating judge (art. 458(1) CCP).[162] Any gathered evidence will follow the same path backwards.

This brief overview demonstrates that the legal framework regarding transborder inquiries and the gathering of overseas evidence constitutes a complex and fragmented landscape. This puts the person concerned right from the outset at a disadvantage in terms of legal certainty. Moreover, the equality of arms is seriously compromised, since the Greek Code of Criminal Procedure does not provide for the obligation of the authorities to inform the persons concerned of ongoing proceedings in the context of a mutual legal assistance request for the gathering of evidence, thereby eliminating the person's possibilities to participate effectively.[163] In terms of the protection of the accused during the legal assistance proceedings, the solution of applying the general provisions of the CCP that regulate the gathering of evidence is more convincing than the recourse to the protection of administrative law (solely based on the involvement of executive authorities).[164] That said, the Directive on the

---

[160] See Triantafyllou (2009), p. 67.

[161] See thereon Triantafyllou (2009), pp. 69–71.

[162] The procedure is simplified with regard to requests within the Schengen Agreement framework, where the communication is directly between the judicial authorities, without the intervention of the Ministry of Justice.

[163] See Triantafyllou (2009), pp. 203–211.

[164] See Triantafyllou (2009), pp. 211–216.

European Investigation Order (EIO), which, as of 22 May 2017,[165] replaced the existing fragmented system of transborder gathering of evidence within the EU with a new comprehensive one, covering almost all investigative actions,[166] is a promising development.

7 Requirements of Personal Participation and *In Absentia* Proceedings. The Perspective of Supranational and International Human Rights Law

7.1 The Perspective of International Human Rights Law. Critical Remarks on Domestic Law in the Light of the European Convention

Greece has ratified the European Convention for the Protection of Human Rights and Fundamental Freedoms[167] and, since 1985, has acknowledged the right of individual application to the European Commission and the European Court of Human Rights. With Law 2865/2000, a new provision was added to art. 525 CCP that allows the complete re-trial of a case if the ECtHR declares that the Greek state has violated any of the rights provided in the ECHR (e.g., violation of fair-trial guarantees).

From among the rules and principles of supra-statutory force provided for in the ECHR and its protocols, the right to a fair trial as defined in art. 6(1, 3) ECHR and interpreted in the case law of the ECtHR is of major importance for national judicial practice.[168] The core guarantees in this provision enhance the protection of the dignity of the criminally accused person by providing him or her with defence rights such as the right to a fair hearing within a reasonable time by a tribunal established

---

[165] See art. 34 EIO Directive. The Directive will replace the FD on the European Evidence Warrant and the corresponding provisions of the European Convention on Mutual Assistance in Criminal Matters, the Convention Implementing the Schengen Agreement (CISA), the Convention on Mutual Assistance in Criminal Matters between the Member States of the EU, and the FD on the Execution of Orders Freezing Property or Evidence. See Ambos (2018), pp. 456–461 with further references.

[166] Excluded are the provisions regarding joint investigation teams (art. 3 and recitals 7 and 8 of the EIO Directive) and cross-border surveillance pursuant to art. 40 CISA (recital 9 EIO Directive).

[167] Law 2329/1953. The ECHR was denounciated from 1970 to the end of the military dictatorship period (1967–1974), but was re-accessed and re-ratified with the Legislative Decree 53/1974. See also above, Sect. 1.

[168] The following rules are also of significance to national criminal law: the due process guarantees in the context of deprivation of liberty (art. 5(2)–(5) ECHR); the presumption of innocence (art. 6(2) ECHR); the right to an effective remedy and the prohibition of discrimination regarding the enjoyment of Convention rights in the national territory (arts. 13–14 ECHR); and finally, the procedural safeguards relating to the expulsion of aliens, the right of appeal in criminal matters, and the *ne bis in idem* principle (ECHR Protocol No. 7). See also the respective provisions included in the ICCPR and the Charter of Fundamental Rights of the European Union.

by law, the right to silence, and the right not to incriminate oneself, as well as extensive information rights and the right to effective legal assistance and participation in criminal trials. Over the years, the Greek legal order has finally succeeded in complying, for the most part, with these requirements of international human rights law.[169]

With regard to the presence of the accused at trial, art. 6(3)(c) ECHR, as it is interpreted by the ECtHR, precludes the deprivation of the accused of his/her right to be effectively defended by counsel, even in those cases where the accused, in spite of having been properly summoned, does not appear (even in the absence of an excuse).[170] In this sense, the possibility provided for in art. 432(2) CCP of conducting felony trials in the absence of the accused who is or considered to be a person of known residence and who was lawfully summoned without the appointment of a defence counsel to represent him/her being obligatory, raises human rights issues given particularly the gravity of felony cases. Similar human rights issues raises the possibility provided for in arts. 428–429 CCP of conducting misdemeanour trials in the absence of the accused and without his/her representation by a counsel.[171] This is especially true considering that the routine application of the provision of art. 428 CCP—which provides for the exceptional summons of the accused as a person of unknown residence (art. 156 CCP)—has become the practice of choice in Greek courts whenever the accused is not found at his/her domicile.[172]

7.2 The Perspective of EU Law. Developments in Domestic Law as a Result of EU Law

The many laws ratifying and implementing international and European legal acts regarding issues of mutual legal assistance and cooperation in criminal matters play a central role in the criminal procedure system of Greece. They include, on the one hand, laws focusing on particularly serious crimes or offences with a cross-border dimension,[173] and especially on issues of mutual legal assistance in investigating and prosecuting such crimes (e.g., European Arrest Warrant, Europol and Eurojust,

---

[169] This is especially true with regard to the information rights of the accused, the right to access the case file, the right to an effective defence and to be represented by a defence counsel, and the right to confront witnesses. For more examples and critical remarks, see Margaritis (2014), pp. 845–857.

[170] See ECtHR, *Lala v. the Netherlands*, judgment of 22 September 1994, Appl. No. 14861/89, para. 33; *Pelladoah v. the Netherlands*, judgment of 22 September 1994, Appl. No. 16737/90, para. 40; *Kari-Pekka Pietiläinen v. Finland*, judgment of 22 September 2009, Appl. No. 13566/06, para. 31; *Neziraj v Germany*, judgment of 8 November 2012, Appl. No. 30804/07, para. 19.

[171] See already the analysis above, Sect. 5.2.

[172] See Karras (2005), pp. 414–415, 926–927; Margaritis (2014), p. 848.

[173] See also art. 83(1) TFEU.

joint investigation teams).[174] On the other hand, procedural rights have become more important at the EU level, especially after the Lisbon Treaty entered into force, as is demonstrated by the increased number of secondary legislative acts of the EU adopted in recent years in this regard. In this context, the following Directives are of particular importance:

– Directive 2010/64/EU on the *right to interpretation and translation* in criminal proceedings[175];
– Directive 2012/13/EU on the *right to information* in criminal proceedings[176];
– Directive 2012/29/EU on the *rights, support, and protection of victims* of crime[177];
– Directive 2013/48/EU on the *right of access to a lawyer* in criminal proceedings[178];
– Directive 2016/343/EU on the *presumption of innocence* and the r*ight to be present* at the trial in criminal proceedings[179];
– Directive 2016/800/EU on *procedural safeguards for children* who are suspects or accused persons in criminal proceedings.[180]

From the above, the first two Directives have been transposed into the Greek legal order by Law 4236/2014 and the next two by Law 4478/2017. Of great importance in this respect are the provisions of art. 99A CCP regarding the information rights of the suspect or the accused and the Letter of Rights enhancing and complementing the protection vested by pre-existing provisions.[181] Moreover, based on European provisions, arts. 233, 236, 236A, and 238B CCP regulate extensively the rights of suspected or accused persons to have the linguistic means to participate in the criminal proceedings (as this is required for *effective* participation), providing,

---

[174] See, e.g., Laws 3251/2004, 2865/2000, 2605/1998, 3294/2004, 3295/2004, 3663/2008.

[175] Directive 2010/64/EU of the European Parliament and of the Council of 20 October 2010 on the right to interpretation and translation in criminal proceedings, OJEU L 280/1-7, 26 October 2010.

[176] Directive 2012/13/EU of the European Parliament and of the Council of 22 May 2012 on the right to information in criminal proceedings, OJEU L 142/1-10, 1 June 2012.

[177] Directive 2012/29/EU of the European Parliament and of the Council of 25 October 2012 establishing minimum standards on the rights, support and protection of victims of crime, and replacing Council Framework Decision 2001/220/JHA, OJEU L 315/57-73, 14 November 2012.

[178] Directive 2013/48/EU of the European Parliament and of the Council of 22 October 2013 on the right of access to a lawyer in criminal proceedings and in European arrest warrant proceedings, and on the right to have a third party informed upon deprivation of liberty and to communicate with third persons and with consular authorities while deprived of liberty, OJEU L 294/1-12, 6 November 2013.

[179] Directive (EU) 2016/343 of the European Parliament and of the Council of 9 March 2016 on the strengthening of certain aspects of the presumption of innocence and of the right to be present at the trial in criminal proceedings, OJEU L 65/1–11, 11 March 2016.

[180] Directive 2016/800/EU of the European Parliament and of the Council of 11 May 2016 on procedural safeguards for children who are suspects or accused persons in criminal proceedings, OJEU L 132/1-20, 21 May 2016.

[181] See already thereon the analysis above, Sect. 5.1.

inter alia, for the right to a qualified interpreter, to have all important documents translated, and the obligation of the state to meet the interpretation and translation costs irrespective of the outcome of the proceedings.[182]

8   Concluding Remarks

The Greek Code of Criminal Procedure, despite many systemic disadvantages, either from the beginning or due to the many major and minor amendments and re-amendments through no fewer than 30 different legal acts since the 1980s, shows a general trend towards respecting the defendant's rights and complying with the constitutional (liberal and protective) orientation of the criminal trial, and with the state's primary obligation to respect human dignity and the fundamental rights of the individual.[183] This has been demonstrated in the analysis above. The accused, in particular, has a central role in the criminal proceedings with extended rights to participate and influence the outcome of the criminal trial, from the very beginning of the proceedings when he/she is merely a suspect to the very end when the final judgment is enforced. The accused also has considerable opportunities to obstruct *in absentia* trials and to challenge *in absentia* judgments. These participation rights of the accused are further enhanced through bilateral treaties, international conventions, and other legal instruments signed and agreed upon within the framework of the Council of Europe and the EU. Greece has ratified or implemented, though sometimes with significant delays due to deeper structural deficiencies of the Greek legal order, most of the major legal acts with regard to the procedural safeguards of the defendant, while the judiciary finally seems to keep up and comply with the case law of the European Court of Human Rights and the requirements of international human rights law.

Yet, one cannot overlook the existing shortcomings, especially those resulting from the adoption of international and supranational legal instruments and the transnational nature of proceedings of mutual legal assistance, as well as from the practical deficiencies of the Greek legal system in general. As for the former, potential issues are inherent to the type of instrument and therefore not limited to a specific legal system but are relevant for any legal order in which they are implemented. For instance, based on the principle of mutual recognition, legal assistance instruments present a systemic defect in that they require mutual recognition while sometimes lacking the basic prerequisite of mutual recognition, i.e., the existence of common minimum standards in all the affected legal orders regarding both the technical and

---

[182] See arts. 233–238B CCP.

[183] The legislation introduced in the last 30 years led to an inconsistent, unsystematic, and unclear "patchwork" of procedural provisions. For more details, see Billis (2013), pp. 273–278.

procedural rules as well as the fundamental human rights guarantees.[184] The second category of problems is also intrinsic, resulting directly from the very nature of transnational proceedings, which involve at least two jurisdictions, two languages, and so on and so forth. This fact puts the person concerned at a disadvantage right from the outset, by requiring him/her to confront transnational investigations or prosecutions without always institutionally providing him/her with the possibility of an effective (transnational) defence.[185]

Nevertheless, there are reasons to be optimistic about these issues, especially in view of the efforts made within the EU to enhance the protection of fundamental rights and overcome the current shortcomings.[186] This, however, is not the case in terms of the practical problems of the administration of justice in Greece. An extremely overloaded judicial system, lacking both human and technical resources, has proved to be the actual enemy not only for the suspect and the accused[187] but also for every person involved in it, and for justice itself. A far-reaching structural reform of the Greek system of criminal procedure, beyond a mere re-codification or consolidation of existing scattered provisions and addressing all fundamental and systemic questions anew, is urgently needed.

References

Ambos K (2016) Treatise on international criminal law. Volume III: international criminal procedure. Oxford University Press, Oxford

Ambos K (2018) European criminal law. Cambridge University Press, Cambridge

Anagnostopoulos I, Magliveras K (2000) Criminal law in Greece. Kluwer Law International and Sakkoulas, The Hague

Androulakis N (2012) Themeliodeis Ennoies tis Poinikis Dikis [Θεμελιώδεις Έννοιες της Ποινικής Δίκης] (Fundamental concepts of the criminal trial), 4th edn. P.N. Sakkoulas, Athens

Billis E (2013) National characteristics, fundamental principles, and history of criminal law in Greece. In: Sieber U et al (eds) National criminal law in a comparative legal context, vol. 1.2, introduction to national systems: Australia, Côte d'Ivoire, Greece, South Korea. Duncker & Humblot, Berlin, pp 187–290

Billis E (2015) Die Rolle des Richters im adversatorischen und im inquisitorischen Beweisverfahren. Duncker & Humblot, Berlin

---

[184] See thereon Ambos (2018), pp. 451–452 with further references.

[185] See thereon Ambos (2018), pp. 460–461.

[186] See Ambos (2018), chapters II and IV.

[187] See for instance, the statistics from the ECtHR on the ECHR violations by article and by State for 2014 and 2015 (available at http://www.echr.coe.int/Documents/Stats_violation_2015_ENG. pdf, and http://www.echr.coe.int/Documents/Stats_violation_2014_ENG.pdf, both accessed last on 31.7.2018), where Greece's convictions for excessively long proceedings form almost one fifth of the total violations by 47 Member States. A slight improvement can be seen in the same statistics for 2016 (available at http://www.echr.coe.int/Documents/Stats_violation_2016_ENG.pdf, last accessed 31.7.2018), where Greece's convictions on the same grounds form only one seventh of total violations (16 of a total of 106 violations by 47 Member States).

Billis E (2017) Introduction to the basic characteristics and fundamental principles of the criminal law and penal code of Greece. In: Billis E (ed) The Greek Penal Code. English translation by Vasiliki Chalkiadaki and Emmanouil Billis. Introduction by Emmanouil Billis. Duncker & Humblot, Berlin, pp 1–62

Chalkiadaki V, Billis E (2017) English translation of the Greek Penal Code. In: Billis E (ed) The Greek Penal Code. English translation by Vasiliki Chalkiadaki and Emmanouil Billis. Introduction by Emmanouil Billis. Duncker & Humblot, Berlin, pp 63–226

Christianos V (2008) Application of community law in Greece. In: Kerameus K, Kozyris P (eds) Introduction to Greek law, 3rd edn. Kluwer Law International and Ant. N. Sakkoulas, Alphen aan den Rijn, pp 65–77

Dagtoglou P (2008) Constitutional and administrative law. In: Kerameus K, Kozyris P (eds) Introduction to Greek law, 3rd edn. Kluwer Law International and Ant. N. Sakkoulas, Alphen aan den Rijn, pp 23–64

Karras A (2005) Epitomi Ermineia Tou Kodika Poinikis Dikonomias [Επίτομη Ερμηνεία Του Κώδικα Ποινικής Δικονομίας] (Commentary on the code of criminal procedure), 2nd edn. Ant. N. Sakkoulas, Athens

Karras A (2011) Poiniko Dikonomiko Dikaio [Ποινικό Δικονομικό Δίκαιο] (Criminal Procedure Law), 4th edn. Nomiki Vivliothiki, Athens

Margaritis M (2014) Apotimisi tis epidrasis tou dikaiou tis ESDA sto elliniko poiniko dikonomiko kai ousiastiko dikaio [Αποτίμηση της επίδρασης του δικαίου της ΕΣΔΑ στο ελληνικό ποινικό δικονομικό και ουσιαστικό δίκαιο] (Remarks on the impact of the ECHR on Greek law). In: Kotsalis L (ed) Evropaiki Simvasi Dikaiomaton tou Anthropou & Poiniko Dikaio [Ευρωπαϊκή Σύμβαση Δικαιωμάτων του Ανθρώπου & Ποινικό Δίκαιο] (ECHR & Criminal Law). Nomiki Vivliothiki, Athens, pp 845–857

Mylonopoulos C (1993) Greece. In: Van Den Wyngaert C (ed) Criminal procedure systems in the European community. Butterworths, London, pp 163–183

Spinellis D (1986) The civil action. In: Van Dijk J et al (eds) Criminal law in action. Gouda Quint, Arnhem, pp 405–418

Spinellis D (2008) Criminal law and procedure. In: Kerameus K, Kozyris P (eds) Introduction to Greek law, 3rd edn. Kluwer Law International and Ant. N. Sakkoulas, Alphen aan den Rijn, pp 459–487

Spinellis D, Spinellis C (1999) Greece. In: The European Institute for Crime Prevention and Control, affiliated with the United Nations (ed) Criminal justice systems in Europe and North America. HEUNI, Helsinki. http://www.heuni.fi/en/index/publications/nationalcriminaljusti-ceprofiles/greece.html. Last accessed 31 Aug 2018

Spyropoulos P, Fortsakis T (2009) Constitutional law in Greece. Kluwer Law International and Ant. N. Sakkoulas, Alphen aan den Rijn

Triantafyllou G (2009) Diethnis Dikastiki Syndromi Stin Poiniki Apodiksi [Διεθνής Δικαστική Συνδρομή Στην Ποινική Απόδειξη] (International Legal Assistance in Criminal Evidence). P.N. Sakkoulas, Athens

Report on Hungary

Anett Erzsébet Gácsi, Krisztina Karsai, and Zsolt Szomora

Abstract This paper describes the legal position and the participation of private persons in criminal procedures under Hungarian law, with special regard to the defendant and the defence counsel. The defendant's procedural rights and duties are analysed in connection with the two phases of the criminal procedure: the investigation and the trial. The defendant's position as a party at the trial has sufficient guarantees under Hungarian criminal procedural law, his/her position in the investigation phase should however be strengthened, a more efficient defence should be ensured (e.g. regarding the defence counsel's presence at the first interrogation of the defendant; the defendant's and his/her counsel's presence at sessions where decision on his/her pre-trial detention is made; the defendant's and the counsel's access to the documents of the case).

Special attention is paid to the *in absentia* procedures, which is provided as a special form of procedure in the Code on Criminal Procedure of Hungary. The practical experiences show that this type of procedure lasts significantly longer than procedures where the defendant is present. The delay of the procedure is, in great part, the consequence of the guarantees provided for *in absentia* procedures.

Abbreviations

Btk	Hungarian Criminal Code
CCP	Hungarian Code on Criminal Procedure (from 1998 to 2017)
CJEU	Court of Justice of the European Union
EAW	European Arrest Warrant
ECHR	European Convention on Human Rights

A. E. Gácsi · K. Karsai · Z. Szomora (✉)
Institute of Criminal Law and Criminal Science, University of Szeged, Szeged, Hungary
e-mail: karsai.krisztina@juris.u-szeged.hu; szomora.zs@juris.u-szeged.hu

© Springer Nature Switzerland AG 2019
S. Quattrocolo, S. Ruggeri (eds.), *Personal Participation in Criminal Proceedings*, Legal Studies in International, European and Comparative Criminal Law 2, https://doi.org/10.1007/978-3-030-01186-4_8

ECtHR   European Court of Human Rights
EU   European Union
EUCCM   Cooperation in Criminal Matters between the Member states of the
           European Union
ICCM   International Cooperation in Criminal Matters
new CCP   New Hungarian Code on Criminal Procedure (from 2018)

1 Constitutional Requirements of the Involvement of Private Parties in Criminal Justice

In Hungary, no specific constitutional provisions exist concerning the involvement of private parties in criminal justice. The relevant requirements can be derived from the general clause "right to a fair trial" under Art. XXVIII par. 1. Fundamental Law.[1]

> Every person shall have the right to have any charge against him or her, or any right and duty in litigation, adjudicated by a legally established independent and impartial court in a fair public trial within a reasonable period of time.

The provision cited above *prima facie* refers to the defendant in criminal cases, just like it is the case with Art. 6 par. 1 ECHR, the constitutional safeguard of a fair trial however applies to all private parties involved in criminal proceedings.[2]

2 Personal Participation of Private Parties and Legal Assistance

The Act on Criminal Procedure (a büntetőeljárásról szóló törvény—Act Nr. XIX of 1998, hereinafter referred to as CCP) divides the subjects of the procedure into two groups: authorities and private parties, the latter being the defendant, the defence counsel, the victim, the private accuser,[3] the civil party,[4] the substitute private accuser,[5] other interested parties,[6] representatives, aides and supporters (Arts 42–59 CCP.). It has to be pointed out that the CCP. does not label the witness and the

---

[1] The current Constitutional Charta of Hungary, called Fundamental Law, entered into force on 1 January 2012.

[2] Cf. Bárd (2016), pp. 113–121.

[3] In case of criminal offences subject to private prosecution (e.g. criminal defamation, violation of private secrets).

[4] The victim who has suffered financial damages resulting from the criminal offence and enforces a civil claim against the defendant in criminal proceedings.

[5] In case the public prosecutor terminates the procedure or drops the charge, the victim may act as a substitute private accuser and have the case adjudicated by the court.

[6] Anyone whose right or lawful interest may be directly affected by the decision made in the course of criminal proceedings.

forensic expert as private participants, provisions applying to them are included in the rules on the means of evidence, their qualification as private parties is still undebatable.

Personal participation prevails as general rule in the criminal procedure, and exercising procedural rights and duties through representatives is regarded as exception. *Exercising rights through a representative* is usually provided as a possibility, but, in certain cases, the involvement of a representative is mandatory (e.g. the substitute private accuse in general, or the private accuser in case s/he is legally incapacitated or has limited legal capacity).

The defendant has the right to act for his defence on his/her own (personal defence) or by a defence counsel (formal defence) who can be retained by the defendant or appointed by the authorities. A defence counsel can be involved in any stage of the proceedings and his procedural rights constitute duties as well. Therefore, the rights of the defence counsel cannot be regarded as being transferred from the defendant but as independent procedural rights that can generally be exercised in the interest of the defendant but, with some exceptions, also against his/her will.[7] Some cases laid down in the CCP require mandatory participation of the defence counsel. A defendant must be represented by counsel (Art. 46 CCP):

- if the criminal offence is punishable with imprisonment of five or more years;
- if the defendant is detained;
- if the defendant is deaf, mute, blind or—regardless of his/her legal responsibility—mentally disabled;
- if the defendant does not speak Hungarian or the language of the procedure;
- if the defendant is unable to defend himself/herself personally for any other reasons;

  or

- if it is expressly stipulated in other Articles of the CCP (e.g., trial of third instance, criminal procedure against a juvenile; trial in absentia, waiver of trial or expedited hearing).

The *victim*, who can also act as complainant, private accuser, civil party, can exercise his/her rights in person or through a representative. Authorizing a lawyer as representative is mandatory for a substitute private accuser. Among the private parties in the criminal procedure, it is the *other interested party* who can also authorize a representative. Such representative may be a lawyer or a relative of full age (Arts 56–58 CCP).

---

[7] E.g. the defence counsel is entitled to lodge an appeal even against the will of the defendant (no positive mandate required and the possibility of negative mandate is excluded; Art. 324 CCP). However, the same is not possible concerning the extraordinary legal remedies (no positive mandate required and but there is the possibility of negative mandate; Arts 409 par. 2 and 417 par. 1 CCP).

3 Personal Participation of the Accused in Criminal Proceedings

The central figure of criminal proceedings is the *defendant* against whom the criminal procedure has been instituted. The defendant is used as an umbrella term under Hungarian criminal procedural law for the following different positions:

- *reported person*: until the investigating authority's decision on the institution of criminal proceedings is made (known only in legal literature)[8];
- *a person reasonably susceptible of having committed a criminal offence*: in special situations where the communication of the suspicion cannot take place due to objective obstacles (known only in legal literature);
- *suspect*: in the course of the investigation (Art. 43 par. 1 CCP);
- *accused*: in the course of the court procedure (after the indictment has been filed) (Art. 43 par. 1 CCP);
- *convict*: after the final sentence imposing penalty or certain preventive measures under substantive criminal law (Art. 43 par. 1 CCP);
- *finally acquitted*: after the final sentence acquitting the accused has been passed (known only in legal literature).

3.1 General Features of Personal Participation: Absolute Individual Right of Duty of Diligence?

The defendant being the subject and not the object of the procedure possesses a broad range of procedural rights and must fulfill several obligations as well. In our view, his rights and duties are in close connection with the issue of personal participation; the brief outline of the defendant's legal position is set out below.

The defendant's rights can be a) those serving his/her gaining knowledge about the case; b) serving the effective influence on the procedure; c) the special rights of the detained defendant; d) other rights. With some differences, these rights can be exercised both during the pre-trial and the trial phase.

Ad a) The defendant's *rights to gain knowledge about the case* (Art. 43 par. 2 CCP) are the following: (1) The defendant is entitled to receive information on the suspicion and the charge, on later changes thereof and on any other change as well. (2) The defendant has the right to be present at many actions or procedural events, which right nevertheless has a different extent in the course of the investigation and the trial (will be discussed in detail below). It has now to be emphasized that the personal participation has to be regarded as a right in both procedural phases, which right can be subject to certain limitations. It can be preliminary noticed that a scientific dispute has emerged also in Hungarian legal literature on the issue whether the

---

[8] Herke et al. (2012), p. 99.

presence at the trial is a right[9] or an obligation[10] of the defendant. In our opinion, this has to be conceived as a right of the defendant, also considering the fact that, the defendant can wave of the right to be present in certain special forms of court proceedings. The defendant has (3) the right to read the documents of the case and (4) the right to put questions, which rights can be exercised to a different extent in the pre-trial and the trial phase (will be discussed in detail below). Finally, s/he has the right to be informed by the authorities about his/her rights and duties during the whole scope of criminal proceedings. This right is independent of whether or not the defendant has a defence counsel.

Ad b) The defendant's *rights to effectively influence the procedure* (Art. 43 par. 2 CCP) are the following: (1) S/he has to be given sufficient time and possibility to prepare for the defence. (2) S/he has the right to present facts and data serving his defence in any phase of the procedure; (3) to file motions for procedural actions; (4) to make observations on the procedural actions; and (5) finally, the right of legal remedy.

Ad c) In addition to these rights, the CCP specifically provides *detained defendants' right* of contact and communication (Art. 43 par. 3 CCP) with his/her defence counsel and his/her relatives. The former underlies no limitation or control, while the latter underlies control and can even be limited or prohibited to ensure the success of the criminal procedure.

Ad d) *Other important rights* of the defendant are the following: the right to involve a defence counsel; to make a statement (testimony) and to refuse to make a statement (right to silence); to use his/her native tongue and make use of an interpreter; human dignity and personality rights; the right of personal protection.

The defendant's duties can be divided into two groups: those in connection with the defendant's personal participation in procedural actions (in which cases s/he has the duty to be present—this will be discussed in detail below; participatory obligations to do, not to do or tolerate actions); and his duty to inform the authorities about the change of his residence and address (Art. 43 par. 5 CCP).

3.2 Personal Participation in the Pre-trial Inquiry (with Particular Regard to the Interim Decisions on Coercive Measures)

The Hungarian criminal procedure is of a mixed character, combining the advantageous elements of inquisitorial and adversarial criminal procedures. The pre-trial phase and, in particular, the investigation can be described as more inquisitorial since its secrecy, scriability and the lack of immediacy are decisive features of the

[9] Bárd (2005), p. 217.
[10] Erdei (2011), p. 296.

investigation phase. Obviously, the general functional principles such as the presumption of innocence or the right to defence prevail also in that pre-trial stage.

3.2.1 Personal Participation

As already mentioned above, the defendant's *being present at procedural actions* belongs to the most fundamental rights. However, this right is more restricted *during the investigation* compared to the trial phase where the right to be present prevails generally. If the CCP provides, the defendant can be present at the inspection (of objects or sites), the presentation for identification, reconstruction (of evidence), the search, the hearing of the expert (Arts 149, 184 and 185 CCP.). On the contrary, s/he cannot be present at the interrogation of other defendants and witnesses provided that the interrogation of the latter has not been motioned by him/her or the defence counsel. In terms of certain procedural actions, the CCP prescribes the defendants obligation to be present: when the suspicion is being communicated to him/her and s/he is being interrogated thereafter (Art. 179 par. 1); if s/he has been subpoenaed to be present at procedural actions; when coercive measure are being enforced except s/he has been allowed to be absent (e.g. another person can stand in for his/interest during search—Art. 149 par. 5.). In case the suspect can be present at a procedural action conducted in the course of investigation, s/he can file motions and make observations on the action or its outcome.

As previously mentioned above (see letter B), the defendant can act both in person or by way of his/her defence counsel. In case the defendant's being detained, the involvement of a defence counsel is mandatory (see also above; Art. 46 CCP). Consequently, mandatory defence is provided when the defendant is under arrest or in pre-trial detention (on the decisions connected to pre-trial detention, see C.II.2. below). It has however to be stressed that *mandatory defence in the pre-trial phase is not equal to the defence counsel's duty to be present at investigative and other procedural actions.* It is therefore possible the defence counsel, who has been notified of the action, still not be present when coercive measures are being enforced or the defendant's being heard before making judicial decision on pre-trial detention. Since the defence counsel is not obliged to be present, mandatory defence during the investigation provides for a mere safeguard that the *defence counsel can be present and act* in the interest of the defendant.[11] Thus, should the defendant be under detention, the defence counsel has to be notified of the date and place of the defendant's first interrogation in a way, which *actually enables* him/her to exercise his procedural rights and to be present at the defendant's interrogation. If this notification is not given in a sufficient way and time, the defendant's statement must be

---

[11] A survey carried out by the Hungarian Helsinki Committee in 2015 reveals the fact that officially appointed defence counsels rarely attend hearings and interrogations during the investigation and, if they are present, their activity proves to be low. The analysis of case files has showed that defence counsels were absent in 33% of the very first pre-trial detention hearings, and did not attend 66% of further hearings. Fazekas et al. (2015), pp. 37–38.

excluded as evidence [Decision of the Constitutional Court Nr. 8/2013. (III. 1.) AB]. Consequently, if the notification is given properly, the absence of the defence counsel does not result in the exclusion of the defendant's statement.

Access to the documents of the case is also an issue relevant to personal participation. In the course of the trial, both the accused and the defence counsel have an unlimited access to documents (Art. 193 par. 1 CCP) unlike it is the case during the investigation. Before 1 January 2014, the right to read the documents had been restricted to a too great extent: the defendant had had an unrestricted access to the expert opinion and only and exclusively to such records, which had been made about investigative actions, at which the suspect and the defence counsel could be present (cf. right above). Other documents could be inspected by the suspect and his/her counsel only if this was not disadvantageous for the interests of the investigation (Art. 186 par. 2 CCP).

On the one hand, these rules on the access to the documents had to be amended in order to ensure conformity with the Directive 2012/13/EU of the European Parliament and the Council on the right to information in criminal proceedings. On the other hand, several decisions of the ECtHR stated that Hungary's legal provisions and practices concerning the access to information violated the ECHR.[12] The most important changes after 2014 are as follows:

– First, if the public prosecutor files a motion for ordering pre-trail detention, the defendant and his/her counsel have to be presented with the copy of documents on which the public prosecutor grounds the motion.
– Second, if the public prosecutor files a motion for the continuation of the pre-trial detention, the defendant and his/her counsel have to be presented with the copy of documents that have been produced since the last decision on pre-trial detention was made have (Art. 211. par. 1a CCP).

It however has to be noticed that the CCP modifications are still not in complete conformity with the aforementioned EU Directive. The CCP still makes possible that the authority not present the defendant and his/her counsel with the documents that can make questionable the existence of a ground for pre-trial detention. This represent a violation of the principle of *equality of arms*, which must prevail also in the course of the investigating judge's proceedings.

3.2.2 Decisions on Pre-trial Detention

In this part of the paper, we are going to summarize the rules on the decisions on pre-trial detention (ordering, continuation, upholding and review) made both prior to and after the filing of the indictment. This makes the process and sequence of

---

[12] ECtHR, *X.Y. v. Hungary*, judgment of 19 March 2013, Appl. No. 43888/08; ECtHR, *A.B. v. Hungary*, judgment of 16 April 2013, Appl. No. 33292/09; ECtHR, *Baksza v. Hungary*, judgment of 23 April 2013, Appl. No. 59/196/08; ECtHR, *Hagyó v. Hungary*, judgment of 23 April 2013, Appl. No. 52624/10.

decisions on pre-trial detention visible. It has to be preliminary emphasized that, in the course of investigation, judicial sessions where decisions on pre-trial detention are made are not public (unlike trial hearings after the filing of the indictment when such decisions are also made). However, the right to an effective defence can only be ensured if the defendant (and his/her counsel) can attend these sessions.

In the course of the investigation, it is the investigating judge who can order pre-trial detention upon the motion of the public prosecutor and holding a session where *the suspect is present*. The detention can last for a maximum of 1 month when ordered for the first time. If the public prosecutor files a motion for the continuation of the detention, the investigating judge can decide on the continuation for 3 months each but for a maximum total period of 1 year. It has to be stressed that *the investigating judge is not obliged to hold a session in every case when deciding on the continuation of the detention*. A session shall be hold only if (1) in the public prosecutor's motion for continuation, new circumstances are referred to as grounds for pre-trial detention; or if (2) 6 months have passed since the pre-trial detention was ordered for the first time; (3) in other special cases (e.g. ordering a bail) (Art. 210. par. 1 CCP).

If the public prosecutor files a motion for the *continuation over 1 year*, the decision falls within the competence of the County Courts and *requires holding a session*. The County Court can order continuation for 2 months each before the filing of the indictment.

After the filing of the indictment and in the preparatory phase of the trial (i.e. before opening the public hearing), the court of first instance can decide on pre-trial detention either ex officio or on the public prosecutor's motion. If the court orders or upholds pre-trial detention or house arrest, *s/he has to hold a session only if new circumstances are referred to in the motion* to order/uphold pre-trial detention. Furthermore, if the trial has been commenced and adjourned, the court can decide on pre-trial detention in an *in camera session*, i.e. without the defendant's and the defence counsel's being present (Art. 309. par. 1 CCP). In our view, this provision of the CCP violates both the Fundamental Law and the ECHR [cf. Decision of the Constitutional Court 10/2007. (III. 7.) AB].

After the pronouncement of the first-instance judgement and if an appeal has been lodged against it, the court rules on pre-trial detention or other coercive measure *at the public hearing*. The detention can last until the second-instance judgment has been passed, the necessity of it has however to be reviewed every 6 months. It is though critical that the review of the detention is performed *in camera*, without the defendant's being heard.

3.3   Personal Participation in Proceedings in Camera

3.3.1   The Principle of Publicity and Its Limitations

The principle of publicity prevails only in the trial phase under Hungarian procedural law. From the point of view of publicity, four different forms of court procedure can be distinguished: trial (*tárgyalás*), public hearing (*nyilvános ülés*), hearing (*ülés*) and in camera session (panel session) (*tanácsülés*) (Art. 234 CCP.). This represents also *a sequence of hierarchy concerning procedural guarantees*. It has to be emphasized in advance that court practice has elaborated the limitations to transition from one form of procedure to another one: once a second-instance trial or public hearing has been commenced, the transition to an in camera session is prohibited (Curia Decision 2003. 934. BH).

The principle of publicity can to the greatest extent be realized in a trial or public session. The *trial* is the primary form of court procedure and aims at taking of evidence (Art. 234 par. 1 CCP). The first-instance court rules on the defendant's criminal liability after taking of evidence in a trial (some exceptions can be made in special procedures; see below). If the court of second-instance carries out evidentiary actions, it also has to open a trial. Holding a trial at third-instance is excluded.

Public hearing is the secondary form of court procedure, it is however the most typical in second- and third-instance proceedings where no evidentiary actions take place. It has to be emphasized that the trial and the public hearing *make no difference in terms of personal participation*.

Publicity is limited in case of holding a *hearing*, which embodies a procedural action of preparatory character. As a main rule, no evidentiary actions may take place at a hearing (except the investigating judge in certain cases). The CCP provides three main types of hearing: hearings held by the investigating judge; preparatory hearing (after the filing of the indictment and before opening the trial) and personal hearing (in proceedings subject to private accusation). *Only the parties can be present at a hearing*: the public prosecutor (private accuser, substitute private accuser), the defendant and the defence counsel, and those subpoenaed or notified can attend it (Art. 234. par. 4 CCP).[13]

Publicity and personal participation is excluded in case of *in camera sessions* (or in other words, panel sessions). Only the members of the court and the keeper of the minutes can be present, taking of evidence is excluded (Art. 234 par. 5 CCP). Two main types of in camera sessions can be distinguished: first, a panel session held after the trial or public hearing in order to pass the judgment; second, so-called *ex actis* session in simple cases. The latter is now precisely defined in the CCP, which lists the cases that can be dealt with by in panel sessions. A panel session can embody also a part of the trial, the public hearing or the hearing.

---

[13] This means that the victim or civil party can only be present if s/he has been subpoenaed or notified of the hearing, which, for example is never the case when hearing on pre-trial detention is held.

3.3.2 Closed Trial (in Camera Trial)

The *CCP* exceptionally provides for cases, in which the trial (or public session) or a part of it can be declared closed to public.[14] In case an *in camera* trial is held, the participation of the parties is not limited, that is, also the victim, the private party and their representatives can be present. Furthermore, the so-called "trusted person" can also be present at an in camera trial: should the defendant have no defence counsel or should the victim have no representative, s/he can denominate a person who is actually being present and won't be heard at the trial.

3.3.3 In Camera Session

As mentioned above, the private parties' participation is not possible at an in camera session. It was generally critical in Hungary that the CCP had not provided for clear rules on when a case *on second instance can be adjudicated at an in camera session*, which did not comply with the maxims following from legal certainty and fair trial. Article 360 paragraph 1 included the following general clause: the presiding judge rules, within 30 days after receiving the files, on whether the case will be dealt with at a trial, a public hearing or in camera session. No further provisions were given in the CCP. It is not surprising that the ECtHR dealt with cases in which the rules on the in camera session were contested.[15]

The Constitutional Court examined the provision of the CCP cited above and declared it unconstitutional in its Decision 20/2005. (V. 26.) AB, also stating that the Hungarian Parliament had omitted to provide precise rules on the forms of court procedures at higher instances, which omission leads to an unconstitutional situation. The Constitutional Court found that the rights of all private parties in criminal proceedings had been violated by this general rule because, first, the parties were not to be notified of a in camera session being held, second, no minutes were kept at an in camera session. Since no requirements and limitations to the presiding judge's decision on the form of the court procedure were laid down in the CCP, also the possibility of approving the first-instance decision, or, furthermore, issuing a reformatory decision was given to the second-instance court, without hearing any of the parties, i.e. at in camera session. The decision of the Constitutional Court also emphasized that that both the international conventions, the case of the ECtHR and the CCP regards the whole scope of the court procedure as a consistent and uniform procedure, i.e. the effective participation of the private parties cannot be restricted to the first-instance court proceedings. An opposite approach would transform the

---

[14] We are not going to describe these cases here since the topic of the report mainly concentrates on the personal participation of private parties.

[15] ECtHR, *Csikós v. Hungary*, judgment of 5 December 2006, Appl. No. 37251/04; ECtHR, *Talabér v. Hungary*, judgment of 29 September 2009, Appl. No. 37376/05; ECtHR, *Sándor Lajos Kiss v. Hungary*, judgment of 29 September 2009, Appl. No. 26958/05; ECtHR, *Goldmann and Szénászky v. Hungary*, judgment of 30 November 2010, Appl. No. 17604/05.

court procedure at higher instance into an inquisitorial phase again, in which the exclusion of the defendant's and the defence counsel's participation would to a far greater extent be possible than in the investigation phase. This absurd consequence following from Art. 360 CCP infringed the Constitution.

3.4 Personal Participation in Alternative Proceedings

Alternative proceedings under Hungarian law are the following: mediation procedure and postponement of the indictment, both falling into the discretionary power of the public prosecutor. Should the public prosecutor file the indictment, the court can still order a mediation procedure.

3.4.1 The Mediation Procedure

The institution of mediation in criminal proceedings was enacted in 2006 by the modification of the *Btk* (Criminal Code) and CCP. The mediation procedure aims at being conducive to the compensation of the consequences of the criminal offence and to the perpetrator's behaving legally in the future. In the course of mediation, the persons concerned have to aim at reaching an agreement between the suspect and the victim; this agreement serves as the basis for the active repentance of the suspect.[16]

The legislature provided for the model of mediation procedure *primarily in the investigation phase*, prior to the filing of the indictment. However, the possibility of the court's ordering a mediation procedure either in the preparatory phase of the trial or even after opening the trial follows from certain provisions of the CCP. It has to be stressed that a mediation procedure cannot take place in *in absentia* procedure and in *in audito reo* procedure.[17]

The public prosecutor can order mediation procedure either *ex officio* or upon the defendant's, his/her counsel's, or the victim's motion. As for the personal participation of the parties, the public prosecutor can hear both the defendant and the victim when examining if the conditions of the mediation procedure exist. The public prosecutor can ask for the written opinion of the probationary officer and can hear the officer, too.

---

[16] The procedural prerequisites of mediation are as follows: (1) the conditions of active repentance under the Criminal Code exist; (2) the suspect has confessed the commission of the criminal offence prior to the filing of the indictment and has declared to be ready and able to compensate the victim in such a way for the damages or other harmful consequences caused by the criminal offence that the victim will feel satisfied by that compensation; and (3) both the suspect and the victim have consented to the mediation procedure.

[17] Opinion of the Criminal Board of the Curia (Supreme Court of Hungary) 3/2007 BK.

The details of mediation procedure are ruled in a separate Act of Parliament (Act CXXIII *on mediation in criminal procedure*). The central element of the procedure is the so-called mediatory meeting, which can be attended by the following persons: the defendant and his/her representative (who can also be his/her defence counsel in the criminal procedure); the victim and his/her representative; maximum 2 other persons denominated by the defendant and the victim each, which persons can speak for the affected party. The mediator can hear the defendant and the victim either when they are simultaneously present or without the other party's being present. Article 221/A par. 5 CCP provides important guarantees in case the mediation is not successful, that is, the parties cannot come to an agreement so the public prosecutor shall file the indictment: first, no declarations and statements made by the defendant and the victim in the course of mediation may be used as evidence in the criminal procedure; second, the outcome of the mediation procedure cannot be used to the detriment of the defendant.

3.4.2 The Postponement of the Indictment

The public prosecutor is entitled to postpone the indictment in case of criminal offences that are not serious.[18] The postponement means that the suspect will conditionally not be indicted for a probationary period.[19] The indictment can be postponed only if the conditions to file the indictment exist and no grounds for the termination of the procedure have occurred. If the suspect pleads innocence or disagrees with the postponement of the indictment due to any other grounds, s/he may file an objection; this obliges the public prosecutor to file the indictment. This possibility to objection follows from the basic principle of the right to a fair hearing in court (Article 3 CCP); that is why, the defendant can oblige the public prosecutor to launch the court procedure.

In line with the postponement of the indictment, the public prosecutor may order the probationary supervision of the suspect and may set behavioural rules or other obligations for him/her. Before setting these behavioural rules and obligations, *the public prosecutor must hear the suspect and also the victim if the obligations affect the rights of the victim as well* (e.g., the suspect has to compensate the victim for the damages). It must be clarified in the course of the hearing whether the suspect is willing and able to meet the rules and obligations the public prosecutor plans to set.

---

[18] The conditions of the general type of the postponement are as follows: (1) the criminal offence is punishable with imprisonment up to 3 years; (2) the gravity of the criminal offence and the extraordinary mitigating circumstances shall be considered; and (3) the postponement of the indictment is likely to have a positive impact on the future conduct of the suspect. If all these circumstances are given, the indictment may be postponed for a period between 1 and 2 years.

[19] Bárd (2007), p. 230.

3.5   *Personal Participation at Trial*

The defendant's presence at the trial is closely related to the maxim of fair trial. His/her presence, in other words, his/her personal participation embodies a precondition for his/her being able to exercise the rights following from the fair trial principle. An opposite view conceives the defendant's participation at trial not as a right but as on obligation.[20] In our opinion, the defendant's participation has to be interpreted as his/her right, which can be backed by the mere fact that s/he can even waive of his presence at trial [cf. Decision of the Constitutional Court 14/2004. (V. 7.) AB].

On the other hand, the personal participation of the defendant constitutes not only a right but also a rule that helps the court find the facts. The Hungarian criminal procedure, being similar to other procedural systems in continental Europe, strives to find the "objective truth", which can serve as a reason for Hungarian law's general insisting on the defendant's being presence. This still not excludes the interpretation of the participation as a right.

3.5.1   Personal Involvement in the Evidence-Gathering

The trial under Hungarian law has a *monistic structure*; i.e. the trial of first instance represents a unified procedure, in which the decision is made whether or not the facts constitute a criminal offence, they have been realized by the defendant, the defendant is punishable and what penal sanction shall be imposed.[21]

The Principles of Verbalism and Immediacy

The trial is based on three important principles: that of publicity (see C.III.1), immediacy and verbalism.

Immediacy means that the court can base its judgement only and exclusively on evidence it has directly examined during the trial. Immediacy represents the general rule, some exceptions are though possible (e.g. the defendant's former statement can be read out at the trial).

The principle of *verbalism* is not laid down in the CCP explicitly either but follows from the single rules on trial: the court can pass its judgment only on the ground of an oral procedure, in which the defendant, his/her counsel, the accuser and other participants of the procedure are heard. The general rule excludes the possibility of passing a judgment based merely on documents that have been produced in the course of investigation.

---

[20] Dissenting opinion of Judge Pettiti in the case ECtHR, *Poitrimol v. France*, judgment of 23 November 1993, Appl. No. 14032/88. In recent Hungarian literature, see Erdei (2011), p. 296.

[21] On the monistic and dualistic trial systems, see in detail Bárd (1987), pp. 132–160.

Presence and Filing Motions at the Trial

The principle of immediacy covers the requirement that the parties are present at the trial,[22] the trial is conducted *inter praesentes*.[23]

As already mentioned above, the defendant's presence at the trial can be conceived as a right, even if the CCP provides that the defendant must be present at the trial [Art. 240 par. 3]. His/her presence makes possible that his/her procedural rights can now be exercised on a full scale opposed to the investigation phase. Regarding the order of evidentiary actions, Art. 286 par 1. CCP lays down that taking evidence at the trial must be started by the hearing of the defendant. This rule has a compulsory character even if the defendant's statement cannot be regarded as a primary means of evidence.[24] It has to be noted as well that, under Hungarian criminal procedural law, the participation of the public prosecutor at the first-instance trial is also compulsory [following from the Constitutional Court Decision 72/2009. (VII. 10.) AB].

However, the CCP lays down exceptions to the defendant's obligatory presence, too. The legal provisions are fairly chaotic, they nevertheless can be divided into three main groups:

(1) *The defendant, without previous notice, doesn't attend the trial* [Art. 281 par. 2, 5-9 CCP]. If the defendant has properly been subpoenaed, an order for his/her immediate transport to the court can be issued. Should this be not possible or not be successful, the trial can be held in the defendant's absence as well but the evidentiary procedure may be closed only if the court passes a judgment of acquittal or termination. Otherwise the trial must be adjourned. Should the transportation or the warrant against the defendant lead to no success, the public trial cannot be continued and an *in absentia procedure* has to be instituted [see E.I. and II.]. If the defendant turns up, the trial can be continued by reading out the records taken at the first trial date. If there is need, witnesses and experts can be heard again.

(2) *Special cases, in which the trial can be held in absence of the defendant* [Art. 281. par. 4, Art. 247 par. 1-2 CCP]. First, when a decision about the defendant's compulsory psychiatric treatment has to be made and the defendant cannot attend the trial due to his mental state or s/he is not capable of exercising his/her rights. Second, when the trial is conducted against more defendants, a part of the trial not affecting a certain accused can be held even s/he is not present (partial absence). Third, when the maintaining of the order requires the defendant's removal from the court room. The court continues the trial after the removal but, at latest, orders the accused to return in the court room before closing the evidentiary procedure and presents him/her with the evidence taken in

---

[22] Erdei (2011), p. 218.

[23] Irk (1913), p. 28.

[24] Art. 118 par. 2 CCP stipulates that other means of evidence needs to be taken as well, even if the defendant pleads guilty.

his/her absence (partial absence). If the accused does not cease his/her disorderly conduct, the trial can be continued and closed in his/her absence but his/her defence counsel being present.

(3) *The defendant's absence on notice* (Art. 279 par. 3 CCP). This possibility was enacted in the CCP in 2011, meaning that the judge can inform the accused that the trial can be conducted in his/her absence provided that s/he previously notifies the court of his/her not attending. The participation of his/her defence counsel is mandatory in such a case. Owing to the judicial practice, this notification of absence is not an absolute right of the accused but its exercisability is dependent on the judge's discretion.

The possibility of filing motions can be given through the presence of the defendant and his/her counsel (cf. C.I., Art. 243, Art. 285 par. 1-4 CCP). The accused deserves an unrestricted right to file motions concerning any question that falls in the competence of the court. The court has to pass a formal a decision on each motion, and such decisions are as a main rule subject to appeal unless the CCP excludes the possibility of legal remedy (Art. 347 par. 1 CCP).

3.5.2 Personal Contributing to the Fact Finding

In certain cases, the defendant has an obligation to cooperate (see C.I.): s/he has to undergo expert examination except medical surgery (Art. 106. par. 1 CCP); s/he has an obligation to actively cooperate in case of inspection (of objects or sites), the presentation for identification or reconstruction (of evidence) (Art. 123 par. 4 and Art. 75 par. 4 CCP). S/he has to fulfil the authority's request connected to search or body search (Art. 149 par. 4 and Art. 150 par. 3 CCP). In any other respect, s/he can decide if s/he wants to actively participate in the proceedings and to actively contribute to the fact finding: whether or not s/he makes a statement, asks questions from those heard, makes remarks on the authorities' procedural conducts.

The institution of final speeches is strongly connected to fact finding. Final speeches are held both by the accuser and the defence (both the defence counsel and the accused him/herself). In the court procedure at first instance, final speeches can be held after the closing of evidentiary procedure (Art. 313 CCP); the parties can reflect on the totality of the evidentiary actions, they can debate and evaluate the facts found. In this respect, final speeches represent the only possibility to influence the court's decision.

If the court deems necessary, *the evidentiary procedure can be re-opened* after the final speeches due to the facts and evaluations given in them (Art. 320 CCP). This possibility is against the requirement of speedy trials, it yet is essential to flawlessly ensure a fair trial. Taking new evidence serves the fact finding not to remain unsubstantiated, and subsequently, new final speeches can be made reflecting the outcome of the new evidence taken. The number of the re-openings of the evidentiary procedure is not limited by the CCP, so this possibility could in an extreme case lead to the abuse of law. It still has to be kept in mind that the re-opening is never mandatory but it is up to the court's discretion.

3.6   Personal Participation in Higher Instance

The system of trial jurisdictions comprises the Municipal Courts (járásbíróság), the County Courts (törvényszék), the Regional High Courts of Appeal (ítélőtábla) and the Curia as the Supreme Court (Kúria). The criminal courts of first instance are the Municipal Courts (called District Courts in Budapest) and the County Courts (called Metropolitan Court in Budapest). The criminal courts of second instance are the County Courts and the Regional High Courts of Appeal. Appeals against the judgments of the Municipal Courts bring the case to the County Courts; appeals against the first-instance judgments of the County Courts bring the case to the Regional High Courts of Appeal. There are twenty County Courts (nineteen County Courts and the Metropolitan Court) and five Regional High Courts of Appeal (in the cities of Budapest, Szeged, Pécs, Debrecen and Győr). Exceptionally and in a limited scope, a second appeal has been permissible since the CCP amendment in 2006. The criminal courts of third instance are the Regional High Courts of Appeal (in case of offences falling within the competence of Municipal Courts) and the Curia (in case of offences falling within the competence of County Courts).

While an appeal can be lodged for nearly any reason after the first-instance decision, a second appeal may only be lodged if the accused was convicted in first instance and acquitted by the appellate court, or inversely, that is, the decisions of the first and second instance courts differ concerning the guilt of the defendant (Article 386 CCP).

3.6.1   Presence in Higher Instances

Appeals can be dealt with at in camera session, public hearing or trial. Appeals can be adjudicated at an *in camera session* if the case does not require a contradictory procedure since it can be adjudged on the basis of the documents. Following from the Constitutional Court Decision 20/2005 (V. 26.) AB, the cases in which the appeal can be adjudged in camera are exclusively listed in Art. 306 CCP (declaring the appeal for inadmissible, transferring the case to the competent court, suspending the case etc.). Beyond these administrative actions not affecting the merits of the case and in order to serve to goal of speediness, CCP also provides the possibility for an in camera decision if the appeal was lodged only for the favour of the defendant and the facts laid down in the first-instance judgement are well substantiated, i.e. no further evidence need to be taken.[25] But in such cases, the possibility of

---

[25] The fact that an appeal was lodged only in favour of the defendant triggers the *prohibition of reformatio in peius* in higher instances.

requesting a public hearing or a trial must be given to the defendant and his/her counsel so they can participate in person. An *in camera* decision on the merits of the case may only be made if such a request is missing.

The general form of court procedure in second instance is *public hearing*. The court holds public hearing if the case cannot be dealt with in camera and a trial is not necessary. If the defendant has properly been subpoenaed, the public hearing can be hold despite his/her being absent. A judgment on the appeal can also be passed if the outcome of the public hearing doesn't make the hearing of the defendant necessary (Art. 362 par. 3 CCP). The public prosecutor's attending the public hearing is not compulsory (Art. 362 par. 2 CCP).

The legal conditions for opening a *second-instance trial* are as follows: (1) the case cannot be dealt with in camera; (2) evidence needs to be taken, which is not possible at a public hearing; (3) any other cases where the presiding judge decided to open a trial (Art. 363 par. 2). The defendant must be subpoenaed at least 5 days before the trial date. Should the defendant notify the court of his/her not willing to attend the trial or if no appeal has been lodged to the detriment of the defendant, the trial can be hold despite his/her absence (Arts 364–365 CCP).

The court of third instance generally adjudges the second appeal at a public hearing. The rules on the form of court procedure at second instance apply to the procedure of third instance as well, with the exception that holding a trial and taking evidence in third instance is not allowed.

3.6.2   The Defendant's Statement in Higher Instances

The defendant has the right to make a statement at any stage of the procedure so s/he has to be provided with the possibility of making a statement if s/he decides so (Art. 117 par. 5 CCP).

Invoking this right, the defendant or his/her counsel often files an evidentiary motion *in second instance* so that the defendant who previously remained silent can now make a statement or s/he can modify his/her statement made in first instance. Since it is the first-instance court's duty to take every evidence necessary to find the facts of the case, the appellate court is entitled to review what the first-instant court has done but not to supplement with what the first-instance court has failed to do. Consequently, a motion for the defendant's making a statement can usually not be accepted in the second-instance procedure. Evidentiary actions can be carried out in the second-instance procedure only exceptionally, that is, if the first judgement is unsubstantiated: (1) if the facts of the case are not clarified; or (2) the court of first instance has failed to establish the facts of the case or established them insufficiently; or (3) the established facts of the case are contrary to the contents of the documents; or (4) from the facts established, the court of first instance has drawn erroneous conclusions (Art. 353 par. 1 CCP). The defendant make can a statement in the appellate court procedure only if one these cases exists.

As already mentioned above, evidentiary actions are generally excluded in the court procedure of *third instance*, i.e. the defendant can never make a statement.

3.7 Special Rules in the Field of Serious Organized Crimes

The so-called special procedures under Hungarian criminal procedural law will be discussed below (see E.). One of these special procedures is strongly related to organized crimes: *high-priority procedures*. The form of high-priority procedures was enacted in the CCP in 2011 and its special rules apply to criminal offences committed in office or in a criminal organization (Arts 554/A-O CCP). High-priority procedure shows differences in three respects compared to general procedures: (1) the procedure is accelerated; (2) personal participation and coercive measures; (3) means of evidence; the two latter obviously affecting the private parties' participation.

The defendant's position in high-priority procedure is the same as in the general procedure but it has not always been the case. At the time this procedure was introduced in the CCP in 2011, special rules originally applied to arrest and the right to defence. The general highest term of arrest of 72 h had been expanded to 120 h. Furthermore, the public prosecutor could forbid the suspect to consult his/her defence counsel in the first 48 h of the arrest. This measure of the public prosecutor was not even subject to legal remedy. It has also to be stressed that this prohibition had applied only to the communication between the suspect and his/her counsel; if the suspect had been heard within the first 48 h following his arrest, the defence counsel could be present. The Constitutional Court of Hungary examined these rules and annulled them due to being against the Constitution and international treaties as well [Decision 116/2011 (XII. 20.) AB].[26]

Beyond the participatory rights of the defendant, also those of the victim have to be mentioned here because the victim is granted an additional right when s/he makes his/her final speech in high-priority procedure: s/he can express his/her opinion also regarding the facts of the case unlike in general procedures. In proceedings conducted under general rules, the victim can only speak out on the guilt of the defendant [see D) below].

As for the means evidence and evidentiary actions, the general rule on hearing the defendant and the witnesses is the cross examination in high-priority procedures unlike in general procedure.

The other special procedure relevant to organized crime is the *waiver of trial*.

4 Personal Participation of Private Parties Other Than Defendants (in Particular, the Contribution of the Victim to the Fact-Finding)

Among the other private parties, it is the victim who has an outstanding role in the criminal procedure.

---

[26] On the evaluation of the Constitutional Court Decision, see Tóth (2012), pp. 10–19.

The *victim* can qualify either as a main or an accessory participant in the procedure depending on his/her actual position in a procedure (see A). In most cases, the victim qualifies as an accessory participant, i.e. s/he exercises his/her rights on the side of the public prosecutor, not independently however. On the contrary, if the victim acts as private prosecuting party or substitute private prosecuting party, s/he qualifies as a main, independent participant of the procedure exercising the functions of the accusation.

During previous decades of the twentieth century, the role of the victim became more and more limited to the role of the "most important witness" ("primus inter testes").[27] The CCP currently in force has laid down another concept and strives at strengthening the procedural position of the victim, which also follows from the European tendencies and expectations. The victim has an obligation to testify except obstacles of testimony exist, and s/he also has the obligation to tell the truth. During the hearing of the victim as a witness, his/her rights can be supported by a lawyer retained by him/her, and s/he has also to right to mental, language or other kind of support, which can be provided by a person denominated by the victim (Art. 184 par. 9 CCP).

In terms of the fact finding, the following rights of the victim shall be highlighted: a) the right of presence; b) the right of access to records; c) filing motions and making remarks.

Ad a) The victim's *right to be present* is pretty limited in the course of the investigation: s/he can be present at the hearing of the expert; the inspection (of objects or sites); the reconstruction (of evidence); the presentation for identification (Art. 184 par. 1 and Art. 185 par. 1 CCP). Besides the victim, his/her representative and a full-aged person denominated by him/her can also be present (Art. 184. par. 9 CCP). The latter person can only be excluded if the authority regards his/her presence as against the interests of the procedure. In the course of the court procedure, the victim can be present at the vast majority of the procedural actions: the trial or public hearing in first, second or third instance or when evidence is taken by a delegated judge of the court of trial. But she cannot be present at *in camera* sessions or when a witness under special protection is being heard.

Ad b) The victim's right to inspect the documents has the same scope as his/her right of presence. After the closure of the investigation, s/he also has a full access to the records but only after the defendant and the defence counsel have already inspected the documents. The victim has an unlimited access to the records and documents in the course of the court procedure.

Ad c) The victim's right to file motions and pass remarks shows a special "shrinking" character during the trial while the defendant's and the defence counsel's position is getting stronger.[28] While the important decisions and orders are communicated to the victim during the investigation and s/he usually can file legal remedies against them, this is no longer the case in the course of the trial: the victim has no right to appeal against the judgement of the case. While the defendant and the

---

[27] Király (1962), p. 5.
[28] Herke et al. (2012), p. 107.

defence counsel have the right to hold final speeches on the merits of the case, the victim's final speech is restricted to the guilt of the defendant, i.e. whether the victim finds the defendant guilty or not (Art. 316 CCP). This declaration has a mere symbolic character, it does not in fact influence the court. In case the victim acts as a main participant in the procedure (private prosecuting party or substitute private prosecuting party), his/her situation and access to legal remedies is rather different: s/he exercises the rights of the public prosecutor as a party in trial.

5   *In Absentia* Proceedings

The provisions of the so-called *special procedures* are placed in separate Chapters in the CCP. The special procedures also aim at the examination of the defendant's criminal liability but they provide organisational and procedural frameworks that are different to that of the general type of procedure. The special procedures can be divided into different groups as well, one of these groups is based on the special personal features or situation of the defendant: juveniles' criminal procedure, military criminal procedure, procedure against persons granted immunity and *in absentia* procedures. The latter belongs also to another group of procedures which aim at simplifying and accelerating criminal proceedings (such as expedited hearing, fast track court procedure, waiver of trial).[29] *In absentia* proceedings have been enacted in the CCP in 2000.

5.1   *Information Rights and Conditions of Waiver of Personal Participation in Criminal Proceedings*

In the course of general criminal proceedings, the defendant is required to stay or reside at a place that is known by the authorities. In case the defendant's whereabouts are unknown, criminal proceedings have to be suspended as a general rule. On the contrary, if the public prosecutor files a motion for *in absentia* procedure, the criminal procedure won't be suspended. Since the defendant is absconding, Hungarian literature characterizes proceedings *in absentia* also as proceedings *in contumaciam*.[30]

Since the essence of *in absentia* proceedings is the absence of the defendant, which makes him/her impossible to exercise defence and his/her participatory rights, a core element of the constitutional guarantees is missing. In order to provide a balance required constitutionally, first, the involvement of a defence counsel is mandatory; second, before the final judgement has been delivered, the first-instance trial must be repeated upon request; third, after the final judgement has been

---

[29] On these special procedures, see in detail, Karsai and Szomora (2015), pp. 204–207.
[30] Király (2003), p. 556.

delivered, the trial must be reopened upon request [Constitutional Court Decision 14/2004 (V. 7.) AB].

There are two basic types of *in absentia* proceedings: (1) the defendant's whereabouts are unknown; (2) the defendant is staying abroad at a place known by the authorities. The conditions of these two types will be presented right below.

5.2 Default Proceedings and Subsequent Remedies (e.g. Retrial or Judicial Review in a Higher Instance)

Ad 1) The rules that apply to defendants whose whereabouts are unknown are different a) during the investigation, b) at the time the indictment is filed and c) in the court procedure.

Ad 1a) As a rule, the investigation is not hindered by the defendant's absence. If the criminal offence is punishable with imprisonment and the defendant cannot be found, an arrest warrant shall be issued, evidence has to be collected and secured, and, a defence counsel shall be appointed (Art. 527 CCP pars 1 and 2).

There had been a controversy in practice for a long time on how to deal with cases in which the defendant could not be informed of the suspicion due to his/her absence, that is, the suspect person could not be involved in the proceedings in a formal way. Different decisions were made on whether or not the communication of the suspicion is a precondition of *in absentia* proceedings. Since the turn of the millennium, the legal practice has been unanimous that *in absentia* proceedings can be instituted also without the absconding defendant's being informed of the suspicion or his/her being heard (Supreme Court Decision 2002. 392 BH).

Ad 1b) If the defendant could not be found and arrested after the issuance of the warrant and the documents of the investigation are presented to the public prosecutor, s/he can decide on filing the indictment to the court provided that no other obstacles of the procedure occur and the gravity of the offence calls for pressing charges. Summons and notifications as well as other documents addressed to the defendant shall be served on the defence counsel (Art. 527 pars 3 to 6).

Ad 1c) If the defendant's place of stay became unknown subsequent to the filing of the indictment, and defendant's absconding can reasonably be assumed, the court shall issue and arrest warrant. If the warrant leads to no success within 15 days, the public prosecutor may file a motion for the continuation of the procedure *in absentia*. The private or substitute private prosecuting party may not file a motion for *in absentia* procedure. If a defence counsel has previously not been retained, the court shall appoint one.

In case the defendant can be found before the judgement is delivered, the records of the trial shall be read out in the presence of the defendant and, if necessary, the evidentiary procedure has to be reopened (Art. 531 par. 1 CCP).

In case the defendant can be found after the first-instance judgment has been delivered, s/he can file a motion for repeating the trial instead of an appeal. In the course of the repeated trial, the court has the possibility to read out the minutes of the previous trial instead of hearing the witnesses and the expert anew. On the ground of the repeated trial, the court can uphold its original decision or annul it and deliver a new judgement. The defendant shall be notified that if s/he escapes from the repeated trial, the *in absentia* judgement will be uphold without re-examination (Art. 531 CCP).

In case the defendant can be found during the procedure in second instance, the court of second instance holds a trial, hears the defendant and, if necessary, takes the evidence presented by the defendant. On the ground of the outcome of the trial, the appellate court can affirm or amend the first-instance judgement, or annul it and order the first-instance trial to be repeated. In case the defendant can be found during the procedure in third instance, the appellate court annuls the first- and second-instance decisions and orders the court of first instance to repeat the trial (Art. 531 CCP).

In case the defendant can be found after the final judgement has been delivered, the defendant can request for retrial. The re-opening of the trial is mandatory in such a case (Art. 531 CCP).

Ad 2) *In absentia* proceedings can be instituted also against defendants who are absent but their place of stay is known. The public prosecutor can file a motion for an *in absentia* procedure if the defendant cannot or won't be extradited or surrendered on the ground of an international or European arrest warrant, and the criminal procedure has not been transferred to the country of residence either. If the trial has already been commenced, the court can decide on the continuation of the trial *in absentia* also without the public prosecutor's request.

It is worth mentioning that, according to statistics, hardly any *in absentia* proceedings are conducted in Hungary.[31] It has particularly been the case since the 2011 enactment of the trial in absence on the defendant's notice (see C.V above). It has however to be stressed that despite similar features of *in absentia* proceedings and the trial in the defendant's absence on notice, the latter can though violate the constitutional guarantees. The CCP makes without no differentiation possible that the defendant notifies the court of his/her absence in any case, and, no provisions have been enacted on how and when the defendant can file this notification, that is, the procedural framework of this notification is missing.[32]

5.3   Inaudito reo *Proceedings*

The CCP, among special procedures, provides for the so-called fast track court procedure as well, which can be regarded as equal to *inaudito reo* proceedings. This special procedure was enacted in the CCP in 1900.

---

[31] A Legfőbb Ügyész országgyűlési beszámolója az ügyészség 2015. évi tevékenységéről, p. 22 (http://ugyeszseg.hu/pdf/ogy_besz/ogy_beszamolo_2015.pdf).

[32] Ujvári (2011), p. 535.

At the motion of the prosecutor—or in a case based on private prosecuting, ex officio—the court can conduct the fast track procedure for offences punishable by a maximum of 5 years' imprisonment by the Criminal Code. Fast track procedure means that no trial is held, the court adjudicates the case only and exclusively on the ground of the indictment and the documents produced during the investigation. Further special circumstances are the following according to Articles 543–550 CCP:

- the defendant is not held in pre-trial detention;
- the facts of the case are simple;
- the accused has confessed the commission of the offence (confession of facts);

and

- the aims of the penalty can be attained without a trial as well (concerning the personality, the life, the motivations of the defendant etc.).

A sentence for imprisonment exceeding 2 years may not be imposed without a trial; if the court finds that the circumstances indicate the imposing of a longer imprisonment, the trial must be held. This limit of 2 years of imprisonment is strongly connected with the sentencing rules laid down in the Criminal Code, according to which an imprisonment exceeding 2 years may not be suspended. The 2-year limit laid down in the CCP correlates with the possibility of suspending the penalty under the *Btk*. Thus, the CCP does not allow for imposing a non-suspended imprisonment without a trial, that is, as a result of a fast track court procedure.

The ruling of the court (which is not considered to be a judgment) must be delivered within 30 days following the arrival of the case at the court. The legal remedy against the court ruling is not called an appeal but a request for trial. In case of submitting a request for trial, an ordinary trial shall be held according to the general rules. The judgment passed as a result of the trial can be subject to appeal according to the general rules as well.

Fast track court procedures violate the principle of verbalism, immediacy and publicity. The defendant is still granted sufficient guarantees as no fast track court procedure can be conducted without his/her pleading guilty, and s/he can request for a trial without limitation. When opening the trial, the court is not bound by its decision previously made *inaudito reo*; a more serious penalty can however not be imposed unless the public prosecutor filed an appeal to that end. If the defendant requests for a trial, his/her participation at the trial is mandatory. If s/he remains absent, his request shall be deemed withdrawn (Art. 550 par. 2 CCP).

According to 2015 statistics, the Public Prosecutor's Office filed a motion for fast track court procedure *in every third criminal procedure*. The efficacy of this form of procedure is proven by the high number of final judgements: no trial was requested, that is, the fast track procedure decisions became final in the case of 15.125 defendants.[33]

---

[33]A Legfőbb Ügyész országgyűlési beszámolója az ügyészség 2015. évi tevékenységéről, pp. 21–22 (http://ugyeszseg.hu/pdf/ogy_besz/ogy_beszamolo_2015.pdf).

6 Participatory Rights in Transnational Criminal Justice

In Hungary, the CCP does not contain rules on procedures with transnational elements, there are two separate acts of the Parliament which address the different issues on cooperation with other countries in criminal matters. The general rules of mutual assistance with other countries in criminal cases are set out in Act 38 of 1996 on International Cooperation in Criminal Matters (ICCM). Equivalent rules for the European Union are set forth by Act 180 of 2012 on Cooperation in Criminal Matters between the Member states of the European Union (EUCCM). Both separate acts are to apply in line with CCP due to their speciality—in the cases not specified in the separate Acts, the CCP has to be applied as the general law.

The implementation of the Framework Decision on the European Arrest Warrant[34] was carried out by the EUCCM, while the rules on general extradition procedure are laid down in the ICCM. According to the Hungarian concept, the surrender procedure is a special form of extradition.

The EAW rules in the EUCCM are in line with the FD, in addition, the Hungarian law provides an interpretative section on the catalogue offences, which is a genuine Hungarian content.[35] This solution has advantages from the aspects of legality but, on the other hand, it restricts the flexible application of EAW rules in some cases.

6.1 Participatory Safeguards in EAW Proceedings

6.1.1 Participatory Rights Concerning the Decision on Surrender

According to Art 4 EUCCM, the Metropolitan Court has an exclusive competence to decide on surrender as executing judicial authority, the case shall be dealt with by a single judge.

If the person has been arrested in Hungary, the arrest can last until 72 h, and a trial shall be conducted on the EAW and on the execution of the surrender within this time. The concerned person shall be assisted by a defence counsel at the trial. The decision shall be made within 60 days form the day of the arrest of the concerned person. The EUCCM does not contain other specific rules on the trial, it refers to the applicability of the CCP, therefore, the CCP shall be applied in all surrender cases, the participatory rights of the concerned person can be derived from the general rules as explained above.

---

[34] 2002/584/JHA: Council Framework Decision of 13 June 2002 on the European arrest warrant and the surrender procedures between Member States.

[35] The law establishes interpretative bridges between the vague terms of the catalogue offences listed in the FD and the Hungarian Criminal Code. For example the terms "sexual exploitation of children and child pornography" shall be understood as "misuse of pornography", "sexual violence" and many other different offences provided for by the Hungarian Criminal Code.

6.1.2   *In Absentia* Proceedings in the Country of Trial and Its Relevance in the Surrender Procedure

The EUCCM excludes the surrender of the requested person if the basis of issuance of the EAW is an *in absentia* decision (for the purpose of execution of sanctions; Art. 5 par. 5). But there are numerous exemptions defined in paragraph 6 of the same Article, which, on the one hand, allow the application of EAW under certain circumstances and, on the other hand, provide guaranties in accordance with the case law requirements set out by the CJEU.[36]

Under the EUCCM, the surrender shall not be excluded if

a) the person was summoned directly in due time and was informed of the scheduled date and place of the trial or, by other means, actually received official information of the scheduled date and place of that trial and was informed that a decision may be delivered if he or she does not appear in court;

b) the requested person being aware of the scheduled trial has authorized a defence counsel, or the counsel has been appointed by the court (and the requested person did not complain against the person of the counsel appointed) to defend him or her at the trial, and the counsel actually attended the trial;

c) after being served with the decision and being expressly informed about the right to a retrial or an appeal,[37] the person expressly stated that he or she does not contest the decision or did not request a retrial or appeal within the applicable time frame;

d) the person was not personally served with the decision but s/he will be personally served with it without delay after the surrender and will be expressly informed of his or her right to a retrial or an appeal, and will be informed of the time frame within which he or she has to request for such a retrial or appeal, as mentioned in the relevant European arrest warrant. In this case, the concerned person has the right to get a file of the decision before the execution of the EAW.

6.2   *Participatory Safeguards in Trans-Border Inquiries and the Taking of Overseas Evidence*

The Hungarian criminal procedure has the general character of a continental civil law system; hence the rules of evidence serve other goals than in the Anglo-Saxon criminal procedure. The evidentiary procedure is conducted to find the truth of the facts because the criminal responsibility of a person must be founded upon the factual truth.

The Hungarian CCP represents a mixture of elements of the two main procedural systems concerning evidence; the main rule is that using evidence to prove the truth

---

[36] In particular, see the CJEU, Dworzecki judgement (C-108/16 PPU., 24. May 2016).

[37] In an appellate or retrial procedure, the person shall have the right to participate, and the procedure shall allow the merits of the case to be re-examined, including fresh evidence, which may lead to the original decision being reversed.

is free, but the CCP lists the means of proof and the rules of exclusion of evidence. The obligation of using certain evidence in special cases (e.g., in case of homicide, two experts must give opinions on the cause and circumstances of the death) belongs also to the heritage of the strict system of evidence. Furthermore, the evidence and the result of the evidentiary process shall be judged freely. The CCP does not attribute more or less persuasive evidentiary power (and probative value) to certain pieces of evidence; the judge alone is entitled (and in parallel obliged) to determine the weight of the evidence and then to form his or her conviction.

Generally, the evidence issues with transnational character are not different from those without any international links:

Foreign evidence gathered in the course of police cooperation and pre-trial judicial legal assistance become part of the case (file) in form of documents (documentary evidence). Even the hearing of witnesses or experts carried out by foreign authorities on a request of Hungarian judicial authorities will be part of the Hungarian criminal procedure in form of a document. The evidentiary procedure follows the principle of immediacy, which means that the persuasion of the judge shall only result from what the judge himself/herself has seen and heard during the trial. The court observes the evidence directly; the accused, the witness and the expert are heard (the expert's opinion is examined) by the court. Therefore, using the statement of foreign witnesses in form of minutes does not meet the principle of immediacy. In such cases the court will summon the witness to the Hungarian trial or will submit a request for witness hearing by a judge.

7 Requirements of Personal Participation and *In Absentia* Proceedings. The Perspective of Supranational and International Human Rights Law

7.1 *The Perspective of International Human Rights Law. Critical Remarks on Domestic Law in the Light of the European Convention*

See details in Sect. 5.

7.2 *The Perspective of EU Law. Developments in Domestic Law as a Result of EU Law*

In connection with the EAW, the EUCCM has been changed last year and the amendments came into force on 1 January 2017. The recent case law and the 2009/299/JHAA framework decision (of 26 February 2009) set requirements which had not been implemented into the Hungarian legal environment before, the latest amendments meet the requirements flown from EU law and jurisdiction.

8   Changes Introduced by the New Code on Criminal Procedure

From the 1st of January 2018, a new Code on Criminal Procedure will become effective in Hungary (Act Nr. XC of 2017 on the Criminal Procedure). The new Code reforms the system of the procedure and certain legal institutions in many aspects; one of the major amendments is related to the division of the tasks, i.e. procedural functions in the course of the procedure[38] and aims at this principle's more consequent prevailing. Unlike the CCP currently in force, Articles 164 and 593 of the *new* CCP make clear that only the public prosecutor is required to collect evidence and to file motions for the court examining these pieces of evidence. If s/he fails to do so, the court does not have to gather and evaluate evidence that is to support the indictment. The court's not collecting necessary evidence without evidentiary motions will not make its judgement of acquittal unsubstantiated, therefore the court of second instance cannot quash the first-instance judgment.

The more consequent division of the procedural tasks necessarily results in *strengthening the defence's position*, primarily affecting the rules of mandatory defence and the position of the appointed defence counsel. Should the ground for mandatory defence occur in the course of a procedural action, the defence counsel must be appointed immediately (Art. 46 *new* CCP). Following from this main rule, provisions applying in the phase of investigation make clear that, in such a case, the questioning of the suspect shall be postponed in order to make the attendance of the defence counsel possible (Art. 387. par. 2 *new* CCP). This new rule amends the critical situation under the current CCP, which allowed the questioning of the suspect even if the defence counsel already appointed and notified was actually not present (see above C.II.1). In case the defence is not mandatory, the defendant can still file a motion for having a counsel appointed by the authorities. In the trial phase, the court shall without discretion appoint a counsel upon the request of the defendant. In the investigation phase, the authorities shall however do so only if his/her financial situation does not enable him/her to retain a defence counsel.[39]

On the other hand, the *new* CCP sets up a new system of the *defendant's co-operation*, defines his/her position more clearly as a party. Two basic forms of cooperation are provided. The first type makes possible that the public prosecutor, the defendant and the defence counsel make, without the involvement of the court, a formal settlement on the defendant's guilty plea. In this case, the court will proceed under the rules of "Settlement procedure", in which the legality of the settlement

---

[38] I.e. Prosecution, defence and sentencing shall be separate functions in criminal proceedings.

[39] In our view, this differentiation between the phases of the procedure does not serve the equality of arms. See in details, Gácsi (2017).

shall be examined, it shall consequently be approved or refused but its content cannot be changed by the court.

The other type of co-operation can apply after the filing of the indictment, during the preparation of the trial. This kind of co-operation doesn't result in a formal settlement, it rather means the defendant's accepting his/her situation. In this case, the judgment can be made at the preparatory session of the court, a trial shall be hold exceptionally only. As for both types of co-operation, the facts and their legal qualification shall be determined by the public prosecutor and cannot be subject to settlement. A settlement can be made on the sanctions and supplementary issues. The new and dominant role of the defendant's co-operation is reflected in Art. 524 of the *new* CCP as well: in case s/he pleads guilty in the course of the trial, it can be regarded as if s/he had confessed during the preparatory session, and the trial can from then on be conducted in a simplified way.

As pointed out above (see C.I), a dispute has emerged on the issue whether *the presence at the trial* is a right or an obligation of the defendant. There has been a general demand of the authorities and the courts that the defendant's presence in the trial phase and in connection with coercive measures including the deprivation of liberty be conceived as a *right of the defendant*. This interpretation is also in harmony with the Directive (EU) 2016/343 of the European Parliament and of the Council. Therefore, the *new* CCP rules on the presence of the defendant following from this paradigm, his right to be present at the trial. If sufficient guarantees are provided, the defendant can waive of his/her right to be present; this broadens his/her right of disposition in his/her own case, the fairness of the trial can be assured, and the timeliness of the procedure can also be benefited.

Important changes are going to be introduced regarding the defendant's *access to the documents of the case during the investigation*,[40] not least due the reforms affecting the defendant's co-operation. The current rules on the generally limited access and ad hoc permissions to read the documents will be replaced by an opposite rule: full access and ad hoc limitations (Art. 100 par. 9 *new* CCP).

References

Bárd K (1987) A büntetőhatalom megosztásának buktatói – Értekezés a bírósági tárgyalás jövőjéről. KJK, Budapest

---

[40] These changes stay in connection with the significant reshaping of the system of investigation: a so-called divided investigation model will be introduced in the *new* CCP. The first phase of the investigation will be the detection, in which the facts and the person of the perpetrator have to be detected to an extent, which allows a decision to be made on the reasonable suspicion. If the reasonable suspicion has been communicated to the suspect, the second phase, the examination can be opened, where the public prosecutor can decide about the closure of investigation (Art. 348 *new* Be). The contradictory character of the examination phase is increased compared to the undivided investigation under the CCP.

Bárd K (2005) Tárgyalás a vádlott távollétében – emberijog-dogmatikai analízis. In: Ligeti K (ed) Wiener A. Imre Ünnepi Kötet. KJK-Kerszöv, Budapest, pp 209–230

Bárd K (2007) The development of Hungarian Criminal Procedure between 1985 and 2005. In: Jakab A et al (eds) The transformation of the Hungarian Legal Order 1985–2005. Kluwer Law International, The Netherlands, pp 214–233

Bárd K (2016) A sértettek eljárási jogai a nemzetközi bíróságok gyakorlatában. In: Hack P et al (eds) Kodifikációs kölcsönhatások. Tanulmányok Király Tibor tiszteletére. ELTE Eötvös Kiadó, Budapest, pp 114–140

Erdei Á (2011) Tanok és tévtanok a büntető eljárásjog tudományában. ELTE Eötvös Kiadó, Budapest

Fazekas T et al (2015) Az előzetes letartóztatás gyakorlata: az alternatív kényszerintézkedések és a bírói döntéshozatal vizsgálata. Budapest

Gácsi AE (2017) Quo vadis fegyverek egyenlőségének elve? In: Görög M – Hegedűs A (eds) Lege duce, comite familia: Ünnepi tanulmányok Tóthné Fábián Eszter tiszteletére, jogászi pályafutásának 60. évfordulójára. Iurisperitus Bt., Szeged pp 127-140

Herke C et al (2012) A büntető eljárásjog elmélete. Dialóg-Campus Kiadó, Budapest-Pécs

Irk A (1913) A magyar büntető perjog vezérfonala. Dunántúl Egyetemi Könyvkiadó és Nyomda R.-T., Pécs

Karsai K, Szomora Z (2015) Criminal law in Hungary. Kluwer Law International, The Netherlands

Király T (1962) A védő és a védelem a büntetőügyekben. KJK Kerszöv, Budapest

Király T (2003) Büntetőeljárási jog. Osiris Kiadó, Budapest

Tóth M (2012) Az Alkotmánybíróság határozata a kiemelt ügyek egyes eljárási szabályairól. Jogesetek Magyarázata 3:10–19

Ujvári Á (2011) A vádlott tárgyaláson való jelenléte a Be. 279. § (3) bekezdésének tükrében, avagy a Be. új jogintézménye: a vádlott bejelentett távolléte. In: Gál IL (ed) Tanulmányok Tóth Mihály professzor 60. születésnapja tiszteletére. Pécsi Tudományegyetem Állam- és Jogtudományi Kara, Pécs, pp 531–536

Report on Italy

Annalisa Mangiaracina

Abstract The right to take part personally in criminal proceedings, although not expressly provided at a Constitutional level, is an expression of the principle of a fair trial upheld by Article 6 of the ECHR and translated into Article 111 of the Italian Constitution. In the course of years, the CCP, also following some condemnations by the Strasbourg Court, underwent several modifications aimed at implementing principles and conditions affirmed by the ECHR that can legitimate proceedings *in absentia* of a defendant.

This study is structured into different parts. In the first, an analysis of national rules concerning the participation of a defendant and other private parties at each stage of proceedings is provided. It reveals that the right to participation is less guaranteed in proceedings—such as proceedings in front of the Supreme Court—where the technical character of questions involved do not require the personal contribution of parties, the activity of a defence lawyer being sufficient. A matter of concern is the recent reform regarding participation by means of videoconference: according to our legislators "video" participation should become a rule for certain categories of defendants, therefore undermining the right to self-defence.

In the second part, the structure of *in absentia* proceedings, following a reform introduced in 2014, is examined. Notwithstanding good intentions of legislators, it remains possible to celebrate proceedings *in absentia* also in cases where it is not certain that a defendant has received notice of the request for committal to trial. In this regard, the remedy is appreciable, although not fully satisfactory, introduced by the same legislators, and recently modified, which works after a conviction against an inculpable absent has become *res judicata*, by which judgment is quashed and the case file is forwarded to the first instance judge, with the possibility to request special proceedings (such as a summary trial and an application of penalty upon request of the parties).

In the third part, the right to participation in the field of transnational criminal justice is analysed, where new instruments adopted at EU level, such as the EIO,

A. Mangiaracina (✉)
Department of Law, Palermo University, Palermo, Italy
e-mail: annalisa.mangiaracina@unipa.it

© Springer Nature Switzerland AG 2019   229
S. Quattrocolo, S. Ruggeri (eds.), *Personal Participation in Criminal Proceedings*, Legal Studies in International, European and Comparative Criminal Law 2, https://doi.org/10.1007/978-3-030-01186-4_9

recently implemented in Italy, represent a lost opportunity in order to make effective the principle of equality of harms, from the perspective of the defence.

Abbreviations

CCas	Court of Cassation
CConst	Constitutional Court
CCP	Code of Criminal Procedure
CISA	Convention implementing the Schengen Agreement
CJEU	Court of Justice of the European Union
DirEIO	Directive on the European Investigation Order
DirPIRPT	Directive on certain aspects on the presumption of innocence and the right to be present at trial in criminal proceedings
EAW	European Arrest Warrant
ECHR	European Convention on Human Rights
ECMACM	European Convention on Mutual Legal Assistance in Criminal Matters
ECtHR	European Court of Human Rights
EIO	European Investigation Order
EU	European Union
EU-CMACM	Convention on Mutual Legal Assistance in Criminal Matters between the Member States of the European Union
FdEAW	Framework Decision on the European Arrest Warrant
FdEEW	Framework Decision on the European Evidence Warrant
ICCPR	International Covenant on Civil and Political Rights
PC	Penal Code
RICCP	Rules Implementing the Code of Criminal Procedure

1 Constitutional Requirements of the Involvement of Private Parties in Criminal Justice

It is noteworthy that any provision of the Italian Constitution expressly recognises the right of private parties to participate in a trial. Regarding a defendant, this lack of regulation does not mean that their contribution in criminal proceedings is irrelevant. The first provision to consider is Article 24 (2) which states that the "defence is an inviolable right at every stage and instance of legal proceedings". The vagueness of this formula, poses a risk of restrictive interpretation by jurisprudence. With the aim of defining the concept of defence, the Constitutional Court, in many rulings, and in the course of time, has recognised that the right to a defence has a twofold value: on the one hand, it corresponds to the right to be assisted by a lawyer, and on the other hand, to the right to "self" defence. Concerning the latter, it has been defined "as the whole of activities that the defendant can put in place to influence the development of a trial and contribute to a safe search of the truth".[1] First of all, self-defence is realised through the participation of a defendant at a trial and the possibility to give their personal contribution to the fact-finding process. However, being a right characterised by the freedom of exercise—otherwise it would not be a real defence—it can be exercised also through negative conducts: as affirmed by the Constitutional Court the "right" to defence cannot be transformed into a "duty".[2] In particular, the lack by the defendant of a duty to cooperate with the subjects of the criminal process find a regulation, at national level, in the right to not answer during the interview (in front of the public prosecutor or the judiciary police) or the examination and also in the right to be absent.

The right to participate in a trial has acquired a new meaning after the Constitutional reform of Article 111, operated by Constitutional Law no. 2/1999, that has led to the introduction of the principle of "adversary hearings" (*contradictoire*) as a core principle of the criminal system. According to Article 111 (3) the defendant "(…) shall have the right to cross-examine or to be cross-examined before a judge the persons making accusations and to summon and examine persons for the defence under the same conditions as the prosecution, as well as the right to produce all other evidence in favour of the defence (…)". The first part of this rule recognises the right to confrontation in front of a judge—to be distinguished by the right to the counter-evidence that belongs also to the public prosecutor (as provided by Article 495 CCP)—as a proper right of the defendant[3]; while the second part, recognises to the defendant the right to evidence, as an explanation of the principle of equality of harms. To make these rights effective, Article 111 (3)—in line with Article 6 (3), lett. a) ECHR and Article 14 (3), lett. a) ICCPR—recognises the right of the suspect/defendant to be informed of the charges against them and of their rights as soon as possible. Moreover, in affirming that "The guilt of the defendant cannot be established on the basis of statements by persons who, out of their own free choice, have always voluntarily avoided undergoing cross-examination by the defendant or the defence counsel" (§ 4), the Constitution has clearly stated that the right to confrontation must be exercised by persons against whom statements can be used at the trial, i.e. the defendant.

Within this framework, an interpretation aimed at privileging the objective appearance of the principle of *contradictoire*,[4] deemed as the best method of ascertainment of the facts as well as "an objective guarantee that responds to a public interest", would entail imposing upon the defendant an obligation to participate at a

---

[1] CConst, 18 December 1973, no. 186; CConst, 23 April 1975, no. 99.

[2] CConst, 15 July 1994, no. 301.

[3] Galantini (2011), p. 5.

[4] On the objective and subjective appearance of the principle of *contradictorie*, see, among others, Conti (2000), p. 197 ff.

trial. This approach has not been followed by the Constitutional Court[5] which, as regards the defendant's participation at a trial, has affirmed that the principle of *contradictorie* is a part of the right of defence: is the right of defence which must prevail, being the consent of a defendant one of the exceptions to the principle of adversary hearing.[6]

2 Personal Participation of Private Parties and Legal Assistance

Among Italian scholars, it is common to make a distinction between "parties" and "subjects" of criminal proceedings. The meaning of the expression "party of the trial" is strictly related to the concept of action: parties are persons who exercise (it is the public prosecutor) or serve the criminal action and the civil action, when the latter is exercised within criminal proceedings.

The first private party of the proceedings is the defendant. The Italian criminal procedure code has translated some fundamental rights recognised by the Italian Constitution into normative provisions. The most important of which is the right to a defence (Art. 24 (2)), which, as noted before, acquires a twofold value. On the one hand, it corresponds to the right to the assistance of a lawyer (the defendant can appoint a maximum of two lawyers), who may be chosen by the defendant (Art. 96 CCP) or appointed by the State (Art. 97 CCP) and it is deemed an inalienable right. Indeed, our code has opted for the compulsory technical defence as a form of objective guarantee. In case the defendant has not appointed a lawyer, it is the proceeding authority who has to appoint a lawyer chosen from a list. On the other hand, the right to a defence, as a personal defence, corresponds to the right of a defendant to choose how to exercise it, for instance, being absent during a trial.

Among "parties", a further distinction needs to be made between parties who are necessary, such as the public prosecutor and the defendant, and parties who are potential, with their participation in the trial the consequence of a discretional choice. Among the latter, first of all should be mentioned the person who has suffered a damage as a consequence of the crime (Art. 74 CCP). This person has the power to join the proceedings assuming the role of civil plaintiff (*parte civile*), in order to exercise the civil action for restitutions and for compensation for damages against the defendant and (eventually) the person who has a civil liability for the conduct of the defendant (*responsabile civile*, Art. 83 CCP). Regarding this, it is notable that our procedural criminal code has confirmed the distinction between the person who has suffered the crime (victim) and the person who has suffered harm as a result of the offence (injured person).[7] As a consequence of this distinction, the

---

[5] CConst, 21 March 2007, no. 117. See Negri (2014a, b), p. 124 f.

[6] Art. 111 (5) Const.

[7] Gialuz (2017), p. 33.

victim (Art. 90 CCP) may not acquire the *status* of a party in the proceedings. If the victim wishes to play a role in proceedings they must join proceedings as a civil plaintiff (Art. 75 CCP).

Following the exercise of the civil action within the criminal proceedings, another party can join the proceedings: the person who has a civil liability, based on law, for the damages provoked by the conduct of the defendant, such as parents of the minor author of the crime (Art. 83 CCP). Another potential party is the person who, having a particular relationship with the defendant, has a civil liability for the payment of the fine, should the defendant be insolvent (*civilmente obbligato per la pena pecuniaria*, Art. 89 CCP).

The first stage of the criminal proceedings where the right to participate as a civil plaintiff can be exercised is the preliminary hearing (Art. 416 CCP and following), being formally exercised the criminal action against the (possible) author of the crime who will assume the role of "accused". The request for committal to trial submitted by the public prosecutor, along with the notice of the day, time and place of the hearing shall be served by the judge on the "accused" and the "victim" of whom the identity and the address for service are specified in the documents (Art. 419 (1) CCP). Should the victim—a person who is also an injured person—decide to join criminal proceedings, they have to submit a written statement that must contain, under penalty of inadmissibility, several elements and in particular: the name of the lawyer and reference to the letter of attorney; the list of reasons justifying the request; the signature of the lawyer (Art. 78 CCP). Civil plaintiffs, as well as persons who have civil liability for damages and for fines, cannot stand trial personally, but through a lawyer (no more than one) with the special power of attorney, who represents parties along all the stages of the criminal proceedings (Art. 100 CCP). The statement to join the proceedings as civil plaintiff produces its effect at every stage and level of the proceedings. It should be highlighted that, attendance during a trial of private parties is not necessary as well as that of a lawyer who represents them, except at the end of the trial. Indeed, during the final discussion, the lawyer of the civil plaintiff has to submit written conclusions regarding the amount of damages requested (Art. 523 (2) and 82 (2) CCP).

3   Personal Participation of the Accused in Criminal Proceedings

3.1   General Features of Personal Participation: Absolute Individual Right or Duty of Diligence?

As noted before the Italian Constitution does not expressly provide for the right to personally participate in criminal trials. Notwithstanding the lack of any specific provision, the right to take part personally in criminal proceedings is strictly linked with other "fair trial" guarantees expressly recognised. According to our Constitution, as interpreted by the Constitutional Court, the right to confrontation in a condition of equality, in front of a judge third and impartial (Art. 111 (3) Cost.), implies that the participation of a defendant at a trial is an individual right. That being so, any consequence can derive from the choice of the defendant to not be present or by the refusal to contribute to the fact-finding process at the trial.[8] There is the possibility for the judge to force the defendant to appear at the trial, but only where their participation is necessary to gather evidence different from the examination (Art. 490 CCP)[9]; this exclusion is justified by the consideration that the examination of the defendant is possible only if they consent or require this means of evidence.

3.2   Personal Participation in the Pre-trial Inquiry with Particular Regard to the Interim Decisions on Coercive Measures

Regarding the participation of a person under investigation in the pre-trial inquiry, the attention should be focused on two proceedings: the discontinuing proceedings, instituted when a public prosecutor is not willing to prosecute (Art. 409 CCP) and the proceedings aim to challenge a coercive measure (Art. 309 CCP). For the possibility of the person under investigation to be examined during the special evidentiary hearing named "*incidente probatorio*", see *below*, Sect. 3.5.2.

Following Legislative decree no. 28 of 16 March 2015, a role has been recognised to a person under investigation within discontinuing proceedings[10] where a public prosecutor is not willing to prosecute a case being a person not punishable because an offence is of minor nature, according to criteria provided by Article 131-*bis* PC.[11] In this regard, a public prosecutor has the duty to notify the person under investigation and a victim of the request for the dismissal of the case also if the latter has not requested to be informed in their criminal complaint or after the filing of a criminal complaint. Both the person under investigation and the victim, are granted a look at the case file and the possibility to oppose the request, within 10 days since the serving of the request. Unlike the opposition submitted by victims within the

---

[8] At this regard see below, Sect. 3.5.2.

[9] See also Art. 399 CCP.

[10] Art. 408 CCP and ff.

[11] See Art. 411 (1*bis*) CCP. Among Italian scholars see Daniele (2015), p. 51 ff. When the public prosecutor deems the criminal complaint to be unfounded (Art. 408 (1) CCP), or there exists procedural obstacles to prosecute, or the offence has lapsed or where the act is not a criminal offence at all (Art. 411 (1) CCP), a different procedure applies that does not involve the person under investigations, unless the judge for preliminary investigations fixes a hearing. The hearing is fixed when the judge doubts the correctness of the request of the public prosecutor, or if establishes that the victim has a point in their complaint to new substantial circumstances that raise further investigation. For more details see Novokmet (2016), p. 95 ff.

traditional discontinuing proceedings,[12] the person under investigation and the victim have merely to express the reasons for disagreement with the request.[13] Concerning the victim, it is evident their personal interest in a different outcome of proceedings; regarding a person under investigation, the interest is strictly related to the effects of this type of decision. Thus, because the dismissal, requiring that a crime has been committed, although of minor nature, could be used in further proceedings by the judicial authority to assess the habitual of the offender, as an element that would prevent a new application of this specific ground for dismissal. Following an admissible opposition, the judge has to fix a hearing to decide upon a request; it is expressly provided that a decision be adopted by the heard parties.[14] In any case, parties will be heard only if they appear; indeed their participation is not mandatory.

During preliminary investigations, the judge for the preliminary investigation, under request of the public prosecutor, can apply coercive measures (such as custody or house arrest) against a person who is seriously suspected of committing a criminal offence (Art. 273 CCP). According to Article 274 CCP, these measures can be imposed if there are some specific needs to protect, such as: (a) a real and concrete threat to obtaining or the genuine character of the evidence; (b) when the defendant has escaped or the danger that he escapes is real and immediate; (c) when, due to the circumstances of the fact and the defendant's personality, there is a real and immediate danger that serious crimes or other criminal offences may be committed, similar to which they have been proceeded for. All the stages of proceedings are kept secret, and the decision on the request is adopted by the judge *de plano*. The system provides some remedies which work after the application of the measure. Against a coercive measure, applied by the judge for the first time, an interested person and their lawyer can make a request for review (*riesame*) within 10 days of the performance or service of the contested measure (Art. 309 CCP). In contrast, any other decision regarding the defendant's liberty must be challenged by means of the appeal (Art. 310 CCP). The jurisdiction to hear the request for review lies with a judicial review Tribunal (*Tribunale della libertà*), represented by the Tribunal sitting en banc, of the provincial capital of the Court of Appeal in whose district the judge who issued the contested measure is based. The request for review, which provides an overall re-examination of the grounds for pre-trial measure, has been partially amended by Law no. 47 of 16 April 2015, enacted with the aim, among others, to increase the right of participation of a person interested.[15] As noted above, these measures are applied by the judge in secret, so that the request for review is the first opportunity given to a person interested in exercising the right of defence on the basis of full knowledge of all the material collected by the prosecutor during the investigations: to make this right effective, until the date established for the hearing, the case file remains available to the defence, who can examine it and make copies.

---

[12] Art. 410 (1) CCP. See *Below*, Sect. 4.

[13] Regarding a victim see CCas, V, 25 October 2017, no. 49046.

[14] Art. 411 (1 *bis*) CCP. On this provision see CCas, V, 5 September 2016, no. 36857.

[15] See, among scholars, La Rocca (2016), p. 486 ff.; Maggio (2015), p. 89.

The request for review, to be lodged by the defendant, within 10 days since the performance of the measure, or by his lawyer within 10 days since the service of the order of the measure, according to § 6 of Article 309 CCP can be motivated and, according to the new phrase added by the legislator in 2015, the defendant may ask to personally appear in front of the Tribunal. This provision must be read in conjunction with the period added in § 8-*bis* where it is written that a defendant who has requested to participate in the hearing has the right to appear. This rule is aimed at avoiding some interpretations of the previous provisions that excluded the right to personally participate in the hearing in the case of defendants detained outside the district of the Tribunal. That was because according to the general rule provided by Article 127 CCP—recalled by Article 308 (8) CCP—participation was not deemed as necessary: within the model described by Article 127 CCP,[16] the interested party has the right to be heard if they appear, while, where they are detained outside the Tribunal's district and make a request, they have the right to be heard, before the hearing, by the judge of surveillance (Art. 127 (3) CCP). It is to say that also in the case of a person detained in the same district of the Tribunal, according to jurisprudence, the request to appear, although with the lack of a specific normative term, had to be formulated "without delay" (Art. 101 (2) RICCP) and often was not accepted.[17] It was because the concept of timeliness led to a wide discretion of the judicial authority.

Following the reform, the Tribunal has not any discretionary power in front of the request to take part in the hearing. With § 8-*bis* being a special rule—in relation to Article 127 CCP—it is not possible to delegate the hearing of the person who is detained outside the district of the Tribunal to the judge of surveillance of that place. The only exception is applicable in cases provided by Article 146-*bis* RICCP, where the participation in the trial is guaranteed through a video-conference.[18] Concerning subjects and terms for the request to appear, jurisprudence has clarified that it can also be presented by a lawyer appointed by the State and it is to be submitted "together with the request for review". According to jurisprudence[19] this "strict" term does not prejudice the right of defence because a few days before the hearing in front of the Tribunal the defendant has the possibility to defend during the interview of "guarantee"[20] performed by the judge within—respectively—5 or 10 days from the imposition of the detention measure, depending on whether pre-trial detention or other measures are involved. As a consequence of this reasoning, the right to defence at the hearing has a minor relevance because it is subordinated to the will of the defendant who can also decide to make spontaneous statements at the hearing and in almost cases these declarations are a mere repetition of what a defendant said

---

[16] *Below*, Sect. 3.3.

[17] CCas, II, 5 November 2014, no. 6023.

[18] *Below*, Sect. 3.7.

[19] CCas, I, 6 October 2015, no. 49882; CCas, II, 11 March 2016, no. 13707; *contra* CCas, II, 3 April 2017, no. 36160, that has excluded the necessity to submit the request together with the request for review.

[20] Art. 294 CCP.

during the interview. These arguments are not persuasive, not considering that during the interview a defendant does not have any knowledge of the investigation file and finally restrict the right to participate to the right to make spontaneous statements. Lastly, it is worthy of mention in the perspective to recognise to the detained the right to appear in case of legitimate impediment as well as the right to better prepare their defence, the new provision of § 9-*bis*, according to which under request personally submitted by a defendant within 2 days since the notification of the advice of the hearing, the Tribunal can postpone the hearing from a minimum of 5 days until a maximum of 10 days if there are justified reasons.[21]

Another remedy provided by the criminal procedure code, to challenge the decision of the court proceedings relating to an instance of revocation or amendment of precautionary measure already in place, is the appeal (Art. 310 CCP). The appeal is available to a Public prosecutor, a defendant and their lawyer and, unlike the request for review must be motivated. At the appeal stage, general rules provided by Article 127 CCP apply[22]: in the lack of a specific recall to rule provided by § 8-*bis* of Article 309 CCP, the right of a defendant detained in a different place to take part at the hearing seems to be excluded. The last remedy is the recourse to the Supreme Court (Art. 311 CCP) that may be used by an interested person, his lawyer and a public prosecutor against measures issued by the Tribunal in charge of a complaint as a result of the complaint or appeal against a precautionary measure. A person interested and their lawyer may also appeal immediately to the Supreme Court but only for breaches of law against decisions which apply a coercive measure. A decision is adopted by the Supreme Court following provisions provided for in Article 127 CCP.

It is to note that a defendant (and a public prosecutor) can ask at any time for a revocation or modification of a measure in place (Art. 299 CCP). The request is decided by a judge without a hearing[23]: he has a duty to hear a public prosecutor who has to express their opinion within 2 days, otherwise a judge can autonomously take a decision. However, before deciding, a judge may question the person under investigation. If the request for revocation or substitution is based on new reasons or reasons different from those already evaluated, the judge is obliged to question the person subjected to the measure who requested to be heard (Art. 299 (3-*ter*) CCP).

---

[21] CCas, S.U., 20 July 2017, no. 47970, para. 5.

[22] See Sect. 3.3.

[23] A different procedure, aimed at involving the victim, is provided by Article 299 (3) CCP where a request for revocation or substitution concerns measures provided for in Articles 282-*bis* (Injunction to stay away from the family house), 282-*ter* (Injunction to stay away from the places attended by the victim), 283 (Prohibition and obligation of abode), 284 (House arrest), 285 (Precautionary detention in prison) and 286 (Precautionary detention in a healthcare centre) CCP, applied in proceedings for offences committed with violence against the victim.

3.3   *Personal Participation in Proceedings* **In Camera**

In the criminal procedure code, there is a general provision concerning proceedings *in camera*: Article 127 CCP.[24] These proceedings have two main characteristics: the absence of a public (§ 6) and, more importantly, participation of parties and of other persons interested is eventual, being heard only if they appear at a hearing. As a general model, they apply in different contexts: but it should be said that in some cases rules provided by Article 127 CCP are integrally applied, while on the other there are some differences, mainly related to the orality principle (the latter is the case, above mentioned, of a hearing following a request for review). According to the general rule, a public prosecutor, parties and their lawyers are heard at a hearing if they appear; it is to underline that in the notice of the hearing it is not provided that the defendant has the right to participate at the trial. A specific provision concerns the participation of a defendant who is detained in a place outside the district of the judge: if this person requires to be heard, they must be heard the day before a hearing, by a judge of surveillance of a place where it is restricted (§ 3). It means that a hearing is held by a judge who is not the person legitimate to take a decision on the case, so waiving the principle of immediacy. According to § 4 of Article 127 CCP the postponement of a hearing is subjected to some conditions: (a) a legitimate impediment of a defendant; (b) the request by a defendant to take part in proceedings; (c) a defendant must not be detained in a place other than where a judge of that hearing is. Regarding the second condition, although any advertisement is provided in the advice for a hearing, according to jurisprudence, a defendant has to express their will 5 days before a hearing: the term corresponds to that provided by § 2 for the submission of briefs. According to jurisprudence, unlike rules which apply at a preliminary hearing (Art. 420-*ter* CCP) and at a trial (Art. 484 (2-*bis*)), any relevance has the impediment of a lawyer to proceedings held *in camera*.[25]

3.4   *Personal Participation in Alternative Proceedings*

As a general principle, participation of a defendant in alternative proceedings is not mandatory. Alternative proceedings provided by the Italian criminal procedure code can be broken down into two general categories: proceedings that eliminate a trial and proceedings that jump a summary hearing. In the first category, it mentions a summary trial (*giudizio abbreviato*, Art. 438 CCP) and the application of a penalty

---

[24] In general, on proceedings *in camera*, see Di Chiara (1994), passim; Fonti (2008), p. 43 ff.

[25] At this regard it is to note that the Supreme Court, following an interpretation based on the respect of Art. 111 Constitution, has recognised the relevance of a legitimate impediment within an appeal against a judgment adopted following a summary trial (CCas, S.U., 21 July 2016, no. 41432), and within proceedings before the Sentence Supervision Tribunal *ex* Art. 678 CCP (CCas, I, 3 May 2017, no. 27074).

under request (*applicazione della pena su richiesta delle parti*, Art. 444 CCP). Regarding a summary trial, it is a special proceeding requested by an accused personally or through their lawyer with the power of attorney, at a preliminary hearing. A defendant renounces to the guarantees of a trial and, as an advantage, in case of conviction, has the right to a reduction of a penalty in the measure of one third if the judgment concerns a crime and of a half in case of a misdemeanour (Art. 442 (2) CCP). As said before, a summary trial is requested and celebrated within the preliminary hearing, so general rules relating to this hearing apply. A damaged party who has already join proceedings as a civil plaintiff could not accept the abbreviated proceedings (Art. 441 (2) CCP). As a consequence, civil proceedings instituted for compensation of damages will not be suspended (Art. 441 (4) CCP), as generally provided for by Article 75 (3) CCP when civil proceedings are initiated after a civil-law complaint has been lodged before a criminal court. Furthermore, a damaged party does not risk any binding effects of the criminal judgment on the civil proceedings initiated by them or in their interest (Art. 652 (1) CCP).[26]

At this stage, attendance of a public prosecutor and a lawyer of a defendant is mandatory, but not of a defendant requiring a summary trial, being in this case represented by their lawyer. Neither is the personal participation necessary by a defendant, in case of a summary trial subjected to the condition of gathering new evidence (Art. 438 (5) CCP), both at the moment of a request—that can be submitted by a lawyer with the power of attorney—both at the moment of the gathering of evidence. Personal participation of a defendant at a summary trial could become relevant should a public prosecutor, after the gathering of evidence requested by a defendant or admitted *ex officio* by the judge, change a criminal charge[27]: in this case a defendant may ask to proceed through an ordinary trial (Art. 441-*bis* CCP). Regrettably, according to jurisprudence, a defendant who is absent at a hearing, being represented by their lawyer, does not have the right to be personally informed of a change, being sufficient that changes are communicated to their lawyer, in application of Article 423 CCP related to a preliminary hearing.[28] This interpretation poses some problems, depriving a defendant of the right of defence: following this interpretation, they could be convicted of an offence they would have preferred to challenge at a trial, with the guarantees accorded by Article 111 of the Constitution.[29]

Regarding the application of penalty upon request of the parties (Art. 444 CCP), the will or the consent by a defendant to conclude an agreement related to a penalty with a public prosecutor can be expressed personally or through their lawyer with the power of attorney. Any role has a civil plaintiff within the agreement. Moreover, once delivered the application of penalty, the defendant shall only be ordered by the

---

[26] For considerations on this regard see Ruggeri (2017), p. 66 ff.

[27] On this institute, as it works at different stage of criminal proceedings, see Cassibba (2016), p. 177 ff.

[28] CCas, V, 3 February 2015, no. 23983.

[29] See Negri (2014a, b), p. 260 f.; Cassibba (2016), p. 220.

judge to pay costs incurred by a civil plaintiff, unless there are valid grounds for full or partial compensation (Art. 444 (2) CCP). These proceedings are normally requested during a preliminary hearing,[30] within the time limit set to formulate the conclusions (Art. 446 (1) CCP). Should a judge deem the opportunity to verify the voluntariness of the request or of the consent, they can request the personal appearance of a defendant (Art. 446 (5) CCP). The application of a penalty upon request can be requested by parties also during preliminary investigations to the judge for preliminary investigations (Art. 447 CCP). In this case the judge fixes a hearing for a decision,[31] that is celebrated *in camera*. At a hearing, a public prosecutor and a lawyer are heard if they appear (Art. 447 (2) CCP), not being their participation mandatory. A victim, according to jurisprudence,[32] is not among subjects that have to receive notice of the hearing. Regarding a damaged party, at this stage, cannot still join proceedings as a civil plaintiff.

Within the category of proceedings that skip a preliminary hearing there is a direct trial (*giudizio direttissimo*) and an immediate trial (*giudizio immediato*). A direct trial is available in different situations, each involving strong evidence of a defendant's culpability. The first situation involves defendants caught and arrested in the act of committing a crime. Under such circumstances, a prosecutor may bring a defendant before a trial judge within 48 h to have an arrest ratified and the matter set for immediate trial (Art. 449 (1) CCP). Should an arrest not been ratified by a trial judge it remains possible to immediately celebrate the trial if the defendant and the public prosecutor consent. The third application concerns situations in which an arrest has been ratified by the judge for preliminary investigations: in this case the prosecutor brings the defendant before the trial judge within 30 days since being arrested, unless this may create a prejudice for investigations. The fourth situation permits an immediate trial under *giudizio direttissimo* involving defendants who have made a full confession to a public prosecutor. When this occurs, a prosecutor requests a *giudizio direttissimo* within 30 days of recording the crime in the crime register, unless this may create a prejudice for investigations. Another situation is provided for when a person has been urgently removed from a family house according to Article 384-*bis* CCP: the judiciary police, under request of a public prosecutor, can summon the person for a direct trial and the ratification of an arrest within the following 48 h, unless this may create a prejudice for investigations. A few concerns arise, with regard to the Constitutional frame, the possibility for a public prosecutor, when proceeding to the *giudizio direttissimo*, to impose the presence at a trial of a defendant who has been arrested or subjected to the application of a precautionary measure (Art. 450 (1) CCP). In fact, there are many scholars[33] who think that a

---

[30] See Article 448 (1) CCP, regarding conditions for the submission of the request in front of the first-instance judge.

[31] CCas, VI, 4 April 2017, no. 23049, that has affirmed the duty to fix a hearing.

[32] CCas, V, 8 June 2016, no. 30941. Thus, because a victim cannot intervene in the agreement. See Trib. Torino, 28 January 2014, www.penalecontemporaneo, 3 March 2014, last accessed 31.7.2018, according to which whether a victim has knowledge of the hearing can intervene and submit briefs.

[33] Chiliberti et al. (1994), p. 485. On the debate among scholars see Negri (2014a, b), p. 294 ff.

public prosecutor can obtain, also with coercion, the presence of a defendant at a trial because Article 451 (4) CCP requires the public prosecutor bring an accusation against an accused present at a trial. This point of view undermines the fact that the participation at a trial is not a duty but the result of a free choice. Should a defendant decide not to participate at a trial, to proceed with these special proceedings it would be necessary to adopt a decree for committal to trial.

An immediate trial is intended for use in situations in which evidence against a defendant is very strong (Art. 453 CCP). The criminal procedure code provides that within 90 days of commencing investigation of a crime, where an inquiry has revealed conclusive evidence against a defendant and after a defendant has been interrogated or asked to give a statement, a public prosecutor, unless the request may prejudice the investigations, may ask a judge for preliminary investigation to set the matter for trial without holding a preliminary hearing (Art. 453 (1) CCP). According to the criminal procedure code, it is sufficient that a person has been put in the condition of being heard: should not appear at a fixed interview, a public prosecutor can ask for an immediate trial, unless a defendant did not appear for a reason of a legitimate impediment or because it was not founded. A public prosecutor may ask for an immediate trial also for an offence that has led to the application of a coercive measure, unless the request may prejudice the investigations (Art. 453 (1-*bis*) CCP). There is no hearing upon request; a judge for preliminary investigation merely reviews the records of the investigation,[34] which a prosecutor submits for review, and rules within 5 days. Should a judge for preliminary investigations rule to proceed with an immediate trial, within 15 days since the serving of the decree fixing the trial, a defendant may ask for a summary trial or the application of a penalty under request or the probation. Otherwise, it will be celebrated a trial following ordinary rules, including provisions related to the *absentia*, as is made clear by reference to Article 429 (1) and (2) CCP by Article 456 (1) CCP.

The last special proceedings to mention, introduced by the Italian legislator by Law no. 67 of 28 April 2014, with the main aim of speeding up the trial, is the probation of proceedings for adults (Art. 464-*bis* CCP).[35] In cases provided for in Article 168-*bis* PC, proceedings can be suspended when the defendant requests to be given a probation period to repair the harmful or dangerous consequences of the offence committed and, where possible, to compensate the injured party for the damages caused. It can be requested by a defendant during preliminary investigations (in this case it is necessary the consent of a public prosecutor), or at a preliminary hearing, or at a first hearing in front of a single judge (§ 2); the will can be expressed by a defendant personally or through their lawyer with the power of attorney. As well as for the application of a penalty under request, should a judge deem the opportunity to verify the voluntariness of the request, the personal appearance of the defendant may be required (Art. 464-*quater* (2) CCP). During the suspension

---

[34] The judge has to check respect of terms: CCas, S.U., 26 June 2014, no. 42979.

[35] See CConst, 21 February 2018, no. 91, that has recognised the compliance of these proceedings with the Constitution.

of proceedings pending probation, it could be necessary to gather an evidence that it is not possible to defer at the end of the period of probation. At this regard, Article 464-*sexies* CCP provides that the Tribunal shall, upon request of a party, in compliance with the rules applying at a trial (i.e. the *contradictorie*), gather two types of evidence: non-deferrable evidence and evidence that may lead to dismissal of the defendant.

It is to note that during the suspension of proceedings pending probation, according to Article 464-*quinquies* (3) CCP, the Tribunal may modify the original prescriptions imposed on a defendant, provided that the new prescriptions comply with the aims of probation. In this case the Tribunal has to decide after hearing the defendant and the public prosecutor, but is not required the consent of a defendant. By contrast, the consent is necessary at the hearing fixed to decide on probation, where the Tribunal intends to add information to or modify the treatment plan (Article 464-*quater* (4) CCP. A participatory right, although in accordance with the model of proceedings *in camera* regulated by Article 127 CCP, is recognised to a defendant (and also to a victim) at the end of the probation period, should the Tribunal declare that the suspension is revoked.[36]

Concerning the penal order procedure provided for in Article 459 CCP, see *below*, Sect. 5.3.

3.5 Personal Participation at Trial

3.5.1 Personal Involvement in the Evidence-Gathering

The possibility of the defendant contributing to evidence-gathering appears in very clear terms from the formulation of Article 111 (3) of our Constitution which, like the ECHR, ensures to the accused the right either to examine or to 'have examined the witnesses against him'. As a general principle, evidence is admitted upon request of a party[37] and the judicial authority only in exceptional cases, expressly provided by the law, may gather evidence at his own initiative.[38] Any part interested in the gathering of evidence, at least 7 days prior to the date set for the trial, must file with the Tribunal Registry, a list of persons to be examined (witnesses, experts, persons referred to in Article 210 CCP), specifying the circumstances on which their examination must be based, so to inform other parties of proceedings. The party who intends to request the gathering of the records of evidence from other criminal proceedings must submit an explicit request upon filing the list.[39]

Regarding the gathering of oral evidence at a trial, it is based on the cross-examination. As noted above, defendants do not have the right to defend themselves

---

[36] Art. 464-*octies* CCP.

[37] Art. 190 (1) CCP.

[38] Art. 507 (1) CCP.

[39] Art. 468 (1 and 4-*bis*) CCP.

personally but through legal assistance: so cross-examination of incriminating witnesses, such as examination of defence witnesses, experts, private parties, is an activity restricted to a lawyer. At this regard, a defendant who participates in a trial, has the right to sit close to their lawyer during proceedings. In recognising the importance of the personal contribution of a defendant, Italian criminal procedure code acknowledges a defendants' right to be present, at their own request, at the hearing of witnesses, experts and technical advisors of the parties, examined in their domicile in exceptional cases.[40] Remarkably, in the case of special evidentiary hearing, where evidence is gathered following the procedure set for a trial, the criminal procedure code allowed the person under investigation (and also the victim) to participate at the hearing when a witness or a different person must be examined, while in other cases it is necessary an authorisation.[41]

The evidence taken in other proceedings is subjected to a special regulation aimed at strengthening the right to *contradictorie*.[42] In particular, evidence gathered at a special evidentiary hearing or at a trial can be taken, but the records of statements may be used against the accused only if the lawyer has taken part in evidence gathering.[43] As a general rule, without prejudice to Article 190-*bis* CCP, the parties maintain the right to obtain, under Article 190 CCP which regulates the admission of evidence, the examination of persons whose statements have been taken as evidence, where the evidence is repeatable.[44]

A question that raises concern among scholars[45] is related to the introduction by Law no. 479 of 16 December 1999 of a mechanism, based on the consent, allowing for the parties to agree that specific pieces of evidence gathered by either the police or the prosecutor or the defence and contained in the investigative dossier, are inserted into the trial file,[46] so being usable by the judge for the decision. At this regard, lawyers can reach an agreement with the prosecutor and the other parties also where their clients have not provided them with the special power to do so and even regardless of whether the defendants were in any case informed on this important decision. As a result, the decision of the judge could be based on the content of

---

[40] Art. 502 (2) CCP.

[41] Art. 401 (3) CCP.

[42] Ferrua (2017), p. 5, according to whom evidence could be used if is in favour of the defendant.

[43] Art. 238 (2-*bis*) CCP.

[44] Art. 238 (5) CCP.

[45] Ruggeri (2017), p. 92 ff.

[46] Agreements can be reached at the end of a preliminary hearing, after the decree for committal to trial, when the two files are set up (Art. 431 (2) CCP), or at the moment of request for evidence (Art. 493 (3) CCP). According to Art. 500 (7) CCP, regarding the use of out-of-court statements aimed at challenging the witness's credibility during a trial, upon agreement of the parties, the statements contained in the investigative dossier that had been previously made by the witness can be included in the trial dossier.

the investigative dossier, without any consideration for the real will of a defendant,[47] especially in case of a defendant who is absent.

It should be noted that according to Article 490 CCP a judge can authorise the coercive participation of a defendant at a trial for the gathering of evidence different from their examination. In the lack of a specification, the rule has been interpreted in the sense that a judge can use this power also for the confrontation between defendants.[48] The same rule applies at the special evidentiary hearing where a person under investigation is absent without pleading a legal impediment and their presence is necessary to gather evidence.[49] Still remaining in the area of the "coercive" contribution of a defendant, Article 224-*bis* CCP should be mentioned, concerning the decision of a judge on expert evidence involving actions affecting personal freedom. If the collection of expert evidence requires either actions affecting personal freedom, such as the sampling of hair or mucosa from the oral cavity of a living person to determine their DNA profile, or medical checks and the person to be examined by an expert does not provide their consent, the judge shall, also *ex officio*, issue an order to direct that such actions be nonetheless performed, if they are deemed essential to prove events. This rule is aimed at reaching a balancing between protection of personal freedom and interest of justice in ascertain crimes.

Lastly, it is to say that the power to collect evidence by a defence lawyer[50] can be exercised at every stage of criminal proceedings, included a trial. Are also admitted preventive investigations (Art. 391-*nonies* CCP). In any case, it is forbidden participation of a defendant, as well as of a victim and other private parties, at the interview performed by a defence lawyer following Article 391-*bis* CCP with whoever is able to provide information relevant for the reconstruction of the facts.

3.5.2   Personal Contribution to the Fact-Finding

A defendant present at a trial is not obliged to actively participate: should they decide to take an active role, they can give their contribution in a different manner. After the opening of a trial, a defendant is advised by a judge that at every stage of the trial they can make spontaneous statements under the condition that they are related to the charge and does not hinder the trial[51]: if during these statements a defendant does not respect the mentioned conditions, the judge can admonish a defendant and should they persist will be interrupted. A special rule applies if a preliminary hearing has been celebrated *in absentia*: a defendant can require to

---

[47] See CConst, 4 June 2001, n. 81. The Italian Constitutional Court, in declaring the inadmissibility of the question, has affirmed that lawyers, thanks to their knowledge in legal matters, can make the most proper decision in the interest of their clients.

[48] Art. 211 CCP.

[49] Art. 399 CCP.

[50] Art. 391-*bis* and following CCP.

[51] Art. 494 CCP.

make spontaneous statements during a stage that comes before the opening of a trial. Regarding a preliminary hearing, the defendant can exercise the right to defence, through spontaneous statements or an interview[52]: under request of a party, the interview will take place applying rules on cross-examination.[53]

The privileged tool to acquire the contribution of a defendant at a trial is the examination,[54] that is in the availability of a party. Indeed, a defendant—like other private parties—can be heard during a trial through the cross-examination if they make a specific request or consent to the request made by other parties of a trial. As a general rule, a defendant is not obliged to answer truthfully—not being a witness—and during an examination could refuse to answer some questions: but the refusal must be recorded in the record of the hearing.[55] Thus, demonstrates that the silence opposed by a defendant can be assessed as an argument of evidence: it means that a judge could not deem a defendant reliable.[56] A defendant could also report information on facts they have been heard from other persons, but are not obliged to indicate the person or the source that informed them, such as for the witness.[57] Regarding the procedural aspects, examination of a defendant (and of other private parties) takes place after the examination of witnesses by the public prosecutor (and by civil plaintiffs). This rule[58] is justified by the necessity to avoid that a defendant can inspire their statements by declarations of defence witnesses who are heard after a public prosecutor's witnesses. For the sake of completeness, it can be said that a person under investigation can be examined also during preliminary investigations or within a preliminary hearing through the evidentiary hearing (*incidente probatorio*). According to Article 392 (1) lett. c) CCP, a public prosecutor and a person under investigation can ask for the special evidentiary hearing to proceed for the examination of a person under investigation on conducts concerning criminal responsibility of other persons. Being gathered in respect of the adversarial procedure, evidence becomes part of a file for a trial (*fascicolo per il dibattimento*). However, as a general principle, with the aim of guaranteeing the right of defence, evidence gathered in the context of the special evidentiary hearing shall be used at trial exclusively against defendant whose lawyer have participated in evidence gathering.[59]

---

[52] Art. 421 (2) CCP.

[53] Arts. 498 and 499 CCP.

[54] Art. 208 CCP.

[55] Art. 209 (2) CCP.

[56] See CCas, II, 21 December 2017, no. 57152: in assessing the evidence gathered, the judge may also consider the silence opposed by the defendant on circumstances useful for the defence.

[57] Art. 195 CCP.

[58] Art. 150 RICCP.

[59] Art. 403 (1) CCP.

3.6 Personal Participation in Higher Instances

It is to note that different rules apply for proceedings of second and third instance.

Regarding an appeal stage there are two different proceedings: one held in public and another *in camera*. When an appeal has to be celebrated in a public hearing, rules specifically provided in Articles 601–605 CCP must be read in conjunction with rules that apply at a first stage, because of the clause provided in Article 598 CCP.[60] The Court of Appeal has to ascertain regular attendance of parties in a trial and in the notice regarding the date of a hearing in appeal it is expressly specified that should a defendant not appear, a trial will be celebrated according to rules provided by Articles 420-*bis*, 420-*ter* and 420-*quinquies* CCP (Art. 601 (3) CCP). The attendance of a defendant has a relevance especially in case of renewal of the trial evidentiary hearing by the Court.[61]

More complex is the regulation of an appeal celebrated *in camera* (Art. 599 CCP) because there is a general recall by § 1 to Article 127 CCP, that concerns the model of proceedings *in camera*, with some exceptions. According to Article 599 CCP an appeal is celebrated *in camera*—a model aimed at guaranteeing the speed of a trial—only where it has as an object the kind or the measure of a penalty, also with reference to comparisons among circumstances, or the applicability of generic lenient circumstances. The same procedure applies in case of appeal against judgments adopted within a summary trial (Art. 443 CCP), as well as against agreement on the arguments for appeal also with waiver ("*concordato anche con rinuncia ai motivi di appello*"), regulated by Article 599-*bis* CCP.[62] A trial is postponed if there is a legitimate impediment of a defendant who has expressed the will to appear (§ 2): if a defendant has expressed the will to appear and is not led to a trial, the consequence is that the trial and the judgment adopted will be nulled. As it is evident, Article 599 (2) CCP is deemed a special rule with respect to Article 127 (4) CCP where a further condition is provided, whereby a defendant must not be detained outside the district of the judge. This interpretation, as underlined by jurisprudence, favors the right to participation of a defendant. For the same reason, the second condition that the request of being present must be lodged within the term of 5 days before a trial provided by Article 127 (2) CCP does not apply. Also in this regard, the special rule of Article 599 CCP prevails, that does not establish any term for the expression of will to appear.[63] Regarding the term, although there is not a term fixed by law to express the will to appear, this does not exclude that the request has to be

---

[60] According to this article "The provisions concerning the first-instance trial shall be observed in the appeal trial, if applicable, without prejudice to the provisions of the following Articles".

[61] Art. 603 CCP. Following case-law of the ECtHR, Italian legislators have introduced, by Law no. 103 of 23 June 2017, the so-called "Orlando Reform", a new § 3-*bis* in Art. 603 CCP, so structured: "If the public prosecutor appeals against a judgment of dismissal on grounds concerning the evaluation of oral evidence, the appeal court shall order the renewal of the trial evidentiary hearing". See, among others, Bronzo (2017), p. 409 ff.

[62] Introduced by Law no. 103/2017. For a comment see Marandola (2017), p. 389 ff.

[63] CCas, S. U., 24 June 2010, no. 35399; CCas, Sez. III, 17 November 2015, no. 4077.

made—unless a defendant is inept, as it is in a case they have been restricted a few days before a trial—in a way that is possible to led them to a trial.[64] A defendant who is detained, has the duty to communicate to the Court of Appeal their will to appear, with the consequence that the legitimate impediment, included the *status detentionis*, is irrelevant if the defendant does not fulfill their duty to communicate the impediment and the will to appear. Within an appeal *in camera*, a defendant, under detention or under measures that restrict their personal freedom, has the right to require the authorization to appear at a trial and in front of the request, there is a duty for a judge to led them to the trial, with the celebration of a trial in the absence of a defendant being prohibited. Should an Appeal judge renew the evidence, a Court will hear evidence *in camera*, with the necessary participation of the public prosecutor as well as of the lawyer. If lawyers are not present when the renewal is ordered, the Appeal Court shall set a new hearing and order that a copy of the decision be notified to the public prosecutor and served on the lawyers.

Regarding participation of a lawyer within proceedings held *in camera*, according to jurisprudence, in case of an appeal against a judgment adopted within a summary trial, it is relevant the legitimate impediment of a lawyer who has decided to take part in a trial but is unable to appear due to vis major, unpredictable events or illness.[65] In this case, there is no doubt that a different reasoning by the Court, would have prejudiced the right of defense.

The Court of last instance is the Italian Court of Cassation, based in Rome, whose task is to ensure the exact observance and uniform interpretation of law, the unity of law, and the division of competence between different jurisdictions. It is important to underline that the Court of Cassation does not take cognizance of the merits of the case, its purpose being to state whether law has been correctly applied on the basis of fact already definitively assessed in decisions referred to it. Indeed, the model of participation of a defendant in front of the Court of Cassation is conditioned by the consideration that this body deals with questions of judicial character that do not require the personal contribution of a defendant. The impossibility for the Court of Cassation to assess the merit of the case legitimate the exclusion of personal participation of a defence. Following the reform introduced by Law no. 103/2017, aimed at reducing the amount of applications to the Supreme Court, the application for appeal to the Court cannot be signed by the defendant personally, but under penalty of inadmissibility, by lawyers recorded in the special register of the Court of Cassation (Art. 613 (1) CCP).[66]

In front of the Court of Cassation there are two proceedings: one held *in camera* and another in public. Regarding the first, Article 611 CCP is the general rule which applies in case of appeals against decisions not adopted in a trial (such as an appeal against the pronounce there are no grounds for prosecution issued by a judge of a

---

[64] CCas, II, 22 June 2016, no. 28780; CCas, S.U., 24 June 2010, n. 35399.

[65] CCas, S.U., 21 July 2016, no. 41432.

[66] According to CCas, S.U., 21 December 2017, no. 8914, this is a general principle to apply against every type of decision.

preliminary hearing and confirmed by the Court of Appeal[67]): an exception applies for judgments adopted at the end of a summary trial, being special proceedings that can be used also for serious crimes where complexity of matter would require personal participation of a defence. Article 611 CCP also applies at a preliminary stage, where the President of the Court of Cassation finds a reason for inadmissibility of the appeal to the Court itself. In such a case, the President shall assign the recourse to a specific chamber of the Court of Cassation. The President of the chamber shall set the date for the decision; then the Court Registry shall inform the General Prosecutor and the lawyers about the filing of the case and the date of the hearing, celebrated following Article 611 CCP. The reform introduced by Law no. 103/2017 where provides (Art. 610 (1)) that notice of the hearing shall contain the specification of the cause for inadmissibility identified from the grounds for the appeal to the Court of Cassation, listed in Article 606 (1) CCP, should make effective the right of defence, although exercised in a written form, at this relevant stage of proceedings.

The main characteristic of these proceedings is the written debate among parties. Indeed, the notice of the hearing must be communicated to the General Prosecutor and defence 20 days before a hearing, with the possibility to submit new grounds of appeal and briefs 15 days before the hearing and to reply through briefs 5 days before. No participation of the parties is provided for. New proceedings "without any formal procedure" have been introduced by Law no. 103/2017 in Article 610 (5-*bis*) CCP. According to the new text, the Court of Cassation has to adopt these proceedings for the declaration of inadmissibility of the appeal to the Court in the cases provided for in Article 591 (1), a), exclusively as regards to the lack of entitlement to lodge an appellate remedy, b), c), except for the non compliance with Article 581, and d). The same procedure applies for the inadmissibility of the appeal against judgments adopted following an application of penalty upon request of parties (Art. 444 CCP), as well as delivered in accordance with the new Article 599-*bis* CCP. According to scholars,[68] the lack of a written debate in these proceedings may create a deep crisis of Article 111 (2) of the Constitution, where it is required, as a general method of the jurisdiction, the "adversary proceedings" further to Article 24 (2) of the Constitution, regarding the right of self-defence.

If the proceedings are held in public (Art. 614 CCP), it is provided that parties can appear through their defence who represent them. This participation, only eventual for the defence, finds its *ratio* in the consideration that all parties have to introduce questions to be discussed in advance; also briefs have to be presented 15 days before the hearing. This procedure leads to the consideration that a defendant cannot find an opportunity of participation with the development of the hearing. It should be recognised the right to be present at the hearing, if the Supreme Court should change the juridical qualification of the offence, with negative consequences for a defendant.

---

[67] See Art. 428 (3 *ter*) CCP, as introduced by Law no. 103/2017.
[68] See De Caro (2017), p. 240 f.; Marafioti and Del Coco (2018), p. 100.

3.7   Special Rules in the Field of Serious Organised Crimes

In Italy, the need to fight against mafia crimes have led legislators to the introduction of a "double-track" regime, that in the course of the years has extended to different categories of crimes (such as sexual offences).[69] Our criminal procedure code provides special rules for serious organised crimes, at different stages: investigations, trial, sentencing and imprisonment. Regarding the trial, the right of a defendant to confrontation with a witness is subject to the limits laid down by Article 190-*bis* (1) CCP. Following this rule, in proceedings regarding one of the crimes referred to in Article 51 (3-*bis*) CCP (such as mafia organized crimes, drug trafficking organised crimes), should a request be made for the examination of a witness, or one of the persons referred to in Article 210 and should such a person have already provided statements during the special evidentiary hearing or at a trial in the cross-examination, with the person against whom the same statements will be used or have provided statements whose records have been gathered under Article 238 CCP, the examination by the judge shall be admitted only if it concerns facts or circumstances other than those included in the previous statements or if it is requested by the court or a party by virtue of specific needs. A provision, that, unlike general rule (Art. 190 CCP), leaves a significant margin of discretion to the competent authorities in deciding on the admission of the oral evidence. Should the request be rejected, the judge, for the purposes of deliberation, will use previous statements made in front a different judicial authority.

Regarding participation at a trial, security concerns against mafia suspects have conducted legislators to the introduction of the possibility of ensuring the participation at a trial of certain categories of defendants by means of videoconference (Art. 146-*bis* RICCP, introduced by Law no. 11 of 7 January 1998).[70] Recently, by Law no. 103/2017, legislators have significantly modified Article 146-*bis* RICCP, transforming the recourse to participation by means of a videoconference in rule rather

---

[69] See, for instance, Art. 190-*bis* (2) CCP.

[70] The first provision was introduced by Legislative decree no. 306 of 8 June 1992, converted into Law no. 356 of 7 August 1992—Art. 14-*bis* RICCP—aimed at protecting the security of "collaborators of justice" who are examined at a trial. According to this provision videoconferences can also be used—unless a judge considers personal participation as necessary—when within proceedings for offences provided for in Art. 51 (3 *bis*) or 407 (2) subparagraph (a) no. 4 of CCP, defendants must be examined in related proceedings (Art. 210 CCP), against whom are pending proceedings for one of the offences provided for in Art. 51 (3 *bis*) or 407 (2) subparagraph (a) no. 4 of CCP; and also for examination of undercover agents. The ECtHR, regarding Art. 146-*bis* RICCP, as originally structured, has excluded any violation of Article 6 ECHR in a judgment concerning Italy. See ECtHR, *Viola v. Italy*, Judgment of 5 October 2006, Appl. no. 45106/04, para. 76: "participation by videoconference in the appeal hearings during the second set of criminal proceedings did not put the defense at a substantial disadvantage as compared with the other parties to the proceedings, and that the applicant had an opportunity to exercise the rights and entitlements inherent in the concept of a fair trial, as enshrined in Article 6".

than in exception, for certain categories of detainees (being under the application of a precautionary measures or final conviction).[71]

The regulation is linked to proceedings concerning one of the offences provided in Article 51 (3-*bis*) and Article 407 (2) subparagraph (a) no. 4 of CCP (crimes such as mafia organised crimes, drugs trafficking organised crimes, terrorism crimes and other serious crimes). Indeed, following § 1, a defendant who is detained for crimes above mentioned, "participates" at a trial by means of a videoconference,[72] even where not detained in relation to those proceedings, and also within criminal or civil hearings where the defendant has to be heard as a witness. The same rule applies to the participation at a trial, as a defendant, of a person under protection programmes or measures, including urgent and temporary measures (§ 1-*bis*). With the aim of mitigating the mandatory nature of aforementioned rules, it is provided that, except for proceedings brought against a detainee who has been the subject of the measures provided for in Art. 41-*bis* ("hard prison regime") of Penitentiary Law no. 354 of 26 July 1975, as subsequently amended, the judge "may" decide, by reasoned decree, also upon request of parties, the personal participation of persons above mentioned, where it is deemed as "necessary". The vagueness of this clause, in the lack of normative criteria, gives to the judge a wide margin of discretion in excluding personal participation.

As noted above, for a defendant in a "hard prison regime", participation by means of a videoconference is mandatory and cannot be derogated.[73] Regarding this, it is worthy to mention a judgment of the Assise Court of Palermo[74] that, within a trial named "trattativa Stato-mafia", rejected the request of defendants, detained for mafia offences, to participate in the examination as witness of the previous Head of the Italian Republic, that took place at the Quirinale. According to the decision, a videoconference could not apply in this specific case because the activities took place outside the place where the trial is normally celebrated.

The third hypothesis, now optional, introduced by § 1-*quater*, provides that a judge, except in cases provided by §§ 1 and 1-*bis*, may order participation by means of a videoconference, in the following cases: (a) where there are serious requirements of security; (b) where proceedings are particularly complex and participation at a distance is deemed necessary in order to avoid delays; (c) where the person to

---

[71] Lorusso (2017), p. 1 ff.; Curtotti (2017), p. 509 ff., also for an overview of this instrument.

[72] According to the previous § 1, participation at a trail of a defendant who is detained in a prison, in relation to proceedings concerning one of the offences provided for in Art. 51 (3 *bis*) and Art. 407 (2) subparagraph (a) no. 4 of CCP, is ensured by means of a videoconference in the following cases: (a) where there are serious requirements of security or public order; (b) where proceedings are particularly complex and participation at a distance is deemed necessary in order to avoid delays; (c) where proceedings is brought against a detainee who has been the subject of the measures provided for in Art. 41 *bis* ("hard prison regime") of Penitentiary Law no. 354 of 26 July 1975, as subsequently amended.

[73] As clarified by CCas, IV, 12 April 2018, no. 22039, the application of the "hard prison regime" cannot be referred to the past.

[74] Assise Palermo, 9 October 2014, Bagarella and others, in www.penalecontemporaneo.it. 21 October 2014, last accessed 31.7.2018. On this judgment see Negri (2014a, b), p. 1 ff.

be heard as a witness is detained in a penitentiary institute. Lastly, § 4-*bis*, provides that, within proceedings celebrated by means of a videoconference, the judge, upon request, may consent to the parties and their defence lawyer, "to take part by means of a videoconference, bearing costs of the videoconference". This provision makes evident the needs to reduce judicial costs, that is on the basis of the reform.[75]

The same rules apply, according to Articles 45-*bis*, 134-*bis* RICCP and 7 (8) of Legislative decree no. 159 of 6 September 2011 ("Special plan against the mafia and delegation to the Government on anti-mafia legislation"), as amended by Law no. 103/2017, to the participation of the above-mentioned categories of defendants, within proceedings held *in camera* and within a summary trial celebrated in public and within preventive proceedings ("*procedimento di prevenzione*") for the examination of witnesses.

Regarding the entry into force of mentioned rules, it has been postponed to February 2019, except for provisions concerning persons detained for crimes such as association for terrorism ends, including international or for subversion of the democratic order (Art. 270 *bis* § 1 CP), promoting, directing or organizing association of mafia-type (Art. 416-*bis* (2)) and association for drug trafficking (Art. 74 (1) d.P.R. no. 309 of 1990), that have entered into force the last 3 of August.

4 Personal Participation of Private Parties Other Than Defendants (in Particular, the Contribution of the Victim to the Fact-Finding)

In the Italian criminal procedure code, the term "victim" is not a technical one and is used occasionally (such as in Article 498 (4-*ter*) CCP where the term "minor victim of crime" is used), while other positions are recognised, such as the person injured by a crime (*persona offesa dal reato*)—who is a mere subject and not a party—the bodies and associations representing the interests injured by a crime (Art. 93 CCP), as well as a person damaged by a crime (Art. 74 CCP), who has the power of joining the proceedings assuming the role of a civil plaintiff. Thus premise, in this section the term victim will be used as corresponding to a person injured by a crime (Art. 90 CCP).

It is to say that a specific role is recognised to the victim when, at the end of preliminary investigations, a public prosecutor makes a request to dismiss a case to a judge for preliminary investigations (Art. 408 CCP). The notice of a request dismissing a case shall be served by the public prosecutor on a victim who, in a criminal complaint or after its submission, has expressed an intention to be informed if the case is dropped (for crimes committed with violence against a person the notice is served also if a victim did not express an intention to be informed: this rule, aimed at widening the participation of victims, according to jurisprudence, is applicable to

---

[75] Lorusso (2017), p. 5.

crimes such as persecutory acts and cruelty against family[76]). The right to inform the victim is strictly related to the right of opposition. Indeed, following Article 410 CCP, a victim can oppose a request to dismiss the case, within 20 days—or 30 days for crimes committed with violence against a person as well as for burglary and snatching pursue—indicating, under penalty of inadmissibility, the purpose of further investigations and the related element of evidence to collect. Moreover, should be considered that an opposition can also be presented by a victim of the crime who has not asked to be notified of the request for dismissal, but who became aware of it *aliunde*. The judge for preliminary investigations shall decide on the objection by way of a hearing *in camera* (Art. 409 CCP) to be held before the judge and in the presence of parties (public prosecutor, person under investigation, victim and respective lawyers). The attendance of parties is not mandatory, the model of hearing *in camera* provided for by Art. 127 CCP being applicable. The victim, if participates in a hearing, can make their reasons, be heard and seek to obtain possible alternatives to closure of proceedings: the continuation of investigations or, even, the formulation of a charge. Finally, the criminal procedure code, as modified by law no. 103/2017,[77] regarding the victim[78] provides the possibility to object the decision that discontinue the case adopted by the judge, within 15 days of the day they are informed of the decision, through a petition (*reclamo*) to the Tribunal sitting as a single judge (Art. 410-*bis* (3)). The aim of the objection against the decree (*decreto*) is denouncing failure to observe Article 408 (2) and (3-*bis)* and Article 411 (1-*bis*) CCP, regarding failure to serve or an untimely serving of the notice of the request to discontinue or of the request to discontinue due to the seriousness of the offence, or case where after an opposition is submitted, the judge does not decide on its admissibility or declares the opposition being inadmissible, where victim complied with Article 410 (1) CCP. The objection against the order (*ordinanza*) is aimed at denouncing failure to observe Article 127 (5) CCP and, in other words, failure to serve or an untimely serving of the notice of the date of the hearing or failure to observe their rights to participate in a hearing. The decision on the objection is adopted by the single-judge Tribunal by way of an unappellable order, without any right for the parties to intervene. Parties have to be informed at least ten days in advance, of the hearing set for the delivery of the decision and may submit briefs no later than five days prior to the hearing (Art. 410-*bis* (3) CCP).

Regarding the right of victims to be heard, it is interesting to note that our code provides a special evidentiary hearing (*incidente probatorio*) that can take place during preliminary investigations or a preliminary hearing (Art. 392 CCP), under request by a public prosecutor or by the defense of a person under investigation, to

---

[76] CCas, S.U., 29 January 2016, no. 10959. The same rule applies for the offence referred to in Art. 624-*bis* PC-Italy (burglary and snatching purse).

[77] Art. 409 (6) CCP, regarding the victim provided the possibility to appeal for cassation against the dismissal order, but only with the aim of denouncing failure to observe Art. 127 (1) and (3) CCP and, in other words, failure to serve or an untimely serving of the notice of the date of the hearing or failure to observe their rights to participate in a hearing.

[78] The CCP refers to "the person concerned", so including a person under investigation.

a judge for preliminary investigations (or of a preliminary hearing) who decides on the admissibility of a request. This procedure, originally introduced with the aim of ensuring the gathering of evidence that might disappear or deteriorate if its gathering were postponed to the trial, has in the course of time changed its function, as revealed in § 1-*bis* of Article 392 CCP. According to this provision—as amended by several legislative interventions—with reference to proceedings for crimes pursuant to Articles 572, 600, 600-*bis*, 600-*ter* and 600-*quater*, also if concerning child sexual abuse material of Articles 600-*quater*.1, 600-*quinquies*, 601, 602, 609-*bis*, 609-*quater*, 609-*quinquies*, 609-*octies* 609-*undecies* and 612-*bis* c.p. (cruelty within the family, paedophilia, human trafficking, virtual pornography, sexual violence, serious sexual violence, sexual acts with children, corruption of children, group sexual violence, solicitation and persecutory acts), a public prosecutor, also at the request of a victim, or a person subjected to preliminary investigations can ask for a special evidentiary hearing to proceed, even outside the sphere of the hypotheses provided by § 1 of the above-mentioned Article 392 CCP and, therefore, without the otherwise necessary indication of the circumstances that establish the non-deferability of the evidence at a trial, as if the same is presumed to be *ex lege* in that it is implied by the nature of significant crimes and by the subjective conditions of the particular declaratory evidence: a child and an adult victim of a "specific" crime. A further change was made by Legislative decree no. 212 of 15 December 2015, adopted to implement Directive 2012/29/EU, "establishing minimum standards on the rights, support and protection of victims of crime and replacing Council Framework Decision 2001/220/JHA". It has introduced a new sentence in § 1-*bis* that expand the special procedure. Indeed, even outside the sphere of the above-mentioned crimes, when the victim is in condition of particular vulnerability,[79] the public prosecutor, also on the request of the same victim, or the person subjected to preliminary investigations can ask for the special evidentiary hearing to proceed. The aims are manifold: fostering a rapid removal of the traumatic experience and, at the same time, to avoid alteration or dispersion of a testimony given by a vulnerable person, through the formal establishment of evidence at a time closer to a criminal episode. With the aim to protect a victim, once evidence has been taken during the special evidentiary hearing, a victim should not repeat their examination during a trial. Indeed, Article 190-*bis* (1-*bis*) CCP admits an examination at a trial "only if it regards facts or circumstances different from those that are the object of previous declarations or if the judge or one of the parties should consider it necessary on the basis of specific needs". This rule, originally limited to children under 16 years of age, pending crimes of sexual violence and paedophilia, has been recently extended to the victim in condition of particular vulnerability. A defect of the procedure is the absence of a direct legal right, by a victim of a crime in general and by a person with specific needs in this case, to ask a judge for them to be

---

[79] See Art. 90-*quater* CCP.

admitted: although it is a measure guaranteeing a victim, it can only be activated following a plea by a public prosecutor or by a person subject to investigations.[80]

During a trial, a victim of crime, under request of a party of proceedings can be heard as a witness through cross-examination. In this way victims have the power of making a direct contribution to the ascertainment of facts, and their statements have to be assessed by a judge as proof. Except in particular cases (it is for instance the case of a victim who is a relative of a defendant: this person may abstain from giving evidence at trial, according to Article 199 (1) CCP), victims cannot abstain from giving evidence and cannot refuse to carry out their role in court. It means that victims have the duty to appear in front of the Court, to answer questions and to answer truthfully, a duty whose violation is punishable as a criminal offence. When victims join proceedings as civil plaintiffs, if they have not been called as witnesses, they can in any case ask or consent to be examined as a private party (Art. 208 CCP). In this case, a civil plaintiff will be examined first, followed by a person who has a civil liability for damages and by a person who has a civil liability for payment of a fine (Art. 503 CCP); otherwise, if they do not join proceedings as a civil plaintiff, in the capacity of simple person, victim of a crime, they only have the right to indicate evidence, except in front of the Supreme Court, but not the right to have it admitted. It remains the possibility for a victim at every stage and level of proceedings to present briefs (Art. 90 (1) CCP). Moreover, only a civil plaintiff can dispute the judgment in relation to their application for compensation which may have been rejected (Art. 576 CCP). A victim, as well as a civil party and the organisations and associations that participated under Articles 93 and 94 CCP, have a mere power of making a plea to a public prosecutor to lodge an application for appellate remedy to any criminal effect (Art. 572 CCP).

A specific role has the victim within special proceedings of suspension with probation (Art. 464-*bis* CCP), introduced, as said before, by Law no. 67/2014. First of all, the motion by a defendant to suspend procedures by putting on probation must contemplate a program which, *inter alia*, must envisage "prescriptions of behavior and other specific commitments that the defendant assumes also for the purpose of avoiding or attenuating the consequences of the crime, considering to this end compensation for damages, reparatory actions and restitutions", as well as "actions aimed at promoting, where possible, mediation with the injured person" (Art. 464-*bis* (4) lett. b) and c) CCP). What is relevant is that a victim must be heard and informed both of the hearing and where a decision on the suspension is taken (Art. 464-*quater* (1) CCP), both of a hearing where a judge has to take the decision of cancellation of a offence due to a positive result of a probation (Art. 464-*septies* (1) CCP). Moreover, a victim has an autonomous power to challenge the decision on probation, where they have not been informed of the hearing or, in case of appearance, have not been heard (Art. 464-*quater* (1) and (7) CCP).

---

[80] See Todaro (2015), p. 116.

5 *In Absentia* Proceedings

5.1 *Information Rights and Conditions of Waiver of Personal Participation in Criminal Proceedings*

As a general principle, in Italy attendance of the defendant at a trial is not mandatory. It is to premise that by Law no. 67/2014,[81] Italian legislator has introduced relevant changes to the previous system, based on the "*contumacia*",[82] with the aim of reinforcing the right of participation of defendants: according to the intention of the legislator a trial *in absentia* should be possible only where a defendant has been personally informed of a trial or has waived their right to participate in an unequivocal manner or there are situations that consent to infer knowledge of a trial from the knowledge of a proceedings. In case a defendant is untraceable (Art. 159 CCP) the trial should be suspended (Art. 420-*quater* CCP).[83]

The first stage of criminal proceedings where right to participation can be exercised is a preliminary hearing (*udienza preliminare*). A notice of preliminary hearing served on a defendant[84] on an order of a judge, closed to a request for committal to trial filed by the public prosecutor, contains, among others, information about date and place of the hearing and consequences of non-appearance (Art. 419 (1) CCP). Indeed, it is specified that in case of non-appearance rules provided for by Articles 420-*bis*, 420-*ter* and 420-*quinquies* CCP will apply. The recall of these provisions can make it difficult for a defendant to really understand the consequences of non-appearance because these rules govern different institutions. The first regulates situations that legitimise to proceed *in absentia* of a defendant; the second regulates the legitimate impediment to appear by a defendant and their lawyer; the third, cases where judges have to suspend proceedings, in front of the impossibility to trace a defendant. If it is so, the mentioned warning risks of being only an apparent guarantee, should case law consider that its lack does not make void the notice of a preliminary hearing, as happened with the previous provision.

At the first hearing the judge has to check that all parties—public prosecutor, defendant, their lawyer and (eventually) the person who is claiming damages as consequence of a crime—have been regularly summoned. While a hearing must be attended by a public prosecutor and a defence (Art. 420 (1) CCP), any obligation to appear is by a defendant. Hence, if a defendant, who is free or detained, and is regularly summoned does not appear at the hearing, under certain conditions, it is possible to hold the hearing *in absentia*. The first condition is that a defendant has

---

[81] On the reform see, among others, Tonini and Conti (2014), p. 509 ff.; Marcolini (2014), p. 135 ff.; Di Paolo (2014), p. 175 ff.; Negri (2015), p. 197 ff.; Belluta (2015), p. 249 ff.; Ciavola (2015), p. 197 ff. More recently see Ruggeri (2017), p. 57 ff.

[82] See Negri (2014a, b), Mangiaracina (2010), Moscarini (1997) and Ubertis (1984).

[83] Quattrocolo (2014a, b) (2), p. 235 ff.

[84] Failure to serve a notice is a cause of an absolute nullity: CCas, S.U., 24 November 2016, no. 7697.

expressly waived the right to participate: a clear situation where it is proved, beyond any reasonable doubt, the knowledge of a hearing (Art. 420-*bis* (1) CCP). If a legitimate impediment to appear does not exist (Art. 420-*ter* CCP), the judge can also hold the hearing *in absentia* if the defendant has been summoned in person, a means that gives the certainty of the knowledge of a trial (§ 2).

The criminal procedure code, following the 2014 reform, provides other situations that legitimise the judge to proceed *in absentia* where the knowledge of the preliminary hearing is deduced from knowledge of some acts of preliminary investigations. As noted by scholars,[85] since the drafters of Law 67/2014 deemed it sufficient that defendants were in any case informed of a pre-inquiry against them, it may happen that the court proceedings are instituted even though it is certain or highly probable that the defendant was not aware of the court summons. Assuming that a defendant has been regularly summoned (although not personally) and there are not situations of legitimate impediment, the hearing can be conducted *in absentia* where there are three (alternative) knowledge indices provided by the legislator: (a) the declaration or election of domicile; (b) the case of a defendant who has been subjected to arrest,[86] detention or precautionary measures; (c) the appointment by a defendant of a lawyer. According to jurisprudence, the first situation[87] recurs also if the domicile has been elected to the defence appointed *ex* officio, being a presumption of knowledge of the trial, in reason of a duty on the defendant to maintain contacts with a lawyer on the development of proceedings.[88] This interpretation has raised concerns for the protection of the right to have an effective knowledge of criminal proceedings,[89] being the only condition that can legitimate a renounce to participate by the defendant. Thus, it is welcomed the new § 4-*bis,* introduced in Article 162 CCP by Law no. 103/2017, according to which "selection of the court-appointed lawyer's address as the address for service shall produce no effect if the proceeding authority does not receive the lawyer's consent together with the statement of address for service". This rule should reinforce relation between a defendant and their defence appointed by the court.

---

[85] Ruggeri (2017), p. 58.

[86] If the aim of the rule is to ascertain a firm knowledge of the proceedings, the case of the arrest not followed by the validation by the judge for preliminary investigations is problematic. On this point see Moscarini (2014), p. 250.

[87] The declaration or election of domicile for the purpose of notification, is made to a judge, a public prosecutor, or police during the first act of preliminary investigations that requires participation of the person under investigation or of the defendant not detained (Art. 161 CCP).

[88] See CCas, V, 7 July 2016, no. 36855, that has rejected the request of "rescissione del giudicato".

[89] The Italian Constitutional Court, 5 October 2016, no. 31, has declared the inadmissibility of the question of unconstitutionality of arts. 161 and 162 CCP, for the breach of arts. 2, 3, 21, 24, 111 and 117 Cost, the latter in relation to arts. 14 ICCPR and 6 ECHR, where it is not provided the personal serving of the request for committal to trial in case where the domicile is elected at the defence appointed by the judiciary police. For a critical comment see Alonzi (2017), p. 213 ff.

The second index provided by law is related to the application of measures such as arrest, detention or a precautionary measure that, according to scholars,[90] in the absence of any normative specification could also be a real measure. The last of the above-mentioned indices—the appointment of a counsel—responds to the legislative choice to valorize the relationship between a defendant and their counsel, which is based on trust. Already in 2005, by § 8-*bis* of Article 157 CCP, introduced by Legislative decree no. 17 of 21 February 2005,[91] converted into Law no. 60 of 22 April 2015, concerning notifying a defendant who is not under detention, the Government has provided that once the first notification has been served, according to the sequence of acts provided for by Article 157 CCP, further notification will be sent to the defense, if appointed. This provision has two exceptions: a general one, provided for in the *incipit* of § 1 of Article 157 CCP concerning the election or declaration of domicile by a defendant in a different place; and a special one that is the declaration to a competent authority by a lawyer to refuse notification of the act.

Turning to the indices of knowledge, Article 420-*bis* (2) CCP, provides a sort of "safety clause" that gives the possibility to a judge to consider acts of the proceedings other than those mentioned above. Indeed, where emerges with certainty that the defendant has "knowledge of proceedings" or "voluntary has escaped" knowledge of the whole proceedings or of part of it, the judge can hold the hearing *in absentia*. Regarding the first situation, it is doubtful whether the appointment of a lawyer by the State can be included. The answer should be negative: the appointment of a lawyer by the State cannot be deemed equivalent to the appointment of a lawyer by the person. Remarkably, the Supreme Court, adopting an interpretation in conformity with principles established by the ECtHR, has excluded that the "knowledge of proceedings" coincides with the knowledge of an act performed by the judiciary police before the recording of the *notitia criminis* by the public prosecutor, such as a photographic surveys.[92]

Concerning the second situation, according to jurisprudence of the Supreme Court, it is possible to consider cases where any notice (*avviso*) related to the proceedings has been personally received by the defendant. The case of a defendant is also included, who expressly invited, has refused to declare or to elect domicile.[93] In all these situations, a defendant who is absent is represented by their own lawyer, if already appointed, or by a court-appointed lawyer.[94]

The 2014 reform led to the introduction, by Article 420-*quater* CCP, of the suspension of the proceedings in cases of non-traceable defendants, an institute

---

[90] Quattrocolo (2014a, b), p. 98.

[91] The Legislative decree was adopted following condemnations by the ECtHR in the following cases: ECtHR, *Somogyi v. Italy*, judgment of 18 May 2004, Appl. no. 67972/01; ECtHR, *Sejdovic v. Italy*, judgment of 10 November 2014, Appl. No. 56581/00.

[92] CCas., I, 2 March 2017, no. 16416; CCas, VI, 23 June 2017, no. 39563.

[93] CCas, II, 27 October 2015, no. 2291.

[94] Is also represented by their lawyer, a defendant who, initially present, turned away from the courtroom hearing (Art. 420-*bis* (3) CCP).

accepted in full by scholars.[95] In particular, if the defendant is not present at a preliminary hearing, with the exception of the cases set out in above mentioned Article 420-*bis* and in Article 420-*ter* CCP and the cases of nullity of the service, the judge shall order that the notice is served personally on the defendant by the judiciary police, more adequate to trace the accused. When this is impossible, the judge will order the suspension of criminal proceedings, unless there are conditions to pronounce a judgment of dismissal, according to Article 129 CCP. Following a mechanism used in another context (Art. 72 CCP, regarding the incapacity of the defendant), where the judge has decided for the suspension, at the end of the first year, from or before the decision of suspension if deemed as necessary, he will order new searches for the defendant, in order to serve the notice. Article 420-*quinquies* (2) CCP lists in detail the situations which are able to demonstrate the knowledge of the proceedings by the defendant, that impose the revocation of the order, and among these latter is mentioned the appointment of a lawyer.

The decision adopted by the judge to hold a hearing *in absentia* is not definitive, being possible for the defendant to appear during the celebration of the preliminary hearing (Art. 420-*bis* (4) CCP). Should a defendant appear before the final decision of a preliminary hearing, a judge will revoke a decision (*ordinanza*) to proceed *in absentia* and if a defendant proves that an *absentia* was caused by an innocent lack of knowledge of the trial, a judge will postpone the hearing and the defendant will have an opportunity to exercise the right of defence through the request for the admission of acts and documents according to Article 421 (3) CCP. The late appearance of a defendant at a trial of first instance, gives them the right to request the admission of evidence according to the general rule provided for by Article 493 CCP.[96] In any case, all the acts of proceedings performed before an appearance remain valid, although a defendant can require the renewal of evidence. The same provision applies if a defendant proves that their absence was due to an absolute impossibility to attend due to unforeseeable circumstances, force majeure or legal impediment and the evidence of the impediment arrived late without culpability. A judge has to revoke the decision to proceed *in absentia* also in the event the previous judge had to suspend proceedings according to Article 420-*quater* CCP. The rules examined until now also apply at a trial in force of Article 484 (2-*bis*) CCP and, in particular, during the stage of introductory acts of a trial.[97] Before the opening of a trial if a defendant gives evidence that the *absentia* during the preliminary hearing was provoked by situations described by Article 420-*bis* (4) CCP, they can request special proceedings such as a summary trial or the application of a penalty under request (Art. 489 CCP).

---

[95] Regarding subjects interested see Quattrocolo (2014a, b) (2), p. 238 ff.

[96] This rule, although referred to at the trial of first instance, has been inserted in the context of a provision which applied at the preliminary hearing.

[97] These rules do not apply to the proceedings of execution of the final judgment provided for by Art. 666 CCP: see Constitutional Court, 16 June 2016, no. 140.

5.2 Default Proceedings and Subsequent Remedies (e.g., Retrial or Judicial Review in a Higher Instance)

As noted above the system introduced by Law no. 67/2014 provides that the lack of firm evidence that a defendant knew the trial—because the notice of the trial was not summoned personally—is compensated by evidence of knowledge of "proceedings" (to read as "acts of preliminary investigations"). Thus, implies the risk that a trial (and a preliminary hearing) can be held *in absentia* although a defendant did not receive notice of it. To manage these situations, Law no. 67/2014 has provided some remedies which operate during proceedings or after the pronouncement of a final judgment, aimed at allowing a defendant to exercise the right of defence and access to special rewards proceedings. At an appeal stage, in virtue of § 5-*bis*, added in Art. 604 CCP, when a trial is held *in absentia* and there is evidence that the judge had to apply Article 420-*ter* CCP (concerning the impossibility to appear) and postpone the hearing, or Article 420-*quater* CCP (concerning the impossibility for the judiciary police to personally serve notice of the preliminary hearing to the defendant) and suspend proceedings, the Court of Appeal quashes the judgment and forwards the case file to a first instance judge. The same rule applies where a defendant proves that they did not know about proceedings without culpability. In both cases, a defendant, in front of a judge of first instance, can request special proceedings such as a summary trial or application of a penalty under request and, despite the lack of a specific provision, also probation.[98]

A similar provision applies in front of the Supreme Court. Indeed, under the same conditions provided by Article 604 (5-*bis*) CCP the Supreme court can quash a judgment and forward a case file to a first instance judge (Art. 623 lett. b) CCP).

Within the general reform on proceedings *in absentia* realised by Law no. 67/2014, the legislators introduced a new extraordinary remedy, named "*rescissione del giudicato*" which works after a judgment has the *status* of *res judicata*. This remedy was regulated by Article 625-*ter* CCP, then has recently been annulled by Law no. 103/2017 and replaced by Article 629-*bis* CCP, among rules on the reopening of a trial. A convicted or person subjected to a security measure as an effect of a final judgment, whose trial has been heard *in absentia*, may request to have the *res judicata* quashed if demonstrate that their *absentia* was caused by an innocent absence of knowledge of the trial. The request is under a term: 30 days since the knowledge of proceedings. The competence to decide on the request lies with the Court of Appeal (while in the previous text with the Supreme Court)[99]; should a

---

[98] This provision is deemed not complete: Diddi (2014), p. 222.

[99] After enforcing the new provision, some interpretative questions were posed, which were subsequently resolved by the Supreme Court (CCas, S.U., 17 July 2014, no. 36848). Regarding the burden of proof, the Supreme Court has clarified that although the burden of proof is on a requesting person, who has to attach documents, it is not prohibited for the Supreme Court to collect integrative documents, being in some cases necessary with the aim of clarifying ambiguities or filling gaps or verifying correspondence of documents with acts of the trial. Another question solved by the Supreme Court, in the absence of a specific provision, concerned procedures to

request be accepted a judgment is quashed and a case file is transmitted to a first instance judge. The main value of this provision is that the defendant has the right to request the summary trial or the application of a penalty upon request by the parties in front of the first judge, despite expiry of time (as well as probation). Regrettably, defendants have to prove that the unawareness of the proceedings was not due to their negligence. At this regard, it is appreciable, concerning procedures to apply, the reference to Article 127 CCP. The kind of decision that the Court of Appeal has to take and the collection of documents, require the possibility for parties to give their contribution through participation, although optional, at the hearing. By virtue of the explicit recall of Article 635 CCP it is possible for a Court to suspend the execution of the penalty. Should the Court of Appeal reject a request of "rescissione" the right to appeal to the Supreme Court is expressly recognised.

Some problems have been posed by the new remedy of "*rescissione del giudicato*" in the relationship with the application of leave to appeal out of time,[100] a traditional remedy provided for in case of conviction *in absentia*. Although § 2 of Article 175 CCP has been changed by Law no. 67/2014, it would have been applicable to transitional situations. Indeed, according to Article 15-*bis* of Law no. 67/2014, if the ruling of a judgment of first instance has been pronounced before the entry into force of the new law, previous rules still apply. It implies a reference to Article 175 (2) CCP that, in the text before enforcement of Law no. 67/2014, it was structured so: "In the event of a conviction in absentia (…) the defendant may request the reopening of the time allowed for appeal against the judgment, unless he had effective knowledge of the proceedings or of the judgment and has voluntarily refused to appear or to appeal against the judgment. The judicial authorities shall carry out all necessary checks to that end".[101] On this point, the Supreme Court[102] has affirmed the following principle: "Once admitted a request to reopen the time allowed for an appeal against a judgment *in absentia*, in the text in force before the enforcement of Law no. 67/2014, a defendant who did not have an effective knowledge of a trial, can ask a judge of appeal for special proceedings (such as a summary trial)". According to the Court, the reopening of time allowed for an appeal would be inefficient should not be recognised to the defendant the right of defence, of which the possibility to require special proceedings is an expression. Indeed, according to previous rules, if a request to reopen the time for an appeal was successful, a defendant was deprived of the first instance trial and also of the possibility to request special proceedings. Moreover, the possibility for a renewal of evidence at an appeal stage was under a burden of proof on a defendant.[103] Previous wording of Article

---

apply. According to the Supreme Court the decision is adopted *de plano* when a request will probably be rejected; otherwise the Supreme Court can decide *in camera*, following Article 611 CCP, that does not recognise the right to participation. For an analysis of this exceptional remedy see Spagnolo (2018), p. 141 ff.

[100] Art. 175 (2) CCP.

[101] Bargis (2015), p. 10.

[102] CCas, S.U., 29 September 2016, no. 52274.

[103] Ubertis (2008), p. 109 ff.

603 (4) CCP, not amended by Law no. 60/2005, was: the judge orders renewal of a trial evidentiary hearing "if the accused, who was absent by default in the first-instance trial, requests so and demonstrates that they were unable to appear due to unforeseeable circumstances, force majeure or because they were unaware of the decree of summons, provided that they he cannot be held responsible for it, or the summon for the first-instance trial was served on a lawyer in the cases mentioned in Articles 159, 161, 164 and 169, and they have not voluntarily avoided to be informed about documents regarding proceedings". Article 603 (4) CCP has been annulled by Law no. 67/2014.

Finally, a conviction can be quashed through another extraordinary remedy, "*revisione*".[104] Should the Supreme Court confirm the judgment, a convicted, having exhausted internal remedies, can only apply to the Court of Strasbourg. If the Court of Strasbourg ascertains violation of Article 6 ECHR (or other Conventional rules), the convicted person can request the reopening of a trial, in accordance with a judgment of the Italian Constitutional Court[105] which has declared the partial unconstitutionality of Article 630 CCP insofar as it does not include decision by Strasbourg assessing human rights violations among the exceptional circumstances allowing a review of a final conviction. Thus, Article 630 CCP should now be read as including Strasbourg's decisions assessing the violation of a Convention right among the exceptional cases for review.

5.3   Inaudito Reo *Proceedings (e.g., Penal Order Procedure)*

Among the special proceedings provided by the Italian criminal procedure code, it is worth mentioning proceedings by penal order (Art. 459 CCP), that can lead to a conviction without a defendant having an opportunity of being heard and often even without knowing that a formal charge has been brought against them. Indeed, during preliminary investigations, within proceedings for offences punishable *ex officio* or by lawsuit of a victim, should a public prosecutor deemed possible to apply a fine—also as a substitute for a custodial penalty—they may ask to the judge for preliminary investigations to issue a penal order, resulting in a 50% fine reduction. This stage of proceedings is in secret: a judge for preliminary investigations can accept (or reject and transmit the file back to a public prosecutor) a request (or issue a sentence of not to proceed *ex* Article 129 CCP) within proceedings *inaudita altera parte*. Once a penal order has been issued, it is communicated to a public prosecutor and notified to a person convicted, their court appointed lawyer or their lawyer and also to a person who is obliged to the civil payment of a fine. The penal order contains, among other elements, the exposition of facts, of circumstances and rules of

---

[104] Art. 630 CCP admits the recourse to this extraordinary remedy in several cases.

[105] CConst, 7 April 2011, no. 113. For a comment on this judgment see, among others, Gialuz (2011), p. 3308 ff.

law violated; the advertisement that the convicted person and the person obliged to pay a fine can lodge an opposition (Art. 460 CCP). This opposition, to lodge within 15 days from notification of an order, constitutes the first opportunity for a defendant to react against a conviction issued against them without a trial hearing. Otherwise the penal order becomes final upon expiry of a period of 15 days from its service. With an opposition, a convicted person may access special proceedings such as a summary trial, an application of a penalty under request, suspension with probation (as an effect of Constitutional Court, 6 July 2016, no. 201) or to an immediate trial or require the payment of fine on the spot (*oblazione*). A special guarantee is provided for the person convicted by Article 460 (4) CCP: if it is not possible to serve the penal order because somebody convicted cannot be found at their residence or domicile, a judge revokes the penal order and sends a file back to a public prosecutor. A matter of concern about this procedure—starting from the premise that lodging and opposition and requiring an immediate trial can lead to a *reformatio in peius* of a previous conviction—is that an opposition can be lodged not only by a defendant but also by their legal counsel on their initiative, and also by a lawyer appointed by the Court.[106]

6 Participatory Rights in Transnational Criminal Justice

6.1 Participatory Safeguards in EAW Proceedings

It is to premise that significant steps forward the protection of the right of a defendant to participate and to legal assistance, within the EAW proceedings, have been made in virtue of national law aimed at implementing Directives adopted following the Roadmap for strengthening procedural rights of suspected or accused persons in criminal proceedings of 2009.[107]

6.1.1 Participatory Rights in the Decision on Surrender

Italy has implemented the Framework Decision on the European Arrest Warrant[108] by Law no. 69 of 22 April 2005, making a distinction between passive proceedings and active proceedings. Regarding the first, the forum which pronounces on the EAW (and also on extradition request) is the Court of Appeal, whose jurisdiction is fixed according to classic territorial criteria (fixed residence, domicile, temporary

---

[106] CCas, VI, 13 November 2014, no. 51079. Criticism has been expressed by Ruggeri (2017), p. 62 ff. As underlined by the Author, the "lawyer's initiative may depart from the accused's intentions and can entail the permanent loss of some important opportunities".

[107] See Siracusano (2016), p. 10.

[108] FD EAW 2002/584/JHA, 13 June 2002.

residence, place of arrest). The Court of Appeal of Rome has a residual competence. Regarding the procedure, except cases where it is the judiciary police that perform the arrest, the Ministry of Justice forwards, without delay, the EAW enacted by the competent authority of a Member State, to the President of the Court of Appeal which is territorially competent (Art. 9 (1)). The President of the Court, called the Court of appeal, and heard the General Prosecutor, by an order, which must be reasoned 'on pain of nullity', then decides whether to apply preventive measures, taking into account, in particular, the need to prevent a suspect from absconding, as required by Article 12 of the Framework Decision (Art. 9 (4)). In implementing Directive 2013/48/EU, "on the right of access to a lawyer in criminal proceedings and in the European arrest warrant proceedings, and on the right to have a third party informed upon deprivation of liberty and to communicate with third persons and with consular authorities while deprived of liberty", by Legislative Decree no. 184 of 15 September 2016,[109] a new § 5-*bis* has been added in Article 12. It provides that at the moment of an execution of the mentioned order, the judiciary police inform requested persons that they have the right to appoint a lawyer in the issuing Member State. When requested persons exercise or wish to exercise the right to appoint a lawyer in the issuing Member State, the President of the Court of Appeal shall promptly inform the competent authority in the issuing Member State. Art. 9 § 6 of the implementation Law states that measures restricting personal freedom cannot be ordered if there is sufficient reason to believe that grounds exist for a refusal to surrender. By virtue of application of Art. 719 CCP, a requested person, their lawyer and a public prosecutor are all permitted to appeal against an order of the President of the Court of Appeal to the Court of Cassation on grounds of violation of a law. According to Article 10 (1) of Law no. 69/2015, where preventive measures are ordered, a requested person shall be heard by the President of the Court (or by a judge delegated) within 5 days after their execution in the presence of their legal counsel appointed by them or by the State. The President, on this occasion, informs a requested person in a language that they know, of the content of the EAW and of the execution procedure, and of the possibility of consenting to surrender to the issuing judicial authority and of renouncing the possibility of not carrying out of criminal proceedings, convicted or deprived of personal freedom for offences committed prior to their surrender other than that for which they surrendered. A lawyer must be informed of these activities at least 24 h in advance. A hearing at which a request is decided upon shall take place *in camera* within a period of 20 days after execution of preventive measures. The decree that establishes the hearing must be communicated to a General Prosecutor and notified to a requested person and to their lawyer at least 8 days before a hearing.

Special rules apply in the event that the judiciary police performs an arrest on their own initiative: it is provided that an officer who has arrested a person, informs the person, in a language that they can understand, of the EAW and its content and deliver a communication, written in a clear and precise manner, that informs a

---

[109] For a comment see Siracusano (2017), p. 235 ff.

person about the possibility to consent to a surrender and advise the person about the possibility to appoint a lawyer and of the right to be assisted by an interpreter (Art. 12 (1)). With the aim of reinforcing the right to an effective defence a, new § 1-*bis* has been added, following Legislative decree no. 184/2016, that replies to the content of the above-mentioned Article 9 (5 *bis*). Within 24 h since receiving the official report by the police, the President of the Court of Appeal or a judge of the Court, informed the General Prosecutor, heard a person under arrest in a language that is known by the said person and, if it is necessary, with the attendance of an interpreter and of a lawyer (Art. 13 (1)). A hearing of a requested person is mainly aimed at receiving the consent to surrender, which, once expressed, is irrevocable (Art. 14) and making the procedure faster: in this case the Court of Appeal will decide on the execution of the EAW within 10 days, heard the General Prosecutor, the lawyer and the person requested if they appear. Except this case, under Article 17 of Law no. 69/2005, the decision on the request is adopted by the Court of Appeal heard the General Prosecutor, the lawyer and, only if appears, person requested and, if present, person who represents the requesting State. The decision must normally be made within 60 days after an execution of an order restricting personal freedom, which corresponds to the time limit defined by Article 17 (3) of the Framework Decision. If a decision within this period is impossible due to force majeure, the President of the Court of Appeal shall inform the Minister of Justice, who in turn shall inform the issuing authority 'also through Eurojust'. Article 22 of the implementing Act provides for a judicial remedy before the Court of Cassation against a decision of the Court of Appeal on a surrender. On the basis of this provision, the only way to question the legality of an arrest warrant, a person requested, their lawyer and General Prosecutor can raise objections on the grounds related either to its merit or to a law. The Court of Cassation has to decide within rigid time limits applying rules related to proceedings *in camera* (§ 2). The Italian regulation fills a gap in the Framework Decision. The only procedural protection demanded by the FdEAW is a right to be informed (Art. 11) and to be heard by a judicial body in case a requested person opposes surrender (Art. 14). In terms of (even) minimum defence rights, to be incorporated into every national legal order, the Framework Decision is thus very minimalistic. The Italian implementing Act by providing for a '*ricorso per Cassazione*', in particular complies with Article 111 (7) of the Constitution, which gives everybody the right to bring an action before the Court of Cassation against measures *de libertate*. However, the Italian implementing Act goes further than this, as an appeal against a decision to surrender can be based not only on grounds of law, but also factual grounds.[110]

---

[110] See Marin (2008), p. 263.

6.1.2   In Absentia *Proceedings in the Trial Country and Its Relevance in the Surrender Procedure*

Adopting a solution in line with an extradition system, the FdEAW in its original content, introduced, among guarantees to be given by the issuing State for a requested person (Art. 5), a specific condition related to a trial celebrated *in absentia*. Indeed, where the EAW had been issued for the purpose of executing a sentence or a detention order imposed by a decision rendered *in absentia* and if a person concerned had not been summoned in person or otherwise informed of a date and place of a hearing which led to a decision rendered *in absentia*, an executing authority had the possibility to subject a surrender under the condition that an issuing judicial authority "gives an assurance deemed adequate to guarantee the person who is the subject of the EAW that he or she will have the opportunity to apply for a retrial of the case in the issuing Member State and to be present at the judgment". This provision was transposed in Article 19 (a) of Law no. 69/2005, headed "Guarantees requested to the issuing State", which applies when Italy is the executing State. The different solutions provided by various FDs implementing the principle of mutual recognition to final decisions were not satisfactory. The necessity to provide clear and common ground for non-recognition of decisions following a trial *in absentia* execution, brought the European legislator to adopt FD 2009/299/JHA, amending, among others, FD EAW, "thereby enhancing the procedural rights of persons and fostering the application of the principle of mutual recognition to decisions rendered in the absence of the person concerned at trial".[111] Through the new Article 4-*bis* and the annulment of Article 5 (1), trial *in absentia* exits an optional ground for non-recognition of the EAW, if a person concerned did not appear in person at a trial. However, executing Member States may surrender a person under certain assurances given by a requesting judicial authority related to the respect of some guarantees yet provided or to be provided in favour of a defendant tried *in absentia*.[112] In transposing the content of the above-mentioned FD, by Legislative decree no. 31 of 15 February 2016, a certain margin of discretion seems to be recognised by the Court of Appeal, as demonstrated by the use of the verb "may".[113] According to the new text of Article 19 (a), when the EAW has been issued with the aim of executing a penalty or a security measure adopted following a judgment *in absentia*, and the person interested did not appear in person at the trial resulting in the decision,[114] the Appeal Court may deliver the person if the certificate declares one of the following conditions: (1) the interested person was summoned in due time and personally, being informed in a unequivocal manner both of the scheduled date and place of the trial which has brought to the judgment *in absentia*

---

[111] Zanetti (2017), p. 94 ff.

[112] On this provision see CJEU, 26 February 2013, *Melloni*, Case C-399/11, para. 52.

[113] CCas, VI, 19 May 2016, no. 21773. Some scholars still consider the new condition as mandatory being unchanged the *incipit* of Article 19: see, for instance, Bigiarini (2016), p. 1004.

[114] On the interpretation of the concept "trial resulting in the decision", see CJEU, 10 August 2017, *Tupikas*, Case C-270/17 PPU; CJEU, 10 August 2017, *Zdiaszek*, Case C-271/17.

both of the possibility that a decision may be handed down if he/she does not appear at a trial; (2) the interested person, being aware of the proceedings, was defended by the legal counsellor, appointed by the person concerned or by the State; (3) the person interested, after being served with the decision and being expressly informed about the right to a retrial or an appeal in which the person has the right to participate and which allows the merits of the case, including fresh evidence, which may lead to the original decision being reversed, expressly stated that he/she does not contest the decision, neither requested the retrial or appeal; (4) the person interested was not personally served with the decision but will be personally served with it without delay after the surrender and will be expressly informed of terms within to exercise his/her right to a retrial or an appeal in which the person has the right to participate and which allows the merits of the case, including fresh evidence and which may lead to the original decision being reversed. It is to underline that there are some relevant differences between the content of the FD EAW and the Italian law aimed at implementing it. Regarding the first condition, it is significant that it has not been provided that a person was informed of a scheduled trial "by other means": within our criminal procedure code it is not possible to use "other means" to summon a defendant at the beginning of a trial. The second condition related to the possibility that a concerned person was represented by a lawyer appointed by the said person or by the State, poses some troubles if interpreted in the sense that the representation by the lawyer appointed by the State to execute the EAW is sufficient. According to scholars,[115] this condition can be satisfied when, being a defendant absent at a trial, not only they have appointed a lawyer but they have renounced to participate at a trial and being represented by their lawyer. Another difference is related to the use of the phrase, by Italian legislator, "being aware of the proceedings" (n. 2) that is wider than the European text where it is provided that a person "being aware of the scheduled trial".

As said before these rules apply when Italy is the executing authority. When the Italian judicial authority is requesting the surrender of persons who are abroad, the only change concerns the format to complete when the request is enacted, a format that is substituted with the one attached to the Legislative decree.

6.2   Participatory Safeguards in Transborder Inquiries and the Taking of Overseas Evidence

Within the Italian legislative picture concerning the taking of overseas evidence, a defence is a subject often neglected. In Italy, since Law no. 367 of 7 December 2000, with the aim of realising the principle of equality of harms, it has been expressly regulated the right to a defence of all private parties of criminal proceedings to collect, independently from the prosecution, some forms of evidence (such

---

[115] Alesci (2016), p. 49.

as interviews with persons who have knowledge of facts of a case) at every stage of the proceedings; but, according to jurisprudence, a lawyer wishing to collect evidence located in a foreign country must submit a formal request to a public prosecutor (during preliminary investigation) or to a judge (during a trial), who will act through the instrument of letters rogatory.[116] Indeed, the defence are not among the subjects who can issue letters rogatory—a traditional instrument of mutual assistance to gather evidence located abroad—with the consequence that the defence has to reveal the strategy to a public prosecutor (or to a judge) should it be necessary to collect evidence abroad. Moreover, any obligation neither a public prosecutor nor a judge has to perform the request.

Thus premise, it is to say that in Italy the obtaining of overseas evidence has been mainly regulated by the 1959 Council of Europe's European Convention on Mutual Assistance, based on the respect of the *lex loci*. This Convention had already provided for a form of intervention also of private parties in the execution of letters rogatory (Art. 4 (1)), so developing the so called 'participatory' or 'joint letters rogatory' (*rogatorie partecipate* or *concelebrate*).[117] However, the possibility of joint letters rogatory is based on the consent of the foreign country and only allows for mere presence at the evidence-gathering without any possibility of investigations conducted by the Italian authorities and without any law enforcement powers on foreign territory.[118]

Italy has not enacted instruments of legal assistance, such as the Second Additional Protocol to the 1959 Convention on Mutual Assistance and the 2001 Additional Protocol to the 2000 EU Convention. Only recently, by Legislative decree no. 52 of 5 April 2017, Italy has implemented the 2000 EU Convention, that has represented, at EU level, a significant step forward in the development of judicial cooperation in criminal matters. Although the 2000 EU Convention has been replaced (as well as 1959 Convention and CISA),[119] from 22 of May 2017, by Directive of 3 April 2014, on the EIO in criminal matters, transposed in Italy by Legislative decree no. 108 of 21 June 2017 (entered into force on 28 July 2017),[120] it will apply to judicial assistance relations with Member States that are not bounded by the Directive on the EIO,[121] and also with States that have signed the 2000 EU Convention, but are not members of the EU, such as Island and Norway. Moreover, it will apply to relations with States that adhere to the Directive, for certain investigative acts not regulated by Directive on the EIO, such as sending and service of procedural documents[122]—unless it concerns the EIO itself or acts aimed at its

---

[116] CCas, I, 29 May 2007, no. 23967.

[117] Marchetti (2005), p. 179 ff.

[118] Ruggeri (2017), p. 190.

[119] It has also replaced FD 2003/577/JHA, of 22 July 2003, on the execution in the EU of orders freezing property or evidence, as regard freezing of evidence, and FD 2008/978/JHA, of 18 December 2008, on the EEW.

[120] See Mangiaracina (2018), p. 158 ff.

[121] Ireland and Denmark are not bound by Directive. Ireland has not ratified EU-CMACM.

[122] Arts. 5 and 6 of Legislative decree no. 52/2017 (Art. 5 EU CMACM).

execution—spontaneous exchange of information between competent authorities[123] and relationship between administrative authorities.[124]

Following Article 696 (3) CCP,[125] national rules and, in particular, book XI of the CCP, headed "Jurisdictional relationship with foreign authorities" apply only when the matter is not regulated by the supranational source or it is not regulated in a different way. Concerning methods of obtaining evidence, as said before, the main instrument remains letters rogatory, regulated by Article 723 and following of the CCP.[126]

Regarding letters rogatory requested by the foreign authority the competence to rule on the execution is shared between the Minister of Justice and the Public prosecutor towards the Tribunal of the capital district of the place where it is necessary to gather evidence, while in the past the judicial authority was the Court of Appeal.[127] Should a letters rogatory concern investigative acts to be gathered in front of a judge or acts that according to Italian law have to be performed by a judge, a Public prosecutor shall transmit their request to the judge for preliminary investigations (Art. 724 (2) CCP).

Concerning modalities to be followed for the execution of the request by Italian authorities, as a general principle, assistance is provided pursuant to national rules: however, where requested, Italian authorities are generally committed to applying foreign procedure, unless they infringe the fundamental principles of the State (Art. 725 (1) CCP).[128] This rule is aimed at avoiding the evidence collected abroad becoming inadmissible because of non-compliance with the *lex fori*, while at the same time preventing the *lex fori* from being imposed in the executing State if it is not compatible with the basic principles of the executing State. Following the new text of Article 725 (3) CCP, Italian judicial authority can authorise the participation of "representatives" (*rappresentanti*) or "agents" (*incaricati*) of the requesting State to the gathering of evidence. The wording of this Article seems to exclude participation of private parties.

In the field of active letters rogatory, the possibility to request respect for domestic formalities provided by Italian law as a condition to use the evidence in foreign investigations still applies only where an international instrument in force in Italy allows it (Art. 727 (9) CCP): Italian authorities can only request the application of

---

[123] Art. 9 of Legislative decree no. 52/2017 (Art. 7 EU-CMACM).

[124] Arts. 3 and 4 of Legislative decree no. 52/2017.

[125] As modified by Legislative decree no. 149 of 3 October 2017, that has significantly changed book XI of CCP.

[126] See Marchetti (2005), p. 41 ff.

[127] According to previous Article 724 CCP, on the jurisdictional authority lied the competence on the *exequatur*. Any role had the defence in the proceedings of *exequatur*, ruled by Art. 724 CCP where it was provided only the participation of a General Prosecutor. According to jurisprudence it was not possible to challenge a decision on the *exequatur*: CCas, I, 29 November 2006, no. 40415. For an analysis of the new rules concerning request of mutual assistance see Piacente (2018), p. 32 ff.

[128] A similar provision is, for instance, in Article 4 (1) 2000 EU-CMACM.

the domestic rules affecting the admissibility at trial of the evidence taken. Article 729 CCP then specifies that the execution by the foreign State of a letters rogatory with a different modality than the one mentioned following Article 729 (9) CCP, implies the exclusion of acts so gathered where the sanction is expressly provided for by the law. This provision should avoid the use of discretionary interpretation on the part of the requesting authority. Indeed, notwithstanding the importance of participation of defense in the gathering of evidence abroad, the Supreme Court has affirmed that respect for the *lex loci* of the requested State ceases if these rules are in contrast with mandatory rules of public order or morality, rules that cannot be identified with the content of the criminal procedure code and, in particular, with rules concerning defence rights.[129] In a judgment[130] the jurisprudence justified this approach invoking two arguments: the need to apply the minimum standard protection provided by the ECtHR case law and the exemption clause of "objective impossibility" (Art. 111 (5) Const.), as a means for admitting overseas evidence collected outside an adversarial procedure.[131] This reasoning, following above mentioned rules, should be rejected.

Specific rules have been introduced by Legislative decree no. 149/2017 concerning hearing and participation by means of a videoconference, where provided for by international agreements, of a person under investigation, a defendant, a witness and an expert. It is specified that the hearing and the participation of a person under investigation or of a defendant, by means of videoconference require the consent. In case of active letters rogatory there is a recall to Article 205-*ter* RICCP (Art. 729-*quater* (2)). According to the latter provision, in case of participation at a trial by a defendant who is detained abroad and cannot be transferred to Italy, the recourse to the video-conference is possible, when provided for by international agreements and according to these rules. Another condition is the consent of a defendant. Should a defendant deny their consent, the mere detention abroad cannot be deemed a legitimate impediment to participate in a trial, according to Article 420-*ter* CCP and, as a consequence, a judge is not obliged to postpone a trial. The videoconference can be used also for the participation at a trial of witnesses and experts, following modalities provided for by international agreements. In the lack of specific rules, it applies Article 147-*bis* RICCP, where applicable.

---

[129] CCas, III, 16 December 2014, n. 17379.

[130] CCas, I, 28 April 2009, no. 19343.

[131] Ruggeri (2017), p. 600.

7 Requirements of Personal Participation and *In Absentia* Proceedings. The Perspective of Supranational and International Human Rights Law

7.1 The Perspective of International Human Rights Law. Critical Remarks on Domestic Law in the Light of the European Convention

The case law of ECtHR[132] has brought significant changes in Italian legislation regarding participation at a trial of a defendant. First of all, in 2005 and with a more comprehensive reform, in 2014, through the introduction of a new procedure for a defendant who is absent at a trial. But the picture is not still in conformity with principles of ECHR. Putting aside the lack of a national reform concerning the serving of procedural acts, the possibility for a judge, according to Article 420-*bis* (2) CCP, to declare a defendant absent when emerges with certainty that they have knowledge of the proceedings, although a notice of a trial was not summoned personally and a defendant has not waived his right, or voluntary escaped from knowledge of proceedings, open a wide discretion to the judge not in conformity with the principle that a trial can be held *in absentia* only in cases where it is certain that a defendant had knowledge of a trial and renounced to exercise their right. Especially the second part of the above-mentioned rule poses some trouble regarding a "fugitive" (*latitante*).[133] According to the case law of ECtHR,[134] it could not be inferred merely from the *status* of "fugitive" (*latitante*), that a defendant has waived their right to appear at a trial and defend themselves. Furthermore, a person charged with a criminal offence must not be left with the burden of proving that they were not seeking to evade justice or that their absence was due to *force majeure*. It means that the *status* of "fugitive" cannot be included among the conditions to proceed *in absentia*. It should be necessary to identify other elements which demonstrate knowledge of proceedings.

---

[132] ECtHR, *Sejdovic v. Italy*, judgment of 1° March 2006, Appl. no. 56581/00; ECtHR, *Sejdovic v. Italy* (fn 78).

[133] See Quattrocolo (2014a, b) (2), p. 242.

[134] ECtHR, Grand Chamber, *Sejdovic v. Italy*, judgment of 1° March 2006, Appl. no. 56581/00, para. 87–88.

7.2   The Perspective of EU Law. Developments in Domestic Law as a Result of EU Law

From the perspective of judicial cooperation, it is worth noting that national legislation aimed at implementing Directives adopted following the 2009 Roadmap has strengthen the participatory guarantees of a person subjected to the EAW.[135] In implementing Directive 2013/48/UE, through Legislative decree no. 184/2016, it is provided that a person requested must be informed of the faculty to appoint a lawyer in the issuing State. To make effective this provision, Article 29 RICCP has been modified, concerning lists of lawyers appointed by the State, providing the availability of lawyers of detained or arrested persons abroad in execution of an EAW within the active procedure, with the aim of promptly identifying a lawyer in an issuing State who can assist a lawyer appointed in an executing State.[136] But it is to say that some shadows still remain. By Legislative decree no. 101/2014, aimed at implementing Directive 2012/13/EU, it is provided that judiciary police have to deliver to a person requested a communication written in a clear and complete manner, that informs a person about the possibility to consent to delivery, to appoint a defence lawyer and of being assisted by an interpreter (Art. 12 (1)). As underlined by legal scholars,[137] the requested person is still unaware of consequences of the delivery as well as of the refusal opposed to the delivery, or, in the latter case, of the right to be heard by a judicial authority. Concerning the right to an interpreter, Italian legislator, in implementing Directive 2013/64/EU on the right to interpretation, has not modified national law implementing the FD EAW: a matter of concern is the lack of a remedy against the decision adopted by the national authority to refuse the appointment of an interpreter.

From the perspective of the right to the equality of harms, we can find a new approach in the Directive on the EIO. At this regard, the text of the Directive provides that "the issuing of an EIO may be requested by the suspected or accused person, or by a lawyer on his behalf" and that the request by the defendant may be filed "within the framework of applicable defence rights in conformity with national criminal procedure" (Art. 1 (3)). In implementing the European Directive, by above mentioned Legislative decree no. 108/2017, Italy has opted for a "minimal" solution, that does not satisfy the right to the equality of harms. Indeed, according to Article 31 of Legislative decree no. 108/2017, the lawyer of a person under investigation, of a defendant or of a person proposed for the application of a preventive financial measure, may request to the public prosecutor or to the judge, depending on the stage of proceedings, the issuing of an EIO with the specification, under penalty of inadmissibility, of the investigative measure and reasons that justify the measure itself. It means that such a request entail disclosure of the defensive strategy before official discover take place. Moreover, the competent judicial authority

---

[135] Arasi (2017), p. 132 ff.

[136] Quattrocolo (2016).

[137] Ruggeri (2015), p. 148, footnote 100.

of the proceedings is not bound by the defense lawyer's request and national legal system does not provide a remedy against refusal. It is certainly positive the provision according to which if the request is refused, the public prosecutor adopts a reasoned decree (Art. 31 (3), while the judge issues a decision (*"ordinanza"*) after having heard parties (Art. 31 (4)).[138] What is negative is that against both kind of decisions is not provided any remedy. In practice, there is not any significant difference with the procedure applicable to letters rogatory.

In Legislative decree no. 108/2017 is not regulated the performing of defense investigation activity abroad: a matter, as noted above, specifically regulated at national level. Except for investigative acts that require the authorization by the judge (such as the access to private places), the defense should be legitimate to gather abroad information through a consultation with whoever is able to provide information relevant for the reconstruction of the facts, by means of an undocumented interview.[139] Where it is requested a written statement, it should be necessary to respect rules provided for by the Italian CCP (Art. 391-*ter* CCP), being respect for these rules under penalty of exclusion of evidence by the trial. In case the person should refuse to cooperate with the defense, the impossibility to apply national rules (Art. 391-*bis* (10) and (11) CCP),[140] would impose the recourse to an EIO, with the possibility, above mentioned, of a refusal opposed by the public prosecutor or by the judge.

In the specific context of an EIO, a difference procedure applies where the request of the defense concern the issuing of a seizure. In this case, it is to apply Article 368 CCP: if the public prosecutor, believes that the seizure requested by the person concerned—in this case the person under investigation, his/her lawyer—must not be carried out, he shall forward the request, along with his opinion, to the judge for preliminary investigations.

Alongside the lack of a national remedy against the refusal to issue an EIO, another weak point of national legislation—although, at this regard, perfectly in line with the content of Directive—is the consideration that a victim is not among subjects who may request the issuing of an EIO. As a consequence, victim could only submit a request to the public prosecutor who is not obliged to issue the EIO, neither to give a formal explanation of his refusal.

Also regarding participation of the lawyer of a person under investigation or accused or of private parties in the gathering of evidence abroad, rules introduced at national level are not satisfactory. Art. 29 of Legislative decree no. 108/2017 provides that public prosecutor—by agreement with the executing authority—can

---

[138] Belfiore (2018), p. 407.

[139] On this topic see Grifantini (2016), p. 5.

[140] According to § 9 when the person who is able to provide information relevant for the reconstruction of the fact has exercised the right to silence or not to render any statements, the Public prosecutor, upon request of the lawyer, shall set the examination of such person within seven days of the request. As an alternative, according to § 11, the lawyer shall be entitled to request to proceed to the gathering of testimony or to the examination of the person who exercised the right above mentioned, by means of special evidentiary hearing (Art. 392 (1) CCP).

participate directly or through on or more officials of the judiciary police in the execution of the EIO. With this aim the public prosecutor can also promote the setting up of a joint investigation team (in this case it applies Legislative decree no. 34 of 2016). Also, the judge who issued an EIO may request the execution authority to participate in the execution of the EIO. Unfortunately the article does not require the participation of a lawyer or of private parties: a defect underlined by scholars also with regard to the content of DEIO. This underestimates the role of the defence in ensuring that foreign procedural formalities are properly applied.[141]

The absence of defence lawyer during the execution of an EIO may invalidate the whole execution procedure, i.e. admissibility of evidence in the proceedings in the issuing Member States where participation of lawyer is an essential requirement under national law. It is the case, for instance, where the evidence to gather is an oral evidence, such as the hearing of a witness. To avoid this risk the issuing authority may indicate participation of the defence lawyer during the execution of an EIO as a procedure to which the executing authority shall comply with (a possibility recognised by Article 33 (1) of Legislative decree no. 108/2017). In this case, the problem is that participation of defense lawyer would depend on a discretionary decision of the issuing authority; moreover, the indication of formalities and procedures to comply with in the execution of an EIO is not compulsory for the executing authority, who could refuse the request if it is deemed in contrast with fundamental rights of the executing State, a general "clause" that leaves a great discretion to the executing authority.

Also, where Italy is the executing State, Article 8 of Legislative decree no. 108/2017 does not provide any participation of private parties.

8   Concluding Remarks

Significant steps forward the protection of the right to participate in a trial have been made in virtue of jurisprudence of the ECtHR as well as of the Directives adopted following the 2009 Roadmap. Concerning the obtaining of evidence overseas, in implementing Directive on the EIO our Government has lost the opportunity to reinforce the right of defence to all the parties in proceedings. Lastly, in the context of judicial cooperation, Directive 2016/1919 of 26 October 2016 on legal aid is welcomed, to be implemented by 25 May 2019, which concerns also persons who are the subject of EAW proceedings. According to Article 5 of the Directive, the executing Member States shall ensure that requested persons, who are the subject of EAW proceedings for the purpose of conducting a criminal prosecution and who exercise their right to appoint a lawyer in the issuing Member State in accordance with Directive 2013/48/EU should have the right to legal aid in that Member State for the purpose of such proceedings in the executing Member State, in so far as legal

---

[141] See Ruggeri (2013), p. 301.

aid is necessary to ensure effective access to justice, as laid down in article 47 of the EU Charter of Fundamental Rights. This would be the case where a lawyer in the executing State cannot fulfil their task, with regards to the execution of an EAW, effectively and efficiently without the assistance of a lawyer in the issuing State. Moreover, Member States shall ensure a remedy under national law in the event of a breach of their rights. From the perspective of the Italian criminal procedure system, a few concern poses the ruling of the CJEU of 24 May 2016[142] which has pointed out that Article 4a (1) (a) (i) of FD 2002/584, as amended by FD 2009/299, must be interpreted "as meaning that a summons (…) which was not served directly on the person concerned but was handed over, at the latter's address, to an adult belonging to that household who undertook to pass it on to him, when it cannot be ascertain from the European Arrest warrant whether and, if so, when that adult actually passed that summons on to the person concerned, does not itself satisfy the condition set out in that provision". Indeed, such a method of service does not allow it to be unequivocally established that the person received the information. This judgment could have an influence on the system related to proceedings *in absentia* as structured by the legislator in 2014, which still poses doubts on its compatibility with the case law of ECtHR and, after the mentioned judgment, also with the CJEU.

Regarding the right to participation, it is to say that the content of the Directive on the strengthening of certain aspects of the presumption of innocence and the right to be present in a trial in criminal proceedings of 9 March 2016, aimed at establishing common minimum rules among Member States, is not completely satisfactory. The Directive allows criminal proceedings to be carried out without the competent authorities having fulfilled their obligation of personally informing defendants, if the latter are granted the opportunity of a subsequent remedy aimed at a full review of a conviction. Regarding this, the Directive provides that a new trial—or another remedy—has to allow "a fresh determination of the merits of the case, including examination of new evidence and which may lead to the original decision being reversed" (Art. 9).[143] As underlined by scholars,[144] these measures of "compensation" would not be sufficient, if a defendant lost certain defence measures such as the access to special proceedings. From this perspective, Italian legislation provides a higher standard of protection. Moreover, the Directive allows Member States to maintain proceedings of certain stage thereof to be conducted in writing and without a trial hearing "provided that this complies with the right to a fair trial" (Art. 7 (6)): this rule poses serious risks in respect of the principles of ECHR, as well as principles of our Constitutional system. In any case, the right to participate, according to the scope of application of the rules, should not be excluded at a "trial which can result in a decision on the guilt or innocence of a suspect or accused person (…)". The problem still remains regarding proceedings—such as

---

[142] CJEU, 24 May 2016, *Dworzecki*, C-108/16 PPU.

[143] For an analysis of Directive and its impact on Italian proceedings *in absentia* Alonzi (2016), p. 1 ff.

[144] Ruggeri (2016), p. 47.

penal order procedure—where, as noted before, a conviction is adopted by a judge without any participation of a person convicted.[145] A clarification on this provision will be necessary if the aim of the Directive is to reinforce cooperation among Member States, in the respect to defence rights.

References

Alesci T (2016) Il d.lgs. 15 febbraio 2016, n. 31: il riconoscimento dei provvedimenti assunti in absentia. In: Masrandola A (ed) Cooperazione giudiziaria internazionale. Giuffré, Milano, pp 46–52

Alonzi F (2016) La direttiva UE sul diritto dell'imputato di partecipare al giudizio e la disciplina italiana sul processo in absentia. www.legislazionepenale.eu, 21 September 2016, pp 1–30, Last accessed 31 July 2018

Alonzi F (2017) La Corte costituzionale si pronuncia sul diritto alla conoscenza della vocatio in iudicium da parte dell'imputato. Giurisprudenza costituzionale, pp 213–221

Arasi S (2017) Per uno spazio giuridico europeo irrobustito dai diritti processuali: mandato di arresto europeo e reciproco riconoscimento delle decisioni in absentia. Processo penale e giustizia 1:132–153

Bargis M (2015) La rescissione del giudicato ex art. 625 ter c.p.p.: un istituto da rimeditare. www.penalecontemporaneo.it, 16 January 2015. Accessed 31 July 2018

Belfiore R (2018) Su alcuni aspetti del decreto di attuazione dell'ordine europeo di indagine penale. Cassazione penale, pp 400–410

Belluta H (2015) Le impugnazioni come rimedi ripristinatori: verso il giusto processo in assenza dell'imputato. In: Daniele M, Paulesu PP (eds) Strategie di deflazione penale e rimodulazione del giudizio in absentia. Giappichelli, Torino, pp 249–277

Bigiarini A (2016) Mandato di arresto europeo e reciproco riconoscimento delle sentenze penali nei processi in absentia. In: Kalb L (ed) Cooperazione giudiziaria: le novità del recepimento delle fonti sovranazionali, Diritto penale e processo, special issue, pp 999–1006

Bronzo P (2017) La nuova ipotesi di rinnovazione dell'istruzione dibattimentale in appello. In: Baccari GM, Bonzano C, La Regina K, Mancuso EM (eds) Le recenti riforme in materia penale. Cedam, Padova, pp 409–423

Cassibba F (2016) L'imputazione e le sue vicende. Giuffré, Milano

Chiliberti A, Roberti F, Tuccillo G (1994) Manuale pratico dei procedimenti speciali. Giuffré, Milano, pp 1–484

Conti C (2000) Le due anime del contraddittorio. Diritto penale e processo, pp 197–202

Ciavola A (2015) Alcune considerazioni sulla nuova disciplina del processo in assenza e nei confronti degli irreperibili. Diritto penale contemporaneo, Rivista trimestrale 1:196–218

Curtotti D (2017) Le modifiche alla disciplina della partecipazione al dibattimento a distanza. In: Baccari GM, Bonzano C, La Regina K, Mancuso EM (eds) Le recenti riforme in materia penale. Cedam, Padova, pp 509–521

Daniele M (2015) L'archiviazione per tenuità del fatto fra velleità deflattive ed equilibrismi procedimentali. In: Quattrocolo S (ed) I nuovi epiloghi del procedimento penale per particolare tenuità del fatto. Giappichelli, Torino, pp 41–64

De Caro A (2017) Il ricorso per cassazione. In: Scalfati A (ed) La riforma della giustizia penale. Giappichelli, Torino, pp 223–248

Di Chiara G (1994) I procedimenti in camera di consiglio. Giuffré, Milano, pp XXII–546

---

[145] On this point Ruggeri (2015), p. 138.

Di Paolo G (2014) La revoca dell'ordinanza che dispone il giudizio in assenza. In: Vigoni D (ed) Il giudizio in assenza dell'imputato. Giappichelli, Torino, pp 175–207

Diddi A (2014) Novità in materia di impugnazioni e restitutio in integrum. In: Vigoni D (ed) Il giudizio in assenza dell'imputato. Giappichelli, Torino, pp 209–234

Ferrua P (2017) Il contraddittorio tra declino della legge e tirannia del diritto vivente. In: Ferrua P, Negri D (eds) Le erosioni silenziose del contraddittorio. Giappichelli, Torino, pp 1–25

Fonti R (2008) Il procedimento in camera di consiglio. In: Spangher (ed) Trattato di procedura penale. Utet, Torino, vol I, t. II, pp 43–85

Galantini N (2011) Giusto processo e garanzia costituzionale del contraddittorio nella formazione della prova. www.penalecontemporaneo.it, 7 September 2011, Last accessed 31 July 2018

Gialuz M (2011) Una sentenza "additiva di istituto": la Corte costituzionale crea la "revisione europea". Cassazione penale 51(10):3308–3320

Gialuz M (2017) The Italian code of criminal procedure: a reading guide. In: Gialuz M, Luparia L, Scarpa F (eds) The Italian code of criminal procedure. Cedam, Padova, pp 17–55

Grifantini F (2016) Ordine europeo di indagine penale e investigazioni difensive. Processo penale e giustizia 6:1–9

La Rocca N (2016) Misure cautelari (profili innovativi). Digesto Discipline penalistiche, Aggiornamento. Utet, Torino, pp 462–499

Lorusso S (2017) Dibattimento a distanza vs. "autodifesa"?. www.penalecontemporaneo.it, 17 May 2017, Last accessed 31 July 2018

Maggio P (2015) I controlli. In: Bene T (ed) Il rinnovamento delle misure cautelari. Analisi della legge n. 47 del 16 aprile 2015. Giappichelli, Torino, pp 83–127

Mangiaracina A (2010) Garanzie partecipative e giudizio in absentia. Giappichelli, Torino

Mangiaracina A (2018) L'acquisizione "europea" della prova cambia volto: l'Italia attua la direttiva relativa all'ordine europeo di indagine penale. Diritto penale e processo, pp 158–180

Marandola A (2017) Il ritorno del concordato sui motivi d'appello. In: Baccari GM, Bonzano C, La Regina K, Mancuso EM (eds) Le recenti riforme in materia penale. Cedam, Padova, pp 389–408

Marchetti MR (2005) L'assistenza giudiziaria internazionale. Giuffré, Milano

Marcolini S (2014) I presupposti del giudizio in assenza. In: Vigoni D (ed) Il giudizio in assenza dell'imputato. Giappichelli, Torino, pp 135–173

Marin L (2008) The European arrest warrant in the Italian Republic. Eur Constit Law Rev 4:251–273

Marafioti L, Del Coco R (2018) Le eterogenee incursioni nel ricorso per cassazione. In: Bargis M, Belluta H (eds) La riforma delle impugnazioni tra carenze sistematiche e incertezze applicative. Giappichelli, Torino, pp 83–114

Moscarini P (1997) La contumacia dell'imputato. Giuffré, Milano

Moscarini P (2014) Una riforma da tempo necessaria: l'abolizione della contumacia penale e la sospensione del processo contro l'imputato irreperibile. In: Conti C, Marandola A, Varraso G (eds) Le nuove norme sulla giustizia penale. Cedam, Padova, pp 239–271

Negri D (2014a) La presenza personale dell'imputato alla testimonianza del Presidente della Repubblica: un diritto fondamentale non confiscabile. www.penalecontemporaneo.it, 21 October 2014. Accessed 31 July 2018

Negri D (2014b) L'imputato presente al processo. Una ricostruzione sistematica. Giappichelli, Torino

Negri D (2015) Il processo nei confronti dell'imputato "assente" al tortuoso crocevia tra svolgimento e sospensione. In: Daniele M, Paulesu PP (eds) Strategie di deflazione penale e rimodulazione del giudizio in absentia. Giappichelli, Torino, pp 197–247

Novokmet A (2016) The right of a victim to a review of a decision not to prosecute as set out in Article 11 of Directive 2012/29/EU and an assessment of its transposition in Germany, Italy, France and Croatia. Utrecht Law Rev 12(1):86–108

Piacente N (2018) Overview of Italian legislation and case law on judicial cooperation. Diritto penale contemporaneo, Rivista trimestrale 9:25–68

Quattrocolo S (2014a) Il contumace cede la scena processuale all'assente mentre l'irreperibile l'abbandona. Diritto penale contemporaneo, Rivista trimestrale 2:97–106

Quattrocolo S (2014b) La sospensione del processo nei confronti dell'imputato non comparso e la revoca della relativa ordinanza. In: Vigoni D (ed) Il giudizio in assenza dell'imputato. Giappichelli, Torino, pp 235–255

Quattrocolo S (2016) Interventi minimi in materia di diritto di accesso al difensore: la recente trasposizione della direttiva 2013/48/UE. www.eurojus.it, 15 October 2016. Accessed 31 July 2018

Ruggeri S (2013) Horizontal cooperation, obtaining evidence overseas and the respect for fundamental rights in the EU. From the European Commission's proposals to the proposal for a directive on a European Investigation Order: towards a single tool of evidence gathering in the EU? In: Ruggeri S (ed) Transnational inquiries and the protection of fundamental rights in criminal proceedings. A study in memory of Giovanni Grevi and Giovanni Tranchina. Springer, Heidelberg, pp 279–310

Ruggeri S (2015) Procedimento penale, diritto di difesa e garanzie partecipative nel diritto dell'Unione europea. Diritto penale contemporaneo, Rivista trimestrale 4:130–160

Ruggeri S (2016) Inaudito reo proceedings, defence rights, and harmonisation goals in the EU. Eucrim 1:42–51

Ruggeri S (2017) Audi Alteram Partem in criminal proceedings. Towards a participatory understanding of criminal justice in Europe and Latin America. Springer, Basel

Siracusano F (2016) Procedure di cooperazione giudiziaria e garanzie difensive: lungo la strada, a piccoli passi. www.archiviopenale.it, n. 3, pp 1–14, Last accessed 31 July 2018

Siracusano F (2017) Il diritto all'assistenza del difensore nel procedimento di esecuzione del mandato d'arresto europeo. In: Negri D, Renon P (eds) Nuovi orizzonti del diritto alla difesa tecnica. Giappichelli, Torino, pp 207–245

Spagnolo P (2018) La rinnovata fisionomia della rescissione del giudicato. In: Bargis M, Belluta H (eds) La riforma delle impugnazioni tra carenze sistematiche e incertezze applicative. Giappichelli, Torino, pp 141–166

Todaro G (2015) The Italian system for the protection of victims of crime: analysis and prospect. In: Luparia L (ed) Victims and criminal justice. European standards and national good practices. Wolters Kluwer, Torino, pp 101–117

Tonini P, Conti C (2014) Il tramonto della contumacia, l'alba radiosa della sospensione e le nubi dell'assenza "consapevole". Diritto penale e processo, pp 509–519

Ubertis G (1984) Dibattimento senza imputato e tutela del diritto di difesa. Giuffré, Milano

Ubertis G (2008) L'adeguamento italiano alle condanne europee per violazione dell'equità processuale. In: Balsamo A, Kostoris RE (eds) Giurisprudenza europea e processo penale italiano. Giappichelli, Torino

Zanetti E (2017) Diritti e processo in absentia. In: Ruggieri F (ed) Processo penale e regole europee: atti, diritti, soggetti e decisioni. Giappichelli, Torino, pp 93–111

Report on Luxembourg

Valentina Covolo

Abstract In the last decade, Luxembourg law governing *in absentia* proceedings was subject to legislative reforms intended to enhance the rights of suspects and accused persons. In particular, the amendments adopted in 2008 and 2017 aimed to make national criminal procedure compliant with the ECtHR case law. Against this background, the present contribution aims to analyse legal framework governing *in absentia* and *inaudito reo* proceedings in Luxembourg.

Abbreviations

CA	Cour d'appel
CCP	Code of Criminal Procedure
Ch.c.C.	Chambre du conseil de la Cour d'appel
CSJ corr.	Cour Supérieure de Justice, chambre correctionnelle
CSJ crim.	Court Supérieure de Justice, chambre criminelle
ECHR	European Convention on Human Rights
ECtHR	European Court of Human Rights

1 Constitutional Requirements of the Involvement of Private Parties in Criminal Justice

The Constitution of Luxembourg contains few provisions related to the involvement of private parties in criminal proceedings. Among these, Article 12 of the Constitution guarantees the right to liberty and security, while specifying some procedural safeguards that aim to enable the arrested person to defend himself against arbitrary

V. Covolo (✉)
University of Luxembourg, Faculty of Law, Economics and Finance,
Luxembourg, Luxembourg
e-mail: valentina.covolo@uni.lu

© Springer Nature Switzerland AG 2019
S. Quattrocolo, S. Ruggeri (eds.), *Personal Participation in Criminal Proceedings*, Legal Studies in International, European and Comparative Criminal Law 2, https://doi.org/10.1007/978-3-030-01186-4_10

deprivation of liberty. According to the provision, no one can be arrested without a reasoned judge's order that must be served at the time of arrest or at the latest within 24 h. In addition, the arrested person has the right to be informed without delay about the available remedies for regaining his liberty.[1] Other constitutional provisions enshrine fundamental rights of private parties that criminal proceedings may impair, such as the guarantee of a tribunal established by law[2] or the inviolability of the home,[3] without mentioning, however, specific participatory rights of accused persons, suspects or victims.

It should, however, be stressed that Luxembourg jurisprudence adopted over the years a monist approach towards the legal status of international treaties in domestic law.[4] A consequence thereof are the frequent references by criminal courts to the European Convention of Human Rights (ECHR) and the related case law of the Strasbourg Court.[5] In doing so, Luxembourg judges give direct effect to the fundamental rights guaranteed under the Convention and most particularly to the procedural safeguards of Articles 5 and 6, which prevail over national legal provisions. A leading example is the right of access to a lawyer.

2 Personal Participation of Private Parties and Legal Assistance

Under Luxembourg law, the personal participation of private parties in criminal proceedings is closely linked with the right to legal assistance. However, their relationship varies depending on the person and the stage of the proceedings in question. Legal assistance is first to be understood as the right to appoint, to be assisted and represented by a counsel of one's own choosing. In recent years, emphasis was given to the right of suspects and accused persons and its special significance in the pre-trial stage of criminal proceedings. In 2011, a note of the General Public Prosecutor extended the scope of the right to legal assistance with the aim to comply with the ECtHR judgement in *Salduz*.[6] In March 2017, the national legislature adopted a statute implementing *inter alia* Directive 2013/48/EU on the right to access a lawyer in criminal proceedings.[7] The reform of Luxembourg Code of Criminal Procedure (CCP) thereby codified the judicial practice and further

---

[1] Art. 12 Luxembourg Constitution.

[2] Art. 13 Luxembourg Constitution.

[3] Art. 15 Luxembourg Constitution.

[4] Gerkrath (2019).

[5] Petschko et al. (2013), pp. 449–472, at 450.

[6] Note of the General Public Prosecutor, 13 May 2011, implementing guidelines for the compliance with the ECtHR, *Salduz v. Turkey*, judgement of 27 November 2008, Appl. No. 366391/02.

[7] Law of 8 March 2017 strengthening procedural guarantees in criminal matters, Mem. A No. 346, 30.03.2017.

strengthened the guarantee of legal assistance. In particular, Article 3-6 CCP grants the right to access a lawyer to any person deprived of his liberty or subject to an arrest warrant, the person against whom the prosecutor requests the opening of a judicial investigation (*inculpé*), the individual who undergoes questioning in the investigation stage of the criminal proceedings as well as to the accused who appear in front of a Trial Court (*prévenu*).[8] In addition, Luxembourg law expressly acknowledges the right of victims to be assisted and represented by a lawyer.[9]

Thus defined, the right to legal assistance interplays with two further guarantees. On the one hand, access to a lawyer may be guaranteed through free legal aid. Under Luxembourg law, the latter is granted to both the defendant and other private parties who lack sufficient resources or where serious reasons related to the social, family and material situation of the person justify the granting of legal aid.[10] On the other hand, the personal participation of private parties in criminal proceedings does not necessarily imply mandatory legal assistance. Indeed, the procedural safeguard enshrined in Article 6, para 3 c) ECHR shall not preclude the possibility for the suspect to defend himself in person. In this respect, Luxembourg law requires first that the suspect or accused expressly waives his right to legal assistance.[11] National Courts interpret such a requirement in the light of the ECtHR case law, notably by verifying whether the person was sufficiently informed in order to reasonably foresee the consequences of the waiver.[12] In contrast, legal assistance is, under certain circumstances, mandatory. In accordance with the European Court of Human Rights (ECtHR) case law, Luxembourg law requires the compulsory appointment of a lawyer where legal assistance is necessary in the interests of justice[13] and, particularly, in order to ensure the proper defense of the accused's interests.[14] This is for instance the case for minor defendants questioned by the Examining Magistrate (*juge d'instruction*) at the preliminary stage of criminal proceedings.[15] Likewise, private parties must be represented by a lawyer in the proceedings before the Court of Cassation (*Cour de cassation*).[16]

Lastly, physical attendance of private parties at trial is not an absolute requirement despite the crucial importance of the right to be heard in criminal proceedings. Although the legislator may discourage unjustified absences, the non-appearance of the defendant at a court hearing cannot as such deprive him of the right to legal

---

[8] Art. 3-6 (1) CCP.

[9] Art. 4-1 (3) CCP.

[10] Law of 10 August 1991 on the profession of lawyer, Mem. A No. 58, 27.08.1991.

[11] Art. 81(8) CCP.

[12] CSJ Ch.c.C., 8 July 2013, No. 369/13, 370/13, 371/13, 372/13 and 374/13.

[13] ECtHR, *Lagerblom v. Sweden*, judgement of 14 January 2003, Appl. No. 26891/95, para 50.

[14] ECtHR, *Correia de Matos v. Portugal*, judgment of 1 April 1999, Appl. No. 48188/99.

[15] Art. 81(4) CCP.

[16] Law of 18 February 1885 related to appeals and proceedings before the Court of Cassation, Mem. A No. 23, 18.04.1885.

assistance.[17] Thus interpreted by the ECtHR, the right to legal assistance of persons sentenced *in absentia* found expression in the 2008 Act related *inter alia* to the appearance of the accused in court.[18] Since its entry into force, Luxembourg CCP clearly states that where the accused does not appear in person, a lawyer shall be given the opportunity to present his defense.[19] In such a case, the legal counsel is further entitled to represent his client's interests with regard to the imposition of a sentence, by requesting a social inquiry[20] or agreeing with an order suspending the sentence.[21] The trial proceedings conducted in the presence of the defendant's lawyer are deemed adversarial.[22]

3 Personal Participation of the Accused in Criminal Proceedings

3.1 General Features of Personal Participation: Absolute Individual Right or Duty of Diligence

Among the strongest expressions of participatory rights in criminal proceedings is the right of the accused to be heard and to be present at trial. The scope of those procedural guarantees perfectly illustrates the dual nature of such participatory rights. Indeed, rules related to the appearance of the accused at trial shall find a balance between defense rights and the need for the judge to hear the defendant in order to reach his personal opinion and pronounce an individualized sanction.[23] This was among the objectives of the 2008 statute reforming *in absentia* proceedings.[24] Under Luxembourg law, the accused duly notified who does not appear at trial has two options. First, if the defendant presents a valid excuse for his absence, he can request the adjournment of the hearing. The validity and reasonableness of the excuse is assessed by the Court.[25] Second, as indicated above, the physical absence

---

[17] ECtHR, *Van Geyseghem v. Belgium*, judgement of 21 January 1999, Appl. No. 26103/95, para 33.

[18] Law of 27 June 2008 modifying Articles 116, 126, 127, 152, 185, 188, 620 and 621 Code of Criminal Procedure, Mem. A No. 97, 09.07.2008.

[19] Art. 185 (1), para 3 CCP.

[20] Art. 620 CCP.

[21] Art. 621 (1) CCP.

[22] Art. 185 (1) para 4 CCP.

[23] Franchimont et al. (2009), p. 709.

[24] Law of 27 June 2008 modifying Articles 116, 126, 127, 152, 185, 188, 620 and 621 Code of Criminal Procedure, Mem. A No. 97, 09.07.2008.

[25] Art. 185(1) CCP. It should be noticed that the provision applies to Criminal Courts having jurisdiction over offences punished by imprisonment. Separate provisions govern *in absentia* proceedings before the Trial Courts having jurisdiction over minor offences not punished with imprisonment (*juge de police*). See Art. 149 *et seq.*

of the accused does not prevent him to be represented at trial by a lawyer, who must be able to present his client's defense.[26]

The right to legal assistance already shows that the defendant who fails to appear at trial shall not face adverse procedural consequences that would impair the fairness of the proceedings.[27] Thus, any 'sanction' against an unjustified absence must be strictly circumscribed in order to guarantee an effective defence. Where the accused duly notified does not appear in person without presenting a valid excuse or he is not represented in court by a lawyer, the judgment is delivered *in absentia*.[28] In such circumstances, Luxembourg law guarantees the right to a new trial.[29] By contrast, if the defendant does not appear in person at the first hearing but is represented by a legal counsel, the competent tribunal can deliver, in exceptional circumstances, an order to appear in court, which is not open to appeal.[30] In this specific case, the subsequent judicial decisions are automatically considered as the result of an adversarial proceeding.[31] If the defendant summoned to appear is not present at hearings but represented by a lawyer or absent and non-represented by a legal counsel, he will not be entitled to a retrial. Nevertheless, even though the lack of diligence on the part of the accused summoned into court deprived him of the right to a new trial before the same tribunal, he still has the right to lodge an appeal with a second instance court.

3.2   Personal Participation in the Pre-trial Inquiry

Besides cases of *flagrante delicto* offences, Luxembourg criminal procedure distinguishes two categories of pre-trial inquiries. On the one hand, the police conducts preliminary investigations (*enquête préliminaire*) under the supervision of the Public Prosecutor.[32] The purpose is to establish the facts and collect information needed for the competent prosecuting authority to decide whether prosecution should be initiated.[33] As a general rule, the preliminary investigation does not contemplate the possibility to enforce coercive measures.[34] If the Prosecutor decides to prosecute the case, he can either request the Examining Magistrate to authorize

---

[26] Art. 185 CCP.

[27] ECtHR, *Poitrimol v. France*, judgement of 23 November 1993, Appl. No. 14032/88, para 35.

[28] Art. 185 (2) CCP.

[29] Art. 187 CCP.

[30] Art. 185 (3) and (4) CCP.

[31] Ibid.

[32] Art. 46 CCP.

[33] Indeed, Luxembourg criminal justice system adopts the principle of discretionary prosecution (*opportunité des poursuites*). Art. 23 CCP.

[34] Vogel (2009), p. 60.

specific investigative measures (*instruction simplifiée*)[35] or refer the case to Examining Magistrate, who will lead further investigations (*instruction*).[36] This second category of judicial inquiries is mandatory for serious crimes (*crimes*) and optional for offences punished by lower imprisonment sentences (*délit*) depending on the need to take coercive investigative acts.[37] It is during the judicial investigation that the rights of the suspects and, thereby, his personal participation find the strongest expression during pre-trial proceedings, given the particular intrusive character of the investigative acts that the Examining Magistrate can order.

A first example are the procedural safeguards guaranteed in case of arrest and detention. Under Luxembourg law, the Examining Magistrate can summon the suspect to appear (*mandat d'amener*) or deliver an arrest warrant (*mandate d'arrêt*). The former measure can be enforced if there is a risk of the accused fleeing, suppression of evidence or if the whereabouts of the accused are unknown.[38] The latter applies where the accused is fugitive or not resident in Luxembourg, provided that the offence he is suspected of having committed is punishable by imprisonment.[39] In both situations, the use of coercion implies a set of procedural safeguards that primarily aims to protect the arrested person against arbitrary deprivation of liberty. At the time of arrest, the suspect receives a copy of the warrant.[40] If the person cannot be captured, the police notifies him of the arrest warrant at his last place of residence.[41] Warrants must be reasoned in a detailed manner by reference to the factual circumstances of the case and in the light of the legal requirements for arrest and detention,[42] in order to guarantee the right of the arrested person to be informed. Moreover, the arrested person must be brought before the Examining Magistrate for questioning within 24 h after arrest.[43] Besides the right to legal assistance,[44] the first hearing before the Examining Magistrates determines the timing and the application of two further defense rights. First, the judge conducting the questioning informs the suspect about the charges against him.[45] Secondly, the arrested person and his lawyer have access to the entire case file at the latest 30 min before the questioning.[46]

---

[35] Art. 24-1 (1) CCP. More specifically, when conducting a preliminary investigation of minor offences punished by imprisonment not exceeding 1 year, the Public Prosecutor may request the Examining Magistrate to order searches, seizures, the hearing of a witness or an expertise.

[36] Art. 50 CCP.

[37] Art. 49 CCP.

[38] Art. 91 CCP.

[39] Art. 94-1 CCP.

[40] Art. 97 para 2 CCP.

[41] Art. 102 CCP.

[42] Art. 94 and 94-1 CCP.

[43] Art. 93 CCP.

[44] Art. 3-6 CCP.

[45] Art. 81(1) CCP.

[46] Art. 85 (1) CCP.

After the first questioning of the accused, the Examining Magistrate can order a pre-trial detention (*mandat de dépôt*) if there are strong indications that the suspect accused has committed a criminal offence and the presumed facts would give rise to at least 2 years of imprisonment.[47] In addition, one of following grounds must be met: danger of flight, risk of suppression of evidence or risk that the accused will commit further offences.[48] Luxembourg law does not set forth a maximum length of pre-trial detention, nor does it provide a system of *ex-officio* judicial review at regular intervals. Indeed, the CCP only foresees an 'information procedure' that simply requires the Examining Magistrate to inform the competent Public Prosecutor about the continued detention. The latter has than the possibility to request the Pre-trial Chamber of the competent District Court to order interim relief (*mise en liberté*), if the conditions for continued detention are no longer fulfilled.[49] However, the person held in pre-trial detention can at any time submit to the Pre-Trial Chamber a request for interim release, at intervals of at least 1 month.[50]

Secondly, Luxembourg criminal procedure provides for the participation of the accused in connection with coercive investigative measures. For instance, home searches are undertaken in the presence of the person whose home is searched, his lawyer or, failing that, two witnesses designated by the police.[51] The same rule applies to searches of persons (*fouilles corporelles*) and of wallets and luggage (*fouilles de portefeuilles et baggage à main*).[52] As for the active participation of the accused in the evidence-gathering, Luxembourg law does not recognize, properly speaking, a procedural right to gather evidence. Admittedly, the accused can undertake acts that may contribute to his defense, with the exception of investigative measures that would imply coercion. However, the defendant has the possibility to request the Examining Magistrate to undertake certain acts, such as for instance witness questioning[53] or the appointment of an expert.[54] The decision by which the Examining Magistrate (*ordonnance du juge d'instruction*) dismisses the request is of judicial nature[55] and, therefore, can be appealed before the Pre-Trial Chamber of the competent District Court.[56] By contrast, the decision whereby the Examining Magistrate orders an investigative act without however following upon an application or a claim are considered administrative acts, which are subject to limited judicial review.[57] Nevertheless, pleas of illegality concerning investigative orders can be

---

[47] Art. 94 para 1 CCP.

[48] Art. 94 para 2 CCP.

[49] Art. 94-3 CCP.

[50] Art. 113 and 116 (1) CCP.

[51] Art. 34 CCP.

[52] For a detailed analysis, see Petschko et al. (2013), pp. 460–461 (fn 5).

[53] Art. 69 (3) CCP.

[54] Art. 87 (2) CCP.

[55] Vogel (2009), p. 133.

[56] Art. 133 CCP.

[57] Vogel (2009), p. 133.

raised before the Pre-trial Chamber, which has only the power to annul the challenged act and therefore exclude the use of evidence gathered via the execution of an investigative measure that was declared void.[58]

3.3 Personal Participation in Proceedings In Camera

The principle of an oral and public hearing is enshrined in both the Luxembourg Constitution and Article 190 of the CCP. However, the Trial Court may order the holding of the hearings *in camera* (*huis clos*) if the publicity of proceedings would jeopardize public order or public morals.[59] The decision, however, does not affect the public pronouncement of the judgment,[60] nor the right of the accused and his lawyer to be present at trial.[61]

3.4 Personal Participation in Alternative Proceedings

Luxembourg law further endeavors to ensure the personal participation of the defendant in alternative proceedings. Indeed, since 2015,[62] the Public Prosecutor and the defendant can conclude a plea bargaining agreement (*jugement sur accord*) at any stage of the criminal proceedings before the Trial Court rules on the case.[63] The negotiated proceeding only applies to minor offences punishable by a fine or imprisonment not exceeding 5 years. Where an accused person pleads guilty to the charges against him, he or the Public Prosecutor can suggest the conclusion of an agreement.[64] The latter establishes the facts that the accused acknowledged, the legal characterization of those facts as well as primary and ancillary penalties to be imposed.[65] Once validated by the District Court, the agreement will have the effect to terminate the prosecution of the case as far as the charges it refers to are concerned. If a judicial investigation has been opened, the Examining Magistrate will report his opinion on the agreement.[66]

Not only may the defendant take the initiative in negotiated proceedings. Luxembourg law also provides for his active participation in the subsequent stages

---

[58] Art. 126 CCP.

[59] Art. 190 (2) and 222 CCP.

[60] Art. 190 (3) CCP.

[61] Art. 185 (1) CCP.

[62] Law of 24 February 20115 modifying the Code of Criminal Procedure with the aim to introduce the "*jugement sur accord*", Mem. A No. 33, 04.03.2015. For a detailed analysis, De Geest (2014), pp. 51–56.

[63] Art. 563 para 2 CCP.

[64] Art. 564 para 1 CCP.

[65] Art. 565 CCP.

[66] Art. 568 and 569 CCP.

of the plea-bargaining agreement procedure. It should first be underlined that the accused enjoys the right to legal assistance throughout the entire proceeding[67] and has access to the case files, either immediately[68] or, if a judicial investigation was ongoing, under the conditions set forth under Article 85 CCP.[69] Most significantly, the 2015 law requires the presence of the accused at the hearing before the Court called upon to declare the person guilty and validate the agreement.[70] Indeed, the attendance of the accused is of fundamental importance to guarantee the fairness of the negotiated justice procedure.[71] First, the Public Prosecutor summons the person with whom the agreement was reached to appear before the competent Court.[72] The attendance of the accused is governed by the same rules that apply to the presence of the defendant at the trial in ordinary criminal proceedings.[73] Consequently, not only can the accused be represented by his legal counsel,[74] also the procedures related to judgements delivered *in absentia* laid down in Article 185 CIC apply.[75] At the hearing, the President of the District Court verifies the identity of the accused and questions him about the charges on which he agreed.[76] The defendant and his lawyer can submit to the court further observations and conclusions.[77] Thus, the presence of the accused enables the competent court to undertake a judicial, although limited, review of both the culpability of the defendant for the charges that are object to the agreement and the legality and appropriateness of the proposed penalty.[78]

The proceeding may lead to two different outcomes. If the District Court does not raise objections, it sentences the accused to the penalties set forth in the agreement by delivering a reasoned judgment.[79] Where the Court holds that the culpability is not established, the proposed penalty is not appropriate or that the legal qualification of the facts or the sanction are vitiated by errors of law, it declares that the agreement has lapsed.[80] The accused can still appeal against the judgement delivered by the District Court by means of ordinary remedies provided under Luxembourg criminal procedure.[81]

---

[67] Art. 564 para 2 CCP.

[68] Art. 564 para 4 CCP.

[69] Art. 564 para 5 CCP.

[70] Art. 570 *et seq.* CCP.

[71] On the scope of Article 6 of the ECHR with regard to alternative proceedings and the judicial review to be undertaken by the trial court, see ECtHR, *Natsvlishvili and Togonidze v. Georgia*, judgement of 29 April 2014, Appl. No. 9043/05, para 92.

[72] Art. 570 CCP.

[73] Art. 572 CCP.

[74] Art. 185 CCP.

[75] See *infra*, Sect. 5.

[76] Art. 573 CCP.

[77] Art. 573 CCP.

[78] Art. 575 (1) CCP.

[79] Art. 575 (2) CCP.

[80] Art. 575 (3) CCP.

[81] Art. 576 CCP.

3.5 Personal Participation at Trial

3.5.1 Personal Involvement in Evidence-Gathering

As previously mentioned, Luxembourg law does not formally acknowledge the right of the defendant to gather evidence. The underlying reason lies in the central role that inquisitorial systems traditionally assign to the judge.[82] During the pre-trial stage of criminal proceedings, the Examining Magistrate is empowered to take all investigative acts, which he considers necessary to establish the truth. The defendant may, however, request him to undertake certain investigative measures.[83] Similarly, Trial Court judges play an active role in the evidence-gathering. Indeed, it is for the President of the Criminal Court to steer and conduct the debates, while being obliged to seek both incriminating and exculpatory evidence.[84]

As a consequence, the active participation of the defendant at trial must be analyzed in the light of the right to present his defense, rather than to collect and adduce evidence. A telling example is the right of the defendant to call or present witnesses.[85] Luxembourg CCP requires trial and especially first instance courts to hear the witnesses for and against the accused—in particular where the former was not previously confronted with the latter[86]—if their testimony is necessary in order to establish the truth.[87] This encompasses the witnesses called by the prosecution, the accused and to some extent the victim who constitutes a "*partie civile*". Under certain circumstances, the judges have also the possibility to subpoena witnesses.[88]

Nevertheless, the right enshrined in Article 6 §3, d) ECHR to have witnesses examined is not absolute. Luxembourg criminal procedure provides for two restrictions.[89] On the one hand, if the hearing is manifestly impossible—because for instance of the witnesses' death—, the Court gives reading of their written statements.[90] On the other hand, the Trial Court verifies whether the hearing of the witness called by the defense is likely to contribute to establishment of the truth. In other words, the judge assesses the appropriateness and usefulness of the hearing.[91] This second aspect is particularly source of case law as regards appeal hearings.[92] Indeed, under Luxembourg criminal procedure, appeals on the merits lodged in

---

[82] On the different role of the judge with regard to evidence-gathering in inquisitorial and accusatorial systems, see Pradel (2008), pp. 262–263.

[83] See Sect. 3.2.

[84] Vogel (2009), p. 262.

[85] Art. 190-1 and 153 CCP.

[86] Vogel (2009), p. 262.

[87] Art. 190-1 (3) CCP.

[88] Art. 157 CCP.

[89] CSJ corr. 6 December 2011, No. 586/11 V.

[90] Art. 158-1 CCP.

[91] Vogel (2009), p. 369.

[92] Art. 210 CCP.

front of a second instance Court do not necessarily imply a fresh and complete examination of the case.[93] Thus, Appellate Courts are not required to hear all witnesses called by the defense, who have already testified before the first instance tribunal.[94] However, if the Court of Appeal holds that the hearing is manifestly unnecessary, the decision rejecting the defendant's submission must be duly reasoned in order to avoid arbitrary exclusion of testimonial evidence.[95] The opportunity to hear witnesses called by the defense implies an assessment *in concreto* on whether the particular circumstances of the case constitute an obstacle to the hearing or indicate that the statements the witness will made would lack evidential value. For instance, the Appellate Court may reasonably refuse to hear a witness where the defendant fails to indicate precise reasons for the need to take such an act, as well as the consequences he would draw from it.[96] In a similar way, the Trial Court is entitled to assess whether the questions asked to a witness are relevant in order to establish the truth and it can stop the hearing if it considers that all relevant questions have been asked.[97]

3.5.2 Personal Contribution to the Fact-Finding

At the trial stage of criminal proceedings, the defendant's contribution to the fact-finding is first guaranteed through the right to be heard in person. Indeed, the entitlement to an oral hearing gives the accused an opportunity to comment on the contested facts and to put his case forward. Under Luxembourg law, Article 190-1 CCP provides that the President of the competent Court verifies the identity of the accused and gives reading of the decision to commit for trial.[98] The provision further requires the Trial Court to question the accused, who subsequently presents his defense.[99] According to the case law, the fact that the judge interrupts the hearing of the accused or of the witnesses called by him does not breach the right to a fair trial, provided that the accused had the opportunity to provide all relevant clarifications and effectively comment on all facts against him.[100]

The right to be heard and to give evidence in person is inherent to the adversarial character of the hearing. In this respect, the personal contribution of the defendant lies in the adversarial discussion of evidence and cross-examination of witnesses presented by the prosecution. In case of re-characterization of the charges, Luxembourg Courts ascertain whether the defendant had an effective opportunity to

---

[93] CSJ corr. 18 November 2015, No. 511/15X.
[94] Vogel (2009), p. 397.
[95] CSJ corr. 12 March 2012, No. 141/12 VI.
[96] CSJ corr. 28 April 2015, No. 158/15 V.
[97] Vogel (2009), p. 397.
[98] Art. 190-1 (2) CCP.
[99] Art. 190-1 (3) CCP.
[100] CSJ corr. 4 April 2011, No. 186/11 VI.

take a position on the new characterization of the facts, as well as to prepare and present his defense.[101] The right to be heard also encompasses evidence and arguments put forward by the victim.[102] Finally, Article 190-1 CCP grants the defendant the right of reply (*droit de réplique*) after the closing arguments presented by the prosecutor.[103] The right to speak last does not contradict the presentation beforehand of the defense pleadings, but aims to guarantee the opportunity for the accused to effectively challenge the arguments put forwards by the Public Prosecutor.[104]

3.6   Personal Participation in Higher Instances

Under Luxembourg CCP, judicial review by higher instances corresponds first to appeals brought against a first instance judgement.[105] Appeals shall be lodge with a Court of second instance, which has jurisdiction on the merits of the case. As a consequence, Luxembourg law provides the right of the defendant to be heard in Appellate Courts.[106] However, appeal proceedings do not imply a full re-examination of the case.[107] Therefore, the competent court may refuse, under certain conditions outlined above, to hear a witness called by the defendant and already heard by the first instance Court.[108] It is worth noting that the accused who brings the action has the possibility to submit new arguments on appeal, with the exception of those that must be raised *in limine litis* before the first instance Court, such as for instance the *exceptio obscuri libelli*.[109]

Judgments that have become final may further be challenged with the Court of Cassation.[110] Contrary to the proceedings before Criminal Courts of second instance, appeals in cassation (*pourvoi en cassation*) are limited to points of law.[111] Such a restricted scope of review has an impact on the personal participation of the accused in cassation proceedings. Indeed, Luxembourg law does not guarantee the right for the defendant to be present nor to be heard in the Court of Cassation. This is in line with the ECtHR case law insofar as an appeal on cassation constitutes proceedings

---

[101] CSJ corr. 13 February 2007, No.101/07 V.

[102] CSJ corr. 23 January 2007, No. 51/07 V.

[103] Art. 190-1 (3) CCP. See also CSJ corr. 21 October 2015, No. 421/15 X.

[104] CSJ corr. 4 April 2006, No. 190/06 V.

[105] Depending on the seriousness of the offence prosecuted and therefore the competent court delivering the contested judgement, the right to appeal is enshrined in Articles 172, 199 and 221 CCP.

[106] Art. 210 CCP.

[107] CSJ corr. 18 November 2015, No. 511/15X.

[108] See Sect. 5.1.

[109] Vogel (2009), p. 277.

[110] Art. 416 CCP.

[111] Art. 408 CCP.

involving only questions of law, which intervene only after a public hearing is held in lower instances.[112]

3.7 Special Rules in the Field of Serious Organized Crime

To date, Luxembourg law does not provide specific rules affecting the participation of the accused in criminal proceedings related to organized criminality. The most intrusive measures are allowed in investigations related to a list of serious crimes, among which is organized crime.[113] It should, however, be noted that the Parliament is discussing a bill of law strengthening the investigative tools Luxembourg authorities can use to detect and prosecute terrorism.[114] The proposal is likely to affect the rights of the suspects and accused and, therefore, their participation in criminal proceedings.

4 Personal Participation of Private Parties Other Than Defendants

Luxembourg law provides for specific provisions related to the participation of the victim in criminal proceedings. The most striking example are the procedural guarantees conferred to the *partie civile*. The latter designates the victim of a criminal offence, within the meaning of domestic criminal provisions, who lodges a complaint claiming damages with the Examining Magistrate at the pre-trial stage of proceedings (*constitution de partie civile par voie d'action*)[115] or brings an action for compensation before the Criminal Court at trial (*constitution de partie civile par voie d'intervention*).[116] In both cases, the complaint must indicate the prejudice allegedly suffered by the victim and include a request for compensation. The action for damages thereby instituted by the *partie civile* is referred to the Criminal Court having jurisdiction to establish the guilt or innocence of the accused.[117]

At the pre-trial stage of proceedings, the complaint lodged with the Examining Magistrate has a twofold procedural consequence. One the one hand, the judge conducting the investigation is under the duty to start judicial inquiries (*instruction*), except if the facts set out in the complaint cannot be prosecuted or do not

---

[112] ECtHR, *Hermi v. Italy*, judgement of 18 October 2006, Appl. No. 18114/02, para. 61.

[113] For instance, undercover investigations. Art. 48-17 CCP.

[114] Bill of law No. 6921 adapting the criminal procedure to the needs related to the fight against terrorism, Doc. 6921/00, 2 December 2015.

[115] Art. 56 CCP.

[116] Art. 147 para 2 CCP.

[117] Art. 3 CCP.

constitute a criminal offence.[118] On the other hand, once the complaint is duly filed, the victim is accorded the status of a full party to the criminal proceedings. Consequently, he/she enjoys procedural guarantees akin to the rights of the defendant,[119] such as the right to information and the right to legal assistance.[120] Most importantly, the *partie civile* can access the case file after the first hearing of the accused by the Examining Magistrate.[121] In a similar way, the *partie civile* plays an active role in the pre-trial inquiry. Like the defendant, he/she has the possibility to be present during the questioning of the accused[122] and can request the investigative judge to hear a witness[123] or to appoint an expert.[124] The *partie civile* has notably the possibility to request the Examining Magistrate to ask questions to the witness who is confronted with the accused.[125]

When the Examining Magistrate closes the investigation (*instruction*), the *partie civile* can refer the case to the Pre-Trial Chamber of the competent District Court that has jurisdiction to commit the case to trial if the public prosecutor fails to do so.[126] At the trial stage of proceedings, the *partie civile* takes part in the court hearings. He/she has the right to call witnesses and make submissions to the Court.[127] Being a party to the proceedings, the *partie civile* cannot, however, be heard as a witness on oath.[128] Finally, the *partie civile* as the right to appeal against the decision on civil law claims brought before the competent Criminal Court.[129]

5 *In Absentia* Proceedings

5.1 *Information Rights and Conditions of Waiver of Personal Participation in Criminal Proceedings*

According to Article 185 CCP, the accused who has been duly summoned must appear in court.[130] The provision aims to guarantee not only the right to be heard, but above all the right of the accused to be present at trial. This presupposes that the

---

[118] Art. 57 CCP.

[119] Vogel (2009), p. 19.

[120] Art. 4-1 CCP.

[121] Art. 85 (1) CCP.

[122] Art. 81 (8) CCP.

[123] Art. 69 CCP.

[124] Art. 88 CCP.

[125] Art, 82 CCP.

[126] Art. 127 (3) CCP.

[127] Art. 153 CCP.

[128] CSJ corr. 28 April 2015, No. 158/15 V.

[129] Art. 202 CCP.

[130] Art. 185 (1) para 1 CCP. The provision refers to criminal proceedings before Courts having jurisdiction over offences punished by imprisonment not exceeding 5 years (*Chambre correctionnelle*

defendant has been informed, in due time, of the trial and the consequences of non-appearance.[131] For this purpose, Luxembourg law sets forth procedural requirements for the validity of summons related to both the timing and content of the notification.

On the one hand, summons to appear in court must be notified at least 8 days before the holding of the trial.[132] The time-limit is extended where the defendant does not reside in the country.[133] The defendant has, however, the possibility to renounce beforehand the time-limit of the notice.[134] In addition, Article 146 paragraph 4 CCP provides specific rules in case the above-mentioned time requirements are not respected. If the defendant does not appear in court, the trial court will declare the notification void.[135] If, on the contrary, the accused is present at trial, the judge will not annul the summon to appear, but might postpone the hearing upon request of the defendant.[136]

On the other hand, the content and forms of the notification are subject to a set of legal requirements. In particular, summons to appear must provide the defendant, in a language that he understands, with detailed information about the charges, including the nature and legal characterization of the offence.[137] The Trial Court ascertains whether the information provided was accurate and sufficient for the accused to prepare and present an effective defense (*exception obscuri libelli*).[138] Further irregularities may result from a lack of indications concerning the date and place of the hearing, as well as from the non-compliance with other formal requirements, such as for instance the signature of the competent prosecuting authority.[139]

Where duly summoned, the accused shall appear in person or be represented by a mandated lawyer, who must have the opportunity to present his client's defense. In both cases, the trial is deemed to be adversarial.[140] Thus defined, the rule enshrined in Article 185 of the Luxembourg CCP repealed the absolute duty to appear in

---

du tribunal d'arrondissement). It also applies to Criminal Courts called upon to rule of most serious crimes (*Chambre criminelle du tribunal d'arrondissement*). Art. 222 CCP.

[131] Art. 8 Directive (EU) 2016/343 of the European Parliament and of the Council of 9 March 2016 on the strengthening of certain aspects of the presumption of innocence and of the right to be present at the trial in criminal proceedings, OJ L 65/1.

[132] Art. 146 para 1 CCP.

[133] Art. 146 para 2 CCP.

[134] Art. 146 para 3 CCP.

[135] Art. 146 para 4, 1) CCP.

[136] Art. 146 para 4, 2) CCP.

[137] Vogel (2009), pp. 293 ff.

[138] *Ibidem*, p. 293.

[139] Procedural requirements and related nullities that apply to summons to appear in court are laid down under Articles 381 *et seq.* CCP.

[140] Art. 185 CCP. The provision refers to criminal proceedings before Courts having jurisdiction over offences punished by imprisonment not exceeding 5 years (*Chambre correctionnelle du tribunal d'arrondissement*). It also applies to tribunals competent for misdemeanors (*Tribunal de police*) and most serious crimes (*Chambre criminelle di tribunal d'arrondissement*). See respectively art. 152 CCP; CSJ crim. 21 May 2014, No. 18/14.

person incumbent on the defendant prosecuted for an offence punished by imprisonment.[141] Indeed, the 2008 reform of *in absentia* proceedings[142] was adopted with the aim to enable the accused who does not appear in person at his trial to be assisted by a lawyer and, thereby, to ensure the compliance of Luxembourg law with the case law of the ECtHR.[143] As a result, the defendant may adopt under the procedures in force one of the following options.

The accused can first exercise his right of personal appearance. Where he is unable to be present in Court, he shall provide an excuse for his absence, the validity and reasonableness of which is assessed by the court.[144] In the absence of more detailed statutory provisions, the Court verifies whether it was absolutely impossible for the accused, either because of his physical of psychical situation, to attend the trial.[145] The case law requires for instance that the medical certificate presented by the accused provides concrete and detailed reasons for his absence.[146] In such circumstances, the defendant has the possibility to request the adjournment of the hearing. By contrast, where no valid excuse is presented, the judgement is delivered *in absentia* unless the accused appoints a counsel, who presents his defense at trial.[147]

In other words, Luxembourg law deems the trial adversarial whereas the defense of the absent accused is presented by a lawyer of his choosing. This condition is fulfilled if the legal counsel is commissioned by his client to present his defense and has an effective opportunity to submit his case to court. Effective legal representation is at the very heart of the interpretation held by Luxembourg Criminal Courts of Article 185 (3) CCP. According to the provision, where the defendant who was present during the 'introductory hearing' (*audience d'introduction*) does no longer appear in person and neither is represented by a lawyer, the trial shall be considered adversarial.[148] The case law constantly specified that this provision applies only in exceptional circumstances, i.e. if the defendant does not appear in person or through legal representation after the judgment is reserved, provided that his counsel took stance on the facts and effectively presented his client's defense in court.[149] Hence, the adversarial character of criminal proceedings presupposes the effective possibility for the accused or his lawyer to present his defense on the merits.[150]

---

[141] Conseil d'Etat, Opinion of 13.2.2007, Bill of law No. 5597 modifying Articles 116, 152, 185 and 188 of Luxembourg Code of Criminal Procedure and repealing Articles 127 (5) and 186 of the above-mentioned code.

[142] Law of 27 June 2008 modifying Articles 116, 126, 127, 152, 185, 188, 620 and 621 Code of Criminal Procedure, Mem. A No. 97, 09.07.2008.

[143] Conseil d'Etat, Opinion of 13.2.2007, cited above.

[144] Art. 185 (1) para 1 CCP.

[145] CSJ corr. 29 June 2004, No. 227/04 V.

[146] CSJ corr. 5 May 2006, No. 215/06 V; CSJ corr. 11 December 2007, No. 586/07 V.

[147] CSJ corr. 13 November 2007, No. 521/07 V.

[148] Art. 185 (3) CCP.

[149] CSJ corr. 22 November 2011, No. 552/11 V.

[150] CSJ corr. 5 June 2013, No. 313/12 X.

Legal representation at trial does obviously not preclude the right to personal appearance at court, nor is the accused who does not appear under the obligation to appoint a legal counsel. However, Luxembourg Courts held that the defendant, who still fails to appoint a lawyer after repeated adjournments of the hearing, is using stalling tactics with the aim to delay the trial and therefore should be judged *in absentia*.[151]

Finally, Luxembourg law grants the competent trial court the power to order the defendant to appear in person.[152] Luxembourg judges make use of this power under exceptional circumstances, more specifically in cases in which only the lawyer appears at the first hearing and requests the opportunity to submit the accused's defense.[153] The order to appear is taken by the Trial Court in the form of a judgment, which is not open to appeal.[154] If, in spite of the order, the accused does not appear in court, the final judgement to be adopted is deemed to be adversarial, even when the accused does not appoint a lawyer to present his defense in the subsequent hearings.[155]

5.2   Default Proceedings and Subsequent Remedies

Besides the above-mentioned hypothesis in which the trial is deemed to be adversarial, Article 185(2) CCP provides that a judgement is delivered *in absentia* when neither the accused appears at trial nor does he appoint a lawyer who presents his defense. The rule applies to both first instance judgements and decisions rendered on appeal.[156] In such circumstances, the defendant has the right to lodge an objection (*opposition*) against the enforcement of the judgement delivered *in absentia* within 15 days after having received notice thereof.[157] In order to guarantee the effectiveness of the remedy provided under Article 187 CCP, the provision sets forth as a prior condition that the person convicted *in absentia* must have been informed of the judgement. If the convicted person is not notified in person or if no measures are taken to enforce the judgement which indicate that he was informed, the time limit to lodge an objection is extended until the expiration of the limitation period for the execution of the sentence.[158]

---

[151] CSJ corr. 20 March 2012, No. 162/12 V; CSJ corr. 10 July 2015, No. 310/15 V.

[152] Art. 185 (4) CCP.

[153] CSJ crim. 17 December 2014, No. 45/14.

[154] Art. 185 (4) CCP.

[155] Art. 185 (4) para 3 CCP.

[156] Art. 208 CCP.

[157] Art. 187 para CCP.

[158] Art. 187 para 4 CCP.

The objection has the effect of preventing convictions following a trial in the absence of the accused to acquire force of *res judicata*.[159] Indeed, if the defendant lodges an objection, the judgement delivered *in absentia* shall be deemed null and void.[160] By contrast, acquittal decisions do not fall within the scope of Article 187 CCP.[161] With regard to the scope of review, the provision grants the person convicted *in absentia* the right to a new trial before a Court of same instance. The latter undertakes a fresh determination of the merits of the case and a full assessment, including the examination of new evidence, which may lead to the original decision being reversed.[162] Thus defined, the objection brought against *in absentia* convictions differs from the right to appeal against first instance judgements, which can be instituted by both the defendant and the Public Prosecutor before Courts of second instance.[163] Likewise, the judgement delivered as a result of an objection procedure can still be appealed by the defendant to higher courts. In such circumstances, the competent Appellate Court has, however, no jurisdiction to review the decision by which the first instance judge declared the objection admissible. Such a power would otherwise run counter to the prohibition of *reformation in pejus*.[164]

Despite its fundamental importance, the right to a new trial is not an absolute right. On the contrary, the procedural guarantee benefits the accused who shows a certain diligence. The defendant who lodges an objection shall notify both the *partie civile* and the Public Prosecutor.[165] The latter shall then summon the defendant to appear in court.[166] However, where the accused duly summoned still fails to appear or does not appoint a lawyer to present his defense, the objection is dismissed.[167] Hence, the right to a new trial is not intended to protect the defendant who repeatedly and deliberately fails to be present at trial (*itératif défaut*).[168] In such a case, the person convicted *in absentia* is not entitled to institute a second objection procedure (*opposition sur opposition ne vaut*).[169]

---

[159] Vogel (2009), p. 304.

[160] Art. 187 para 1 CCP.

[161] CSJ corr. 39 March 2009, No. 172/09 VI.

[162] Vogel (2009), pp. 307–308.

[163] Art. 199 *et seq.* CCP.

[164] CSJ corr. 20 February 2013, No. 98/13 X.

[165] Art. 187 para 1 CCP.

[166] Art. 188 para 1 CCP.

[167] Art. 188 para 2 CCP.

[168] CSJ corr. 24 November 2009, No. 516/09 V.

[169] CSJ corr. 15 May 2007, No. 250/07 V.

5.3   Inaudito reo *Proceedings*

Besides *in absentia* proceedings, Luxembourg law sets forth a penal order procedure (*ordonnance pénale*).[170] The latter belongs to the category of *inaudito reo* proceedings, since it rules out *"any participation on the part of the defendant prior to the decision-making, while giving the accused the right to challenge the conviction by means of a special remedy having the form of an opposition"*.[171] Given the exception to the personal participation of the defendant at criminal trial that the penal order procedure implies, Luxembourg law accurately restricts its scope of application. From a substantive point of view, a penal order can apply to minor offences punished by a fine (*contraventions*) or offences punished by short term imprisonment (*délits*) for which the Public Prosecutor requires the imposition of a fine only.[172] Further procedural requirements may obstacle the adoption of a penal order, namely when the victim is a party in the criminal proceedings (*partie civile*), when the case is referred to the Examining Magistrate, the residence of the accused is unknown, when the damage caused to a third party is not compensated or when goods must be returned and were not.[173]

Where the case falls within the above-defined scope of application, the Public Prosecutor shall first inform the defendant, who can access the materials of the case file within 1 month.[174] Only after the expiration of this period, the Prosecutor can request the imposition of a fine of which he sets the amount.[175] The penal order shall then be filed at the registry of the competent Court[176] that can either disagree or agree with the sanction proposed by the Prosecutor. In the former hypothesis, the case is brought to court according to the ordinary criminal procedure.[177] In the latter, the penal order imposes the fine set by the Public Prosecutor,[178] who notifies the decision to the accused.[179]

The notification serves two main functions. First, it guarantees the right of the sentenced person to be informed. To this end, Article 399 CCP lists the information that the penal order must indicate, including a description of the facts, their legal characterization and the sanction imposed. Secondly, the notification is the prerequisite enabling the person subject to a penal order to bring an action against it. In this respect, the order must provide precise information about the remedies available

---

[170] Art. 394 *et seq.* CCP.
[171] Ruggeri (2016), p. 43.
[172] Art. 394 CCP.
[173] Art. 395 CCP.
[174] Art. 396 CCP.
[175] Art. 396 b) CCP.
[176] Art. 397 CCP.
[177] Art. 398 para 2 CCP.
[178] Art. 398 para 1 CCP.
[179] Art. 400 CCP.

to the defendant.[180] On the one hand, the effects of a penal order are assimilated by law to those of a judgement delivered *in absentia*.[181] Therefore, the defendant may lodge an objection against the penal order according to the procedure laid down in Article 187 CCP.[182] On the other hand, this first remedy does not preclude the possibility for the accused to appeal against the penal order before a second instance Court.[183]

6 Participatory Rights in Transnational Criminal Justice

6.1 Participatory Safeguards in EAW Proceedings

6.1.1 Participatory Rights in the Decision on Surrender

The Framework Decision 2002/584/JHA on the European Arrest Warrant (EAW) was implemented in Luxembourg by the Law of 17 March 2004.[184] National implementing provisions guarantee the participation of any person subject to an EAW executed by the Luxembourg judicial authorities throughout the surrender procedure. As with the rights of suspects and accused persons in national criminal proceedings, the 2017 Act implementing the ABC Directives further strengthened the procedural guarantees afforded to the surrender person.[185]

At the time of arrest, the person subject to an EAW has first the right to be provided with a written letter of rights in a language that he understands.[186] The information provided encompasses the right of access to a lawyer in Luxembourg and in the issuing State, the right to interpretation and translation, the possibility of consenting to surrender and renouncing entitlement of the 'speciality rule' and the right to be heard by a judicial authority.[187] As with national arrest warrants, the person arrested on the basis of an EAW is presented within 24 h to the Examining Magistrate, who verifies his identity and takes the decision on whether the requested

---

[180] Art. 399 CCP.

[181] Art. 401 CCP.

[182] See *supra*, Sect. 5.2.

[183] Art. 399 b) and 402 CCP- CCP.

[184] Modified Law of 17 March 2004 related to the European arrest warrant and surrender procedures between the Member States of the European Union, Mem. 2004, p. 588. Hereinafter Law implementing the EAW.

[185] Law of 8 March 2017 strengthening procedural guarantees in criminal matters, Mem. A No. 346, 30.03.2017.

[186] Art. 7 para 2 of the 2004 law implementing the EAW.

[187] Art. 7 para 2 of the 2004 law implementing the EAW.

person should remain in detention.[188] The individual has the right to request legal assistance[189] and can at any time submit a request for interim release.[190]

According to the Framework Decision, the arrested person can consent to surrender and renounce expressly the 'speciality rule' before the competent magistrate of the Prosecution Office.[191] In order to ensure a free and informed consent, Luxembourg law grants the requested person the right to linguistic and legal assistance. On the one hand, if the arrested person does not understand French or German, the assistance of an interpreter must be provided throughout the entire surrender procedure, namely from the arrest until the surrender or the refusal to surrender.[192] On the other, the 2017 reform enhanced the right of access to a lawyer in proceedings for executing a EAW in order to fully comply with Article 10 of Directive 2013/48/EU.[193] In this regard, Luxembourg law also guarantees the right for the arrested person to appoint a lawyer in the requesting State.[194] The role of that counsel is to assist the lawyer in the executing Member State by providing that him with information and advice with a view to the effective exercise of the rights of requested persons.

Where the person does not consent to surrender, the case is referred to the Pre-trial Chamber of the competent District Court, which has jurisdiction to order surrender.[195] The requested person and his lawyer are informed about the place and date of the hearing at the latest 48 h before it takes place.[196] The information thus provided are the necessary preconditions that enable the requested person to exercise his right to be heard in court guaranteed under Article 12, paragraph 3 of the 2004 law. In a similar way, the decision adopted by the Pre-trial Chamber is given to the requested person,[197] who has the right to appeal against surrender to the competent higher Court.[198]

---

[188] Art. 8 Law implementing the EAW.

[189] Art. 8 para 1 Law implementing the EAW.

[190] Art. 9 Law implementing the EAW.

[191] Art. 10 Law implementing the EAW.

[192] Art. 7-1 (5) of the 2004 Law implementing the EAW.

[193] Before the legislative reform, Luxembourg law implementing the EAW granted the requested person the right of access to a lawyer where he/she is heard by the Luxembourg executing authorities and in connection with remedies related to the execution of a EAW. In particular, the presence of a lawyer was mentioned in relation to the hearing before the examining magistrate to establish the arrested person's identity (*intérrogatoire d'identité*), where the arrested person indicates that he consents to surrender or renounces his entitlement to the "speciality rule", the hearing before the pre-trial chamber competent to rule upon the execution of the EAW and the appeal against the latter's decision, as well as in the procedure executing a EAW for the purpose of prosecuting other than for which the surrender was requested.

[194] Art. 7-1 of the 2004 law implementing the EAW.

[195] Art. 12 para 12 Law implementing the EAW.

[196] Art. 12 para 3 Law implementing the EAW.

[197] Art. 12 (4) Law implementing the EAW.

[198] Art. 13 Law implementing the EAW.

6.1.2 *In Absentia* Proceedings in the Trial Country and Its Relevance in the Surrender Procedure

In 2015, Luxembourg introduced a specific ground for refusal related to EAWs issued for the purpose of executing a decision rendered *in absentia*.[199] Indeed, Article 5 (9) of the 2004 law implementing the Framework Decision 2002/584 opposes to the surrender of a person who did not appear in person at the trial resulting in the decision referred to in the EAW, unless one of the following conditions are fulfilled. Firstly, the requested person received in due time official information of the scheduled date and place of that trial in the issuing Member State and was informed that a decision may be handed down if he/she does not appear at the trial. Secondly, he or she had given a mandate to a legal counsellor and was indeed defended by that counsellor at the trial. Thirdly, after being served with the decision and being expressly informed about the right to a retrial or an appeal, the requested person expressly stated that he or she does not contest the decision or did not request a retrial or appeal within the applicable time frame.[200]

In addition, Luxembourg law allows the surrender of persons sentenced *in absentia* provided that the issuing Member States guarantees their right to retrial or appeal against the judgement delivered in his absence. In particular, Article 19 of the 2004 law implementing the EAW requires the issuing judicial authority to give an assurance deemed adequate to guarantee to the person who is the subject of the EAW that he or she will have an opportunity to apply for a retrial of the case in the issuing Member State (*droit d'opposition*) and to be present at the judgement.[201]

6.2 Participatory Safeguards in Transborder Inquiries and the Taking of Overseas Evidence

Procedures governing the cross-border gathering of evidence are less protective of participatory safeguards, in particular with regard to defense rights. It should first be noted that Luxembourg has not yet implemented the Directive 2014/41/EU regarding the European Investigation Order,[202] which provides procedural requirements—although limited—aimed at protecting the rights of suspects and accused persons.[203] Considering the comprehensive legal framework for the cross-border gathering of

---

[199] Art. 22 Law of 12 April 2015 modifying the law implementing the European arrest warrant, Mem. A No. 74, 17.04.2015.

[200] Art. 5 (9) Law implementing the EAW.

[201] Art. 19 Law implementing the EAW.

[202] Bill of law No. 7152/00 implementing Directive 2014/41/EU on the European Investigation Order and modifying the CCP.

[203] Directive 2014/41/EU of the European Parliament and the Council of 3 April 2014 regarding the European Investigation Order in criminal matters, OJ L 130, 1.5.2014, p. 1.

evidence that the directive aims to establish[204] and the current lack of implementation in Luxembourg law, two general remarks arise. First, participatory rights might vary depending on the specific provisions provided in the international instrument of judicial cooperation on which the request for assistance is based. Secondly, Luxembourg Criminal Procedure does not formalize the possibility for the defendant to seek evidence abroad, as it does not formally acknowledge a right of the accused to collect evidence in national criminal proceedings.[205] As a consequence, participatory rights in transnational inquiries mainly consist in legal remedies available to the defendant in the issuing and executing States.

In this perspective, two situations must be distinguished. On the one hand, private parties can be involved in procedures governing the execution by Luxembourg authorities of requests for assistance. In this regard, the law of 2000 concerning judicial cooperation in criminal matters grants any person who is subject to the investigation and also third parties holding a legitimate interest to submit written conclusion before the Pre-trial Chamber of the competent Court regarding alleged procedural irregularities in the execution of international letters rogatory.[206] Written submissions can also contain restitution claims.[207] The judicial review undertaken by national courts is, however, limited to executing acts taken by Luxembourg competent authorities. By contrast, a person cannot challenge before Luxembourg courts the legality of the request for assistance addressed by the issuing authorities of another country.[208]

Secondly, considering that a large majority of cross-border investigations concern requests for judicial assistance executed by Luxembourg authorities,[209] only limited case law clarifies participatory rights of private parties in respect of requests for assistance issued by Luxembourg authorities for the purpose of collecting overseas evidence. As regards the advisability of investigative acts, the defendant has the possibility to request the Examining Magistrate to issue a request for assistance in order for foreign authorities to take coercive measures and collect evidence. The Examining Magistrate assesses freely the necessity and appropriateness of the measure.[210] Nonetheless, the decision rejecting the defendant's request can be challenged by the defendant before the competent Court, as it is the case for national inquiries.[211] As regards the review on legality, the request for judicial assistance issued by Luxembourg authorities constitutes a procedural investigative act within the meaning of Article 48-2 CCP. Therefore, procedural flows affecting the legality

---

[204] Recital 7 Directive 2014/41/EU.

[205] See Sect. 3.2, Personal participation in the pre-trial inquiry.

[206] Art. 9 (4) Law of 8 August 2000 concerning judicial cooperation in criminal matters, as modified by the law of 27.10.2010, Mem. A No. 13, 21.1.2011.

[207] Ibidem.

[208] CA, 1st February 1989, No. 6/89.

[209] Report of Judicial authorities (2015), p. 61. www.justice.public.lu/fr/publications/index.html, last accessed 31.7.2018.

[210] CSJ Ch.c.C. 24 April 2012, No. 252/12.

[211] See Sect. 3.2, Personal participation in the pre-trial inquiry.

of such an act are subject to nullities and can be declared void by the Pre-Trial Chamber of the competent District Court. Recently, national courts specified that a time-limit for lodging a request for annulment (*demande en nullité*) applies to any ground for nullity, whatever violation of national or international rules is alleged.[212]

7   Requirements of Personal Participation and *In Absentia* Proceedings. The Perspective of Supranational and International Human Rights Law

7.1   *The Perspective of International Human Rights Law. Critical Remarks on Domestic Law in the Light of the European Convention*

To date, no applications before the ECtHR have challenged the compliance of *in absentia* or *inaudito reo* proceedings under Luxembourg law, nor has the Court held Luxembourg State liable for violations of the right to an oral hearing and the right to be present at trial. It should be recalled, however, that the 2008 law modifying the *in absentia* proceedings was precisely adopted with the aim to comply with the case law of the Strasbourg Court. Indeed, before its entry into force, the accused was under the duty to appear in person at trial as long as he was facing an imprisonment sentence. Where absent, the judgement was delivered *in absentia*.[213] The 2008 reform emphasized the freedom for the defendant to decide whether to appear in person at trial in the light of the ruling *Van Geysem v. Belgium*. Pursuant to the ECtHR judgement, "*a defendant, in spite of having been properly summoned, does not appear, cannot – even in the absence of an excuse – justify depriving him of his right under Article 6 § 3 of the Convention to be defended by counsel*".[214] As a result, the Luxembourg law of 2008 guarantees the right to legal assistance of the accused who does not appear in person at trial.[215]

As regards the interpretation of Article 6 of the Convention with regard to proceedings ruling out the accused's involvement, Luxembourg law seems to comply with the case law of the ECtHR. First, the person sentenced in absentia can subsequently "*obtain from a court which has heard him a fresh determination of the merits of the charge, in respect of both law and fact, where it has not been established that he has waived his right to appear and to defend himself or that he*

---

[212] CSJ crim. 19 February 2013, No. 3/13.

[213] Conseil d'Etat, Opinion of 13.2.2007, Bill of law No. 5597 modifying Articles 116, 152, 185 and 188 of Luxembourg Code of Criminal Procedure and repealing Articles 127 (5) and 186 of the above-mentioned code, p. 2.

[214] ECtHR, *Van Geysem v. Belgium*, judgement of 29 January 1999, Appl. No. 26103/95, para 33.

[215] Art. 185 CCP.

intended to escape trial.[216] Indeed, Article 187 CCP guarantees the right to a new trial before a Court of the same instance, without precluding subsequent appeals lodged with higher instances. Secondly, Luxembourg law assimilates the imposition of penalties resulting from *inaudito reo* proceedings to judgements delivered *in absentia* and thus grants to the defendant the right to lodge an objection under the same conditions laid dawn in Article 187 CIC.[217]

7.2   The Perspective of EU Law. Developments in Domestic Law as a Result of EU Law

While the right to be present at trial under the ECHR does not raise specific points of criticism by the legal doctrine, it is worth recalling that to date Luxembourg did not transpose Directive 2016/343/EU on the strengthening of certain aspects of the presumption of innocence and of the right to be present at trial in criminal proceedings.[218] Nonetheless, no in-depth reform of the rules governing *in absentia* proceedings is expected to arise from the implementation into Luxembourg law of the EU Directive. Indeed, Luxembourg law already guarantees the right to a new trial provided under Article 9 Directive 2016/343/EU, given that the objection procedure under Article 187 CCP allows a fresh determination of the merits of the case by a Court of same instance, which can quash the conviction delivered *in absentia*. However, the right to a new trial guaranteed under the Directive refers to the 'original decision' delivered *in absentia*, without distinguishing, as Luxembourg criminal procedure does, between convictions and acquittals.[219] Likewise, no reform of the penal order procedures is to be foreseen, considering that the right to be present at trial guaranteed by the 2016 Directive would only apply to national proceedings if one or more hearings are held.[220]

Finally, although the 2017 Act implementing Directives A, B and C harmonizing the rights of suspects and accused persons in criminal proceedings was not intended to modify *in absentia* proceedings nor penal order proceedings, two amendments to the legal framework are worth mentioning. Firstly, the appearance notice indicating time and place of the trial hearings shall also indicate the consequences of non-appearance and the subsequent remedies available to persons sentenced *in absentia*.[221] Secondly, the 2017 Act explicitly acknowledges the possibility to lodge an

---

[216] ECtHR, *Sejdovic v. Italy*, judgement of 1 March 2006, Appl. No. 56581/00, para 81.

[217] Art. 401 CCP.

[218] Directive (EU) 2016/343 of the European Parliament and of the Council of 9 March 2016 on the strengthening of certain aspects of the presumption of innocence and of the right to be present at the trial in criminal proceedings.

[219] Art. 9 Directive 2016/343/EU.

[220] Recital 41 Directive 2016/343/EU.

[221] New Article 184 CCP.

objection against a conviction delivered *in absentia* by second instance Courts. The reform codified thereby the judicial practice, which consistently held that the defendant can also lodge objections against judgements delivered on appeal in the absence of the accused.[222]

References

De Geest H (2014) Le jugement sur accord au Grand-Duché du Luxembourg: c'est à l'oeuvre qu'on reconnaîtra l'artisan. JurisNews Droit pénal des affaires 3–4:51–56

Franchimont M, Jacobs A, Masset A (2009) Manuel de procédure pénale. II ed. Larcier, Brussels

Gerkrath J (2019) The constitution of Luxembourg in the context of EU and international law as 'Higher Law'. In: Albi A (ed) The role and future of national constitutions in Europe and global governance. Springer, Heidelberg

Petschko M, Schiltz M, Tosza S (2013) Luxembourg. In: Ligeti K (ed) Toward a prosecutor for the European Union, vol 1. Hart Publishing, Oxford and Portland, pp 449–472

Pradel J (2008) Droit pénal comparé. Dalloz, Paris

Ruggeri S (2016) *Inaudito reo* proceedings, defence rights and harmonisation goals in the EU. Responses of the European Courts and new perspectives of EU law. Eucrim 1:42–51

Vogel G (2009) Lexique de procedure pénale. Larcier, Brussels

---

[222] Bill of law No. 6758 strengthening procedural safeguards in criminal matters, doc. 6758/00, 17 February 2015, p. 52.

Report on Portugal

Vânia Costa Ramos and Bárbara Churro

Abstract Following an introduction to the system of criminal proceedings established in Portugal, this chapter describes the participatory rights of private parties (accused, defence lawyer and victims) in Portuguese criminal proceedings. It covers pre-trial, trial and appellate stages and cross-border cases. It is shown that victims have a broad intervention in Portuguese criminal proceedings. The accused is also vested with a broad range of participatory rights and enjoys a robust right to legal assistance. However, such rights remain quite limited in pre-trial stages. The chapter also considers the law in force concerning *in absentia* trials, which makes them into a commonplace occurrence rather than a measure of last resort. This essentially derives from a combination of the obligation to make a Statement of Identity and Residence, combined with expedited means of serving procedural documents based on a legal fiction of knowledge by the accused, as well as a narrowly designed obligation for the judge to postpone the trial only where he/she believes that the presence of the accused is absolutely indispensable from the outset of the trial hearing. This system is not balanced by the establishment of a right to a re-trial or to lodge an appeal allowing for a fresh determination of the merits of the case, including the right to present new evidence, which makes it hardly compatible with European Law, in particular the case law of the European Court of Human Rights and the newly approved Directive 2016/343/EU. European Law may therefore require that domestic law is reformed in this regard.

This text reflects the personal views of the authors, if not stated otherwise, and not the views of the institutions where they exercise their functions.

V. C. Ramos (✉)
Research Centre for Criminal Law and Criminal Sciences, University of Lisbon, Faculty of Law, Lisbon, Portugal

Alameda da Universidade, Cidade Universitária, Lisbon, Portugal
e-mail: vaniacostaramos@carlospintodeabreu.com

B. Churro
Portuguese Constitutional Court, Lisbon, Portugal
e-mail: bchurro@tribconstitucional.pt

© Springer Nature Switzerland AG 2019
S. Quattrocolo, S. Ruggeri (eds.), *Personal Participation in Criminal Proceedings*, Legal Studies in International, European and Comparative Criminal Law 2, https://doi.org/10.1007/978-3-030-01186-4_11

Abbreviations

CCP	Portuguese Code of Criminal Procedure
CJEU	Court of Justice of the European Union
CPLP	Convention on Mutual Legal Assistance in Criminal Matters among the Member States of the Community of Portuguese Speaking Countries
ECHR	European Convention for the Protection of Human Rights and Fundamental Freedoms
ECtHR	European Court of Human Rights
PC	Penal Code
PConst	Portuguese Constitution
SCJ	Supreme Court of Justice
SIR	Statement of Identity and Residence

1   The Involvement of Private Parties in Criminal Justice

1.1   The Structure and Stages of Portuguese Criminal Proceedings

In 1926 a military movement instituted a dictatorship, named National Dictatorship and later *Estado Novo*. The dictatorship moulded criminal law and criminal procedure law to serve its narrow political views. In what concerns criminal procedure law, the authoritarian regime approved a new code, which entered into force in 1929 and "intensified the inquisitorial nature of the proceedings and softened the defence guarantees, mainly as regards political crimes".[1] This was particularly obvious in the investigation stage where, until 1945, the same judge would lead the investigation and would be responsible to try the case.

However, following the 1974 Revolution, the enactment of a democratic Constitution and the accession to the European Convention on Human Rights (ECHR) in 1976 "demanded new penal laws, fully compliant with respect for fundamental rights".[2] Changes to the system were introduced with the 1982 Penal Code (PC) and the 1987 Code of Criminal Procedure (CCP).[3]

The CCP entered into force on 1 June 1987 and instituted a more adversarial system, providing stronger safeguards for the accused in criminal proceedings.[4] The

---

[1] Silva (2007), p. 25.

[2] Caeiro and Costa (2013), p. 541.

[3] Decree-Law 7/87, of 17 February 1987. Some of the main features of this new Code, such as the power of the public prosecutor to lead the investigation stage, were subject to a preventive constitutionality analysis by the Constitutional Court in its judgment no. 7/87 of 1 January 1987, available at http://www.tribunalconstitucional.pt/tc/acordaos/19870007.html, last accessed 31.7.2018.

[4] In the words of Caeiro and Costa (2013), pp. 540–541, "the main features of the model adopted are: (i) an accusatorial system that ensures equality of arms between prosecution and defence;

Portuguese criminal procedure system does not fit into a purely accusatorial model, but is instead a procedure with an accusatorial structure complemented by the principle of judicial investigation in the field of gathering and production of evidence. The law explicitly states that the Court must, either on its own initiative or at the request of a "subject of the procedure", order the production of all evidence that are deemed as necessary in order to discover the truth and make the right decision in the case.[5]

Strictly speaking, it is not a system of parties, in which the court retains complete control of the case and has the duty to take guidance not only from evidence presented by the defence and prosecution/victim, but also from the results of its own efforts in the search for the truth.[6] Therefore, when using the term "private parties" in this text, it must be taken into account that it does not correspond to the domestic expression used to describe the participants in the proceedings, each of whom is a "subject of the procedure" (*sujeito processual*).

Portuguese criminal proceedings follow the legality principle: as a rule, a report on a criminal offence always leads to the opening of an inquiry and, provided sufficient evidence[7] is gathered, the prosecution has virtually no discretion to decide whether or not to bring charges against someone.[8]

Criminal proceedings are divided into: (i) ordinary or common proceedings (*processo comum*); (ii) abbreviated proceedings (*processo abreviado*); (iii) summary proceedings (*processo sumário*); and (iv) expedited proceedings (*processo sumaríssimo*).[9]

Ordinary criminal proceedings consist of three stages (two pre-trial stages and a trial stage), possibly followed by an appeal stage. The pre-trial stages are the inquiry (*inquérito*) and the judicial pre-trial stage (*instrução*).[10]

---

however it is not a procedure of "parties": in the first place, the prosecution must abide by a principle of objectivity, investigating *à charge et à decharge*, and, if that is the case, pleading for the acquittal of the accused, or appealing on his behalf; in the second place, the court has the power to take the measures that are deemed necessary to discover the truth, irrespective of the contributions of the prosecution and the defence; (2) a full-fledged right of defence; (3) the conferral upon the judge of the power to order (or, at least, ratify) measures that interfere more seriously with fundamental rights".

[5] Art. 340 CCP.

[6] Beleza and Costa Pinto (2007), p. 172.

[7] "Sufficient evidence is the evidence on the basis of which it is reasonable to believe that a sanction or security measure would be imposed on the accused should he/she face trial" (Art. 283(2) CCP).

[8] Alternative measures set out in CPP are deviations from this principle, although according to Caeiro and Costa (2013), p. 548 and footnote 46, they do not qualify as instances of opportunity since they do not involve a discretionary power. See also. Caeiro and Costa (2013), pp. 547–548. See below, Sect. 3.4.

[9] See below, Sect. 3.4.

[10] About the procedural stages, see Antunes (2016), pp. 59–107; 157–198; Silva (2014), pp. 9–17 (and the whole volume); Mendes (2013a), pp. 53–103; Caeiro and Costa (2013), p. 543–545. The latter use the term "bringing someone to judgment" to describe the judicial pre-trial stage.

The inquiry[11] is led by the Public Prosecutions Office (*Ministério Público*), assisted by criminal police bodies, and comprises a set of legal steps aiming at investigating the alleged commission of a criminal offence, identifying its perpetrators and determining their responsibility and at finding and gathering evidence for the purpose of deciding whether or not to prosecute.[12] Prosecutors must act under strict criteria of legal objectivity and impartiality. Their role is to collaborate with the Court in order to find the truth, i.e. they also have a duty to collect evidence favourable to the suspect.[13] During the inquiry, any procedural acts which interfere with fundamental rights must be authorized, ordered or conducted by an investigating judge, upon request by the prosecutor.[14]

The judicial pre-trial stage[15] is a facultative screening stage. It will only take place if requested: (i) by the accused, in order to challenge the prosecutorial indictment or private indictment; or (ii) by the assistant to the prosecution,[16] where the proceedings do not depend on private indictment, in order to challenge the closing of the case by the Public Prosecutions Office. This stage is presided over by the investigating judge (*juiz de instrução*), assisted by the criminal police bodies. The investigating judge cannot later take part in the trial, for the sake of impartiality.[17] This stage is not open to the public, but it is organized in an adversarial manner—i.e. accused, prosecutor and assistant may take part and intervene in all procedural acts. This stage comprises the evidence gathering or production acts deemed relevant by the investigating judge and also a mandatory pre-trial hearing (*debate instrutório*), which is adversarial and conducted orally. After the pre-trial hearing, the investigating judge evaluates whether or not there is sufficient evidence to indict the accused.

The trial stage[18] is presided over by one judge or a panel of three judges, the latter for more serious crimes. Trials by jury (a mixed jury composed of three professional judges and four laypersons) are possible in certain cases, but are extremely rare. The single judge (or presiding judge) takes an active role in the trial proceedings, having the power to direct the entire trial hearing. The questioning of the accused, the assistant, the civil parties and the experts is conducted by the judge(s). The prosecution, the assistant's lawyer and the defence lawyer may, at the end of the questioning, suggest further questions to be asked by the judge. The presiding judge also has the power to investigate and may order the gathering or production of both inculpatory

---

[11] Art.s 262 to 285 CCP.

[12] Art.s 262 (1) and 263 CCP. See Caeiro and Costa (2013), pp. 545–547, describing the authorities competent for investigation and prosecution.

[13] In the words of Germano Marques da Silva, investigation is unilateral in the sense that the acts undertaken are those which the Public Prosecution deems necessary or suitable, but from the viewpoint of the search for the truth, it should rather be classified as "omni-comprehensive"—Silva (2014), p. 89.

[14] Art. 32 (4) PConst and Art.s 267 and ff CCP.

[15] Art.s 286–310 CCP. There is no preliminary judicial stage in special procedure forms.

[16] See below, Sect. 4.

[17] Art. 40 (b) CCP.

[18] Art. 311 to 380 CCP.

and exculpatory evidence *ex officio*—which is done quite often. Trial hearings are public, save when, in order to safeguard personal dignity or public morals or to ensure the Court's normal operations, the Court decides otherwise by written order.

1.2 Definition of Private Parties

As outlined above, the term "private parties" does not correspond to the domestic expression used to describe the active procedural participants, but will be used for the purposes of this text to describe private persons with active involvement in criminal proceedings, i.e. those who have participation rights which enable them to influence the outcome of the criminal limb of the proceedings. Many entities and individuals take part in the proceedings. Hence we should distinguish private parties from those who collaborate but are not allowed to intervene in an active way in the proceedings (mere participants) from those who have an active participation in the *civil limb* of the proceedings.[19]

Having this definition in mind, the private parties in Portuguese criminal proceedings are (i) the accused; (ii) the assistant and (iii) the defence lawyer.

1.3 Constitutional Requirements of the Involvement of Private Parties in Criminal Justice

The Portuguese Constitution (PConst)[20] lays down the fundamental framework of the participation of private parties in criminal justice.

Drawing on Art. 6 ECHR, Art. 20 PConst, under the heading "access to law and to effective judicial protection", lays down **the right to a fair trial, to legal remedy and to legal assistance**. It reads "[e]veryone is guaranteed access to the law and the courts in order to defend his/her rights and interests that are protected by law, and justice may not be denied to anyone due to lack of sufficient financial means" (§1); "[s]ubject to the terms of the law, everyone has the right to legal information and advice, to legal counsel and to be accompanied by a lawyer before any authority" (§2) and finally "[e]veryone has the right to secure a decision in any suit in which he is intervening within a reasonable time limit and by means of fair process" (§4).

---

[19] See Silva (2013), p. 152, adopting the distinction drawn by Dias (1988) p. 1 and ff. clearly distinguishing those participants that undertake single actions the procedural contents of which are exhausted in the undertaking of such actions from those who hold autonomous rights that allow them to mould the progress of the proceedings and to influence its final outcome—the "subjects of the procedure", which include the Court, the Public Prosecution, the Accused, the Assistant and the Defence Lawyer.

[20] Available in English on http://www.en.parlamento.pt/Legislation/CRP/Constitution7th.pdf, last accessed 31.7.2018.

In the scope of criminal proceedings, Art. 32 PConst, which is a concretion of Art. 20, lays down the fundamental principles of criminal procedure, including the rights of private parties, both accused and victim, under the heading "[s]afeguards in criminal procedure".

Among these are the rights of the accused to enjoy the widest procedural safeguards, including the right to appeal (§1); the presumption of innocence and the right to be tried promptly (§2); the right to be assisted by a lawyer of the accused's choice (§3); the right to adversarial proceedings (§5); the right to be present (§6); the right to have evidence obtained by means of torture, coercion, an infringement of bodily of moral integrity of the person, abusive interference in private life of the home, in correspondence and telecommunication excluded from proceedings (§8).[21]

The 1997 Constitutional Amendment introduced a legal provision in Art. 32 concerning the rights of victims which reads: "[v]ictims have the right to intervene in the proceedings, as laid down by law" (§7).

Fundamental rights bind all public authorities and private entities and are directly applicable (Art. 18§1 PConst). They may only be restricted in order to safeguard other constitutionally protected rights or interests and by means of explicit previous laws and as long as their essential content remains unaffected (Art. 18§§2 and 3 PConst). Courts are obliged not to apply unconstitutional provisions (Art. 204 PConst) and must construe any legal provisions in conformity with constitutional rights or principles.[22]

2   Personal Participation of Private Parties and Legal Assistance

The fundamental rights outlined in the previous section and their exercise are defined in precise terms by legislation that implements the constitutional mandate, in particular the Code of Criminal Procedure, but also in the Victim Statute,[23] the

---

[21] Other relevant protections are laid down in Art. 32§9 (right to the "*natural judge*"); Art. 29§5 (right not to be punished or tried twice); Art. 27 and 28 (the right to liberty, limitations to that right and the right to have detation reviews by a judge and to compensation for unlawful deprivation of liberty); Art. 31 (*habeas corpus*), etc.

[22] "Constitutional provisions have a triple role: a guaranteeing role, allowing a direct control of legislation, as well as its enforcement by the courts (through constitutional review); a conforming one, as they determine and impose upon the legislator a certain scope of procedural matters; and finally, an interpretative role, through which constitutional solutions may be invoked in the process of finding the correct answer to concrete problems. They may even be used to fill in *lacunae* within procedural legislation"—Beleza and Costa Pinto (2007), p. 171.

[23] Appended to Law 130/2015, of September 4. There are also special regulations for the victims of violent crimes and of domestic violence: Law 104/2009, of September 14, on compensation to victims of violent crimes; Law 112/2009, of September 16, on prevention of domestic violence and protection and assistance to its victims; Decree-Law 120/2010, of October 27, on the Commission on the Protection of Crime Victims.

Regulation on Procedural Costs[24] and the Law on Access to Law and to the Courts.[25] In the next sections we will outline the main traits of the participatory rights of private parties.

2.1 The Accused[26]

The Portuguese Code of Criminal Procedure distinguishes between the "suspect" (*suspeito*) and the "accused" (*arguido*). Only the latter falls into the above-mentioned definition of private party. As will be shown, it is the acquisition of the status of accused that grants a person specific defence rights and duties, as well as institutional guarantees. This is why qualifying someone as either a suspect or an accused is a matter of major relevance, since until that moment a suspect—or any person—is a mere intervener in the proceedings.[27]

A "suspect" is defined by Art. 1(e) CCP as a "person in respect of whom there is evidence that he/she has committed or is preparing to commit a criminal offence, or took part in that commitment or is preparing to take part in it". Until formally entitled with the status of accused, the position of the suspect in the proceedings is more alike that of an ordinary witness. He is not allowed to intervene in the proceedings, *maxime* in the investigation stage, namely requesting for evidence to be gathered or for the opening of the judicial pre-trial stage.[28] Like any person, the suspect has two main rights[29]: (i) he/she cannot be compelled to answer self-incriminating questions or to provide self-incriminating evidence; and (ii) he/she has the right to be assisted by a lawyer. Moreover, the suspect has the right to request to be considered as an "accused", which entitles him/her to the full range of rights granted to the latter.[30]

Although the CCP does not contain a notion of "accused",[31] its definition may be drawn from the provisions that shape the status of the accused, i.e. his/her rights and

---

[24] Decree-Law 34/2008, of February 26.

[25] Law 34/2004, of July 29.

[26] About the accused see Antunes (2016), pp. 36–44; Mendes (2013a), pp. 123–131; Silva (2013), pp. 297–320.

[27] Antunes (2016), pp. 36–37.

[28] At later stages of the proceedings, this distinction becomes faint; a trial must be conducted against an accused.

[29] Art.s 132(2) and (3) CCP. Cf. on the suspect's the right against self-incrimination, Mendes (2013a), pp. 123–125.

[30] Art. 250(8) CCP. Caeiro and Costa (2013), p. 550, state that "[t]he suspect, as such, has no formal status in the Portuguese criminal procedure. Therefore, he has no special procedural rights of duties"—we believe the authors are referring only to the non-existence of a special status of suspect, but not purporting that suspects have no rights at all.

[31] See Caeiro and Costa (2013), pp. 550–551.

duties within the criminal proceedings (Art.s 60 and 61[32]), and also from the provisions that lay down the requirements for the formal acquisition of that status (Art.s 57, 58 and 59[33]).

According to Art. 60 once a person acquires the status of accused he/she is ensured the exercise of procedural rights and duties, without prejudice to the enforcement of coercive and patrimonial guarantee measures or evidence gathering acts, as provided for by law.

Some of these rights and duties are scattered across the CCP, but their essence, which constitutes the status of the accused, is contained in Art. 61.[34]

According to this provision,[35] the accused has the following rights: (i) to be present in all procedural acts that directly concern him/her; (ii) to be heard by the court or the investigating judge whenever they must hand down a decision that personally affects him/her; (iii) to be informed on the charges against him/her prior to making any statements before any entity; (iv) to silence and against self-incrimination[36]; (v) to appoint a defence lawyer of his/her choice or to ask the court to appoint him/her one; (vi) to be assisted by a defence lawyer in any procedural acts where he/she takes part and to consult in confidence with such lawyer including while in detention; (vii) to intervene in the inquiry and judicial pre-trial stage, submitting evidence and making applications for the carrying out of any acts which he/she deems necessary; (viii) to be informed on his/her rights by the judicial authority or criminal police body before which he/she must appear; (ix) to appeal, under the law, against any decisions made to his/her detriment.

The status of the accused implies, on the other hand, the following duties[37]: (i) to appear before the judge, prosecutor or criminal police body whenever required by law and after having been duly summoned; (ii) to answer truthfully questions addressed by the competent authority about his/her identity; (iii) to make a statement of identity and residence (*termo de identidade e residênica*) as soon as he/she acquires the status of accused; (iv) to undergo evidentiary acts and suffer coercive and patrimonial guarantee measures, as specified by law and as ordered and implemented by a competent authority.

The accused is considered to be a "subject of the proceedings" as opposed to an "object of the proceedings"—i.e. the accused is not a collaborator of judicial or

---

[32] A non-official translation of these provisions is available in English on http://www.gddc.pt/codigos/code_criminal_procedure.html, last accessed 31.7.2018.

[33] A non-official translation of these provisions is available in English on http://www.gddc.pt/codigos/code_criminal_procedure.html, last accessed 31.7.2018.

[34] On the rights of the accused in more detail see also Caeiro and Costa (2013), pp. 577–585.

[35] Art. 61(1) CCP.

[36] Art. 61(1)(d) explicitly refers to the right to silence only, but it is construed in conformity with the PConst as containing a broader right against self-incrimination—see, for example, Judgment of the SCJ 14/2014 (harmonising case-law) of May 24, 2014, published in the Official Gazette on 21 October 2014, Series I, available at https://dre.pt/application/file/a/58512485. This judgment ruled, by 9 votes to 6, that compelling the accused to provide handwriting samples for the purposes handwriting analysis fell within the scope of the protection of the right against self-incrimination, but considered that it was a constitutionally admissible restriction of such right.

[37] Art. 61(3) CCP.

police authorities in the search for the truth and the achievement of justice,[38] but rather an intervener vested with defence rights which he/she may exercise if he/she wishes to do so and in a manner as he/she determines.

When does a "suspect" become an "accused"? The latest at the end of the inquiry, if an indictment is brought against a person, or if there has been a request by the assistant to open the judicial pre-trial stage against that person.[39] During the investigation the formal acquisition of the status of accused (*constituição de arguido*) is mandatory as soon as: (i) a person makes statements before any judicial authority or criminal police body during an inquiry started against him/her, where there are reasonable grounds to suspect that such person has committed a criminal offence; (ii) a coercive or patrimonial guarantee measure must be imposed on a specific person; (iii) a suspect is arrested under the terms and for the purposes of Art.s 254 to 261 of the Criminal Procedural Code; (iv) a police report has been drawn up identifying a person as an alleged offender and such person has been informed on the content thereof, unless the report is manifestly ill-founded.

In addition to those cases, the CCP also requires that where in the course of an interview with someone other than an accused person a reasonable suspicion that such interviewed person committed a criminal offence arises, the authority conducting the interview shall immediately suspend it and declare that person as an accused person. This may also occur upon request of such a person whenever investigations conducted for purposes of confirming a suspicion personally affect him/her.[40]

The formal acquisition of the status of accused is undertaken by means of notification to the person concerned stating that as of that moment he/she has the status of accused in criminal proceedings and is entitled to the rights and bound by the duties laid down in Art. 61 CCP, which are listed on a "letter of rights and duties" (*termo de constituição de arguido*) that is given to that person. If necessary, an oral explanation of those procedural rights and duties shall be given. Furthermore, the letter also contains the particulars of the case files and the identification of the defence lawyer, if one has been appointed.[41]

If a person is not declared as an accused in contravention of these provisions, or, although declared as one, the legal formalities have not been complied with, any statements made by that person (as well as any secondary evidence causally linked thereto) cannot be used.[42]

Legal entities may also be held liable for criminal conduct, provided that such responsibility is explicitly established in a statute. Portugal has introduced criminal liability for legal entities in 1984, albeit on an exceptional basis, in the field of tax and customs criminal law, and of economic crimes. However, in 2007 a general provision was introduced in the Criminal Code (Article 11), establishing corporate

---

[38] Mendes (2007), pp. 602–609.

[39] Art. 57(1) CCP.

[40] Art. 59 CCP and 250 (8) CCP.

[41] Art. 58(2) and (4) CCP.

[42] Art. 58(5) CCP.

criminal liability for a vast number of crimes. Surprisingly, the legislator did not introduce any procedural rules for legal entities in their capacity of accused persons, which may create many hurdles—and even issues of unconstitutionality—since it is necessary to apply by analogy, in an adapted manner, provisions which were made for natural persons, such as those concerning service of papers and coercive measures.

2.2 The Defense Lawyer and the Right of the Accused to Legal Assistance[43]

The defence lawyer is considered a private party of his/her own who exercises the rights conferred to the accused, which do not need to be exercised in person,[44] but he/she also has rights of his/her own, such as the right to communicate with the client in person and in confidence even while in detention.[45] The defence lawyer can intervene in any stage of the proceedings and his/her status is protected by professional immunities and privileges.

The defence lawyer is, however, not a mere assistant or representative of the accused, but an organ of the administration of justice who acts in the exclusive interest of the defence, despite the absence of a manifestation of will of the accused asking for representation, or even against the will of the accused.[46] It is in the interest of justice that criminal defence is effective.[47] The role of the lawyers as an essential element to the administration of justice is even constitutionally established in Art. 208 PConst. In fact, the defence lawyer "exercises a role of general interest guaranteeing the lawfulness of proceedings with the aim of ensuring Justice and also helping the accused to vindicate his rights and legal interests".[48] This two-folded role is therefore, on one hand, a role of guarantee and control of the lawfulness of procedural acts and, on the other hand, a role of legal technical assistance to the accused.

The Constitution states that the accused has the right to be assisted by a counsel of his/her choice and specifies that the law shall determine in which cases and stages

---

[43] About defence lawyers, see Antunes (2016), pp. 44–47; Mendes (2013a), p. 13; Silva (2013), pp. 321–354. Silva (2013), pp. 345–354 is the only author who seeks to define what is a "criminal lawyer" is from a practical rather than a legal viewpoint, reflecting on what characteristics such a lawyer should have, based on his empirical observations over decades and exchanges of views with other defence lawyers.

[44] Art. 63. This is the case of making statements—only the accused can make statements on his/her behalf.

[45] Art. 78 Law 145/2015, of September 9.

[46] Antunes (2016), p. 45.

[47] Mendes (2013a), p. 131; Silva (2013), p. 326.

[48] Silva (2013), pp. 322–323.

such assistance is mandatory.[49] The law requires legal assistance in many instances.[50] In fact, one could state that there are few instances in which the accused intervenes in criminal proceedings without the assistance of a defence lawyer—mainly when police authorities question the accused without having him/her arrested and during some evidence gathering acts if the accused speaks Portuguese and is above 21 years of age.[51]

Mandatory assistance stems from the acknowledgment that the accused finds him/herself in a vulnerable position, either on procedural or on personal grounds. Accordingly, the CCP mandates legal assistance in the following situations—notwithstanding any other provisions requiring legal assistance—considered of "procedural vulnerability": (i) interrogation of an accused who is deprived of his/her liberty; (ii) interrogations conducted by judicial authorities; (iii) in pre-trial hearings and in trial hearings; (iv) in the appeal stages; (v) during the gathering of witness statements that may be used in court later ("statements for future memory"); (vi) in trial hearings taking place in the absence of the accused.[52] In addition to those, due to the "personal vulnerability" of certain persons, the CCP requires legal assistance in any procedural acts other than the formal declaration as accused (*constituição de arguido*), whenever the accused has any visual, hearing or speech impairment or is illiterate, cannot speak or understand the Portuguese language, is under 21 years old, or if doubts concerning his/her mental capacity to stand trial are raised.[53]

Certain acts can only be undertaken by the defence lawyer, such as the application to lodge an appeal, to open or to close arguments during trial or present oral pleadings in the appellate stages.[54]

Financial legal aid is available for the accused in any criminal case, irrespective of the severity of the offences he/she has been charged with. There is a means test

---

[49] If the accused cannot afford a lawyer (or does not have a lawyer of his choice), he/she has the right to request for one to be appointed by the state.

[50] The Portuguese regime of mandatory assistance has been challenged frequently at international level. Until 2006 it had been deemed as compatible with international law, namely the ECHR. But in 2006, the United Nations' Human Rights Committee decided that there had been a violation of Art. 14, paragraph 3 (d), of the International Covenant on Civil and Political Rights since Portuguese Criminal proceedings foresaw no exceptions to mandatory legal assistance, irrespective of the severity of the charges and the complexity of the case and of the characteristics of the accused (Correia de Matos v. Portugal, Comm. 1123/2002, U.N. Doc. A/61/40, Vol. II, at 175 (HRC 2006), available on http://www.worldcourts.com/hrc/eng/decisions/2006.03.28_Correia_de_Matos_v_Portugal.htm, last accessed 31.7.2018.

There is also an application to the European Court of Human Rights pending decision of the Grand Chamber in case Correia de Matos v. Portugal, application no. 56402/12 (see http://hudoc.echr.coe.int/eng?i=001-147105, last accessed 31.7.2018).

[51] In this case the accused may oppose to his/her statements being used in a later stage.

[52] Art. 64(1)(a) to (c) and (e) to (g) CCP.

[53] Art. 64(1)(d) CCP.

[54] Art.s 339, 360 and 423 CCP.

established in the Law on Access to Law and to the Courts,[55] and in further legal aid regulations.

In practice, however, irrespective of meeting the means test, or not, the accused always benefits from legal assistance. Even if the accused has not been granted financial legal aid, he/she always enjoys the benefit of legal assistance by a lawyer appointed *ex officio*, if a private lawyer has not been instructed by him/her. This lawyer is paid for by the state[56] and the accused will only bear the respective costs if he/she is convicted. In such cases where a legal aid lawyer is appointed to represent the accused, the latter is not free to choose his/her own lawyer. One will be drawn randomly from a roster by a computer system managed by the Portuguese Bar Association.

Defence lawyers enjoy broad privileges and immunities in the discharge of their functions, following the constitutional mandate that considers them as an element essential to the administration of justice.[57] The Law on Organization of the Judiciary[58] and the Law on the Portuguese Law Bar Association[59] implement the constitutional mandate. Lawyers may not be prevented from exercising their role and enjoy all privileges and immunities needed to exercise it in an unbiased, independent and responsible manner, namely those of: (i) protection of professional secrecy; (ii) the right to provide legal assistance freely and not to be sanctioned for the exercise of any acts in conformity with the professional rules; (iii) the right to special protection of communications with the client and to the protection of secrecy of any documents concerning the exercise of the rights of defence; (iv) the right to special regulations concerning scaling, listing and searches conducted in their professional premises, as well as concerning seizure of documents.[60] Professional secrecy concerning legal assistance in criminal proceedings is absolute—there are no exceptions to the confidentiality of communications between defence lawyer and client.[61] Defence lawyers themselves also have the right to communicate, in person and in confidence, with their clients while the latter are in detention.[62]

On a final note it should be stressed that, as mentioned above, the accused has the right to communicate with his/her defence lawyer at all times and in confidence, including while in detention. In the first legislative draft of the CCP there was a provision derogating from the right to access to a lawyer in cases of terrorism, violent or highly organized criminality, which would allow for the public prosecutor to prevent the communication of the detained person with his/her lawyer before the

---

[55] Law 34/2004, of July 29.

[56] The fees legal aid lawyers receive are very modest.

[57] Art. 208 CCP.

[58] Law 62/2013, of August 26, 2013.

[59] Law 145/2015, of September 9, 2015.

[60] Art. 13 Law 62/2013, of August 26, 2013, and Art.s 66(3), 69, 72, 75, 76, 77, 78, 79, 80, 88, 89, 92 and 113 Law 145/2015, of September 9, 2015.

[61] See Art.s 143(4), 179(2) and 187(5) CCP.

[62] Art. 78 Law 145/2015, of September 9.

arraignment. This was found to be incompatible with Art. 32§3 PConst, since the right to legal assistance encompasses, in the view of the Constitutional Court, not only the right to the presence of a lawyer, but also the right of the accused to communicate with his/her lawyer.[63]

2.3   Victims and the Right to Legal Assistance

Victims[64] in Portugal enjoy a broad right to legal assistance. This is in line with the right of every person to have access to law, laid down in Art. 20§2 PConst mentioned above. This constitutional provision ensures that "[s]ubject to the terms of the law, everyone has the right to legal information and advice, to legal counsel and to be accompanied by a lawyer before any authority". This provision, which, as other constitutional rights, is directly applicable, enables all persons to assert their right to legal assistance before any authority, which obviously encompasses authorities conducting or assisting in criminal proceedings.

Victims may instruct a lawyer to represent them in criminal proceedings, irrespective of the capacity in which they intervene.[65] In certain instances—if the victim is an "assistant"[66]—legal assistance is mandatory. In private prosecution cases, for instance, the absence of the victim's lawyer at trial may result in a dismissal of the proceedings.[67]

Financial legal aid is available for victims of crime, but, contrarily to the accused, victims are required to make an application for financial legal aid as soon as they intervene in criminal proceedings, or as soon as their lack of financial means arises. An *ex officio* lawyer will not be appointed if the social security services deny the application for legal aid. In such cases where a legal aid lawyer represents the victim, he/she is not free to choose his/her own lawyer, since one will be drawn out of a roster randomly by a computer system managed by the Portuguese Bar Association.

In contrast to the accused, who is allowed to file applications himself,[68] victims may only do so if they have not instructed a lawyer to act on their behalf. Whenever a lawyer is representing a victim, all procedural applications must be signed by the lawyer unless the lawyer is impeded and the act is subject to an expiration deadline.[69]

---

[63] Constitutional Court judgment no. 7/87 of January 1, 1987, available on http://www.tribunalconstitucional.pt/tc/acordaos/19870007.html, last accessed 31.7.2018.

[64] See below Sect. 4 for the definition of victims in Portuguese criminal proceedings.

[65] See below Sect. 4. Art.s 67-A(4), 70, 76 and 132(4) CCP; Art. 13 of the Victim Status, appended to Law 130/2015, of September 4, 2015.

[66] See below Sect. 4.

[67] Art. 330(2) CCP.

[68] See Sect. 3.1.

[69] Art. 98(2) CCP.

3 Personal Participation of the Accused in Criminal Proceedings

3.1 General Features of Personal Participation: Absolute Individual Right or Duty of Diligence?

According to the CCP, as outlined above, the presence of the accused is not only a right, but also a duty.

Art. 61(1) CCP states that the accused is entitled to be present at his/her own trial and to participate in the proceedings being conducted against him/her. As a right, the presence requirement is inevitably connected to the benefits granted to the accused by having the opportunity to participate in the proceedings.[70]

By being present, the accused is able to convey his/her side of the story to the court, either by making statements, or by submitting memorandums undersigned personally, or applications made by his/her lawyer. It should be noted that, even though defence is mandatory at trial stage, the accused is always able to make applications on his/her own. These applications, as long as they are connected to the subject matter of the proceedings or aim at safeguarding the accused's fundamental rights, must remain in the case files.[71]

But Art. 61(3) CCP states that an accused has the duty to "appear before the judge, prosecutor or criminal police body whenever required by law and after being duly summoned". Because presence is also seen as a duty, the CCP establishes different mechanisms in order to ensure that the accused will appear at his/her trial. Failure to appear may lead to the issuing of arrest warrants and to the imposition of sanctions on the accused such as fines, or the suspension of the accused's civil and political rights as a sanction for his/her disobedience in failing to appear for trial (*contumácia*).

As will be outlined below, the system that the CCP introduced by the 2000 amendment relies almost entirely on a duty of diligence of the accused: the accused has the right (but also the duty) to be present. Therefore the accused has a right to be informed on the date of his/her trial, but this will be made by expedited postal means to the address given at the moment when the accused first faces the criminal proceedings and it is incumbent upon the accused to inform the authorities on any changes of address, a duty which non-compliance is "sanctioned" with the possibility to conduct the trial *in absentia* in a legally admissible manner, according to our domestic provisions, as explained below.

---

[70] See also Summers (2007), p. 67.
[71] Art. 98(1) CCP.

3.2   Personal Participation in the Pre-Trial Inquiry with Particular Regard to the Interim Decisions on Coercive Measures

3.2.1   Participation in the Pre-Trial Inquiry in General

The Constitution states criminal proceedings have an "accusatorial structure" and the trial hearing is of an adversarial nature, in the sense that all parties have a right to intervene, to make applications and to examine and cross-examine.[72] The CCP then implements this mandate across several legal provisions, which regulate the intervention and participation rights of the parties.

In addition to that, the CCP also confers participation and intervention rights to the accused during the inquiry and the judicial pre-trial stage,[73] including the right to make applications for the gathering of evidence—this is essential since "private investigations" are traditionally not allowed and may be seen as an illegitimate interference with the investigation.[74] This is a clear inquisitorial trait of Portuguese criminal proceedings. As rightly pointed out by Silva (2013), the practice of criminal defence is generally limited to "seek[ing] to discredit, at the argumentative level or through cross-examination, the evidence presented by the prosecution, which appears to us as manifestly insufficient in order to guarantee an effective defence and the equality of arms between prosecution and defence".[75]

During the inquiry there is a limited right of participation—the accused is in general entitled only to be present during procedural acts that directly aim at him/her, such as a search to his/her premises or his/her questioning. There are no regulations concerning the participation of the accused in other evidence-gathering acts, which could lead us to think that—since the rule is that the inquiry is public, unless judicial secrecy has been applied—the accused (or the defence lawyer) would be given opportunity to be present during, for example, questioning of witnesses by the

---

[72] Art. 32(5) PConst.

[73] Art. 61(1)(g) CCP.

[74] About this topic, see Monge (2016), pp. 173–189; Silva (2013), pp. 338–343. Caeiro and Costa (2013), pp. 578–579, refer to this right and to "the (Absence of a) Right to Undertake Investigation Measures". This is a tendency also observed in other European states, e.g. Bulgaria: "[t]he use of private detectives for the collection of evidence is practically unknown and, apart from the questioning of witnesses, there is little other new evidence that could be presented by the defence at trial"—Grozev (2012), p. 100. In white-collar and complex criminality such investigations tend nonetheless to become the rule and to receive acceptance or, at least, not to be seen as illegitimate interference with the investigation. Cape et al. (2010), pp. 44–45, state that "[existing research shows that inquisitorially-based criminal justice systems often prohibit active defence at the pre-trial phase and merely allow reactive defence: only when the results of the official (pre-trial) investigation are made know to the accused is he in a position to propose further investigations such as the questioning of (additional) witnesses or counter-investigation by an expert I…] In some jurisdiction investigation by the accused or his lawyer is even regarded as obstructing the course of the official investigations."

[75] Silva (2013), pp. 338–339.

police. In practice this does not occur. In fact, neither the accused, nor his/her lawyers are informed on when such acts will take place (even if it concerns witnesses indicated by the defence).[76] If the inquiry is not secret, the defence lawyer may nevertheless consult the case files at any time. It is also possible to request the gathering of further relevant evidence. Applications made by the defence asking for evidence to be gathered are generally decided by the Public Prosecution—that is obliged to investigate *à charge et à décharge*. This is one of the basic principles the system is built upon and according to which the Public Prosecution itself would safeguard the rights of the defence at the investigation stage. In practice, however, investigations are often one-sided.[77] This may be understandable, as it is in the nature of persons charged with the investigation of criminal offences to be inclined to act with a view to proving who has committed an offence, rather than the opposite.

There are no restrictions to the right to request investigation measures, but there is no right to actually have those measures ordered. Nonetheless, the decision on whether such measures should be ordered is not merely discretionary and should be determined by the law, in particular by the assessment on whether such evidence may be relevant to the investigation or to the defence.[78] If applications presented by the defence during the inquiry are rejected, there is no immediate legal remedy available. The defence will have to wait for the judicial pre-trial stage or the trial stage to renew his/her applications. What if the Public Prosecution rejects an application made for the collection of evidence, which could perish? In that case, the defence may invoke a "safety valve". The Constitution states that the "instruction" must be conducted by a judge who can delegate the acts that do not contend directly with fundamental rights (Art. 32(4) PConst). The constitutionality in view of this provision of attribution of the competence to lead the investigation to the Public Prosecution Office has been accepted by the Constitutional Court, subject to the condition that any procedural acts that contend directly with fundamental rights must be ordered or approved by a judge (e.g. ordering coactive measures, intercept of communications, etc.). Hence, since the rejection of an application for the collection of perishable evidence would undermine the rights of the defence in a way that could not be compensated at a later procedural stage, the investigating judge must have jurisdiction to decide on an application presented with the goal of challenging such a refusal, in direct application of Art. 32(4) PConst and Art. 268(1)(f) CCP.

---

[76] See Caeiro and Costa (2013), p. 555.

[77] Cf. other states, e.g. Bulgaria, "[t]he right of defendants to request investigation has been effectively limited. While the accused has the right to request the collection of specific evidence, it is up to the investigation authority to allow or refuse such motions, and lawyers interviewed for this report have noted a clear reluctance of the investigating authority to do so"—Grozev (2012), p. 99.

[78] Similarly Caeiro and Costa (2013), p. 579, state that "there are no restrictions to the right to request investigation measures itself, but the authorities are not bound to grant them. Nonetheless, the decision whether or not to do so is not discretionary and should be taken according to legal criteria".

An important rule in our criminal proceedings is that whenever a criminal investigation against an identifiable person is pending, this person must be interrogated at the latest before the decision on whether to bring and indictment, or not.[79] This interrogation allows the accused to gain knowledge of the charges against him/her and also, if he/she wishes to convey his/her side of the story to the Public Prosecution. The Supreme Court has ruled that the omission of this interrogation before the indictment is brought, save in exceptional cases where it was not possible to find the accused or serve him/her, is sanctioned by nullity, which implies the annulation of the consequential acts.[80]

One significant point should be stressed: as a rule, testimonial evidence gathered during the inquiry cannot be used in trial over the objection of the accused, save in exceptional cases (e.g. the witness is deceased). This would compensate the lack of intervention of the accused in the evidence gathering acts during the inquiry. In cases where it is known that testimony will likely not be given live in trial (e.g. witness lives abroad, suffers from lethal illness, is a child victim of sexual offences[81]) and therefore it will be necessary to use the statements gathered in the pre-trial stage, the law foresees special safeguards. The testimony is thus obtained in line with special regulations concerning "statements for future memory". According to these regulations the accused—if known—must be informed that the witness interview will take place and has the right to be present. In addition to that, the defence lawyer must always be present, subject to nullity—i.e. evidence cannot be used.[82]

During the judicial pre-trial stage, the participation rights of the accused are stronger than during the inquiry—he/she has the right to participate in all procedural acts, as well as the defence lawyer. However, the right to request the production of evidence is still more limited than during trial, since the judge may dismiss any applications to produce evidence that he/she considers to be dispensable to find the truth and there is no right to appeal against that decision.

3.2.2 Participation in the Pre-Trial Inquiry Concerning Decisions on Coercive Measures

Decisions on coercive measures (i.e. precautionary measures aiming at safeguarding the purposes of the criminal proceedings, such as the presence of the accused at trial, the gathering and integrity of the evidence and the prevention of the commission of crimes by the accused, or severe disturbance of the public order[83]) during the pre-trial inquiry are handed down by the investigating judge.[84]

---

[79] Art. 272(1) CCP. See Caeiro and Costa (2013), p. 554.

[80] Judgment of the SCJ of 23.11.2005 (harmonising case-law), published in the Official Gazette on 2 January 2006, Series I, (retrieved on http://www.stj.pt/index.php/jurisprudencia-42213/fixada/criminal-83968/366-criminal2006).

[81] Art. 271(1) and (2) CCP.

[82] Art.s 271, 294, 320 and 356(2)(a) CCP.

[83] These are the purposes recognized by the CCP in Art. 204.

[84] Art.s 194(1) and 268(1)(b) CCP.

Coercive measures during the inquiry are requested by the Public Prosecution and applied by the investigating judge. The accused must always be given the opportunity to state his/her position on the imposing of such coercive measures before a decision is taken. This may take place by means of written applications, but the usual scenario (if the Prosecutor seeks a coercive measure more severe than the statement of identity and residence) is that the accused is detained and brought to the presence of the investigating judge for an "arraignment" hearing, which is called "first judicial interrogation of the accused in detention".[85] During this interrogation, in which the accused must be represented by a defence lawyer, the accused has the right to be informed and to have access to the evidence sustaining the charges against him/her, save when such information may jeopardize the investigation, inhibit the search for the truth or create a risk to the life, bodily or mental integrity or liberty of those involved in the proceedings or of the victims.[86] If the accused decides to make a statement on the facts during this interrogation, the questions will be put to him/her by the investigating judge. Defence and Prosecution may request clarifications at the end of the judge's questioning.[87] These statements may be used against the accused during trial and he/she will be informed about that before making any statements.[88] The assistant or the victims are not present at this interrogation.[89]

If the inquiry has not been placed under judicial secrecy, the accused may have access to the files during this questioning. In practice, at least in cases that are not highly complex, the defence lawyer should request such access. After being informed about the charges and the evidence, if the defence lawyer so requests, a recess will be made to allow the defence to consult the case files. If the inquiry has been placed under judicial secrecy, then it is highly likely that the above-mentioned exception will apply and the accused will either have no access to the case files whatsoever, or very limited access to them. The CCP establishes that the decision imposing a coercive measure more severe than the statement of identity and residence must include a reference to the evidence in the case files sustaining the charges and that only the evidence about which the accused was informed at the beginning of his/her interrogation may be used to ground the decision. Furthermore, it states that the accused has the right to access to such evidence during his/her interrogation and up to the deadline for lodging and appeal against such decisions. Nevertheless, these rights on information and access to the evidence are subject to limitations in the above-mentioned conditions: jeopardy for the investigation; inhibition of search for the truth; creation of a risk to the life, bodily or mental integrity or liberty of those involved in the proceedings or of the victims.[90] If

---

[85] Art.s 141 and 194(1) and (4) CCP. About the concepts of "arrest" and "detention" in Portuguese criminal proceedings, see Caeiro and Costa (2013), pp. 551–554.

[86] Art. 141(4)(e) and 194(6)(b) and (8) CCP.

[87] Art. 141(2), (5) and (6) CCP.

[88] Art.s 61(1)(d), 141 4(a) and (b) and 357(1)(b) CCP.

[89] Art. 141(2) CCP.

[90] Art. 141(4)(e) and 194(6)(b), (7) and (8) CCP.

coercive measures are applied during the judicial pre-trial stage, the accused will have full access to the case files.

During the first interrogation, the accused and his/her lawyer are also allowed to make applications for submitting evidence relevant to the search of the truth and the decision on coercive measures.[91] Witnesses may be heard, but that is a very exceptional occurrence that usually takes place in order to obtain evidence about the personal or professional situation of the accused. The defence must bring the witnesses to the court, since the interrogation will not be postponed due to an application for interviewing a witness.

In exceptional circumstances, if it is impossible to find or to question the accused, coercive measures can be applied without the accused being heard beforehand.[92] This may happen if there has been an indictment and the accused cannot be found and the prosecutor requests the application of a coercive measure at the end of the indictment. In this situation, if the accused does not have a private defence lawyer in the case, one will be appointed by the state and the application for imposing the coercive measure will be sent to the accused's lawyer in order for him/her to convey their views on the application of such a measure.

However, in the cases where it is not possible to find the accused, at the same time the indictment is brought, the Public Prosecution will request that the judge issues an arrest warrant in order to bring the accused before a judge as soon as he/she is found in order for a coercive measure to be applied. This application does not always[93] state explicitly which coactive measure is sought to be applied. The defence lawyer will be informed on this application.

Concerning remedies against the imposition of coercive measures during the inquiry: the accused may lodge an appeal to the Court of Appeals (without the possibility of adding new evidence)[94]; he/she may request that the investigating judge alters the decision due to a change in the circumstances (attenuation of the risks, new evidence weakening the charges, etc.).[95] If pre-trial detention has been imposed, the accused may lodge an extraordinary *habeas corpus* petition to the Supreme Court, limited to cases of flagrant unlawfulness of detention (conduct is not a crime; pre-trial detention is not possible for the crime; authority who ordered detention has no power to do so; detention is maintained in unlawful facilities; detention is maintained beyond time limits established in the CPP).[96]

---

[91] This is not explicitly established but derives from the general provisions on the rights of intervention (Art. 61(1) CCP) and on the duty of the investigating judge to take into account whichever evidence is relevant to decide on the coercive measures (Art. 340(1) applied by analogy). And it does happen in practice.

[92] Art. 194(4) CCP.

[93] In our opinion, incorrectly.

[94] Art. 219 CCP.

[95] Art. 212 CCP.

[96] Art.s 220 and 222 CCP and 31 PConst.

3.3 *Personal Participation in Proceedings* in camera

According to Art. 206 PConst, court hearings are public, except where in order to safeguard personal dignity or public morals or to ensure its own normal operation, the Court itself decides otherwise in a written order that sets out the grounds for its decision. The Criminal Procedure Code also states that trials are public under penalty of nullity except in cases specifically provided for by law. The reading of the judgment is always public.[97] The principle is granted as a guarantee against arbitrariness concerning the application of law, in order to safeguard the principle of transparent justice.

After the indictment, the accused has full access to the whole case files. Before the indictment, the rule is the publicity, but the law allows the Public Prosecutor to apply secrecy, subject to approval by the investigating judge. The accused, the victim or the assistant can also request secrecy.[98] If declared, then the accused will only have access to the elements of the case files that are used to substantiate the grounds of application of coactive measures, such as pre-trial detention.[99] But only during the arraignment and the deadline to lodge an appeal against the application of such a measure (30 days). In practice this is not always straightforward, since it is a "novelty" introduced in 2007.

3.4 *Personal Participation in Alternative Proceedings*

The concept of plea-bargaining as such does not actually exist in the Portuguese legal system—a system that is founded on the legality principle. Concerning the initiation of a criminal investigation, no plea-bargaining or "deal" is possible. If there is evidence that a crime might have been committed, an inquiry will be open. Nonetheless, there are some alternative routes for dealing with criminal proceedings. During the inquiry four possibilities are open to the Public Prosecution as an alternative to issuing an indictment and bringing the case to trial with a full oral hearing: (i) mediation; (ii) provisional suspension of the proceedings; (iii) closure in cases of exemption of penalty[100]; and (iv) *processo sumaríssimo* (expedited proceedings).

Mediation[101] takes place between the victim and the accused him/herself in the presence of the mediator, following a decision made by the Public Prosecutor to send the proceedings to mediation. The criminal defence lawyer may also take part

---

[97] Art.s 321 and 87(5) CCP.

[98] Art. 86 (1) to (3) CCP. There are only two exceptions which are the file on witness protection (but in the case that the identity of the witness is concealed, then the Bar Association appoints a lawyer who is supposed to ensure the rights of defence) and the file concerning the undercover agent.

[99] Art. 194(8) CCP.

[100] About these alternative measures, see Caeiro and Costa (2013), pp. 568–571.

[101] Caeiro and Costa (2013), pp. 569–570.

in mediation proceedings. The result will be an agreement between accused and victim, which then must be approved by the Public Prosecutor. The Criminal Mediation Regime[102] states that the participants may freely determine the terms of the agreement, subject to one exception: sanctions which deprive the suspect of his/her liberty or require the fulfilment of duties that offend his/her dignity or exceed a length of 6 months cannot be agreed upon. There is no right to trigger mediation "as of right", but the accused has the right to make an application for mediation to take place. If an agreement is reached, the case will be closed (the effect is equivalent to withdrawal of the complaint by the victim).[103]

The provisional suspension of proceedings[104] is a mechanism that allows the Public Prosecution, as an alternative to the indictment, to make a proposal for the suspension of proceedings subject to compliance with certain duties by the accused (moral satisfaction of the victim, compensation, treatment, etc.). The application of this measure requires the agreement of the accused, which will be given either during an interrogation, or in writing following notification of the Public Prosecution proposal.[105]

If the accused complies with those duties, the case will be closed and cannot be reopened (the effect is equivalent to the closure of the case without charges—there will be no criminal record, but thereafter the accused may not benefit of this mechanism in future criminal proceedings for crimes of a similar nature.

The criminal defence lawyer and the accused may play an active role by requesting the Public Prosecution to apply this mechanism, and also proposing the conditions and negotiating with the victim's lawyer concerning moral or pecuniary compensation, or the content of the duties (if the victim has requested to be an assistant, his/her consent is necessary[106]). Evidently, the fulfilment of the requirements that allow for the application of this mechanism may be demonstrated by evidence adduced by the accused during the investigation.[107]

Closure in cases of exemption of penalty[108] allows the Public Prosecution to refrain from indicting the accused in those situations for which the Penal Code foresees the possibility of a conviction without applying a sanction on the defendant. These are cases of lower guilt and minor wrongdoings, in which there has been compensation for damages and there are no preventive needs that hinder the

---

[102] Art. 6(1) and (2) Law 21/2007, of June 12.

[103] Art. 5(4) Law 21/2007, of June 12. However, if the agreement is not fulfilled within the deadline agreed, the complaint may be renovated within 1 month.

[104] Art.s 281 and 282 CCP. This mechanism may also be applied during the judicial pre-trial stage—Art. 307(2) CCP. See also Caeiro and Costa (2013), p. 569.

[105] Art. 281(1)(a) CCP.

[106] Art. 281(1)(a) CCP. If the crime under investigation is of domestic violence, the provisory suspension of the proceedings will be determined as long as the victim makes an application to that effect and the accused has no convictions for crimes of a similar nature, and has not benefited from the mechanism for crimes of a similar nature.

[107] See Sect. 2.2.

[108] Art. 280 CCP. See Caeiro and Costa (2013), pp. 568–569, using the expression "filing of the procedure in case of possible exemption of penalty".

non-application of the penalty. The effect is equivalent to closing the case without charges.

Apart from the Penal Code, there is a significant number of special regulations that allow the Public Prosecution to use this mechanism—e.g. tax crimes allow for exemption of penalty if the tax returns have been properly corrected and all taxes and interest due have been paid before the indictment has been brought[109]; legislation on drug trafficking allows for the exemption of a penalty for those suspects who cooperate with the authorities in gathering substantial evidence to identify or capture other suspects, in particular if these are members of criminal associations, groups or organizations[110]; a similar provision for terrorist organizations can be found in the Penal Code[111]; in corruption cases the exemption of penalty may be applied to the *whistle blower* who reported the crime within 30 days of its perpetration, as long as this is made before the institution of criminal proceedings, or to the person that promises/accepts an undue benefit and withdraws/refuses it before performing the correspondent action.[112]

In all of these situations, the defence lawyer may intervene providing advice to the client on possible cooperation and/or requesting for the application of the diversion mechanism. Especially when the application depends on the cooperation of the accused in the gathering of evidence, the role of the defence in providing evidence is highly significant. The consent of the accused is not a requisite of the exemption of sanction, but it will often be given since the defence usually has an active role in applying for this regime. The general rules on the inquiry applies—the accused must always be interviewed before the decision to close the inquiry, therefore he/she will have the possibility to be heard.[113]

Processo sumaríssimo[114] (expedited proceedings) is the only legal framework in Portuguese criminal proceedings whereby a sanction may be imposed on an accused without an oral and public trial hearing having taken place. The Public Prosecution, after having heard the accused, or upon his/her request, may apply to the judge for the imposition of the sanction by means of expedited proceedings. This application describes the person that is being accused, the facts, the applicable legal provisions, the evidence and the reasons why a sanction of deprivation of liberty should not be imposed in the instant case. It further proposes a sanction and, if applicable, an amount for compensation to the victim. The judge, if the application is admissible,[115] then

---

[109] Art.s 22 and 44 General Regulations on Tax Infringements (*Regime Geral das Infracções Tributárias*)—Law 17/2001, of June 5.

[110] Art. 31, Law 15/93, of January 22.

[111] Art. 29 (4), PC.

[112] Art. 374-B Penal Code. The Law on corruption in international commerce and in the private sector does not foresee "whistle blowers" (Law 20/2008, of April 21, Art. 5), but its applicability on the basis of the Penal Code could perhaps be sustained.

[113] See Sect. 3.2.1.

[114] Art.s 392–398 Code of Criminal Procedure.

[115] It will not be admissible if it is applied outside of the legally permitted cases, or if the indictment is ill founded (the facts are not a crime), or if the judge finds that the sanction is inappropriate—

serves it on the accused,[116] who may accept it or may oppose to it. If he/she opposes, then the case will be dealt with by following another procedural form.[117] The accused may trigger the application of the *processo sumaríssimo*. Nevertheless this is rather unusual and therefore the prosecutorial proposal is typically not negotiated previously with the accused or his/her lawyer. This type of alternative "negotiated" proceedings is used most commonly for offences of driving under the influence of alcohol, or without a driving permit.

Some dissimilarity among these four possibilities of diversion should be pointed out. Regarding the maximum applicable sentence threshold, closure in cases of exemption of penalty may only be applied to crimes punished with a sentence of up to 6 months imprisonment, or in other cases specifically listed in statutory law (such as the above-mentioned cases of drugs trafficking, corruption, etc.).[118] The other diversion mechanisms may in general be applied to crimes punishable with a sentence of up to 5 years imprisonment.[119] From a different perspective, these diversion mechanisms—except closure in cases of exemption of penalty—have a particular characteristic: the victim (although subject to differing degrees[120]) is also a part of the agreement and may oppose it. Mediation in particular may only take place in private or semi-private crimes (i.e. crimes regarding which the commencement of proceedings and further prosecution depends on the victim submitting a formal complaint and bringing a private indictment against the accused—the latter only in private crimes) against persons or against property. Concerning the competent authority, apart from mediation, a judge must approve the application of diversion mechanisms.[121] Mediation agreements must be approved by the Public Prosecution only.[122] If the judge does not accept the application of the diversion mechanisms as proposed, the proceedings will continue, but the judge may not preside over the trial.[123] It should be highlighted that only convictions in *processo sumaríssimo* will be written on the defendant's criminal records[124] and are hence equivalent to a final judgment. The other decisions will also be registered, but this register is only available to courts and to prosecution authorities and it does not have the value of a previ-

---

Art. 395(1) CCP. In the latter case the judge may propose a different sanction.

[116] Concerning the issue of trials *in absentia* in the scope of *processo sumaríssimo*, see below Sect. 5.3.

[117] See Sect. 1.1.

[118] Art.s 280 CCP and 74 CP.

[119] Art.s 281(1) and 392(1) CCP and 2(3)(a) Law 21/2007, of June 12.

[120] The agreement of the victim is always required in mediation. In the provisory suspension of the procedure, it will only be required if the victim requested his/her admission as an assistant. See Sect. 4.

[121] Art.s 281(1) and 392(1) CCP.

[122] Art. 5(4) and (5) Law 21/2007, of June 12.

[123] Art. 40(e) CCP.

[124] Although even in these situations it is possible to exceptionally request the judge not to order the transcript of the decision in the criminal records, for employment purposes.

ous conviction, but is an impediment to the starting of new criminal proceedings for the same facts.

For the purposes of this contribution, there are some final important aspects to note. Firstly, with the exception of *processo sumaríssimo*, the accused does not always have a defence lawyer at this stage. He/she may request the appointment or instruct one privately, but the appointment is neither automatic nor compulsory.[125] This means that during the investigation, when facing the possibility of accepting diversion mechanisms, the accused does not necessarily enjoy the advice of a criminal defence lawyer. Secondly, as may be inferred from the description of these alternative measures, they normally involve a certain degree of participation of the accused, by conveying his/her view of the facts, bringing evidence and sometimes explicitly requesting the application of said measures. Practice also shows that these measures are usually applied when the accused has made admissions on the acts he/she has been charged with, since that is generally viewed by the Public Prosecution as demonstrating that there is no preventive need to pursue a "classic" criminal case. Finally, the participatory rights of the accused in these alternative proceedings during the inquiry are not different from those described above.[126]

Other than these four diversion mechanisms, criminal proceedings in Portugal may take place, as outlined above, in a more expedited manner, in the framework of abbreviated proceedings (*processo abreviado*) or summary proceedings (*processo sumário*).[127]

As a general principle, these special forms involve: reducing the acts performed in trials and the terms under which they take place to the indispensable minimum required to come to a final decision; restrictions on the possibility of adjourning the trial hearing itself, on the use of evidence and the time limits during which it can be produced, and on appeals; and increasing the oral aspect of procedural acts. In the criminal field, these forms of procedure are linked to small and medium criminality (punishable with imprisonment up to 5 years), and normally are used when the facts are immediately verified because the agent was caught "red-handed"—in *flagrante delicto*—or similar, which makes it possible to dispense with other formalities and the more in-depth investigation that would normally occur in the investigation and fact-finding phases of common criminal proceedings. The accused has the same participatory rights as in common proceedings, but will usually have to produce his/her evidence and defence in a swifter manner.[128] It should be noted that in summary proceedings, since the accused has necessarily been caught red-handed, he/she (if not kept in detention) will be immediately summoned to appear in court the following day, or on Monday if caught during the weekend, and informed that, if he/she does not appear the trial may take place without his/her presence.[129]

---

[125] Save for the cases described in Sect. 2.2. where defense is mandatory.

[126] See Sect. 3.2.

[127] Art.s 381 and ff. CCP.

[128] In summary proceedings, either immediately, or within 15 days—Art. 383(2) CCP.

[129] Art. 385(2)(a) CCP.

3.5   Personal Participation at Trial: Involvement in Evidence Gathering and Personal Contribution to Fact-Finding

Notwithstanding his/her position as a "subject of the proceedings", as opposed to civil proceedings, where the accused sits next to counsel, the accused in criminal proceedings is physically placed in the middle of the courtroom, in front of the bench, behind a "fence" and far from the defence lawyer.

The first evidence adduced in trial hearings is the statement of the accused. He/she may decide to make a statement, or not. The exercise of the right to silence may not jeopardize the position of the accused—negative inferences are not allowed. But it may not benefit him/her either. As put by Dias (1974), the exercise of the right to silence may not be used as evidence of as a presumption of guilt (*exclusionary rule*). Nor it may be used, once guilt has been proven, for purposes of sentencing.[130] This being said, it should be noted that despite the legal proscription of using the exercise of the right to silence against the accused, from a practical *de facto* viewpoint, silence may disfavour the position of the accused, if as a consequence the court is not informed about circumstances that would justify or excuse the offence, totally or partially. In exercising his role, the defence lawyer should consider this possibility and try to bring such circumstances to the attention of the court by other means of evidence.

On the other hand, if the accused makes a statement—which is made without giving an oath—and the Court does not believe his/her accounts, it may use such statement against the accused. Hence, although legal scholars describe the statements of the accused as being of a hybrid nature, both as a means to obtain evidence and a means of defence,[131] at this stage it is indisputable that such statements will be used in evidence, and they may be used against the accused.

If the accused decides to make a statement and gives a confession at the beginning of the trial hearing, he/she may benefit from a mitigation of the sentence and procedural costs and the remainder of the evidence might be dispensed, thereby speeding up the trial. This does not dispense the Court with assessing the reliability of the accused's confession. If there are doubts about the reliability, the full trial will take place. Although the accused may make statements at any time during the trial hearing, a confession or an admission of the facts will generally only have mitigating effects if made at the outset of the trial, before experts and witnesses make their statements. The accused's personal contribution to the fact-finding is thus given a significant weight. Therefore, it is essential for the accused to define his/her strategy in this regard together with the defence lawyer.

As explained above, legal assistance is mandatory. Therefore, the accused exercises his/her rights mainly via the defence counsel. It is the defence lawyer who has the right to examine or cross-examine witnesses, for example. The accused does not sit near his/her defence lawyer, but rather in a special section of the courtroom, in

---

[130] Dias (1974), pp. 448–449.
[131] See Antunes (2016), p. 41; Dias (1974), pp. 444–445; Neves (1968), pp. 165–179.

the centre, facing the bench. The defence lawyer typically sits on a special table on the right hand side of the courtroom. He/she is allowed to stand and approach the accused in order to exchange views and even to ask for a recess in the hearing in order to consult with the accused. But as one may imagine it is not quite feasible to exchange views with the client during the trial hearing under such circumstances.

The accused may also be compelled to participate in a line up, to be finger-printed, and to have blood extracted from his/her veins against his/her will, or to produce handwriting samples, all of which are procedures that often assist in his/her conviction and punishment. Although falling in the scope of protection of the right against self-incrimination, these limitations have been considered constitutionally admissible.[132]

A final note on the statements made by the co-accused should be addressed at this stage. In Portugal it is quite common to try all persons accused of the same facts, or of facts that are connected, in the same trial. In the last decade there has even been some strong criticism of the so-called "mega trials"—where over 50, sometimes even over 100 accused persons, were tried together, or some cases where, despite the number of accused persons being lower, the trial took over 2 years. The statements made by the accused may be used against the co-accused, as long as the former does not refuse to answer the questions put to him/her by the court or during cross-examination by the defence counsel of the co-accused.[133] It is disputed whether it is admissible to convict a person solely on the basis of the statements of the co-accused, without any need for corroboration by other evidence, but the case-law of the SCJ accepts such evidence without corroboration, although it does underline that in order to ascertain the reliability or credibility of such evidence, corroboration is of importance.[134]

3.6   Personal Participation in Higher Instances[135]

As a rule, in Portuguese criminal proceedings there is no production of evidence in appellate stages.[136] Therefore, the accused is not summoned and is not allowed to make a statement. In fact, although the accused may be present during the appeal

---

[132] See Judgment of the SCJ 14/2014 (harmonising case-law) of May 24, 2014, published in the Official Gazette on 21 October 2014, Series I, available at https://dre.pt/application/file/a/58512485, last accessed 31.7.2018.

[133] Art. 345(4) CCP.

[134] E.g. Judgment of the SCJ of 12 June 2008, case no. 08P694, available at http://www.dgsi.pt/jstj. nsf/954f0ce6ad9dd8b980256b5f003fa814/6082ccff48a8006980257421003b9252?OpenDocum ent, last accessed 31.7.2018; Judgment of the Court of Appeals Porto of 5 February 2014, case no. 1/07.8GASTS.P1, available at http://www.dgsi.pt/jtrp.nsf/c3fb530030ea1c61802568d9005cd5bb/ cb2a6d4be3ca614f80257c84004d0211?OpenDocument, last accessed 31.7.2018.

[135] About this topic, see Barreiros (2014), pp. 89–90.

[136] Art. 430(4) CCP.

hearing (which is exceptional), the hearing will take place without his/her presence and will not be postponed due to the absence of the accused. Actually, in practice, the rule is that the accused is not present at the appeal hearing at all. Therefore the participation of the accused in higher instances is limited to the intervention of his/her defence counsel. The only exception is the right to present memorandums signed by the accused, already referred to above.[137]

3.7 Special Rules in the Field of Serious Organized Crimes

There are no special rules concerning participation rights in the field of serious organized crimes. The rights of the accused and of victims remain the same. As outlined above the first draft legislative proposal for the CCP contained a provision derogating from the right to have access to a lawyer in cases of terrorism, violent or highly organized criminality, which would allow for the public prosecutor to impede communication between the detained person and his/her lawyer before the arraignment, which was found to be unconstitutional.[138]

There are procedural differences, but rather in terms of other fields, such as gathering of evidence and freezing of assets, for example. In practical terms it should, nevertheless, be underlined that in criminal proceedings concerning serious organized crime the intervention of private parties during the inquiry, especially that of the accused, is more limited since, normally, judicial secrecy will apply and therefore there will be no access to the case files before the final decision about bringing an indictment, which makes it more difficult, in practical terms, to intervene. Notwithstanding, if an accused is remanded to pre-trial detention, there is, in principle, access to the elements of the cases which grounded such a decision.[139]

4 The Position of Victims, the Assistant and Their Personal Participation

Criminal proceedings are about identifying the person or legal entity responsible for the commission of a crime. The victim *per se* is not at the centre of the proceedings. However, this does not mean that the victim's interests cannot be taken into account in criminal proceedings.

There was a classic definition in the CCP of "person who suffered harm" (*ofendido*), i.e. the holder of the legal interest protected by the criminal law that has been

---

[137] See above text accompanying note 71.

[138] Constitutional Court judgment no. 7/87 of January 1, 1987, available at http://www.tribunalconstitucional.pt/tc/acordaos/19870007.html, last accessed 31.7.2018. See above Sect. 2.2.

[139] See above Sect. 2.2.

infringed by the suspect or accused.[140] The "person who suffered harm" is not a "private party" in the sense defined above, since he/she cannot exercise a decisive participatory influence in the outcome of the proceedings.[141] Victims do have the right to participate, but this is a limited right, which only becomes fully-fledged when they request to be accepted as assistants. The concept of "victim" as such was not used in the CCP, or, when it was—in particular in special legislation—it was in a criminological sense. In 2015 a new Title was introduced in the CCP, headed "Victim", containing one single provision, Art. 67-A CCP, by Law 130/2015 of September 4, which also approved the "Victim Status" appended to that law.[142] According to Art. 67-A, a victim is any person who, as a result of a crime, was directly harmed or affected in their physical integrity, honour, health or property. If the victim has passed away, is a minor or lacks mental capacity he/she may be represented by his/her closest relatives. Legal entities can be harmed by criminal activity, and may become private parties in criminal proceedings, but they are not "victims" for the purposes of that provision.

In order to enforce his/her rights the victim has various possibilities, which depend on his/her will to take a more or less active part in the proceedings. Natural persons or legal entities that suffer harm as a result of criminal activity have had the legal capability to adopt an active role in Portuguese criminal proceedings for many years—the tradition of recognising a role for the victim goes back to the nineteenth century.[143] This role may be exercised under different legal positions, each with a specific regime attached thereto: as a mere victim-witness (*vítima-testemunha*), as a complainant (*queixosa*), as a civil claimant (*demandante civil*) or as an assistant, i.e. collaborator of the Public Prosecution (*assistente*).

Firstly, a victim can be a mere witness or complainant. For example, a victim who was subject to an armed robbery can intervene during the investigation stage and in the trial, in order to convey his/her account of the facts of the crime. In this case, the intervention of the "*vítima-testemunha*" (victim-witness) is passive. Even so, the victim has several rights, including the right to be assisted by a lawyer during any procedural act, and if lacking financial means, to request financial legal aid from the social security services.[144] However, the lawyer can only accompany and

---

[140] Art. 113(1) PC and 68(1)(a) CCP.

[141] Nevertheless such persons could request to be accepted as "assistants" to the prosecution, in which case they would become private parties as outlined below.

[142] Antunes (2016), p. 53–53, justly criticizes this legislative amendment, stating that it withdraws the criminological categorization of the concept and blurs the procedural distinction of the various roles which the victim may adopt within criminal proceedings ("person who suffered harm", assistant or civil claimant), in favour of "political correctness".

[143] Silva (2013), p. 278, note 10, states that the current structure dates back to 1852 (concerning the right to make prosecution conditional to a complaint) and 1832 (concerning the possibility of the victim to lodge an accusation in concurrence with the Public Prosecution).

[144] Other rights are: (i) to ask for compensation for travelling expenses; (ii) to ask for protection, in case of fear that the author of the crime could harm him/her because of testifying; (iii) if the court is not located in her/his area of residence, to ask to testify by videolink at the court of the residence district during the trial; (iv) to benefit from victim support services (both social and psychological

advise the witness, he cannot take an active role or intervene during the pre-trial proceedings or the trial hearing.

In certain cases, in which the start of criminal proceedings depends on the victim reporting the crime and asking for criminal proceedings to be initiated,[145] the victim is called a complainant. The complainant does not automatically have an active role in the proceedings. If the victim remains as a simple complainant he/she will have the same degree of participation in proceedings as a mere witness. The complainant has, nonetheless, the right to withdraw his/her complaint until the judgment in first instance has been handed down, which will lead to the closure of the case without further prosecution, if the accused agrees to the closure.[146]

Victims have a right to challenge the closure of the investigation by making an application to the prosecutor with hierarchical oversight over the prosecutor who decided to close the case.[147] Victims will be informed on the decision to close the investigation in order to be able to exercise such a right.[148] The advice of a lawyer at this stage is, in our opinion, essential, since the victim has to decide whether this means of reaction is adequate, or whether he/she should rather make an application to open the judicial pre-trial stage, which requires that the victim intervenes in his/her capacity of assistant, as described below.

The second possibility is for the victim to participate in criminal proceedings as a civil claimant.[149] If a victim is seeking damages, he/she can (and usually he/she must) claim them directly in the criminal proceedings. Authorities are obliged to inform any victims who suffered damages of their right to claim civil damages as soon as they are aware of their existence. For the purposes of the definition of private parties set out above, **the civil claimant is not a private party**, since his/her powers are limited to the civil limb of the case. For example, if the accused has requested the screening of the indictment by means of opening the judicial pre-trial stage, the civil claimant—who will by then have lodged his/her claim within the criminal case—will have no intervention and may not challenge a decision not to indict.

A third possibility for a victim who wants to have a more active role is to request to take part in the proceedings as an assistant,[150] i.e. a form of collaborator of the

---

support); (v) to be informed about whether or not the accused was indicted; (vi) to be informed on his/her rights—see Art.s 11 and ff. of the Victim Status, appended to Law 130/2015, of September 4, 2015.

[145] Art. 49 CCP.

[146] Art. 116(2) CCP.

[147] About this possibility, see Caeiro and Costa (2013), p. 571.

[148] Art.s 277(3) and 278(2) CCP.

[149] Art. 71 CPP. About the civil parties in criminal proceedings, see Antunes (2016), pp. 53–55; Mendes (2013a), pp. 137–139; Silva (2013), pp. 355–363.

[150] Art. 68–69 CPP. About the assistant and its distinction from other categories, see Antunes (2016), pp. 47–53; Mendes (2013a), p. 123–125; Silva (2013), pp. 275–295; Dias (2004), pp. 55–65.

Public Prosecution. In this position, the victim or harmed person is a private party as defined for the purposes of this text.[151]

Other than "victims" or "persons who suffered harm", in certain crimes the law allows for any citizen or for associations to intervene in criminal proceedings as assistants: it is a sort of "popular" accusation, or "popular criminal prosecution". This is the case e.g. in crimes of corruption[152] or against the environment.[153]

As an assistant the victim may take part in the proceedings by providing evidence and making interventions in various key-moments of the proceedings. In order to become an assistant, it is necessary to pay a court fee in advance (currently €102). Legal assistance is mandatory.[154] As outlined above the assistant may apply for financial legal aid in case of insufficient financial means.[155]

Further to the general rights of victims, the assistant has a broad range of rights (information, intervention, hearing, appeal)[156]: (i) to intervene in the inquiry and judicial pre-trial stage, submitting evidence and making applications for the carrying out of any acts which he/she deems necessary and to be informed on the rulings concerning such applications; (ii) to indict independently of the Public Prosecution and, in cases of private crimes, even where the Public Prosecution has not filed and indictment; (iii) to appeal, even where the Public Prosecution has not done so, thereto having access to the indispensable elements of the case files, subject to regulations concerning judicial secrecy.[157]

The rights to participate and to request the production of evidence in the investigation stage are difficult to be put in practice by the assistant and his/her lawyers. The way proceedings are conducted is very formal and a true "collaboration", in the sense of teamwork, with the Public Prosecution seems to be rather the exception. The investigation is seen as a domain of the Public Prosecution and the participation rights of the assistant are not seen as a right to effectively follow the course of the investigation, having permanent access and information, or to be heard at all times. It is possible to have access to information frequently, and to make applications for the gathering of evidence, but generally this must be done by means of formal applications by the assistant's lawyer which, after consulting the case files in order to gain

---

[151]Antunes (2016), p. 48, states that admission as an assistant is connected to the acknowledgment of the status of "subject of the procedure" as opposed to a mere participant 36–37. The victim may be both civil claimant and *assistente* at the same time, intervening in the criminal and civil parts of the criminal proceedings.

[152]Art. 68(1)(e) CCP.

[153]Art.s 1, 2, 3 and 25 Law 83/95, of August 31, 1995.

[154]Art. 70 CPP.

[155]See above Sect. 2.3.

[156]Art. 69 CCP.

[157]Other rights are scattered across the CCP, for example, if the Public Prosecution doesn't file an indictment against the suspect of crime, the assistant can request that the judge of investigation indict the accused; the assistant also has the right to oppose to the application of measures alternative to the indictment, such as "closure without charges" upon the fulfilment of certain obligations, or to influence the content of these obligations—Art. 281(1)(a) CCP. The assistant is also allowed to request trial by jury—Art. 13 CCP.

information on the *status* of the investigation, may submit formal applications which will be object of a formal decision and reply by the Public Prosecution. There are cases in practice where the collaboration of the assistant with the Public Prosecution or police is more intense, but we find that to be the exception that confirms the rule. Furthermore, at the investigation stage the victim has limited rights in terms of challenging decisions of the Public Prosecution rejecting his/her applications—these are essentially the same as the ones faced by the accused and described above.[158]

One of the most relevant rights of the assistant is to challenge the prosecutorial closure of the case before an investigating judge, as outlined above. It means that a case may be brought to trial even where the Public Prosecution found that there was no sufficient evidence to do so, as long as the assistant challenged that decision and an investigating judge then concluded that there was sufficient evidence after all. During the judicial pre-trial stage, the assistant has the right to submit new evidence and to request the production of evidence to supplement the investigation.[159] This also applies when the judicial pre-trial stage has been opened upon request of the accused.

During the trial stage, the assistant has fully-fledged rights to intervene. Not only will he/she give a statement, like any other victim in general, but his/her lawyer may be present throughout the trial and has the right to examine and cross-examine prosecution and defence witnesses, as well as to request clarifications concerning the statements made by the accused, other victims, experts, etc.[160] The assistant also has the right to request the production of his/her own evidence, which may be different from that of the Public Prosecution.[161] At the end of the trial, the assistant may appeal against acquittals, as well as against convictions (as long as the appeal is not limited to sentencing, in which case the assistant has no standing to appeal).[162] The assistant's lawyer will also be able to make opening and closing arguments before the court.[163]

Looking at the rights conferred to the assistant, one can say that he/she is a private party who, at least after the indictment, has a position that is equal in arms to that of the accused and the prosecution and has autonomous rights that allow her/him to influence and determine the course and outcome of proceedings, including the fact-finding activity of the judicial authorities. Notwithstanding, the law describing him/her as a "collaborator of the Public Prosecution, to which activity their intervention in the proceedings is subordinated, unless otherwise provided by law" (Art. 69(1) CCP), the assistant does have a high degree of autonomy and rights to challenge or not to follow the decisions of the Public Prosecutor, as just described.

---

[158] See above Sect. 3.2.

[159] Art.s 287(1)(b) and (2), 289, 302, 401(1)(b) CCP.

[160] Art.s 345(2), 346, 347(1), 347-A(1), 349, 350(1) CCP.

[161] Art.s 284(2)(b) and 283(3)(d) to (f); Art. 341.

[162] Art. 401(1)(b) CCP.

[163] Art.s 339(2) and 360(1) CCP.

Therefore the assistant is not at all a mere subordinate of the Public Prosecution but rather a private party of its own right.[164]

5   *In Absentia* Proceedings

5.1   In Absentia *Proceedings in Portugal: An Exception in Law-in-Books, a Commonplace in Law-in-Action*

The Portuguese Code of Criminal Procedure states as a general principle that the accused must be present at his/her own trial. However, following certain amendments introduced trials *in absence* of the accused are permitted—which shall only take place in exceptional and specific circumstances—and due to a number of specific ingredients that we will later explain, trials *in absentia* have become increasingly a commonplace.[165]

It is worth noticing that before the entry into force of Law 59/98, of August 25, 1998 the postponing of hearings due to the failure of the accused to appear was one of the main causes of paralysis of the criminal justice system. The way this circumstance undermined the speedy administration of justice and the efficiency of the criminal justice system was so problematic that it gave rise to a very deep amendment of the criminal procedural system.[166]

This concern was so serious that it led to an amendment to the Constitution itself, as well as to the Code of Criminal Procedure. Regarding the former, amendments introduced with the 1997 revision of the Constitution in Art. 32§6 were specifically intended to make it possible to hold trials in the absence of the accused, "as long as compliance with the rights of defence is ensured". Several amendments were also

---

[164] Dias (2004), p. 55, explains that the position of subordinated collaborator must be understood in the sense that criminal proceedings are of public nature and that the holder of the power of criminal prosecution is the Public Prosecution Service. But the assistant has autonomous powers that mould the outcome of proceedings and allow him to diverge from the Public Prosecution and these powers are not exceptional. Mendes (2013a), p. 133, also considers that the exceptions to subordination are so frequent that it is inadequate to characterise the assistant as a mere collaborator of the Public Prosecution. Silva (2013), p. 277, on the other hand considers that in public and semi-public crimes the assistant is a collaborator of the Public Prosecution in seeking the just outcome for the case, even though such collaboration is indirect after the indictment—presenting a perspective different of that of the Public Prosecution is in his view notwithstanding a form of indirect collaboration. In private crimes, such a position is more blurred. However, he recognises on p. 279 that the assistant is only a true collaborator of the Public Prosecution during the inquiry and that only during that stage is its activity subordinated to that of the Public Prosecution.

[165] Mendes (2014), p. 1070, even states that trials *in absentia* are nowadays the rule; Barreiros (2014), pp. 81–82; Cunha (2010), p. 257, states that the legislator has created a system that strongly seeks to ensure the presence of the accused, but that creates the danger that trials *in absentia* become a rule rather than *ultima ratio*, which would be more adequate to the system. There are no known statistics on the number of trials *in absentia*.

[166] Beleza (1998), pp. 54–55, gives an example of a trial that had around 17 adjournments.

introduced in the latter with the aim of making it more difficult to postpone a trial due to the failure of the accused to appear. An example can be found in the provisions concerning summons proceedings, namely the Statement of Identity and Residence (SIR). We will come back to this issue later on.

In the first place, we should note that the CCP does not contain a provision defining what a trial *in absentia* is. This is important because Member States' legal systems seem to adopt different criteria as to what should be regarded as the absence of the accused for the purpose of considering that there was a trial *in absentia*. In other words, it is relevant to identify in which cases the CCP considers that there was an absence of the accused for the purpose of considering that the trial was held *in absentia*.

In the CCP archetype, there are four constellations of cases referring to the accused's absence in the main hearing. These can be grouped into two, one in which the absence derives from the initiative of the court and another one in which the absence derives from the initiative of the accused.[167] According to the CCP, the trial hearing must take place—or it may continue—notwithstanding the absence of the accused in four constellations:

(1) if the accused, properly summoned and thereby informed of the scheduled date and place of the trial, fails to attend;
(2) upon request or consent of the accused who is relieved from the duty to appear at the hearing, namely because he/she his too ill or too old to attend the court, or if he/she lives abroad;
(3) if the accused, having been present at the beginning of the hearing, later voluntarily absents himself;
(4) where the court decides to temporarily exclude the accused from the hearing, or certain periods thereof, even though the accused is willing to be present.

Although those four situations involve the absence of the accused, for the purpose of being regarded as an exception to the rule of the presence of the accused at his/her own trial the CCP only regards as trial *in absentia* those constellations in which *the whole trial* was held in the absence of the accused, i.e. constellations (1) and (2).

The other constellations, namely when the accused made an initial appearance before the court and later voluntarily absents himself from the hearing, or fails to appear when an interrupted main hearing is continued, or when he is removed from court, pending the hearing, by order of the presiding judge, are not considered by the CCP as "real" trials *in absentia*.

Concerning safeguards that should surround the trial *in absentia* there is a difference between constellations (1) and (2). In fact, the CCP only establishes special rules for the first case. The reason for that is that only in the former situation the Court has had absolutely no contact with the accused. In situation (2) the Court

---

[167] Following Albuquerque (2011), p. 860 who divides the constellations of trials *in absentia* into two groups, one of the initiative of the court and the other of the accused.

knows that the accused is aware of the proceedings and of the date of the hearing and has authorized that it takes place in his/her absence. Instead, in the first group we only have the "formal" presumption that the accused has been duly summoned. This circumstance is also what explains why there are different rules concerning the service of the judgment. In fact, only in the first case there are special safeguards concerning the service of the judgment and the moment from which the deadline to lodge an appeal against such a decision starts counting—service has to be made in person and the deadline does not start counting until service is made in person to the accused. In constellation number (2), as is the case in trials held in the presence of the accused, service is deemed to have been made through service on the defence lawyer and the deadline to lodge an appeal starts counting from the day the judgment is handed down. This is because one can take for granted that in constellation (2) the accused is aware of the trial hearing and voluntarily chose not to be present and to be represented by the defence lawyer with whom he/she is in contact. Hence, it is not necessary to have special concerns regarding the service of the decision and this is why there is no special rule for that purpose.

We should also note that Portuguese system allows trial *in absentia* for any kind of offence, irrespective of the severity of the crime or the applicable sanction. In any case, a lawyer appointed by him/her or by the state, as legal defence is mandatory in Portuguese criminal trials, must represent the absent accused person.

Let's take a closer look at those constellations of trial *in absentia*.

Art. 333 states that "where the accused duly served to appear is not present at the time fixed for the hearing to begin, the presiding judge takes the necessary and legally admissible measures in order to secure the accused's appearance. The hearing shall not be adjourned unless the court considers that the accused's presence for the beginning of the hearing is absolutely indispensable to finding the material truth".[168]

According to this provision, three conditions must be met in order to enable a trial in the absence of the accused. Firstly, the accused must fail to appear at the beginning of the hearing; secondly, the accused must have been duly summoned[169]; and thirdly—a negative condition—his/her presence *from the beginning of the trial hearing* must not be deemed to be absolutely indispensable to the search for the material truth.

This means that pursuant to the terms of that provision, notwithstanding the accused's absence, if those requirements are fulfilled, the adjournment of the begin-

---

[168] In its Judgment no. 465/2014 of 23 June 2004, available at http://www.tribunalconstitucional.pt/tc/acordaos/20140465.html, last accessed 31.7.2018, the P Const Court found no unconstitutionality in Art. 333 CCP, considering that there was no violation of Art. 32(6) of the P Const.

[169] If the accused has not been duly summoned—which generally only occurs where the accused did not make a SIR, he will be declared an "absconder" (*contumaz*), the proceedings will be suspended and the accused is prevented of requesting his personal ID or passport, he is prohibited to conclude any private contracts, his assets may be frozen and arrest warrants will be immediately issued, etc.—see Art.s 335 to 337 CCP. The counting of the deadline of statute of limitations due to the passage of time is also suspended.

ning of the trial is void, so the hearing must begin—and it may continue until a judgment is made—without his/her presence.

As mentioned before, the only situation—which allows the presiding judge to postpone the beginning of the trial to a later session—is if the accused's presence *from the beginning of the trial hearing* is deemed to be absolutely indispensable to the search for the material truth. What cases should be regarded as such is at the discretion of the Court. However, we should point out that in practice there are very few circumstances falling within what can be regarded as "absolutely indispensable to finding the material truth from the beginning of the trial hearing". This is one of the factors that explains why trials *in absentia* in Portugal, instead of being an exception, have become a commonplace.

Additionally, it should be stressed that whilst the CCP states that the presiding judge must determine appropriate measures to bring the accused before the Court, few measures can be deemed appropriate or effective to ensure the presence of the accused in a timely manner. It is possible to issue an arrest warrant, but it will not be executed right away. This means that—in practice—in the majority of situations, notwithstanding the accused's absence, there are no grounds for adjournment and the trial hearing must be held and will proceed. The SCJ has even ruled (by 8 votes to 7) that where the Court is satisfied that the accused's presence is not necessary for the search of the truth it may close the trial hearing the same day, unless the defence lawyer requests an adjournment.[170]

This applies irrespective of whether the accused providing a sufficient and timely justification for his/her non-appearance at the beginning of trial, namely if he is unable to appear due to health issues. In both situations, unless the judge deems his/her presence to be "absolutely indispensable to the search for the material truth from the beginning of the trial hearing", which may be the case in very few and rare situations, the beginning of the trial shall not be adjourned. The only difference between failure to appear with or without justification is that in the latter a coercive fine may be imposed and an arrest warrant may be issued.

This means that in both cases the hearing will take place according to the same rules which are laid down for the trial in the presence of the accused, with the following particularities: the persons present thereto shall be heard pursuant to the order set forth in Art. 341(b)(c), notwithstanding any adjustment deemed necessary to the list of witnesses previously produced; the accused maintains his/her right to make statements until the closure of the hearing. If the closure takes place on the first date, the lawyer chosen by the accused or the defence counsel appointed by the court may ask for the accused to be heard on the second date fixed by the judge pursuant to Art. 312(2).[171] If, at the next trial session, the accused again fails to

---

[170] Judgment of the SCJ 9/2012 (harmonizing case-law) of March 8, 2012, published in the Official Gazette on 10 December 2012, Series I, available on https://dre.pt/pesquisa/-/search/190575/details/maximized.

[171] According to Art. 312(2) CCP, when setting a date for the trial hearing, the presiding judge, besides the day, time and venue for the main hearing, shall also set a second date for the main hearing to take place in case of adjournment under Art. 333(1) CCP, or for the accused to be heard at

appear, the hearing will proceed and be concluded in his/her absence, meaning that the proceedings will have taken place entirely in absence of the accused. The same will happen when the lawyer does not make a request to adjourn the hearing to the second date.

Another factor that may explain the large number of trials *in absentia* in Portugal may be found in the way by which the accused's awareness of the trial is ensured. As will be shown, summons proceedings are themselves part of the problem.

In order to exercise the right to appear in person at the trial, the accused must be aware of the date scheduled for the trial. This is the reason why, as above mentioned, in accordance with Art. 333, a trial *in absentia* can only take place in case the accused has been duly summoned.

This is quite problematic if we take into account the summons proceedings commonly used in Portugal. Unfortunately, due to the means through which the vast majority of documents are served in the current CCP, it is very difficult to find a situation where the accused is not considered "duly summoned".

Every person who is a suspect in a criminal case in Portugal must make a Statement of Identity and Residence (SIR) (*termo de identidade e residência*).[172] Once a person has signed a SIR, service of documents concerning the criminal case will be made at the address stated, unless he/she informs the court by means of an application delivered in person, or by registered mail, that he/she moved to a new address.[173]

Service at that address is made by postal delivery without acknowledgment of receipt. The postman/postwoman will deposit the letter in the post-box and fill in a "post-card" in which he/she states the date on which he/she deposited the letter on the said address.[174]

Service of the "order setting up the trial date" is made using this procedure. The problem of using such a procedure to serve the accused in a criminal case on the date and place of his/her trial is that this means of service does not clearly prove that the accused has received the letter and is unequivocally aware of the date of his/her trial. It is a mere legal fiction that the accused has become aware of his/her trial, since the postman deposited the letter in his/her post-box at the address given on the SIR.

In addition to that, an accused will often have an officially appointed lawyer (that will have made no applications whatsoever to the Court and frequently has no contact with the client at all) and will not have been present at the initial questioning of the accused during the pre-trial stage, when the SIR had just been given. Even in that case the accused may be—according to Portuguese law, validly—tried in *in absentia*. In fact, when signing a SIR, the accused is also informed that, as long as he/she has been duly served, the trial may be held *in absentia* and a defence lawyer

---

the request of his lawyer or defense counsel appointed under Art. 333(3) CCP.

[172] Art. 196(1) CCP.

[173] Art. 196(3)(c) and 113(1)(c) CCP.

[174] Art. 113(3) to (5) CCP.

will represent him/her. And as long as the person has not informed the authorities of a new place of residence and the postman has deposited the letter in the post-box, then the accused may be tried in his/her absence.

This is quite problematic if we take into account that criminal proceedings in Portugal take years. It is common for an investigation not to be closed until a year after it was opened (in a simple case). But this can take even longer. It can take years, sometimes a decade. Therefore demanding that a person keeps informing the authorities on changes of residence indefinitely, subject to being tried *in absentia,* seems disproportionate.

Additionally, the SIR is frequently signed without a lawyer being present. Whether the person properly understood the consequences of the SIR is never established unequivocally—even highly literate people have difficulties in understanding the legal jargon and the consequences—i.e., the prejudice for their defence—of being tried in their absence. In practice, the SIR has become a mere bureaucracy—one among many papers (placement as an accused, minutes of interrogation and search or seizure, consent to search or DNA gathering, detention papers, etc.) that the accused is required to sign during his/her first contact with criminal justice authorities, usually the police. This is fairly criticized by some, as such a bureaucracy triggers obligations which violation is then punished with a severe sanction of a valid trial *in absentia,* irrespective of the reasons why service was not made, making it a kind of *public vendetta* system.[175]

Finally, in the most striking cases in the past, some courts have considered that the accused had been served despite factual information to the contrary in the case files (for instance, when the letter had been returned to the sender or when there was information that the person no longer lived at the given address). There is some case law stating that if the court knows that the accused could not have received the letter, then the presumption of service "in person" is rebutted and the trial may not be conducted *in absentia.* A trial conducted in such circumstances would be null, but the nullity has to be invoked before the case becomes final, otherwise the trial *in absentia* is validated. But this case law is far from being dominant.

The problems posed by the summons formalities are particularly problematic because they increase the probability of trials held *in absentia* in situations where the accused was unaware of the trial and therefore unable to access the Court and exercise his/her participation rights.

The second constellation of cases of trials *in absentia* is not as problematic.[176] In constellation (2) identified above, trials *in absentia* are allowed in situations where there is an impossibility or a great inconvenience for the accused to be present, namely because the accused has health issues or is too old to attend the court, or if he/she lives abroad. In these circumstances, or others similar, the accused may request or may consent that the hearing take place without his/her presence. Contrary to what happens in constellation (1), when such a request is made or when the con-

---

[175] Barreiros (2014), p. 87; Beleza (1998), pp. 58–59.

[176] Art.s 333(4) and 334 (2) CCP.

sent of the accused was collected, the trial will follow the ordinary rules established for trials conducted in the presence of the accused. The only specific rule provided for this constellation of cases is that if in the course of the hearing the presiding judge turns out to deem the accused's presence absolutely indispensable to finding the material truth he/she shall order that the accused appears and interrupt or—if necessary—adjourn the trial hearing.[177]

In the third and fourth constellations, the CCP considers that they are not "real" trials *in absentia*. And, in fact, in these cases it is known—and not only presumed— that the accused is aware of the hearing and voluntarily—even if due to practical circumstances such as illness or age—opted not to be present. Or the accused, being present, has disturbed the trial hearing in such a manner (by obstructing the normal course of the hearing of by interfering or threatening the witnesses) that the Court may legitimately exclude him/her from the trial (although it will then make an oral summary of everything that happened during that period).

5.2   Default Proceedings and Subsequent Remedies (e.g. Retrial or Judicial Review in a Higher Instance)

Under current Portuguese law, the existing legal remedy (if the decision has not become final, in which case there are only very limited, extraordinary remedies) for the accused tried *in absentia* is the right to lodge an appeal. There is no right to a re-trial under Portuguese Law.[178]

The appeal does not allow for the presentation of new evidence and is strictly limited to a review of the decision of the Court of first instance and errors of fact[179] and law that the latter might have made. There is no new instance before which the evidence is produced *ex novo*, or which permits the submission of new evidence by the defence.

Appellate proceedings are decided solely on the basis of the case files. A renewal of the evidence produced in the first instance can take place, but only in very exceptional cases, and even in those cases it is at the discretion of the court whether or not to order the renewal. It is irrelevant for this decision to know whether the trial was conducted *in absentia* or not. Furthermore, it is important to stress that renewal of evidence strictly refers to the opportunity to newly hear evidence already heard in the first-instance proceedings. If renewal is allowed, the hearing follows the rules stated for the first instance trial and the accused may be heard. However, we should

---

[177] Art. 334 (3) CCP.

[178] This right existed between 1998 and 2000 in Art. 380-A CCP.

[179] The Court of Appeals may analyze the evidence in the case files and hear the recordings of the trial hearing in order to reevaluate the decision on the facts, but the power to reevaluate is interpreted in a restrictive fashion—i.e. it is not a new trial, but only a control on whether the decision taken is acceptable considering the evidence.

emphasize that, in practice, these situations are extremely rare.[180] Therefore, we can conclude that the CPP does not grant the accused a right to be present, to participate effectively and to fully exercise the rights of the defence in appellate stages. His/her limited participation rights have to be exercised by the defence counsel.

5.3   Inaudito reo *Proceedings (e.g. Penal Order Procedure)*

As mentioned above, *processo sumaríssimo* is the only type of criminal proceedings where a guilty verdict can be achieved in writing and without any oral and public trial hearing.[181] Nonetheless, since the procedure guarantees that the accused is heard before a decision is made, participatory rights are granted to the defendant.

Before presenting an application, the Public Prosecution must hear the accused, *ex officio* or upon his/her request.[182] This step will allow the accused to gain knowledge of the charges against him/her and also, if he/she wishes to, to put forward his position concerning the proceedings.

The application, as already mentioned, must describe the accused person, the facts, the applicable legal provisions, the evidence and the reasons why a sanction of deprivation of liberty should not be imposed in the case in question. It must also propose a sanction and, if applicable, an amount for compensation to the victim.[183]

If the judge deems the application admissible, he/she must appoint a lawyer to defend the accused, if he/she does not have one of his/her choice, and then serve the application on both the accused and the appointed lawyer. The accused must be served in person and thereby informed of the right to file a statement of opposition, of the means to do so and of the time limit for lodging that statement of opposition against the application and also of the consequences of presenting, or not presenting, the statement of opposition.[184]

If, duly served, the accused does not present a statement of opposition, the conviction will become final and will be handed down in writing and is hence equivalent to a final judgment.[185]

If he/she opposes it, then the case will be dealt with following another procedural form. The accused may also trigger the application of the *processo sumaríssimo* as mentioned in Sect. 3.4.[186]

---

[180] We have heard that there have been few cases of renewal of evidence but we have not been able to find any published appellate decisions where this has taken place—therefore we cannot be sure that it has ever occurred, at least in recent years.

[181] See Sect. 3.4.

[182] Art. 392(1) CCP.

[183] Art. 394(1)(2) CCP.

[184] Art. 396(1) (2)CCP.

[185] Art. 397(1)(2) CCP.

[186] Art. 395(2) CCP.

The existing legal remedy is the right to lodge an appeal in the terms described above concerning the common proceedings. As said before, there is no right to a re-trial under Portuguese Law.

Since the application must be served in person and must contain information concerning the means of reaction, the time limit for doing so and the implications of presenting or not presenting a statement of opposition, there is a guarantee that a conviction cannot become final if the accused has not truly understood the information received and the consequences of the option not to make a statement of opposition.

In fact, as long as the accused is duly served and thereby made aware that presenting an opposition means that another form of proceeding, with a public hearing, will therefore follow, we can assume that if he/she chooses not to oppose, there is an unequivocal waiver of the guarantee of a public hearing. From this perspective, since the accused has been granted the option to benefit, or not, from a public hearing—and chose not to do so—although there is no public hearing, we believe the proceedings comply with the right to a fair trial, since the right to be heard is assured before a conviction becomes final. The ECtHR has on several occasions acknowledged the lawfulness of criminal proceedings held without a public hearing, provided that the accused persons were in a position to unequivocally waive this guarantee and that this does not run counter any public interest.[187] These findings should make the adoption of simplified written procedures conditional on the fact that the accused either was given the possibility to wave his/her right to a court hearing or could have access to an effective subsequent remedy.

Finally, we should point out that the recent Directive 2016/343/EU, on the strengthening of certain aspects of the presumption of innocence and of the right to be present at the trial in criminal proceedings, states that "the right to be present at the trial can be exercised only if one or more hearings are held". The Directive, while establishing strict limits for the institution of trial hearings in the accused's presence, leaves Member States discretion to provide for "proceedings conducted in a simplified manner following, solely or in part, a written procedure or a procedure in which no hearing is provided for" as long as these proceedings comply with the right to a fair trial.[188]

---

[187] Ruggeri (2016), p. 46.
[188] Art. 8 (6). Ruggeri (2016), p. 45.

6 Participatory Rights in Transnational Criminal Justice

6.1 Participatory Safeguards in EAW Proceedings

6.1.1 Participatory Rights in the Decision on Surrender (and in Portugal as Issuing State)

EAW proceedings in Portugal take place before the Court of Appeals.[189] The Law describes the "normal" procedure as receiving the EAW and having it analysed by the Public Prosecutor and the Judge Rapporteur at the Court of Appeals who will then issue an arrest warrant. The alternative would be arrest pursuant to a SIS II or Interpol Red Notice, which is valid for purposes of arrest by any high-ranking police authority in Portugal.[190] However, in practice, the rule is that the person sought is detained pursuant to one of these notices, rather than after the EAW having been analysed by the Public Prosecutor.[191]

EAW proceedings always include a first "arraignment" which has to take place within 48 h and is conducted by the Judge Rapporteur at the Court of Appeals.[192] The person sought will then be informed about his rights to oppose, to surrender and to the benefit of specialty, and about the possibility of waiving those rights. The person will also be informed about the content of the EAW.[193] An interpreter will be appointed if the person does not understand Portuguese.[194] At this hearing, the Court will also decide whether to grant bail or not.[195]

The Directives on the Right to Legal Assistance (2013/48/EU) and to Legal Aid (2016/1919/EU), which include provisions on EAW proceedings, have not been implemented in Portugal. However, since legal assistance is mandatory, a lawyer will always be appointed if the person does not instruct one.[196] The lawyer may communicate with the person in detention at all times and in confidence and, if necessary, shall request another interpreter for conversations with the client. EAW proceedings are considered criminal in nature and the CCP applies subsidiarily, with the necessary adaptations.[197]

---

[189] Art. 15, Law 65/2003, of August 23.

[190] Art.s 4(4) and (5), 5(2) and 29 Law 65/2003, of August 23, and 1(d) CCP.

[191] Art. 16, Law 65/2003, of August 23.

[192] Art. 18, Law 65/2003, of August 23. If detention occurs on a Friday afternoon, the detainee will be brought before an investigating judge for validation of his detention, in order not to exceed 48 h before judicial verification of the detention—Art. 19, Law 65/2003, of August 23.

[193] Art.s 17 and 18(5), Law 65/2003, of August 23.

[194] Art. 17(3) Law 65/2003, of August 23.

[195] Art. 18(3), Law 65/2003, of August 23.

[196] Art. 18(4), Law 65/2003, of August 23.

[197] Art. 34 Law 65/2003, of August 23, and Art. 92(3) CCP and 61(1)(f) CCP and 78 Law 145/2015, of September 9.

The provisions on "dual defence" and on legal aid in the issuing state have not been implemented. From the perspective of Portugal as Issuing State, there is always a right to have a lawyer appointed by the state at any moment in the proceedings. Therefore, access to a lawyer is granted. In fact, if the person has already been indicted, then there must be a defence lawyer appointed in the case.[198] Unfortunately, this information and the contact details are usually not included in the EAW forms. In terms of best practices, it would be advisable for the contact details to be included.

If the person has not yet been indicted, then a lawyer will only be appointed once the person is removed to Portugal, after a decision to surrender has been handed down in the Executing State. Since detention in both Executing and Issuing State should be seen as a *continuum*, practice should also change and bring forward the moment in which the lawyer is appointed to immediately after the detention in the Executing State has been communicated to our Issuing Authority. This way the defence lawyer in the Issuing State could, among others, immediately exercise the right of access to the case files established in Art. 7 Directive 2012/13/EU.

These minor practical changes would probably make it possible to improve one of the most significant shortcomings of defence in EAW cases, at least in the situations where Portugal is the Issuing State: the difficulties of putting a dual defence into practice. Given the sort time required to present a defence in an EAW case and the geographic, legal and linguistic barriers between defence lawyers in both states, the indication of the details of the defence lawyer on the EAW form would be quite helpful.

Furthermore, difficulties in defending EAW cases arise from the fact that there is no specialization. Any lawyer registered for legal aid services in the area of the Court of Appeals for criminal law may be appointed. Since payment of fees according to legal aid rates is very low and lawyers tend to have few of these cases, investment in training on the EAW is not incentivized.[199] This could only be solved by improving the legal aid rates in general and by creating a specialized section for EAW cases in the legal aid application procedure for lawyers, as well as an indication of the lawyers' linguistic abilities. Other than that, even if lawyers are available to take on an EAW case at legal aid rates, they cannot do it, nor can the client ask for their appointment, since there is no free choice of lawyer in legal aid cases.[200] At a more general European level there is still a difficulty for lawyers to find a suitable lawyer in the other Members States who can communicate in the same language and has knowledge about EU Criminal Law and procedure.[201]

---

[198] See Sect. 2.2.

[199] See the JUSTICE study of 2012, http://www.ecba.org/extdocserv/projects/EAW/JUSTICE_ EAW.pdf, last accessed 31.7.2018, which includes a chapter on Portugal. The European Criminal Bar Association has recently created a new practical tool for lawyers with little experience in EAW cases: ECBA Handbook on the EAW for Defense Lawyers—How to defend a European Arrest Warrant Case—an e-book and web app (also on mobile platform) accessible free of charge at http://handbook.ecba-eaw.org/, last accessed 31.7.2018.

[200] See Sect. 2.2.

[201] The European Criminal Bar Association has a list of Members who are criminal practitioners on

When Portugal acts as Executing State, proceedings after the first hearing are generally written, unless witnesses are heard. This is rather exceptional. Since the facts or evidence underlying an EAW, even if for the purposes of criminal proceedings, are not subject to analysis by our Courts, witnesses are usually not heard. Documents may be submitted and are usually accepted. The exception might be the cases where evidence about the liaison to Portugal is needed for the purposes of refusing the conviction EAW and executing the sentence in Portugal, or to demand a guarantee of a return to serve the sentence in Portugal in EAW for criminal proceedings. This being the case, the normal course of an EAW case is that after the first hearing, if there is no consent, the defence lawyer presents the defence, the Public Prosecutor replies (this reply is not always sent to the defence lawyer) and then the Court makes a decision.[202] "Although the law foresees that it all happens at the first hearing, the practice is that a deadline for lodging a defence is given and the Public Prosecutor will also lodge a written reply. Then, unless oral evidence is to be procuded, there is no oral hearing or pleadings. There is, however, conflicting case law on this point. At least in one case the Supreme Court of Justice has ruled that there should be an oral hearing.[203] The decision on maintaining detention or other bail measures and the decision on surrender are subject to appeal at the Supreme Court of Justice.[204] If a matter of normative constitutionality is raised, an appeal to the Constitutional Court may also be lodged.[205]

6.1.2   *In Absentia* Proceedings in the Trial Country and Their Relevance in the Surrender Procedure

The Framework Decision on the European Arrest Warrant (FD 2002/584/JHA) was implemented in Portugal by Law 65/2003, of August 23, which entered into force on 1 January 2004.

Regarding trials *in absentia*, Portugal has chosen, like most Member States, to make surrender of a person subject to an EAW conditional to providing the assurances established in Art. 5 FD 2002/584/JHA. Hence, if the issuing state has not provided assurances or, if having provided them, these were deemed insufficient, refusal to surrender was mandatory, not facultative as stated in the Framework Decision.

---

the website: http://www.ecba.org/contactslist/contact-details.php?idreg=20150052, last accessed 31.7.2018. Other NGOs may assist in finding lawyers, such as Fair Trials https://www.fairtrials.org/.

[202] Art.s 21 and 22 Law 65/2003, of August 23.

[203] Judgment of the CSJ, 10.02.2017, case no. 795/16.0YRLSB, available at www.dgsi.pt (last accessed 31.7.2018).

[204] Art.s 24 Law 65/2003, of August 23.

[205] From the perspective of Portugal as Issuing State, all remedies available against a national arrest warrant are available also against EAWs, namely the ones referred to above concerning coercive measures. See Sect. 3.2.2.

Other than that, Art. 13(a) Law 65/2003 implemented Art. 5(1) Framework Decision almost verbatim. We say "almost verbatim" since our law added to the right to a retrial in the final section the possibility of "lodging an appeal". This "oversight" was already present in the Portuguese version of the Framework Decision which, when compared to the other language versions, such as the English, the French and the Spanish versions, added that option.

The changes introduced by FD 2009/299/JHA to FD 2002/584/JHA have been transposed into domestic law by Law 35/2015, of May 4, which replaced Art. 13(a) Law 65/2003 by Art. 12-A, which now regulates the issue of trials *in absentia* in the issuing state. Art. 12-A replicates Art. 4-A FD 2002/584/JHA, as amended by FD 2009/299/JHA, with the exception the first section of lit. a) and the final section of lit. c) and d).

The body of no. 1 reaffirms that the fact that the trial took place without the presence of the person sought is grounds for optional refusal. Thereafter it states the cases where, exceptionally, notwithstanding the absence of the accused in his/her trial, surrender may not be refused. There are some inconsistencies in the implementation of the Framework Decision. In our domestic law, the expression "in due time" in lit. a) was eliminated, as well as the reference to the right to participate in the new trial, or appeal, in lit. c) and d).

The preparatory works for Law 35/2015[206] include no reference to this inconsistency, leaving open the reasons why those references have been eliminated, and whether that was unintentional. Assuming that it was an oversight, we believe that it could be overcome by interpretation consistent with EU Law.

Directive 2016/343 has not yet been implemented into domestic law. The implementation of the minimum rules will involve changes into domestic law. Upon expiration of the deadline for implementation into domestic law, on April 1, 2018, the domestic courts will be obliged to interpret domestic law in consistency with the text and purpose of the Directive, or to disapply domestic law that contravenes EU Law.

As outlined above, our current system of criminal procedure does not establish the right to a new trial or to an appeal following the terms and in the situations included in lit. c) and d) of Art. 4-A FD 2002/584/JHA, as amended by FD 2009/299/JHA.[207]

Accordingly, the Portuguese courts have been confronted with an awkward situation: they have to request from their counterparts an assurance that is required by European law and the Law of other Member States as a condition for the mutual recognition of trials *in absentia*, but that our domestic law does not grant.

Our Supreme Court has had to rule in several cases about EAW issued for the surrender of persons tried *in absentia*. Under the initial version of Law 65/2003— before the implementation of FD 2009/299/JHA[208]—in the judgments of

---

[206] Available at http://www.parlamento.pt (last accessed 31.7.2018).

[207] See Sect. 5.2.

[208] Before the implementation of FD 2009/299/JAI, there was conflicting case law concerning the

10.11.2011,[209] 27.05.2009[210] and 09.01.2008,[211] the Portuguese judicial authorities requested from the issuing states—Bulgaria, Romania and France—that these provide assurances that their legal system would grant the persons convicted *in absentia* the right to a new trial. In the first judgment, the SCJ ordered surrender subject to a resolved condition, reserving the right to consider the decision to surrender revoked and to order the return to Portugal of the person surrendered, should the Bulgarian authorities violate the conditions established concerning the right to a new trial. In the two latter cases, the SCJ also considered that the guarantees were sufficient and ordered surrender.

In another judgment, of 18.09.2013,[212] the SCJ reversed the decision of the Court of Appeals and ordered surrender, grounding its decision, among other aspects, in the fact that the Romanian authorities had stated on the EAW form that the accused had been informed in person of the date and place of the trial. The SCJ considers that the information provided by the issuing state in the EAW form, namely the indication of the applicable domestic provisions granting the right to a new trial, are sufficient for ruling on the adequacy of the assurances provided.[213] This case law has recently been confirmed by a judgment of the SCJ of 30.03.2016.[214]

6.2 Participatory Safeguards in Transborder Inquiries and the Taking of Overseas Evidence

The gathering of evidence overseas is regulated in Portugal in the Code of Criminal Procedure (Art.s 229 to 233) and in Law 144/99, of August 31 (International Judicial Co-Operation in Criminal Matters[215]). These domestic provisions apply only where

---

implications of the Framework Decision in domestic EAW proceedings: in the Judgment of 10.11.2011, case no. 763/11.8YRLSB.S1, the SCJ ruled that despite the lack of implementation, according to the *Pupino* case law, there was an obligation to interpret domestic law in accordance with the FD. In the Judgment of 18.09.2013, case no. 1191/11.0YRLSB.S1, the SCJ states that FD 2009/299/JAI is not in force in Portugal because it had not been implemented, according to the terms of Art. 34(2)(b) TEU.

[209] Judgment of the SCJ of 10.11.2011, case no. 763/11.8YRLSB, available at www.dgsi.pt (last accessed 31.7.2018).

[210] Judgment of the SCJ of 27.05.2009, case no. 1043/09.4YRLSB, quoted in Graça (2014), pp. 137–138.

[211] Judgment of the SCJ of 09.01.2008, case no. 4856/07, available at www.dgsi.pt (last accessed 31.7.2018).

[212] Judgment of the SCJ of 18.09.2013, case no. 1191/11.0YRLSB.S1, available at www.dgsi.pt (last accessed 31.77.2018).

[213] In addition to the judgments quoted, see Judgment of the SCJ of 06.07.2011, case no. 552/11.0YRLSB.S1, available at www.dgsi.pt (retrieved on 15.07.2017).

[214] Judgment of the SCJ of 30.03.2016, case no. 1642/15.5YRLSB, available at www.dgsi.pt (last accessed 31.7.2018).

[215] Mainly Art.s 145 and ff. and the general provisions in Art.s 1 to 30. Available in English at http://

international conventions or EU Law do not establish the applicable rules.[216] Within the European Union, Law 88/2017, of August 22 (European Investigation Order[217]) applies. In addition to these, Law 109/2009, of September 15, implementing the Council of Europe Cybercrime Convention applies to the gathering of electronic evidence.[218]

There is little case law in this field, but there is certainly a trend for change in this respect, since cross-border cases are growing and practitioners are becoming more aware of these issues.[219]

When Portugal acts as an issuing or requesting state, evidence acts requested from foreign authorities must indicate the formalities that are requisites for the constitutional validity of evidence, otherwise the evidence received risks not being proper for use in the Portuguese courts.[220] The gathering of evidence must respect the fundamental principles of our Constitution, and the PConst exclusionary rule established in Art. 32§8 is applicable. Many of the rules established in the CCP and other domestic laws implement constitutional rights and prohibitions and therefore their violation might also entail the exclusion of the evidence thus obtained (e.g. provisions concerning the right to silence, legal assistance, protection of privacy of communications, moral and physical integrity). Controversies in this respect will usually relate to determining whether a certain provision is, or not, a concretion of a fundamental right. This will apply even where evidence is gathered abroad. Until recently there was no explicit provision mandating that the Portuguese requesting authorities should request compliance with such formalities, but it derives from the system of exclusionary rules established in the Constitution, the CCP and other laws implementing the Constitutional mandate.[221] Law 88/2017 on the EIO establishes that "the EIO will indicate, if applicable, the formalities and procedures especially

---

www.gddc.pt/legislacao-lingua-estrangeira/english/lei144-99rev.html, last accessed 31.7.2018.

[216] Art. 299 CCP and Art. 3(1) Law 144/99, of August 31. The most important Conventions in this regard are the European Convention on Mutual Assistance in Criminal Matters and its Protocols (ETS 030, 099, 182), the Schengen Convention and the Convention on Mutual Legal Assistance in Criminal Matters among the Member States of the Community of Portuguese Speaking Countries (CPLP Convention).

[217] Until the approval of the Law implementing the European Investigation Order, the 2000 Convention on Mutual Legal Assistance in Criminal Matters among the Member States of the European Union applied.

[218] Art.s 20 and ff. Available in English at https://www.anacom.pt/render.jsp?contentId=985560, last accessed 31.7.2018.

[219] See Ramos (2013), pp. 555–562 for a list of cases on the validity of evidence obtained abroad.

[220] See Caeiro and Costa (2013), pp. 576–577. This request is permitted under Art. 9(2) Directive 2014/41/EU on the European Investigation Order; Art. 4(2) CPLP Convention; Art. 8 of the Second Additional Protocol to the European Convention on Mutual Assistance in Criminal Matters. The EIO and the European Convention establish that the requested or executing state *shall* comply with the requirements of the *forum* state that the action sought is not contrary to fundamental principles of its law. The CPLP states that the requested state *may* comply.

[221] More evidence of this is that Art. 85 Law 144/99, of August 31, states that, when Portugal accepts a transfer of criminal proceedings to Portugal, the judge shall validate the foreign acts, except those which are not "admissible".

required for the gathering of the examination of the evidence, according and with reference to the applicable legal rules, requesting that they are followed by the executing authority, in order to safeguard the validity and effectiveness of the evidence". This provision should be construed as requiring such an indication whenever the formalities and procedures are constitutionally mandated either directly or indirectly by laws implementing the constitutional mandate (i.e. the validity requirements applicable and protected by exclusionary rules were the evidence to be gathered in Portugal).

If Portugal acts as a requested or executing state, the normal rule is that Portuguese Law will apply to the gathering of evidence.[222] This includes the protection of any privileges, such as those concerning privacy, professional secrecy, state secrecy, witness privileges and any other types of secrecy established in domestic law.[223] However, domestic law foresees the applicability of the requesting state's law upon explicit request by the said state, or if international law foresees such applicability. Foreign law will not be applied if it impinges upon the fundamental principles of Portuguese Law or causes severe damages to those involved in the proceedings.[224] Law 88/2017 on the EIO explicitly states that such procedures will only apply to the extent that "the prerequisites and requirements of national law concerning evidence in the framework of similar national proceedings".[225]

Mutual legal assistance may be granted even in the absence of dual criminality, but if it entails coercive measures, the requisite of dual criminality applies and the gathering of evidence will take place according to the Portuguese law.[226] Further to that, measures interfering with fundamental rights, which may only apply in criminal proceedings concerning certain crimes (e.g. interception of communications), will only be executed if they could have been ordered in a similar domestic procedure.[227] If the requested acts aim at gathering evidence exempting a person of his/her criminal liability, then mutual assistance involving coercive measures may still be granted, even in the absence of dual criminality.[228] Mutual legal assistance will

---

[222] Art. 146(1) Law 144/99, of August 31; Art. 8(1) Law 88/2017, of August 22; Art. 9(1) Directive 2014/41/EU; Art. 4(1) CPLP Convention; Art. 3 European Convention on Mutual Assistance in Criminal Matters. See Caeiro and Costa (2013), pp. 555–567, on the requisites of such measures in Portuguese criminal proceedings.

[223] Art. 11 Law 144/99, of August 31. See also Art. 22(1)(b) and (c) Law 88/2017, of August 22; Art. 11(a) and (b) Directive 2014/41/EU.

[224] Art. 9(2) Directive 2014/41/EU; Art. 4(2) CPLP Convention; Art. 8 of the Second Additional Protocol to the European Convention on Mutual Assistance in Criminal Matters.

[225] Art. 18 (2) Law 88/2017, of August 22.

[226] Art. 147(1) Law 144/99, of August 31. Art. 2 CPLP Convention. This Convention requires a minimum threshold for searches, seizures, examinations or expert evidence and that the conduct is also punishable in the requesting state with a prison sentence of at least 6 months. Art. 5(a) and (c) European Convention on Mutual Assistance in Criminal Matters and reservation made by Portugal.

[227] Art.s 11(1) and 160.-C Law 144/99, of August 31, and Art. 126 CCP.

[228] Art. 147(2) Law 144/99, of August 31; Art. 2(2) CPLP Convention.

not be granted if it entails the undertaking of actions not permitted by Portuguese law, or which would be subject to disciplinary or criminal sanctions.[229]

In the scope of application of the EIO, dual criminality applies only limitedly, but it does apply to intrusive or coercive measures, to which the requisite of "dual admissibility" of the measure also applies—i.e. these measures may only be executed if that would have been possible in similar domestic proceedings.[230] It also applies if the issuing state is exercising extraterritorial jurisdiction and the executing state would have territorial jurisdiction.[231]

The CCP and Law 144/99, of August 31, have virtually no regulations on the intervention of private parties in mutual legal assistance for the gathering of evidence. However, the CCP applies. This means that the rights of intervention of private parties outlined in this contribution apply equally in the scope of mutual legal assistance. The Law implementing the European Investigation Order (EIO) explicitly states that the EIO may be issued upon an application made by the "subjects of the procedure", which includes not only the accused, but also the assistant. In practice, however, at least until now, this intervention suffers from relevant limitations.

The first limitation is a legal one. The only explicit regulations are contained in Art.s 152(7) Law 144/99 and 230(2) CCP. These two provisions state that rogatory letters will only be issued if the competent Portuguese judicial authority "deems that such is necessary in order to obtain evidence of any fact that is *essential* either *to the prosecution or to the defence*." (emphasis added). This higher threshold does not apply to most decisions determining the gathering of domestic evidence, which may be ordered as long as it is *relevant* or *necessary* to the object of proceedings.[232] This limitation may be seen as an unjustified limitation of the rights of the defence, or of the victim acting as an assistant, in particular if applied within the context of the European Investigation Order and the European Union. Law 88/2017 contains no provisions in this regard. It does state that an EIO will only be issued if necessary, adequate and proportionate to the aims of the relevant proceedings, but it does not state that they *must* be issued in the same conditions as would apply to an order for gathering domestic evidence, if requested by the private parties. We believe that in the context of the European Union, where there is freedom of movement—meaning that evidence may also be anywhere in the EU—and there are no fixed rules concerning jurisdiction in criminal matters—meaning that criminal proceedings will not necessarily be conducted where relevant evidence is located, and accused persons should be treated equally, the threshold for gathering evidence in other EU Member States should be equal to that for domestic evidence.[233]

---

[229] Art. 146(3) Law 144/99, of August 31.

[230] Art.s 22(1)(a)(d)(h) and (2), 38(6), 39(6), 40(2), 41(3)(a), 42(5), 43(3) Law 88/2017, of August 22; Art.s 11(1)(c)(g)(h) and (2), 26(6), 27(5), 28(1), 29(3(a), 30(5), 31(3) Directive 2014/41/EU.

[231] Art. 22(1)(f) Law 88/2017, of August 22; Art. 11(1)(e) Directive 2014/41/EU.

[232] See Art.s 124(1), 262 (1), 340(1) and (4)(b) CCP.

[233] Whether this principle applies to a larger extent outside of the EU, in particular among States with intense cooperation, such as within the Council of Europe, should also merit consideration.

The second limitation, which is also legal, is that confidentiality of proceedings—at least during the investigation stage—will apply in mutual legal assistance if requested by the requesting state.[234] This means that, despite having rights of intervention in theory, they will be limited in a majority of cases by a broader application of judicial secrecy. Accordingly, if a foreign state requests confidentiality during the investigation stage, the accused and the victim will either not know at all that there was a request for gathering the evidence or, even when they do gain knowledge about it, because of the law or practical contingencies (e.g. arrests, seizure, freezing of accounts, interviewing the victim or the defendant), the exercise of their participation rights will be limited due to lack of access to the case files of the cooperation request.

This brings us to the practical limitations. The first important practical limitation is that, where the accused or the victim were not aware of the request for gathering evidence in Portugal before it has been executed and returned to the requesting or issuing state, they can only exercise their rights in Portugal in a very limited manner. Although—assuming that the time limits thereto are respected—they would be able, for example, to complain about the validity of the gathering of the evidence, in practice that is made very difficult since the whole case files concerning the execution of the request are sent back to the requesting or issuing state. Sometimes it is possible to have access to some elements in Portugal, but only to some of the formal letters in response to the requests, and to some of the evidence, when this evidence has been gathered previously in the framework of other Portuguese criminal proceedings. In any event, even where it is possible to make an application requesting the declaration of invalidity of certain acts of gathering evidence in Portugal at the request of a foreign state, there are no explicit binding international rules that would make the Portuguese exclusionary rules applicable in the foreign proceedings.[235] Therefore, the effectiveness of such *ex post facto* complaints is virtually null.

The second practical limitation has to do with the difficulties involving dual defence. If the defence (or the victim) need to intervene in the gathering of evidence in Portugal upon a foreign request, they necessarily need to have the assistance of foreign lawyers. Here the difficulties outlined above in respect of EAW proceedings apply equally,[236] with the further limitation that there is no international legally binding instrument stating clearly that there is a right to dual defence. This limitation is highly relevant when Portugal is the *forum* state. Nothing in Portuguese law prevents the validity of the evidence being challenged, also according to the laws of

---

[234] Art. 149 Law 144/99, of August 31; Art. 30 Law 88/2017, of August 23. Art. 5 CPLP Convention. Art. 25 of the Second Additional Protocol to the European Convention on Mutual Assistance in Criminal Matters.

[235] Portugal has a Constitutional exclusionary rule on Art. 32§8 PConst, and several exclusionary rules throughout the CCP and other laws. The fruit of the poisonous tree doctrine applies, with the limitations of the "*attenuation of the taint*", "*inevitable discovery*" and "*independent source*". On this topic see Mendes (2013b); Caeiro and Costa (2013), pp. 573–576.

[236] See Sect. 6.1.1.

the executing or requested state. In practice, though, defence lawyers are not able to challenge this without having to resort to foreign lawyers, which involves costs. This means that in the overwhelming majority of cases the issue will not be litigated, since the financial situation of the accused does not permit the lawyer to instruct foreign defence lawyers.[237] Some on-going cases involving white-collar criminality might produce a change in the landscape of litigation in this field in the coming years.[238]

There are also practical limitations involving participation in acts for the gathering of evidence abroad: although nothing prevents defence lawyers from participating in such acts, at least in those instances where Portuguese law would permit that, the practical limitations for lawyers to intervene abroad, either directly or with foreign defence lawyers, are often insurmountable due to non-existence of proper legal aid and lack of financial resources of the accused (or of the assistant). Concerning testimonial evidence, these limitations may be alleviated through the use of video links rather than requests for interviews conducted by the executing or requested state.

On a final note in this section, we believe that with the application of the EIO the litigation of cross-border evidence in Portugal will grow. But its applicability also entails added complexity since it requires knowledge not only of domestic and international cooperation law, but also of the constitutional, institutional and fundamental rights law of the EU, as well as of secondary EU law and of the procedural requisites and mechanisms to invoke these provisions in domestic cases. Given the limitations in terms of effective defence in cross-border cases, it seems that change is required in order to provide the accused (and the victims) with the effective legal assistance and remedies they are entitled to.

---

[237] The number of available cases of the higher courts confirms this practical view—see Ramos (2013), pp. 555–562.

[238] In the scope of cases concerning Brazil as a requesting state and Portugal as a requested state (*Operation Car Wash/Operação Lava Jato*), the Advisory Board of the General Attorney's Office has recently produced an opinion which also covers (albeit partially) the issue—See Opinion 2/2016 available at https://dre.pt/application/file/74179268. And some legal opinions by academics instructed by the accused have been produced—see Canotilho and Brandão (2016) on the *ordre public* as a limitation to international cooperation in the scope of Operation Car Wash and the plea bargaining agreements.

7 Requirements of Personal Participation and *In Absentia* Proceedings. The Perspective of Supranational and International Human Rights Law. Critical Remarks on Domestic Law in the Light of the European Convention and EU Law

The right of an accused person to appear in person at the trial is included in the right to a fair trial provided for in Art. 6 of the European Convention for the Protection of Human Rights and Fundamental Freedoms (ECHR), as interpreted by the European Court of Human Rights (ECtHR). The ECtHR has also declared that the right of the accused person to appear in person at the trial is not absolute and that under certain conditions the accused person may, of his/her own free will, expressly or tacitly but unequivocally waive that right.[239]

As mentioned above, the Portuguese Constitution acknowledges the fundamental nature of such a right, which is included in the rights of the defence.[240] Given that the presence of the accused person is essential for the existence of a fair and equitable trial, as stated in Art. 6(1) and (3)(c) ECHR, the ECtHR only allows for a judgment to be handed down *in absentia* when the accused expressly waived such right: such a waiver is, however, only valid if established in an unequivocal manner and if made voluntarily, knowingly and intelligently.[241]

The ECtHR also establishes that when a trial in the absence of the accused person has been carried out improperly, he/she will have the right to request a new trial or to appeal, which includes the possibility of a fresh determination of the merits of the case, as well as the submission of new evidence.[242]

Directive (EU) 2016/343 of 9 March 2016, on the strengthening of certain aspects of the presumption of innocence and of the right to be present at the trial in criminal proceedings, lays down minimum requirements governing, among others, the right to be present at one's trial.

One of the most relevant features of the Directive gears towards the harmonization of the conditions under which it is possible to hold a trial in the absence of the accused person (in other words, the conditions under which it can be assumed that there has been a valid waiver of such right), as well as the accused's right to request a new trial if the conditions set out above are not fulfilled.

The Directive allows for the possibility to hold the trial in the accused's absence, provided that the accused has been informed, in due time, of the trial and of the consequences of non-appearance; or having been informed of the trial, that person

---

[239] See, for example, Recital 1 of Framework Decision 2009/299/JHA, of 26 February 2009.

[240] Art. 32§§1 and 6 PConst.

[241] ECtHR, *Colozza v. Italy,* Judgment of February 12, 1985, application no. 9024/80; *Sejdovic v. Italy* [GC], Judgment of March 1, 2006, application no. 56581/00.

[242] ECtHR, *Sejdovic v. Italy* [GC], Judgment of March 1, 2006; *Poitrimol v. France,* Judgment of November 23, 1993, application no. 14032/88.

has given a mandate to a lawyer that was appointed by that person or by the state.[243] The Directive moreover states that if it is not possible to comply with these conditions, because a suspect or accused person cannot be located despite reasonable efforts having been made, Member States should ensure that the accused has the possibility to challenge the judgment through the right to request a new trial or another legal remedy, such as an appeal which allows for new evidence to be presented.[244]

These conditions were inspired by the jurisprudence of the ECtHR.

Looking at the Portuguese criminal procedure system in light of the Directive, as interpreted by the courts and legal literature, there might be the need to amend Portuguese law concerning the right to be present at one's trial, since the Directive particularly requires that, for the trial to be held in the absence of the accused, he/she should have been summoned in person and thereby informed of the scheduled date and place of the trial, or, by other means, actually been given official information of the scheduled date and place of that trial, in such a manner that it was unequivocally established that he/she was aware of the scheduled trial.

In this respect, the summons proceedings established in the current CCP seems insufficient to ensure such actual knowledge, which is more problematic to the extent that Portuguese law does not offer a remedy through the right to a retrial or an appeal with the possibility to present fresh evidence.

As mentioned above, in the Portuguese system, in case the accused person made a SIR and has not indicated a change of address via registered letter during the proceedings, all subsequent notices will be sent to the stated address with simple proof of deposit, which includes the service of the court's order setting the date for the trial.

Currently, that notice is made by means of simple postal delivery, which does not make it possible in any case to verify whether the accused was informed of the trial, since it does not prove whether that person was effectively aware of it. In the light of this, it cannot be inferred *per se* whether or not the accused waived his/her right to be present at the trial in an unequivocal, voluntary, knowing and intelligent manner or whether that person deliberately sought to evade justice. Indeed, when the SIR is made during the investigation phase, the service of documents by simple postal delivery does not even ensure that the accused person is aware of the existence of an indictment against him/her.

Accordingly, when there is no proof that the accused person was effectively aware of the trial, holding the trial in his/her absence on the basis of the notice sent to the accused, by means of simple postal delivery, to the address mentioned in the SIR may not satisfy the conditions set forth in Art. 8(2) of the Directive.

Indeed, in line with the jurisprudence of the ECtHR, Member States must exercise a duty of care that obliges them to adequately search for the whereabouts of the accused before they can conduct the trial in his/her absence. A simple notice, which

---

[243] Art. 8(1) and (2).
[244] Art. 8(4) and 9.

would in any case only be susceptible of demonstrating awareness of the trial but not enough to waive the right to be present, is not sufficient. This is even more evident if the correspondence has been deposited in the letter-box but is returned with an indication that the accused is not residing at the address in question, or when there is information in the case file revealing that the accused might not have been aware of such notification (in particular, for individuals living abroad). In these cases, the burden of proof that is incumbent upon the court is clearly not met.

Recent case law of the CJEU seems to confirm that our system does not meet the requirements of EU Law. In the *Dworzecki* case, the CJEU underlined that it is a requisite of Art. 4a(1)(a)(i) Framework Decision 2009/299/EU to demonstrate that the person actually knew about the date and place of the trial and that such information was provided enough in advance for the person to organize his/her defence effectively. And that "the fact that the summons was handed over to a third party who undertook to pass it on to the person concerned, whether or not that third party belonged to the household of the person concerned, cannot in itself satisfy those requirements".[245]

In any case, holding the trial in the accused's absence as a penalty for having violated the obligation stemming from the SIR to provide the new address if it changed seems to be a drastic consequence which is disproportionate to the seriousness of the breach in question, particularly when there is a possibility that the accused will receive a high prison sentence.[246]

In fact, our criminal procedural system acknowledges the possibility of holding the trial in those circumstances in which the accused person might not have been aware of the trial and, for this reason, it requires that the service of the judgment or conviction take place by means of personal contact with the accused, pursuant to Art.s 333(5) and (6) CCP.

Our criminal procedural system would not be incompatible with the Directive if it would grant the right of the accused to request a new trial or the right to lodge an appeal on questions of fact which would allow for a fresh determination of the merits of the case, alongside the possibility to present his/her defence at this procedural stage and to request and produce new evidence, as prescribed in Art.s 8(4) and 9 of the Directive.

Actually this was the case under Law 59/98 of August 25, 1998 and more precisely its Art. 380-A. The latter conferred the right to a new trial to persons accused

---

[245] Judgment of 24 May 2016 in case C-108/16 PPU, *Dworzecki*, §47.

[246] Cunha (2010), pp. 257–258, rightly points out that "sanctioning the accused, for whichever reason, with a loss of his rights of defence, in total or partially, does not seem to be a valid principle in a state governed by the rule of law (very much the opposite, it is a true denial of rule of law)". Barreiros (2014), p. 88, actually compares it to the system in place during the dictatorship—in which a judgment handed down *in absentia* would never become final before being served to the accused is person—the current system instituted by the democracy "is far behind the former one in terms of safeguarding the rights and the dignity of the institutions: the presumption of service, the fiction of knowledge, the dispensability of presence, the disregard of personification, the degrading of the act of the trial and the pushing over of sentencing into the category of routines of repressive bureaucracy are in force, and all is valid, effective and enforceable, in sum, tolerated".

of having committed offences that were punishable with a sentence of more than 5 years; in the remaining cases, the said right was granted only if the accused wished to submit new evidence.[247]

In the current CCP however the existing legal remedy does not allow for the presentation of new means of evidence and is strictly limited to a review of the decision of the court of first instance and of the errors of fact and law that it might have made. There is no new instance before which the whole evidence is adduced *ex novo*, or which at least permits the submission of new evidence provided by the defence. Thus, although the ECtHR (and the provisions of the Directive) do not impose retrial as a sole condition, since they specifically refer to "another legal remedy, which allows a fresh determination of the merits of the case, including examination of new evidence, and which may lead to the original decision being reversed", it cannot be said that the remedy prescribed in Portuguese law complies with those standards.

It may be thus necessary to reform the existing criminal procedural framework.[248]

If Portuguese criminal procedural law remains unchanged after the deadline for implementing the Directive has elapsed, on April 1 2018,[249] then the national provisions contrary to Art.s 8 and 9 of the Directive must be set aside and Art. 9 can be invoked directly to establish the right to request a new trial. In case of doubts concerning the interpretation or validity of the Directive, there will also be an obligation to refer cases to the Court of Justice of the European Union for a preliminary ruling. Until then, the publication of the Directive imposes the obligation to interpret the national law in conformity with the norms laid down in the Directive, as far as the former contributes to the fulfilment of the aims of the Directive.

---

[247] Text available at http://www.pgdlisboa.pt/leis/lei_mostra_articulado.php?artigo_id=199A0380A&nid=199&tabela=lei_velhas&pagina=1&ficha=1&so_miolo=&nversao=9#artigo (last accessed 31.7.2018).

[248] Antunes and Costa (2015), pp. 42–43 and 45, commenting on the Directive Proposal also states that the Portuguese system of trials *in absentia* following the combination of SIR and service by means of simple postal delivery without acknowledgement of receipt may raise problems of compatibility with the Directive Proposal since it is not a procedure that allows to establish unequivocally that the accused is aware of the order setting out the trial date and since there is no right to a re-trial.

[249] So far, none of the "suspects' procedural rights directives" whose implementation deadline has elapsed has been implemented in Portugal. The Government alleged that national law already complies with the Directives. This is mostly correct, but there are some issues in particular with interpretation and translation (quality, scope of interpretation at trial and non-existence of certified translators or a list), and possibly with some obligations set out in the right to information directive. Concerning legal assistance and legal aid, the formal rules in Portugal guarantee a broad right to legal assistance—as outlined in Sect. 2. But there might be some issues concerning substantive effectiveness of the defense and the free choice of lawyers when these are appointed by the state.

8 Concluding Remarks

Although they are constitutionally designed as proceedings of an adversarial structure, safeguarding the widest rights of defence and mitigated by an investigation principle, Portuguese criminal proceedings remain characterized in pre-trial stages by strong inquisitorial traits. In particular, the role of the defence is still designed in a passive-reactive fashion and therefore the participation rights in those stages are limited. In cross-border cases, there are significant limitations to participation rights, in particular from a practical viewpoint.

At the trial stage, although the presence of the accused is described in the Constitution and in the Code of Criminal Procedure as the rule, it has turned out to be the exception in many cases. Trials *in absentia* have become a commonplace, the service of the accused and his/her presence or participation is becoming a bureaucratic aspect of the case. And non-compliance with the Statement of Identity and Residence is sanctioned with a trial *in absentia* without any compensation measures, such as granting the accused the right to request a new trial or to appeal and bring fresh evidence to the consideration of appellate courts.

This situation seems to be incompatible with European Law and the entry into force of Directive 2016/343 of 9 March 2016 may force the legislator and the judiciary to change the current legal framework or case law.

References

Albuquerque P (2011) Comentário do Código de Processo Penal à luz da Constituição da República e da Convenção Europeia dos Direitos do Homem, 4.ª Ed., Universidade Católica Editora, Lisbon

Antunes M (2016) Direito Processual Penal. Almedina, Coimbra

Antunes, M, Costa FJ (2015) Comentário à Proposta de diretiva sobre a presunção de inocência e o direito de comparecer em tribunal em processo penal. In: Caeiro P (ed) org. A Agenda da União Europeia sobre os Direitos e Garantias da Defesa em Processo Penal: a "segunda vaga" e o seu previsível impacto sobre o direito português. Instituto Jurídico/FDUC, Coimbra, pp 21–46

Barreiros J (2014) Presença e ausência do arguido no julgamento penal. JURISMAT 4:79–90

Beleza T (1998) Julgamento de Ausentes: o Tempo (celeridade) e o espaço ("ausência") na reforma da lei processual. UAL, Lisbon, pp 49–60

Beleza T, Costa Pinto F (2007) Criminal procedure. In: Ferreira de Almeida C, Cristas A, Piçarra N (eds) Portuguese law – an overview. Almedina, Coimbra, pp 167–180

Caeiro P, Costa M (2013) The Portuguese System. In: Ligeti K (ed) Toward a prosecutor for the European Union, vol 1. Hart, Oxford, pp 540–585

Canotilho G, Brandão N (2016) Colaboração premiada e auxílio judiciário em matéria penal: a ordem pública como obstáculo à cooperação com a operação lava jato. RLJ 4000:16–38

Cape E et al (2010) ECHR and the right to effective defence. In: Effective criminal defence in Europe. Intersentia, Antwerp

Cunha J (2010) Julgamento à Revelia. In: III Congresso de Processo de Processo Penal, Manuel Monteiro Guedes Valente, ed. Almedina, Coimbra, pp 243–258

Dias A (2004) A tutela do ofendido e a posição do assistente no processo penal português. In: Palma MF (coord) Jornadas de Direito Processual Penal e Direitos Fundamentais. Almedina, Coimbra, pp 55–65

Dias F (1974) Direito Processual Penal. Coimbra Editora, Coimbra

Dias F (1988) Sobre os sujeitos processuais no novo Código de Processo Penal. In: Jornadas de Direito Processual Penal: o Novo Código de Processo Penal. CEJ, org. Almedina, Coimbra, pp 3–34

Graça A (2014) O Regime Jurídico do Mandado de Detenção Europeu. Coimbra Editora, Coimbra

Grozev Y (2012) Bulgaria. In: Cape E, Namoradze Z (eds) Effective criminal defence in Eastern Europe. LARN/Soros Foundation, Moldova

Mendes A (2014) Anotação ao artigo 332. In: Gaspar AH, Cabral S, Costa M, Mendes O, Madeira P, da Graça H (eds) Código de Processo Penal Comentado. Almedina, Coimbra

Mendes P (2007) Estatuto de arguido e posição processual da vítima. RPCC 4:601–612

Mendes P (2013a) Lições de Direito Processual Penal. Almedina, Coimbra

Mendes P (2013b) Comparative exclusionary rules, Portuguese and Brazilian perspective. http://carlospintodeabreu.com/en/text-0-0-54-152-comparative-exclusionary-rules-portuguese-and-brazilian-perspective (acceded on 16.09.2017)

Monge S (2016) A investigação levada a cabo pela Defesa. In: Valente MMG (ed) V Congresso de Direito Penal e de Processo Penal. Almedina, Coimbra, pp 173–189

Neves A (1968) Sumários de Processo Criminal (1967–1968), n.e. (typed and copied by João Abrantes), Coimbra

Ramos V (2013) Problemas da obtenção de prova em contexto transnacional – introdução. RPCC 4:547–568

Ruggeri S (2016) Inaudito reo proceedings, defense rights, and harmonisation goals in the EU, responses of the European Courts and new perspectives of EU law. EUCRIM, pp 42–51

Silva CN (2007) Portuguese legal history. In: Ferreira de Almeida C, Cristas A, Piçarra N (eds) Portuguese law – an overview. Almedina, Coimbra, pp 15–28

Silva G (2013) Direito Processual Penal Português, vol I. UCP, Lisbon

Silva G (2014) Direito Processual Penal Português, vol III. UCP, Lisbon

Summers S (2007) Fair trials. Hart, Oxford

Report on Romania

Flaviu Ciopec and Magdalena Roibu

Abstract In Romanian criminal proceedings, the accused cannot claim an absolute individual right to be present at trial, which would imply considerable efforts on the part of judicial authorities to make it effective. Failure to bring the accused to trial does not lead to a stay of proceedings—as an expression of an absolute nature of such right—but allows the trial to continue if judicial authorities prove that they have performed a duty of diligence in this respect, e.g. the defendant has been lawfully summoned and the procedure has been complied with. The presence of the defendant to court, in person or through a representative or a counsel of his/her own choosing or appointed *ex officio*, if the latter contacted the person they represent, shall redress any irregularity related to the summoning procedure. The court proceedings may take place in the absence of the defendant, if the latter is missing, avoids proceedings or has changed his/her address without informing thereupon the judicial authorities and if his/her new address remains unknown. Court proceedings may also occur in the absence of the defendant, when, even though lawfully served the summons, the defendant provides no justification for his/her absence from the trial of the case.

The Romanian procedural law provides an extraordinary remedy by which a person who was tried *in absentia* and convicted by a final ruling may request the retrial of his/her case in a term of 1 month calculated from the day he/she was informed, by any official notification, that a trial had been held against him/her. Unlike the other extraordinary remedies, the application for retrial of the case does not aim at challenging the unlawful or unfounded nature of the decision ruled *in absentia,* but instead the defendant seeks to give effectiveness to his/her right to participate personally to trial and exert his/her right to defense.

The ECtHR case-law on *in absentia* trials involving Romania is very sparse. The situation looks very much alike when it comes to the case-law generated by preliminary rulings filed by Romanian judges to the European Court of Justice on the conformity of *in absentia* proceedings with EU law. This means that compliance with

F. Ciopec (✉) · M. Roibu
Faculty of Law, West University of Timișoara, Timișoara, Romania
e-mail: flaviu.ciopec@e-uvt.ro; magdalena.roibu@e-uvt.ro

© Springer Nature Switzerland AG 2019
S. Quattrocolo, S. Ruggeri (eds.), *Personal Participation in Criminal Proceedings*, Legal Studies in International, European and Comparative Criminal Law 2, https://doi.org/10.1007/978-3-030-01186-4_12

the European standards in the area of proceedings held *in absentia* could not take place by means of judicial practice, a situation which is not specific only to Romania. Therefore, it is necessary that harmonization may be achieved within the law-making process. Currently adopted legal instruments at the EU level aim at such ambitious endeavor.

Abbreviations

APW	All ports warning
CCP	New Code of Criminal Procedure
DIICOT	Department for the Investigation of Organized Crime and Terrorism
EAW	European Arrest Warrant
ECHR	European Convention on Human Rights
ECtHR	European Court of Human Rights
(f)CCP	Former Code of Criminal Procedure
GEO	Government's Emergency Ordinance
ICCPR	International Covenant on Civil and Political Rights
NPC	New Penal Code
RCC	Romanian Constitutional Court

1 Constitutional Requirements of the Involvement of Private Parties in Criminal Justice

In most jurisdictions, involvement of private parties in criminal justice is subject to usually codified rules of procedure. The change of a strictly procedural rule into a constitutional standard is an idiosyncratic legal reaction to a specific historical or traditional background. If such a change occurs, an explanation should righteously follow.

The Romanian Constitution (adopted in 1991, reviewed in 2003) does not contain express provisions related to the participation of persons to criminal proceedings. The fundamental law states in art. 126 (2) that: "the jurisdiction of courts and the *rules of proceedings* are regulated only by law". This text was interpreted[1] in the sense that only the lawmaker has the absolute prerogative to set out the rules of court proceedings, including the conditions which allow access of parties before the courts. Since the Constitution actually points to the law as the key source which enables access to the criminal justice system, this explains the *absence of constitutional requirements* in the matter.

---

[1] Plenary of the Romanian Constitutional Court, Decision no. 1 of 8 February 1994, para. II, published in the Official Journal no. 69 of 16.03.1994.

However, this statement should not imply that the Romanian legal system completely disregards the presence of private parties to trial, a paramount standard in criminal justice, since the very same Constitution recognizes the preeminence of international covenants and treaties on fundamental human rights over national law (art. 20 in the Constitution). Thus, Romania has ratified the International Covenant on Civil and Political Rights (hereinafter ICCPR) in 1974 and its provisions are directly applicable in Romanian legislation.[2]

Therefore, art. 14 (3d) of the ICCPR which expressly provides the personal participation to trial as a minimal guarantee in repressive proceedings, conceptually qualifies as a standard above national ordinary criminal laws. Nevertheless, the ICCPR has been a "wax museum exhibit" in Romanian criminal case-law, since the courts have applied it only by exception. This attitude has also affected the effectiveness of personal participation to trial as a functional standard.

That is why the issue has been approached from a different perspective, namely that of the *free*[3] *access to justice* principle (art. 21 of the Constitution[4]).

Given that *access to justice* has not been provided precisely in the chapter dedicated to fundamental rights and freedoms, but in a section on common rules applicable to the latter, it has *not* been qualified as *a fundamental right, but* as *a principle* which governs fundamental rights and freedoms,[5] alongside with other principles, i.e. the principle of universality (art. 15), the non-retroactivity of the law (art. 15), the equality of rights (art. 16), the nationality of public offices (art. 16), the primacy of international regulations in the matter of human rights (art. 20) or the exceptional character of the restrictions of rights and freedoms (art. 53).

As the doctrine[6] has stated, access to justice implies the opportunity for every person to file a lawsuit, of his/her own will, even if such lawsuit may be unfounded in fact or in law, with the duty for the state to settle it in an authorized court. Art. 21 of the Romanian Constitution cohabits with art. 6 of the European Convention on Human Rights (hereinafter the ECHR), ever since it has been part of national legislation, i.e. the day the Convention was ratified.[7] Although art. 6 of the Convention does not expressly refer to the access to justice as a fundamental right (an unfortunate mistake of the drafters of the ECHR), this does not mean that said text fails to provide implicit safeguards for it. It was the Court's merit in stating that the right to a fair trial[8] is not limited to legal proceedings which are already pending, but, in

---

[2] As regards the international law of human rights Romania adopted the monist legal system, which implies that ratification is sufficient in order to transpose the international treaty into the national legal order, with no further formality (e.g. a special transposition law).

[3] Since access to justice has no absolute nature, the term "free" should be avoided.

[4] "Everyone is entitled to refer to justice for the protection of their rights, freedoms and legitimate interests. No law shall restrict the exercise of such right".

[5] Iancu (2003), p. 99.

[6] Chiriță (2006), p. 176.

[7] Romania ratified the ECHR by Act no. 30 of 31 May 1994.

[8] In the Romanian Constitution, the right to a fair trial is subsumed to the free access to justice section, which could allow the inference that it belongs to the latter, an approach which is different

addition, it secures a right of access to the courts for every person wishing to commence an action in order to have his civil rights and obligations determined.[9]

Unlike art. 6 of the ECHR, which refers strictly to a "violation of civil rights and obligations" or a "criminal charge", art. 21 of the Romanian Constitution is *more widely applicable*. This means that for those areas of law to which art. 6 of the ECHR does not apply, access to justice shall be allowed under the Romanian fundamental law.

In order to have access to justice appropriately respected, the State must *impose two standards*: effectiveness and accessibility.

On the one hand, the two standards have different meanings, depending on whether they refer to criminal or non-criminal matters. On the other hand, criminal matters need to be treated distinctively, in accordance with the perspective of the accused or the victim.

In criminal justice, from the perspective of the accused, *effectiveness* implies:

- a duty by the State to impose that the examination of any criminal charge which a person is confronted with be decided by a court,[10] since it is inconceivable that criminal liability could be incurred in the absence of a ruling by a judge (*nulla poena sine judicio*)
- a duty by the State to set up criminal courts with complete jurisdiction over a case on the merits, both *de facto* and *de jure*[11]
- a duty by the State to allow access to all procedural means by which justice is done[12] which in criminal matters signifies a real and effective possibility of the accused to protect him/herself from the charges: the right to plead for his/her case, the right to have free legal assistance, the right to enjoy all facilities for the preparation of his/her defense, the right to file a legal remedy, etc.
- a duty by the State to ensure any accused the double degree of jurisdiction, exclusively in criminal matters.

Unlike civil matters, where *accessibility* does not have an absolute character, in criminal matters there are no limitations, therefore it is unfair that an accused who does not wish to initiate criminal proceedings should be imposed conditions in order to benefit from ruling by a judge (e.g. compliance with certain formalities, observance of timeframes, payment of certain amounts of money, etc.). Consequently, in criminal justice, accessibility does not raise sensitive issues.

From the perspective of the victim,[13] access to justice is more strictly settled. The ECHR does not guarantee the victim a right of access to a criminal court (to initiate

---

from the ECHR view, whereby access to justice is part of the right to a fair trial. The inversion could be explained by that the "fair trial" standard has been introduced in the Constitution only since 2003, while free access to justice was prior to it.

[9] ECtHR, *Golder v. The United Kingdom*, decision of 21 February 1975, Appl. no. 4451/70 para 25.

[10] Vasiescu and Călin (2013), p. 10.

[11] Chiriță (2008), pp. 266–270.

[12] Muraru and Ciobanu (2008), p. 190.

[13] Chiriță (2008), pp. 83–84.

criminal proceedings), which makes art. 6 inapplicable, yet it can be applied if criminal proceedings were initiated and the victim of the offense chose to participate to trial as a civil party. As to the civil damages required by the victim, the right of access to justice is recognized, since the litigation aims at the exercise of certain civil rights and obligations (under art. 6 ECHR).

To sum up the afore-mentioned, participation of parties to criminal proceedings is *constitutionally determined, but only indirectly*, by resorting to the principle of access to justice.[14]

As noted above, a key element of access to justice is the right of any person to appear and plead his/her case before a judge (*effectiveness*). This means that a person whose rights and interests were exposed as a result of his/her direct participation to criminal proceedings, shall be entitled to take part to such proceedings. The possibility to plead for the personal case before a court implies precisely the opportunity to participate to that case, a constitutional guarantee which is activated by the access to justice principle.

Taking into account this reasoning, the Romanian Constitutional Court (hereinafter RCC) has ruled on several cases in criminal matters, related to the access to justice. In a much debated decision,[15] the Court stated that "everyone who is dissatisfied with the solution given by the Public Ministry to his/her petition shall have the right, based on art. 21 of the Constitution, to refer to justice, for the protection of his/her rights, freedoms and legitimate interests [...]. Therefore, the provisions of art. 278 in the Code of Criminal Procedure (...) are unconstitutional since they block the access of persons who are dissatisfied with the solutions given to their petitions by the Public Ministry, to refer to justice. This right shall mainly apply to those decisions by which the prosecutor chooses to end a criminal law conflict, whether real or apparent, such as decisions not to prosecute, not to pursue formal charges or to cease prosecution". Aware of the fact that "it would be necessary that the lawmaker intervene and provide for the right of persons to further refer to the authorized court when dissatisfied with the solution given to their petition against the measures of the prosecutor", the Court concluded that art. 21 of the Constitution shall be directly applicable until an amendment *de lege lata* of the (f)CCP.

Following this decision, which acknowledged the possibility of the victim to intervene into the trial stage of criminal proceedings, the RCC adopted another decision related to the rights of the victim in a trial started at his/her own initiative. The Court referred[16] to the provisions of art. 129 of the Constitution: "against the rulings of courts, the interested parties and the Public Ministry shall exert the legal remedies, as provided under the law" and held that "this constitutional provision

---

[14] There is also the opinion whereby the right to personally attend the trial is a corollary of the right to defense, of equality of arms, of contradictory and open-court debates—cf. Deleanu (2006), p. 558.

[15] The Romanian Constitutional Court, Decision no. 486 of 2 December 1997, published in the Official Journal no. 105 of 06.03.1998.

[16] The Romanian Constitutional Court, Decision no. 100 of 9 March 2004, para. 4, published in the Official Journal no. 261 of 24.03.2004.

covers two situations: (a) the first recognizes the right of any party to a trial, regardless of its subject-matter, as well as the right of the Public Ministry, to exercise legal remedies against court rulings considered to be unlawful or unfounded; (b) the second establishes that the exercise of legal remedies shall follow the rules provided by the law. In other words, the first situation refers to the fundamental right, provided by art. 21 of the Constitution, to benefit from free access to justice. Therefore, this situation belongs to substantial law. The second situation refers to procedural law rules which cannot interfere with the essence of the right granted by the first situation. Thus, when it comes to the conditions in which legal remedies can be exerted, the lawmaker shall provide for the timeframes within which they can be filed, the formal standards for using such remedies, their contents, the court where the remedy should be filed, the type of jurisdiction and trial rules, the solutions that may be ruled and other similar issues [...]. Yet the lawmaker can neither suppress the substantial right of an interested party to exert legal remedies nor can he restrict the exercise of such right, except in the derogatory cases set out by art. 53 of the Constitution. It is true that, although art. 129 of the Constitution guarantees the exercise of legal remedies *"under the law"*, this constitutional provision does not mean that *"the law"* could annul or restrict the exercise of the rights or freedoms expressly granted by the Constitution". Therefore, the disposition set out in art. 326 (1c) (f)CCP, which allowed the victim to file an appeal only *"in those cases where the public action is initiated upon a prior complaint"* was declared unconstitutional, and, as a result, it opened the possibility for the victim to file an appeal, regardless of whether the public action is initiated *ex officio* or upon a prior complaint.

In case of a criminal trial initiated *ex officio*, with no interference from the victim, the Court stated that[17] "since constitutional provisions contain no distinction, it results that free access to justice does not refer exclusively to the introductory lawsuit filed in the first instance, but also to a further referral to superior courts, which are competent under the law to rule on the superior stages of a trial, including on legal remedies, since the defense of the rights, freedoms and legal interests of individuals logically implies an opportunity to challenge those judgments that are deemed unlawful or unfounded. Consequently, to restrict the right of the parties to the same trial from exerting legal remedies implies a limitation of the very access to justice [...]." Therefore, the RCC stated that the dispositions of art. 362 (1d) (f)CCP are unconstitutional as long as they do not allow the civil party and the party incurring civil liability to file an appeal also on the criminal side of proceedings. This reasoning was deemed[18] as "slightly far-fetched", since it places the civil party in a position to challenge the criminal side of the court judgment, such as the legal qualification of the act or the amount of the penalty, which seems unnatural.

The three decisions were ruled in the context of the former Code of Criminal Procedure, enacted in 1969, which has been presently repealed, starting on the 1st

---

[17]The Romanian Constitutional Court, Decision no. 482 of 9 November 2004, para. 2, published in the Official Journal no. 1200 of 15.12.2004.
[18]Chiriță (2008), p. 399.

of February 2014. They aimed at highlighting the nonconformity of certain provisions of the (f)CCP with the constitutional principle of access to justice, thus attempting to reestablish the balance of criminal proceedings in favor of certain persons who were denied the right to participate to a criminal trial due to the absence of a legal provisions that may allow them to exert legal remedies against a judgment which could potentially harm their legitimate rights and interests. Such persons (the victim, the civil party or the party incurring civil liability) *were unable to defend their case* before the criminal court, although they were interested in doing it, *due to procedural rules* that restricted their access to justice instruments (complaints, legal remedies). In all situations, the RCC eventually intervened, sometimes after much hesitation, in order to rule on the lack of conformity of such provisions with the fundamental law and to *allow an extended participation* of all interested persons to criminal proceedings.

The entry into force of the New Code of Criminal Procedure (hereinafter CCP) gave the Constitutional Court the chance to reaffirm its above-analyzed case-law in a new context.

As regards the text of art. 488 CCP, which used to provide an exclusive right of the defendant and the prosecutor to challenge the judgment of a court which ruled on the validity of a plea bargain, the RCC noticed[19] that "free access to justice and the right to a fair trial do not mean that these rights are guaranteed only in first instance courts, but also in the courts competent to rule during later stages of a trial, since the safeguard of rights and freedoms of participants to a criminal trial also implies their legal possibility to challenge the judgments which infringed their rights and freedoms. From this perspective, the absence of regulations which allow the victim, the civil party and the party incurring civil liability to challenge, *on the criminal side of proceedings*, the judgment ruled according to art. 485 CCP, breaches art. 21 (2) and (3) of the fundamental law, as well as the provisions of art. 6 of the ECHR". Taking into account the aforementioned arguments, the Court noticed that the jurisdiction which tried the case on the merits should rule on the plea bargain only after the victim, the civil party and the party incurring civil liability were lawfully summoned and heard. The Court dismissed the text of art. 484 (2) as unconstitutional, since it excludes the victim, the civil party and the party incurring civil liability from participating to the proceedings in which the plea bargain was validated.

The protection of the victim, the civil party and the party incurring civil liability was addressed also on the occasion of a new decision[20] ruled by the RCC which stated that "[…] the access, preparation and exercise of a challenge (opposition) as a legal remedy in the preliminary hearing (on evidence) procedure represents an aspect of the free access to justice, a fundamental right protected by art. 21 of the Constitution […]. Under these circumstances, restricting the number of persons

---

[19] The Romanian Constitutional Court, Decision no. 235 of 7 April 2015, para. 46, 51 and 69, published in the Official Journal no. 364 of 26.05.2015.

[20] The Romanian Constitutional Court, Decision no. 631 of 8 October 2015, para. 31 and 34–35, published in the Official Journal no. 831 of 06.11.2015.

who can exert the challenge (opposition) as a legal remedy in the preliminary hearing procedure - to the prosecutor and defendant only, leads to the breach of the right of free access to justice, enshrined by art. 21 of the fundamental law and by art. 6 of the ECHR, *a right that belongs also to* the victim, the civil party and the party incurring legal liability, given that, as the Court previously stated, the outcome of the preliminary hearing procedure on legal issues related to how evidence was supplied and the investigative acts were conducted by the authorities, has a direct influence on the judgment on the merits and may be decisive for the culpability or innocence of the defendant and/or for the protection of rights of formerly mentioned persons".

For the same reasons, the RCC ruled[21] a similar decision in the situation of the absence of legal remedies against preventive measures on assets ordered by the preliminary chamber judge (in the preliminary hearing procedure) or by the court, when judging either on the merits or on appeal, considering that said absence is contrary to the access to justice.

More recently, the RCC debated[22] the unconstitutionality of the provisions of art. 434 (1) CCP which read: "An appeal on law shall be exerted against the decisions ruled by the courts of appeal as appellate courts". Upon deliberation, the RCC, by majority of votes, allowed the plea of unconstitutionality and concluded that "a solution which excludes the possibility that decisions passed by the High Court of Justice as appellate court may be subject to an appeal on law is contrary to the Constitution". The Court considered that the challenged provisions do not provide a remedy in case of breach of the law and lead to a gap in legislation in case of illegal decisions ruled by the High Court of Justice as an appellate court—those by which the merits of a case was solved—on the one hand, by depriving the prosecutor of the instruments necessary to exert his specific role in a criminal trial, and, on the other hand, by depriving the parties from a chance to defend their legitimate rights, freedoms and interests.

2 Personal Participation of Private Parties and Legal Assistance

The Romanian doctrine,[23] following the model adopted by the procedural law, distinguishes two situations related to legal assistance during criminal proceedings: legal assistance as such, and legal representation.

---

[21] The Romanian Constitutional Court, Decision no. 24 of 20 January 2016, published in the Official Journal no. 276 of 12.04.2016.

[22] The Romanian Constitutional Court, Decision no. 540 of 12 July 2016, para. 24, published in the Official Journal no. 841 of 24.10.2016.

[23] Udroiu (2016), pp. 782 and 802.

The first situation refers to the performance of legal services by a lawyer, of one's own choosing or appointed *ex officio*, in the presence of the assisted person, in order to protect his/her rights, freedoms and legitimate interests. The other situation implies the performance of professional services by a lawyer, *in the absence* of a party or other person involved in a trial, acting in their name and on their behalf. The distinguishing criterion is therefore clear: *legal assistance as such is associated with the participation of the assisted person* to criminal proceedings, while *legal representation occurs in the absence of the person*.

The CCP has made a clear distinction between the parties to a trial and other persons involved in it. Thus, the parties[24] are the defendant (acting on the criminal side of the trial), the civil party, as well as the party incurring civil liability (acting on the civil side of proceedings). The victim is not a party, but a person involved in the trial, just like the suspect. The difference between the parties and the other persons involved in the trial is rather scholastic and formal, since the criminal procedure law provides that the other persons involved in a trial have the same rights as the parties to it (art. 33 CCP). However, it is commonsensical that the victim should not be a party, due to the fact that he/she does not exercise the public (criminal) action in any circumstance, given that the Prosecutor's Office is completely dominant over that. Under the law, a person can become a party to a criminal trial only by exerting the criminal (public) action, which is not the case with the victim. In case of the prosecutor, the afore-mentioned rule does not apply. Although the prosecutor is in total charge of the public action, he/she does not become a party to trial, but preserves the status of judicial authority (art. 30 CCP).

According to art. 88 CCP, in a criminal trial the lawyer shall *assist or represent all the parties*, including the victim and the suspect, with *no restriction*. In a broad sense, performing legal assistance implies that the lawyer has the right to solicit *access to the case file*, throughout the entire criminal trial (art. 94 CCP) and to *assist to any act of investigation*, except for those situations where special methods of surveillance and investigation are used (i.e. phone tapping, access to a computerized system, audio-video or photo environmental monitoring, use of undercover agents, controlled delivery, localization or surveillance by technical means, obtainment of data on financial transactions, tracking data of registered correspondence, etc.), as well as in case of strip search or vehicle search upon commission of a flagrant offense (art. 92 CCP). The lawyer is also entitled to *assist to home search*, as well as to *participate to the hearing of any person* by the liberty and custody judge, to file applications, complaints, and to submit statements of defense. During the trial stage, the lawyer of the defendant, the victim, the civil party or the party incurring civil liability shall exert all the rights of the assisted party, except for those which said party can personally exert (art. 93 CCP).

---

[24] "The parties are those persons who exert or against whom a judicial action is exerted" (art. 32 (1) CCP).

Under the former (f)CCP, as regards art. 172 (1) related to the right of the lawyer to assist to any act of investigation, only if "*the presence of the suspect or defendant for whom the lawyer performs the defense*" is ensured, the RCC stated[25] that this situation represents a conditioning and a limitation of the lawyer's right to assist to investigation activities, and thus a breach of the right of the suspect/defendant to have his/her defense guaranteed.

Pursuant to art. 96 CCP, throughout the criminal proceedings, all the parties and other persons involved in the trial can be represented, except for the cases when their presence is compulsory (e.g. the defendant is under arrest) or when such presence is *deemed necessary* by a judicial authority. The presence of a person in court is guaranteed by serving summons or apprehension warrants on the former. The court may refuse[26] to rule on the case only in the presence of the party's representative and in the absence of the interested party and shall order the appearance of said party.

At this point we would like to refer to a former case-law[27] of the RCC which decided that: "[…] the solution adopted by the European Court of Human Rights which concluded to the violation of art. 6 section 1 and section 3 d) of the ECHR in those cases where the law obstructs representation of the defendant during the stages of legal remedies – is also applicable to art. 174 (1a) (f)CCP which *does not allow representation* of the defendant when the case is tried by the court of first instance […], when the offense is punishable by an imprisonment term of more than one year".

Starting on the adoption of this decision, representation of the defendant and, by extension, of the other parties, has become a rule in the Romanian criminal trial. Thus, even in those cases where representation of the defendant is prohibited by the law since he/she is under arrest and his/her presence to trial can be assured at any time, representation becomes still possible as a sort of remedy granted by the law— for those situations when the defendant cannot be brought before the court,[28] as he/she is hospitalized and motionless or his/her transport is obstructed due to force majeure or to a state of necessity (art. 204, 225, 235, and 242 CCP).

The same situation occurs in case of supplying evidence in the letters rogatory procedure, where an arrested defendant shall be compulsorily represented (art. 200 (8) CCP).

On a different occasion, referring to the dispositions of art. 402 (3) of the former Code for criminal procedure, according to which the arrested person is brought to

---

[25] The Romanian Constitutional Court, Decision no. 1086 of 20 November 2007, para. 6, published in the Official Journal no. 866 of 18.12.2007.

[26] Udroiu (2015), pp. 284–285.

[27] The Romanian Constitutional Court, Decision no. 145 of 14 July 2000, para. 3, published in the Official Journal no. 665 of 16.12.2000.

[28] Neagu (2007), p. 223.

court when a case is subject to legal review only if the court deems it necessary, the RCC stated that[29] "indeed, the condition *only if the court deems it necessary* [...] is contrary to the provisions of art. 24 in the Constitution, which guarantee the right to defense, since it invalidates paragraph (2) of the same text, pursuant to which all throughout the trial, the parties have the right to be assisted by counsel, whether of their own choosing or appointed *ex officio*. [...]. The Court notices that both the activity of investigation and the defense of the citizens 'rights (notably the right to defense) imply an effective exercise of the right to defense, with no restrictions and assessments by the court whether the presence of the arrested person is necessary upon preliminaries of a trial in which a case is subject to legal review. Consequently, his/her presence is compulsory, so that his/her right to defense be effectively guaranteed".

In case of criminal proceedings initiated against a *legal entity*, its legal representative shall speak on its behalf when it comes to performing procedural acts. If for the same criminal act or joined acts, the public action was initiated also against the legal representative of the entity, the latter appoints an attorney-in-fact in order to represent it at trial. If the legal entity did not appoint an attorney-in-fact, the latter would be appointed, depending on the trial stage, by the prosecutor in charge of the investigation, by the preliminary chamber judge or by the court, from among the insolvency practitioners, licensed under the law (art. 491 CCP).

In the event that a *large number of persons* (e.g. in cases of fraud offenses), who do not have contrary interests, become civil parties in criminal proceedings, these may appoint a person to represent their interests within the criminal proceedings (art. 20 CCP). If civil parties did not appoint a joint (common) representative, for the proper conducting of criminal proceedings, the prosecutor or the court may appoint a counsel to represent the interests of the former. The court resolution or the prosecutor order shall be notified upon the civil parties, who have to inform the prosecutor or the court if they refuse to be jointly represented by such counsel. All acts of the proceedings communicated to the representative or of which such representative took knowledge are presumed to be known by the represented persons. The absence of civil parties shall be covered by the presence of the representative/counsel, which shall be deemed sufficient in court proceedings.

The afore-mentioned shall apply accordingly in the event of a large number of victims (art. 80 CCP).

Parties or other persons involved in a trial, who have conflicting interests, may not be assisted or represented by the same counsel (art. 88 CCP). If this occurs, any acts of proceedings shall be null and void.[30]

---

[29] The Romanian Constitutional Court, Decision no. 348 of 18 December 2001, published in the Official Journal no. 63 of 29.01.2002.

[30] Mateuţ (2007), p. 645.

3 Personal Participation of the Accused in Criminal Proceedings

3.1 General Features of Personal Participation: Absolute Individual Right or Duty of Diligence?

As a matter of principle, art. 1 (2) CCP provides that criminal procedure law aims at ensuring an *efficient exercise of the duties* of judicial authorities, by *guaranteeing the rights* of parties and the other participants in a criminal trial, *in order to comply with the provisions* of the Constitution, the founding treaties of the European Union, the other regulations of the European Union in criminal procedure matters, as well as the covenants and treaties on the fundamental human rights, ratified by Romania.

Although the reference from art. 1 CCP related to efficiency is singular within the contents of the code, it could represent a guiding line for the entire criminal trial structure of the code. The Explanatory Memorandum of the new code uses this term 14 times, which is sufficient to create the impression that is has not been used randomly.[31] A righteous question would be[32]: what does efficiency mean in terms of criminal proceedings? A higher percentage of convictions or an increased percentage of acquittals? Or a faster justice?

From the contents of the afore-mentioned art., it can be concluded that efficiency is primarily associated with the exercise of the duties incumbent on judicial authorities and only secondarily with the procedural safeguards granted to parties at trial. Therefore, we consider that this text is symptomatic for the way in which the Romanian criminal trial shapes out. Thus, from the standpoint of judicial authorities, efficiency is ensured by imposing duties of diligence rather than by granting an absolute protection of individual rights, as this implies ensuring certain guarantees that are incompatible with the standard of efficiency.

As shown in what follows, the accused *cannot claim an absolute individual right* to be present at trial, which would imply considerable efforts on the part of judicial authorities to make it effective. Failure of bringing the accused to trial does not lead to a stay of proceedings—as an expression of an absolute character of such right— but allows the trial to continue if the judicial actors prove that they have performed their *duty of diligence*. This solution is in accordance with the idea of efficiency which has been tackled above.

---

[31] Ciopec (2014), p. 37.
[32] Ionescu (2011), p. 87.

3.2 Personal Participation in the Pre-trial Inquiry (with Particular Regard to the Interim Decisions on Coercive Measures)

3.2.1 Essentials

Under Romanian criminal procedure law, the investigation stage serves to collect the evidence necessary to establish if an offense was committed, to identify potential offenders and hold the latter liable, in order to decide whether they should be indicted or not (art. 285 CCP). To achieve the scope of the investigation, once a criminal act was reported, the authorities are bound to search for and assemble data and information related to the existence of the offense and the identification of offenders, as well as to collect and supply evidence (art. 306 (1) CCP).

When the report (complaint) complies with the conditions required by the law, the investigation authorities decide, by an order, to initiate the investigation with a focus on the act that has been committed or whose commission is being prepared, even if the offender is mentioned in the report or is known (art. 305 (1) CCP). When there is evidence leading to the reasonable suspicion that *a certain person has committed the act* which entailed initiation of the investigation and there is no circumstance which may obstruct initiation or exercise of the public action, the investigation authorities order continuation of the inquiry to his/her regard, and thus the person becomes a suspect[33] (art. 305 (3) CCP).

A person who has acquired the status of a suspect shall be informed about this before his/her first hearing and, at the same time, he/she shall be made aware of the criminal act(s) which he/she is suspected of, the nature of the charges, as well as his/her rights during the trial, a written record being drawn to this effect (art. 307 CCP).

The public action is initiated by order of the prosecutor, during the investigation, when the former notices that there is evidence leading to the conclusion that *a certain person has committed an offense* and there is no circumstance which may obstruct the initiation of public action (art. 309 (1) CCP). Notice of initiation of the public action is served upon the defendant[34] by the investigation authorities who call the former for a hearing.

Once the public action is initiated and the investigation authorities discover new criminal acts, data leading to the participation of other persons to the act, or circumstances that may modify the nature of the charges, they shall decide, by an order, to extend the investigations or to change the initial qualification of the act (art. 311 CCP). The judicial authority who ordered the extension of investigations or the change of the legal qualification of the act is bound to inform the suspect about the new acts that determined the extension.

---

[33] "When, given all the data and evidence of the case, there results a reasonable suspicion that a person has committed a criminal act, that person shall become a suspect" (art. 77 CCP).

[34] "The person against whom the public action was initiated shall become a party in a criminal trial and shall be called a defendant" (art. 82 CCP).

The prosecutor, either referred to by the judicial police, upon extension of investigations, or acting by his own motion (*ex officio*) may order the extension of public action to the new criminal acts that were discovered.

In short, *the most important stages of a criminal investigation* are:

- initiation of the investigation with focus on the criminal act (*in rem*)
- continuation of the investigation with focus on a person (initiation of the investigation *in personam*)
- initiation of the public action
- extension of investigations or of the public action.

Finally, pursuant to art. 312 CCP, in case a forensic medical report concludes that the suspect or defendant suffers from a serious disease that precludes him from taking part to proceedings, the judicial police shall submit their recommendations and the case file to the prosecutor so that he may order stay of investigation.

The order to stay investigation shall be served on the parties, the victims and the suspects. During the stay of investigation, the judicial police shall continue to perform all the activities whose completion is not hindered by the absence of the suspect or defendant, in compliance with the right to defense of the parties or the other persons involved in the trial. On resumption of the investigation, the activities completed during the stay can be repeated, if possible, upon request of the suspect or defendant. The judicial police are bound to check periodically, but no later than 3 months from the stay of investigation date, whether the ground which led to the stay still persists.

3.2.2 The Duty to Inform

In all cases, the person subject to investigation, whether a suspect or a defendant, shall be called before the judicial authority, in order to be informed about the accusation(s). Under such circumstances, with no exception, *the authorities shall ensure the participation of the investigated person to proceedings.* Usually, the person's participation shall be ensured by *serving a summons* on him/her, according to art. 257 CCP, under the form of a written summons, a phone call, a fax call, an electronic mail or other system of electronic messaging (but only if these latter methods are consented by the person under investigation). The summons shall be served on the suspect or the defendant at their *place of residence* or at the *address indicated* in their personal statements. In order to serve the summons on the suspect/defendant, the prosecutor has a right of direct access to the electronic database of the state administration authorities (art. 267(1) CCP), such as the Local Register Office, the Passport Office or the National Driver License Office.

If the place of residence is unknown, the summons shall be served on the suspect or defendant at their *place of work,* by the human resources department within the institution where they are employed. If even this address is unknown, a summons shall be served by posting a notification at the *venue of the judicial authority.* The persons in custody shall be served the summons at the *detention place*, the sick persons shall be served the summons in *hospitals or social assistance centers*, and the members of the military shall be served the summons by the *commander of the unit* to which they belong. In case of the suspect or defendant who lives abroad, the summons shall be served on him/her in accordance with the international law rules applicable in the relations with the state of reference. In the absence of such rules, the summons shall be served by *registered mail*. The staff of diplomatic missions, of consulates, as well as the Romanian citizens who work within international organizations, the family members that co-habit with them, during their stay abroad, as well as the Romanian citizens who are abroad for business, including the family members who accompany them, shall be served a summons by the *employer* which sent them abroad.

The suspect or the defendant can be served the summons at the *office of a lawyer* of his/her own choosing, if he/she did not appear in court after the first summons was served with the respect of legal procedures (art. 259 (4) CCP).

A person can be brought before the investigation authority or the court by using an *apprehension warrant*, when, although previously summoned, the person did not appear, without justification, and the former's hearing or presence is necessary. The same applies when it was impossible to properly serve the summons on the person or when the circumstances clearly indicate that the person avoids being served with the summons (art. 265 (1) CCP). The suspect or defendant can be brought before the judicial authorities by an apprehension warrant even before being summoned, if such measure is necessary in order to solve the case.

The investigation authorities can continue the inquiry *without hearing the defendant*, when the latter fails to appear for no reason, avoids the proceedings or is missing (art. 309 (5) CCP). By interpreting the above-mentioned provisions, it results that *criminal investigations can be instituted* in absentia, *in case of a defendant* (!) *who fails to appear, avoids the proceedings or is missing*. Based on his failure to appear before judicial authorities, on his avoidance of proceedings or his missing, it can be inferred that the defendant gave up his/her right to be present and participate to the inquiry.

In order to reach this conclusion, the following stages have to be respected:

- to call the defendant, which implies a duty of the judicial agent to summon the former and issue an apprehension warrant against him/her;
- if the first stage fails, the judicial agent must check if there is a case of compulsory assistance by counsel, when a lawyer shall have to be appointed *ex officio* in order to represent the defendant;
- if even the second stage fails, the judicial agent must verify if the defendant appointed a lawyer of his own choosing, in order to represent him/her at trial.

Only when such proceedings are finalized, may a judicial organ assume that the defendant waived his/her right to participate to proceedings.

Surprisingly, the law does not stipulate *similar provisions* such as the above-mentioned, *in case of a suspect*. Apparently, it seems that the hearing of a suspect is compulsory in all cases, so it would be legally impossible to continue the investigations against a suspect, without his/her hearing. In concrete terms, such a conclusion, although correct in theory, becomes relative in practice.

On the one hand this occurs because, as shown above, the suspect can be brought before the judicial authorities by an apprehension warrant even before a summons is served on him/her, so even before the suspect is notified of an inquiry conducted against him/her. This hypothesis is different from the one where the *defendant* is brought by an apprehension warrant, since the status of defendant cannot be granted before that of a suspect, so that the defendant could anticipate an impromptu summoning before the judicial agent, being aware of this risk from the very moment he/she is informed of his/her suspect status. For the suspect, the summoning by means of an apprehension warrant may be a total surprise, since previously the person had no status whatsoever in the criminal file and could not possibly predict the acquirement of such status, as long as the initiation of the investigation *in rem* is not made public. Thus, it becomes possible to conduct an investigation without the suspect being warned about it, and, consequently, without his/her participating to proceedings. It is also true that the suspect-to-be can anticipate, in certain cases, the aggravation of his/her legal status. Thus, there is a practice of judicial authorities to summon a person as a witness during the investigation, disloyally making use of the duty of a witness to testify. The witness makes statements in order to avoid potential charges for perjury and discloses information that may contribute to his/her own future incrimination. The Romanian law, in opposition with the ECHR, does not recognize the witness a right to remain silent, but provides only that statements made as a witness shall not be used against the person (art. 118 CCP). In such a situation, a diligent witness may anticipate that he/she shall become a suspect.

On the other hand, the status of a suspect does not entail legal consequences as serious as does the status of a defendant (e.g. a suspect can be neither arrested, nor placed under judicial control), therefore the investigation can perfectly be performed without the immediate hearing of the suspect (an argument *a fortiori*: if the absence of the defendant is no obstacle, there is even less reason why the absence of the suspect should matter).

Therefore, it is possible to infer that *the presence of the suspect to proceedings is not deemed essential for the continuation of investigations.*

The above inference is sustained by the fact that the criminal procedure law *does not provide for a timeframe* that needs to be respected by judicial authorities, between the moment they initiate the investigation *in rem* and the moment they summon the person to be heard as a suspect. This is justified by the fact that in order to have a suspect, it is necessary to *reach a certain standard*, namely to have evidence which leads to the reasonable suspicion that a person committed the act for which the investigation was initiated. Or, the respective evidence must be discovered and supplied in order to have a reasonable suspicion. Judicial authorities shall exclusively assess when the reasonable suspicion has arisen, so that it may justify the labeling of a person as a suspect. Until an individual is not personally subject to the inquiry, the performance of investigations strictly *in rem* cannot possibly generate adverse effects against that person.

Following issuance of an order which transformed the person into a suspect, can the judicial agent continue the investigation without that person being aware of the inquiry conducted against him/her? Such practice, justified by the *need to preserve secrecy of the investigation*, may substantially prejudice the rights of the investigated person, by denying his/her right to participate to the inquiry. In case of the victim, the law has prescribed his/her right to be informed about the stage of criminal investigations, upon express request (art. 81 (1-d) CCP). Neither the suspect nor the defendant can benefit from such right.

As long as the investigation authorities can continue their activity without hearing the defendant in those situations in which the latter fails to appear for no reason, avoids proceedings or is missing, *a contrario,* if it is proven that the defendant does not avoid proceedings, the investigation cannot be conducted in his/her absence. The hearing implies however being made aware of the act, the legal qualification of the act, and, implicitly, the criminal file against the defendant. Similarly, the status of suspect must be notified to the person, prior to his/her becoming a defendant. These formalities compel the judicial agent to admit certain limits to the non-public exercise of the investigation. The limits consist precisely in a *legal ban on the continuation of the inquiry in the absence of the defendant, when the latter is available.* The breach of such interdiction represents a prejudice to the rights of the defendant, which may lead to the invalidation of all acts of investigation, under art. 282 CCP, since such breach can only be remedied by annulling the act(s).

In order to avoid the sanction of nullity (invalidation), judicial authorities are bound to perform a duty of care, namely inform the person and ensure his presence to criminal proceedings. The judicial agent is bound to notify the person about the investigation against him/her, thus respecting his/her right to defense, while the latter has a correlative duty to appear before the judicial agent, whenever he/she might be called. The writ of summons must warn as to the consequences of the failure to appear before judicial authorities (art. 258 (1-h) CCP), namely the possibility to issue an apprehension warrant or even to draw up a proposal for preventive arrest, when the person avoids the proceedings (art. 108 (2-a) CCP).

We need to explain further when the duty of care is activated.

It is true that, as a matter of principle, art. 10 CCP (on the principle of defense) provides that a suspect has the right to be informed *promptly* about the act which is being investigated and its legal qualification. The term *promptly*, which is *no longer used in the article dedicated to the rights of the suspect* (art. 83 (1-a[1]) CCP) has the only meaning that the notification must take place immediately after the prosecutor has issued or confirmed[35] the order to initiate the investigation *in personam.* The term *promptly* has its counterpart in art. 6 paragraph 3a) of the ECHR which refers

---

[35] The measure ordered by the judicial police is subject, in a 3-day term, to the confirmation by the prosecutor who supervises the investigation—art. 305 (3) CCP, as amended by the Government's Emergency Ordinance (hereinafter GEO) no. 18/2016, published in the Official Journal no. 389 23 May 2016.

to the right of any accused to be informed *promptly*,[36] in a language which he understands and in detail, of the nature and cause of the accusation against him. A similar
provision is to be found in art. 14 paragraph 3a) of the International Covenant on
Civil and Political Rights.[37] A person facing a *criminal charge*, in the European
sense of the term, cannot be left a long time without knowing the nature and cause
of the suspicion against him/her, for two reasons: in order to ensure his/her legal
security and to allow him/her to prepare an adequate defense.[38]

Once the law on the application of the CCP[39] was adopted, the authors of the
Explanatory Memorandum to said law stated that they transposed the dispositions
of art. 3 (right to information about rights), art. 4 (letter of rights on arrest), art. 6
(right to information about the accusation), art. 7 (right of access to the materials of
the case) and art. 8 paragraph 2 (right to challenge in case of refusal to provide
information) of the Directive 2012/13/EU of the European Parliament and of the
Council on the right of information in criminal proceedings.[40] Both art. 3 and art. 6
expressly refer to a right to be promptly informed of the accusation.

In practice, the *lack of acting promptly*, as required by the Romanian criminal
procedure law *entails no sanction*, since such conduct is not associated with an
effective sanction. Therefore, it becomes perfectly possible to perform an investigation, in the absence of a person who is not informed about the inquiry. The suspect
does not have a specific right to participate to the investigation stage, since such a
right is at the discretion of judicial authorities. In the absence of a duty assorted
with a sanction against the judicial agent, which may constrain the former to
promptly inform the person about a pending criminal case against him, *there is no
effective right in this sense*. The person under investigation must wait for the moment
when he/she is informed about the inquiry.

Theoretically, it can be argued that such a situation should not prejudice, under
any circumstances, the legal status of the investigated person. In practice, almost all
evidence can be supplied[41] without the participation or notification of the person
who is already a suspect. Therefore, is there a risk that the largest part of the investigation be conducted without the suspect being aware of the criminal file?

Not only is such a situation possible, but sometimes there is even an interest of
judicial authorities in keeping the suspect into the dark. As shown above, when a
person is informed about his/her status as a suspect, this entails the preparation of

---

[36] "Promptly" in the original English version or *"dans le plus court délai"* in the original French
version.

[37] Ratified by Romania by Decree 212 of 20 November 1974.

[38] Bârsan (2005), p. 552.

[39] Act no. 255 of July 19th 2013 published in the Official Journal no. 515, 14 August 2013. The
Explanatory Memorandum is available at http://www.senat.ro/legis/PDF%5C2013%5C13L010EM.
pdf, last accessed 31.7.2018.

[40] Published in the Official Journal of the European Union no. L42/1 of 01.06.2012.

[41] In the Romanian Code for criminal procedure investigation is still conducted following the rules
of the inquisitorial trial system. The evidence supplied during this stage can be, under certain conditions, used at trial.

the defense by the former, which consists either in accessing the case file, or in assisting to all the activities (except for a few notable situations) of criminal investigation. Given such possibilities of reaction, the absence of the suspect substantially facilitates the supplying of evidence (e.g. the hearing of a witness). Hence derives *the interest of judicial authorities to postpone the notification of the suspect,* as much as possible, in order to obtain evidence.

Thus, it becomes rather clear that neither the moment prior to the status of a suspect, which reinforces the reasonable suspicion, nor the moment subsequent to it, which guarantees the notification of the suspect about the aim of the investigation, is *protected from the risk of discretion.* Judicial authorities shall not comply with the duty to inform the suspect immediately after they ordered the initiation of the investigation *in rem* or *in personam. Keeping the person confused brings a huge advantage to the inquiry, but implies a gross mistake by not assuring participation of the suspect to the criminal trial.*

From a different perspective, the person who knows that he/she is suspect shall *deliberately* avoids appearing before the authorities (as part of the defense strategy) or fails to appear, for no justified reason. The procedural law has not provided for such situations, but the conclusion can only be that the absence of a suspect in such situation does not impede the investigation.

3.2.3 Interim Decisions on Coercive Measures

In case of preventive measures, the presence of the suspect or the defendant depends on the nature of the adopted measure.

Thus, in case of house arrest (art. 219 CCP), if the defendant is not present before the judge, this does not impede the latter to rule on the proposal for arrest. The same solution applies to judicial supervision when, even if the defendant is not present at trial, his/her absence does not hinder the adoption of the measure, except for the case when the defendant is in custody. In this situation, assuring the presence of the defendant is compulsory (art. 212 CCP).

In case of detention orders of medical nature, the detention of a patient for observation is not conditioned by the presence of a defendant who was legally summoned (art. 246 CCP).

Nonetheless, the ruling on the proposal for preventive arrest shall take place *only* in the presence of the defendant (art. 225 (4) CCP). In exceptional situations, it is possible to issue an *arrest warrant by default,* namely when the defendant fails to appear for no justified reason, is missing, avoids the proceedings or for other reasons, such as his state of health, force majeure or necessity, which makes it impossible for him/her to appear or to be brought before the judge (art. 231 CCP).

Similarly, the extension of the arrest period during the investigation stage can be ordered only in the presence of the defendant (art. 235 (2n) CCP). When the arrested defendant is hospitalized and due to his/her state of health, he/she cannot be brought before the liberty and custody judge, or when, due to force majeure or necessity, he/she is in a motionless state, the proposal shall be examined in the absence of the defendant, but only in the presence of his/her lawyer, who shall plead in his/her defense.

The interlocutory judgments ruled by the liberty and custody judge in the matter of preventive measures can be contested by the defendant. The challenge (opposition) shall be ruled upon in the presence of the defendant, except for the case when he/she fails to appear for an unjustified reason, is missing, avoids the proceedings or for other reasons, such as his/her state of health, force majeure or necessity, which makes it impossible for him/her to appear or to be brought before the judge (art. 204 (7) CCP). There shall be also considered as present a defendant who is deprived of freedom and who, by his/her consent and assisted by a lawyer, either of his/her own choosing or appointed *ex officio*, and, if the case may be, assisted by an interpreter, participates to the ruling upon the challenge (opposition) *by videoconference, while being at his detention place.*

The ruling upon a proposal for temporary placement in a healthcare facility[42] takes place only after the hearing of the suspect or defendant, if his/her healthcare state allows it, while assisted by a lawyer of his/her own choosing or appointed *ex officio.* When the suspect or defendant is already hospitalized in a healthcare unit and he/she is in a motionless state, the liberty and custody judge shall conduct the hearing of the former in that unit, in the presence of the lawyer (art. 248 CCP).

If the forensic psychiatric expert examination committee deems that a more complex examination is necessary, which requires the medical admission of the suspect or defendant to a specialized medical institution, and he/she refuses such admission, the committee shall notify the investigation authorities on the need to adopt an involuntary admission measure (art. 184 (5) CCP). The ruling on the proposal for involuntary admission to a specialized medical institution shall take place only in the presence of the suspect or defendant, except when he/she is missing, avoids proceedings or when, due to his/her state of health, force majeure or necessity, he/she is unable to appear before the judge.

3.3   Personal Participation in Proceedings *in Camera*

In camera proceedings are a very sensitive issue of a criminal trial, since they imply a non-public procedure, which by itself may question personal participation. It is to be noted though that non-public procedures do not always entail a restriction of personal participation, as it is perfectly normal that a proceeding *in camera* may be conducted in the presence of all interested parties (e.g. proceedings related to preventive measures).

The reform of the criminal trial system in Romania, as a consequence of a CCP, has brought about a new stage in criminal jurisdiction matters, namely the preliminary

---

[42] "A suspect or defendant who is mentally ill or chronic user of psychoactive substances may be temporarily placed in a healthcare facility if adoption of such measure is necessary in order to annihilate a clear and present danger for public safety" (art. 247 CCP).

chamber trial, which our Constitutional Court has considered as a new procedural institution, which belongs neither to the criminal investigation, nor to the judgment, being the expression of a different stage in criminal proceedings.[43]

According to art. 54 CCP, the preliminary chamber judge shall have jurisdiction to:

(a) verify if the indictment was lawfully drawn up by the prosecutor;
(b) verify if the evidence was lawfully supplied and if the investigation activities were legally performed by the judicial police and the prosecutor;
(c) rule on the petitions against the prosecutor's decisions not to refer the case before the court or decisions not to initiate prosecution.

All the above-stated proceedings, although they do not involve the merits of the case, are extremely important, since the preliminary chamber judge rules on certain issues that may prove decisive for the manner in which the case shall be tried on the merits.

The preliminary chamber has been envisaged as an intermediate procedure, between the investigation and the judgment stage, and initially it took place *in camera*, without the participation of the petitioner, the prosecutor or other persons, who could only file written submissions to the judge. The preliminary chamber proceedings have developed in the purest inquisitorial manner,[44] which has generated a wave of reactions in the legal *milieu*, up to the highest level. The Constitutional Court gave a strong response against the manner in which criminal proceedings were conducted *in camera*, ruling on several cases (8 decisions) by which it *sanctioned the absence of the parties or other interested persons*, as contrary to the fundamental law.

Thus, in a first decision,[45] the RCC stated that "as it results from art. 341 (2) CCP, copies of the petition shall be served on the prosecutor and the parties. According to art. 32 CCP the parties to a trial are only the defendant, the civil party and the party incurring civil liability. From this perspective, the Court notices that the victim and the suspect, as persons directly involved in a trial cannot prepare their defense against the arguments of the petitioner, since they are not served with a copy of the petition. Or, in case the public action was not initiated, the persons directly involved in a trial are deprived of the right to a fair trial by the fact that being unaware of the contents of the petition, they cannot defend their legitimate rights. Therefore, these inconsistencies can be remedied only if the preliminary chamber judge *shall rule on the petition within an oral and contradictory debate*".

Additionally, the Court notices that "a fundamental aspect of the right to a fair trial is the fact that the investigation stage must have a contradictory nature and that there should be an equality of arms between the accusation and the defense [...]. Or,

---

[43] The Romanian Constitutional Court, Decision no. 641 of 11 November 2014, para. 27, published in the Official Journal no. 887 of 05.12.2014.

[44] Ionescu (2011), p. 93.

[45] The Romanian Constitutional Court, Decision no. 599 of 21 October 2014, para. 40–43, published in the Official Journal no. 886 of 05.12.2014.

from this standpoint, the Court observes that, in the absence of contradictory debates, the petitioner, the civil party, the party incurring civil liability, the suspect or the victim—not only are they denied the right—which a defendant actually enjoys—to file requests and objections to the lawfulness of the evidence supplied or the investigation activities performed—but they can challenge under no circumstance such objections and requests, precisely because art. 374 (7) CCP provides that evidence supplied during the investigation and not challenged by the parties shall not be resupplied during the inquiry of the court. Therefore, if *the interested parties were summoned to court*, they would have the chance to participate to the debates, and, consequently, would benefit from the right to express their opinions and respond not only to mutually relevant issues, but also to potential questions raised by the preliminary chamber judge".

At the same time, the Court retains that "the interest of the defendant to be summoned to preliminary chamber proceedings and debate the petition in a contradictory procedure is obvious, since, according to art. 341 (7-2c) NCPP, the preliminary chamber judge may rule the beginning of trial. Therefore, when a court—such as the preliminary chamber judge—has jurisdiction to examine the well-founded nature of a petition by checking the evidence which leads to the conclusion that there are no grounds to prosecute, then the court, for reasons related to the fairness of the procedure, shall not rule on the petition without directly assessing the statements of the person who pleads against having committed the offense. Consequently, *the presence of the defendant is indispensable* at this stage of proceedings, when the preliminary chamber judge must decide on whether or not to begin the trial, as well as on the lawfulness of the manner in which evidence was supplied and the investigation activities were conducted".

"Moreover, in those cases where the public action was initiated, the aim of the proceedings by which the judge rules on the petitions against the prosecutor's decisions not to refer the case before the court or not to initiate prosecution, consists not only in checking the admissible and well-founded nature of said decisions, but also in verifying the lawfulness of evidence and the investigation activity. According to art. 341 (11) CCP, evidence that was excluded by the judge at this stage shall not be taken into account upon judging the case on the merits, if the preliminary chamber judge ruled the beginning of trial. Or, as long as the evidence represents the essence of each criminal trial, and the investigation authorities must collect evidence both in favor and against the suspect or the defendant, it is obvious that the outcome of these proceedings has a direct influence on the equity of later proceedings, including on the trial itself. Hence derives the necessity to ensure the presence of both the defendant and the prosecutor to the ruling upon the petition by the preliminary chamber judge, since striking a balance between the rights of the accusation and those of the defense is the core of a fair trial, which is also based on the equality of arms".

Thus, from the perspective of oral and contradictory debates, as essential elements of the equality of arms and the right to a fair trial, the Court noticed that the *law should provide the possibility* of the parties, the victim, the suspect and the prosecutor *to effectively debate the submissions filed to the preliminary chamber judge*.[46] Therefore, the Court concluded that the provisions of art. 341 (5) CCP related to the ruling on the petition *"without participation of the petitioner, the prosecutor and the other interested persons* is contrary to the right to a fair trial, with a view to its component of oral and contradictory debates. In order to make such guarantees effective, it is necessary to serve summons on these persons to be present in court".

The *dictum* of the Constitutional Court was reaffirmed in a later decision[47] where it was stated that the proceedings within the preliminary chamber[48] do not follow the rules of an oral procedure in which the parties may sustain their arguments, but by written submissions filed by the defendant and answered by the prosecutor's office. Based on these reasons, the Court allowed the plea of unconstitutionality and stated that the solution contained by art. 345 (1) and art. 346 (1) CCP, by which the preliminary chamber judge shall rule on the indictment *"without participation of the prosecutor and the defendant"* is unconstitutional, since it denies participation of the prosecutor, the defendant, the civil party and the party incurring civil liability in a procedure which takes place *in camera*, before the preliminary chamber judge. The Court notices that, judging by the standards of a fair trial, it is sufficient to ensure the parties the possibility to take part to this procedural stage, since the judge may rule conclusion of proceedings even in the absence of parties, as long as they have been legally summoned to appear in court.

For the same reasons, the RCC declared[49] unconstitutional art. 341 (10) CCP according to which the preliminary chamber judge from the superior court shall, *"in the absence of the prosecutor and the defendant"*, rule upon the challenge (opposition) against the solution given by the preliminary chamber judge of the inferior court to the objections raised against the way the evidence was supplied and the criminal investigation was conducted.

Moreover, the Court noticed[50] that the provisions of art. 549[1] CCP on the declaration of a document as null and void are unconstitutional since, "these proceedings take place before the preliminary chamber judge and the case shall be judged in summary proceedings, based on the written submissions filed by the interested parties, thus disregarding the principles of an oral, open court and contradictory debate, whereby the prosecutor and the parties to a trial have the right to find out about all the documents and observations filed to the judge and to sustain their case before the latter".

---

[46] In this situation, the preliminary chamber judge has jurisdiction to perform the prerogative set out at art. 54 c CCP, as stated above.

[47] The Romanian Constitutional Court, Decision no. 641 of 11 November 2014, para.43–49, quoted above.

[48] In this situation, the preliminary chamber judge has jurisdiction to perform the prerogative set out at art. 54 a-b CCP, as stated above.

[49] The Romanian Constitutional Court, Decision no. 663 of 11 November 2014, published in the Official Journal no. 52 of 22.01.2015.

[50] The Romanian Constitutional Court, Decision no. 166 of 17 March 2015, para.45, published in the Official Journal no. 264 of 21.04.2015.

Similarly, the RCC allowed[51] the plea of unconstitutionality of the dispositions set out in art. 335 (4) CCP, and deemed that the legislative solution whereby the preliminary chamber judge shall rule *"in the absence of the prosecutor and the suspect or, if the case may be, the defendant"* upon resumption of the criminal investigation is contrary to the Constitution.

Besides the preliminary chamber, which represents a role-model for the *in camera* proceedings, there are other examples of situations when these proceedings apply.

Abstention and challenge of judges procedure (art. 68 CCP) is a non-public procedure, where the access of parties and other persons involved in a trial is not allowed as a matter of principle. Yet, the judge/panel of judges who rule on the abstention or challenge *may decide to hear those persons* if deemed necessary. The reason for such a hermetic procedure is the fact that it is largely a matter of justice administration which does not leave room for contradictory debates. This explains the fact why there is no legal remedy against the interlocutory judgment ruled in the case.

The application for protection of a witness during the trial stage (art. 128 CCP) can be filed by the prosecutor of his own motion, by the witness him/herself, as well as by any party to a trial or even by the victim. None of the persons who apply for protection participates *in camera,* except for the prosecutor. Ruling on an application in a non-contradictory session may affect the balance of proceedings, given that the protection of a witness by granting him/her the "anonymous" status decisively damages the right to defense.

As related to the extraordinary remedies (namely the extraordinary annulment and the extraordinary review), since they all involve a preliminary exam on their admissibility which used to take place *in camera,* without the participation of the parties or other interested persons, the RCC ruled on the unconstitutionality of such proceedings.

Thus, the Court decided[52] that "the legislative solution provided by art. 459 (2) CCP, whereby the preliminary admissibility of the request on extraordinary review (of the judgment) shall be examined by the court *"without serving summons on the parties"* is unconstitutional, since it breaches art. 21 (3) of the Constitution and, consequently, the parties must be summoned to a proceeding where the prosecutor participates, in order to ensure the possibility of the former to be involved in this trial stage".

Similarly, the Court stated[53] that "The exclusion of the defendant, the civil party, the party incurring civil liability and the victim from this preliminary stage of the extraordinary annulment (of a judgment) and the ruling upon the request of

---

[51] The Romanian Constitutional Court, Decision no. 496 of 23 June 2015, published in the Official Journal no. 708 of 22.09.2015.

[52] The Romanian Constitutional Court, Decision no. 506 of 30 June 2014, para. 33, published in the Official Journal no. 539 of 20.07.2015.

[53] The Romanian Constitutional Court, Decision no. 542 of 14 July 2015, para.17, published in the Official Journal no.707 of 21.09.2015.

preliminary examination only in the presence of the prosecutor leads to a disadvantageous position at trial for the parties and the victim as compared with that of the prosecutor. This occurs since neither the parties nor the victim can have access to or file submissions against the legal or factual allegations of the prosecutor, including the exclusion of certain evidence and the potential stay of execution of the judgment which is subject to extraordinary annulment".

As regards the *preliminary exam of the appeal on law* (art. 440 CCP), envisaged as an intermediate proceeding and destined to facilitate the workload of the Supreme Court and prevent the filling of ill-founded requests, the Court has not made any ruling yet. During said exam, a single judge shall conduct the proceedings, in the absence of any persons, since the preliminary exam is deprived of its contradictory essence.

Finally, by another decision,[54] the RCC allowed the plea of unconstitutionality of the provisions set out in art. 488^4 (5) CCP and stated that the legislative solution whereby the *challenge against the duration of a criminal trial* shall be judged "*in the absence of the parties and the prosecutor*" is contrary to the fundamental law.

3.4 Personal Participation in Alternative Proceedings

According to the Romanian procedural law, alternative proceedings to an ordinary trial consist of plea bargaining (during the investigation stage), the plea of guilty before the court and mediation in criminal matters.

Plea Bargaining (Art.s 478–488 CCP) The defendant may conclude a plea bargain with the prosecutor, whereby the defendant is bound to admit the commission of the offense and to accept the charges on which the public action was initiated, such bargain aiming at the nature and amount of the sentence, as well as the manner in which the sentence shall be executed. The defendant must sign the bargain personally, which implies his/her presence upon signing. However, upon negotiations, his/her presence is not necessary, since the former can be represented by a lawyer whose attendance is mandatory by law.

The plea bargain thus concluded is subject to a review by the court. The proceedings shall take place in open court, with the participation of the defendant, the prosecutor, the victim, the civil party and the party incurring civil liability. The presence of the victim and the party incurring civil liability was imposed as a result of a decision passed by the RCC,[55] whereby the Court stated that the legislative solution provided by art. 484 (2) CCP contravenes to the Constitution, insofar it excludes the victim and the party incurring civil liability from the hearing before the court.

---

[54] The Romanian Constitutional Court, Decision no. 423 of 9 June 2015, published in the Official Journal no. 538 of 20.07.2015.

[55] Decision no. 235 of 7 April 2015, quoted above.

Plea of Guilty (Art.s 374, 375, 396 CCP) When the public action was not initiated for an offence punishable by life imprisonment, the presiding judge shall inform the defendant that he may solicit that the judgment should be based only on the evidence supplied during the investigation stage and on the written submissions of the parties and the victim, if the defendant fully admits all the charges filed against him, with the benefice of reducing by one-third the limits of the penalty provided by law in the case of imprisonment, whereas in the case of a fine, by one-fourth. If the defendant solicits that the judgment should take place by the rules of this procedure, the court shall hear him, and after the closing remarks of the prosecutor and the other parties, shall rule on the request. Recently, it was passed an amendment to the procedural law which allows the defendant to admit charges against him by submitting an affidavit as evidence. In this case, if the defendant submits an affidavit as evidence, his presence in court is no longer necessary.

Mediation (Act No. 196/2006[56] on Mediation and Mediators) As a matter of principle, parties to a dispute may resort their conflict to a mediator. In case only one party appears before the mediator, the latter, upon request of this party, shall draw up a written invitation for the other party, in order to inform him/her of the mediation and the fact that in a 15-day term, he/she can agree on the mediation. The invitation shall be conveyed by any means which assure acknowledgment of the receipt. The requesting party shall provide the mediator with all the data necessary to contact the other party. In case one party finds it impossible to appear before the mediator upon convocation, the mediator, at the request of this party, can set up a new date in order to inform said party of the mediation and the agreement to mediate. In case the party agrees on the mediation, the parties under dispute and the mediator shall sign a mediation agreement. If one of the parties conveys a written and express refusal to mediate, does not respond to the invitation mentioned above, or does not appear twice at the dates fixed for the conclusion of the mediation agreement, the mediation shall be deemed unaccepted.

These general provisions of law are applicable also to criminal cases, both to the criminal side of proceedings, and to the civil side. As concerns the criminal side of proceedings, the provisions on mediation shall apply only in those cases of offenses where the defendant shall be exonerated of criminal liability if he/she reconciles with the victim or if the victim withdraws the complaint against the defendant. The parties and the other persons involved in a criminal trial cannot be coerced into accepting the mediation. In criminal cases, mediation proceedings must be conducted so as to respect the rights of any party or person involved in the trial to be assisted by counsel, and, if the case, to benefit from the services of an interpreter. The report concluded according to law, by which the mediation proceedings are closed, must indicate if the persons who were subject to mediation benefited from the assistance of a lawyer or the services of an interpreter and, in the contrary case, the report must mention that the former expressly gave up these services.

---

[56] Published in the Official Journal no. 441 of 22.05.2006.

Since mediation represents an alternative way of criminal dispute resolution, the presence of parties is essential so that the mediator may be able to identify their common denominator in an effort to conclude a transaction (not filing a preliminary complaint or withdrawing a preliminary complaint) which leads to the end of a criminal trial. Or, the circumstance that the parties do not actually participate, but are represented, even if this is done by a professional, is not capable of generating this effect.

3.5   Personal Participation at Trial

3.5.1   Essentials

The first instance trial may take place only if the defendant is lawfully summoned and the procedure has been complied with (art. 353 (1) CCP). The defendant and, if the case may be, his/her legal representative, are summoned *ex officio* by the court. The presence of the defendant to court, in person or through a representative or a counsel of his/her own choosing or appointed *ex officio, if the latter contacted the person they represent*, shall cover any irregularity related to the summoning procedure.

The defendant may appear in court and participate to court proceedings even if he/she was not summoned to appear or did not receive the summons, whereas the presiding judge is under a duty to determine his/her identity (art. 358 (2) CCP).

The defendant, present in person, through representative or through counsel, to any court hearing, as well as the party who was served the summons in person, through their representative or by the clerk in charge with receiving the mail, were lawfully summoned to appear to court hearing shall not be summoned for the subsequent hearings, even if they were absent from any of such hearings, except for the situations when their presence is mandatory (art. 353 (2) NCPP). The personnel of the army and the detainees shall be summoned *ex officio* to each court hearing.

The presiding judge is under a duty to check, upon opening the court sitting, which of the defendants are present (art. 358 (1) CCP). In the case of the defendants who are absent, the presiding judge shall check whether they were served the summons and whether they provided any justification for their absence.

If the defendant is not present in court, this does not obstruct the trial of the case. If the court deems that the presence of the defendant is necessary, it may order that the defendant be brought by an apprehension warrant. Thus, it is compulsory to bring before the court a defendant who is detained (art. 364 (1) CCP). It shall be considered as present to court a defendant deprived of liberty who, by his/her own consent and/or in the presence of the counsel of his/her own choosing and in the presence of an interpreter, attends the trial by videoconference, at the place of detention.

Even though criminal proceedings can be held irrespective of the presence of the defendant, however, if there are certain exceptional situations which prevent the attendance of the defendant and they are duly justified, the court shall order stay of the trial. One such case is provided under art. 367 CCP (Stay of court proceedings), whereby: "(1) When, based on a forensic medical report, the court finds that the defendant is severely ill, which prevents him from participating at the trial, the court, in an interlocutory judgment, shall order the stay of proceedings until the health of the defendant will allow him/her to take part at the trial. (2) When there are several defendants and the grounds for the stay relate only to one of them and when it is not possible to severe the case, the whole procedure before the court shall be stayed". Criminal proceedings shall resume *ex officio*, as soon as the defendant is able to take part at trial. The court is bound to check regularly, but no later than 3 months, if the grounds that caused the stay of court proceedings are still valid.

The mandatory bringing of a defendant in custody before the court does not apply to a defendant who is deprived of freedom abroad.[57] Ensuring the presence of a defendant who is in such a situation would be possible only if there were conventional provisions between Romania and the foreign state, which may allow the temporary transfer of the defendant. The European Convention[58] of Mutual Assistance in Criminal Matters, adopted at Strasbourg, on 12th of April, 1959, and its Additional Protocols, allow the transfer of the person in custody only if the former is a witness or for purposes of confrontation, which excludes the transfer of the person in custody in order to take part to the trial as a defendant (art. 11).

The court proceedings may take place *in the absence of the defendant*, if the latter is missing, avoids proceedings or changed his/her address[59] without informing thereupon the judicial authorities and, following the controls carried out, his/her new address remains unknown.

The court proceedings may also take place *in the absence of the defendant*, when, even though lawfully served the summons, the defendant provides no justification for his/her absence from the trial of the case.

All throughout the trial, the defendant, including when deprived of liberty, may apply, in writing, to be tried *in absentia*, as represented by a counsel of his/her own choosing or appointed *ex officio*. In case the detained defendant applied to be tried *in absentia,* the court may order, upon request or of its own motion, that the defendant submit his/her conclusions or argue his/her case by videoconference, in the presence of the counsel of his/her own choosing or appointed *ex officio*.

The defendant who participates to the court hearing is under a duty to respect discipline in court. When a defendant disturbs the court hearing or disobeys the measures taken, the presiding judge shall warn him/her to keep order in court, whereas if the misconduct repeats itself or the insubordination is severe, the presiding judge *shall order to have him/her removed from the court room* (art. 359 (4)

---

[57] Zainea (2006), p. 98.

[58] Romania ratified the Convention by Act no. 236 of 21 December 1998.

[59] Art. 108 (1–b) and art. 259 (2) NCPP—the defendant must inform the court in writing, within a 3-day term, of any change of address, while being drawn the attention that, for failure to comply with this duty, the summons and any other documents served to the first address shall remain valid and shall be deemed as brought to his/her attention.

CCP). A defendant who was removed from the courtroom shall be recalled into the room before initiation of debates. The presiding judge shall inform the defendant on the essential acts performed in his/her absence and shall read the statements of persons heard in court. If the defendant continues to disturb the court hearing, the presiding judge may order again to have him/her removed from the courtroom, while the debates shall take place in their absence.

If the defendant still keeps on disturbing the court hearing also upon court ruling, the presiding judge may order that the former be removed out of the courtroom, in which case, the court ruling shall be notified to the defendant.

The option of the defendant to attend the trial or not shall not prevent the court, as shown above, from trying the case. At the same time, though, the absence of the defendant is not a reason for aggravating his/her legal situation, and the court cannot infer negative consequences from the absence of his/her attendance. Nonetheless, there are certain unfavorable consequences that derive from his/her absence. Thus, the proportionate sentencing made by the court, especially the infliction of non-custodial sentences, depends on the consent of the defendant, i.e. whether he/she agrees to perform community work. The Romanian Penal Code conditions access of the defendant to the adjournment of penalty infliction (art. 83 1c RPC) and to the suspended sentence assorted with probation (ar. 91 1c RPC) on such consent, so that upon lack of consent due to the absence of the defendant from trial, the court cannot order the formerly mentioned measures, even if the other requirements provided by the law are fulfilled. The alternative of an affidavit consisting of a personal statement given before a notary public has been regarded distrustfully by the courts, therefore absence from trial can constitute a legitimate aggravation of the legal situation of the defendant, since the court has no option left but to inflict a custodial sentence on him/her.

3.5.2 Personal Involvement in Evidence-Gathering

The Romanian criminal procedure law was substantially amended when it comes to the proceedings on obtaining evidence, given that all procedural dispositions on evidence contained in secondary (special) legislation were taken over by the CCP. The transfer of these provisions occurred by introducing into the new legislation rules on evidence gathering that apply to certain types of offenses (e.g. organized crime, drug trafficking, human trafficking, etc.). This transfer has thus generated two types of proceedings used to obtain evidence: the ordinary (classic) ones, which pre-existed in the code, and the special ones, imported from secondary (special) legislation. In order to preserve a mark of their imported origin, the CCP has integrated them in a distinct chapter (Chapter V, art.s 138–154 CCP) of Title IV on evidence.

Apparently, the reshaping outlined by the CCP seemed to have positive effects, avoiding an over-layering of provisions, thus leading to a more coherent law on evidence. In fact, the adverse effects surpassed the reshaping work. This has happened due to the fact that, as a result of their integration in the CCP, the special proceedings of evidence gathering, initially applicable only to certain matters, have insidiously become common rules. What used to be applied exclusively in the area of organized crime, for example, is currently applicable to other areas which have nothing in common with organized crime (e.g. offenses against the patrimony in general). This phenomenon could be easily termed as "banality of evil", since the proceedings of collecting evidence, invasive on human rights and freedoms, which are justifiable in the context of serious crimes, have invaded the domain of obtaining evidence. The situation is almost irreversible, since these proceedings assure some comfort to the investigating authorities, and they shall not be given up to very easily, which leads to a complete ignorance of the warnings as to their destructive effects on human rights and freedoms.

This situation has entailed important consequences. One of these consists in that the initiation of methods aimed at obtaining certain evidence has grown to be decided in the absence of all parties, including the defendant. Thus:

a. *obtaining data* generated or processed by providers of public electronic communications *networks* or providers of electronic communication *services* intended for the public, other than the content of communications (art. 152 CCP). This procedure takes place in the absence of any person, the liberty and custody judge being called for to authorize a procedure used for evidence finding, applied to a very sensitive matter. The presence of interested persons would considerably lessen the "surprise" effect of this procedure of obtaining evidence as well as the efficiency of the searched data (traffic analysis and location data).
b. *deciding physical examination without the consent of the examined person* (art. 192 CCP). This procedure allows the liberty and custody judge to disregard the absence of consent by the examined person, with a view to obtaining evidence which may be found on or inside the body of that person.

Another consequence of this situation is that evidence-finding proceedings have become increasingly non-public, while still allowing the prosecutor to take part to these, which leads to a trial misbalance, such as the procedure for the issuance of an electronic surveillance warrant (art. 140 CCP), the procedure for the issuance of a home search warrant (art. 158 CCP) or the procedure on computer data storage search (art. 168 CCP).

3.5.3   Personal Contribution to the Fact-Finding

The Romanian criminal trial has been shaped, since the very emergence of modern legislations, by the predominantly inquisitorial system. This system aims mainly at finding the truth.

In this sense, art. 5 CCP states that judicial authorities *are under an obligation* to ensure, based on evidence, the finding of truth about the facts and circumstances of the case, as well as about the suspect or defendant. Consequently, the aim of the trial is too important to be left at the discretion of parties and represents an essential obligation of judicial authorities. The latter have jurisdiction to establish the facts on which trial decisions shall be based. *The defendant is slightly involved in this process.*

When it comes to public (criminal) action, the burden of proof is mainly on the prosecutor (art. 99 CCP). In its turn, the court may decide to supply evidence on its own motion, when it deems it necessary for its intimate conviction (art. 100 (2) CCP) or the finding of truth and the fair resolution of the case (art. 374 (10) CCP).

The defendant has the right, not the obligation, to solicit supplying of evidence to judicial authorities. In case evidence is supplied, such evidence must show the facts and circumstances that need to be proved, the means that support the evidence, the place where these means can be found, and as concerns the witnesses and the experts, their identity and address. The circumstance that the defendant indicates the facts which must be proved does not mean that the former contributes to the establishment of facts, but only that he helps the court to assess of the pertinence, conclusiveness and utility of the evidence.

Similarly, if the defendant, on the occasion of his closing argument, points out to new facts or circumstances, essential for solving the case (art. 389 (2) CCP), this does not amount to a contribution to the establishment of facts. The only effect is that the court is bound to order resumption of court inquiry and debates so that the newly revealed facts may be established.

From another perspective, in criminal trials, the absence of the defendant cannot be valued as admittance of facts as it occurs in civil proceedings where the conduct of a party who refuses to subject him/herself to a cross-examination may be deemed by the court as a full recognition in favor of the other party (art. 358 Romanian Code of Civil Procedure). This interpretation directly challenges the presumption of innocence since the mere absence of the defendant would lead to reversal of said presumption.[60]

In fact, in the most inquisitorial manner, the judge is the only person competent to legally establish the facts. According to art. 393 (1) CCP, the panel of judges shall deliberate first on questions of fact, then on questions of law. The deliberation shall be secret and shall occur only in the presence of the panel members before whom the debates took place, and no other person whatsoever shall be present (art. 392 CCP).

Nevertheless, when the victim, the civil party and the party incurring civil liability are heard by the court, the defendant can directly conduct the cross-examination on their own, as an expression of his contribution to fact-finding (art. 380 CCP). This prerogative which is a genuine feature of the adversarial model, is substantially restricted by judge's historical propensity to master, in a purely inquisitorial manner the entire trial.

A situation whereby the defendant only apparently contributes to fact-finding could be that in which he/she requires a summary judgment based on a plea of guilty (*nolo contendere*). Thus, the court may solve the case only based on evidence supplied during the investigation stage, *if the defendant solicits this and fully admits to*

---

[60] Ciopec (2005), p. 151.

all charges held against him/her and *if the court deems that evidence is sufficient* for the finding of truth and a fair verdict to the case (art. 374 (4) CCP).

The situation is only apparent, since a plea of guilty does not necessarily mean that the defendant is the one who determines the facts. The defendant's request for summary proceedings only opens the possibility of such proceedings, and is not an obligation for the court. The latter may allow or dismiss the request. If the court dismisses the solicitation, it shall initiate its own inquiry into the facts. Nonetheless, when the solicitation of the defendant is dismissed and the court does its own inquiry, and, following such inquiry, there shall result the same factual situation as the one admitted by the defendant, in case of conviction or adjournment of penalty enforcement, the defendant shall be granted the benefit of having entered a plea of guilty (the decrease by a third of penalties' latitude in case of imprisonment, and by a fourth, in case of fines, according to art. 396 (10) CCP).

3.6 Personal Participation in Higher Instances

In the hierarchical system of Romanian courts, the higher instances are the Court of Appeal, having jurisdiction over each of the 15 territorial divisions and the High Court of Justice. The appellate courts rule on the appeal as an ordinary legal remedy against judgments passed by county courts (*judecătorii*) and tribunals (*tribunale*). The High Court of Justice rules on judgments delivered by the courts of appeal as first instance courts.

In all cases, the trial on appeal shall take place by serving summons on the parties and the victim. This measure has been envisaged in order to ensure presence of said persons to trial, although the case can follow its course even in their absence. If the defendant is placed in detention, his presence at the trial on appeal is compulsory. This personal participation serves not only for reasons of defense, but also for the mandatory hearing of the defendant by the judge.

When these procedural rules are breached, the law provides for sanctions leading the invalidation of the judgment, namely by filing an extraordinary annulment against the unlawful summoning of parties (art. 426 a CCP), the absence of the defendant when his/her participation is compulsory (art. 426 e CCP) or the non-hearing of the defendant, although he/she was present at trial (art. 426 h CCP).

As regards the appeal on law, an extraordinary remedy that can be judged exclusively by the High Court of Justice, the parties must be summoned at trial and their potential absence does not affect the course of proceedings.

From the above-mentioned rules, there is only one exception, namely that an appeal filed against interlocutory judgments which, as provided under the law, may be challenged separately, shall be tried *in camera*, in the absence of parties, who can file written submissions (art. 420 (12) CCP). However, even in such situations, the court may deem necessary to try the case in open court. The hypothesis of interlocutory judgments which are tried separately is very limited.[61] An example could be the inter-locutory judgments whereby the legitimate rights of any natural or legal person have been directly harmed, but strictly as concerns the dispositions of the judgment which caused such harm (art. 409 (1f) CCP)—e.g. confiscation of certain assets which do not belong to the defendant or the party incurring civil liability.

3.7 Special Rules in the Field of Serious Organized Crimes

Romanian procedural laws on organized crime have been comprised in three main sources, namely Organized Crime Act,[62] DIICOT Act[63] (Department for the Investigation of Organized Crime and Terrorism, a subsidiary of the Public Ministry) and the CCP. The first two sources do not deal with special rules on personal partici-pation, therefore we shall refer to the provisions of the adjective law.

Thus, art. 113 (1) CCP states that when the legal requirements on the status of threatened or vulnerable *witness* or on the need to protect private life and dignity are met, the investigation authorities may order measures of protection *for the victim or the civil party*, according to art.s 124–130 CCP, which shall apply to the case.

The procedural law therefore extends the protection measures, usually granted to the vulnerable or threatened witness, to the victims of organized crimes. It thus allows that, both during the investigation stage, and the trial stage, the authorities may order specific measures, such as the hearing without the actual presence of the victim/civil party, meaning audio-video transmission devices (video-link) with their voice and image distorted (art.s 126–127 CCP).

The law presumes to be victims of organized crimes—children, persons who are dependent on the perpetrator, victims of terrorism, human trafficking, sexual vio-lence or exploitation, victims of offenses committed for reasons of hate, prejudice, discrimination which could derive from their individual features, disabled victims, as well as victims who suffered a substantial damage as a result of the seriousness of the crime.

Since the absence of the victim/civil party from the hearing may cause a great deal of stress to the defense, the law has provided an appropriate procedural guaran-tee for such a circumstance, namely that the conviction shall not be based, to a decisive extent, on the statements of persons with protected status (art. 103 CCP).

---

[61] Grădinaru (2015), p. 1052.

[62] Act no. 39 of 21 January 2003, published in the Official Journal no. 50 of 29.01.2003.

[63] Act no. 508 of 17 November 2004, published in the Official Journal no. 1089 of 23.11.2004.

4 Personal Participation of Private Parties Other Than Defendants (in Particular, the Contribution of the Victim to the Fact-Finding)

In the Romanian criminal trial, the victim does not enjoy too much attention, and the statement made in the doctrine, whereby "the victim is a great actor in a minor role"[64] is still topical.

This marginal role can be explained by two reasons. First, it is due to the fact that the victim does not have a decisive contribution to the initiation of criminal investigation, since the investigation authority preserves its prerogative to start the inquiry *ex officio*, regardless of the victim's complaint. Second, even though the victim reports the offense to the investigation authorities, its role shall cease at this point, due to the monopoly exerted by the Public Ministry on the investigation stage. Ever since 2006, the victim has lost his/her prerogative to initiate a private criminal action which could have excluded the prosecutor as a state representative. Presently, the victim has no longer the status of party to the criminal trial.[65]

Nonetheless, there are certain situations where the victim intervenes in the course of criminal proceedings. Thus, in a case where criminal investigations have already been *conducted ex officio* and it is noted that a preliminary complaint is required, the criminal investigation agent shall call upon the victim and ask whether he/she wishes to file such a complaint. In the event of an affirmative answer, the criminal investigation authority shall continue its investigations. In the contrary case, it shall submit its documents to the prosecutor, accompanied by a proposal to dismiss the case.

The CCP has not set out a right of the victim to participate to the criminal investigation, but *a duty* to appear before the judicial authorities, whenever called upon, for instance upon the hearing of the victim. As a protection measure for the threatened or vulnerable victims, the law has provided the possibility that such victims can be heard without being physically present before the judicial authority, but through audio-video transmission devices, with their voice and image distorted (art. 113 with reference to art. 126 CCP).

When there occurs a risk that a victim might not be available for hearing during trial, the prosecutor can ask the liberty and custody judge to hear that victim before the trial (art. 308 CCP). The liberty and custody judge, if he deems such request well-founded, shall immediately set a date and place for the hearing and summon the parties. The statement of the victim, made during the anticipated hearing procedure, shall be able to be used with no limitations, as evidence at trial.

As concerns the involvement of the victim in fact-finding, similarly with the situation of the defendant, the victim does not usually participate to such proceedings. However, in the case of confrontation, when it is noted that there are contradictions

---

[64] Paşca (2011), p. 97.
[65] Roibu (2014), p. 84.

between the statements of persons heard in the same case (including the victim), judicial authorities shall proceed to their confrontation, if this is necessary to clarify the case. Confronted persons are heard about the facts and circumstances in respect of which the previously made statements contradict each other. Criminal investigation authorities or the court may agree that the confronted persons ask each other questions (art. 131 CCP). This last situation actually proves the role of victim in fact-finding, since the victim performs a sort of cross-examination of the other person subject to interrogation.

However, if the contradictions arise between the statements of the victim and those of the defendant, it is highly improbable that a confrontation might be ordered, due to the potential emotional reactions that these proceedings might entail on the victim who is thus forced to re-experience the criminal act.

During the trial stage, the victim and the parties are compulsorily summoned to trial, but may solicit both orally or in writing, that the case be tried *in absentia*, and in such a situation they shall no longer be summoned to the next court sessions, but instead they may be represented by counsel (art.s 365–366 CCP). When the defendant is heard by the court, the victim, the civil party and the party incurring civil liability can directly conduct the cross-examination on their own, as an expression of their contribution to fact-finding (art. 378 (f)CCP).

Nevertheless, in judicial practice, this prerogative, which derives from the adversarial system, is considerably limited by the judge's habit to control the proceedings, which is due to a long-lasting inquisitorial tradition.

5 *In Absentia* Proceedings

5.1 *Information Rights and Conditions of Waiver of Personal Participation in Criminal Proceedings*

In order to assure a fair and lawful trial, "it is of capital importance that a defendant should appear" at trial,[66] since "the duty to guarantee the presence of the accused in the courtroom, either during the original proceedings or in a retrial after he/she emerges" represents a core requirement of art. 6 of the European Convention.[67]

Even if a trial held in the absence of the accused is not in itself incompatible with art. 6 of the ECHR, no doubt that there is a denial of justice when a person convicted *in absentia* cannot subsequently have his/her case retried as to the well-founded reasons of the charges, both in fact and in law, except for the situation when it was

---

[66] ECtHR, *Poitrimol v. France*, judgment of 23 November 1993, Appl. no. 14032/88, para. 35.
[67] ECtHR, *Stoichkov v. Bulgaria*, judgment of 24 March 2005, Appl. no. 9808/02, para. 56.

established unequivocally that the accused waived his/her right to be present at trial and defend him/herself[68] or that the accused "sought to escape trial".[69]

In the CCP, art. 466 provides an extraordinary remedy by which a person who was tried *in absentia* and convicted by a final ruling may request retrial of his/her case in a term of 1 month, calculated from the day he/she was informed, by any official notification, that a trial had been held against him/her.

Unlike the other extraordinary remedies, the application for retrial of the case does not aim at challenging the unlawful or unfounded nature of the decision ruled *in absentia,* but instead, the defendant seeks to give effectiveness to his/her right to participate personally to trial and exert his/her right to defense.

This difference entails two practical consequences. The first is that upon examining the application for retrial the court shall not look into the lawful or well-founded nature of the final decision ruled in the case, and the second is that if the court allows the application, this does not imply that it shall necessarily conclude to a miscarriage of justice done by the court which ruled the conviction. Both from the ECHR perspective, and from the national law standpoint, a trial held *in absentia* is not in itself contrary to the exigencies of a fair trial and, therefore, the court which tried the case on the merits is not "culpable" for the development of the trial *in absentia*.

If it can be stated unequivocally that the accused waived his/her right to participate personally to trial, then a re-hearing of the case is no longer necessary, since the state cannot be bound to incur social and material costs entailed by the option of the accused not to exert his/her procedural rights at the appropriate moment in time.

Art. 466 paragraph 2 CCP[70] sets out two main conditions of admissibility which govern the re-hearing of a case when the trial was held *in absentia*. These conditions are as follows:

5.1.1 The Person Was Not Summoned to Trial and Was Not Notified Thereof, in Any Other Official Manner, About the Criminal Proceedings Against Him/Her

The negative condition imposed by the Romanian lawmaker, namely that the defendant was not summoned at trial, has led to interpretation dilemmas in legal practice.

---

[68] ECtHR, *Einhorn v. France*, decision of 16 October 2001, Appl. no. 71555/01, para. 33.

[69] ECtHR, *Medenica v. Swizerland*, judgment of 14 June 2001, Appl. no. 20491/92, para. 55.

[70] Art. 466 (2) CCP: Retrial in case of *in absentia* proceedings against the convicted person—The following shall be deemed as tried *in absentia*: the convicted person who was *not summoned* to trial and was *not notified* thereof in any other official manner, respectively, the person who even though aware of the criminal proceedings in court, was *lawfully absent* from trial and *unable to inform* the court thereupon. The convicted person who appointed a counsel, or a representative of his/her own choosing, shall not be deemed tried *in absentia* if the latter *appeared* at any time during the criminal proceedings in court and neither shall the person who, after having been lawfully served with the conviction decision, did *not file an appeal*, waived filing an appeal or withdrew the appeal.

The dominant solution in court practice was that the summoning of the defendant in accordance with the legal provisions in force at the time when the trial was held should not lead to the conclusion that the accused avoided the proceedings or, even worse, that he/she actually knew about the trial against him/her.

Regardless of the lawful summoning of the defendant, taking into account the ECtHR case-law, what is of real importance upon assessing whether a defendant was tried *in absentia* is that he/she was not informed personally of the proceedings against him/her, so he/she did not know about the trial.

Looking into the second part of the above-mentioned condition, it can be noticed that it refers to any official way by which the defendant was notified about the trial.

This text sets out a difference from the European Convention standard, since the ECtHR[71] did not exclude the possibility that, in the absence of an official notification, "certain established facts might provide an unequivocal indication that the accused is aware of the existence of criminal proceedings against him/her and of the nature and the cause of the accusation and that he/she does not intend to take part in the trial or wishes to avoid prosecution. This may be the case, for example, where the accused states publicly or in writing that he does not intend to respond to summons of which he has become aware through sources other than the authorities".

These examples must be clearly distinguished from the situation when the defendant escapes from the crime scene for fear of being prosecuted, where it is unreasonable to presume that the accused was aware of a trial and of the well-founded nature of the criminal charges against him/her and therefore he/she waived his/her right to appear in person before the court.

By comparing the above-stated examples, it appears that the national lawmaker has imposed a superior standard of protection for the accused, as compared to that of the European Convention, so domestic provisions shall apply with priority, pursuant to art. 20 (2) in the Romanian Constitution.

According to art. 602 CCP, the meaning of "official notification" is to be found in the definition given by art. 178 (2) of the New Penal Code (hereinafter NPC), namely a notification issued by a legal person to which art. 176 NPC[72] refers or from a person indicated by art. 175 (2) NPC.[73]

The Romanian doctrine[74] has criticized the judicial practice solution by which the courts considered that even other notifications, warnings or notices which do not have an official nature can be held against the defendant, such as, for instance, the fact that the defendant was prosecuted, tried and convicted together with several

---

[71] ECtHR, *Stoyanov v. Bulgaria*, judgment of 31 January 2012, Appl. no. 39206/07, para. 31.

[72] Art. 176 NPC: The term "public" designates everything relating to public authorities, public institutions or other legal entities managing or exploiting public assets.

[73] Art. 175 (2) NPC: At the same time, for the purposes of criminal law, the following shall be deemed a public officer: any person who performs a public-interest service, which they have been vested with by the public authorities or who shall be subject to the latter's control or supervision with respect to supplying such public service.

[74] Constantinescu (2015), p. 1168.

other defendants, most of whom were his/her relatives, and consequently the former did know about the criminal proceedings against him/her.

The doctrine concluded that no such unofficial notification can be invoked against the defendant tried *in absentia*.

5.1.2 The Person Who, Even Though Aware of the Criminal Proceedings in Court, Was Lawfully Absent from Trial and Unable to Inform the Court Thereupon

This case refers to the situation in which the defendant was aware of the trial, but was lawfully absent from the proceedings in court and could not possibly inform the court of such absence. Such circumstances may occur during the trial of first instance or on appeal, when events beyond the will of the defendant prevent him/her from participating to trial, for example an emergency surgery, a placement in custody in some other state, etc.

Said circumstances do not have to qualify as *force majeure*, but the "prevention" must be an invincible, objective circumstance which could not have been foreseen in any other way, such as a state of war, a flood, a massive snowfall, an epidemic or any other occurrence which led to the interruption of traffic on the way between the court premises and the whereabouts of the defendant. In case the defendant was unable to attend proceedings, he/she must inform the court of such objective impossibility. If he/she does not fulfill this duty, and the case is tried *in absentia*, the defendant is culpable and loses the right to challenge the court decision if it is unfavorable for him/her.[75]

5.1.3 Special Case of Application for Retrial

Art. 466 (3) CCP provides a special situation when a person can apply for retrial of the case, namely when a person, convicted by a final decision, was tried *in absentia* and against that person an authority of a foreign state ordered *the extradition* or *the surrender* as a result of a European Arrest Warrant (hereinafter EAW). In this particular situation, the application for retrial can be filed within a term of 1 month, calculated from the day in which, after repatriation of said person, the conviction decision was served upon him/her.

According to art. 4a d) of the Council Framework Decision 2002/584/JHA of 13 June 2002 on the European arrest warrant and the surrender procedures between Member States[76]—as amended by Council Framework Decision 2009/299/JHA of 26 February 2009, which enhances the procedural rights of persons and fosters application of the principle of mutual recognition to decisions rendered in the

---

[75] High Court of Justice, Criminal Chamber, Decision no. 1642 of 27 April 2010, http://www.scj.ro, last accessed 31.7.2018.

[76] Published in the Official Journal of the European Union L19 of 18.07.2002.

absence of the person concerned at the trial,[77] "The executing judicial authority may also refuse to execute the European arrest warrant issued for the purpose of executing a custodial sentence or a detention order if the person did not appear in person at the trial resulting in the decision, unless the European arrest warrant states that the person, in accordance with further procedural requirements defined in the national law of the issuing Member State, was not personally served with the decision but:

- will be personally served with it without delay after the surrender and will be expressly informed of his or her right to a retrial, or an appeal, in which the person has the right to participate and which allows the merits of the case, including fresh evidence, to be re-examined, and which may lead to the original decision being reversed; and
- will be informed of the time frame within which he or she has to request such a retrial or appeal, as mentioned in the relevant European arrest warrant".

On the other hand, a person shall *not be deemed* as tried *in absentia,* when one of the following circumstances occur:

a. **The person appointed a counsel or a representative of his/her own choosing**

The law presumes that the convicted person who appointed a lawyer or a representative of his/her own choosing was aware of the trial, and by agreeing to be represented in court he/she waived the safeguards provided by art. 6 of the ECHR. Nonetheless, the appointment of a lawyer or a representative is not sufficient, the former persons being bound to appear in court whenever called upon during the trial. The second requirement imposed by the law seems unjustified, since the presence of the lawyer or the representative to trial is just an aspect of the manner in which the defense is conducted, as the defendant may appoint the lawyer only to file written submissions.

What is indeed important for this special procedure is the fact that the defendant was aware of the criminal charges against him/her and he chose to exert the right to defense by appointing a lawyer or a representative.

The ECtHR stated that when a defendant appointed lawyers to represent him in court, "the fact that lawyers were later replaced by lawyers appointed by members of his family does not alter the clear finding that he knew about the criminal proceedings against him. By choosing to leave the country, the applicant must be considered to have intentionally and unequivocally waived his rights under art. 6 of the Convention and could reasonably have foreseen the consequences of his conduct".[78]

b. **The person, after having been lawfully served with the conviction decision, did not file an appeal, waived filing an appeal or withdrew the appeal**

The law additionally presumes that a convicted person shall not be deemed as tried *in absentia* if he/she was lawfully served with the conviction decision and,

---

[77] Published in the Official Journal of the European Union L 81/24 of 27.03.2009.

[78] ECtHR, *Sulejmani v. Albania*, decision of 19 June 2012, Appl. No. 16114/10, para. 22.

subsequently did not file an appeal, waived filing an appeal or withdrew the appeal.

It must be noted that not all circumstances in which the decision is served are legally relevant, but only the circumstance where the conviction decision is served *personally* on the defendant, since only such situation may lead to the conclusion that the defendant unequivocally waived his/her rights under art. 6 of the Convention. For example, if the conviction decision is served on a relative co-habiting with the defendant, although the service was lawful, the application for retrial filed after the appeal term has expired cannot be dismissed on this ground.

In judicial practice[79] there has been examined the situation in which the defendant, who was not lawfully summoned to the trial of first instance and was absent during the proceedings before the court of first instance, personally files an appeal and subsequently is absent from the debates on appeal. For the next court session, the same defendant files an application to adjourn proceedings, which is allowed by the tribunal. At a later court session, to which the defendant was lawfully summoned, the former neither appeared before the judge, nor invoked an impediment for his/her absence. Therefore, taking into account that the defendant could require a review of the charges against him/her during the appeal stage, the court deemed that his/her application represents a waiver of his/her right to be personally present in court, since he/she foresaw the consequences of such waiver, namely the trial of the case based only on the evidence already contained in the case file.

The serving of the decision on the defendant implies a procedure which takes place prior to the moment when the decision becomes final, and not a subsequent procedure accomplished after the enforcement of the penalty execution warrant or after the surrender of the defendant based on a EAW.

In a recent case,[80] the national courts were called for to analyze the situation of a person tried *in absentia,* against whom there had been issued a penalty execution warrant and also a EAW. Following surrender of the person by the authorities of Cyprus and after serving the conviction decision on the defendant, the latter filed an application for retrial of the case. The court dismissed the application, stating that the defendant, after being lawfully served with the conviction decision, should have filed an appeal, since the extraordinary remedy provided under art. 466 CCP cannot be exerted *omisso medio.* In explaining its legal reasoning, the court added that the appeal is an ordinary remedy, while the retrial, in case of *in absentia* decisions, is an extraordinary remedy which means that in order for courts to allow such exceptional remedies, the defendants must file an appeal first, which did not occur in the given case.

---

[79] Court of first instance of the 6th district in Bucharest, Criminal Chamber, Decision no. 171 of 17 March 2014, available in Constantinescu (2015), p. 1169.

[80] Court of Appeal of Timișoara, Criminal Chamber, Decision no. 20 of 15 January 2015, available in Constantinescu (2015), p. 1170.

The solution of the court is criticizable, since in the given case the conviction ruled by the court of first instance was final under art. 551 (2) CCP and, consequently, in the event the defendant had indeed filed an appeal, his/her application would have certainly been dismissed as untimely.

c. **The convicted person applied to be tried *in absentia***

According to art. 364 (4) CCP, "throughout court proceedings, the defendant, including when he/she is deprived of freedom, may apply, in writing, to be tried *in absentia*, and shall be represented by a counsel of his/her own choosing or appointed by the court".

Such application of the defendant to be tried *in absentia* demonstrates an unequivocal waiver of his/her right to be present in the courtroom, and therefore, the defendant cannot subsequently file an application for retrial of the case.

5.2 Default Proceedings and Subsequent Remedies (e.g. Retrial or Judicial Review in a Higher Instance)

5.2.1 Application for Retrial of the Case[81]

The Competent Court

As a rule, a person tried *in absentia* by a court of first instance shall continue to be tried *in absentia* also during the stage of appeal filed by the Public Ministry or the parties. In such a situation, the convicted person shall file an application for retrial before the court of first instance which tried the case *in absentia*, and the decision ruled as a result of allowing the application for retrial shall be subject to appeal. When the defendant lodges an appeal against the decision passed by a first instance court, following a trial *in absentia*, and he/she is lawfully absent from the trial on appeal and cannot inform the appellate court of such absence, the court competent to rule on the application shall be the appellate court.

---

[81] Art. 467 CCP: Application for retrial of the case.

(1) The application for retrial of the case can be submitted by the person tried *in absentia* and shall be filed to the court that tried the case *in absentia*, either as a court of first instance, or as an appellate court.

(2) When the person tried *in absentia* is deprived of liberty, the application may be filed to the penitentiary, which shall refer it as soon as possible to the competent court.

(3) The application shall be drawn up in writing and shall prove fulfillment of the requirements provided under art. 466.

The Final Conviction Decision Rule

The application for retrial can be filed only after a final conviction decision was ruled, according to art.s 551–552 CCP. Pursuant to art. 466 (5) CCP an application for retrial may be filed also against final decisions[82] by which courts ruled waiver of penalty enforcement or adjournment of penalty enforcement (deferment), since based on art.s 396 (3) and (4) CCP, the former solutions can be ruled only if the court concludes that the criminal act exists, it constitutes an offense and was committed by the defendant.

Even if in case of minor offenders Romanian courts order decisions whereby educational sanctions are imposed on the former, from a procedural perspective such solutions represent conviction decisions as well therefore minor defendants tried *in absentia* can also apply for retrial of their case.

Given the rule that an application for retrial is duly filed only if a final conviction decision was ruled, we may infer that such application becomes inadmissible in case the courts rule the acquittal or the cease of the criminal trial.

It is interesting to note what happened in practice in a situation of trial *in absentia*, when, although the court stated that the defendant was guilty, due to the statute of limitations of criminal liability, the same court was bound to rule cease of the criminal trial, in accordance with the provisions in the Code of Criminal Procedure. The question which arises is that if in such a case the person tried *in absentia* can apply for retrial.

In the case of a Romanian applicant,[83] tried *in absentia* by the tribunal and the court of appeal, the former invoked art. 13 of the previous Code of Criminal Procedure, whereby he was allowed to ask for a continuation of the trial, despite the occurrence of statute of limitations as regards his criminal liability, in order to be declared innocent and obtain an acquittal. So, the applicant expressly demanded the Court of Appeal to examine the well-founded nature of the charges against him, which the court did but stated at the same time that the evidence in the file leads to the conclusion that the defendant is culpable of the act for which he was tried.

The approach of the European Court of Human Rights to the case was that a potential lack of response by the Romanian Court of Appeal could have been interpreted as denial of justice, contrary to art. 6 of the European Convention, but deemed that the national court was not bound to conclude to the innocence of the defendant. Moreover, the defendant's culpability had been ruled only at a formal level. Consequently, the ECtHR dismissed the application as inadmissible.

This approach is criticizable, because even in a case where a court only formally refers to the culpability of the defendant, yet, due to the intervention of the statute of limitations of criminal liability, it rules the cease of the criminal trial, the defendant tried *in absentia* should be able to apply for retrial.

---

[82] High Court of Justice, Preliminary Ruling no. 22 of 9 June 2015, published in the Official Journal no. 486 of 02.07.2015.

[83] ECtHR, *Ganga and the Trade Union of Independent Jurists of Romania v. Romania*, decision of 10 April 2012, Appl. no. 28906/09, para. 43.

Formal Requirements of the Application for Retrial[84]

Art. 467 (3) and (4) CCP states that the application for retrial shall be done in writing and shall prove meeting of requirements that govern a trial conducted *in absentia*. To this end, the convicted person is compelled to point to the case file and the conviction decision, as well as to expose the reasons for which he/she considers that he/she was tried *in absentia*.

When the convicted person supplies evidence that consists of documents (for example a copy of the passport which proves that when the writ of summons was lawfully served on the defendant, he/she was in a foreign country), he/she is bound to attach them to the application and to certify them as true copies of the original.

Art. 467 (2) CCP provides that a person deprived of freedom may file the application to the penitentiary administration, which shall refer it as soon as possible to the competent court. Taking into account the dispositions of art. 270 CCP,[85] the application for retrial shall be considered to have been submitted in due time if it is filed to the detention facility before expiry of the term, regardless of the moment when it was registered at the competent court.

Art. 468 CCP[86] sets out the preliminary measures to be ordered before the application for retrial is examined by the court.

An interesting issue in judicial practice has been the procedure to be followed in case a person who must be brought to trial is detained in a penitentiary abroad.

A possible solution to this intricate problem is that the person represented by a lawyer, either of his/her own choosing or appointed *ex officio* may request that the admissibility in principle of his/her application be examined *in absentia*, according to art. 364 (4) CCP.

Thus, even if this text is applicable to the trial stage, it becomes obvious that if a defendant may waive his/her right to participate to proceedings where the well-founded nature of the charges against him/her is examined, for all the more reasons

---

[84] Iugan (2016), pp. 124–132.

[85] Art. 270 CCP: Procedural acts regarded as completed within the timeframe provided under the law—(1) Any document filed within the timeframe required by law, to the detention facility or to the military base or to the post office via registered mail shall be regarded as having been completed within timeframe. Registration or certification by the detention facility, marked on the document that was filed, the receipt from the post office, as well as registration or certification by the military base, marked on the document that was filed, shall serve as evidence of the filing date.

[86] Art. 468 CCP: Preliminary measures

(1) When the application for retrial of the case is received, a date is set for the hearing when the admissibility shall be examined in principle, and the presiding judge orders that the case file be attached, as well as that the parties to trial and other persons involved be summoned to appear in court.

(2) When the person who filed the application for retrial is deprived of liberty, even in another case, the presiding judge shall order that the former be notified as to the date of the court hearing and shall take preliminary measures to appoint a counsel *ex officio*.

(3) The person deprived of liberty shall be brought to court for trial.

he/she should be able to waive the right to be present in court upon examination of an extraordinary remedy.

A refuse to examine the application for retrial in the absence of the convict would generate unfavorable consequences on the convict's situation, since he/she would not be able to obtain the annulment of the conviction decision which could be precisely the reason of his/her deprivation of freedom in the foreign state. Such a situation would actually be a hypothesis when the right to be personally present to criminal proceedings is used against the convicted person.

In case the convict deprived of freedom wants to be brought to trial, but his/her transportation would generate unjustified costs due to the long distance between the penitentiary and the court of first instance or it is not possible (e.g. the convict serves a custodial sentence in Spain) the presence of the convicted person can be assured by videoconference, based on art. 106 (2) and (3) CCP.[87]

In case of a person located outside the Romanian territory, the videoconference hearing shall be ordered by a request for international judicial assistance, based on art. 178 of Act no. 302/2004 on international judicial cooperation in criminal matters.

The admissibility in principle of the application for retrial is examined by the court after the parties and other persons involved in the trial have been lawfully summoned.

Unlike the other extraordinary remedies, whose admissibility in principle is analyzed *in camera*, the application for retrial is debated in open court. One cannot help noticing the inconsistency of the Romanian lawmaker in this matter, since the application for retrial is the only extraordinary remedy whose admissibility in principle is examined in open court.

The participation of the prosecutor is compulsory.

At this preliminary stage, evidence that consists only in documents may be submitted, as it is results from the provisions of art. 467 (4) CCP; other evidence may be supplied only after the application has been allowed in principle and the case is ready for retrial.

Taking into account that the application for retrial is expressly qualified as an extraordinary legal remedy, a judge who participated to the trial of the case in first instance or on appeal, leading to the decision of conviction *in absentia* shall become incompatible to rule on the application for retrial.

The compulsory legal assistance by counsel, provided under art. 90 CCP[88] does not apply to the preliminary stage of the admissibility in principle, since the applicant is not a suspect or defendant, but has the legal status of a convicted person.

---

[87] Art. 106 CCP: (2) A detained person may be heard at the detention facility through videoconference, in exceptional situations and if judicial authorities decide that this does not obstruct the proper conducting of the trial or the rights and interests of the parties.

(3) In the situation set by paragraph (2), if a person subject to hearing finds him/herself in any of the situations set by art. 90 (i.e. the cases of compulsory assistance by counsel), the hearing may be conducted only in the presence of their counsel at the detention facility.

[88] Art. 90 CCP: Legal assistance is compulsory:

During this procedure, the court shall analyze if the following requirements are met:

i. the application was filed in due time and the person was convicted by a final decision rendered *in absentia;*
ii. the application is grounded on proceedings conducted *in absentia* and is supported by justified reasons, according to art. 467 (5), which can be completed until the first hearing or within a short term established by the court;
iii. a previous application for retrial was dismissed and the convicted person did not invoke the reasons set forth in the new application, in other words the convict is compelled to indicate from the start all the reasons that support his/her allegations of a trial *in absentia*, since filing of an additional application shall be considered an abuse of procedural right and shall be accordingly sanctioned as inadmissible.

Art. 469 (2) CCP[89] provides that the court vested with an application for retrial may order stay of execution of the imprisonment penalty which was ruled in the

---

(a) when a suspect or defendant is underage, is admitted to a detention facility or an educational center, when he/she is detained or arrested, even in a different case, and when in respect of such person a detention order was ruled, remanding them to a healthcare facility, even in a different case, as well as in other situations provided by law;
(b) when a judicial authority deems that a suspect or defendant could not prepare the defense on his/her own;
(c) in the course of trial, in cases where the law provides the penalty of life imprisonment or imprisonment exceeding 5 years for the committed offense.

[89] Art. 469 CCP: Court examination of the application for retrial

(1) The court shall hear the arguments of the prosecutor, the parties and the other persons involved in the trial, and examine whether:

(a) the application was submitted within the timeframe provided under the law and by one of persons provided under art. 466;
(b) legal grounds were relied upon to lead to a retrial of the case;
(c) the reasons which support the application had not been indicated in a prior application, which a court of last resort ruled upon.

(2) The application shall be examined by priority and when the convicted person is serving a sentence of imprisonment ruled in the case whose retrial is applied for, the court may totally or partially order stay of execution of the sentence and provide the reasons thereof and may order the convict to observe one of the duties provided under art. 215 paragraphs (1) and (2). When the service of the prison sentence has not commenced, the court may order the convict to observe one of the duties provided under art. 215 paragraphs (1) and (2).
(3) If the court finds that the requirements provided under paragraph (1) are fulfilled, it shall rule by an order that the application for retrial be allowed.
(4) If the court finds that the requirements provided under art. 466 are not fulfilled, it shall rule by a sentence that the application for retrial be dismissed.
(5) The court interlocutory judgment whereby the application for retrial has been allowed may be challenged jointly with the merits of the case.
(6) The court sentence that has dismissed the application for retrial shall be subject to the same legal remedies as the court decision rendered *in absentia.*
(7) When the application for retrial is allowed, this may result in the automatic (*ope legis*) annulment of the decision ruled in the absence of the convicted person.

case subject to examination. Stay of execution may be ordered from the very moment when the application for retrial is randomly distributed to the court (by a computer program) and up to the moment when court shall rule on the admissibility in principle of the application. Following this stage, the stay of execution is no longer possible, since, if the court allows the application, the conviction decision is automatically (*ope legis*) annulled, based on art. 469 (7) CCP; if the court dismisses the application, it shall rule divestiture of jurisdiction.

The stay of execution can only be ordered with respect to a custodial sentence which is effectively served, ruled in the case that is subject to the application for retrial. Therefore, the duties incumbent on the convicted person as a result of the adjournment of penalty enforcement (deferment) or of a suspended sentence assorted with probation cannot be subject to a stay of execution; furthermore, the effect of the stay of execution cannot apply to penalties or preventive measures ordered in other cases in which the same person was involved.

If the application for retrial is filed to the court which tried the case in first instance, the dismissal of said application shall be ordered by a decision which is subject to appeal.

If the convicted person files the application for retrial to the court which tried the case on appeal, the application shall be dismissed by a final decision.

By this final decision which dismisses the application for retrial, the court shall compel the convicted person to pay the judicial fees incurred by the state, based on art. 275 (2) CCP, and, additionally, to pay the judicial expenses incurred by the parties, pursuant to art. 276 (6) CCP.

If the court concludes that the requirements provided under art. 469 (1) CCP are met, it shall allow the application for retrial of the case which took place in the absence of the convicted person. According to art. 469 (5) NCPP, the interlocutory judgment thus rendered cannot be challenged by a separate procedure, but only jointly with the merits of the case.

Once the application for retrial has been allowed, this entails a series of important effects:

1. **the *ope legis* annulment of the conviction decision**[90]

    This effect is imposed by the lawmaker and cannot possibly be censured by the court. Upon ruling, the decision of conviction rendered in the absence of the defendant loses its *res judicata* power and its binding force. Thus, the person tried *in absentia* no longer has the status of a convict, but becomes a defendant

---

(8) The court shall retry the case and shall examine it also with respect to the parties that did not file any application. The court may also rule on their situation, without creating a more difficult situation for the former.

(9) Once the court has allowed the application for retrial, on its own motion or upon request by the prosecutor, the court may order that one of the preventive measures provided under art. 202 paragraph (4), letters b) to e) be taken.

[90] Dan (2012), p. 64.

and the conviction decision cannot be used in order to determine if it is a case of recidivism or concurrent offenses.

The loss of the binding force of the conviction decision ruled *in absentia* shall entail annulment of all subsequent procedural acts issued with the aim to enforce said decision.

Having regard to the various manners in which the penalty is executed, the court which has allowed the application for retrial, shall:

i. annul the penalty execution warrant and the prohibition to leave the country;
ii. rule withdrawal of the EAW, pursuant to art. 94 (1) of Act no. 302/2004 on international judicial cooperation in criminal matters, if such a warrant has been issued;
iii. inform the International Cooperation Police Center within the Romanian General Police Department in order to delete the alert on person from the Schengen Information System (SIS);
iv. order the notification of the Romanian General Police Department in order to revoke the all-ports warning (APW), according to art. 526 CCP.

A person's deprivation of freedom, based on a conviction decision that was annulled, does not constitute lawful detention in the sense of art. 5 (1a) of the European Convention, due to the lack of a legal ground strong enough to oppose the principle of legal certainty (security).[91]

2. **Another essential effect of the allowance of the application for retrial is a fresh new exam of the well-founded nature of the charges against the defendant.**

Even if not all the defendants of a case were tried *in absentia*, according to art. 469 (9) NCPP, the court shall retry the case and shall examine it also with respect to the convicted persons that did not file any application. Therefore, it is to be inferred that the extension of the effects entailed by the retrial of the case is automatic and mandatory, such a conclusion being also backed up by the provisions of art. 469 (7) NCPP which refer to the annulment of the decision rendered *in absentia,* and not to the annulment of the solution rendered with respect to the person tried *in absentia*.

Given the practical effects of art. 469 (8) CCP, in order to avoid retrial of the case also in respect of those defendants who were present to criminal proceedings, it is recommendable that the court rule severance of the case as regards the defendants who were tried *in absentia*, thus a new case file being formed.

3. **A further beneficial effect triggered by the allowance of the application for retrial is set out in art. 155 (5) NPC, whereby "The admission in principle of the application for retrial of a criminal case causes a new statute of limitations term of criminal liability to run".**

The above-mentioned provision does not actually set out a classic case of interruption of the statute of limitations on criminal liability, since in case of an

---

[91] ECtHR, *Sâncrăian v. Romania,* judgment of 14 January 2014, Appl. no. 71723/10, para. 72–79.

application for retrial, the limitation period did not even begin, as the previous trial (where the person was tried *in absentia*) ended up with a final decision. In other words, the limitation period flow is interrupted by the final decision of conviction, a moment after which the statute of limitations on the execution of the sentence shall begin. That is why the period which passed before the conviction decision was rendered shall not be taken into account, but a new limitations period shall begin from the moment the application for retrial was allowed.

4. **A less advantageous effect of the allowance of the application for retrial consists of the possibility of the court to order a preventive measure**[92] **against the defendant, during retrial of the case (art. 469 (9) CCP).**

Within the same interlocutory judgment by which the court has allowed the application for retrial, it may order that a preventive measure be taken against the defendant. Such order is immediately binding; when the order was ruled by a court of first instance, it can be challenged under the terms of art. 206 CCP.[93]

In case of persons against whom an execution of penalty warrant has been issued, the court, by the same interlocutory judgment, may order annulment of that warrant. If, however, preventive arrest has been ordered, an arrest warrant shall be issues for a term of 30 days which begins on the very day the judgment has been rendered. Thus, the defendant shall not be effectively released, since the preventive arrest is still in force, but on different grounds. If the application for retrial is allowed during the appeal stage, the preventive measure that shall be ordered by a decision which is final (including with respect to the preventive measure).

The Application for Retrial Timeframe

The application for retrial of the case can be filed within a term of 1 month, calculated from the day when the convicted person was informed, by any official notification, of the criminal trial against him/her. The timeframe was significantly reduced, as compared with the initial form of the CCP, which provided a term of 6 months within which the application could be filed. This term has a peremptory nature, therefore if it is not complied with, the person can no longer apply for retrial.

---

[92] In art. 202 (4), the CCP sets out the following categories of preventive measures: custody; judicial control; judicial bail; house arrest; pre-trial arrest.

[93] Art. 206 CCP: Legal remedies against court judgments ordering preventive measures during the trial

(1) Against court judgments by which preventive measures have been ordered in first instance, the defendant and the prosecutor may file a challenge, within 48 h of their ruling by the court or, if the case, of their service on the parties. A challenge shall be filed to the court having rendered the contested judgment and shall be submitted, together with the case file, to the superior court, within 48 h of its registration.

5.2.2 Retrial of the Case[94]

By interpreting the provisions of art. 467 (1) and art. 470 CCP (now repealed), it results that the retrial of the case regards only the *trial* stage of criminal proceedings (either in first instance or on appeal), and not the stage of criminal investigation, as well. Taking into account that the investigation represents a distinct stage of criminal proceedings, a person *tried in absentia* cannot obtain a retrial of the case and, additionally, the re-initiation of investigation.

At the same time, the preliminary chamber is a new stage of criminal proceedings, and not a separate stage of the trial phase.

This procedure consists in the control over the jurisdiction and the lawful referral of the case to the competent court, as well as in the judicial review over the lawfulness of the evidence supplied and the acts performed during the investigation stage. Thus, the preliminary chamber procedure represents a sort of *filter procedure* between the two important stages of the criminal trial, namely the criminal investigation and the trial.[95]

Once a case is subject to retrial and the conviction decision is annulled, the defendant cannot apply for a resumption of the preliminary chamber procedure,[96] since this latter stage is distinct from a trial stage. Therefore, the lawfulness of evidence and the procedural acts conducted during the investigation cannot be challenged by a defendant who obtained a solution of retrial.

Although the defendant is unable to obtain the resumption of the investigation, as a matter of principle, his/her procedural rights are guaranteed during the trial stage by re-supplying the evidence and the former's possibility to submit new evidence; nonetheless, the defendant's impossibility to challenge the lawfulness of the evidence collected against him/her during the investigation may lead to a breach of the fair trial. It is well-known that the use of statements obtained by torture or inhuman/degrading treatment (by violation of art. 3 of the European Convention) in order to establish the facts of a case entails a qualification of the entire trial as unfair. Additionally, the impossibility of the defendant to obtain exclusion of the evidence collected by breach of his/her right to remain silent or to be assisted by counsel may also entail an unfair trial.

The defendant's impossibility to challenge the legality of investigation is criticizable also from the perspective of art. 16 (1) in the Romanian Constitution which grants equal rights of citizens before the law. Thus, the lawmaker has instilled a different treatment for persons who find themselves in the same legal situation, namely they were all indicted in a criminal case. The circumstance whereby a defendant was tried *in absentia* is no reasonable ground for a creating a distinct treatment for the former, since, as a rule, that trial conducted in his/her absence is not imputable on the defendant.

---

[94] Art. 470 CCP: The case shall be retried according to the rules of procedure applicable to the trial stage for which the retrial of the case was ordered.

[95] Ciopec and Roibu (2016), p. 7.

[96] High Court of Justice, Ruling in the interest of the law no. 13 of 3 July 2017, published in the Official Journal no. 735 of 13.09.2017.

So, from this perspective, art. 470 CCP instills a discriminating legal treatment that may lead to a suppression of the right to defense of the person tried *in absentia* and tends to transform the retrial of the case in a mere judicial formality.

Once the application for retrial has been allowed, the court which judges the case on the merits shall fix a term for the next session, in open court, and the parties and other persons involved in the trial shall be summoned to appear.

Given that the principle of *non reformatio in pejus* is set out by art. 469 (8) CCP as regards the extension of the effects (brought about by the retrial of the case) upon defendants who did not apply for retrial, all the more reasons for not aggravating the legal situation of the person tried *in absentia*, after his/her application for retrial was allowed.

As concerns the application for retrial of the case filed to the appellate court, if it is grounded on the reason that the defendant was lawfully absent from trial and could not inform the court thereof, the appellate court shall dismiss the application as inadmissible.

Consequently, retrial of the case by the appellate court, following the rules of this extraordinary remedy (the retrial) is not possible, and yet the defendant may file another similar remedy, namely the extraordinary annulment, based on art. 426 a) CCP.[97]

5.3   *Inaudito Reo Proceedings (e.g. Penal Order Procedure)*

Romanian legislation is not familiar with these proceedings, the only available remedy is the one tackled with above, in case of *in absentia* trial.

6   Participatory Rights in Transnational Criminal Justice

6.1   *Participatory Safeguards in EAW Proceedings*

The CCP contains no provisions on transnational criminal justice, such dispositions being settled in a separate regulation, Act no. 302/2004[98] on international judicial cooperation in criminal matters which has the outward appearance of a mini code. This act operates a distinction between extradition and EAW proceedings.

---

[97] Art. 426 CCP: Cases of extraordinary annulment

An application for extraordinary annulment may be filed against final rulings of criminal courts, in the following cases: (a) when the court proceedings on appeal were conducted without lawfully summoning a party or when, even though lawfully summoned, the party could not appear in court and inform the court thereupon.

[98] Republished in the Official Journal of Romania no. 377 of 31.5.2011.

If extradition of a person is requested in order to have him/her serve a penalty imposed by a judgment[99] ruled *in absentia* against that person, Romania (as Requested State) may refuse extradition for this purpose, if it deems that the trial procedure has disregarded the right to defense acknowledged to any person suspected or accused of having committed an offence. However, extradition shall be granted if the Requesting State provides safeguards deemed as sufficient to guarantee the person whose extradition is requested the right to a new trial that would give effectiveness to his/her right to defense.

The extradition decision entitles the Requesting State either to try the case again, in the presence of the convict, if the latter has no objections or, if otherwise, to pursue the extradited person. When the Romanian state notifies the person whose extradition has been requested about the judgment ruled against him/her *in absentia*, the Requesting State shall not take this announcement as a notification that entails effects upon the criminal proceedings in this latter State, such as the running of a term for demand of the retrial of the case (art. 32 (2) of Act no. 302/2004). There are similar provisions for the case when Romania acts as Requesting State, thus if the extradition is requested for a person convicted *in absentia*, and the Requested State informs the pursued person of the decision rendered *in absentia*, such a notice shall not generate effects on the Romanian criminal proceedings (art. 66 (13) of said Act).

It must be noted that the absence of the defendant from a trial which was held in a foreign court contravenes the legal order of Romania, a sufficient reason to prevent extradition. The Romanian State shall agree with extradition only in case the Requesting State guarantees compliance with the rule that the case shall be retried in the presence of the interested party.[100] In its turn, when Romania has ruled a conviction *in absentia* and acts as Requesting State, retrial of the case shall be ensured by the competent department within the Ministry of Justice, upon solicitation of the Requested State (art. 69 of said Act).

In case the Romanian state must enforce a European Arrest Warrant based upon a conviction decision ruled *in absentia*, the following rules shall apply (art. 92 of the Act):

(1) When the convicted person was not present at trial, the court shall check the documents and the proceedings of the file, in order to ascertain whether:

  (a) the convicted person was notified in due time, by written summons served in person or by telephone notification, fax, e-mail or by any other such means, as to the day, month, year or place where he/she should appear and of the fact that a judgment may be ruled if he/she does not appear for the trial; or

---

[99] Romania is part of the European Convention on the International Validity of Criminal Judgments, adopted at The Hague on 28 June 1970 (ratified by Act no. 35 of 17th of April 2000). A judgment in absentia for the purposes of this Convention means any judgment rendered by a court in a Contracting State after criminal proceedings at the hearing of which the sentenced person was not personally present (art. 21 paragraph 2).

[100] Ciopec (2006), p. 164.

(b) the convicted person, being aware of the day, month, year and place where he/she should appear, mandated the counsel of his/her own choosing or appointed *ex officio* to represent him/her in court, and legal representation and defense before the court were effectively performed by the counsel; or

(c) once the conviction decision was personally served and the convicted person was informed that, under the law, the case may be re-tried or that the conviction decision may be subject to legal remedies and that it may be revised, including based on new evidence, and if any remedy is allowed, the conviction decision may be annulled, the convicted person either expressly waived to have the case re-tried or to take legal action, or did not request the case to be re-tried or did not initiate, within the period provided by law, that legal action.

(2) When the documents of the file reveal that the convicted person was not personally served with the conviction decision, the issuing court shall inform the executing judicial authority of Romania that:

(a) within 10 days after the surrendered person has been placed, as the case may be, in a detention and provisional arrest center or in a penitentiary, the conviction decision shall be personally served upon the former;

(b) upon serving the conviction decision on the surrendered person, he/she shall be informed that he/she have the right, to have the case retried or to take any other legal action (file a legal remedy such as review of the conviction decision or apply for its annulment).

Also, in case of the EAW to be executed in Romania, there shall apply the same grounds for non-execution of the warrant,[101] as stated above. Where the EAW has been issued for the purposes of executing a sentence or a detention order imposed by a decision rendered *in absentia* and if the person concerned has not been summoned in person or otherwise informed of the date and place of the hearing which led to the decision rendered *in absentia*, surrender may be subject to the condition that the issuing judicial authority gives an assurance deemed adequate to guarantee the person who is the subject of the EAW that he or she shall have an opportunity to apply for retrial of the case in the issuing Member State and to be present at trial (art. 97 of Act 302/2004).

6.2 Participatory Safeguards in Trans-Border Inquiries and the Taking of Overseas Evidence

As concerns cross-border inquiries, Act no. 302/2004 recognizes the use of the following proceedings of international judicial cooperation in criminal matters[102]:

---

[101] Streteanu (2008), p. 13; Muntean (2007), p. 115.

[102] Radu (2009), pp. 81–82.

(a) locating and identifying persons and objects; hearing suspects or defendants, victims and other parties, witnesses and experts, as well as confrontation; searches, seizure of objects and documents, special and extended confiscation; on-site investigations and case reconstruction; expert opinions, technical-scientific reports and forensic reports; transmission of information needed in a particular proceeding, audio and video tapping and recording, examination of archived documents and special files;
(b) transmission of exhibits to be supplied as evidence;
(c) transmission of documents or files;
(d) hearing by videoconference;
(e) exchange of information with no prior request;
(f) controlled delivery;
(g) using undercover investigators;
(h) using joint investigation teams;
(i) cross-border surveillance;
(j) identification of proceeds of crimes.

Said Act addresses all the above-mentioned regulations *in extenso*, but contains no reference whatsoever to *in absentia* proceedings. The only mention available is that Romanian judicial authorities shall decide whether to take part in such cooperation proceedings based on the Romanian laws. Given that Romanian law is open to recognize all procedural safeguards which accompany *in absentia* cases, no doubt they shall become applicable in cross-border proceedings as well.

7 Requirements of Personal Participation and *In Absentia* Proceedings. The Perspective of Supranational and International Human Rights Law

7.1 The Perspective of International Human Rights Law. Critical Remarks on Domestic Law in the Light of the European Convention

The ECtHR case-law on trials *in absentia* involving Romania is very sparse. There are two possible explanations for this scarcity. In the former Code of criminal procedure, which was in force until 2014, the procedure of retrial of persons convicted *in absentia*, was introduced[103] rather late, namely in 2003, and up to that moment there was no remedy for such situations. This was a peculiar circumstance, since

---

[103] Art. 522¹ former CCP: Retrial of persons tried in absentia in case of extradition or surrender based on EAW—(1) When there is a request as to the extradition or surrender based on an EAW of a person tried and convicted *in absentia*, it is possible for the case to be retried by the court which tried the case in first instance, upon application of the defendant.

Romania had already ratified the ECHR in 1994. It is obvious that the introduction of such procedure in the CCP was entailed by the pressure of harmonizing national legislation with the ECHR requirements. As in similar situations, the adaptation was merely formal, simply in order to comply with the European standards, without the intention to make a genuine amendment, therefore judicial practice proved rather insensitive to the enforcement of such a procedure.

Furthermore, the new text inserted in art. 522^1 of the former Code of criminal procedure could not be an effective remedy as long as it left retrial of the case at the courts' discretion and did not impose a duty on the former in this respect. Thus, even if the court, following an application filed by the person convicted in absentia, notices that the latter was indeed absent upon his/her trial and conviction, the court has only the possibility to retry the case, which is in total breach[104] of art. 13 of the ECHR whereby "everyone whose rights and freedoms are violated, shall have an effective remedy before a national authority". The fact that there were no legal criteria that the courts should have observed made the procedure unpredictable and inaccessible, and hence the scarcity of its use.

As shown above, the CCP introduced a procedure which is to a high extent compatible with the ECHR exigencies, but which, is still at the beginning of its application. So far, we have no knowledge of an application filed before the ECtHR based on the provisions of the new code.

As concerns former legislation, in the case of *Boroancă v. Romania*,[105] the ECtHR recalls its constant case-law in the matter[106] (*Colozza v. Italy*, § 29; *Somogyi v. Italy*, para. 66; *Medenica v. Switzerland*, § 55; *Sejdovic v. Italy*, para. 82, etc.), where it stated that "a procedure which occurred in the absence of the accused is not in itself incompatible with art. 6 of the ECHR. It must nonetheless be stated that there is a denial of justice when a person convicted *in absentia* cannot subsequently have his/her case retried as to the well-founded reasons of the charges, both in fact and in law, except for the situation when it was established unequivocally that the accused waived his/her right to be present at trial and defend him/herself or that the accused sought to escape trial".

In the afore-mentioned case, the Court concluded that there was no violation of the applicant's right to a fair trial. The Court stated that the restart of the term of appeal against the conviction *in absentia,* once the accused was given the possibility to be present before the appellate court and request that new evidence be supplied, led to the possibility of a new ruling on the well-founded nature of the charges, both in fact and in law. It noted that the applicant had been notified about the criminal investigation against him/her, that he/she took part in the police inquiry and was regularly served the summons at the address that he/she indicated. As a result of

---

[104] Dan (2012), p. 61.

[105] ECtHR, *Boroancă v. Romania*, judgment of 22 June 2010, Appl. no. 38511/03, para. 66–68.

[106] For an analysis of the constant ECtHR case-law please refer to Renucci (2009), pp. 510–511; Sudre (2006), p. 299; Gouttenoire (2011), pp. 312–314.

return of the summons due to a change of address, he/she was lawfully summoned at two other addresses.

Consequently, the applicant did not find himself in a situation of total absence from the trial against him/her and had the opportunity to have his/her case retried in an ordinary procedure.

In another case[107] the Court observed that "the first question is whether the applicant was officially notified of the criminal proceedings against him. The Court had already held that informing someone that a prosecution is being brought against him is a legal act of such importance that it must be carried out in accordance with procedural and substantive requirements capable of guaranteeing the effective exercise of the accused's rights; vague and informal knowledge cannot suffice". As regards the question of whether the authorities acted diligently and made sufficient and adequate efforts to trace the applicant (who left the country before the start of the proceedings against him) and establish his/her whereabouts so that they might notify him/her of the criminal proceedings, the Court noted that "the investigating authorities tried to contact the applicant at the beginning of the investigation. They show that the investigating authorities went to the applicant's last place of residence several times. However, there was no evidence that the applicant was served with a summons at his last place of residence or at any other address after the initiation of the criminal investigation [...]. In the light of the above considerations and in the absence of any official notification addressed to the applicant, the Court is not convinced that the latter had knowledge of the trial against him at the beginning of the proceedings. However, it appears that after his conviction by the first-instance court, the applicant became aware of the criminal proceedings. He lodged an appeal against his conviction and chose to be represented by the same lawyer who had been appointed by the court to represent him before the first-instance court [...] Moreover, the Court notes that after the dismissal of his appeal the applicant came back to Romania of his own free will and attended all the hearings before the High Court of Cassation and Justice in the proceedings concerning the appeal on points of law".

As a conclusion, the Court stated that the proceedings as a whole may be said to have been fair if the defendant was allowed to appeal against the conviction *in absentia* and was entitled to attend the hearing in the court of appeal, thus opening up the possibility of a fresh factual and legal determination of the charges.

In its early case-law[108] in the matter, the ECtHR considered that the fact that the applicant was defended by a counsel appointed *ex officio*, did not amount to a waiver, by the accused, of his/her right to be present at trial. More specifically, the Court argued that "the appointed counsel had knowledge neither of the file contents nor of his client, and did not have the necessary time to prepare the defense, especially due to the fact that the Supreme Court ruled on the appeal on law in one single court session. Therefore, the defense ensured by the counsel appointed *ex officio*

---

[107] ECtHR, *Coniac v. Romania*, judgment of 6 October Appl. no. 4941/97, 2015, para. 51, 53–54, 56.

[108] ECtHR, *Gaga v. Romania*, judgment of 25 March 2008, Appl. no. 1562/02, para. 54–58.

could not possibly be interpreted as efficient and adequate". In the light of the afore-mentioned, the Court concluded that "the applicant who was tried by the Supreme Court and in relation to whom it had not been proved that he intended to avoid proceedings or unequivocally waived his right to appear in court, actually had not been granted the possibility to have his case fairly retried, following his hearing, in compliance with the right to defense, as concerns the well-founded nature of the accusations against him". In consequence, the Court concluded to a violation of art. 6 of the ECHR.

7.2   The Perspective of EU Law. Developments in Domestic Law as a Result of EU Law

Since Romania has become a member of the EU in 2007 and acknowledged the jurisdiction of the Court of Justice in Luxembourg, Romanian nationals could claim protection against the violation of fundamental rights before said Court, based on the Charter of Fundamental Rights of the European Union.

Until now, the case-law consisting of preliminary rulings filed by Romanian courts has been scant in all matters in general terms, and in criminal matters it has been almost inexistent, in particular terms. So far, there have not been identified rulings of the Luxembourg Court related to *in absentia* proceedings derived from Romanian case-law. Thus, compliance with the European standards in the area of proceedings held *in absentia* could not take place by means of judicial practice, a situation which is not specific only to Romania. Therefore, it is necessary that harmonization may be achieved at the level of legislation. The European lawmaker understood this necessity, and that is why two legal instruments have been adopted, i.e. a Framework-Decision in the area of Justice and Home Affairs and a Directive following the enforcement of the Treaty of Lisbon.

These are the Council Framework Decision[109] 2009/299/JHA of 26 February 2009 amending Framework Decisions 2002/584/JHA, 2005/214/JHA, 2006/783/JHA, 2008/909/JHA and 2008/947/JHA, thereby enhancing the procedural rights of persons and fostering the application of the principle of mutual recognition to decisions rendered in the absence of the person concerned at the trial and, respectively, Directive[110] 2016/343/EU of the European Parliament and of the Council of 9 March 2016 on the strengthening of certain aspects of the presumption of innocence and of the right to be present at the trial in criminal proceedings.

---

[109] Published in the Official Journal of the European Union L 81/24 of 27.03.2009.
[110] Published in the Official Journal of the European Union L 65/1 of 11.03.2016.

When it comes to the first European instrument, Romania transposed it,[111] by adopting Act no. 300/2013[112] which amended Act no. 302/2004 on international judicial cooperation in criminal matters. As to the second act, according to its provisions, it is to be transposed by Member-States by April 1st 2018. So far, the Romanian Ministry of Justice has not adopted any draft aimed at the transposition of said Directive. Nevertheless, a draft Act is pending in Parliament proceedings, after a recent constitutional review of the said draft Act (12.10.2018).

8 Concluding Remarks

The Romanian Constitution does not contain express provisions related to the participation of persons to criminal proceedings, yet this attendance is constitutionally determined, but only indirectly, by resorting to the principle of access to justice. This means that a person whose rights and interests were exposed as a result of his/her direct participation to criminal proceedings, shall be entitled to take part to such proceedings, a constitutional guarantee which is activated by the access to justice principle.

According to the New Romanian Code of Criminal Procedure (CCP), in a criminal trial the lawyer shall assist or represent all the parties, including the victim and the suspect, with no restriction. It implies that a counsel shall meet no impediments to perform legal services even in case of *in absentia* proceedings.

In Romanian criminal proceedings, the accused cannot claim an absolute individual right to be present at trial, which would imply considerable efforts on the part of judicial authorities to make it effective. Failure to bring the accused to trial does not lead to a stay of proceedings—as an expression of an absolute nature of such right—but allows the trial to continue if judicial authorities prove that they have performed a duty of diligence in this respect.

When referring to *interim* decisions on coercive measures, all rulings on preventive arrest shall take place only in the presence of the defendant, unlike other custodial orders.

As regards the preliminary chamber proceedings (the hearing on evidence), the Romanian Constitutional Court gave a strong feedback against the purely inquisitorial manner in which such proceedings used to be conducted *in camera*, ruling on several cases by which it sanctioned the absence of the parties or other interested persons, as contrary to the fundamental law. As a major effect of these decisions, the summoning of all parties to preliminary chamber proceedings became compulsory.

Related to trial proceedings, these may take place only if the defendant has been lawfully summoned and the procedure has been complied with. The presence of the defendant to court, in person or through a representative or a counsel of his/her own

---

[111] A presentation of the developments of national law, as a result of the transposition of EU law were discussed in section 6 of the present study.

[112] Published in the Official Journal of Romania no. 772 of 11.12.2013.

choosing or appointed *ex officio*, if the latter contacted the person they represent, shall redress any irregularity related to the summoning procedure. The court proceedings may take place in the absence of the defendant, if the latter is missing, avoids proceedings or has changed his/her address without informing thereupon the judicial authorities and if his/her new address remains unknown. Court proceedings may also occur in the absence of the defendant, when, even though lawfully served the summons, the defendant provides no justification for his/her absence from the trial of the case.

The defendant is slightly involved in the process of fact-finding, due to the traditionally inquisitorial approach to finding the truth in a criminal case. It is commonly considered that the aim of the trial is too important to be left at the discretion of parties and represents an essential obligation of judicial authorities.

The CCP has not set out a right of the victim to participate to the criminal investigation, but a duty to appear before judicial authorities, whenever called upon. Still, the victim preserves an essential prerogative, namely to challenge before a judge the decisions issued by the prosecutor (e.g. decisions not to prosecute or to cease prosecution). During the trial stage, the victim is imposed no restrictions on his/her participation.

The Romanian procedural law provides an extraordinary remedy by which a person who was tried *in absentia* and convicted by a final ruling may request the retrial of his/her case in a term of 1 month calculated from the day he/she was informed, by any official notification, that a trial had been held against him/her. Unlike the other extraordinary remedies, the application for retrial of the case does not aim at challenging the unlawful or unfounded nature of the decision ruled *in absentia,* but instead the defendant seeks to give effectiveness to his/her right to participate personally to trial and exert his/her right to defense.

From the perspective of transnational criminal justice, the absence of the defendant from a trial which was held in a foreign court, contravenes the legal order of Romania, a sufficient reason to impede extradition or to refuse surrender based on a European Arrest Warrant (EAW). The Romanian state shall agree with the extradition or the execution of the EAW only if the Requesting State guarantees compliance with the rule whereby retrial of the case must occur in the presence of the interested party.

The ECtHR case-law on *in absentia* trials involving Romania is very sparse. The situation looks very much alike when it comes to the case-law generated by preliminary rulings filed by Romanian judges to the European Court of Justice on the conformity of *in absentia* proceedings with EU law. This means that compliance with the European standards in the area of proceedings held *in absentia* could not take place by means of judicial practice, a situation which is not specific only to Romania. Therefore, it is necessary that harmonization may be achieved within the lawmaking process. Currently adopted legal instruments at the EU level aim at such ambitious endeavor.

References

Bârsan C (2005) The European convention on human rights. Comments by articles. Rights and freedoms, vol I. C.H. Beck, Bucharest

Chiriță R (2006) Paradigms of the access to justice. How free is the access to justice? Pandectele Române 1:176–214

Chiriță R (2008) Right to a fair trial. Universul Juridic Publisher, Bucharest

Ciopec F (2005) *In absentia* proceedings. Traditional and topical trends. Ann Fac Law Timișoara 1:148–151

Ciopec F (2006) Retrial in case of extradition. Ann Fac Law Timișoara 1:162–168

Ciopec F (2014) The new Romanian code of criminal procedure. J East Eur Crim Law 1:33–52

Ciopec F, Roibu M (2016) The new Romanian code of criminal procedure – cosmetics or surgery? La legislazione penale 1:1–12

Constantinescu VHD (2015) Application for retrial of the case. *In absentia* proceedings. In: Udroiu M (ed) Criminal procedure code. Comments by articles. C.H. Beck, Bucharest, pp 1162–1181

Dan R (2012) Retrial after conviction in absentia, an illusionary procedure…A study on the compatibility of the institution referred by art. 522¹ of the Romanian criminal procedure code with the ECHR standards. Crim Law Writ 4:49–65

Deleanu I (2006) Constitutional institutions and procedures - in Romanian law and comparative law. C. H. Beck, Bucharest

Gouttenoire A (2011) Right to attend one's own trial. In: Sudre F et al (eds) Great rulings of the European Court of human rights. Rossetti Publisher, Bucharest (Romanian translation)

Grădinaru D (2015) The appeal. In: Udroiu M (ed) Criminal procedure code. Comments by articles. C.H. Beck, Bucharest, pp 1049–1069

Iancu G (2003) Fundamental rights, freedoms and duties in Romania. All Beck Publisher, Bucharest

Ionescu D (2011) On the new approach on trial and the new code of criminal procedure. A few simple matters. Crim Law Writ 1:66–97

Iugan AV (2016) Retrial of the criminal case. Universul Juridic, Bucharest

Mateuț G (2007) Companion to criminal procedure. General part, vol I. C.H. Beck, Bucharest

Muntean CS (2007) The European arrest warrant. A legal instrument able to replace extradition. Crim Law Writ 1:91–121

Muraru I, Ciobanu VM (2008) Free access to justice. In: Muraru I, Tănăsescu ES (eds) Romanian constitution - comments by articles. C. H. Beck, Bucharest, pp 175–194

Neagu I (2007) Companion to criminal procedure law. General part. Global Lex Publisher, Bucharest

Pașca V (2011) Criminal law studies. Universul Juridic Publisher, Bucharest

Radu FR (2009) International and European cooperation in criminal matters. Wolters Kluwer, Bucharest

Renucci J-F (2009) Companion to European law of human rights. Hamangiu Publisher, Bucharest (Romanian translation)

Roibu M (2014) The rights of the victim in the Romanian new code of criminal procedure. Ann Fac Law Timișoara 2:83–93

Streteanu F (2008) A few comments on the European arrest warrant. Crim Law Writ 1:1–16

Sudre F (2006) European and international law of human rights law. Polirom Publisher, Iași (Romanian translation)

Udroiu M (2015) Legal assistance and representation at trial. In: Udroiu M (ed) Criminal procedure code. Comments by articles. C.H. Beck, Bucharest, pp 261–286

Udroiu M (2016) Criminal procedure. General part, 3rd edn. C.H. Beck, Bucharest

Vasiescu M, Călin RM (2013) Access to court. In: Human rights dictionary – completed by case-law. C.H. Beck, Bucharest, pp 9–21

Zainea M (2006) Personal participation of the defendant to trial. Decisions ruled *in absentia*. Leg Cour J 7–8:94–104

Report on Spain

María Luisa Villamarín López

Abstract Personal participation in criminal proceedings is widely protected in the Spanish criminal procedural regime not only in the Criminal Procedural Law but also at a constitutional level. Accused persons are fully protected by a wide variety of procedural rights applied in all stages of the criminal proceeding, enjoying a status in accordance with the high European parameters. Spain has a very specific regime regarding participation of accusations in criminal procedure in so far as citizens, under certain circumstances, can bring criminal actions before the courts even if they are not victims. And, finally, the Spanish system has also been peculiar in the treatment of *in absentia* proceedings although its criteria has changed as a result of the transposition of European instruments and the application of the European case-law.

Abbreviations

CC	Spanish Criminal Code
CFREU	Charter of Fundamental Rights of the European Union
ECHR	European Convention of Human Rights
ECtHR	European Court of Human Rights
JCC	Judgment of the Spanish Constitutional Court
LAJG	Legal Aid Law
LECrim	Criminal Procedural Law
LOPJ	Organic Law of the Judicial Power
SC	Spanish Constitution (1978)

M. L. V. López (✉)
Department of Procedural Law, University Complutense Madrid, Faculty of Law, Madrid, Spain
e-mail: mlvillamarin@der.ucm.es

© Springer Nature Switzerland AG 2019
S. Quattrocolo, S. Ruggeri (eds.), *Personal Participation in Criminal Proceedings*, Legal Studies in International, European and Comparative Criminal Law 2, https://doi.org/10.1007/978-3-030-01186-4_13

1   Constitutional Requirements of the Involvement of Private Parties in Criminal Justice

Since its first Constitution of 1812, Spain presents a remarkable singularity in relation to the participants in the criminal procedure, given that private subjects are allowed to intervene in the process to prosecute whether they have been offended by the crime—private accusers ("*acusadores particulares*")—or if, without having been, they are interested in defending the legality—public accusers ("*acusadores populares*")—.[1] Although the participation of the non-offended was initially limited to a few crimes, the current Criminal Procedure Law, passed in 1882, enshrined this model and generalized it in the terms that we will analyze later.

Notwithstanding that both types of private accusations are recognized in the current Constitution of 1978, their constitutional support is nonetheless diverse. While the actions of those who have been injured or offended by the crime (so-called "private accusers") is protected by the right to effective judicial protection of article 24(1) SC, inasmuch the exercise of criminal action in this case seeks to protect their legitimate interests, public action is just understood as one of the manifestations of citizen participation in the Administration of Justice provided for in art. 125 SC, and therefore does not share the nature of fundamental right. However, despite the fact that their constitutional basis is different, both parties enjoy the same fundamental right from the moment they bring the criminal action into court: the right to effective judicial protection of article 24(1) SC, which the Spanish Constitutional case-law has called "*ius ut procedatur*", which consist of a "right to initiate a process", to demand that it should be substantiated in accordance with the requirements of the fair trial and to be constituted as accusatory parties provided that the procedural and material requirements provided by law are fulfilled. In this sense, if it were judicially established that these requisites do not concur, its content would be exhausted just with a reasoned judicial decision of denial of the requested protection.[2] Therefore, this "*ius ut procedatur*" does not entitle the accusers to request the process to be followed up to sentence only because the procedural requirements are fulfilled—as it happens in the civil procedure—and much less gives them a fundamental right to convict the accused.[3]

In line with the international human rights law (arts. 6 ECHR and 14 ICCPR), the Spanish Constitution recognizes both these accusers and the accused a series of common guarantees covering their actions before the criminal courts. Thus, article 24 SC provides for the following: the right to obtain the effective protection of the Courts in the exercise of their legitimate rights and interests, which includes, among others, the right to a motivated resolution; the right of access to the ordinary judge

---

[1] See art. 255 of the Constitution of 1812, art. 98 of the Constitution of 1869, and art. 29 of the Constitution of 1931.

[2] JCC 34/2008, of 25 February.

[3] Spanish Supreme Court Judgment of 26 June 2014, no. 6224/2014.

predetermined by law; and the right to a public trial without undue delays and with full guarantees.

Logically, along with these common rights, the accused must be specially protected to prevent an abusive or arbitrary exercise of the governmental *ius puniendi* that unnecessarily may disturb innocent people. For this reason, the same provision of the Constitution provides for a series of specific guarantees to protect the accused in criminal proceedings. In particular, article 24(2) SC provides for the following fundamental rights: the right to the defense and assistance of a lawyer; the right to be informed of the charges brought against them; the right to the use of evidence appropriate to their defense; the right not to make self-incriminating statements and not to declare themselves guilty and, finally, the right to be presumed innocent. They also enjoy the recognition of another set of rights recognized by the Constitution as fundamental, such as the secrecy of communications [art. 18(3)], the inviolability of the home [art. 18(2)] and the right to personal liberty [art. 17], which are specially protected in such a way that they can only be restricted in the course of criminal proceedings in very precise cases established by law and, generally, with judicial authorization.

2 Personal Participation of Private Parties and Legal Assistance

In Spain, with the exception of procedures on non serious offences [art. 967(1) LECrim], the parties who may intervene in a criminal procedure must have legal assistance. The defendants have a fundamental right to legal advice, recognized in the Constitution as a manifestation of the right to defense [arts. 17 and 24 SC] and developed in detail in the Spanish Criminal Procedural Law [arts. 118 and 520 LECrim]. The Spanish Constitutional Court has understood that this right guarantees the presence of a lawyer not only during the activities carried out before the court but also before the police, even if the defendants choose not to declare, in order to avoid activities carried out on defendants that could interfere with their right of defense (in particular, statements). It has also affirmed that this right is closely linked with the accusatory principle and the equality of arms between the parties, in order to avoid situations of lack of defence[4] and, for this reason, it should be effective.[5] The presence of a lawyer from the very first moment a person is formally charged is not only a guarantee but also a duty of the defendants so that they cannot waive this right either at the trial stage or during the investigation stage [arts. 118 and 767 LECrim]. Legal advice is required by law from the moment they are arrested or the moment that the proceedings result in a charge being laid against them. In this sense if defendants do not choose their own lawyer, a duty lawyer from

---

[4] JCC 38/2003, of 27 February.
[5] JCC 13/2000, of 17 January.

the Bar of Lawyers should be appointed either by the Police, the State Prosecution Service or the judicial authorities. Once they are legally assisted, they have the right to interview with their lawyers confidentially, except if they are "incommunicados" by the judicial authority in the cases of serious offences as provided by the Criminal Procedural Law.

The accusers must also be assisted by legal professionals from their first intervention in the procedure. In principle, if there is a plurality of accusations, each would act independently with their own lawyer, although exceptionally the judge may require them to act with only one "when the good order of the process or the right to a process without undue delay may be affected" [art. 109(bis)(2) LECrim].

Although the Constitution does not refer to court advocates ("procuradores"), they are also required to intervene in criminal proceedings according to article 543 LOPJ. While the lawyers direct and advise their clients legally and defend them in court, court advocates represent them within the course of the proceedings. Their fees are also included in the procedural costs.

When the private parties do have insufficient means to afford the trial costs, they can ask for legal aid, according to art. 3 of the Legal Aid Law.[6] As an exception, regardless of their resources, free legal aid is granted for victims of gender violence, terrorism, human trafficking and abuses or their successors [art. 2(lit)(g) LAJG].

3 Personal Participation of the *Accused* in Criminal Proceedings

3.1 General Features of Personal Participation: Absolute Individual Right or Duty of Diligence?

The participation of the accused in criminal proceedings is a right derived from the fundamental guarantee of defence and it means that nobody can be condemned without being previously heard. This right does not only determine the status of the accused during the trial but also his role in the investigation stage. From the moment he is linked to the proceedings, he is recognised the right not only to know what is happening with the course of the proceedings but also to intervene in any activity carried out in the pre-trial, as we will see below, except if, as it occurs in exceptional cases, he is declared "incommunicado".

If he decides not to exercise this right and not to appear before the court, the investigation may continue until the decision to open or not the next stage is taken. But it is different when the trial begins because in that moment it is a must to have a person whom all the indictment or accusations documents can be addressed and therefore he must be necessarily present at the court. In words of the article 786(1) LECrim, "attendance by the accused and the defence lawyer is compulsory at the

---

[6] "Ley de Asistencia Jurídica Gratuita"; onwards, LAJG, 1/1996, 10 January.

oral trial". As a result, if he does not go to court when summoned, the proceedings must be suspended until he voluntary or involuntary appears.

Only in the context of abbreviated proceedings and non-serious offences his intervention could be deemed as a duty of diligence because, as analysed in the next section of this chapter, if his absence is unjustified, given certain circumstances provided in articles. 786(1)(II) and 971 LECrim, the trial may be held against him.

3.2   Personal Participation in the Pre-trial Inquiry (with Particular Regard to the Interim Decisions on Coercive Measures)

Although since the Constitution of 1978 the accused has been covered by several guarantees that have allowed him to participate actively in many of the activities that take place in the first phase of the process, since the reform of 2015 (which adapts Spanish law to the European standards on rights of the accused, which will be dealt in Section G.II of this work) was passed, his status has been even reinforced.

The person who has been attributed a criminal offense, arrested or not, shall have the right to intervene in the course of the investigation from the first moment after being notified of the existence of the case, being able to carry out all the activities provided for in the law to guarantee their right of defence. For that purpose, "he may be informed of the facts ascribed to them, of any relevant change in the subject of the investigation and of the grounds on which the accusation was based" and he is recognized also the right to "examine the proceedings sufficiently in advance" and, "at, any event, prior to all statement being taken". As has been pointed out previously, legal assistance is required for all actions, so a lawyer will be appointed *ex officio* in case the defendant does not have a lawyer in which he trusts. The only limitation to this right to access to the procedure takes place when, "to avoid a serious risk to the life, liberty or physical integrity of another person" or to "prevent a situation that could seriously compromise the outcome of the investigation or the process", the judge declares the secrecy of the process, that may last for a maximum of one month; in this case, he can only have access to what affects his personal freedom [art. 302 LECrim].

His intervention during the investigation phase is wide, and he can request the actions he deems necessary for his defense to be carried out, being able to participate in them. In particular, as far as the investigative measures are concerned, he can intervene both during the development of ordinary measures (its own taking of evidence, confrontation, statement of experts, witnesses) and in those limiting fundamental rights. With regard to his own declaration, he may request it whenever he wishes or as many times as the investigating judge desires, in presence of his lawyer, preserving his right to silence.

Finally, as regards precautionary measures, the detained person has broad powers to intervene in the phase of the adoption of these measures and is always allowed to appeal those adopted. In case of detention, he may request *habeas corpus*, an instrument provided for in Organic Law 6/1984, of May 24. This procedure governs non-judicial arrests carried out in irregular manner or prolonged beyond the time limits provided by law, and constitutes an effective and fast instrument for the detainee to be brought before a court to discuss his situation.

For the adoption of remand in custody, it is foreseen that the person who has been detained by the Police will be brought to justice within a maximum period of 72 h. The hearing will be held before the judge to order this precautionary measure. The detainee, assisted by his lawyer, may express what he deems appropriate regarding the request for imprisonment made by the accusations and/or the Public Prosecutor's Office, and may even be tested on the necessary issues to resolve the petition [art. 505 LECrim]. If he does not agree with the decision taken, he can challenge the decision by means of an appeal with a preferential treatment [art. 507(1) LECrim].

3.3   Personal Participation in Alternative Proceedings

3.3.1   Fast-Track Procedure

Since 2002 defendants can be judged quicker thanks to a new procedural modality called fast-track proceeding for certain crimes ("*juicio rápido para determinados delitos*") in which the investigation stage is especially accelerated. This procedure may be applied for crimes punished with a penalty which does not exceed 5 years of prison or 10 years if it is of other nature, when the investigation is presumed to be simple (art. 795.1.3ª LECrim), when it is a flagrant crime (art. 795.1.1ª LECrim) or when they are less serious crimes (as mentioned in the list in art. 795.1.2ª LECrim).

In order to be able to follow this procedural track it is necessary that the judicial police, for as long as necessary or, at any event, during the arrest, carry out a series of urgent actions foreseen in article 796 LECrim, which include the following: (a) inform the accused of their right to appear before the duty court assisted by a lawyer; (b) if the person is not arrested, it will be summoned to appear in the duty court, pointing out the consequences if he does not appear; (c) the witness will also be summoned; (d) request for the medical report, for the analysis of the substances seized, if necessary, and in cases of road traffic crimes, for the breath analyzer test. Having received the police statement with the information taken from these activities, the duty court has to carry out urgently the following duties: (a) obtain the criminal record of the detainee; (b) obtain expert records; (c) take a statement from the detainee before the court; (d) take a statement from the witness; (e) if necessary, order a confrontation between witnesses, witnesses and the person under investigation or the persons under investigation among themselves; (f) summon the persons who should appear before him. In case these activities are considered not sufficient, he must transform this track into the abbreviated procedure. If the judge considers all these legal measures sufficient and considers the investigation stage finished, he shall order to continue to the next phase: the intermediate stage, where the judge will examine if the oral trial should be carried out and, if so, where the statements from the accusation and the defense may be submitted. The oral trial, in case it may take place, may follow the general rules of the abbreviated proceedings, including the one referred to the accused participation; that it is to say, his appearance is necessary to carry out the trial only if the crimes are of those punished with more than 2 years of imprisonment.

There is a possibility to transform an abbreviated procedure into a fast-track procedure if the accused, assisted by his lawyer, admits the facts in judicial presence when he was accused of a crime punished by a sentence included in the limits of this quicker procedure [art. 779(5) LECrim].

3.3.2 Guilty Plea

As it occurs in most of the modern criminal justice systems, Spanish law provides for the possibility of early termination of the process by guilty plea ("*acuerdo de conformidad*"). This modality is allowed both in the ordinary proceedings [arts. 655 and 668 LECrim] and abbreviated procedure [arts. 782 and 784 LECrim] and in fast-track procedure, in which guilty pleas have a special incentive, in so far as the sentence is reduced by one third [art. 801 LECrim].

In ordinary proceedings, guilty plea can be provided in Spanish proceedings at two different times: after the presentation of the defense statement or at the beginning of the oral trial. In any case, the judge must verify both the correctness of the legal qualification of the facts and of the punishment requested, as well as, above all, the freedom of the accused to give consent to guilty plea: the judge must ensure that he has personally lent it (it does not serve by its defense; in case of juridical persons, that has been validly rendered its representative), voluntarily and with full knowledge of its consequences. In order for the trial not to continue, all the accused persons must agree with the guilty plea [art. 697 LECrim].

3.3.3 "Acceptance by Decree Procedure" ("Procedimiento por aceptación de decreto")

For a restricted area of very frequent but not severe crimes, the Spanish Criminal Procedural Law foresees from 2015 a new type of procedure called "acceptance by decree" ("*procedimiento por aceptación de decreto*"), in which the Public Prosecutor, instead of presenting to the court a complaint about the facts, directly formulates a sanction proposal that, if accepted by the accused and authorized by the court, becomes a judicial decision, putting an end to criminal proceedings in advance. It can be carried out even if the suspect has not yet been heard before the court. Three requirements must be fulfilled [art. 803.bis.a LECrim]: (1) it must be a crime punishable by a fine, works for the benefit of the community or with imprisonment not exceeding one year and which may be suspended according to article 20 CC; (2) the Public Prosecutor should understand that the applicable penalty is a fine or work for the benefit of the community and, where appropriate, a penalty of deprivation of the right to drive motor vehicles and mopeds; (3) that there should not be private accusation (*"acusador particular o popular"*) in the case.

The defendant will be called to appear before the judge in case he authorizes this decree when these three requirements are fulfilled. A lawyer must always assist him, otherwise the procedure will be suspended. At the hearing, which will be recorded in full by audio-visual means, it will be checked whether the accused understands the meaning of the decree and its consequences and will be asked about his acceptance. If so, the decree will become a final judicial decision, and no further appeal may be filed against it. If he does not appear or does not accept it, the procedure will continue its course through the corresponding procedure [art. 803.bis.h LECrim].

3.4   Personal Participation at Trial

3.4.1   Personal Involvement in the Evidence- Gathering

During the investigation stage, Spanish criminal proceedings are based on the principle of *ex officio* investigations. The judiciary lead the task of searching for relevant evidence. In contrast, during the trial, the parties must decide which evidence they are interested in and they make an application in this regard to the court. Therefore, the general rule is that each party decides the evidence that should be submitted to the court, who would decide over its admissibility [art. 728 LECrim]. The only exception is provided in article 729 LECrim. The court may order evidence *ex officio* in the three following cases: (a) confrontation of witnesses among themselves or with the accused or between them; (b) sources of evidence not proposed by any of the parties, which court deems necessary for the verification of any of the facts that have been the subject of the writing of qualification; (c) evidence of any kind offered by the parties in the act to establish any circumstance that may influence the probative value of a witness's statement, if the tribunal considers them admissible.

Once proposed by the parties, the court has the duty to allow the evidence submitted by them to be heard, except if the evidence is useless, irrelevant or unlawful [art. 11 LOPJ]. During the evidence taking, the parties may intervene regardless of who proposed them.

3.4.2   Personal Contribution to the Fact-Finding

The fact-finding has a similar treatment to the evidence-gathering in the Spanish system. Although during the investigation stage the judge has to look for the facts that define the core of the process, once the oral trial is opened, the object of discussion is determined by what was introduced by the parties in their indictments and defense. Specifically, the accused is asked to submit a written defense answering the charges formulated by the accusation. He may state his intention to accept the facts and its legal qualification as articulated by the accusation or to accept a new indictment signed jointly by the accusations and the accused together with their lawyers. Prior to the hearing, the accused is given an opportunity to plead guilty, as studied before. Once the evidence is heard, the parties must state whether they confirm or amend the conclusions set out in the written statements.

Before finishing the trial, the accused has a right to the last word in case he wants to add something to the proceedings.

3.5   *Personal Participation in Higher Instances*

Within the right to effective judicial protection, article 24 SC recognizes a right to remedies, although it is not absolute in the sense that an appeal against any and all of the judicial decisions issued cannot be risen, although, once these are provided for in the law, they must be interpreted in the most favourable sense to the interests of the appellants.[7] However, by imperative of article 14.5 of the International Covenant on Civil and Political Rights, the Spanish Constitutional Court has traditionally understood that it was required to provide a way of appeal against any criminal conviction. Given that, the Spanish Criminal Law provides always for an appeal in this case but in some types of proceedings only with one instance, since the remedy did not open a second phase (this was the case with the judgments of Provincial Courts given in the ordinary proceedings). After years of scholar discussions, the Spanish Parliament considered that the International Covenant obliged to generalize the second instance in the criminal procedural system, a task undertaken recently and which has been enshrined in the last reform of the LECrim of 2015. In this way, every condemned person will have the possibility to file an appeal to a superior court, regardless of the type of proceeding for which he has been tried. It is understood that the defendant is guaranteed the immediacy in the assessment of his evidence in the case.

Convicted also enjoy in the area of remedies another privilege called "*reformatio in peius*". In cases where they are the only party who appeal the judicial decision, the privilege prevents the situation in which he was left in the appealed decision from worsening because he could not be imposed a higher penalty than the one set in the judgment under appeal.[8] The reason is that it is understood that the opposite would violate the requirements of the accusatory principle and, therefore, the right of defense.

---

[7] JCC 140/1985, of 21 October.

[8] See art. 902 LECrim in relation to appeals, although applicable to other actions by JCC 17/1989, of 30 January, and 40/1990, of 12 March.

In addition to the ordinary and extraordinary remedies legally regulated, the LECrim also provides that in cases of clear and severe injustice anyone who has been convicted by a final judgment (and even if the deceased, his spouse, ancestors or descendants, in order to rehabilitate his memory) can challenge the decision, passing over the authority of *res judicata*. Consider, for example, if a person has been condemned twice for the same crime (*non bis in idem*). The mechanism used in these cases is called "*revisión*" and, provided for in articles 954 and following LECrim, the Supreme Court may study the case and, if it appreciates the motive alleged, will annul the judgment rendered, ordering, if necessary, the new investigation of the case.

## 3.6	Special Rules in the Field of Serious Organized Crimes[9]

As it is well known, Spain has suffered for decades the scourge of terrorism by the organized group ETA so that from the beginning of democracy had to find instruments to react within the rule of law against this type of crime. One of the first measures taken during the Transition was the creation in 1977 of the "National Court",[10] institution attributed the centralized knowledge of all causes for crimes of terrorism committed in Spain, including minors [art. 65 LOPJ]. In addition to these measures of an organic nature, substantive and procedural rules specially designed to combat this type of crime have also been adopted since the beginning of democracy. As far as the involvement of those accused of terrorism in criminal proceedings is concerned, special mention should be made of the rights of "persons integrated or related to armed bands or terrorist or rebel individuals", most of them introduced by Organic Law 4/1988, of 25 May.

Firstly, measures related to their personal liberty should be pointed out. Suspects may be subject to a more severe detention regime, since they may remain in police hands, without prior judicial hearing, for a longer period of time. Thus, compared to the general 72 h maximum limit fixed by law for the police to bring the detainees to court, taking into account the greater complexity of anti-terrorist operations, article 520(bis) (2) LECrim allows its extension 48 h more if it is justified and authorized by a judge. The general term of the detainees' special "incommunicado" detention regime may also be extended, which, when compared to the five days provided for as a general rule, could even reach ten in such cases [art. 509.2 LECrim].[11]

Secondly, some specialties are envisaged as to the way in which investigations that may affect fundamental rights are carried out. In particular, two specialties stand out. Firstly, in matter of searches and seizures, the LECrim foresees (art. 553) that, contrary to the general rule requiring judicial authorization, when these types

---

[9] For more information on these special rules see Bachmaier Winter (2012).

[10] "*Audiencia Nacional*"; passed by Royal Decree 1/1977, of January 4.

[11] See in detail Bernardo San José y Padura Ballesteros, in Bachmaier (coord.), 2012.

of crimes are traced, if an exceptional or urgent need exists, the police may proceed to search the domiciles of those who are held responsible for them "under their own authority"; that is to say, without prior judicial authorization. Secondly, when the object of the investigation is terrorism, article 579(1) LECrim allows the judge to order seizure, opening and examination of postal and telegraphic private correspondence, including faxes and money orders that the accused sends or receives, "if there are indications that discovery or verification of some fact or circumstances relevant to the case will be obtained by these means". And, even, "in the event of urgency" to persecute one of these crimes, the Minister of Internal Affairs or, in default, the Secretary of State for Security, may order these measures [article 579(3) LECrim], being obliged to notified immediately the measure taken to the competent judge and, at any event, within a maximum time limit of 24 h, justifying their decision.

Thirdly, art. 384 (bis) LECrim contains a special regulation in regard to the accused' status, since it provides that, when an order for prosecution is final and provision imprisonment is ordered for one of these crimes, "the accused who may held a public duty will automatically be suspended from its exercise whilst imprisonment last".

4   Personal Participation of Private Parties Other Than Defendants (in Particular, the Contribution of the Victim to the Fact-Finding): "acusadores particulares", "acusadores populares", "actores y responsables civiles"[12]

In Spain, the State Prosecution Service does not have exclusive powers to instigate criminal proceedings and exercise criminal action, but also certain private individuals. Specifically, as already mentioned above, all victims can do so, entering the process as "private accusers" ("*acusadores particulares*"), as well as certain particular subjects, provided they comply with certain legal requirements, acting as "public accusers" ("*acusadores populares*").

Within the category of "private accusers", the Criminal Procedural Law allows the participation of those persons harmed or injured by the crime; that is, those who have directly suffered the commission of the offence ("direct victims" in terms of art. 2 of Law 4/2015, of the Statute of the Victim), as well as their closest relatives or their heirs if they are missing by death or disappearance ("indirect victims"). Since their right to participate is based on the existence of a legitimate interest in the prosecution of the person responsible for the punishable act, any person directly affected by the crime, whether natural or legal person, Spanish or foreign, public or private, may be a private prosecutor. The Spanish legislature has recently extended

---

[12] See in detail Chozas Alonso (2015).

the legitimacy to be private accusers in 2015, allowing extraordinary associations and legal entities to defend victims' rights, subject to their authorization [art. 109 (bis) (3) LECrim].

The victims' participation in the criminal process has traditionally been extensively regulated in the Criminal Procedure Law, although their position and rights have been reinforced after the approval of Law 4/2015, of 27 April, that deals with the Statute of the victim of the crime, transposing Directive 2012/29/UE, of 25 October 2012, into Spanish law. Since their first contact with the authorities, victims have the right to be informed of their rights and of the possibility of requesting assistance and support measures, to denounce the facts, to be legally advised, to be informed of all decisions affecting their rights, if necessary, to appeal against decisions (even in the execution phase: art. 13 of Law 4/2015), and, if it so wishes, to be a party in the proceedings, in which it may enter without the need to file a complaint ("querella") or to set up a bond. From that moment, he must be informed of any resolution issued in the course of the case [art. 7 of Law 4/2015]. They can access the proceedings at any time prior to the classification of the crime in the ordinary procedure and before the beginning of the trial in the abbreviated proceedings. Once they are a party, victims can carry out each and every one of the actions of the phase in which the process is taking place: to take cognizance of the action [arts. 302.I, 771.1 and 776.3 LECrim]; intervene in the practice of the activities that are taking place, and, if necessary, request new ones [arts. 302.I, 311 and 312 LECrim] and introduce sources of evidence; request the adoption of precautionary measures. Once the investigation phase is completed, he may request the proceeding to be dismissed if there is no reason to continue or, on the contrary, if the oral trial should be opened, exercising the accusation during the course of the oral trial, using the appropriate evidence. During the proceedings, and, in particular, when making statements or taking evidence on their person, special protection is provided for their fundamental rights, in particular for their right to privacy [art. 22 of Law 4/2015].

In addition to victims, the Constitution allows persons who have not been offended or harmed by the crime to bring criminal actions before the courts.[13] As mentioned above, this figure is an example of citizen participation in the Administration of Justice [art. 125 SC] and, at the same time, it is a tool to control possible abuses in the exercise of criminal action by the Public Prosecutor Service, especially in cases in which crimes of special public or political relevance are pursued, having in mind that in Spain the Public Prosecutor Office depends on the Executive Power [art. 124.4 SC]. This right to bring criminal actions, recognized by the Constitutional Court to both natural and legal persons,[14] is limited to Spaniards

---

[13] On "*acusadores populares*" see also Banacloche Palao (2008), p. 9; Giménez García (2009), and Pérez Gil (1997).

[14] For example, in JCC 241/1992, of 21 December, 34/1994, of 31 January and 59/1998, of 16 March.

of legal age who have not previously been convicted of an offense of calumnies and conditioned to request to be part of the process by means of a written complaint (called "querella"; see art. 270.I LECrim) and to a provision of a bond that should be proportionate and justified [art. 280 LECrim]. Also, unlike what happens with the private accusation, the "*acusador popular*" has to constitute a deposit to appeal and, as a rule, his expenses are not included within the costs of the process.

Once these requirements have been met, the "*acusador popular*" has traditionally enjoyed identical powers as the private accuser in the course of the procedure. However, in recent years the Supreme Court has limited its scope of action. In 2007 the Court understood that it was not possible to agree to open the oral trial by the mere request of the private prosecution,[15] a doctrine confirmed in 2013 by the Constitutional Court in Sentence 205/2013, of 5 December. However, this interpretation was qualified in a judgment of 8 April 2008 (Case Atutxa), which clarified that this limitation did not operate in the case of offenses relating to supra individual interests in which, by their very nature, there is no possibility that they may have been offended or harmed by the crime.

There are also two other possible private persons who can intervene in the criminal process: the civil actor and the civil responsible. Although normally accusers brings jointly the civil with the criminal action in the same criminal process—and the person against whom the criminal accusation is directed is also usually the one who responds to the civil action–, in our criminal system the intervention of the offended or injured by the crime is also allowed to exercise only the civil action, being called in this case "civil actor"; likewise it is also provided that a person may intervene solely to deal with civil liability ("civil responsible").

Civil actors can request to be part of the proceedings, to be legitimized to intervene throughout his course, although their powers are restricted to what affects civil liability; in fact, these issues are processed separately from the principal cause. Civil responsible is thus declared by the Penal Code in articles 116 to 122, either directly (persons who commit the crime, finally held or not criminally accountable for it [arts. 116 and 118 CC] and insurers up to the limit established or contractually agreed compensation [art. 117 CC]), or, falling those held criminally accountable, subsidiarily (parents or guardians for the crimes committed by their legal aged sons but still subject to their parental rights and cohabiting with them; natural o legal persons owing publishing houses, magazines, radio or television channels or similar for crimes committed using the media they own; natural or legal persons owning vehicles liable to third parties, for the crimes committed in use of these by their authorized persons [art. 120 CC]; public entities for damage caused by public agents, employees or authorities criminally accountable for malicious or negligent crimes [art. 121 CC]).

---

[15] Case Botín, Judgment of the Spanish Supreme Court of 17 December 2007 (JUR\2008\189).

5 *In Absentia* Proceedings[16]

5.1 Information Rights and Conditions of Waiver of Personal Participation in Criminal Proceedings

In order to explain the extent of the intervention of the accused, a distinction must be made between the two main stages of the criminal procedure.

The investigation phase can be carried out without difficulties even if the possible perpetrator of the punishable offense remains unknown and, in fact, the activities carried out during this stage have frequently the purpose of ascertaining their identity. However, from the moment the suspect is identified and the offense is attributed to him, the accused enjoy the full right of defense and, in order to be able to benefit from all of its content, it is envisaged that the information of rights is given in an understandable and accessible way, taking into account his particular circumstances (age, nationality, ability, etc.). Specifically, he must be informed of the following rights [arts. 118 and 520 LECrim]: (a) the right to remain silent, and to give no statement if he chooses not to answer any question; (b) the right to not testify against himself and to not confess guilt; (c) the right to a lawyer, to request the presence of his lawyer at all judicial hearings, with permission to act in all corresponding recognition of identity; (d) the right to inform a family member or any other person of the place where they are being held at any given time; foreign persons have also the right to inform their country's consular office about the foregoing circumstances; (e) the right to be assisted by an interpreter, free of charge, when the accused person is foreign and neither understands nor speaks; (f) the right to be examined by a forensic doctor; (g) the right to meet in confidence with a lawyer both before and after providing a statement.

However, if the person charged decides not to assert his defense mechanisms during the investigation stage and does not observe the court's request ("*requisitoria*"), he will be declared in default and the proceeding will continue without him until this phase is completed, moment in which the course of the proceedings must be suspended and the records filed [art. 840 LECrim].

Once the trial is opened, his the situation is completely different. As a general rule, if the accused is not present before the court, the hearing cannot be held because it is understood that, by virtue of the requirements of the principle of hearing, no one should be convicted of a criminal offense without having been effectively heard. However, Spanish classical doctrine states that, if the person charged has been duly informed and does not appear because he does not want to, there should be no failure of this principle, but his presence would still be necessary, based on the fact that he is one of the pieces of evidence and part of the object of the process. Thus, if the accused is declared in default, the proceedings must be suspended and the writs filed (art. 841 LECrim) until he appears or is taken by force to

---

[16] On *in absentia* proceedings see Gutiérrez Berlinches (2008), p. 203.

court. This suspension implies, for the purpose of time limits, that its calculation of the prescription shall be restarted once again, invalidating "the time elapsed" [art. 132(2) CC].

5.2 Default Proceedings and Subsequent Remedies (e.g., Retrial or Judicial Review in a Higher Instance)

However, the general rule requiring the presence of the accused in the trial has two exceptions in two cases of prosecution of minor crimes: first, in the area of the abbreviated procedure when the judge or court, at the request of the prosecutor or the accuser, and after hearing the defense, consider that "there are sufficient elements for the prosecution", provided that the penalty requested does not exceed 2 years of deprivation of liberty or, if it is of different nature, when its duration does not exceed 6 years [art. 786 LECrim]; the second, in the area of proceedings for minor offenses, whenever the judge, *ex officio* or at the request of a party, does not deem necessary the statement of the accused [art. 971 LECrim]. In his first appearance, the suspect or accused must be informed of the consequences that in these cases may be absent from the trial [arts. 775.1 and 962.1 LECrim].

Decisions adopted *in absentia* may be reviewed throughout an exceptional procedure known as "annulment" (*"anulación"*), which the accused may raise to attack firm decisions within the 10-day period provided for the appeal (regulated in arts. 790 and following LECrim), counting from the time the convicted person became aware of the judgment, and subject to the same requirements of the appeal [art. 793.2 LECrim]. Given that this is an extraordinary mechanism for challenging final decisions, the judgment ruling on the annulment cannot resolve the substance of the case, but must restrict itself to withdraw the challenged judgment and, therefore, the evidence is limited. This was stated by the Supreme Court in its non-jurisdictional Agreement of February 25, 2000: "it will be limited to verifying whether the sentencing court has scrupulously observed the legal requirements of the trial *in absentia*, since any other question has been raised by the legal representation of the convicted through appeal cassation (...). In case of non-compliance with these requirements, the judgment will be declared null and void in respect of the absentee, which must be repeated before the competent court".[17]

---

[17] In the same sense, Judgment of the Supreme Court of 19 July 2002 (RAJ 1371/2002).

5.3   Inaudito Reo *Proceedings (e.g., Penal Order Procedure)*

Although Law 41/2015 has introduced into the criminal procedure a new process called "acceptance of decree" ("*proceso por aceptación de decreto*"), by way of a criminal "fast track" procedure, it is not foreseen in any case that this decree issued by the Public Prosecutor may be converted into a conviction if the subject does not appear to accept the proposal of sanction contained therein [arts. 803bis.g and 803bis.h LECrim].

6   Participatory Rights in Transnational Criminal Justice

6.1   Participatory Safeguards in EAW Proceedings

6.1.1   Participatory Rights in the Decision on Surrender

EAW proceedings are provided in Spain by the Law 23/2014, of 20th November, of mutual recognition of judicial decisions in criminal matters within the EU. We will try to summarize in this section the main participatory rights of the accused within this proceeding.

If the person claimed in Spain is found, the detention is practiced by the police, who will read the detainee's rights and notify him of the reasons for the arrest, which is reflected in the police report of the detention. Notified the detention to the Central Investigation Court ("Juzgado Central de Instrucción"), he will communicate the same to the issuing judicial authority, indicating the period available to send the European arrest warrant, to the Prosecutor of the National Court and to the Section of International Legal Cooperation of the Ministry of Justice.

The detained person must be placed at the disposal of the Central Investigation Court, directly or through the Court of Instruction of the party in which he was detained, within 72 h of the arrest. The judicial authority must inform the arrested person of the existence of the European arrest warrant, its content, the possibility of irrevocable consent to the surrender and of his rights [art. 13.3 of the Law].

Within a period of 72 h after being at the court disposal, the hearing referred to in article 14 of the Law will be held (as foreseen for the declaration of the detained by the Law of Criminal Procedure) before the Central Investigation Court, with the assistance of the Public Prosecutor, the lawyer of the detained person and, if applicable, the interpreter. The detained person will be heard on the provision of his irrevocable consent to the surrender and on his resignation to avail himself of the principle of specialty. The Central Investigation Court shall ensure that his consent to surrender and his waiver of the specialty principle have been freely provided and with full knowledge of its consequences, especially its irrevocable character.

If the requested person admits his surrender, it shall be issued a comprehensive minute subscribed by the detained person, the secretary, the representative of the

Public Prosecutor's Office and the judge shall be issued, where t shall be also recorded his waiver to the principle of specialty.

If the defendant is Spanish and the European order has been issued for the purpose of executing a custodial sentence or security measure, he will be asked if he agrees to serve the sentence in the issuing State; in case the European order has been issued for the purpose of bringing a criminal action, he will be asked if he wants to be returned to Spain to comply with the custodial sentence or security measure that can be pronounced against him in the issuing State. In both cases, a statement of consent will be recorded in the minutes as indicated. The parties may propose at this hearing the evidence needed to prove the concurrence of causes of refusal or conditioning on surrender.

In the course of this hearing, after listening to the the Public Prosecutor, the judge will decide on the personal situation of the defendant [art. 17 of the Law], being able to order provisional detention or provisional release, adopting any precautionary measures considered necessary to ensure full availability of those affected and especially those provided for in the Law on Criminal Procedure, taking into account the circumstances of the case and the purpose of ensuring the execution of the European order. There is nothing to prevent the prosecutor from requesting the imprisonment in writing at the same time as he requests that the surrender be ordered. Neither should there be an obstacle for the judge to order pre-trial detention at the beginning of the hearing.

The decision of the Central Investigation Court on the personal situation of the defendant could be appealed before the Criminal Chamber of the National Court.

The case must be submitted in Spanish and, if not, the procedure will be suspended until the European order duly translated into Spanish is transmitted.

Pending the procedure, the judicial authority of the issuing State may request, either that the person sought be given a declaration, or that it be temporarily delivered to the issuing State. In both cases, the Central Investigation Court may also consider the possibility of using videoconference, under the conditions agreed with the executing judicial authority, for the practice of the pertinent procedural activity that the Spanish detainee's right to legal assistance, not to confess guilty and not to testify against himself, and to be assisted by an interpreter must be respected.

It is possible for the Central Investigation Judge to order the temporary transfer of the person claimed pending the decision on the delivery. The conditions and duration of the transfer shall be those agreed with the issuing judicial authority. In any case, the requested person must return to Spain to attend oral hearings.

Finally, regarding the surrender of the defendant, the Spanish law establishes that it may be done by the agent of the Spanish authority, in the place and date fixed, which must be previously communicated to the authority designated by the issuing judicial authority.

The delivery must be verified within 10 days after the date of the resolution, although the period can be extended by 10 more days if the delivery cannot be verified for reasons beyond the control of the issuing or executing State. Exceptionally, the issuing authority may suspend delivery on serious humanitarian grounds until it ceases to exist.

The National High Court will inform the issuing judicial authority of the period of deprivation of liberty suffered, for the deduction of the penalty or measure imposed. When the person claimed has pending proceedings or a sentence pending compliance with the Spanish jurisdiction for a fact other than that which motivates the European arrest warrant, the Spanish judicial enforcement authority, even if it has resolved to comply with the order, may suspend delivery of the person claimed until the termination of the process or the final compliance with the sentence [Article 21 of the Law].

Under these conditions, the temporary delivery allows the requested person to be sent provisionally to the judicial issuing authority that issued the order, thus avoiding that the delivery may be delayed by pending internal processes or compliance with the sentence imposed. To this end, the issuing judicial authority may submit a request to the executing judicial authority by any means allowing a written record in conditions that allow the executing State to establish its authenticity. The conditions for temporary delivery shall be formalized in writing with the judicial authority of the issuing State and shall be binding on all Spanish judicial authorities. Alternatively, it may be useful to use videoconference under the conditions agreed with the issuing judicial authority, for the practice of the relevant procedural actions and that the Spanish law allows to carry out without the physical presence of the respondent.

At the request of the issuing or *ex officio* authority, the executing authority shall intervene and deliver, in accordance with domestic law, objects that constitute evidence or subject to the offense, without prejudice to the rights that the Spanish State or third parties may have purchased on them [art. 22 of the Law]. In this case, once the trial is concluded, it will be returned. The objects must be delivered even if the European order cannot be executed due to the death or evasion of the claimed person. When the goods are subject to embargo or confiscation in Spain, the executing authority may deny the delivery or carry it on a temporary basis, if necessary for the pending process. The expenses incurred in Spanish territory shall be borne by the Spanish State (art. 4 of the Law).

6.1.2 In Absentia Proceedings in the Trial Country and Its Relevance in the Surrender Procedure

For years, the Spanish Constitutional Court has claimed that the safeguards provided for in the Spanish legislation that we have discussed up to now should also be preserved when a foreign element is present, even if they were Member States of the European Union.[18] In particular, with regard to the instrument of the European arrest warrant, the Court has held on several occasions that the fact that neither the European Framework Decision on it nor the Spanish Law implementing it, the Law 3/2003, of 14 March, consider as a condition for the surrender of the accused that

---

[18] See JCC 91/2000, 30 March and 134/2000, 16 May, *inter alia*, concerning extradition proceedings between Spain and Italy.

the laws of the executing State necessarily establish a retrial does not prevent Spain from being able to requiring it since it is a fundamental right Fundamental provided in article 24 SC. In particular, it considered that "the right of the accused to be present at the oral hearing is not only a requirement of the principle of contradiction, but the instrument that makes possible the exercise of the right of self-defense to answer the factual allegations that, referred to their own conduct, constitute the accusatory claim" and, consequently, if that right is not respected, a violation of the right to fair trial occurs.[19] For many years, a great majority of the Spanish literature criticized this position of the Spanish Constitutional Court, considering it "weak", clearly debatable under article 24 SC, and of very dubious compatibility with the principles of trust and mutual recognition of the Union, thesis joined occasionally by some Magistrate of this Court. This interpretation was supported even after the adoption of Framework Decision 2009/299/JHA, of 26 February, which expressly "provides in essence that, once the person convicted *in absentia* was aware, in due time, of the scheduled trial and was informed that a decision could be handed down if he did not appear for the trial or, being aware of the scheduled trial, gave a mandate to a legal counselor to defend him at the trial, the executing authority is required to surrender that person, with the result that it cannot make that surrender subject to there being an opportunity for a retrial of the case at which he is present in the issuing Member".[20] For example, in its Judgment 199/2009, of 28 September, the Spanish Constitutional Court still maintained a position that was already in clear confrontation with the wording of the aforementioned European Law of 2009, as understood by two of the judges who issued the resolution in individual votes. In particular, they pointed out that this "interpretation violates the third pillar system of sources" (…) "This principle of equivalence and sufficiency in protection is particularly clear and enforceable within the European Union, which only makes sense as a political and legal project on the basis of legitimate expectations in the Community institutions and in the other Member States. In short, and for what now matters, a State, in principle, cannot impose on others their parameter of protection of fundamental rights, and should move in their relations with other Member States within the common substantive and procedural framework".

This controversial interpretation given by the Spanish Constitutional Court has brought on some conflicts in recent years with at least three European countries: Romania,[21] France[22] and Italy.[23]

Having in mind this situation, the Spanish Constitutional Court decided to send a question to the Court of Justice of the European Union, arising three requests for a preliminary ruling. The Spanish national court considered the binding nature of

---

[19] See, for example, in JCC 177/2006, of 5 June.

[20] Article 4 (a)1 of the Framework Decision, introduced by the Framework Decision 2009; article summarized in Judgment C-399/11, explained below.

[21] JCC 199/2009, of 28 September.

[22] JCC 177/2006, of 5 June and 37/2007, of 12 February.

[23] JCC 86/2011, of 9 June.

fundamental rights when applied 'externally' is attenuated, since only the most basic or elementary requirements may be linked to Article 24 of the Spanish Constitution and give rise to a finding of 'indirect' unconstitutionality. "Nevertheless, a decision of the Spanish judicial authorities to consent to extradition to countries which, in cases of very serious offences, allow convictions *in absentia* without making the surrender conditional upon the convicted party being able to challenge the same in order to safeguard his rights of defense, gives rise to an 'indirect' infringement of the requirements deriving from the right to a fair trial, in that such a decision undermines the essence of a fair trial in a way which affects human dignity". And, consequently, the European Court of Justice is also asked if Article 4a(1) of Framework Decision 2002/584/JHA must be interpreted as precluding national judicial authorities, in the circumstances specified in that provision, from making the execution of a European arrest warrant conditional upon the conviction in question being open to review, in order to guarantee the rights of defense of the person requested under the warrant" and, going even further, if that provision is not incompatible with Article 47 of the Charter and if, in that case, Article 53 of the Charter should be applied, allowing "a Member State to make the surrender of a person convicted *in absentia* conditional upon the conviction being open to review in the requesting State, thus affording those rights a greater level of protection than that deriving from European Union law, in order to avoid an interpretation which restricts or adversely affects a fundamental right recognized by the constitution of the first-mentioned Member State".

The Court of Justice of the European Union, in its well known Judgment of 26th February 2013,[24] gave a very clear answer to those questions, rejecting all arguments introduced by the Spanish Constitutional Court. It explained that article 4 (a) of the Framework Decision must be interpreted "as precluding the executing judicial authorities, in the circumstances specified in that provision, from making the execution of a European arrest warrant issued for the purposes of executing a sentence conditional upon the conviction rendered *in absentia* being open to review in the issuing Member State". And, in its opinion, this article not only does not infringe on fundamental rights provided in article 47 CFREU but also pursues the harmonization of the conditions of execution of European arrest warrants in order to "enhance the procedural rights of persons subject to criminal proceedings whilst improving mutual recognition of judicial decisions between Member States". Consequently, the Court explained that

> allowing a Member State to avail itself of article 53 of the Charter to make the surrender of a person convicted in absentia conditional upon the conviction being open to review in the issuing Member State, a possibility not provided for under Framework Decision 2009/299, in order to avoid the adverse effect on the right to a fair trial and the rights of the defense

---

[24] Case *Melloni*, C-399/11, of 26 February 2013.

guaranteed by the constitution of the executing Member State, by casting doubt on the uniformity of the standard of protection of fundamental rights as defined in that framework decision, would undermine the principles of mutual trust and recognition which that decision purports to uphold and would, therefore, compromise the efficacy of that framework decision.

This judgment forced the Spanish Constitutional Court to review its traditional doctrine and, in this sense, in its Judgment of 13 February 2013,[25] it noted that the fact that the accused is condemned *in absentia* without any subsequent possibility of applying for a retrial does not constitute a violation of the right to a fair trial [art. art. 24 SC]) when the failure to appear at the trial is stated to have been decided voluntarily and unequivocally despite having been summoned in person or officially informed of the scheduled date and place or the trial, if he is been effectively represented by a legal counsel instead of appearing in person.

6.2 Participatory Safeguards in Transborder Inquiries and the Taking of Overseas Evidence

Spanish Law 23/2014, of 20 November, in its Title X, incorporates the content of the European regulations on transmission and execution of evidence abroad.[26] The rule governs the Spanish petitions on the request of the Spanish authorities to obtain evidence in other Member States [arts. 187 to 194], as well as the execution by the Spanish authorities of foreign petitions [arts. 195 to 200]. The competence, its scope of application and the requirements for issuing these orders are regulated in detail, although there is no specific provision that addresses the role of the accused in the practice of these tests, so we understand that they will be of application in each case the general rules on evidence. As far as the guarantees of the accused are concerned, art. 194 regulates the processing of personal data and limits its use to "procedures in which that resolution may be agreed, to others directly related to it or exceptionally to prevent an immediate and serious threat to public security"; in other cases, authorization from the "competent authority of the executing State or directly from the person concerned". Regarding the execution of foreign petitions by Spanish authorities (which may be agreed at the request of part or ex officio), art. 195 establishes that there will be no double-check control and that, if there are several means, it is necessary to employ the one that least restricts individual freedom.

---

[25] JCC 26/2014.

[26] For more details see Escribano Mora (2015), pp. 507 ff.

7 Requirements of Personal Participation and *In Absentia* Proceedings. The Perspective of Supranational and International Human Rights Law

7.1 The Perspective of International Human Rights Law. Critical Remarks on Domestic Law in the Light of the European Convention

Most of Spanish scholars have argued that no international law forced Spain to defend at all costs the necessary presence of the accused in the oral trial in order that it could be carried out. In fact, it does not seem that such a conclusion can be drawn from art. 10 of the Universal Declaration of Human Rights ("Everyone is entitled in full equality to a fair and public hearing by an independent and impartial tribunal, in the determination of his rights and obligations and of any criminal charge against him") or from art. 14(3)(d) of the International Covenant of Civil and Political Rights ("To be tried in his presence, and to defend himself in person or through legal assistance of his own choosing").[27]

Within the scope of the European Convention on Human Rights, as is well known, it is understood that the right to be present at trial is part of the basic content of article 6, as the European Court of Human Rights had held on numerous occasions. Serve as an example the following declaration in case *Medenica*:

> The Court has previously stated that it is of capital importance that a defendant should appear, both because of his right to a hearing and because of the need to verify the accuracy of his statements and compare them with those of the victim – whose interests need to be protected – and of the witnesses.[28]

Nevertheless, the European Court has reiterated that this right is not absolute, thus leaving a considerable margin for the admissibility of trials in absence in the different national legislations.

However, the Spanish courts have not taken these considerations very much into account. On the contrary, the Spanish Constitutional Court has continued defending its doctrine on the basis of the ECtHR case law.[29] Thus, for example, citing the cases *Sejdovic* and *Colozza*, it pointed out that the European Court has stated that "a denial of justice nevertheless undoubtedly occurs where a person convicted *in absentia* is unable subsequently to obtain from a court which has heard him a fresh determination of the merits of the charge, in respect of both law and fact, where it has not been established that he has waived his right to appear and to defend himself"[30] and, following

---

[27] See for all Torres Muro (2013), p. 350; Cedeño Hernán (2010), p. 12.

[28] ECtHR. *Medenica v. Switzerland*, judgment of 14 June 2001, Appl. No. 20491/92.

[29] Cf., for example, JCC, order 86/2011, of 9 June.

[30] ECtHR, *Sejdovic v. Italy*, judgment of 1 March 2006, Appl. No. 56581/00; ECtHR, *Colozza v. Italy*, judgment of 12 February 1985, Appl. No. 9024/80. More recently, cfr. also ECtHR, *Demeboukov v. Bulgaria*, judgment of 28 February 2008, Appl. No. 68020/01.

the *Poitrimol* case, that waiver "must, if it is to be effective for Convention purposes, be established in an unequivocal manner and be attended by minimum safeguards commensurate to its importance".[31] This approach of the Spanish Constitutional Court has been harshly criticized by Spanish scholars for being not only discordant, but even contrary, to the ECHR and the ECtHR case law.[32]

The truth is that since the Judgment of the Court of Justice of the European Union of 26 February 2013 analyzed before, the Spanish Constitutional Court has been forced to revise its traditional doctrine. Interestingly, constitutional case law still invokes the same ECtHR case law to which it referred so far, but now to support its new approach, favoring the possibility of imposing a sentence "without the appearance of the accused and without further possibility of remedying his lack of presence in the criminal proceedings, if he waives his right voluntarily and unequivocally and was effectively defended by counsel appointed".[33]

7.2 The Perspective of EU Law. Developments in Domestic Law As a Result of EU Law

Since the Tampere European Council in 1999, the European legislature has improved criminal cooperation between Member States in various regards, in many of them dealing with aspects relating to the involvement of the parties in the process. Specifically, the EU institutions have been concerned with establishing measures to protect victims, including powers of intervention and participation in the process, and to establish common minimum rights for all suspects and defendants in the proceedings within the European Union.

The Spanish legislature was forced to adapt its system to these new European laws, with very good results so far, improving to a very good extent the level of protection of the rights and guarantees of citizens who are immersed actively or passively in criminal proceedings.[34]

With regard to the protection of victims, the Spanish Parliament has incorporated into Spanish law the Directive 2012/29/EU (25 October 2012, establishing minimum standards on the rights, support and protection of victims of crime, and replacing Council Framework Decision 2001/220/JHA) by Law 4/2015, of 27 April, of the Statute of the victim, and by the amendment of article 730 LECrim.

Regarding the rights of suspects and accused persons, three have been the areas in which legislative changes have already taken place.

---

[31] ECtHR, *Poitrimol v. France,* judgment of 23 November 1993, Appl. No. 14032/88.

[32] See, for example, Torres Muro (2013), p. 355; Cedeño Hernán (2010), p. 11; Torres Pérez (2010), p. 452.

[33] JCC 26/2014, of 13 February 2014.

[34] See in detail on this topic Aguilera Morales (2016).

Firstly, the regulation of the right to interpretation and translation has been improved as a consequence of Directive 2010/64/EU, of 20 October 2010. In fact, new articles 123 to 127 of the Spanish Criminal Procedural Law recognize all charged or accused who does not speak or understand Spanish or the official language in which the proceedings are held (Catalan in Catalonia, Basque in the Basque Country or Galician in Galicia) or with sensory disability the right to be assisted free of charge by an interpreter during all proceedings, including police interrogation, and to translate in writing the essential documents to guarantee the right of defense.

Secondly, the transposition of Directive 2012/13/EU, of 22 May 2012, has also improved access to information in criminal proceedings in the Spanish law. Thereby, all accused have the right to be informed about the acts ascribed to them and also about any relevant change in the subject of investigation and the grounds on which the accusation was based (art. 118(a) LECrim)and, as an outstanding novelty, they have the right to examine the proceedings in sufficient time to safeguard the right of defense [art. 118(1)(a) LECrim)].[35]

Finally, as a consequence of the transposition of the Directive 2013/48/UE, of 22 October 2013, the Spanish law has reinforced the right of access to a lawyer [arts. 118(1)(d) and 520(c) LECrim], in particular the right to have a private interview with their lawyer, even prior to making statements to police, prosecutors o judicial authorities [art. 520.6.d) LEcrim].

Despite all these that has been achieved in recent years, there are still two recent Directives to be transposed into Spanish law: Directive 343/2016/EU, of 9 March 2016, on the strengthening of certain aspects of the presumption of innocence and of the right to be present at the trial in criminal proceedings, and Directive 2016/800/EU, of 11 May 2016, on procedural safeguards for children who are suspects or accused persons in criminal proceedings. In particular the first one is going to force a change in the traditional criteria of the Spanish case law on two subjects: (a) "*in dubio pro reo*", because the article 6.2 of the Directive does not allow any exceptions in the application of that procedural rule, as was contemplated in Spain for the circumstances of modification of criminal responsibility; (b) on the exercise of the privilege against self-incrimination, because, according to article 7, courts are prohibited from extracting any negative inferences from the silence of the accused, as occurred in the Spanish courts in recent years (for example, the most recent, from the Constitutional Court, Judgments 9/2011, of 28 February; 26/2010, of 27 April; also from the Supreme Court: Judgments 592/2010, of 20 May (RAJ 2010/8145); 84/201, of 18 February (RAJ 2010/3500)), supporting this interpretation of the privilege in the doctrine sustained for years by the ECHR.[36]

This change of criteria seems to confirm that the Spanish Constitutional Court had exceeded for many years by setting the requirements of trials *in absentia* and that it had made a biased understanding of the ECHR case law which, fortunately, has been recently abandoned.

---

[35] Also recognized when they are kept in detention: arts. 505.3 and 520 LECrim.

[36] For all, ECtHR, *John Murray vs. United Kingdom*, judgment of 8 February 1996, Appl. No. 18731/91, and *Saunders vs. United Kingdom*, judgment of 17 December 1996, Appl. No. 19187/91.

8 Concluding Remarks

From this chapter it could be worked out that the possibilities for intervention of private persons in the Spanish process are very broad and, although it has been somehow limited in recent years, our system remains as a benchmark in European criminal procedural law. Regarding the guarantees of the main characters in criminal proceedings (victims and accused persons), it could be considered that the Spanish procedural regime complies with the international standards and, in particular, with the European parameters. However, it is clear that one of our weakest points was precisely the maintenance of reluctance to accept trials in absence in other countries, an obstacle that, as analyzed above, has been overcome in recent years thanks to the intervention of the European courts.

Let us trust that this high level of guarantees and safeguards for the protagonists of the criminal process continues both at national and European level despite the continuing terrorist attacks that our countries are undergoing and that are questioning the viability of our current system of freedoms and rights that have taken us so many years to build.

References

Aguilera Morales M (2016) Justicia penal y Unión Europea: un breve balance en clave de derechos. In: 8883 Diario La Ley (16 December 2016), Section IV

Bachmaier Winter L (ed) (2012) Terrorismo, proceso penal y derechos fundamentales. Marcial Pons, Madrid

Banacloche Palao J. (2008) La acusación popular en el proceso penal: propuestas para una reforma: Revista de Derecho Procesal, pp 9–54

Cedeño Hernán M (2010), Vulneración indirecta de derechos fundamentales y juicio en ausencia en el ámbito de la orden europea de detención y entrega. A propósito de la STC 199/2009, de 28 de septiembre. Revista General del Derecho Europeo, pp 1–15

Chozas Alonso JM (ed) (2015) Los sujetos protagonistas del proceso penal. Dykinson, Madrid

Escribano Mora A (2015) El exhorto europeo de obtención de pruebas y la orden europea de investigación. In: González Cano MI (ed) Cooperación judicial penal en la Unión Europea. Tirant lo Blanch, Valencia, p 507

Giménez García J (2009) Reflexiones sobre la acción popular en el proceso penal desde la jurisprudencia de la Sala Segunda del Tribunal Supremo. Eguzkilore 23:317–323

Gutiérrez Berlinches A (2008) La celebración del juicio oral en ausencia del acusado: sus ventajas e inconvenientes. Revista de Derecho Procesal, pp 203–256

Pérez Gil J (1997) La acusación popular. Comares, Granada

Torres Muro I (2013) La condena en ausencia: unas preguntas osadas (ATC 86/2011, de 9 de junio) y una respuesta contundente (Sentencia del Tribunal de Justicia de la Unión Europea de 26 de febrero de 2013). Revista Española de Derecho Constitucional 97:343–370

Torres Pérez A (2010) Euroorden y conflictos constitucionales: a propósito de la STC 199/2009, de 28 de septiembre de 2009. Revista Española de Derecho Europeo 35:441–471

Part III
Personal Participation in Court Proceedings and *In Absentia* Trials in Comparative Criminal and Civil Justice

Participatory Rights in Comparative Criminal Justice. Similarities and Divergences Within the Framework of the European Law

Serena Quattrocolo

Abstract This chapter is devoted to comparing the results of the national reports on the basis of the Attachment. The comparison aims to cast light on similarities, if existing, and divergences between the different domestic jurisdictions. The comparative process moves from a hypothesis to be assessed: whether it is possible to argue that the ECHR and the EU legislation have shaped a common core of rules, regulating the participatory rights in criminal proceedings regardless the different legal traditions. To respond to this question, the chapter highlights the most relevant differences between the selected member states, with regard to the specific topics that have been addressed by the study, which is based on a multidisciplinary pattern and encompasses also specific EU law-, ECHR-, constitutional law- and criminal law-based analysis of participatory rights.

As the reader has seen in the first part of this Section, each national summary approached the Attachment with a different attitude, based on the individuals' legal tradition and personal sensitivity. Thus, some remarks are not 'universal', but try to highlight, at least, 'common trends'.

In fact, the identification of 'common trends' is the major result of this comparative study. However, a great number of divergences also emerged, demonstrating that, even though the ECtHR case-law and the recent 'ABC directives' of the EU had a strong impact on the national orders, some major differences still exist in the inner concept of what *in absentia trial* is and how it must be regulated, in compliance with fundamental rights. Nevertheless, it stems from this comparison that the values underpinning the parties' personal contribution to the proceedings are facing a general crisis. In particular, the defendant's non-participation, for different reasons and in various manners, is a growing phenomenon, now affecting even jurisdictions that have historically emphasized the importance of such personal participation.

S. Quattrocolo (✉)
Department of Law, and Political, Economic and Social Sciences, University of Piemonte Orientale, Alessandria, Italy
e-mail: serena.quattrocolo@uniupo.it

© Springer Nature Switzerland AG 2019
S. Quattrocolo, S. Ruggeri (eds.), *Personal Participation in Criminal Proceedings*, Legal Studies in International, European and Comparative Criminal Law 2, https://doi.org/10.1007/978-3-030-01186-4_14

Abbreviations

AFSJ	Area of Freedom Security and Justice
CCP	Code of Criminal Procedure
CJEU	Court of Justice of the European Union
CoE	Council of Europe
Const.	Constitution
CPS	Crown Prosecution Service
EAW	European Arrest Warrant
ECHR	European Convention on Human Rights
ECtHR	European Court of Human Rights
EIO	European Investigation Order
EU	European Union
FD	Framework Decision
ICC	International Criminal Court
ICCPR	International Covenant on Civil and Political Rights
JHA	Justice and Home Affaires
MLA	Mutual Legal Assistance
MS	Member State of the EU
PACE	Police and Criminal Evidence Act
TFEU	Treaty on the Functioning of the European Union
US	United States of America

1 Preliminary Remarks. Constitutional Requirements of the Involvement of Private Parties in Criminal Justice

The main aim of this study was to offer readers a comprehensive overview of a number of European Union jurisdictions. The national rapporteurs were asked to incorporate the specific topic of private parties' participation in criminal proceeding, within a general summary of their domestic system.[1] Thus, the reader is provided with a wide legal framework, allowing her to appreciate the prominence of adversarialism within each domestic system.

---

[1] The main inspiration for this work is based on what still remains the most ambitious project in European comparative criminal procedure, M. Delmas-Marty's *Procédures pénales d'Europe*. However, the basis and the means of this study are narrower. The main tool of the comparative section was the form that the reader can find in the Attachment. There were no round ups, but almost individual discussions to clarify some specific aspects. If the goal of that pioneer research was to compare rules, systems, tools and practices, our main focus was the rules regulating participatory rights. Of course, the national rapporteurs enriched their reports with references to the systems and to the most popular trends in domestic practice.

However, to prevent falling into what G.P. Fletcher calls the "reportorial trap",[2] this section aims to compare the outcomes of national investigations. It is recognised that one of the major challenges and limitations of comparison in law is characterised by the choice of a proper approach.[3]

On the one hand, Fletcher himself harshly criticised the common attitude to "suppress difference", aspiring to find convergence between jurisdictions, rather than divergence.[4] On the other hand, comparative studies in criminal law have been criticized because of an opposite approach. It has been argued that "criminal law and criminal procedure instead remained consigned within the boundaries of contrastive comparison, one that limits itself to the analysis of differences".[5] However, recent phenomena, such as the establishment of the ICC and, in particular, the evolution that occurred within the EU, from the former "third pillar" system to the new settlement of competences (articles 82 and 83) in the consolidated TFEU, have ultimately enhanced an integrative approach in the comparative study of criminal law and procedure.[6]

Such an ambition is appealing, in this context. Is it possible to draw from these national overviews the common core of private parties' participation in criminal proceeding in the European Union area? Each domestic jurisdiction is a member of both the Council of Europe and the European Union: within these two organisations, the European countries unquestionably experienced a converging normative trend. Thus, a legitimate expectation could be to detect a merging landscape. But if it is true that "the priority of alterity must act as a governing postulate for the comparatist",[7] the approach adopted here tries to overcome, at least, any *praesumptio similitudinis*.[8]

In presenting the method of this work, I must acknowledge some preconditions. If "the comparative method is founded upon the actual observation of the elements at work in a given legal system", I made this observation on the basis of a hypothesis.[9] The question I moved from is the existence of a common core of principles and regulations among the countries of the CoE, with regard to participatory rights. For instance, this does not mean that I had an expectation to find it. As a consequence, the analysis of the results will place much value on diversity for two main reasons.

---

[2] Fletcher (1998), p. 691.

[3] For an historical overview of the extensive debate on the meaning of 'comparative law' and its methods, see Ancel (1971), esp. pp. 30 ff.

[4] Fletcher (1998), p. 694.

[5] Grande (2013), p. 192. According to this Author, comparison in criminal law and procedure for a long time simply meant to learn from a distance a good or bad example of a foreign law, if not passively to accept the hegemony of a foreign legal system.

[6] Grande (2013), p. 193 f.

[7] Legrand (1997), p. 124.

[8] Zweigert and Kötz (1998), p. 40.

[9] Sacco (1991), p. 25.

Firstly, diversity can endorse a valuable critical review of each domestic jurisdiction, inspiring a reconsideration[10] of the entire subject of private parties' right to be present at the proceedings.

Secondly, the aspiration to achieve, within the AFSJ, a major approximation in the protection of individuals' fundamental rights within criminal proceedings demonstrates the enduring differences that still exist between member states. If ECHR and EU law provide minimum standards of protection, it is important to assess whether divergences between member states are still rooted in a lack of minimum protection or, actually, highlight a greater appreciation of the value of personal presence by some jurisdictions.

In light of this approach, each of the points listed in the Attachment will be considered diachronically. Convergent trends will be summarised firstly, whilst, if present, relevant dissimilarities will be explicitly identified in opposition to the general trend, if existing.

The conclusions will summarise the *status quo*. Without expecting to find it, we will assess whether a common core of the private parties' right to be present exists or not[11]: if yes, to what extent it is due to the influence of ECHR and EU law; if not, how inter-/supranational law could still enhance the achievement of a common minimum standard of protection in this field.

The first point of this study aims at identifying whether the domestic jurisdictions list the right of the private parties to be present in criminal justice amongst their constitutional guarantees.[12]

A short foreword could be useful. Although the Attachment does not expressly dwell on the classic distinction between monist and dualist systems, this issue is clearly related to the first point of this comparative-law study. In considering constitutional provisions setting forth the protection of the private parties' right to participate in criminal justice, an important preliminary remark concerns the structure of each jurisdiction, either monist (e.g.: international law and the domestic legal systems constitute a unified normative system, in which international law has supremacy over state law) od dualist (e.g. the national and international law systems exist independently and the first must incorporate the latter into a piece of domestic legislation). Assuming that 'monism' and 'dualism' are not pure and absolute concepts (as in realty we see occasions where the influence of the two concepts converge),[13] those countries that tend to incorporate international treaties automatically, at the highest layer of the legal order (like Luxembourg), mostly refer to the ECHR as the main source of constitutional guarantees for the private parties' position. The other domestic systems, tending to dualism, appear to rely on national statutory provisions: of course, the interpretation and implementation of those provisions were

---

[10] Grande (2003), p. 147.

[11] Zweigert and Kötz (1998), p. 33: "all one can do is to take a method as a hypothesis and test its usefulness and practicability".

[12] The topic of participatory rights will be expressly analysed from the point of view of constitutional law in another part of this work. In particular see Pollicino and Bassino, in this volume.

[13] Sperduti (1977), pp. 31 ff.

deeply influenced by the European Convention and the Strasbourg Court's decisions, albeit somewhat indirectly. This second group is certainly the largest one, as the majority of the countries show a progressive adjustment of existing original provisions to align with the European Court's increasing focus on the parties' right to be present at criminal proceedings.

Two general trends arise from the national overviews. A very small group of countries, Portugal and Spain,[14] demonstrates an explicit constitutional recognition of the private parties' right to be involved in criminal proceedings.

Art. 32 of the Portuguese Constitution clearly stipulates a comprehensive list of rights of the accused, one of which being the right to be present (par. 6) at procedural acts (the lawmakers chose a negative form, establishing that the law shall define the cases in which personal presence can be dispensed with). Moreover, pursuant to a 1997 amendment, par. 7 of the same provision sets forth that victims have the right to intervene in criminal proceedings.

As to Spain, Constitutions traditionally guarantee an individual's right to prosecute offences, either as *acusador particular* (being the victim of the crime), or *acusador popular* (without being the victim). Although providing different standards of protection, Spanish constitutional law acknowledges the procedural role of these private parties, as well as their right to take part in the proceedings. The defendant's right to be present does not appear to enjoy the same acknowledgment. However, *acusadores* and accused benefit from a common list of guarantees in front of the court, which are listed in articles 24, 18 and 17 of the 1978 Constitution, but are not directly related to their personal presence at the procedural acts.

With the exception of these member states, the others show, as mentioned, a progressive incorporation of the ECtHR interpretation of art. 6(1) into pre-existing constitutional provisions, via the implementation of statutory amendments or the 'evolution' in the courts' interpretation. Among them, some jurisdictions, inspired by a monist system, do not allow for specific constitutional principles, but rely on the ECHR direct application, in particular of article 6. This seems to be the case with Luxembourg, where the increased emphasis of the jurisprudence towards a monistic approach to international treaties brought the courts to a direct application of the ECHR and the related Strasbourg case-law. Austria granted the ECHR a constitutional status, allowing national courts to apply the Convention directly, and the Constitutional Court to repeal any national law infringing it.[15] Similarly, article 28 of the Greek Constitution provides for the direct application of the ECHR, so that the latter prevails over any contrary statutory provision, but not over the Constitution

---

[14] See Costa Ramos and Churro, in this volume, Sect. 1; Villamarin López, in this volume, Sect. 1.

[15] Interestingly enough, it seems that the Austrian system incorporated the ECHR by transforming the violations of the Convention into infringements on domestic procedural law: the party, whose participatory right (directly granted by the Convention) has been infringed upon, must promptly challenge it, in order not to be prevented by a time limit from doing so. The issue of transforming conventional violations into domestic procedural violations was discussed in Italy as well: see Kostoris (2011), pp. 474 ff.

itself. The latter, however, provides individuals with the right to seek protection by courts and to be heard by a judge (art. 20).

In the other cases, "access to justice", "right to defence" and "fair trial" appear to be the main principles through which European countries recognise and protect the individuals' participatory rights. With a wide range of solutions, each having variable force, the constitutional apparatus of any jurisdiction encompasses the individuals' right to participate in criminal justice, as a complementary condition for other guarantees.

France has in article 16 of the Declaration of the Rights of Man and Citizen a solemn statement of every private party's right to access to justice, having their case heard by a judge. Based on this principle, the *Conseil Constitutionnel* increased the participatory rights of the *partie civile*, levelling out her position and that of the accused.

England and Wales display a multifaceted framework, because of their tradition of unwritten formal constitution. If it is true that since "the most important provision relating to participatory rights is of course the *Human Rights Act 1998*",[16] access to justice is generally considered to be a pillar of common law and of other statutes with constitutional relevance. However, the fact that Parliament theoretically could, at any stage, legislate contrary to the fundamental principles of human rights does not deprive those principles of their power. Access to justice also seems to be the key to granting constitutional protection to participatory rights in Romania.

In Germany, the State's obligation to respect human dignity, set forth by the Constitution, is considered to be the fundamental source for the accused's participatory rights. However, it is from the right to a fair hearing that the defendant's personal right to impact her trial derives. Both in Italy and Hungary, the defendant's right to be involved in criminal proceedings is embedded in the principle of fair trial, even though, in Italy, before the constitutional amendment of 1999 (incorporating into article 111 Cost. many of the article 6 ECHR guarantees), participatory rights were protected under the umbrella of the right to defence (art. 24 Cost.). In Bulgaria, the right to defence, for individuals and legal entities is still considered to be the root of any participatory right.

In view of the considerations reported in the national summaries, it appears that none of the twelve countries fully overlooks participatory rights at the constitutional level. However, there are important differences that can be summarised. Firstly, the main difference is between constitutional systems providing—either expressly or indirectly—also for protection of the victims' and *parties civiles*' participatory rights, and systems affecting only the accused's rights. Private parties, other than the accused, still struggle to find open acknowledgment, at the constitutional level, for their right to be involved in criminal justice.

Secondly, whilst few Constitutions, among those of the jurisdictions taken into account, expressly mention the parties' presence and participation, in the remaining ones such guarantees derive from an evolutionary interpretation given by the Constitutional Courts to pre-existing principles. This phenomenon could directly

---

[16] Leader, in this volume, Sect. 1.

impinge on the very existence of the guarantees themselves. In fact, the Courts' evolutionary interpretation, although generally influenced by the ECtHR case-law, might always be overruled. In particular political situations, the risk of a restrictive overruling is more probable than the implementation of a restraining constitutional amendment.

2   Personal Participation of Private Parties and Legal Assistance

Point B of the Attachment covers a wide range of issues. The approach was deliberately general, in order to allow the authors to focus on the most relevant features of individuals' participation in criminal proceedings in their jurisdictions. In this section, several crucial aspects emerged from the national summaries. Reading and comparing them gives the impression of a huge jigsaw puzzle, whose pieces do not fit together. At a first glance, differences seem to prevail over similarities, and it is not easy to find common patterns underpinning the different systems. However, there are some recurrent features, from which it is possible to progress.

The first remarkable characteristic is the distinction, present in many member states, between parties and other participants who are involved in criminal proceedings. Some jurisdictions emphasise a strong distinction between these two roles. At least formally, the parties have a stronger position, which implies a wider range of procedural rights, while the other 'participants' have less opportunity, either under the participatory guarantees or the evidence strategy. In Bulgaria, for instance, scholars distinguish between 'participants', 'subjects' and 'parties'.[17] It is possible to say that all criminal justice systems provide at least one specific feature underpinning the distinction between parties and participants. This is the strength of each individual's interest in the proceedings. In fact, the parties usually are those who have a direct interest in the decision that will be delivered. On the contrary, other participants, such as witnesses, expert-witnesses and other individuals barely bringing their personal or professional knowledge to the proceedings have no interests in the outcome of the proceedings. Thus, not all jurisdictions treat them as parties to the proceedings. Although this distinction is generally confirmed by the national reports, in several countries the position of the victim does not seem to tally with it. According to a traditional approach, the victim is often viewed similarly to the other witnesses, even though her interest in the ruling of the case is crucial. Only those who are party to the proceedings can exercise a decisive participatory influence on the outcome of the criminal trial while the victim usually has not such power,[18]

---

[17] Petrova, in this volume, Sect. 1.

[18] Although Directive 2012/29/EU directly aimed at granting victims a wider and clearer role in criminal proceedings then the one they usually have, the national rule-makers were not bound to confer victims the role of a party in the criminal trials.

unless she claims a specific position, either filling a complaint for damages or assuming a prosecutorial role.

As a matter of fact, member states provide very different domestic regulations on this issue, some of them granting certain private subjects a prominent role as assistants of the public prosecutor. It is important to focus on this aspect as a first relevant example of the existing divergence between the several jurisdictions considered by this study. Bulgaria, England and Wales, Germany, Hungary, Portugal and Spain acknowledge the role of private individuals—essentially victims, but not exclusively—as "complementary" prosecutors, sometimes assisting, sometimes challenging the prosecutor's decisions.[19] This can lead to situations in which the proceedings may reach the trial stage even if the prosecutor decided to drop the case (Portugal,[20] or Bulgaria, where in "privately actionable cases" no pre-trial stage is offered and the file goes straight to trial). Other countries, for instance, such as Italy, do not recognise any prosecutorial role to individuals or entities other than the public prosecutor. Among the jurisdictions allowing for private prosecution, we can observe significant differences regarding the right to access legal aid: in some cases (e.g. Portugal and Spain), the "private prosecutor" is allowed access to financial help, via legal aid; in other cases, such an opportunity is denied (e.g. England and Wales).

Occasionally, the national rapporteurs also focused on legal entities, specifying whether and how they can participate in criminal proceedings. Although this point has not been addressed in all reports, it appears that only in Romania, Portugal, England and Wales can the legal person be made the object of criminal proceedings, that is to say can be accused of the perpetration of a crime, assuming the role of suspect/defendant. Generally speaking, legal entities are more often assimilated to the other private parties, namely the 'civil claimant' or the 'civil responsible' (for the damages or the fine).[21]

The second pattern is related to the strength of the defence rights granted to the parties and the other participants. From this perspective, the distinction between

---

[19] As to private prosecution in the different jurisdiction, it is worth highlighting that the role of individuals in such a context significantly varies from State to State. The relationship with the public prosecution can be tailored in several different ways, sometimes leading to a kind of complete 'independence' of the private accusation from the prosecutor's decisions (like in Portugal, provided that an investigative judge approves it, or in Bulgaria, with the "privately actionable cases"), sometimes dispatching the private action under the control of the CPS (England and Wales).

[20] With the exception of private crimes, where the assistant can lodge a private accusation that will move directly to trial if the pre-trial judicial stage is not requested by the accused. On the contrary in public and semi-private crimes, the investigative judge must confirm the 'private prosecution' (which is the application to open the pre-trial judicial stage; application in which it is up for the assistant to outline the facts that will build the basis of the possible 'judicial indictment').

[21] In Italy, for instance, an insurance company can be held responsible for the damages caused by the defendant in negligent road injuries cases; an employer must pay the criminal fine instead of her employee, if the latter is insolvent and it is demonstrated that she perpetrated the crime in the interest (even putative) of the employer.

parties and subjects is not always crucial. In some jurisdictions, the subjects have the same defence rights as the parties. In fact, regarding the second topic of this section, attention should be drawn not only to the distinction between parties and subjects, but also between the suspect/defendant and the other private parties. Although this is not a general feature, in many countries the defendant is permitted much stronger defence rights (e.g., in Austria). However, the twelve summaries display different layers of flexibility in regulating her right to defence. Two clarifications can help us summing up the different domestic approaches. Firstly, several differences depend on the way the various jurisdictions conceive of the 'defence': even though defence is always a defendant's right, it is sometimes considered also to entail a duty. Secondly, a crucial distinction is often drawn between pre-trial and trial phase: the countries examined place different emphasis on granting the accused defence rights during the proceedings. Usually, the level of protection depends on how deeply and crucially the acts of that phase will impact on the adjudication of the case. We shall analyse these two topics separately.

In some way, it is possible to 'measure' how wide the access to a lawyer is in the various jurisdictions. As has already been mentioned, some countries consider the right to legal assistance to be a duty for the defendant. In fact, there are countries in which the suspect/accused does not have the right to self-representation. In Italy, defendants must be assisted by a lawyer in all criminal trials regardless of whether they are charged with extremely serious or petty crimes. This stems from the principle of the general interest of justice: both the prosecutor and the trial court need to interact with a professional subject, i.e. the lawyer, who is not influenced by personal emotions and interests, as is instead the defendant. Thus, Italian law tailors this right as a duty, providing for mandatory legal assistance for any suspect or defendant, regardless of the seriousness of crime and the defendant's potential to waive her right. It stems from this constitutional law principle that the rule-maker must provide the accused with a lawyer appointed *ex officio*, whenever she does not have a counsel of her own choosing.[22] Bulgaria and Portugal seem to share the concept of mandatory legal assistance.[23] On the contrary, other jurisdictions have a different concept of the 'interest of justice', also impinging, but the other way around, on the right to access a lawyer. In several cases, the *ex officio* appointment of a lawyer for less well-off defendants is submitted to the interest of justice (e.g. England and Wales, where the 'interest of justice test' covers: kind of

---

[22] Art. 97 CCP-Italy sets forth a system of *ex officio* appointment (by the judge or by the prosecutor) for any act of the procedure to which the lawyer must assist. Lawyers willing to be appointed *ex officio* enter a system run by each Bar Order: based on an annual calendar they will serve periods of availability. They cannot refuse the *ex officio* appointment (with the exception of some special cases). *Ex officio* appointment, in Italy, is not related, in any way, to the defendant's means. The system of legal aid is completely separated from the ex officio appointment. A less well-off defendant should first apply for legal aid; if she meets the means test, she will be granted legal aid and she will be allowed to appoint a lawyer of her choice. If, for any reason, she does not appoint one, there will be an ex officio assignment.

[23] Petrova, in this volume, Sect. 2.

case, history of the offender, seriousness of the consequences. See also, Austria,[24] Germany[25]).

The issue of mandatory legal assistance represents one of the basic features of each domestic order. The Italian model seems to be almost unique and is based on absolute mandatory attendance of the lawyer at trial and at a list of investigation acts that the latter must attend. Usually, the results of the investigation (by the prosecutor, the police or the defence) are not admissible as such at trial: the parties have full access to the investigation file, even though only after the completion of the investigative phase, but the trial judge cannot access it. The majority of the other jurisdictions (except Portugal) accept self-representation at trial, although specifying a list of cases in which the lawyer's presence is mandatory, either at trial or during the investigation (see, e.g. France, Luxembourg). In some cases, a recent increase in investigative acts requiring the mandatory presence of a lawyer was inspired by the ECtHR case-law.[26] In many of these jurisdictions, investigative acts have a greater impact on the trial phase. However, it does not seem possible to conclude that there is a precise pattern behind this strategy. Traditional approaches and reforms have overlapped in recent decades, especially under the influence of the European Convention and the EU Directive 2013/48 imposing the increased prominence of the issue of access to a lawyer.

The study pointed out some landmarks. Firstly, there is often concurrence, in the domestic systems, of *ex officio* appointment and access to legal aid. The interest of justice, the mandatory presence of a lawyer and the defendant's socio-economic position may often results in concurring requirements for *ex officio* appointment. Secondly, with specific regard to the presence of a lawyer in the trials held *in absentia*, the general trend is to consider it mandatory or at least possible. As a rule, Greece also provides for such possibilities; however, Greek law includes also a regulation that stipulates that a defendant who is formally and lawfully summoned but fails to appear and to appoint a lawyer will not be *ex officio* represented at trial.[27]

A third problematic issue is the relationship between the private parties and the lawyer. From this angle, several topics are relevant within the twelve countries.

Following the distinction drawn in the previous paragraph, some jurisdictions grant lawyers a specific set of rights and powers other than that of their clients (see Hungary).[28] In some cases, the lawyer's rights and the defendant's rights overlap, but the former exercises them on her own and not on behalf of the latter. The French case is particularly interesting, as the *Conseil Constitutionnel* had to intervene twice to grant two private parties—namely, the accused and *partie civile*—the right to

---

[24] Golser, in this volume, Sect. 2.

[25] Vogel, in this volume, Sect. 2.

[26] ECtHR, *Salduz v. Turkey*, judgment of 27 November 2008, Appl. No. 36391/02. See France, with the '*garde à vue* saga' and Luxembourg, where the Salduz case, even if not binding for that State, inspired main amendments.

[27] Billis and Gkaniatsos, in this volume, Sect. 2.

[28] Gácsi et al., in this volume, Sect. 2.

personally access a piece of information contained in the file, without the assistance of a lawyer.[29] Moreover, in France the lawyer's presence is mandatory to grant effectiveness to the defendant's choice of a summary proceeding, the *comparution sur reconnaissance préalable de culpabilité*. In other countries the lawyer can exercise the client's rights, on her behalf, but holds a specific set of guarantees deriving from her professional privileges (e.g. Austria, Italy, Portugal). This issue is of the utmost importance taking into account the distinction between assistance and representation by a lawyer, a topic in which the member states show very different regulations. Representation is not always included in the mandate stemming from the appointment: in Germany, e.g., the lawyer can represent her client only if the latter authorised her and in the cases allowed by the law, with the exception of the cases that imply a waiver of the defendant's fundamental rights. In such cases, the defendant—who must be assisted by a lawyer—cannot be represented by the latter, but must express her will personally.

The issue of the lawyer's powers of representation, deriving straight from their appointment, is crucial in cases of *in absentia* proceedings. In such situations, the defendant is not personally present and the lawyer must be able to represent her: otherwise, the defendant's prerogatives cannot be exercised. However, there are cases in which the defendant, who failed to appear and to appoint a lawyer of her own choice, will be tried *in absentia*, without the presence and representation of a lawyer. This happens in Greece,[30] provided that the defendant was regularly summoned (otherwise she has the right to be retried) and in Luxembourg, where, however, the defendant has the right to be re-tried, if she appears.[31]

3 Personal Participation of the Accused in Criminal Proceedings

3.1 General Features of Personal Participation: Absolute Individual Right or Duty of Diligence

As a preliminary note, it is important to stress that personal participation undergoes different limitations depending on specific stages of the proceedings. In most jurisdictions, participation becomes stronger at the judicial stage, while investigations tend to be almost secret. In every country, the concept of 'participation' entails a previous charge and the commencement of the trial. In particular, the French report lingers over this distinction, focusing on the general postponement of personal participation after the completion of the investigation, as will be expressly addressed in Sect. 3.2.

---

[29] Drevet, in this volume, Sect. 2.

[30] See fn. 27.

[31] Art. 187 CCP-Luxembourg.

The distinction between right and duty perhaps marks the most conventional approach to the defendant's participatory rights adopted in the literature. However, the results of this study show that, nowadays, this distinction is decreasingly explicit, displaying rather a collection of different situations in which several divergent interests merge.

England and Wales offer an almost paradigmatic example, highlighting the interesting evolution from a resolved, traditional approach, providing for mandatory presence, to the current multifaceted regulation, which allows for alternative forms of participation and also absence. The defendant's duty to be present in court seems to reflect the idea of the authority of the law over the body of the accused, which still influences some of the courtroom rules, such as the use of the dock in all criminal trials.[32] Some scholarship couples the duty to be present with the right to confrontation, even though many authors in England and Wales underline that the latter is weaker than it is in continental Europe and in the US. In any case, the obligation to attend court hearings has undergone a trend of progressive limitation in this jurisdiction. On the one hand, two cases of absence are provided: nowadays, in England and Wales, *in absentia* trials are permitted for indictable offences; secondly, the defendant can be removed from court in case of disruptive behaviour. On the other, an alternative form of participation has been introduced via technological devices, providing for remote participation of accused remanded in custody (or defendants), for bail hearings, but also pre-trial and sentencing hearings. For at least a decade, the discussion on video-link participation has gained the ECtHR's attention[33]: in fact, remote participation *is* a limitation of the defendants' participatory rights, which must be balanced with general interests, like the prevention of organised crime.[34]

The evolution that has taken place in England and Wales from an 'obligation to be present' to less strict provisions, allowing both absence and remote participation, provides a paradigmatic example of the vagueness of the concept of 'participatory rights'.

In fact, not only is presence not absolutely mandatory in those countries considering it a right, but, as seen above, it is not absolute even where it is considered to be an obligation.[35] Several countries, other than England and Wales, consider participation both a right and a duty: Austria, Germany, Luxembourg, Portugal and Spain show such a twofold attitude and impart appropriate consequences for absence. In Austria, the defendant must cover the cost of rescheduling the hearing. In Germany, the defendant's presence is deemed necessary to uncover the truth, which is the aim of any criminal proceeding and if the defendant is not able to prove sufficient justification for non-appearing, she can be arrested for the duration of the trial. In Luxembourg, courts can deliver, in some cases, an order to appear. In

---

[32] See Quattrocolo and Ruggeri in Part I of this volume, Sect. 2.1.

[33] The leading case is, still, ECtHR, *Marcello Viola v. Italy*, judgment of 5 October 2006, Appl. No. 45106/04.

[34] See Sect. 3.2.

[35] See England and Wales (Leader, in this volume, Sect. 3.1) and Spain, with regard to abbreviated proceedings and non-serious offences (Villamarin López, in this volume, Sect. 3.1).

Portugal, failure to appear can result in arrest, fines, suspension of civil and political rights, while in Spain, it results in the suspension of the proceedings (with the exception of abbreviated proceedings and non-serious offences). In conclusion, in those countries considering presence a as duty (or also as duty), absence is not a legitimate defence strategy, as it is considered to be in Italy, for instance. On the contrary, if participation is primarily a right and not a duty (see Hungary and Greece), the defendant should be able to waive it, without negative consequences (except those deriving directly from her absence, that she accepted with the waiver). Impressively enough, in Bulgaria *in absentia* trials can be the consequence of a defendant's free choice or of her poor health not allowing her to physically take part in the hearings).

However, we saw that, even where presence is considered to be a right, this right is not absolute. Firstly, like England and Wales, many other countries (see Italy, Germany, Austria, e.g.) allow for removal of the defendant from the courtroom, in the case of disruptive behaviour. Secondly, many jurisdictions allow for remote participation, even if for different reasons. Thus, England and Wales and Germany prescribe remote participation in the interest of truth and witnesses. In Italy, the original purpose of the lawmakers was to prevent inmates from contacting their criminal organisation during the hearings; however, a very recent reform, namely Law 103/2017, largely extended the video-link participation, beyond the context of organised crime and, within the this field, also to defendants at liberty.[36]

The multifaceted nature of the defendant's presence can offer a justification for the inconsistency among the regulations of European countries of *in absentia* trials. Personal participation reflects the inner workings of each country's criminal justice system. The purpose of the proceedings; the nature of the defendant's role (is she the subject of the proceeding or rather the object of it?); the intensity of the state's punitive power is reflected into the national rules on the defendant's presence in trial. Considering the national results on this point, it is possible to argue that criminal proceedings nevertheless have heterogeneous goals throughout the European continent: personal participation of the defendant reflects divergent historical approaches that still underpin the domestic systems of criminal justice, expressing a different balance between public authority and individuals' role.

3.2   Personal Participation in the Pre-trial Inquiry (with Particular Regard for the Interim Decisions on Coercive Measures)

As set forth in the previous paragraph, the relevance of participatory rights increases with the development of the proceedings. In approaching the general topic of the right to participation, some of the reports highlighted very limited allowances for it

---

[36] Signorato (2017), p. 5 f.; Daniele (2017b), p. 2.

during the investigation, for both the defendant and the victim. However, this specific area of regulation displays, today, the effects of two recent Directives, namely Directive 2012/29/EU and Directive 2012/13/EU, the former establishing minimum standards on the rights, support and protection of victims of crime (replacing Council Framework Decision 2001/220/JHA), the latter allowing for right to information in criminal proceedings. Both legal instruments had a significant impact on an aspect that is strictly related to personal participation, this is to say information. In many cases I could find an express reference to these directives, and even where they are not explicitly mentioned, the right to be informed about one's own rights proves to be a basic ground for exercising the right to be present.

As a result, lack of information seems to hinder the defendant's proactive participation in the proceedings instituted against her. This happens in England and Wales, particularly. *Leader* clearly emphasises that the majority of the defendants at the magistrates' court enter a guilty plea, at a very early stage of the proceedings.[37] In fact, an early plea of guilty is encouraged by a sentence reduction: the sooner the guilty plea, the higher the reduction of the sentence. Such a mechanism affects the defendant's interests, as she often lacks information about the charge and her position in the proceedings, at the time when she is asked to decide, especially in those (many) cases where there may have been no appointment of a lawyer.

Personal participation in pre-trial inquiry is often affected by the results of a traditional civil-law mechanism, which is still allowed for by some member states: the two-track investigation—consisting of a police inquiry and a judicial investigation—is still prevalent in France and Luxembourg. The judicial investigation provides more opportunity for personal participation.

The comparative-law examination of the selected countries outlined a widespread trend of excluding the accused's participation in the interview of witnesses during the investigation (either by police and prosecutor).[38] Several countries (Austria, Germany, Greece, Italy, Portugal) allow for an (fully accomplished or summary) 'adversarial examination' of the witness who may not be available for the trial (to come). In such cases, the defendant and[39] her lawyer can attend the hearing and interact with the witness. Beyond this (anticipating a typical trial activity), there is no common regulation, in the domestic jurisdictions, of the investigative acts that the accused can attend personally. She *must* be present in searches and inspections of her own body and premises but, each domestic regulation lays out its own sequence of investigative acts and the subsequent right of the accused (and her lawyer) to take part into it or not. It is worth stressing that in some countries, defendants can not only largely participate in investigative acts (Greece, Spain), but can also request investigative measures to be performed in their interest by the police or prosecutor (e.g. Greece, Luxembourg, Portugal, France during the judicial

---

[37] Leader, in this volume, Sect. 3.1.

[38] As to Italy, the regulation of witnesses' interview during the investigation has been often amended, with special regard to vulnerable people (see, e.g. art. 351 co. 1-ter CCP); however, amendments never encompassed the form of confrontation with the suspect.

[39] Or her lawyer, e.g., in Greece.

investigation; in Italy, where many of the investigative acts are secret, a considerable set of rules regulates the defendant's and victim's right to hold their own private investigations: requesting the prosecutor to perform an act on their behalf [or, at least, in their interest] is scarcely a residual option).

Interestingly, some jurisdictions allow for personal participation of the defendant in the procedure on the dismissal of the case. In Italy, where prosecution is mandatory, the competent judge for the pre-trial inquiry can, *ex officio* or after the victim's objection against the prosecutor's request for dismissal, order a closed hearing, of which the suspect must be notified.

The twelve summaries, moreover, provide a very interesting overview on the personal participation in incidental proceedings on remand into custody and further pre-trial measures. Firstly, some jurisdictions allow for appearance and confrontation before the coercive measure is decided. This happens in France, in Spain, in Romania (only for certain types of measures), and in Austria. On the contrary, participation seems to be the general rule in custody review proceedings. The study demonstrates that it is permitted[40] extensively, even though there is widespread acceptance of 'remote participation'. In many countries, the accused remanded in custody should appear at the hearing (bail hearing and first hearing, in England and Wales; Germany, for pre-trial detention review) via video-link from the remote place of detention. As argued above, this can hamper the individual's opportunities for being granted bail (see England and Wales),[41] or other alternative measures in her favour. Legal scholarship has on several occasions stressed that videoconference may hinder the defendant's rights, or may at least negatively impact their sense of being afforded an effective self-defence.[42] In particular, *Leader* observes that appearing from a prison may affect how a defendant is perceived by the court, impinging on the defendant's presumption of innocence.[43]

Several fundamental rights are involved here. On the one hand, Article 5(3) ECHR stipulates that

> Everyone arrested or detained in accordance with the provisions of paragraph 1 (c) of this Article shall be brought promptly *before a judge* or other officer authorised by law to exercise judicial power.

Does the term *before* necessarily imply a physical presence or is video-link participation compliant with the provision? ECtHR case law on Article 5(3) focuses on the prerogatives of the judge or "other officer"—their independence from the prosecutor or other political bodies—rather than on the place or method of the interview. Even though the Court, in *Schiesser v. Switzerland*,[44] ruled that "the procedural

---

[40] But, in Austria, the appeal against a coercive measure is decided by the court without a hearing. Golser, in this volume, Sect. 3.1.

[41] Leader, in this volume, Sect. 3.1.

[42] However one of the very first study made in the US by Terry and Surette (1986), p. 34 showed a high satisfaction between defendants with their appearance with videoconference.

[43] See also Vogler (2012), p. 89.

[44] ECtHR, *Schiesser v. Switzerland*, judgment of 4 December 1979, Appl. No. 7710/76.

requirement places the 'officer' under the obligation of hearing himself the individual brought before him", case-law does not provide for further interpretation of the terms "hearing himself" and it is not possible to dismiss the possibility that a video-link can satisfy this requirement.

As to the participation in the trial stage, the ECtHR case-law on the defendant's right to be personally present has since *Colozza v. Italy* been the foundation of the whole doctrine of the Court about *in absentia* judgments.[45] The Court has always reiterated that the system of guarantees provided by Article 6 ECHR (and, in particular, para. 3) entails personal presence in court, to hear and follow the proceedings and to give confidential instructions to the lawyer. However, as said, in the case of *Marcello Viola*, the Court stipulated that in the interest of victims and witnesses, and to prevent other serious crimes, the video conference participation of the defendant, being charged with extremely serious organised crimes is compliant with the principles of Article 6 ECHR. Even though "admittedly, it is possible that, on account of technical problems, the link between the hearing room and the place of detention will not be ideal, and thus result in difficulties in transmission of the voice or images",[46] nothing hampered, in that specific case, the applicant's fundamental rights.[47] It is worth noting that the substance of this decision is based on the balance between the fundamental relevance of the defendant's personal presence and the need to fight organised crime in an efficient way. On the contrary, the national reports refer to video-link participation regardless of the nature of the accusation, and certainly not in the realm of organised crime. Do such situations concur with the view expressed by the ECtHR in the abovementioned judgment? In fact, the sacrifice of the defendant's rights does not seem to be balanced against other relevant interests. However, it must be remarked that the ECtHR adjudicated other cases based on the claim of violation of Article 6(1) and (3) ECHR, due to the defendant's video-link participation. In particular, in *Gennadiy Medvedev v. Russia*,[48] the applicant, sentenced to 16 years of imprisonment for murder and other crimes, complained about the infringement of his right to personally take part in the hearing (appeal), because of the domestic Court's decision to allow his presence only by video-link. The decision delivered by the European Court, even though formally referring to the *Marcello Viola* case, disregarded the results of that judgment, rooted, as said, in the balance between the sacrifice of the defendant's rights and the institutional goal to defeat organised crime. In the Russian case, the issues were not related to organised crime and the Strasbourg Court simply drew on the fact that there was no evidence of a poor quality of the video-link (as the applicant did not provide evidence of this). It stems from that decision (which seems not to have been cited in subsequent Strasbourg case-law) that the only condition that can be considered reducing the defendant's right to personal participation is the quality of the

---

[45] ECtHR, *Colozza v. Italy*, judgment of 12 February 1985, Appl. No. 9024/80, para. 27.

[46] ECtHR, *Marcello Viola v. Italy* (fn. 32), para. 74.

[47] Chiavario (2008), p. 235.

[48] ECtHR, *Gennadiy Medvedev v. Russia*, judgment of 14 April 2012, Appl. No. 34184/03.

video-link, regardless of any other standard. It would be interesting to confront the Court with this (apparent) inconsistency, in order to assess if and how the Court's perception of defendant's video-link participation changed over time. In the opinion of the Court, is still video-link an exceptional restriction of fundamental rights to be balanced with other capital interests or is it a useful and efficient IT means,[49] to speed up the proceedings, provided that it has a good video and audio quality? In light of the Court's (hypothetical) assessment it would be possible to scrutinise the compliance of many of the national jurisdictions, allowing the defendant's participation via video-link participation, with the Convention.

Concluding on this point, it can be argued that the national overviews give the impression of there being a wide range of investigative acts which the accused person can attend. This conclusion is somewhat wider than the expectation, suggesting a progressive reduction of secrecy in investigations, at least from a formal point of view. In any case, it is evident that, even if allowed to participate, the defence is often deprived of a previous access to the file and this impinges negatively on the effectiveness of their participation.

Moreover, the defendant's presence during the pre-trial stage seems to be increasingly hampered within the proceedings reviewing the lawfulness of restrictive measures, as a result of the growing reliance on video-link participation.

3.3   *Personal Participation in Proceedings* **In Camera**

In camera proceedings seem to be subject to a range of different regulations in the twelve scrutinised countries. For the purpose of this investigation, *in camera* proceeding are intended as non-public hearings,[50] which can either occur in a courtroom, where public access is prohibited, or in a judicial authority's office. In any case, the sense in which the term is (generally intended and) used here is that it potentially enables the parties to confrontation, excluding from the range of *in camera* proceedings, *de plano* decisions, in which there is no hearings[51] (see. e.g., the Hungarian *in camera* sessions).[52] Some member states are completely reluctant to the idea of *in camera* proceedings in criminal matters: Austria and Spain do not allow for it at all, while in Germany, the Constitutional Court repeatedly excluded the constitutionality of those types of *in camera* proceedings, in which evidence is not disclosed to the accused.[53]

---

[49] See Van der Vils (2012), pp. 13 ff. about the European E-justice Action Plan 2009–2013 and other EU regulation focusing on video-link participation of witnesses and experts but also defendants, if personally agreed.

[50] See the definition in IATE (InterActive Terminology for Europe, www.iate.europa.eu).

[51] Ruggeri, in Part V of this volume, Sect. 2.3.

[52] Gácsi et al., in this volume, Sect. 3.3.

[53] Vogel, in this volume, Sect. 3.3.

With these exceptions, it is possible to argue that almost all the scrutinised member states provide for proceedings *in camera*, especially before the beginning of the trial, which is public by principle. The grounds to choose *huis clos* may be different,[54] but there is a certain convergence on the fact that the exclusion of the public should not impinge on the defendant's rights to be present (see e.g. England and Wales, Luxembourg and Italy, where, as a rule, the parties are heard if they appear at the *in camera* hearing). It is exactly in light of these considerations that the Romanian Constitutional Court repeatedly ruled against provisions excluding an oral and adversarial debate in front of the preliminary chamber. However, some peculiarities emerge from the national reports. In Greece, the judicial councils hold *in camera* proceedings during the pre-trial stage in which the accused does not have the right to participate, but can only enter written statements. England and Wales demonstrates a wide range of other restrictions that can be requested by the prosecutor in addition to a motion for *in camera*, such as an application for the non-disclosure of sensitive materials and an application for the defendant to remain anonymous. *Leader* recalls a very famous terrorism case, the *Incedal* case, in which the Director of Public Prosecution had requested all these motions. Only after a challenge from The Guardian newspaper and others was the name of the defendant disclosed and some parts of the trial were opened to journalists. Adjudicating that challenge, the England and Wales Court of Appeal reiterated that the defendant's rights are unchanged whether the case is heard in open court or *in camera*. However, *Leader* deems such a statement overly optimistic, not only because the defense in the *Incedal* case underwent serious restrictions, but because the Courts in England and Wales made it clear that the interests of national security can override the right to open trial and to disclosure.[55]

It is worth noting that the parties themselves may have a role in establishing non-public hearings. In France, for example, some types of proceedings held by the Investigation Chamber are public (challenges of remand in custody; extradition and EAW); as to the remand in custody proceedings, the parties can ask for *huis clos*, because publicity may jeopardise the investigation, or hinder the presumption of innocence or even harm a person's dignity. Moreover, even if the power to decide *huis clos* rests in the judge's hands, before the criminal courts, the victim *partie civile* may ask for *in camera* proceedings in some cases listed by Article 306 CCP-France (and the defendant can do the same, indirectly: if the victim does not oppose, the court can freely decide whether to allow it). The parties also have a role in lodging an *in camera* motion in Portugal and in Italy.[56]

Concluding on this point, the twelve member states proved to have quite different regulations on *in camera* proceedings, some of them rejecting it completely. As to the parties' involvement in those jurisdictions (the majority) providing for *in*

---

[54] See *below*.

[55] Leader, in this volume, Sect. 3.2.

[56] In particular, see under Sect. 3.4, the defendant's choice for a diversion proceeding may depend on the fact that she prefers an *in camera* proceeding, avoiding *strepitus fori*.

camera proceedings, it is reasonable to say that the domestic regulation does not seem to affect their participatory rights, with the exception of Greece, where, as a rule, no personal presence is allowed before the judicial councils, in *in camera* proceedings. On the contrary, rather than compressing it, *huis clos* seems to fall within the interests of the parties that, in many cases, can enter a motion for it.

3.4   Personal Participation in Alternative Proceedings

Another relevant problem are proceedings allowing the judicial authority to adjudicate the case under a set of criteria that are different from the ones regulating the trial. In the jurisdictions that do not provide for mandatory prosecution, diversion proceedings may be alternative to prosecution and/or to sentencing.

Of course, alternative proceedings encompass negotiated justice, which represents, however, only one form of simplification. In fact, it is possible to argue that today[57] any national (or even international) system of criminal justice provides for alternative proceedings,[58] based on the need to have faster and simpler ways to adjudicate on a criminal charge in specific situations[59]: e.g. when the offence is petty; when the evidence is clear[60]; when the defendant pleads guilty; when the perpetrator is arrested; and so on. The literature about negotiated justice is burgeoning and there is no room here to linger over it, for many reasons. Firstly, negotiation is in itself a complex phenomenon, as it is considered to be the outcome of the general crisis of social rules and of traditional legal rules[61]: this gave ground to extensive research, both legal and sociological, that cannot be considered in this essay. Secondly, as said, negotiation covers only one possible ground for alternative proceeding. On the one hand, scholars tend to include into the concept of negotiation only procedures based on an arrangement, a mutual exchange between the parties, implying a mutual sacrifice to achieve a common goal. However, in many jurisdictions the legislation provides for 'adhesive proceedings',[62] in which one party takes the initiative for the alternative proceeding and the other barely accepts (even implicitly), or not at all, the conditions imposed upon, without negotiating them.[63] In any case, the result is a waiver of the defendant's procedural rights. Moreover, European countries often

---

[57] Even though settlement of dispute was a common feature of early medieval process, both on the continent and in England: Damaška (2004), p. 1020.

[58] Pradel (1995), p. 537; Maffei (2004), p. 1050.

[59] Damaška (2004), p. 1019: "the full adjudicative process is in decline everywhere".

[60] *Ibid.*, p. 1023.

[61] Ost (2002), p. 24.

[62] Pursuant the definition by Tulkens (2002), p. 643.

[63] Damaška (2004), p. 1019.

allow for accelerated proceedings based on a high standard of proof: e.g., when there has been an arrest *in flagrante delicto* or a confession.[64]

The national reports, in Section I, offer an interesting overview of the various domestic regulations. This discussion focuses on the parties' participation and of course not on the different characteristics that the alternative proceedings have in the twelve jurisdictions.

Regardless of the distinctions set forth above, some common features appear to affect the majority of the alternative proceedings described by the rapporteurs. The most common ground for holding such a proceeding is the motion or the consent of the defendant: in almost all of the scrutinised jurisdictions the law provides for at least one kind of alternative proceeding based on the defendant's agreement (Austria, Bulgaria, England and Wales, Greece, Hungary, Italy, Luxembourg, Portugal, Romania, Spain). Moreover, in many countries, another set of alternative proceedings is based on the perpetrator's arrest or apprehension (Italy, Spain, Portugal, Greece).

Both these features directly impinge on the presence of the parties at the proceedings. Firstly, the proceedings based on a defendant's request or agreement imply the personal participation of the aforementioned in the procedure. She must express her consent to the specific conditions regulating the alternative proceedings. In fact, in the 'mediation type' proceedings, there must be a settlement between offender and victim. In the 'plea bargaining type' proceedings there must be an admission of guilt [but not in the Italian 'patteggiamento'[65]]. In the alternative proceedings based on a transaction between the prosecutor [or the police], who refrains, suspends or reduces the charge, and the offender there must be an arrangement for the conditions to be respected by the latter: to pay a fine (*transaction pénale*, in France)[66]; to follow behaviour prescriptions (*messa alla prova*, in Italy,[67] the postponement of the indictment, in Hungary[68]; the provisional suspension and the closure in case of exemption of penalty in Portugal). In all these situations, the personal participation of the parties involved (perpetrator and, possibly, victim) is not only encouraged, but is mandatory, in order to ascertain the terms of the agreement. There are some exceptions (in Italy, only the defendant's lawyer presence is mandatory: the client can attend but is not forced to; in France, the *composition pénale* and the *transaction pénale* do not denote the undertaking of a hearing).

The national summaries prove that formality in the personal participation of the parties in alternative proceedings is directly related to the period in which the diversion operates. Several jurisdictions provide for very early agreements, between the police and the offender: in such cases the personal participation does not attain the

---

[64] See Pradel (1995), p. 539.

[65] Langer (2004), p. 51; Maffei (2004), p. 1061.

[66] Art. 41-1-1 CCP-France. See, however, the recent repeal by the Conseil d'Etat: Drevet, in this volume, Sect. 3.4.

[67] Art. 464-bis CCP-Italy.

[68] Gàcsi et al., in this volume, Sect. 3.4.2.

form of formal participation in a hearing. Moreover, mediation proceedings are usually based on an out-of-court contact between the victim and the offender, in order to enhance a dialogue to restore justice and often do not even result in a court hearing.[69]

Secondly, those alternative proceedings based on arrest or apprehension of the perpetrator logically imply the personal presence of the defendant at the hearing, being in custody. In Italy, where participation is a right and not a duty, the arrested defendant is permitted to waive her right to participate in the hearing (*giudizio direttissimo*).

In many jurisdictions, the prosecutor takes the initiative to start a written proceeding, by entering a request to the judge. After revising the legal conditions (that tend to differ between the many states), the competent judge delivers a strongly reduced fine, *inaudita altera parte*. This common pattern seems to inspire different legislations: The defendant can accept a reduced fine, avoiding challenging the decision; or she may decide to challenge it and undergo a fully adjudicative procedure, with no reduction of the subsequent punishment.[70] In the general scheme of these proceedings (investigator's request/judge's decision/defendant's acceptance), the parties' personal participation is completely neglected.[71] As to the Italian penal order procedure (*decreto penale di condanna*),[72] there has been discussion about its compliance with the Constitution, especially after the 1999 reform, which amended Article 111 of the Constitution, providing for adversariness as a basic feature of criminal proceedings.[73] As explained, in Italy the exceptions to this general rule must be grounded in the personal (and conscious) consent of the defendant to the non-adversarial procedure. Is the waiver of the right to challenge the judicial decision a "consent", pursuant to the definition provided for by the Constitution? The Italian Constitutional Court has always assessed the compliance with the Constitution, clearing the way for a wider application of this (extremely) alternative proceeding.[74]

Likewise, Spain has recently introduced a new proceeding (*procedimiento por aceptación de decreto*) that can be applied in a restricted area of very common and frequent crimes. The prosecutor can propose a low punishment (fine/social work/ imprisonment up to 1 year, which can be suspended). In case of acceptance by the defendant, the decision cannot be appealed and the sentence is enforceable.

---

[69] However, Directive 2012/29/EU sets forth a very wide definition of 'restorative justice', which is considered to be the paradigm of mediation: in fact, Article 2(1)(d) stipulates that "restorative justice' means any process whereby the victim and the offender are enabled, if they freely consent, to participate actively in the resolution of matters arising from the criminal offence through the help of an impartial third party". See Mannozzi (2016), pp. 1517 ff.

[70] Or, e.g. in Italy, the defendant can challenge it and request another 'special proceeding, such as *patteggiamento, giudizio abbreviato, messa alla prova*.

[71] Ruggeri (2017), p. 350.

[72] Art. 459 CCP-Italy.

[73] Ruggeri (2008), in particular pp. 155 ff.

[74] CConst. 2003/32.

However, because of the strong impact of such procedure on the fair trial guarantees, the defendant must appear in front of a judge and accept the decree personally, proving aware of the consequences of it.[75]

To partially conclude on this point, it can be argued that despite the wide variety of alternative proceedings regulated by domestic legislation, personal involvement of private parties within these seems to be characterised by some common trends. From a general viewpoint, there is a relatively high level of personal participation of defendants, victims and prosecutors. In fact, the majority of the alternative proceedings are based on a settlement: (*a*) about the consequences of the offence, between the offender and the victim, who may undergo a restorative procedure; (*b*) about the charge or the punishment, between the prosecutor and the offender, who may take part in a negotiation about these features. However, it is worth underlining that many jurisdictions tolerate a trend of genuine suppression of the parties' participatory rights in a common pattern of summary proceedings, based on an *inaudita altera parte* judicial decision,[76] applying a reduced fine. The opportunity for challenging such a decision rests on an implicit guarantee of the defendant's right to recover her participatory rights.

3.5 Personal Participation at Trial

The issue of personal participation at trial has been partially examined under C I, where we dealt with the problem of whether participation is to be viewed as a right or a duty.

Here also, the focus is not on the participatory rights at trial of the sole defendant, but of private parties in general. Comparing the national reports on this point offers a sense of general convergence, which is mainly due to the significant impact of ECtHR case-law on the privilege against self-incrimination and the equality of arms,[77] especially with regard to the admission of evidence. However, some relevant differences emerge, reflecting traditional national approaches, underpinned by deep cultural differences.

3.5.1 Personal Involvement in Evidence-Gathering

Even though this issue was not dealt with in all reports, one of the main forms of defendant's participation in fact-finding is her own interview or statements. The defendant's examination is strictly related to her right to remain silent. From a

---

[75] See Villamarin López, in this volume, Sect. 3.3.3.

[76] See *infra* Sect. 5.3.

[77] In light of the right 'to make one's voice heard', see Ruggeri, in Part V of this volume, Sect. 4.3 and in Part VI of this volume, Sect. 4.2.4.

general viewpoint, it seems that all jurisdictions comply with the fundamental right of the defendant not to be forced into self-incrimination. It stems from this remark that none of the criminal justice systems examined provide for a defendant's mandatory duty to reply to questions about her personal responsibility and to tell the truth. Nevertheless, two features are worth noting. Firstly, several jurisdictions granting the right to silence display different regulations about the consequences of it. Secondly, many of the summaries (Portugal, Italy, Romania, Hungary) expressly focus on the fact that coercion can be used to oblige the defendant to give evidence that implies her presence (taking samples for DNA profiling; line-ups, body searches etc.).

In Austria, the defendant's interview is the first step of the evidence-gathering procedure, offering her the chance—but not the duty—'to show her point of view on the facts of the case'. It seems that in other countries also the defendant's personal statement or examination is also always permitted, even if it is not mandatory and the defendant has the right to refuse to answer. In Portugal, the code of criminal procedure provides for the defendant's interview, but the timing is not regulated: it is usually performed at the end of the investigative phase, after all the pieces of evidence are taken, as the person should have a chance to convey his or her views before the decision about the indictment. Hungary, where the defendant's presence at trial is mandatory, displays a similar provision, coupled, however, with a peculiar rule: the defendant's statements cannot be a primary means of evidence, but must be supported by other elements, even if she pleads guilty.[78] In Spain, the defendant is asked to submit a written response to the charge, before the beginning of oral examinations. Interestingly enough, in Germany, the absent defendant can authorise her lawyer to give statements and to respond to questions of the court about the charge on her behalf and in her name.[79]

Generally speaking, the majority of the countries proved cautious in drawing inferences from a defendant's silence. However, England and Wales represent a remarkable exception. Firstly, as *Leader* underlines, introducing defence counsel within the English trial had the effect of silencing the defendant. Nowadays, the defendant has a largely passive role in evidence-gathering and fact-finding, unless she opts for self-representation. Secondly, recent amendments allowed the defendant to give statements under oath, and the judge to draw inferences from her silence. This puts England and Wales in a quite unusual situation, which does not seem to be shared by other jurisdictions. Notwithstanding these peculiarities, England and Wales may appear compliant with the ECHR. On the one hand, it is true that the privilege against self-incrimination is fundamental at the initial stage of the proceedings, especially during the police interview; practically speaking, waiving the right to silence during the trial stage may be less risky. On the other, the ECtHR has never totally rejected inferences drawn from the defendant's silence[80]: in the leading

---

[78] Art. 118(2) CPP-Hungary.

[79] Vogel, in this volume, Sect. 3.5.2.

[80] Chiavario (2001), p. 198.

case of *John Murray v. UK*[81] the Court held that the defendant's right to silence is not an absolute one, in particular at the trial stage "when the trial court seeks to evaluate the evidence against him".

French law appears clearly inspired by the abovementioned ECtHR jurisprudence, stipulating that neither can the defendant's silence be considered an admission of guilt, nor can it be the sole or prevalent basis for the conviction. For this reason, the defendant in the French trial must be granted the right to renew her previous statement and, *Drevet* underlines, the judge "cannot substitute the accused's silence by the declarations she made before".[82] Italy probably shows the largest tolerance for the defendant's right to silence. Even though, at the beginning of the 2000s, a stricter regulation was passed, the defendant in her own proceedings and the defendants in connected proceedings still have the right to remain silent. The competent authority for their first investigative interview must inform them that they can remain silent. If they voluntarily give statements, the latter will be used against them (at any stage of the proceedings). If they voluntarily give statements about other defendants, they will be treated as witnesses (under oath), only with regard to those specific statements, and as a rule, they will be provided with legal assistance. At the trial, all the parties are allowed to decide whether to undergo cross-examination. No provision expressly allows the judge to draw inferences from the parties' decision to remain silent: however, if they agree to undergo the examination, their refusal to answer one or more of the questions must be reported in the record (art. 209 CCP-Italy). This implies that the judge can draw inferences from it.[83]

As to the request and admission of evidence by the parties, apparently there are not patent violations of the principle of the equality of arms. This means that the domestic reports do not highlight rules or practices compressing one party's right to have her evidence admitted under the same conditions provided for the other parties. Some of the jurisdictions, however, display interesting provisions related to this topic, owing to different traditions.

The Luxembourgish system is still influenced by the traditional inquisitorial approach, based on the central role of the judge in providing for evidence. In fact, as *Covolo* notes, the "active participation of the defendant at trial must be analysed in the light of the right to present his defense, rather than collect and produce evidence".[84] The judge has the main role in managing the evidence-gathering, while

---

[81] ECtHR, *John Murray v. UK*, judgment of 8 February 1996, Appl. No. 18731/91, para. 47

[82] Drevet, in this volume, Sect. 3.5.

[83] However, there are divergent opinions in the literature: some authors (Orlandi 1990, p. 506 f.; Mazza 2008, p. 214; Patané 2006, pp. 216 ff.) disagree about the power of the judge to draw inference from the defendant's silence. For the mainstream opinion, reported in the text, Lavarini (2012), p. 37.

[84] Covolo, in this volume, Sect. 3.4. The questionnaire did not expressly focus on the defense's investigation (that in some country is extensively admitted: see art. 391-*bis* ff. CCP-Italy) and the reports did not provide general information about the topic, that, however, would be very interesting for a comparison.

the defendant acquires some opportunity of asking for the admission of evidence during the appellate proceedings.

The German regulation seems to be based on an intermediate setting, in which the court is mainly entitled (and even required) to gather evidence, but the defendant has the right to request for the gathering of further pieces of evidence or to provide personally for it. The defendant can submit her request to take evidence for the Court's evaluation, based on a (rather long) list of criteria: the court rejects the request whether it is inadmissible, superfluous, irrelevant, "wholly inappropriate or unobtainable",[85] when the request is made to delay the proceedings or is based on facts that can certainly be assumed as true. Moreover, there may be a restriction on the parties' requests for the examination of more experts—unless the skills of the first expert are criticized—and for *in loco* inspections. Despite this long list of limitations, the defendant has a much broader opportunity to provide evidence herself, summoning[86] or producing it directly at trial. In such cases, the Court can reject the evidence only on the basis of a shorter list of criteria.

Italy, on the other hand, having adopted an adversarial approach in 1988,[87] demonstrates a system almost solely based on the parties' initiative in collecting and asking for evidence. Every party has the right to have her evidence admitted under the same rules and the defendant and prosecutor have the right to counterevidence. The trial court may order evidence only if it is absolutely necessary to adjudicate the case.[88]

Greece provides an interesting regulation of the duty to disclose evidence. During the preparatory proceeding for the most serious crimes, the prosecutor's office must disclose its evidence to the defendant, both witness and documents. Also the *partie civile* is required to disclose her evidence before the trial, while the defendant is not bound to this.

3.5.2 Personal Contribution to the Fact-Finding

As to the parties' personal contribution to fact-finding, the majority of the reports are based on some common patterns: right to personally questioning witnesses and experts; right to give final statements and have the final word; duty to participate in acts implying their personal presence; confessing or pleading guilty. However, it is arguable to find an exact distinction between point 3.5.1 and 3.5.2 of this topic: in fact, some aspects addressed in the two sections are overlapping. This is the case

---

[85] Vogel, in this volume, Sect. 3.5.1.

[86] It is worth noting that the defendant must cover personally (in advance) all the expenses incurred by the witness or expert.

[87] For some interesting overviews on the Italian reform, Langer (2004), pp. 47 ff.; Illuminati (2005), pp. 567 ff.

[88] See Art. 507 CCP-Italy, even though, in reality, courts tend to be much more activist with regard to the gathering of evidence. Cf. Belluta (2006), pp. 143 ff.

with the parties' examination—especially the defendant's one—that has been considered under both.

As to the right to question witnesses, Austria, Germany and Greece display a very interesting rule, providing the defendant with the chance to submit a statement after each witness' cross-examination. On the contrary, some jurisdictions do not allow the defendant to personally examine the witnesses, but rather her defendant or the judge (France, Bulgaria and Portugal, where the defendant is not allowed to sit beside her counsel and the latter has the right to effectively examine witnesses). In Romania, personal cross-examination by the defendant is allowed whenever the victim and the other private parties testify.

Not every summary deals with the topic of the defendant's right to have the last word. However, in the jurisdictions that provide for it (Greece, Hungary, Italy, Luxembourg), the final statement is considered to be a means of influencing the fact-finding.[89]

As to the role of confession and guilty pleas for the purposes of fact-finding proceedings, many of the authors underline that it is rare that the defendant's statements are accepted by the court as the truth. This is to say that, on the one hand, such acknowledgment of responsibility may be not sufficient for a conviction (Hungary). On the other hand, in those jurisdictions providing for alternative proceedings based on a plea of guilt, the court must review the defendant's statement and may decide not to allow the alternative proceeding itself (Romania); in some cases (Portugal), the court may decide to accept a very early guilty plea, at the beginning of the trial hearing, applying a reduced sentence, because of the relevant reduction of time in examining witnesses and experts. However, the court must always evaluate the reliability of the confession, taking into account the evidence in the case-file.

To conclude this point, all the twelve member states highlight a landscape of different specific rules and procedures related to evidence. It is widely acknowledged that evidence is the least harmonised part of criminal procedure through Europe. The ECtHR itself displays self-restraint when the parties' allegations focus on evidence, and especially on admissibility.[90] However, the sense stemming from comparing these twelve domestic jurisdictions is that the parties' personal contribution to evidence-gathering and to fact-finding is crucial. The national regulations still linger over it, resulting in very detailed rules, demonstrating that this personal contribution is still potentially very important.

---

[89] Though, some study argued that the last word in court may hinder the defendant's position: Englich et al. (2005), pp. 705 ff.

[90] Which is, according to the ECtHR, "a matter for regulation under national law" (*Al Khawaja and Taheri v. UK*, judgment of 15 December 2011, Appl. nos. 26766/05, 22228/06, para. 126).

3.6   Personal Participation in Higher Instances

With regard to participatory rights in higher instances, the jurisdictions involved in this study display a wide range of solutions, ranging from a general provision imposing mandatory presence of the defendant and the prosecutor in all appellate proceedings (Bulgaria), to several forms of *in camera* or *de plano* decisions, excluding personal participation. For the sake of clarity, it is worth setting forth some remarks, both of terminology and of concept. Firstly, many reports refer to non-public proceedings or hearings to which neither the public nor the parties are admitted. Within this range of situations, and pursuant to the terminology used before in this study, it is possible to draw a distinction between *in camera* hearings—usually allowing parties' presence but not the public—and *de plano* procedures, in which the court delivers upon one party's request, without hearing the parties or the defendant (but this last option would almost be in breach of the equality of arms, art. 6 ECHR).[91] Secondly, it should be borne in mind that almost all the continental systems reported here stipulate the right of the prosecutor to challenge the judgment (sometimes both acquittal and conviction), taking advantage of the same remedies provided for the defendant.

With the purpose of highlighting similarities, it is possible to say that, where participatory rights are restricted, it is almost on the basis of the very nature of the remedy. This is to say that, according to the ECtHR established doctrine,[92] appellate procedure in law may be held without the participation of the defendant: in the case of *Ekbatani v. Sweden*,[93] the Court stressed, after the Commission, that the defendant's right to be present and to defend herself personally must be balanced with the "special features of the proceedings involved". In fact, "leave-to-appeal proceedings and proceedings involving only questions of law, as opposed to questions of fact, may comply with the requirements of Article 6 (art. 6), although the appellant was not given an opportunity of being heard in person by the appeal or cassation court".[94] Thus, the grounds for limiting participatory rights can rest on the object of the adjudication. Similarly, in some of the jurisdictions covered by this study, restrictions on the defendant's right to participate are justified by the fact that the challenged decision was delivered within an alternative proceeding. In fact, diversion, at first instance proceeding, is often based on the waiver of public trial (e.g. see Italy, with *giudizio abbreviato*).[95]

Generally speaking, many of the summaries refer to a very common distinction within the European continental tradition, between second instance courts (usually

---

[91] Ruggeri, in Part V of this volume, Sect. 2.3.

[92] *Ibid.*, Sect. 2.4.

[93] ECtHR, *Ekbatani v. Sweden*, judgment of 26 May 1988, App. No. 10563/83, para. 27–33.

[94] *Ibid.*, para 31. See also ECtHR, *Fejde v. Sweden*, judgement of 29 January 1991, App. No. 12631/87, para. 67–69; *Kremzow v. Austria*, judgement of 21 September 1993, App. No. 12350/86, para. 65–69; *Botten v. Norway*, judgment of 19 February 1996, App. No. 16206/90, para. 39.

[95] Art. 443 CCP-Italy.

called courts of appeal), hearing a fresh consideration of the facts, and supreme courts (often called cassation courts, after the French *Tribunal de cassation*),[96] delivering a decision in law. In light of this distinction, it is possible to argue (in compliance with the abovementioned ECtHR doctrine) that the defendant's presence is more likely to be allowed in appellate proceedings, rather than in supreme courts proceedings. According to the results of the study, all the countries acknowledge the general right of the parties to be present in the appeal hearings. However, this is just a rough assumption as many domestic regulations stipulate that the appeal courts may, in some conditions, adjudicate *in camera* and, in particular, without the parties' participation (*de plano*). Moreover, in some countries, the defendants' presence is mandatory or *de facto* mandatory. Within that general framework, we can distinguish between three groups of situations: specific cases of mandatory presence; cases preventing the parties' (or the defendant's) presence; finally, cases tolerating the defendant's absence.

Concerning the first group, it has been noted that in Bulgaria both the defendant and the prosecutor must be present, either before the appeal court and the Supreme Court. In Romania, detained defendants must be present at the appeal proceedings. Moreover, Germany offers a hybrid example, as the Court must dismiss the appeal lodged by the defendant, if the latter and her counsel do not appear without excuse. In fact, unexcused absence is considered as an implicit waiver of the appeal, demonstrating that the defendant is no longer interested in it. Thus, it can be affirmed that the presence of the defence is a mandatory condition for the appeal to be adjudicated by the court (at least as far as the defendant's appeal is concerned). Furthermore, if counsel attends the hearing, but the Court deems the defendant's personal presence necessary, the appeal can be dismissed whenever the latter does not appear without a sufficient excuse.

As to the second group, in Greece, convicted defendants serving a sentence outside of the Court's district are not allowed presence in the hearing, and they can only submit written statements. Article 306 of the Hungarian CCP stipulates the conditions in which the appeal can be adjudicated *de plano*. One group of conditions is grounded in 'technical' issues, such as inadmissibility, incompetency, suspension of the case and so forth. But a second ground for *de plano* appellate procedure is listed: in case the appeal is lodged only by the defendant (and not also by the prosecutor), and the Court is not asked to take new evidence, the decision can be delivered without contradictory procedure. However, in such cases, the defendant and her lawyer may expressly ask for a public hearing, in order to be able to participate.

Interestingly enough, the third group covers a range of very different situations. In Portugal, the defendant may be present at the appellate procedure, but she is not summoned for the hearings. Her absence is not a ground to postpone the case, as the

---

[96] The *Tribunal de cassation* was created in 1790, to take over the task originally performed by the *Conseil des parties*, abolished during the French Revolution. The *Tribunal de cassation* was ancillary to the lawmaker, a warden of respect and compliance with the law. Every year, it had to report to the Parliament about the number of quashed judgments (cassations): see Vincent et al. (2005), p. 395.

only relevant subject is her counsel. As a result, defendants never appear in appeal proceedings. In Italy, the general concept of defendant's presence being a right and not a duty applies also to remedies. The defendant who is not interested in taking part into the appeal hearings is free to avoid it. She will always be represented by a counsel, either of her choice or appointed *ex officio*. Appeal proceedings are sometimes decided *in camera*,[97] this is to say without a public hearing, in which the parties are heard if present (if the defendant's absence in the appeal hearing is excused, the proceeding must be postponed). Also detained defendants have the right to be present in the appellate procedure, if willing to, provided that they expressly ask for it.[98] Moreover, a noteworthy example can be found in Germany, where the Court can adjudicate the appeal proceeding promoted by the prosecutor without the presence of the defendant and her lawyer, if their absence is not excused and the defence's presence is not necessary to "uncover all the relevant facts".[99] The defendant and her lawyer are not prevented from participating in the hearing, but their presence is not necessary. On the contrary, if the defendant's presence is necessary to adjudicate, then she can be brought before the court and even arrested.

As to Supreme Court proceedings, focusing only on questions of law, some jurisdiction excludes the parties' right to participation (Austria), ruling on the basis of written statements and submissions; or the defendant's right to personal presence (Greece; Germany, in the *Revision*, if the defendant is not at liberty; Luxembourg); in Hungary, the so-called *court of third instance* adjudicates in a public hearing. However, the defendant, who may be present, is not allowed to give statements, as there is not a fresh evaluation of the facts, but only a decision in law. In Italy, the Supreme Court may adjudicate either in public or *de plano*. The general rule is that *de plano* procedure is adopted when the Court must review an interlocutory judicial decision (not adjudicating on the merit of the case); however, the very same procedure is adopted when reviewing a decision delivered in a summary trial (*giudizio abbreviato*).[100] The court rules on the basis of the parties' written submissions. In case of public procedure, the private parties cannot appear in person and are represented by their counsels. Romania displays a very similar regulation, providing for a *de plano* procedure for reviews upon interlocutory decisions. In England and Wales the appellant's presence is not required in the higher courts. Only Bulgaria exhibits a rule of mandatory presence of the parties before the Supreme Court.[101]

---

[97] Pursuant to a recent reform (law 103/2007), the Court of appeal can hold an *in camera* hearing (art. 599-bis CCP-Italy) when the parties find an agreement on the requests submitted to the court (the agreement covers some of the requests, which will be accepted by the court, while the other requests are waived).

[98] Mangiaracina, in this volume, Sect. 3.6.

[99] Vogel, in this volume, Sect. 3.6.

[100] It is a diversion proceeding, in which the defendant waives her right to be adjudicated on the basis of evidence taken in court, within an adversarial procedure. As a rule, a single judge— namely, the competent judge for the pre-trial inquiry—rules upon the investigations file.

[101] See Petrova, in this volume, Sect. 3.6.

In sum, we can conclude that in all jurisdictions, regardless of their peculiar cultural background, the personal contribution that the parties can offer within the remedies proceedings is limited. The parties, especially the private parties, are able to introduce information, elements of description of the merits. The very nature of remedies implies, however, a progressive detachment from the merits of the case, culminating in a technical review of questions of law. Such nature cannot but relegate parties' personal participation, as a non-relevant feature, especially in Supreme Court procedures.

3.7   Special Rules in the Field of Serious Organised Crimes

Most European jurisdictions provide for some specific procedural rules regarding serious organised crimes. Some countries have a long tradition of counter-organised crime policies, like Italy, with mafia, Spain and UK with ETA and IRA terrorism. It is common knowledge that the basic European Union freedoms also allowed free circulation of organised crime, unfortunately. Thus, almost every country provides now for some special provision aimed to counteract sophisticated criminal organisations.

Mostly, the special rules to which the national reports refer can be divided into investigative tools and trial tools. Within the former, highly intrusive investigation measures are encompassed, based on more lenient conditions for: wire-tapping, room-bugging and other kinds of interception (Greece, Italy, Austria); taking of DNA-profile samples (Greece); seizures and freezing measures (Portugal, Italy, Spain); arrest or pre-trial detention (France, Spain, Italy); undercover police operations (Austria, Italy, Greece). Within the latter (trial measures), every jurisdiction takes into account the peculiar position of victims of organised crime. As a consequence of the duty to implement Directive 2012/29/EU, member states stipulate special rules for the examination of witnesses being (vulnerable) victims of organised crime. Pursuant to this purpose, the selected jurisdictions allow for anonymous statements, video-recorded or video-link statements (Austria, Germany, Greece, Romania). Moreover, *huis-clos* hearings may be decided by the court, in the interest of witnesses, also in organised crime proceedings (Austria, Italy). In such a context, some member states provide for measures directly impinging on the defendant's participatory rights. In particular, as noted, Italy has specific provisions[102] stipulating the defendants' video-link participation at trial: this peculiar regulation, although recently extended, has at its core counter-mafia policies, suggesting a severe restriction on the defendant's right to be present in court and to confront the accusations. Furthermore, the lawyer must decide whether to sit in the courtroom or in the remote location, with her client: this may hinder her ability to intervene in the debate. Thus, almost defence counsels generally prefer to sit in court, leaving their

---

[102] Arts. 45-*bis*; 146-*bis*; 147-*bis* CCP-Italy.

clients alone (they should be able to talk confidentially, through a protected telephone line), or assisted by a colleague of them. As mentioned here above, both the Constitutional Court and the European Court of Human Rights endorsed these measures, ruling that this restriction on the defendant's rights is balanced with the public interest to oppose organised crime. Germany provides for a more lenient provision, allowing the removal of the defendant from the courtroom during the victim's examination.

In conclusion, except the Italian regulation, which seriously affects the defendant's participatory rights,[103] most of the other jurisdictions adopted special rules for organised crime that do not directly hamper the defendant's participation in the proceedings.

However, it is worth underlining that, although reflecting the need for the protection of vulnerable subjects, measures such as anonymity, videotaped witnesses and video-link examination affect the defendant's right to confrontation and, as a consequence, her contribution to fact-finding. Nevertheless, such balance among conflicting interests seems to fit properly within the framework of a fair trial, both in view of the ECtHR case-law and EU law.

4 Personal Participation of Private Parties Other Than the Defendant (in Particular, the Contribution of the Victim to the Fact-Finding)

This section of the study focuses mainly on the victim, whose role and position within criminal proceedings was already addressed in many of the previous points.

As mentioned above, the person having suffered a crime can be considered a sort of convergence point for very different legal approaches. On the one hand, the EU Directive 2012/29 aimed at harmonising a number of victim's rights, as well as some aspects of her role in criminal proceedings (above all, the concept of 'particular vulnerability'). On the other hand, in several jurisdictions, the victim tends to reconcile the twofold limbs of a case, the criminal and the civil-law side, having suffered from both a violation of a fundamental right and an economic loss. In fact, almost all the domestic legal systems represented here (except England and Wales) display full acceptance of the French traditional model of *partie civile*, allowing the person who has undergone damages deriving from the perpetration of a crime, to assume the role of plaintiff or claimant within criminal proceedings aimed at prosecuting that offence. Moreover, the victim is, and always will be, a crucial source of evidence, although she is not neutral as witnesses theoretically are.

Nevertheless, despite the recent Directive and the existence of such a broad, traditional convergence between the continental jurisdictions (enhanced by the ECtHR

---

[103] See the long list of limitations in Mangiaracina, in this volume, Sect. 3.7.

case-law),[104] this section of the comparative study highlights many interesting peculiarities. On the grounds of the method applied, some common patterns will be
highlighted firstly; then, specific national rules, contrasting the common patterns,
will be singled out.

An initial area of regulation regarding the position of victims within the proceedings deals with their role in reporting the offence.

Most European jurisdictions acknowledge the victims' right to make a complaint. However, interestingly enough, few authors linger over the victims' right to
be informed about the process and involved in the development of the investigation.
Although such a point is expressly addressed by the EU Directive 2012/29, only the
Austrian, the English and the French reports refer to the victims' access to information since the very beginning of the proceedings, especially when the victim is supposed to submit a complaint. Psychological support is provided, if needed. *Billis
and Gkaniatsos*,[105] also, refer to such measures, but with regard to the evidence-
gathering procedure rather than the investigative phase. In several countries, the
complainant, *per se*, is not considered to be a party of the proceeding (Portugal,
Italy), unless she gains an additional role, e.g., of *partie civile* or private
prosecutor.

This leads to a second relevant aspect. Albeit with different conclusions, the
twelve jurisdictions can almost be divided into two groups: the first group, applying
the French model of *partie civile*, and the second group acknowledging the victims'
subsidiary role in supporting the public prosecution or instituting an independent
one.

France, Italy and Luxembourg can be included in the first group. *Drevet* high
lights the concept of *partie civile* as one of the most distinctive features of French
criminal procedure. In all of these jurisdictions, *parties civiles* almost enjoy the
same rights the other parties are entitled (some powers may be reserved to the prosecutor and the defendant; however, when a right is generally provided to all 'the
parties', the *partie civile* is certainly entitled). In particular, *parties civiles* have the
right to gather evidence and have it admitted by the court. Within this context, an
interesting French case-law established that the general principle of loyalty in gathering evidence is not applicable to the *partie civile*.[106]

In Italy, the aggrieved party can claim for compensation after the institution of
the court proceedings by lodging a private-law complaint. Once the claim is admitted, the *parte civile* (following the Italian definition) enjoys all the rights acknowledged to the parties. Other aspects of her position are relevant at a previous stage:
during the investigation, she is entitled the right to information (art. 90-*bis* and
90-*ter* CCP-Italy), about (among others): how to submit a complaint; the existence
of an investigation and its development; the prosecutor's request to drop the case;
the offender's arrest or pre-trial detention; the access to legal aid. Generally speak-

---

[104] Ruggeri, in Part V of this volume, Sect. 3.2.

[105] Billis and Gkaniatsos, in this volume, Sect. 4.

[106] Cass. crim. 4th February 2015, no. 01-85559, Bull. 131.

ing, we can argue that the victim holds a relevant twofold role in the Italian criminal proceedings, as a complainant and source of evidence: in fact, she can oppose the prosecutor's decision to drop the case, provided that she can prove that more investigations are needed. On the contrary, both in France and Luxembourg, the *partie civile* has the power to initiate prosecution on her own: this feature allows us to draw distinctions within the first group. In Luxembourg, after the completion of the pre-trial investigation, the *partie civile* can refer the case to the pre-trial chamber if the prosecutor fails to do it.

In France, since the very beginning of the twentieth century, the case-law of the *Cour de cassation* accorded the plaintiff—having undergone a direct and personal harm from the offence—a *voie d'action*, that is to say the power to start the criminal proceedings. *Mauro* recently referred to the victim as the all-powerful party of the French criminal procedure,[107] alluding to the fact that she can submit the case to the investigating judge or to the trial court, forcing the prosecutor to endorse the prosecution. Statistics show that a great number of criminal cases pending before the Paris courts (between 25 and 40%, with a peak of 80% in economic and financial offences) were opened on the grounds of a compensation claim by the *partie civile*. Even more impressive are the figures relating to the success of such actions: 80% of cases opened by the *partie civile* were dropped by the investigating judge,[108] after having 'wasted' time and public means.[109]

Germany and Spain are in the second group. *Vogel* highlights the peculiarities of the German 'private accessory prosecutor', who can support the prosecution for some types of crimes. This prosecutor has a wide range of rights and powers, either in evidence gathering and in challenging decisions on her own. Hungary provides for a double regime. The victim can qualify as independent or subsidiary prosecution. In the first case, she enjoys a long list of rights, especially in the trial phase, in which she can be excluded from hearings only in few cases. As seen above, Spain displays, possibly, the most interesting set of regulation, allowing for a "joint ownership" of the prosecuting power. With the vest of *acusador particular* and *acusador popular*, a private citizen having suffered (the former) or not (the latter) a damage as a consequence of a criminal activity is allowed to indict the defendant and to enjoy a lot of procedural rights. As *Villamarin López* remarks, this is due to the fact that the Spanish prosecution office is submitted to the control of the Ministry of Justice and the Government: private prosecution provides for public oversight of criminal policies. Spanish private accusers are also allowed to submit a complaint for damages. However, this does not imply that the person claiming for damages must take on the role of *acusador particular*. Under Spanish law, it is possible to bring a compensation claim within the criminal proceeding, without assuming the burden of private prosecution. Of course, the civil-law claimant has limited powers,

---

[107] Mauro (2015), p. 146.

[108] Figures are cited by Magendie (2004). Mr. Magendie used to be the President of the Tribunal de Grande Instance, Paris. He was repeatedly asked by the Ministry of Justice to monitor the situation of courts, either of first instance and appeal.

[109] Mauro (2015), p. 148.

confined within the civil limb of the matter, which is treated separately from the main case (criminal liability).

Austria, Greece and Portugal fit into both groups. In Austria, on the one hand, victims can claim for compensation by intervening in criminal proceedings as claimants (the court adjudicates on such claim, unless this negatively affects the delay of the proceedings); on the other, some petty offences can be prosecuted only if the victim herself prosecutes them, on her own. In Greece, the *partie civile* has the right to insert her claim for compensation within the criminal proceedings. However, she is also allowed to stand in trial and to support the prosecutor with the criminal charge, to a limited extent. In Portugal, the victim can play different roles within the proceedings. In addition to complainant and witness, the victim can be a civil claimant, lodging a complaint for compensation. In such case her powers are limited to the civil limb of the proceedings: this prevents her from taking part in the pre-trial judicial investigation. Moreover, the victim can ask to be admitted as an assistant to the prosecutor. In such a case, the assistant, instead of cooperating in a real team with the prosecutor, is able to act autonomously, e.g. with different requests for evidence. As *Costa Ramos and Churro* argued, she is a truly private party rather than a prosecutor's assistant.

Concerning Bulgaria, the 2005 regulation of victims' participation proved in contrast with efficiency.[110] As to Romania, *Ciopec and Roibu* refer that the victim's position is irrelevant within the criminal proceedings. Her role is essentially related to her contribution to fact-finding and evidence gathering as a witness. This is the third topic that deserves a comparative-law examination of the national summaries.

All European jurisdictions consider the victim a crucial source of evidence. Thus, a wide range of regulations was introduced with a view to harmonising the public interest to obtain evidence from the victim, with the question of her vulnerability. Such a trend has developed slowly in the past decades, firstly under the influence of the initial, timid, approach of the ECtHR to the victim's aspiration to a fair trial[111] (that would lately result in the CoE Lanzarote Convention, protecting child victims of sexual exploitation and abuse). Secondly, many EU Directives and Framework Decisions addressed the topic of secondary victimization, urging the member states to pass regulations providing for anticipation of victims' statements;

---

[110] Petrova, in this volume, Sect. 4.

[111] See ECtHR, *Doorson v. The Netherlands*, judgement of 26 March 1996, Appl. no. 20524/92, para. 70: "it is true that Article 6 (art. 6) does not explicitly require the interests of witnesses in general, and those of victims called upon to testify in particular, to be taken into consideration. However, their life, liberty or security of person may be at stake, as may interests coming generally within the ambit of Article 8 (art. 8) of the Convention. Such interests of witnesses and victims are in principle protected by other, substantive provisions of the Convention, which imply that Contracting States should organise their criminal proceedings in such a way that those interests are not unjustifiably imperilled. Against this background, principles of fair trial also require that in appropriate cases the interests of the defence are balanced against those of witnesses or victims called upon to testify". For a general human rights-oriented overview of this case-law, see Ruggeri, in Part VI of this volume, Sect. 4.3.

for means to grant anonymity or at least to prevent personal contact between the victim and the offender; for psychological support.[112] Directive 2012/29/EU represented the culmination of such a path. Thus, the summaries from Austria, Bulgaria, England and Wales, Greece, Hungary, Italy, Portugal and Romania expressly address the topic of the victim-witness, reporting a range of specific domestic provisions aiming to protect the abovementioned interests. Interestingly enough, where the victim has the chance to intervene as *partie civile* (this is to say as a claimant for damages), she is prevented from giving statements under oath (Luxembourg, Italy, where she can be interviewed either as a victim, under oath, or as *parte civile*, without oath: Art. 208 CCP-Italy).

As to the power of the victim to challenge the court's decision, the domestic reports display diverging conclusions. However, in general, it is possible to argue that where the victim assumes the role of private party, in the guise *of partie civile* or of 'private/assistant prosecutor' (France, Germany, Italy, Luxembourg, Portugal), she has the right to challenge the court's decision.[113] Usually, where she vests the role of *partie civile* (Luxembourg and Italy), her appeal is reserved to the civil limb of the decision, while in those countries in which she assumes the role of 'prosecutor, she has a wider right to appeal, also with regard to the criminal-law limb.

5 *In Absentia* Proceedings

The attention comes now to the domestic regulation of *in absentia* proceedings. Having previously lingered over the parties' right to be present in the different phases of the proceedings, here the focus is on the sets of domestic regulations that allow for general or special procedures without the defendant's participation.

Other chapter contributions within this research will deal with the ECtHR and EU approach to this topic. Thus, I will not specifically dwell upon that matter, even though the questionnaire, in this part, is deeply influenced by the ECtHR case-law regarding the compliance of *in absentia* trials with paragraphs 1 and 3 of Article 6 ECHR. Point E of the Attachment is divided into three parts, the first dealing with the information of the defendant about the proceeding and the consequences of waiving her right to be present. The second refers to the remedies against *in absentia* decisions: in fact, if the defendant's absence is not based on an 'unequivocal waiver', but on a miscommunication or a misunderstanding, the person convicted *in absentia*

---

[112] For a comprehensive overview of the path that brought to Directive 2012/29/EU see Morillo and Bellander Todino (2017), pp. 3–14.

[113] In some jurisdictions, the victim has the right to give final statements before the court adjudicates the case (England and Wales, Hungary, Greece), even though she is not a party and such power does not always match with the chance to lodge an appeal of the decision. Where the victim is a party, she is automatically entitled to draw arguments.

must be entitled to lodge an appeal or any other effective remedy, allowing for the reopening of the case.[114]

The third part of point E focuses on *inaudito reo* proceedings, if any. Drawing on the ECtHR general doctrine about the defendant's participatory rights,[115] this section of the study aims at casting light on a form of extreme summary proceedings. Actually, the examination of national legal systems showed that many jurisdictions recur to *in camera* proceedings, without the parties' participation, especially when petty offences and fines are at stake. This is clearly due to the need for quick and effective adjudication of the plainest cases. However, there may be a breach of the conventional right to be present if the domestic regulation does not provide for some sort of remedy, allowing the convicted to exercise her right to a fair trial.

The present comparison will examine these three aspects.

However, first and foremost, the national reports demonstrate a crucial fact. All the criminal justice systems examined in this study allow for the exceptional carrying out of (at least) some criminal proceedings without the defendant's personal participation. As a matter of fact, none of the jurisdictions avoid, completely, a 'judgement without defendant'. I will highlight differences and peculiarities displayed by the different regulations in selecting the cases in which defendants can be tried in their absence. This analysis shows, in compliance with the ECtHR case-law, that the defendant's right to be present in her trial is not an absolute one. There are cases and reasons overarching the defendant's participatory right, allowing the courts to deliver a judgment even when the defendant did not appear in court. As to this issue, the twelve jurisdictions displayed a common approach.

Secondly, comparison highlighted a lack of a common concept of *in absentia* trial. In fact, some jurisdictions do not consider the proceedings in which the defendant is represented by a counsel as *in absentia* trials in a strict sense.[116] In such cases, that the accused's interests are defended by her lawyer seems to be enough to exclude real conditions of *absentia* (France as to the Criminal courts—Greece, Luxembourg, Portugal, Romania). Actually, in several countries, the absent defendants represented by their lawyer are 'considered to be present'. Such a situation formally allows those proceedings to be classified as non-*in absentia*.[117] However, an important remark must be made. In fact, such issue is strictly related to the institutional role vested by the lawyer in each jurisdiction, as addressed under points A and B of this questionnaire. On the one hand, appointing a counsel of her own choice is often considered to be an indication of the defendant's personal knowledge of the criminal proceedings against her (but we will see—hereinafter, Sect. 5.1— that the lawyer's appointment may occur during the investigation, much time before

---

[114] ECtHR, *Somogyi v. Italy*, Judgment of 18 May 2004, Appl. No. 67972/01, para. 71. For a general overview of the ECtHR case-law on *in absentia* trials within this research, see Ruggeri, in Part V of this volume, Sect. 3.1.1.2, as well as Bachmaier, in this volume, Sect. 2.4.

[115] Ruggeri, in Part V of this volume, Sect. 3.1.1.

[116] From a human rights viewpoint, it is doubtful that legal assistance and personal presence in court can be considered as alternative: Ruggeri, in Part VI of this volume, Sect. 4.2.3.

[117] About Greece, see Billis and Gkaniatsos, in this volume, Sect. 5.

the effective prosecution starts). On the other hand, some jurisdictions provide for mandatory (or almost mandatory, at least in most serious cases) assistance of a lawyer, who can be appointed *ex officio*, if need be. This assumption entails several consequences.

The assistance and representation by a lawyer do not necessarily imply the defendant's awareness of the trial against her, as counsel may have been appointed *ex officio*. However, ECtHR case-law distinctly states that one of the two basic conditions for *in absentia* proceedings being in compliance with the Convention is the defendant's "sufficient knowledge of his prosecution and of the charges against him".[118] Thus, the knowledge of the proceeding—allowing the defendant to appoint a lawyer—is a precondition of *absentia* and not an element excluding it. For this reason, cases in which the defendant appointed a lawyer of her own choice should still be considered as *in absentia* proceedings, even though the presence of a counsel grants a minimum standard of adversarialism (allowing the defence to present the Court with its point of view on the facts).

By examining the whole range of contribution that the parties can personally make in criminal proceedings, one of the main purposes of this comparative analysis is to demonstrate that presence is not simply the opposite of absence. Thus, even though the majority of the jurisdictions tend, by a *fictio legis*, to consider the defendant present in trial if represented by her lawyer, such cases must be classified *in absentia*, because the defendant is not personally taking part in the proceeding, of which she must have a formal knowledge.[119] Without such information, there cannot be a fair trial and there is a violation of art. 6 ECHR.[120] It should be clear, so far, that *in absentia* proceedings are not characterised by a situation of ignorance, of unawareness of the prosecution by the defendant. On the contrary, they imply a conscious and unequivocal decision to waive the wide range of participatory rights that have been examined here above. For the same reason, we can agree to leave out from the area of *in absentia* procedures the situations in which the defendant is temporarily excluded from the courtroom because of her disruptive behaviour.[121]

Here, we assume that the defendant's absence does not imply a denial of the right to be represented by a lawyer of her own choice, or appointed *ex officio*. In fact, the Strasbourg Court[122] reiterated that "A person charged with a criminal offence does not lose the benefit of this right merely on account of not being present at the trial". The contracting States are free to regulate this aspect with a certain margin of appreciation, as Article 6(3)(c) ECHR does prescribe specific manners for exercising such a right, but they must guarantee effective assistance of the absent defendant.

---

[118] ECtHR, Grand Chamber, *Sejdovic v. Italy*, judgment of 1 March 2006, Appl. no. 56581/00, para. 101.

[119] See below, Sect. 5.1.

[120] Ruggeri, in Part V of this volume, Sects. 2.1 and 4.1 ECtHR, Grand Chamber, *Pélissier and Sassi v. France*, judgment of 25 March 1999, Appl. no. 25444/94, para. 52.

[121] See Costa Ramos and Churro, in this volume, Sect. 5.1.

[122] ECtHR, *Mariani v. France*, 31 March 2005, Appl. No. 43640/98, para. 40 and, previously, *Van Pelt v. France*, 23 May 2000, Appl. No. 31070/96. Cf. Ruggeri, in Part V of this volume, Sect. 4.2.

What falls out of the scope of Article 6(3)(c) are the shortcomings that may occur within the attorney-client relationship:

> the competent national authorities are required under Article 6(3)(c) to intervene only if a failure by legal aid counsel to provide effective representation is manifest or is sufficiently brought to their attention in some other way.[123]

As a consequence of such interpretation, France was forced to change their domestic regulation, firstly with a judicial overruling by the *Court de cassation* and secondly with a new law (Perben II), providing for mandatory lawyer's hearing in case of the defendant's (unexcused) absence.

In the following sections, we will focus on the national regulations to assess how far they comply with the reported ECtHR interpretation of Article 6(3)(c) ECHR. We will point out the cases in which the absent defendant is not represented by a lawyer, trying to understand if the remedies provided for are suitable to prevent an infringement of the Convention.

5.1   Information Rights and Conditions of Waiver of Personal Participation in Criminal Proceedings

Form this angle, the majority of the jurisdictions display the effects of the recent implementation of the EU Directive 2012/13 on the right to information about rights. However, this Directive does not linger over the right of the accused to be informed about the consequences of a possible waiver of participatory rights. The investigation phase is often secret, under the control of the police, or the prosecutor or the investigating judge. As we noted above, participatory rights are very few and weak, during the investigation: consequently, no information is provided about a possible waiver of the right to be present at trial. Among the countries involved, only Bulgaria seems to have a form of early information about *in absentia* trials, as the prosecutor is charged with an information duty during the pre-trial stage. Usually, such information is attached to the summons to appear before the court, which is served after the prosecution has started. Some national overviews focus on the importance of properly serving the acts of the proceeding and, in particular, the summons to the trial hearing. In fact, the possibility of summoning the defendant personally or by post presupposes that the judicial authority exactly knows the defendant's whereabouts. To this end, suspects are often requested to give a statement about their current address at the beginning of the investigation (Italy, Portugal), or to choose an address at which they wish to receive the acts of the proceedings. Attached to the statement, there is the duty to inform the judicial authority about any change of such address. The Portuguese and Italian reports underline how the effectiveness of the serving process is crucial to the actual information of the

---

[123] ECtHR, *Daud v. Portugal*, judgement of 21 April 1998, Appl. no. 22600/93, para. 38.

defendant about the proceeding against her.[124] *Costa Ramos and Churro* emphasize that it is pure legal fiction to consider the accused informed of the trial, when the summon is served by post, with no need of acknowledgment of receipt, as is the case in Portugal.

As a matter of fact, all European countries take it for granted that the first precondition for *in absentia* trials is to effectively inform the defendant about the proceedings against her. Nonetheless, we can assume that in all jurisdictions the notification process remains an ancillary and secondary practical performance, almost neglected by literature and scholarship, despite being crucial to such an aim. None of the authors (except *Mangiaracina*, although referring to a minor amendment)[125] mentions recent reforms or improvements of the rules on court summons. Thus, the basic condition for *in absentia* trials, the one shared by all the countries considered here, this is to say the defendant's information about the trial, seems to be inevitably related to the topic of notification, which is not the object of improving research or legal reform. Few authors refer to rules requiring personal summons, in general: even where present (Austria), such provisions do not rule out exceptions.

England and Wales recently display a very peculiar approach to the requirement that the defendant be personally summoned to appear in court. In fact, in Magistrates' Courts proceedings the court shall proceed in the absence of the defendant (if over 18) "unless it appears to the court to be contrary to the interest of justice to do so". This provision was passed with the Criminal Justice and Immigration Act 2008, and prevents the court from proceeding only where there is "an acceptable reason" for the defendant's failure to appear. What constitutes an 'acceptable reason' is doubtful and *Leader* refers to a debate within the case-law.[126] It is clear, however, that in Magistrates' Court, *in absentia* proceedings, without control over the defendant's awareness of the prosecution against her, are becoming more commonplace, whilst they were traditionally exceptional. Anticipating the topic of the following paragraph, it is worth noting that there is a specific remedy based on the issue of unawareness: within 21 days of the trial, the defendant having been convicted *in absentia* by a Magistrates' Court can lodge a statutory declaration stating that she was unaware of the prosecution against her, until it took place. The effect of the statement is that the hearing "must be treated as it had not taken place at all".[127]

This issue is strictly related to another relevant aspect. In cases in which the defendant's whereabouts are unknown—i.e., where she is untraceable—the summons cannot be served and the accused is clearly unaware of the prosecution against her. The selected jurisdictions display different approaches to this situation, even though not every report deals with the matter of untraceable defendants. Some of

---

[124] For a similar reference, see also Vogel, in this volume, Sect. 5.1.

[125] Mangiaracina, in this volume, Sect. 5.1.

[126] For a human rights-oriented critique of what can be considered a viable waiver of the defendant' right to be involved in the proceedings, Ruggeri, in Part VI of this volume, Sect. 3.2.2.

[127] Section 37.11 Criminal Procedural Rules (England and Wales).

them provide for the undertaking of the trial *in absentia*,[128] while others stipulate a suspension of the proceedings, until the person is found.[129] Some countries provide for a kind of previous 'contact' between the judicial authority and the suspect: before being summoned to the trial, the defendant must be interviewed (Austria, Germany) or is required to submit a statement of identity and residence (Portugal, Greece, Italy). This 'personal contact' should reduce the risk of difficulties in properly summoning the defendant to the trial. However, the earlier the contact with the authority, the lower the standard of information about the proceeding, especially when such 'contact' occurs during the investigation.

None of the jurisdictions seems to limit *in absentia* cases to the explicit waiver of rights (which is, however, expressly considered a ground to proceed in the defendant's absence: see Austria; France, where the defendant can send a letter of waiver to the criminal court; Germany; Italy, Portugal, Romania). Although such an event certainly indicates that the two crucial ECtHR standards[130] (awareness of the prosecution and of the consequences of absence; unequivocal waiver)[131] are met, the jurisdictions tend to accept also non-explicit waiver. The example of England and Wales is paradigmatic.[132] In the proceedings before Crown Courts, *in absentia* trials have been permitted since 2001, under two conditions, namely that the defendant has waived the right to attend, and the trial must be fair notwithstanding the defendant's absence. *Leader* refers to the existence of concerning courtroom practices in assessing the effective knowledge of the prosecution by the defendant. English courts tend to be satisfied by the evidence that the defendant received a standardised written information about consequences of non-attendance. Once more, the problem here is to verify the defendant's effective knowledge of the proceedings and of the consequences of the waiver of her right to be present and case-law accepts a rather low standard of proof. Hopefully, the second standard, the overall fairness of the proceeding, largely prevents *in absentia* proceedings against defendants who are not represented by a lawyer. In such cases, the absence of both the defendant and a lawyer, prevents the defence from presenting its account on the events. Such a low standard does not satisfy the condition of the overall fairness of the proceedings.

The second common feature is that the proceeding is held *in absentia* only if the defendant's absence is not covered by an excuse: all reports refer of a wide range of excuses, like *force majeure*, preventing the defendant from participating in person. If an excuse occurs, the proceedings should stop and cannot be treated as *in absentia* ones. The legal systems seem to attach two different consequences to such excuses.

---

[128] Hungary, Italy until 2014 and Romania, according to the 'indulgent' interpretation of "official notification" endorsed by the judicial practice: see Ciopec and Roibu, in this volume, Sect. 5.1.

[129] Bulgaria, with a discretionary decision by the judge, if she deems it contrary to the aim of discovering the truth to go on without the defendant's presence; France, before the *Cour d'Assize*; Italy; apparently Greece, for felonies; Spain, although with two exceptions.

[130] Ruggeri, in Part V of this volume, Sect. 3.1.2.

[131] Bachmaier, in this volume, Sect. 2.2.

[132] See also Greece, Italy, Romania. These national reports refer to non-explicit—but hopefully, unequivocal—waiver of the defendant's participatory right.

On the one hand, they usually constitute a ground for postponing the trial hearing (however, see Portugal, where failure to appear with justification is not a reason to adjourn the beginning of the trial, but only a way to escape the fine that can be applied in case of non-justified absence). On the other, excuses justify recourse to special remedies against *in absentia* decision (or at least, convictions).[133] Of course, a high level of discretion in the judicial decision accepting or rejecting such justification is common to the twelve member states (Bulgaria, England and Wales, Luxembourg; see also Germany, with special regard to the case of the defendant having impaired his physical condition, on purpose, so as not to be able to stand in trial). As has been noted, what is considered to be a viable excuse for absence from the trial hearing is almost a matter of judicial practices. All jurisdictions appear to have a rich case-law about such excuses. The summaries are almost general on this point and, thus, it is not possible to compare exactly the conditions justifying the defendant's absence in the domestic case-law. However, in some of them (especially Germany and Italy) it is commonplace for courts to accept justifications that tend to exclude the fault of absent defendants. As a matter of fact, domestic courts apply somewhat objective and strict criteria to assess whether the absence is due to a defendant's negligence or, rather, to an external, non-personal condition, which prevented her from participating. It seems that the discussion about a valid medical certificate to justify absence is a very common issue: what kind of illness really prevents the defendant from taking part consciously in the trial? Even though this topic does not have a core relevance in academic debates about *in absentia* trials, several reports (Austria, Germany, Italy)[134] demonstrate that the indisposing nature of the illness is crucial to the matter of defendant's absence justification.

It is interesting to note that there is another common condition governing *in absentia* trials. Almost all jurisdictions have the judicial power to order the defendant to appear in court, even under coercive measures. Such power to impose personal participation is usually related to fact-finding, although with different standards of intensity. In some countries, such as Greece and Portugal, legislation refers to the search for truth; Austrian and German law invokes the need for fact-finding; English law requires an "interest of justice"; in Italy, art. 490 CCP-Italy allows the judicial power to order, coercively, the defendant's presence with the specific aim of taking evidence. Although admitting *in absentia* trials, many legal orders take the 'general interest in assessing the fact and uncovering the truth' into account and consider it a sufficient ground to overcome the defendant's unwillingness to participate, forcing her to appear in court.

In conclusion, it can be argued that none of the jurisdictions considered here totally refuses *in absentia* trials: thus, in all of them there are, at least, some exceptional cases in which the court is allowed to proceed without the defendant (see Spain, with one case within the constellation of abbreviated proceedings and one in

---

[133] See below, Sect. 5.2.

[134] See also Italy. There is a huge case-law in Italy about the requirements of medical certificates excusing absence. Cf. Varraso (2017), pp. 3017 f.

the area of proceedings for minor offences). From this angle, it is worth noting that several countries amended their statutes in the last decades, introducing (England and Wales, Hungary), or deeply reforming their regulations on *in absentia* trials (France, Luxembourg, Italy, Portugal). Some of the authors account for such statutes to the outcome of the impact of the ECtHR case-law (France, Italy,[135] Luxembourg), which has cleared out the requirements for an *in absentia* procedure to be compliant with the Convention. As a result of such reforms, we found several common features, which we enumerated here above. Nevertheless, some crucial differences emerge from this section of the study.

Firstly, some jurisdictions specify areas of criminal affaires in which *in absentia* is excluded. Such areas may be based on a personal feature, like age (excluding juveniles, or offenders under the age of 21: Austria; Spain), or on the seriousness of the offence (Bulgaria; Germany; Greece; Spain; in England and Wales, France the rules for *in absentia* trials are different, according to the major or minor seriousness of the offence). Other jurisdictions set general rules for the defendant's absence, not related to a personal condition or to a specific group of offences (Hungary, Italy, Portugal, Romania).

Secondly, some jurisdictions are influenced by the concurrent relationship between the defendant's role and her lawyer's role. In some cases, their roles overlap, and this allows the counsel to give statements and undergo the interview on behalf of her client (Austria, Germany). However, as anticipated, the presence of a counsel representing the absent defendant allows the court to consider the trial as an adversarial one, limiting *in absentia* to the cases in which the defendant did not appoint a lawyer (France, Criminal Courts; Greece, Luxembourg, Romania). Such a feature merges with the domestic rules about non/mandatory appointment of a lawyer, uncovering situations in which *in absentia* trials seem to take place without *ex officio* appointment of a lawyer, in breach of the abovementioned ECtHR interpretation of Article 6(3)(c) ECHR. In France, if the defendant appointed a lawyer, the judgment is not *in absentia*, but *contradictoire à signifier* and will be served to the defendant, allowing her to lodge a complaint. Thus, *in absentia* decisions are delivered without the previous appointment of a lawyer *ex officio*. Similarly, in Greece, where no *ex officio* appointment seems to be provided in the case in which the defendant did not appoint her lawyer. In Luxembourg the distinction between *in absentia* and adversarial judgments seems to be characterised by the participation of a lawyer chosen by the defendant, who is able to present the defendant's point of view on the facts. Thus, the main difference is not in the appointment of a counsel of one's own choice or a court-appointed lawyer, but in the counsel's mandate to take a position and put forward his client defence at the court hearing. Romania seems to share this very same distinction. As noted, in England and Wales, before the Crown courts, the criterion of the overall fairness of the proceedings seems to prevent *in absentia* trials in cases of non-represented defendants. However, *Leader*

---

[135] Although there are doubts about compliance of the new regulation with the Convention, especially because it puts on the defendant's shoulders the burden of proving the she had no culpability in having been absent. See Quattrocolo (2014), pp. 105 f.

stresses that it is theoretically possible for a trial to proceed in the absence of a defendant who has waived her rights to representation. Such a situation is also likely to be more frequent before the Magistrates' Courts.

These remarks confirm the observations made in the introduction of this comparative essay, in which we highlighted a relationship between participatory rights of private parties and defendants, in particular, and adversarialism of criminal proceedings. The analysis demonstrates that the selected European countries examined display different levels of compliance with such concept. Without formally disregarding it, and despite considering, formally, *in absentia* trials an exception, they tolerate courtroom practices deeply reducing and affecting the level of adversarialism. Where the control on the defendant's effective information about the prosecution is loosened, the risk of compromising the fairness of the proceeding is high: in such situation, the absence of legal representation may seriously jeopardise the minimum standard of fairness of the whole *in absentia* proceeding.

5.2   Default Proceedings and Subsequent Remedies

In the previous paragraph, we anticipated the most relevant features of default proceedings, while drawing a scheme of common elements connecting the twelve jurisdictions, under the focal point of conditions for the waiver of the defendant's participatory rights.

However, it is worth recalling that once the conditions for absence are met, the default proceedings are usually undertaken *"as the defendant was present"*. One of the main differences, as highlighted above, lies in the lawyer's role. We singled out cases in which the absent defendant is not represented by a counsel, possibly hampering the minimum standard of procedural fairness, as stressed by the ECtHR. On the other hand, the ECtHR attaches much attention to the available remedies, when considering the overall fairness of *in absentia* proceedings.[136] The case-law on this point is burgeoning and clearly sets out the obligation for the contracting states to provide for a remedy allowing fresh determination of the facts, in case the defendant's absence was unintentional. In fact, despite the national court's evaluation, the defendant may have been unaware of the prosecution against her; or, her waiver may not have been unequivocal, as she may not have been properly informed of the

---

[136] "The resources available under domestic law must be shown to be effective where a person charged with a criminal offense has neither waived his right to appear and to defend himself nor sought to escape trial": ECtHR, *Somogyi v. Italy* (fn. 105), para. 67.

consequences of her absence.[137] Thus, the Strasbourg Court is often called upon to analyse the functioning of the national remedies.[138]

What stems from the twelve member states is that *in absentia* decisions—in particular, *in absentia* convictions—are often submitted to special remedies. This is to say that defendants can lodge a challenge even against a final decision.

Eleven among the twelve national jurisdictions provide for special remedies (or *also* special remedies) against final decisions, which are tailored to the specific features of *in absentia* proceedings. In fact, the aim of challenging a default decision is to complain against the *in absentia* proceeding, having taken place *without* the legal requirements (the conditions we singled out in the previous paragraph). Such situation implies that the defendant's rights were infringed, because she was not able to participate in the proceeding, exercising the whole range of participatory rights that we examined above, in violation of Article 6(1) ECHR. Moreover, special remedies can have two different aims. They may purely enable the defendant to appeal a final decision (because she did not know about the prosecution against her and was not able to timely challenge the decision). Or they may quash the default decision, allowing for the repetition of the proceeding *with* the opportunity of the defendant's participation.

This second option is permitted by the majority of the countries examined. Actually, in many cases, the jurisdictions provide for remedies against both non-final and final decisions (Austria, Bulgaria, England and Wales, France—only in criminal courts—[139] Germany; Greece—depending on some distinction based either on the seriousness of the crime and on the fact the defendant was considered traceable or untraceable   ).

Italy, after the recent reform in 2014, combines both kinds of remedies. Like in Germany, the commencement of a default proceeding in violation of the defendant's participatory rights is always considered a ground for nullity of the first instance decision, to be challenged by an ordinary appeal. If the default decision becomes final, there is an extraordinary remedy: the decision will be quashed and the defendant will be retried based on fresh evidence. Romania provides for a special application for retrial, once the default decision becomes final[140]: the decision delivered as

---

[137] ECtHR, *Colozza v. Italy* (fn. 42), para. 29; ECtHR, *Einhorn c. France*, decision of 16 October 2001, Appl. No. 71555/01, para. 33; ECtHR, *Krombach v. France*, judgment of 13 February 2001, Appl. No. 29731/96, para. 85; ECtHR, *Battisti v. France*, decision of 12 December 2006, Appl. No. 28796/05.

[138] Bachmaier, in this volume, Sect. 2.4.

[139] It is doubtful whether *Cour d'Assize* proceedings comply with the ECHR. In fact, the defendant cannot challenge a conviction held *in absentia*. The only way for the convicted person to have the decision quashed is to be arrested or surrendered to the competent authority, as annulment is the automatic consequence of the arrest or surrender. However, the ECtHR set fort doubts about the surrender being a fair condition to impose on the defendant, in order to get the chance to be retried at her presence: see ECtHR, *Krombach v. France*, para. 87; and even earlier, ECtHR, *Khalfaoui v. France*, judgement of 14 December 1999, Appl. No. 34791/97, para. 42–45.

[140] Ciopec and Roibu, in this volume, Sect. 5.2 highlight the fact that, formally, the remedy can only be lodged against final convictions and not also against final acquittals. This deprives the absent defendant of the right to seek for a more favourable acquittal.

a result of the retrial may be subject to an ordinary appeal. Similarly, Spain relies on a special procedure, called "*anulación*", which only aims at assessing whether or not the conditions for *in absentia* trial were fulfilled. The merits of the case are to be treated by the first instance court, with the retrial. Interestingly, Portugal does not provide for retrial in case of violation of the defendant's participatory rights. *Costa Ramos and Churro* emphasise that Portuguese law does not provide the defendant with effective remedies. In fact, the existing remedy against the default decision is an ordinary appeal, before it becomes final. Remedies against final decisions seem to be ineffective, according to the domestic report. Moreover, the real problem of Portuguese legislation is that new evidence is not allowed at the appeal stage: the appellate proceeding is ruled on the basis of the result of the first instance proceedings, in which the defendant did not participate. The chances for gathering new evidence are exceptional and this makes such remedy a non-effective means of granting the defendant's personal participation.

Such regulation looks very much in contrast with either the ECtHR case-law and the EU law. The EU Directive 2016/343, although not imposing to member states a specific model of remedy against *in absentia* decisions, states that such remedy must "ensure a fresh reassessment of the merits of the case, including the examination of new evidence as well as the reversal of the conviction" (art. 9).[141]

Some of these remedies are submitted to strict deadlines. In Austria, the objection to a guilty verdict rendered *in absentia* must be lodged within 2 weeks (the deadline starts from the personal service of the verdict).[142] In England and Wales, the defendants convicted *in absentia* by the Magistrates' Courts (rule 37.11) may lodge a statutory declaration, within 21 days from the decision,[143] stating that they were unaware of the prosecution against them. Such statement grants a retrial, as the first decision had not been delivered. However, *Leader* has pointed out the very low rate of remedies lodged under this provision, demonstrating that the majority of the people convicted *in absentia* are not aware of their right. As noted, French law combines ordinary means (the appeal) and extraordinary means, such as the *opposition*; the defendant may choose between the two and she has only 10 days to lodge the opposition (running from the notification of the default judgment or from the moment she became aware of the decision). Ten days is also the timeframe to file a request for *anulación*, in Spain, starting from the moment the defendant became aware of the judgment against her. As to Italy, a new remedy—namely, a 'revocation'—against final convictions (art. 629-*ter* CCP-Italy) must be submitted to the court of appeal within 30 days from the moment the defendant became aware of the *in absentia* decision; also, the Romanian application for retrial must be filed within

---

[141] It was noted that such guarantees may not be sufficient to restore the defendant's right to a fair trial. In fact, if the remedy is not tailored to the model of retrial, the defendant may definitively loose some strategic chance (e.g. bargaining a plea with the prosecutor, to reduce the sentence; asking for taking evidence). Cf. Ruggeri (2016), p. 47. See also Bachmaier Winter, in this volume, Sect. 4.3.

[142] See Golser, in this volume, Sect. 5.2.

[143] Courts may extend the time allowed.

1 month. In Luxembourg, the *opposition* (very similar to the French one) must be lodged within 15 days and it prevents the decision from becoming final. As to Portugal, we already emphasised that the ordinary appeal must be lodged within the general deadline, before the decision becomes final.

Against this background, we can conclude that remedies against *in absentia* decision are all submitted to strict deadlines (from around 10 to 30 days), notwithstanding that the domestic regulations show some important differences in the moment at which this period starts. When the timeframe runs from the day the decision was delivered, the chances to successfully lodge an appeal are fewer, as the defendant may remain unaware of the *in absentia* prosecution for a relatively long period. From this angle, it is worth noting that the Strasbourg Court displayed reluctance towards very short deadlines to file remedies against *in absentia* decisions. In the case of *Sejdovic v. Italy*, the Court criticised the term of 10 days, in force at the time of the facts.[144] The Court, considering the overall effectiveness of the remedy, emphasised the difficulties that a convicted person being detained abroad may have in respecting a timeframe of only 10 days, to file a motion for a leave to appeal.[145]

However, the European jurisdictions examined did not strongly take this remark into account, and very short deadlines are still allowed for in the case of domestic remedies against *in absentia* decisions.

5.3 Inaudito reo *Proceedings (e.g. Penal Order Procedure)*

To some extent, the topic of *inaudito reo* proceedings has been previously addressed in our inquiry. In fact, where the questionnaire approached the subject of *in camera* proceedings (C III), many authors dealt with special proceedings in which the judge can adjudicate *de plano*, without a hearing either public or *huis clos*. The penal order turned out to be an almost common pattern.

As a matter of fact, *inaudito reo* proceedings provide for a decision delivered in the absence of the defendant (and all the parties). The main difference, of course, is that in the trials *in absentia* the defendant *has* the right to be present, but waives it, while here she *has no* right to participate.[146] As such, these "fast-track" procedures would be definitively in breach of the fundamental principles of fair trial, under ECHR, ICCPR and EU Charter of Fundamental Rights. What makes them (at least) apparently compliant is the provision of a remedy aimed at quashing the *inaudito reo* decision and at granting the defendant an ordinary, adversarial trial.

As recently noted by the EU Court of Justice in the *Covaci* case, the service of a penal order often "represents the first opportunity for the accused to be informed of

---

[144] ECtHR, *Sejdovic v. Italy* (fn. 108), para. 103.

[145] In that case, the remedy in force in Italy at the time was a bare extension of the deadline to lodge an ordinary appeal against the default decision, having become final.

[146] Ruggeri (2016), p. 42, and hereinafter, in Part VI this volume, Sect. 3.3.

the accusation against him"[147]; thus, the defendant's initiative does not aim at a new judgment by a higher court but allows her to obtain a trial hearing in which she can take part.[148] Clearly, this procedure entails that after the completion of the pre-trial investigation, the prosecutor (or the police) adjudicates (or requests the judge to adjudicate) the case on the basis of the sole information gathered by the investigative authorities. So far, such proceedings are clearly in breach of the basic features of the fair trial. However, as said, their compliance with such common principles of human rights law, must be considered together with the subsequent remedy. Considering this, our inquiry covers, first, the legal requirements for *inaudito reo* decisions and, second, the remedies against such decisions.

Inaudito reo proceedings belong to the continental civil-law tradition,[149] as is confirmed by this comparative-law study. Only the English and the Romanian summaries gave a negative answer to point E.III. of the Attachment.[150] The other jurisdictions provide for at least one form of *inaudito reo* proceeding, usually grounded in the reduced seriousness of the offence, or more precisely, the reduced sentence. Most European countries submit such proceedings to clear limits. Usually, *inaudito reo* proceedings are applicable when a fine or a suspended (short term) imprisonment sentence is deemed just by the judge. In France, Greece, Italy, Luxembourg, and Portugal the basic requirement for applying such proceedings is the application of a fine.[151] As to France, the fine applied with *inaudito reo* decisions cannot be higher than 5000 Euros. In some other jurisdictions, the *inaudito reo* proceedings may lead to the application of a suspended imprisonment sentence (see Hungary, up to 2 years).[152] In particular, in Austria and Germany,[153] defendants who are not represented by a lawyer can only be sentenced to a fine through *inaudito reo* proceedings; on the contrary, defendants being represented may also be sentenced up to 1 year of suspended imprisonment.[154] Spain recently introduced a very peculiar proceedings, which is only partly *inaudito*. Actually, the investigating magistrate, upon a request by the prosecutor, can issue a 'proposal of punishment'. The defendant must be summoned to appear in front of the investigating magistrate, with the assistance of a

---

[147] C-216/14, para. 60.

[148] Ruggeri (2016), p. 44.

[149] *Ibid.*, p. 42.

[150] As to Spain, see Villamarin López, in this volume, Sect. 3.3.

[151] As to Italy, the fine can be the punishment provided for the offence by the penal code or the result of the conversion of a short-term punishment into a fine.

[152] The general limit is that the fast track procedure cannot be applied for offenses punished *in abstracto* with more than 5 years of imprisonment.

[153] Vogel, in this volume, Sect. 5.3, emphasizes that for a penal order to be issued, the judge does not need to be sure of the defendant's guilt beyond any reasonable doubt. In cases of doubts, however, the judge can always divert from the *inaudito reo* model and open a main hearing. Moreover, the penal order can be issued as a form of diversion from the main hearing, in petty or medium seriousness offenses.

[154] The general limit is that the offense must not be punished, *in abstracto*, with more than 3 years of imprisonment.

lawyer of her choice or appointed *ex officio*. The judge must inform the defendant of the effects of accepting the decree and must assess her effective will to agree on the proposed punishment. In case of acceptance, the decree is converted into a final and enforceable conviction.[155]

It is worth noting that some domestic regulations set more specific requirements, relating to a sort of previous contact between the offender and the judicial authority. For example, Hungarian law provides for a list of further conditions, allowing for the application of a fast-track procedure: the defendant must be at liberty; she must have confessed the crime; the facts of the case must be simple; a trial must be superfluous. Interestingly, the penal order is not considered to be a formal judgment (like in Italy). In Luxembourg, the defendant has the right to access the case file before the penal order being issued. In fact, the prosecutor must inform the defendant of this right and wait for the expiration of the timeframe of 1 month, during which the defendant may access the file. As to Portugal, the prosecutor must interview the accused before asking the judge to issue a penal order. In all these events, the defendant is not completely unaware of the proceeding against her, having had previous contact with the authority. Of course, the penal order is always issued without a previous adversarial hearing. Nevertheless, such contact with the investigating authority can grant some room for the defence to set forth its point of view on the facts.

In some jurisdictions, the penal order must be served personally (Portugal). In other countries, the issuing of a penal order is submitted to the condition that the defendant is formally traceable (Germany, Luxembourg, Italy). In particular, in Spain the defendant must appear personally before a judge in order to accept the *decreto*, demonstrating that she fully understands the consequences of it. As emphasized by the CJEU, serving the penal order is the means by which the defendant is informed of the accusation against her. Therefore, this information must comply with the requirements set out in Article 6 of Directive 2012/13/EU.

Even though the authors were not asked to refer to this specific issue, it seems that usually penal orders are not applicable to juvenile (Italy) and young offenders, under 21 (Austria).

In Luxembourg, penal order procedures cannot be applied if damages occurred to the *partie civile*. In Italy, the civil limb falls completely out of the regulation of penal orders: in fact, even if the fast track decision becomes final, it will not affect the (possible) civil decision about the recovering of damages. The European Court has recently dealt with the topic of participation of the private parties, other than the defendant, in *inaudito reo* proceedings in its decision issued in the case of *Gray v. Germany*.[156] The Strasbourg case-law, however, did not take a clear position on the matter, excluding that, in this specific case, there had been a violation of the victim's next of kin's participatory right.[157]

---

[155] Villamárin López, in this volume, Sect. 3.3.3.

[156] ECtHR, *Gray v. Germany*, judgment of 22 May 2014, Appl. No. 49278/09.

[157] Ruggeri (2016), p. 49.

As to the remedies allowed by the domestic jurisdictions, the most interesting features are: the timeframe to lodge the opposition; the consequences of it, possibly preventing the judicial authority from sentencing the defendant to a higher penalty, at the end of the ordinary trial; the need for the defendant's personal participation in the ordinary trial.

The delay for filing the opposition is usually quite short: 8 days, in Greece (but it must be noted that the penal order, after having become final, can be challenged by the ordinary means of appeal); 2 weeks or 15 days in Germany,[158] Italy and Luxembourg[159]; 4 weeks in Austria; 30 or 45 (for misdemeanours) days in France. Bulgaria provides for reopening of the proceedings within 6 months. Here, however, the competent judge is the Court of cassation and its mandate is limited to matters of law: thus, it seems that the Bulgarian law does not provide for a remedy granting the fresh determination of the facts, if the case was previously adjudicated through a penal order. As to the timeframe for lodging the opposition, the CJEU recently ruled on the matter, in three important decisions.[160] The Court emphasized that regardless of the defendant's whereabouts and her language, the convicted person must be able to benefit from the timeframe established by law in its entirety.

Some authors expressly remark that national legislation generally prevents a *reformatio in peius*. Thus, even though the penal order is quashed because of the opposition, the judge of the following main hearing still cannot sentence the defendant to a higher penalty. In Austria and Hungary, this is expressly provided by statutory law, although in Hungary, the prosecutor can lodge a specific appeal, allowing him to ask for a harsher sentence. On the contrary, in Italy, *reformatio in peius* is part of the risk that the defendant must face if she decides to oppose the penal order. Whether to oppose or not, is a decision almost based on the comparison between the amount of the fine imposed by the order and the sentence that could be imposed after the opposition, in the ordinary trial (the defendant may, with the opposition, request different special proceedings, such as the plea bargaining or the abbreviated procedure). Unfortunately, only few summaries reported such information.

As noted in the introduction of this paragraph, the main feature of penal orders is a decision delivered *inaudito reo*. Thus, the opposition enables the defendant to have her participatory rights fulfilled by way of expressing her point of view on the facts in an potentially adversarial and public hearing. As a matter of fact, the defendant's presence is crucial within the trial following the opposition. On the one hand, accepting the penal order means to waive, implicitly, one's right to be heard, in an adversarial context, by the judge, before the decision is delivered. On the other hand, the opposition implies the defendant's intention to take part in her trial: it is

---

[158] In the case of Covaci (CJEU, judgment of 15 October 2015, C-216/14), the CJEU seems to be aware of the risk of discrimination, represented by the German limit of 15 days, especially when the defendant does not reside within the jurisdiction: Ruggeri (2016), p. 45.

[159] As the Greek one, the Luxembourgish regulation stipulates that, once the penal order has become final, it can be challenged by the ordinary means of appeal.

[160] CJEU, *Covaci* (fn. 145); CJEU, *Tranca, Reiter and Opria*, judgment of 22 March 2017, joined cases C-124/16, C-188/16 and C-213/16; *Sleutjes*, judgment of 12 October 2017, C-278/16.

plausible that some jurisdictions consider the defendant's personal participation to the following trial a condition to proceed. In Germany, the defendant has the right, albeit not the duty, to be present in court, for the main hearing, however, if the defendant is absent with no plausible justification and is not even represented by a lawyer, the case shall be dismissed and the penal order will regain effect and become final. In Hungary, the defendant's participation at the trial is mandatory: if she does not appear in court, her request for retrial is dismissed.

Since the opposition aims at granting the defendant to the full exercise of her fair trial rights, it is a common feature that the decision delivered at the end of the trial, following the opposition, can be challenged with the ordinary means of appeal. It is up to the defendant to take this into account when deciding whether or not to challenge the penal order. If she opposes, there will be an ordinary proceeding, leading to a first instance decision that may be challenged by a means of appeal. The fast-track procedure will be substituted by a possibly long proceeding, which may be barred by a statute of limitation. This issue deserves special consideration, especially because the offenses for which a penal order can be issued are usually punished with less serious penalties and thus have shorter timeframe for statute of limitation (e.g., in Italy).

Concluding on this point, it is worth noting that *inaudito reo* proceedings are very common within the twelve countries considered in this study. The aim of reducing time and costs by a fast track procedure is tempting and domestic lawmakers seem to be satisfied with the balance between penal order and possible subsequent opposition.[161] On the one hand, *inaudito reo* decision entails a complete restriction on the fair trial rights; on the other, the opposition allows for an almost full recovery of such rights. Furthermore, the European Court of Human Rights and EU law have never really challenged, so far, these proceedings. The Strasbourg Court has had few opportunities of ruling upon this topic. Recently, the CJEU had to deliver several decisions related to *inaudito reo* national proceedings. Neither in the case of *Covaci*, nor in the following cases of *Tranca, Reiter and Opria* and of *Sleutjes* did the Luxembourg court take a strong critical position on the topic; the EU law rules only for mandatory information of the defendant about her right to oppose and the timeframe for doing so (coupled with linguistic assistance, if necessary). Moreover, the recent Directive 2016/343/EU, on the strengthening of certain aspects of the presumption of innocence and of the right to be present at trial did not prevent *inaudito reo* proceedings. Article 8, combined with recital No. 41, underpins *de plano* proceedings, in which the decision is delivered without a previous hearing. In fact, the defendant's right to be present is granted "only if one or more hearings are held" (Recital 41). Thus, it is possible to argue that the current European framework does not impose amendments of,[162] or restrictions on, the existing legislation on penal order procedures. According to the most recent EU legislation, there

---

[161] Though this was criticized some scholars. Cf. Ruggeri (2016), p. 48.

[162] With the exception of the Bulgarian case, where the remedy provided covers only matters of law and not of fact.

may even be room for those jurisdictions that do not allow for such procedures to introduce *inaudito reo* decisions, with the effect of speeding up prosecutions for less serious crimes.

6   Participatory Rights in Transnational Criminal Justice

The principle of mutual recognition, being the cornerstone of the AFSJ,[163] harnessed the attention of the member states' judicial authorities and of the CJEU on the respect of participatory rights. In particular, the circulation of criminal decisions within the AFSJ brought the matter of executing *in absentia* convictions to the general attention.

On the one hand, even under the 1957 European Convention on Extradition, previously in force, shortcomings had occurred between some of the member states, because of the different (or apparently different) approach to the defendant's right/duty to be present at her trial. Actually, Article 3 of the Second Additional Protocol (1978), provided for non-mandatory ground for refusal of extradition whenever the conviction held *in absentia* did not respect the minimum rights of the defence. Within the general framework of such Convention, bilateral relationships between Italy and Spain became tense before the entry into force of Framework Decision 2002/584/JHA, with specific regard to execution of surrenders of persons having been convicted in default in Italy.

On the other hand, it is well known that Article 5 of the EAW Framework Decision expressly considered the matter of *in absentia* final decisions,[164] allowing the executing State to submit the surrender of the person to the condition of a retrial of the case in the defendant's presence. Moreover, the Framework Decision 2009/299/JHA enacted a new Article 4a into the EAW Framework Decision, while converting the case of Article 5 into a non-mandatory ground for refusal.

In the following paragraphs, therefore, I shall examine how European jurisdictions enacted the EAW provisions into their legislation, case-law and practices. Furthermore, since the mutual trust lies at the core of the whole system of the AFSJ, the matter of the parties' personal participation into MLA practices may affect also the constellation of the trans-border taking of evidence.

---

[163] Klip (2015), p. 394.

[164] The defendant having not been personally summoned or informed about the place and time of the hearing could be surrendered at the condition of reopening the proceedings or having a new trial.

6.1 Participatory Safeguards in EAW Proceedings

6.1.1 Participatory Rights in the Decision on Surrender

Concerning the execution of an EAW issued by a foreign judicial authority, the jurisdictions involved in this study seem to guarantee a common standard of participation. The national reports firstly highlight the information for the person arrested because of the EAW. Almost all of them deal with the initial information about the warrant, as well as the right to access to a lawyer and to an interpreter. Moreover, two crucial aspects characterise the first part of the "passive" procedure.[165] First, the execution of the EAW implies the arrest of the person, whom must be brought before a judge within a short period of time. This is the first moment of contact with the judicial authority, in which the person can actively take part in the surrendering procedure. Secondly, the person must be interviewed in order to assess whether she wants to consent to surrender. The authority gathering the possible consent (usually one person, not a court) may not be the same decision-maker ruling upon the execution of the EAW (usually a court: see Germany; Italy). As to the subsequent decision about the execution of EAW, it is usually delivered by a court after a hearing, sometimes public (see, e.g. Greece), sometimes *huis clos* (see, e.g., Italy). However, some of the jurisdictions provide for a non-oral procedure (Germany, where the hearing is exceptional; Portugal[166]; in Bulgaria, the requested person can waive her right to take part personally in the hearing): in this event, the person, with the assistance of her lawyer and interpreter, can submit written allegations.

As to the participation of the requested person in the decision on whether to execute the EAW, one interesting aspect is the right to appoint a lawyer in the issuing country. Not all EU countries have yet implemented the provision of Article 10(4) of EU Directive 2013/48 on the right to access to a lawyer (see Greece and Portugal). As *Costa Ramos and Churro* emphasized, such a limitation can hinder the opportunity for the requested person and her lawyer to actively participate in the decision upon surrender.

It is apparent (see, in particular, England and Wales and Italy) that national courts engage in inquiring the existence of possible grounds for refusing the EAW execution, especially with regard to the respect of fundamental rights. In comparison to Framework Decision 2002/584/JHA, national courts (and lawmakers) have attributed themselves the power to refuse extradition in a larger number of cases. This wider inquiry implies the possibility of the requested person taking part personally in the decision-making process with a view to allowing the competent court to gather the necessary information.

---

[165] In the m.l.a. tradition, 'passive' identifies the process of executing a EAW issued by a foreign authority; 'active' is related to the issuing of the EAW.

[166] For some new interesting trend in case-law, see Costa Ramos and Churro, in this volume, Sect. 6.2.

Thus, the personal involvement of the sought individuals in the decision on surrender appears crucial for several reasons. Not only does it enable her to consent to surrender and waive the speciality principle, but also to inquire about possible grounds for refusal. Interestingly, the jurisdictions covered by this study display a different attitude towards consent to be surrendered. Even though not all the summaries cover such a topic, there are several different approaches. In Austria, e.g., the person having agreed to the surrender may challenge the decision delivered by the court (within 3 days) to execute EAW.[167] In France, the Court's decision to execute the EAW cannot be challenged by the requested person who agreed with surrender.[168]

6.1.2   *In Absentia* Proceedings in the Trial Country and Its Relevance in the Surrender Procedure

As to the role that *in absentia* convictions can play into the executing authority's decision to surrender, the majority of the jurisdictions displayed compliance with Framework Decision 2009/299/JHA. Actually, almost every country implemented the consolidated version of the EAW Framework Decision, providing for a new non-mandatory ground for refusal. Greece, however, has not fully implemented this legal instrument yet: thus, according to the Greek legislation, the national court can submit the execution of an EAW to the guarantee of the right to retrial, but cannot refuse the execution.

The other national systems have amended their implementation laws, taking into account the four exceptions set forth by Article 4a of the consolidated version of the EAW Framework Decision (Bulgaria provides for a general provision, based on the respect of fair trial in the foreign *in absentia* proceeding[169]). Some of the authors remark that the national version amended the text of Article 4a, on the basis of some national peculiarities (Italy, Portugal). In particular, Portuguese law does not provide for retrial after *in absentia* convictions: *Costa Ramos and Churro* underline the peculiar situation of the Portuguese courts, which must provide to their counterparts an assurance that is not foreseen by the domestic law.

In addition, England and Wales implemented Framework Decision 2009/299/JHA, providing that the EAW can be executed if: the defendant was present in trial; she was voluntarily absent; she was non-voluntarily absent but she has the right to a retrial with the guarantees of personal presence, new evidence, and the assistance of a lawyer.

The Spanish summary offers a very interesting point of view on this topic. In fact, *Villamarín López* outlined the approach of the Spanish Constitutional Tribunal with regard to the matter of executing EAW based on *in absentia* convictions.

---

[167] See Golser, in this volume, Sect. 6.1.1.

[168] See Drevet, in this volume, Sect. 6.1.1.

[169] See Petrova, in this volume, Sect. 6.1.2.

Spanish constitutional case-law always displayed a critical attitude towards such warrants, considering them non-compliant with the standard of fair trial granted by the Constitution, in particular, with regard to the case of defendants having been convicted *in absentia* as a result of a voluntary and unequivocal waiver of their participatory rights. Domestic courts often had to face the matter, especially with regard to Italian, French and Romanian EAWs. Thus, the Constitutional Court decided to lodge a preliminary ruling to the CJEU, which led to the well-known decision in the case of *Melloni v. Ministerio Fiscal* (C-399/11). As it has been emphasised in another part of this volume,[170] the Luxembourg Court ruled that the national standards of protection cannot jeopardise the guarantees established by the EU law, in the areas in which the Union holds a competence. The Spanish report dealt with this issue from the viewpoint of domestic law, which provides a genuine overview on the inconsistency generated by the Luxembourg ruling within Spanish constitutional case-law.[171]

6.2 Participatory Safeguards in Trans-Border Inquiries and the Taking of Overseas Evidence

As to the participatory rights in trans-border inquiries and, in general, in MLA requests, comparison sketches a multifaceted situation.

Firstly, it is worth noting that, until the EIO Directive is fully implemented, the conditions for execution of MLA requests will be submitted, even within the EU area, to a multitude of regulations. Moreover, as each jurisdiction is bound to respect the existing international treaties and covenants with third parties, national courts will have to deal with very different sets of regulation. It may be argued that it is almost impossible to find a general regulation. In fact, the traditional approach, still adopted by the 1959 CoE European Convention on Mutual Assistance, is based on

---

[170] Ruggeri, in Part VI of this volume, Sect. 2.1.

[171] The 'Melloni case' has been compared with recent affaire of C-42/17, apparently concluding the so-called 'Taricco case' (CJEU, Grand Chamber, 5 December 2017, M.A.S. and M.B., C-42/17, and previously CJEU, 15 September 2015, Taricco, C-105/14). In a similar situation, the Italian Constitutional Court lodged a preliminary ruling based of the national standard of protection of the principle of legality, in relation with the statute of limitation for offenses punishing the VAT avoidance. In such case, however, the Luxembourg Court concluded by recognising that national courts are bound to set aside national legislation in contradiction with the EU, "unless that disapplication entails a breach of the principle that offences and penalties must be defined by law because of the lack of precision of the applicable law or because of the retroactive application of legislation imposing conditions of criminal liability stricter than those in force at the time the infringement was committed". About the 'Taricco case' see Pollicino and Bassini (2017). As a consequence of the CJEU decision delivered in the case C-42/17, the Italian Constitutional Court recently (10 April 2018) ruled that the Italian judges and courts are not bound to apply the CJEU decision of 15 September 2015, C-105/14, which concluded for setting aside arts. 160 and 161 CCP-Italy.

the application of the requested country's national law.[172] Some authors refer to a general application of the domestic criminal procedural law (England and Wales with P.A.C.E., Portugal). Thus, all the participatory guarantees listed in the national reports must also be applied in MLA passive procedures. *Billis and Gkaniatsos* underline very severe conditions for the person concerned, who is not entitled to be informed of the existence of an on-going MLA procedure, having no opportunity for taking part actively in evidence-taking.[173]

In fact, within the EU area, the implementation of the 2000 Brussels Convention[174] led to the general application of the law of the requesting country, unless this is not compliant with the fundamental principles of the requested country (see Art. 4 of the Convention).[175]

If such a provision enhanced the circulation of evidence and investigative acts, it seems that it did not play a relevant role in fostering the defendant's participatory rights. In fact, the application of the law of the requesting State may help the defendant, against whom the evidence is supposed to be used. The application of a familiar regulation grants control over the piece of evidence taken abroad. However, there seems to be a general lack of regulation of private parties' initiative in taking evidence abroad (Italy, Luxembourg, Portugal).[176] In fact, only the domestic judicial authority can send a MLA request to a foreign judicial authority, for the taking of evidence or investigative acts. Hopefully, such a critical situation could be partly overturned with the implementation of the EIO. Although Directive 2014/41/EU does not expressly cover such a provision, the national implementation acts may provide for the right of the defence to request the judicial authority for an investigation order. This is the case with the Italian Legislative Decree 108/2017, which implemented the EIO legislation,[177] as Article 31 expressly provides for a request by the defendant's counsel. The latter must describe the specific piece of evidence sought and the reasons supporting the request. It is the prosecutor, or the proceeding judge, who is called to rule upon this request, being instead required to give reasons in cases of rejection.

---

[172] Hopefully, the Additional Protocols amended such rule, allowing the requesting authority to proactively participate in the taking of investigative acts and evidence. Cf. Chiavario (2017), p. 1104.

[173] This is also often the case in Portugal, unless by the nature of the acts the person has to be informed (a search of the house of the accused for example).

[174] In 2016, Italy also implemented the Convention was already binding for most EU countries since a long (moreover, in 2004, Island and Norway had already signed an agreement for the application of some parts of such convention in the MLA relationships with EU member states: 22004A0129(01).

[175] For the exceptions foreseen by Romania, see Ciopec and Roibu, in this volume, Sect. 6.2.

[176] Mangiaracina, in this volume, Sect. 6.2; Covolo, in this volume, Sect. 6.2; Costa Ramos and Churro, in this volume, Sect. 6.2.

[177] For a general overview of this Italian legislation, see Daniele (2017a), pp. 108 ff.

7 Requirements of Personal Participation and *In Absentia* Proceedings. The Perspective of Supranational and International Human Rights Law

The final part of the form submitted to the authors aims at summarising the relationships between domestic law and the twofold system of European law. Considering the several topics that have been examined, are the national regulations of participatory rights consistent with the European Convention on Human Rights and the EU primary and secondary law? Actually, the reader may have the impression, before reading any further, that the answers has already been given. In fact, addressing the various topic of the attachment, the authors often relied on the patterns offered by the ECtHR case-law and EU law. Amendments and evolutions in the different legislations have almost always been presented in light of the criteria set forth by the Strasbourg Court or EU institutions. Meanwhile, authors often highlighted aspects of their national jurisdictions that are not compliant—and cannot be compliant—with European standards.

In general, both the European Convention and the EU law deeply affected, albeit in different ways, the national regulations of *in absentia* trials. The trends highlighted by the rapporteurs may be very divergent, having different backgrounds and having produced heterogeneous consequences. Nevertheless, they all testify to the process of a growing sensitivity towards participatory rights. On the one hand, the importance of providing the defendant with official information about her own trial and to assess the unequivocal waiver of her right to be present at trial; on the other, the existence of an effective remedy against decisions delivered in the violation of the abovementioned guarantees. In this context, the movement towards implementation of EU 'Road-map' directives added important elements to the defendant's right to information and access to a lawyer, promptly and confidentially. Unfortunately, the recent directive 2016/343/EU has not yet been generally implemented. However, many rapporteurs referred to this legal instrument, in some cases emphasizing its structural shortcomings, in other cases its general compliance with the new legislation.

Ultimately, in view of the second part of this volume,[178] it is interesting to see how the authors examined the relationship between their jurisdictions and the second layer of European law. Beyond these general remarks, it is quite difficult to detect common trends among the countries, with regard to their relationships with the ECHR and the EU law. The authors pointed out specific issues that, in their opinion may be in breach of the ECHR or the EU legislation, the latter having been partially implemented or not yet implemented. There is no doubt that, today, the most peculiar situation is that of England and Wales, which are currently facing Brexit, on the one hand, and possibly the repeal of the Human Rights Act 1998,

---

[178] See Quattrocolo and Ruggeri, in Part VI of this volume.

implementing the ECHR domestically.[179] However, comparing the situation of the twelve member states under this viewpoint inspires some final remarks.

8   Concluding Remarks

Although the reader probably noted a low level of uniformity among the domestic regulations of *in absentia* proceedings, the national reports suggest a pattern of harmonisation. It is evident that many decades of ECtHR case-law and the recent EU legislation created a general framework of basic procedural rights that surround the specific topic of *in absentia* trials. In fact, according to the ECtHR doctrine, the major conditions for a potentially lawful *in absentia* trial are: official information of the defendant about her trial; unequivocal waiver of the right to be present; availability of an effective remedy. However, these three aspects are strictly related to a wider framework of basic guarantees. Being formally and promptly informed, in a language and in a manner that is accessible to every defendant is a basic requirement underpinning the first condition set forth by the ECHR. Moreover, access to a lawyer is fundamental in establishing whether there has been a conscious and unequivocal waiver of the defendant's right to be present at her trial.

In light these considerations, it is possible to argue that in the majority of the countries represented in this study, the impact of the ECHR and EU law created a basic layer of guarantees that underpin the enactment of *in absentia* trials. Of course, accordance with ECtHR decisions and implementation of the EU law are not universal and the individual summaries display situations of persisting inconsistency, regardless of the frequency and intensity of the European standards' violation. In particular, what stems from some of the national pictures (especially France, Germany, Hungary—where the brand-new code, entered into force since January 2018, provides for major access to the investigation file, although with the purpose to allow early plea bargaining—Italy and Portugal), is a need for further transparency during the investigation and pre-trial phase. As *Drevet* underlines in her conclusions, a more effective access to the file during the initial stage of the proceeding would strengthen compliance of *in absentia* proceedings to the fair trial standards.[180]

Moreover, a more basic trend of harmonisation stems from the overview on the member states. *In absentia* trials, instead of being a reducing phenomenon, are becoming more and more frequent, all over Europe. The last decades testify to a growing trend of reduction of defendants' personal participation at trials: growing on the basis of figures and numbers; growing on the basis of the number of jurisdictions admitting it (and allowing for judicial cooperation upon requests issued on the basis of *in absentia* convictions). Such a trend derives, firstly, from a deep change in

---

[179] For more details, see Quattrocolo and Ruggeri, in Part VI of this volume.
[180] Drevet, in this volume, Sect. 8.

social habits, as more and more people freely and frequently move to other countries, not to evade justice, but for personal and professional reasons. The value of personal participation at the hearings is balanced with other values or interests, that may be considered preeminent by the defendant. This may, of course, sound at odds with those jurisdictions, like the German one, being inspired by the goal of assessing the truth. In fact, considering such an aim, the defendant's personal presence appears fundamental and *Vogel* emphasises the uneasiness of the German Constitutional Court in dealing with the increasing trend of *in absentia* proceedings, at a European level.[181] Actually, the very recent Hungarian reform appears to be inspired, instead, by more 'contemporary' philosophy, having established that the defendant's personal presence at trial is a right and not a duty.[182]

Secondly, the huge crisis that globally affected the economy impinged also on the costs of criminal justice. To participate personally and actively in one's own proceedings may imply huge expenses that defendants are not able to face: appointing a lawyer, even only to understand the charge and the consequences of self-representation implies a cost that may be too high. Meanwhile, the need to face the crisis by enhancing efficient policies urged national governments to cut public expenses, including in the area of criminal justice. In this context, delivering a decision regardless of the defendant's awareness of the proceeding, and her unequivocal will to waive her right to be present, may represent a result in terms of efficiency (see *Petrova*'s concluding remarks on this point).[183] This seems to be the context in which even the English common law culture moved towards a greater entertainment of *in absentia* proceedings.

Thus, the results of this study may contribute to focusing attention on the conditions of *in absentia* trials. Far from being a receding phenomenon, the enactment of trial without the defendant's personal participation is going to become an even more widespread practice (see in particular England and Wales and Portugal reports). Regardless of the reasons for this occurrence, the main issue, in the near future, seems to be the establishment of a clear and precise pattern of guarantees and, especially, remedies. This is the trend clearly underpinning the recent Dir. 2016/343/EU,[184] insisting more on remedies against *in absentia* decisions, rather than on the fulfilling of informative measures, preventing 'non-voluntary' situations *in absentia* trials. As *Mangiaracina* notes in her concluding remarks, the directive could have set higher standards of protection, instead of emphasising the issue of remedies.[185] It is probable that the political convergence on strengthening remedies is the result of the two abovementioned trends. In actuality, ensuring an effective summoning system in a context of ever faster free movement of people may be unattainable.

---

[181] Vogel, in this volume, Sect. 8.

[182] Gácsi et al., in this volume, Sect. 8.

[183] Petrova, in this volume, Sect. 8.

[184] Though *Ruggeri* remarks that, in the case of *Mariani v. France*, the ECtHR displayed a similar attitude, proving satisfied with the bare availability of an effective remedy against *in absentia* decisions. Cf. Ruggeri, in Part VI of this volume, Sect. 2.2.

[185] Mangiaracina, in this volume, Sect. 8.

And although IT technologies may appear to be the solution for such a shortcoming, collapsing systems of justice may consider such a solution too expensive, in these times of very slow recovery from economic crisis. As *Ciopec and Roibu* note in their concluding remarks, failure to bring the defendant to Court does not lead to a stalling of the proceedings: with the judicial authorities having satisfied a minimum level of diligence in this respect, the proceedings can move on, provided that a remedy is available in case the defendant claims her own ignorance about the proceedings against her.

In light of these remarks, and without anticipating other Parts of this book, it is possible to argue that, so far, the ECtHR has built up a twofold scheme for compliance of *in absentia* trials to the Convention: the Strasbourg Court always attached the same importance to both official information and unequivocal waiver—as preconditions for the defendant's decision not to exercise her participatory rights—and the availability of an effective remedy against *in absentia* decision, in case the defendant claims that she did not know about the proceedings. Within this consolidated framework, Directive 2016/343/EU appears to almost push harmonization on the second aspect, requiring the MS to display more diligence in providing possible remedies rather than in bringing defendants to trial. It is likely that a different method would probably require major efforts on the administrative and bureaucratic side. Nevertheless, burdening the member states with the duty of successfully and effectively informing the defendant of her trial, allowing her to exercise her participatory rights, would have been more consistent with the philosophy of the Roadmap and of the previous directives.

References

Ancel M (1971) Utilité et méthodes du droit comparé, Eléments d'introduction générale à l'étude comparative des droits. Editions Ides et Calendes, Neuchâtel

Belluta H (2006) Imparzialità del giudice e dinamiche probatorie *ex officio*. Giappichelli, Torino

Chiavario M (2001) Diritto processuale penale. Profilo istituzionale, 3rd edn. Utet, Torino

Chiavario M (2008) La videoconference comme moyenne de participations aux audiences pénales. Revue Trimestrielle des Droits de l'Homme:223–237

Chiavario M (2017) Diritto processuale penale. Utet giuridica, Torino-Milano

Damaška M (2004) Negotiated justice in international criminal law. J Int Crim Just:1018–1039

Daniele M (2017a) L'ordine europeo di indagine penale entra a regime. Prime riflessioni sul d. lgs. n. 108 del 2017. www.penalecontemporaneo.it. Accessed 31 July 2018

Daniele M (2017b) La partecipazione a distanza allargata. www.penalecontemporaneo.it. Accessed 31 July 2018

Englich B, Mussweiler T, Strack F (2005) The last word in court – a hidden disadvantage for the defence. Law Hum Behav:705–722

Fletcher G (1998) Comparative law as a subversive discipline. Am J Comp Law 46:683–700

Grande E (2003) Uno sguardo oltre il confine. La comparazione giuridica al di là del diritto privato. In: Bertorello V (ed) Io comparo, tu compari, egli compara: che cosa, come, perché? Giuffré, Milano, pp 153–156

Grande E (2013) Comparative criminal justice. Cambridge companion of comparative law, pp 191–209

Illuminati G (2005) The frustrated turn to adversarial procedure in Italy. Wash Univ Global Stud
    Law Rev:567–581
Klip A (2015) European criminal law, 3rd edn. Intersentia, Antwerp
Kostoris R (2011) La revisione del giudicato e i rapporti tra violazioni convenzionali e invalidità
    processuali secondo le regole interne. La legislazione penale:471–480
Langer M (2004) From legal transplant to legal translation: the globalization of plea bargaining
    and the Americanization thesis in criminal procedure. Harv Int Law J 45:1–65
Lavarini B (2012) L'esame delle parti. Giappichelli, Torino
Legrand P (1997) The impossibility of legal transplant. Maastricht J Eur Comp Law 4(2):111–124
Maffei S (2004) Negotiation on evidence and negotiation on sentence: adversarial experiments in
    Italian criminal procedure. J Int Crim Just:1050–1069
Magendie JCl (2004) Célérité et qualité de la justice. La gestion du temps dans le procès. Rapport
    au Garde des Scaux. www.presse.justice.gouv.fr. Accessed 31 July 2018
Mannozzi G (2016) Le alternative alla detenzione: profili critici e prospettive di riforma - le aper-
    ture alla giustizia riparativa nell'ambito delle misure alternative alla detenzione. Giurisprudenza
    Italiana: 1517 ff
Mauro C (2015) Dell'utilità del criterio della non punibilità per particolare tenuità del fatto in un
    sistema di opportunità dell'azione penale. Esperienze francesi. In: Quattrocolo S (ed) I nuovi
    epiloghi del procedimento per particolare tenuità del fatto. Giappichelli, Torino, pp 143–169
Mazza O (2008) Esame delle parti private. In: Enciclopedia del Diritto, Annali II, t. 1. Giuffré,
    Milano, pp …
Morillo F, Bellander Todino I (2017) The victims' rights directive: origins and expectations. In:
    Bargis M, Belluta H (eds) Vittime di reato e sistema penale. Giappichelli, Torino, pp 3–14
Orlandi R (1990) Art. 209. In: Chiavario M (ed) Commento al nuovo codice di procedura penale,
    vol II. Utet, Torino, pp 502–507
Ost F (2002) Les lois conventionnellement formées tiennent lieu de conventions à ceux qui les ont
    faites. In: Gérard F, Ost F, Van de Kerchove M (eds) Droit négocié, Droit imposé? Presses
    Universitaires Saint Louis, Bruxelles, pp 17–107
Patané V (2006) Il diritto al silenzio dell'imputato. Giappichelli, Torino
Pollicino O, Bassini M (2017) Defusing the Taricco bomb through fostering constitutional toler-
    ance: all roads lead to Rome, in Vervssungsblog. Accessed 5 Dec 2017
Pradel J (1995) Droit pénal Comparé. Dalloz, Paris
Quattrocolo S (2014) Il contumace cede la scena processuale all'assente, mentre l'irreperibile
    l'abbandona. Riflessioni a prima lettura sulla nuova disciplina del procedimento senza impu-
    tato. www.penalecontemporaneo.it. Accessed 31 July 2018
Ruggeri S (2008) Il procedimento per decreto penale. Giappichelli, Torino
Ruggeri S (2016) Inaudito Reo proceedings, defence rights, and harmonisation goals in the
    EU. Responses of the European Courts and new perspectives of EU law. Eucrim 1:42–51
Ruggeri S (2017) Audi Alteram Partem in criminal proceedings. Springer International Publishing,
    Cham
Sacco R (1991) Legal formants: a dynamic approach to comparative law. Am J Comp Law:1–34
Signorato S (2017) L'ampliamento dei casi di partecipazione a distanza tra logiche efficientistiche
    e menomazioni difensive. www.lalegslazionepenale.eu. Accessed 31 July 2018
Sperduti G (1977) Dualism and monism: a confrontation to be overcome. Ital Yearb Int Law
    (3):31–49
Terry WC, Surette R (1986) Media technology and the courts: the case of closed circuit video
    arraignments in Miami, Florida. Crim Just Rev:31–36
Tulkens F (2002) Negotiated justice. In: Delmas-Marty M, Spencer J (eds) European criminal
    procedures. Cambridge University Press, Cambridge, pp 641–687
Van der Vils EJ (2012) Videoconferencing in criminal proceedings. In: Braun S, Taylor J (eds)
    Videoconference and remote interpreting in criminal proceedings. Intersentia, Antwerp,
    pp 13–31

Varraso G (2017) Art. 420-ter. In: Canzio G, Bricchetti R (eds) Codice di procedura penale. Giuffré, Milano, pp 3012–3032

Vincent J, Guinchard S, Montagnier G, Varinard A (2005) Institutions judiciaries. Organisation, juridictions, gens de justice. Dalloz, Paris

Vogler R (2012) England and Wales. In: Ruggeri S (ed) Liberty and security in Europe. A comparative analysis on pre-trial precautionary measures in criminal proceedings. V&R Press (Universitätsverlag Osnabrück), pp 87–103

Zweigert K, Kötz H (1998) An introduction to comparative law. Oxford University Press, Oxford

Personal Participation and *In Absentia* Trials in Civil Proceedings Imposing Pecuniary Penalties Within the European Judicial Area

Elena D'Alessandro

Abstract This chapter explores the role of personal participation in civil proceedings imposing civil pecuniary penalties within the European judicial area. It also deals with the civil trial in absentia in order to determine whether a civil default judgment rendered in a EU Member State shall be considered, in itself, as a penalty against a defendant who deliberately fails to appear at the hearing.

Abbreviations

CPC	Civil Procedure Code
CJEU	Court of Justice of the European Union
ECHR	European Convention on Human Rights
ECtHR	European Court of Human Rights
EU	European Union
EUCFR	European Charter of Fundamental Rights
ICPC	Italian Civil Procedure Code

1 Theoretical Framework

According to the common understanding, there is a clear difference between criminal and civil justice.

Criminal-law actions are brought by the State when a public offence has been committed, whereas civil cases are promoted by a private party (the plaintiff) seeking to vindicate his own rights against another civilian (the defendant).

E. D'Alessandro (✉)
Department of Law, University of Turin, Turin, Italy
e-mail: elena.dalessandro@unito.it

© Springer Nature Switzerland AG 2019
S. Quattrocolo, S. Ruggeri (eds.), *Personal Participation in Criminal Proceedings*, Legal Studies in International, European and Comparative Criminal Law 2, https://doi.org/10.1007/978-3-030-01186-4_15

Criminal proceedings are strictly related to punishment and imprisonment, while civil proceedings are often related to compensation for damages as a consequence of the breach of a behaviour that the law imposes on everyone with regard to other's rights.

However, the two systems are not diametrically and totally opposed as it might seem, because civil proceedings can often also serve as a vehicle for punishment, through the imposition of 'civil pecuniary penalties'.

A 'civil pecuniary penalty' aims at punishing the losing party for his offensive conduct, basically in tort cases, and at deterring him and others like him from similar wrongdoing in the future.

The most well-known examples of civil pecuniary penalties are the American punitive damages awarded by juries in tort cases,[1] and accepted by the mid-nineteenth century.

Until 2008 the amount of punitive damages, freely determined by the jury due to the lack of a clear frame prescribed by the law and therefore unpredictable, usually went beyond the amount of compensatory damages.

In the famous case *BMW North America v. Gore*[2] (1996), Dr. Gore purchased a new BMW auto from an authorized Alabama dealer, subsequently discovering that the car had been repainted. Consequently, he brought a suit for fraud asking for compensatory and punitive damages against the American distributor of BMW.

At trial, the jury returned a verdict finding BMW liable for compensatory damages of $ 4000, in addition assessing $ 4 million in punitive damages, then reduced to 2 million by the Court of appeal. Because of its magnitude, the US Supreme court considered that the 2 million punitive damages award was "grossly excessive" in relation to the State's legitimate interests in punishing unlawful conduct and deterring its repetition.

Twelve years later, in 2008,[3] in the case *Exxon Shipping Co. v. Baker*, the US Supreme Court, in a 5-3 decision, found that a 1:1 punitive-compensatory ratio was a fair upper limit in maritime cases. Therefore, it ruled that the punitive damages awarded to the victims of the Valdez oil spill against Exxon Shipping must be reduced from $ 2.5 billion to $ 500 million.

Focusing now on Europe, it can be observed that, although the awarding of punitive damages by an EU court seems not to be permitted by the Recital 32 of the Rome II Regulation,[4] many European Member States deal with 'other' forms of civil pecuniary penalties. Indeed, penalty payments are popular.

---

[1] On the doctrine of punitive damages see e.g., Morris (1931), p. 1173 ff.; Meurkens (2014), p. 42 ff.; Polinsky and Shavell (1988), pp. 869–962; Sharkey (2003), pp. 347–453; Sunstein et al. (1998), pp. 2071–2153; D'Alessandro (2007), p. 383 ff.

[2] US Supreme Court, *BMW of North America, Inc. v. Gore* 517 U.S. 559 (1996).

[3] US Supreme Court, *Exxon Shipping Co. v. Baker*, 554 U.S. 471 (2008).

[4] Von Hein, Article 26, in: Callies (2015), p. 810; Stone (2007), p. 177. However, the idea of recognizing American decision awarding punitive damages has been accepted in Spain (*Tribunal Supremo, Sala de lo Civil*, judgement of 13 November 2001), France (*Cour de cassation*, judgments of 1 December 2010, No. 0913303, and 7 November 2012, No. 11-2387) and Italy (Italian Court of Cassation, Joint Sections, judgment of 5 July 2017, No. 16601, *Foro italiano*, 2017, 2639, with a comment by D'Alessandro, Riconoscimento di sentenze di condanna a danni punitivi: tanto tuonò che piovve.

In France,[5] Belgium,[6] Spain[7] and Poland[8] penalty payments (*'astreintes'*) against the debtor, who can be a natural or a physical person, have become a very efficient means of enforcement of pecuniary claims.

In term of contents, penalty payments are orders of payment of a sum of money for each day of delay issued against a natural or a physical person, usually (but not always, as indicated below) paid to the claimant, rather than to the State.

In Italy, a system of penalty payments inspired by French/Belgian experience was introduced in 2009, by way of Law 69/2009, which added a new article 614-*bis* within the CPC, titled "Performance of obligations to do or not to do".[9]

According to article 614-*bis* ICPC:

1. By the judgment against the defendant, except where this is manifestly unjust, upon motion of a party, the court may establish the amount of money due by the party having an obligation to perform, for any breach, delay or failure to observe the duty. The judgment against the defendant is enforceable [...]
2. The court determines the amount of the sum under the first paragraph, taking into account the value of the dispute, [...] the predictable damage, and any other useful circumstance.

Regarding Italy, two other forms of civil penalties should be considered:

---

[5] According to articles L. 131-1 to L. 131-4 of the French Code of Civil Enforcement Proceedings. For a brief overview on French *astreintes,* in English language, see: Kennet (2000), p. 291; Tallon, Contract Law, in: Bermann and Picard (2008), p. 234 ff.; Herzog and Weser (1967), p. 559.

[6] As mentioned by the Advocate general Spuznar, in his opinion delivered on 16 April 2015, Case C-14 (ECLI:EU:C:2015:233), paras 12–18:

> Penalty payments are governed by Articles 1385 *bis* to 1385 *nonies* of the *Code judiciare.* Article 1385 *bis* of the Judicial Code provides: 'On the application of one of the parties, the court may order the other party to pay a sum of money, known as a penalty payment, if the principal obligation laid down in the judgment has not been performed, without prejudice to damages, where appropriate. ...'. Article 1385 *ter* of the Judicial Code is worded as follows: 'The court may set the penalty payment at a fixed amount or at an amount determined by unit of time or by breach. In the last two cases, the court may also set an amount above which the order to pay the penalty payment shall cease to have effect.' Article 1385 *quater* of the Judicial Code provides: 'The whole amount of the accrued penalty payment is payable to the party who obtained the order. That party may pursue recovery of the penalty payment on the basis of the order imposing it. ...'. Article 1385 *quinquies* of the Judicial Code is worded as follows: 'The court that imposed the penalty payment may also cancel it, suspend its accrual for a stipulated period or reduce its amount, on application by the party ordered to pay the penalty, if he is permanently or temporarily entirely or partially unable to perform the principal obligation. The court may not cancel or reduce the penalty payment if it has accrued before the circumstances causing the inability arise.' Since the enforceable instrument permitting recovery of the penalty payment is the judicial decision imposing that penalty (Article 1385 *quater* of the Judicial Code), the beneficiary does not need to have the penalty payment quantified prior to enforcement. If the debtor challenges enforcement, the creditor of the penalty payment must produce evidence to establish the breaches alleged. It will then be for the court dealing with the enforcement proceedings to decide whether the conditions for payment of the penalty are satisfied.

[7] See Articles 709 and 711 of the Spanish CPC ("Ley 1/2000, de 7 de enero, de Enjuiciamiento Civil').

[8] Pursuant to Article 1050 and 1051 of the Polish CPC.

[9] *See* e.g. Ferrari and Bocharova (2015), p. 13.

- *Article 96(3) ICPC.* In order to discourage the use of litigation, Law 69/2009 added a new paragraph to Article 96 of the ICPC. The new paragraph empowers the courts, even on their own motion, to order the losing party to pay—to the opposing party—a further and equitable amount of money besides the costs.[10]
- Italian case-law[11] tends to consider Article 96(3) ICPC a (civil) penalty against abuses of process.
- No statutory limits to the amount of awardable money are provided, so the courts have a complete discretion in sanctioning vexatious litigation.
- *Legislative Decree 7/2016.* In 2016, Legislative Decree No. 7 of 15 January was enacted to reduce the number of penal cases pending, decriminalizing a number of minor crimes, such as insult, forgery in a private deed, appropriation of property. These still remain civil torts.

Instead of criminal sanctions, infringements in those fields will incur in civil monetary penalties to be paid to the State.[12] More precisely, in the course of a civil proceedings for damages relating to a tort brought by the plaintiff—i.e., the offended person—the court, on its own motion, may order the losing defendant to pay, in addition to compensatory damages, a civil statutory penalty (depending on the case: up to 8000 or 12,000 €) to the State, possible by instalments.

Other examples of civil penalties paid to the State, rather than to the creditor, can be traced in Finnish[13] and German law.[14]

---

[10] See *e.g.* Lupoi (2012), pp. 25–51.

[11] See, in particular, Italian Constitutional Court, judgment of 1 June 2016, No 152.

[12] See *e.g.* Bove (2016) and Lavarini (2016), pp. 845–863.

[13] See the Opinion of the Advocate-General Spuznar, delivered on 16 April 2015, p. 3.

[14] See:

  (i) Paragraph 888 (*Actions that may not be taken by others*), in the English official translation of the German CPC, available at https://www.gesetze-im-internet.de/englisch_zpo/englisch_zpo.html

  (1) Where an action that depends exclusively on the will of the debtor cannot be taken by a third party, and where a corresponding petition has been filed, the court of first instance hearing the case is to urge the debtor to take the action in its ruling by levying a coercive penalty payment and, for the case that such payment cannot be obtained, by coercive punitive detention, or by directly sentencing him to coercive punitive detention. The individual coercive penalty payment may not be levied in an amount in excess of 25,000 euros. The stipulations of Chapter 2 regarding detention shall apply mutatis mutandis to coercive punitive detention. (2) No warning shall be issued regarding the coercive measures. (3) These rules shall not be applied in those cases in which a person is sentenced to provide services under a service agreement).

  (ii) Paragraph 889 (*Statutory declaration in lieu of an oath pursuant to civil law*):

  (1) In cases in which, in accordance with the stipulations of civil law, the debtor has been sentenced to making a statutory declaration in lieu of an oath, this declaration shall be made before the local court (Amstgericht, AG) as the court responsible for execution, in the district of which the debtor has his place of residence in Germany or, should he not

Under German law, in particular, if someone fails to observe an obligation not to act, it is possible to impose monetary penalties and even imprisonment not exceeding 6 months. Notwithstanding the fact that imprisonment is a typical criminal sanction, the CJEU, in the case *Realchemie Nederland BV v. Bayer CropoScience AG*,[15] held that:

> Even if, according to Paragraph 890 German CPC, the fine at issue in the main proceedings is punitive and the reasoning in the order imposing it explicitly mentions the penal nature of that fine, the fact remains that, in those proceedings, there is a dispute between two private persons.[16]

That is precisely the reason why such German penalties have been considered as having a civil-law character, and thus have been included in the meaning of "civil and commercial matters" listed in Article 1 of the Brussels I Recast Regulation (Regulation No. 1215 of 2012) on jurisdiction, recognition and enforcement of judgments, like the aforementioned civil pecuniary penalties in favour of a creditor.

In a wider perspective, it is generally acknowledged that judicial decisions ordering pecuniary penalties in favour of a creditor, when rendered by a civil court in a Member State, are capable of recognition and enforcement within the European Judicial area according to Article 55 of the Brussels I Recast Regulation,[17] which deals with judgments ordering a payment by way of a penalty "in civil and commercial matters".

---

have such a place of residence, where the debtor has his place of abode, and otherwise before the local court as the execution court, in the district of which the court of first instance hearing the case has its seat. The stipulations of sections 478 to 480 and section 483 shall apply *mutatis mutandis*; (2) Should the debtor fail to appear at the hearing determined for the statutory declaration in lieu of an oath to be made, or should he refuse to make such a statutory declaration in lieu of an oath, the execution court shall proceed as set out in section 888.

(iii) Paragraph 890 (*Forcing the debtor to cease and desist from actions, or to tolerate actions*):

(1) Should the debtor violate his obligation to cease and desist from actions, or to tolerate actions to be taken, the court of first instance hearing the case is to sentence him for each count of the violation, upon the creditor filing a corresponding petition, to a coercive fine and, for the case that such payment cannot be obtained, to coercive detention or coercive detention of up to six (6) months. The individual coercive fine may not be levied in an amount in excess of 250,000 euros, and the coercive detention may not be longer than a total of two (2) years; (2) The sentence must be preceded by a corresponding warning that is to be issued by the court of first instance hearing the case, upon corresponding application being made, unless it is set out in the judgment providing for the obligation; (3) Moreover, upon the creditor having filed a corresponding petition, the debtor may be sentenced to creating a security for any damages that may arise as a result of future violations, such security being created for a specific period of time) of the German CPC.

[15] CJEU, *Realchemie Nederland BV v. Bayer CropScience AG*, judgment of 18 October 2011, case C-406/09.

[16] *Ibid.*, para 41.

[17] As well as in the EFTA States, according to Article 49 of the 2007 Lugano Convention.

The brief analysis carried out hitherto shows that proceedings imposing civil pecuniary penalties are considered full-fledged 'civil proceedings'.

Even though the idea of punishment does not depend on the nature of the proceedings in which it is inflicted,[18] the changing of label, from criminal-law to civil-law "sanction", seems to have significant consequences in terms of procedural guarantees,[19] due to the differing procedural standards applied in civil and criminal matters.[20]

A first practical consequence is that in civil proceedings, in Europe, there is no right to a jury trial.

A second consequence relating to the burden of proof rules is that in a civil-law action imposing a sanction the plaintiff needs to prove that the defendant has committed the offence on the balance of probabilities, whereas in criminal proceedings, in principle, the prosecution has to prove guilt beyond any reasonable doubt.

A third consequence, whose analysis will be the prime scope of paragraph 2 of this study, relates to the role of personal participation in civil actions imposing civil pecuniary penalties within the European judicial area.

A further question, which paragraph 3 of this chapter aims to address, concerns the so-called 'in absentia civil trials'. The relevant question is whether a civil default judgment rendered in proceedings pending in a Member State in the absence of the defendant shall be considered, in itself, as a civil penalty against a party who fails to appear at the hearing without any valid reason, such as the absence of service or errors deliberately committed in serving him/her with the claim form (failure of a defendant to appear before a civil court as sanctionable abuse of process).

2 Personal Participation in Civil Proceedings Imposing Civil Pecuniary Penalties

In civil proceedings, the value of self-representation is not universal. Whereas in common law jurisdictions, such as in England and Wales, parties are in principle free to represent themselves before a court (this way taking a direct part in the

---

[18] US Supreme Court, *One 1958 Plymouth Sedan v. Pensylvania,* 380 US 693 (1965).

Even the ECtHR, in order to determine what falls into the notion of criminal law, is looking at the very nature of the sanction, as well as the degree of severity of the penalty that in the worst case the person is liable to incur. A penalty which falls into the notion of criminal law, according to the case-law of the ECtHR, shall comply with the guarantee requirements set in Article 6 ECHR. In addition, the proportionality between the punishment and the personal behaviour of the defendant must be guaranteed.

See, on this point, as for the relationship between the ECHR and national administrative sanctions, ECtHR, *Grande Stevens and Others* v. *Italy,* judgment of 4 March 2014, Appl. Nos. 18640/10, 18647/10, 18663/10, 18668/10 and 18698/10; ECtHR, *Nykänen* v. *Finland,* judgment of 20 May 2014, Appl. No. 11828/11; ECtHR, *A and B* v. *Norwey,* judgment of 15 November 2016, Appl. No. 24130/11 and 29578/11.

[19] See Charney (1974), p. 478 ff.

[20] For a general overview see Kuckes (2006), p. 1 ff.

proceedings) and self-representation is treated as a fundamental right,[21] in most European civil law countries, self-representation in civil actions is not permitted.

In continental Europe, a civil litigant is not entitled to self-represent himself at an oral hearing, as representation by counsel is, in principle, mandatory,[22] and often perceived by the parties as a right. Parties without sufficient financial means to pay their counsels must have access to legal aid.

Because of legal technicalities of civil procedure, in principle parties are merely able to take part in proceedings indirectly, through their counsels. They may exercise their right to comment on all relevant points of fact and law and to offer evidence supporting their position only in an indirect way, through their counsels. However, sometimes the personal attendance of any party at the hearing is allowed.

With regard to the ban of self-representation in civil law jurisdictions, some exceptions are provided.[23]

In France, pursuant to Article 18 of the local CPC, self-representation is only permitted before courts of a lower instance (commercial courts, family courts, juvenile courts), unless otherwise established.

No specific rules are provided for representation in proceedings imposing civil penalties before courts of a lower instance, so that the general rule of Article 18 seems to be applicable.

In Germany, representation by counsel is mandatory, except in the circumstances listed in § 79 (1) of the German CPC, according to which:

> (…) Parties asserting a third-party monetary claim, or a monetary claim assigned to them for the purpose of collecting the claim on another's account, must be represented by counsel as attorneys-in-fact unless they are authorised, pursuant to the stipulations of subsection 2, to represent the creditor, or unless they are collecting a claim of which they were the original creditor.

Adjustments are also provided when the German civil-law action aims at imposing civil (pecuniary) penalties.

Although representation by counsel is in principle mandatory according to § 78 of the German CPC, when the civil-law action aims at imposing a civil penalty, the potential recipient must be heard in person prior to the decision being delivered (§ 891 German CPC), thus ensuring him the guarantee of personal participation in the proceedings.[24]

---

[21] On close examination, however, self-representation in UK civil proceedings is often perceived as a weakness in complex civil cases, as shown by the growing phenomenon of the 'McKenzie Friends'. McKenzie friends are non-lawyers offering assistance and seeking to appear as advocates on behalf of litigants who are self-represented, to make effective their right of defense. On this topic see Assy (2015), pp. 127 ff.

[22] This is also the position taken by the ECHR. On this point, for a critical approach, see Settem (2015), pp. 319 ff.

[23] For instance, self-representation is permitted within continental Europe by the European small claims regulation, established by the EU Regulation No. 861/2007.

[24] On § 891 German CPC see Gruber (2016); Lackmann in: Musielak and Voit (2016), 2016.

In Italy, parties need to be represented by counsel, except for civil and commercial claims concerning very small amounts of less than 1.100 €, which falls under the competence of the justice of the peace (*giudice di pace*). In such cases, parties may personally appear before the judicial authority.

In addition, according to article 86 ICPC, a counsel may represent himself in any civil proceedings, without any other counsel's assistance.[25]

However, unlike in Germany, either prior to the decision imposing a sanction according to articles 96(3) and 614-*bis* ICPC or in relation to tort proceedings covered by Legislative Decree 7/2016, there is no duty for the court of hearing in person the potential recipient of the civil penalty.

As personal participation in Italian civil proceedings, including civil proceedings imposing pecuniary penalties, shall be granted by virtue of article 117 ICPC only if ordered by the court on its own motion (and at its discretion) or jointly requested by the parties, under no circumstances the defendant has a 'right' of personal appearance.

3   *In absentia* Trials: Default Judgment as a Civil Penalty Against the Defendant Who Deliberately Failed to Appear?

All the Member States taken into consideration in paragraph 2—France, Germany, Italy, England and Wales—provide sanctions for the failure to respond to the institution of a civil-law action or for the failure to appear at the hearing.

In France, Germany, England and Wales, the behaviour of the defendant failing to respond to the bringing of a civil-law action is qualified as an admission of the facts by non-denial (*ficta confessio*). If the defendant fails to respond, this way showing his lack of interest for the proceedings, every allegation of fact contained in the claim form shall be deemed to be admitted. More precisely:

In England and Wales, when the defendant deliberately fails to file an acknowledgment of service or to raise a defence within the time limit set by the court, after the applicant has served the claim form and the particular of claims, a default judgment in favour of the plaintiff may be rendered prior to the oral hearing, if the claim is for a specified sum of money or for an amount of money to be decided by the court.[26]

When such requirements are fulfilled, the claimant shall apply in order to have the judgment delivered by administrative process to the court office "without

[25] See e.g. Luiso (2015), pp. 230 ff.

[26] Or if it is a claim for delivery of goods, where the claim form gives the defendant the alternative of paying their value: see Andrews (2013), pp. 239 ff.

troubling a judge".[27] In other words: the court has no power to evaluate on its own motion either the formal validity or the substance of the claim.

Considering those characteristics, from the perspective of the present chapter, an English default judgment, in itself, seems to be a 'civil penalty' against a defendant, who deliberately fails to file an acknowledgment of service or to defend himself in the proceedings.

However, such a 'civil penalty' has been considered by the CJEU consistent with the fundamental guarantee of the fair trial as stated in article 6 ECHR and in article 47 EUCFR.

In the case *Trade Agency*[28] the CJEU held that, even if an English judgment given in default of appearance

> which does not contain any assessment of the subject-matter, basis and merits of the action, is a restriction on a fundamental right within the legal order of that Member State [....] [...] fundamental rights do not constitute unfettered prerogatives and may be subject to restrictions, provided that the restrictions in fact correspond to objectives of general interest pursued by the measure in question and that they do not constitute, with regard to the objectives pursued, a manifest and disproportionate breach of the rights thus guaranteed.[29]

As a consequence, a court of a Member State in which enforcement is sought, pursuant to the Brussels I (Recast) Regulation on recognition and enforcement of judgments within the European Judicial area

> may refuse to enforce a judgment given in default of appearance which disposes of the substance of the dispute but which does not contain an assessment of the subject-matter or the basis of the action and which lacks any argument of its merits, [for breach of fair trial] only if it appears to the court, after an overall assessment of the proceedings and in the light of all the relevant circumstances, that that judgment is a manifest and disproportionate breach of the defendant's right to a fair trial referred to in the second paragraph of Article 47 EUCFR, on account of the impossibility of bringing an appropriate and effective appeal against it.

The European legislator has shared the CJEU's view in article 7(3) of Regulation No. 861/2007, establishing a European Small Claims Procedure, according to which:

> If the court or tribunal has not received an answer from the relevant party within the time limits laid down in Article 5(3) or (6), it shall give a judgment on the claim or counterclaim.

---

[27] Andrews (2013), p. 239. In case-law see *Football Dataco Ltd v. Smoot Enterprises* LTD [2011] EWHC 973 (Ch); [2011] 1 WLR 1978, at para 16 (Briggs J.):

> Default judgment is not, in any circumstances, a judgment on the merits [...] The essential distinction between default judgment and a judgment on the merit is that the court is not when asked to give default judgment called upon to form any view about the merits of the claimant's claim, whether as a matter of fact or law.

[28] CJEU, *Trade Agency Ltd v. Seramico Investments Ltd,* judgment of 6 September 2012, case C-619/10.

[29] *Ibid.*, paras 54–55.

A few years before, another English civil sanction relevant to our topic, the so-called 'debarment',[30] was brought to the attention of the CJEU in the case *Gambazzi*.

Mr. Gambazzi, a Swiss lawyer, appeared in proceedings pending before the English High Court of Justice but was precluded from continuing because he failed to comply with the obligations imposed by an earlier order. He was sanctioned with the exclusion from the proceedings (debarment)[31] and the court entered judgment as if Mr. Gambazzi was in default. Consequently, he argued that his right to a fair trial was breached and, therefore, the English decision was unrecognizable within the European Judicial area, and, in particular, in Italy where he had assets, due to the ground of refusal of recognition of infringement of procedural public policy [art. 27(1) of the Brussels Convention of 1968].

The question was referred to the CJEU by the Court of appeal of Milan (Italy).

In the course of the preliminary proceedings before the CJEU, the Government of the United Kingdom explained that the aim of such civil sanction (debarment) was to ensure the fair and efficient administration of justice. On this regard, the CJUE held that:

> Such an objective is capable of justifying a restriction on the rights of the defence [...]. Such sanctions may not, however, be manifestly disproportionate to the aim pursued, which is to ensure the efficient conduct of proceedings in the interests of the sound administration of justice.

> With regard to the sanction adopted in the main proceedings, the exclusion of Mr Gambazzi from any participation in the proceedings, [...] is [...], the most serious restriction possible on the rights of the defence. Consequently, such a restriction must satisfy very exacting requirements if it is not to be regarded as a manifest and disproportionate infringement of those rights.[32]

The CJEU also clarified that it is for the national court to assess if that is the case but it is for the Luxembourg Court to explain the principles that it has defined by indicating the general criteria with regard to which the national court must carry out its assessment.[33]

The national court of the Member State of enforcement, which was the Court of appeal of Milan,[34] after having done the analysis suggested by the CJEU, declared the English 'default judgment' recognizable and enforceable in Italy, as not contrary to local procedural public policy.

---

[30] CJEU, *Marco Gambazzi v. Daimler Chrysler Canada Inc. and CIBC Mellon Trust Company*, judgment of 2 April 2009, Case C-394/07.

[31] For general background concerning the "debarment" in English civil procedure see, e.g., Regan (2016), pp. 18 ff.

[32] CJEU, *Marco Gambazzi v. Daimler Chrysler Canada Inc. and CIBC Mellon Trust Company* (fn. 30), paras 31 ff.

[33] *Ibid.*, paras 40–45.

[34] Court of appeal of Milan, judgment of 14 December 2010, *Int'l Lis*, 2011, 146–152.

The decision rendered by the Court of appeal of Milan was subsequently confirmed by the Italian Court of Cassation.[35]

In Germany, if the defendant deliberately fails to defend himself in civil proceedings, every allegation of facts contained in the claim form submitted by the plaintiff shall be deemed to be admitted (§ 331 German CPC).[36]

However, the court has to decide the case with a previous consideration of procedure and merits, so that a default judgment in favour of the plaintiff can be only given when:

(i) The facts alleged by the plaintiff are sufficient to support the claim for relief (the so-called *Schlüssigkeitsprüfung*), and:
(ii) The court finds the claim procedurally regular (*e.g.* the court has jurisdiction over the claim);
(iii) The plaintiff has *locus standi* and a genuine interest in bringing proceedings;
(iv) The claim form complies with the formal requirements listed in the German CPC.

In short, it seems that the German default judgment, unlike the English one, cannot be considered as a purely civil-law sanction aimed at punishing the defendant for his deliberate absence in the proceedings. In principle, even a decision on the merit in favour of the defendant may be pronounced, as the court maintains its power to evaluate not only the formal validity but also the substance of the claim (*Schlüssigkeitsprüfung*).

In France, pursuant to Article 471 of the local CPC, if the defendant does not appear and has not been served personally, the court, on its own motion, may order a renewal of the service.[37] The court may also inform the interested party, by ordinary letter, of the consequences of his failure to appear.

After doing so, even if the defendant deliberately continues failing to appear, the court shall decide the case on the merits (Article 472 French CPC).

More precisely, if the defendant voluntarily fails to appear, every allegation of facts contained in the claim form submitted by the plaintiff shall be deemed to be admitted. However, the court shall find in favour of the plaintiff only if it finds the claim well founded (i.e., if the facts alleged by the plaintiff are sufficient to support the claim for relief) and 'procedurally regular'. It means that a default judgment cannot be entered merely because the defendant was absent. In light of this, even the French default judgment cannot be considered as a purely civil sanction aimed at punishing the defendant merely for his absence in the proceeding.

Our brief investigation ends with Italy, which provides even more guarantees in favour of the defendant, who deliberately fails to appear in civil proceedings.

---

[35] Italian Court of Cassation, judgment of 6 March 2013, No. 11021.

[36] Prütting (2016); Murray and Stürner (2004), pp. 317 ff.

[37] Douchy-Oudot (2013–2015) and Crifó (2009), pp. 204 ff.

In Italy, pursuant to articles 291–294 ICPC, devoted to default proceedings (*contumacia*),[38] when a defendant fails to appear and consequently does not file a defence, the court has to declare him/her in default[39] but cannot give a judgment on the claim for the plaintiff. A defendant who has been declared in default (*contumace*) by the court is presumed to challenge the plaintiff's claim (*ficta contestatio*), so that the plaintiff has to prove his assertions.

As a consequence, an Italian default judgment does not amount to an uncontested claim[40] and for that reason cannot be qualified as a civil penalty against a defendant who fails to appear before the court.

Nevertheless, notwithstanding the existence of any contrary provision of national law, an Italian default judgment shall be regarded as an 'uncontested' claim within the meaning of the second subparagraph of Article 3(1)(b) of Regulation (EC) No. 805 of 21 April 2004 creating a European Enforcement Order for uncontested claims. In fact, as stated by the CJEU in the case *Pebros Servizi s.r.l.*,[41] in order to ensure a high degree of uniformity in interpretation of EU legal instruments, the meaning of the word "uncontested", must be assessed without any reference to national procedural law. Consequently, a final condemnatory decision rendered '*in contumacia*' can be certified as a European enforcement order for uncontested claims according to Regulation No. 805 of 2004.

4 Conclusions

At the very beginning of the present chapter, the purpose of this research was presented as the investigation around two main issues.

The first issue was the role of personal participation in civil proceedings imposing penalties within the European judicial area.

The analysis conducted, as expected, has revealed fragmentation: while in European common law countries, such as England and Wales, personal

---

[38] For an English language overview on the Italian '*contumacia*'' cf. Crifó (2009), pp. 227 ff.

[39] As the procedure '*in contumacia*' (default proceedings) covers only a party's failure to make an appearance declared by the court with an order, a party who has made an appearance but has failed to attend a hearing cannot be considered '*contumace*', but merely absent (absent defendant). The rules on '*contumacia*' are not applicable in case of mere absence.

[40] Is also worth mentioning that a party who has been declared '*in contumacia*' may appear, at any time, in the course of the proceeding, taking the case as it finds it. As observed by Cappelletti and Perillo (1965), p. 300, "in the absence of a statutory recognized excuse for his lateness, a party who has made a late appearance may generally neither introduce a counterclaim nor offer any evidence, make any motion or perform any procedural act that a party who has made a timely appearance would be precluded from performing at this stage of the case". If the proceeding has been ended with a final judgment, the party who has been declared '*in contumacia*' may request a retrial, after having proved that she/he had no previous knowledge of the proceedings.

[41] CJEU, *Pebros Servizi S.r.l. v. Aston Martin Lagonda Ltd*, judgment of 16 June 2016, Case C-511/14.

representation in civil actions is permitted, in European continental countries representation by counsel is, in principle, mandatory in civil proceedings. With the only exception of Germany, no special rules are provided for proceedings imposing civil pecuniary penalties, with the aim of ensuring to the defendant/potential recipient the right to be heard in person prior to the civil sanction being imposed. In this respect, seems that a person liable to a "sanction" is entitled to a stronger protection in criminal proceedings than in civil cases.

The second issue consisted in evaluating whether default judgments in civil proceedings within the European judicial area are, in fact, civil penalties for deliberate failure to appear as a sanctionable abuse of process.

The analysis took into consideration England, France, Germany and Italy.

The study has revealed that, given its characteristics, only the English default judgment can be considered a pure civil sanction against the defendant who fails:

(I) To file an acknowledgment of service, or
(II) To appear and defend himself at the hearing without a valid reason, or
(III) To comply with a court's order for disclosure.

Despite that, as stated by the cited case-law of the CJEU, if the defendant has been properly served with the claim form,[42] such a civil penalty is compatible with the right to a fair trial[43] guaranteed in Article 6 ECHR and in article 47 EUCFR, as the possibility of a court appearance has been guaranteed to the defendant, who voluntarily waived such a right, deciding not to appear before the state court.

References

Andrews N (2013) Andrews on civil processes, vol I. Intersentia, Cambridge

Assy R (2015) Injustice in person. The right to self-representation. Oxford University Press

Bermann G, Picard E (2008) Introduction to French law. Kluwer International, Alphen aan den Rijn

Bove M (2016) Sull'introduzione di illeciti con sanzioni pecuniarie dal punto di vista del processualcivilista (note a margine del d.lgs. n. 7 del 15/1/2016). http://www.lanuovaproceduracivile.com/sullintroduzione-di-illeciti-con-sanzioni-pecuniarie-dal-punto-di-vista-del-processualci-vilista-note-a-margine-del-d-lgs-n-7-del-1512016/. Accessed 21 Feb 2017

Callies GP (2015) Rome regulations. Commentary, 2nd edn. Kluwer Law International, Alphen aan den Rijn

Cappelletti M, Perillo JM (1965) Civil procedure in Italy. Martinus Nijhoff, The Hague

Charney J (1974) Need for constitutional protection for defendants in civil penalty cases. Cornell Law Rev 59:478–517

Crifó C (2009) Cross border enforcement of judgment. Wolters Kluwer, Alphen aan den Rijn

D'Alessandro E (2007) Pronunce americane di condanna al pagamento di *punitive damages* e problemi di riconoscimento in Italia. Rivista di diritto civile, 383–406

---

[42] And has a remedy against the judgment aiming at demonstrating possible mistakes made by the court.

[43] As stated in Article 6 ECHR and in Article 47 EUCFR.

D'Alessandro E (2017) Riconoscimento di sentenze di condanna a danni punitivi: tanto tuonò che piovve. Foro italiano, 2639–2642

Douchy-Oudot M (2013–2015) Jugement par défaut et opposition. Juris Clausseur Procédure civile, fasc. 540

Ferrari F, Bocharova N (2015) The *astreinte* in the Italian and Russian administrative (judicial) and civil proceedings. Russian Law J 3:13–45

Gruber U (2016) § 891. In: Münchener Kommentar zur ZPO, 5 Auflage. https://beck-online.beck.de. Accessed 21 Feb 2017

Herzog P, Weser M (1967) Civil procedure in France. Springer, The Hague

Kennet W (2000) The enforcement of judgments in Europe. Oxford University Press, Oxford

Kuckes N (2006) Civil due process, criminal due process. Yale Law Policy Rev 25:1–61

Lavarini B (2016) I profili processuali dei recenti provvedimenti di depenalizzazione. Archivio penale:845–863

Luiso FP (2015) Diritto processuale civile, I, 8th edn. Giuffrè, Milano

Lupoi MA (2012) Recent developments in Italian civil procedure law. Civil Proced Rev 3:25–51

Meurkens RC (2014) Punitive damages. Wolters Kluwer, Deventer

Morris C (1931) Punitive damages in Tort cases. Harv Law Rev 44:1173–1191

Murray P, Stürner R (2004) German civil justice. Carolina Academic Press, Durham, NC

Musielak HJ, Voit W (2016) ZPO, 13th edn. Beck, Munich

Polinsky M, Shavell S (1988) Punitive damages: an economical analysis. Harv Law Rev 111:869–962

Prütting H (2016) § 331. In: Münchener Kommentar zur ZPO, 5th edn. https://beck-online.beck.de. Accessed 5 Nov 2018

Regan D (2016) Much ado about nothing. New Law J 166:18

Settem OJ (2015) Applications of the "Fair Hearing" Norm in ECHR Article 6 (1) to civil proceedings. Springer, Cham

Sharkey CM (2003) Punitive damages as social damages. Yale Law J 113:347–453

Stone P (2007) The Rome II regulation on choice of law in Tort. Ankara Law Rev 4:95–130

Sunstein CR, Kahneman D, Schkade D (1998) Assessing punitive damages (with notes on cognition and valuation in law). Yale Law J 107:2071–2153

Part IV
A Critical Assessment of *In Absentia* Trials. The Viewpoint of Constitutional and Substantive Criminal Law

Personal Participation and Trials *In Absentia*. A Comparative Constitutional Law Perspective

Oreste Pollicino and Marco Bassini

Abstract Personal participation in criminal proceedings is subject to a very different consideration among the various legal orders as an inviolable duty of the defendant rather than as a waivable right of the same. Depending on how the latter is framed, states may either permit or ban or subject to some limitations trials *in absentia*. The purpose of this essay is to provide a comparative overview focusing on the attitude of some legal orders towards trials *in absentia* in order to determine whether the US and European constitutionalism had an impact on the framing of these principles in the various legal orders. Particularly, it is argued that, in the absence of any black-or-white distinction, the dichotomy between common law and civil law systems would not provide an appropriate perspective to capture the existence of different attitudes between the understanding of personal participation as a duty and as a right.

Abbreviations

CJEU   Court of Justice of the European Union
ECHR   European Convention on Human Rights
ECtHR   European Court of Human Rights
EU   European Union
ICCPR   International Covenant on Civil and Political Rights

Marco Bassini is author of paras. 1–4 and para. 7; Oreste Pollicino is author of paras. 5–6.

O. Pollicino (✉) · M. Bassini
"Angelo Sraffa" Department of Legal Studies, Bocconi University, Milano, Italy
e-mail: oreste.pollicino@unibocconi.it; marco.bassini@unibocconi.it

© Springer Nature Switzerland AG 2019
S. Quattrocolo, S. Ruggeri (eds.), *Personal Participation in Criminal Proceedings*, Legal Studies in International, European and Comparative Criminal Law 2, https://doi.org/10.1007/978-3-030-01186-4_16

1   Introduction

There is an inherent tension between the understanding of personal participation of the accused in criminal proceedings as a part of the right to defense which defendants can avail themselves of or waive and the alternative view that sees personal participation as a duty of the defendant that is required for the fairness of judicial procedures.

This tension, as noted,[1] has grown up as a consequence of the larger and larger movement of persons across European and non-European countries whose constitutional legal orders may encapsulate different views of the nature of personal participation. This tension has come to the attention, among others, of the European courts, which released some important judgments on this matter.

The difference between these alternative 'genetic codes' of personal participation seems to be able to represent reliable bearings to explore the constitutional law profiles stemming from trials *in absentia*. It also offers a challenging perspective to speculate on a very topical issue (as the *Taricco*[2] and *Melloni*[3] cases show very well), i.e. whether the expansion of European criminal law is compatible with the existence of heterogeneous standards of protection in the constitutions of Member States; and, if any, whether a degree of constitutional pluralism in this regard is tolerable.

Behind this dichotomy between the understanding of personal participation as a right rather than as a duty lies a different view of the relevant constitutional interest that claims protection[4]: the right to defense of the accused person, in the first scenario; the general interest to a fair administration of justice in the latter.[5]

From a comparative perspective, it is difficult to draw a clear line between the jurisdictions that consider personal participation as a duty of the defendant and those which instead allow *in absentia* trials. A commonly accepted idea is that civil law systems fall within the latter category, while common law systems generally prevent trials from taking place without the defendant's personal participation. Some scholars,[6] however, have called into question this 'conventional' distinction that seems to be rather weak and even opaque in light of the existence of significant exceptions in both the categories. Thus, from a methodological standpoint, the most appropriate option is to separately examine the approach of European constitutionalism and US constitutionalism, against the background of international law. Both models are worth comparing since, even if it would be improper to refer to an

---

[1] Quattrocolo (2016), p. 30.

[2] CJEU, *Melloni c. Ministerio Fiscal*, judgment of 26 February 2013, Case C-399/11.

[3] CJEU, *Ivo Taricco and others*, judgment of 8 September 2015, Case C-104/15.

[4] Vigoni (2014) and Ianovska (2015).

[5] For a view on the relationship between administration of justice and human rights, see Weissbrodt (2009).

[6] See Pradel (1995) and also Mangiaricina (2010). See also Bachmaier Winter, in this volume, Section 1.

American and European criminal procedure, convergences can be observed within these systems depending on the impact of rather commonly shared constitutional principles. Exploring these multi-layer systems will permit to put the different understandings of personal participation in criminal proceedings in connection with the relevant constitutional background. Without prejudice to the above, and despite the said difficulties to draw a red line between common law and civil law systems, the comparative assessment will move from a joint analysis of the US and UK system and then focus on other European models reflecting most of the characteristics of the latter. Although this choice may apparently be in contradiction with the assumption that there is no clear-cut distinction in the consideration of personal participation as a duty rather than a right, the relevant developments are very telling. They reveal, in effect, that despite some common grounds the actual understanding of personal participation relies more on the relevant constitutional background.

As the comparative overview below will bring to light, in fact there is not a black-or-white distinction; rather, various degrees can be identified in the grey area between the right to appear and the duty to appear, even though very rarely constitutions mention personal participation expressly. As a consequence, courts have played a very pivotal role. In particular, the case law of the European Court of Human Rights had an impact with respect to the interpretation of the right to fair trial. The Court of Justice of the European Union, on the other hand, had to face the challenges that Member States posed to EU law by virtue of the enlargement of its scope of action in the criminal field. The famed case *Melloni*, in this respect, provides an example of the inherent tension between the safeguard of domestic standards of protection and the commitment to an openness to EU law.

2 Personal Participation in International Law

It is of utmost importance, prior to exploring the approaches of the European and American constitutionalism, to consider how personal participation is regarded at the level of international law.

The International Covenant on Civil and Political Rights frames personal participation as a fundamental right of the defendant. Article 14(3)(d) in particular provides that, in the determination of any criminal charge against him, everyone shall be entitled "to be tried in his presence, and to defend himself in person or through legal assistance of his own choosing". Personal participation is expressly ranked among a series of 'guarantees' that benefit any defendant in criminal proceedings. It is worth noting that the explanations released by the Human Rights Committee, in General Comment no. 13, refer to trials held 'exceptionally' *in absentia* for justified reasons, recommending in such cases "strict observance of the rights of the defense", that is all the more necessary. Unfortunately, since there is no definition of the notion of "justified reasons", the actual margin for derogating the ban of holding *in absentia* trials is uncertain.

Interestingly enough, the Statute of the International Criminal Court reflects a similar consideration of personal participation[7]: trials *in absentia* are prohibited except for under special circumstances.[8]

At the level of international law, therefore, the understanding of personal participation as a right of the defendant, i.e. as a guarantee to the benefit of the same, is widely accepted.

It is worth noting that while this qualification seems to be consistent with the nature of human rights covenant of the ICCPR, it is probably unexpected under the Statute of the International Criminal Court, whose purpose is mainly to set up procedural mechanisms then protect directly human rights.

3 Article 6 of the European Convention on Human Rights and Its Judicial Interpretation

Looking at 'regional' international law, the European Convention on Human Rights has played an important role[9] in framing the approach of the Contracting Parties to personal participation on the side of fundamental rights.[10]

Even though Article 6 of the ECHR does not mention any ban of trials *in absentia*, personal participation is regarded as a fundamental right that may exceptionally be subject to certain limitations. This provision establishes a set of minimum rights that everyone charged with a criminal offense is entitled to, most of which are *de facto* incompatible with the absence of the defendant in the trial. Framing personal participation as a fundamental right of the defendant mirrors the assumption that the right to appear before the court constitutes a requirement of the principle of equality of arms, as pointed out by some commentators.[11]

---

[7] As reported by Triffterer (1999), p. 806, three different perspectives confronted in 1998, at the time the Rome Statute was drafted. The first view, that eventually has prevailed, was that *in absentia* trials were impermissible; a second perspective discouraged *in absentia* trials as the defendant would have had the right to a new trial by appearing before the Court; the third approach was that it was practically impossible, in some cases, to force defendants to appear before the Court.

[8] Trials *in absentia* are also prohibited by the statutes of other international tribunals, including the International Criminal Tribunal for the Former Yugoslavia, the International Criminal Tribunal for Rwanda and the Sierra Leone Special Court.

[9] On the approach of the European Convention and mostly of the Strasbourg Court see Ruggeri, in Part V of this volume 18, and Bachmaier Winter, in this volume, Section 2.

[10] However, according to Bassiouni (1993), only the constitution of Malta, among the states that are parties to the Convention, refers to personal participation, albeit indirectly. Article 39(1) of the Constitution of Malta provides that "Whenever any person is charged with a criminal offence he shall, unless the charge is withdrawn, be afforded a fair hearing within a reasonable time by an independent and impartial court established by law". The Author counted 25 national constitutions to enshrine personal participation as a fundamental right.

[11] Negri (2008), p. 671. See ECtHR, *Ekbatani v. Sweden*, judgment of 26 May 1988, Appl. No. 10563/83.

It is not by chance that, while carrying out its review, the ECtHR has paid important attention to profiles which are intertwined with the personal participation in trials. Some judgments of the ECtHR, in fact, focused on both the preliminary activities prior to the commencement of the trial, where the defendant must enjoy sufficient resources (including time and information) to substantiate his defense, and on the consequences of sentencing the defendant *in absentia*.

First of all, Article 6(3)(c) provides that everyone charged with a criminal offense has the right "to defend himself in person or through legal assistance". Additionally, litt. (d) and (e) of the same paragraph set forth the right to examine or have examined witnesses and the right to have the free assistance of an interpreter. The European Court of Human Rights delivered a landmark decision on the interpretation of Article 6 in *Colozza v. Italy*.[12] The Court found that "although personal participation is not expressly mentioned in paragraph 1 of Article 5, the object and the purpose of the Article taken as a whole show that a person "charged with a criminal offence" is entitled to take part in the hearing. Moreover, sub-paragraphs (c), (d) and (e) of paragraph 3 guarantee to "everyone charged with a criminal offence" the right "to defend himself in person", "to examine or have examined witnesses" and "to have the free assistance of an interpreter if he cannot understand or speak the language used in court" and it is difficult to see how he could exercise these rights without being present".[13]

Thus, the ECHR does protect personal participation as a part of the right to defense, i.e. the right of any person charged with a criminal offense to be subject to a fair trial. This guarantee is not explicit but personal participation is assumed to be a prerequisite to enjoy the "minimum rights" set forth by Article 6(3).

In the same and other judgments, the ECtHR has specified that the right to personal participation is not an absolute one and may nevertheless be subject to restrictions. However, when legislation of Contracting States allows trials *in absentia* some conditions have to be met.[14]

First of all, it must be established that the defendant had an actual knowledge of the existence of a trial and the relevant charges. In this respect, the ECtHR has reviewed legislation of Contracting Parties that did not properly manage to ensure that the accused was duly noticed of his charges.[15]

As further condition, the "waiver of the exercise of a right guaranteed by the convention must be established in an equivocal manner",[16] also *per facta concludentia*, provided that the same are explicit.[17] It is then necessary that the documents

---

[12] ECtHR, *Colozza v. Italy*, judgment of 12 February 1985, Appl. No. 9024/80.

[13] *Ibid.*, para 27.

[14] See Quattrocolo (2016), p. 32.

[15] See in particular ECtHR, *Somogyi v. Italy*, judgment of 18 May 2004, Appl. No. 67972/01, where the European Court found that Italy had violated Article 6 of the Convention. The case arose out of a trial *in absentia* that resulted in the conviction of the defendant, who had not been served with the notice of the preliminary hearing that was given wrongly to another person.

[16] ECtHR, *Somogyi v. Italy* (fn. 15), para 28.

[17] ECtHR, *Hu v. Italy*, judgment of 28 September 2006, Appl. No. 5941/04.

of the file show without uncertainty that the accused person waived the right to appear and defend himself before the court. The ECtHR also specified that the waiver must be in conditions to reasonably foresee the consequences of his choice.[18]

Alternatively, it must be established that the intention of the person was to escape justice.

In any cases, with respect to the consequences of a possible trial *in absentia* that resulted in sentencing the defendant, the ECtHR stated that if the legislation of Contracting State does not ban trials *in absentia*, the defendant, once become aware of the proceedings, must be able to obtain "from a court which has heard him, a fresh determination of the merits of the charge".[19] According to the ECtHR, automatic retrial and trial reopening are the most appropriate remedies for a Contracting State to take in case a trial *in absentia* resulted in sentencing the defendant. In this respect, however, the ECtHR said that the Contracting Parties, within their respective margin of appreciation, are free to determine the remedies which are a better fit for this purpose, provided that the same are compatible with the Convention and the rights enshrined therein.

If the analysis were to stop at this layer, one could definitely and easily conclude that personal participation is regarded by the ECHR as a fundamental right of the defendant only.

Interestingly, the ECtHR has also put the two different understandings of personal participation in connection each other. In fact, in the view of the ECtHR, the right to take part to trial in person must be reconciled with the public interest of justice. The latter may prevail, for instance, when the "impossibility of holding a trial by default may paralyze the conduct of criminal proceedings, in that it may lead, for example, to dispersal of the evidence, expiry of the time-limit for prosecution or a miscarriage of justice". Under these circumstances, the striking of a reasonable balance is necessary.

Furthermore, extending the scope of the analysis to the Second Additional Protocol to the European Convention on Extradition, a different consideration of personal participation comes up.

Article 3 of the Second Additional Protocol introduced a specific ground for the refusal of extradition that refers to the absence of the person whose surrender is requested in the relevant proceedings. Accordingly, the requested party is entitled to refuse the surrender if the proceedings that resulted in the judgment did not respect the minimum rights of defense to which any person charged with a crime is entitled to. The surrender can be granted, in any ways, if proper assurance is given by the requesting party that the claimed person will enjoy retrial.

These provisions reflect the existence of diverging standard of protection applicable in the various Contracting Parties. The same problem, as will be said, it is at the heart of the *Melloni* saga, where the CJEU found that the application of a higher

---

[18] In *Hakansson and Sturesson v. Sweden*, judgment of 15 July 1987, Appl. No. 11855/85, the ECtHR specified that the choice of the defendant to waive his right to appear personally before the Court must not be in contrast with a compelling public interest.

[19] ECtHR, *Colozza v. Italy* (fn. 12), para 29.

level of protection granted by a Member State's Constitution to the right to defense shall not compromise the primacy, unity and effectiveness of EU law.

In this respect, the personal participation of the defendant emerges in a different light, i.e. as a condition to fulfill the general interest of justice. This regard is, indeed, pretty weak, as the holding of a trial *in absentia* does not automatically preclude extradition: the surrender can be refused on the basis of an assessment of the requested party on the respect of the minimum rights of defense. However, the introduction of this ground is very telling, at least is so much as the power to refuse the surrender is in the hands of the requested party, i.e. a state, then an entity that by definition pursues the general interest. Here, in other words, it is actually not the accused person to waive his right to personally appear before the court but rather the state to consider that the general interest of justice would be harmed if extradition were allowed following a judgment rendered *in absentia.*

The comparative overview will show how, although the Convention holds different ranks in the Contracting States" legal orders, whether constitutional or not, the interpretation of Article 6 of the ECHR constituted a key reference for domestic legislators and courts.

4   Trials *in absentia* in Common Law Systems

As pointed out above, drawing a red line between the systems that tolerate *in absentia* trials and those which, on the contrary, ban trials held without the presence of the accused constitutes a misleading and probably wrong approach. The United States are often referred to as guardian of personal participation of the defendant in criminal proceedings. Accordingly, the attitude of each legal system reflects the understanding of personal participation as either a part of the essence of the right to defense or a duty of the defendant to guarantee fair administration of justice.

Looking at the historical evolution of the procedural model, the presence of the accused has been regarded since the very beginning as necessary, given that criminal proceedings were framed consistently with civil lawsuits, according to an adversarial system. Particularly, the methods used to seek justice required the physical presence of the defendant. Even with the advent of the trial by jury personal participation of the defendant was required.[20] Therefore, there is an inherent connection between the participation of the accused person and the purpose of the trial: at least at the origins, in common law systems, the presence of the defendant was a mandatory requirement to fulfill the general interest of justice. Personal participation has therefore been embodied, in the US, in the scope of the due process, that receives constitutional protection under the Fifth, Sixth and Sixteenth Amendment to the US Constitution. The presence of the defendant was meant as a condition for the valid exercise of jurisdiction and was thus conceived as "absolute and

---

[20] Tassara (2009).

nonwaivable".[21] Over the time, this rule has been subject to some exceptions, that became more and more common as courts, at the end of the nineteenth century, started to share the view that in non-capital cases, where the defendant was not in custody, he was entitled to voluntarily absenting himself once the trial had begun in his presence. This rule was eventually accepted by the Supreme Court in the judgment *Diaz v. United States*, dated 1912.[22]

Interestingly enough, the Supreme Court took the same position as in cases where the defendants had absconded after the commencement of the trial. This holding was then embodied by Rule 43 of the Federal Rules of Criminal Procedures, introduced in 1946 and amended on several occasions.

Pursuant to Rule 43, the defendant must be present at the following stages: the initial appearance, the initial arraignment and the plea; every trial stage, including jury empanelment and the return of the verdict; and sentencing. Some exceptions apply, as the presence can be discontinued by the accused. Rule 43(c) reads as follows:

> A defendant who was initially present at trial, or who had pleaded guilty or nolo contendere, waives the right to be present under the following circumstances:
>
> (a) when the defendant is voluntarily absent after the trial has begun, regardless of whether the court informed the defendant of an obligation to remain during trial;
> (b) in a noncapital case, when the defendant is voluntarily absent during sentencing; or
> (c) when the court warns the defendant that it will remove the defendant from the courtroom for disruptive behavior, but the defendant persists in conduct that justifies removal from the courtroom.

If the defendant waives the right to be present, the trial may proceed to completion, including the verdict's return and sentencing, during the defendant's absence.

In 1993 the Supreme Court delivered another landmark decision in *Crosby v. United States*. The Supreme Court had the chance to extend the scope of the permissible holding of trials *in absentia*. Since the language of Rule 43 leaves the doors open to other exceptions in addition to those listed therein, the Supreme Court had to face a case where the defendant was absent at the beginning of the trial and eventually convicted. The District Court and the Court of Appeals had found that the defendant, Mr. Crosby, had voluntarily waived his constitutional right to be present during the trial.[23]

The Supreme Court reversed. The initial presence of the defendant, in the view of the Supreme Court, is necessary to assure that any waiver is indeed "knowing".

---

[21] Starkey (1978), p. 724.

[22] The Supreme Court ruled that "Where the offense is not capital and the accused is not in custody, the prevailing rule has been, that if, after the trial has begun in his presence, he voluntarily absents himself, this does not nullify what has been done or prevent the completion of the trial, but, on the contrary, operates as a waiver of his right to be present and leaves the court free to proceed with the trial in like manner and with like effect as if he were present". 223 U.S. 442 (1912).

[23] After having been arrested and sentenced to imprisonment by the District Court, Crosby appealed and claimed that Federal Rule of Criminal Procedure 43 prohibited to try *in absentia* a defendant who was not present at the beginning of the trial.

The judgment took a different road from *Diaz*, where the defendant had waived to his right to appear only during the trial and the Court had had no chance to tackle the case of a failure to appear for the commencement of trial. Accordingly, in *Crosby v. United States* the Supreme Court held that sentencing *in absentia* a defendant who did not appear at the beginning of the trial is not permitted.

Why did the Supreme Court accept to derogate from the general ban to hold trials *in absentia* only to a certain degree? One could wonder which is actually the rationale of the distinction between cases where the accused was present at the commencement of the trial and cases where he was not. Criminal trials *in absentia* have been defined as "jarring" to the American sensibilities.[24] In fact, the constitutional status of the defendant "furthers basic and profound societal values".[25] According to *Shapiro*, "these interests demand a more searching standard for the relinquishment of the right than a waiver analysis alone". Thus, in this view, the complexity of the legal implications of personal participation of the accused may not be reduced to an analysis of the act by which he has waived the constitutional right to appear before the court. There is an underlying "imperative that justice be administered in an appropriate and orderly manner". These concerns do reflect the assumption that personal participation is not only a waivable right of the defendant but rather amounts to a very distinguishing feature of procedural model for the fair administration of justice. This remark is backed by the historical evolution of the procedures: although the defendant is no longer tested by fire or boiled water nor required to dwell, his presence is nevertheless considered crucial for carrying out a set of activities that may have an impact on correct holding of the proceedings, and may particularly influence the determination of the truth. Requiring the presence of the defendant at the beginning and at the end of the trial, in the view of *Shapiro*, would be satisfactory assuming a perspective where the only relevant interest at stake lies with the right to defense of the accused.

It is then suggested that the US Supreme Court should not only focus on the voluntary, knowing and intelligent absence of the defendant but go beyond, taking an approach able to reconcile the different and more complex significances that are embodied in the requirement of the personal participation of the accused in criminal proceeding Criticism is expressed that most of the judgments of the US Supreme Court attached consideration particularly to the position of the defendant within the proceedings, disregarding the broader scope behind the prerequisite of personal participation.[26] Just in a few cases the Supreme Court paid specifically attention to the broader reach of this expectation from a constitutional perspective. In the same *Diaz v. United States* decision, for example, the Court said that in case of felony personal

---

[24] Shapiro (2012).

[25] *Ibid.*

[26] The author notes, among others, that the Supreme Court in *Crosby* quoted a Supreme Court of Pennsylvania case dated 1851, namely *Prine v. Commonwealth,* where the purpose of the personal participation of the defendant was said to incline "the hearts of the jurors to listen to his defense with indulgence".

participation is treated by common law courts "as being scarcely less important to the accused than the right of trial itself".[27]

Looking at the European context, neglecting any similarities between the US and the UK as common law systems would most likely lead to misleading conclusions. It is therefore a helpful perspective to explore the legal status of trials *in absentia* in the UK. Particularly, in England trials *in absentia* were banned until 2001 with the sole exceptions where the defendants absconded in the course of the trial.

In the landmark decision *Regina v. Jones*[28] the House of Lords was requested to hear an appellate claim against the judgment of the Court of Appeal. The question raised before the House was "Can the Crown Court conduct a trial in the absence, from its commencement, of the defendant?". In the first instance proceeding, the appellant, Mr. Jones, accused of a robbery, had not been arrested nor surrendered by the date of the trial.

The question had been affirmatively answered by the Court of Appeal, that highlighted how "the discretion to proceed with a trial in the absence, from the beginning, of the defendant is one to be exercised with extreme care and only in the rare case where, after full consideration of all relevant matters, including in particular the fairness of a trial, the judge concludes that the trial should proceed".

The House of Lords observed that the law of England and Wales had recognized for many years the right of a defendant to attend his trial; in trials on indictment, personal participation was even mandatory. This consideration reflected the importance of personal participation in respect of the role of jury, and then for the sake of a fair administration of justice. Over the years, however, courts had to exceptionally face with cases where the defendant, once appeared at the beginning of the trial, could not stay until the end as a consequence, among others, of illness or voluntarily absconding. Under these circumstances, it became well-established that courts had discretion to determine whether to continue the trial or to delay it to a later date. This discretion, according to the House of Lords, is "to be exercised with great caution and with close regard to the overall fairness of the proceedings; a defendant afflicted by involuntary illness or incapacity will have much stronger grounds for resisting the continuance of the trial than one who has voluntarily chosen to abscond".

Also, the House of Lords noted that the ECtHR "never found a breach of the Convention where a defendant, fully informed of a forthcoming trial, has voluntarily chosen not to attend and the trial has continued". Therefore, it dismissed the appeal.

In his leading opinion, Lord Bingham of Cornhill highlighted that was no reason to discriminate between the continuation of trial in the absence of the defendant and the beginning of trials that had not yet commenced.[29]

---

[27] 223 US 442, 455 (1912).

[28] [2002] UKHL 5.

[29] Interestingly enough, albeit conceding that the point was not decisive at all, he maintained that "the inconvenience to witnesses of attending to testify again on a later occasion, and the waste of time and money, are likely to be greater if the trial is stopped than in the case of a trial that has

Lord Bingham argued that, if a defendant voluntarily absents himself, there is no reason in principle why his refusal to comply with an obligation and to enjoy his right to appear before the court may have the effect of suspending the criminal proceedings against him until he chooses to surrender or is apprehended. In his view, in fact, the accused who voluntarily chooses not to avail himself of the right to appear cannot subsequently complain about the loss of the benefits deriving from the personal participation in the trial. Even considerations of practical justice suggest to take this view.[30] Under such circumstances, the fairness of the trial cannot be called into question.

This way, trials *in absentia* were reconciled with the severe common law tradition. Since then, the holding of criminal proceedings *in absentia,* despite the important caveat made by Lord Bingham, has become quite common. The approach of the House of Lords reflects a specific understanding of personal participation as a waivable right of the defendant, while it seems that a limited regard is attached to the alleged duty of the defendant to appear for the sake of the fair administration of justice, since the same does no longer depend only on the physical presence of the defendant. As the next chapters will highlight, this approach is quite similar to that of some civil law systems. Accordingly, once again, drawing a red line between common law and civil law systems on the basis of their attitude to trials *in absentia* would probably fail to catch the very essence of their respective understanding of personal participation.

5   Trials *in absentia* in Civil Law Systems. The Influence of EU Law

Europe is definitely the most interesting playground where to see the different understandings of personal participation in action across various states, each one with its own specific constitutional background. As the *Melloni* judgment shows very well, the existence of different degrees of protection is not easy to reconcile

---

never begun". In *Crosby v. United States*, the US Supreme Court noted that "the costs of suspending a proceeding already under way will be greater than the cost of postponing a trial not yet begun. If a clear line is to be drawn marking the point at which the costs of delay are unlikely to outweigh the interests of the defendant and society in having the defendant present, the commencement of trial is at least a plausible place at which to draw that line".

[30] According to Lord Bingham "it is only necessary to consider the hypothesis of a multi-defendant prosecution in which the return of a just verdict in relation to any and all defendants is dependent on their being jointly indicted and jointly tried. On the eve of the commencement of the trial, one defendant absconds. If the court has no discretion to begin the trial against that defendant in his absence, it faces an acute dilemma: either the whole trial must be delayed until the absent defendant is apprehended, an event which may cause real anguish to witnesses and victims; or the trial must be commenced against the defendants who appear and not the defendant who has absconded. This may confer a wholly unjustified advantage on that defendant".

with European integration, particularly when it comes to criminal law, a field where EU law has recently extended its reach.

As it is well known, criminal law has been immune from the influence of EU law for a while. Only recent developments, from the entry into force of the Amsterdam Treaty to that of the Lisbon Treaty, led to a progressive "communitarisation of criminal law".[31]

The Charter of Fundamental Rights of the European Union does not expressly mention the right to appear before the court. However, Article 48(2) provides that "Respect for the rights of the defence of anyone who has been charged shall be guaranteed", while Article 47(2) establishes that "Everyone is entitled to a fair and public hearing within a reasonable time by an independent and impartial tribunal previously established by law. Everyone shall have the possibility of being advised, defended and represented". Like Article 6 of the ECHR, the Charter does not refer to personal participation, but covers a number of situations that are compatible with the presence of the defendant.

A first act of utmost importance lies with the Council Framework Decision 2009/299/JHA—that amended the European Arrest Warrant Framework Decision[32]— "enhancing the procedural rights of persons and fostering the application of the principle of mutual recognition to decisions rendered in the absence of the person concerned at the trial".

By the approval of the Decision, it was said, the European institutions were creating the conditions for the right to personal participation enshrined in the ECHR to be actually protected through an "indirect way"[33]: on the one hand, in fact, the Decision aimed at facilitating the execution of custodial sentences or detention orders following a trial where the person did not appear; on the other one, however, the Decision introduced through Article 4a some grounds to refuse the execution of such decisions. Then, as highlighted by *Chelo*,[34] the purpose of this Decision, far from harmonizing Member States" national legislation,[35] was in fact to circumscribe the execution of decisions rendered *in absentia* in accordance with the requirements set forth by the ECtHR. In other terms, the goal of the Council Framework Decision was to prevent Member States to give execution to judgments resulting from trials *in absentia* where the minimum conditions laid down by the case law of the Strasbourg Court were not met.[36]

---

[31] See Mitsilegas (2010) and Pollicino (2008a), pp. 219 ff.

[32] 2002/584/JHA: Council Framework Decision of 13 June 2002 on the European arrest warrant and the surrender procedures between Member States.

[33] See Chelo (2015), p. 5.

[34] *Ibid.*

[35] See in this respect Böse (2011).

[36] See Recital 8: "Under this Framework Decision, the person's awareness of the trial should be ensured by each Member State in accordance with its national law, it being understood that this must comply with the requirements of that Convention. In accordance with the case law of the European Court of Human Rights, when considering whether the way in which the information is provided is sufficient to ensure the person's awareness of the trial, particular attention could, where

The coming into force of this Framework Decision was definitely an important step to incorporate said criteria in EU law, even though Member States were already subject to the influence of those standard in their capacity as Contracting Parties to the Convention.[37]

However, the Decision did only constitute a starting point that stimulated deeper discussion among the European institutions on the legal status of suspects and accused persons in criminal proceedings. More recently, Directive 2016/343 ("on the strengthening of certain aspects of the presumption of innocence and of the right to be present at the trial in criminal proceedings") has entered into force, following a resolution of the Council dated 30 November 2009, (which had outlined a road-map for strengthening procedural rights of suspected or accused persons in criminal proceedings without mentioning personal participation at all), and the subsequent adoption of a package of legislative proposals by the Commission in November 2013.[38] The enactment of the said Directive in this respect is very telling, as it demonstrates that mutual trust among Member States in the specific field of judicial cooperation was still limited, notwithstanding the existence of the binding standard encapsulated by the ICCPR and the ECHR common to all the European countries.

Article 8 of the Directive is specifically focused on the right to be present at the trial.

First of all, this provision establishes the obligation for Member States to guarantee that suspects and accused persons have to right to appear before the court. Therefore, it comes up that at least at EU law level personal participation is regarded as an individual fundamental right, rather than a duty imposed to guarantee the fair administration of justice.

Also, Article 8 lays down the conditions under which a trial can be held in the absence of the suspect or accused person and, accordingly, a decision on the guilt or innocence taken *in absentia* can be enforced against the defendant. Either "the suspect or accused person has been informed, in due time, of the trial and of the consequences of non-appearance"; or "the suspect or accused person, having been informed of the trial, is represented by a mandated lawyer, who was appointed either by the suspect or accused person or by the State".[39]

In case none of these conditions is met, Member States can nevertheless allow that a decision *in absentia* is taken and enforced provided that the suspects or accused persons are informed of the decision and of the possibility to challenge the

---

appropriate, also be paid to the diligence exercised by the person concerned in order to receive information addressed to him or her".

[37] Article 2, in particular, amended the Framework Decision 2002/584/JHA by inserting a new Article 4(a). In this regard cf. Schneider, in this volume.

[38] See Bachmaier Winter, in this volume.

[39] As some commentators have pointed out (see among others Chelo 2015, p. 10), the reference to the fact that the defendant must be generally 'informed' of the trial prior to appointing a lawyer to represent him seems to be unsatisfactory since no formal requirement for such information is given and Member States may feel legitimate to take and enforce decisions *in absentia* on the basis of the simple knowledge of the existence of a trial that the defendant may in any ways obtain. This option would be most likely in contrast with the case law of the ECtHR, requiring the suspect or accused persons being properly and duly informed on the trial and the relevant charges.

same (to bring appeal) and of the right to a new trial or a remedy that Member States guarantee.

The existence of such a detailed provision reflecting a certain understanding of personal participation is likely to generate a quite significant impact on regulation of criminal proceedings of each Member State, it remaining understood that the latter are allowed to take measures reflecting a higher degree of protection of the position of the suspect or accused. The comparative framework below will support understanding the attitude that Member States will have toward these legislative developments.

6 Comparative Framework

Against this background, exploring how Member States consider personal participation in criminal proceedings reveals the existence of an important grey area where the constitutional protection of the relevant interests at stake may assume different degrees.

At the outset, a pivotal role is played by the European Courts, the most appropriate actors to detect and sometimes resolve cases of constitutional clashes like those deriving from the intertwining of varying standards of protection.

6.1 Spain

Spain is a very interesting case study to explore the constitutional consideration of personal participation of the accused in criminal proceedings, most notably in light of the interaction between the domestic and the European Union legal orders. Among the Member States, Spain is the jurisdiction where trials *in absentia* are subject to the most severe restrictions.

Personal participation in criminal proceedings is deemed in fact to be a part of the right to defense, which enjoys broad constitutional protection under Article 24 of the Spanish Constitution.[40]

---

[40] 1. All persons have the right to obtain effective protection from the judges and the courts in the exercise of their rights and legitimate interests, and in no case may there be a lack of defense.

2. Likewise, all have the right to the ordinary judge predetermined by law; to defense and assistance by a lawyer; to be informed of the charges brought against them; to a public trial without undue delays and with full guarantees; to the use of evidence appropriate to their defense; not to make self-incriminating statements; not to plead themselves guilty; and to be presumed innocent. The law shall specify the cases in which, for reasons of family relationship or professional secrecy, it shall not be compulsory to make statements regarding allegedly criminal offences.

Spanish legislation differentiates the consequences of the absence of the defendant between the investigations phase and the trial. In the former case, if the defendant does not appear before the court investigations will continue; on the contrary, the presence of the defendant is required in the subsequent stage, i.e. when the trial begins, since "attendance by the accused and the defense lawyer is compulsory at the oral trial" pursuant to Article 786 of the *Ley de Enjuiciamiento Criminal*. If the defendant fails to appear during the trial, the latter is suspended until the defendant is apprehended or appears before the court. More in detail,[41] under these circumstances, the defendant is served with another notice (*requisitoria*) specifying the charges at hand in the trial and the date by which the defendant must appear before the court. The same act contains the order sent to the police for carrying out the search of the defendant. If the defendant fails to appear within the assigned term, he is declared "*rebelled*", unless his absence was due to a legitimate impediment.[42]

Only in case of abbreviated proceedings or proceedings for minor offense the defendant is not required to appear before the court.

Abbreviated proceedings are applicable if the offense at hand is punished by no more than 9 years of imprisonment or an equivalent sanction. When it comes to abbreviated proceedings, the presence of the defendant can be derogated from, if the penalty requested by the prosecutor or the accuser does not exceed 2 years of imprisonment (or 6 years, in case a sanction of another nature applies).

The presence of the defendant is not required, as well, in proceedings for minor offenses, unless the court does consider the statement of the same to be necessary.

However, a special procedure for the review of the judgments taken *in absentia* is established, in accordance with the case law of the ECtHR requiring "fresh determination" of the merits of the case.

In light of the foregoing, personal participation of the defendant is deemed to be both a right of the defendant and a duty of him. The duty of the defendant to appear before the court in ordinary proceedings reflects a specific understanding of personal participation as a duty to protect (also) the underlying general interest of fair administration of justice. Even though there is no explicit constitutional ban of trials *in absentia*, the necessary presence of the defendant is aimed at guaranteeing that criminal proceedings serve the supreme interest of justice and ensuring that the trial is actually *fair*. This conclusion does not seem to be called into question by the existence of derogations applying to some abbreviated proceedings and to proceedings for minor offenses. It is worth stressing that even in such cases the court is entitled to exert its discretionary assessment and require, if necessary, the presence of the defendant.[43] The Spanish Constitutional Tribunal confirmed the twofold nature of personal participation as right and duty, stressing that the presence of the defendant before the court "is not only a requirement of the principle of

---

[41] See also Vigoni (2014), pp. 60–61.

[42] See Villamarín López, in this volume, Section 5.1.

[43] *Ibid.*, Section 5.2.

contradiction, but the instrument that makes possible the exercise of right of self-defense".[44]

Against this background, the very heart of the Spanish case study lies with the *Melloni* saga, which brought to light the existence of a high risk of clashes between constitutional standards in the field of criminal law.

This case shows better than any other the difficulty of reconciling different views and constitutional understandings of personal participation across various jurisdictions. The Spanish Constitutional Tribunal has followed a very conservative approach over the time, by taking the view that the same safeguards relating to the ban of trials *in absentia* should apply also in the relationship with other Member States, in particular when it comes to executing European arrest warrants for the surrender of the defendant. Despite the absence in EU law and in the national legislation of any provision subjecting the surrender of the defendant convicted *in absentia* to the existence of retrial in the requesting State, the Court found itself legitimate to require so in light of the strong protection of the right to defense afforded by Article 24 of the Constitution.[45] This critical position caused increasing tension with other Member States, to which surrender of defendants was refused.[46]

This difference of views between the Spanish *Tribunal Constitucional* and the CJEU resulted in the *Melloni* case, as noted above. The Spanish Constitutional judges asked the Court of Justice whether this practice was compatible with the European Arrest Warrant Framework Decision and thus whether Member States were allowed to make conditional the surrender of defendants convicted *in absentia* upon the right to retrial or review. The end of the story is well-know, and will be more in detail commented on later.

6.2 Germany

Like Spain, Germany adopts a quite restrictive approach in respect of the holding of criminal trials *in absentia*.[47] The Basic Law does not establish any specific ban; however, Article 103 provides for that "in the courts every person shall be entitled to a hearing in accordance with law" and the Code of Criminal Procedure lays down

---

[44] STC 177/2006.

[45] See in this volume the contributions of Villamarín López, Section 6.1.1; Demetrio Crespo and Sánz Hermida, Section 3.1; Schneider, Section 3.3.1.2 and 3.3.2. As noted therein, this approach did not change even after the coming into being of the Council Framework Decision 2009/299/JHA that limited the grounds for refusal of the execution of an European Arrest Warrant and excluded, accordingly, that the requested State could make the surrender of a person convicted *in absentia* conditional if that person had been informed in due time of the trial and of the consequences of the refusal to appear before the court or had appointed a lawyer to defend himself in the trial.

[46] Namely Romania (JCC 199/2009), France (JCC 177/2006, and 37/2007) and Italy (JCC 86/2011, in the *Melloni* case).

[47] See Vogel, in this volume, Section 5.

detailed rules on personal participation of the defendant in criminal proceedings. The relevant provisions reflect the strong consideration attached to the presence of the defendant in the trial, conceived as a duty in the best interest of justice. Criminal proceedings *in absentia*, as a consequence, are permissible only under limited conditions.

As a general rule, Article 230 of the Code of Criminal Procedure provides for that if the defendant fails to appear at the commencement of the trial, the court may take the necessary steps to force him to do so, unless his absence is due to legitimate reasons. Additionally, the Code of Criminal Procedure requires the defendant being regularly present over the course of the trial, except for the case where he has been examined on the relevant charges and the court finds his presence to be no longer necessary. This provision reflects the understanding of the personal presence of the defending as a cornerstone of the epistemic goals behind the procedure, i.e. the acquisition of evidence. For the sake of this objective, the presence during the trials appears to be a duty of the defendant more than just a right of the same. However, a strong connection emerges between the different profiles of the personal participation of the defendant.

The defendant can also be deprived of the possibility to appear before the court in case he abuses his right to defense. Article 231(a) and (b) of the Code of Criminal Procedure permit the trial to be held *in absentia*, respectively, (i.) if the defendant deliberately acts in order to be unable to appear and thus to obstacle or delay the trial (ii.) or if his conduct violates the rules governing the procedure. Under these circumstances, the balance between the right to defense and the interest of justice is in favor of the latter, as the presence of the defendant is supposed to not bring any contribution to the research of the truth, while it ultimately obstacles that goal.

Apart from these cases, where the conduct of the defendant is in contrast with the correct exercise of this right to defense,[48] the requirement of personal attendance can be derogated from in other situations for procedural reasons.

First, the defendant can be authorized by the court to leave the trial in case the activities carried out in the course of the same concern co-defendants. In this case, the derogation mirrors the lack of a specific interest to exercise the right to personal participation by the defendant, while the general interest of fair administration of justice is not impaired at all.[49]

In addition to the above, the absence of the defendant in the trial is permitted pursuant to Article 232 of the Code of Criminal Procedure if the relevant proceedings meet certain conditions. The scope of these exceptions includes the proceedings for offenses which are not punished with imprisonment and those which are punished either with no longer than 6 months imprisonment or with a fine or other penalties. In the former case, the defendant must have been served with the notice of the trial and warned that the trial could continue even in absence of the defendant. If the defendant was unable to appear, he is entitled to ask the retrial to challenge the

---

[48] See Vigoni (2014), p. 64.
[49] *Ibid.*, p. 66.

final judgment rendered *in absentia*. In the latter case, the defendant is entitled to be examined by the court, once he has been informed of the trial, of the relevant charges and of the consequences of his absence.

However, the very strong consideration of personal participation is mirrored by the mandatory presence in the course of *in absentia* trials of a defense attorney that represents the defendant.[50]

As specified below, also in Germany a crucial role was played by courts, and in particular by the Federal Constitutional Tribunal, that in December 2015 invalidated the execution of an European arrest warrant because of the violation of human dignity, protected by Article 1 of the German Basic Law, that constitutes a crucial element of the constitutional identity.[51] Even though it did not result in a preliminary reference, the case became part of the *Solange* saga (and named *Solange III*) to highlight the connection between the respect of the constitutional identity in the execution of an European arrest warrant and the control that the German Constitutional Tribunal reserved itself on the equivalence to national standards of the level of protection afforded by EU law to fundamental rights.[52]

6.3   Austria and the Netherlands

Among the various Contracting States, Austria and Netherlands offer interesting examples on the influence of the Convention on the development of the standard of protection of the right to personal participation in criminal proceedings. These States have a very special and distinguishing relationship with the Convention.

In Austria, the Convention is regarded as directly applicable federal constitutional law. The ECHR does then enjoy a constitutional rank and can be enforced as parameter of constitutional review by the *Verfassungsgerichtshof*. Accordingly, as long as a statutory provision conflicts with Article 6 of the ECHR, it has to be considered unconstitutional.[53]

The Austrian legal order encapsulates a twofold consideration of personal participation in criminal proceedings: on the one hand, it constitutes an individual fundamental right; on the other one, at least in part, it also represents a duty of the defendant, for example before first instance and appeal courts. Accordingly, trials *in absentia* are subject to very restrictive conditions, as an exception to the general rule that obliges the defendant to be present. The Convention has proved to be quite influential in respect of the rules of the Code of Criminal Procedure governing personal participation, that also require the defendant having enough time for preparing

---

[50] Article 234 of the Code of Criminal Procedure.

[51] 2 BVerfG 2735/14 (*Solange III*).

[52] See 2 BvL 52/71 (*Solange*) and 2 BvR 197/83 (*Solange II*). See also 2 BvE 2/08 (*Lissabon-Urteil*) and 2 BvR 2728/13 (*Gauweiler*). More recently, Claes and Reestman (2015).

[53] Öhlinger (1990).

his defense, being properly informed of the charges—even in the pre-trial phase—and personally served with the relevant notice. In case the defendant fails to appear before the court, except for legitimate reasons, the trial has to be rescheduled at his expenses. *In absentia* trials are permissible only in proceedings for offenses that are punished by no more than 3 years imprisonment. Once the defendant has been heard by the court, the judge can decide whether the presence of the same is necessary or not. Decisions rendered at the end of trials held *in absentia* are subject to review if the defendant was prevented from appearing before the court because of unavoidable impediments or in case the conditions for judgments to be handed down *in absentia* were not met.

Despite trials in the absence of the defendant are considered an exception, in accordance with the interpretation of Article 6 of the Convention given by the ECtHR, some problems may arise[54] in connection to the implementation of the mechanism of the European Arrest Warrant. In particular, the execution of sentence resulting from *in absentia* trials is permitted under certain conditions. Among others, the execution is permitted if the requesting State ensures that the requested State will be noticed the judgment rendered *in absentia* without delay after the surrender and the defendant will be informed of his rights to a retrial or to a new examination on the facts of the case. This provision may raise some uncertainties as to its compatibility with Article 6 of the ECHR, requiring the defendant "to be informed promptly, in a language which he understands and in detail, of the nature and cause of the accusation against him". These conditions may perhaps not be fulfilled in case of posthumous release of the judgment and service of the defendant with the relevant information. As noted,[55] Austria is thus bound to surrender defendants convicted *in absentia* in other Member States without having received the judgment or properly informed the defendant. These remarks support that view that interstate relationships concerning the execution of European arrest warrants constitutes the leading playground for clashes between the different constitutional understandings of personal participation. The problem, as pointed out above, does not only refer to the qualification of personal participation as a right rather than a duty of the defendant; in addition to that, clashes may arise if a different degree is protection is afforded by the respective constitutions of Member State: the Spanish case and the approach of the *Tribunal Constitucional* are very telling.

In the Dutch legal system, the Fundamental Law[56] provides that "The constitutionality of Acts of Parliament and treaties shall not be reviewed by the courts".[57] Accordingly, the judiciary[58] cannot assess the conformity of the statutory provisions with the Constitution, but it can do with respect to the ECHR, which basically play

---

[54] As noted by Golser (2017).

[55] *Ibid.*

[56] Formally, the "Constitution of the Kingdom of the Netherlands of 2008", available at https://www.government.nl/documents/regulations/2012/10/18/the-constitution-of-the-kingdom-of-the-netherlands-2008. See Article 120.

[57] See for some remarks, Martinico (2017).

[58] See de Poorter (2013) and van der Schyff (2010).

the role of a "Shadow Constitution". It cannot be than surprising than that the ECHR enjoy has constitutional rank and applies directly pursuant to Article 93 of the Constitution.[59] The Dutch legal order provides an example of monistic approach in respect of the incorporation of international law. In the Netherlands, trials *in absentia* have been regarded as an alternative to contradictory proceedings, even though they are subject to stricter requirements. Particularly, courts must comply with the formalities that are necessary to make sure that the defendant is served with a notice of the trial (and the relevant place and data) and informed of the specific charges. The defendant was allowed to be replaced by his defense attorney, at the outset only in limited circumstances. Over the time, courts approached *in absentia* trials by permitting defense attorney to appear not to represent but rather to replace their clients when there were grounds that the defendant wished to appear but did not manage to do so because of compelling reasons. The "compelling reasons" test, thus, became the general rule to assess whether the defense attorney was entitled to speak on behalf of his client, as if he were present.[60] Article 6(3)(c) of the ECHR, as said above, establishes the right of the defendant to be assisted by a defense attorney. In fact, in the absence of compelling reasons, courts were used to not allow the lawyer to speak on behalf of the client and to replace the same, according to a "clear-cut bipolar approach" that was challenging in light of the direct application of Article 6 of the ECHR.[61]

It is not by chance that this attitude was brought to the attention of ECtHR in the case *Lala v. the Netherlands*. The application grew out of the refuse of the Dutch Court of Appeal to allow the defense attorney of Mr. Lala to speak on behalf of him after the same had refused to appear before the first instance court, that convicted him *in absentia*. Mr. Lala had refused to appear because of the risk of facing arrest as a result of another sentence handed out to him in another proceeding. The Court of Appeal had found that there were no compelling reasons justifying the defense attorney to speak in the absence of the defendant, so that Mr. Lala was given no opportunity to defend in the appeal proceeding and before the Supreme Court of the Netherlands. The European Court held that a violation of Article 6(3)(c) had occurred, by taking the view that

> it is also of crucial importance for the fairness of the criminal justice system that the accused be adequately defended, both at first instance and on appeal, the more so if, as is the case under Netherlands law, no objection may be filed against a default judgment given on appeal. In the Court's view the latter interest prevails. Consequently, the fact that the defendant, in spite of having been properly summoned, does not appear, cannot – even in the absence of an excuse – justify depriving him of his right under Article 6 para. 3 (art. 6-3) of the Convention to be defended by counsel.

---

[59] Provisions of treaties and of resolutions by international institutions which may be binding on all persons by virtue of their contents shall become binding after they have been published.

[60] See, more in detail, Stamhuis (2001).

[61] *Ibid.*, p. 722.

Interestingly enough, the arguments of both the ECtHR and the Dutch Government mentioned the public interest to fair administration of justice. The right to defense was seen, thus, as a prerequisite of the proper functioning of the trial (even though, as it comes up from another judgment of the ECtHR,[62] deprivation of a counsel also impacts the right of the specific profile that is inherent to the defendant's status, of the right to be heard). New legislation[63] entered into force as a consequence of the *Lala* judgment with a view to expressly amending the existing (restrictive) practice concerning the right of the defendant to be replaced by his defense attorney. Defense attorneys are then entitled to speak on behalf of the defendant who does not appear, pursuant to the Code of Criminal Procedure, once the notification procedures have been properly completed and the defendant is informed of the charges, in addition to the time and date of the trial.

This way, the significant degree of openness to international law, namely to the European Convention, has permitted to 'leverage' the standard of protection of the right to defense, encompassing now specific situations where the defendant avails himself of the right to not participate in criminal proceedings without waiving, however, the right to defense.

6.4 France

If the Dutch case shows the shifting of personal participation away from the paradigm of a duty to a fundamental right perspective (namely, that of the right to defense), the understanding behind the French legal order is even more reflecting the latter view.

Trials *in absentia*, in France, have been regarded for a while as a possible option where certain circumstances were met, but not a as a threat to the right to defense. Like in Italy, a specific regulation was once established by the Code of Criminal Procedure in case the defendant did not appear before the court (procedure *par contumace*). As noted by some commentators, the case law of the ECtHR has played a pivotal role in promoting significant changes to legislation that was found to impair the status of the defendant absent in criminal proceedings.[64]

Against this scenario, the landmark decision in *Krombach v. France*[65] had an impact on the specific procedure *par contumace*, that has been eventually repealed. Two profiles, in particular, were found to determine a violation of the Convention: the lack of any remedy to obtain the review of the decisions rendered *in absentia* and the exclusion of the assistance of a defense attorney in case the defendant failed

---

[62] See ECtHR, *Poitrimol v. France,* judgment of 23 November 2003, Appl. No. 14032/88, and Ruggeri, in Part V of this volume, Section 2.2.

[63] See Article 278 and 279 of the Code of Criminal Procedure.

[64] See Vigoni (2014), p. 34.

[65] ECtHR, *Krombach v. France*, judgment of 13 February 2001, Appl. No. 29731/96.

to appear. On the latter profile, also the decision in *Poitrimol v. France*[66] stressed that the right to defend himself through the assistance of a lawyer has to be guaranteed even if the defendant does not appear before the court.

Currently, trials can be held in the absence of the defendant before the Assize Court and the Criminal Court, even though an *ad hoc* procedure no longer exists.[67] Comparing the French model to the Dutch one, it is worth noting that until 2004 if the defendant did not appear before the court without legitimate reasons there were no chances to hear the defense attorney on behalf of the client. The ruling of the European Court in *Van Pelt v. France*[68] found such restriction in contrast with the right to fair trial, similarly to the *Lala v. the Netherlands* case. Accordingly, the legislation was amended[69] with a view to introducing the right of the defendant to be heard through his defense attorney. The defendant can apply for being tried *in absentia* and ask to be represented by his attorney before the *Tribunale de police* and the Criminal court. Before the Assize Court, instead, it is up to the court to determine whether the absence of the defendant is attributable to him or not.[70]

But the very crucial aspect that reflects the concept of personal participation as a fundamental right of the defendant probably lies with the existence of different remedies to review decisions taken *in absentia*, according to the "fresh determination" requirement posed by the European Court. Judgments handed down by the Criminal court can be subject to appeal or opposition, the latter being a remedy limited to decisions *in absentia* and aimed to nullifying the same. Judgments issued by the Assize Court, instead, are automatically void once the defendant appears or is apprehended or surrounded before the sentence expires.

The case law of the Strasbourg Court, then, has significantly contributed to framing the French model, that historically proved to be not so much reluctant to *in absentia* trials, even though the purpose of judgments delivered in the absence of the defendant has been considered largely symbolical.[71]

6.5   Italy

In Italy, the 'history' of the right to personal participation is inextricably intertwined with that of a pivotal constitutional reference, namely Article 111 of the Constitution and, generally speaking, with the (changing and sometimes unpredictable) attitude of the Italian constitutional order towards supranational law.

---

[66] ECtHR, *Poitrimol v. France*, judgment of 23 November 2003, Appl. No. 14032/88.

[67] See De Caro (2014), pp. 2–3.

[68] ECtHR, *Van Pelt v. France*, judgment of 23 May 2000, Appl. No. 31070/96.

[69] See Article 279(1) of the Code of Criminal Procedure.

[70] See more in detail Drevet, in this volume.

[71] See De Caro (2014), p. 3.

Article 111 in fact encapsulates, in its current version, a set of principles that in the case law of the European Court of Human Rights are meant as the essence of fair trial. These principles were not included in the scope of Article 111 until the beginning of 2000, when a constitutional reform adopted in 1999 entered into force with a view to expanding the constitutional guarantees relating to the so-called "fair trial".[72] The constitutional amendment that introduced the principles developed by the ECtHR came up at the end of a very confrontational interaction, almost a conflict, between the Italian Constitution Court and the Italian Parliament.[73] While the lawmakers were attempting to introduce certain principles, the Constitutional Court repeatedly struck down the relevant legislation by reason of a conflict with the prior text of Article 111 of the Constitution.[74] Eventually, the Parliament took the road to introduce these principles directly in the constitutional text.

The current version of Article 111 of the Constitution provides that

> In the criminal process, all individuals charged with a criminal offence have the statutory right to be notified promptly and confidentially of the nature and cause of the charges made against them; they shall be given adequate time and conditions to prepare their defense; they have the statutory right to examine, or have examined, the witnesses testifying against them in court and to obtain the attendance and examination of witnesses on their behalf under the same conditions as witnesses against them, and to obtain all other evidence on their behalf; they shall be assisted by an interpreter if they cannot understand or speak the language used during the trial.

Therefore, personal participation is clearly framed as a fundamental right of the defendant. Article 111 also establishes that "The criminal process is governed by the adversarial principle for the determination of evidence. Guilt shall not be established on the basis of statements made by anyone who has freely chosen not to submit to questioning by the defendant or the defendant's counsel".

Finally, paragraph 5 reads as follows: "The law shall govern the cases in which the determination of evidence is not subject to adversarial process whether because of the consent of the defendant, or where it is objectively proven to be impossible, or as a result of proven unlawful conduct".

These and other paragraphs were inserted by the aforementioned constitutional fair trial reform of 1999 and were not contained in the previous version of Article 111, that not even mentioned the fair trial principle.

Against that background, a first question of constitutionality was raised before the Constitutional Court in 1998 to challenge the provisions of the Code of Criminal Procedure allowing the trial to be held *in absentia* in respect of the so-called 'untraceable defendants' (*imputati irreperibili*), that is, defendants who did not appear and could not be noticed of both the existence of an indictment to trial and the specific charges. The Constitutional Court[75] rejected the question on the basis of

---

[72] See Constitutional Amendment Law 2/1999. For an overview on the consequences of the constitutional amendment see *ex multiis* Marzaduri (2000).

[73] See, generally, on the influential role of the Italian Constitutional Court, Bognetti (1974).

[74] See Galantini (2011).

[75] Italian Constitutional Court, judgment of 10–11 December 1998, No. 399.

a textual interpretation of the ECtHR judgment in *Colozza v. Italy,* where the European Court had specified that for the right to defense to be guaranteed it was sufficient, in case of trial held *in absentia,* that the defendant was provided with the possibility of a retrial. The existence of *ex post* remedies (retrial or review of the case) was considered by the Italian Constitutional Court as an alternative to the *a priori* ban of trials *in absentia.*

In the view of the Constitutional Court, then, the Italian State must adopt either a general prohibition of holding trials in the absence of the defendant or measures allowing the latter to remove the consequences of his absence in the trial.

In 2006 a new question on the same provisions was referred to the Constitutional Court by the Court of Pinerolo,[76] that expressly mentioned the 1998 decision and observed that a different position could be taken by the constitutional justices in light of the amendment to Article 111 that had expressly introduced the right to fair trial.

According to the Court of Pinerolo, as consequence of the amendments to Article 111, the Constitution provides even stricter limits on the model of criminal procedure than those deriving from the ECtHR case law. In particular, the reform resulted in a significant strengthening of the adversarial principle, that is expressly established as a requirement of fair trial. On this assumption, the Court of Pinerolo noted that the relevance attached to the adversarial principle (particularly in respect of the determination of the evidence) is of such nature that the personal participation of the defendant does no longer come into question as a fundamental right, but rather also as an essential requirement for the *legality* of the trial.[77]

Thus, in the opinion of the Court of Pinerolo, the Constitution requires that, in case the defendant does not appear before the court and has not been served with a notice of the trial and the relevant charges, the trial must be suspended until the defendant is actually noticed of the existence of the trial. No relevance, instead, should be paid to the arrangement of various remedies established with a view to making possible the retrial and review of the decision rendered *in absentia.* The Constitutional Court did not follow the opinion of the referring Court of Pinerolo and by judgment no. 117/2007[78] rejected the question. The Constitutional Court did not specifically take position on the value of the adversarial principle, but only said that the latter constitutes in any cases a profile of the right to defense. It is not by chance that, to the extent paragraph 5 of Article 111 allows the legislator to lay down some derogations from the principle of *contradictoire* along the lines set forth by constitutional law, this option nevertheless relies on the consent that must be given by the defendant. In the view of the constitutional judges, furthermore, the

---

[76] Court of Pinerolo, order of 31 January 2006.

[77] The Court observed, in particular, that the adversarial principle embodied by the fair trial model is no longer just a guarantee for the defendant, since it amounts to an epistemic guarantee that serves to the purpose of shaping criminal trials in accordance with the pursuit of general public interests of fair administration of justice.

[78] For a comment, see Negri (2008).

ECHR does not grant the defendant greater guarantees with respect to trials held *in absentia*.

In the meanwhile, the reference to the Convention embodied in Article 117(1) of the Constitution was subject to an extensive interpretation by the Constitutional Court, inaugurated with the well-known 'twin judgments' no. 348 and no. 349 of 2007.[79] Article 117(1) of the Constitution, as amended in 2001,[80] does provide for that "Legislative powers shall be vested in the State and the Regions in compliance with the Constitution and with the constraints deriving from EU legislation and international obligations". In the 'twin judgments' the Court detailed the status of the ECHR in the Italian legal order and specified that the respective provisions constitute an "interposed parameter" to review the compatibility with the Constitution—namely, through the 'channel' of Article 117(1)—of any statutory provision.

Furthermore, legislation governing trials *in absentia* was significantly amended as result of an extensive reform that took place in 2014, through Law No. 67, that entered into force with a view to making the domestic constitutional order as much adherent as possible with the principles laid down by the European Court of Human Rights.[81] However, the results of these efforts were not satisfactory. Article 420-*bis* of the code of criminal procedure provides that trials are held *in absentia* if the defendant, whether in custody or not, does not appear before the court and has waived the right to be present. In addition to that, Article 420-*bis* sets forth a series of circumstances under which, if the defendant does not subsequently appear, he is assumed to have waived his right to be present before the court and is represented by his defense attorney, including: the statement of an address for service; the arrest, the detention or the adoption or pre-trial precautionary measures; the appointment of a defense attorney; the personal service of the defendant with the notice of the commencement of the trial; or any other circumstances on the basis of which it is certain that the defendant is aware of the trial or has voluntarily ignored the existence of the trial and the relevant stages. Then, the same rule is governing the cases where the absence of the defendant in the trial grounds on an explicit refusal of the latter and cases where the defendant is assumed to have waived his right to appear. In this respect, the goal of the national law-makers was to strike a balance between the need to not obstacle the holding of trials in the absence of the defendant and the need to ensure that the conditions from which the acceptance *per facta concludentia* of the trial *in absentia* is presumed are clear and coherent.

However, this provision has raised some criticism among commentators as the circumstances on which this presumption relied actually were really various and encapsulated different rationales. It is not by chance that recently another question of constitutionality has been raised before the Constitutional Court. The Court of

---

[79] See, among others, Pollicino (2008b), Rossi (2009), Fontanelli and Biondi Dal Monte (2008).

[80] For a comprehensive analysis of the relationship between the Italian Constitutional Court and the ECHR, see among others Pollicino (2015).

[81] See Mangiaracina, in this volume, Section 5.1.

Asti[82] challenged in particularly the compatibility with Article 3 (principle of equality) and Article 117 of the Constitution (requiring respect of the obligations deriving from international and European law) of Article 420-*bis* to the extent it included among the presumptive circumstances the statement of the public defender's address as address for service. According to the referring Court, in fact, the act of establishing the address for service in case of appointment of a court-appointed lawyer is a routine practice occurring generally when the first stages of the proceedings take place, thus in most of the cases a long time before the beginning of the trial. As a consequence, when the trial begins the relevant notice is served to the court-appointed lawyer, who most likely will face difficulties to reach the defendant out. Under these circumstances, in the view of the Court of Asti, the presumption established by Article 420-*bis* would most likely fail as the statement of the address for service does not reflect an actual knowledge by the defendant of the existence of the trial. The very problem of this provision, according to the Court of Asti, lies with the exclusion of any room for a discretionary assessment by the court on the actual degree of awareness or knowledge by the defendant regarding the trial. In fact, Article 420-*bis* requires the court to continue the trial without any alternative. In such scenario, presuming that the defendant is aware of the trial would be difficult to reconcile with the case law of the European Court, which requires the defendant to be informed of the date and place of the trial and of the relevant charges. Also, this provision seems to be in contrast with Article 8 of Directive 2016/343 that requires, if the defendant is represented by a mandated lawyer, that he has been informed of the trial.[83] The Constitutional Court declared the question inadmissible on procedural grounds by judgment no. 31/2017. However, the Court, albeit very shortly, focused on the key requirement of proper notice of the trial. According to the constitutional judges, the ECtHR does not require the defendant being served personally with the notice of the commencement of the trial. In the view of the Constitutional Court, the only obligation deriving from the said case law is to establish a series of rules on the basis of which the absence of the defendant in the trial is presumed as a consequence of a knowing and aware refusal to appear before the court. The determination of these criteria is subject to the sole lawmakers' discretion and cannot be interfered with by the Constitutional Court that would most likely enter into the political domain of these choices, since no constitutionally-mandated solution would be applicable in this case.

In light of all the foregoing, the Italian legal order seems, at least apparently, to frame personal participation in criminal proceedings as a fundamental right, rather than a duty of the defendant.

---

[82] Court of Asti, order of 10 November 2015. See also Ciavola (2016).

[83] Interestingly enough, the Court of Asti observed that even though the purpose of the reform adopted by Law 67/2014 was to avoid the delaying of criminal trials concerning the so-called "ghost defendants", in accordance with the principles developed by the Court of Strasbourg, the law actually fails to reach said goal, by facilitating the increase of judgments rendered *in absentia* in cases where the defendant, whether guilty or innocent, is not aware at all of the existence of a trial.

This view is also confirmed by the constitutional case law that considers the right to defense as an expression of the free determination and responsibility of the defendant and, ultimately, as an expression of his freedom to take the most appropriate steps to face the relevant criminal charges. The same Constitutional Court had already clarified, in some dated judgments, that the protection of the adversarial principle does not require the defendant being necessarily present at the trial.[84] Then, according to the Constitutional Court it is not the adversarial principle *per se* that must be ensured, but rather the sole opportunity for the defendant to appear to exercise his right to defense. The same conclusions, as noted,[85] cannot be called into question even after the reform of Article 111.

However, the chance to clarify once again this point, that may be a driving factor for future (and necessary) reforms in the Italian procedural law, was unfortunately missed by the Constitutional Court more recently.

7   Final Remarks

The influence of EU law on the criminal law and the criminal procedure of Member States has been growing over the last years, in particular following the entry into force of the Lisbon Treaty.[86] The abolition of the third pillar led to a further 'communitarisation' of European criminal law, that nonetheless was seen with suspicion and with some degree of resistance by some Member States. The first decisions handed down by the Court of Justice in this field unveil the existence of a growing tension, as result of the strict connection that criminal law has with a set of constitutional values entrenched in domestic constitutions that are not common to all the Member States. The existence of different understandings of some of these core values and interests has further given rise to stances of constitutional resistance, where Member States acted in their capacity of guardians of the respective constitutional identity. The extension of the scope covered by EU criminal law probably matches the objective of a more effective contrast of crimes taking place on a larger and larger scale but brings about some issues with respect to the existence of varying standards of protection and constitutional guarantees. While the extension of EU criminal law would require a common ground to work at its best, Member States are reluctant to accept that certain constitutional values are subject to a lower degree of protection and thus subject to 'degradation'. As is well-known, the Italian Constitutional Court and the German *Bundesverfassungsgericht* rank among the most 'suspicious' courts in respect of European integration in the specific field of

---

[84] In the judgment no. 9 of 14 January 1982, the Italian Constitutional Court declared unconstitutional Article 428 of the Code of Criminal Procedure to the extent it did not permit the suspension of the trial once the defendant, after having been examined, had no longer appeared on legitimate grounds.

[85] See Mangiaricina (2010), p. 8.

[86] See Mitsilegas (2016). See also Mitsilegas (2010).

fundamental rights. It is not by chance that through, respectively, the counter-limits doctrine and the equivalence test, these courts *de facto* reserved themselves the last say on the respect of the essence of the fundamental rights protected by domestic constitutions in EU law. The interaction between courts, therefore, constitutes a key factor to be considered while looking at the current degree of openness of Member States to the extension of European criminal law, insomuch as the latter calls into question the degree of protection afforded to certain fundamental values. Trials *in absentia* and the debate on the nature of personal participation as a fundamental right or a duty of the defendant are not immune from these developments. On the contrary, the very landmark decision in the field of European criminal law, namely *Melloni*, brings to light the difficulties of reconciling the requirements for EU law to apply in uniform way across Member States (i.e. the primacy of EU law) and the safeguard of the higher standards of protection entrenched in national constitutions. To the extent certain Member States permit trials *in absentia* and others ban the same, a transnational constitutional law issue arises.

Recently, the *Taricco*[87] saga has renewed attention on the different scope of protection that Member States and EU law may grant to certain rights or principles. In *Taricco*, the Court of Justice found that the narrow limitation periods established by the Italian Criminal Code for the crime of VAT fraud should be disapplied by national courts in case prosecution of serious frauds is time-barred in a significant number of cases. The Italian Constitutional Court, however, found this judgment in contrast with Article 25 of the Constitution, which embodies a strong protection of the principle of *nulla poena sine lege* preventing retroactive application of criminal law *in peius* and reserving to the Parliament rule-making powers in this field. The very heart of the clash in *Taricco* lies with the different consideration of limitations periods in the Italian legal system and in EU law: in the former, limitation periods are regarded as substantive criminal law and thus subject to the principle of *nulla poena sine lege*, while in the latter they are a matter of procedural law. On these grounds, the Court of Justice held that strict limitation periods are in contrast with Article 325 TFEU, that requires Member States adopting appropriate measures to safeguard the financial interests of the Union; also, it noted that disapplying limitation periods does not infringe the principle of legality enshrined in Article 49 of the Charter. The Italian Constitutional Court referred a new question before the Court of Justice, by stressing the existence of a constitutional impediment preventing the enforcement in Italy of *Taricco* that, in any ways, would not call into question the primacy of EU law. A new decision is now awaited from the Court of Justice and is expected to mark a turning point with respect to the extension of the scope of European criminal law and its relationship with the constitutional standards of protection of each Member State.[88]

---

[87] See among others Bassini and Pollicino (2017a, b), Rossi (2017) and Faraguna (2017).

[88] It is worth noting that in *Taricco* the relevant parameter on which the decision of the Court of Justice is grounded, namely Article 325 TFEU, has nothing to do *per se* with criminal law; its interpretation, however, is seen as having a significant impact on Member States' criminal legislation.

The European Arrest Warrant Framework Decision has been the playground[89] of the clash between the stronger constitutional protection of personal participation entrenched in the Spanish constitutional law, resulting in the need of additional guarantees to surrender defendants convicted *in absentia*, and the primacy of EU law. The Court of Justice, held that Member States can apply higher standards of protection unless it does not compromise the unity, primacy and effectiveness. Requiring to make conditional the surrender upon circumstances additional to that provided for by the Framework Decision, in the view of the Court of Justice, constituted an obstacle to the application of EU law, notably in field based on mutual trust among Member States. The same problem can be seen emerging now in the *Taricco* saga, where the claim of the Italian Constitutional Court to apply the principle of legality according to a broader construction may be interpreted by the Court of Justice as an obstacle to the primacy of EU law. The Italian Constitutional Court, in its order asking a new preliminary reference, drew a distinction between *Melloni* and *Taricco,* trying to identify in the latter a case where a "constitutional impediment" prevented to give full effects to the judgment of the Court of Justice without challenging the primacy of EU law. Another element that is often referred to when it comes to the core values of the constitutional legal order lies with the national (or constitutional) identity. In *Taricco*, the Italian Constitutional Court took into account for the first time the concept of constitutional identity,[90] although in a pretty shy way, to substantiate its claim that the decision of the Court of Justice was not enforceable. The Constitutional Court speculated on Article 4(2) TEU and questioned whether the constitutional identity clause herein established may constitute a sound basis for the refusal to apply the decision of the Court of Justice. This was the first attempt of the Italian Constitutional Court to refer to the notion of constitutional identity that, on the contrary, is very often referred to by the German *Bundesverfassungsgericht.* In fact, the German Basic Law recognizes the national identity as a limit to constitutional review and qualifies the same as a counter-limit to the application of EU law. On 15 December 2015, as noted, the German Federal Constitutional Tribunal took a landmark decision in the *Solange III* case.[91] The BVG invalidated the extradition of an American citizen to Italy, where he had been convicted *in absentia* in 1992, on the basis of a European arrest warrant. The applicant complained that he had never been informed of the trial and had no chance to obtain retrial or the review of the judgment *in absentia.* The Court held that under these circumstances the warrant violated Article 1 of the Basic Law, protecting human dignity. This conclusion was reached on the grounds of the identity-review that the BVF undertook since the respect of human dignity is part of the constitutional identity of Germany and, as such, a limit to the application of EU law.

---

[89] See more generally Pollicino (2008c).

[90] See particularly Fabbrini and Pollicino (2017).

[91] Cf. Hong (2016) and Sarmiento (2016). See Demetrio Crespo and Sánz Hermida, in this volume, Section 3.1; Ruggeri, in Part VI of this volume, Section 2.1.

As correctly observed,[92] the *Solange III* decision indeed relied on an extensive interpretation of the European Arrest Warrant Framework Decision and did not come to the conclusion that EU law was infringing upon the constitutional identity. According to this Framework Decision, as amended in 2009, the executing judicial authority cannot refuse to execute a warrant to enforce a judgment *in absentia* if the warrant states that the person that was not personally served with the decision will be personally served with it without delay after the surrender and will be expressly informed of the right to a retrial, or an appeal. These conditions, in the view of the *Bundesverfassungsgericht*, were not met by the Italian law and the German authorities were therefore authorized to refuse the surrender. As pointed out,[93] since the BVF found that there was no need for interpretation, the Court of Justice was not asked to give a preliminary ruling. However, the answer would have been most likely the opposite one, since in *Melloni* the Court noted that even a domestic provision with constitutional rank may not undermine the effectiveness of EU law.

The fact that the BVF did not enforce the identity clause is probably good news from the perspective of the European cooperative constitutionalism. However, the approach of the Court of Justice is well-know, and would have probably resulted in a judgment very similar to *Melloni*, following which the Spanish Constitutional Court, definitely in a weaker position than the German Constitutional Tribunal, was forced to step back and revisit its conservative approach *vis-à-vis* the trials *in absentia*. It is likely that the clash that occurred in *Melloni* between a Member State seeking to enforce its domestic higher constitutional standard of protection and the Court of Justice, guardian of the primacy of EU law, materializes in *Taricco*, most notably after the very conservative opinion delivered by Advocate General Bot, that firmly suggested the Court not to take any step back.

Who is going to win this fight?

Indeed, the existence of various understandings of the same constitutional values (e.g., right to defense, principle of legality), which are protected by national constitutions according to a different scope, is difficult to be qualified as a factor that *per se* obstacle the primacy of EU law. The extension of the scope of action of EU criminal law led to find out that, unlike other areas of law, Member States may have very different approaches, sometimes hard to harmonize and even to reconcile with EU law. Who is going to self-restrain, then? Both is probably the right and most politically-correct answer. The European Union shall take into account that extending its competences in the field of criminal law requires probably a more tolerant view, in accordance with the idea of constitutional pluralism. In this respect, revisiting *Melloni* or at least the criteria on which the *Melloni* test relies could be an option. After all, requiring Member States to waive their constitutional traditions (without calling into question the notion of constitutional identity) for the sake of primacy of EU law clashes with the idea that European integration has been fostered by the expansion of fundamental rights and their protection.

---

[92] Faraguna (2016).

[93] *Ibid.*

On the other hand, Member States should probably take seriously the extension of the scope of action of the EU criminal law. If this is a desirable result, it seems that a price has to be paid in terms of constitutional guarantees. If, on the contrary, the price to be paid is deemed to be too much high, to leave the camp appears to be the only alternative.

References

Bassini M, Pollicino O (2017a) The Taricco Decision: a last attempt to avoid a clash between EU law and the Italian Constitution. http://verfassungsblog.de/the-taricco-decision-a-last-attempt-to-avoid-a-clash-between-eu-law-and-the-italian-constitution. Accessed 14 Nov 2017

Bassini M, Pollicino O (2017b) The opinion of advocate general bot in Taricco II: seven "deadly" sins and a modest proposal. http://verfassungsblog.de/the-opinion-of-advocate-general-bot-in-taricco-ii-seven-deadly-sins-and-a-modest-proposal. Accessed 14 Nov 2017

Bassiouni MC (1993) Human rights in the context of criminal justice: identifying international procedural protections and equivalent protections in national constitutions. Duke J Comp Int Law 3:235–298

Bognetti G (1974) Political role of the Italian Constitutional Court. Notre Dame Law Rev 49:981–999

Böse M (2011) Harmonizing procedural rights indirectly: the framework decision on trials in Absentia. N C J Int Law 37:489–510

Chelo A (2015) Le "istruzioni sovranazionali" sui limiti al processo in absentia: dalle pronunce della Corte europea dei diritti dell"Uomo al diritto di partecipare al processo nella normativa dell"Unione europea. Archivio penale, pp 1–13

Ciavola A (2016) Assenza dell"imputato e dubbia sintomaticità dell"elezione di domicilio presso il difensore d"ufficio: una lettura costituzionalmente orientata. Archivio penale, pp 1–20

Claes M, Reestman J (2015) The protection of national constitutional identity and the limits of European integration at the occasion of the Gauweiler Case. Germ Law J 18:917–970

De Caro A (2014) Processo in absentia e sospensione. Una primissima lettura della legge n. 67 del 2014. Archivio penale, pp 1–28

de Poorter JCA (2013) Constitutional review in the Netherlands: a joint responsibility. Utrecht Law Rev 9:89–105

Fabbrini F, Pollicino O (2017) Constitutional identity in Italy: European integration as the fulfilment of the constitution. EUI Working Papers LAW 2017/06, pp 1–15

Faraguna P (2016) Solange II: il BVerfG colpisce ancora. Quaderni costituzionali, pp 123–126

Faraguna P (2017) The Italian Constitutional Court in re Taricco: "Gauweiler in the Roman Campagna". http://verfassungsblog.de/the-italian-constitutional-court-in-re-taricco-gauweiler-in-the-roman-campagna. Accessed 14 Nov 2017

Fontanelli F, Biondi Dal Monte F (2008) The Decisions No. 348 and 349/2007 of the Italian Constitutional Court: the efficacy of the European Convention in the Italian legal system. Germ Law J 9:889–932

Galantini N (2011) Giusto processo e garanzia costituzionale del contraddittorio nella formazione della prova. Diritto penale contemporaneo, pp 1–13

Golser F (2017) Personal participation in criminal proceedings. Austrian report

Hong P (2016) Human Dignity and Constitutional Identity: The Solange-III-Decision of the German Constitutional Court. http://verfassungsblog.de/human-dignity-and-constitutional-identity-the-solange-iii-decision-of-the-german-constitutional-court. Accessed 14 Nov 2017

Ianovska O (2015) Participation of an accused in proceedings: right or obligation. Law Ukrain, pp 26–33

Mangiaricina A (2010) Garanzie partecipative e giudizio in absentia. Giappichelli, Torino

Martinico G (2017) Studio sulle forme alternative di judicial review: il caso dei Paesi Bassi e della Svizzera. Federalismi.it, pp 1–27

Marzaduri E (2000) Commento all'art. 1 legge costituzionale 2/1999. La Legislazione penale, pp 762–804

Mitsilegas V (2010) European criminal law and resistance to communautarisation after Lisbon. New J Eur Crim Law 4:458–480

Mitsilegas V (2016) EU criminal law after Lisbon rights, trust and the transformation of Justice in Europe. Hart, London

Negri S (2008) Giudizio in absentia e garanzie processuali internazionali: note a margine della sentenza della Corte cost. n. 117/2007. Diritto penale e processo, pp 665–679

Öhlinger T (1990) Austria and Article 6 of the European Convention on Human Rights. Eur J Int Law 1:286–291

Pollicino O (2008a) Incontri e scontri tra ordinamenti e interazioni tra giudici nella nuova stagione del costituzionalismo europeo: la saga del mandato d''arresto europeo come modello di analisi. Eur J Leg Stud 2:220–268

Pollicino O (2008b) Constitutional Court at cross road between constitutional parochialism and cooperative constitutionalism. Eur Const Law Rev 4:363–382

Pollicino O (2008c) European arrest warrant and constitutional principles of the member states: a case law-based outline in the attempt to strike the right balance between interacting legal systems. Germ Law J 9:1313–1355

Pollicino O (2015) The European Court of Human Rights and the Italian Constitutional Court: No "Groovy Kind of Love". In: Siegler K (ed) The UK and of European Court of Human Rights - a strained relationship? Hart, London, pp 362–378

Pradel J (1995) Droit pénal compare. Dalloz, Paris

Quattrocolo S (2016) Assenza e irreperibilità dell''imputato. Enciclopedia del diritto, Annali IX. Giuffré, Milano, pp 29–57

Rossi LS (2009) Corte costituzionale (Italian Constitutional Court): Decisions 348 and 349/2007 of 22 October 2007, and 102 and 103/2008, of 12 February 2008. Common Mark Law Rev 46:319–331

Rossi LS (2017) How could the ECJ escape from the Taricco Quagmire?. http://verfassungsblog. de/how-could-the-ecj-escape-from-the-taricco-quagmire. Accessed 14 Nov 2017

Sarmiento D (2016) The German Constitutional Court and the European Arrest Warrant: the latest twist in the judicial dialogue. http://eulawanalysis.blogspot.it/2016/01/the-german-constitu-tional-court-and.html. Accessed 14 Nov 2017

Shapiro EL (2012) Examining an underdeveloped constitutional standard: trial in Absentia and the relinquishment of a criminal defendant's right to be present. Marquette Law Rev 96:591–625

Stamhuis E (2001) In Absentia trials and the right to defend: the incorporation of a European human rights principle into the Dutch criminal justice system. Vic Univ Wellington Law Rev 32:715–728

Starkey JG (1978) Trial in absentia. St John's Law Rev, 721–745

Tassara L (2009) Trial in Absentia: rescuing the "Public Necessity" requirement to proceed with a trial in the defendant's absence. Barry Law Rev 12:153–171

Trifterer O (1999) Commentary on the Rome Statute of the International Criminal Court: observers' notes, article by article. Beck-Hart-Nomos, Baden-Baden

van der Schyff G (2010) Constitutional review by the judiciary in the Netherlands: a bridge too far? Germ Law J 11:275–290

Vigoni D (2014) Panorama europeo in tema di giudizio senza imputato. In: Vigoni D (ed) Il giudizio in assenza dell'imputato. Giappichelli, Torino, pp 31–71

Weissbrodt D (2009) The administration of justice and human rights. City Univ Hong Kong Law Rev 1:23–47

In Absentia Proceedings in the Framework of a Human Rights-Oriented Criminal Law. The Perspective of Substantive Criminal Law

Eduardo Demetrio Crespo and Ágata María Sanz Hermida

Abstract The legislative regulation of *in absentia* proceedings presents important difficulties in order to guarantee the effectiveness of the criminal system without undermining the fundamental rights of citizens. Therefore, in general, the lawfulness of the *in absentia* proceedings has traditionally been linked to the respect of certain limits or conditions such as respect for the rights of the accused to the defence, to a fair trial or to an effective judicial protection. Trials held *in absentia* also can affect other fundamental guarantees such as, for example, the *individual guilt* principle or the protection of human dignity, as noted by the German *Bundesverfassungsgericht* in its decision of 15 December 2015. However, not all national statutes on trials *in absentia* sufficiently respect these limits, particularly those of a substantive criminal law nature, which has caused problems in European law instruments of judicial cooperation to recognize or execute decisions *in absentia*. In this context, a lively discussion arises on the primacy of Union law or the possibility that Member States can refuse the execution of foreign decisions because of the need to protect their citizens on the grounds of the *individual guilt* principle and human dignity. This discussion is extremely relevant, as it concerns the definition of the standards of protection of fundamental rights in the Member States and in the EU without, in our view, the claimed effectiveness of European cooperation being able to ground a lower protection. This highlights the need for an in-depth discussion on the incorporation of main criminal law principles and their dogmatic implications for harmonization in the EU criminal justice.

Abbreviations

AFSJ	Area of freedom, security and justice
BVerfG	*Bundesverfassungsgericht* (German Constitutional Court)

E. Demetrio Crespo (✉) · Á. M. Sanz Hermida
Faculty of Legal and Social Sciences, Castilla-La Mancha University, Toledo, Spain
e-mail: Eduardo.Demetrio@uclm.es; Agata.Sanz@uclm.es

© Springer Nature Switzerland AG 2019
S. Quattrocolo, S. Ruggeri (eds.), *Personal Participation in Criminal Proceedings*, Legal Studies in International, European and Comparative Criminal Law 2, https://doi.org/10.1007/978-3-030-01186-4_17

559

CJEU   Court of Justice of the European Union
CFR   Charter of Fundamental Rights of the European Union
EAW   European Arrest Warrant
ECHR   European Convention on Human Rights
ECtHR   European Court of Human Rights
EU   European Union
GG   *Grundgesetz* (Basic Law of Germany)
LECrim   *Ley de Enjuiciamiento Criminal* (Spanish Criminal Procedure Code)
SC   Spanish Constitution
STC   Judgment of the Spanish Constitutional Tribunal
TC   Spanish Constitutional Tribunal
TFEU   Treaty on the Functioning of the European Union

1 Introduction

The right of the accused to be present during the proceedings is one of the basic principles of any criminal justice system, a principle that reaches its maximum expression at the hearing when the evidence that may discredit the presumption of innocence is examined. Personal attendance is an essential fundamental guarantee that must be respected in the legal systems of all social and democratic States based on the rule of law. This safeguard is strictly linked with the recognition of the right to a fair trial and the guarantees of defence (the right to defence and assistance by a lawyer; to be informed of the charges brought against them; to a public trial; to the use of evidence appropriate to their defence, etc., under art. 24 SC and art. 6 ECHR).

However, like any other fundamental right or freedom, the right to be present at trial does not have an absolute character. Consequently, its recognition does not necessarily imply the constitutional-law ban on *in absentia* trials, but the subjection of any limitation of the right to be present to its regulation by law, which must always respect the essential content—hard core of the right—and the requirements of the principle of proportionality. In this sense, the lawfulness of the trial in the absence of the defendant—as a restriction on the fundamental rights and guarantees mentioned above—has been linked to the guarantee of specific limits or conditions serving certain interests worthy of protection in criminal justice. Among the main safeguards, we should mention the right of the suspected person and the accused to be informed of the charges, as well as on the date and consequences of the choice of not being present at trial. Another important guarantee is that the defendant, even though he does not attend the trial, must be effectively defended by a lawyer, where required, and that the enforceability of the conviction rendered *in absentia* is subject to the possibility of a subsequent appeal. The ECHR defines this appeal as the possibility of the person concerned being able to obtain, from a court which has heard him, a "fresh determination of the merits of the charge".[1] (*Colozza case*, ECHR, 12

---

[1] ECtHR, *Colozza v. Italy*, judgment of 12 February 1985, Appl. No. 9024/80, § 29.

February 1985). In this respect, the Spanish Constitutional Tribunal has pointed out that

> what is in no way compatible with the absolute content of the right to a fair trial [art. 24(2) SC] is the conviction *in absentia* without the aforementioned possibility to remedy the deficiencies that the absence of the trial may have caused in the criminal proceedings followed by very serious crimes (STC 91/2000, of 30 March).

The limits or conditions are linked to the procedural safeguards such as the right to a fair trial, to obtain an effective protection from the judges or to the defense. However, along with these limits or conditions, other issues should be taken into account, such as the severity of the facts that may be prosecuted *in absentia*[2] or others relating to the conditions of effective enforcement of that decision in the issuing State. These last aspects directly affect the limits of the punitive power, namely, the *individual guilt* principle and, ultimately, the necessary respect for human dignity.

In this context, some important questions arise. Is the *individual guilt* principle an unavoidable principle that requires the attendance of the accused in all criminal trial? How can the *individual guilt* principle be protected in cases where the accused is tried *in absentia*? Taking into consideration the legal context of the EU, could cooperation between States be denied in cases where the executing State considers that the legal regulation of the requesting State does not respect the *individual guilt principle* or that the conditions of enforcement in the requesting State may breach the prohibition of inhuman or degrading treatment or the human dignity? What would the basis for such denial be? Can a Member State summon its greater degree of protection of rights of the suspect or accused as a reason for refusing criminal cooperation under the principles and foundations of the *area of freedom, security and justice*?

These issues have been the subject of a number of decisions by the highest judicial Courts, highlighting the difficult balance, which exists in the area of criminal justice to meet both the effectiveness of the system and the guarantee of the citizens' rights. On the other hand, the different standards of protection in the Member States sometimes result in significant tensions that need to be addressed by satisfying in an appropriate manner the necessary agility and effectiveness of the criminal cooperation system, and the due respect for the adequate protection of fundamental rights of the accused within the human rights framework. In particular, we should ascertain whether, although in an exceptional and restricted way, the Member States,

---

[2] It is necessary to bear in mind that the description that has been made of the trial *in absentia* focuses on the 'commonplace' elements in some States, so some legal systems could address other aspects. Indeed, the Spanish system allows for trials *in absentia* under exceptional circumstances and in relation to criminal cases regarding offences with low severity. Thus, article 786(1) LECrim establishes the following conditions: the unjustified absence of the accused; the request for non-suspension by the accusation and heard the defence; and the limit that the penalty requested does not exceed 2 years of deprivation of liberty or, if different, when its duration does not exceed 6 years. In the case of trials for minor offences, article 971 LECrim allows the trial in the absence of the accused not appearing voluntarily, and who have been duly informed, unless the judge, *ex officio* or a requested character, considers that the accused must be heard. On Spanish default proceedings see Villamarín López (2017) and, in this volume, Sect. 5.2.

when proceeding with an instrument of cooperation, can/should have certain powers of control in the protection of fundamental rights and which control parameters should be used to determine the content of the human rights; or whether, on the basis of the principle of mutual trust and primacy of EU law, they are deprived of these reviewing powers even if this can put at risk the protection of human rights. We will deal with these aspects in the following sections.

2 The Framework: The Protection of Fundamental Rights in the European Union

2.1 Universal Values as Values of the Union

After World War II, some decisive changes in an international society influenced the transition from classical to contemporary international law. The latter is characterized by the formation of an international legal system that protects human rights.[3] The *Universal Declaration of Human Rights* of 10 December 1948 is recognized by the Member States of the Council of Europe in the *European Convention for the Protection of Human Rights and Fundamental Freedoms* of 4 November 1950. Subsequently, on 16 December 1966, the *International Covenant on Civil and Political Rights* was adopted in New York, to which many of the EU Member States also belong.

At the same time and after the end of WWII, the European states approved their constitutional texts and incorporated a wide catalog of fundamental rights and freedoms. Thus, the recognition and protection of the so-called 'basic human rights' in Europe operated through two types of different legal mechanisms: an internal mechanism (constitutional rules and development legislation) and an international mechanism (international Conventions and Treaties), with the diversity of extension, application, and effectiveness that this implies.

The EU did not have any legal instrument of its own establishing a catalog of fundamental rights and a system of guarantees aimed at protecting them, which would harmonize the different European systems. Therefore, the setting of such objective encountered several hurdles.[4] In this context, the *Charter of Fundamental*

---

[3] Pastor Ridruejo (2017), pp. 59 ff.

[4] To be sure, the recognition of fundamental rights in the EU is part of a larger phenomenon, which is the consolidation of the *area of freedom, security and justice* whose evolution, moreover, will not be analyzed in detail in the context of the present discussion. Here it is worth observing that the achievement of a coordinated criminal law policy with a transnational scope is a necessity that has been imposed by the evolution of relations between States and, specifically, by the evolution of the EU. Indeed, the increasing internationalization of human relations together with the idea, reinforced after World War II, of the protection of 'universal' legal rights has revealed the limitations of the State's *ius puniendi* and the need to establish instruments of collaboration with other States. From this perspective, cooperation among States plays an essential role in the fight against crime; the principle of mutual recognition of judicial decisions is its cornerstone; the approximation of

Rights of the European Union (CFR) was drawn up and formally proclaimed it in Nice by the European Parliament, the Council and the Commission in December 2000.[5] The EU Charter, however, became legally binding with the entry into force of the Lisbon Treaty in December 2009 with the same legal status as the Treaties.[6]

The EU has faced the dilemma of whether or not to enact a catalog of fundamental rights and guarantees, since, on the one hand, it contributes to the enshrinement of these rights within the European area, providing security and the same legal value.[7] On the other, the fact that fundamental rights were already incorporated into other international Treaties or Conventions, including the ECHR, raises the question of whether this normative reiteration is necessary. This question becomes even more relevant if we take into account that the meaning and scope of the rights acknowledged by the CFR need to be "the same as those conferred on the said Convention" [art. 52(3) CFR] and that the provisions of the EU Charter cannot be interpreted as limiting or adversely affecting the human rights and fundamental freedoms, including those established in the ECHR (art. 53 CFR).[8] In addition, we must take into consideration that Strasbourg case-law keeps the ECHR's rights and guarantees alive and dynamic by providing them with an expansive and amplifying effect and by extending and updating their content, strength, and scope.[9]

---

legislations, its mechanism of facilitating the achievement of those objectives; and finally, the protection of human rights, the guarantee of its proper functioning. At the EU level, this necessary collaboration was accelerated in the 1990s when significant advances began to be made in this area: first, with the Maastricht Treaty (1991), and later with the Treaty of Amsterdam (1996), which enacted the establishment of an *area of freedom, security and justice*, as a priority objective of the EU, into a broad political program prepared by the Tampere European Council in 1999 and developed in the Treaty of Nice (2001). This area is based on the need for cooperation between States in criminal matters but with the ambitious objective of overcoming their traditional understanding in favor of achieving a "common sense of justice in the Union". Reaching, however, that common sense of justice is not an easy task in a space in which national legal systems are very different. Therefore, the EU has taken steps to achieve this objective from different perspectives such as the delimitation of the areas of action or the adoption of measures to favor the development of the principle of mutual recognition of judicial decisions, whose effectiveness depends, among other parameters, on the protection of the rights and guarantees of the individuals affected.

[5] DOCE, series C, No 364 of 18 December 2000. See Salcedo (2001).

[6] See below. Lisbon Treaty by virtue of which the European Union Treaty and the Treaty constituting the European Union are modified, signed in Lisbon on 13 December 2007, whose article 6 states: "1. The European Union recognizes the rights, freedoms and principles set out in the Charter of Fundamental Rights of the European Union of 7 December 2000, as adapted on 12 December 2007 in Strasbourg, which will have the same legal value as the Treaties".

[7] In this respect, the Commission ruled that the *Green Paper on procedural safeguards for suspects and defendants in criminal proceedings throughout the European Union*, COM (2003) 75 final. In this paper, the Commission concluded that the recognition of fundamental rights or guarantees in this area, although being consistent with those already included in the ECHR, is intended to ensure that the defined rights are applied in a more coherent and uniform manner throughout the European Union, thereby avoiding discrepancies in relation to operational safeguards in the various Member States.

[8] See among other references Llorens (2001), pp. 85 ff.; Fernández Tomás (2002), pp. 108 ff.

[9] Sanz Hermida (2003), pp. 188 ff.

The CFR Preamble states expressly that

> the Union is founded on the indivisible and universal values of human dignity, freedom, equality, and solidarity and is based on the principles of democracy and the rule of law.

This provision entails the acknowledgment of a catalog of rights—and freedoms—that States must respect and promote 'when they apply the right of the Union' [art. 51(1) CFR]. Although their exercise may be limited by law, this must respect their essential content and the guarantees inherent in the principle of proportionality [art. 52(1) CFR]. Their interpretation will be carried out, as the case may be, in accordance with the provisions of the ECHR [art. 52(3) CFR], which does not prevent the Union law from granting more extensive protection [art. 52(3) CFR]. At any rate, the provisions of the Charter may not be construed as limiting or jeopardising human rights and fundamental freedoms (art. 53 CFR), or exceeding the prohibition of the abuse of law (art. 54 CFR).

The inclusion of a wide range of criminal law rights within the list of Fundamental Rights must be highlighted such as: the right to life (art. 2) and the integrity of the person (art. 3); the prohibition of torture and inhuman or degrading treatment or punishment (art. 4); the right to freedom and safety (art. 6); respect for private and family life (art. 7); the principle of equality and the prohibition of discrimination (arts. 20 et seq.); the right to effective remedy and to an independent and an impartial judge (art. 47), the presumption of innocence and the right of defence (art. 48), the principles of legality and proportionality of criminal offences and penalties (art. 49) or the right not to be tried or punished twice in criminal proceedings for the same criminal offence (art. 50).

At any rate, the fundamental rights and freedoms regarding criminal justice recognized in the Charter should be considered as 'minimum standards or guarantees' in a double sense: on the one hand, because the CFR itself establishes that their scope can be extended; on the other hand, because this does not prevent the Member States from maintaining or introducing a higher level of protection in this area.[10]

From these observations it follows that the fundamental rights acknowledged by the European Union can be applied in criminal law both vertically, acting as limits to criminal law action, and horizontally, as grounds for developing a criminal-law response to their infringement by third parties.[11] It should also be recalled that the implementation of these provisions will be carried out by the institutions, bodies, agencies of the Union and by the Member States "only when they are implementing Union law" [art. 51(1) CFR] so the Charter does not broaden the scope of application of EU law [art. 51(2) CFR].

---

[10] *Ibíd.*, p. 190.
[11] Ugartemendia Eceizabarrena (2010), pp. 116, 125 ff.

2.2 Fundamental Rights in the Development of the Area of Freedom, Security, and Justice

The road towards achieving the area of freedom, security, and justice has been slow and progressive, based on the need to speed up and simplify cooperation in criminal matters. This also requires harmonization that contributes to the strengthening of the principle of mutual recognition, the cornerstone of cooperation, as coined in Tampere.

However, developments in this area have always encountered a fundamental obstacle, which is the consideration by States of criminal matters as an exclusive domain of state sovereignty,[12] despite the existence of roots and principles shared by the Member States.[13] All this, in general, is reflected by the scenario that has led to the construction of a 'European criminal law'. This has to face, on the one hand, the sovereign tension (a relevant discussion concerns the areas of sovereignty that can be 'given up' and those that are to be deemed 'intangible') and, on the other, the need for a certain degree of integration and/or harmonization in order not to leave unanswered the demands that globalization poses at the level of transnational crime.[14] The latter goal must be pursued, moreover, in a manner that avoids the risk of universal standardization, which aims at levelling out and suppressing any diversity between criminal law systems with the consequent risk of hegemony.[15]

In fact, European criminal law must satisfy the principles of the primacy, subsidiarity and/or proportionality and complementarity in order to attempt to attenuate the disorder and instability generated by the complexity of the national legal system. It should be acknowledged, however, that even the fulfilment of such principles does not succeed in eliminating what *Delmàs-Marty* calls "discontinuities". In addition to the 'legalistic solution', there is also another solution concerning the values concerned with human rights, namely the 'humanistic solution'. This aims to

---

[12] For further details, cf. Demetrio Crespo (2006), pp. 501 ff.

[13] See Nieto Martín (2005).

[14] On this link see, among other references, Vogel (2005), pp. 115 ff.

[15] Delmàs-Marty et al. (2009), pp. 545 ff., in her ambitious schema on the models of harmonization, raises the hypothesis of an epistemological mutation beyond the mutation of the same reality that materializes, at a quantitative level, by the proliferation of rules and, at a qualitative level, by a number of discontinuities and contradictions that are produced in different areas. The author stresses that, while the latter is apparent to everybody, the former is progressively transforming our way of conceiving of criminal law, since it means moving from a simple (or modern) concept to a more complex or post-modern concept of criminal law action. In any case, it would be an unfinished mutation since we would find ourselves in an intermediate or transitory phase in which the two basic models coexist. One clinging to the idea of completeness and coherence assumed by the unity of traditional systems, and another model enabling the use of both forms of interaction, the vertical and the horizontal one, as a mixed form of harmonization, which, unlike the former, appear as incomplete or discontinuous. While the former would respond to the mechanistic model of physics preponderant in the imaginary of jurists for a long time, the latter would be better explained by the thermodynamic background of biology, which is based upon the multiple unit as a whole in tension.

increase coherence through 'cross-interpretation games' such as those resulting from the rulings of the ECtHR and the CJEU, on the one hand, and the pronouncements by the constitutional courts of the Member States, on the other.

These considerations should lead us to scrutinise the effectiveness of harmonization in relation to the guarantees inherent to the protection provided by the fundamental rights. Although the legal systems of Member States belong to different legal traditions, they all share a common respect for the great democratic principles. In fact, the jurisprudence of the ECHR has played an important role in the process of mutual approximation of domestic legislations. Legal scholarship points out that the process of erosion of the purely state-based elements of the European penal systems, as well as of criminal law science, coincided with the birth of the Council of Europe. Its aim was to reinforce the bonds between the old continent countries, in order to prevent the tragic conflicts, which resulted from mutual intolerance and the opposition between European states. In particular, the jurisprudence of the ECtHR has contributed to the emergence of a 'common law of guarantees' with which the criminal law of the Member States must comply. Therefore, even if a federalism does not exist in Europe, the transnationalism that characterises European criminal law helps overcome the absolute supremacy of national parliaments.[16]

The EU's expectations regarding the development of the AFSJ should be understood within this context. On the one hand, article 83 TFEU provides for a list of serious cross-border crimes, which could be extended by a unanimous decision of the Council and which could support the future European Public Prosecutor's Office provided for in article 86 TFEU. Paragraph 2 of this article, moreover, provides for a mechanism of 'minimum rules' in order to bring together the criminal law in respect of both types and penalties and sanctions whenever this is essential to ensure the effective implementation of a Union policy in an area having undergone harmonization measures. On the other hand, judicial cooperation in criminal matters is based on article 82 TFEU on the principle of mutual recognition of court rulings and judgments. Paragraph 2 of this article also lays down some minimum standards on specific issues of criminal procedure law, such as the mutual admissibility of evidence, the rights of victims and the rights of individuals during the criminal proceedings. All this is further accompanied by the limit set by the so-called 'non-regression clause' according to which the Member States not only can improve the protection standards that result from the minimum rules but can also establish commitments of non-reduction of the achievements of their legal systems.

---

[16] Bernardi (2004), pp. 7 f.; Gómez-Jara Díez (2005), pp. 153 f.; Gómez-Jara Díez (2006), pp. 279 f.; Nieto Martín (2010), pp. 353 f.

3   The Protection of Fundamental Rights in the Recognition and Enforcement of Judgments Ordered *In Absentia*

3.1   *Absolute Content and Constitutional Identity, an Insurmountable Limit in the Protection of Human Rights?*

It is clear that the way in which *in absentia* trials are regulated in the domestic legal systems of the States has important repercussions of not only domestic nature, namely in order to assess the strength of the standards of protection of the fundamental rights of the accused, but also of a transnational and international nature, as they have a direct impact on the functioning of the instruments of judicial cooperation in criminal matters. The various international treaties and other legal instruments of judicial assistance in Europe,[17] as well as a number of pronouncements by the highest courts of the Member States, provide clear examples of the transnational effects of *in absentia* trials. Legal instruments of judicial cooperation have generally focused on the formal control of compliance with the aforementioned conditions to allow for the recognition and enforcement of judgements in cases of trials and/or convictions rendered *in absentia*.[18] This approach was followed in order to determine whether or not the essential content of the right to a fair trial and defence has been fulfilled in the indicated terms. The reasons for non-recognition and/or non-execution constitute an exhaustive list and, in their transposition, EU States have little room for manoeuvre, although the fundamental rights of the accused must be respected in any case.[19]

---

[17] Cf. the European Convention on Extradition of 13 December 1957 or the Council Act of 27 September 1996, adopted in accordance with Article K.3 of the Treaty on European Union by which the Convention on extradition between the Member States of the European Union is established, as well as Framework Decision 2002/581/JHA of 13 June on the European Arrest Warrant; Framework Decision 2009/299/JHA of 26 February amending the Framework Decisions 2002/584/JHA, 2005/214/JHA, 2006/783/JHA, 2008/909/JHA and 2008/947/JHA, designed to strengthen the procedural rights of individuals and to promote the application of the principle of mutual recognition of judgements rendered following trials carried out without appearance of the accused.

[18] Thus, for the purposes of this study, the aspects related to the trial *in absentia* within the European Arrest Warrant, in particular, are included in article 4-*bis* (as a result of the wording given in article 2 of Framework Decision 2009/299/JHA) and are summarized in Recital 10 of the aforementioned Framework Decision as follows: "The recognition and execution of a decision rendered following a trial at which the person concerned did not appear in person should not be refused where the person concerned, being aware of the scheduled trial, was defended at the trial by a legal counsellor to whom he or she had given a mandate to do so, ensuring that legal assistance is practical and effective. In this context, it should not matter whether the legal counsellor was chosen, appointed and paid by the person concerned, or whether this legal counsellor was appointed and paid by the State, it being understood that the person concerned should deliberately have chosen to be represented by a legal counsellor instead of appearing in person at the trial. The appointment of the legal counsellor and related issues are a matter of national law".

[19] In this respect, the argument 15 of Framework Decision 2009/299/JHA, based upon the fact that the grounds for non-recognition by the States are optional. Stated that if they were incorporated

Nevertheless, the decisions of some constitutional courts have highlighted the significant objections that can be made to deny cooperation, precisely by exceeding what has been called in some cases the 'absolute content'[20] of fundamental rights or 'constitutional identity'.[21] These expressions entail a set of minimum guarantees or inalienable rights that under no circumstances can be disregarded or left unapplied by the States and that must be ensured in any case.

The Spanish Constitutional Tribunal already highlighted the idea of an absolute content of fundamental rights and guarantees, although it referred to the extradition system in force before the European arrest order came into operation in its STC 91/2000, of 30 March.[22] In this decision, the Spanish constitutional judges invoked the argument of the 'absolute content' of fundamental rights when projected *ad extra*, viewed as the binding or invulnerable minimum that every legal statute must guarantee precisely. Because of its universal validity, this core aims at safeguarding those rights and that minimum which "belong to the person as such and not as a citizen or, in other words [...] those contents that are essential for guaranteeing human dignity". To be better understood, for the Spanish Constitutional Tribunal, while the domestic public authorities must unconditionally abide *ad intra* by the fundamental rights as they have been established by the Constitution, the absolute content of the fundamental rights when projected *ad extra* has a reduced binding effect, relating to their most basic or elemental requirements.[23] According to this doctrine, when national authorities (including the judiciary) recognize, approve or validate a resolution adopted by a foreign authority, they may cause an 'indirect' breach of some

---

into the internal legal systems, the States should be governed by the right to a fair trial while taking into account the overall objective of the Framework Decision of reinforcing the procedural rights of the individuals and facilitating the judicial cooperation in criminal matters. Article 1(2) highlighted that the Framework Decision "cannot have the effect of modifying the obligation to respect fundamental rights and legal principles provided for in Article 6 of the Treaty, including the right of defence of persons charged in criminal proceedings, and any corresponding obligations to the judicial authorities in this respect will remain immutable".

[20] Expression used by the Spanish Constitutional Tribunal. See STC 91/2000, of 30 March.

[21] Expression used by the BVerfG in the judgement of 15 December 2015, which will be subject to a more detailed examination in the following paragraphs.

[22] In this decision, the Spanish Constitutional Tribunal ruled on the lawfulness of the request for an extradition by Italy to serve prison sentences for very serious crimes performed in a trial held in the absence of the accused without the possibility of a subsequent challenge allowing him to be present. The applicants argued that there was a possible breach of the right to defence, to a fair trial, to equality in the application of the law, and the prohibition of inhuman or degrading treatment or punishment; infringement on the right to a fair hearing.

[23] Cuerda Riezu (2003), p. 28, clearly explains the reasoning of the Spanish Constitutional Tribunal as follows: "In order to assess a breach of a fundamental right provided for in our Constitution, which is directly committed by a foreign public authority and indirectly attributable to a Spanish public authority, it is necessary to have a qualified illegality or, if it is preferred, a challenge to a reduced content of our fundamental rights, which would be a content which would become the common denominator in the international arena. This gives rise to an expansive effect of the fundamental rights included in the Spanish Constitution, based on the doctrine initiated by the ECHR on the basis of its judgement of 7 July 1989 ordered in the *Soering case*, a doctrine that was subsequently developed by the European Court itself".

of the fundamental rights, if that resolution could be considered as jeopardising a fundamental right in the aforementioned terms (i.e., without respecting the absolute content of the right to be projected *ad extra*).[24]

The Spanish Constitutional Tribunal further developed this doctrine in STC 26/2014 of 13 February, which introduced a substantial change compared to STC 91/2000, in the well-known *Melloni* case. This decision has had a great impact since, on the one hand, it was the basis for the first request for a preliminary ruling in this problematic area referred to by a constitutional court before the CJEU and was settled by the Grand Chamber's judgment of 26 February 2013, which we will refer to hereinafter. On the other hand, because it clarified the jurisprudence of the Spanish Constitutional Tribunal in relation to the absolute content of a fundamental right, which was also intended to have an important influence on the understanding of the instruments of criminal cooperation within the AFSJ. According to the Spanish TC, in order to determine the absolute content of a fundamental right—in cases where it is projected *ad extra*—it is necessary to determine the control model. The 2014 ruling refers to the ECHR, as well as to the Charter of Fundamental Rights of the EU, which, particularly as interpreted by the competent bodies established by those legal instruments, provide essential elements when determining the meaning of the absolute content. Taking those considerations of the Constitutional Tribunal into account, the *Melloni* case entailed accepting, in accordance with the aforementioned CJEU's judgment of 26 February 2013, that EU law harmonized the conditions for the execution of a European Arrest Warrant. The conclusion of this judgment was the impossibility of applying the higher level of protection set by domestic law, but only the standards of fundamental rights protection recognized in articles 47 and 48(2) of the EU Charter.

In its 2014 judgment, the Spanish Constitutional Tribunal clarified its doctrine on the scope of the absolute content that should no longer be determined by fundamental rights as there are established in the Constitution (control model used in STC 91/2000), but in conformity with the provisions of article 10(2) of the Spanish Constitution,[25] which in turn are to be interpreted according to EU law. This approach has been criticized for not fully accepting the principle of primacy of EU law.[26]

---

[24] We should also bear in mind that the Spanish Constitutional Tribunal stated in its STC 177/2006 of 5 June, or STC 199/2009, of 28 September, that this doctrine on indirect breaches of the right to the proceedings with full guarantees was also applicable within the framework of international surrender procedures established in the European Union by the Council Framework Decision 2002/584/JHA on the European Arrest Warrant, which was implemented in Spain by Law 3/2003 of 14 March.

[25] Article 10(2) of the Spanish Constitution states: "The provisions regarding the fundamental rights and freedoms recognized by the Constitution shall be interpreted in accordance with the Universal Declaration of Human Rights and the international treaties and agreements on the same matters ratified by Spain".

[26] This reasoning has been criticized mainly in relation to the vote by Judge Adela Asúa, who made the following statement: "I consider unsatisfactory the legal grounds based on the majority judgement. That reasoning may encourage the view that this Court does not recognize the primacy of

The judgement of the German Constitutional Court of 15 December 2015[27] has in turn raised again the relevant criminal-law issue concerning the *different levels of protection of human rights* provided for by the domestic legal system, on the one hand, and the European criminal law, on the other.[28] The main question was whether, in certain cases of application of the European Arrest Warrant, the principle of *individual guilt* and, hence, human dignity itself can be affected.[29]

The German Constitutional Court makes a qualitative leap in the field of international surrender in cases of convictions rendered *in absentia*, in that it not only took into consideration not only the procedural law conditions established in this instrument of cooperation, but also invoked arguments of a substantive criminal law nature regarding the *individual guilt* principle which is inherent in the right to individual dignity. The rendering of a conviction to a very serious crime after a trial *in absentia* in a State that does not have a system of review of such judgments allowing the submission of new evidence should not permit the recognition of the surrender order as it does not respect the aforementioned *individual guilt* principle. An interesting aspect of this decision of the German Constitutional Court is the legal basis for this new control, which relates to the idea of 'constitutional identity'. This idea is also to be understood as a set of inalienable rights, as acknowledged in the Constitution, which rights, being linked to human dignity, cannot be disregarded. The concept of 'constitutional identity', according to this High Court, is also inherent in article 4(2) TEU and does not violate the principle of loyal cooperation in the sense established in the article 4(3) TEU. Only in order to clarify this reasoning, the German constitutional judges point out that the constitutional identity does not entail a substantial risk for the uniform application of Union law, since the powers of control reserved to the Federal Constitutional Court must be exercised with caution, in a way open to European integration, in exceptional cases and under strict conditions.[30] According to this judgment, the Federal Constitutional Court, if

---

Union law and that it adopts a defensive position of its legal autonomy *vis-à-vis* that law, bypassing the primacy of Union law through interpretive operations, which it believes, can control in accordance with article 10(2) EC. The idea that this jurisdiction does not apply the Union rights, but rather the fundamental rights of the Spanish Constitution, although properly interpreted in such a way as to coincide inevitably with the level of protection recognized in the Union, is a rather unconvincing fiction".

[27] German Constitutional Court (BVerfG), decision of 15 December 2015, 2 BvR 2735/14, BVerfGE 140, 317.

[28] Cf. Díez Picazo and Nieto Martín (2010); Ambos (2017), p. 111.

[29] On the individual guilt principle in the European Union from the substantive point of view cf. Demetrio Crespo (2010), pp. 371–388.

[30] In a similar line, the Constitutional Court of Hungary, in the recent judgement of 30 November 2016 (Decision 22/2016, XII.5.), although in this decision it referred to cases of collective expulsion and right of asylum. This Court also considers that, despite the decisions of the European Court of Justice on the primacy of EU law, Member States are not obliged to breach their national constitutional obligations to carry out their cooperation commitments within the EU. Therefore, it states the possibility of control by the State of the lawfulness of the act based on the protection of the national identity. All this within the limits we have referred to: in exceptional cases and when EU acts might violate fundamental rights such as human dignity. A detailed commentary on that judgement can be found in Mohay and Tóth (2017).

necessary, "will base its review of the European act in question on the interpretation of that act provided by the Court of Justice of the European Union in a preliminary ruling pursuant to 267(3) TFEU".

The BVerfG's purpose was to ensure the control of 'constitutional identity' resulting from article 23(1) third paragraph in relation to articles 79(3) and 1(1) GG with regard to the inalienable and unlimited protection of human rights. Furthermore, this judgment stresses that the *individual guilt* principle belongs to the constitutional identity and must thus be preserved in the case of a request for international surrender aimed at the execution of a conviction rendered in the absence of the accused. Thus, German authorities cannot contribute to the violations of human dignity by other States,[31] similarly to what the Spanish Constitutional Tribunal stated in the aforementioned STC 91/2000.[32]

This raises again the delicate alternative between cooperation or dissociation. In these terms, for instance, *Classen* considers the *dissociation model* unconvincing, as is clearly prevailing in the BVerfG case-law, in which the protection of fundamental rights at the national and European level are excluded in their respective scopes of application.[33] According to this author, the BVerfG should have made use of the possibilities of cooperation provided for by the EU law in order to improve the protection of fundamental rights in force within the scope of application of the Union's law. *Classen* sees in the controls of identity a harmful 'sensationalism' that has resulted in an equivalent media reaction. In this sense, he adds that the BVerfG was well-known in the past for "its bark being worse than its bite", stressing that it should have limited itself to its successful reflections on the real problem. His conclusion is convincing: on the whole, the BVerfG controls too little within the scope of application of EU law, while its reasoning on constitutional identity seems to be too fundamentalist.[34] The key phrase of the BVerfG ruling is that, if after the completion of the investigations the court is convinced that the minimum standard of protection set by the *Grundgesetz* is not met, the sought surrender should not be granted.[35] As *Satzger* states, the second Chamber of the BVerfG declares that the checks on constitutional identity are legal, which would enable the German authorities and courts to reject a European Arrest Warrant.[36] In this case, however, the constitutional judges would paradoxically have avoided this path as they came to the result that the German court had to deny surrender because of a correct interpretation according to the European law on the grounds for refusal set forth by the

---

[31] Cf. Kromrey and Morgenstern (2017), p. 106; Classen (2016), p. 304; Ewer (2016), p. 335; Finke (2016), p. 327; Meyer (2016), p. 332; Sachs (2016), p. 373; Satzger (2016), p. 514; Sauer (2016), p. 1134.

[32] Cf. Martín Rodríguez (2014), p. 603; Punset Blanco (2017), p. 189.

[33] Classen (2016), p. 311.

[34] Classen (2016), p. 312.

[35] BVerfG_2 BvR 2735/14, para 75: "If, after conclusion of the investigations, the court becomes aware that the minimum standards mandated by the Basic Law will not be complied with by the requesting state, the court must not allow the extradition".

[36] Satzger (2016), p. 516.

EAW Framework Decision.[37] *Satzger* also observes that, though in these cases the individuals concerned can obtain constitutional-law protection through constitutional identity checks, the Chamber itself emphasizes that in this way *strict legal requirements must be met*. In addition, he concludes that it is not at all clear to what extent these requirements exceed those of an "ordinary *amparo*".[38]

3.2 The Absolute Content of Fundamental Rights in the CJEU

The decisions analysed hitherto highlight the existence of certain sticking points about the difficult balance between the effectiveness of surrender procedures and the need for mutual trust between Member States, on one hand, and the protection of fundamental rights in the field of international cooperation, on the other. This problem also concerns the interpretation that the CJEU had made so far which is based on the supremacy of the EU Law and the existence of a high degree of trust between the Member States, which is a prerequisite for the effectiveness of cooperation. The principle of mutual trust requires each EU country, mainly within the AFSJ, to assume that, except in extraordinary circumstances, all Member States fulfil EU law, particularly the fundamental rights recognized by Union's law. These considerations, transposed into the field of recognition and enforcement of an EAW, should therefore require the Member States to provide cooperation. Thus, they can only refuse to execute an EAW in the cases of mandatory grounds for non-execution, exhaustively listed in article 3, and in those of optional grounds for refusal established in articles 4 and 4-*bis* of the EAW Framework Decision, as indicated by the CJEU in the *Melloni* case. In addition, according to Luxembourg case-law, the execution of the EAW can only be subject to the conditions defined in article 5 of the EAW Framework Decision.

However, the most recent judgment of the CJEU in the case *Aranyosi and Căldăraru,* settled by Grand Chamber on 5 April 2016, opens a door to the possibility of some control by Member States, in order to avoid any detrimental consequences for the absolute content of fundamental rights. The control model of the 'absolute content' must necessarily refer to the CFR and the ECHR. Indeed, the CJEU in *Aranyosi and Căldăraru* refers to the possibility of limiting the principles of mutual recognition and trust between the Member States "in exceptional circumstances".[39] These would be supported by the provisions of article 1(3) FD EAW in the sense that this Framework Decision cannot have the effect of modifying the obligation to respect the fundamental rights that are mainly provided for in the EU Charter. In the instant case, a possible breach of the prohibition of inhuman or degrading treatment or punishment established in article 4 of the Charter was at stake. This right, as

---

[37] On the previous problems regarding the BVerfG's interpretation of the EAW Framework Decision cf. Demetrio Crespo (2006), pp. 1–4.

[38] Satzger (2016), p. 519.

[39] Opinion of the Court (Full Court), 18 December 2014, EU:C:2014:2454, para 191.

stated by the CJEU, is absolute, being strictly linked to the respect for human dignity, as established in article 1 of the Charter. The CJEU again refers to the 'absolute nature' of certain rights, which is based on the provisions of the CFR and is confirmed by the provisions of article 3 ECHR. Articles 1 and 4 of the Charter, as per article 3 of the ECHR, establish in this manner one of the fundamental values of the European Union and its Member States. Therefore, under any circumstances, even in the cases regarding the fight against terrorism and organized crime, the ECHR prohibits in absolute terms torture and inhuman or degrading treatment or punishment, irrespective of the behavior of the person concerned. Thus, when the executing judicial authority has evidence that there is a real risk of inhuman or degrading treatment of the persons detained in the issuing Member State, the former must request supplementary information that be provided by the issuing judicial authorities. The executing judicial authority must postpone its decision on the surrender of the individual concerned until it obtains the supplementary information that allows it to discount the existence of such a risk. In this regard, as *Satzger* points out,[40] the type of control exercised by the CJEU in relation to possible violations of human dignity can be described with the following conceptual pair:

1. *Abstract danger* related to the objective, reliable, accurate and duly updated elements[41] on the detention conditions in the issuing Member State, which demonstrate the existence of systemic or generalized deficiencies affecting certain groups of persons or certain places of detention.
2. *Specific danger*: once such a risk has been ascertained, the executing judicial authority will still have to verify, accurately and precisely, whether there are serious and well-founded reasons to believe that the person concerned will be at risk because of the detention conditions that he or she would endure in the issuing Member State.

4   Conclusion

The recognition and enforcement of criminal decisions ordered *in absentia* in the EU have shown that serious objections of a constitutional and criminal law nature can still be raised against these proceedings such objections if effective cooperation is to be achieved within a legal framework that is intended to guarantee the fundamental rights of citizens. Despite the progress made in criminal cooperation within the AFSJ, the existence of general law instruments based on essentially formal controls aimed at simplifying the recognition and enforcement of criminal decisions results, on many occasions, in the introduction of provisions that do not always

---

[40] Satzger (2016), p. 520.

[41] These elements might result mainly, as the CJEU points out in the said judgement, from international court decisions, such as ECHR judgements, from judicial decisions of the issuing Member State or from decisions, reports or other documents drawn up by Council of Europe bodies or from the United Nations system.

provide a response which sufficiently guarantees the protection of the fundamental rights of citizens. Beyond the interpretation that is to be given to the relationship between the *concepts of equivalence and trust* with which the principle of mutual recognition operates and which after a close examination seem to be rather opposed, the rut in which most EU law instruments (such as European Arrest Warrant) have fallen is attributed to the absence of a mechanism to ensure the equivalent protection of the fundamental rights of European citizens despite the favorable effect of it through the jurisprudence of the CJEU.[42]

The evolution that will take place from now on must clarify how some basic principles like that of primacy or direct effectiveness of the EU law operate with others that can eventually be in contradiction with the first ones, like those of absolute content, constitutional identity and judicial protection of fundamental rights, which is not easy. Some constitutional courts from various Member States have claimed their own autonomy regarding the level of protection that their respective Constitutions provide to their citizens. As we have seen, the situation does not substantially change with the Treaty of Lisbon, given that according to the current legislative set-up, the transposition of directives that weaken the standards of human rights protection provided by domestic law will lead citizens to apply for protection before constitutional courts. As *Kromrey and Morgenstern* pointed out,[43] it is clear that, from the perspective of the individuals and the protection of their fundamental rights, judgments such as the BVerfG—2BvR 2735/14, despite having raised several criticisms, marked important steps forward. At the same time, the process of harmonization requires, before anything else, an in-depth discussion on the main criminal law principles, including the dogmatic implications of the *individual guilt* principle, which is rooted more than any other principle in the idea of human dignity.[44]

References

Ambos K (2017) Derecho penal europeo. Aranzadi, Cizur Menor (Navarra)

Bernardi A (2004) L'Europeizzazione del Diritto e della Scienza Penale. Giappichelli, Torino

Classen CD (2016) Zu wenig, zu fundamentalistisch – zur grundrechtlichen Kontrolle "unionsrechtlich determinierter" nationaler Hoheitsakte. Zeitschrift Europarecht 3:304–312

Cuerda Riezu A (2003) De la extradición a la "euro orden" de detención y entrega. Con un análisis de la doctrina del Tribunal Constitucional Español. Centro de Estudios Ramón Areces, Madrid

Delmàs-Marty M, Pieth M, Sieber U (2009) Los caminos de la armonización penal. Tirant lo Blanch, Valencia

Demetrio Crespo E (2006) El caso Darkazanli. Acerca de la declaración de nulidad por el Bundesverfassungsgericht de la norma de transposición de la Orden de Detención Europea. Diario Jurídico La Ley 6441:1–4

---

[42] García Rivas (2010), p. 94.

[43] Kromrey and Morgenstern (2017), p. 124.

[44] For all, Ruggeri (2016), pp. 42 f.

Demetrio Crespo E (2010) El principio de culpabilidad: ¿un Derecho Fundamental en la Unión Europea? In: Díez Picazo LM, Nieto Martín A (eds) Los Derechos Fundamentales en el Derecho penal europeo. Aranzadi, Cizur Menor (Navarra), pp 371–388

Díez Picazo LM, Nieto Martín A (eds) (2010) Los Derechos Fundamentales en el Derecho penal europeo. Aranzadi, Cizur Menor (Navarra)

Ewer W (2016) Was garantiert eigentlich die "Ewigkeitsgarantie"? Das Bundesverfassungsgericht lotet behutsam den unantastbaren Kerngehalt des Grundgesetzes aus. Anwaltsblatt 4:335–336

Fernández Tomás A (2002) La Carta de Derechos Fundamentales de la Unión Europea. Tirant lo Blanch, Valencia

Finke J (2016) Neuer status quo und offene Fragen – Anm. Zum Urteil BVerfG. Onlinezeitschrift für Höchstrichterliche Rechtsprechung zum Strafrecht 100:327–331

García Rivas N (2010) La tutela de las garantías penales tras el Tratado de Lisboa. In: Díez-Picazo LM, Nieto Martín A (eds) Los Derechos Fundamentales en el Derecho penal europeo. Aranzadi, Cizur Menor (Navarra), pp 91–114

Gómez-Jara Díez C (2005) Constitución Europea y Derecho penal: ¿Hacia un Derecho penal federal europeo? In: Bacigalupo Sagesse S, Cancio Meliá M (eds) Derecho penal y política transnacional. Atelier, Barcelona, pp 153–208

Gómez-Jara Díez C (2006) ¿Federalismo jurídico-penal en la Constitución Europea? Un diálogo con el Prof. Silva Sánchez. In: Bajo Fernández M et al (eds) Constitución Europea y Derecho penal económico. Ramón Areces, Barcelona, pp 279–294

Kromrey H, Morgenstern C (2017) Die Menschenwürde und das Auslieferungsverfahren. Zeitschrift für internationale Strafrechtsdogmatik 2:106–124

Llorens MP (2001) La Carta de los derechos fundamentales de la Unión Europea. Publicacions Universitat de Barcelona, Barcelona

Martín Rodríguez PJ (2014) Sentencia 26/2014, de 13 de febrero, en el recurso de amparo 6922-2008 promovido por Don Stefano Melloni. Revista de Derecho Comunitario Europeo 48:603–622

Meyer F (2016) Das BVerfG und der Europäische Haftbefehl – ein Gericht auf Identitätssuche. Onlinezeitschrift für Höchstrichterliche Rechtsprechung zum Strafrecht 100:332–339

Mohay Á, Tóth N (2017) Decision 22/2016. (XII.5.) ab on the interpretation of article E) (2) of the fundamental law. Am J Int Law 111(2):468–475

Nieto Martín A (2005) Fundamentos constitucionales del Derecho penal. Revista General de Derecho Penal 3:1–70

Nieto Martín A (2010) El Derecho penal europeo: una aproximación a sus problemas actuales. In: Serrano-Piedecasas JR, Demetrio Crespo E (eds) Cuestiones actuales de Derecho penal empresarial. Colex, Madrid, pp 353–383

Pastor Ridruejo JA (2017) Curso de Derecho internacional público y organizaciones internacionales, 21st edn. Tecnos, Madrid

Punset Blanco R (2017) Derechos Fundamentales y primacía del Derecho Europeo antes y después del caso Melloni. UNED. Teoría y Realidad Constitucional 39:189–212

Ruggeri S (2016) *Inaudito reo* proceedings, defense rights, and harmonisation goals in the EU. Eucrim. The European Criminal Law Associations' Forum 1:42–51

Sachs M (2016) Grundrechte: Identitätskontrolle bei Anwendung von Unionsrecht. Auslieferung eines Ausländers nach Europäischem Haftbefehl auf Grund eines Abwesenheitsurteils. Juristische Schulung 1:373–378

Salcedo C (2001) Notas sobre el significado político y jurídico de la Carta de Derechos Fundamentales de la Unión Europea. Revista de Derecho Comunitario Europeo 9:7–26

Sanz Hermida A (2003) El futuro espacio europeo de justicia penal. Revista del poder judicial 71:175–191

Satzger (2016) Grund- und menschenrechtliche Grenzen für die Vollstreckung eines Europäischen Haftbefehls? – "Verfassungsgerichtliche Identitätskontrolle" durch das BVerfG vs. Vollstreckungsaufschub bei "außergewöhnlichen Umständen" nach dem EuGH. Neue Zeitschrift für Strafrecht 36(9):514–522

Sauer H (2016) "Solange" geht in Altersteilzeit – Der unbedingte Vorrang der Menschenwürde vor dem Unionsrecht. Neue Juristische Wochenschrift. 16:1134–1142

Ugartemendia Eceizabarrena JI (2010) La eficacia vertical y horizontal de los Derechos Fundamentales de la Unión Europea sobre el ámbito penal. In: Díez Picazo LM, Nieto Martín A (eds) Los Derechos Fundamentales en el Derecho penal europeo. Aranzadi, Cizur Menor (Navarra), pp 115–147

Villamarín López ML (2017) La Directiva Europea 2016/343, de 9 de marzo, sobre presunción de inocencia y el derecho a estar presente en el juicio. InDret. Revista para el análisis del Derecho. 3:1–39

Vogel J (2005) Derecho penal y globalización. Anuario de la Facultad de Derecho de la Universidad Autónoma de Madrid. 9:113–126

Part V
Participatory Safeguards and *In Absentia* Proceedings in International Human Rights Law and EU Law

Personal Participation in Criminal Proceedings, *In Absentia* Trials and *Inaudito Reo* Procedures. Solution Models and Deficiencies in ECtHR Case-Law

Stefano Ruggeri

Abstract Notwithstanding the failure of the drafters of the European Convention to enact a general provision regarding the right to be present at trial, Strasbourg case-law, by means of a comprehensive view of the right to a fair hearing, has long recognised the possibility of personal participation of defendants in criminal proceedings. This acknowledgment, however, has not led to the Court excluding the lawfulness of restrictions on this fundamental guarantee by means of procedures, such as default proceedings, which rule out any involvement of the accused. It would, however, be oversimplifying to affirm, that the contribution of European case-law was circumscribed to the right to merely be present at trial and its limitations.

This study provides a systematic examination of the way the Strasbourg Court has reinterpreted the participatory safeguards over almost four decades. This allows us to observe the development of the qualitative conditions of personal involvement of defendants in criminal proceedings, and the forms in which they can give their contribution to fact-finding. Further developments, moreover, can be expected in the near future. On the one hand, the rising focus of the European case-law on the protection of fundamental rights of individuals other than the accused, such as vulnerable witnesses and victims, poses the question of whether and to what extent the Convention's participatory safeguards can also be extended particularly to the aggrieved parties. The Court has until recently dealt with this question only in specific fields, such as that of *inaudito reo* procedures. On the other, the delicate field of transnational criminal justice increasingly poses specific challenges, which make the approach now followed by European case-law in relation to the accused's participatory rights somehow outdated especially in the EU area of freedom, security and justice.

S. Ruggeri (✉)
Department of Law 'Salvatore Pugliatti', Messina University, Messina, Italy
e-mail: steruggeri@unime.it

© Springer Nature Switzerland AG 2019
S. Quattrocolo, S. Ruggeri (eds.), *Personal Participation in Criminal Proceedings*, Legal Studies in International, European and Comparative Criminal Law 2, https://doi.org/10.1007/978-3-030-01186-4_18

Abbreviations

ACHR   American Convention of Human Rights
CCP   Code of Criminal Procedure
ECHR   European Convention on Human Rights
EComHR   European Commission of Human Rights
ECtHR   European Court of Human Rights
EU   European Union
IACtHR   Inter-American Court of Human Rights
ICCPR   International Covenant on Civil and Political Rights

1   Premise

Unlike other human rights charters,[1] the European Convention of Human Rights includes the personal involvement in criminal trials neither among the general features of the right to a fair hearing nor among the specific safeguards of the person charged with an offence. Nevertheless, the Strasbourg Court has long recognised this fundamental guarantee as a milestone of the general right to a fair trial. This acknowledgment, however, has not led it to rule out the lawfulness of criminal proceedings that in different ways exclude the involvement of defendants from fact-finding or restrict their personal contribution to a significant extent.

The great attention attached by the European Court to default proceedings over more than three decades might suggest that Strasbourg case-law has looked at participatory rights in terms of the right to be present at trial and the exceptions from this fundamental guarantee allowed by the Convention. The contribution of European case-law to a reconstruction of this problematic area, however, has been of utmost importance in a much more complex way. The systematic approach to the accused's personal participation in criminal proceedings as a feature of the general right to a fair trial has led the Court to recognise precise duties of diligence not only on the part of the competent authorities but also of the defendant, which does not allow us to look at this fundamental safeguard under the European Convention in terms of an absolute right. Furthermore, Strasbourg case-law was recently called upon to examine the delicate issue of *inaudito reo* proceedings, providing conclusions that somehow differ from those reached in the field of *in absentia* proceedings, and which also extended the problem of personal participation to individuals other than the accused. Yet the Court has not limited itself to dealing with the right to be simply present at trial. The most significant contribution of European case-law

---

[1] The International Covenant on Civil and Political Rights, in particular, explicitly grants defendants the right to be tried in their own presence, a guarantee significantly enshrined in the same provision that ensures to defendants the right to defend themselves or to obtain the assistance of a lawyer. Cf. Art. 14(3)(d) ICCPR.

was perhaps to lay down conditions that put defendants in a position to decide whether and to what extent to take part personally in criminal proceedings, and to the qualitative requirements that should govern their personal involvement in fact-finding in criminal matters.

This study analyses the developments that have taken part in Strasbourg case-law with a view to addressing the extent to which private parties can claim a right to be present in criminal trials under the European Convention, as well as the conditions under which their participation can be restricted or postponed, or criminal proceedings can even be held *in absentia*. Moreover, I shall also address the safeguards acknowledged by the European Court for defendants being able to take part personally in criminal proceedings and the ways in which they can give their own contribution to fact-finding and make their voices heard in criminal trials.

2 The Right to Be Personally Involved in Criminal Proceedings and the Overall Fairness of Criminal Proceedings

2.1 The Right to Be Present at Trial and the Need for a Systematic Approach to the Guarantee of a Fair Trial

It has been observed that, although the European Convention does not expressly provide for the right to personally participate in criminal proceedings, Strasbourg case-law has long dealt with the delicate issue of the right to be present at trial. Various factors contributed to this result.[2] Not only did the non-exhaustive nature of the fair trial guarantees listed in Article 6(3) ECHR facilitate a systematic view of this fundamental safeguard as an expression of the general right to a fair trial, but furthermore a number of guarantees explicitly recognised by the Convention either set the necessary conditions for the accused being able to take part in the proceedings or are structured in such a way that they clearly presuppose the possibility of doing so.

The very first safeguard acknowledged to the person charged with an offence, focusing on the right to be informed about the accusation in detail and in a language that the accused can understand, demonstrates the attention paid by the drafters of the European Convention to the need to ensure simple information, which the addressee of a criminal trial is personally able to understand in its legal and even linguistic aspects. Moreover, the provision allowing the accused either to "defend himself in person or through legal assistance of his own choosing",[3] even though it

---

[2] The leading case was the 1985 judgment *Colozza v. Italy*. See ECtHR, *Colozza v. Italy*, judgment of 12 February 1985, Appl. No. 9024/80.

[3] Art. 6(3)(c) ECHR.

cannot be seen as a real alternative,[4] reveals the clear favour of the European Convention towards the accused's personal involvement in fact-finding. Against this framework, furthermore, a systematic examination of other procedural safeguards shows that some of them are fully consistent with the personal involvement of the accused in criminal proceedings or in specific phases. For instance, the right to examine or have examined prosecutorial witnesses[5] presupposes the accused being put in a position to be personally confronted with his accuser.

Beyond the specific safeguards of the accused, moreover, the general acknowledgment of the right to a 'fair hearing' requires that the individuals charged with a criminal offence be put in a fair condition to be heard personally, to expose their arguments and to challenge the arguments put forward by other parties.[6] The right to personal participation in criminal proceedings takes on more specific meanings where defendants are restricted in their fundamental freedoms. In cases of restrictions on liberty, moreover, the physical presence of the arrested or detained person not only serves the purposes of criminal proceedings but is also viewed as a necessary condition of the lawfulness of the ongoing procedure. Significantly, the individuals concerned, regardless of the legal initiatives that they can undertake to challenge the measure applied, must be brought to the judicial authority and 'release may be conditioned by guarantees to appear for trial'.[7]

2.2 Right or Duty to Personal Participation in Criminal Proceedings Under the European Convention? The Case of Defendants Equipped with Legal Knowledge

The systematic approach adopted by European case-law to the right to be present at trial as an expression of the general guarantee of a fair hearing highlights its main nature as an individual right under the Convention. Accordingly, the Strasbourg Court has long acknowledged the defendants' right to waive their right to participate in the proceedings.[8] Yet, since its earlier jurisprudence, European case-law has pointed out that the waiver decision must be provided with specific guarantees.[9] The Court, in particular, requires defendants to waive their right to be present at trial, if not explicitly, in an unequivocal manner, after being made aware of the consequences of their decision.

---

[4] Below, Sect. 4.2.

[5] Art. 6(3)(d) ECHR.

[6] Ubertis (2009), p. 49.

[7] Art. 5(3) ECHR.

[8] In *Colozza v. Italy*, however, the Court left open the question of whether the right to personal participation could be waived. Cf. Trechsel (2005), pp. 255f.

[9] ECtHR, *Neumeister v. Austria*, judgment of 27 June 1968, Appl. No. 1936/63.

One of the most significant aspects of this jurisprudence, furthermore, is the clear attempt to relativize the scope of the waiver decision, and by this means also the individual nature of the right to be present at trial. Almost all criminal justice systems, as noted, allow the competent authorities to compel the physical presence of the accused to serve specific purposes of criminal proceedings, and in this context the European Convention also recognises the lawfulness of alternatives to deprivation of liberty, provided they can ensure the accused's appearance at trial. Nevertheless, the Court has never given entirely favourable consideration to the waiver of personal participation in criminal proceedings, which still remains the preferred solution in particular situations. The most remarkable case is that of defendants who have a personal expertise in legal issues.[10] The disfavour of Strasbourg case-law towards the decision not to personally participate in the proceedings goes so far as to acknowledge the lawfulness of some sort of sanction by the competent authorities[11] in order to "discourage unjustified absences".[12] To be sure, the Court has not yet given very clear indications in this respect.[13] As a matter of principle, the Court rules out national law adopting drastic measures to obtain the defendant's presence by coercive means, *e.g.* by requiring that defendants should undergo pre-trial imprisonment to challenge a conviction issued against them.[14] National authorities also cannot sanction defendants who choose not to take part personally in the proceedings by depriving them of the right to appoint a lawyer of their own choosing—a decision that, according to the Court, must remain unimpeded.[15] On close examination, this approach does not highlight the importance of legal assistance as such but reveals the existence of a core content of the right to personal involvement in criminal proceedings which cannot be restricted. As we shall see, this core content allows us to look at the alternative between legal assistance and self-defence from a different perspective.

2.3 Participatory Rights in Closed Hearings

These conclusions, however, do not apply to the overall course of criminal proceedings according to Strasbourg case-law. Certainly, ECHR law does not confine the right to personal participation solely to the trial phase. A delicate issue is whether and to what extent participatory rights are to be protected in closed hearings. Until recently, *in camera* hearings in criminal proceedings were largely used for the

---

[10] In *Franquesa Freixas v. Spain*, the Court regarded with disfavour the defendant's choice not to defend himself precisely because he was a lawyer. Cf. ECtHR, *Franquesa Freixas v. Spain*, decision of 21 November 2000, Appl. No. 53590/99.

[11] Trechsel (2005), p. 256.

[12] ECtHR, *Poitrimol v. France*, judgment of 23 November 1993, Appl. No. 14032/88, § 35.

[13] Negri (2014), pp. 149ff.

[14] ECtHR, *Poitrimol v. France* (fn. 12), para 38.

[15] ECtHR, *Lala v. The Netherlands*, judgment of 22 September 1994, Appl. No. 14861/89.

purposes of interim decisions and to solve procedural issues. International human rights law, by way of acknowledging the right to a public hearing, does not appear to leave any room to the use of closed hearings to deal with the merits of a criminal case. In the light of this, the domestic arrangements of those contracting states that left to the competent authority a great margin of discretion in deciding whether a case or a specific instance should be adjudicated in a public hearing or *in camera* led to various interventions by Strasbourg case-law, which on several occasions declared the inconsistency of such solutions with the European Convention. An emblematic example is that of the Hungarian code of criminal procedure, which left in the hands of the president of the competent court the delicate decision on whether an appeal ought to be deal with *in camera*, in a public session or a hearing. This solution has for more than one decade led to several convictions of Hungary by the Strasbourg Court.[16] Furthermore, European case-law has dealt with closed hearings in relation to other criminal justice systems, developing a wide jurisprudence that, while acknowledging the importance of the general right to a public hearing, has progressively recognised various exceptions.[17]

In the last decade, however, new developments in the field of terrorism-related crimes have led to a significant evolution of European case-law as well.[18] In the 2009 landmark judgment *A. et al. v. United Kingdom*,[19] the Grand Chamber had already justified the use of closed hearings in the field of security law. Six years later, the Court for the first time extended these findings to the area of criminal justice by stressing that the *habeas corpus* safeguards must be adapted to the specific challenges relating to terrorist crimes. Thus, the ordinary requirements set by Article 5(1)(c) ECHR

> should not be applied in such a manner as to put disproportionate difficulties in the way of the police authorities in taking effective measures to counter organised terrorism in discharge of their duty under the Convention to protect the right to life and the right to bodily security of members of the public.[20]

It is true that according to this decision, Article 5(4) ECHR still requires the national authorities to disclose adequate information to enable the detained individuals to know the nature of the allegations against them and have the opportunity to produce exculpatory evidence. Moreover, the detainee and his lawyer should be put in a position to effectively participate in the court proceedings concerning continued detention. However, the Court also made it clear that the Convention "cannot require disclosure of such material or preclude the holding of a closed hearing to

---

[16] ECtHR, *Goldmann and Szénászky v. Hungary*, judgment of 30 November 2010, Appl. No. 17604/05. For further references to ECtHR case-law see Gácsi et al., in this volume, Sect. 3.3.3.

[17] For in-depth examination of Strasbourg case-law see Di Chiara (2009), pp. 293 ff.

[18] For a critical analysis of these developments see Vogel (2016).

[19] ECtHR, Grand Chamber, *A. et al. v. United Kingdom*, judgment of 19 February 2009, Appl. No. 3455/05.

[20] ECtHR, *Sher et al. v. United Kingdom*, judgment of 20 October 2015, Appl. No. 5201/11, para 149.

allow a court to consider confidential material".[21] This conclusion—along with confirming, as we shall see, the lawfulness of national arrangements aimed at the disclosure of confidential evidence solely to a 'special advocate'—turned out to justify the conduct of *in camera* hearings to deal with substantial issues, such as *fumus delicti*.

2.4 The Right to Be Present Before a Higher Instance

Another difficult problem is whether and under which conditions the accused can claim his right to be present in a higher instance. Strasbourg case-law has traditionally dealt with this question from the viewpoint of the right to effective defence in the appeal proceedings. As a matter of principle, the European judges have acknowledged the guarantee of personal participation before a higher instance by stressing that the human rights protection provided by the Convention must potentially be extended to legal remedies. Of course, this right holds different features depending on the characteristics of the different procedures before higher instances, as defined by national law. Where appeal aims at both a factual and a legal review of the decision, the proceedings must, as a rule, be held in oral and public form,[22] especially if defendants have material arguments against the judgment issued at first instance, or are interested in requesting the collection of further evidence. On the contrary, if appeal only aims at a legal revision of the decision without engaging the higher court in further factual inquiries, the appeal proceedings can be conducted in written form and without the defendants' participation.[23]

These findings are clearly inspired by those European countries in which the appeal on a point of law is structured in such a manner as to require the defendants to be represented in court by a lawyer (who must often be specifically entitled to appear before a higher court).[24] Yet the Court's reasoning can be problematic from a human rights perspective, since it deprives defendants of the possibility of giving their contribution to the decision-making in a higher instance. Furthermore, the approach adopted does not appear to be consistent with European case-law, which, as noted, has expressed clear preference for the personal participation of the accused equipped with legal knowledge.[25] Certainly the appeal proceedings may entail negative consequences for the accused persons, since Protocol No. 7 to the European Convention does not protect them from the risk of *reformatio in pejus*.[26] On close examination, even the appeals on a point of law can lead to this result and therefore worsen the appellant's position. Therefore, the simple fact that the competent

---

[21] *Ibid.*

[22] ECtHR, *Constantinescu v. Romania*, judgment of 27 June 2000, Appl. No. 28871/95.

[23] ECtHR, *Döry v. Sweden*, judgment of 11 November 2002, Appl. No. 28394/95.

[24] See, *e.g.*, Art. 613(1) CCP-Italy.

[25] Above, Sect. 2.2.

[26] Trechsel (2005), p. 362.

authority is called upon to examine the legal foundation of the case is not a sufficient ground for excluding the accused's participation. It is worth observing, moreover, that the Strasbourg Court, while allowing for appeal proceedings to be held without involving the defendants, does not engage in assessing whether their defence rights were properly protected before a higher instance. Instead, the European judges usually scrutinise this point in the case of derogation from the right to a public hearing at first instance.[27]

3 The Problem of *In Absentia* and *Inaudito Reo* Proceedings

3.1 *Requirements of a Fair Trial in Cases of* In Absentia *Proceedings*

3.1.1 Conditions of Lawfulness of Default Proceedings Under the European Convention

Despite the acknowledgment of the right to be present at trial, we have anticipated that the European Court has never gone so far as to consider criminal proceedings entailing significant restrictions on this right or even ruling out any involvement of the accused as incompatible with the Convention. As far as *in absentia* trials are concerned, the adoption of this flexible approach was certainly due to the need to adapt the Convention's standards to the features of the criminal justice systems of those contracting states (especially of continental Europe) that largely allow for default proceedings to be held against the accused. On close examination, there are no unequivocal provisions in the European Convention which forbid such procedures. The acknowledgment of the lawfulness of *in absentia* trials is not unconditional, however, since these procedures must fulfil strict conditions and specific safeguards must be met to ensure the overall fairness of the proceedings.

Strasbourg case-law has always attached great weight to the grounds for non-appearance in court, distinguishing the cases which, as noted, stem from the accused's free decision to waive his right to be present at trial from those in which there are no clear indications as to his intentions. The examination of the latter cases reveals the attention paid by the Court to the need for the addressee of a criminal enquiry not to be charged with the burden of proving the reasons for their lack of awareness of the proceedings, nor especially with the burden of proving that non-appearance in court was due to *force majeure* or other unforeseeable circumstances.[28] Since the *Colozza* case, the Court has made it clear that the national authority are responsible for informing the defendants about the charges filed against them. It is worth observing that the competent authorities cannot be released from responsibility even in the case of conduct of the accused that could be relevant

---

[27] ECtHR, *Liebreich v. Germany*, judgment of 8 January 2008, Appl. No. 30443/03.
[28] ECtHR, *Colozza v. Italy* (fn. 2), para 30.

in the field of administrative law, such as the failure to communicate a change of residence.[29]

In spite of these findings, the European Court has always been quite cautious while scrutinising whether the obligation to inform the accused about the charges was infringed. Even if the competent authorities failed to serve the defendants of the institution of criminal proceedings against them, this does not automatically affect the lawfulness of the procedure conducted *in absentia*. To justify this result, since the *Colozza* case, the Court has required the accused to be granted a proper opportunity to access a retrial or a remedy aimed at allowing a new decision on the merits of the case. This approach, which was further developed by subsequent jurisprudence, also found wide acceptance in EU law in the field of both domestic and transnational criminal justice. The European Court has however laid down specific requirements for subsequent remedies. Thus, if national law does not provide for mechanisms capable of granting defendants knowledge of the proceedings, the overall fairness of the procedure is not undermined if defendants are given, either upon request or by the court, "a fresh determination of the merits of the charge [...]".[30] It is noteworthy that in the *Colozza* judgment, the Strasbourg judges did not limit itself to acknowledging the right to be present at the retrial or in the appeal proceedings instituted against the conviction issued *in absentia*, but already required that the new examination of the case be made "from a court which has heard" the accused.[31] This reveals the awareness by the European Court of the need for a fair hearing as a necessary precondition of decision-making.

The Court's approach reveals the clear attempt to strike a compromise solution aimed at saving the lawfulness of those national arrangements that provide for subsequent mechanisms in order to ensure a judicial review by a higher court of convictions issued *in absentia*. European case-law, however, highlights a formalistic understanding of the right to be present at trial, which stretches the guarantee of personal participation in criminal proceedings to such a point that it turns out to blur the right to a fair hearing. Yet, the condition of a "fresh determination of the merits of the case" in a retrial or in a higher instance may not be sufficient to erase the shortcomings of a procedure held *in absentia*, particularly where national law limits the right to adduce exculpatory evidence in a higher instance.[32] Even though no limitations are provided for, the fact-finding made during the default

---

[29] ECtHR, *F.C.B. v. Italy*, judgment of 28 August 1991, Appl. No. 12151/86.

[30] ECtHR, *Colozza v. Italy* (fn. 2), para 29.

[31] *Ibid.*

[32] This case occurred in Italy after the Law 60/2005, which adapted the rules on the so-called '*restituzione in termini*'—a legal tool granting defendants leave to appeal out of time against a conviction held *in absentia*—to the requirements set forth by European case-law. Thus, despite opening the door of second instance, moreover, Law 60/2005 failed to amend the conditions for the exercise of the right to evidence in the appeal proceedings. As a consequence, defendants could only have evidence obtained in the second instance by proving that they had been unaware of the initiation of criminal proceedings. Cf. Negri (2005), p. 268. This result was eliminated by Law 67/2014, which abolished the default proceedings, while defining a new procedure *in absentia*. On this legislative reform see Quattrocolo (2014), Mangiaracina, in this volume, Sect. 5.

proceedings in the first instance may still have serious consequences on fundamental rights, at least where the competent authorities for the retrial or the higher instance can use the pieces of evidence taken without the accused's contribution unconditionally. Furthermore, subsequent remedies and even a retrial may not be able to compensate the person convicted through default proceedings for the lost opportunities, such as the possibility of requesting a more favourable procedure or a bargaining decision. Nor can one overlook the adverse effects that the initiation of the criminal trial can produce, due to the tools available in the current phase of the information society, as to the image of both the defendants and their families. In the light of this, it is debatable that the accused's presence at trial can be deemed equivalent to his involvement in a subsequent trial or a higher instance.

On close examination, the Court's approach, which is open to the different ways in which the right to be present at trial, provided that defendants are granted the opportunity to participate in a (subsequent) fair hearing, does not provide clear indications on the exact contents of right to a retrial. Remarkably, the European Court has on several occasions pointed out that the propriety of the national approach largely depends on the circumstances of the concrete case, which must be assessed by the European Court on the basis of the effectiveness given to the right to a defence in domestic proceedings.[33] In this way, therefore, the Strasbourg Court made itself the ultimate instance for scrutiny of the appropriateness of domestic arrangements.

On a deeper level still, Strasbourg case-law attaches very scant attention to the justification of *in absentia* proceedings. Yet, even though national authorities may have applied all the available means to make defendants aware of the institution of criminal proceedings, this does not make a criminal law action absolutely necessary, especially where the grounds for the accused's absence remained unclear. It is true that, particularly when serious crimes are at stake, a prompt prosecution can best satisfy the needs of a social defence policy and can avoid further shortcomings, *e.g.* by reducing the risk that relevant evidence may get lost or that the genuineness of evidence subject to high risk of deterioration may be altered. However, these undisputable advantages are largely outweighed by the risks arising from conducting a criminal law action in the defendant's absence.

In the *Colozza* judgment, the European Court was already aware that the institution of criminal proceedings in the defendant's absence must satisfy a public interest, since it held that "the impossibility of holding a trial by default may paralyse the conduct of criminal proceedings, in that it may lead, for example, to dispersal of the evidence, expiry of the time-limit for prosecution or a miscarriage of justice".[34] It is surprising, however, that the public interest factor justifying the initiation of a criminal prosecution becomes blurred in the event that defendants are given the opportunity of a retrial or a subsequent remedy. Furthermore, allowing for the institution of default proceedings irrespective of the existence of specific prosecutorial needs

---

[33] ECtHR, Grand Chamber, *Öcalan v. Turkey*, judgment of 12 May 2005, Appl. No. 46221/99, para 210.

[34] ECtHR, *Colozza v. Italy* (fn. 2), para 29.

entails a clear underestimation by Strasbourg case-law of the defendants' contribution to fact-finding.

3.1.2　Default Proceedings and International Surrender Procedures

This approach was not limited solely to domestic proceedings but has also conditioned the evolution of European case-law in the field of international cooperation. The problem of *in absentia* trials has long had enormous relevance particularly in relation to extradition procedures, and there is no doubt that the solutions elaborated by the 1978 Second Additional Protocol to the Council of Europe's Convention on Extradition have had great impact on the developments that have taken place in EU law, since the 2002 legislation on the European arrest warrant. This Protocol was the first multilateral international law instrument in Europe, which enabled the requested country to discretionarily reject a request for surrender aimed at the enforcement of a sentence or detention order imposed by a judgment issued *in absentia*, where it considered that the minimum defence rights due to any person charged with a criminal offence had not been satisfied in the relevant proceedings. On the contrary, refusal of surrender was excluded where the requesting state offered sufficient assurance to guarantee to the individuals concerned the right to a retrial aimed at safeguarding their defence rights.[35] By excluding denial of surrender when the requesting country gives proper assurance that the sought individuals can obtain a retrial aimed at safeguarding their defence rights, the 1978 Protocol clearly favoured a system that releases the requested state from the obligation to assess the respect for the minimum defence rights at the first instance, provided that the accused will potentially have the opportunity of a subsequent remedy.

European case-law confirmed this approach in the field of transnational criminal justice, giving rise to a further softening of its jurisprudence developed on national trials held *in absentia*. Remarkably, in the 1991 *F.C.B.* judgment the Court already relied on the mechanism of a retrial without, however, inquiring into whether this solution could allow a fresh determination of the merits on the basis of new evidence.[36] Fifteen years later, the *Battisti v. France* case provided the Court with the opportunity of redefining the question of whether under the European Convention, a proceeding conducted *in absentia* in the requesting country can hinder international cooperation and what guarantees the requested country should ensure to the sought person.[37] The European judges rejected the recourse lodged by Mr. Battisti against the 2005 ruling of the French *Conseil d'Etat*, which had deemed the Italian default proceedings compatible with the requirements of a fair trial. The Court therefore confirmed that the applicant had not unlawfully been deprived of his right

---

[35] Art. 3(1).

[36] ECtHR, *F.C.B. v. Italy*, judgment of 28 August 1991, Appl. No. 12151/86.

[37] ECtHR, *Battisti v. France*, decision of 12 December 2006, Appl. No. 28796/05. On this decision cf. Galgani (2013), pp. 174f.

to be present at trial, on the basis of the main argument that Mr. Battisti had been duly informed of the criminal proceedings instituted in Italy and that his choice of appointing two lawyers to defend him in court demonstrated his decision to waive his right to participate personally in the court proceedings.

It might be argued that the Court simply confirmed its jurisprudence developed in relation to domestic cases, according to which defendants can also implicitly waive their right to be present at trial, provided that they were informed of the institution of criminal proceedings. Furthermore, the focus on the assistance by one or two lawyers may seem to fulfil the requirement of 'minimum defence rights', set forth by the 1978 Additional Protocol. Nevertheless, it cannot seriously be affirmed that legal assistance in itself always ensures effective defence if defendants were not put in a position to decide whether to personally participate in criminal hearings and especially if they were not duly informed on the consequences that their decision to appoint a lawyer might have upon a future surrender procedure. It was precisely this requirement that lacked in the proceeding against Mr. Battisti. Moreover, this case reveals a further departure from the general approach followed in relation to national cases. On close examination, the defendant's information about the proceedings and his choice to appoint two lawyers to represent him at trial should not necessarily be interpreted in the terms acknowledged by the European judges, since neither the knowledge of criminal proceedings nor the decision to appoint a lawyer of one's own choosing logically demonstrate the waiver of personal participation. The *Battisti* judgment, therefore, highlights the dangerous assumption that the knowledge of the proceedings and the appointment of a lawyer can act as surrogate to the requirement, long recognised by Strasbourg case-law, of unequivocal waiver of personal participation.

Furthermore, this complex case allows us to examine another delicate issue, that is, whether and to what extent the European jurisprudence on *in absentia* trials can influence the international cooperation policy of non-contracting countries. Despite the far-reaching scope of European case-law, it would probably be an exaggeration to affirm that the authorities of a non-member state could not question the worldwide authority of the Strasbourg Court.[38] This especially applies to countries such as Brazil (where Mr. Battisti had fled long before the European Court's ruling), which must abide by different international human rights case-law, namely Inter-American case-law, whose standards of protection sometimes significantly differ from those of the Strasbourg Court. Furthermore, it cannot be argued that Brazil was required to surrender Mr. Battisti because the extradition treaty between Italy and Brazil excluded the refusal of extradition solely on the grounds that proceedings were conducted *em revelia* in the requesting country. Certainly, this clause calls for overall examination of the concrete circumstances of the case at stake.[39] It should also be taken into consideration, moreover, that this treaty, like other bilateral agreements on extradition, was signed at a time in which Brazil still allowed for criminal proceedings to be carried out *em revelia*. It is worth noting that, when Brazil first

---

[38] In this sense see instead Galgani (2013), p. 175.
[39] *Ibid.*

refused extradition (2010), Brazil had not only long dropped the proceedings *em revelia*, but had also already enacted various mechanisms in domestic trials, aimed at avoiding the conduct of a criminal law action against defendants unaware of the proceedings.[40]

3.2   Inaudito Reo *Procedures and the Right of the Aggrieved Parties to Give Their Personal Contribution to Fact-Finding*

Compared to the comprehensive case-law regarding *in absentia* trials, there has until recently been almost no jurisprudence regarding the *inaudito reo* proceedings in criminal matters. Notwithstanding some similarities, *inaudito reo* procedures significantly differ from *in absentia* trials, posing somewhat diverse human rights concerns. From the viewpoint of the phase preceding the decision-making, *inaudito reo* proceedings not only usually rule out the accused's participation but are also carried out without trial or any court hearing. Therefore, the guilty verdict normally takes the form of an order rather than a judgment, as highlighted by the emblematic case of penal order procedures. Yet, unlike *in absentia* trials, *inaudito reo* proceedings do not exclude the accused's participation at all, but only prior to decision-making, on the assumption that a subsequent challenge will ensure a trial hearing compensating him for the previous loss of defence opportunities.

The case *Gray v. Germany* provided the Strasbourg Court with the opportunity of examining the lawfulness of these proceedings.[41] In the case at hand, the applicants complained under Article 2, read in conjunction with Article 1 ECHR, that shortcomings in the British health system in connection with the recruitment of *locum* doctors and supervision of out-of-hours *locum* services had led to their father's death as a consequence of medical malpractice by a German *locum* doctor.[42]

---

[40] Brazilian Law 9.721/1996 dropped the default proceedings (*em revelia*), which took place in any case of defendants who, duly summoned, did not appear in court without justification. See Art. 366 CCP-Brazil (before 1996). Yet the 1996 reform, although requiring the defendants to be summoned personally, maintained the possibility of criminal proceedings being conducted against absent defendants who either failed to appear in court without a justified reason or failed to communicate their new residence. This legislation also did not drop the possibility of defendants being summoned by edict (*citação por edital*). Since the likelihood that defendants summoned by edict become aware of the proceedings initiated against them is surely low, Law 9.721/1996 provided for the suspension not only of criminal proceedings but also of the time limit laid down for the prosecuted offence. The only procedural activities allowed in this lapse of time are the collection of urgent evidence and the possibility of the competent judge remanding defendants into custody pursuant to Article 312 CCP-Brazil. More precisely, the time limit is first suspended after the judicial authority receives the *denúncia*, and will be subsequently suspended if the defendant did not appear in court. See Art. 366 CCP-Brazil.

[41] ECtHR, *Gray v. Germany*, judgment of 22 May 2014, Appl. No. 49278/09.

[42] *Ibid.*, para 3.

Although the case did not primarily concern the right to a fair hearing, the complaint focused on two important aspects of penal order proceedings. In particular, the applicants challenged the lawfulness of the summary proceedings instituted in Germany in that (*a*) they had not "involved a proper investigation or scrutiny of the facts of the case or the related evidence", and (*b*) "the German authorities had failed to inform them of the proceedings and had thus deprived the deceased's next of kin of any possibility to get involved and participate in the latter".[43] These complaints highlighted the problematic nature of the penal order procedure from a rather innovative perspective, which relates to the need for proper investigation and the possibility for the aggrieved parties to be involved in a criminal law action. The former aspect concerned the phase prior to the rendering of the guilty verdict, while the latter related to the trial phase, in which under German law, the applicants could have joined the prosecution as plaintiffs. This result did not materialise, however, since the penal order was not challenged and the applicants only learned of the procedure after the conviction had already become final.

The Court's focus, therefore, shifted the problem of participation in criminal proceedings to individuals other than the accused. The Strasbourg judges rejected the complaint relating to Article 2 ECHR, while incidentally providing, however, some indications on these *inaudito reo* proceedings. Concerning the failure to involve the applicants in the proceedings, the Court recognised that German law neither requires the aggrieved parties to be informed of a penal order procedure nor enables them to challenge the conviction with a view to joining the prosecution as plaintiffs.[44] Remarkably, European case-law also excluded that the obligation to involve them can derive from Article 2 ECHR, as conversely acknowledged in relation to situations in which the responsibility of state agents in connection with a victim's death had been at stake.[45]

The reasoning used to support this conclusion is rather unconvincing. Like in *Hugh Jordan v. United Kingdom*, the Strasbourg judges did not rule out that, as far as medical negligence is concerned, "the next of kin of to the victim must be involved in the procedure to the extent necessary to safeguard his or her legitimate interests",[46] provided that the "circumstances surrounding the death were suspicious or unclear".[47] In this respect, however, the Court quite uncritically relied on the Government's argument that "the circumstances of the case had been sufficiently established in the course of the investigative proceedings".[48] Therefore, "a participation of the applicants in a potential main hearing, even if it might have a cathartic effect for the victim's next of kin, could not have further contributed to the trial court's assessment of the case".[49]

---

[43] *Ibid.*, para 61.

[44] *Ibid.*, para 87.

[45] *Ibid.*

[46] ECtHR, *Hugh Jordan v. United Kingdom*, para 109.

[47] ECtHR, *Gray v. Germany* (fn. 35), para 87.

[48] *Ibid.*, para 91.

[49] *Ibid.*

This approach cannot be properly understood without an overall consideration of the Court's reasoning, which comes to the conclusion that "the applicants have not specified which aspect" of the offender's "responsibility for medical negligence causing the applicants' father's death has not been sufficiently clarified".[50] This functional approach leads to somehow paradoxical results. Following the Court's arguments, the European Convention should protect the right of the aggrieved parties to be involved in a criminal inquiry only as long as they can demonstrate the usefulness of their contribution in a public hearing.

Although a functional reasoning is not rare in Strasbourg case-law,[51] this turns out to weaken the humanitarian function of the right to be involved in criminal proceedings. It is not easy to understand how the aggrieved parties can hold the right to take part in criminal proceedings but cannot claim it unless they can adduce evidence to shed light on unclear points of fact-finding. Moreover, stating that "in the sphere of medical negligence the procedural obligation imposed by Article 2 does not necessarily require the provision of a criminal-law remedy",[52] the Court makes it clear that the European Convention cannot grant the injured party a subsequent remedy if this is not provided for by national law. This approach, however, shifts the problem of fact-finding entirely to the stage after decision-making, without facing the lawfulness of the penal order procedure in such delicate cases. Therefore, the main question raised by the aggrieved parties—namely, whether "in an unusual and sensitive case like the present one the prosecution authorities' decision to apply for a conviction"[53] through a summary proceeding that excludes their involvement was justified—remained unanswered.

4 The Personal Involvement of Private Parties in Criminal Proceedings and the Qualitative Requirements of a Fair Trial

4.1 The Requirement of Personal Information

4.1.1 Information About the Charge and Linguistic Safeguards

It has been noted that, despite the great relevance that *in absentia* proceedings have had in Strasbourg case-law, its contribution to the acknowledgment of the right to fairly be involved in criminal proceedings cannot be reduced to simple presence at

---

[50] *Ibid.*

[51] For a functional approach to the relationship between the right to be informed about the accusation and the right to a defence, see ECtHR, *Mattoccia v. Italy*, judgment of 25 July 2000, Appl. No. 23969/94.

[52] ECtHR, *Gray v. Germany* (fn. 35), para 91.

[53] *Ibid.*

trial. A close examination of the European jurisprudence allows us to draw up the qualitative requirements of a fair trial that involves private parties in fact-finding.

Certainly, the granting of proper information is the first condition of effective participation in criminal hearings. In this respect, the European Convention ensures to any person charged with an offence two main safeguards, namely information on the accusation and information on the evidence available. While the former safeguard cannot be restricted solely to the court proceedings following the preferment of the indictment,[54] the Convention acknowledges the latter, albeit not explicitly, in different ways, particularly by means of the provision regarding the right to have time and the necessary facilities to prepare one's own defence.[55] Doubtless, there is a strict link between these two safeguards, for the setting up of a proper defence strategy logically presupposes the knowledge of the charges.[56] The utmost importance of the guarantee of information about the charge is such that denying the possibility of knowing the meaning of the act with which the accused was charged gives rise to a "Kafkaesque situation".[57]

It is worth observing that European case-law does not merely require defendants to be provided with any information on the charge but also stresses the need for detailed information on the nature and type of the charge in a language the accused can personally understand. As noted, the European Convention stands out among other international human rights instruments in that it attaches specific attention to the linguistic understanding of the charge. Significantly, the Court examined this delicate question for the first time in a transnational case, namely *Brozicek v. Italy*.[58] In this case, the point at stake was not just the lack of information but the lack of information that the defendant could understand. According to the European judges, this jeopardised his right to take part effectively in criminal proceedings, which were carried out by default.

Notwithstanding this systematic approach, European case-law has often been quite flexible in acknowledging the scope of this fundamental guarantee. The European Court, in particular, has not always viewed the right to information as entailing the obligation of national authorities to make defendants aware of the charges preferred against them,[59] provided that they could obtain information by other means. From this it follows that information on the charge was sometimes seen as a weak guarantee for the individuals concerned rather than as the obligation

---

[54] Kühne (2009), Rn. 496. In a different sense cf. Trechsel (2005), p. 198f., according to whom the right to information should be interpreted as relating to the act through which the court proceedings are instituted.

[55] Art. 6(3)(b) ECHR. In this sense see Trechsel (2005), p. 200f.

[56] In the *Haxhia* case, however, the European Court ruled out that the notification of the accusation should necessarily entail the disclosure of supporting evidence to enable the accused to prepare for trial. See ECtHR, *Haxhia v. Albania*, judgment of 8 October 2013, Appl. No. 29861/03.

[57] Trechsel (2005), p. 193.

[58] ECtHR, *Brozicek v. Italy*, judgment of 19 December 1989, Appl. No. 10964/84.

[59] In *Mattoccia v. Italy* (fn. 44), however, the Court held that information 'rests entirely on the prosecuting authority's shoulders'.

for the competent authorities to inform them (and keep them informed) of the accusation.[60] Moreover, the aforementioned functional perspective, in particular, led the Court to conclude that the negative consequences for the defence of the reclassification of the offence can be compensated for in a higher instance.[61] This perspective has made the Court lose sight of the importance for the accused to be properly informed in the light of an overall consideration of the right to a fair hearing and the contribution that the defence can give to fact-finding. It is noteworthy that the Court followed a more rigid approach in relation to further fair trial requirements such as the impartiality of the judge,[62] which cannot be granted or integrated in further instances. Yet the failure to adopt here a similar perspective has not enabled Strasbourg case-law to exploit the potentials of the right to the information on the accusation.[63]

4.1.2 The Right to Access Relevant Evidence and Its Limitations Under the European Convention. The Problem of Special Advocate Procedures

The guarantee of information about relevant evidence highlights further important features of the accused's right to personal involvement in criminal trials. Indeed, as a matter of principle, defendants should be granted personal access to relevant pieces of information in order to set up an effective defence strategy. This acknowledgment, however, is not unlimited. In a 1993 judgment, the Court already held that national law can restrict the access to the file solely to the lawyer, a solution that can be justified in the case of risks to the ongoing inquiry, particularly in the field of organised crimes.[64]

Moreover, we saw that in recent years Strasbourg case-law not only further developed this approach in the field of security law, but also extended it to criminal proceedings. In the *Sher et al.* case, the Court allowed for the use of closed hearings to deal with substantial issues,[65] while confirming the lawfulness of national arrangements aimed at disclosing confidential evidence solely to a 'special advocate' in the field of criminal justice. From this result the way is short to a decision on guilt based (albeit partially) on confidential evidence examined by informants through a special advocate procedure, which leads us to reflect whether this solution can satisfy the requirements of the right to confrontation.

---

[60] Trechsel (2005), p. 204.

[61] ECtHR, *Sipavicius v. Lithuania*, judgment of 21 February 2002, Appl. No. 49093/99, paras 27 et seqq.

[62] ECtHR, *De Cubber v. Belgium*, judgment of 26 October 1984, Appl. No. 9186/80.

[63] In these terms cf. Trechsel (2005), p. 194.

[64] ECtHR, *Kremzow v. Austria*, judgment of 21 September 1993, Appl. No. 12350/86.

[65] ECtHR, *Sher et al. v. United Kingdom* (fn. 20).

4.2 Taking Part Personally in Criminal Proceedings and the Right to Legal Assistance: A Real Alternative?

It has been observed that the provision granting the accused the right either to "defend himself in person or through legal assistance of his own choosing", while showing the clear favour of the Convention towards the accused's personal involvement in criminal proceedings, does not set a real alternative between two separate guarantees. Indeed, legal defence can have various features according to the characteristics of national criminal justice. Therefore, the drafters of the Convention enacted such a broad provision, aimed at satisfying the needs of those European countries that do not allow for self-defence in the criminal process, requiring the competent authorities to appoint a lawyer where defendants have not chosen their own counsel. Yet there is little doubt that the decision to appoint a lawyer of one's own choosing is also a form of direct participation in criminal proceedings, which can have a significant incidence on the defence strategy. In this respect also, the right to know and understand the charge constitutes a necessary precondition for defendants being able to choose the most appropriate lawyer to deal with their case. That the competent authority can appoint the defence lawyer without the defendant having had the possibility of choosing his own counsel,[66] therefore, is debatable under the European Convention. Furthermore, defendants must in principle be granted the opportunity of giving their own contribution even where a lawyer represents them in court. Remarkably, all criminal justice systems provide for specific decisions that personally lie with the interested party. Moreover, the accused should be given the possibility of being involved even in procedural activities that can be carried out by the lawyer, such as the cross-examination of a prosecutorial witness, if he wishes to do so.

4.3 The Right to Give One's Own Contribution to Evidence-Gathering and the Right to Make One's Voice Heard Fairly

One of the most significant expressions of the right to be personally involved in criminal proceedings is the possibility for defendants to take part in the collection of prosecutorial evidence by being confronted with their accuser. Remarkably, in *Mattoccia v. Italy* the Court pointed out the strict link between the right to information and the right to exercise an effective defence by holding that insufficient information can negatively affect the guarantees listed not only in lit. *b*) but also in lit. *d*) of Article 6(3) ECHR.[67] The possibility of the accused contributing to evidence-gathering appears in very clear terms from the formulation of the latter provision,

---

[66] Trechsel (2005), p. 244.

[67] *Ibid.*, p. 201.

which, like that of other international human rights instruments,[68] ensures to the accused the right either to examine or to 'have examined the witnesses against him'.

At first glance, this solution reflects the alternative between self-defence and legal assistance, allowing for the examination of incriminating witnesses by the defence lawyer in countries that do not enable defendants to cross-examine prosecutorial witnesses. On close examination, the drafters of the European Convention aimed at striking a compromise between two main forms of confrontation existent in the European countries, which broadly correspond to cross-examination, typical of common-law countries, and the continental tradition of witness examination conducted by a third body (presiding judge of the tribunal, investigating magistrate, etc.).[69] From this interpretation it follows that the Convention ensures a broad protective umbrella, allowing for both direct and indirect examination of incriminating witnesses, the latter being open, moreover, to different arrangements, provided that the defence rights are properly satisfied and effective confrontation in the accused's interests is ensured.

It is precisely from this viewpoint that this broad interpretation of the European Convention's provision on the right to confrontation, following the Strasbourg jurisprudence, can lead to highly problematic results in the light of the perspective adopted in this study. Concerning the personal involvement in the taking of prosecutorial evidence, it is worth observing that in *Isgrò v. Italy*, the Court ruled out a violation of the Convention, even though the witness had been examined by the accused, not assisted by counsel.[70] There is no doubt that this solution, underestimating the importance of the lawyer's presence, largely frustrates the humanitarian goal of the right to confrontation.[71]

Even more delicate problems arise in case of judicial examination. This solution would be highly problematic under other international human rights instruments. In particular, the Pact of San José, despite not requiring the contracting states to enable defendants to examine their accusers personally, reveals a clear favouring of personal involvement of the defence in obtaining the appearance of prosecutorial witnesses and therefore in the taking of incriminating evidence.[72] As noted, the broad formulation chosen by the drafters of the European Convention does not necessarily require the involvement of the defence but is also compatible with forms of examination conducted by an independent authority. To be sure, judicial hearing often provides the best solution so as not to jeopardise fundamental rights of other individuals involved in criminal inquiries. Yet there is little doubt that judicial examination cannot grant the defence the same opportunities as direct confrontation. On close examination, the lawfulness of any form of indirect confrontation depends on the room left to the defence. Even a judicial hearing might not satisfy the requirements of effective

---

[68] Art. 14(3)(e) ICCPR.

[69] In this sense cf. Trechsel (2005), p. 311; Maffei (2012), p. 17; Spencer (2014), p. 48.

[70] ECtHR, *Isgrò v. Italy*, judgment of 19 February 1991, Appl. No. 11339/85, para 36.

[71] Trechsel (2005), p. 310.

[72] Art. 8(2)(d) ACHR.

confrontation, even though the defence lawyer is allowed to forward questions to the witness through the judge. Doubt, in particular, arises as to whether a court-appointed lawyer, who has never had the opportunity to contact the accused, can properly represent him in the examination of key prosecutorial witnesses or co-defendants. Moreover, it is debatable whether effective confrontation takes place if the defence lawyer's is only allowed to put a few additional questions, after the witness has been long examined by the judicial authority.[73]

Further concerns arise in the field of transnational criminal justice. According to a solution long rooted in European case-law, in cases of letters rogatory,

> confrontation is not only complied with if the accused or his defence counsel have the opportunity of putting questions to the witnesses themselves, but also if they can request that certain questions are put to the witness by the court.

The former European Commission on human rights first reached this conclusion in the 1986 case *P.V. v. Federal Republic of Germany*,[74] as it held that defendants must at least be given the possibility of formulating written questions to be addressed to the witness abroad. The Strasbourg Court confirmed this approach in *Solakov v. the Former Yugoslav Republic of Macedonia*. Thus, from the conclusion that the applicant had "not expressly given any questions that he would have liked to be put to the witnesses"[75] it can be inferred that the Court deemed the solution of written questions to be consistent with the specific challenges posed by transnational evidence-gathering.[76]

This approach, however, raises several human rights concerns. To start with, the focus of the *Solakov* judgment on the need for the accused expressly giving the questions to be forwarded to the witness being examined on commission may seem to offload onto defendants the burden of formulating in advance the questions as a means of being involved in the taking of incriminating evidence abroad. This is tantamount to saying that the right to participate in the confrontation with the accuser is only protected by the Convention as long as the accused is able to anticipate the questions he wishes to be put to prosecutorial witnesses or co-defendants. Yet this approach is not consistent with the very notion of cross-examination, which is often shaped by European countries in such a way that it does not charge with this task the party called upon to cross-examine witnesses but the party that requested their hearing.[77] This also has its practical justification, particularly in cases of inter-

---

[73] Jackson and Summers (2012), p. 349.

[74] EComHR, *P.V. v. Federal Republic of Germany*, decision of 13 July 1987, Appl. No. 11853/85.

[75] ECtHR, *Solakov v. the Former Yugoslav Republic of Macedonia*, judgment of 21 October 2001, Appl. No. 47023/99, para 62.

[76] In this sense Trechsel (2005), p. 311 f.

[77] Italian law, for instance, requires all parties to specify, the latest 7 days before the trial first hearing, the personal data and the circumstances on which the witnesses, co-defendants and experts they wish to summoned will be examined in open court. Cf. Art. 486 CCP-Italy. This duty, instead, does not lie with the parties called upon to cross-examine them.

national cooperation: it is hard to imagine how written questions can be defined in advance in the field of letters rogatory.

Moreover, it is questionable who holds responsibility for putting the accused in a fair position to this preventive participation, namely what country and which authorities are called upon to inform him about the possibility of formulating written questions and about the circumstances on which the witness will be heard. The *Solakov* judgment raised serious doubts as to the feasibility of this solution. Thus, the applicant's lawyers were summoned only 1 week before the trip and the court summons contained 'no detailed information about the venue or exact date of the questioning, the number and names of the witnesses to be heard, or the questions that the investigating judge wished to put to them'. Under these circumstances, it was very unlikely that the applicant or his lawyers could arrange a clear defence strategy and therefore, the acknowledgment of the possibility for the accused to formulate written questions in advance was rather rhetorical.

The European Commission had already had the opportunity for examining this delicate issue in the 1973 case *X., Y. and Z. v. Austria*. At that time, the Government argued that neither Austrian law nor the 1959 European Convention on Mutual Legal Assistance allowed for private parties to put questions during testimonial examinations taken through letters rogatory. The defence replied to this argument by holding that even in cases of questioning conducted by the judicial authority, Article 6(3)(d) ECHR requires that defendants be put in a position to formulate their own questions. Yet, according to the defence, this should entail the defence's presence at the hearing on commission. Thus,

> it would have been impossible to formulate in advance questions of the defence to be included in the letters rogatory, since this is exclusively feasible if the witness heard was a defence witness, unlike the present one. Questions to a prosecution witness usually emerge, according to the applicants, at the moment when he is heard.[78]

These arguments demonstrate that a broad interpretation of Article 6(3)(d) ECHR can be sustained if the accused is granted the opportunity of being fairly involved in the taking of incriminating evidence. By declaring the application inadmissible, the Commission, however, did not address this point at that time, nor has the Court until now departed from the approach adopted in the *P.V.* decision.

4.4 Restrictions on Freedom, the Right to Be Personally Informed and the Guarantee of a Fair Hearing

It has been observed that the adoption of measures interfering with fundamental rights makes it necessary not only to ensure a formal oversight of their lawfulness but also to provide the individuals concerned with the opportunity of making their voice heard fairly. Under the American Convention of Human Rights, the

---

[78] EComHR, *X., Y. and Z. v. Austria*, decision of 5 February 1973, Appl. No. 5049/71.

application of restrictions on liberty requires a constant check of the physical integrity and the general conditions of the individuals concerned.[79] The European Convention also attaches particular weight to the personal involvement of the arrested or detained person in the proceedings instituted with arrest or detention. This enhances the guarantee of judicial intervention, which can 'lead to the detection and prevention of life-threatening measures or serious ill-treatment which violate the fundamental guarantees contained in Articles 2 and 3 of the Convention'.[80]

Significantly, in *Fox, Campbell and Hartley v. United Kingdom*, the Court pointed out that "any person arrested must be told, in simple, non-technical language that he can understand, the essential legal and factual grounds for his arrest".[81] On close examination, the requirement of simple and understandable information not only provides the individuals concerned the ability to undertake proceedings against the measure applied, as highlighted by the earlier European case-law,[82] but also to face the hearing before the judicial authority to which they must promptly be brought under Article 5(3) ECHR. In the light of this, it is surprising that in the *Fox, Campbell and Hartley* case, the Court allowed for the applicants to be granted a "bare indication of the legal basis for the arrest" at the time of the arrest, on the assumption that they were later informed of the reasons for their suspected of being terrorists during their police interrogation.[83] This result was debatable, providing the arrested person with no substantial information to cope with police questioning. Although it is rather obvious that granting information only during police questioning increases the vulnerable condition of the applicants, making them unable to set up a defence strategy, the Court found no violation of Article 5(2) ECHR. Even more worryingly from the perspective of this study, the *Fox, Campbell and Hartley* judgment satisfied itself with the fact that the arrested individuals could understand on their own the grounds for arrest or detention.[84] Subsequent case-law further

---

[79] Remarkably, the Inter-American Court has on several occasions stressed that forced disappearances put individuals in a condition of extreme vulnerability by depriving them of the ability to defend themselves, especially when constant violations of human rights are tolerated by the State. See IACtHR, *Radilla Pacheco v. Mexico*, judgment of 23 November 2009, Series C No. 209, paras 138 et seqq. This has led the Court to view the requirement that the accused personally appear in court and be examined by an independent authority not just as a separate guarantee but as the means of assessing (and sometimes avoiding) multiple infringements on the Convention. In these terms cf. Casal (2014), p. 197.

[80] ECtHR, *Kurt v. Turkey*, judgment of 25 may 1998, Appl. No. 24276/94, para 123.

[81] ECtHR, *Fox, Campbell and Hartley v. United Kingdom*, judgment of 30 August 1990, Appl. No. 12244/86 12245/86 12383/86, para 40.

[82] In *X. v. United Kingdom*, the link between the knowledge of the grounds for arrest and the right to undertake proceedings was so exclusive in the earlier case-law that the Court found no ground to ascertain a violation of the Convention under paragraph 2 if paragraph 4 was infringed. See ECtHR, *X. v. United Kingdom*, judgment of 5 November 1981, Appl. No. 7215/75.

[83] ECtHR, *Fox, Campbell and Hartley v. United Kingdom* (fn. 75), para 41.

[84] *Ibid.*

developed this viewpoint: for instance, in the *John Murray* case, the Grand Chamber deemed it lawful that the arrestee could infer the reasons from the questioning.[85]

Doubtless, the link between information rights and the guarantee of a fair hearing becomes even stricter where the judicial authority is called upon to scrutinise the lawfulness of arrest or detention either *ex officio* or on request of the interested party. The Strasbourg Court, however, has developed a somewhat different case-law in relation to these two situations. Concerning the judicial oversight required by paragraph 3 of Article 5 ECHR, the European judges have long recognised the need to provide the individuals deprived of liberty with the opportunity of being heard in person by a judge not only in cases of police arrest but also when restriction on freedom was ordered by the judicial authority and even in the presence of the defendant's lawyer.[86]

The right to be heard fairly by an independent authority holds particular importance in the case of long-term restrictions on freedom. In cases of remand detention in particular, the delicate question arises whether the detainee should be confronted alone with the competent authority or whether he has the right to legal assistance. In the latter case, the further question arises whether or not the Convention allows for the detainee to await judicial hearing without having the possibility to communicate with his counsel.[87] The Convention provides no indication as to whether the accused has the right to be assisted by a lawyer either after or during the judicial hearing. Therefore, the earlier European case-law had given a negative response to this question.[88] The Strasbourg Court, however, departed from this approach in the *John Murray* case. By examining the guarantee at hand in conjunction with the general right to a fair hearing, the European judges found a breach of the Convention because the applicant was denied access to a lawyer during the first 48 h of his police detention.[89] As far as legal assistance during the questioning is concerned, the Court held in the same ruling that Article 6 ECHR in principle requires that "the accused be allowed to benefit from the assistance of a lawyer already at the initial stages of police interrogation". The Court, however, softened this conclusion by clarifying that this right "may be subject to restrictions for good cause. The question, in each case, is whether the restriction, in the light of the entirety of the proceedings, has deprived the accused of a fair hearing".[90] It took

---

[85] ECtHR, Grand Chamber, *John Murray v. United Kingdom*, judgment of 8 February 1996, Appl. No. 18731/91. Cf. Trechsel (2005), p. 461.

[86] ECtHR, *McGoff v. Sweden*, judgment of 26 October 1984, Appl. No. 9017/80. Cf. Trechsel (2005), p. 506.

[87] This question holds particular importance in those European countries, such as Italy, which still allows the competent authorities to restrict communication between counsel and the defendant subject to remand detention (or in house arrest) before the first judicial hearing. See Art. 294 CCP-Italy.

[88] ECtHR, *Schiesser v. Switzerland*, judgment of 4 December 1979, Appl. No. 7710/76.

[89] Trechsel (2005), pp. 514f.

[90] ECtHR, *John Murray v. United Kingdom* (fn. 85), para 63.

several years before European case-law recognized, in the 2010 *Brusco* case, the right of detained defendants to be heard in presence of their lawyer.[91]

The Court followed a somehow different approach in relation to *habeas corpus* proceedings under Article 5(4) ECHR. Notwithstanding the broader scope of this fundamental guarantee than that of the right to judicial review under paragraph 3, there is still no consistent case-law regarding the delicate question of whether the competent court must grant the person arrested or detained a fair opportunity to be heard in person prior to decision-making, and which safeguards must be ensured to the individuals concerned. Whereas there is extensive case-law on this requirement in relation to the situations of Article 5(1)(c) ECHR,[92] the Court has not given an explicit response on whether the arrested person must be personally examined in the other situations of paragraph 1. The reasoning used in this regard in *Sanchez-Reisse v. Switzerland*[93] was rightly deemed to be rather "cryptic".[94]

Of course, the right to be personally heard must be balanced with the requirement of speediness of the procedure. In general terms, the Court acknowledges that *habeas corpus* must satisfy the requirements of a fair trial insofar as an adversarial procedure and full respect for the *par condicio* principle are ensured.[95] In *Keus v. The Netherlands*, the European judges released the national authorities from responsibility in a case in which the decision was issued in the absence of the person against whom an arrest warrant was ordered, notwithstanding that it could not be executed because the person concerned was fugitive.[96] In this ruling, however, the Court, relying on Dutch law, justified the failure to inform the lawyer, during the period in which the applicant was a fugitive, about the hearing and the decision to extend the applicant's confinement.[97] It took 15 years before European case-law recognised that both the detainee and the counsel must in principle be informed of the hearing.[98] From this it does not follow, however, that the Convention requires the person concerned to be always heard. In *Varbanov v. Bulgaria*, the Court suggests that the personal participation of the detained person can be unnecessary where "some form of representation" is guaranteed.[99] Unfortunately, European case-law has not yet clarified what representation should exactly be necessary. It is quite clear that the possibility of effectively challenging the lawfulness of the deprivation of freedom are very low if the person concerned is left alone.[100]

---

[91] ECtHR, *Brusco v. France*, judgment of 14 October 2010, Appl. No. 1466/07.

[92] See among others ECtHR, *Wloch v. Poland*, judgment of 19 October 2000, Appl. No. 27785/95.

[93] ECtHR, *Sanchez-Reisse v. Switzerland*, judgment of 21 October 1986, Appl. No. 9862/82.

[94] In these terms cf. Trechsel (2005), pp. 480f.

[95] ECtHR, *Garcia Alva v. Germany*, judgment of 13 February 2001, Appl. No. 23541/94, para 39.

[96] ECtHR, *Keus v. The Netherlands*, judgment of 25 October 1990, Appl. No. 12228/86.

[97] *Ibid.*, para 25.

[98] ECtHR, *Fodale v. Italy*, judgment of 1 June 2006, Appl. No. 70148/01.

[99] ECtHR, *Varbanov v. Bulgaria*, judgment of 5 October 2000, Appl. No. 31365/96, para 58.

[100] Trechsel (2005), p. 486.

5　Conclusions

Notwithstanding the failure of the drafters of the European Convention to enact a general provision regarding the right to be present at trial, Strasbourg case-law, by means of a comprehensive view of the right to a fair hearing, has long recognised the possibility of personal participation of defendants in criminal proceedings. This acknowledgment, however, has not led to the Court banning restrictions on this fundamental guarantee by means of procedures, such as default proceedings, which rule out any involvement of the accused.

It would be an oversimplification to affirm, moreover, that the contribution of European case-law was circumscribed to the right to merely be present at trial and its limitations. A systematic examination of the way the Strasbourg Court has reinterpreted the fair trial safeguards over almost four decades allows us to observe the development of the qualitative conditions of personal involvement of defendants in criminal proceedings, and the forms in which they can give their contribution to fact-finding. Further developments, moreover, can be expected in a near future. On the one hand, the rising focus of European case-law on the protection of fundamental rights of individuals other than the accused, such as vulnerable witnesses and victims, poses the question of whether and to what extent the Convention's participatory safeguards can also be extended particularly to the aggrieved parties—a question until now dealt with only in specific fields, such as that of *inaudito reo* procedures. On the other, the delicate field of transnational criminal justice increasingly poses specific challenges, which make the approach now followed by European case-law in relation to the accused's participatory rights somewhat outdated, especially in the EU area of freedom, security and justice.

References

Casal JM (2014) Article 7. In: Steiner C, Uribe P (eds) Convención Americana sobre Derechos Humanos. Comentario. Konrad Adenauer Stiftung, Berlin, pp 180–206

Di Chiara G (2009) "*Against the administration of justice in secret*": la pubblicità delle procedure giudiziarie tra Corte europea e assetti del Sistema italiano. In: Balsamo A, Kostoris RE (eds) Giurisprudenza europea e processo penale italiano. Giappichelli, Torino, pp 293–308

Galgani B (2013) Extradition, political offence and the discrimination clause. In: Ruggeri S (ed) Transnational inquiries and the protection of fundamental rights in criminal proceedings, A study in memory of Vittorio Grevi and Giovanni Tranchina. Springer, Heidelberg, pp 167–191

Jackson JD, Summers SJ (2012) The internationalisation of criminal evidence: beyond the common law and civil law traditions. Cambridge University Press, Cambridge

Kühne H-H (2009) In: Kühne H-H, Miehsler H and Vogler T, Article 6. In: Pabel K, Schmahl S (eds) (2013) Internationaler Kommentar zur Europäischen Menschenrechtskonvention. Carl Heymanns, Köln et al

Maffei S (2012) The Right to Confrontation in Europe. Absent, anonymous and vulnerable witnesses. Europa Law Publishing, Groningen

Negri D (2005) Commento all'art. 1 Decreto-legge 17/2005. La Legislazione penale, pp 260–291

Negri D (2014) L'imputato presente al processo. In: Una ricostruzione sistematica. Giappichelli, Torino

Quattrocolo S (2014) Il contumace cede la scena processuale all'assente, mentre l'irreperibile l'abbandona. Riflessioni a prima lettura sulla nuova disciplina del procedimento senza imputato. www.penalecontemporaneo.it. Accessed 30 Apr 2014

Spencer JR (2014) Hearsay evidence in criminal proceedings, 2nd edn. Hart Publishing, Oxford

Trechsel S (2005) Human rights in criminal proceedings. Oxford University Press, Oxford

Ubertis G (2009) Principi di procedura penale europea, 2nd edn. Raffaello Cortina, Milano

Vogel B (2016) "In camera"-Verfahren als Gewährung effektiven Rechtsschutzes? Neue Entwicklungen im europäischen Sicherheitsrecht. Zeitschrift für die internationale Strafrechtsdogmatik, pp 28–38

In Absentia Trials and Transborder Criminal Procedures. The Perspective of EU Law

Anne Schneider

Abstract *In absentia* trials have proven to be a challenge for EU criminal law. This chapter focusses on the solutions that have been developed in order to deal with different standards on *in absentia* trials in transborder criminal proceedings. The main focus of this chapter is on judicial cooperation. This includes in particular the execution of a European Arrest Warrant issued for the enforcement of a judgment resulting from an *in absentia* trial and the enforcement of foreign judgments resulting from *in absentia* trials. The explicit, written grounds for refusal will be analysed. It will also be discussed whether, and if so, to what extent written grounds for refusal are supplemented by unwritten ones. In this context, Directive 2016/343/EU will also be examined. In addition, the chapter will touch upon *in absentia* trials in the context of the transnational *ne bis in idem* principle.

Abbreviations

BVerfG	*Bundesverfassungsgericht* (German Constitutional Court)
BVerfGE	Official selection of decisions and judgments by the senates of the BVerfG
BVerfGK	Official selection of decisions by the chambers of the BVerfG
CFR	Charter of Fundamental Rights of the European Union
CISA	Convention implementing the Schengen Agreement of 14 June 1985 between the Governments of the States of the Benelux Economic Union, the Federal Republic of Germany and the French Republic on the gradual abolition of checks at their common borders

A. Schneider (✉)
Department of Criminal Law, Criminal Procedure and White Collar Crime,
University of Mannheim, Mannheim, Germany
e-mail: anne.schneider@uni-mannheim.de

© Springer Nature Switzerland AG 2019   605
S. Quattrocolo, S. Ruggeri (eds.), *Personal Participation in Criminal Proceedings*, Legal Studies in International, European and Comparative Criminal Law 2, https://doi.org/10.1007/978-3-030-01186-4_19

CJEU	Court of Justice of the European Union
EAW	European Arrest Warrant
ECHR	European Convention of Human Rights
ECtHR	European Court of Human Rights
EIO	European Investigation Order
EU	European Union
FD EAW	Council Framework Decision 2002/584/JHA of 13 June 2002 on the European Arrest Warrant and the surrender procedures between Member States, amended by Council Framework Decision 2009/299/JHA of 26 February 2009
FD *in absentia* trials	Council Framework Decision 2009/299/JHA of 26 February 2009 amending Framework Decisions 2002/584/JHA, 2005/214/JHA, 2006/783/JHA, 2008/909/JHA and 2008/947/JHA, thereby enhancing the procedural rights of persons and fostering the application of the principle of mutual recognition to decisions rendered in the absence of the person concerned at the trial
GG	*Grundgesetz* (Basic Law, the German Constitution)
LG	*Landgericht* (District Court)
OJ	Official Journal of the European Union
TEU	Treaty on European Union
TFEU	Treaty on the Functioning of the European Union

1 Introduction

With (still) 28 Member States, the European Union has lots of different legal systems to take into account when designing legal instruments. In European Criminal Law and Criminal Procedure, one issue that has proven to be controversial is trials that have been held in the absence of the defendant (*in absentia* trials). The following chapter will start by explaining why *in absentia* trials present a problem for the EU (Sect. 2). Then, it will be examined to what extent *in absentia* trials are recognized as a ground for refusal in the context of judicial cooperation (Sect. 3). This will be the major part of the chapter. Finally, the *ne bis in idem* principle in case of *in absentia* trials will be dealt with (Sect. 4).

2 *In Absentia* Trials and Mutual Recognition

Article 82(1) TFEU explicitly states that judicial cooperation in criminal matters in the EU shall be based on the principle of mutual recognition of judgments and judicial decisions. The principle of mutual recognition forms the core of many legislative acts in the field of criminal law.[1] It means that judicial decisions of one Member State are also effective in other Member States and thus have "extraterritorial effects" without a substantive examination of the decision.[2] Under this principle, the Member States are supposed to rely upon the legal systems of their fellow Member States. Mutual recognition is thus based on mutual trust.[3]

However, this trust in the legality of other Member States' decisions can be easily shattered, and it has certainly been severely tested in the case of *in absentia* trials. *In absentia* trials are judicial decisions that are issued in legal proceedings at which the person concerned was not present.[4] As the national reports in the first volume of this book show, the Member States' ideas on the admissibility of *in absentia* trials differ considerably.[5] It follows that a Member State that puts much emphasis on the defendant's personal participation in criminal proceedings could potentially mistrust decisions that have been adopted in *in absentia* trials.

The European Union has acknowledged this problem and come up with several solutions. The Framework Decisions on mutual legal assistance, such as the Framework Decision on the European Arrest Warrant, already contained different rules on dealing with *in absentia* trials. However, in 2009, the Council adopted a Framework Decision in order to approximate the rules on *in absentia* trials.[6] This Framework Decision does not harmonize the rules on the admissibility of *in absentia* trials, but aims at defining common grounds for non-recognition of cooperation instruments in cases where the defendant has not been present at trial.[7] Therefore, it solely applies in the context of mutual legal assistance, which is the major policy area of the EU in criminal matters. The rules on *in absentia* trials are based on the jurisprudence of the European Court of Human Rights.[8] As the Framework Decision on *in absentia* trials amends other framework decisions in the field of legal cooperation, it will not be analysed separately, but be discussed in the context of each measure of judicial cooperation.

---

[1] See Böse (2011b), p. 492; Mitsilegas (2006), p. 1278.

[2] Wasmeier (2014), § 32, para 37.

[3] See, also, Albers and Beauvais (2013), p. 15; Korenica and Doli (2016), p. 542.

[4] Art. 1(3) of Council Framework Decision 2009/299/JHA of 26 February 2009 amending Framework Decisions 2002/584/JHA, 2005/214/JHA, 2006/783/JHA, 2008/909/JHA and 2008/947/JHA, thereby enhancing the procedural rights of persons and fostering the application of the principle of mutual recognition to decisions rendered in the absence of the person concerned at the trial, OJ L 81/24 (in the following: FD *in absentia* trials).

[5] See, on the different national laws, also Bartels (2014), p. 43; Klitsch (2009), p. 11; Paul (2007), p. 41.

[6] FD *in absentia* trials (fn. 4).

[7] Böse (2011b), p. 504.

[8] Böse (2011b), p. 503 f. See, on the jurisprudence of the ECtHR, Ruggeri, in Part V of this volume.

In 2016, the EU adopted Directive 2016/343/EU,[9] which also deals with the right to be present at criminal trials. Article 8 of Directive 2016/343/EU lays down the conditions under which criminal trials can be held in the absence of the accused person. If these conditions have not been met, the accused has the right to a new trial (Article 9). In contrast to Framework Decision 2009/299/JHA, the new Directive does not only apply in case of cooperation in criminal matters, but aims at harmonizing the standards for holding *in absentia* trials throughout the European Union. The provisions of the Directive will be discussed in detail elsewhere in this volume.[10] Accordingly, the Directive will only be touched upon insofar as it is of interest for transborder criminal procedures, i.e. for the matter of judicial cooperation.

3   *In Absentia* Trials and Mutual Legal Assistance

It has already been explained above that *in absentia* trials can become an encumbrance if the prosecuting Member State requires legal assistance. In the following paragraphs, the treatment of *in absentia* trials in different areas of mutual legal assistance will be analysed. The analysis will start with an overview on the new Directive 2016/343/EU. It will then go on to look at the provisions dealing with *in absentia* trials in specific legal instruments. As *in absentia* trials typically only provide problems when they have led to a decision, the analysis will not cover legal assistance in the pre-trial phase. This means that, for instance, the European Investigation Order will not be discussed here.[11] Instead, the analysis will concentrate on post-trial assistance, starting with the most important legal instrument, the European Arrest Warrant.[12] Then, unwritten rules on *in absentia* trials will be discussed.

3.1   *The Impact of Directive 2016/343/EU*

Before analysing the regime of legal cooperation, it is important to examine which impact Directive 2016/343/EU has. As explained above, this Directive sets minimal standards for *in absentia* trials. It grants the defendants the right to be present at their own trial [Article 8(1)], but allows for exceptions under certain circumstances

---

[9] Directive 2016/343/EU of the European Parliament and of the Council of 9 March 2016 on the strengthening of certain aspects of the presumption of innocence and of the right to be present at the trial in criminal proceedings, OJ L 65/1.

[10] See Bachmaier Winter, in this volume.

[11] See, on *in absentia* arguments in the pre-trial phase, *e.g.*, ECtHR, *Ait Abbou c. France*, judgment of 2 February 2017, Appl. No. 44921/13.

[12] According to Mitsilegas, this is the "most-analysed" instrument of the European Union, Mitsilegas (2006), p. 1283.

[Art. 8(2)]. The Directive also states clearly under which circumstances the suspect or accused person has the right to a new trial (Article 9).

Although the rules do not directly affect judicial cooperation, they have an impact on mutual legal assistance. The Directive should have been transposed into national law by 1 April 2018 [Article 14(1)]. As this time-limit has expired by now, Articles 8 and 9 of the Directive become binding in all Member States, whether they have been transposed into national law or not, because the rules are precise enough to be directly applicable.[13] This means that the Directive can then be taken into account when interpreting other EU legislation such as the FD *in absentia* trials.

Moreover, a binding directive granting rights to the suspect or accused person can well be relevant in determining the European public order (see *below*, Sect. 3.3.1.1). The acknowledgement of *in absentia* trials by EU law means that this form of trial gains even more recognition throughout the EU and thus becomes more and more accepted.[14] This effect could also lessen the chances of objecting to judicial cooperation in the case of *in absentia* trials on the basis of national constitutional law if the violation of national constitutional law does indeed constitute an accepted ground for refusal (see, on this question, *below*, Sect. 3.3.2). If a Member State does comply with the minimum rights provided by Directive 2016/343/EU, it will be harder to argue that the protection of the absentee's right is insufficient. This is because such an argument would show that the EU Directive—that was drafted under participation of the Member States—offered insufficient protection.[15] On the other hand, Member States might argue that the low standard of defendant's rights in the EU enables them to invoke specific constitutional guarantees against (further) participation in the EU. Whether or not arguments based on national constitutional law will have a chance of success in transborder criminal proceedings in the future will be discussed below (Sect. 3.3.2).

However, this use of Directive 2016/343/EU will only be possible when the Directive has been transposed by all Member States or when it will have become binding, i.e. in April 2018. Until then, the Member States cannot rely on other Member States to adhere to the Directive.[16] This means that they cannot count on national laws on *in absentia* trials having been shaped with regard to Directive 2016/343/EU. Nonetheless, as the timeline for transposing the Directive into national law is rather short, it makes sense to take the new Directive into account when analysing European law on judicial cooperation. As the new Directive is an expression of the European legislator's wish for further harmonization of the rules on *in absentia* trials, it should be considered even now when interpreting other EU

---

[13] Böse (2017), p. 759 f.; Brodowski (2016), p. 417. See, in more detail, Rönnau and Wegner (2013), p. 566 f.

[14] This has been a point of criticism with regard to the FD *in absentia* trials, see Burchard (2013), § 14, para 52; Heger and Wolter (2015), Article 4a RbEuHb, para 668; von Heintschel-Heinegg (2014), § 37, para 55.

[15] See the similar argument in opinion of AG *Bot, Melloni*, 2 October 2012, C-399/11, para 72.

[16] See also Brodowski (2016), p. 417.

law.[17] This is even more important because the new Directive strengthens the defendant's rights. Therefore, the Directive will be taken into account when interpreting rules on *in absentia* trials in the context of mutual cooperation.

3.2   Grounds for Refusal in Legal Instruments

3.2.1   European Arrest Warrant

In the case of the EAW, *in absentia* trials usually become important when they form the basis of a sentence or detention order that shall be executed in the issuing Member State.[18] An example for this situation is the *Krombach* case.[19] Dieter Krombach was a German doctor suspected of having killed his stepdaughter who was a French national. While the German authorities refused to indict Krombach for lack of evidence, he was tried and convicted in France *in absentia*.[20] In order to execute this judgment, the French authorities could nowadays have recourse to the European Arrest Warrant.[21] In this situation, the question arises whether the executing Member State (in the *Krombach* case Germany) can refuse to execute the European Arrest Warrant if it serves to execute a judgment that was delivered in absence of the defendant in the issuing Member State (in the *Krombach* case France).[22] In order to answer this question, the provision on *in absentia* trials, Article 4a FD EAW, will be examined first. Then, it will be discussed whether unwritten grounds for refusal exist.

Since 2009, the FD EAW contains a special provision on *in absentia* trials in Article 4a.[23] Article 4a allows the Member States to refuse the execution of an EAW under certain circumstances in case of *in absentia* trials, i.e. it constitutes an optional ground for refusal. This has been criticized as being in contrast with the requirements of the ECHR, which—at least in some cases—oblige the Member States to

---

[17] See the similar argument in Rönnau and Wegner (2013), p. 563. On the effects of directives that are in force but must not yet have been transposed, see Hofmann (2015), § 15, para 3 ff.

[18] See Art. 1(1) of Council Framework Decision 2002/584/JHA of 13 June 2002 on the European Arrest Warrant and the surrender procedures between Member States, OJ L 190/1, amended by Council Framework Decision 2009/299/JHA of 26 February 2009, OJ L 81/24 (in the following FD EAW).

[19] ECtHR, *Krombach v. France*, judgment of 13 February 2001, Appl. No. 29731/96. See, also, Böse (2011b), p. 490 f.

[20] Cour d'Assises Paris, third section, judgment of 9 March 1995, No. 2556/92. See, on the facts, Netzer (2009), p. 752 f.

[21] The original judgment was delivered before the Framework Decision on the European Arrest Warrant entered into force in 2002, see Netzer (2009), p. 752.

[22] This was not the only issue under dispute in the *Krombach* case, which raises many questions in the field of international cooperation. For an overview, see Netzer (2009), p. 752.

[23] This provision has become binding from 28 March 2011 or at the latest 1 January 2014 [Art. 8(1)&(3) FD EAW].

refuse extradition.[24] However, one has to consider that—from the perspective of EU law—Article 4a aims at solving a specific problem, namely that a Member State does not feel comfortable executing an EAW that is based on an *in absentia* trial. Its main purpose is thus not the protection of defence rights, but defining clear rules on when execution of a European Arrest Warrant can be refused and when not.[25] The defendant's right to be present at trial is guaranteed by Directive 2016/343/EU.

Article 4a applies to EAWs issued for the execution of custodial sentences or detention orders "if the person did not appear in person at the trial resulting in the decision". The person that is referred to in Article 4a is the person that is now requested under the EAW, i.e. the defendant of the *in absentia* trial. The terms "custodial sentence" and "detention order" refer to decisions in criminal matters that can become final.[26] This can be read from other language versions that use terms that point at final decisions,[27] but also from paragraphs c and d of Article 4a(1) that point at the right to a retrial or an appeal.[28] In contrast, Article 8(2) Directive 2016/343/EU refers to a "trial which can result in a decision on the guilt or innocence of the suspect or accused person", which is a much clearer description of what is understood to be problematic in *in absentia* trials in criminal matters.

Recently, the CJEU has further defined what constitutes a "trial resulting in the decision", which is an autonomous concept of EU law.[29] In *Tupikas*, the Court had to decide whether an EAW that did not contain information about the appeals procedure had to be executed. It reiterated that a "trial resulting in the decision" referred to a final decision. In cases where there have been different (appeal) procedures, a "trial resulting in the decision" is

> [...] the instance which led to the last of those decisions, provided that the court at issue made a final ruling on the guilt of the person concerned and imposed a penalty on him, such as a custodial sentence, following an assessment, in fact and in law, of the incriminating and exculpatory evidence, including, where appropriate, the taking account of the individual situation of the person concerned.[30]

If the appeals procedure contains a new assessment of the facts and the law, as is often the case (*e.g.* in Germany), it is the decision of the appellate court only that counts for the purpose of Article 4a FD EAW. This means that Article 4a FD EAW does not apply, if the requested person was absent from the first instance proceedings, but attended the appeals trial.[31] In a second judgment taken on the same day,

---

[24] Bartels (2014), p. 104 f.; Böse (2011b), p. 507. On the ECHR, see Ruggeri, in Part V of this volume, Sect. 3.1.2.

[25] See Recitals 4, 6 FD *in absentia* trials.

[26] Bartels (2014), p. 192 f.

[27] Cf. *e.g.* the German version: "*Freiheitsstrafe, freiheitsentziehende Maßregel der Sicherung*"; the Italian version: "*pena, misura di sicurezza privativa della libertà*"; the Danish version: "*frihedsstraf, frihedsberøvende foranstatning*".

[28] Bartels (2014), p. 192 f.

[29] CJEU, *Tupikas*, judgment of 10 August 2017, C-270/17 PPU, para 65.

[30] *Ibid.*, para 81.

[31] *Ibid.*, para 85.

the Court had to decide on a case where the requested person had been absent from a decision on the amendment of custodial sentences that had been handed down in separate trials.[32] The Court held that this decision determining the sentence was part of the "trial resulting in the decision" if the judge had any discretion on the sentence.[33] This shows that both the finding of guilt and the sentencing are relevant parts of the trial.

According to Article 4a(1) FD EAW, a Member State may refuse to execute a European Arrest Warrant based on an *in absentia* trial unless the EAW states that the requirements of one of the four situations defined in Article 4a(1) are met. This means that the EAW itself must contain information on how the requirements have been met in order to be enforceable.[34] This mechanism has been criticized as allowing too much leeway to the issuing Member State.[35] However, the executing Member State can ask for further information if the information provided is insufficient (Art. 15 para. 2 FD EAW).[36] This means that there is a way of reviewing the information provided by the issuing Member State.[37] If the issuing Member State does not provide sufficient information, execution may be refused.[38] It should also be noted that the requirements in Article 4a(1)(a-d) FD EAW apply alternatively, i.e. that execution of the EAW cannot be refused if one of the requirements is fulfilled.[39] In this case, the executing Member State must surrender the person.[40] This shows that—in contrast to the former rule in Article 5(1) FD EAW (old version)—the executing State cannot make execution conditional upon the granting of a new trial in the scenarios that are part of Article 4a(1)(a-b) FD EAW.[41]

Article 4a(1)(a) FD EAW

Article 4a(1)(a) FD EAW allows the execution of EAWs after *in absentia* trials if the defendant, i.e. the requested person, either was summoned in person and thereby informed of the scheduled place and date of trial, or by other means received official information about the place and date of trial. In any case, the defendant must have received the information "in due time", that is sufficiently in time to prepare a

---

[32] CJEU, *Zdziaszek*, judgment of 10 August 2017, C-271/17 PPU.

[33] *Ibid.*, para 90, 96.

[34] See point d) of the Annex to the EAW, FD EAW.

[35] Bartels (2014), p. 206.

[36] Böse (2011b), p. 508.

[37] *Ibid.*

[38] CJEU, *Zdziaszek* (fn. 32), para 104.

[39] Reinbacher and Wendel (2016), p. 336.

[40] CJEU, Grand Chamber, *Melloni v. Ministerio Fiscal*, judgment of 26 February 2013, C-399/11, para 40 et seqq.

[41] Opinion of AG *Bot*, *Melloni* (fn. 15), para 57 et seqq.

defence (Recital 7 FD *in absentia* trials), and must have been notified about the possibility that a decision could be taken in his absence.[42]

The conditions set down in Article 4a(1)(a) FD EAW ("summons", "by other means having received official information") are autonomous concepts of EU law.[43] The requirement that the person must have been summoned in person means that he or she must him- or herself have received official summons.[44] This means that the summons cannot be served to a third party.[45] In the *Dworzecki* case, the CJEU rightly refused to consider the defendant to have been summoned when the summons was handed over to the defendant's grandfather.[46] Nor can it be assumed that the person has been summoned, even if the applicable national law generally recognizes such a fiction.[47] The burden of proof lies with the issuing Member State.[48]

The alternative requirement that the person has been officially informed by other means is less precise.[49] Indeed, it was argued by the national governments in *Dworzecki* that it sufficed as official information to inform another adult living at the defendant's address.[50] However, any ambiguity as to what constitutes official information is countered by the strict rule of evidence in Article 4a(1)(a)(i) FD EAW. Thereby, it must be unequivocally established that the requested person was aware of the date and place of trial.[51] Any doubts in this respect lead to grounds for non-execution under Article 4a(1)(a) FD EAW. The CJEU has stated explicitly in *Dworzecki* that it is up to the authorities of the issuing state to supply information that shows that the defendant was indeed aware of the date and place of trial.[52] If they fail to do so and the summons has been handed over to a third person, the requirements of Article 4a(1)(a)(i) FD EAW are not fulfilled.[53] This also means that Article 4a(1)(a) FD EAW does not apply if the requested person has fled to another Member State before being informed of the trial.[54] In this case, there is no awareness of time and place of trial. However, this situation is governed by litera d (see *below*, Sect. 3.2.1.4).

---

[42] See, also, Wahl (2015), p. 73.

[43] CJEU, *Dworzecki*, judgment of 24 May 2016, C-108/16 PPU, para 32.

[44] *Ibid.*, para 45. See also ECtHR, *Colozza v. Italy*, judgment of 12 February 1985, Appl. No. 9024/80, para 28.

[45] Bartels (2014), p. 196; Paul (2007), p. 243.

[46] CJEU, *Dworzecki* (fn. 43), para 33 et seqq.

[47] Opinion of AG *Bobek*, *Dworzecki*, 11 May 2016, C-108/16 PPU, para 57; Böse (July 2012), § 83 IRG, para 12; Böse (2017), p. 756.

[48] Bartels (2014), p. 195.

[49] This is criticised by Bartels (2014), p. 196 f.; Klitsch (2009), p. 18; Ruggeri (2016), p. 597.

[50] CJEU, *Dworzecki* (fn. 43), para 40.

[51] See ECtHR, Grand Chamber, *Sejdovic v. Italy*, judgment of 1 March 2006, Appl. No. 56581/00, RJD 2006-II, para 99.

[52] CJEU, *Dworzecki* (fn. 43), para 49.

[53] *Ibid.*, para 54.

[54] Böse (2011b), p. 505. Different Bartels (2014), p. 196 f., who apparently sees this as a problem.

The CJEU's decision in *Dworzecki* gives a convincing interpretation of Article 4a(1)(a)(i) FD EAW. However, it should be noted that Article 8(2)(a) of Directive 2016/343/EU does not use the same terms as Article 4a(1)(a)(i) FD EAW. Instead, it suffices if the person was "informed" of the trial. What is meant by "informed" can be gathered from Recital 36: "Informing a suspect or accused person of the trial should be understood to mean summoning him or her in person or, by other means, providing that person with official information about the date and place of the trial in a manner that enables him or her to become aware of the trial."[55] This definition is similar to the one in Article 4a FD EAW, but not identical. In the FD EAW, it must be *unequivocally* established that the person was indeed aware of the trial. Under the new Directive, the person must only have been enabled to become aware of the trial. Whether the person was in fact aware of the trial must not be proven under the new law. This means that the burden of proof is lower under the new Directive than under the FD *in absentia* trials.[56]

What does this mean for judicial cooperation? It has already been explained that the new Directive could be used for interpreting the rules in the existing instruments. However, if the Member States have made use of this optional ground for refusal, the EAW must comply with the requirements set down in Article 4a(1)(a) FD EAW in order to be executed, no matter what is written in Directive 2016/343/EU. The required standard of proof in Article 4a(1)(a) FD EAW is quite clear. Moreover, the CJEU has upheld this strict standard of proof in *Dworzecki* despite the fact that Directive 2016/343/EU was already in force. This goes well with the assessment of AG *Bobek* in *Dworzecki* that Article 4a FD EAW constitutes common minimum standards.[57] Accordingly, the Member States still have to unequivocally establish the awareness of the trial if they issue an EAW after an *in absentia* trial and do not want to risk the refusal of the execution. Insofar, the Member States would be well advised to adapt their Criminal Procedure Law to Article 4a EAW and not Article 8 Directive 2016/343/EU.

In this context, it should be noted that Article 3 of the Directive on the right of access to a lawyer gives every defendant a right to legal representation, including those that fall within the situation described in Article 4a(1)(a) FD EAW. This means that the defendant cannot be deprived of his right to be defended by a lawyer, even if he or she was ordinarily summoned.[58]

Article 4a(1)(a) FD EAW does not state what happens if the person has been aware of the trial but could not attend it for reasons that he or she had no control over. An example is that the requested person is in prison and the prison authorities refuse to surrender the person for trial.[59] In this situation, the person cannot be

---

[55] See also Ruggeri (2016), p. 597.

[56] Cf. also opinion of AG *Bobek*, *Dworzecki* (fn. 47), para 74 with reference to the ECHR.

[57] *Ibid.*, para 36.

[58] Torres Pérez (2014), p. 313.

[59] See ECtHR, *Hokkeling v. The Netherlands*, judgment of 14 February 2017, Appl. No. 30749/12. See also Wahl (2015), p. 73.

assumed to have waived her right to be present at trial.[60] Accordingly, this situation should not fall within the ambit of Article 4a(1)(a) FD EAW.

Article 4a(1)(b) FD EAW

Article 4a(1)(b) FD EAW obliges the Member States to execute an EAW if the absent defendant was aware of place and date of the trial and has given mandate to a "legal counsellor" to defend him or her. A "legal counsellor" is a defence lawyer.[61] The counsellor can either have been appointed by the absentee or by the state. However, the defendant must explicitly have given mandate to the lawyer to defend him- or herself in his/her absence. The recognition of state appointed lawyers has been criticized as being in breach with the defendant's right to choose his or her own legal assistance [Art. 6(3)(c) ECHR], particularly because the Member States are not required to appoint the counsel of choice in the context of Article 4a FD EAW.[62] However, since the Directive on the right of access to a lawyer has by now become binding, Article 4a must be interpreted in this context. Article 3 of Directive on the right of access to a lawyer, which contains the right of access to a lawyer in criminal proceedings, is interpreted in the light of Article 6 ECHR and thus includes the right to choose a lawyer.[63] It can be assumed that *in absentia* trials have met the requirements set down in the Directive on the right of access to a lawyer and therefore of the Article 6 ECHR in this respect. Anyway, the defendant can always refuse to give mandate to the state appointed counsel, which would be at odds with Article 4a(1)(b) FD EAW.

In any case, the mandate of the lawyer alone does not suffice for the purpose of Article 4a(1)(b) FD EAW. The lawyer must actually have defended the absentee.[64] In *Melloni*, one of the arguments was that the lawyers who had defended Mr. Melloni on appeal had no longer been mandated to do so.[65] The CJEU did not address the question of whether the trial had been fair under these circumstances, but stated that Article 4a(1)(b) FD EAW was generally conform with the CFR.[66] Considering that Mr. Melloni had withdrawn the mandate of the lawyers who

---

[60] ECtHR, *Hokkeling v. The Netherlands* (fn. 59), para 60; Ruggeri (2016), p. 597; Wahl (2015), p. 73.

[61] See the German version "*Rechtsbeistand*", which is also used in Directive 2013/48/EU of the European Parliament and of the Council of 22 October 2013 on the right of access to a lawyer in criminal proceedings and in European arrest warrant proceedings, and on the right to have a third party informed upon deprivation of liberty and to communicate with third persons and with consular authorities while deprived of liberty, OJ L 294/1. See also the Italian version "*difensore*".

[62] Bartels (2014), p. 201 f.

[63] Schneider (December 2016), III D 18, para 25.

[64] Cf. ECtHR, *Poitrimol v. France*, judgment of 23 November 1993, Appl. No. 14032/88, para 28 et seqq.

[65] CJEU, *Melloni* (fn. 40), para 16.

[66] *Ibid.*, para 47 ff.

defended him, the Court ought to have raised the question of whether the requirements of Article 4a(1)(b) FD EAW were still fulfilled.[67] This is doubtful: Article 4a(1)(b) FD EAW makes it clear that it is the mandated lawyer that must defend the person, not any other qualified lawyer.[68] Insofar, the Member State should have explained why it has accepted a defence by lawyers whose mandate has been withdrawn.[69]

Moreover, the absentee again must have been aware of the scheduled trial. Whether the strict standards set down in Article 4a(1)(a) FD EAW apply, which refer to an official notification, is unclear.[70] Some of the language versions use the same words in lit. a and b,[71] while others do not.[72] Considering that the presence of a mandated lawyer proves that the absentee knew about the trial beforehand, any form of information should suffice. In contrast, if a lawyer is only appointed by the state authorities at trial, there is no mandate for defending the absentee and thus no room for the application of Article 4a(1)(b) FD EAW. Even the presence of a mandated lawyer is insufficient if the defendant has not deliberately chosen to have himself defended by the lawyer while absent from the trial.[73]

Article 4a(1)(c) FD EAW

Article 4a(1)(c) FD EAW deals with the situation that the absent defendant has been served with the decision and informed of his or her right to be granted a new trial or an appeal, but either explicitly stated that he or she did not want a retrial or failed to apply for a new trial or appeal within the prevised time frame. The text does not explicitly state that the Member State has to grant a retrial. However, the formulation implies that the Member State must indeed grant this right, i.e. it does not have discretion.[74] Now, a right to a new trial is incorporated in Article 9 Directive

---

[67] Gaede (2013), p. 1281.

[68] See, also, Ruggeri (2016), p. 597 f.

[69] Gaede (2013), p. 1281.

[70] Bartels (2014), p. 201.

[71] For instance, the English ("*aware*"), German ("*Kenntnis*"), Spanish ("*conocimiento*"), Danish ("*var klar*"), French ("*connaissance*"), Italien ("*essere al corrente*"). This generally refers to the second variant stated in Article 4a(1)(a) FD EAW.

[72] For instance, the Dutch and Swedish versions.

[73] Recital 10 FD *in absentia* trials. See also Böse (2011b), p. 506.

[74] See German Constitutional Court (BVerfG), decision of 15 December 2015, 2 BvR 2735/14, BVerfGE 140, 317, para 88. An English version of the judgment can be found at http://www.bundesverfassungsgericht.de/SharedDocs/Entscheidungen/EN/2015/12/rs20151215_2bvr273514en.html (last access on 6 November 2017); agreeing Classen (2016), p. 305; Kühne (2016), p. 302; Reinbacher and Wendel (2016), p. 336; Eßlinger and Herzmann (2016), p. 862; Satzger (2016a), p. 516 f.

2016/343/EU and thus will be mandatory for all Member States from April 2018 on.[75]

Article 4a(1)(c) FD EAW specifies what kind of trial is accepted: the retrial or appeal must allow for the re-examination of the merits of the case and the reversal of the original decision, and the defendant must have the right to participate in the new trial.[76] The re-examination of the merits of the case refers to the facts of the case and includes new evidence. The provision does not explicitly state whether a re-examination of legal issues must also be possible.[77] However, it would be impractical to allow for a revision of facts without a revision of their legal evaluation. Moreover, the reason for granting a new trial is to enable the defendant to use his or her defence rights (Recital 11 FD *in absentia* trials).[78] This purpose would be defeated if the defence could not raise legal issues. In addition, questions of law might well arise when considering the evidence, which is something that must be guaranteed at the new trial. All in all, it does not make sense to restrict the new trial to matters of fact. Furthermore, it should be noted that the new trial is possible even if the original decision has *res judicata*.[79] However, the Member States are not obliged to reverse the original decision.[80]

Article 4a(1)(c) FD EAW requires the decision to have been served. "Served" is a different verb from "summoned" and thus does not refer to the strict criteria for a "personal summons".[81] This means that it is in principle possible to serve the decision to an authorised person if national law allows so.[82] However, the requested person must be expressly informed about his or her right to a retrial.[83] Considering that this information is crucial for the defence rights of the requested person, the person him- or herself ought to be informed directly, not by proxy.

This is even more true when taking into account the two other requirements for enforcing an EAW based on an *in absentia* trial: the requested person must have either explicitly stated that he or she does not contest the decision or not requested a new trial or filed an appeal within the applicable time frame. If national law allows a request for a new trial only during a limited period of time, the beginning of this time frame is important. A similar problem arose in the *Covaci* case.[84] In this case, the German courts wanted to issue a penalty order (*Strafbefehl*) in the absence of the defendant. As the defendant's domicile was abroad, he had authorised a Court official to receive documents on his behalf. The penalty order was to be served to the

---

[75] See also JHR/LB (2016), p. 218.

[76] See ECtHR, Grand Chamber, *Sejdovic v. Italy* (fn. 51), para 82.

[77] Bartels (2014), p. 203 f.

[78] See also Art. 9 sent. 2 of Directive 2016/343/EU.

[79] Hauck (2009), p. 146.

[80] Bartels (2014), p. 204.

[81] Bartels (2014), p. 205.

[82] See CJEU, *Covaci*, judgment of 15 October 2015, C-216/14, para 62 et seqq.

[83] See ECtHR, Grand Chamber, *Sejdovic v. Italy* (fn. 51), para 86 et seq.

[84] CJEU, *Covaci* (fn. 82). See also Ruggeri (2016), p. 601.

authorised person, starting the 2 week time frame for objection, and then sent along by the authorised person to the defendant. The Court held that it was possible to authorise another person to receive important documents. However, the time period for objection should not be shortened.[85] The Court bases this assessment on Article 6 of Directive 2012/13/EU on the right to information in criminal proceedings.[86] According to this provision, the defendant must be informed about the accusation. Although a penalty order is also a decision, it is—in cases like the one of Mr. Covaci—the only way to inform about the accusation. The Court comes to the conclusion that defence rights and the principle of non-discrimination demand the full time period for objections to be available to the defendant.[87] Although Article 4a(1)(c) FD EAW does not necessarily include situations where the defendant was not informed about the accusation, it also refers to Article 6 ECHR and the defence rights. The situations are thus similar. Accordingly, a waiver of the right to a retrial can only be assumed if the defendant had the full prescribed period of time for consideration.[88] This means that it does not suffice for the purpose of Article 4a(1)(c)(ii) FD EAW that the decision was served to an authorised person.

Article 4a(1)(c) FD EAW does not oblige the Member State to inform the convicted person about the period of time for applying for a new trial. From the point of view of defendant's rights, this is a severe shortcoming.[89] It is doubtful whether the requirements of a fair trial are met if the person was not informed about the period for applying for a retrial. Certainly, he or she cannot be deemed to have waived the right to a retrial if there was no information about it.

In this respect, it should also be noted that Articles 8 and 9 of Directive 2016/343/EU neither refer to an explicit time frame for demanding a new trial, nor acknowledge the possibility of a waiver. Therefore, it is highly doubtful whether the Member States will be able to refuse to grant a new trial for these reasons in the future. This is certainly true for the time frame which is neither mentioned in the text nor in the recitals of the Directive. One might thus argue that the Member States have to grant the right enshrined in Article 9 of the Directive any time. In contrast to a time limit, the waiver is mentioned in Recital 35, which claims that the right to presence is not absolute but can be disposed of by the defendant. Nonetheless, the recitals are not legally binding. Moreover, other directives on the defendant's rights include explicit provisions on waivers which are subjected to procedural guarantees.[90] The fact that Directive 2016/343/EU lacks such guarantees suggests that a waiver of the right to a new trial is not possible. If this were true, Article 4a(1)(c) FD EAW would be bereft of its meaning because a new trial could never be excluded. By refusing to ask

---

[85] CJEU, *Covaci* (fn. 82), para 68.

[86] OJ 2012 L 142/1.

[87] CJEU, *Covaci* (fn. 82), para 65.

[88] Cf. Wahl (2015), p. 74.

[89] See also Bartels (2014), p. 205.

[90] See Art. 9 of the Directive on the right of access to a lawyer, Article 3(8) of the Directive 2010/64/EU of 20 October 2010 on the right to interpretation and translation in criminal proceedings, OJ 2010 L 280/1.

for a new trial, the convicted person could block his or her extradition and thus prevent the enforcement of the judgment. This scenario shows that the Member State must be allowed to set a reasonable time limit for the new trial, even though this is not mentioned in the Directive.

Article 4a(1)(d) FD EAW

Article 4a(1)(d) FD EAW deals with the situation that a decision has been taken in the absence of the defendant and has not yet been served. This situation arises when the defendant has fled before being summoned.[91] In this case, the issuing Member State must promise that the requested person will be served with the decision after surrender and will be informed about the right to a new trial. Moreover, in contrast to lit. c, the person must also be informed about the time frame for the request [Article 4a(1)(d)(ii) FD EAW].

The rule on *in absentia* trials in Directive 2016/343/EU is slightly different. According to Article 8(a) sent. 2 of the said Directive, the persons shall be informed of their right to a new trial when they are apprehended and informed of the decision. The Directive does not deal with transborder proceedings and therefore refers only to one Member State. However, in transborder criminal proceedings, the requested person is usually apprehended in the executing Member State, which is not the state whose courts have rendered the decision. Nonetheless, if the requested person is arrested on the basis of an EAW in order to be surrendered to the issuing Member State, he or she has to be informed about the EAW and its contents [Art. 11(1) FD EAW]. This includes information about the decision that forms the basis of the EAW [Article 4a(1)(c) FD EAW]. The same result can be got from Article 6(2) of Directive 2012/13/EU on the right to information in criminal proceedings. As Article 8(4) sent. 2 of Directive 2016/343/EU links the information about the new trial to that about the decision that was rendered *in absentia*, the executing Member State must inform about the new trial, too, when the requested person is apprehended. This is an earlier point of time than the one mentioned in the FD EAW (surrender). This means that, from 2018 on, the Member States will be obliged to give this type of information when the requested person is apprehended. Considering that the requirements of Article 4a(1)(d) FD EAW are mandatory, the requested person will effectively have to be informed twice, by both the issuing and the executing Member States.

Article 4a(2) FD EAW obliges the Member State to hand over a copy of the judgment that forms the basis of the EAW if requested. This obligation is not part of Article 8 Directive 2016/343/EU. The judgment must be translated if necessary [Art. 3(2) Directive 2010/64/EU].[92] The same goes for the EAW [Art. 3(6) Directive

---

[91] See Recital 39 of Directive 2016/343/EU.

[92] See ECtHR, Grand Chamber, *Sejdovic v. Italy* (fn. 51), para 89 et seq. See also Bartels (2014), p. 206.

2010/64/EU] and the information about a new trial.[93] Insofar, the requested person will be well informed about his or her rights.

3.2.2 Enforcement of Foreign Judgments

Custodial Sentences

In absentia trials can also become relevant in the framework of international cooperation when the judgment resulting from such a trial shall be executed not by the Member State that has rendered the judgment but by another Member State. In this case, the Member State does not request the surrender of the convicted person, but forwards the judgment to another Member State and requests enforcement. There are several legal instruments in the area of legal assistance that deal with the enforcement of foreign decisions in criminal matters, depending upon the nature of the sanction.

The Framework Decision on custodial sentences or measures involving deprivation of liberty[94] is one of those instruments. Like the FD EAW, it has been amended by the FD *in absentia* trials and now contains an explicit rule on how to deal with decisions resulting from *in absentia* trials in Article 9(1)(i). This rule is almost the same as Article 4a(1)(a-c) FD EAW (see Sects. 3.2.1.1, 3.2.1.2, 3.2.1.3) and also constitutes only an optional ground for refusal. However, there is no equivalent to Article 4a(1)(d) FD EAW. This is because this provision obliges the Member States to guarantee a new trial after surrender. As there is no surrender in the cases that are covered by the FD custodial sentences, naturally this situation cannot occur. The lack of a provision similar to Article 4a(1)(d) FD EAW also means that the enforcement of the sentence can be refused if the decision was not served to the defendant and he or she was neither summoned nor defended by a mandated legal counsel [cf. Article 9(1)(1)(i-iii) FD custodial sentences]. In these cases, the issuing Member State can only take recourse to the EAW in order to achieve the surrender of the requested person and grant him or her a new trial or appeal.

---

[93] Schneider (December 2014), III D 17, para 26.

[94] Council Framework Decision 2008/909/JHA of 27 November 2008 on the application of the principle of mutual recognition to judgments in criminal matters imposing custodial sentences or measures involving deprivation of liberty for the purpose of their enforcement in the European Union, OJ 2008 L 327/27, amended by Council Framework Decision 2009/299/JHA of 26 February 2009, OJ L 81/24.

Financial Penalties

The Framework Decision on financial penalties[95] has also been amended to include a provision on *in absentia* trials. According to Article 7(2)(i), the executing Member State can refuse the execution of a decision stating a financial penalty if the person against whom the decision is directed did not appear at trial, unless the person was summoned, defended by a mandated legal counsel or has waived its right to a new trial after being served with the decision [Art. 7(2)(i)(i-iii)]. These exceptions are exactly the same as those in Article 4a(1)(a-c) FD EAW. As with custodial sentences, enforcement is not possible if the person was not summoned or informed and the decision has not been served.[96] In written procedures, which are fairly common in case of financial penalties, the decision must not be enforced if the person was not informed about his or her right to contest the case and the applicable time limits [Art. 7(2)(g)].

Conditional Judgments and Probation Decisions

The FD *in absentia* trials has also introduced a new ground for refusal into the Framework Decision on conditional judgments and probation decisions.[97] Article 11(1)(h) of the Framework Decision is the same as Article 9(1)(i) of the Framework Decision on custodial sentences, Article 7(2)(i)(i-iii) of the Framework Decision on financial penalties and Article 4a(1)(a-c) FD EAW.[98] This makes sense because these types of judgments are closely related.

Confiscation Orders

Article 8(2)(e) of the Framework Decision on confiscation orders[99] contains an optional ground for the non-recognition of confiscation orders that result from an *in absentia* trials. Again, it is the same as Article 4a(1)(a-c) FD EAW.

---

[95] Council Framework Decision 2005/214/JHA of 24th February 2005 on the application of the principle of mutual recognition to financial penalties, OJ 2005 L 76/16, amended by Council Framework Decision 2009/299/JHA of 26 February 2009, OJ L 81/24.

[96] See *above*, Sect. 3.2.2.1.

[97] Council Framework Decision 2008/947/JHA of 27 November 2008 on the application of the principle of mutual recognition to judgments and probation decisions with a view to the supervision of probation measures and alternative sanctions, OJ 2008 L 227/102, amended by Council Framework Decision 2009/299/JHA of 26 February 2009, OJ L 81/24.

[98] See Sects. 3.2.1.1, 3.2.1.2, 3.2.1.3, 3.2.2.1 and 3.2.2.2.

[99] Council Framework Decision 2006/783/JHA of 6 October 2006 on the application of the principle of mutual recognition to confiscation orders, OJ 2006 L 328/59, amended by Council Framework Decision 2009/299/JHA of 26 February 2009, OJ L 81/24.

In its proposal for a Regulation on freezing and confiscation orders,[100] the Commission suggested an optional ground for non-execution in Article 9(1)(g). The provision is basically the same as Article 8(2)(e) of the Framework Decision on confiscation orders. However, the ground for refusal in the proposal only applies to confiscation orders that are "linked to a final conviction". This refers to confiscation orders under Article 4(1) of Directive 2014/42/EU.[101] This provision links confiscation orders to a final conviction, explicitly including *in absentia* proceedings.[102] However, Article 4(2) of Directive 2014/42/EU allows non-conviction based confiscation orders under certain circumstances, *e.g.* in case of flight of the addressee of the order. Execution of such a non-conviction based confiscation order cannot be refused under the proposed Article 9(1)(g).[103] If the proposal is accepted without changes, this leads to the odd situation that the enforcement of a confiscation order that is linked to an *in absentia* trial can be refused while the enforcement of a confiscation order that is not even linked to a criminal conviction must take place. Considering that the reasons allowing a non-conviction based confiscation order often correspond to those allowing a trial in the defendant's absence (*e.g.* in case of flight), the defendant's position is better when the Member State allows *in absentia* trials than when it does not.[104] One has to hope that the proposal will be amended in order to introduce a similar rule for non-conviction based confiscation orders.

3.3   Unwritten Grounds for Refusal

Apart from the explicit ground for refusing the execution of an EAW or a judgment in cases of *in absentia* trials, there is also a discussion about whether the execution can be refused in other cases on the basis of the European public order and fundamental rights or national constitutional law.

---

[100] Regulation of the European Parliament and of the Council on the mutual recognition of freezing and confiscation orders, COM(2016) 819 final.

[101] Directive 2014/42/EU of the European Parliament and of the Council of 3 April 2014 on the freezing and confiscation of instrumentalities and proceeds of crime in the European Union, OJ 2014 L 127/39.

[102] See also Recital 15 of Directive 2014/42/EU.

[103] See COM(2016) 819 final, p. 13.

[104] For example, if the defendant has fled abroad, Germany does not allow *in absentia* trials, but non-conviction based confiscation orders (§ 76a German Criminal Code). These orders must be executed under the proposal, whereas an order that was linked to an *in absentia* trial does not necessarily have to be executed.

3.3.1 European Public Order and Fundamental Rights

When considering this question, it is first important to have a look at what rules can be found in the European public order and fundamental rights on *in absentia* trials. In a second step, the question will be considered of whether such an argument can be used in order to refuse the execution of measures in judicial cooperation.

The Content of the European Public Order and Fundamental Rights

It is not easy to figure out which rules on *in absentia* trials form part of the European public order, or, more generally, what constitutes the European public order. However, it seems to be clear that the ECHR forms the core of the European public order.[105] This means that the execution of EAWs or judgments resulting from *in absentia* trials must be conform with human rights, particularly Article 6 ECHR.[106] Moreover, EU fundamental rights such as the right to an effective remedy and to a fair trial (Article 47 CFR[107]) and the presumption of innocence and right of defence (Article 48 CFR) also play a part in shaping the standard on *in absentia* trials. Like all guarantees in the CFR, these provisions may not be interpreted in a way that provides lower standards than the ECHR.[108] A higher protection is still possible [Article 52(3) sent. 2 CFR]. Nonetheless, so far, there is no evidence that the CJEU has interpreted Articles 47, 48 CFR in a broader way in order to enhance the scope of the EU fundamental rights in comparison with the ECHR in the field of *in absentia* trials.[109] Therefore, it can be assumed that the guarantees in EU primary law are similar to the ECHR.

Since the EU has recently adopted Directive 2016/343/EU which stipulates minimum rights for *in absentia* trials, the question arises of whether this Directive has an impact on the EU public order. At first glance, this question might sound strange: can a directive, i.e. EU secondary law, really be considered part of the European public order? However, in case of Directive 2016/343/EU, the crucial point is that this Directive is meant to set common minimum standards as defined by the ECHR. The purpose of the Directive is "to enhance the right to a fair trial in criminal proceedings by laying down common minimum rules concerning […] the right to be present at the trial".[110] This shows that the Directive is directly linked to those guarantees that are part of the European public order (see also Recital 1). If EU law

---

[105] See also Burchard (2013), § 14, para 52.

[106] Bartels (2014), p. 184. See also Böse (2015), p. 137. On the ECHR and *in absentia* trials see Ruggeri, in Part V of this volume, Sect. 3.1.1.

[107] Charter of Fundamental Rights of the European Union, OJ 2016 C 202/289.

[108] Art. 52(3) sent. 1 CFR. See also the Explanations relating to the Charter of Fundamental Rights, OJ 2007 C 303/17, Art. 52.

[109] See CJEU, *Melloni* (fn. 40), para 47 ff.; Opinion of AG *Bot*, *Melloni* (fn. 15), para 83 et seq. This is criticized by Torres Pérez (2014), p. 314.

[110] Recital 9 of Directive 2016/343/EU.

stipulates minimum standards about what constitutes a fair trial in case of *in absentia* trials, these standards become binding for the Member States.[111] Due to the importance of the fair trial principle for the European public order, these standards thus form part of the public order, too. This reasoning does not only apply to Directive 2016/343/EU, but to all other legal instruments that are concretizations of EU fundamental rights and the ECHR.

In consequence, an *in absentia* trial can constitute a violation of the European public order if it either is contrary to the guarantees in the ECHR or violates Articles 8 and 9 of Directive 2016/343/EU.[112] As judicial cooperation helps to enforce a judgment that results from an *in absentia* trial, such cooperation must also be seen as a violation of the European public order.

Obligation to Refuse?

Having said that helping to enforce a judgment resulting from an *in absentia* trial, be it the judgment itself or an EAW, can constitute a violation of the European public order, it must be asked whether the Member States can still choose whether they want to refuse judicial cooperation or not. It has already been explained that *in absentia* trials constitute optional grounds for refusing the enforcement of a judgment or the execution of an EAW (see Sect. 3.2). In *Dworzecki*, the CJEU pointed out that, even though the requirements of Article 4a(1)(a) FD EAW were not met, the Member State could take different criteria into account because Article 4a was an optional ground for refusal.[113] This is undoubtedly true: if the Member States can choose to execute an EAW issued for the enforcement of a judgment resulting from an *in absentia* trial without any further safeguards, they can also choose to set lower safeguards than those envisaged in Article 4a FD EAW.[114] Still, the Member States' obligation to respect the ECHR can even now oblige them to avail themselves of the optional ground for refusal.[115]

However, since April 2018, the situation has changed. Articles 8 and 9 of Directive 2016/343/EU oblige the Member States to allow *in absentia* trials only under specific circumstances. *In absentia* trials that do not adhere to the principles set down in the Directive will violate EU law after the Directive has become binding. If the Member States enforce judgments resulting from (now illegal) *in absentia*

---

[111] See also Meyer (2016), p. 338.

[112] The content of the ECHR and Directive 2016/343/EU will not be described here but will be discussed elsewhere: see Ruggeri and Bachmaier Winter in this volume.

[113] CJEU, *Dworzecki* (fn. 43), para 50 et seqq. See also CJEU, *Zdziaszek* (fn. 32), para 106 et seqq.

[114] For example, under German law, extradition cannot be refused if the defendant has absconded in order to avoid being summoned to trial (§ 83 no. 3 IRG), see Böse (July 2012), § 83 IRG, para 13.

[115] See BVerfG, 2 BvR 2735/14 (fn. 74), para 92 et seqq.; Böse (2015), p. 142; Rung (2016), p. 148; Torres Pérez (2014), p. 314.

trials, they support the infringement of EU law and thus act themselves contrary to their obligations under EU law [see Article 4(3) TEU]. This means that from April 2018 on, the Member States are obliged to refuse the execution of EAWs or judgments that have not respected the common minimum standards contained in Articles 8 and 9 of Directive 2016/343/EU.[116] Therefore, the optional ground for refusal in case of *in absentia* trials will become mandatory from then on. Accordingly, it can be said that the new Directive constitutes an obligation to refuse extradition or the enforcement of the judgment.

The Admissibility of the European Public Order as Ground for Refusal with Regard to *In Absentia* Trials

Having found out that there are indeed guarantees on *in absentia* trials in the European public order, the question remains whether this is a valid argument in the context of judicial cooperation for refusing the execution of an EAW or the enforcement of a judgment.

The problem is that the framework decisions in the field of judicial cooperation contain a specific list with grounds for refusal. As the idea of mutual recognition is to limit grounds for refusal, the CJEU has repeatedly stressed that the lists are exclusive and thus state the only grounds for which refusal of recognition is allowed.[117] Considering that most legal instruments include an explicit ground for refusal in case of *in absentia* trials, it must be doubted whether there really is a need for recognizing an unwritten ground for refusal based on the European public order (see below). Nonetheless, as unwritten grounds for refusal have in fact been discussed in the context of *in absentia* trials, the question of whether the European public order can serve as a ground for refusal will be discussed here.

Only few legislative measures list a violation of fundamental rights as ground for refusal.[118] Among these is Article 20(3) FD financial penalties, which allows the Member States to oppose the recognition and execution of a decision if the certificate gives rise to fundamental rights issues. Although the executing Member State has to consult the issuing Member State in this case, it is up to the executing State's discretion to decide on whether it wants to oppose the execution of the decision. In this case, it is clear from the text of the Framework Decision that the European public order constitutes a ground for refusal. Insofar, the admissibility of this argument is not in question.

---

[116] See, also, Böse (2017), p. 759, for cases of flight.

[117] See, e.g., CJEU, Grand Chamber, *Aranyosi and Căldăraru*, judgment of 5 April 2016, C-404-15 and C-659/15, para 80; Opinion of AG *Bot, Aranyosi and Căldăraru*, 3 March 2016, C-404/15 and C-659/15 PPU, para 129. See also Böhm (2017), p. 78; Satzger (2016a), p. 514.

[118] See *e.g.* Art. 20(3) FD financial penalties; Art. 11(1)(f) of Directive 2014/41/EU on the European Investigation Order.

Still, the FD on financial penalties is the only Framework Decision in the field of judicial cooperation that can boast of a ground for refusal based on the European public order, apart from the EIO Directive that is not important in case of *in absentia* trials.[119] However, some of the other framework decisions point at the importance of the ECHR and the EU fundamental rights in a more general way.[120] In the *Radu* case, which dealt with alleged infringements of, among others, Article 6 ECHR, AG Sharpston argued that a Member State could refuse the execution of an EAW if human rights have been or will be infringed as a result of the surrender procedure.[121] This view was taken up by the CJEU in the more recent judgment *Aranyosi and Căldăraru*.[122] In this preliminary ruling, the Court was called upon to decide on whether an EAW must be executed even if there is concrete evidence that the requested person will suffer detention in an inhumane and degrading way in the issuing State. The FD EAW does not explicitly allow Member States to refuse execution in case of bad detention conditions. Nonetheless, the Court held that surrender procedures could be "brought to an end" if there was "objective, reliable, specific and properly updated evidence" that there were systematic deficiencies in detention conditions and there was a real risk that the requested person would suffer from these deficiencies.[123] Bringing surrender procedures to an end effectively means (in this context) refusing to surrender the requested person and this, in turn, means that the CJEU has stipulated a new ground for refusal for bad detention conditions.[124] The CJEU's judgment in *Aranyosi and Căldăraru* thus shows that EU fundamental rights can be invoked as a ground for refusal.[125]

It is unclear to what extent the principles of *Aranyosi and Căldăraru* apply to other fundamental rights than the prohibition of inhuman and degrading treatment (Article 4 CFR, Article 3 ECHR).[126] The reasoning in *Aranyosi and Căldăraru* can well apply to other fundamental rights issues. Still, it has been argued that only absolute rights, such as those contained in Article 15(2) ECHR, can form the basis of this new unwritten ground for refusal.[127] This view comes from the CJEU's judgment

---

[119] Notably, such an exception is missing in the FD EAW, Korenica and Doli (2016), p. 546; Schallmoser (2012), p. 156.

[120] See, *e.g.*, Art. 1 para. 3 FD EAW. On this argument, opinion of AG *Bot, Aranyosi and Căldăraru* (fn. 118), para 72 et seqq.

[121] Opinion of AG *Sharpston*, 18 October 2012, C-396/11—*Radu*, para 97. See also Böse (2015), p. 139.

[122] CJEU, *Aranyosi and Căldăraru* (fn. 118).

[123] *Ibid.*, para 104. On the different steps that must be undertaken before bringing procedures to an end Brodowski (2016), p. 429 et seq.; JHR/LB (2016), p. 220 et seq.; Reinbacher and Wendel (2016), p. 341 f.; on the burden of proof Korenica and Doli (2016), p. 550. See also, in detail, Kromrey and Morgenstern (2017), p. 119 ff.

[124] Brodowski (2016), p. 431.

[125] See also Korenica and Doli (2016), pp. 543 ff., 547; O'Leary (2016), p. 37.

[126] See Brodowski (2016), p. 431 f.

[127] Korenica and Doli (2016), p. 547. See, also, Hong (2016), p. 561.

which explicitly refers to absolute rights and Article 15(2) ECHR.[128] If this assessment is true, only few rights can give rise to the procedure laid down in *Aranyosi and Căldăraru*.[129]

With regard to *in absentia* trials, the effect of *Aranyosi and Căldăraru* is rather limited. This is because most legal instruments of judicial cooperation provide for an explicit ground for refusal in this case (see Sect. 3.2). Therefore, the question is not if the recognition of decisions can be refused at all in case of *in absentia* trials, but if the existing ground for refusal covers all situations in which the European fundamental rights demand a refusal. This depends on whether the exceptions to the right to refuse enforcement apply or not.[130] This is a matter of the interpretation of the FD *in absentia* trials and the corresponding provisions and also a matter of the compatibility of EU secondary law with primary law.[131] Accordingly, the CJEU took the correct approach when assessing the compatibility of Article 4a FD EAW with Articles 47 and 48 CFR in *Melloni*, whatever one may think of the result of its assessment.[132] If the grounds for refusal do not take into account the rules of the European public order on *in absentia* trials and therefore the Member States are obliged to grant judicial cooperation in cases where this would infringe the European public order, this obligation is in breach of EU primary law and thus void. Judicial cooperation would thus be halted until the EU changes the legal instrument accordingly. Therefore, there is no need to fall back on unwritten grounds for refusal in case of *in absentia* trials.

This unwritten ground for refusal could only become important for *in absentia* trials if the EU drafted legal instruments in the matter of judicial cooperation without including a ground for refusal for *in absentia* trials. In this situation, the principles of *Aranyosi and Căldăraru* could be activated in order to refuse judicial cooperation when the standards of the EU are not respected (see Sect. 3.3.1). If one restricts *Aranyosi and Căldăraru* to absolute rights, this could be a problem in case of *in absentia* trials because the right to be present at trial can be waived and is thus not absolute. Nor is it referred to in Article 15(2) ECHR. However, the rights that can be invoked under *Aranyosi and Căldăraru* can well be broader than those contained in Article 15(2) ECHR. The CJEU does not state that only the rights contained in Article 15(2) ECHR can constitute an unwritten ground for refusal, but refers to Article 15(2) ECHR in order to strengthen the argument for using Article 4 CFR as such a ground.[133] In this context, it should be noted that EU law contains rights and guarantees which cannot be waived. These guarantees shape EU fundamental rights and have a direct impact on the CFR. Accordingly, they can be

---

[128] CJEU, *Aranyosi and Căldăraru* (fn. 118), para 84 et seq., 86.

[129] These are: Art. 2 (Right to Life), Art. 3 (Prohibition of Torture), Art. 4 para. 1 (Prohibition of Slavery) and Art. 7 (No Punishment without Law).

[130] See Rung (2016), p. 148.

[131] See, in detail, Wahl (2015), p. 71.

[132] CJEU, *Melloni* (fn. 40), para 47 ff. On the result, see the criticism in Gaede (2013), p. 1281 f.

[133] CJEU, *Aranyosi and Căldăraru* (fn. 118), para 86.

regarded as more precise characterizations of the CFR which show the boundaries for the Member State's discretion. An example for this is provided by Articles 8 and 9 of Directive 2016/343/EU. These provisions do not leave discretion to the Member States as to whether they want to protect the right to presence at trial or not and to what extent they should allow a waiver. This means that they contain the absolute core of the right to presence at trial, which is a subcategory of the right to a fair trial. These provisions are so precise that they have become directly applicable since 1 April 2018. Therefore, a violation of these principles should give rise to a new ground for refusal under *Aranyosi and Căldăraru*.

Besides, it is unlikely that the CJEU would uphold an obligation that leads to an infringement of EU law. If EU legislation contained an obligation for judicial cooperation that was in breach with Directive 2016/343/EU, the new legislation would be contrary to Articles 47 and 48 CFR.[134] Therefore, the obligation in the new legislation would also be void and could be challenged before the CJEU (see *above*).

3.3.2 National Constitutional Law

It can also be questioned whether the execution of an EAW or the enforcement of a foreign judgment can be refused on the basis of the national constitutional law of a Member State. The CJEU has taken a clear stand on this topic in *Melloni*.[135] Mr. Melloni had been arrested in Spain under an EAW issued by Italy for the execution of a judgment resulting from an *in absentia* trial.[136] The Spanish authorities considered themselves bound to execute the EAW under Article 4a(1)(b) FD EAW. However, Spanish constitutional law demanded a guarantee that the extradited person would be granted a new trial in Italy, which was not a requirement under Article 4a(1)(b) FD EAW. In its preliminary reference, the Spanish Constitutional Court now wanted to know, among other things, whether it could introduce such a condition in order to comply with the fundamental rights guaranteed by the Spanish constitution.[137] It based this question on Article 53 CFR, which refers to the Member States' constitutions and could be interpreted to mean that these constitutions applied if they offered higher protection than EU law.[138]

The CJEU rejected this argument. The reason given was that

> [...] that interpretation of Article 53 of the Charter would undermine the principle of the primacy of EU law inasmuch as it would allow a Member State to disapply EU legal rules which are fully in compliance with the Charter where they infringe the fundamental rights guaranteed by that State's constitution.[139]

---

[134] See Recital 9 of Directive 2016/343/EU.

[135] CJEU, *Melloni* (fn. 40).

[136] See, in detail, Herzmann (2015), p. 445; Torres Pérez (2014), p. 308; de Boer (2013), p. 1083.

[137] CJEU, *Melloni* (fn. 40), para 55.

[138] *Ibid*., para 56.

[139] *Ibid*., para 58.

The effectiveness of EU law takes precedence over the national fundamental rights. The Court also points out that these particular concerns have been addressed in the FD *in absentia* trials and that this Framework Decision contains the consensus among the Member States on when the execution of an EAW should be refused.[140] In consequence, arguments based on the national constitution cannot be used to refuse the execution of an EAW.

Understandably, the *Melloni* decision has not met with much approval by the national constitutional courts. The Spanish Constitutional Court that had referred the *Melloni* case to the CJEU did in fact change the interpretation of its constitutional law in order to comply with the preliminary ruling, albeit grudgingly.[141] However, it also reiterated that the Spanish Constitution would take precedence in case of an irreconcilable conflict.[142] In December 2015, the German Constitutional Court stated in a decision on the execution of an EAW in case of *in absentia* trials that the provision on human dignity in the German Constitution [Article 1(1) GG] obliged the Member States to refuse extradition if there was danger of a violation of human dignity.[143] This was in spite of the CJEU's ruling in *Melloni* to which the BVerfG explicitly referred.[144] The reasoning of the BVerfG is based on Article 79(3) GG, which forbids changes to Articles 1 and 20 GG (so-called "eternity guarantee").[145] When exactly an extradition violates Article 1 GG remains to be seen.[146] In a later case, the BVerfG rejected the argument that the possibility to evaluate the silence of the defendant in a negative way, which is the rule in English law, gave the right to refuse extradition because the English law did not go against the core of the principle against self-incrimination.[147] Considering that German Criminal Procedure allows trials in the absence of the defendant under certain circumstances (see §§ 230 ff. StPO), it can be doubted whether the BVerfG would consider *in absentia* trials to violate the core of human dignity.[148] In the respective cases on *in absentia* trials, the constitutional courts have avoided a conflict with EU law by interpreting the provisions in question in a way that was conform with EU law. However, these examples show that the national constitutional courts are not willing to sacrifice crucial constitutional guarantees for the sake of the primacy of EU law.

---

[140] *Ibid.*, para 62 et seq.

[141] STC 26/2014 of 13 February 2014, available at www.tribunalconstitucional.es (last access on 23 February 2017). See also Herzmann (2015), p. 448; Torres Pérez (2014), p. 319.

[142] See Herzmann (2015), p. 451; Torres Pérez (2014), p. 319 f.

[143] BVerfG, 2 BvR 2735/14 (fn. 74), para 83.

[144] *Ibid.*, para 82.

[145] *Ibid.*, para 40 ff. See, in more detail, Brodowski (2016), p. 421; Kühne (2016), p. 299; Kromrey and Morgenstern (2017), p. 112 ff.; Satzger (2016a), p. 516.

[146] For possible examples of a conflict, see Satzger (2016a), p. 522.

[147] See BVerfG, judgment of 6 September 2016, 2 BvR 890/16, para 37 ff.

[148] Safferling (2014), p. 551. See, e.g., on extradition and *in absentia* trials, BVerfG, Neue Juristische Wochenschrift 1991, 1411; BVerfGK 3, 27 (32 f.); BVerfGK 3, 314 (317 f.). Cf. also BVerfGE 63, 332 (334).

Nevertheless, from a European point of view, the *Melloni* judgment is convincing with regard to national constitutional law.[149] The principle of mutual recognition would not work if any Member State had the option to refuse the execution of an EAW because national law offered a higher protection than the FD EAW. The whole point of the FD EAW was to harmonize the law on international surrender among Member States in order to prevent arbitrary decisions. This goal would be undermined if national constitutional law were accepted as a ground for refusal. Therefore, the idea to develop a common standard on what constitutes grounds for refusal should be upheld. However, the conflicts between the CJEU and the national constitutional courts show that the idea of harmonizing grounds for refusal, albeit convincing, was badly executed. Mandatory requirements under national constitutional law should have been discussed when drafting the Framework Decision in order to find a compromise that is acceptable to all parties concerned. Nothing would have prevented the EU to adopt stricter rules or even explicitly refer to national constitutional law. It is the Member States' responsibility that they have not voiced their concerns at the right time.

It is not easy to find a solution for these conflicts, which refer to the relationship of EU and national fundamental and human rights in general. However, in my opinion, it would not be the best approach to allow national courts to invoke new grounds for refusal. This is because these rules would completely depend on the will of the executing Member State and thus be unforeseeable for both the requested person and the other Member States. The applicable standards would not be clear at all. Therefore, arguments based on national constitutional law should not be permitted. However, the EU ought to make sure that human rights are protected by EU law. The ECHR, the CFR and the directives shaping the ECHR provide sufficient ground for arguments based on the EU public order and for introducing a human rights perspective in transborder proceedings. They can be referred to when interpreting the written grounds for refusal for *in absentia* trials. Furthermore, the Member States that are dissatisfied with the legislation on *in absentia* trials can propose a change of legislation. *Melloni* has been criticized for its lax interpretation of Charter rights.[150] The recent development in *Aranyosi and Căldăraru* is therefore an important step towards a higher protection of human rights and a necessary complement to the ban of national constitutional law as a ground for refusal.

3.4 Conclusions

In absentia trials have proven to be a controversial issue in judicial cooperation and a threat to the mutual recognition of decisions. This is why the EU has adopted FD *in absentia* trials and thus introduced optional grounds for refusal in several legal

---

[149] Böse (2015), p. 141 f.; Wahl (2015), p. 75. Similarly Satzger (2016a), p. 515 f.

[150] See, *e.g.*, Böse (2015), p. 142; von Heintschel-Heinegg (2014), § 37, para 57.

instruments. These are similar in case of the execution of an EAW and the enforcement of judgments, which are the most relevant constellations.

The provisions on *in absentia* trials must be interpreted with reference to other EU law such as the directives on defendant's right, particularly Directive 2016/343/EU which sets common minimum standards for *in absentia* trials and will become binding by April 2018. From that day on, the Member States will be obliged to refuse the execution of an EAW or the enforcement of a judgment if the requirements of Articles 8 and 9 Directive 2016/343/EU are not met. Moreover, the provisions should be interpreted in light of the CFR and the ECHR.

The European public order is defined by the CFR, ECHR and the Directives on defendant's rights. If the provisions on *in absentia* trials cannot be interpreted in a way that is conform with the European public order, the Framework Decision is contrary to primary law and therefore void. Only if there is no explicit provision on *in absentia* trials applicable, the question arises of whether a ground for refusal can stem from a violation of the European public order. After the CJEU's judgment *Aranyosi and Căldăraru*, this question must be answered in the affirmative. This at least applies to a violation of Article 8 and 9 of Directive 2016/343/EU.

In contrast, national constitutional law does not allow refusing the execution of an EAW or the enforcement of a judgment. This view has been challenged by several constitutional courts of the Member States which have claimed the right to preserve fundamental rights that form the core of the Member State's constitution. However, in case of *in absentia* trials, the potential conflict has not yet evolved. This might be because the provisions on the ground for refusal in case of *in absentia* trials cover most situations that were discussed controversially and therefore conflicts can be solved by means of interpretation.

Nonetheless, solving conflicts by interpretation bears a risk. Considering that it is the national court's task to apply EU law in case of judicial cooperation, it is entirely possible that the Member States will use their own constitutional guarantees for the interpretation of EU law by stealth. The BVerfG judgment shows how this could be done: first, the BVerfG states the similarity of the German constitution and EU guarantees on *in absentia* trials, then it goes on to interpret Article 4a FD EAW in light of these guarantees, and finally it states that this interpretation is an *acte claire* and does not need to be referred to the CJEU.[151] This approach has been severely criticized. Scholars have pointed out that it is easy to interpret open guarantees like those in the ECHR and CFR any way one would like, and that this is why there are courts—the CJEU and the ECtHR—that have the final word on interpretation.[152] In addition, the interpretation of Art. 4a FD EAW can hardly be called obvious, so the matter should have gone to the CJEU.[153]

[151] BVerfG, 2 BvR 2735/14 (fn. 74), para 67 et seqq.
[152] Böhm (2017), p. 78; Kühne (2016), p. 302.
[153] Kühne (2016), p. 302; Reinbacher and Wendel (2016), p. 343 f.; Rung (2016), p. 149 f.; Satzger (2016a), p. 519.

What will happen to judicial cooperation and *in absentia* trials in the future? It is likely that there will be more and more cases in which the interpretation of the provisions on *in absentia* trials is questioned, especially in the light of Article 6 ECHR, Articles 47 and 48 CFR. It is also possible that the ECtHR will be called upon in order to decide on the compatibility of national law implementing EU framework decisions and the ECHR.[154] After *Aranyosi and Căldăraru*, it is also probable that the European public order will be invoked as an unwritten ground for refusal. Whether the Member States' constitutional courts will refuse judicial cooperation on the basis of national constitutional law—a clear breach of the principle of sincere cooperation—remains to be seen, but is not very likely considering that the respective arguments could also be made under the label of the European public order. Time will tell how EU law will shape the guarantees on *in absentia* trials.

4   *In Absentia* Trials and *ne bis in idem*

Judgments resulting from *in absentia* trials can also present problems with respect to the *ne bis in idem* principle enshrined in Articles 50 CFR and 54 CISA. The first question is whether a judgment resulting from an *in absentia* trial constitutes a final decision in the sense of Articles 50 CFR and 54 CISA. In its *Bourquain* judgment, the CJEU answered this question in the affirmative: as the wording of Art. 54 CISA does not exclude *in absentia* trials and as this provision is not dependent on a harmonization of the rules on *in absentia* trials, judgments resulting from these trials are final decisions.[155] Considering that these judgments are meant to be a final decision on the merits of the case, this assessment is convincing.

However, Article 54 CISA only forbids a second prosecution if the penalty (in case of a conviction) "has been enforced, is actually in the process of being enforced or can no longer be enforced". Typically, judgments resulting from *in absentia* trials have been delivered in the absence of the defendant because the defendant has absconded and could not be found. This usually means that enforcement of the judgment is difficult. Therefore, this type of judgments has often not been enforced. Can other countries then start new criminal proceedings, disregarding the existing unenforced judgment? In view of Article 54 CISA, the answer should be yes. However, Article 50 CFR, which also contains the *ne bis in idem* principle, does not restrict *ne bis in idem* to judgments that have been enforced, are being enforced or can no longer be enforced. This discrepancy between the two provisions has led to the question of whether the so-called "execution condition" still applies after Article 50 CFR has become binding primary law.[156]

---

[154] Wahl (2015), p. 76.

[155] CJEU, *Bourquain*, judgment of 11 December 2008, C-297/07, para 33 ff.

[156] This question has been extensively discussed. See, e.g., Böse (2011a), p. 504; Eckstein (2012), p. 521 ff.; Merkel and Scheinfeld (2012), p. 208 ff.; Satzger (2016b), § 10, para. 57 ff.; Schomburg and Suominen-Picht (2012), p. 1191 f.; Swoboda (2011), p. 264; Zöller (2016), p. 326.

This question was the subject matter of the CJEU's judgment in *Spasic*.[157] Mr. Spasic had been sentenced by the Italian courts *in absentia* to a custodial sentence and a fine for fraudulent activities and counterfeiting of money. Mr. Spasic had paid the fine, but the custodial sentence had not been enforced. The German authorities planned to prosecute him for the same facts and asked the Court whether this prosecution was barred by Articles 50 CFR and 54 CISA. The CJEU held that the execution condition also applied to Article 50 CFR.[158] Article 52(1) CFR allows limitations to fundamental rights if they are provided by the law, as is the case with Article 54 CISA.[159] Article 54 CISA is also proportionate.[160] Therefore, a new trial is possible if the execution condition has not been met. In this respect, the Court held that the enforcement of one penalty—the fine—did not suffice, so that *ne bis in idem* did not apply.[161]

In consequence, judgments resulting from *in absentia* trials do not automatically bar second prosecutions if they have not been enforced. This result seems at first glance to be at odds with the extensive possibilities that exist in EU law for judicial cooperation, especially in case of *in absentia* trials. Therefore, it has been suggested that it is not proportionate to start new criminal proceedings if it would be possible to enforce the first judgment.[162] If the Member States are trying to enforce the first judgment by means of an EAW or by asking for enforcement in another Member State, the judgment is "in the process of being enforced" and therefore falls within the *ne bis in idem* principle enshrined in Article 54 CISA. Accordingly, the problem only arises if the Member State of the first judgment does not bother to try to enforce the judgment or if the second Member State can refuse cooperation, *e.g.*, because the *in absentia* trial did not comply with the requirements of the European public order set down in provisions such as Article 4a FD EAW (see Sect. 3).

In the latter case, barring a second prosecution would mean that the convicted person could live in freedom without being threatened by a sanction in any Member State other than the convicting one. It is understandable that such a result ought to be avoided, because no one has the right to trust in not suffering the consequences of a legal conviction.[163] Insofar, a complete ban on second prosecution would lead to an area of freedom, but not to an area of security and justice.[164] Therefore, a second prosecution should, in principle, be possible if the enforcement of the first judgment is not possible under EU law.[165]

---

[157] CJEU, Grand Chamber, *Spasic*, judgment of 27 May 2014, C-129/14 PPU.

[158] *Ibid.*, para 74.

[159] *Ibid.*, para 54 et seq.

[160] *Ibid.*, para 60 et seqq.

[161] *Ibid.*, para 75 ff.

[162] Gaede (2014), p. 2991.

[163] See Gaede (2014), p. 2991. See also Zöller (2016), p. 330.

[164] See, also, Satzger (2016b), § 10, para 57.

[165] Safferling (2011), § 12, para 85. Critical Böse (2011a), p. 509.

However, in case of *in absentia* trials, it is worth looking at the reasons for why the enforcement of the judgment can be refused.[166] As has been shown above (Sect. 3.2), EU law contains, by now, specific provisions on when judicial cooperation can be refused. When the person has neither been summoned nor defended by a mandated lawyer, the enforcement of a judgment or the execution of an EAW is still possible if the person is informed about his or her right to a new trial [see, *e.g.*, Art. 4a(1)(c-d) FD EAW]. This is also the content of Articles 8 and 9 of Directive 2016/343/EU. Accordingly, the impossibility to enforce a judgment resulting from an *in absentia* trial only arises if the Member States are not willing or unable to grant a new trial.[167] Since 1 April 2018, the deadline for the transposition of Directive 2016/343/EU, this is in breach of Articles 8 and 9 of Directive 2016/343/EU. The Directive clearly states when and under which conditions judgments resulting from *in absentia* trials can be enforced [see Art. 8(3-4) of Directive 2016/343/EU]. A judgment that does not fulfil these requirements, thus blatantly violating EU law and international human rights standards, should not have the consequence that any other state can prosecute again.[168] Otherwise, the individual would carry the burden of the Member State's failure to comply with EU law. This would lead to the strange consequence that the individual could claim damages from the Member State of the first judgment for making him or her suffer a second trial in another Member State because judicial cooperation was not possible for a violation of human rights. Instead of allowing such a construction, it would be more humane to refuse a second trial altogether. This would put more pressure on the first Member State and thus ensure the effectiveness of EU law better. The respective Member State would then be liable for breach of its obligation to transpose Articles 8 and 9 of the Directive under the infringement procedure (art. 258 TFEU).

If the Member State has not even tried to have the judgment enforced, the question is whether it is really proportionate to have the defendant suffer a second trial. One should keep in mind that criminal proceedings require time and money and limit the personal freedom of the defendant considerably. Even if the defendant was absent from the first trial, this does not mean that he or she has not invested time and money in his or her defence. Moreover, the defendant could well have experienced other restrictions on his or her fundamental rights (*e.g.* seizure of assets). In this respect, it would be better from the point of cost-effectiveness and human rights if the Member States consulted each other in order to achieve the enforcement of the first judgment.[169] The CJEU sees the possibility of consultation but does not consider consultations to be as effective as a new trial, particularly because judicial cooperation is dependent on a decision of the Member State.[170] But should not the

---

[166] For an example, see the German *Boere* case, LG Aachen, Strafverteidiger 2010, 237. On the facts, Swoboda (2011), p. 252.

[167] See, also, Swoboda (2011), p. 263. Böse seems to take it for granted that the Member State could grant a new trial, Böse (2011a), p. 510 f.

[168] Similarly Böse (2011a), p. 510 f.

[169] Gaede (2014), p. 2991; Meyer (2014), p. 274 ff.; Weißer (2014), p. 593.

[170] CJEU, *Spasic* (fn. 158), para 69.

Member States be obliged to try for enforcement of the first judgment in order to protect the *ne bis in idem* rights of the defendant?[171] Could not fundamental rights of the defendant limit the Member States' discretion? These are questions that should have been addressed in *Spasic*. Insofar, the judgment leaves a lot to be desired.[172]

Such a solution would also solve the problem of partial enforcement that arose in *Spasic*. If Germany had consulted with Italy in order to get Italy to send the judgment and certificate over to Germany (or, earlier, Austria) for enforcement of the custodial sentence, Mr. Spasic could have given consent to the enforcement of the judgment instead of having to suffer a second trial. In case of refusal of consent and if an Italian EAW was not a solution, a new trial would have been justified. Nonetheless, on the basis of the CJEU's interpretation of the execution condition, it makes sense to demand the full execution of the judgment.[173]

5 Final Remarks

As has been shown, *in absentia* trials have proven to be a severe trial for the still young EU Criminal Law and Criminal Procedure. Many important decisions in the area of EU criminal law and fundamental rights had to do with *in absentia* trials. The decisions by the Spanish and German Constitutional Court on the EAW have shown that *in absentia* trials could also become the crack that brings the wall of mutual recognition down. Therefore, the EU had to come up with solutions on how to deal with this particular form of trial in transborder criminal proceedings.

In the area of judicial cooperation, the EU has chosen to explicitly address the problem in legal instruments. Although the legislation on *in absentia* trials has been criticized for its vagueness, a legal solution opens the way to an interpretation in the light of EU fundamental rights and thus paces the way for arguments based on defendant's rights. The new development of EU human rights doctrine in *Aranyosi and Căldăraru* helps at assuring that individual's rights are respected even in case of *in absentia* trials. This is especially important if one takes into consideration that the EU Directives on defendant's rights shape the EU public order, and therefore a violation of these Directives can easily be claimed before the CJEU. In case of *in absentia* trials, Articles 8 and 9 of Directive 2016/343/EU are particularly important. Therefore, the solution found in the area of judicial cooperation is adequate, albeit not perfect.[174]

---

[171] Meyer (2014), p. 276; Zöller (2016), p. 334 f.

[172] See, in more detail, Meyer (2014), p. 274 ff.

[173] Meyer (2014), p. 278; Weißer (2014), p. 593; Zöller (2016), p. 332.

[174] Most criticism refers to the fact that the EU provisions do not exactly match the jurisprudence of the ECHR, see Bartels (2014), p. 190; Klitsch (2009), p. 17; Wahl (2015), p. 71.

With regard to the *ne bis in idem* principle, the assessment is different. The solution found by the CJEU does not sufficiently take into account the elaborate means of judicial cooperation that exist in the EU. It seems odd that the EU has on the one hand adopted explicit provisions on when execution of a judgment can be refused, on the other hand completely leaves it to the Member States to ask for enforcement. Admittedly, this problem does not only arise in case of *in absentia* trials, but in all cases where Member States refrain from undertaking the execution of their own judgments. Nevertheless, from the point of view of defendant's rights, this is a disappointing result. It must be hoped that the EU will come up with a better solution. Such a solution could be an explicit obligation to try to enforce judgments before a second prosecution is allowed (see Sect. 4).[175] In cases where standards on *in absentia* trials from the EU public order have been breached, second prosecution should not be possible.

Recently, the EU has at least adopted minimum rules on the question of under which circumstances judgments resulting from *in absentia* trials can be enforced. These provisions have the effect that the grounds for refusal in case of *in absentia* trials have become mandatory on 1 April 2018 (see Sect. 3.3.1.2). However, they also state when a judgment cannot be enforced. This could help in shaping the *ne bis in idem* guarantee if the CJEU decided to follow the differentiating approach that is favoured here (which, admittedly, is not likely). In any case, Directive 2016/343/EU will provide new challenges in case of *in absentia* trials and thus initiate further solutions.

References

Albers P, Beauvais P (2013) Procedural aspects and instruments for enhancing mutual trust between Member States. In: Albers P, Beauvais P, Bohnert J-F, Böse M, Langbroek P, Renier A, Wahl T (eds) Towards a common evaluation framework to assess mutual trust in the field of EU judicial cooperation in criminal matters. Ministerie van Veiligheid en Justitie, The Hague, pp 14–30

Bartels S (2014) Die Auslieferung zur Vollstreckung eines Abwesenheitsurteils in Europa. Dr. Kovač, Hamburg

Böhm KM (2017) Aktuelle Entwicklungen im Auslieferungsrecht. Neue Zeitschrift für Strafrecht: 77–84

Böse M (2011a) Die transnationale Geltung des Grundsatzes "ne bis in idem" und das "Vollstreckungselement": Zugleich Besprechung von BGH, Beschluss vom 25.10.2010. Goltdammer's Archiv für Strafrecht 158:504–513

Böse M (2011b) Harmonizing procedural rights indirectly: the framework decision on trials in absentia. N C J Int Law Commercial Regul 37:489–510

Böse M 27th installment (July 2012) In: Grützner H, Pötz PG, Kreß C (eds) Internationaler Rechtshilfeverkehr in Strafsachen, 3rd edn. C.F.Müller, Heidelberg

---

[175] Another solution could be the prevention of conflicts of jurisdiction. See, e.g., the suggestion in Böse et al. (2014), p. 381.

Böse M (2015) Human rights violations and mutual trust: recent case law on the European Arrest Warrant. In: Ruggeri S (ed) Human rights in European criminal law: new developments in European legislation and case law after the Lisbon Treaty. Springer, Cham, pp 135–145

Böse M (2017) Neue Standards für Abwesenheitsverfahren in "Fluchtfällen"? Zu den Auswirkungen der Richtlinie 2016/343/EU auf die Auslieferung und Vollstreckungshilfe in der Europäischen Union. Strafverteidiger 37:754–760

Böse M, Meyer F, Schneider A (2014) Conflicts of jurisdiction in criminal matter in the European Union, Volume II: rights, principles and model rules. Nomos, Baden-Baden

Brodowski D (2016) Die drohende Verletzung von Menschenrechten bei der Anerkennung Europäischer Haftbefehle auf dem Prüfstand: Die zweifelhafte Aktivierung der Verfassungsidentität durch das BVerfG und eine Kurskorrektur in der Rechtsprechung des EuGH. Juristische Rundschau 2016:415–432

Burchard C (2013) § 14 Auslieferung (Europäischer Haftbefehl). In: Böse M (ed) Europäisches Strafrecht. Nomos, Baden-Baden, pp 537–571

Classen CD (2016) Zu wenig, zu fundamentalistisch - zur grundrechtlichen Kontrolle "unionsrechtlich determinierter" nationaler Hoheitsakte: Anmerkung zum Beschluss des BVerfG vom 15.12.2015, 2 BvR 2735/14. Europarecht 51(3):304–313

de Boer N (2013) Addressing rights divergences under the Charter: *Melloni*. Common Mark Law Rev 50:1083–1103

Eckstein K (2012) Grund und Grenzen transnationalen Schutzes vor mehrfacher Strafverfolgung in Europa. Zeitschrift für die gesamte Strafrechtswissenschaft 124:490–527

Eßlinger S, Herzmann K (2016) Die verfassungsgerichtliche Identitätskontrolle und ihre Konkretisierung durch die Entscheidung 2 BvR 2735/14 – "Identitätskontrolle I" als Vorbote von "Solange III"? Juristische Ausbildung 2016:852–864

Gaede K (2013) Minimalistischer EU-Grundrechtsschutz bei der Kooperation im Strafverfahren. Neue Juristische Wochenschrift 18:1279–1282

Gaede K (2014) Transnationales "ne bis in idem" auf schwachem grundrechtlichen Fundament. Neue Juristische Wochenschrift 67:2990–2992

Hauck P (2009) Richterlicher Anpassungsbedarf durch den EU-Rahmenbeschluss zur Anerkennung strafgerichtlicher Entscheidungen in Abwesenheit des Angeklagten? Juristische Rundschau 2009:141–147

Heger M, Wolter K (2015) In: Ambos K, König S, Rackow P (eds) Rechtshilferecht in Strafsachen. Nomos; Facultas; Helbing Lichtenhahn, Baden-Baden, Wien, Basel

Herzmann K (2015) Das spanische Verfassungsgericht und der Fall Melloni: Konsequenzen des EuGH-Urteils aus Sicht seines Adressaten - zugleich Anmerkung zu Tribunal Constitucional de España, STC 26/2014, v. 13.2.2014. Europäische Grundrechte-Zeitschrift:445–453

Hofmann C (2015) § 15 Die Vorwirkung von Richtlinien. In: Riesenhuber K (ed) Europäische Methodenlehre, 3rd edn. C.H. Beck, München, pp 326–346

Hong M (2016) Human dignity, identity review of the European arrest warrant and the Court of Justice as a listener in the dialogue of courts: Solange-III and Aranyosi. Eur Constit Law Rev 12:549–563

JHR/LB (2016) Editorial. Eur Constit Law Rev:213–222

Klitsch S (2009) Der neue EU-Rahmenbeschluss zu Abwesenheitsverurteilungen - ein Appell zur Revision. Zeitschrift für Internationale Strafrechtsdogmatik:11–21

Korenica F, Doli D (2016) No more unconditional "mutual trust" between the Member States: an analysis of the landmark decision of the CJEU in Aranyosi and Caldararu. EHRLR:542–555

Kromrey H, Morgenstern C (2017) Die Menschenwürde und das Auslieferungsverfahren. Zeitschrift für Internationale Strafrechtsdogmatik:106–124

Kühne HH (2016) Auslieferung nach Abwesenheitsverurteilung (Italien) – "Solange III". Strafverteidiger: 299–302

Merkel R, Scheinfeld J (2012) Ne bis in idem in der Europäischen Union - zum Streit um das "Vollstreckungselement". Zeitschrift für Internationale Strafrechtsdogmatik:206–213

Meyer F (2014) Transnationaler ne-bis-in-idem-Schutz nach der GRC Zum Fortbestand des Vollstreckungselements aus Sicht des EuGH: zugleich Besprechung zu EuGH HRRS 2014 Nr. 484. Höchstrichterliche Rechtsprechung in Strafsachen: 269–278

Meyer F (2016) Das BVerfG und der Europäische Haftbefehl – ein Gericht auf Identitätssuche. Höchstrichterliche Rechtsprechung in Strafsachen:332–340

Mitsilegas V (2006) The constitutional implications of mutual recognition in criminal matters in the EU. Common Mark Law Rev 43:1277–1311

Netzer F (2009) Krimi, Tragödie und Lehrbuch-Klassiker - der Fall Krombach. Zeitschrift für Internationale Strafrechtsdogmatik:752–758

O'Leary S (2016) Courts, charters and conventions: making sense of fundamental rights in the EU. Irish Jurist 56:4–41

Paul C (2007) Das Abwesenheitsverfahren als rechtsstaatliches Problem. Peter Lang, Frankfurt a.M

Reinbacher T, Wendel M (2016) Menschenwürde und Europäischer Haftbefehl - Zum ebenenübergreifenden Schutz grundrechtlicher Elementargarantien im europäischen Auslieferungsverfahren. Europäische Grundrechte-Zeitschrift:333–343

Rönnau T, Wegner K (2013) Grund und Grenzen der Einwirkung des europäischen Rechts auf das nationale Strafrecht: ein Überblick unter Einbeziehung aktueller Entwicklungen. Goltdammer's Archiv für Strafrecht:561–582

Ruggeri S (2016) Right to personal participation in criminal proceedings and in absentia procedures in the EU area of freedom, security and justice. Zeitschrift für die gesamte Strafrechtswissenschaft 128:578–605

Rung J (2016) Grundrechtsschutz zwischen Verfassungsidentität und der Melloni-Rechtsprechung des EuGH: Besprechung von BVerfG, 15.12.2015 - 2 BvR 2735/14. Europäisches Wirtschafts- und Steuerrecht:145–150

Safferling C (2011) Internationales Strafrecht. Springer, Cham

Safferling C (2014) Der EuGH, die Grundrechtecharta und nationales Recht: Die Fälle Åkerberg Fransson und Melloni. Neue Zeitschrift für Strafrecht:545–551

Satzger H (2016a) Grund- und menschenrechtliche Grenzen für die Vollstreckung eines europäischen Haftbefehls? "Verfassungsgerichtliche Identitätskontrolle" durch das BVerfG vs. Vollstreckungsaufschub bei "außergewöhnlichen Umständen" nach dem EuGH. Neue Zeitschrift für Strafrecht 36:514–522

Satzger H (2016b) Internationales und Europäisches Strafrecht, 7th edn. Nomos, Baden-Baden

Schallmoser N (2012) Europäischer Haftbefehl und Grundrechte: Risiken der Verletzung von Grundrechten durch den EU-Rahmenbeschluss im Licht der EMRK. Manz, Wien

Schneider A 37th installment (December 2014) In: Grützner H, Pötz PG, Kreß C (eds) Internationaler Rechtshilfeverkehr in Strafsachen, 3rd edn. C.F.Müller, Heidelberg

Schneider A 40th installment (December 2016) In: Grützner H, Pötz PG, Kreß C (eds) Internationaler Rechtshilfeverkehr in Strafsachen, 3rd edn. C.F.Müller, Heidelberg

Schomburg W, Suominen-Picht I (2012) Verbot der mehrfachen Strafverfolgung, Kompetenzkonflikte und Verfahrenstransfer. Neue Juristische Wochenschrift 65:1190–1194

Swoboda S (2011) Paying the debts - late Nazi trials before German courts: the case of Heinrich Boere. J Int Crim Just 9:243–269

Torres Pérez A (2014) Melloni in three acts: from dialogue to monologue. Eur Constit Law Rev 10:308–331

von Heintschel-Heinegg B (2014) § 37 Europäischer Haftbefehl. In: Sieber U, Satzger H, von Heintschel-Heinegg B (eds) Europäisches Strafrecht, 2nd edn. Nomos, Baden-Baden, pp 661–676

Wahl T (2015) Der Rahmenbeschluss zu Abwesenheitsentscheidungen: Brüsseler EU-Justizkooperation als Fall für Straßburg? Eucrim:70–76

Wasmeier M (2014) § 32 Von der herkömmlichen Rechtshilfe zur gegenseitigen Anerkennung - Entwicklungslinien der strafrechtlichen Zusammenarbeit. In: Sieber U, Satzger H, von

Heintschel-Heinegg B (eds) Europäisches Strafrecht, 2nd edn. Nomos, Baden-Baden, pp 569–591

Weißer B (2014) Anmerkung zu EuGH (Große Kammer), Urt. v. 27.5.2014 - C-129/14 PPU. Zeitschrift für das Juristische Studium:589–594

Zöller MA (2016) Das transnationale europäische Doppelbestrafungsverbot - Luxemburgum locutum, causa finita? Goltdammer's Archiv für Strafrecht 163(5):325–335

New Developments in EU Law in the Field of *In Absentia* National Proceedings. The Directive 2016/343/EU in the Light of the ECtHR Case Law

Lorena Bachmaier Winter

Abstract This study analyses the rules for trials *in absentia* included in the Directive 2016/343 with the aim of assessing their impact in the protection of fundamental rights in criminal proceedings in the European Union. The aim is further to check if the requirements defined by the Strasbourg Court—included in the FD EAW and in this Directive—provide sufficient safeguards for the defence rights in trials *in absentia*. This seems to be the consensus at the EU level and up to now the European Court of Justice has seen no necessity to go beyond those minimum requirements. However, the risks of trials *in absentia* cannot be underestimated and therefore it should be examined whether the EU should not have aimed at establishing a higher standard than the one set out by Strasbourg.

Abbreviations

AFSJ	Area of Freedom, Security and Justice
CJEU	European Court of Justice
DEIO	Directive on a European Investigation Order
DPIRPT	Directive on certain aspects on the presumption of innocence and the right to be present at trial in criminal proceedings
ECHR	European Convention Human Rights
ECtHR	European Court of Human Rights
EU	European Union
FD EAW	Framework Decision on the European Arrest Warrant

L. Bachmaier Winter (✉)
Faculty of Law, University Complutense Madrid, Madrid, Spain
e-mail: L.Bachmaier@der.ucm.es

© Springer Nature Switzerland AG 2019
S. Quattrocolo, S. Ruggeri (eds.), *Personal Participation in Criminal Proceedings*, Legal Studies in International, European and Comparative Criminal Law 2, https://doi.org/10.1007/978-3-030-01186-4_20

641

1   Introduction

In 1995 Jean Pradel[1] already stated that legal opinion conventionally distinguishes between common law systems, where it is assumed that judgments *in absentia* are not possible, and European continental civil law systems,[2] where they are. However, this distinction is somewhat artificial. First because under common law systems trials *in absentia* are exceptionally allowed, and this exception is very similar to the requirement to authorize them in EU continental civil law systems, namely: if the defendant having been personally summoned willingly fails to appear at trial or absconds.

On the other hand, in EU continental civil law systems, although convictions *in absentia* of the defendant are generally possible, many countries have traditionally limited the enforcement of the judgment, so that the convicted could not be serving sentence until the new trial or review proceedings had taken place.[3] Other legal systems, even allowing trials *in absentia* to be held, they considerably limit their scope, as in Germany where a trial without the defendant's presence can only take place if the penalty does not entail deprivation of liberty (Article 232 StPO); or Spain, where these type of trials are possible only if the defendant's presence is not deemed necessary by the judge, the defendant's lawyer is present, and the maximum penalty provided for the offence is not higher than 2 years imprisonment, which in practice entails an automatic suspension of its enforcement (Article 786 LECRIM). In general, in most EU countries, judgments *in absentia* are possible, and regarding petty offences they are long ago not an oddity. However, the rules on trials *in absentia* are far from being harmonized at the EU level.

More than two years have passed since the Directive (EU) 2016/343 on the strengthening of certain aspects of the presumption of innocence and of the right to be present at the trial in criminal proceedings, of 9 March 2016 was adopted.[4] This Directive seeks to continue advancing in the establishment of a single Area of freedom, security, and justice with an adequate protection of the fundamental rights of suspects and defendants in criminal matters. Although regulating the presumption of innocence and introducing further rules for the harmonization of the *in absentia*

---

[1] Pradel (1995), pp. 525–526. A very interesting comparative analysis can be seen in Paul (2007), tracing a comparison between the criminal trials in absentia in Germany, the England, France, The Netherlands and Austria.

[2] Jean Pradel uses the expression "Romano-Germanic legal systems", which is equivalent to the one used here as "European-continental civil tradition".

[3] This is why the European Convention on the International Validity of Criminal Judgments of 1970 intended to ensure that the penalty imposed in one State could be enforced in another State. See European Convention on the International Validity of Criminal Judgments, European Treaty Series No. 70, The Hague 28 May 1970.

[4] OJ L65, 11 March 2016. The time limit for transposition of this Directive is 1 April 2018 (Art. 14 DPIRPT).

national criminal proceedings was not foreseen in the Roadmap approved in 2009,[5] later there was agreement that some action should be taken in particular with regard to the right to be presumed innocent.[6] Some difficulties in the implementation of the Framework Decision on the European Arrest Warrant, which became specially visible in the *Melloni* case,[7] also led the EU institutions to adopt the Framework Decision 2009/299,[8] thus providing a clear legal framework on trials *in absentia* and its impact in the refusal of EAW. Practice on the EAW made clear that for a better international cooperation more harmonization and equivalent minimum standards in ensuring the right to be present at trial and have a new trial or the judgment reviewed in the national proceedings should be fostered.

This study will analyse the rules for trials *in absentia* included in the Directive 2016/343 in order to assess their impact in the protection of fundamental rights in criminal proceedings in the European Union. My aim is further to analyse if the requirements defined by the Strasbourg Court—included in the FD EAW and in the Directive—really constitute a sufficient safeguard for the defence rights in trials *in absentia*. This seems to be the consensus the Member States have expressed when they put forward the reform of the EAW FD in 2009[9] and also when approving the EU Directive 2016/343 with 25 Member States voting in favour.[10] On the other hand the CJEU has seen no necessity to go beyond those minimum requirements.[11] However, the risks of trials *in absentia* cannot be underestimated and therefore it should be examined whether the EU should not have aimed at establishing a higher standard than the one set out by Strasbourg.

To that end, the case law of the ECtHR in this regard will be studied, although only in so far it is necessary to assess the development of the EU law in this field and

---

[5] Council Resolution on a Roadmap for strengthening the procedural rights of suspected and accused persons in criminal proceedings, OJ C 295, 4 December 2009.

[6] On 11 December 2009 the European Council made the Roadmap part of the Stockholm programme "An open and secure Europe serving and protecting citizens", OJ C 115, 4.5.2010, and a specific mention to the presumption of innocence was included. A proposal for a Directive on the presumption of innocence was presented the 27 November 2013 (COM(2013) 821. On the long way until the adoption of this Directive, see the detailed description of the steps taken and the difficulties encountered in the negotiations in Cras and Erbeznik (2016), pp. 25–27. On the text of the proposal of the Directive and the amendments introduced thereof see also Ruggeri (2017), pp. 373–374.

[7] On the Melloni case, see, for example, Bachmaier Winter (2015), pp. 153 ff.; and Bachmaier Winter (2016), pp. 160 ff.; Böse (2015), pp. 139–142.

[8] Council Framework Decision 2009/299/JHA of 26 February 2009, amending the Framework Decisions 2002/584/JHA, 2005/214/JHA, 2008/909/JHA and 2008/947/JHA, thereby enhancing the procedural rights and fostering application of the principle of mutual recognition to decisions rendered in the absence of the person concerned at the trial, OJ L 81/24, 27 March 2009. On the Framework Decision 2009/299/JHA see Wahl (2015), pp. 71 ff.

[9] See Tinsley (2012), p. 27.

[10] Cras and Erbeznik (2016), p. 34.

[11] Vervaele (2012), pp. 48 and 52; Martín Rodríguez (2013), p. 33.

the Directive 2016/343.[12] Secondly the precise wording of the Directive will be analysed to check in how far it departs or confirms the Strasbourg approach in ensuring the rights of defendants in trials *in absentia*. The differences between the rules on trials *in absentia* provided within the ambit of the international judicial cooperation and the execution of EAW and those provided in the Directive and the possible impact from the latter upon the former, will only be mentioned when needed within the scope of this study. A closer analysis on these issues is carried out in another Chapter of this volume.[13]

Finally it will be assessed whether the Directive has just followed the long established principles set out in the Strasbourg case-law, in which case the added value would only be found in the legal instruments to ensure the compliance with such rules, namely through the action of the EU Commission and the competence of the European Court of Justice.

The very interesting issues related to the proceedings *inaudito reo*, closely connected to the trials *in absentia*, will not be discussed here, as these types of proceedings are expressly excluded from the scope of application of the Directive [Article 8(6) and Recital 41 DPIRPT].[14] The temporary exclusion of the defendant from the trial will neither be dealt here, mainly because the Directive does not set any rules on them.[15]

2 Trials *In Absentia* in the ECtHR Case Law

2.1 The Right to Be Present at One's Trial and Judgments In Absentia

The right to be present at one's own trial is a fundamental right recognized expressly in Article 14(3)(d) of the United Nations International Covenant on Civil and Political Rights,[16] in contrast to the ECHR that does not identify expressly the right to be present at one's trial. However, this does not mean that this right is not protected under the ECHR.[17]

---

[12] For an analysis of ECtHR case law see Ruggeri, in Part V of this volume.

[13] See Schneider, in this volume.

[14] For a comprehensive analysis on these proceedings with an interesting comparative law approach, see Ruggeri (2017), p. 59 ff. and also Ruggeri (2016b), pp. 42 ff. Cf. also Ruggeri, in Part V of this volume, Sect. 3.2.

[15] See Article 8(5) DPIRPT, stating that the rules of Article 8 shall apply without prejudice to national rules on trials where the defendant is kept out of the court room when this is necessary for securing "the proper conduct of the criminal proceedings".

[16] ICCPR, Article 14.3: "In the determination of any criminal charge against him, everyone shall be entitled to the following minimum guarantees, in full equality: (d) To be tried in his presence, and to defend himself in person or through legal assistance of his own choosing; (…)".

[17] See generally Kostoris (2017), pp. 155–158.

Although it is not mentioned explicitly under Article 6(1) ECHR, compliance with the fair trial rights implicitly require that the right to be present is guaranteed. This has been the view taken by the ECtHR case-law, precisely in the *Colozza* case: although the right to be present "is not expressly mentioned in paragraph 1 of Article 6, the object and purpose of the Article taken as a whole show that the person charged with a criminal offence is entitled to take part in the hearing".[18] Moreover, sub-paragraphs (c), (d), and (e) of paragraph 3 guarantee "the right to everyone charged with a criminal offence the right to defend himself in person, to examine or have examined witnesses and to have free assistance of an interpreter (...) and it is difficult to see how he could exercise there rights without being present".[19]

The right to be present at one's own trial is of capital importance for the interests of a fair and just criminal process and the duty to guarantee the right of a criminal defendant to be present at one's own trial—either during the original proceedings or in the retrial—ranks as one of the essential requirements of Article 6 ECHR.[20] The personal attendance of the defendant does not take on the same crucial significance for an appeal hearing as it does for the trial hearing and it depends on the special features of the proceedings involved.[21] But even where the court of appeal has jurisdiction to review the case both as to facts and as to law, Article 6 does not always require a right to a public hearing, still less a right to appear in person.[22] However, when such hearing is foreseen and the defendant can challenge the conviction and present evidence before the appellate court, depriving him from the right to be present at such a hearing, amounts to a violation of the Convention.[23]

As to the meaning of a judgment rendered *in absentia*, within this study it will be considered as any judgment rendered by a court after criminal proceedings at the hearing of which the sentenced person was not personally present. The Directive further reduces the scope of application to the trial where the decision on guilt or innocence is to be taken [Article 8(2) DPIRPT].

---

[18] On the need for a systematic approach to the right to personal participation in criminal proceedings see Ruggeri, in Part V of this volume, Sect. 2.1.

[19] ECtHR, *Colozza v. Italy*, judgment of 12 February 1985, Appl. No. 9024/80, para 27. See also ECtHR, *Lala v. The Netherlands*, judgment of 22 September 1994, Appl. No. 14861/89, para 33; *Poitrimol v. France*, judgment of 23 November 1993, Appl. No. 14032/88, para 35; *Zana v. Turkey*, judgment of 25 November 1997, Appl. No. 18954/91, para 68; *De Lorenzo v. Italy*, judgment of 12 February 2004, Appl. No. 69264/01; *T. v. Italy*, judgment of 12 October 1992, Appl. No. 14104/88, para 26; *F.C.B. v. Italy*, judgment of 28 August 1991, Appl. No. 12151/86, para 33.

[20] ECtHR, *Stoichkov v. Bulgaria*, judgment of 24 March 2005, Appl. No. 9808/02, para 56.

[21] ECtHR, *Helmers v. Sweden,* judgment of 29 October 1991, Appl. No. 11826/85, paras 31–32; *Hermi v. Italy*, judgment of 18 October 2006, Appl. No. 18114/02, para 60. See Mangiaracina (2010), pp. 30 ff.; Paul (2007), pp. 222–238. On this topic see also Ruggeri, in Part V of this volume, Sect. 2.3.

[22] ECtHR, *Hermi v. Italy* (fn. 21), para 62.

[23] ECtHR, *Belziuk v. Poland,* judgment of 25 March 1998, Appl. No. 23103/93, a case of an attempted car theft where the defendant was present at first instance and convicted to 3 years imprisonment, but was deprived of his right to be present at the appellate hearing.

Judgments *in absentia* are allowed because of the difficulties—if not impossibility—it entails in many cases to bring the defendant in front of the court, precisely when he evades the action of justice. But this happens also when the whereabouts or the residence of the accused are unknown and after efforts remain unknown. If such presence cannot be granted, after taking all legal measures to ensure it, many legal systems allow trying a person without his presence. Of course, it can be presumed that, if the defendant was duly summoned of the criminal complaint, knowing the date and hour of the trial and the consequences of not appearing, his absence to appear is willing. However this presumption is *iuris tantum*, because despite a correct summons for trial, the accused might not have received it, may have not understood the content and consequences or, despite having knowledge and understanding, was impeded to appear at court and inform thereof.[24] On the willingness of the waiver to be present at trial, will be discussed in more detail below.

This is why special safeguards are to be put in place to ensure that judgments *in absentia* do not infringe upon the fundamental principle of the right to be present, the right to be heard and the right of defence. The safeguards, additionally to the rules on the summons and serving process, are to be provided by ways of remedies: once the defendant appears or is found, he has to be given enough opportunity to explain the reasons of his non appearance; and in case these are justified, he has to be heard and has to be given teh opportunity to present evidence, either by way of an ordinary remedy, if the appeal provides for such possibility, or by granting the right to a new trial.

These remedies will apply in those cases where the summons where done correctly, and nevertheless they were not effective or another reason hindered the defendant's appearance at trial. If the summons were not served according to the law, and such infringement was not cured by the knowledge of the defendant, such judgment should be declared void: in these cases an appeal or a new trial should not be enough remedy for a breach of the right to be present at trial and be heard.

The right to set aside or review a judgment *in absentia* will not be effective if the information on the existence of such sentence does not reach the convicted person. Special provisions are to be included as to the way to notify the person on the judgment, the timeframe to challenge such judgment and finally, the scope of the remedy.

If the judgment rendered *in absentia* has been confirmed or pronounced after opposition by the person sentenced (review on the merits and/or re-trial of the case), or after the convicted defendant has been served with the judgment and confirmed his intention not to oppose to it, the final sentence is not considered anymore *in absentia*. This means, no further extraordinary remedies are to be provided, because such judgment is not based anymore on a presumption that the right to be heard has been respected, but actual proof that the defendant has really had knowledge of the proceedings and has been provided with adequate opportunities to defend himself.

---

[24] In the same sense Wahl (2015), p. 73.

And no further safeguards or reservations regarding the enforcement of the conviction sentence should apply.

In short, if a decision has been rendered in full observation of the fundamental principles of the European Convention of Human Rights, in particular, Article 6 ECHR, the fact that the judgment was rendered *in absentia* should not preclude its enforcement.

The CoE Resolution (75)11 of 21 May 1975[25] already included recommendations to the Member States of the Council of Europe regarding the criminal proceedings held in the absence of the defendant. This text underlined that the presence of the

> accused at his trial is of vital importance from the point of view both of his right to be heard and of the need to establish the facts and, if need be, pass the appropriate sentence; whereas exemptions should be granted only in exceptional cases (Recital 2 and recommendation 3).

But it also stated that "the systems adopted by several Member States to avoid judgments in the absence of the accused and their consequences do not always appear to be effective when, for example, the accused is resident abroad" (Recital 5). The 9 recommendations included in this text are still completely appropriate: they point out the way any defendant should be summoned; the information on the consequences of his non-appearance; the differentiation between the person who has been properly served with the summons and those who where not served properly, establishing for the latter a remedy to get the sentence annulled. Finally, it also mentions specifically the cases where the right to re-trial should be granted, specifically under recommendation 9:

> A person tried in his absence, but on whom a summons has been properly served is entitled to a retrial, in the ordinary way, if that person can prove that his absence and the fact that he could not inform the judge thereof were due to reasons beyond his control.

2.2 The Waiver of the Right to Be Present at Trial

The Strasbourg Court has repeatedly stated that it is of capital importance that a defendant should appear at trial, both because of his right to a hearing and because of the need to verify the accuracy of his statements and compare them with those of the victim and of the witnesses, and the States should legislate in such a way that unjustified absences are discouraged.[26] However the Court has also said that this

---

[25] Council of Europe Resolution (75)11, *On the criteria governing proceedings held in the absence of the accused*, adopted by the Committee of Ministers on 21 May 1975 at the 245th meeting of the Ministers' Deputies.

[26] See ECtHR, judgment of 14 June 2001, *Medenica v Switzerland*, Appl. No. 20491/92, para 54; *Poitrimol v. France* (fn. 19), § 35; *Krombach v. France*, judgment of 13 February 2001, Appl. No. 29731/96. On the conditions of waiver under the European Convention, as well as on the duty of participation, see also Ruggeri, in Part V of this volume, Sect. 2.2.

right is not absolute and that the defendant can waive this right. In *Kwiatkowska v. Italy* the Court expressly held that

> neither the letter nor the spirit of Article 6 of the Convention prevents a person from waiving of his own free will, either expressly or tacitly, the entitlement to the guarantees of a fair trial.[27]

However, such a waiver has to be unequivocal and voluntary[28] and before an accused can be said to have implicitly, through his conduct, waived an important right under Article 6 of the Convention it must be shown that he could reasonably have foreseen what the consequences of his conduct would be.[29]

Indeed recognising the unequivocal and willing character of such waiver, when it is made in an express form, usually should not pose any difficulties. Nevertheless in practice in the criminal proceedings it is at odds that the defendant appears before the court to manifest his will to waive the right to be present at the hearing.[30] Most often the waiver is deduced from facts that reasonably show a will of the defendant to stay away from the trial.

This may be the case, for example, where the accused states publicly or in writing that he does not intend to respond to summonses of which he has become aware through sources other than the authorities, or succeeds in evading an attempted arrest,[31] or when materials are brought to the attention of the authorities which unequivocally show that he is aware of the proceedings pending against him and of the charges he faces.[32]

It is for the procedural rules to define which are those circumstances that allow presuming that the absence of the defendant can be interpreted as a waiver of his right to be present at trial. Usually if the defendant has been summoned personally and informed of the date of the trial and the consequences of his absence, his non-appearance can be interpreted as a waiver of his right. However, the non-attendance by itself is not a waiver.

But the Court has also held that where a person charged with a criminal offence has not been notified in person, it cannot be inferred merely from the fact that he has been declared a fugitive—relying on a presumption with an insufficient factual basis—, that he has waived his right to appear at the trial and defend himself.[33] Even

---

[27] ECtHR, *Kwiatkowska v. Italy*, judgment of 30 November 2000, Appl. No. 52868/99.

[28] See also ECtHR, *Colozza v. Italy* (fn. 19), para 28; *Poitrimol v. France* (fn. 19); *Zana v Turkey* (fn. 19), para 70.

[29] ECtHR, *Jones v. the United Kingdom*, judgment of 9 September 2003, Appl. No. 30900/02.

[30] One of such cases where the defendant had clearly expressed his will not to attend to the trial and wished to be tried *in absentia*, was the *Poitrimol v France* case.

[31] See, among others, ECtHR, *Iavarazzo v Italy*, judgment of 4 December 2001, Appl. No. 50489/99.

[32] In *T v. Italy* of 12 October 1992, Appl. No. 14104/88, it was proved by way of a letter sent to his wife, that the defendant had been aware of the proceedings, but nevertheless this was not considered to amount to an unequivocal waiver of the right to be present.

[33] ECtHR, *Colozza v. Italy* (fn. 19), para 28; *Sejdovic v. Italy*, Grand Chamber, judgment of 1 March 2006, Appl. No. 56581/00, para 58: "An applicant who had never been officially informed of the

more, such person shall not be left with the burden of proving that he was not seeking to evade justice. As the Strasbourg Court pointed out in *Somogyi v. Italy*, "Article 6 of the Convention imposes on every national court an obligation to check whether the defendant has had the opportunity to apprise himself of the proceedings against him"[34] and in particular where this is disputed on a ground that does not immediately appear to be manifestly devoid of merit.

In *Somogyi v. Italy*, an arms trafficking case where a Hungarian citizen was sentenced *in absentia* to 8 years imprisonment by an Italian court, the applicant contested that he had not been given the opportunity to reopen the case and set aside the judgment rendered in his absence. In this case Mr. Somogyi had been given notice of the trial by post sent to his address in Hungary. Upon receiving the reply slip acknowledging receipt of the notice, the Rimini District Court proceeded to trial *in absentia* and to appoint a lawyer for the defendant. The applicant alleged that the signature in the postal receipt slip was not his, that the name on it was not correct and that the address was mistaken. None of these allegations were considered to set aside the sentence by the Italian courts. The Strasbourg Court, however, ruled in favour of the applicant stating that such allegation was not *prima facie* without foundation (§ 70), and thus the waiver of the right to be present had not been unequivocally established. Therefore, not giving the defendant the chance to reopen the case had caused a violation of Article 6(1) ECHR.

In *Stoichkov v. Bulgaria*,[35] where the defendant had a broad previous criminal record, and was accused in 1988 of rape, the court found that the criminal proceedings against the applicant—which were conducted in absentia and the reopening of which was refused in 2001—to have been "manifestly contrary to the provisions of Article 6 or the principles embodied therein" (§ 53). The defendant, despite having been represented by a court-appointed lawyer, had never been notified of the proceedings. The Court analysed whether the requirement of Article 6 ECHR to ensure the right of the accused to be present during the proceedings against him is so basic as to render proceedings conducted *in absentia* where the reopening has been refused, a "flagrant denial of justice".

This judgment is very interesting, because once recognised that such conviction *in absentia* amounted to a flagrant denial of justice, it also stated that this would "unavoidably lead to the conclusion that the applicant's ensuing deprivation of liberty to serve the sentence imposed in these proceedings cannot be considered justified under Article 5. 1 (a) ECHR". In this case, the Court also found a violation of Article 5 of the Convention derived from the breach of Article 6 of the trial *in absentia*.

---

proceedings against him, could not be said to have unequivocally waived his right to appear at his trial". And the possibility to have a re-trial only upon showing that he was wrongly deemed fugitive, was considered by the Strasbourg Court as not providing enough guarantees. This was an extradition case, where the applicant was accused of murder in Italy, was declared fugitive and later was detained in Hamburg.

[34] ECtHR, *Somogyi v. Italy*, judgment of 18 May 2004, Appl. No. 67972/01, para 72.

[35] ECtHR, *Stoichkov v. Bulgaria* (fn. 20), Appl. No. 9808/02.

2.3 Absence of the Defendant and Legal Assistance at Trial

The waiver of the right to be present at trial is the first requisite that has to be complied to try a defendant in his absence. If there are no facts that allow inferring that the defendant has waived such right, the trial should not take place. Once this can be established—in an unequivocal way—the absence of the defendant should not lead to a lack of defence. This is why it is required that his defence is taken over by a defence lawyer and the Court has repeatedly found violation of Article 6(1) ECHR where the absent defendant had been denied the assistance or representation of a lawyer.[36] Following recommendation 5 of the CoE Resolution (75)11: "Where the accused is tried in his absence, evidence must be taken in the usual manner and the defence must have the right to intervene".

If the defendant is not present, but knowing the date and hour for the trial, has appointed lawyer of his own choice, it is deemed that he knows about the trial—and thus the presumption of the waiver could be established—, and it also can be presumed that he is adequately defended against the accusation.

This was the case in *Medenica v Switzerland*,[37] a doctor practising in Switzerland who was accused of fraud, intimidation and forging documents, causing the Yugoslavian welfare institutions substantial losses. After being released on bail, he moves to the USA where he continues working as an oncologist. The defendant did not appear at trial in Switzerland, alleging a restraining order from the USA that he could not leave the country, because otherwise his patients would remain without doctoral treatment. His two lawyers defended him at trial. He was convicted to 4 years imprisonment, plus exclusion from Swiss territory for 10 years. After conviction the defendant sought to set aside the sentence *in absentia*, but the appeals were dismissed by the national courts.

The Strasbourg Court in this judgment stressed that, as far as the defendant had been summoned and was assisted by lawyers of his own choosing

---

[36] ECtHR, *Poitrimol v. France* (fn. 19), paras 32–38; *Lala v. Netherlands* (fn. 19), paras 30–34; *Pelladoah v. The Netherlands*, judgment of 22 September 1994, Appl. No. 16737/90, paras 37–41, this one concerning a criminal appeal by way of re-hearing, where the defendant's lawyer was not allowed to intervene; *Van Geyseghem v. Belgium*, judgment of 21 January 1999, Appl. No. 26103/95, paras 33–35: this case dealing with the right to be represented by lawyer in the absence of the defendant during appellate proceedings. The case is of particular interest, because the defendant had properly served at first instance, but did not appear and was convicted in absentia. She moved to set aside the judgment and was tried again. During the appellate proceedings against this second conviction, albeit having been served, she did not appear, but was represented by counsel. The counsel was not allowed to make submissions regarding the time-barred prosecution. Not allowing the defence counsel to act was found a violation of the fair trial rights under Article 6 ECHR. The Court further considers that the conduct of the defendant in the case did not amount to abuse of process. See also ECtHR, *Krombach v. France* (fn. 26), paras 83–90.

[37] ECtHR, *Medenica v. Switzerland* (fn. 26).

regard being had to the margin of appreciation allowed to the Swiss authorities, the applicant's conviction in absentia and the refusal to grant him a retrial at which he would be present did not amount to a disproportionate penalty.[38]

The Court considered that the grounds given to refuse the setting aside of the sentence rendered *in absentia* were not arbitrary, and that the defendant had not proved that the reasons for his non-appearance where sufficiently justified. The Court in this case found no violation of Article 6(1) ECHR. The *Medenica* judgment is relevant because it shows that the right to have the sentence *in absentia* set aside and be granted a re-trial is not an absolute right, but only a remedy if the absence was unwilling or justified—no waiver principle determined—and the defendant was not represented adequately at trial. Consequently, if defence rights were effectively ensured during trial, despite the personal absence of the defendant, the Court has found no violation of the fair trial rights, even if the re-opening of the case to set aside the conviction sentence is denied. In such case, if the defendant does not prove that there were reasons beyond his control to appear in court, the right to a new trial can be denied.

However, it should already be noted that the fact that the Court in *Medenica* did not find a breach of Article 6 of the Convention, because of the specific circumstances of the case, cannot be interpreted *sensu contrario*: that a new trial is not to be granted in those cases where the defendant knew about the trial and was represented by lawyers of own choice. It shall be checked later how has the EU law dealt with these elements.

In *Stoichkov v. Bulgaria*,[39] the trial was also held *in absentia* and the convicted defendant had been represented by a duty lawyer. This case differs from the previous one in that the defendant had never been summoned, and thus the willingness of the waiver of the right to be present cannot be fully deduced. Apart from it, the defence had been taken over by a duty lawyer, and not of own choice.

In *F.C.B. v. Italy*,[40] a murder case, where the defendant had not been duly notified to be present at the appeal hearing, and was sentenced to 24 years imprisonment, although being represented by lawyer, the Court held that the waiver of his right to be present at trial had not been unequivocal. The circumstances were the following: the family was notified and the lawyer was notified, so the Italian courts draw the conclusion that the waiver to be present before the Milan Court of Appeal was willing. However, seeking to set aside the sentence, the defendant stated that he had been in solitary confinement in a prison in The Netherlands and had not been aware of the date of the hearing. The Court held in this case that

> The applicant's conduct may give rise to certain doubts but the consequences which the
> Italian judicial authorities attributed to it are (...) manifestly disproportionate, having

---

[38] *Ibid.*, para 59.
[39] ECtHR, *Stoichkov v. Bulgaria* (fn. 20).
[40] ECtHR, *F.C.B. v. Italy* (fn. 17).

regard to the prominent place which the right to a fair trial holds in a democratic society within the meaning of the Convention.[41]

As it was not fully established that the defendant had been summoned, the Court found in this case violation of Article 6(1) and 6(3)(c) ECHR.

Four elements are to be considered to ensure that trials *in absentia* do not violate Article 6 ECHR: the summons to trial upon the defendant (or eventually to appellate proceedings hearing); the appointment of lawyer; the effective defence carried out by the defence lawyer; and the absence of good cause for the non-appearance of the defendant at his own trial. However it is uncertain if the Strasbourg Court when assessing the violation of the right to be present—taking together Article 6(1) and 6(3) ECHR—uses the counterbalancing technique or rather the defect-curing argumentation.[42] Whatever the possible incoherencies in the reasoning techniques there might be, it is true that the Strasbourg Court has established a consistent protection of the rights of defendants to be present at trial, with almost all of the judgments decided in favour of the applicant.[43]

2.4 Right to Have the Case Re-opened and Sentence In Absentia *Set Aside*

Although proceedings that take place in the accused's absence are not in themselves incompatible with Article 6 of the Convention, a denial of justice nevertheless undoubtedly occurs where a person convicted *in absentia* is unable subsequently to obtain from a court which has heard him a fresh determination of the merits of the charge, in respect of both law and fact, where it has not been established that he has waived his right to appear and to defend himself or that he intended to escape trial.[44] The Convention leaves the Member States broad discretion as regards the choice of the legal means to ensure compliance with the requirements of Article 6 ECHR, as it is not the role of the Court to define legislative measures but to determine whether such national mechanism are adequate to achieve the result called for by the Convention. In particular, the procedural means offered by domestic law and practice must be shown to be effective where a person charged with a criminal offence has neither waived his right to appear and to defend himself nor sought to escape trial.[45] Thus, it is up to the national laws to chose the proceedings to grant the re-

---

[41] *Ibid.*, para 35.

[42] On the patterns of reasoning used by the Court when assessing the infringements of Article 6 and determining the fairness of the proceedings, see critically Goss (2014), pp. 139–160.

[43] Most of the judgments analysed here indeed find in favour of the applicant tried *in absentia*, exception made of the case *Medenica*. In this sense, see also Paul (2007), p. 294.

[44] See ECtHR, *Colozza v Italy* (fn. 19), § 29; *Krombach v. France* (fn. 26), § 85; *Somogyi v. Italy* (fn. 34). See also Ruggeri, in part V of this volume, Sect. 3.1.1.

[45] ECtHR, *Stoichkov v. Bulgaria* (fn. 20).

hearing of the case: either provide for a new trial, a specific review of the trial with a re-hearing and possibility for a fresh determination of the facts, or an ordinary appellate procedure but not limited to a *revisio prior instantiae*. The ECtHR case law does not impose a specific procedural mechanism to be adopted by the Member States, as long as new evidence and a fresh assessment of the facts and the legal issues is ensured.

The Court has further held that a denial of justice occurs when a person convicted *in absentia*, where it has not been unequivocally established that he has waived his right to appear and to defend himself, is not granted subsequently the possibility to present his case before the court and have a fresh determination of the merits of the charge, in respect of both law and fact. This conclusion is in line with the established case law confirming that the right of an accused to participate in person in the proceedings is a fundamental element of a fair trial.

The Court has also held that the re-opening of the time allowed for appealing against a conviction *in absentia*, where the defendant was entitled to attend the hearing in the court of appeal and to request the admission of new evidence, entailed the possibility of a fresh factual and legal determination of the criminal charge, so that the proceedings as a whole could be said to have been fair.[46] This explains also why a new trial is not always required to counterbalance the unwilling absence of the defendant: when the defendant was deprived of his right to be present during the appellate hearing, a new trial might not be necessary to cure such infringement, but the reopening of the time to file the appeal might be enough.

3 The Scope of Application of the Directive 2016/343

According to Article 2 of the Directive 2016/343 it only applies to "suspects or accused persons in criminal proceedings". This provision is completely clear and only applies to trials "which can result in a decision on the guilt or innocence of a suspect or accused person" [Article 8(2) DPIRPT]. It is unclear if the right to be present is focused on the court main hearing—trial in English—or it extends to other stages of the proceedings, due to the diverse concepts used in the different languages of the Directive: in fact, *Hauptverhandlung* or trial is not the same as *processo* or *juicio*. Although I share the view that the wording is unclear, I am inclined to consider that the Directive is addressing mainly the right to be present at the trial in the sense of *Hauptverhandlung*, not aiming to ensure directly participatory rights in all hearings held during the pre-trial stage, but only at those stages of the proceedings where a decision on guilt is to be taken.[47]

---

[46] ECtHR, *Jones v. the United Kingdom*, decision of 9 September 2003, Appl. No. 30900/02.

[47] On the linguistic differences of this provision see Ruggeri (2017), p. 371, who pointed out the implications of an interpretation that restricts the scope of application of the procedural safeguards laid down by Directive 2016/343. Thus, interpreting the right to personal attendance as relating to the sole trial phase rules out all those alternative proceedings, such as bargaining procedures and

Two judgments of the CJEU are to be applied here to interpret the scope of application of the Directive 2016/343, both relating to the execution in the Netherlands of an European arrest warrant and the meaning of "trial resulting in the decision" within Article 4(1)(a) FD EAW. In the *Tupikas* case,[48] where the EAW had been issued by the Regional Court of Klaipeda of Lithuania, the CJEU concludes that the meaning of trial in that provision covers the instance in which the decision on the guilt was finally adopted.[49]

The same day, in the *Zdziaszek* case[50]—another EAW issued by the Regional Court of Gdansk to enforce a conviction judgment, where the second instance was held *in absentia*—, the CJEU interprets that the meaning of "trial resulting in the decision" in Article 4(1)(a) FD EAW:

> must be interpreted as covering the appeal proceedings that led to the decision which, after a new examination of the merits of the case in fact and in law, finally determined the guilt of the person concerned and imposed the penalty upon him, such as a custodial sentence, even though the sentence handed down was amended by a subsequent decision.[51]

Regarding the types of proceedings to which this Directive is applicable, it does not take the same path as the European Investigation Order Directive (DEIO), where its Article 4 defines the types of proceedings for which the EIO may be issued. Following this rule, the EIO Directive applies to criminal proceedings that take place before a judicial authority "in respect of a criminal offence under the national law of the issuing State" (Article 4a DEIO). But additionally to criminal proceedings, it may also be issued within proceedings brought before an administrative authority for infringements "which are punishable under the national law of the issuing State by virtue of being infringements of the rules of law" if these administrative proceedings can "give rise to proceedings before a court having jurisdiction, in particular, in criminal matters".

It is not suggested that the present Directive should have extended its material scope beyond in the same sense as the EIO Directive, but it might be worth to ques-

---

the abbreviated proceedings, which not only aim at a decision on guilt, albeit in the pre-trial stage, but were also often structured by national lawmakers in a way that requires the competent authority to hear the accused and verify his eventual waiver of personal attendance.

[48] CJEU, *Tadas Tupikas*, judgment of 10 August 2017, C-270/17 PPU.

[49] See § 100: "Where the issuing Member State has provided for a criminal procedure involving several degrees of jurisdiction which may thus give rise to successive judicial decisions, at least one of which has been handed down *in absentia*, the concept of 'trial resulting in the decision', within the meaning of Article 4a(1) FD EAW must be interpreted as relating only to the instance at the end of which the decision is handed down which finally rules on the guilt of the person concerned and imposes a penalty on him, such as a custodial sentence, following a re-examination, in fact and in law, of the merits of the case".

[50] Judgment *Slawomir Andrezj Zdziaszek*, judgment of 10 August 2017, C-271/17 PPU.

[51] See § 82. Moreover, the Court also rules that the concept of "trial" in Article 4(1)(a) FD EAW also covers "subsequent proceedings, such as those that led to the judgment handing down the cumulative sentence at issue here, at the end of which the decision that finally amended the level of the initial sentence was handed down, inasmuch as the authority which adopted the latter decision enjoyed a certain discretion in that regard" (§ 111).

tion what is the reason for this different approach. Although European Parliament proposed to extend the scope also to administrative offences' proceedings complying the so-called 'Engel criteria',[52] the Council and the Commission opposed to this on the basis that this would cause substantial confusion, and that the other Directives on procedural rights of suspects and defendants were also limited to criminal proceedings as interpreted by the CJEU[53] "without prejudice to the case-law of the ECtHR" (Recital 11 DPIRPT). Opting for this solution clearly avoids complex interpretations on the scope of application, and thus I consider it might be the most reasonable approach, precisely with regard to trials *in absentia*.

As to the scope of application *ratione personae*, the Article 2 of the Directive explicitly restricts it to "natural persons who are suspects or accused persons" (see also Recital 12). The explanation for excluding legal persons from the scope of application is given under Recitals 13 and 14: recognizing that the rights flowing from the presumption of innocence do not accrue to legal persons in the same way as they so to natural persons "it would be premature to legislate at Union level on the presumption of innocence with regard to legal persons" (Recital 14). In a Joint Position Paper in 2014, Fair Trials International noted that this leaves "their protection to existing safeguards, while acknowledging that the case law of the ECtHR has not clearly recognised the right of silence for legal persons".[54] Given that legal persons can clearly be affected by the mutual recognition agenda, this is an opportunity missed in terms of clarifying and enhancing protection.[55]

On the other hand, taking into account that not all EU Member States provide for the criminal liability of legal persons, including them into the scope of application rather than promoting an harmonized application it could result in a patchwork application of it.[56] This is the reason why it was finally not included.

While these arguments might be justified when it comes to the rights enshrined in the presumption of innocence, it is not so evident when speaking about the right to be present at one's own trial, which should apply indistinctly to natural and to legal persons. Although the practice on trials *in absentia* is focused on natural persons, precisely because their capability of absconding or changing much more easily their abodes, the right to be present at trial when the accused is a legal person should also

---

[52] ECtHR, *Engel and Others v. the Netherlands*, judgment of 8 June 1976, Appl. Nos. 5100/71 5101/71 5102/71 5354/72 5370/72, § 82: 1) the classification of the offence in national law, 2) the nature of the offence, and 3) the degree of severity of the penalty imposed on the offender. See also *Öztürk v Germany*, judgment of 21 February 1984, Appl. No. 8544/79; *Lauko v Slovakia*, judgment of 2 September 1998, Appl. No. 26138/95.

[53] See Cras and Erbeznik (2016), p. 29.

[54] Joint position paper on the proposed Directive on the strengthening of certain aspects of the presumption of innocence and of the right to be present at trial in criminal proceedings, November 2014, https://www.fairtrials.org/wp-content/uploads/Presumption-of-Innocence-Position-Paper.pdf (Accessed on 17 January 2017), § 12.

[55] In the same sense, see also Lamberigts (2016), pp. 36–41.

[56] See Cras and Erbeznik (2016), p. 28.

be ensured.[57] Following the expansion of the protection of the Convention to legal persons done by the Strasbourg Court, most notably to companies charged with criminal offences, it is not clear why the right to be present should not be also guaranteed at the EU level to legal persons facing criminal proceedings. The Court has stated, although not directly related to trials *in absentia*, that the fair trial rights enshrined in Article 6(3) ECHR also apply to companies and other private law legal persons.[58] Therefore it is hard to figure out what is the reason for excluding the application of Articles 8 and 9 of the Directive 2016/343 to legal persons. I do not see this issue as premature, but rather that while the focus was put on the presumption of innocence, the safeguards for trials *in absentia* of legal persons were simply disregarded.

Finally, the rules on trials *in absentia* "shall be without prejudice to the national rules that provide for proceedings or certain stages thereof to be conducted in writing" [Article 8(6) DPIRPT]. In other words, where the national procedural rules do not provide for a hearing, the rules of this Directive on the right to be present do not apply (Recital 41).

4   EU Law on Trials *In Absentia* and the Directive 2016/343

4.1   Requirements for Holding a Trial **In Absentia**

Following strictly the case law of the ECtHR, Article 4a(1)(a) FD EAW, as introduced by the aforementioned Framework Decision 2009/299/EU,[59] excludes the possibility of refusing the enforcement of an EAW based on the fact that the judgment has been rendered *in absentia* if two conditions are met: the defendant knew the date and place of the trial (either because he was summoned personally or it can be by other means unequivocally established that he was aware) and was informed about the consequences. These provisions are not aimed at setting uniform standards on how the trials *in absentia* should be conducted or regulated at the national level, but only seek to ensure that certain grounds for refusal are not interpreted in a way that might run counter the principle of mutual recognition or even obstruct the international judicial cooperation.[60] However, indirectly, Article 4a FD EAW sets out which are the minimum standards to be complied when holding a trial *in absentia*,[61] and if those standards are complied, none of the EU countries can invoke such circumstance as a ground for refusing the enforcement of an EAW.

---

[57] On the application of the ECHR to legal persons, most notably companies, see Van Kempen (2011), p. 373.

[58] ECtHR, *Forum Oil and Gas Oy v Finland,* judgment of 12 November 2002, Appl. No. 32559/93, quoted by Van Kempen (2011), pp. 373–374.

[59] For the examination of the solutions adopted by the 2009 legislation see in this volume Schneider, in this volume.

[60] On the international cooperation in criminal matters in the EU and the mutual recognition principle, see generally Satzger (2018), pp. 204 ff.

[61] On the indirect harmonizing effect of EU law, see Böse (2011), pp. 489 ff.

Apart from the two requirements (personal summons or awareness by official means and information of the consequences of non-appearance),[62] Article 4a(1)(b) FD EAW establishes a further presumption of the waiver to appear if following conditions are met: "being aware of the scheduled trial, had given a mandate to a legal counsellor, who was either appointed by the person concerned or by the State, to defend him or her at the trial, and was indeed defended by that counsellor at the trial".

Paragraphs (c) and (d) of Article 4a(1) FD EAW define situations where the EU legislator already establishes the right of the person convicted *in absentia* to challenge the judgment or to the re-trial of the case. We will focus here on paragraph (b), because it may pose higher risks for the defence rights.

The two conditions set out in Article 4a(1)(b) FD EAW—knowledge of the trial and defence by legal counsel—might be reasonable for presuming the waiver of the defendant to be at the trial and thus to presume that the fundamental right to a public hearing of Article 6 ECHR has been respected. The requirements are adequate to establish the presumption and also to make an assessment *a posteriori* on the possible violation of the rights of Article 6(1) y 6(3)(c) ECHR, as the Strasbourg Court does.

In a similar way, although with other wording and less precision, Article 8(2) of the EU Directive 2016/343 provides for the possibility to render judgments in absentia if following requirements are met:

(a) the suspect or accused person has been informed, in due time, of the trial and of the consequences of non-appearance; or

(b) the suspect or accused person, having been informed of the trial, is represented by a mandated lawyer, who was appointed either by the suspect or accused person or by the State.

Both texts, as can be seen, are almost identical, despite the fact that under Article 4a FD EAW the safeguards in the summoning are higher ("summoned in person" or "unequivocally established that he was aware of the scheduled trial"), than under Article 8(2) of the Directive PIPT ("has been informed"). And both follow the two main requisites established by the ECtHR case law. Recital 36 underlines that informing a suspect or accused of the trial "should be understood to mean summoning him or her in person", but also by "other means" providing official information that enables him to become aware of the trial. This allows wide margin of discretion to the national law to establish how shall be the notice of the proceedings and the trial be done to the defendant to ensure his right to be present, which may be subject to criticism.[63]

Notwithstanding the correctness of establishing such a presumption of unequivocal waiver—the waiver principle[64]—it cannot be overlooked that despite knowing

---

[62] Critical with the lack of precision of these terms used in Article 4 FD EAW Wahl (2015), pp. 72–73.

[63] See also Ruggeri (2016a), p. 597.

[64] See Tinsley (2012), p. 25.

about the trial and being represented by lawyer, there may be a breach of the fundamental right to be present at trial, as happened in the case *Mariani v. France*[65]: the defendant knew about the date of the trial before a French court, and was represented by lawyer before the trial, however he had not waived his right to be present, but was impeded to appear due to the fact that he was serving a custodial sentence in an Italian prison.

This is just an example of a situation that occurs in practice more often than imagined and that shows that knowing when the trial is taking place and being represented by lawyer are reasonable elements to establish an acceptable presumption, but do not always prove the willingness of the waiver.[66]

On the other hand if every waiver of a right should be based on the free will of its holder, it is questionable if it can be said that there is a willing waiver of the right to be present at trial, if the appearance at trial will imply being detained and remanded in custody. This explains why the ECtHR has stated that the mere condition of being fugitive does not by itself mean that the defendant waives his right to defend himself at trial,[67] because for applying the presumption of unequivocal waiver, the defendant must have knowledge of the trial. Free will in criminal proceedings undoubtedly has a different meaning than in civil proceedings. And there can only be a waiver of the right, if previously one has been informed of the charges, the proceedings or the date and time of the trial.

However, as practice shows, it often occurs that before criminal charges are brought before a suspect, he absconds and becomes untraceable. This is why the right to be present at trial is to be balanced with other interests. The Strasbourg Court has agreed that, when the circumstances so require, the right to take part in person in the hearing has to be reconciled through the striking of a "reasonable balance" with the interests of justice. The impossibility of holding a trial *in absentia*, for example when the defendant has fled, may halt the conducting of criminal proceedings, and this may lead to disappearance or destruction of evidence, expiry of the time-limit to prosecute or even a miscarriage of justice.

Does EU law and Article 8(2) of the Directive 2016/343 provide for this "reasonable balance"? To that end, the assistance of the lawyer should be analysed in more detail.

---

[65] *Mariani v. France*, judgment of 31 March 2005, Appl. No. 43640/98.

[66] In the same sense Tinsley (2012), p. 29, citing information of Fair Trials International. For other infringements of fundamental rights in EAW proceedings see also Heard and Mansell (2011), pp. 136–144; Sullivan (2009), pp. 37–44; Martín Rodríguez (2013), p. 36.

[67] *Sejdovic v. Italy* (fn. 33).

4.2 Legal Assistance and Right of Defence in Trials In Absentia: *The Need for the Defence to Be Effective?*

As seen above, trials *in absentia* are allowed under Article 8(2)(b) of the Directive 2016/343 if the suspect or accused person, having been duly informed of the trial, is represented by lawyer, either of his own choice of appointed by the State. This provision does not include any reference to the effectiveness of such defence.

However, to strengthen the safeguards of the right of defence in trials *in absentia*, Article 4a(1)(b) FD EAW additionally requires that the defence is effective "and was indeed defended by the counsellor at trial".

The question to analyse here is whether the cases where a defendant has been duly given notice of the trial and is represented by lawyer, do not exclude the possibility of a violation of Article 6 ECHR.

Article 8(2)(b) of the Directive sets a lower standard as Article 4a(1)(b) FD EAW, as the former does not mention the level of protection set out by the ECtHR requiring that the right to legal assistance shall be effective and not merely formal.[68] It would have been convenient that the Directive had adopted a similar wording as Article 4a 1 (b) FD EAW, but not having done so does not mean that the ECHR standards are not applicable here too. Article 8(2)(b) of the Directive 2016/343 only States under which circumstances a trial *in absentia* can be held, but it does not say that complying with those conditions ensures the fulfilment of the fair trial rights in any event. Allowing the holding of trials *in absentia* without expressly requiring the effective exercise of the defence is to a certain extent logical, because the effectiveness of the defence can eventually only be assessed *ex post*, while the proceedings *in absentia* are to be granted precisely *ex ante* to hold the trial.

Having said this, it shall be seen now how the effectiveness of the legal assistance and the defence influences the specific safeguards to be granted in trials *in absentia*. As a rule, the control on the effectiveness of the defence is meant to be applied to the duty appointed lawyers, as it is taken for granted that when the defendant appoints a lawyer of own choice such decision is based on the trust upon his professional skills and that he will perform the mandate according to best practices. Although this might not be always the case—and there are also malpractice cases of lawyers appointed by the defendant himself—in practice the problems related to the effectiveness of the defence appear mostly with regard to duty appointed lawyers.

What is considered an "effective legal defence"? What are the criteria to measure such effectiveness? The ECtHR has established that for a defence to be effective the States shall ensure that the lawyers are provided with all the necessary information to carry out the defence in the most adequate way.[69] But the Strasbourg Court, when

---

[68] ECtHR, *Artico v. Italy*, judgment of 13 May 1980, Appl. No. 6694/74; *Kamasinski v. Austria*, judgment of 19 December 1989, Appl. No. 9783/82, §§ 63–71; *Imbrioscia v. Switzerland*, judgment of 24 November 1993, Appl. No. 13972/88.

[69] ECtHR, *Goddi v. Italy*, judgment of 9 April 1984, Appl. No. 8966/80; *Öcalan v. Turkey*, of 12 March 2003, Appl. No. 63486/00. On the right to counsel and the parameters for assessing the

adjudicating on precise cases and assessing *ex post* if there has been a violation of the ECHR, does not aim at setting general rules or definitions on the content of an effective defence by a lawyer.

For instance in the case *Artico v. Italy*, the ECtHR stated that the non-appearance of the lawyer and the lack of active involvement in the defence, could not be considered as an effective defence, and therefore violation of Article 6 ECHR was found. Beyond this, the ECtHR has not required for the defence to be effective that the lawyer shows a certain level of dedication or professional competencies. As it is said in *Sejdovic v. Italy*[70]—another case against Italy related to a trial in absentia with presence of duty appointed lawyer—

> a State cannot be held responsible for every shortcoming on the part of a lawyer appointed for legal aid purposes or by the accused. It follows from the independence of the legal profession from the State that the conduct of the defence is essentially a matter between the defendant and his counsel, whether appointed under a legal aid scheme or privately financed.

In this context, the following affirmation of the ECtHR is relevant:

> The competent national authorities are required under Article 6(3)(c) to intervene only if a failure by legal aid counsel to provide effective representation is manifest or is sufficiently brought to their attention in some other way.[71]

The position of the Strasbourg Court is clear: it starts from the premise that duty appointed lawyers—within the system of legal aid or out of it—, will provide an effective defence and the quality of their services will be granted by the States by ruling on the conditions for exercising the legal profession.

However, it is well known that not every Member State controls the quality of the duty appointed lawyers in the same way, and in the vast majority of cases, only if the duty appointed lawyer manifestly infringes upon his obligations and does not comply with his functions—for example by not appearing to hearings—, will be removed and another lawyer will be appointed.[72] Moreover, in compliance with the principle of judicial impartiality, many legal systems, especially those where the criminal procedure is more adversarial, the judge will be barred to intervene in the debates to counteract the ineffective defence of a duty appointed lawyer.

What would happen if, knowing about the trial despite not having been correctly summoned, a defendant stays away from the trial and is represented by a duty appointed lawyer? Such a situation fits in principle into the wording of Article 8(2)(b) Directive 2016/343 and Article 4a(1)(b) FD EAW, save that the expression "given mandate" is understood in the sense of a personal act of the defendant giving powers of representation to the duty appointed lawyer. But it can nevertheless run counter the rights of Article 6 ECHR.

---

effectiveness of the legal assistance under the Convention, cf. the comprehensive study by Coster van Voorhut (2017), in particular pp. 153 ff.

[70] ECtHR, *Sejdovic v. Italia* (fn. 33), § 90.

[71] See ECtHR, *Daud v. Portugal*, judgment of 21 April 1998, Appl. No. 22600/93, § 38.

[72] Plekksepp (2012), p. 473.

Moreover, there is another element that can negatively affect the "effectiveness" of the defence: there might be no fluent communication between the defendant in absentia and the duty appointed lawyer. In such cases, can it be really presumed that the defence will be exercised effectively?

In sum, the right to have an 'effective' defence in practice is more illusory than real, as only when a lawyer blatantly infringes his obligations, the relevant trial court or the State—directly or through the Lawyer's Chambers—will intervene to grant the 'effectiveness' of the defence. And when the communication between the absent defendant and the State appointed lawyer is not established, the effectiveness of the defence is more than debatable.

Taking into account these circumstances, it is clear that even having knowledge of the trial and being represented by lawyer, does not unequivocally prove that the defendant waives his right to be present, it neither ensures that the rights of defence are fully respected.[73] In my view the criticism is not to be directed to Article 8(2) of the Directive, but rather to Article 9 DPIRPT, which only requires the Member States to ensure the right to a new trial when "the conditions laid down in Article 8(2) were not met". This will be discussed next.

4.3 Right to a New Trial

Legal systems that allow the carrying out of criminal trials *in absentia* enable the defendant to set aside or review the conviction judgment rendered in his absence. The ECtHR has also held that

> the proceedings that take place in the accused's absence will not of themselves be incompatible with the Convention if the accused may subsequently obtain, from a court which has heard him, a fresh determination of the merits of the charge (...).[74]

Such retrial or appeal must fully comply with the demands of Article 6 of the ECHR, among them the right to confront previous evidence, including the cross-examination of witnesses, to present new evidence and to contest the merits of the case.

Aware that providing for the possibility of reopening the case tried *in absentia* is necessary to counterbalance the unavoidable risks that these type of judgments entail, the EU Directive 2016/343 includes a specific article on such right.

Article 9 of Directive 2016/343 reads as follows:

> Member States shall ensure that, where suspects or accused persons were not present at their trial and the conditions laid down in Article 8(2) were not met, they have the right to a

---

[73] In the same sense also Ruggeri (2016a), pp. 597–598 pointing out that: "A reductive interpretation of this provision (Art. 8) would allow those national solutions to be maintained that couple the institution of default proceedings with the appointment of lawyer by the court".

[74] Cf. ECtHR, *Medenica v. Switzerland* (fn. 26), § 54; *Colozza v. Italy* (fn. 19), § 29; and *Poitrimol v. France* (fn. 19), § 31.

new trial, or to another legal remedy, which allows a fresh determination of the merits of the case, including examination of new evidence, and which may lead to the original decision being reversed. In that regard, Member States shall ensure that those suspects and accused persons have the right to be present, to participate effectively, in accordance with procedures under national law, and to exercise the rights of the defence.

According to Article 8(4) DPIRPT when the person convicted *in absentia* was not previously informed and could not have a lawyer present because he could not be located "despite reasonable efforts", the States shall ensure that when they are apprehended they are informed of the possibility and time to challenge the sentence rendered *in absentia*.

The information on the remedies is a pre-requisite to be able to exercise them, and thus it is welcome that the Directive has expressly included such obligation. However, the precise meaning of what shall be deemed "reasonable efforts" made for locating the defendant can be interpreted in many variegated forms. In practice, many breaches of the right to be heard and be present at trial stem precisely from those efforts made before a person is considered non traceable, in many cases simply because they have changed address.[75] Closer attention should be paid in the future by the CJEU to ensure that, only after really meaningful efforts, a personal summon to the defendant can be substituted by another less reliable form of giving notice of the trial.

On the other hand, serving notice of the sentence is not a prior requisite for the enforcement of the judgment rendered in absentia [Article 8(3) DPIRPT], if the conditions under Article 8(2) have been met: the defendant, upon being apprehended or found, will have the opportunity to challenge the conviction sentence, but the fact that it was rendered *in absentia*, following the EU Directive, will not prevent its enforcement. For this purpose, the judgment *in absentia* is deemed final.[76]

Although the Directive aims at establishing "common minimum rules on the protection of procedural rights (…) to strengthen the trust of Member States in each others criminal justice systems" (Recital 10), Article 9 DPIRPT does not foster much harmonization. It requires to provide a new trial or remedy with "fresh determination of the merits of the case" when the waiver principle is not fully established, but the regulation of such mechanisms is left to the national procedural rules. The harmonization is thus minimum. At least it shall ensure that when the waiver

---

[75] See ECtHR, *T v. Italy*, judgment of 12 October 1992, Appl. No. 14104/88, where the defendant was accused of rape and notified in Italy and Saudi Arabia, his last known addresses. However, the summons did not reach the defendant, as by the time he was served in Saudi Arabia, he had already moved to Sudan. As this fact could have been easily found out, because the defendant registered in the Italian consulate upon arrival, the Court found that the before declaring him not traceable the efforts made had not been enough (§§ 28–30). This case is also relevant as it expressly recognizes that the defendant was aware of the proceedings, but *nevertheless*, the Court states that "vague and informal knowledge cannot suffice" to establish the waiver in an unequivocal manner (§ 28).

[76] See Ruggeri (2016a), p. 599, comparing this provision with the original proposal for a Directive, under which the enforcement was made dependent on the information of the subsequent remedies.

was not unequivocal,[77] the judgments rendered *in absentia* should grant a full review of the case, with new evidence and fresh determination of the merits. This was already set out by the ECtHR, but having EU legal instruments will increase its compliance by each of the Member States.

Regarding the content of Article 9 DPIRPT, ensuring the possibility of the exceptional remedy against sentences rendered *in absentia* only in cases where the conditions under Article 8(2) DPIRPT were not met, to my mind, is clearly not enough, even if the text under Recital 34 might allow a broader interpretation of this provision.[78] In any event, as Recitals are not binding, it has to be admitted that the way Article 9 is drafted it does not only not promote the strengthening of the protection of human rights in criminal proceedings in the EU AFSJ, but it does not even follow the principles set out in the case-law of the ECHR, as seen above: in consequence, Article 9 of the Directive is to be considered providing 'less than minimum' safeguards. It may be argued that these minimum rules do not prevent national States to provide higher safeguards, and even they do not make void the EU Member States' obligations to follow the case law of the ECtHR. While this is clearly true, then the question is why the EU legislature has opted for such a low standard of harmonization, going even lower than that established by the Strasbourg case law.

It should be discussed if not enabling the defendant to request the re-opening or review of a judgment rendered *in absentia*, even when he knew the date of the trial and was represented by lawyer, really complies with the fundamental right to defence. As seen above, despite fulfilling those requirements, there might be situations where the defendant should be granted the opportunity to state the reasons why he was deprived of his right to be present at trial or why his rights of defence where infringed upon even though a lawyer represented him in court. I am not stating that the right to a new trial shall be ensured in all cases, but excluding it when certain conditions are met, implies assuming important risks for the protection of fundamental rights. This has been confirmed by the numerous applications to the ECtHR related to trials *in absentia* and in particular in the cases *Mariani v. France* or *Sejdovic v. Italy*.

This issue was also discussed within the execution of the EAW, namely in the *Melloni* case. The preliminary reference filed by the Spanish Constitutional Court claimed that when amending the FD EAW in 2009, instead of establishing a higher level of protection in the execution of EAWs, the EU legislature opted for strengthening the efficiency of the surrender proceedings at the cost of possibly lowering the level of protection in transnational proceedings granted by the Spanish Court. At the time the Spanish authorities had to decide on the surrender of Mr Melloni to Italy, the restrictions for reopening a case tried in absentia amounted to a practical denial of such a right. It has to be recalled that before the amendment carried out in Italy in 2014, the Italian code of criminal procedure established that if the judgment

---

[77] The adjective "unequivocal" is not be found in Article 9 of the Directive, but under Recital 35.

[78] Recital 34 DPIRPT: "If, for reasons beyond their control, suspects or accused persons are unable to be present at the trial, they should have the possibility to request a new date for the trial within the time frame provided for in national law".

delivered *in absentia* had been served on the defendant's officially assigned counsel, an application for challenging the final conviction judgment rendered *in absentia* could be granted only if two conditions were satisfied: that the convicted person could establish that he had not had effective knowledge of the judgment, and that he had not deliberately refused to take cognisance of the procedural steps. In short, the Italian rules did not provide for review the sentence delivered in absentia in a case falling under Article 4a(1)(b) FD EAW. While the *Melloni* case was pending, Italy passed a legal reform of its code of criminal procedure, broadening the scope of review of judgments *in absentia*.[79]

Despite the undeniable risks present in every trial *in absentia*, the CJEU did not consider the right for reviewing or reopening judgments *in absentia* should be integrated in Article 47 of the EU Charter. It strictly applied the theory of equivalence set out in Article 52(3) of the Charter and thus renounced to establish a higher level of protection within the EU than the one provided by the ECHR.[80] By doing this also avoided analysing more deeply the content of Article 4a(1)(b) FD EW and the possibility of considering it contrary to the Charter. What is really missing in this judgment are solid legal reasons on the right to a fair trial and the right to defence in trials *in absentia*.[81] The CJEU simply refers to the criteria established by the CJEU in the *Trade Agency* judgment—a civil case, where the right to a fair trial and to a public hearing has clearly a different scope—and follows the lead of the case law of the ECtHR, which is just mentioned, but not analysed.[82] It seems that it is taken for granted that insofar Article 4a(1)(b) FD EAW follows the same criteria established by the ECtHR, there is no need to enter into a deeper analysis.

While the approach of the CJEU can be considered reasonable if viewed from the perspective of the effectiveness of the international judicial cooperation, it cannot be praised from the point of view of creating a common space of justice where the mutual trust is to be based on a high standard of human rights. Although mutual trust is used as a driver of integration[83] and is deemed to already exist,[84] its full

---

[79] Law 67/2014. On the Italian reform of *in absentia* trials, see among others, Mangiaracina (2014), p. 556 ff.; Quattrocolo (2014), pp. 97 ff.; Vigoni (ed) (2014); Ruggeri (2017), pp. 55 ff.

[80] On the meaning and scope of Article 52 of the EU Charter of Fundamental Rights, see Borowsky (2002), p. 577 ff.

[81] In the same sense also De Visser (2013), pp. 584–585.

[82] Critical also is Gaede (2013), p. 1281. Of the opposite opinion is Maguery (2013), p. 285, who considers the reliance on the Strasbourg doctrine without further analysis as appropriate, taking into account the expertise and prestige of the ECtHR.

[83] See Herlin-Karnell (2013), p. 447.

[84] Practice shows that not all Member States adhere to the same level of protection of fundamental rights, as it is shown in the Report from the Commission to the European Parliament and the Council On the implementation since 2007 of the Council Framework Decision of 13 June 2002 on the European arrest warrant and the surrender procedures between Member States, of 11 April 2011, COM/2011/175 final. On the shaky foundations of mutual trust see also Tinsley (2013), pp. 463–466.

acceptance and smooth functioning require its reinforcement by means of the enhancement of the level of protection of the fundamental rights.[85]

Against this background, the Directive 2016/343 should have strived for a higher standard of protection in criminal trials held *in absentia* and inviting the Member States to provide for adequate rules on reviewing judgments *in absentia* would have been welcomed. I would have considered more appropriate to stick to the wording of the Resolution 75 (11) of the Council of Ministers of the Council of Europe,[86] whose recommendation 9 reads:

> A person tried in his absence, but on whom a summons has been properly served is entitled to a retrial, in the ordinary way, if that person can prove that his absence and the fact that he could not inform the judge thereof were due to reasons beyond his control.

Bearing in mind that in certain occasions, there will be "reasons beyond the control" of the absent defendant to appear in court or even inform of his non-appearance, disregarding such situations when regulating the right to new trial, seems to me unsatisfactory—even if this is provided under Recital 34 DPIRPT. Moreover, it is sad to see that the EU legislature has to take action to 'strengthen' the protection of human rights, whereas since 1975 there has already been a Council of Europe Recommendation—soft law—defining the standards and safeguards to be applied in criminal trials *in absentia*. But it is also sad that the rules passed now in the EU Directive 2016/343 to strengthen those protections, in fact only ensure a lower protection than those approved in 1975. I am fully aware that negotiations at the EU level—with the particularities of 27 (or 28) legal systems—is nothing but easy, and that achieving to pass a new Directive like this can be seen as a resounding success. Nevertheless, someone has to point out that these rules are quite poor from the perspective of enhancing the protection of human rights and that Europe should aim at providing higher standards.

5 Concluding Remarks

Specific EU instruments to protect the rights of suspects and defendants in criminal proceedings have to be welcomed. The decision to insert in the Directive 2016/343—dedicated mainly to ensure the presumption of innocence—two provisions related to the right of the defendant to be present at his own trial and to the minimum safeguards to be preserved in trials *in absentia*, merits undoubtedly a positive assessment. Having EU law in this regard will ensure that these safeguards are more effectively respected in all Member States, and action can be taken by the CJEU if any of them infringes upon these rules.

---

[85] See also Heard and Mansell (2011), pp. 146–147.

[86] Resolution (75) 11 of the Council of Ministers of the Council of Europe, on the criteria governing proceedings held in the absence of the accused, 21 May 1975.

Article 8(2) DPIPT, as previously Article 4a(1)(b) FD EAW, correctly reflects the elements required by the ECtHR for allowing judgments to be rendered in the absence of the defendant. Whereas the solutions elaborated by the EU legislation are adequate and reasonable, however, it has to be recalled that these elements cannot operate as an irrefutable presumption that there has not been a violation of fair trial rights. Practice shows that even complying scrupulously with all the conditions set out in Article 8(2) DPIRPT or Article 4a(1)(b) FD EAW, the fair trial rights of the absent defendant might have been violated. In other words, despite all reasonable safeguards that are designed to allow holding trials *in absentia*, the risk of violating the rights of defence can never be fully excluded.

This is why the rules on the right to a new trial should be drafted in such a way that they could encompass also a new trial when enough cause is shown that the right to be present might have been violated, despite the presumption of its waiver. Article 52(3) of the Charter confirms that the EU may raise standards beyond those of the ECHR but it cannot permit States to fall below them (taking also into account the non-regression clause laid down in Article 13 of the Directive 2016/343). The ECHR is thus the core baseline for any assessment of the efficacy of new standards. And those standards are not adequately reflected in the rules on trials *in absentia* in this Directive, even if they are mentioned in the Recitals.

Although one can be disappointed for the lack of ambition in improving the guarantee of defence rights and in particular for the meagre results on the protection of fundamental rights in trials *in absentia* provided in this Directive, its added value cannot be overlooked. And it is to be expected that the Directive will aid not only in advancing towards mutual trust, but also in reducing the number of applications before the Strasbourg Court.

References

Bachmaier Winter L (2015) Más reflexiones sobre la sentencia Melloni: primacía, diálogo y protección de los derechos fundamentales en juicios in absentia en el derecho europeo. Rev. Española de Derecho Europeo 56:153–181

Bachmaier Winter L (2016) Dealing with European legal diversity at the Luxembourg Court: Melloni and the limits of European pluralism. In: Colson R, Field S (eds) EU criminal justice and the challenges of diversity. Legal cultures in the area of freedom, security and justice. Cambridge University Press, Cambridge, pp 160–178

Borowsky M (2002) Artikel 52. In: Meyer J (ed) Kommentar zur Charta der Grundrechte der Europäischen Union. Nomos, Baden-Baden, pp 577–592

Böse M (2011) Harmonizing procedural rights indirectly: the framework decision on trials in absentia. N C J Int Law:489–510

Böse M (2015) Human rights violations and mutual trust: recent case law on the European Arrest Warrant. In: Ruggeri S (ed) Human rights in European criminal law: new developments in European legislation and case law after the Lisbon Treaty. Springer, Heidelberg, pp 135–145

Coster van Voorhut J (2017) Ineffective legal assistance. Redress for the accuse in Dutch criminal procedure and compliance with ECHR case law. Brill, Leiden

Cras S, Erbeznik A (2016) The directive on the presumption of innocence and the right to be present at trial. Genesis and description of the new EU-measure. Eucrim 1:25–35

De Visser M (2013) Case note: dealing with divergences in fundamental rights standards. Maastricht J 20(4):576–588

Gaede K (2013) Minimalistischer Grundrechtschutz bei der Kooperation im Strafverfahren. Neue Juristische Wochenschrift:1279–1282

Goss R (2014) Criminal fair trial rights. Article 6 of the European Convention of Human Rights. Hart Publishing, Oxford

Heard C, Mansell D (2011) The European arrest warrant: the role of the judges when human rights are at risk. New J Eur Crim Law 2(1):133–147

Herlin-Karnell E (2013) European criminal law as an exercise in EU 'experimental' constitutional law. Maastricht J 20(3):442–464

Kostoris R (2017) Manuale di Procedura Penale Europea, 3rd edn. Giuffrè, Milano

Lamberigts S (2016) The directive on the presumption of innocence. A missed opportunity for legal persons? Eucrim 1:36–41

Maguery T (2013) European Union fundamental rights and member states action in EU criminal law. Maastricht J 20(2):282–301

Mangiaracina A (2010) Garanzie partecipative e giudizio *in absentia*. Giappichelli, Torino

Mangiaracina A (2014) Il "tramonto" della contumacia e l'affermazione di un'assenza "multiforme". La Legislazione Penale 4:556–592

Martín Rodríguez P (2013) Crónica de una muerte anunciada: comentario a la sentencia del Tribunal de Justicia de 26 de febrero de 2013, Stefano Melloni, C-399/11. Revista General de Derecho Europeo 30:1–45

Paul C (2007) Das Abwesenheitsverfahren als rechtstaatliches Problem. Peter Lang, Frankfurt a.M.

Plekksepp A (2012) Die gleichmässige Gewährleistung des Rechts auf Verteidigerbeistand. Duncker & Humboldt, Berlin

Pradel J (1995) Droit pénal compare. Dalloz, Paris

Quattrocolo S (2014) Il contumace cede la scena processuale all'assente, mentre l'irreperibile l'abbandona. www.penalecontemporaneo.it. Accessed 30 Apr 2014

Ruggeri S (2016a) Right to personal participation in criminal proceedings and in absentia procedures in the EU area of freedom, security and justice. Zeitschrift für die gesamte Strafrechtswissenschaft 128:578–605

Ruggeri S (2016b) *Inaudito reo* proceedings, defence rights, and harmonisation goals in the EU. Eucrim 1:42–51

Ruggeri S (2017) *Audi Alteram Partem* in criminal proceedings. Towards a participatory understanding of criminal justice in Europe and Latin America. Springer International Publishing, Cham

Satzger H (2018) Internationales und Europäisches Strafrecht. Nomos, Baden-Baden

Sullivan G (2009) Fair trials international case notes. The European arrest warrant: abuse of process as a bar to extradition. New J Eur Crim Law, Special edition: 37–44

Tinsley A (2012) Note on the reference in case C-399/11 Melloni. New J Eur Crim Law 3(1):19–30

Tinsley A (2013) Protecting criminal defence rights through EU law: opportunities and challenges. New J Eur Crim Law 4(4):461–480

Van Kempen PH (2011) The recognition of legal persons in international human rights instruments: protection against and through criminal law. In: Pieth M, Ivory R (eds) Corporate criminal liability. Emergence, convergence, and risks. Springer, Heidelberg, pp 355–389

Vervaele J (2012) The European arrest warrant and applicable standards of fundamental rights in the EU. Rev Eur Adm Law 2:37–54

Vigoni D (ed) (2014) Il giudizio in assenza dell' imputato. Giappichelli, Torino

Wahl T (2015) Der Rahmenbeschluss zu Abwesenheitsentscheidungen: Brüsseler EU-Justizkooperation als Fall für Straßburg? Eucrim:70–76

Part VI
Models for Solution in Human Rights Law and Guidelines for a Participatory Approach to Criminal Justice

Participatory Rights in Criminal Proceedings. A Comparative-Law Analysis from a Human Rights Perspective

Stefano Ruggeri

Abstract The present study provides a comparative-law examination of the requirements concerning the involvement of private parties in criminal proceedings, as well as the national procedures that rule out any participation of the accused. This research cuts across the solutions emerged from EU law and international human rights law, comparing them with the requirements set forth by domestic law from a constitutional and substantive criminal law perspective. The results of this analysis highlight a complex scenario. A systematic view not only of the procedural safeguards enshrined in the European Convention, but also of the constitutional and criminal law requirements make it extremely difficult to maintain the traditional schemes applied to criminal proceedings conducted against absent defendants, justified on the perspective of a retrial or a remedy that is often unable to compensate the accused for the opportunities lost. Doubtless, the solutions provided by the Strasbourg Court on *in absentia* trials had large influence not only on national legislation and case-law practices but also on the rapid evolution of EU law in the field of transnational and domestic criminal justice. Yet the legislative instruments adopted at all these levels are not always in line with the European jurisprudence. Further human rights concerns arise from the proceedings held *inaudito reo*, which, depending on the solutions provided by domestic law, can often not even ensure a subsequent remedy corresponding to the accused's intentions.

A comparative analysis of the developments that have occurred in international, domestic and supranational law in the last years, moreover, allows us to reconstruct a problematic area, which goes far beyond the issues of *in absentia* trials and *inaudito reo* procedures, thus posing a number of difficult challenges arising from a participatory understanding of criminal proceedings. The examination of the Strasbourg case-law and EU law, in particular, enables us to define the qualitative requirements that should be satisfied with a view to ensuring effective participation in criminal proceedings. Along these lines, the present study has firstly examined the fair trial safeguards that the accused should be granted, by focusing on four main

S. Ruggeri (✉)
Department of Law 'Salvatore Pugliatti', Messina University, Messina, Italy
e-mail: steruggeri@unime.it

© Springer Nature Switzerland AG 2019
S. Quattrocolo, S. Ruggeri (eds.), *Personal Participation in Criminal Proceedings*, Legal Studies in International, European and Comparative Criminal Law 2, https://doi.org/10.1007/978-3-030-01186-4_21

issues, namely (*a*) the information rights, (*b*) the right to understand and to be understood in the criminal trial, (*c*) the relationship between legal assistance and the right to self-defence, and finally (*d*) the right to make one's voice heard fairly. Furthermore, the increasing tendency to enhance an overall consideration of criminal proceedings by international human rights law and EU law suggests further broadening the research area. Therefore, this investigation was extended to the analysis of whether and to what extent individuals other than defendants, who are also (and often coercively) involved in criminal proceedings, also have the right to be heard fairly and to make their own contribution to fact-finding.

Abbreviations

ACHR	American Convention of Human Rights
BVerfG	*Bundesverfassungsgericht* (German Federal Constitutional Court)
CCass	*Corte di Cassazione* (Supreme Court)
CConst	Constitutional Court
CCP	Code of Criminal Procedure
CFR	Charter of Fundamental Rights of the European Union
DAL	Directive on the right of access to a lawyer in criminal proceedings
DICP	Directive on the right to information in criminal proceedings
DIT	Directive on the right to interpretation and translation in criminal proceedings
DLA	Directive on legal aid for suspects and accused persons in criminal proceedings and for requested persons in European arrest warrant proceedings
DPIRPT	Directive on certain aspects on the presumption of innocence and the right to be present at trial in criminal proceedings
DVR	Directive on the rights, support and protection of victims of crime
EAW	European arrest warrant
ECHR	European Convention on Human Rights
ECtHR	European Court of Human Rights
EU	European Union
ICCPR	International Covenant on Civil and Political Rights
LECrim	*Ley de enjuiciamiento criminal* (Spanish law on criminal procedure)
PC	Penal code

1   Introductory Remarks

The analysis conducted hitherto allows us now to examine comparatively the requirements concerning the involvement of private parties in criminal proceedings and the national procedures that exclude or considerably restrict participation. For this purpose, the present study cuts across the standards acknowledged by EU law and international human rights law with the requirements set forth by domestic law with specific regard to constitutional law and substantive criminal law. In this framework, particular attention will be devoted to case-law, with special reference being made to the solutions elaborated by constitutional case-law, as well as by Strasbourg and Luxemburg jurisprudence.

This comparative research poses the difficult challenge of scrutinising whether and to what extent different standards of protection of fundamental rights acknowledged in a similar way at different legal levels can co-exist—and therefore whether a human rights pluralism is tolerable and even desirable—in the European judicial area. On a first level, the different approaches followed by the Constitutions of European countries to the personal involvement of private parties in criminal proceedings (not to mention the judicial proceedings having punitive character) reveal the high tension produced by constitutional pluralism,[1] which has determined significant clashes between EU member states. One of the main fields in which these clashes have emerged is surely that of international surrender procedures. This field was historically characterised by conflictual inter-state and judicial relationships, to the extent that international law agreements were needed to circumscribe governmental and judicial discretion.[2]

Yet the sole perspective of constitutional law, despite being of the utmost importance, does not suffice to grasp the complexity of this problematic area. It is precisely the co-existence of different approaches to the problem of *in absentia* trials, both in the field of domestic criminal justice and transnational cooperation within the EU area, that also led to strong confrontation between domestic (constitutional) courts and Strasbourg as well as, more recently, Luxembourg case-law. This confrontation, which is far from having reached a satisfactory conclusion, has brought to light two main scenarios that may result from the different treatment of fundamental rights by several legal orders, namely (*a*) the prevalence of individual systems of human rights protection over the others and (*b*) the mutual approximation of different systems towards common patterns. The former scenario calls for uniform solutions at different law levels, while revealing a fragmentary view of the systems of human rights protection, each one aiming to provide the best balance of the conflicting interests. The latter, instead, promotes solutions that have by definition relative relevance, as they are intended to provide the most appropriate response

---

[1] Pollicino and Bassini, in this volume, Sect. 1.

[2] It is worth mentioning that the 2002 EAW legislation was somehow anticipated by the bilateral extradition treaty between Italy and Spain, signed in 2000 with a view to providing an alternative to the ordinary extradition proceedings. See among others Grevi (2000).

to the challenges posed by concrete cases in relation to the human rights requirements set forth by domestic (constitutional) law as well as supranational and/or
international human rights law.

Recent history, moreover, shows that these scenarios do not constitute rigid alternatives, as both of them have strongly characterised the inter-judicial relationships
over the last years. As far as domestic and international human rights law are concerned, we have witnessed the alternation of both the models of one-sided prevalence and mutual adaptation. In Europe, not only has the Strasbourg Court strongly
contributed to the evolution of a participatory understanding of different national
criminal justice systems but significant changes have also taken place in European
case-law, which significantly departs from the lines laid down by the findings of the
Colozza judgment. All these developments highlight today a highly complex view
of participatory rights in criminal proceedings, which goes far beyond the physical
attendance in court of the accused. The examination of Strasbourg case-law, in particular, reveals the clear attempt to reconstruct the scope of the participatory safeguards with a view to providing a better balance between the Convention's
requirements and the fair trial conditions set by constitutional law. At a deeper level
still, European jurisprudence displays a picture in which the defendant's right to
participate in criminal proceedings must be redefined in the light of the overall challenges inherent in a fair trial, which encompass the state-related interest in efficient
prosecution, as well as the right of the aggrieved parties to contribute to fact-finding
and the need to give a voice to individuals other than those who, despite not being
formally party to the proceedings, are (often forcefully) involved in them.

These preliminary observations demonstrate that human rights pluralism can
certainly not be viewed in terms of relationship between static entities in that it
involves protection systems that are in constant evolution and whose mutual relationships must thus be examined in a diachronic way. For the sake of clarity, this
study firstly analyses the developments that have recently characterised the two
aforementioned scenarios. Secondly, I shall comparatively examine the conditions
under which *in absentia* trials can be held and decisions *inaudito reo* can be issued
in the European judicial area. Ultimately, I shall compare the models for solution
that have emerged from the analysis of the human rights systems examined in this
research in order to highlight the qualitative requirements that should be met to
satisfy the right of the individuals involved in criminal proceedings to make themselves heard and contribute to the ascertainment of the facts.

2   Participatory Guarantees and *In Absentia* Trials in Criminal Justice. Two Possible Scenarios in the Multilevel Relationships Between Different Systems of Human Rights Protection

2.1   *The Logic of Prevalence of Individual Systems of Human Rights Protection Over the Others*

It has been observed that participatory rights in criminal proceedings—and especially the problem of *in absentia* trials both in domestic and transnational criminal justice—have been the playground for strong confrontation between different systems of human rights protection, and that such confrontation has firstly highlighted the tendency of individual legal orders to prevail over others and to achieve one-sided arrangements. Certainly, this tendency reveals a conception of the relationships between legal systems that is strongly based on hierarchy. Yet, as noted, confrontation should no longer be seen as occurring between static entities, as statutory law provisions are constantly subject to interpretation processes. Consequently, prevalence can also flow from "transjudicial dialogue".[3]

Without a doubt, the *Melloni* judgment has provided one of the most emblematic examples in the last years.[4] A huge amount of commentary was written about this decision in several countries. It is well-known that in its response on the Spanish request for preliminary ruling, the Luxembourg Court pointed out that a broad interpretation of both Framework Decision 2009/299/JHA and the Fundamental Rights Charter, would frustrate the milestone of the judicial cooperation in the EU area, namely the mutual recognition principle. The main argument used by the European judges was the need to preserve the uniform application and, deeper still, the primacy of EU law. The inevitable price for not frustrating the mutual recognition principle governing the judicial cooperation within the EU area, therefore, was a restrictive interpretation of Article 53 CFR, which ruled out the possibility of national authorities invoking the requirements of their own constitutional law to achieve a stronger protection of the fundamental rights at stake in the specific case.[5]

Legal scholarship has strongly criticised this approach from the viewpoint of both constitutional and criminal law.[6] The main criticism was perhaps that the *Melloni* judgment provided a lax interpretation of EU (primary) law,[7] which revealed

---

[3] This expression was used by Vogler (2014), p. 182, who developed the approach of Slaughter (1994), pp. 99 ff.

[4] CJEU, Grand Chamber, *Melloni v. Ministerio Fiscal*, judgment of 26 February 2013, C-399/11.

[5] On the relationship between EU law and constitutional law in the *Melloni* judgment see, from different perspectives, Demetrio Crespo and Sánz Hermida, in this volume, Sect. 3.1; Pollicino and Bassini, in this volume, Sects. 5 and 6.1; Schneider, in this volume, Sect. 3.3.2.

[6] See among others Ruggeri (2015), pp. 10 ff.; Böse (2015), pp. 141 f.

[7] Böse (2015), p. 142.

a closed view of the European Union as having a self-sufficient legal system aimed at saving its supremacy over domestic law in order to ensure its own existence.[8] A look at the reaction by the Spanish Constitutional Tribunal to this preliminary ruling[9] might seem to confirm that the Luxembourg judges achieved the prevalence of EU law over national law and one-sided adaptation by the domestic court. Yet the reasoning of the 2014 ruling of *Tribunal Constitutional* highlights the clear attempt to justify the solution adopted on the basis of Strasbourg case-law. By relying on the doctrine that allows for unequivocal waiver of the right to personal involvement in criminal proceedings, provided that the accused is ensured legal assistance, the Spanish court ruled out the requirement of a retrial being always a necessary condition to save the fairness of a procedure held *in absentia* in the requesting country. In this way, however, the Constitutional Tribunal also indirectly invoked Strasbourg case-law, which, while generally allowing *in absentia* trials in cases of unequivocal waiver of participation, requires the contracting states to ensure legal assistance even where defendants should in principle take part in the judicial proceedings and their absence is unjustified.[10]

One could wonder why the Spanish constitutional judges chose this reasoning. The simplest explanation might be that they felt the need to support the decision to depart from its jurisprudence of 2000, which had stressed the "absolute content of the right to a fair trial",[11] on the basis of the long-developed jurisprudence of the Strasbourg Court.[12] On close examination, it can be doubted that the *Melloni* judgment truly aimed at sustaining the self-sufficient primacy of EU law over any other legal order, since Framework Decision 2009/299 does not only contain a general reference to the European Convention[13] but also and more specifically requires national law to comply with the Strasbourg case-law regarding the means to ensure the knowledge of the scheduled trial.[14] Yet in this case the fact that notice of the proceedings was sent to the two lawyers of Mr. Melloni was clearly not enough to ensure his awareness of the proceedings, as it did not put him in a position to decide whether to attend the court hearing in person. Moreover, there was no clear evidence that he decided not to participate in the court proceedings. To be sure, even the appointment of a lawyer of one's own confidence does not in itself demonstrate the accused's waiver of his right to take part personally in criminal proceedings. In this case, however, the lawyers who defended Mr. Melloni on appeal no longer represented him, since he had withdrawn their mandate. This in turn casts doubts as to the fulfilment of the requirements set forth by the 2009 EU legislation, which, although not requiring the proof of the unequivocal waiver of personal participation,

---

[8] Ruggeri (2015), pp. 10 ff.

[9] STC 26/2014.

[10] Ruggeri, in Part V of this volume, Sect. 2.2.

[11] Cf. Demetrio Crespo and Sánz Hermida, in this volume, Sect. 1.

[12] In this sense see also Villamarín López, in this volume, Sect. 7.1.

[13] Recital No. 1.

[14] Recital No. 8.

conditioned the accused's surrender on the fact that he was truly defended by a counsel who, no matter whether appointed by the state or by himself, was mandated to do so.[15]

It might be argued, therefore, that the decision of the Spanish Constitutional Tribunal, while complying with the Luxembourg judgment, aimed at bringing to light its inconsistencies and particularly the inability of the EU legislation to properly achieve one of its own main goals, namely orienting the international cooperation in the European judicial area towards the requirements set forth by Strasbourg case-law. Furthermore, we might perhaps assume that the Spanish constitutional case-law also aimed to demonstrate that the Luxembourg Court's approach inevitably weakened EU law as well. As noted, some specific requirements posed by the EU legislation—especially the requirement that a lawyer mandated by the sought person defend him at trial—were ignored by the Court of Justice.

It may therefore be doubted that the *Melloni* judgment could be justified even from the perspective of EU law[16]; and this doubt is enhanced by the examination of EU primary law. We have seen that legal scholarship has also raised several criticisms against this judgment, mainly because it provided a weak interpretation of the EU Charter, starting with the principle of the strongest protection of fundamental rights enshrined in Article 53 CFR. Yet the logic of prevalence turned out to frustrate EU primary law at a deeper level still. There is little doubt that the requirement of Article 4(2) TEU that the Union respect the national identity of member states should also be extended to the constitutional identity of EU countries, which not only relates to the state apparatus but also to the overall system of fundamental rights protection.[17]

Furthermore, Article 67 TFEU—far from generically recognising the common area of freedom, security and justice as being based on fundamental rights—acknowledges that this area can only exist as long as the strongest protection of fundamental rights is ensured. This demonstrates that, where individual rights are at stake, EU law also should not leave any room for rigid forms of respect for individual legal systems as traditionally interpreted. In this context, the *Melloni* judgment may also appear to have overlooked that the principle of sincere cooperation of Article 4(3) TEU, requiring the Union and the member states to assist each other in carrying out tasks flowing from the treaties, advocates a transcultural understanding of the relationship not only with the European Convention but furthermore with national (constitutional) law.

In the light of this, we can even doubt that the Luxembourg Court's attempt to impose the supremacy of the EU legislation over constitutional law also entailed a self-referential view of EU law as a system of human rights protection closed to any

---

[15] Schneider, in this volume, Sect. 3.2.1.2.

[16] In this sense see instead Schneider, in this volume, Sect. 3.3.2.

[17] On this argument, which was, however, not taken into consideration by the Luxembourg Court in the *Melloni* judgment, see Ruggeri (2015), p. 23.

other legal order. On the contrary, there seem to be good reasons to conclude that the *Melloni* judgment aimed at defending the solutions laid down by Framework Decision 2009/299/JHA as being able to provide a satisfactory development of the balances among conflicting interests set forth by the Strasbourg case-law. This attempt, however, was only apparently successful. The aforementioned arguments lead us to conclude that the submission to the Court of Justice's ruling by the Spanish Constitutional Tribunal, bringing to light the deficiencies of the *Melloni* judgment, was intended to provoke a reaction by subsequent case-law. It is worth observing that the Spanish judges, despite departing from the approach followed in the 2000 constitutional decision, still invoked the requirement, underlined since then, that the core contents of the right to a fair trial also be fulfilled in cases of transborder cooperation in order to ensure full respect for the constitutional principle of human dignity.

It is worth observing that the focus on human dignity also lies at the heart of a decision issued in December 2015 by the German Federal Constitutional Court, which expressly challenged the *Melloni* doctrine.[18] I shall deal with this decision while examining the feasibility of a substantive criminal law approach to the problem of *in absentia* trials.[19] Moreover, this important decision also deserves attention in the context of the present discussion, as it provides a rather different example of the logic of prevalence over other systems of human rights protection. Thus, prevalence does not necessarily entail the forced adaptation of national (constitutional) law to the standards imposed upon by supranational (or international) law, but can also take place in the opposite direction. In this decision, the German constitutional judges allowed refusal of execution of a European arrest warrant that, despite fulfilling the safeguards set by EU law in relation to proceedings held *in absentia*, can infringe on the fundamental requirements of human dignity and the rule of law, which form part of the "inalienable constitutional identity" under Article 79(3) in conjunction with Article 1(1) of the German Basic Law. It is noteworthy that the reference to the constitutional identity clearly shifted the focus on the aforementioned limit of EU law action, as laid down by the Treaty of the European Union.

Interestingly, the 2015 German decision also largely inherited the criticisms promoted by the Spanish constitutional ruling of 2014. A different reaction, however, distinguishes the two approaches. The German constitutional judges, although invoking the so-called "eternity guarantee" of the Basic Law, decided not to request a preliminary ruling by the European Court of Justice. It might be argued that this decision was reasonably justified by the fact that German criminal procedural law "allows trials in the absence of the defendant under certain circumstances", which would cast doubt on the fact that *in absentia* trials could truly "violate the core of

---

[18] BVerfG, decision of 15 December 2015, Az. 2 BvR 2735/14. On this decision see Vogel, in this volume, Sect. 1; Pollicino and Bassini, in this volume, Sect. 6.2; Demetrio Crespo and Sánz Hermida, in this volume, Sect. 3.1; Schneider, in this volume, Sect. 3.3.2.

[19] Below, Sect. 3.2.1.

human dignity".[20] Yet we might perhaps also assume that the approach adopted by the German Constitutional Court constituted another way to provoke a reaction—this time, however, by the Luxembourg Court, which was given the opportunity for a re-examination of its previous position. One might even see in the 2015 ruling the attempt to pursue a more ambitious goal, which, as noted, highlights another expression of the logic of prevalence. It appears to me that the German constitutional court didn't just arrogate for itself the control on the "equivalence to national standards of the level of protection afforded by EU law to fundamental rights",[21] but also aimed at promoting this equivalence by the Luxembourg case-law, thus seeking adaptation (at least in relation German law) by EU law.

It is well-known that considerable developments have since then taken place in the relationship between domestic law and EU law. While constitutional courts do not appear to yield ground and again promote centralised models for solution of normative conflicts even in cases of self-executing EU law provisions,[22] the examination of the Luxembourg case-law reveals the clear attempt of the Court of Justice to come closer to the requirements set forth by constitutional law.[23] Notwithstanding these developments, there seems still to be no clear indications by supranational case-law regarding the lawfulness under EU law of criminal trials that rule out the involvement of the individuals concerned prior to decision-making. This does not mean, however, that Luxembourg case-law has not at all evolved from the *Melloni* doctrine. It is true that there is no case-law against the possibility of criminal decisions issued after excluding the intervention of private parties and especially of the accused. Yet we shall see that the judgments rendered by the EU Court of Justice in the cases *Covaci*[24] and *Dworzecki*[25] highlight a clear tendency to enhance the information rights in the trials held *inaudito reo* and *in absentia*.[26] As far as *inaudito reo* procedures are concerned, this tendency has been further developed by the subsequent judgments in the cases *Sleutjes*[27] and *Tranca, Reiter and Opria*.[28]

---

[20] For references to German constitutional case-law in relation to the problem of *in absentia* trials in the field of extradition cf. Schneider, in this volume, Sect. 3.3.2.

[21] In this sense see Pollicino and Bassini, in this volume, Sect. 6.2.

[22] See the recent judgment 269/2017 of the Italian Constitutional Court.

[23] See especially the solutions adopted in the *Aranyosi and Căldăraru* case. Cf. CJEU, Grand Chamber, *Aranyosi and Căldăraru*, judgment of 5 April 2016, C-404-15 and C-659/15. Even more significant developments are apparent in the *Taricco* saga, if one compares the rigid solutions of the 2015 ruling (CJEU, Grand Chamber, *Taricco and others*, judgment of 8 September 2015, C-105/14) with the more flexible findings of the judgment issued in December 2017 (CJEU, Grand Chamber, *M.A.S. and M.B.*, judgment of 5 December 2017, C-42/17).

[24] CJEU, *Covaci*, judgment of 15 October 2015, C-216/14.

[25] CJEU, *Dworzecki*, judgment of 24 May 2016, C-108/16 PPU.

[26] See below, Sects. 3.2.3.1 and 3.3.

[27] CJEU, *Sleutjes*, judgment of 12 October 2017, C-278/16.

[28] CJEU, *Tranca, Reiter and Opria*, judgment of 22 March 2017, C-124/16, C-188/16 and C-213/16.

2.2 Mutual Approximation of Different Systems of Human Rights Protection, as the Best Means of Balancing the Conflicting Interests Posed by Specific Cases

The strong confrontation that has taken place among different legal orders (and different jurisprudences) in relation to participatory rights in criminal proceedings, as noted, has also revealed a second scenario, characterised by the mutual approximation of diverse systems of human rights protection towards common patterns. The issue of *in absentia* trials has surely been one of the fields in which transjudicial dialogue has led to considerable changes both in domestic and international human rights law, even though they have not always followed a straightforward path. It is not a coincidence that the landmark decision *Colozza v. Italy* was issued in relation to the Italian criminal justice, which at that time widely allowed for default proceedings. In this fundamental judgment, the European Court, after deducing by the general guarantee of a fair trial the accused's right to take part in criminal hearings, recognised the lawfulness of *in absentia* trials—if provided for by national law—on the condition that the defendant can later obtain "a fresh determination of the merits of the charge".[29]

This Solomon-like solution allowed for Strasbourg jurisprudence permeating criminal justice systems which are characterised by a very different tradition. The developments that have taken place in Italian law over three decades provide a clear example of this phenomenon. As far as Italy is concerned, however, it took several years before this approach could positively affect domestic law. It is true that, although the 1987 Delegation Law for the new code laid down a general requirement of compliance with the European Convention,[30] this did not suffice to orient the new Italian criminal justice system towards the indications provided by Strasbourg case-law. Notwithstanding the *Colozza* case, the 1988 codification therefore reproduced the old default proceedings, without, moreover, drawing a clear distinction between two main situations highlighted by the European Court, namely the case of non-attendance due to the accused's waiver of personal participation and that in which criminal proceedings are instituted without any clear indication of the defendant's willingness. An inevitable ambiguity thus remained inherent in the rules on default proceedings, which applied both to defendants possibly unaware of the institution of criminal proceedings and to those who chose not to participate in the proceedings. Furthermore, the 1988 code also did not comply with the need to ensure the opportunity of a retrial to the defendants convicted *in absentia*, but only a tool aimed at granting them leave to appeal out of time against the conviction (*restituzione in termini*), while offloading onto them the burden of proving that they remained unaware of the proceedings without fault.

Nevertheless, it took almost two decades before a reform of this problematic area was carried out in Italy. Yet this hurried reform, made under the pressure of two new

---

[29] ECtHR, *Colozza v. Italy*, judgment of 12 February 1985, Appl. No. 9024/80, para 29.
[30] Art. 1 Law 81/1987.

convictions by the Strasbourg Court,[31] led neither to the abolition of default proceedings nor to in-depth change of their structure. Thus, Law 60/2005 only amended the rules on leave to appeal out of time against a conviction *in absentia*, freeing defendants from the burden of proving their unawareness of the proceedings.

It is more than doubtful that this reform satisfied the requirements set forth by the *Colozza* case, particularly that of a fresh-determination of the merits of the case. Thus, defendants convicted *in absentia* were not ensured the opportunity of a retrial but only had a facilitated access to the second instance, characterised, however, by considerable limitations compared to the first instance. Not only was there no possibility of applying for alternative proceedings in the second instance, but furthermore the appeal proceedings maintained the original structure of a scrutiny of the judgment rendered *in absentia*, a scrutiny based mainly on the written records of evidence already collected. Moreover, despite opening the door of second instance, Law 60/2005 failed to amend the conditions for the exercise of the right to evidence in the appeal proceedings, with the result that defendants convicted in default proceedings could only have evidence obtained in the second instance by proving that they had been unaware of the initiation of criminal proceedings.[32]

In sum, the solutions provided in 2005 ensured a very weak protection to the right to effective participation in proceedings,[33] and a rigorous application of the original case-law of the European Court would probably have sufficed to find an infringement of the Convention. By upholding the conviction of Italy in the *Sejdovic* case, the Grand Chamber however provided a rather ambiguous response about the 2005 reform,[34] stressing that it was still premature, in the absence of case-law on the new legislation, to draw conclusions on its ability to avoid future infringements of the Convention.[35] The developments that took place in Italian case-law after 2005 revealed the dangerous backslide towards solutions close to those reached before this reform.[36] In the 2008 *Cat Berro* decision, however, the Court confirmed the adequacy of the 2005 legislative reform to grant the defendants tried *in absentia* the full satisfaction of their right to a retrial.[37] It might be argued that this result aimed at avoiding future clashes with Italy in this delicate field. Yet, along with aforementioned arguments on the limitations of the appeal proceedings, a close examination of the rules on judicial service also would probably have enabled the

---

[31] Cf. ECtHR, 1st Chamber, *Sejdovic v. Italy*, judgment of 10 November 2004, Appl. No. 56581/00; and ECtHR, *Somogyi v. Italy*, judgment of 18 May 2004, Appl. No. 67972/01.

[32] Cf. Art. 603 CCP-Italy (version 2005). On this point cf. critically Negri (2005), p. 268.

[33] Carini (2008), p. 283.

[34] Chiavario (2005), p. 256.

[35] ECtHR, Grand Chamber, *Sejdovic v. Italy*, judgment of 1 March 2006, Appl. No. 56581/00.

[36] In several decisions the Supreme Court, while deeming the notification at the law firm equivalent to a personal notification, charged defendants again with the burden of proving the reasons for which they had remained unaware of the notification made at their legal domicile. See CCass, judgment of 12 December 2007, *Ciarlantini*, in CED rv. 239207; CCass, judgment of 10 May 2006, *Gherasim*, in Rivista penale (2007), p. 234.

[37] ECtHR, *Cat Berro v. Italy*, decision of 25 November 2008, Appl. No. 34192/07.

European Court to draw different conclusions on the Italian reform of 2005. Since the rules on court summons were not at all amended, defendants were still not always in a position not only to decide whether to waive their right to personal participation, but also, after the decision being held *in absentia*, whether to request to be relieved from the effects of the expiration of the time to challenge the conviction.

From the viewpoint of the present discussion, it is also worth observing that both national courts and the European Court somewhat changed their jurisprudence over the years. In particular, it is interesting to note that, while Italian case-law has in the recent years started interpreting the new rules in the light of the Strasbourg jurisprudence,[38] the Strasbourg Court has become more and more flexible as to the requirements of subsequent remedies. In *Mariani v. France*, the European judges seemed to focus solely on whether the defendant was given the opportunity of applying for a retrial.[39] The Court followed a similar approach in relation to other fair trial safeguards, such as those of independence and impartiality of the judicial authority. For instance, in *Öcalan v. Turkey*, the Court stressed that, although in these cases also the

> "most appropriate form of redress would be for the applicant to be given a retrial", [...] the "specific remedial measures, if any, required of a respondent State in order to discharge its obligations under Article 46 had to depend on the particular circumstances of the individual case and be determined in the light of the terms of the Court's judgment in that case, and with due regard to the [...] case-law of the Court".[40]

These rulings, therefore, seem to demonstrate that the suitability of the subsequent remedy largely depends on the circumstances of each concrete case, which should be assessed in the light of the degree of effectiveness of the right to a defence in domestic proceedings. This can also explain the approach followed in the *Sejdovic* and especially in the *Cat Berro* case, in which the Court, while deeming the legislative solutions adopted by Italy in 2005 consistent with the Convention, further weakened its own jurisprudence, going far beyond the approach adopted in *Jones v. the United Kingdom*.[41] In this decision, the European judges had already admitted that a subsequent remedy can also be "the reopening of the time allowed for appealing against a conviction *in absentia*"; this, however, on the condition that the "defendant was entitled to attend the hearing in the court of appeal and to request the admission of new evidence, [...] so that the proceedings as a whole could be said to have been fair".[42] Five years later, dealing with the *Cat Berro* case, the European

---

[38] These developments are apparent particularly in the case-law of the Italian Supreme Court. After the 2005, some decisions followed a different approach than that adopted by the Sections indicated in footnote 36, offloading onto the competent authority the task of demonstrating the interruption of any contact between the defendants and their lawyers, if the conviction issued *in absentia* was notified at the law firm chosen by the defendants as their legal domicile. Cf. CCass, judgment of 1 March 2006, *Bidimost*, in CED rv. 233614.

[39] ECtHR, *Mariani v. France*, judgment of 31 March 2005, Appl. No. 43640/98.

[40] ECtHR, Grand Chamber, *Öcalan v. Turkey*, judgment of 12 May 2005, Appl. No. 46221/99.

[41] ECtHR, *Jones v. the United Kingdom*, decision of 9 September 2003, Appl. No. 30900/02.

[42] In this sense cf. Bachmaier Winter, in this volume, Sect. 2.4.

judges accepted that the defendants' right to personal participation can also be satisfied by a mechanism that allows them to accede to a second instance, notwithstanding that it considerably restricts their right to adduce exculpatory evidence.[43] This result materialised in Italian law, in which the 2005 reform, as noted, still charged the accused with the burden of proving that in the first instance he had remained unaware of the proceedings without any fault.

It is worth observing that, while the Italian legislature dropped this limitation through Law 67/2014, which abolished the default proceedings and introduced a new procedure *in absentia*,[44] the Strasbourg Court has never reviewed this jurisprudence until now. It might be argued that this development has brought European case-law closer to those domestic criminal justice systems that provide for limitations to the right to evidence in a new higher instance, similar to those established by Italian law before the 2005 reform. In this way, however, the constant reference to a fresh re-determination of the criminal charge, which the European judges have also reiterated in the recent judgment *Moreira Ferreira v. Portugal (No. 2)*,[45] seems to have lost its original ability to link the right to a re-trial or a remedy with the effective fulfilment of defence rights and the possibility of the accused being granted the opportunity denied in the proceedings held in his absence.

3 The Fair Trial Safeguards Due in the Proceedings That Exclude or Restrict Participation of the Defence in a Criminal Law Action

3.1 Premise

Against this background, I shall now compare the models for solution regarding those proceedings that exclude or restrict in a relevant way the involvement of the defendant and other private parties. As noted, it is precisely in the field of *in absentia* trials that we have witnessed significant developments not only in

---

[43] To be sure, in the *Cat Berro* case the Court was not called upon to scrutinise whether the right to evidence could be properly satisfied in the appeal proceedings instituted after the accused's application for leave to appeal against the conviction. However, the European judges examined, albeit incidentally, the merits of the Italian reform by providing a response to the question, left open by the Grand Chamber in the *Sejdovic* case (fn. 35), of whether the 2005 legislation fit the requirements set forth in the European Convention. The response was that this reform enabled the individuals convicted in their absence to obtain a facilitated access to the second instance, which allowed a re-determination of the case and the exercise of the defence rights. In this way, therefore, the Strasbourg case-law accepted a solution that, viewed as a whole, still limited the defendant's right to evidence in the second instance.

[44] On this legislative reform see Mangiaracina, in this volume, Sect. 5. Cf. also Quattrocolo (2014); Vigoni (2014); Daniele and Paulesu (2015).

[45] ECtHR, Grand Chamber, *Moreira Ferreira v. Portugal (No. 2)*, judgment of 11 July 2017, Appl. No. 19867/12.

international human rights law and in EU law, but also in the constitutional models of a fair trial. By largely drawing on the heritage of Strasbourg case-law, EU institutions have recently shown a growing interest in the harmonisation of domestic criminal justice in this problematic area. Along with the general acknowledgment of the right to be present at trial, the EU legislation still appears to aim at the enshrinement of the conditions under which fair criminal proceedings can be held in the accused's absence. It should be acknowledged, however, that the jurisprudence of the European Court of human rights has not remained entirely consistent with its earlier decisions.

Yet, the focus on *in absentia* trials cannot sufficiently reflect the complexity of this this problematic area, which suggests broadening the viewpoint of research in two directions. Firstly, I shall comparatively examine the human rights requirements that must be satisfied in those special proceedings that are structured in a way that not only always excludes the involvement of the defendant, but also jeopardises the interest of private parties other than the accused to contribute to fact-finding. In this context, particular attention will be attached to *inaudito reo* proceedings. On a second level, I will examine the participatory safeguards that human rights law acknowledges in cases of closed and *in camera* hearings.

3.2   Human Rights in Trials Held In Absentia

3.2.1   Human Rights and Criminal Law Principles Endangered by the Conduct of a Criminal Law Action Against Absent Defendants

At first glance, *in absentia* trials do not appear to pose specific problems from the perspective of human rights law. International human rights charters, in general, do not explicitly acknowledge the right to take part personally in criminal proceedings. The International Covenant constitutes an exception, in that it explicitly grants defendants the right to be tried in their own presence.[46] By contrast, neither the European Convention nor other important human rights instruments, such as the American Convention, contain an explicit reference to the right to be present at trial, which does not appear among the general requirements of the right to a fair hearing, nor among the minimum rights of the person charged with a criminal offence. Constitutional law also rarely recognises the right to be present in criminal proceedings in explicit terms. At the EU law level, as noted, the recent Directive 2016/343, after solemnly proclaiming the right to be personally involved in criminal proceedings, focuses on the requirements of trials being held in the absence of the suspects or the accused.

It is worth observing, however, that most of the fair trial safeguards recognised by international human rights instruments were structured in such a way that they

---

[46] Art. 14(3)(d) ICCPR.

not only are compatible with, but also promote, the personal involvement of the defendant in criminal proceedings. It is no coincidence that the drafters of the American Convention placed the right to linguistic assistance at the top of the accused's fair trial rights,[47] while the Rome Convention emphasises the need for detailed information on the charge in a language the accused can understand.[48] These provisions clearly demonstrate the importance that international human rights law attaches to the right of the defendant not just to be formally present at trial but furthermore to follow the procedural activities.

The comparative-law analysis carried in this research provides an overview of all the essential standards endangered by the carrying out of a criminal trial without the personal involvement of private parties. From the perspective of procedural law, there are a number of fundamental rights and principles governing a modern criminal justice, which can be jeopardised by the conduct of a criminal law action without the involvement of the accused, starting with the presumption of innocence. EU law highlights this link in very clear terms by means of the systematic approach adopted by Directive 2016/343, which deals with both certain aspects of the presumption of innocence and the right to be present in criminal trials. There is little doubt that, if defendants are not enabled to decide whether to take part in criminal proceedings, they are also deprived of the opportunity of making their own contribution to fact-finding by countering the proof of guilt that, pursuant to international human rights law instruments[49] and the EU Fundamental Rights Charter,[50] marks the end of their status as innocent individuals. Furthermore, the way in which *in absentia* trials are structured in some European countries reveal that a sort of reproach (if not even disdain) still characterises the treatment of 'contumacy' of those who (choose to) remain away from the procedural scene. It has been noted that Italian law, in spite of the abolition of the default proceedings and the new procedural safeguards granted to absent defendants, still charges them with considerable burdens—particularly with the burden of proving the lack of any negligence—to obtain subsequent remedies,[51] such as the annulment of the conviction in the appeal proceedings[52] or the revocation of the final judgment.[53]

The focus on participatory rights in the light of the parties' contribution to fact-finding helps avoid viewing the right to be personally involved in criminal proceedings as an alternative to legal assistance. Doubtless, there is a strict link between the presumption of innocence, the right to taking part personally in a criminal trial and the proper exercise of defence rights. Remarkably, the International Covenant has enshrined the right to be present at trial in the same provision that ensures defen-

---

[47] Art. 8(2)(a) ACHR.

[48] Art. 6(3)(a) ECHR.

[49] Arts. 6(2) ECHR and 14(2) ICCPR.

[50] Art. 48(1) CFR.

[51] Cf. Mangiaracina, in this volume, Sect. 5.2.

[52] Art. 604(5-*bis*) CCP-Italy.

[53] Art. 629-*bis* CCP-Italy.

dants the right to defend themselves or to obtain the assistance of a lawyer.[54] The EU Charter in turn deals with the presumption of innocence and the right to a defence jointly.[55] In this context, it should also be acknowledged that depriving the accused of his right to follow the procedural activities entails considerable risks for the right to a defence even if a lawyer is present. The European Court had the opportunity for dealing with this delicate issue in *Stanford v. United Kingdom*, in which it rejected the application of a defendant who complained that he could not participate effectively in the proceedings since he had been placed in a glass-fronted dock.[56] Despite acknowledging that the applicant had "difficulties in hearing some of the evidence given during the trial",[57] however, the European judges stressed that he had been sufficiently represented by his counsel. This was surely a rather unfortunate argument, which revealed the Court's underestimation of the importance of the possibility of the defendant following the proceedings personally within the limits of their capacities.[58]

On close examination, the *Stanford* case demonstrates the existence of another risk from a human rights perspective, which concerns the right of the accused to hear and to take part actively in obtaining evidence, particularly if incriminating evidence is at stake.[59] In this respect also, no alternative should be viewed between the right to personal participation and the guarantee of legal assistance, since taking part in the evidence-gathering does not presuppose the accused being entitled to cross-examine incriminating witnesses. Even if national law does not provide for it, it is of utmost importance that a defendant can contribute to evidence-gathering by providing his lawyer with information that can enhance the potentials of legal assistance. To be sure, European case-law has not always provided clear indications on the safeguards due to the accused if legal assistance is ensured. Along with the *Stanford* case, there are several rulings in which the Court satisfied itself with the fact that national law granted solely the lawyer some fair trial rights, such as the right to access the prosecutorial file.[60] It is thus no surprise that Italian courts allowed for the use of testimonial evidence on the sole condition that the defence lawyer could take part in the execution of letters rogatory, even though the accused expressly requested personal participation.[61] Yet there is no doubt that this interpretation frustrates the *audi alteram partem* rule, giving a rather formalistic sense to the right to

---

[54] Art. 14(3)(d) ICCPR.

[55] Art. 48 CFR.

[56] ECtHR, *Stanford v. United Kingdom*, judgment of 23 February 1994, Appl. No. 16757/90.

[57] *Ibid.*, para 25.

[58] Trechsel (2005), p. 253 fn. 41.

[59] Arts. 6(2)(d) ECHR and 14(3)(e) ICCPR.

[60] ECtHR, *Kremzow v. Austria*, judgment of 21 September 1993, Appl. No. 12350/86.

[61] Cf. among others CCass, judgment of 1 December 2010, *De Falco*, in CED rv. 248963. On this case-law see critically Caprioli (2013), p. 446.

be fairly involved in the collection of (oral) evidence, as recognised by the Italian Constitution.[62]

Similar concerns can be raised in the light of the European Convention. It should be noted, however, that the Strasbourg Court adopted these solutions in cases, such as that dealt with in *Stanford v. United Kingdom*, in which the accused's right to take part in the evidence-gathering was restricted, but not completely taken away. There is no doubt that, where a criminal law action is instituted against defendants whose awareness of the proceedings is not proven, the 'difficulties' highlighted in the *Stanford* judgment become almost insurmountable. In such cases, it is apparent that the initiation of a trial *in absentia* turns out to infringe on a fundamental precondition of the *audi alteram partem* rule, namely the right to be informed about the accusation and the institution of criminal proceedings. As noted, the focus of the European Convention on the need for detailed information on the charges in a language that the accused understands reveals the clear attention paid by international human rights law to personal knowledge of the (merits of the) proceedings. Regrettably, the *Melloni* judgment, which satisfied itself with the legal assistance provided by two lawyers who no longer represented the accused in court, did not show interest in preserving the personal involvement of the defendant in criminal proceedings. This inevitably weakened the standard of protection of EU law on condition that a lawyer was present, which paved the way for the approach followed by Directive 2016/343/EU. Thus, notwithstanding the relevance attached by both Directive 2010/64/EU and Directive 2012/13/EU to the need to provide the defendants with information on the charges preferred against them in a language they can understand,[63] the 2016 legislation, departing from the Framework Decision 2009/299/JHA, does not require that a mandated lawyer represent the accused in court, but only that a lawyer—no matter whether mandated by the accused or by the state—is present at trial.[64] Yet it is apparent that "even the presence of a mandated lawyer is insufficient if the defendant has not deliberately chosen to have himself defended by the lawyer while absent from the trial".[65]

Whatever view one may have of the relationship between the aforementioned ruling of the *Bundesverfassungsgericht* and the *Melloni* doctrine of the Luxembourg Court, as well as the decisions of the Spanish *Tribunal Constitucional*,[66] it has been anticipated that this ruling of the German court adopted an unprecedented approach, which raises further concerns about *in absentia* trials from the viewpoint of substantial criminal law. The German constitutional judges pointed out that German criminal law is strongly based on the principle of individual guilt as a part of the inalienable constitutional identity. From this it follows that the possibility of a criminal punishment, which also entails a socio-ethical reproach (*sozial-ethischer*

---

[62] Art. 111(4) Const.-Italy.

[63] Cf. Arts. 3(2) DIT and 6 DICP.

[64] Art. 8(2)(b) DPIRPT.

[65] In this sense Schneider, in this volume, Sect. 3.2.1.2.

[66] Above, Sect. 2.1.

Vorwurf), presupposes that the competent court could ascertain the accused's individual blameworthiness (*individuelle Vorwerfbarkeit*), as a rule, in his presence.[67] Therefore, the German Constitutional Court deduced from the principle of individual guilt the procedural-law consequence that defendants must always be ensured minimum defence safeguards. Significantly, these safeguards—particularly the possibility of contributing to decision-making by presenting "circumstances for consideration to the court, circumstances that may be exonerating or relevant for sentencing"[68]—must also be guaranteed in cases of international surrender procedures.

Doubtless, this approach opens up new perspectives in relation to the problem of *in absentia* trials. To be sure, notwithstanding its strong position, the German court did not rule out the lawfulness of international surrender in all cases of *in absentia*. This decision, however, casts doubts as to whether in the EU area of freedom, security and justice, cross-border cooperation can be provided where in the issuing state the criminal trial was held in the absence of the accused without the proof that he was personally informed of the institution of the proceedings and especially without the proof of his intention not to be involved in them. This raises the question of the extent to which criminal liability can be ascertained in purely objective terms and without the defendant attending court. The comparative-law analysis of European countries reveals that the principle of individual guilt is widely rooted in several criminal law systems. It is noteworthy that Italian constitutional law followed a systematic approach that couples in the same provision the principle of individual guilt and the presumption of innocence.[69] In Greece, even though the Constitution does not expressly deal with the involvement of the accused and other private parties in criminal proceedings, the defendant's participatory rights hold constitutional status by means of the combination of a fundamental procedural law principle with supra-statutory force, namely the presumption of innocence [Art. 6(2) ECHR in combination with Art. 28(1) of the Greek Constitution], with specific constitutional provisions concerned with other guarantees. Among them, we should mention the right to legal protection by the courts and to a judicial hearing, (Art. 20 Const.), as well as the guarantees of 'natural judge' (Art. 8 Const.) and of judicial impartiality and independence (Arts. 87–90 Const.), the due process guarantees in the context of deprivation of liberty and illegal detention (Art. 6 Const.), the public nature of court hearings (Art. 93 Const.) and, most importantly, the general constitutional requirement of respect for human dignity [Art. 2(1) Const.].[70] As noted, the focus on the state's obligation to respect human dignity provides constitutional relevance to the accused's participatory rights under German law too, which "prevents individuals in criminal proceedings from being treated as mere objects".[71] Although Portuguese

---

[67] B VerfG, decision of 15 December 2015 (fn. 18), para 2.a.aa.

[68] *Ibid.*

[69] Art. 27(2) Const.-Italy.

[70] Billis and Gkaniatsos, in this volume, Sect. 1.

[71] In these terms see Vogel, in this volume, Sect. 1.

constitutional law also acknowledges the principle that criminal liability cannot be transferred to other people,[72] it is interesting to note that the 1997 Constitutional Amendment enacted into the Portuguese Constitution a provision that explicitly allows for procedural activities to be carried out in the absence of the accused, while requiring lawmakers to define the cases and provide that defence rights are ensured in these situations.[73]

Furthermore, cutting across the European criminal justice systems highlights that the accused's personal attendance is not only necessary to ascertain the criminal intent and negligence, but also to further issues relevant to the examination of overall individual blameworthiness, such as the defendant's mental state. In the light of this, the possibility of hearing the defendant (and under certain conditions, of carrying out further inquiry about the accused, such as expert evidence) should be deemed a necessary condition of issuing a verdict that not only reflects the objective ascertainment of facts, but also the scrutiny of the individual guilt. It is true that some issues, such as the accused's capacity and mental state, should be examined in relation to the time in which the alleged offence was committed. Yet this does not mean ignoring his conduct at trial, particularly if a relatively short period of time elapsed between the facts and institution of criminal proceedings.

It is worth observing that under Italian law, even in the field of juvenile criminal justice, notwithstanding that minor defendants usually undergo considerable changes in a very short time, judges tend to scrutinise the accused's mental state in a somewhat diachronic way. Thus Italian courts, starting with the general duty of the judge to inquiry into the minor's personality,[74] enable the competent judge to examine the minor's mental state not only on the basis of the accused's behaviour at the time in which the alleged offence was committed but also of the evolution of his personality and his conduct during the proceedings.[75] This jurisprudence raises several human rights concerns as to the systematic approach followed by the Italian legislature, which has extended to the proceedings against minor offenders the new rules on *in absentia* trials introduced by the aforementioned Law 67/2014. This legislative solution entails that not only the trial[76] but also the intermediate phase[77] can be held in the accused's absence in the field of juvenile criminal justice too. It

---

[72] Art. 30(3) Const.-Portugal.

[73] Art. 32(6) Const.-Portugal. See Costa Ramos and Churro, in this volume, Sect. 4.1.

[74] Art. 9 Decree of the President of the Republic 448/1988, which provides a comprehensive statute on the criminal proceedings against minor offenders.

[75] CCass, 29 April 2010, n. 24004, in www.dejure.giuffre.it This jurisprudence relies on a ruling of the Joint Sections of the Supreme Court under Royal Legislative Decree 1404/1934, which laid down the previous statute on juvenile criminal justice. See CCass, Joint Sections, judgment of 26 January 1985, *Tammaro*, in Cassazione penale 1985, p. 1333 ff. For further references and a critical analysis of Italian case-law see Panebianco (2012), pp. 157 f.

[76] Art. 31(1) of the Decree of the President of the Republic 448/1988. See Bargis (2017), pp. 157 ff.

[77] Thus Article 1(1) of the Decree of the President of the Republic 448/1988, which contains a general reference to the ordinary rules on criminal proceedings, allows for provisions of Articles 420-*bis* et seqq. CCP-Italy to be applied to the intermediate phase in the proceedings against minors. Cf. Cesari (2017), pp. 137 ff.

should be taken into account, however, that under Italian law, the criminal proceedings against minor defendants are characterised by the fact that the trial constitutes an exception. The intermediate phase holds a central importance, being the procedural stage in which not only is the investigation of the minor's personality usually carried out, but also a number of important rulings can be issued precisely with a view to avoiding the institution of a public trial (judicial pardon, probation, as well as diversion due to the low severity and occasional nature of the conduct). Therefore, in spite of the general applicability of the rules on the proceedings *in absentia*, Italian law still enables the competent judge to order the minor accused to be brought to court coercively,[78] a judicial power that should however be exercised with great caution and for the purposes of those favourable decisions.[79]

3.2.2 The Different Relevance of the Defendant's Absence Under Human Rights Law: The Free Decision Not to Be Present at Trial and the Failure to Attend a Court Hearing Without Any Clear Indications of the Accused's Intentions

To reduce the risks of infringement on human rights, the carrying out of a criminal law action in the accused's absence must satisfy specific conditions. Since the landmark decision *Colozza v. Italy*, the contribution made by Strasbourg case-law has been of utmost importance in the laying down of such qualitative requirements. A comparison of the European jurisprudence and the developments that have taken place in EU law may seem to highlight a different approach to two main situations, depending on whether or not the failure to attend a court hearing was due to a free decision of the interested party. The former situation relates to the case in which there are clear indications that the defendant waived his right to personal participation, while the latter covers all the situations there is no (unequivocal) decision by the accused, who may in turn have remained fully unaware of the proceedings instituted against him.

On close examination, it can be doubted that Strasbourg case-law draws such a clear division line between the cases in which non-attendance in court stems from the accused's free decision to waive his right to be present at trial and those in which there are no sure indications of his intentions. Therefore, it is debatable that these two situations deserve different treatment under the European Convention. Concerning the former situation, it should be noted that, whereas in its earlier case-law the Strasbourg Court had not made it entirely clear whether defendants could waive their right to personal participation,[80] in the 1990s European judges started relativizing the fact that personal involvement constitutes a right of which

---

[78] Art. 31(1) of the Decree of the President of the Republic 448/1988.

[79] Similarly Cesari (2017), pp. 139 ff.

[80] To be sure, in *Colozza v. Italy*, the Court left open the question of whether the right to personal participation could be waived. Cf. Trechsel (2005), pp. 255 f.

defendants can always freely dispose, particularly when they are provided with legal knowledge that requires them to be present and make their contribution to fact-finding.[81] The Strasbourg Court, however, did not clarify the exact sanctions that the contracting states should adopt to "discourage unjustified absences".[82] Nor is there any trace of a similar approach in Luxembourg case-law, which instead focuses on the existence on a free waiver of participation by the accused.[83] Yet there can be situations in which the decision not to appear in court, despite being unequivocal, neither can be deemed totally 'free' nor reflects the clear intention not to take part in judicial proceedings personally, *e.g.* where the accused's absence is due to the fear of being arrested and remanded into custody.[84]

While the Strasbourg Court has pointed out that the mere condition of being a fugitive does not in itself mean that the defendant waived his right to be present at trial,[85] EU law does not seem to attach specific attention to such situations. Even more worryingly, a comparative examination of Framework Decision 2009/299/JHA and Directive 2016/343/EU displays a picture in which, once the accused has been informed of the institution of criminal proceedings either personally or by other means provided for by domestic law, the appearance of a lawyer, despite not being mandated by the defendant, suffices to save the lawfulness of a domestic criminal trial held *in absentia*. Thus the attendance of a defence lawyer is not only compatible with the default or similar proceedings, as still defined in various countries (*e.g.*, the new Italian proceedings against absent defendants), but furthermore reveals an approach that shows a clear indifference towards the accused's knowledge and intentions. Indeed, it is apparent that the presence of a lawyer does not say anything about whether or not the accused knowingly decided not to make his own contribution to fact-finding, and whether his decision can be deemed to be truly 'free'.

Yet it is apparent that "there can only be a waiver of the right, if previously one has been informed of the charges, the proceedings or the date and time of the trial".[86] On close examination, this fundamental requirement also holds relevance in the cases in which there are no unequivocal indications as to the accused's intentions. This is apparent from the attention paid by Strasbourg case-law to the need that the addressee of a criminal inquiry be charged neither with the burden of proving the reasons for their lack of awareness of the proceedings, nor with the burden of proving that his non-appearance in court was due to *force majeure* or other unforeseeable circumstances. Since the *Colozza* case, the Court has made it clear that, whatever decision the accused wishes to make, the national authority are responsible

---

[81] Cf. Ruggeri, in Part V of this volume, Sect. 2.2.

[82] ECtHR, *Poitrimol v. France*, judgment of 23 November 1993, Appl. No. 14032/88, para 35.

[83] CJEU, *Melloni v. Ministerio Fiscal* (fn. 4), para 49.

[84] In this regard see Böse (2015), p. 142, as well as in this volume Bachmaier Winter, in this volume, Sect. 4.1.

[85] Bachmaier Winter, in this volume, Sect. 4.1.

[86] *Ibid.*

for informing them about the charges filed. According to Strasbourg case-law, the competent authorities cannot be released from this responsibility even in the case of conduct of the accused that could be relevant in the field of administrative law, such as the failure to communicate a change of residence.[87]

In this regard also, EU law has undoubtedly weakened the protection particularly of the individuals involved in international surrender procedures in cases of *in absentia* trials. To be sure, most of the arrangements made by the Framework Decision 2009/299/JHA revealed a clear attempt to enact into the EU area the solutions elaborated by the Strasbourg Court. Nevertheless, the fact that the conditions set forth by Article 4a FD EAW have disjointed relevance leads to the result that, where national law provides a subsequent remedy in line with the requirements laid down by the 2009 legislation, the executing authority does not need to engage in further inquiry as to whether the domestic authority properly fulfilled its duties of diligence in informing the accused of the initiation of criminal proceedings. It is true that Strasbourg case-law also does not engage in examining whether the national authorities fulfilled their informational duties where there are clear indications of the accused's intention to waive his right to appear in court. Yet it is apparent that the same logic should not be applied to the cases of absence whose reasons are unknown. Worryingly, the Directive 2016/343/EU has further developed this approach. Despite the attention paid by this legislation "to the diligence exercised by public authorities in order to inform the person concerned and to the diligence exercised by the person concerned in order to receive information addressed to him or her",[88] the two cases laid down in Article 8(2) also highlight disjointed conditions. From this it follows that, as noted, a criminal trial can be held *in absentia* on the condition that a court-appointed lawyer represents the accused at trial, even though the defendant neither received personal notification nor ever waived his right to personal participation.

3.2.3   Information Safeguards

The Awareness of the Initiation of Judicial Proceedings

Against this background, there can be little doubt that the first requirement to ensure the lawfulness of a trial *in absentia* is that the individuals concerned are made personally aware that judicial proceedings have been initiated against them. Significantly, not only international human rights charters but also some constitutional charters, such as the Italian Constitution, set at the top of fair trial rights information safeguards, which firstly cover the right to be informed about the institution of a criminal law action. We can accept, following the Strasbourg jurisprudence, that a duty of diligence also lies with the accused and that under certain

---

[87] ECtHR, *F.C.B. v. Italy*, judgment of 28 August 1991, Appl. No. 12151/86.
[88] Recital No. 38 DPIRPT.

circumstances, a further inquiry into whether domestic authorities fulfilled their informational obligation might be useless where there is clear evidence that he decided not to take part personally in the trial. Yet, even if a waiver is expressed in explicit terms, it should be examined whether further requirements were properly fulfilled—in particular, whether defendants were also made aware of the charges filed and understood the consequences of their decision to take part or not in the proceedings.[89] Moreover, the European Court has long recognised that notice of proceedings is a formal procedural act and that the obligation to inform is of such importance that it cannot be "complied with passively by making information available without bringing it to the attention of the defence".[90]

It must be acknowledged, however, that the Strasbourg Court has not always been consistent with this jurisprudence. While the European case-law tends to strengthen the informational duties of the national authorities in cases of defendants abroad,[91] it has often followed a functional approach to purely domestic cases, which enhanced the duties of diligence of the accused to the point that it somehow blurred the obligation of the competent authority to inform them about the instituted proceedings and the charges preferred.[92]

This evolution of Strasbourg case-law might perhaps explain why the 2009 Framework Decision had already not required information to be necessarily provided to the accused personally, thus accepting the lawfulness of 'other means' established by national law.[93] In this regard, the developments that have occurred after the Framework Decision 2009/299/JHA reveal a further weakening of human rights protection. Although the 2009 legislation did not necessarily require that the accused be personally served with the proceedings, the reference to 'other means' provided by national law could not be interpreted as allowing for the maintenance of any legal arrangement but only of those that were unequivocally able to make defendants aware of the initiation of the trial. In the context of international cooperation, this acknowledgment entails that the sought person can only be surrendered if the issuing authority provides proper information that he was officially made aware of the proceedings, as pointed out by the Luxembourg Court in the recent *Dworzecki* case.[94] Unfortunately, the 2016 Directive has not reproduced this approach in the field of domestic criminal justice, as *in absentia* trials are allowed on the condition that the accused had the opportunity to be aware of the proceedings.[95] This generic indication is far from ensuring the effective awareness of the institution of criminal proceedings, which can therefore be conducted in the accused's absence on the basis of a real presumption of

---

[89] See below, Sect. 3.2.3.2.

[90] ECtHR, *Mattoccia v. Italy*, judgment of 25 July 2000, Appl. No. 23969/94, para 65.

[91] ECtHR, *T. v. Italy*, judgment of 12 October 1992, Appl. No. 14104/88, paras 28 et seq.

[92] Trechsel (2005), pp. 193 ff.

[93] Art. 4a(1)(a)(i) FD EAW.

[94] CJEU, *Dworzecki* (fn. 25), para 32. On this point see Schneider, in this volume, Sect. 3.2.1.1.

[95] Cf. in this volume Schneider, in this volume, Sect. 3.2.1.1.

knowledge. The 2016 legislation also does not seem to tighten this requirement where legal assistance is provided by a lawyer mandated either by the state or by the defendant. Even if Directive 2016/343 attached relevance to legal assistance on the condition that the accused was informed of the proceedings, this information also remains at a generic level. Consequently, there is nothing to ensure that the defendant truly received notice of the proceedings, mostly because EU institutions did not reproduce the requirement, set forth by the 2009 Framework Decision, that the accused should have mandated the counsel to represent him in court.

The Need to Ensure a Proper Understanding of the Charges Filed and the Consequences of Absence

Certainly, notice of proceedings alone does not suffice to enable defendants to take the difficult decision as to whether and to what extent they can take part in procedural activities personally. Even if *vocatio in judicium* could reach the accused personally, there is nothing to ensure that he has properly understood the charges filed against him as well as the consequences of his choice of remaining absent. This simple observation highlights the limitations of the Strasbourg doctrine of 'unequivocal waiver'. We saw that also in cases of conduct that clearly reflects the accused's intention of not being involved in the proceedings personally and even if waiver is expressed in explicit terms, one should examine whether further qualitative requirements were satisfied—in particular, whether the defendant was made aware of the merits of the case and the consequences of his decision not to attend court. In *Jones v. the United Kingdom*, the European Court showed its awareness of the need for further conditions being met by stressing that

> the applicant, as a layman, cannot have been expected to appreciate that his failure to attend on the date set for the commencement would result in his being tried and convicted in his absence and in the absence of legal representation.[96]

Consequently, the European judges added to the usual requirement of unequivocal waiver another important condition, namely that the accused's waiver should also be 'intentional'. Unfortunately, the Court did not further develop this approach in subsequent rulings, which limited themselves to reproducing the sole requirement of unequivocal waiver.[97] Yet it is apparent that information of the charge does not only allow the setting up of a proper defence strategy, but is also necessary for the purposes of a number of decisions that the accused must take personally. Thus, the knowledge and understanding of the charge are essential conditions for deciding how defence rights should be exercised at trial, thus enabling the accused to decide whether or not to make his own contribution to fact-finding and to decide which

---

[96] ECtHR, *Jones v. the United Kingdom* (fn. 41).
[97] Cf., *e.g.*, ECtHR, Grand Chamber, *Hermi v. Italy*, judgment of 18 October 2016, Appl. No. 18114/02.

lawyer should best represent him in court. The latter decision is of utmost importance where the charges concern criminal law areas that require highly specialised competences (tax crimes, environmental crimes, etc.). In light of this, providing detailed information about the charges in a language that the defendant understands also holds a fundamental relevance by allowing him to make an informed decision; therefore, it is to be welcomed that EU law has also recognised both the guarantees by means of Directives 2012/13 and 2010/64.

Yet it is apparent that, even if the accused understand the scope of the charges, this may not be enough to render his waiver truly 'intentional', if he remains unaware of the consequences of non-attendance in court. Depending on the arrangements provided for by national law, the accused's absence can entail a number of negative consequences,[98] not only where criminal proceedings are instituted with a view to rendering a judgment *in absentia*,[99] but also where domestic law provides for the suspension of both the proceedings[100] and the time limits for prosecuting criminal offences,[101] particularly if the latter suspension runs without a maximum time limit.[102]

But who should take responsibility for granting the accused this information? The competent authority at the time of the institution of the judicial proceedings does not appear to be always the most appropriate one to provide such delicate information, particularly when this authority lacks independence, *e.g.* because it was in charge of the pre-trial investigations or it was responsible for preferring the charges. Notwithstanding the importance of this issue, neither constitutional law nor international human rights law surprisingly provide any specific indications. In the EU area, supranational legislation also does not foresee anything in this regard, as both the Framework Decision 2009/299 and the Directive 2016/343 have failed to deal with this problem in both the fields of international cooperation and of domestic criminal justice. Yet EU institutions are certainly aware that some delicate decisions can only be taken after the person concerned has been informed of the

---

[98] For a comparative analysis of this point in the selected countries see Quattrocolo, in this volume, Sect. 5.2.

[99] This can happen under Italian law pursuant to the new procedure for absent defendants. Cf. Mangiaracina, in this volume, Sect. 5.

[100] Under Spanish law, the judicial order declaring *rebeldía* entails the suspension of the proceedings. See Villamarín López, in this volume, Sect. 3.1.

[101] In Italy, Law 67/2014 reform coupled the suspension of the proceedings with the suspension of the limitation period for the prosecution of the offence, which, however, cannot exceed the maximum time limits laid down in Article 161(2) PC. See Art. 159(1 n. 3-*bis*) PC, introduced by Article 12 of Law 67/2014. It is worth noting that Article 159(1 n. 3-*bis*) PC was declared unconstitutional on the grounds that it allowed for the suspension of the time limits for the prosecution of the offence even in the cases in which it was judicially ascertained that the accused's mental state irreversibly prevented him from taking part consciously in the proceedings. Cf. Constitutional Court, judgment 45/2015.

[102] Outside Europe, this result materialises under Brazilian law, thus posing delicate problems from the viewpoint of constitutional, substantial and procedural criminal law. See Lopes Jr. (2017), pp. 552 ff.

consequences of his absence. It is noteworthy that defendants can waive their right
to interpretation and translation in criminal proceedings after having been granted
legal advice and with full knowledge of the implications of their decision.[103] A similar approach should be established in relation to the decision to waive the right to be
present at trial,[104] and the competent judge seems to be the most appropriate authority to provide the accused with clear information on the merits of the charge filed
and the consequences of his decision not to appear in court personally.

It might be wondered whether defendants with legal knowledge need such safeguards. Whereas they might not understand the language of the proceedings and the
meaning of the court summons, they should be able to understand the scope of the
charges and the consequences of the decision not to be present at trial. As noted, the
European Court has long developed a sort of exception to the general freedom to
waive the right to be present at trial by dealing with the accused with legal knowledge. However, we saw that Strasbourg case-law neither followed a consistent
approach in relation to higher instances aimed at a legal review of the decision, in
which the attendance of the sole defence lawyer may be enough, nor has the Court
ever clarified which sanctions the contracting states should exactly adopt to discourage unjustified absences. At a deeper level still, it should be acknowledged that the
reference to 'legal knowledge' is extremely vague. Who exactly is a person with
legal knowledge and who should ascertain whether the accused has such skills?

Furthermore, it is apparent that the very concept of 'legal knowledge' has a relative meaning. Even if the accused has in-depth knowledge of legal matters in his
country, one cannot realistically expect that he will be able to understand the charges
filed in relation to offences provided for by criminal law provisions of any other
country, as well as the implications of his absence in every criminal justice system.
Therefore, if we assume that the European Convention accepts that under certain
circumstances the accused should appear in court, this obligation cannot be based
on the generic assumption of legal knowledge, nor can he be required to be present
in all phases of criminal proceedings, i.e., also in phases in which, whatever his
competences in legal matters, participation still remains a free choice. The approach
followed by the European case-law should perhaps be circumscribed to the first
hearing, but not in the terms highlighted in the *Poitrimol* judgment. In other words,
it might be acknowledged that international human rights law accepts that all
accused should be required to attend the first court hearing, in which, however, the
competent judge should not generically check their legal knowledge, but should
more specifically scrutinise their understanding of the charges as well as of the consequences of their decision not to be present in court pursuant to the solutions provided for by national law. Of course, this scrutiny should take place at the presence
of the accused's counsel, and the judicial authority should appoint a lawyer *ex officio* to represent the defendant without a counsel of his own choosing, while providing linguistic assistance to defendants who do not understand the language of the

---

[103] Art. 3(3) DIT.

[104] In this sense see Böse (2015), p. 142.

proceedings. If these conditions were met, the eventual waiver would be ensured before an independent authority and could be deemed to be both 'unequivocal' and 'intentional'.

3.2.4 Providing Absent Defendants with Effective Legal Assistance

From a human rights perspective, this systematic approach casts doubts on the lawfulness of implicit waiver, notwithstanding the fact that it is widely recognised by Strasbourg case-law. The vagueness of the notion of 'implicit waiver' led the drafters of Framework Decision 2009/299/JHA to consider the attendance of a lawyer mandated by the accused as expressing his intention not to be present in court, even though there is no logical reason supporting this assumption in all cases. As noted, the Directive 2016/343, despite the clear attempt to extend this approach to domestic criminal proceedings, has failed to reproduce the requirement of a mandate given by the accused. Consequently, EU law also allows the institution of a trial *in absentia* on the condition that a court-appointed lawyer is present in court, even if there is no evidence that the accused decided to be represented by him instead of appearing in court personally. Paradoxically, this solution might allow for member states to maintain (or even introduce) default proceedings, such as those foreseen by Italian law before the 2014 reform, which also provided the accused in default with a court-appointed lawyer.[105]

It might be argued that EU institutions weakened the protection of the defence rights of absent defendants in criminal proceedings in comparison to that provided in relation to international surrender procedures. A close examination of the Luxembourg case-law, however, would probably lead us to relativize this conclusion. As has been observed, the *Melloni* judgment attached no relevance to the fact that Mr. Melloni had withdrawn the mandate given to the two lawyers who defended him on appeal. This approach turned out to blur the requirement, laid down by Article 4a FD EAW, of the mandated counsel representing the requested person as a necessary condition for his surrender to the issuing country.[106] It is true that the 2009 legislation did not require the counsel to be necessarily "chosen, appointed and paid by the person concerned", who should however "deliberately have chosen to be represented by a legal counsellor instead of appearing in person at the trial".[107] In the more recent *Dworzecki* judgment, the Grand Chamber, despite enhancing the protection of the information rights of the individuals tried *in absentia*, did not deal with the condition of a mandated counsel and therefore did not make any step forward in the definition of the relationship between legal assistance and the

---

[105] Art. 420-*quater* CCP-Italy (version before 2014).

[106] Above, Sect. 2.1.

[107] See Recital No. 10 Framework Decision 2009/299/JHA. On this point see Böse (2011), p. 506, as well as Schneider, in this volume, Sect. 3.2.1.2.

participatory rights of absent defendants involved in international cooperation in the EU area.

At any rate, there can be little doubt that the drafters of Directive 2016/343 did not attach the necessary importance to the requirement that legal assistance be not only 'practical' but also 'effective',[108] as required in the field of international surrender procedures.[109] If there is no evidence that the accused was personally summoned to appear in court and was represented by a lawyer appointed by the state whom he never mandated, these are clearly not the necessary conditions for effective defence. A court-appointed lawyer may have huge difficulties in contacting the absent accused, which would clearly impede any communication between them and consequently the possibility of setting up an effective defence strategy. The difficulties further increase in those cases in which not even the lawyer appointed by the state appears in court and national law requires the appointment of a lawyer 'immediately traceable',[110] who might be fully unaware of the case. Unfortunately, the 2016 Directive does not seem to attach specific relevance to the need for constant communication between the absent defendants and their lawyers, which turns out to frustrate legal assistance too.[111]

On close examination, Strasbourg case-law also has not always dealt with this problem in a consistent way. It is true that the European judges have repeatedly held that absent defendants cannot be deprived of legal assistance, which constitutes a guarantee of such importance that, as noted, must also be ensured to the accused with legal knowledge even in cases of unjustified absences. In *Medenica v. Switzerland*, however, the Court satisfied itself with the circumstance that the accused had been summoned to court and was represented by lawyers of his own choosing,[112] thus supporting a sort of presumption of waiver of the right to be present at trial on the basis of the decision to appoint a lawyer chosen by the defendant.[113] In other decisions, the Court has not always followed this approach. For instance, in the case *F.C.B. v. Italy*, examined 10 years earlier, the European judges, although the accused was defended in court by his lawyer, considered this circumstance—as well as the fact that both counsel and the family had been informed of the proceedings—as not reflecting an unequivocal waiver of the right to take part in the trial personally.[114]

A comparative examination of this case-law with the aforementioned solutions elaborated in the *Jones* decision might lead us to conclude that under the European Convention also, the counsel's attendance can compensate for the accused's absence only if there is unequivocal evidence that the latter intentionally chose to be

---

[108] For this concern see extensively Bachmaier Winter, in this volume, Sect. 4.2.

[109] Recital No. 10 Framework Decision 2009/299/JHA.

[110] This solution is provided for by the Italian code. See Art. 97(4) CCP-Italy.

[111] Bachmaier Winter, in this volume, Sect. 4.2.

[112] ECtHR, *Medenica v Switzerland*, judgment of 14 June 2001, Appl. No. 20491/92.

[113] Bachmaier Winter, in this volume, Sect. 2.3.

[114] ECtHR, *F.C.B. v. Italy* (fn. 87).

represented by a legal counsel instead of appearing in person at the trial. If we assume that the European Convention tolerates that the accused can be required to appear at the first court hearing so that the competent charge can verify their understanding of the charges, the assistance of a lawyer will certainly play a role of utmost importance. Thus, defendants should be given the opportunity of expressing before an independent authority whether they are satisfied with legal assistance or whether they have a specific interest in following the proceedings personally.

3.2.5 How Can a Fair Criminal Law Action Be Carried Out Against Absent Defendants Who Were Neither Informed of the Proceedings Nor Waived Their Right to Be Involved in Them?

Granting a Retrial to Defendants Convicted *In Absentia*. Can Subsequent Remedies Compensate for the Lost Participation Before Decision-Making?

At this point, the question arises as to whether and how a fair criminal law action can be carried out against absent defendants who were neither informed of the proceedings nor in any way waived their right to be involved in them. It has been noted that in the *Colozza* judgment, Strasbourg case-law saved the fairness of the proceedings provided that a retrial or a remedy was ensured to the person convicted *in absentia* with the view to enabling him to obtain a new adjudication of the case. Since then, the Court has not limited itself to acknowledging the right to obtain a subsequent mechanism, but has also elaborated some qualitative requirements that such mechanisms must satisfy. Thus, regardless of the solution adopted by national law, the accused must be ensured a mechanism aimed at a fresh determination of the merits of the charge "from a court which has heard" the accused.[115]

While the Strasbourg Court has repeatedly reproduced this approach, a look at the evolution of its jurisprudence over recent years reveals the clear tendency to broaden the potential of subsequent remedies. It has been noted that in the *Jones* decision the Court also accepted the reopening of the time allowed for appealing against a conviction *in absentia*. The European judges confirmed this approach in the *Cat Berro* decision, notwithstanding that the Italian legislative reform of 2005 was not able to compensate the accused for the lost of the first instance by default, particularly because of the restrictions on the right to adduce exculpatory evidence in the appeal proceedings.[116] Moreover, we have seen that in the same period the *Öcalan* judgment pointed out that the suitability of the subsequent remedy largely depends on the circumstances of each concrete case, which should be scrutinised in

---

[115] ECtHR, *Colozza v. Italy* (fn. 29), para 29.
[116] Above, Sect. 2.2.

relation to the degree of effectiveness of the right to a defence in domestic proceedings.[117]

These developments, while blurring the original requirements of the right to a retrial, have also made the Strasbourg Court the ultimate instance for scrutiny of the adequacy of these domestic arrangements. Furthermore, recourse to subsequent mechanisms has progressively enabled the European judges to stretch the guarantee of personal participation in criminal proceedings to such a point that it has turned out to be deemed equivalent to the accused's involvement in a retrial or a higher instance. Doubtless, the adoption of a 'holistic' consideration of the fairness of criminal proceedings has contributed to this result. Yet it should be acknowledged that in this way Strasbourg case-law has often weakened the right to personal participation in criminal proceedings in its humanitarian function. Indeed, it is precisely the need for a comprehensive examination of the fairness of criminal proceedings that should require an in-depth assessment of the risks arising from a criminal law action, especially when defendants suffered from severe restrictions on their fundamental rights as a result of coercive means adopted against them *in absentia* (seizure of assets, etc.). Furthermore, there are damages that cannot be erased by means of a remedy or a retrial, even where a 'fresh determination of the merits of the charge' is ensured. Some defensive opportunities are precluded after the end of the first instance, not to mention the adverse effects that the initiation of the criminal trial can produce, due to the tools available in the current information society, of the image of both the defendants and their families. At a deeper level still, the indiscriminate use of mechanisms subsequent to the rendering of a decision *in absentia* reflects a clear underestimation of the defendants' contribution to fact-finding.

The shortcomings of Strasbourg case-law, moreover, did not remain confined to the sphere of the European Convention, since, as observed, they have also had enormous influence on the developments of EU law. Alongside the aforementioned problems, the approach followed by the drafters of the Framework Decision 2009/299 highlights a general methodological deficiency. Thus, far from requiring a progressive order of conditions for surrender, Article 4a FD EAW enables the requested authority to execute the arrest warrant where at least one of the aforementioned situations occurs.[118] Indeed, each of these situations suffices to justify the accused's surrender, releasing the executing authority from the obligation of inquiring into the others. Therefore, on the sole condition that the accused was informed of the initiation of criminal proceedings, the requested authority needs not ascertain whether he was also given a fair opportunity to consent to a trial being held in his absence, nor whether the accused's absence was the result of his unequivocal decision to waive the right to personal participation.[119]

---

[117] *Ibid.*

[118] Siracusano (2011), p. 96.

[119] Of a different view Siracusano (2011), p. 97, who considered that the granting of proper information could justify a presumption of waiver in the case of the accused's absence. In the light of the approach followed in this study, it can be doubted that the mere absence can be interpreted in

The systematic approach of Article 4a FD EAW also entails serious human rights risks from the perspective of the present discussion. It is questionable that the EU legislation considers the right to personal participation at trial and the possibility of a retrial as fungible requirements. It appears to be a worrisome result that, where defendants were served with the decision rendered *in absentia* and provided they could apply for a retrial, the executing authority does not need to scrutinise whether the competent authorities fully complied with their task of informing the accused about the institution of criminal proceedings. Furthermore, because of the structure of Article 4a FD EAW, each one of the conditions established by EU law does not only enable the executing authority, but also requires it to surrender the sought person to the trial country.[120]

These shortcomings are further aggravated by the fact that EU institutions softened the information requirements in relation to the right to a retrial or a remedy aimed at a review of the judgment rendered *in absentia*. For the purposes of international surrender, it suffices that the individuals convicted *in absentia* were 'served' with the decision and 'expressly' informed on the possibility of a retrial. These terminological differences can have substantial consequences from a human rights viewpoint. While being 'served' with the decision may seem to be compatible with the solution of an authorised person being notified of the judgment rendered *in absentia*,[121] the requirement that defendants be 'expressly' informed of the right to a retrial also does not mean that they were necessarily notified in person. Nor does the 2009 legislation require member states to inform the convicted person about the

---

this way and that so delicate decisions, such as waiver of the right to take part personally in the proceedings, can be presumed.

[120] See in this volume Schneider, in this volume, Sect. 3.2.1.

[121] *Ibid.*, Sect. 3.2.1.3, according to whom the importance of this information for the defence should require the individuals concerned to be "informed directly, not by proxy". Although this solution surely enhances the protection of the sought person, I personally consider this interpretation to be perhaps excessively optimistic. It is true that, in the light of the indications provided by the *Covaci* judgment (below, Sect. 3.3), we might conclude that the possibility of challenging a penal order and the exercise of the right to a retrial after a decision rendered *in absentia* presuppose personal information being ensured to the accused. Yet we shall see that the *Covaci* judgment did not provide the convicted person with sufficient safeguards in order to decide whether or not to lodge an objection. Furthermore, there are considerable differences between a summary procedure aimed at a decision *inaudito reo* and a trial *in absentia*, which differences mainly concern the structure of the two proceedings. Since *inaudito reo* proceedings generally exclude any hearing before the rendering of the guilty verdict, the objection aims at compensating the accused for not being involved in the procedure prior to the conviction. Therefore, it is logical that he is to be granted personal information about this remedy, as confirmed by the Court of Justice in the aforementioned *Sleutjes* judgment (fn. 27, paras 30 et seqq.). Retrial or a remedy subsequent to a decision held *in absentia* should instead constitute exceptional tools where it was impossible to involve the accused in an ordinary criminal trial, which should therefore have been instituted after performing all means aimed at ensuring their 'unequivocal' knowledge of the proceedings. In the field of international cooperation, however, the main problem lies in the fact that both the notice of the proceedings through a means aimed at granting such unequivocal knowledge of the scheduled trial and the information of a retrial, as noted, constitute disjoined conditions of surrender under Framework Decision 2009/299/JHA.

period of time for applying for a retrial or the prescribed remedy.[122] As a consequence of this set-up, there is nothing to ensure that the failure to request a retrial within the established timeframe was the result of a conscious decision. Furthermore, this result can also be caused by the existence of linguistic barriers.[123] Yet, despite the fact that this is certainly not an unlikely situation in the multilinguistic EU area, neither the 2009 legislation nor the 2010 Directive on the right to interpretation and translation require the information on a retrial to be provided in a language the accused can understand.

Seven years after Framework Decision 2009/299/JHA, the intervention of EU law, with a view to laying down the conditions under which domestic criminal proceedings can fairly be held *in absentia*, has further aggravated these shortcomings. By following the approach of the 2009 legislation, the 2013 proposal for a new Directive also allowed for trials *in absentia*, if defendants were expressly informed of the possibility of a retrial or a remedy aimed at ensuring a review of the merits of the case and they did not avail themselves of this tool.[124] On closer examination, this situation was highly problematic. In particular, the proposal made the lawfulness of *in absentia* judgments dependent on two rather heterogeneous conditions, namely (*a*) that the accused expressly decided not to request a retrial or a remedy[125] and (*b*) that he did not "request a retrial or appeal within a reasonable time frame".[126] Equating these two cases, however, was not a good solution: unlike the case in which the accused expressly decides not to request them, the failure to request a retrial or a remedy may reflect the objective circumstance that the available tools were not used rather than being the result of the informed decision not to use them.[127]

Although the 2016 Directive dropped these arrangements, the new provisions still give rise to serious human rights concerns. Thus, even if the accused was not informed of the proceedings or was not represented in court by a lawyer, the judgment rendered *in absentia* can also be executed, provided that the convicted person was made aware of the possibility of challenging the decision or accessing a retrial. Furthermore, serious problems also arise as to the way this information should be provided. By transposing the 2009 solutions into the field of national proceedings, the draft proposal required the accused to be 'expressly' informed of the possibility of a retrial or an appeal.[128] By contrast, the final text does not clarify at all how defendants should be made aware of subsequent remedies, whereas Recital No. 39 allows for information to be provided either in writing or orally, on the sole condition, in the latter case, that information is noted pursuant to the recording procedure

---

[122] Schneider, in this volume, Sect. 3.2.1.3.

[123] Heger and Wolter (2015), p. 349.

[124] Art. 8(3) DPIRPT-proposal.

[125] Art. 8(3)(a) DPIRPT-proposal.

[126] Art. 8(3)(b) DPIRPT-proposal.

[127] Critical remarks on this case were also expressed by the CCBE. Cfr. http://www.ccbe.eu/fileadmin/user_upload/NTCdocument/EN_04042014_CCBE_Res1_1399968822.pdf.

[128] Art. 8(3) DPIRPT-proposal.

set forth by national law. Furthermore, neither this Directive nor other supranational legal instruments provide any indication as to whether the information on the possibility of a retrial or a subsequent remedy should also be ensured in a language that the accused understands, and whether other relevant information—in particular, information about the time limit within which subsequent tools must be applied for—should also be granted.

In one point, however, Directive 2016/343/EU may seem to have improved the approach of the 2009 legislation. Since execution of the conviction on the grounds of subsequent remedies is only allowed where none of the conditions set forth by Article 8(2) have been met,[129] the requirements of the 2016 legislation should not be viewed as fungible. Yet it is precisely the way the first two conditions were structured that raises further concerns.[130] It has been noted that serious concerns arise in relation to both information rights and legal assistance. It is worth observing that in both these regards, considerable changes have occurred from the 2013 proposal to the 2016 Directive, which have further weakened the protection of the defendant's participatory rights.

By reproducing the approach of the 2009 legislation, the 2013 proposal required defendants to be summoned to court either in person or by other means to receive official information of the scheduled trial hearing.[131] These specifications were dropped from the provisions of Article 8 of the Directive, which only requires the accused to be "informed, in due time, of the trial and of the consequences of non-appearance".[132] The two aforementioned situations, although being inserted into Recital No. 36, still provide important interpretative guidelines. Nevertheless, it is noteworthy that, whereas the 2013 proposal required that the information tool adopted by national law be in any case able to unequivocally demonstrate that the accused was aware of the scheduled trial,[133] this requirement does not even appear in the aforementioned Recital No. 36. This casts doubts as to whether the standards of information set forth by this legal instrument can truly ensure that the defendant's absence was due to his unequivocal decision to waive their right to participate in criminal proceedings.[134]

Moreover, the need for unequivocal intention to waive the right to take part personally in criminal proceedings is further blurred by the way in which, as noted, the requirement of legal assistance was structured. In this regard also, the 2016 Directive significantly departed from the approach of the original proposal that, in line with the 2009 legislation, allowed for the initiation of criminal proceedings where the accused, "being aware of the scheduled trial, had given a mandate to a legal

---

[129] Art. 8(3) DPIRPT.

[130] For similar criticisms see Bachmaier Winter, in this volume, Sect. 4.3.

[131] Art. 8(2)(a)(i) DPIRPT-proposal.

[132] Art.8(2)(a) DPIRPT.

[133] Art. 8(2)(a)(i) DPIRPT-proposal.

[134] Recital No. 35 DPIRPT. Furthermore, it is debatable whether the 2016 Directive can be used to attach a reductive meaning to the provisions of Framework Decision 2009/299 in relation to international surrender procedures. On this point see Schneider, in this volume, Sect. 3.2.1.1.

counsellor, who was either appointed by the person concerned or by the State, to defend him or her at the trial, and was indeed defended by that counsellor at the trial".[135] Whereas this provision was shifted to Recital No. 37, Article 8 of the Directive seems to satisfy itself with the objective fact that "the suspect or accused person, having been informed of the trial, is represented by a mandated lawyer, who was appointed either by the suspect or accused person or by the State".[136] It is apparent that the requirement of a mandate given by the accused is not the only possible interpretation of the new provision, which, as noted, could allow for member states to maintain those legal solutions that require in the case of default proceedings the appointment of a court-appointed lawyer.

Ultimately, it should be noted that, while the scrutiny of subsequent remedies presupposes that these requirements were not satisfied, each one of the two conditions laid down by Article 8(2) DPIRPT suffices to justify the enforcement of the judgement. In other words, the way these two conditions were structured makes them fungible in their mutual relationship. This approach renders legal assistance even more of a formal requirement. It is true that the appointment of a lawyer should presuppose the accused being informed about the scheduled trial. Yet, since the 2016 Directive has not clarified how this information should be provided, it is clear that the attendance of a lawyer, whether or not mandated by the accused, is enough to allow for the institution of criminal proceedings, and there is no need for subsequent mechanisms. Worryingly, not only does EU law show no interest in the reasons that lead the accused not to appear in court, but it furthermore precludes access to the retrial, as instead required by Strasbourg case-law.

Balancing Conflicting Interests: The Need for a Public Interest or a Human Rights-Based Ground Justifying Prosecution Against Absent Defendants

These observations cast doubts as to whether subsequent remedies constitute an appropriate solution to satisfy the participatory expectations of defendants tried *in absentia*. As already observed, it is surprising that the Strasbourg Court, despite emphasising the obligation of national authorities to ensure the defendant's knowledge of criminal proceedings, considers his presence at trial to be equivalent to his involvement in a subsequent trial or a higher instance. A close examination of this reasoning, moreover, highlights an even more serious methodological flaw. The fact that national authorities applied all the available means to make defendants aware of the institution of criminal proceedings does not make a criminal law action absolutely necessary, particularly where the grounds for the accused's absence remained unclear. It is true that when serious crimes are at stake, a prompt prosecution can best satisfy the needs of a social defence policy and can avoid further shortcomings, *e.g.* by reducing the risk that relevant evidence may get lost or that the genuineness

---

[135] Art. 8(2)(b) DPIRPT-proposal.
[136] Art. 8(2)(b) DPIRPT.

of evidence subject to high risk of deterioration may be altered. However, these undisputable advantages are largely outweighed by the risks arising from conducting a criminal law action in the defendant's absence.

In the *Colozza* case, the European judges were already aware that the institution of criminal proceedings in the defendant's absence must satisfy a public interest, in that they held that

> the impossibility of holding a trial by default may paralyse the conduct of criminal proceedings, in that it may lead, for example, to dispersal of the evidence, expiry of the time-limit for prosecution or a miscarriage of justice.[137]

This assumption clearly called for proper balance between the accused's right to be present at trial and other relevant interests,[138] notwithstanding that the way in which the Court formulated this argument was clearly oriented towards a solution that favoured the conduct of default proceedings. In order to compensate the accused for the serious shortcomings, therefore, the Strasbourg judges emphasised the need to grant him a subsequent remedy aimed at avoiding the "complete and irreparable loss of the entitlement to take part in the hearing".[139] However, it is apparent from the aforementioned observations that the need for a public interest justifying the initiation of a criminal prosecution becomes blurred, even if defendants are given the opportunity of a retrial or a subsequent remedy.

On close examination, the arguments put forward by the *Colozza* judgment do not exclusively highlight public interests, but can also be viewed from a human rights perspective. Doubtless, the need to avoid the expiry of the time-limit for prosecution is also in the interests of the aggrieved parties, who must be ensured the most effective "conduct of criminal proceedings". Furthermore, 'dispersal of the evidence' calls for prompt collection of information by individuals other than those who are party to the proceedings, who might not be in a position to wait for the accused's attendance indefinitely (*e.g.*, ill witnesses, co-defendants in a dangerous situation, etc.). Indeed, these individuals, being involved in the criminal law action, also have the right to make their voice heard, and there can be little doubt that a human rights-oriented model of criminal justice should also take care of such interests.

A better solution than the (almost) indiscriminate use of subsequent remedies to compensate the accused for the institution of criminal proceedings by default or based on mere presumptions of knowledge, therefore, seems to be a strict scrutiny of the efforts made by the competent authorities and the reasons for a defendant's absence in court. If the domestic authorities properly fulfilled their obligation of ensuring the defendant's knowledge of criminal proceedings, but the reasons for his non-appearance remained unknown, the institution of criminal proceedings should be justified on the basis of a public interest or a specific interest of individuals other

---

[137] ECtHR, *Colozza v. Italy* (fn. 29), para 29.

[138] On the need for a 'reasonable balance' among conflicting interests see also Bachmaier Winter, in this volume, Sect. 4.1.

[139] ECtHR, *Colozza v. Italy* (fn. 29), para 29.

than the accused. In these cases, however, the proceedings should only be initiated in order to collect urgent evidence, being afterwards suspended, as provided for by the national law of various European countries.

A further question is whether suspension of the proceedings can last indefinitely, as well as whether it can be coupled with the suspension of the time limit for prosecuting the alleged offence and how long the latter suspension should be.[140] It is apparent that re-opening the process after decades can mean directing prosecution against a completely different person,[141] which, in the case of conviction, can inevitably frustrate the goal of resocialisation of the criminal being punished. Moreover, while suspension of the time limit for prosecution clearly satisfies the victim's rights, it cannot indiscriminately concern all types of offences, regardless of their seriousness and the severity of the expected sanction. Certainly the indefinite extension of the time limits for prosecuting criminal offences reveals an outdated concept of prescription, which runs counter to the modern right to have the offence forgotten.[142] In the EU area, the Directive 2012/29 attached particular importance to the victim's interest in being forgotten,[143] to the point that it made the victim's right to information conditional on his explicit request. Yet there is little doubt that the interest of the accused—as a presumably innocent person—in not being subject to the risk of a criminal prosecution indefinitely also deserves proper protection.

3.3 The Participatory Rights of the Individuals Involved in Summary Procedures. The Problem of inaudito reo Proceedings

Somewhat different problems arise in relation to a special type of criminal proceedings that ordinarily rules out any form of participation of the accused before the decision on guilt, namely the procedures *inaudito reo*. An emblematic example of these procedures is that of the penal or penalty order proceedings, which in Europe are mainly spread in the countries of Roman-German tradition. In Germany, the so-called *Strafbefehlverfahren* still holds the typical characteristics of a simplified procedure aimed a summary fact-finding without the accused being heard before the guilty verdict and being assisted by a lawyer in the decision on whether or not to challenge the penal order, which becomes final after the expiry of the time-limit prescribed for objection. In Italy, penal order proceedings, despite raising serious constitutional law concerns,[144] have progressively increased their scope of

---

[140] For in-depth comparison of the solutions enacted in Brazil and the statutory arrangements made by Spanish law see Lopes Jr. (2017), pp. 354 f.

[141] In this sense, from the viewpoint of Brazilian law, cf. Lopes Jr. and Badaró (2009), p. 14.

[142] Tourinho Filho (2010), p. 929; Lopes Jr. (2017), p. 553 fn. 18.

[143] Recital No. 29 DVR.

[144] The first doubts regarding the incompatibility with Italian constitutional law were raised under

application. Moreover, a recent legislative reform has for the first time enacted a similar procedure into Spanish law.[145]

For the purposes of the present study, I shall examine whether and to what extent these procedures properly satisfy the requirements set forth by international human rights law and EU law, as well as the conditions of a fair trial laid down by constitutional law. As far as ECHR law is concerned, the Strasbourg Court has never excluded the lawfulness of penal order proceedings.[146] Yet there can be little doubt that, as long as they are structured as purely *inaudito reo* procedures, they do not best fit the fair trial requirements set by the European Convention. Along with the lack of a fair hearing prior to the rendering of the guilty verdict, it is worth observing that European case-law has generally recognised the lawfulness of criminal proceedings held without a public hearing, provided, however, that defendants waived it unequivocally and that this waiver does not run counter to any relevant public interest. These findings should make the adoption of simplified written procedures conditional on the fact that the defendants either were given the possibility to waive their right to a court hearing or can effectively access a subsequent remedy. In light of the aforementioned observations, however, it is debatable whether subsequent mechanisms can truly compensate the accused for the lost opportunities.

These considerations may shed light on the developments that have recently taken place in EU law and especially in the CJEU case-law. As far as EU legislation is concerned, it must be acknowledged that until recently, *inaudito reo* proceedings did not lie at the core of EU criminal law policy. It is surprising, however, that Directive 2016/343, despite aiming to enshrine the right to personal participation in criminal proceedings, allowed for the maintenance of the rather inquisitorial practice of convictions issued by means of summary procedures. Thus, the new rules leave member states free to provide for "proceedings or certain stages thereof" to be conducted not only without involving the accused but even in writing.[147] Yet this reference cannot be interpreted as relating to intermediate and interlocutory proceedings, which anyway fall outside the scope of the Directive. Therefore, the meaning of these exceptions should be defined within the scope of the main provision, which concern the proceedings aimed at a decision on guilt.

On closer examination, *inaudito reo* decisions also pose delicate human rights problems from the perspective of EU law. It is debatable whether this summary

---

the 1930 code. Cf. Tranchina (1961), pp. 516 ff. The solutions enacted by the 1988 code have aggravated the inconsistency with the Constitution and particularly with the constitutional model of fair trial, introduced in 1999. See Ruggeri (2009), pp. 133 ff.

[145] The penal order procedure (*procedimiento por aceptación de decreto*) was enacted by Law 41/2015. See Villamarín López, in this volume, Sect. 5.3.

[146] In *Gray v. Germany*, the Strasbourg Court was called upon to examine German penal order procedures. See ECtHR, *Gray v. Germany*, judgment of 22 May 2014, Appl. No. 49278/09. Although the European judges did not take the opportunity to deal with the problem of the lawfulness of *inaudito reo* convictions in general, they have provided some indications on the particular viewpoint of the participatory rights in these summary proceedings of the aggrieved parties and their relatives.

[147] Art. 8(6) DPIRPT.

proceeding fulfills the right to a "fair and public hearing",[148] as recognised by the EU Charter of fundamental rights. Although this acknowledgment entails the accused's right to be put in a position to make his contribution to decision-making, the drafters of the 2016 legislation did not make any attempt to bring these procedures in line with the fundamental right to a fair hearing. Moreover, Recital No. 41 of the Directive contains a highly worrisome statement, whereby defendants hold the right to be present in the criminal proceedings instituted against them only if national law provides for one or more hearings in relation to a specific procedure. Instead, "if the proceedings are conducted in a simplified manner following, solely or in part, a written procedure or a procedure in which no hearing is provided for",[149] there would be no need to ensure any participatory rights.

If this conclusion were the correct one in absolute terms, procedures aimed at out-of-court decision on the merits of the case could be lawfully carried out in the accused's absence under EU law and any further discussion about respect for fair trial safeguards would be unnecessary. Yet this conclusion cannot be shared. Certainly, the drafters of the 2016 Directive did not take into due account the indications provided by the EU Court of Justice 1 year before in the *Covaci* judgment,[150] which revealed the clear attempt to identify a balance between the need for procedural speediness of summary fact-finding and the search for basic participatory safeguards.

The main question that the Court of Justice was called upon to examine in the *Covaci* case was not whether EU law allows for a person to be convicted through a *inaudito reo* procedure, but whether he has the right to be properly informed of the accusation and should be given a fair subsequent compensation for the defence opportunities that were not ensured to him prior to the rendering of the guilty verdict. In the *Covaci* decision, moreover, this question held particular relevance as it dealt with the case of a foreign defendant who was most in need while deciding whether to apply for a subsequent trial. The conclusions reached by the Luxembourg Court were not entirely satisfactory, displaying a scenario in which non-resident defendants must be granted information on the accusation contained in the penal order and must be ensured either legal or linguistic assistance, depending on whether they choose to lodge written or oral opposition—but not both. Furthermore, neither legal nor linguistic assistance are necessarily due in the period between the service of the decision and the lodging of the objection, but only after the interested person has chosen to challenge the guilty verdict and the form of objection. This is certainly a debatable result, taking into account that in most cases non-resident defendants are also foreigners who are fully unfamiliar with *lex fori*.

Certainly, the main responsibility to ensure full respect for legal and linguistic guarantees lies with national law. Moreover, one should also examine whether further EU legislation grants specific safeguards to the accused convicted through an

---

[148] Art. 47(2) CFR.
[149] Recital No. 41 DPIRPT.
[150] CJEU, *Covaci* (fn. 24).

out-of-court decision. The answer is certainly negative in relation to the two legislative instruments examined by the Court in the *Covaci* case. Nor were specific solutions provided by the 2013 Directive on the access to a lawyer,[151] which, despite requiring member states to protect defendants in such time and in such a manner so as to allow them to "exercise their rights of defence practically and effectively",[152] does not take into account the particular case of a conviction *inaudito reo*. It is true that that the 2013 Directive has a very broad scope of application, which includes "where applicable, sentencing and the resolution of any appeal".[153] However, this reference only concerns the right to legal assistance within the appeal proceedings, a situation that does not fit the case of the objection against a penal order, which does not aim at a review of the conviction by a higher court, but at a new decision on the merits of the case.

In sum, a close examination of the EU legislation does not seem to provide adequate solutions aimed at ensuring some of the most basic procedural safeguards to the individuals tried through proceedings *inaudito reo*. Yet, in the area of freedom, security and justice, it can surely not be tolerated that national law allows the institution of criminal proceedings that exclude the defendant's involvement on the basis of a prosecutorial decision, without giving him the possibility to knowingly decide whether to apply for a subsequent trial.

The developments that have more recently occurred in the case-law of the Court of Justice do not appear to take into account the need to ensure to the accused the fundamental safeguards of linguistic and legal assistance, in order to enable him to take the important decision on whether or not to challenge a guilty verdict rendered against him *inaudito reo*. It is true that the judgments issued in the cases *Sleutjes* and *Tranca, Reiter and Opria* have enhanced the information rights of the individuals convicted through a penal order, while confirming that EU law can only allow these procedures as long as the defendant is properly served with the decision and is ensured a subsequent remedy to challenge it. However, the acknowledgment that the notification of the penal order holds relevance under EU law in terms of information about the accusation[154] inevitably renders this guilty verdict a 'provisional decision'. This systematic approach, which was explicitly confirmed by the *Covaci* judgment,[155] raises complex questions, especially in the light of the solution of the judgment *Tranca, Reiter and Opria*. Thus in this decision, although the Luxembourg judges recognised that optimally the prescribed period for lodging the objection should begin to run from the time when the accused actually became aware of the penalty order,[156] they left the door open for a more flexible solution, which allows

---

[151] Directive 2013/48/EU. See among others Bachmaier Winter (2015), pp. 111 ff.

[152] Art. 3(1) DirAL.

[153] Art. 2(1) DAL.

[154] In the *Sleutjes* judgment, moreover, the Luxembourg judges pointed out the double relevance of the information on the penal order, which "represents both an indictment and a judgment within the meaning of Article 3(2) of Directive 2010/64". Cf. CJEU, *Sleutjes* (fn. 27), para 31.

[155] CJEU, *Covaci* (fn. 24), para 20.

[156] CJEU, *Tranca, Reiter and Opria* (fn. 28), para 41.

for this decision to become final provided that the defendant is given a subsequent tool to challenge it—even the application for leave to appeal against the conviction out of time.[157]

Form these developments it follows that under EU law a decision *inaudito reo* can not only be issued but can even become final on condition that a subsequent mechanism is feasible. Yet how can a 'provisional decision' become *res judicata*? What *res* can be deemed to be fairly *judicata* if the guilty verdict reflects a summary ascertainment of the facts? And can a subsequent mechanism, such as the application for leave to appeal against the conviction out of time, truly ensure a fair opportunity of contributing to fact-finding? Under German law, for instance, the possibility of being restored to the *status quo ante* presupposes that the interested person was prevented from complying with a period through no fault of his own. It is true that constitutional case-law tends to relax this requirement in cases of penal order procedures.[158] Yet who has the burden of proving the lack of fault? Moreover, in what language should the application for leave be filed and which safeguards does EU law grant the accused to decide whether to do so?

Whereas the EU Court of Justice has not yet provided any response to these delicate questions, it should be acknowledged that domestic law has made important steps forward towards a model of *inaudito reo* proceedings that is more consistent with the requirement of a fair trial. In Spain, for instance, a penal order can only become final if the accused appears in court and consents to the proposed sentence through this decision,[159] since the possibility of *res judicata* as a result of a procedure held *inaudito reo* would inevitably jeopardise the constitutional requirement of an effective defence. It is also noteworthy that Spanish law does not leave the accused taking alone this important decision, as he must be ensured the assistance of a lawyer[160] and the competent judge is required to hear him without the attendance of the public prosecutor. This solution allows for direct dialogue between the defendant and the judge, who is also expressly required to verify whether the accused understood the proposed decision and the consequences of his eventual consent.[161] A further safeguard is provided by the fact that the accused's hearing must be videotaped.[162]

Some important developments have also occurred in Italian law under the influence of the 1999 constitutional fair trial reform. Although the Italian legislation does not acknowledge to the accused the possibility of a previous hearing, it is interesting to note that since 2001 the lawyer mandated by the defendant must also be served with the penal order. Where no counsel is mandated, a court-appointed

---

[157] *Ibid.*, paras 47 et seqq.

[158] See among others BVerfGE 37, 93, 96. For further references to German constitutional case-law in this regard see Roxin and Schünemann (2017), para 22/19.

[159] Art. 803-*bis* i LECrim.

[160] Art. 803-*bis* g LECrim.

[161] Art. 803-*bis* h(3) LECrim.

[162] Art. 803-*bis* h(4) LECrim.

lawyer must be notified of the penal order[163] and will therefore assist him in the decision on whether to challenge the guilty verdict. Further significant developments have also occurred in Italian constitutional case-law, which has since 2007 departed from its traditional understanding of penal orders in terms of 'preliminary decisions'.[164] More recently, the Constitutional Court has also abandoned its long-developed doctrine—based on an idea originally elaborated in the field of civil proceedings[165]—of the subsequent eventual involvement of the accused in the procedure instituted by means of the objection (*contraddittorio eventuale e differito*).[166]

To be sure, the doctrine of a subsequent possibility of *contradictoire*—according to which the accused who is convicted without knowing about the institution of the criminal process must be enabled to apply for an 'ordinary *inter partes* procedure' by challenging the penal order—had allowed the Constitutional Court to reject, since its very first ruling on this issue,[167] any doubt on the incompatibility of penal order procedures with the Italian constitution. Surprisingly, this doctrine remained untouched even after the 1999 fair trial reform, which enacted into the Constitution a model of fair criminal justice based on the parties' involvement in the administration of justice and, not less significantly, on the principle of equality of arms.[168] Legal scholarship has also certainly contributed to this result, supporting the lawfulness of penal order procedures under the new constitutional framework on the double assumption that the right to a fair hearing can still be satisfied as long as the decision has not become final, and that the Italian Constitution enables the accused to consent to evidence being taken without an adversarial hearing.[169] Yet it is apparent that the possibility of the accused contributing to fact-finding is inevitably frustrated if a guilty verdict can be rendered in his absence, notwithstanding that the decision has not yet become final. The idea of subsequent consent also cannot be shared, particularly because Italian law enables the defence lawyer—and even a court-appointed lawyer—to challenge a penal order without a special power and regardless of the intentions of the accused. As long as this procedure remains structured in these terms, therefore, it cannot be deemed in line with the Italian constitutional model of a fair trial. The new approach followed by the Constitutional Court, which relies on the principle of reasonable length of the judicial proceedings,[170] also does not provide a convincing justification of penal orders, since the requirement of

---

[163] Art. 460(3) CCP-Italy, as amended by Law 60/2001.

[164] CConst, decision 323/2007.

[165] This approach mixed the doctrine elaborated by two outstanding scholars of civil procedural law during last century, i.e., *Piero Calamandrei*, who advocated the idea of subsequent involvement of the defendant, and *Francesco Carnelutti*, who focused on the eventual nature of his participation. See, respectively, Calamandrei (1926), and Carnelutti (1924), pp. 270 ff. Carnelutti's doctrine was first imported to penal order procedures by *Girolamo Bellavista*. Cf. Bellavvista (1952), p. 47.

[166] CConst, 23/2015.

[167] CConst, 46/1957.

[168] CConst, 8/2003, 32/2003, 131/2003, and 257/2003.

[169] See among others Marzaduri (2000), pp. 767 f.

[170] Art. 111(2) Const.-Italy.

reasonable duration presupposes that a criminal law action already satisfies all the necessary conditions of a fair trial, starting with the right to *contradictoire*.

3.4 Participatory Guarantees in Closed Hearings

A last problematic area covers the participatory rights in closed hearings. In the last years, various types of *in camera* proceedings have increasingly been used not only with a view to ruling on procedural issues, but also in order to solve the merits of the case.[171] Depending on the manner in which domestic law structures specific forms of closed hearings, they can considerably restrict participation of the accused as well as other private parties, or involve them only in an indirect way, and even rule out their involvement at all. In some cases, furthermore, the conduct of a hearing *in camera* depends on the initiative of the interested parties,[172] while in other cases statutory law defines the situations in which a closed session can take place. Notwithstanding that European Constitutions rarely acknowledge the right to a public (criminal) hearing in explicit terms, constitutional case-law has long recognised its constitutional relevance in several countries and in various ways. For instance, the Italian Constitutional Court has since the 1960s acknowledged the public character of judicial proceedings,[173] while including it among the inviolable rights of every person under Article 2 Const.[174] In Hungary, the constitutional reference to the right to a defence led to a declaration of unconstitutionality of the statutory solution that allowed the president of the competent court the delicate to decide whether an appeal ought to be deal with *in camera*, in a public session or a hearing.[175]

This does not mean, however, that the right to a public hearing constitutes a rigid principle and that closed sessions are not covered by constitutional law or are even to be deemed unconstitutional. A close examination of the reasons that led to a declaration of unconstitutionality, as well as of the constitutional law parameters invoked by domestic courts, may seem to demonstrate that in some cases the infringement of the Constitution is not a result of the provision of a closed hearing in itself, but of the implications on other human rights which derive from that provision. For instance, the aforementioned provision of the Hungarian code was declared

---

[171] In Italy, Law 103/2016 has strengthened the possibility of appeal proceedings being held *in camera* by enabling the parties to agree on the acceptance, in whole or in part, of the arguments for appeal. Cf. Art. 599-*bis* CCP-Italy.

[172] Under Italian procedural law, defendants are entitled to apply for the abbreviated proceedings, which aim at a decision on guilt in the intermediate phase and in a closed session, unless a public hearing is requested by all the accused. See Art. 441 CCP-Italy.

[173] The first ruling was the Constitutional Court's judgment 25/1965. For further references to Italian constitutional case-law see Chiavario (1984), pp. 277 ff.; Di Chiara (2009), pp. 294 f.

[174] CConst, judgment 17/1981.

[175] Cf. Art. 360 CCP-Hungary, which was declared unconstitutional by decision 20/2005. See Gácsi et al., in this volume, Sect. 3.3.3.

unconstitutional not only since it left to the judicial authority a great margin of discretion in deciding whether an appeal should be held in public or *in camera*, but furthermore because the parties were not to be informed about an *in camera* session, and worse still, no minutes were to be drawn up of such hearing.[176]

Notwithstanding the explicit acknowledgment of the right to a public hearing in international human rights charters, international courts have not banned the use of closed hearings. Strasbourg case-law is not an exception and, while confirming the relevance of the principle, has over the last decades developed a wide range of possible derogations. It is worth observing that the increasing use of closed proceedings, particularly where prosecution is directed against serious organised crimes and terrorism-related offences, has led to unprecedented developments in international human rights case-law as well. By extending the findings of the landmark judgment *A. et al. v. United Kingdom* to the field of criminal proceedings,[177] in *Sher et al. v. United Kingdom* the Strasbourg Court has recognised the lawfulness of closed hearings especially in the area of terrorism-related criminal law. It is debatable, however, whether the severe implications of these national arrangements— particularly the lack of any communication between the accused and the 'special advocate' who has access to confidential materials—can be tolerated under European Convention, where decisions are at stake which aim at the application of measures seriously interfering on fundamental rights.

It is not an easy task to assess whether and to what extent closed hearings in criminal proceedings are consistent with EU law. It has been noted that, in spite of the explicit right to a fair and public hearing contained in the EU Charter of fundamental rights, the drafters of Directive 2016/343 defined the right to take part in criminal proceedings with a very limited scope of application, which allows for maintenance of summary and written procedures. It is true that Recital No. 41 does not seem to rule out closed sessions, as long as national law provides for one or more hearing. However, the provisions of Article 8 of this Directive cannot always be applied to *in camera* proceedings—certainly not, if a closed hearing does not aim at a decision on guilt or acquittal. Furthermore, it would be difficult to tolerate also under EU law that a hearing is held *in camera* without the lawyer being able to communicate with the accused.

---

[176] For criticisms against the statutory solution cf. Gácsi et al., in this volume, Sect. 3.3.3.

[177] ECtHR, Grand Chamber, *A. et al. v. United Kingdom*, judgment of 19 February 2009, Appl. No. 3455/05.

4 The Qualitative Requirements of a Fair and Effective Participation in Criminal Proceedings

4.1 Premise

Despite the focus by international human rights law and EU law on judicial proceedings that in different ways rule out or considerably restrict participation of the accused, neither Strasbourg case-law nor EU institutions have developed the accused's participatory rights in criminal proceedings with exclusive regard to such procedures. More generally, it would be reductive to think that human rights law only conceives of the right to be involved in criminal hearings in terms of the mere physical attendance of defendants at trial. Certainly, being simply present in a criminal hearing constitutes a formal level of participation, which does not fully satisfy the fair trial requirements of effective involvement in the proceedings. It is of little use for defendants to be present in court if they are not granted a fair opportunity to be heard, make their contribution to fact-finding, and so on. The Strasbourg Court has on several occasions stressed the need to ensure effectiveness of the accused's participation. A clear example was the *Stanford* case, in which, as noted, the European judges pointed out that defendants must be given the right not only to be present but also to hear and follow the proceedings.[178] To a great extent, EU law has inherited from Strasbourg case-law the attention towards the requirement of effective participation. Despite its piecemeal approach, the supranational legislation issued after the Lisbon reform has sought the harmonisation of a minimum set of core safeguards, which should enable the individuals concerned to be involved in criminal proceedings actively.

In some countries, constitutional law recognises specific participatory safeguards, such as the fair trial rights of the accused provided for by Article 111(3) of the Italian Constitution. Moreover, even in the countries whose Constitutions lack an explicit acknowledgment of the right of private parties to be involved in judicial proceedings, participatory rights also hold constitutional relevance by means of general clauses, such as that regarding access to justice, which—for instance, in Romanian constitutional law—must be ensured with the utmost effectiveness.[179] The provisions, albeit differently formulated by European Constitutions, on the right to effective defence also constitutes a fundamental point of reference, which attaches constitutional relevance to the involvement of private parties in judicial (criminal) proceedings.[180]

In Spain, constitutional law has since the 1812 Constitution acknowledged also the proactive role in criminal proceedings of private accusers and public accusers

---

[178] ECtHR, *Stanford v. United Kingdom* (fn. 56).

[179] Ciopec and Roibu, in this volume, Sect. 1.

[180] This reference holds particular relevance in countries, such as Bulgaria, which lacks a set of specific participatory safeguards acknowledged at the constitutional law level. See Petrova, in this volume, Sect. 1.

other than public prosecutors, although their participation has different relevance under the current Constitution—respectively, as a fundamental right (namely the right to effective judicial protection) and as an expression of citizens' involvement in the administration of justice.[181] Portuguese constitutional law also recognises a set of fair trial rights (*inter alia*, the right to legal assistance), which define some essential conditions of effective participation in criminal proceedings.[182] Most interestingly, we have seen that the Portuguese Constitution explicitly allows for procedural acts to be carried out in the absence of the accused, in the cases and pursuant to the safeguards ensured by law.[183]

In several European states (*e.g.*, Austria and Luxembourg), the failure of constitutional law to enact comprehensive provisions on participatory rights in criminal trials was somehow compensated for by the constitutional acknowledgment of international human rights charters like the European Convention and the International Covenant.[184] A similar conclusion also indirectly applies to England and Wales, despite the lack of a written Constitution. Here, a number of participatory safeguards have gained constitutional relevance mainly through the 1998 Human Rights Act, which, by way of domesticating *inter alia* the fair trial guarantees of Article 6 ECHR, enhanced some fundamental safeguards (*e.g.*, the presumption of innocence and the right to confrontation) that were long rooted in English law.[185]

In most European countries, moreover, constitutional case-law has played a relevant role in the reconstruction of a number of participatory guarantees. It is noteworthy that the case-law of the French *Conseil constitutionnel* has also recognised the extent to which constitutional law also protects the right not to take part in criminal proceedings or not to participate in active way.[186] The solutions adopted by constitutional courts and Strasbourg case-law in relation to the same safeguards, however, have not always been consistent with each other. An emblematic example is that of the right of the civil party to appeal before the Supreme Court, a right that French law limited where the public prosecutor failed to lodge an appeal before *Cour de cassation*. That this set-up, which the European judges had considered to

---

[181] Villamarín López, in this volume, Sect. 1.

[182] Costa Ramos and Churro, in this volume, Sect. 1.2.

[183] Art. 32(6) Const.-Portugal.

[184] In Austria, the Rome Convention is deemed to have constitutional rank. See Golser, in this volume, Sect. 1; Bassini and Pollicino, in this volume, Sect. 6.3. In Luxembourg, the adoption of a monist approach by domestic case-law has led to the increasing enactment of the fair trial safeguards acknowledged by Strasbourg jurisprudence. Cf. Covolo, in this volume, Sect. 1. The Romanian Constitution does not only provide for a rule governing the cases of inconsistencies between national law and international covenants and treaties on fundamental human rights, which rule establishes the clear precedence of international law instruments. Furthermore, it requires even constitutional provisions concerning the citizens' rights and freedoms to be interpreted and enforced in line with the Universal Declaration of Human Rights, as well as to the covenants and other treaties Romania is a party to. See Ciopec and Roibu, in this volume, Sect. 1.

[185] Cf. Leader, in this volume, Sect. 1.

[186] See Drevet, in this volume, Sect. 1.

be in line with the European Convention, was declared unconstitutional in 2010 may be explained by the fact that the Strasbourg Court focused on the principle of equality of arms without taking into account the repercussions on the defence rights of the damaged party.[187]

The comparative-law examination of the relevant countries analysed in this research has revealed that the involvement of private parties in criminal proceedings may hold different features depending on several factors, such as the stage of the proceedings and the diverse interests brought in the proceedings by the individuals concerned, and so on. Yet human rights law has, albeit from different viewpoints, demonstrated that some basic conditions must be ensured in any case, setting necessary prerequisites for their effective participation in criminal trials. For the sake of clarity, I shall firstly cut across the model solutions concerned with the accused's involvement in criminal proceedings. On a second level, I shall analyse whether and to what extent private parties other than defendants have the right to take part personally in criminal proceedings, focusing particularly on the guarantees that both the European Convention and EU law recognised to the victim.

4.2 Fair Trial Safeguards to Enable the Accused's Effective Involvement in Criminal Trials

4.2.1 Information Rights for Present Defendants

Information on the Charge

It has been observed that the granting of proper information is a core condition for the accused being able to decide whether to appear in court personally. In this regard, we have also anticipated that notice of the proceedings may not be enough for these purposes, as defendants need to be provided with information on the merits of the case to make an informed decision. Furthermore, being properly informed about the charge holds even greater relevance for defendants who have already chosen to be present at trial by enabling them to decide how to set up the most effective defence strategy.

Doubtless, Strasbourg case-law has contributed to the development of a broad understanding of the information about the charge, which must not only be provided in a form that can be understood but must also be equipped with the necessary details on the legal and factual grounds for the institution of a criminal law action. As far as the legal issues are concerned, however, we saw that the European Court has not always been fully consistent with this acknowledgment, allowing for restrictions on the right to be present in higher instances if appeal only aims at a legal revision of the decision without engaging the competent court in further factual

---

[187] *Ibid.*

inquiries.[188] This approach does not appear to be consistent with the European Convention, which requires simple and detailed information about both legal and factual issues in order to enable the accused's most effective defence.

In *Mattoccia v. Italy*, moreover, European case-law emphasised the link with the right to a defence to such a point that it adopted a rather functional approach to this fundamental guarantee, whereby individuals can only claim before the Strasbourg Court to the extent that they concretely suffered from a restriction on their defence rights.[189] This approach, however, charges the accused with the difficult task of proving a hypothetical situation, that is, whether the defence's opportunities would have been different should proper information have been provided. Furthermore, the Court is also not equipped to inquire into the concrete restrictions suffered by the lack of information and even less able to scrutinise the hypothetical benefits that would have derived from proper information.[190] This doctrine surely weakens the right to information, ensuring to the individuals concerned no certainty about to the extent to which the European Convention protects their information rights. Of course, this doctrine was elaborated in the field of the contentious jurisprudence of Strasbourg and it will not be an easy task for the Court—if requested to give an advisory opinion, as provided for by Additional Protocol No. 16 to the European Convention—to define in advance the limits within which information on the charge should be ensured.

The adoption of a broad concept of the information about the charge, moreover, has also led European case-law to extend its scope of application beyond sole judicial proceedings. To be sure, unlike other international human rights charters, the European Convention links this specific safeguard—among the others generally acknowledged to any person 'charged' with a criminal offence—with the preferment of an 'accusation'.[191] Yet individuals charged with a criminal offence certainly cannot wait until a formal accusation is preferred against them to obtain information on the charge. A literal interpretation of the Convention, furthermore, would frustrate some of its main goals, depriving suspects of the ability to set up a proper defence strategy and to challenge the coercive means often ordered against them in the pre-trial inquiry. The Strasbourg Court has never adopted a rigid interpretation of the right to information on the accusation, instead following a flexible approach that looks at the substantial repercussions of criminal investigations on the suspect's fundamental rights.[192] This approach, therefore, may lead us to conclude that the European Convention also recognises the necessary conditions for the accused being able to take part in procedural activities and particularly in interim decisions

---

[188] ECtHR, *Döry v. Sweden*, judgment of 11 November 2002, Appl. No. 28394/95. See Ruggeri, in Part V of this volume, Sect. 2.3.

[189] ECtHR, *Mattoccia v. Italy* (fn. 90).

[190] In this sense cf. Trechsel (2005), p. 194 f.

[191] Art. 6(3)(a) ECHR. Therefore, some commentators interpreted the right to information as relating to the act through which the court proceedings are instituted. See among others Trechsel (2005), pp. 198 f.

[192] Cf. *inter alia* ECtHR, *Brozicek v. Italy*, judgment of 19 December 1989, Appl. No. 10964/84.

at the pre-trial stage, even though the content of information cannot be the same regardless of the different phases of the proceedings.

A look at EU law reveals that the legislation issued after the entry into force of the Lisbon Treaty has largely inherited the focus of Strasbourg case-law. Directive 2012/13/EU, in particular, does not only require defendants to be provided with detailed information on both the factual and legal issues regarding the accusation, but furthermore emphasises the need for information about the charges to be written in a sufficiently clear manner that all individuals, regardless of their actual knowledge of legal matters, can understand it.[193] This requirement clearly demonstrates the awareness by the EU institutions of the importance of involving defendants personally in the proceedings. Furthermore, following the Strasbourg case-law, EU law has structured the guarantee of information on the charge with the broadest scope by ensuring not only that defendants are given due information on the indictment, but also suspects are given the right to know the preliminary charge.[194] From this approach it follows that the degree of information also varies according to the development of criminal proceedings. Thus, suspects need to be given immediate information on the offence under investigation, which must be sufficiently detailed to ensure the exercise of defence rights and the overall fairness of the procedure.[195] Defendants must be ensured information on the indictment as soon as the court procedure has been instituted and such information must enable them to know the nature and legal classification of the criminal offence, as well as the nature of participation by the accused person.[196]

The need to ensure personal information about the charge is not only relevant at the time in which the court proceedings are instituted, but also in subsequent stages of the proceedings, as is clearly confirmed by a somewhat dynamic understanding of this guarantee by both international human rights case-law and EU law. Doubtless, another important achievement of Strasbourg case-law was the acknowledgment of clear obligations for the competent authorities, which are called upon to inform the accused of any amendment of the charge that make it necessary for the accused to change their defence strategy.[197] In *Pélissier and Sassi v. France*, moreover, the European Court found a breach of the Convention because the decision to amend the legal classification of the charge had not been made through adversarial

---

[193] To ensure the proper fulfilment *inter alia* of the duty of providing information about the charges, the Directive also proposes the adoption of non-legislative means, such as a Letter of rights aimed at providing defendants with information of their rights in a "simple and even non-technical language so as to be easily understood by a person without specific knowledge of criminal procedural law". See Recital No. 38 DICP.

[194] Recital No. 14 DICP.

[195] Art. 6(1) DICP.

[196] Art. 6(3) DICP.

[197] In these terms cf. *Mattoccia v. Italy* (fn. 90), in which the Court clearly stressed that information "rests entirely on the prosecuting authority's shoulders".

argument.[198] This confirms the need also to provide the accused with constant information about the legal issues of the case.

This dynamic approach has undoubtedly had great influence on the development of EU legislation.[199] Furthermore, a functional perspective has also deeply inspired the EU law on the guarantee of information. The conditions of the information due in the pre-trial phase, in particular, were not sufficiently defined at the level of EU law, as detailed information on the offence under investigation is only required to the extent that it ensures the effective exercise of defence rights and fairness in the criminal inquiry. Moreover, amendments of the charge must be communicated only insofar as it is necessary to ensure the fairness of the criminal process. This restrictive approach does not best fit the human rights aims of the EU area. It is difficult to think of a fair criminal proceeding in which defendants are kept in the dark about the changes made to the original accusation issued against them and have therefore to defend themselves against an outdated charge.

Without a doubt, the Strasbourg jurisprudence on the information on the charge has also contributed to the development of a constitutional model of information rights in various countries. Whereas the 1978 Spanish Constitution already recognised the right of defendants to be informed on the accusation preferred against them,[200] the constitutional rank that Austrian law, as noted, reserves to the European Convention entails the acknowledgment of the standards of protection of information rights elaborated by Strasbourg case-law. In Italy, Constitutional Amendment Law 2/2999, while enacting into the Constitution some fair trial rights recognised by the European Convention,[201] explicitly enshrined the accused's right to be informed in detail on the accusation.[202] Remarkably, Italian legal scholarship stressed that this fundamental guarantee should be interpreted in the light of European case-law, which, as noted, did not circumscribe its scope of application to the sole judicial proceedings, but extended it to the pre-trial inquiry where intrusive investigations are to be carried out.[203] The Italian Constitution does not expressly deal with the right to be informed of eventual amendments of the initial charges. Yet, along with the general acknowledgment of the inviolable right to a defence,[204] the requirement that defendants receive information "as soon as possible"[205] also may seem to call for interpretation not limited to the initial charge. Thus, this expression, far from requiring the competent authorities to immediately inform the suspects on

---

[198] ECtHR, Grand Chamber, *Pélissier and Sassi v. France*, judgment of 25 March 1999, Appl. No. 25444/94.

[199] Art. 6(4) DICP.

[200] Art. 24(2) Const.-Spain.

[201] On this constitutional reform see among others Marzaduri (2000), pp. 762 ff.

[202] Art. 111(3) Const.-Italy. In this regard see Mangiaracina, in this volume, Sect. 1.

[203] Marzaduri (2000), p. 777.

[204] Art. 24 Const.-Italy.

[205] Art. 111(3) Const.-Italy.

the charge filed against them, calls for a balance among conflicting interests,[206] banning, however, delays that cannot be justified on the basis of other constitutional interests.

Another question is whether personal information should necessarily be ensured prior to the rendering of the decision on guilt. While the European Convention does not provide any indication in this respect, another important international human rights charter—namely, the Pact of San José—explicitly recognises the right to "prior notification" of the charge.[207] This acknowledgment, which is unique among human rights instruments, enhances the link between the guarantee of information and the right to be fairly heard by a court, as highlighted by Inter-American case-law, which considers it an essential element "for the effective exercise of the right to defense",[208] thus requiring defendants to be notified of the charges issued against them even prior to their first statement.[209] Doubtless, this requirement strengthens the guarantee of information, since it rules out the lawfulness of any procedure aimed at postponing not only the information on the charge, but also the involvement of the accused after the decision-making (like, *e.g.*, penal order procedures existing in some Europe countries). In the EU area, Directive 2012/13 failed to address this issue, which has led the Luxembourg Court to give a rather reductive interpretation of the guarantee of information on the charge. We saw that in the *Covaci* case the Court of Justice confirmed the lawfulness under EU law of the German penal order procedure, on the assumption that the notification of the conviction fulfils the task of informing the accused of the accusation.[210]

Access to the Investigative File

Certainly, the possibility of setting up proper defence strategy also largely depends on the knowledge of the information gathered by the investigative authorities and the access to their file. Although these fundamental safeguards certainly fall within the scope of the guarantee acknowledged by Article 6(3)(b) ECHR, which has a strict link with that of lit. *a*),[211] it is noteworthy that in some cases the European Court excluded that the information of the charges should necessarily entail the disclosure of supporting evidence to enable the accused to prepare for trial.[212] This assumption may also lead us to conclude that the right of paragraph *b*) does not need to fulfil the same requirements set forth in relation to the right to information. From

---

[206] Marzaduri (2000), p. 778.

[207] Art. 8(2)(b) ACHR.

[208] IACtHR, *Barreto Leiva v. Venezuela*, judgment of 17 November 2009, Serie C No. 206, para 128.

[209] IACtHR, *Tibi v. Ecuador*, judgment of 7 September 2004, Serie C No. 114, para 188.

[210] In the *Sleutjes* judgment, the Luxembourg judges deemed the sole information on the objection insufficient. See CJEU, *Sleutjes* (fn. 27).

[211] Trechsel (2005), p. 222.

[212] See among others ECtHR, *Haxhia v. Albania*, judgment of 8 October 2013, Appl. No. 29861/03.

the perspective of the present discussion, this interpretation entails that the European Convention does not necessarily ensure to the accused personal access to prosecutorial and police evidence.

The examination of Strasbourg case-law may seem to support this conclusion, as the European Court allowed the access to the file being restricted solely to the lawyer. The negative impact on the accused's right to be kept informed of the evidence collected by the investigative authorities is enhanced by the possibility of public prosecutors selecting the information to be disclosed to the defence. A number of countries enable the prosecutorial authority to withhold relevant information from the defence,[213] which power can not only be justified on grounds of procedural economy but also for human rights purposes, such as the need to respect the private life of individuals not involved in the ongoing inquiry.[214] In *Edwards v. United Kingdom*, although the European Court proclaimed that prosecutors should "disclose to the defence all material evidence for or against the accused",[215] it accepted the failure by the national authority to provide relevant information on the grounds that this deficiency had been remedied in the second instance. On close examination, the Strasbourg case-law allows for restrictions on the right to know prosecutorial information, provided, however, that such restrictions are kept to a minimal extent and the competent authority adopts proper means to compensate for them.[216]

It is also worth observing that the Strasbourg Court, dealing especially with serious crimes and particularly with terrorism-related offences, recognised the lawfulness of some domestic arrangements aimed at limiting access only to a lawyer, provided, however, that the accused is granted a summary of the information gathered.[217] In *Sher et al. v. United Kingdom*, the Court made it clear that the Convention "cannot require disclosure of such material or preclude the holding of a closed hearing to allow a court to consider confidential material".[218] This approach led the Court not only to extend the possibility of closed hearings to substantial issues, but also to recognise that even in the field of criminal justice, confidential evidence can be disclosed solely to a 'special advocate'. That such advocate cannot have any contact with his client renders the possibility of the accused knowing relevant evidence even more difficult.

It may be argued that these findings have had a strong impact on the developments that have occurred in EU law. The comparative analysis of the formulation of the right to information about the charges and the right to access relevant evidence reveals that Directive 2012/13 allows the information about relevant evidence to be

---

[213] For instance, Italian law allows this result for the purposes of the ordering of wiretapping or other pre-trial measures, such as restrictions on freedom.

[214] Trechsel (2005), p. 225.

[215] ECtHR, *Edwards v. United Kingdom*, judgment of 16 February 1992, Appl. No. 13071/87, para 36.

[216] ECtHR, *Jasper v. United Kingdom*, judgment of 16 February 2000, Appl. No. 27052/95.

[217] For in-depth analysis of this problem cf. Vogel (2016), pp. 28 ff.

[218] ECtHR, *Sher et al. v. United Kingdom*, judgment of 20 October 2015, Appl. No. 5201/11.

provided either to the defendants or to their lawyers.[219] The same logic applies to the documents that are essential with a view to challenging the lawfulness of arrest or detention.[220] It is true that, as a general rule, information must be ensured on all "material evidence in the possession of the competent authorities". Yet EU law recognises that "certain materials may be refused if such access may lead to a serious threat to the life or the fundamental rights of another person or if such refusal is strictly necessary to safeguard an important public interest".[221] In this case, however, the decision to refuse access to certain pieces of evidence either must be taken by a judicial authority or at least is to be submitted to judicial review.[222]

In some countries, constitutional law also recognises to the accused the right to the know the materials of the case, a result that may also be deemed largely due to the increasing role of international human rights law. In Italy, the 1999 Constitutional Amendment Law, by way of enacting the provision of Article 6(3)(b) ECHR, ensured to defendants the right to have the time and the necessary conditions to prepare their defence, which right should be interpreted as entailing the knowledge of the information gathered by the investigative authorities, particularly where coercive measures are at stake.[223] The focus on interference with fundamental rights has led German constitutional case-law also to require that the competent authority for judicial review of coercive or clandestine investigative measures decide on the case after granting the individuals concerned access to the parts of the investigative file which are relevant to assess the lawfulness of the initial authorisation.[224]

4.2.2 Understanding the Language of the Criminal Process

Taking part effectively in criminal proceedings also requires that the accused be put in a position to understand the language of the trial. Otherwise, the right to attend court personally turns out to be a purely formal guarantee. The aforementioned safeguards also would lose most of its protective scope: *e.g.*, the domestic solution of limiting access to relevant evidence to the defence lawyer would be largely frustrated if counsel were not able to communicate with his client.

Both international human rights law and EU law confirm that the granting of linguistic assistance stands out among the essential conditions for the individuals concerned to be able to follow and effectively participate in criminal proceedings. In the American Convention, this right holds a prominent position among other due process safeguards. This approach does not allow for reductive interpretations, calling for the extension of the scope of the linguistic guarantees beyond the court

---

[219] Art. 7(2) DICP.

[220] Art. 7(1) DICP.

[221] Art. 7(4) DICP.

[222] *Ibid.*

[223] Marzaduri (2000), pp. 781 f.

[224] Vogel, in this volume, Sect. 3.3.

proceedings and even in the pre-trial phase, especially where measures of coercion are at stake. Although the European Convention does not follow the same systematic approach, it undoubtedly attaches great relevance to the linguistic safeguards. Remarkably, the information about the accusation must not only be provided in detail but also in a language that the accused understands, which clearly highlights the need to enable defendants to fully understand the charges preferred against them from both legal and linguistic viewpoint.

Doubtless, Strasbourg case-law has had great influence on the evolution of constitutional and EU law in this problematic area too. In some countries, such as Italy, the accused's right to be assisted by an interpreter is enshrined at the constitutional level.[225] As far as EU law is concerned, Directive 2010/64 has devoted increasing attention to the linguistic guarantees in criminal proceedings. The examination of the statutory solutions introduced by the 2010 EU legislation and particularly of the interpretation provided by the EU Court of Justice since the *Covaci* judgment, however, displays a somewhat worrisome picture. It is true that according to the Luxembourg judges, defendants must not only be ensured translation of essential documents, among which indictment is surely to be included,[226] but they also have the right to obtain the assistance of an interpreter to follow the procedural activities that take place in criminal hearings and to communicate with their lawyers. However, while some linguistic versions of Directive 2010/64 adopt a broad expression that ensures information on "any charge or indictment" (*e.g.*, the English text), others adopt formulations that might restrict the scope of application of this fundamental guarantee to the sole accusation with which defendants are brought to court. It is clear that such a restrictive interpretation would not only contradict the broad approach followed by this legislation, which is intended to ensure protection to both suspects and accused, but would also deprive suspects of an essential condition for taking part in criminal activities and even in judicial hearings in the pre-trial phase.

Although there is no specific case-law of the Luxembourg Court on this issue, it is clear that both the *Covaci* jurisprudence and especially the broad approach developed in the *Sleutjes* ruling, which considered the special guilty verdict contained in the penal order in terms of accusation, render the possibility of a restrictive interpretation unlikely. Indeed, both these judgments broadened the protective scope of the safeguards introduced by the 2010 Directive by extending the information on the charges to the notification of the penal order that constitutes the first tool through which defendants can become aware of the charges filed. It has been noted, however, that even personal information may not be enough if further safeguards are not assured. Worse still, since according to Luxembourg case-law legal and linguistic assistance need not be provided jointly to the individuals convicted through a penalty order in the timeframe available to lodge an objection, the requirement of personal notification of the guilty verdict can dangerously backfire, leaving the accused alone to face a decision that can lead to the penal order becoming final. The

---

[225] Art. 111(3) Const.-Italy.
[226] Art. 3(2) DIT.

Solomon-like solution found by the Court of Justice in the *Covaci* case does not exclude the granting of linguistic assistance where the accused decides to lodge a written objection, since the 2010 Directive does not preclude member states from ensuring the translation of further documents that are essential to guarantee the fairness of criminal proceedings.[227] Certainly, this interpretation had the merit of broadening the meaning of 'essential documents' by including documents from the accused, such as written statements and their appeal against the conviction.[228] In this way, however, the Luxembourg judges offloaded onto the national judicial authorities the responsibility to establish, taking into account the characteristics of both the applicable procedure and the case at stake, whether the challenge lodged in writing against a penal order should be considered an essential document for the purposes of its translation.[229]

4.2.3 Legal Assistance and the Accused's Right to Be Present in Court: A Real Out-Out?

In Europe, several countries do not allow for self-defence in criminal proceedings, but require defendants, alongside other private parties, to be represented in court by a counsel appointed either by them or by the state. Under certain conditions, legal aid also has to be granted. Constitutional law widely recognises legal assistance as a fundamental guarantee in judicial proceedings. The Portuguese Constitution stands out among those countries examined in this research, since it not only enshrines the right to access to legal counsel as an essential condition of the general right to effective judicial protection,[230] but also explicitly considers legal assistance as a fundamental element to fair administration of justice.[231] Moreover, Portuguese constitutional law allows for mandatory legal assistance, while charging the legislature with the task of determining the cases and stages in which assistance is mandatory.[232] In other countries, a similar result was achieved by constitutional case-law. In Italy, the problem of self-defence in criminal proceedings led to dramatic consequences at the end of the 1970s, as some individuals charged with terrorism-related offences waived legal assistance as a form of rejection of the institution and judicial protection.[233] Since then, the Constitutional Court has deemed mandatory legal assistance consistent with both the constitutional provision on the right to a defence

---

[227] CJEU, *Covaci* (fn. 24), para 49.

[228] Gialuz (2015), p. 6 f.

[229] CJEU, *Covaci* (fn. 24), para 50.

[230] Art. 20(2) Const.-Portugal.

[231] Art. 208 Const.-Portugal.

[232] See Costa Ramos and Churro, in this volume, Sect. 2.2.

[233] On these cases and the problem of self-defence in Italy see among others Chiavario (1979).

and with international human rights instruments.[234] More recently, the constitutional judges have attempted to enforce this approach by underlining the importance of legal assistance as a necessary condition of a fair criminal trial.[235]

In this regard, international human rights instruments do not define a position in one or another direction. Like other human rights charters, the European Convention not only acknowledges the accused's right to "defend himself in person or through legal assistance of his own choosing", but also grants him the right to "examine or have examined witnesses". Although the latter formulation, in particular, does not necessarily entail the right to have incriminating witnesses cross-examined by counsel,[236] this approach reveals a clear favour of the Rome Convention towards the direct involvement of the accused in criminal proceedings in general, and with a view to specific procedural activities, such as evidence-gathering. Yet, European case-law has not always been consistent with this systematic approach. In *Croissant v. Germany*, the Court found that the legal requirement that a defendant be assisted by counsel at all stages of judicial proceedings could not be deemed incompatible with the Convention.[237] More recently, however, the Strasbourg judges allowed defendants to waive their right to legal assistance, provided, however, that waiver is expressed unequivocally and is "attended by minimum safeguards commensurate to the waiver's importance".[238] From a similar perspective, the United Nations' Human Rights Committee stressed that the failure of Portuguese law to provide for exceptions to mandatory legal assistance, regardless of the severity of the charges and the complexity of the case and of the characteristics of the accused, could not be deemed consistent with Article 14(3)(d) of the International Covenant.[239]

The adoption of such a flexible approach raises two main questions, namely (*a*) which procedural activities allow or even require personal attendance of the accused, and (*b*) whether and how they can make their own contribution to fact-finding if legal assistance is ensured. Concerning the first question, it should be noted that all criminal justice systems (and also countries that exclude self-defence) certainly provide for a number of procedural activities that allow (or even require) the involvement of the accused, as well as decisions that lawyers cannot take alone. In Italy, for instance, the possibility of defendants putting in place certain procedural activities for the purposes of fact-finding was even acknowledged as a right of constitutional relevance.[240] Moreover, the accused's contribution holds specific importance in the field of evidence-gathering, because of the constitutional enshrinement of the accused's right to question or have questioned incriminating witnesses.[241]

---

[234] CConst, judgment 125/1979 and decision 188/1980.

[235] CConst, decision 421/1997.

[236] See Ruggeri, in Part V of this volume, Sect. 6.2.2.1.

[237] ECtHR, *Croissant v. Germany*, judgment of 25 September 1992, Appl. No. 13611/88, para 27.

[238] ECtHR, *Trymbach v. Ukraine*, judgment of 12 January 2012, Appl. No. 44385/02, para 61.

[239] See Costa Ramos and Churro, in this volume, Sect. 2.2.

[240] Cf. Mangiaracina, in this volume, Sect. 1.

[241] Art. 111(3) Const.-Italy.

Over the last decades, however, we have witnessed a clear tendency to reduce the scope of the decisions that require defendants to be personally involved in criminal proceedings. Italian law provides several significant examples. We saw that the 1988 code, departing from the approach of the 1930 codification, allowed for penal orders to be challenged either by the accused personally or by a lawyer, although not being mandated to do so.[242] Italian courts further aggravated this result by acknowledging the lawfulness of an objection filed by a court-appointed lawyer.[243] It is apparent that the lawyer's decision, no matter whether it is to challenge the penal order or not, may depart from the accused's intentions and can entail the permanent loss of some important opportunities. A similar tendency to reduce the personal contribution of the accused to fact-finding can be observed in the field of evidence law. A delicate question is whether defendants must personally waive their right to participation in the gathering of evidence and what role their lawyers can play in this decision. This question has become of utmost importance since Law 479/1999 introduced a flexible mechanism allowing for the parties (including the public prosecutor) to agree that specific pieces of evidence gathered by either the police or the prosecutor or the defence are inserted into the trial file.[244] Again, on the accused's side, lawyers can reach an agreement with the prosecutor and the other parties regardless of whether their clients provided them with the special power to do so, their clients do not even need to be informed on this important decision. Yet evidentiary agreements alter the overall information usable for the decision-making and can therefore heavily impinge on the fact-finding, leading to the use of incriminating evidence.[245] It is more than doubtful whether this solution is in line with the requirements of Italian constitutional law, which enables the legislature to depart from the principle of *contradictoire* if the accused consents to the use of untested evidence.[246]

In more general terms, it is also debatable whether the tendency to reduce the area of the decisions that the accused should take personally is consistent with the requirements of international human rights law. Of course, international charters cannot provide binding indications about the procedural contexts in which the accused can or should be involved personally, as this depends on the specific features of any criminal justice system and the arrangements made by domestic law. However, it might be argued that, at least where procedural activities and investiga-

---

[242] Art. 461(1) CCP-Italy.

[243] CConst, judgment 504/2000. In the same sense see CCass, 4th Section, 29 November 2000, *Kusi Kwaben*. In: Archivio della nuova procedura penale (2002), p. 226.

[244] Agreements can be reached either at the end of the pre-trial phase(s), i.e. at the time in which the two files are set up, or at a later stage of the proceedings. Cf. Arts. 431(2), Art. 493(3) and 500(7) CCP.

[245] Therefore, defendants should be made aware of the consequences of this decision, and should be able to express their intention to consent to the proposal of agreement. In this sense see Marzaduri (2009), pp. 215 f.

[246] Art. 111(5) Const.-Italy. In this regard, Marzaduri (2009), p. 215 f., deems an intervention of the Constitutional Court unnecessary to enable the defendant to personally consent to the use of untested evidence.

tions are at stake that can affect fundamental rights, international human rights law requires that defendants be made aware of the implications of their decisions and defence lawyers should not act without knowing the specific intentions of their clients. This raises the further question of whether international law instruments truly treat legal assistance and self-defence as alternative safeguards. On close examination, human rights law does not provide any indications that allow us to look at these safeguards in such terms. Remarkably, the International Covenant, by way of expressly acknowledging the accused's right to be present at trial, follows an approach that not only systematically couples this guarantee with the right to a defence, but also conceives of personal participation as an additional safeguard to the defence rights.[247] In other words, this legal instrument displays a picture in which defendants are to be granted the necessary conditions for taking part personally in criminal proceedings regardless of whether domestic law allows them to defend themselves or requires them to be assisted by a lawyer.

This conclusion is of utmost importance in the field of evidence-gathering. In particular, the debate about whether the acknowledgment of the right to question prosecutorial witnesses enables national law to empower the accused to cross-examine them personally appears to be somewhat misleading, since defendants can make an essential contribution to fact-finding even if the questions are put by their counsels. Even more, the accused may provide essential information for the purposes of effective cross-examination, information that counsel might ignore. In this regard, it is debatable that Italian case-law allowed for the admissibility of testimonial evidence taken abroad on the sole condition that the defence lawyer could take part in the execution of letters rogatory, even though the accused expressly requested personal participation.[248] There is no doubt that this interpretation frustrates the *audi alteram partem* rule, giving a rather formalistic interpretation of the right to be fairly involved in the collection of oral evidence, which does not seem to be in line with Italian law. Similar problems of constitutionality have arisen in other countries. For instance, French procedural law did not allow for private parties to have access to relevant information, which ought to be communicated solely to lawyer. This set-up has been recently declared unconstitutional in relation to the public prosecutor's requisitions following the end of the investigation and to the Investigation Chamber's decision to order an expertise.[249]

It is questionable whether legal restrictions on the right to know relevant information are consistent with the European Convention and with EU law. We saw that in *Kremzow v. Austria*, the Court allowed for national law to restrict the access to the file solely to the lawyer, and that the more recent judgment *Sher et al. v. United Kingdom* reveals the clear tendency to enhance the use of closed hearings and disclosure of confidential materials to special advocates with no contact with the

---

[247] Thus, the International Covenant ensures to the person charged with a criminal offence the right to "be tried in his presence, *and* to defend himself in person or through legal assistance of his own choosing". Cf. Art. 14(3)(d) ICCPR.

[248] CCass, 1 December 2010, *De Falco*, in CED rv. 248963.

[249] Drevet, in this volume, Sect. 2.

defendant—significantly, not only in the field of security law, but also in criminal proceedings. Yet the 1993 *Kremzow* ruling had already justified the limitations of the right to access relevant evidence in the light of the risks to the ongoing inquiry, and it is more than doubtful that ECHR law can allow such risks to be presumed. As far as EU law is concerned, there are no clear indications in the 2012 Directive on information rights in criminal proceedings. The fact that, as noted, EU law ensures the right to access relevant evidence either to the defendants or to their lawyers, however, should not be seen as a decisive argument to conclude that EU institutions allow for the accused to be kept in dark about essential information on condition that information was provided solely to counsel. This holds true particularly where national law allows for the adoption of procedural arrangements that require the intervention of special advocates who are not permitted to communicate with their client. In some countries, such arrangements can also raise serious problems of consistency with constitutional law. It is worth noting that the provision, contained in the initial legislative project of the Portuguese code of criminal procedure, which allowed for the public prosecutor to impede the communication of the detained person with his lawyer before the arraignment in cases of terrorism, violent or highly organised criminality, was deemed incompatible with the Constitution's acknowledgment of the right to legal assistance that also entails the right of the accused to communicate with his lawyer.[250] From the viewpoint of EU law, it seems that the requirement that the decision to refuse access to certain pieces of evidence either be taken by a judicial authority or at least be submitted to judicial review should be extended to the case under examination.

4.2.4 The Right to Make One's Voice Heard Fairly and the Right Not to Be Heard in Criminal Proceedings

Premise

Doubtless, the right to make one's voice heard fairly stands out among the most precious expressions of the right to be personally involved in criminal proceedings. Yet this right holds different relevance depending on various factors, such as the phases of the proceedings, the competent authorities for questioning, and so on.

Surprisingly, although the right to be fairly heard lies at the heart of the *audi alteram partem* rule, human rights instruments do not generally contain specific provisions on the guarantee of a fair examination. Constitutional law rarely enshrines the right to be heard fairly in judicial proceedings,[251] which should however be deemed acknowledged by the inviolable right to a defence and the principle of

---

[250] Cf. Costa Ramos and Churro, in this volume, Sect. 2.2.

[251] An exception among the Constitutions of the countries examined in this research is that of the German Basic Law, which expressly recognises to every person the right to a court hearing in accordance with law. Cf. Art. 103(1) Basic Law. See Vogel, in this volume, Sect. 1.

(or the right to) *contradictoire*.[252] The European Convention, despite enshrining the general right to a fair hearing, does not acknowledge any safeguards regarding the questioning of the accused, not to mention the possibility of rendering spontaneous statements before the competent authorities. This does not mean, however, that under this human rights charter, a criminal trial can be carried out without the accused being given a fair opportunity of making themselves heard. Remarkably, as noted, the *Colozza* judgment had already stressed that the person convicted *in absentia* should be granted the right to a retrial "from a court which has heard" them.[253]

The need to grant the accused a fair hearing is particularly evident in the field of restrictions on liberty. The requirement that the arrested or detained individuals be promptly brought before a body exercising judicial powers[254] does not aim at an objective oversight of the lawfulness of the coercive measure applied, but requires the competent authority to grant them the opportunity to be heard. Furthermore, the general reference to a 'fair hearing' entails that the individuals charged with a criminal offence be put in a fair condition to be heard, to expose their arguments and to challenge the arguments put forward by other parties.[255] This acknowledgment is even clearer under the American Convention, since two of its four official versions—namely the Spanish and Portuguese versions—formulate the right to a fair hearing as the general right of all the individuals charged with a criminal offence to be fairly heard in the proceedings.[256] This may also explain why in the Pact of San José, as noted, the right of defendants who do not speak or understand the language used in court to be assisted without charge by an interpreter or translator stands out at the top of the minimum fair trial rights.

The systematic importance that international human rights law attaches to the general right to a court hearing, viewed as a listening space, entails that it can certainly not be considered an exclusive prerogative of defendants. Upon close examination, the European Convention also does not simply grant defendants the right to be fairly heard, but recognises their right to be tried in a proceeding that provides a fair hearing of all the involved parties.[257] This means that in Europe international human rights law ensures to defendants the right not only to have access to criminal justice but also to be fairly involved in a proceeding in which all the interests at stake must be mutually balanced and all the parties must also be given the opportunity of making their voice heard. In the last years, international human rights courts have progressively extended the right to be fairly heard to individuals

---

[252] Arts. 24(2) and 111(2) Const.-Italy. See Mangiaracina, in this volume, Sect. 1.

[253] Above, Sect. 3.2.5.1.

[254] Art. 5(3) ECHR.

[255] Ubertis (2009), p. 49.

[256] Art. 8(1) ACHR.

[257] It is noteworthy that the English version of Article 6(1) ECHR acknowledges the right to 'a fair hearing', whereas the French text may seem to adopt a more subjective perspective by granting the accused the right that '*sa cause soit entendue équitablement*'. Most translations into Romance languages have followed the same perspective.

other than the accused and by overcoming the limits of a formal examination. This raises the question of the extent to which international human rights instruments can also protect the right of other individuals—particularly of the victims—to make their voice fairly heard in criminal proceedings.[258] On the accused's side, the comparative examination of international human rights law and EU law allows us to observe three main features of the right to a fair hearing, i.e. (*a*) the right to be fairly examined, (*b*) the right not to be examined and (*c*) the right to give statements in one's favour.

Conditions of a Fair Questioning in the Pre-trial Inquiry

International human rights case-law has not only proclaimed the right to be fairly examined, but has also laid down some qualitative conditions that must be met during the accused's questionings in criminal proceedings. It is worth observing that, as the Strasbourg Court for the first time dealt with the right to an impartial and independent tribunal, it scrutinised the lawfulness of a trial before a court presided over by a judge who had previously acted as a prosecutor in the same case.[259] The requirement of an impartial and independent judge is of utmost importance in the pre-trial inquiry, in which all the individuals involved are in their most vulnerable position where they are questioned by the authorities in charge of investigations. The risk of overwhelming power of the investigative bodies is apparent in the countries in which there is no competent judge for the oversight of the pre-trial investigations and particularly where the police still hold responsibility for the preliminary inquiry. Therefore, since the *John Murray* judgment,[260] the Strasbourg Court has required that suspects be granted the assistance of a lawyer even at the first police interrogation, a guarantee of such relevance that it also entails the right to communicate with counsel prior to the investigative hearing. At the domestic law level, the Spanish Constitution explicitly ensures to every person the right to legal assistance in court proceedings, and it is noteworthy that in the field of criminal justice constitutional case-law extended the scope of this fundamental guarantee to the police hearings.[261]

Doubtless, EU law has followed a similar approach by recognising the right to effective and active participation of the lawyer not only in judicial hearings by also in the questionings conducted by the police or other law enforcement authorities—thus, in such questionings, counsel must be able to ask questions, make statements,

---

[258] Below, Sect. 4.3. On this delicate question see already Chiavario (2001), pp. 938 ff.

[259] ECtHR, *Piersack v. Belgium*, judgment of 1 October 1982, Appl. No. 8692/79. See Trechsel (2005), p. 66 f.

[260] ECtHR, Grand Chamber, *John Murray v. United Kingdom*, judgment of 8 February 1996, Appl. No. 18731/91. See also later ECtHR, *Magee v. United Kingdom*, judgment of 6 June 2000, Appl. No. 28135/95.

[261] Villamarín López, in this volume, Sect. 2.

request clarifications, and so on.[262] Nevertheless, the protection ensured by EU legislation is still far from being fully satisfactory, as there are still no clear rules on some important issues. In particular, EU institutions did not at all clarify what information should exactly be provided to the person being examined. Moreover, extending the right to legal assistance solely to those who become suspects or defendants during a hearing clearly weakens the guarantee of access to a lawyer. Thus, "there is no precise moment where it can be undoubtedly stated that a witness becomes a suspect",[263] and national countries regulate this delicate change of status in very different fashions. Ultimately, the right to access to a lawyer will surely not be sufficient to ensure legal assistance if the accused have no financial means to appoint a lawyer or are in a foreign country, which makes it difficult to find counsel to represent them in court. Following European case-law, legal aid therefore constitutes a necessary condition for the purposes of ensuring effective participation in criminal proceedings, particularly in the case of coercive measures. It is noteworthy that the guarantee of legal aid in the case of deprivation of liberty stands at the top of the situations provided for by the recent Directive 2016/1919/EU.[264]

Procedural Safeguards Against the Use of Coercion in Criminal Hearings and the Enhanced Protection of the *nemo tenetur* Principle in International Human Rights Law

There can be little doubt that the protection against the use of coercion is a fundamental condition of a fair examination in criminal proceedings. In Europe, notwithstanding the lack of explicit acknowledgment of the privilege against self-incrimination among the accused's fair trial rights, Strasbourg case-law has strongly contributed to the elaboration of some essential safeguards against the use of coercive means during questioning.[265] As pointed out by the Strasbourg Court in the *Saunders* case, the right not to be compelled to be examined constitutes, on the accused's side, a clear expression of the presumption of innocence.[266] EU law has recently followed the same approach by enacting specific rules on the *nemo tenetur* principle into Directive 2016/343 on the presumption of innocence and the right to be present at trial. Despite the unquestionable relevance of the right not to undergo coercion to give evidence oneself, the privilege against self-incrimination is not generally provided by the Constitutions of European countries, which has led constitutional courts to provide systematic interpretations to acknowledge it at the constitutional law level. The Spanish Constitution constitutes an exception, as it not

---

[262] Recital No. 25 DAL.

[263] Bachmaier Winter (2015), p. 114.

[264] Art. 2(1)(a) DLA.

[265] For in-depth analysis of the Strasbourg case-law see Arslan (2015), pp. 34 ff.

[266] ECtHR, Grand Chamber, *Saunders v. United Kingdom*, judgment of 17 December 1996, Appl. No. 19187/91.

only expressly recognised the right of the accused not to incriminate themselves, but also linked systematically the *nemo tenetur* principle with the presumption of innocence.[267] In other countries, moreover, constitutional case-law has significantly acknowledged the privilege against self-incrimination as a result of the increasing influence of international human rights charters.[268]

An indisputable merit of European case-law was its constant effort to strengthen the right not to incriminate oneself by progressively broadening the protective scope of the *nemo tenetur* principle in two main ways. On the one hand, the Strasbourg Court acknowledged the privilege against self-incrimination to individuals not under investigation, providing them with protection against the risk of future prosecution. On the other, European case-law extended the scope of the *nemo tenetur* principle to the right to silence as well as, under certain circumstances, the right not to go to the witness box.[269] Redefined in these terms, the privilege against self-incrimination turns out to ensure the right not to be questioned at all, a right, however, that several criminal justice systems only grant those who have assumed the formal status of parties in the proceedings.[270] Interestingly, the European Court also enhanced the privilege against self-incrimination in situations of particular vulnerability for the person examined. The *Gäfgen* judgment, in particular, made it clear that coercive means cannot be allowed in order to obtain incriminating evidence from the individuals concerned—not even if coercion is justified by the need to protect other human rights acknowledged by the Convention, as compulsion used against vulnerable individuals inevitably results in inhuman treatment.[271]

In recent years, moreover, we have witnessed a further enhancement of the protective scope of the privilege against self-incrimination by the European Court. Firstly, Strasbourg case-law, despite long excluding from the area of the *nemo tenetur* principle the use of evidence that could be taken against the will of the person examined,[272] has increasingly acknowledged this fundamental guarantee in relation to information that was not obtained in the context of a hearing but through coercive measures. To be sure, in the *Funke* case, the European Court had already found that the attempt of the competent authority to compel the applicant to hand over documents that could incriminate him infringed the Convention.[273] More recently, the *Jalloh* judgment led to a further development of Strasbourg case-law, which stressed that the use of evidence obtained through interference with the physical integrity of

---

[267] See Vollamarín López, in this volume, Sect. 1.

[268] In France, for instance, the *Conseil constitutionnel* has for the first time in 2016 considered the right to silence as a constitutional principle in the light of the Declaration of the Rights of Man and of the Citizen. See Drevet, in this volume, Sect. 1.

[269] Zacchè (2008), p. 180.

[270] See, for instance, Art. 503(1) CCP-Italy.

[271] ECtHR, Grand Chamber, *Gäfgen v. Germany*, judgment of 1 June 2010, Appl. No. 22978/05, para 107.

[272] See ECtHR, *P.G. and J.H. v. United Kingdom*, judgment of 25 September 2001, Appl. No. 44787/98, in relation to vocal sample with a view to a confrontation.

[273] ECtHR, *Funke v. France*, judgment of 25 February 1993, Appl. No. 10828/84.

the person gives rise to a breach of the Convention also in relation to the *nemo tenetur* principle.[274] This judgment, therefore, opened up unprecedented perspectives for a more modern understanding of the relationship between the *nemo tenetur* principle and the taking of biological materials by coercive means.[275] Nevertheless, it is noteworthy that in the subsequent case *O'Halloran and Francis v. United Kingdom*, the Grand Chamber ruled that the privilege against self-incrimination cannot be infringed upon through the coercive collection of blood sample for the purposes of a DNA analysis.[276]

A second relevant development in Strasbourg case-law concerns the use of evidence taken through coercive means. Interestingly, this development materialised in decisions in which the Court dealt with statements obtained during an administrative investigation. In the *Saunders* case, the European judges, although stressing that the authorities competent for administrative investigations are not bound by the same requirements set for criminal proceedings, had already made it clear that the use of statements obtained under compulsion by an administrative authority can in no way be deemed to be compatible with the right to a fair hearing.[277] It is worth observing that this jurisprudence, which was maintained in *Shannon v. United Kingdom*,[278] contrasts with the approach, based on the sole and decisive evidence doctrine,[279] followed in the *John Murray* case.[280] Doubtless, the *Saunders* doctrine has marked a step of the utmost importance, highlighting that a violation of the Convention does not depend on the probative relevance attached to the information obtained coercively.

The Right to Give Statements in One's Favour and to Make Oneself Heard by the Competent Authority

A final question arises in the context of the present discussion: if the competent authorities decide not to summon the accused to be questioned, do they have a right to make themselves heard in criminal proceedings? Does human rights law grant them a right to be heard without being questioned? In several criminal justice systems, defendants can give spontaneous statements to the competent authority in the

---

[274] ECtHR, Grand Chamber, *Jalloh v. Germany*, judgment of 11 June 2006, Appl. No. 54810/00.

[275] Zacchè (2008), p. 190 f.

[276] ECtHR, Grand Chamber, *O'Halloran and Francis v. United Kingdom*, judgment of 29 June 2007, Appl. No. 15809/02 and 25624/02.

[277] ECtHR, Grand Chamber, *Saunders v. United Kingdom* (fn. 266), para 67.

[278] ECtHR, *Shannon v. United Kingdom*, judgment of 4 October 2005, Appl. No. 6563/03.

[279] See already Trechsel (2005), p. 345, who detected the different approach from that used (prior to the *Al-Khawaja* judgment) in relation to the right to confrontation.

[280] ECtHR, *John Murray v. United Kingdom* (fn. 260).

pre-trial inquiry, and after the court proceedings have been commenced, they cannot be examined without their consent.[281]

International human rights instruments do not provide specific indications on the right of individuals involved in criminal proceedings to give evidence in their favour outside of a formal questioning by the competent authority. Nevertheless, we saw that it lies at the core of the right to a fair hearing that the person charged with a criminal offence should have the opportunity to make his version of the events heard by an independent body. It has also been observed that the American Convention acknowledges the right of any person accused of a criminal offence not just to access a public hearing, but to be heard in public by an independent and impartial tribunal. This acknowledgment should also be read in the sense that the accused, if not summoned to be questioned, must be given the opportunity for giving evidence in his favour. This fundamental requirement can certainly not be deemed extraneous to the system of protection of human rights of the European Convention. We have noted that, despite the great flexibility of Strasbourg case-law on the right to personal participation in criminal proceedings, the European Court has since the 1980s conditioned the lawfulness of the retrial on the fact that the competent court gives a voice to the person convicted *in absentia* prior to the decision-making. Constitutional law also may seem to provide some interesting indications in this regard. For instance, the Italian Constitution, while recognising the European Convention's right of the accused to examine or to have examined incriminating witnesses, also grants them the right to have any further evidence obtained in their favour.[282] Although this formulation does not of course entail an unconditional right to have exculpatory evidence admitted in court,[283] it seems to provide a clear legal basis for the acknowledgment of the constitutional right of the accused to give evidence in their favour.[284]

The main difficulty, however, is to identify the safeguards that should be ensured to the defendant who chooses to appear before the competent authority to give spontaneous evidence. Of course, the most delicate situations arise in the pre-trial inquiry because of the frequent imbalance between the prosecutor and the suspect. In Italy, the suspect's initiative can lead to two different situations, depending on whether the prosecutor informs him of the charge filed. If the suspect receives the information prescribed by the law for prosecutorial questionings,[285] the gathering of sponta-

---

[281] In Italy, the 1988 code enabled the suspect to appear at the public prosecutor's office and to give spontaneous statements. Italian law, moreover, makes it clear that the suspect's conduct does not prevent the application of pre-trial measures. See Art. 374 CCP-Italy.

[282] Art. 111(3) Const.-Italy.

[283] Marzaduri (2000), p. 783 f.

[284] It should be noted, however, that under the Italian constitutional law the accused's right to evidence, along with the right to confrontation, must be satisfied "before a judge". See Art. 111(3) Const.-Italy. Moreover, it is apparent that the prosecutorial and police questionings do not properly fulfil the constitutional requirement of equal treatment of the parties, set forth by Article 111(2) Const.-Italy.

[285] Cf. Arts. 64, 65 and 364 CCP-Italy.

neous statements is deemed equivalent to a prosecutorial examination.[286] The main problem, however, is that the competent prosecutor can discretionarily decide whether or not to provide this information. In the negative case, suspects are kept in the dark on both the prosecutorial charge and the evidence collected by the investigative bodies, and may therefore happen to render statements without proper information. Worse still, Italian law does not require the suspect to be assisted by a lawyer, and prosecutors can therefore gather statements from a clearly advantageous position without the need to provide the information required in the case of a prosecutorial questioning.

It may be surprising that the Italian legislative implementation of the EU Directives 2012/13 and 2013/48[287] has not at all reformed these rules. Yet EU law does not seem to provide any specific protection in relation to the cases under examination. A look at Directive 2013/48/EU, in particular, highlights that the guarantee of previous communication with the lawyer representing the accused and the right to have one's own counsel present and take part effectively in the hearing were recognised solely in case of questioning.[288] Under the European Convention also, there are no statutory indications in this regard. A systematic examination of fair trial safeguards in the light of comprehensive understanding of the right to be heard fairly, however, suggests extending the right both to be informed on the charge and to be assisted by a lawyer also to the case in which the accused takes the initiative in giving evidence before the competent authority. Thus, the possibility of using the statements rendered, along with the broad discretion of prosecutors in deciding whether to provide suspects with the aforementioned information, does not seem to be consistent with the general approach of the European Convention.

4.3   The Participatory Safeguards Acknowledged by Human Rights Law to the Victim and Other Individuals Involved in Criminal Proceedings

Although the traditional understanding of the right to personal participation in criminal proceedings looks at the side of the accused, the complex challenges posed by the *audi alteram partem* rule—viewed from the perspective of constitutional, international human rights and EU law—require us to broaden the focus to other individuals affected by a criminal law action. Doubtless, in a modern view of criminal justice, personal involvement in criminal hearings can no longer be deemed an exclusive prerogative of defendants. It should therefore be examined whether and to

---

[286] Art. 374(2) CCP-Italy.

[287] See respectively Legislative Decree 101/2014 and Legislative Decree 184/2016.

[288] Art. 3(3)(a-b) DAL.

what extent human rights law ensures other individuals involved in criminal proceedings the right to appear in court and make their contribution to fact-finding.

As far as private parties other than defendants are concerned, the question may seem not to make much sense in those countries, such as Italy, which require them to be represented in court by a lawyer whom they mandated with a special power.[289] Yet we saw that legal assistance and personal attendance should not be seen as alternative guarantees. Therefore, even though the special power ensures consistency of the lawyers' activity with the intentions of their clients, legal assistance cannot be intended to rule out the personal involvement of the private parties. Concerning the victim, the main problem lies in the fact that he does not always hold the formal status of a party of the proceedings and his role considerably varies depending on the solutions adopted by domestic law. In some European countries, however, constitutional law also covers the right of the victim to be actively involved in criminal proceedings, as occurs in Romania from the aforementioned viewpoint of the right to access to justice.[290] In France, as noted, the Constitutional Court has recently taken care of the right of the damaged party to take proceedings before *Cour de cassation* without any limit dependent on the initiative of the public prosecutor.[291]

The considerable diversity of national law arrangements concerned with the aggrieved parties in criminal proceedings is probably the reason why EU legislation, despite its increasing attention towards victims' rights, has until now provided scant and not very consistent indications on the victim's right to take part in criminal proceedings. Directive 2012/29/EU, while generally referring to the arrangements of national law as to the role of the injured parties in criminal proceedings, emphasises the need for active participation of the victim, to the extent that the granting of some defence rights (*e.g.*, linguistic understanding of essential documents) largely depends on the victim's active role in criminal justice. This approach raises several questions from a human rights perspective. In particular, what should be meant by 'active participation'? Who should decide whether and to what extent the victim's contribution to fact-finding was sufficiently active?

It is worth observing that the 2012 EU legislation enhanced the information rights of the aggrieved parties, thus highlighting the clear attempt to involve them personally in criminal proceedings. In the Directive on victim's rights, there is a strict link between the guarantee of detailed information and respect for the person injured by the alleged offence, who must be kept informed of development of the criminal inquiry. In this context, EU law attached particular relevance to the need to inform the victim if the decision has been taken not to prosecute the alleged offender. Despite the merits of this solution, information may arrive too late, i.e., when the proceedings have already been discontinued. A better solution, therefore, would be to grant the victim information about the prosecutorial request for termination of the proceedings, in order to enable him to challenge the prosecutorial initiative before a

---

[289] Art. 100(1) CCP-Italy.

[290] Ciopec and Roibu, in this volume, Sect. 1.

[291] Above, Sect. 4.1.

decision has been issued. It is also interesting to note that the right to information has another important feature under EU law from the viewpoint of the victim, namely as the right to forget the offence and to be forgotten. Doubtless, EU institutions devoted great importance to the right not to be informed on the charge and the institution of criminal proceedings, since information is dependent on the explicit request of the victim. Although this arrangement is in principle justified, EU law should have probably required an independent body to scrutinise the voluntariness of the victim's decision not to obtain information, a decision that in turn presupposes awareness of the implications on participatory rights in criminal proceedings.

Another delicate question is whether human rights law grants the victim the right to be heard in criminal proceedings. While neither constitutional law in general nor international human rights law may seem to provide specific indications on this problem, EU law has increasingly focused on the right of the victim to make his voice fairly heard in criminal proceedings. In the *Katz* case, the Luxembourg Court made it clear that, even though national law does not allow victims to render testimonial statements, EU law requires member states to provide them with a proper opportunity to be heard in criminal proceedings. Following this approach, Directive 2012/29/EU enacted a specific provision that explicitly recognises the victim's right not only to give evidence but also to be heard in criminal proceedings.[292] This acknowledgment is of the utmost systematic importance, although it is somewhat blurred by the provision that the right of victims to be heard should be deemed to have been fulfilled where the injured party was allowed to make statements or explanations in writing.[293]

From the perspective of constitutional law, it is worth noting that the 1997 Constitutional Amendment enacted into the Portuguese Constitution a legal provision that ensures to victims the right to intervene in the judicial proceedings, in the terms and in accordance with the conditions laid down by the law.[294] Yet, some negative developments have occurred in constitutional case-law, which reveal a certain tendency to weaken specific participatory rights of the aggrieved parties in criminal proceedings. A clear example is provided by Italian constitutional case-law. We have seen that the Constitutional Court has recently declared the code's regulation on the penal order procedure unconstitutional on the grounds that it enabled the complainant to a preventative opposition to such proceedings in case of offences that can only be prosecuted after a lawsuit by the victim.[295] As noted, this ruling reveals a significant development in constitutional case-law, which has shifted from the traditional understanding of penal order procedures, characterised by a subsequent consent by the accused, towards a new constitutional justification, based on

---

[292] Art. 10 DVR.

[293] Recital No. 41 DVR.

[294] Costa Ramos and Churro, in this volume, Sect. 1.2.

[295] CConst, judgment 23/2015.

the principle of reasonable length of the judicial proceedings in general.[296] From the viewpoint of the present discussion, this decision appears to exasperate the need for a speedy criminal justice, highlighting a conception of criminal proceedings that steps away from the trade-offs developed by the European Court in the last decades. This approach, in particular, seems to ignore the victim's interest in the institution of a criminal trial in which he can participate and his expectation of being fairly heard by an independent court.

Beyond these limits, does human rights law acknowledge a right to be heard and take part in criminal proceedings of individuals other than the private parties, which individuals either are forcefully involved in a criminal law action (*e.g.*, witnesses) or were affected by the offence without being the victim? The examination of international human rights case-law may seem to provide interesting indications in this respect. The Strasbourg jurisprudence on absent and anonymous witnesses, in particular, should not be interpreted exclusively as an attempt to balance the accused's right to confrontation with the state-related need not to waste relevant information. The developments that have taken place in European case-law since the 1990s—particularly, the developments that occurred after the *Al-Khawaja* judgment[297]—highlight the clear focus on the need not only to give a voice to the victim, but also to vulnerable witnesses and undercover agents whose examination in a public hearing could jeopardise them as well as their family members.[298]

More recently, the need to give a voice to the next of kin in criminal proceedings was dealt with in the aforementioned *Gray* judgment, in which the Strasbourg Court provided some indications on penal order procedures from the unprecedented perspective of the aggrieved parties. It has been noted that the Court did not raise doubts about German procedural law, which neither grants the aggrieved parties

---

[296] Art. 111(2) Const.-Italy.

[297] ECtHR, Grand Chamber, *Al-Khawaja and Tahery v. United Kingdom*, judgment of 15 December 2011, Appl. No. 26766/05 and 22228/06. See also ECtHR, 5th Section, *Schatschaschwili v. Germany*, judgment of 17 April 2014, Appl. No. 9154/10. This case was, moreover, referred to the Grand Chamber, which, despite not denying the *Al-Khawaja* doctrine, strengthened the defendant's right to examine incriminating witnesses by holding that confrontation should at least be ensured at the pre-trial stage through a defence lawyer. Cf. ECtHR, Grand Chamber, *Schatschaschwili v. Germany*, judgment of 15 December 2015, Appl. No. 9154/10.

[298] The Strasbourg Court was called upon to examine this issue in *van Mechelen v. The Netherlands*. See ECtHR, *van Mechelen v. The Netherlands*, judgment of 23 April 1997, Appl. No. 21363/93, 21364/93, 21427/93 and 22056/93. In this case, however, the European judges considered the domestic arrangements to be inadequate to compensate the accused for the restrictions suffered on his right to confrontation, although both the defendant und his counsel had been placed in an adjacent room and could follow the witness' examination and ask questions. This result was probably influenced by the fact that the witnesses were police officers. It was a rather unfortunate conclusion, taking into consideration that the Convention's protection of the right to life, physical integrity and security must certainly be ensured to all the persons involved in a criminal law action. It is noteworthy that the Strasbourg Court has broadened the trade-offs concerned with the right to confrontation even beyond the sphere of the parties of the proceedings in a strict sense, taking on the protection of the families of prosecutorial witnesses and their next of kin. In this sense cf. Trechsel (2005), pp. 319 f.

information on a penal order procedure nor enables them to challenge the conviction issued *inaudito reo*. The Court also did not explain why the Convention does not require the contracting states to involve the victim or their relatives in these summary proceedings, as it had instead recognised in relation to situations in which the responsibility of state's agents in connection with a victim's death was at stake. Nevertheless, European case-law recognised that the victim's next of kin must be involved in the proceedings to the extent necessary to safeguard their legitimate interests, particularly where the court procedure aims at the ascertainment of the circumstances of the victim's death. Despite these premises, the conclusion reached by the Court is disappointing: under the European Convention, the victim or his relatives would only have the right to to be involved in the proceedings instituted through the objection lodged against the penal order, as long as they can contribute to the "trial court's assessment of the case".[299] This reasoning, therefore, links the exercise of the participatory rights to the ability of the individuals interested in being involved in criminal proceedings whereby they must demonstrate the usefulness of their contribution for the purposes of fact-finding.

As noted, this functional perspective is a general weak point of the Court's approach to several defence rights. It cannot be accepted that the right to be involved in a criminal trial should be granted *secondum eventum*, and that the individuals concerned can be burdened with the task of proving in advance what contribution they could provide to the ascertainment of the facts. Moreover, where national law does not give the next of kin the formal status of parties of the proceedings, how and in which context should they provide this demonstration in advance? Worse still, in the *Gray* case the Court also ruled out the right to a legal remedy in a procedure that is by definition characterised by the exclusion of private parties prior to decision-making. Thus, the Solomon-like solution provided by the European Court turned out to make the involvement of the victim and his next of kin conditional on the prosecutorial decision to institute a certain type of criminal proceedings or another.

5 Conclusions

The comparative analysis of the participatory rights acknowledged by domestic, international and EU human rights law highlights a complex scenario. A number of constitutional and criminal law requirements, viewed in the light of the overall procedural safeguards enshrined in the European Convention, makes it today extremely difficult to maintain the traditional schemes applied to criminal proceedings held against absent defendants. These schemes were mainly justified by the perspective of a retrial or a subsequent tool, which are, however, often unable to erase the damages suffered from the decision rendered *in absentia* and to truly compensate the accused for the opportunities lost. Further problems arise from the

---

[299] ECtHR, *Gray v. Germany* (fn. 146), para 91.

proceedings *inaudito reo*, which, depending on the solutions provided by domestic law, may not even ensure a subsequent remedy corresponding to the accused's intentions. Doubtless, the solutions provided by the Strasbourg Court on *in absentia* trials not only had large influence on national legislation and practices, but also on the rapid evolution that EU law has undergone in the last decade in the field of transnational and domestic criminal justice. Yet the legislative instruments adopted at the national and EU law level are not always in line with European case-law.

Furthermore, cutting across the developments that have occurred in international, domestic and supranational law allows us to reconstruct a problematic area, which goes far beyond the procedures that exclude the accused from criminal proceedings. A number of difficult challenges arise from a participatory understanding of criminal proceedings. The comparative examination of Strasbourg case-law and EU law, in particular, enables us to define the qualitative requirements that should be satisfied with a view to ensuring effective participation in criminal proceedings. Along these lines, the present study has examined the conditions and fair trial safeguards that should be granted to the accused by focusing on four main issues, namely (*a*) the information rights, (*b*) the right to understand to be understood in the criminal trial, (*c*) the relationship between legal assistance and the right to self-defence, and finally (*d*) the right to make one's voice heard fairly. Moreover, the need to enhance an overall consideration of criminal proceedings by international human rights law and EU law has suggested extending the research area to further relevant issues, which go beyond the sphere of the accused's participatory rights. One of the most delicate questions that human rights law must face in the current era is whether and to what extent private parties other than defendants, as well as other individuals involved in criminal proceedings without being party to them, also hold the right to be heard fairly and contribute to fact-finding.

References

Arslan M (2015) Die Aussagefreiheit des Beschuldigten in der polizeilichen Befragung. Ein Vergleich zwischen EMRK, deutschem und türkischem Recht. Duncker & Humblot, Berlin

Bachmaier Winter L (2015) The EU Directive on the right to access to a lawyer: a critical assessment. In: Ruggeri S (ed) Human rights in European criminal law. New developments in European legislation and case law after the Lisbon Treaty. Springer, Heidelberg, pp 111–131

Bargis M (2017) Il dibattimento e le impugnazioni. In: Bargis M (ed) Procedura penale minorile, 2nd edn. Giappichelli, Torino, pp 154–175

Bellavvista G (1952) Il procedimento penale monitorio, 2nd edn. Giuffrè, Milano

Böse M (2011) Harmonizing procedural rights indirectly: the framework decision on trials in absentia. N C J Int Law:489–510

Böse M (2015) Human rights violations and mutual trust: recent case law on the European arrest warrant. In: Ruggeri S (ed) Human rights in European criminal law. New developments in European legislation and case law after the Lisbon Treaty. Springer, Heidelberg, pp 135–145

Calamandrei P (1926) Il procedimento monitorio nella legislazione italiana. Unitas

Caprioli F (2013) Report on Italy. In: Ruggeri S (ed) Transnational inquiries and the protection of fundamental rights in criminal proceedings. A study in memory of Vittorio Grevi and Giovanni Tranchina. Springer, Heidelberg, pp 439–455

Carini C (2008) Errore e rimedi. In: Digesto delle discipline penalistiche. IV Agg. Utet, Torino, pp 258–291

Carnelutti F (1924) Nota intorno alla natura del processo monitorio. Rivista di diritto processuale civile: 270 ff

Cesari C (2017) Le indagini preliminari e l'udienza preliminare. In: Bargis M (ed) Procedura penale minorile, 2nd edn. Giappichelli, Torino, pp 154–175

Chiavario M (1979) Autodifesa: una questione aperta per una risposta ciivle. ETS

Chiavario M (1984) Processo e garanzie della persona. II) Le garanzie fondamentali, 3rd edn. Giuffrè, Milano

Chiavario M (2001) Il "diritto al processo" delle vittime dei reati e la Corte europea dei diritti dell'uomo. Rivista di diritto processuale: 938 ff

Chiavario M (2005) Una riforma inevitabile: ma basterà? La Legislazione penale, pp 253–259

Daniele M, Paulesu PP (eds) (2015) Strategie di deflazione penale e rimodulazione del giudizio *in absentia*. Giappichelli, Torino

Di Chiara G (2009) *"Against the administration of justice in secret"*: la pubblicità delle procedure giudiziarie tra Corte europea e assetti del Sistema italiano. In: Balsamo A, Kostoris RE (eds) Giurisprudenza europea e processo penale italiano. Giappichelli, Torino, pp 293–308

Gialuz M (2015) Dalla Corte di Giustizia importanti indicazioni esegetiche in relazione alle prime due Direttive sui diritti dell'imputato. www.penalecontemporaneo.it. Accessed 11 Nov 2015

Grevi V (2000) Giustizia, l'accordo tra Italia e Spagna un modello europeo. Correre della Sera (4 December 2000)

Heger M, Wolter K (2015) 2. Hauptteil: Auslieferung – 4. Teil. Recht der EG/EU. In: Ambos K, König S, Rackow P (eds) Rechtshilferecht in Strafsachen. Nomos, Baden-Baden, pp 319–495

Lopes A Jr (2017) Direito Processual Penal, 14th edn. Saraiva, São Paulo

Lopes A Jr, Badaró GH (2009) Direito ao Processo Penal no Prazo Razoável, 2nd edn. Lumen Juris, Rio de Janeiro

Marzaduri E (2000) Commento all'art. 1 legge costituzionale 2/1999. In: La Legislazione penale, pp 762–804

Marzaduri E (2009) La prova negoziata e l'art. 111 Cost.: tra deroga al contraddittorio e valorizzazione dei profili dispositivi dell'accertamento penale. In: Di Chiara G (ed) Eccezioni al contraddittorio e giusto processo. Un itinerario attraverso la giurisprudenza. Giappichelli, Torino, pp 189–224

Negri D (2005) Commento all'art. 1 Decreto-legge 17/2005. La Legislazione penale: 260–291

Panebianco G (2012) Il sistema penale minorile. Imputabilità, pericolosità ed esigenze educative. Giappichelli, Torino

Quattrocolo (2014) Il contumace cede la scena processuale all'assente, mentre l'irreperibile l'abbandona. Riflessioni a prima lettura sulla nuova disciplina del procedimento senza imputato. www.penalecontemporaneo.it. Accessed 30 Apr 2014

Roxin C, Schünemann B (2017) Strafverfahrensrecht, 29th edn. C.H. Beck, Munich

Ruggeri S (2009) Il procedimento per decreto penale. In: Di Chiara G (ed) Eccezioni al contraddittorio e giusto processo. Un itinerario attraverso la giurisprudenza. Giappichelli, Torino, pp 133–188

Ruggeri A (2015) "Dialogue" between European and national courts, in the pursuit of the strongest protection of fundamental rights (with specific regard to criminal and procedural law). In: Ruggeri S (ed) Human rights in European criminal law. New developments in European legislation and case law after the Lisbon Treaty. Springer, Heidelberg, pp 9–29

Siracusano F (2011) Nuove prospettive in materie di processo *in absentia* e procedure di consegna. In: Rafaraci T (ed) La cooperazione di polizia e giudiziaria in materia penale nell'Unione europea dopo il Trattato di Lisbona. Giuffrè, Milano, pp 85–104

Slaughter AM (1994) A typology of transjudicial communication. Univ Richmond Law Rev 29:99–137

Tourinho Filho F (2010) Código de Processo Penal Comentado. I-II vol. 10th edn. Saraiva, São Paulo

Tranchina G (1961) Il procedimento per decreto penale e l'art. 24 della Costituzione. Rivista di diritto processuale: 516 ff

Trechsel S (2005) Human rights in criminal proceedings. Oxford University Press, Oxford

Ubertis G (2009) Principi di procedura penale europea, 2nd edn. Raffaello Cortina, Milano

Vigoni D (ed) (2014) Il giudizio in assenza dell'imputato. Giappichelli, Torino

Vogel B (2016) "In camera"-Verfahren als Gewährung effektiven Rechtsschutzes? Neue Entwicklungen im europäischen Sicherheitsrecht. Zeitschrift für die internationale Strafrechtsdogmatik: 28–38

Vogler R (2014) Criminal evidence and respect for fair trial guarantees in the dialogue between the European Court of Human Rights and national courts. In: Ruggeri S (ed) Transnational evidence and multicultural inquiries in Europe. Developments in EU legislation and new challenges for human rights-oriented criminal investigations in cross-border cases. Springer, Heidelberg, pp 181–192

Zacchè F (2008) Gli effetti della giurisprudenza europea in tema di privilegio contro le autoincriminazioni e diritto al silenzio. In: Balsamo A, Kostoris RE (eds) Giurisprudenza europea e processo penale italiano. Giappichelli, Torino, pp 179–195

Merging the Different View-Points. Concluding Remarks

Serena Quattrocolo and Stefano Ruggeri

Abstract This last chapter is a general overview on the impact of the European law on the domestic regulations of participatory rights. Mostly inspired by a part of the Attachment, submitted to the national rapporteurs, this chapter aims at pointing out two main features. First, the patent impact that the European law, both the ECHR and the EU law, had during the recent decades on national set-ups of participatory rights in criminal procedure. Second, the multifold pattern by which the European law affected local jurisdictions, inducing different reactions and attitudes within the analysed legal contexts. Such a normative evolution happened against a fast-changing background, in which people tend to move more frequently and where presence at trial may be put in balance with new needs and expectations.

Abbreviations

CJEU   Court of justice of the European Union
EAW   European arrest warrant
ECHR   European Convention on Human Rights
ECtHR   European Court of Human Rights
EU   European Union

Although this contribution is the result of a joint discussion, *Stefano Ruggeri* is the author of Sect. 1, while *Serena Quattrocolo* is the author of Sects. 2 and 3.

S. Quattrocolo (✉)
Department of Law, and Political, Economic and Social Sciences, University of Piemonte Orientale, Alessandria, Italy
e-mail: serena.quattrocolo@uniupo.it

S. Ruggeri
Department of Law 'Salvatore Pugliatti', Messina University, Messina, Italy
e-mail: steruggeri@unime.it

© Springer Nature Switzerland AG 2019   743
S. Quattrocolo, S. Ruggeri (eds.), *Personal Participation in Criminal Proceedings*, Legal Studies in International, European and Comparative Criminal Law 2, https://doi.org/10.1007/978-3-030-01186-4_22

1   The Context

As mentioned in the premises of the volume, the main purpose of this study is to approach the topic of parties' personal participation in judicial proceedings from many different angles, introducing several layers of comparison.

The starting point is represented by the national reports, presented separately and then confronted with a comparative method. Thus, the concluding remarks should go back to the domestic realities, to assess how they appear, after having worn the spectacles of an overall comparison.

It is possible to argue that the topic of personal participation has been dealt with in a multifaceted method, inspired to Article 6(3) TEU, having regard to fundamental rights, which, being enshrined in the ECHR and in the constitutional traditions of the member states, establish the general principles of the EU. Actually, the regulation of parties' involvement in criminal proceedings has been scrutinised under the perspective of constitutional law, substantive and procedural criminal law, civil procedural law and, of course, of ECHR and EU law.

Possibly, the last two items have been the *fil rouge* of the whole work, as they tend to gain the role of yardstick in any reasoning about the overall fairness of judicial proceedings. Thus, even in those parts of the text that are not directly based on the analysis of the European law, the authors tend to 'measure', to 'scale' the reality they describe with regard to ECtHR case-law, as well as to the EU framework-decisions and directives, as interpreted by the CJEU.

Throughout this volume, the European law proved to be either an instrument of harmonisation, a goal to be pursued, an inspiration to strengthening the overall fairness of a domestic system and to enhance an effective area of freedom, security and justice. Or, even the symbol of the unavoidable contradiction between long-lasting domestic dogmatic traditions and the non-formal pattern inspiring both the law of the EU and the system of the ECHR...

It is now time to have a general overview on how national scholars consider the European law to having affected their domestic regulation of the parties' personal contribution to criminal proceedings.

2   The Reality of the Domestic Orders Within the Twofold Framework of European Law

2.1   *Critical Remarks on Domestic Law in the Light of the European Convention*

Many of the countries examined in this study were first party to the European Convention on Human Rights and have only lately become EU Member States. Thus, on the one hand, the history of the relationships with the ECHR is much longer than with the EU. On the other hand, countries recently accepted into the EU are still in the process of implementing a relevant body of legislation that is related to *in absentia* trials.

Our starting point is the remark that, even though equally being parties to the Council of Europe and to the Convention, the twelve states analysed here display very different positions, with regard to the influence of the Strasbourg jurisprudence.

Possibly, the most peculiar position (not only with regard to the EU) is now the England and Wales one. *Leader*'s report emphasizes a long list of tendencies in English courts, undermining participatory rights, especially of the defendant. Some of those trends are not recent at all, like the persistent use of the dock in courtrooms. Isolating the defendant from her counsel has been considered in breach of fundamental fair trial rights since long ago.[1] Nevertheless, such use is still the rule, although it is not imposed upon by any legislation and is linked to other practices that hinder the defendants' participatory rights. As mentioned in the Chapter "Participatory Rights in Comparative Criminal Justice. Similarities and Divergences Within the Framework of the European Law" (and not only in relation to England and Wales), the frequent use of video-link with the courtroom is an even more intrusive limitation to the defendants' right to take part, actively, in their proceedings and to have confidential conversation with their counsel. These trends are all related to the urgency for efficiency that has been implemented especially into English criminal justice since 2012, leading to increased emphasis on early guilty pleas. Such a phenomenon is also the result of the legal aid reform, which reduced access to free legal assistance and led many defendants to choose self-representation. Thus, on the one hand, these overlapping trends have indirectly frustrated personal presence. On the other, absence in trials has been increasingly accepted. The Magistrate's Court tends to inquire (if possible) on the reasons for the defendant's absence: regardless of the correctness of the summoning process or *force majeure*, the courts often proceed *in absentia*, rather than rescheduling the hearing. The defendant, who may have been unaware of the trial, can access the remedies explained above. The Crown Court also engages in an inquiry into the reasons for the defendant's absence, but should the trial proceed, there is no automatic right to rehearing, unless it can be demonstrated that the conviction was unsafe.

Against this background, the idea, promoted (but not actively pursued, so far) by the Government, to repeal the 1998 Human Rights Act raises several concerns. Moreover, *Leader* underlines that, even before the Brexit referendum, the English Parliament displayed a major distance from the Strasbourg Court in the affair of

---

[1] There was evidence of challenging the use of docks in the eighteenth and nineteenth century courtroom (see *In the Dock. Reassessing the use of the dock in criminal trials*, in www.justice.org. uk, 2015). However, no massive reactions were enacted, with the exception of some law-reform campaigns, in the 1960s and 1970s of the past century (with the active participation of Baron Jeremy Hutchinson, see Grant 2015, p. 27). Recently see Stone and Blackstock (2017), pp. 4–6; Stone (2015), pp. 7–9; Mulcahy (2013), pp. 1139–1156. Actually, no other reports lingered over the topic of using docks in courtrooms. However, the feeling is that such practice is still very common among the European jurisdictions. Recently, the Strasbourg Court (ECtHR, *Yaroslav Belousov v. Russia*, judgment of 4 October 2016, Appls. Nos. 2653/13, 60980/14) noted that excluding the defendant from the courtroom and, in particular, from her lawyer may amount to a violation of both Article 3 and 6(1) and (3)(b, c) ECHR, hindering her participatory rights.

prisoners' right to vote, revealing the UK's dissatisfaction with the framework of the European Fundamental Rights system. However, even though only speculations are possible at the moment, there is the impression that a possible English Bill of Right could not be dramatically different from the current Human Rights Act. However, repealing the ECHR seems to be a priority only in the Prime Minister's agenda and in the one of a very small minority. What is more likely to happen in the near future is the withdrawal from the Charter of Fundamental rights of the EU and of the CJEU jurisdiction.

As to the other countries, the rapporteurs highlighted many different and interesting points, proving how wide and diversified the impacts of the Strasburg jurisprudence are.

Golser, for instance, focuses on the difficult relationship between the Austrian national law implementing the EAW and the basic principles of Article 6(3)(a) ECHR.[2] In a system that seems to have found a viable balance between the interests of justice and the rights of the defendant, it has been suggested that it would be preferable to surrender requested persons only after having informed them of the charge or the sentence against them and having allowed them to lodge a remedy.

Petrova underlines the major impact of ECHR in the process of democratization of Bulgarian justice and, in particular, criminal justice. With specific regard to *in absentia* trials, the case of *Stoichkov v. Bulgaria*[3] represented an important landmark for the domestic order, ruling on a violation of Article 6(3)(d) ECHR because of a lack of remedies against *in absentia* decisions.[4]

France certainly totals a large number of ECtHR decisions on the matter of *in absentia* trials. *Drevet* draws attention to the fact that the Strasbourg Court case-law succeeded in urging the French law-maker to pass two main reforms. The first related to the matter of the right to be represented by a lawyer, for absent defendants. The second was with regard to the right to appeal against decisions *par contumace*: before the reform, the absent defendant's lawyer was not entitled to lodge an appeal on behalf of her client, whose sole chance to appeal the decision was to surrender. After these crucial reforms, the French criminal procedure seems to *Drevet* to be compliant with the ECHR (but also to the recent directive 2016/343/EU).[5]

Similarly, in Luxembourg one of the main reforms of *in absentia* trials was directly inspired by the ruling of the ECtHR in the case of *Van Geyseghem v. Belgium*.[6] *Covolo* underlines that the 2008 Luxembourgish reform strengthened the right of the absent defendant to be represented by a lawyer. Having emphasised the defendant's right to freely decide whether to appear or not in court, the reform also

---

[2] Golser, in this volume, Sect. 7.1. See also, Demetrio Crespo and Sánz Hermida, in this volume, Sect. 3.

[3] ECtHR, *Stoichkov v. Romania*, judgment of 24 March 2005, Appl. No. 9808/02.

[4] Petrova, in this volume, Sect. 7.1.

[5] Drevet, in this volume, Sect. 7.1.

[6] ECtHR, *Van Geyseghem v. Belgium*, judgment of 21 January 1999, Appl. No. 26103/95.

granted a fresh determination of the facts and of the law in case it is not established that the defendant unequivocally waived her participatory rights. Thus, the national regulation seems to be highly compliant with the Strasbourg standards, also because the guarantees mentioned here apply also in *inaudito reo* proceedings, which are treated under Luxembourgish law as *in absentia* trials.[7]

The German report highlights several crucial aspects in German procedural law, with regard to the ECHR protection of participatory rights. In particular, *Vogel* suggests strengthening the defence's participatory rights during investigation. German law, in particular, does not provide for the appointment of a counsel representing the accused at the pre-trial investigation interview of the witnesses. In fact, in the case of *Schatschaschwili v. Germany*,[8] the Grand Chamber found a violation of Article 6(3)(d) ECHR because of the lack of opportunity for directly cross-examining the witnesses, who did not appear in court at the trial.[9] As to *in absentia* proceedings, *Vogel* emphasizes that the rule providing for dismissal of the appeal (*Berufung*) against *in absentia* decisions, if the defendant does not appear in the court at the second instance proceedings, appears to be in breach of the ECHR. Such an outcome, that is to say the dismissal, should be provided only if the defendant's presence is absolutely necessary to assess the truth. In other cases, it should be possible to admit the representation by a counsel. Moreover, *Berufung* must be dismissed also in case the defendant, initially present, does not attend the following hearings and she is not represented by a lawyer. *Vogel* suggests reconsidering such a provision in view of a more ECHR-compliant approach.[10]

Possibly, the most critical condition, with regard to abiding with the ECHR, is the Greek regulation allowing for the commencement of *in absentia* trials for misdemeanours against untraceable defendants, without the appointment of a lawyer.[11] This point has been previously addressed in the comparative overview of the twelve selected criminal justice systems.[12] To conclude, the complete deprivation of legal assistance in such cases gives rise to serious concerns, since the Strasbourg Court has repeatedly stated the importance of granting legal representation especially when the defendant waived her participatory rights (see, *mutatis mutandis*, the French reform mentioned above). Moreover, Greek law deals with untraceable defendants, who certainly did not unequivocally waive their right to be present at trial. A prompt reform of the Greek regulation (although already providing for remedies against *in absentia* decisions if the defendant appears lately) seems to be the most urgent issue stemming from this study.

---

[7] Covolo, in this volume, Sect. 7.1.

[8] ECtHR, *Schatschaschwili v. Germany*, judgement of 15 December 2015, Appl. No. 9154/10.

[9] Ruggeri, in this volume, Sect. 4.3.

[10] Vogel, in this volume, Sect. 3.6.

[11] Billis and Gkaniatsos, in this volume, Sect. 5.2.

[12] Quattrocolo, in this volume, Sect. 5.

Regarding Hungary, the national rapporteurs underline that, according to figures, hardly any *in absentia* proceedings take place in the country.[13] Thus, the negative impact of possible breaches of the ECHR is neutralised. As to the matter of an unequivocal waiver, the authors report that the domestic code for criminal procedure provides for an explicit communication by the defendant of the decision to waive her right to be present. However, no provision regulates the form or the timing of such a notification, in breach of the national constitution.

Even in Italy, where two significant reforms have been clearly inspired by ECtHR case-law, some doubts still exist about full compliance with the European Convention. On the one hand, *Mangiaracina* stresses that the national case-law still considers fugitives as being informed of the criminal proceeding and, thus, as having unequivocally waived their right to be present, although the Strasbourg Court has openly rejected such conclusion since the case of *Sejdovic v. Italy*.[14] On the other, moving from this example, it is worth noting that the Court repeatedly stated that the defendant should not carry the burden of demonstrating that she did not try to escape justice or her absence was due to *force majeure*.[15] In fact, the 2014 Italian reform introduced a system of *restitutio in integrum* after *in absentia* decisions, which burdens the defendant with the task of proving that she was actually unaware of the proceeding against her. Actually, this may be considered in violation of the Court's interpretation of Article 6(1) and (3) ECHR.

As to Portugal, *Costa Ramos and Churro* have repeatedly stressed a contradiction between the general acknowledgment of the defendant's participatory rights, by the Portuguese Constitution and the current code for criminal procedure. On the one hand, the authors stress the fact that, within the CCP-Portugal framework, the celebration of trials *in absentia* seems to be a sort of penalty for those accused who did not respect the duty to provide an updated addresses and to inform the judicial authority of any change to it. On the other hand, the authors clearly denounce the remedy against *in absentia* decision as highly ineffective. In fact, the new judgment is not based on fresh evidence, but purely on a review of the decision taken *in absentia*.[16]

Romania recently experienced a peculiar situation. Even though the ECHR was ratified in 1994, the harmonisation of the domestic criminal procedure with Article 6 ECHR has been a rather formal and ineffective one. As *Ciopec and Roibu* pointed out, the judicial practice remained rather insensitive to the enforcement of such procedure. As to what concerns expressly *in absentia* trials, the national regulation allowed the courts to decide, case by case, whether to retry or not a defendant having been tried *in absentia* and seeking a remedy against such decisions. The most recent amendments to the code for criminal procedure established a practice that

---

[13] Gácsi et al., in this volume, Sect. 5.1.

[14] Mangiaracina, in this volume, Sect. 7.1.

[15] Ruggeri, in Part VI of this volume, Sect. 3.2.2.

[16] Costa Ramos and Churro, in this volume, Sect. 5.2.

appears to be highly compliant with the ECHR. However, such regulation is far too recent to get feedback from the Strasbourg Court about its abidance to Article 6.[17]

The Spanish report emphasises how far the CJEU's *Melloni* case affected the whole judicial system of *in absentia* trials. In particular, *Villamarín López* stresses that the Spanish Constitutional Court has always paid much attention to ECtHR case-law. When the impact of the *Melloni* judgement forced the Constitutional Court to abandon its previous approach to *in absentia* trials, the Spanish high court went on referring to the very same Strasbourg case-law, now to enhance the new (restrictive) doctrine. However, we should recall *Villamarín López*'s strong criticism towards the Spanish Constitutional Court interpretation (even before the CJEU forced it to abandon it), considering it inconsistent with the ECtHR view.[18]

2.2   *Developments in Domestic Law as a Result of EU Law*

As to the relationship between national jurisdictions and EU law, all the national reports refer to the current situation of implementation. After the Lisbon Treaty, the Roadmap on procedural rights and the Stockholm Programme enhanced an unprecedented stream of harmonisation in criminal procedure. Many of the countries analysed by this study are still struggling to establish a trend of timely implementation of the several Directives adopted by the Council and the Parliament of the EU. At the same time, the implementation of the first directives enhanced the standard of protection of fundamental procedural rights, affecting in many ways the matter of *in absentia* trials. Thus, the twelve summaries tend to distinguish between the benefits provided by the recent implementation of some of the EU directives and the amendments that must be passed by the national lawmakers in order to implement the newest directives, and in particular Directive 2016/343/EU.

As mentioned under paragraph I, the most peculiar situation is the England and Wales one, deeply affected not only by the Brexit referendum but also by the particular position of the UK towards the Chapter V of the TFEU. After the period of the third pillar 'repressive tools' policy, the UK showed reluctance to implement EU criminal justice policies. *Leader* remembers the 2013 announcement of a general repeal of the third Pillar framework decisions: initially, this opt out was due to cover also the EAW FD. However, the final provision opted back into a large number of measures. Since then, the desire of England and Wales to abandon the EU Charter of Fundamental Rights and the whole system of EU legislation in criminal matters became even more evident, not only with the 2016 referendum, but also with the restrictive trend of the Supreme Court in the execution of EAWs. This tendency will play a relevant role in the drafting of the Withdrawal Bill.[19]

---

[17] Ciopec and Roibu, in this volume, Sect. 7.1.
[18] Villamarín López, in this volume, Sect. 7.
[19] Leader, in this volume, Sect. 7.2.

As to the other countries, *Golser* emphasises that, in Austria, the implementation of Directive 2013/48/EU improved confidentiality in client-attorney contacts.[20] It is possible to argue that this directive is the one that affected the national legislation in a major way, under the viewpoint of the effective participation of the accused in criminal proceedings.

Vogel highlights a very interesting issue in the complicated relationship between the German national system of fundamental rights and the EU law. After having summed up the main reforms enacted to implement the Roadmap Directives, he focuses on the specific issue of *in absentia* proceedings, noting that the German Constitutional Court repeatedly displayed criticism towards the 'Melloni doctrine'. In fact, the obligation to respect human dignity, enshrined in Article 1(1) of the German Basic Law is applicable also in the execution of an EAW. Thus, the German authorities must ensure that "the minimum guarantees of the rights of the accused required by the respect for human dignity will also be observed in the issuing MS".[21]

The Greek summary testifies to a slow trend of implementation of the EU procedural acts: at the moment of writing, only Directive 2010/64/EU and 2012/13/EU have been implemented. Nor has the 2009/299/JHA FD been fully transposed. In light of these remarks, Directive 2016/343/EU will represent a huge challenge for Greece. Not only, as mentioned in the previous paragraphs, some specific standards of *in absentia* trials, addressed in the Directive 2016/343/EU are still neglected by the national regulation, but the lack of a complete framework (with the implementation of e.g., of Directive 2013/48) may jeopardise the effect of the transposition.[22]

As to Hungary, the authors refer to the recent implementation of Framework Decision 2009/299/JHA, with no hints on the transposition of the EU Directive 2016/343.[23]

The Italian report does not linger over possible shortcomings in the implementation of Directive 2016/343/EU. *Mangiaracina* gives an overview on the implementation of the Roadmap directives and the directive on the European Investigation Order, which has been recently transposed.[24]

As to Luxembourg, *Covolo* notes that, after the 2008 reform of the domestic criminal procedure code, inspired by ECtHR case-law, the national regulations appear to be compliant with Directive 2016/343/EU. Thus, no major reforms are expected. However, the rapporteur emphasises that the directive provides for retrial of *all in absentia* decisions, in case of unawareness of the defendant or non-unequivocal waiver of the right to be present. On the contrary, the national system allows for retrial only in cases of *in absentia* convictions and not in cases of acquittals.[25]

---

[20] Golser, in this volume, Sect. 7.2.

[21] Vogel, in this volume, Sect. 7.2.

[22] Billis and Gkaniatsos, in this volume, Sect. 7.2.

[23] Gácsi et al., in this volume, Sect. 7.2.

[24] Mangiaracina, in this volume, Sect. 7.2.

[25] Covolo, in this volume, Sect. 5.2.

The Portuguese summary focuses on the persistent shortcomings of national regulation that does not provide for an effective remedy against *in absentia* decisions, based on new evidence. If, on the one hand, this is inconsistent with the ECtHR doctrine, on the other hand this is in contrast with Directive 2016/343/EU. Actually, *Costa Ramos and Churro* note that in case of late implementation, the national courts and judges will be allowed the direct application of Article 9 of the Directive itself, in order to grant the defendant a new and effective trial.[26]

Figures show reluctance of the Romanian courts and judges to submit preliminary rulings to the Court of Justice of the European Union. Consequently, *Ciopec and Roibu* noted, the only form of harmonization experienced by the Romania is implementation by the lawmaker. As to the *in absentia* proceedings, such implementation covered, so far only Framework Decision 2009/299/JHA. At the moment of writing, no initiative has been submitted for the implementation of Directive 2016/343/EU.[27] As noted in the previous paragraph, the Spanish report devotes much attention to the crucial 'Melloni case', which represents a difficult transition in the relationship between the national legal order and that of the European Union. Meanwhile, Spain has regularly implemented the directives on the enhancement of the defendant's and victim's rights. Directive 2016/343/EU has not been implemented yet. The transposition of this legal instrument into domestic law appears to be difficult, not with regard to the part devoted to *in absentia* trials, but in dealing with the presumption of innocence. In fact, on the one hand, the directive sets forth the general rule *in dubio pro reo*, with no exceptions. *Villamarín López* notes that this could be inconsistent with national case-law.[28] On the other hand, Article 7 of the Directive prevents courts from inferring any consequence from the defendant's decision to remain silent: the Spanish Supreme Court acknowledged, decades ago, the ECtHR less stringent doctrine, set forth in *John Murray v. UK* and *Saunders v. UK*,[29] allowing the Courts to consider this aspect in delivering their decision.

3 Concluding Remarks

This quite fragmented overview gives the idea of European law as a multifaceted instrument affecting in many different ways the domestic legal orders.

It emerges clearly from the previous paragraphs, but also from Chapter "Participatory Rights in Comparative Criminal Justice. Similarities and Divergences Within the Framework of the European Law", where the legal systems have been

---

[26] Costa Ramos and Churro, in this volume, Sects. 5.2 and 7.2.

[27] Ciopec and Roibu, in this volume, Sect. 7.2.

[28] Villamarín López, in this volume, Sect. 7.2.

[29] ECtHR, Grand Chamber, *John Murray v. United Kingdom*, judgment of 8 February 1996, Appl. No. 18731/91; ECtHR, *Saunders v. United Kingdom*, judgment of 17 December 1996, Appl. No. 19187/91.

compared, that the European principles regulating personal participation in criminal proceedings may impact on various aspects of the national systems.

We may argue that the absence of uniformity in the regulation of participatory rights was assumed to be the starting point of our analysis. In such context, *Pollicino and Bassini*[30] demonstrated that the existing divergences are not precisely grounded in the dichotomy common law/civil law, and do not respond to rigid dogmatic distinctions. At the same time, the comparative overview pointed out a trend of general convergence towards the growing acceptance of areas on 'non-personal participation', even in those countries that displayed greater reluctance towards *in absentia* proceedings.

The impression is that participatory rights are 'on the move', experiencing a period of basic amendments in almost any country, and this is happening against the background of European law. It does not imply that such movement is a harmonisation trend, in the legal sense of the term. The reality of the different jurisdictions seems to be merging towards a more accepted idea of non-personal presence at trial, provided that some basic guarantees are met, before and after *in absentia* decisions. As I tried to explain in my comparison, this is probably due also to social conditions and changing habits, related to the massive circulation of people within the boundaries of the EU. However, the framework for the evolution towards a larger acceptance of cases in which the parties may not be present at trial has been drawn by the European law. It is in the ECtHR jurisprudence and in the EU legislation, especially in dir. 2016/343/EU that a viable balance can be found, in order to couple the basic participatory rights with the trends of a social context in which people tend to move more frequently and, possibly, to be less interested in criminal proceedings against them.

References

Grant T (2015) Jeremy Hutchinson's case history. John Murray, London

Mulcahy L (2013) Putting the defendant in their place: why do we still use the dock in criminal proceedings? Br J Criminal (6):1139–1156

Stone J (2015) Is it now time to abolish the dock in all criminal proceedings in England and Wales. Archbold Rev 3:7–9

Stone J, Blackstock J (2017) Violating the right to a fair trial? The secure dock in England and Wales. Archbold Rev 7:4–6

---

[30] Pollicino and Bassini, in this volume, Sect. 7.

Printed by Printforce, the Netherlands